S0-ARX-497

PROPERTY AND LIABILITY INSURANCE HANDBOOK

THE IRWIN SERIES IN RISK AND INSURANCE

EDITORS

EDISON L. BOWERS — *The Ohio State University*

DAVIS W. GREGG — *The American College of Life Underwriters*

Boileau, Stalnaker, & Luck *Life Insurance Agency Financial Management*
Brainard *Automobile Insurance*
Dickerson *Health Insurance* Revised Edition
Donaldson *Casualty Claim Practice*
Follmann *Medical Care and Health Insurance: A Study in Social Progress*
Fraine *Valuation of Securities Holdings of Life Insurance Companies*
Goshay *Information Technology in the Insurance Industry*
Gregg *Life and Health Insurance Handbook* Second Edition
Greider & Beadles *Law and the Life Insurance Contract*
Haber & Cohen *Social Security: Programs, Problems, and Policies*
Long & Gregg *Property and Liability Insurance Handbook*
Magee *Life Insurance* Third Edition
Magee *Property Insurance* Third Edition
Magee & Bickelhaupt *General Insurance* Seventh Edition
McGill *Legal Aspects of Life Insurance*
McGill *Life Insurance*
Mehr & Cammack *Principles of Insurance* Third Edition
Mehr & Hedges *Risk Management in the Business Enterprise*
Myers *Social Insurance and Allied Government Programs*
Redeker & Reid *Life Insurance Settlement Options* Revised Edition
Snider *Readings in Property and Casualty Insurance*

PROPERTY AND LIABILITY INSURANCE HANDBOOK

PLANNED AND EDITED BY

JOHN D. LONG

Professor of Insurance, Graduate School of Business, Indiana University

and

DAVIS W. GREGG

President, The American College of Life Underwriters

WITH THE COOPERATION OF

ONE HUNDRED AND THIRTY-TWO OUTSTANDING AMERICAN INSURANCE AUTHORITIES

1965

RICHARD D. IRWIN, INC.

HOMEWOOD, ILLINOIS

First Printing, February, 1965

Library of Congress Catalog Card No. 64–21028

PRINTED IN THE UNITED STATES OF AMERICA

To my parents

John B. Long *and* Effie Y. Long

—who have done so much for me.

J. D. L.

To Leon S. Gregg

—a brother who lit the fire of interest

on my part in insurance

and who himself has achieved greatness

as an insurance practitioner,

and fullness as a whole man.

D. W. G.

PREFACE

The spectrum of property and liability insurance is wide and the elements exceedingly diverse. Moreover, modern society demands heavy use of such insurance. Owning a home, driving an automobile, or operating a business are but a few of many cases in point.

When put together, the various nonlife segments of the insurance industry account for close to half a million full-time employees; assets between $35 and $40 billion; and premiums which may soon reach $20 billion annually. Because of this magnitude and diversity, few efforts have been made to provide in one volume any definitive treatment of the subject. This *Handbook* embodies such an attempt. Since the subject matter has large dimensions, many people necessarily were involved in the writing of this book. In fact, 132 insurance authorities—along with the two principal editors—lent their thinking directly to this project. Seventy-five individuals authored a chapter or an appendix. Fifty-eight served as Consulting Editors.

The basic objective of the Irwin Series in Risk and Insurance, initiated in 1949, has been to create insurance literature useful not only to college and university classes but also to the insurance business itself. We hope that this publication meets this objective. The *Handbook* is designed to be useful to a wide group of people within and outside of the insurance industry. The editors and authors have attempted to develop a substantive treatment of fundamentals sufficiently elementary to be instructive to the beginner but also sufficiently comprehensive to be challenging to the veteran student or practitioner. All of the material has been planned and written in the thought that a good handbook should be a reliable research tool, a handy reference guide, an interesting source of descriptive reading, and a flexible textbook—all in one. This *Handbook*, when used in conjunction with the *Life and Health Insurance Handbook* (now in its second edition) should cover most of the insurance field.

The *Handbook* is divided into nine major sections: Part I—Risk and Insurance; Part II—Fire and Allied Lines Insurance; Part III—Marine and Aviation Insurance; Part IV—Inland Marine Insurance; Part V—Liability Insurance and Related Lines; Part VI—Multiple Line Insurance; Part VII—Suretyship; Part VIII—The Institution of Property-Liability Insurance; and Part IX—Risk Management. Widespread counsel was sought in the effort to arrange the parts, and the chapters within each part, in the most convenient order for teaching and learning. Although each chapter has been designed to constitute a unit, we have included a sprinkling of cross references to facilitate detailed research and study of particular topics. We have prepared also an extensive index of subject matter, an index of names of individuals, an index of names of organizations, and an index of court cases treated in the book. These indexes should prove to be timesavers for many readers. In addition, the 12 appendixes provide a variety of specimen policies and forms plus other useful materials, most of which are not generally available in other textbook sources.

Since with but two exceptions each chapter has been written by a different author, differences in writing style and depth of treatment are readily apparent in this book. While we sought to impose a certain amount of consistency in treatment of subject matter, a conscientious effort was made not to disturb unduly the natural expository style of the 75 Contributing Authors to this volume. In any case, we are extremely pleased to present the writings of these authorities. Some of the contributors are well-known authors in their own rights; others have never had time heretofore to address themselves to manuscripts of this type. If this *Handbook* served no other purpose, it would be well justified simply by providing the mechanism through which the talents of these highly able but extremely busy individuals were brought into focus for the creation of insurance literature.

The outline of chapters for this *Handbook* was a long time in the making and the subject of numerous revisions as suggestions were made by a large number of individuals representing every segment of subject matter treated. Contributing Authors in every case were then chosen from among those persons highly qualified to write on the subjects. We then maintained close contact with each author during the development of his detailed chapter outline. Each manuscript was read and criticized by four or more Consulting Editors, each an expert himself in the subject matter of the chapters he read. Typically, each chapter manuscript went through several drafts before submission to the publisher. In each case we appraised in detail at least three versions of the manuscript as prepared and revised by the author. We read the galley proofs for each manuscript as did also the author. The two of us took responsibility for the page proofs. Despite this elaborate process, the very magnitude of the volume renders the likelihood high that numerous errors remain for which we accept full responsibility.

As would be expected, terminology has presented a major problem in the treatment of numerous property-liability subjects within the same volume. Many words, for example, "contribution," are not accorded the same meaning from one branch of the business to another. Even the name of the *Handbook* posed a problem for us. Initially, it was to be the "Property and Casualty Insurance Handbook," but the Contributing Authors and Consulting Editors indicated an overwhelming preference for the word "Liability" to be used in the title in place of the word "Casualty." While "casualty" is used at numerous places throughout the volume, we have made an effort to avoid using it where "liability" or some other word would make the meaning more clear. Since many of the state tax and regulatory statutes and the federal tax statutes are still couched in terms of "fire and casualty companies," however, the word "casualty" had to be retained for treatment of these subjects. Perhaps the merging of the National Board of Fire Underwriters and the Association of Casualty and Surety Companies into the American Insurance Association signals the official demise of "casualty" as a major generic term in insurance literature.

Another word which proved particularly troublesome for us and which warrants an explanatory comment is "form." The word is used heavily and ambiguously in insurance literature to mean policy, endorsement, total contract, or any one of several other documents such as that for the submission of values as in a "reporting form." In the *Handbook* we attempted to restrict the use of the word to mean the piece of paper which adapts an insurance policy to a particular type of transaction. Examples are the "Dwelling Building(s) and Contents—Broad Form" and "Form 2," the latter of which can be attached to a Homeowners Policy. Despite the narrow intent in the use of this word, a few other meanings doubtless have slipped into the text.

Perhaps by the time this volume requires revision the several working committees operating as parts of the Commission on Insurance Terminology will have made some progress in imputing consistency of meaning to these and other troublesome words. In such a happy circumstance terminology should not prove so frustrating in the revised edition as it has in the present one.

Full acknowledgment of assistance is impossible in a publication of this sort. Primary recognition must be given to the Contributing Authors and Consulting Editors for their direct contributions to this project. Each one has left his mark on this publication. Their names and affiliations are listed on the pages immediately following this preface. Both of us want to thank them not only for their help in preparing and processing manuscripts but also for their counsel and suggestions in the planning and organizing of this book.

We also take pleasure in acknowledging the excellent help we have received from our publisher. Expertise, patience, cooperation, and enthusiasm for this project have characterized each person of Richard D. Irwin, Inc. with whom we have been involved in the preparation of this *Handbook*. Particular appreciation is expressed to Harry H. Bingham whose professional skills have been a comfort to both of us.

Special thanks are given also to Mrs. Helen L. Schmidt at Bryn Mawr and to Mrs. Howard R. Harlow, Mrs. Donald C. Rader, Mrs. Lloyd R. Isaacs, and Mrs. Frank C. Pankiewicz of Bloomington. Each of these competent persons was willing to be employed on an hourly basis as a secretary during numerous long evenings and weekends in order to type and retype manuscripts and handle correspondence on an off-duty basis in their homes. As a rough estimate, this project has involved at least 2,000 letters as well as 77 manuscripts, and numerous appendixes. Without the excellent assistance on the part of these people and others, we could not have completed this project.

In addition, Jerry A. Tignor and Norman F. Mitchell provided inspired intelligent, and highly dependable "backup" research and editorial service. Without their help in keeping correspondence, manuscripts, galley proofs, page proofs, and a multitude of other papers in order and in tracking down and double-checking thousands of miscellaneous items, this book would still be in process.

We would like to use this medium to acknowledge the indirect but highly important contribution made to this publication by H. Jeff Reed. Through the years Mr. Reed has given generously of his wise counsel to John D. Long—counsel both as to the operating realities and the basic nobleness of insurance as a bulwark of society. To the extent that Mr. Reed's precepts and examples have been captured in our editing, this book is the richer.

We both owe debts to our families far in excess of our abilities to repay. Hazel E. Long and Douglas Paul, Martha Susan, and Elinor Jane Long have demonstrated a patience and forbearance far beyond what any reasonable husband and father has a right to expect. Furthermore, they have helped directly with many of the tasks associated with producing a handbook of this type. Mildred Grace Gregg and Mary Cynthia and Davis William have once again shown their colors by suffering through another publication. To Hazel, Millie, and all the children, we express our deepest thanks for your help and for your unflagging enthusiasm for this project.

JOHN D. LONG
DAVIS W. GREGG

BLOOMINGTON, INDIANA
NEWTOWN SQUARE, PENNSYLVANIA
February, 1965

CONTRIBUTING AUTHORS AND CONSULTING EDITORS

LAURENCE J. ACKERMAN, Dean (retired), School of Business Administration, University of Connecticut, Storrs, Connecticut

JOHN ADAM, JR., C.P.C.U., President, Worcester Mutual Fire Insurance Company, Worcester, Massachusetts

LYTTLETON M. BALDWIN, Vice President, The Travelers Insurance Companies, Hartford, Connecticut

RICHARD H. BANCROFT, Vice President, St. Paul Insurance Companies, St. Paul, Minnesota

J. CARROLL BATEMAN, General Manager, Insurance Information Institute, New York, N.Y.

JOHN F. BEARDSLEY, Secretary, Hartford Accident & Indemnity Company, Hartford, Connecticut

SIDNEY G. BEHLMER, Vice President and Secretary, Hartford Fire Insurance Company Group, Hartford, Connecticut

WILLIAM H. BERRY, Vice President and Manager, Pacific Department, Continental Insurance Companies, San Francisco, California

DR. DAVID L. BICKELHAUPT, C.P.C.U., C.L.U., Associate Professor of Insurance, The Ohio State University, Columbus, Ohio

DR. JOHN S. BICKLEY, Professor of Insurance, The University of Texas, Austin, Texas

DR. KENNETH BLACK, JR., C.P.C.U., C.L.U., Regents Professor of Insurance, Georgia State College, Atlanta, Georgia

DR. RALPH H. BLANCHARD, F.C.A.S., Professor Emeritus of Insurance, Columbia University, New York, N.Y.

ROBERT L. BRADDOCK, President, General Reinsurance Corporation, New York, N.Y.

DONALD C. BRAIN, C.P.C.U., Brain & Fritson, Inc., Kansas City, Missouri

DR. CALVIN H. BRAINARD, Professor of Insurance, University of Rhode Island, Providence, Rhode Island

LYMAN B. BRAINERD, President, The Hartford Steam Boiler Inspection & Insurance Company, Hartford, Connecticut

CAMERON BROWN, President, George F. Brown & Sons, Inc., Chicago, Illinois

NORMAN A. BURGOON, JR., Vice President, Fidelity & Deposit Company of Maryland, Baltimore, Maryland

BEN M. BUTLER, President, General Adjustment Bureau, Inc., New York N.Y.

JAMES M. CAHILL, F.C.A.S., General Manager, National Bureau of Casualty Underwriters, New York, N.Y.

DR. JAMES J. CHASTAIN, C.P.C.U., Director of Field Services, American Institute for Property and Liability Underwriters, Inc., Byrn Mawr, Pennsylvania

F. H. CHEGWIDDEN, C.P.C.U., Financial Secretary, General Accident Group of Insurance Companies, Philadelphia, Pennsylvania

GEORGE A. CONNER, Vice President, Fidelity & Deposit Company of Maryland, Baltimore, Maryland

A. HAWTHORNE CRIDDLE, C.P.C.U., Executive Vice President, Ostheimer-Walsh, Inc., Philadelphia, Pennsylvania

JAMES C. CRISTY, Manager—Insurance and Office Services, The Upjohn Company, Kalamazoo, Michigan

BERNARD J. DAENZER, C.P.C.U., President, Wohlreich & Anderson, Ltd. and S & E International, Ltd., New York, N.Y.

HAROLD S. DAYNARD, President, Daynard & Van Thunen Company, Inc., New York, N.Y.

JOHN K. DEEKS, Assistant Secretary, The Aetna Casualty & Surety Company, Hartford, Connecticut

ROBERT F. DEGENER, Vice President and Director, Appleton & Cox, Inc., New York, N.Y.

DR. HERBERT S. DENENBERG, C.P.C.U., Assistant Professor of Insurance, University of Pennsylvania, Philadelphia, Pennsylvania

ROBERT D. DENTON, President, Wolverine Insurance Company, Battle Creek, Michigan

DR. O. D. DICKERSON, C.P.C.U., C.L.U., F.C.A.S., Associate Professor of Insurance, The Florida State University, Tallahassee, Florida

JOHN H. DILLARD, Vice President, Fireman's Fund American Insurance Companies, New York, N.Y.

W. G. DITHMER, C.P.C.U., Regional Director, Insurance Information Institute, Chicago, Illinois

J. DEWEY DORSETT, President, American Insurance Association, New York, N.Y.

MYRON DUBAIN, Vice President, Fireman's Fund American Insurance Companies, San Francisco, California

HENRY K. DUKE, C.P.C.U., C.L.U., Insurance Consultant, Cumberland, Maryland

ROBERT R. DWELLY, A.C.I.I., Marine Manager, Insurance Company of North America, New York, N.Y.

HAROLD G. EVANS, President—U.S. Branch, Accident & Casualty Insurance Company of Winterthur, Switzerland, New York, N.Y.

ARNE FOUGNER, President, Christiania General Insurance Corporation of New York, Tarrytown, N.Y.

ALANSON R. FREDERICKS, General Counsel, Maryland Casualty Company, Baltimore, Maryland

WARREN N. GAFFNEY, General Manager, The Surety Association of America, New York, N.Y.

RUSSELL B. GALLAGHER, Manager, Facilities Analysis, Philco Corporation, Philadelphia, Pennsylvania

DR. ERWIN A. GAUMNÍTZ, Dean, School of Commerce, University of Wisconsin, Madison, Wisconsin

JOSEPH S. GERBER, Attorney-at-Law, Gerber, Berman & Woodruff, Chicago, Illinois

DR. VICTOR GERDES, Professor of Insurance, New York University, New York, N.Y.

WALTER R. GHERARDI, Senior Vice President, Federal Insurance Company and Vice President and Director, Chubb & Son, Inc., New York, N.Y.

HAROLD J. GINSBURGH, F.C.A.S., Senior Vice President (Retired), American Mutual Liability Insurance Company, Wakefield, Massachusetts

ARTHUR C. GOERLICH, President (Retired), The College of Insurance, New York, N.Y.

DR. MARK R. GREENE, Acting Dean, School of Business Administration and Professor of Insurance, University of Oregon, Eugene, Oregon

LEON S. GREGG, Vice President, American General Insurance Company, Houston, Texas

CLAYTON G. HALE, President, The Hale & Hale Company, Cleveland, Ohio

DR. JOHN W. HALL, C.L.U., Professor of Insurance, Georgia State College, Atlanta, Georgia

GEORGE D. HASKELL, Consultant, Peat, Marwick, Mitchell & Company, Chicago, Illinois

CHARLES J. HAUGH, F.C.A.S., Vice President (Retired), The Travelers Insurance Companies, Hartford, Connecticut

DR. BOB A. HEDGES, C.P.C.U., C.L.U., Associate Professor of Finance, University of Illinois, Urbana, Illinois

DR. J. EDWARD HEDGES, C.P.C.U., C.L.U., Professor of Insurance, Indiana University, Bloomington, Indiana

H. RICHARD HEILMAN, Senior Vice President, Insurance Company of North America, Philadelphia, Pennsylvania

BENJAMIN HORTON, C.P.C.U., President, Horton Adjustment Companies, Louisville, Kentucky

DR. S. S. HUEBNER (Deceased), President Emeritus, American College of Life Underwriters and Emeritus Chairman of Board, American Institute for Property and Liability Underwriters, Inc., Bryn Mawr, Pennsylvania

LEWIS V. IRVINE, C.P.C.U., Director of Training, The Travelers Insurance Companies, Hartford, Connecticut

EDGAR E. ISAACS, C.P.C.U., Assistant U.S. Manager, Zurich Insurance Company, Chicago, Illinois

ACIS JENKINSON, 3rd, C.L.U., Director of Education, Insurance Company of North America, Philadelphia, Pennsylvania

CHARLES P. JERVEY, Vice President (Retired), The Travelers Indemnity Company, Hartford, Connecticut

H. CLAY JOHNSON, Executive Vice President, Royal-Globe Insurance Companies, New York, N.Y.

NEWELL R. JOHNSON, General Manager (Retired), American Mutual Insurance Alliance, Chicago, Illinois

DR. DANIEL P. KEDZIE, C.P.C.U., C.L.U., Assistant Vice President and Director of Education, Continental Assurance Company, Chicago, Illinois

ROBB B. KELLEY, C.P.C.U., President, Employers Mutual Casualty Company, Des Moines, Iowa

CHESTER M. KELLOGG, Chairman, Alfred M. Best Company, Inc., New York, N.Y.

AMBROSE B. KELLY, General Counsel, Factory Mutual Insurance Companies, Providence, Rhode Island

DR. SPENCER L. KIMBALL, Professor of Law, University of Michigan, Ann Arbor, Michigan

DR. RICHARD DER. KIP, C.P.C.U., C.L.U., Professor of Risk and Insurance and Associate Dean of The Florida Institute for Continuing University Studies, The Florida State University, Tallahassee, Florida

DR. HAROLD C. KROGH, C.P.C.U., C.L.U., Professor of Business Administration, The University of Kansas, Lawrence, Kansas

RAYMOND D. LACOMBE, Manager, Research Department, American Insurance Association, New York, N.Y.

JACK E. LARSON, Secretary, The Travelers Indemnity Company, Hartford, Connecticut

VESTAL LEMMON, General Manager, National Association of Independent Insurers, Chicago, Illinois

WILLIAM LESLIE, JR., F.C.A.S., Vice President and Actuary, Continental Insurance Companies, New York, N.Y.

FRANCIS A. LEWIS, Marine Secretary, Insurance Company of North America, Philadelphia, Pennsylvania

GEORGE M. LEWIS, C.P.C.U., Manager, The Travelers Insurance Companies, Indianapolis, Indiana

DR. HARRY J. LOMAN, President, American Institute for Property and Liability Underwriters, Inc. and President, Insurance Institute of

America, Bryn Mawr, Pennsylvania and Professor of Insurance, University of Pennsylvania, Philadelphia, Pennsylvania

DR. JOHN D. LONG, C.P.C.U., C.L.U., Professor of Insurance, Indiana University, Bloomington, Indiana

L. H. LONGLEY-COOK, F.I.A., F.C.A.S., A.S.A., Vice President-Actuary, Insurance Company of North America, Philadelphia, Pennsylvania

GERALD L. MAATMAN, Director, Department of Fire Protection and Safety Engineering, Illinois Institute of Technology, Chicago, Illinois

GUY E. MANN, C.P.C.U., Senior Vice President, Aetna Life Affiliated Companies, Hartford, Connecticut

EDWIN A. G. MANTON, President, American International Underwriters Corporation, New York, N.Y.

GEORGE M. MARSHALL, JR., Vice President, Atlantic Mutual Insurance Company and Centennial Insurance Company, New York, N.Y.

CHARLES M. MARTIN, Risk Management Counselor, New York, N.Y.

ROBERT L. MAXWELL, Vice President, The Home Insurance Company, New York, N.Y.

DR. MILTON W. MAYS, Vice President, The Continental Insurance Companies, New York, N.Y.

DWIGHT M. MCCRACKEN, Vice President & General Manager, Loss Prevention Department, Liberty Mutual Insurance Company, Boston, Massachusetts

ROY C. MCCULLOUGH, U.S. Manager, Zurich Insurance Company, Chicago, Illinois

CARL E. MCDOWELL, Executive Vice President, American Institute of Marine Underwriters, New York, N.Y.

THOMAS C. MORRILL, Vice President, State Farm Mutual Automobile Insurance Company and State Farm Fire and Casualty Company, Bloomington, Illinois

H. M. MOUNTAIN, President, Aetna Insurance Company, Hartford, Connecticut

JOSEPH M. MUIR, A.C.A.S., General Manager, Mutual Insurance Rating Bureau, New York, N.Y.

GERALD E. MYERS, C.P.C.U., Insurance Broker and Consultant, Myers-Beatty and Company, Inc., Chicago, Illinois

GEORGE W. NIXON, Vice President, Marine Office of America, New York, N.Y.

DR. GRANT M. OSBORN, C.P.C.U., C.L.U., Director of Economic Research, American Medical Association, Chicago, Illinois

DR. EDWIN S. OVERMAN, C.P.C.U., Dean, American Institute for Property and Liability Underwriters, Inc. and Dean, Insurance Institute of America, Bryn Mawr, Pennsylvania

GILBERT B. OXFORD, Vice President (Retired), Boston–Old Colony Insurance Companies, Boston, Massachusetts

ADRIAN B. PALMER, President, Rollins Burdick Hunter Company, Chicago, Illinois

JOHN C. PARISH, Secretary, St. Paul Insurance Companies, St. Paul, Minnesota

KENT H. PARKER, General Manager, Fire Insurance Research and Actuarial Association, New York, N.Y.

H. F. PERLET, JR., General Counsel, Multi-Line Insurance Rating Bureau, New York, N.Y.

JOHN D. PHELAN, C.P.C.U., President, American States Insurance Companies, Indianapolis, Indiana

M. J. PIERCE, C.P.C.U., Associate Professor of Economics, Olivet College, Olivet, Michigan

J. S. PIERINGER, JR., Vice President and Comptroller, Employers Casualty Company and Texas Employers' Insurance Association, Dallas, Texas

DAVIS T. RATCLIFFE, Insurance Instructor, Mohawk Valley Community College, Utica, N.Y.

GEORGE F. REALL, General Manager, National Council on Compensation Insurance, New York, N.Y.

WILLIAM H. RODDA, C.P.C.U., Manager, Transportation Insurance Rating Bureau, Chicago, Illinois

MATTHEW RODERMUND, F.C.A.S., Vice President-Actuary, Munich Reinsurance Company (United States Branch), New York, N.Y.

DR. WILLIS ROKES, C.P.C.U., C.L.U., Professor of Insurance, University of Omaha, Omaha, Nebraska

GEORGE F. RUTLEDGE, President, George F. Rutledge & Company, Inc., Des Moines, Iowa

LORIN K. SCHOEPHOERSTER, C.P.C.U., C.L.U., Director of Industry Relations, State Automobile Mutual Insurance Company, Columbus, Ohio

EDWIN N. SEARL, Manager, Western Actuarial Bureau, Chicago, Illinois

BRUCE SMITH, Executive Secretary, National Association of Independent Insurance Adjusters, Chicago, Illinois

HERMON D. SMITH, Chairman, Marsh & McLennan, Inc., Chicago, Illinois

ALBERT E. SPOTTKE, Vice President (Retired), Allstate Insurance Company, Skokie, Illinois

DR. ROBERT W. STRAIN, C.P.C.U., C.L.U., Dean, The College of Insurance, New York, N.Y.

WILLIAM A. STRINGFELLOW, C.P.C.U., General Manager, National Association of Mutual Insurance Agents, Washington, D.C.

W. D. SWIFT, Deputy General Adjuster, American Insurance Association, New York, N.Y.

E. ADRIAN TEAF, C.P.C.U., C.L.U., E. Adrian Teaf & Company, Inc., Philadelphia, Pennsylvania

DR. JOSEPH F. TROSPER, C.P.C.U., C.L.U., Professor of Insurance, Southern Methodist University, Dallas, Texas

WILLIAM W. WALTER, Executive Vice President, Associated Aviation Underwriters, New York, N.Y.

THOMAS E. WALTON, JR., Vice President (Deceased), Insurance Company of North America, Philadelphia, Pennsylvania

HAROLD L. WAYNE, General Manager, Inland Marine Insurance Bureau, New York, N.Y.

GEORGE V. WHITFORD, C.P.C.U., Vice President, Reliance Insurance Company, Philadelphia, Pennsylvania

DR. JAMES A. WICKMAN, C.L.U., Associate Professor of Risk and Insurance, University of Washington, Seattle, Washington

FRAZIER S. WILSON, Executive Vice President, Stewart, Smith (Illinois) Inc., Chicago, Illinois

RAYMOND M. WOOLARD, Vice President, Towers, Perrin, Forster & Crosby, Inc., Philadelphia, Pennsylvania

MILES F. YORK, President, Atlantic Mutual Insurance Company and Centennial Insurance Company, New York, N.Y.

CARROLL R. YOUNG, Vice President, The Continental Insurance Companies, New York, N.Y.

FRANK B. ZELLER, U.S. Manager (Deceased), Royal-Globe Insurance Companies, New York, N.Y.

TABLE OF CONTENTS

PART IV: INLAND MARINE INSURANCE

PART VI: MULTIPLE LINE INSURANCE

APPENDIXES

INDEXES

LIST OF ILLUSTRATIONS

Figures

Tables

PART I

Risk and Insurance

Chapter 1

INSURANCE IN SOCIETY

BY HARRY J. LOMAN

The basic role of insurance in the economic and social structure of society is to provide relief from the financial consequences of uncertainty. In turn, this relief from financial loss, and especially from fear of loss, influences the direction and magnitude of economic and social ventures. Consequently, the more subtle role of providing relief from fear of loss is perhaps the feature that has the greatest impact on society. Of course, definitive proof of this service is difficult to obtain. It has been said, however, that irrespective of one's innate capacity, courage, and drive, the constant threat of crushing economic burdens that one might incur through no fault of one's own places a limitation on one's economic independence. Insurance makes possible relief from this kind of harassing threat of financial catastrophe. These observations suggest it is no accident that the institution of insurance has attained its highest development in a society that endeavors to dignify the individual.[1]

THE CONTRIBUTIONS OF INSURANCE TO SOCIETY: A CLASSIFICATION OF THE KINDS OF EVIDENCE

Most economic endeavors are measured in terms of their input and output in physical units and dollar amounts. It is also customary to indicate the number of persons employed by the activity. Sometimes information is also supplied with reference to the impact on other segments of the economy.

This approach by itself is not suitable for an endeavor that deals primarily with intangibles; therefore, it is supplemented here. The characteristics and functions of insurance are divided into those groups which may be analyzed respectively by objective and subjective tests. Further, those yielding to objective testing are subdivided into (*a*) those

[1] These statements encompass all kinds of insurance. This *Handbook*, including the remainder of this chapter, is addressed, however, to property and liability insurance. Consequently, the ensuing discussion of insurance in society is limited accordingly.

measurable in quantitative terms, and (*b*) those provable by observable or factual tests, but not measurable in quantitative terms in the aggregate. Next, those to which subjective testing is applicable are divided according to (*a*) those services demonstrable by deductive reasoning and susceptible to analytic proof, and (*b*) those demonstrable by deductive reasoning but difficult to prove.

CHARACTERISTICS MEASURABLE IN QUANTITATIVE TERMS

The characteristics of insurance capable of being measured are those dealing with (1) the financial magnitude, (2) the number of persons employed, and (3) the dollar volume of claims.

Financial Magnitude

The financial magnitude may be expressed in terms of the assets possessed by all insurers. At the beginning of 1964 the assets of 1,177 nonlife insurance companies in the United States on which data were reported exceeded $35 billion.[2] In 1963, the earned premium income of these companies was about $16 billion. Incurred losses amounted to about $11 billion. Other important figures for 1963 for the same companies were as follows: underwriting expenses over $5 billion; underwriting loss, $157 million; and investment income, slightly under $1 billion.

A study made for the Commission on Money and Credit, published in 1962, showed that assets of the nonlife carriers increased from $400 million in 1898 to $30 billion in 1960 or at an average annual rate of increase of 6.9 percent.[3] (When adjusted to constant dollars, the average rate is 5 percent). This same study showed that the 1939 premium volume was slightly above $2 billion and the 1960 figure almost $15 billion. Since 1951 the average annual increase in premiums has been greater than the increase in the gross national product. This relationship suggests that the property-liability business is a growth industry. (See Chapter 58 for detailed tabular presentations on premium growth.)

The use of some $33 billion of assets is also of tremendous economic importance. Funds are invested in stocks and bonds of private corporations, municipal bonds, government bonds, and mortgages. Thus, insurance companies are a major source of capital funds for both industry and government.

Employment

The first detailed survey of the number of persons engaged in the insurance business was made in May, 1962, as part of the *Current Popula-*

[2] This figure and the others reported in this paragraph came from the *1964 Property Liability Insurance Index, The Spectator, Supplement,* May, 1964.

[3] *Property and Casualty Insurance Companies: Their Role as Financial Intermediaries.* (Englewood Cliffs, N.J.: Prentice-Hall, Inc., 1962.)

tion Survey sponsored by the Institute of Life Insurance.[4] This survey revealed that 1,141,000 individuals had full time positions in insurance, 440,000 of whom were engaged in "nonlife" insurance. A further breakdown of the 440,000 shows 115,000 in sales work, 180,000 in offices of companies issuing policies, 104,000 in agency and brokerage offices, and 41,000 in other offices such as rating and inspection bureaus, trade associations, and so on.

As most of the positions are clerical in nature, about one half of the total number of employees are women. The functioning of the industry, however, does require many special talents from highly skilled personnel. These specialities include lawyers, accountants, engineers, actuaries, underwriters, risk analysts, and managers. The aggregate income figures for property and liability insurance personnel are not available. The number of persons employed, however, makes such income clearly of substantial economic significance to the nation. The insurance industry enjoys an excellent reputation as a source both of exciting careers and of steady employment. Furthermore, insurance personnel in the main are exemplary citizens. Insurance persons commonly are the leaders in charitable, religious, and civic affairs, and their social consciousness is a great asset in any community.

Benefits

The amount of dollar losses incurred annually—in excess of $10 billion at the time of this writing—is the most readily available and certainly a significant measure of the direct dollar benefits derived from property-liability insurers. (Not all of the item of "losses incurred" will be paid to or on behalf of the insureds because an average of 11 to 13 percent of this figure includes the expenses of adjustment.) Another useful summary would be the number of persons who receive benefits, classified by amount received. Unfortunately, such figures are not available. Duplication presents a problem, and even if such figures were obtainable, they could lead to mistaken conclusions. For one reason, many persons never become claimants and the number and identity of those making claims vary from one year to the next. A second reason is that many people benefit indirectly. Third, the benefits derived from the *existence* of the protection may be more significant than payments.

The second and third reasons deserve further explanation. In respect to the second reason, many people are "insured indirectly." For example, the possession and use of both real and personal property without full ownership or unqualified title is ordinarily possible only because the owner, vendor, or lien-holder has been able to protect his interest with the appropriate insurance. Frequently, those who are liable to others for tort damages would be unable to respond if it were not for liability insurance.

[4] *Current Population Survey* (Washington, D.C.: U.S. Department of Commerce, Bureau of the Census, 1962).

Virtually all gainfully employed persons (and indirectly most of their dependents) are covered by workmen's compensation insurance. When these and other examples are combined, it is difficult to find a person who does not benefit in some way by insurance. (Since hospital insurance originated as a casualty line, this line too might be added to the list to support the general statement.) The third reason above deserves extended treatment. Suffice it to say, however, the knowledge that one is protected by insurance affords a peace of mind that has incalculable value.

SERVICES PROVABLE BUT NOT CURRENTLY MEASURABLE IN AGGREGATE QUANTITATIVE TERMS

Insurance renders many services to society which are not currently measurable in aggregate quantitative terms but are provable by observation or other inductive methods.

Accuracy in Predicting Production Costs

The first of these is in the field of economics. The point is that insurance enables managers to improve their accuracy in predicting costs. Writers on economic theory have given considerable attention to the matter of accuracy of production costs, especially in connection with the allocation of the various factors of production. They have given short shrift, however, to the role of insurance in increasing the accuracy of cost predictions as well as in reducing costs. Without insurance, predictions can easily go awry because the element of uncertainty is so potent a factor in any economic undertaking. To the extent that insurance is available to remove uncertainty, it makes possible the substitution of the known for the unknown. In turn this substitution enables an enterpriser to make more efficient allocation of his production facilities and reduces his liquidity needs. Contrariwise, if insurance is not available, the uncertainty may lead to a less efficient use of his capital or to the complete abandonment of the project.

Prevention of Loss

Another observable service is the prevention of loss. It is customary to classify loss prevention as one of the methods of treating risk. However, its development has been so stimulated and directed by insurers that it is appropriate to regard it as a component of the institution. This statement applies to a wide variety of loss prevention activities and not merely—as sometimes implied—to fire prevention.

Prevention of Loss by Fire. The earliest organized efforts to prevent fire losses seem to have been through governmental regulation affecting physical property that contributed to loss. However, the first fire insurance companies stimulated and supported those efforts and thereby improved structural conditions and the quality of protective devices. Some of the early companies also organized fire fighting activities. The active role of the National Board of Fire Underwriters [5] in (1) formulating building codes, (2) recommending standards and specifications for materials and processes, (3) grading cities and towns according to fire defense and physical conditions, (4) investigating arson and incendiarism, (5) compiling statistics of causes of fire losses, (6) making municipal surveys of fire-danger characteristics, (7) providing inspection services, (8) supplying educational material on prevention, (9) engaging in research in this area, and (10) aiding others in their efforts to prevent fire loss is a matter of record for nearly a century. The services of the Underwriters' Laboratories, Inc., in testing with respect to dangerous characteristics of all kinds of materials, substances, and devices, are widely available. The Engineering Division of the Associated Factory Mutuals Insurance Companies has pioneered in industrial direct damage loss prevention and its *Handbook of Industrial Loss Prevention* is a masterpiece. It also conducts plant inspections, recommends standards for materials and protection, and conducts a testing laboratory. The Federation of Mutual Fire Insurance Companies also conducts a fire prevention division with similar activities.

Safety at Sea. The entire maritime industry is served by the safety engineering and loss prevention activities of specialized organizations created and/or sponsored by the insurance industry. Of special significance in this field are the inspection and survey facilities of the United States Salvage Association. This organization reviews architects' plans for hulls, inspects their construction and launching, makes surveys afloat and recommendations for changes that will help to avoid or prevent a loss of property and person. Prevention of loss of cargo through fire, theft, and pilferage is expertly handled by a special committee of the American Institute of Marine Underwriters. This same Institute also makes available its engineering and inspection facilities for terminal operators, stevedores, and repairmen. The engineering inspection services of individual insurance companies are also used extensively for loss prevention purposes in all phases of the maritime industry.

Industrial Safety. Despite the fact the first industrial safety measures were legislative actions providing for factory inspections regarding dangerous machines, much of the broad scale development in industrial safety has been inspired and directed by insurers. The work of the accident prevention department of the Association of Casualty and Surety Companies has won international acclaim and its *Handbook of Industrial*

[5] As of December 31, 1964, the National Board of Fire Underwriters and the Association of Casualty and Surety Companies were merged into the American Insurance Association. The merger reflects the movement of the industry toward multiple line underwriting. In subsequent pages of this *Handbook* many references are made to the work of these organizations. Because the "pre-merger" names are familiar, the references are to the National Board of Fire Underwriters and the Association of Casualty and Surety Companies.

Safety Standards is regarded as an authoritative guide for industrial accident prevention. In 1937 the Association of Casualty and Surety Companies (see footnote 5) absorbed the safety functions of the National Bureau of Casualty and Surety Underwriters which was a successor organization to the "Workmen's Compensation Service and Information Bureau." The latter had been organized by stock insurance carriers in 1910. As early as 1913 this Bureau had developed a volume on *Universal Safety Standards*. Further evidence of the early and continuing role of insurers in industrial accident prevention is found in the Liability Conference of 1896, from which grew the National Workmen's Compensation Service Bureau. This Service Bureau, which is now the Accident Prevention Department of the Association of Casualty and Surety Companies, established a center for safety education at New York University. The Association of Casualty and Surety Companies also vigorously promotes and supports nonindustrial accident prevention. Numerous individual stock and mutual insurers have also made significant contributions.

Highway Safety. The "Highway Safety Action Program" of 1946 was brought into being through the assistance of insurance personnel. In 1959 three of the trade associations representing the major portion of the property-liability companies established an "Insurance Institute for Highway Safety." (They are the Association of Casualty and Surety Companies, the American Mutual Insurance Alliance, and the National Association of Independent Insurers.) This institute initiates, stimulates, and coordinates activities in this field and gives direct financial and technical assistance (1) to carry out balanced traffic safety programs and (2) to promote citizen safety organizations which support the safety program. Among those receiving such aid are: Northwestern University Traffic Institute, American Association of Motor Vehicle Administrators, the National Safety Council, the American Bar Association, the International Association of Chiefs of Police, and the New York University Center for Safety Education. In addition, the Institute has sponsored the National High School Driver Education Award Program.

Medical Rehabilitation. Although insurers did not supply the original impetus to medical rehabilitation, it seems likely that insurance will become the galvanizing force in bringing rehabilitation to a high level of development just as it has in fire prevention, highway safety, and industrial accident prevention. Like other areas of loss reduction, medical rehabilitation provides economic interest to insurers because it reduces insurance losses. This fact was realized by workmen's compensation insurers many years ago. Some of the insurance companies were stimulated to do valuable pioneer work in devising ways of restoring the physically disabled. The American Mutual Insurance Alliance has been outstanding in continuously giving encouragement and support, not only to the economic but also to the humanitarian aspects of rehabilitation. It has been instrumental in popularizing rehabilitation as the restoration of the physically disabled to their place in society. It emphasizes the basic philosophy behind this objective as being the maintenance of the dignity and self-respect of man. As mentioned elsewhere in this chapter, this point should be stressed as a major service rendered by all insurance to society.

Credit Transactions

Insurance has sometimes been called the *sine qua non* of credit transactions. Bankers and other lenders will not loan money on destructible property without insurance protection. In the absence of insurance there would be little or no private financing of homes, automobiles, business properties, merchandise, airplanes, vessels, cargoes, and so forth. The financial world as known today would cease to exist. This illustration points up the fact that insurance performs its services so subtly and silently that proper appreciation of it is possible only if the service is withdrawn.

Public and Private Finance

The service of insurance extends to the field of finance. Insurance companies constitute one of the nation's most important types of institutional investors. This fact comes about primarily through the normal operation of the insurance device which collects in advance from the many who are exposed to risk and accumulates funds to pay the losses of the few that will occur later. In addition, capital and surplus of insurance companies are also substantial. These large funds are invested in public and private security issues, mortgages, and certain other properties, thereby aiding both government and industry.

SERVICES AND RELATIONSHIPS SUSCEPTIBLE TO INDUCTIVE PROOF AND DEDUCTIVE REASONING

Services and relationships under this heading are divided into three main categories as follows: (1) those that have an influence on economic progress; (2) those that have an impact on and a relationship to important areas of the social sciences; and (3) those dealing with the impact of insurance on and relationship with other areas of knowledge. In turn each of these divisions will be subdivided.

Influence on Economic Progress

Large Capital Ventures. Even the largest corporations transfer the bulk of their known insurable risks of any great size to insurers, thereby enabling them to concentrate their specialized talents and skills on the main objectives of their respective enterprises. Of course many of them deliberately assume risk of loss from a variety of hazards, but usually to an extent that is directly commensurate with their financial ability to absorb such losses. However, if they use credit (and the launching of a large capital venture almost invariably requires credit), they are not likely to have any choice because the lenders seldom deviate from their standard practice of demanding insurance. Therefore, it may be concluded that without insurance many planned large ventures would never get started or would be hindered in growth.

Small Capital Ventures. For the small capital ventures, insurance is even more important because the financial margin in these cases is likely to be so slender that assumption of minor risk may be too dangerous, relatively. Then, too, in such cases the lenders of capital are likely to be strict about enforcing their insurance standards.

Individual and Family Units. On account of the relatively greater catastrophe hazard to the small unit or limited exposure, insurance reaches its maximum importance with respect to individuals and family units. Those who have acquired property and responsibility tend to think of this point. Those who wish to avoid worry about a hampering or staggering loss recognize that insurance is indispensable. In addition, individuals and families wishing to use credit to help in their property purchases must insure to satisfy their creditors. The number of family units involved in credit transactions is huge. The 1960 Census of Housing reported 27,862,000 dwelling unit properties of which 15,816,000, or over 56 percent, were mortgaged.[6] In early 1964 consumer installment credit amounted to close to $57 billion.[7] Without insurance these financed purchases would have been impossible.

Interrelationship of Insurance with Other Areas of the Social Sciences

Most persons tend to regard insurance like any service institution, to be used or ignored at will. Seldom is any thought given to its close relationship with other areas of knowledge and action. Nevertheless its extensive ramifications and complications have caused it to be a major influence on many other areas and they in turn have had an impact on it.

Law. One of the best examples of an important interrelationship is found between insurance and law. The writings and discussions on law as related to insurance usually emphasize the fact that law provides the rules and guidelines within which insurance must be conducted. This function of law, of course, extends to all of society's activities. Rules of law cannot be established in a vacuum. Moreover, those interested in the development and preservation of the institution of insurance have made efforts to influence the adoption of rules of law that will aid the functioning of insurance.

[6] *Census of Housing—1960* (Washington, D.C.: U.S. Department of Commerce, Bureau of the Census), Vol. 5, Part 1.

[7] *Survey of Current Business,* Vol. 44 (July, 1964), p. 17.

Inasmuch as the insurance transaction possesses perhaps more distinctive and unusual characteristics than do most other contractual arrangements, it has been involved in the development of many legal doctrines. The point is not that these legal doctrines or concepts originated in insurance but rather that their development has been closely related to the development and use of insurance. In fact, much of their prominence is due to insurance. To name a few: the doctrine of proximate cause, the principle of indemnity, the law of negligence, the doctrine of waiver and estoppel, the effect of warranties and concealment, and the "utmost good faith" doctrine.

The uniqueness of the insurance contract has had a profound impact on legal decisions affecting contract interpretation. This may be attributed to the concurrent existence of the following characteristics. First, even though the insurance coverage may be on tangible property, the contract is personal in nature and is entered into in the utmost good faith by both parties. Second, the contract wording is normally determined by one party, namely, the insurer. Third, the contract is also one-sided in the sense of legal obligation, that is, if the insured has paid the premium, only the insurer has legally enforceable promises to perform (the insured, however, may have to comply with "conditions" in order to enforce the promises of the insurer). Fourth, the contract contains an element of chance because the insurer may become obligated to pay anything from a nominal amount to an enormous sum. Fifth, since the contract is completed only when it expires or all obligations are discharged, it is executory in nature. Such an unusual combination of contractual characteristics requires a variation from the customary rulings and stimulates legal exceptions.

Business Administration. Business executives are fully aware of the availability of insurance to meet some of their risk problems. Top administrators frequently regard the practice of insurance as so specialized and technical that they tend to delegate the responsibility to technicians, but risk and its treatment is properly an area for top-level decisions. As the hazards of the atomic energy and space age multiply and insurance coverages are broadened, more attention is focused on the need for identification and evaluation of risk. Therefore, the modern executive is now aware that he must have a knowledge of the field sufficient at least to evaluate the recommendations of the technicians. The full impact of this change has not yet been felt. However, the alert officials of numerous colleges and universities which prepare persons for business administration are revising their instruction to meet the need.

Insurance had long been referred to as the "handmaiden of commerce." Even though domestic and international trade developed side by side with insurance, this hackneyed phrase grossly understates the case. In the absence of insurance, privately financed international and much local commerce as now conducted, would cease. The enormous value of loaded vehicles or hull and cargo in a single risk produce a catastrophe hazard that can be met only by special and complicated arrangements. Treaty reinsurance of the automatic variety is a common protection answer to the unavoidable concentrations of excessive amounts at risk.

Government Administration. Government administration as related to insurance has three facets: (1) the need for supervision and regulation of a privately rendered technical service which is indispensable to the public; (2) the administration of government operated insurance plans; and (3) the statutory and judicial requirements for certain hazards to be covered by insurance or bonds. Consequently, government administration of insurance is a complex matter ranging from the conduct of individuals to that of large corporations, from the achievement of broad social purposes to minor technicalities, and from the local to the international level. The variety and complexity of the problems encountered in this maze provides a constant source of new examples and new ideas in government administration.

Behavioristic Sciences. It may seem trite to observe that insurance is a potent factor in human behavior because it relieves one from worry and provides peace of mind. However, this relief is the essential link of insurance to the behavioristic sciences. Reaction to risk in situations that can be insured as contrasted with those where insurance cannot be made available affords an excellent area for psychological study and experiment. At the same time these psychological aspects of economic behavior can be of great value in helping to determine the mental health aspects of fear and worry. In recent years, worry has been given much of the blame for our physical ailments, deficiencies, and complaints. The use of insurance also causes the distribution of a society's income to be different from what would otherwise be the case. This point has numerous behavioristic implications.

Relationship of Insurance to Other Areas of Knowledge

The Humanities. Insurance is so commonly considered a prosaic type of business that its association with the humanities is seldom mentioned. Despite this neglect insurance has afforded literature, history, and ethics with some of their choicest illustrations. For example the early marine policy contained quaint wording that packed concisely and precisely in a few paragraphs such meaningful words and phrases that it is truly a literary document. Insurance has often been the basis for intricate, dramatic, and colorful stories. These vary greatly from crimes of arson, bombing, scuttling, and murder with a motive of defrauding insurers, to large payments by insurers to restore handicapped persons to their place in society.

Historical illustrations of the use of the insurance principle go back to Babylonian times when merchants' representatives conveying merchandise to distant lands were relieved of responsibility for the merchandise in their possession if it was lost due to a specified casualty for which they were not to blame. This same release principle enabled the Greeks and Phoenicians to undertake ventures by sea that otherwise would not have occurred or would have been long delayed.

United States history has had dramatic moments when decisive actions were determined by the availability of insurance, especially with reference to marine ventures at the outbreak of a war.

The "utmost good faith doctrine" that is so important in insurance law has blazed a way to higher standards of ethical conduct in business relations generally.

Engineering. The best known contact of insurance with the physical sciences is probably through loss prevention engineering. The loss and damage potential arising from design of structures, the quality and properties of materials, and construction methods must be known by insurers in order to determine the acceptability of, and the rates for, specific risks seeking insurance protection. Hence the need for a testing service such as the Underwriters' Laboratories, Inc., the engineering departments of insurance companies, and other similar organizations referred to in another portion of this chapter. Equally important are the model building codes of the National Board of Fire Underwriters and their essential safety features for school buildings, hospitals, and such; the material and processing guides of the National Fire Protection Association; and the guides for fire-protective devices such as the well-known automatic sprinkler system.

Illustrations of the role of insurance with respect to activities that possess loss or damage potential are countless. An understanding of them is found in the physical sciences. One of the most publicized examples in recent years deals with nuclear energy. As new types of hazards appear, insurers take an active part in attempting to understand them and aid in developing the appropriate protective and safety devices. Uses of the facilities made available by the insurance companies and their service organizations are authentic and comprehensive. It is an unwise regional planner, architect, manufacturer, or processor who does not make extensive use of these facilities.

The Medical Sciences. The medical sciences are usually more closely associated with life insurance than with nonlife insurance. Workmen's compensation and health, however, are two important exceptions. Reducing claims for medical care and disability have stimulated insurers to investigate and act with respect to the causes and remedies for all kinds of disabling injuries and diseases. As mentioned earlier, insurers have been among the primary agencies and motivators of medical rehabilitation.

Researching and solving the problems of life and health preservation and conservation are an over-expanding area of insurance participation and leadership.

Mathematics and Statistics. Mathematicians and statisticians have found insurance a fertile field for the application and development of their theories and techniques. It is well known that the practicability of the insurance device rests upon the mathematical law of large numbers, which is a subdivision of the theory of probability. While this development may seem simple, it actually is quite complicated, partly because the central problem of pricing (ratemaking) in insurance is complicated by two factors: (1) law requires that the rates be adequate, reasonable, and not unfairly discriminatory; and (2) there must be responsiveness to changing conditions because the risks assumed by insurers are not static. Therefore satisfactory statistical sampling that will enable the actuary to apply probability mathematics so as to produce tolerable credibility in his results is a delicate and sophisticated task. Insurance, mathematics, and statistics derive reciprocal benefit from this situation.

SERVICES WHICH CAN BE SHOWN BY DEDUCTIVE REASONING BUT WHICH ARE DIFFICULT TO PROVE IN QUANTITATIVE TERMS

It is not always easy or even possible to produce quantitative evidence of some of the things one firmly believes. Some of the services of insurance are in this category. For example, one of the prime goals of democracy is "equal opportunity" for all citizens. Without the services of insurance this goal is very difficult, if not impossible, to attain.

The preservation of the institution of private property as inherent in the American way of life is possible only if the great majority of citizens can participate in it. If everyone must wait until he has accumulated sufficient cash to share in the ownership of property, the long wait becomes so discouraging that the desire withers. When the risk factors that would prevent financing can be met by insurance, a desire for ownership can be satisfied at the time when it will be most beneficial. The force and significance of this accomplishment may be appreciated more by a comparison of the situation in this country with that of some other countries having an economic philosophy different from the one in this country. In the countries where the masses own little or nothing, government ownership flourishes and dictators control.

Release from worry and fear has been discussed in an earlier section because of its relationship to the behavioristic sciences. It may be classified appropriately also under the heading of this section because it is so commonly appraised through deductive reasoning. On the other hand, proof in quantitative terms is difficult to obtain. Fortunately, this difficulty does not detract from convictions arrived at by logical reasoning.

TREND

In the preceding sections an attempt has been made to show that insurance has been indispensably interwoven into the fabric of a free society. Its essential qualities stem from the fact that in the normal course of human and business affairs there is no identifiable, single, disruptive factor that is more pervasive and at the same time more important than the element of uncertainty. If there is any other element which vitally affects and frequently even dominates decision making to so great an extent, it has not been recognized. Therefore, the rate of progress in the world of business and social affairs is dependent on ways and means of dealing with uncertainty. The function of insurance is to deal with uncertainty.

The various activities of insurers as described in this chapter show how they have performed, inspired, aided, and led, in treating risk by methods that go far beyond the formal definition of insurance. The trend is toward risk and its treatment as an entity. This evolution is rational. As its impact on, and relationship to, other areas of knowledge become better delineated and understood, its guiding principles will be more clearly identified and firmly established. The anatomy of risk will then achieve status as a distinctive discipline. In this atmosphere of an emerging science many ambitious persons with courage and vision will find an opportunity for an exciting career.

SUGGESTED READINGS

Insurance Facts. New York: Insurance Information Institute, 1964.

Magee, John H., and Bickelhaupt, David L. *General Insurance.* 7th ed. Homewood, Ill.: Richard D. Irwin, Inc., 1964. Chap. 2.

Mayerson, Allen L. *Introduction to Insurance.* New York: Macmillan Co., 1962. Chaps. 2, 3.

Chapter 2

RISK AND INSURANCE THEORY

BY JOHN D. LONG

No subject matter is ultimately any stronger or more useful than its underlying theoretical base. The theory developed to date for risk and insurance has numerous dimensions. Some of the theory is fairly precise; other parts of it are still discouragingly vague. Some of the theory relates to risk; other parts to insurance, per se.

Several entire books are devoted primarily to expositions of risk and insurance theory. Numerous insurance textbooks have one or more chapters which treat the "nature of risk and insurance."

This chapter is aimed toward a brief sketch of some of the rudiments of this theory. No particular effort is made here to extend the theory or take issue with it. Rather, the effort is primarily descriptive. The first of the two major sections in this chapter is devoted to a discussion of "risk" in the abstract. Definition of risk, origin of risk, and ways of handling risk are described in turn. The second of the two major sections is addressed to insurance theory.

RISK

"Risk" may well be the most heavily used word in insurance terminology. It is traditionally referred to as the "raw material" of insurance. It is thought of as the base on which the mechanism of insurance squarely rests. It is a "proper" topic for inclusion in a discussion of insurance fundamentals. Yet, there is no widespread agreement as to the meaning of the word. A variety of meanings is imputed. Worse yet, the word is often used in contexts where its meaning is decidedly obscure. Moreover, scholars do not agree among themselves on its reason for being, on what happens to risk when it is treated in any one of several ways, or on the relative social desirability of the several methods of risk treatment.

Concept of Loss

Before definitions of risk are presented, attention is given to the meaning of "loss." This preliminary excursion is necessary because the concept of loss figures so prominently in the several definitions of risk cited.

The meaning of "loss" is not entirely clear. There seems to be little argument that the word refers to the failure on the part of some person, group, organization, or other entity to retain some thing/s in the possession of such entity. For example, a person "loses" his money or a corporation "loses" its franchises. Presumably—but not necessarily—that which was lost had value. Such a presumption becomes a bit shaky, however, when one considers that a tree is said to "lose" its leaves in the fall and a baby duck to "lose" its down. Perhaps "lose" is a poor choice for these two processes. Perhaps loss should be restricted to lack of retention of something of value.

Another interesting complication is what, if anything, a person "loses" if he fails to take advantage of some possibility of gaining had he but followed a particular course. As an illustration, does one lose by failing to buy a given stock when its price is advancing at a time when he had the ability to make the purchase had he felt so inclined?

Still another complication involves expectations. Suppose that Mr. *A* and Mr. *B* agree that *A* will toss a coin and that if it lands on heads *A* will pay *B* \$100 and that if it lands on tails *A* will not pay *B* \$100. Suppose further that *B* is obliged to do nothing for *A*. If *A* tosses the coin and if it does land on tails, the question arises as to whether or not *B* has lost anything. Apparently, he is as well off as before entering the agreement with *A*. One might say, however, that at some point he possessed something of value, namely, the expected value of the gift from *A*. Assuming a fair coin, this value is \$50 (\$100 × .5 probability). With the outcome of the toss, he no longer has this expectation. Many readers, however, may not feel convinced that *B* really suffered a loss. At least they may feel that this situation is significantly different from the one where *B* actually possesses \$50 and loses the whole sum on the fall of a coin. The example is a bit confusing in raising the point about losing an expectation. Still, it does show that risk theory is complicated by the fact that the meaning of loss, itself, is not precisely clear.

The most common meaning attributed to this concept (loss) in the context of risk seems to ignore expectation. Loss generally is thought of as failure to retain possession and enjoyment of something of value. This way of regarding loss, however, does not fit precisely with business interruption insurance. Still, it is close enough to be useful.

Definitions of Risk

The word "risk" is often used to refer to the object of insurance. In subsequent chapters of this *Handbook* this usage is quite common. In this chapter, however, the focus is conceptual and on risk in the abstract. Several different ways of thinking about risk are now reviewed.

Chance of Loss. One short and straightforward definition is simply that risk is "chance of loss." Whether or not there is chance of gain is irrelevant to the existence of risk under this definition (more about this point below). The idea embodied in this concept is that the loss may occur or may not occur and that the outcome is purely fortuitous. Fortuity, in turn, connotes an absence of cause and effect or at least discernible cause and effect. A difficulty with this definition is the ambiguity in the phenomenon of chance. No matter how chance is described, it is a fuzzy concept. According to some points of view, it does not exist at all.

Chance of Gain or Loss. An interesting variation is the definition that risk is a chance of gain or loss. In this way of looking at risk, chance becomes two-dimensional, capable of producing gain as well as loss. Acceptance of this definition—as in the case of the previous definition—depends in part on one's attitude toward the existence of chance.

Risk is often classified to take into account whether or not a gain is possible. Under the usual terminology, risk characterized by both chance of gain and chance of loss is said to be "speculative," whereas risk characterized only by chance of loss is said to be "pure." Insurance traditionally has been associated with pure risk only. On the other hand, normal entrepreneurial risks are thought of as being speculative, carrying both the chance of gain and the chance of loss.

This definition and any other one which embodies the concept of a gain raises a question comparable to the one considered in the section on *Concept of Loss.* The meaning of "gain" is as troublesome as the meaning of loss. The general idea is that one gains when he comes into possession and/or control of something he wants. An abstruse point which clouds the concept a bit, however, is whether or not one gains when he successfully avoids a course of action which would have stripped him of that which he cherishes. For example, does one gain by *not* buying a share of stock before its value declines? Since no "expectation" in the usual sense of the word is involved here, the general approach in much of risk theory is to ignore such considerations.

Uncertainty as to Loss. On another tack, one widely circulated definition simply provides that risk is uncertainty as to loss. While this definition obviates the complexities of chance, it raises questions about the nature of uncertainty. Most of those who have defined risk in this fashion have been vague as to the meaning of uncertainty. The implication is that uncertainty involves an ignorance about whether or not loss will occur—a general feeling of uneasiness and apprehension. The precise meaning intended, however, is not clear at all.

Allen H. Willett (a pioneering student of risk and insurance of an earlier generation) considered uncertainty as being related to risk. He said specifically that risk is the "objective correlative" of subjective uncertainty.[1] He discusses uncertainty as being a psychological influence and implies that it is somehow measurable in degrees. The degree of uncer-

[1] See Allen H. Willett, *The Economic Theory of Risk and Insurance* (Philadelphia: University of Pennsylvania Press, 1951), especially Chapter 1.

tainty in respect to a particular outcome of a given event, however, is not the same in the Willett concept as the degree of probability. He refers to the latter, by the way, as a chance. Uncertainty in his scheme is such that its degree is the highest when the chances are even, that is, when the probability of a particular outcome is one half. Willett makes a point of emphasizing that risk is a condition of the "external" world. He proceeds in somewhat confusing fashion, however, to refer to risk as embodying a degree of uncertainty.

Degree of Probability. Risk, instead of being thought of as the degree of uncertainty about a loss, can be defined as the degree of probability (whether calculable or not) that a loss will occur. Irving Pfeffer takes this position, for example, in suggesting:

> Risk is a combination of hazards and is measured by probability; uncertainty is measured by a degree of belief. Risk is a state of the world; uncertainty is a state of mind.[2]

Calculable Loss Probability. Still another way of regarding risk is to consider it as a condition embracing all loss possibilities where the probabilities are calculable. In this sense risk is not so much a degree of probability of a particular outcome of a given event as a condition where the probability can be calculated.

Back in 1921, Frank H. Knight published his *Risk, Uncertainty, and Profit.*[3] In this treatise he took the position that outcomes of some types of events are calculable while outcomes of other types of events are not. He said in effect that where the outcomes are calculable (that is, where probabilities are known or can be assumed) the situation involves risk. Such events generally are subject to actuarial treatment, according to Knight, and lend themselves to insurance. For many other types of events Knight said that there was no way meaningfully to calculate probable outcomes. These events, he said, are characterized by uncertainty. (Note that this distinction is much different from saying that risk is the degree of uncertainty as to loss and is also much different from the Pfeffer distinction where risk is thought of as being objective and uncertainty as being subjective.)

Knight's risk-uncertainty dichotomy is currently used in much of the modern literature on decision making.[4] Choice among courses of action whose alternative outcomes are subject to probability estimates is defined as decision making under risk. Where the alternative outcomes are not subject to probability estimates the decision making is said to be under

[2] Irving Pfeffer, *Insurance and Economic Theory* (Homewood, Ill.: Richard D. Irwin, Inc., 1956), p. 42. Dr. Pfeffer's excellent book should be placed high on the reading list of anyone seriously interested in risk and insurance.

[3] (Boston: Houghton Mifflin Co., 1921.) See especially Chapters 1 and 2.

[4] See, for example, Duncan Luce and Howard Raiffa, *Games and Decisions* (New York: John Wiley & Sons, Inc., 1958), p. 13.

uncertainty. The diagram in Figure 2–1 may be sufficient to make the distinction clear.

If probabilities can be meaningfully assigned to w, x, y, and z, then the decision-making situation is said to be one of risk. If no probabilities can be meaningfully assigned to w, x, y, and z, the decision-making situation is said to fall in the realm of uncertainty. Insurance in this type of classification obviously is restricted to events involving risk. In fact, one of Knight's purposes in his presentation was to suggest that losses subject to calculable frequencies should be handled by insurance, while losses under uncertainties involved threats to entrepreneurs. These threats, in turn, justified, he suggested, the entrepreneurs' claims to the profits of enterprise as reward for "uncertainty bearing." He emphasized that the contractual claims of others on the income might well mean that no residue for profit would be left.

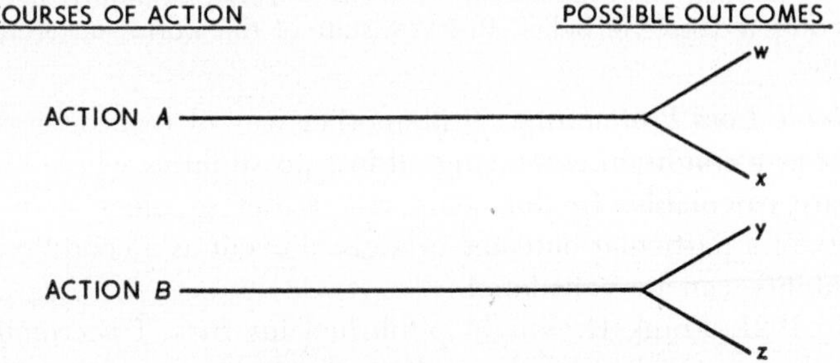

FIG. 2–1. Risk and uncertainty in decision making.

Possibility of Loss. Another way of defining risk is to say that it is simply possibility of loss. Under this definition no attention is given to probability, so long as it is not zero. This probability may range from any value larger than zero to one. At one, loss is certain. When this type of definition is used, one cannot properly say that one situation has more risk than another. A given situation either involves risk or it does not. Risk under this definition is absolute and not susceptible to degree. When risk is defined in this way, some risk situations are subject to insurance, while others are not.

Ignorance as to Loss. An allied definition is the one which stipulates that risk is merely ignorance as to loss. The idea is that, if one does not know whether or not loss will occur in a given time period, he faces risk—regardless of the reason for his ignorance and regardless of what the facts as to loss occurrence may turn out to be. This definition is quite compatible with the concepts of predestination and an ordered universe. It also lends itself quite handily to degrees—the greater the ignorance, the higher the risk. It is quite different from the Knight definition. Whereas Knight limits risk to the realm of calculability, risk under the definition in this paragraph (ignorance as to loss) extends to a complete ignorance of the probabilities of loss and includes the area Knight labeled as uncertainty. This view is similar but not identical to that of regarding risk as uncertainty where uncertainty is defined as an attitude.

Probability Distribution. While numerous other definitions could be added to the list, only one more is suggested here. Risk can be thought of as the distribution of probabilities around a mean. Numerous variations of this idea can be constructed.

One approach is to consider the probability distribution as being reflected by the actual distribution of losses in some recent period.[5] Another is to attempt to arrive at the probability distribution empirically or otherwise and set it up as follows: Suppose that in a certain community there are 10,000 houses. For simplicity, suppose further that they are all of a given size and type of construction and that the only fire losses which occur are total losses. Let the probability of none of the houses burning be p_0; the probability of one house burning be p_1; the probability of two houses burning be p_2; and so on until the probability of 10,000 houses

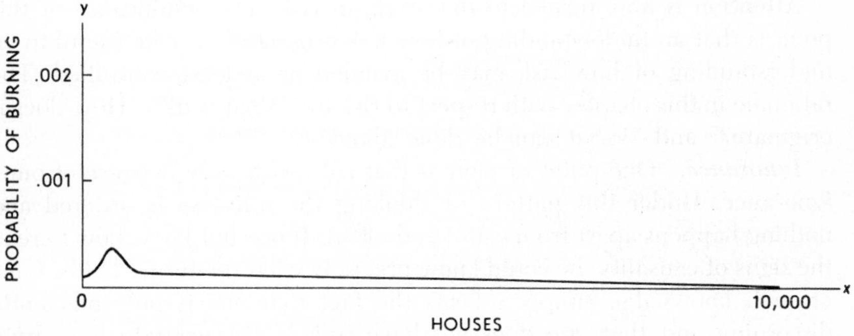

FIG. 2–2. Illustrative loss probability distribution.

burning in the given time period is denoted as $p_{10{,}000}$. Let these probability values be plotted on a graph where the y axis is probability and the x axis is the number of houses. While the shape of the resulting curve depends, of course, on the probabilities assigned, one possible shape (where the curve is *very* close to the x axis as it moves to the right) is shown in Figure 2–2.

For the sake of the discussion here, the shape of the curve is not crucial. The point is that risk is conceived as being reflected by the extent to which the curve is "spread out." The more dispersed the values in the probability distribution, the greater the risk involved in the situation. The same sort of reasoning would apply to the probability distribution built

[5] See, for example, David B. Houston, "The Effectiveness of Rating Classifications," *Journal of Insurance*, Vol. XXVIII (June, 1961), pp. 83–86.

on the basis of actual claims as mentioned above. Readers familiar with statistical terms may be interested in noting that a common measure of dispersion used for the purpose of assessing the degree of risk is the standard deviation. When it can be expressed in this fashion, risk is subject to quantification.

Choice of Definition. When several definitions of risk are offered, the natural question to arise is: "Which one should be used?" The answer can only be that the definition to use is the one which best fits the purpose for using a definition in the first place. Pragmatism—not eternal verity—is the test.

Most traditional insurance theory does not seem to be finely enough developed to require one of the definitions as opposed to the others. In fact, the theory is limited by the very fuzziness of the concept of risk. Many of the writings on insurance theory, however, seem to imply that risk is chance of loss. The probability distribution concept of risk is being used with increasing frequency.

Origin of Risk

Attention is now turned to the origin of risk. The significance of this point is that an understanding of how risk originates may be useful to an understanding of how risk may be avoided or at least controlled. The rationale in this chapter with respect to risk is: "What is it?", "How does it originate?" and "What can be done about it?"

Ignorance. One point of view is that risk exists only because of one's ignorance. Under this pattern of thinking the universe is ordered and nothing happens apart from cause-and-effect. If one but knew how to read the signs of causality, he could know precisely what the future holds. Lack of such knowledge simply reflects the fact that one is not sufficiently discerning and that one does not have sufficiently accurate measuring instruments. Risk exists not because of chance but simply because of ignorance.

This general idea of determinism has been very important over the years in the realm of science. In terms of motion, for example, the premise has been that the position and velocity of a body could be determined precisely if man only knew how to devise instruments which were calibrated finely enough. Precise determination of position and velocity presumably would permit precise and accurate prediction of future position and velocity. In a larger sense this sort of measurement would permit one to perceive fully the future and thus to eliminate risk. The continued existence of risk under this concept is, therefore, attributable to ignorance. The key to treatment of risk is through minimization of ignorance. As a case in point, an assumption made in classical economics in respect to perfect competition is that perfect knowledge exists. The result is that there is no risk in this model.

The idea of determinism may strike some readers as preposterous. Determinism, however, has been and still is a prominent concept in science, religion, philosophy, and other facets of life.

Chance. An altogether different approach to the origin of risk lies in the concept of chance—or fortuity. The phenomenon of chance has confounded man from the beginning. It has caused him to be superstitious, bold, reckless, and conservative all at the same time. On the one hand, it has provoked him to entreat the favor of "Lady Luck" and other apparitions. On the other, it has lent itself with much respectability to the concept of randomness and has thus paved the way for statistical inference and other important statistical tools.

One interesting way to contemplate chance is through the work of a twentieth century physicist, Werner Von Heisenberg. He and others formulated the "principle of uncertainty." (There is that troublesome word again.) Von Heisenberg in working on the quantum theory of matter proved to the satisfaction of his colleagues that a particle of matter does not have a position and velocity determinable simultaneously. Further, the indeterminability exists not because of the absence of sensitive measuring instruments. This indeterminability, rather, stems from the realization that a particle of matter does not have *simultaneously* a position and a velocity. Further, the very attempt to ascertain position or velocity disturbs what would otherwise have been the case and the direction and magnitude of the disturbance may be indeterminate. Put in other words, the measuring process, itself, alters the situation and defeats any effort at perfect measurement and prediction.

The result in the terminology developed in this chapter is that under this viewpoint risk originates in the very nature of things—and not merely through ignorance. No matter how intelligent and perceiving one might be and no matter how finely graduated his measuring instruments, he still could not know and predict because there is no way of knowing what is to happen until it happens. Outcomes may be fortuitous.

One interesting way to sum up the point is to use the colorful example cited a number of years ago by another famous physicist and philosopher.[6] He said in effect that when "a cat looks at a king" the flow of events is indeterminately altered compared to what it would have been otherwise. A comparable illustration can be drawn from the insurance world. It goes as follows: risk can never be eliminated under this viewpoint because the very act of gathering and publishing statistics may alter the loss circumstances compared to what they would have been without the statistical effort.

This explanation may not strike some readers as being any more plausible than the determinism explanation. Nevertheless, it is an

[6] Percy W. Bridgman, "The New Vision of Science," *Harper's Monthly Magazine*, Vol. 158 (March, 1929), pp. 443–51.

alternative explanation of how risk originates. It is useful as a theoretical support for insurance.

Other Comments. Two other concepts are often recognized as being closely related to the origin of risk. Although neither embodies an approach which is necessarily different from determinism or chance as already discussed, these concepts help explain why losses (and gains) occur.

1. *Change.* The first of these two is the concept of change. In a static state, risk—by any definition set forth in this chapter—does not exist. In the pure sense loss can occur only when change takes place. In fact, to say that no change occurs in a static state of affairs is a tautology. In any case, recognition of this point is helpful to an understanding of risk.

2. *Conflict of Interest.* The second of the two concepts is conflict of interest. In respect to virtually any event preferences as to outcome may vary among human beings interested in the event. Commonly, these interests are in conflict. When one or more such persons can exercise partial—but not complete—control over the outcome of the event, risk is present. Whether a loss may occur because of ignorance (determinism) or because of chance (Heisenberg's "principle of uncertainty"), the conflict of interests may introduce numerous additional variables.

Conflict-of-interest situations form the basis for the intriguing study of game theory and several other modern decision theory techniques which also involve absence of certainty.[7] These situations arise in many an insurance context, such as the development of a liability or dishonesty claim or the occurrence of a partial fire loss stemming from arson. Other insurance losses, however, are more nearly "conflicts with nature." Examples are earthquake, flood, or wind losses.

Ways of Treating Risk

The critically important question concerning risk is what to do about it. Only a brief summary of a few of the answers to this question is presented here.

Retention. Perhaps the most common treatment of risk is a passive one under which the individual or group exposed to the risk simply bears it. Sometimes the word "assumption" or the expression "self-assumption" is applied. Since an individual already may be exposed and merely continues in the exposure, retention is perhaps a safer and often a more accurate word. The retention may be by choice or for want of any alternative possibility of risk treatment.

Very little theoretical work has been published on the rationale of risk retention by choice—especially of retention of insurable risks. There are numerous assertions in the literature that generally risk is repugnant or at

[7] Linear programing, on the other hand, involves no uncertainty as to the outcome of alternative courses of action.

least not usually preferred over certainty. The strength of this preference and the precise conditions under which it holds are not known. Furthermore, as many writers point out, many people under various circumstances court risk—pure as well as speculative. Any variety of "Russian roulette" is a case in point.

Many aspects of risk bearing have not been clarified. The question, for example, as to how far one should go in committing some of his assets to the protection of his remaining assets is fundamental. Yet there does not seem to be any objective answer. The question put another way is: How far should an individual or an organization (such as a business firm) go in spending money on insurance premiums? In respect to premiums for a single line or to premiums in the aggregate *some* amount is too much. The determination of the amount is the key matter which needs attention.

In short, some risk is retained because it has to be, while other risk is retained because retention is a more desirable treatment than any alternative course of action. The "rub" is that risk theory is weak on the latter point.

Elimination of Loss Possibility. Some risks are eliminated through elimination of the cause of the loss. When the cost of removing the cause of the loss is lower than some discounted value of the loss contingency, this course of action is manifestly wise. Here again, the point of indifference between removing the cause of loss and retaining the risk may be difficult to establish. Probability complicates the problem. This issue, however, is central to loss prevention in corporate risk management.

A classic example in insurance literature is that installation of lightning rods may be preferable to retaining the full brunt of the lightning risk. In this example or any other when the cost of loss removal is substantially lower than the discounted[8] value of the risk, society obviously benefits by the removal of the cause of loss.

The extent to which this method of treating risk is acceptable at a given time depends in large part on the state of technology. As new techniques are learned which are less expensive than older ones relative to the size of the loss which may be avoided, this treatment of loss becomes more important.

A final comment on this section is that—in accordance with a point made earlier—the action to remove the cause of the loss may, itself, create new loss possibilities. For example, an attempt to predict human behavior so as to remove the cause of a loss may cause such behavior to change and create some new loss possibility. If it does nothing else, this example suggests that removal of loss causes is not necessarily 100 percent effective.

---

[8] One simple but often challenged technique for this discounting is (1) to estimate the present value of the loss on the assumption that it is a certainty and then (2) to multiply such present value by the probability that the loss will occur.

Hedging. Still another way on occasion to treat a risk is to hedge. As the term is used here it simply means "getting on both sides" of a transaction so that there are offsetting gains and losses no matter what outcome attaches to the particular event. While this process permits the hedger to avoid a loss in respect to the given event, it also rules out the possibility of the event yielding him a gain.

A difficulty arises in the fact that few loss possibilities lend themselves to hedging. The commodities markets afford the best opportunities. An individual, for example, can (1) make a contract to sell x units of a given commodity for delivery at a given time, (2) make a contract to buy x units of the same commodity for delivery at the same time, and (3) thus avoid risk in respect to the price of that transaction.

A specific case might work as follows: A middleman might buy grain for cash from a farmer and store it briefly pending sale of it to a miller. Suppose that the middleman buys it for $1.50 a bushel and that his handling costs are 15¢ a bushel. Thus, he needs to sell it to the miller for a price in excess of $1.65 a bushel. Suppose that he normally sells to the miller at a price 20¢ higher than the price at the farm. Suppose further that at the time of this transaction the middleman can and does sell a "futures contract" (in this case a promise to deliver grain at some point in the future beyond the planned date of delivery to the miller of the grain bought for cash) for $1.70 a bushel. Next, suppose that by the time he is ready to sell the cash grain to the miller that the miller's price has declined to $1.60 a bushel. The middleman loses 10¢ a bushel on this transaction compared to what he would have made in the absence of a price change. Suppose that at this point he buys a futures contract for delivery at the same date as the date of the futures contract he sold earlier. Presumably the price per bushel in the futures market will have fallen by about the same amount as the price in the cash market. Thus, the price change in the futures market should about offset the price change in the cash market. The middleman is left in the same situation as if there had been no price changes at all. The results would be similar if the changes had occurred in the opposite direction.

Transfer of the Risk. An obvious risk treatment is to transfer the loss possibility to another person or organization. Such treatment, of course, is successful only to the extent that the transferee has the ability to withstand or otherwise overcome the loss should it occur. Without this ability, the transfer is hollow.

The usual examples cited are investment in a bond (instead of stock), working for another (instead of for one's self), and insistence upon a surety bond (instead of relying solely on the promise of another). As already emphasized, the difficulty is in determining whether or not the transfer is illusory.

Anticipation of Loss. The final risk treatment technique discussed in this chapter is anticipation. As this term is used here it means an effort to ascertain in an aggregate sense loss frequency and loss severity before the losses occur. This anticipation involves some sort of projection or prediction.

While there are numerous approaches, most embody some sort of effort to use the past as a guide to the future. Sometimes sampling techniques are used. For example, experience may suggest that losses of a given type follow a certain distribution as to size—such as the normal (or bell-shaped) curve. Because of the properties of this type of distribution (curve), the arithmetic mean (or some other statistic) of a *random* sample of observations can be used to shed some light on the comparable figure for the universe of (all possible) such observations. Various distributions other than the "normal curve" may work even better. Furthermore, because of the general stability in the outcome of events from one time period to the next, what is learned about a universe in respect to the immediate past may be quite a good description of what will happen in this universe in the near-term future.

No intent exists to conclude this chapter with a discussion of statistics. Rather, the point is that statistical inference and other estimating devices are powerful tools for anticipation of loss. Thus they are pertinent to the treatment of risk. In some circumstances they permit aggregate losses of certain types to be predicted within comfortable tolerances. Risk by almost any definition is thereby affected in some way by this probabilistic knowledge. By some definitions (such as risk being ignorance as to future loss or chance of loss) risk in an aggregate sense is reduced. By other definitions (such as risk being the probability or the standard deviation of the distribution of loss probabilities around a mean) the risk may become calculable whereas previously it was not. Only when risk is defined as possibility of loss does it seem to resist treatment through anticipation.

Insurance is a device based squarely on prediction and thus is an example of treatment of risk through anticipation of losses. Insurance, of course, is the principal risk-treating device discussed in this book. Consequently, specific attention is given to the way the insurance concept fits into risk theory.

INSURANCE AS A DEVICE FOR HANDLING RISK

Insurance is customarily associated with pure risk, that is, with losses but not with gains. Furthermore, insurance, per se, does not necessarily change (although according to the Heisenberg thesis it might) the frequency and severity of losses which occur. Rather, it involves anticipation of losses and a redistribution of the burden of the losses among those participating in the insurance arrangement.

Definitions of Insurance

Many types of activities pass under the label of insurance. In fact, there are many definitions. Most of them, however, involve the idea that insurance is a way of reducing risk and redistributing losses.

One such definition reads as follows: Insurance is an activity involving prediction of losses and a rearrangement of the incidence of such losses. A tighter definition is this: Insurance is a participation by two or more entities in such a way that given losses suffered by one or more of the entities are shared among all the participating entities. (Notice, by the way, that "self-insurance" within one entity is incompatible with this definition.) A still tighter definition is one which stipulates that: Insurance is an activity involving prediction of losses to be suffered by any of two or more entities, collection of funds from all participating entities, and payment of all or part of such collected funds to entities suffering losses stipulated as being subject to the insurance.

Students of the subject can find numerous other definitions.[9] Some of these definitions are quite close to the ones presented here. Others are a bit removed.

Prediction of Losses

The heart of insurance theory—as emphasized earlier—is that under some circumstances loss events can be predicted within a sufficiently narrow margin of error that such losses can be absorbed out of premiums voluntarily paid. The foregoing sentence is long. The concept, however, has several necessary elements: losses, predictability, narrow tolerance, payment of losses, and voluntary premium payment.

Prediction is based on the fact that, while isolated occurrences of the future are unknown and unknowable (because of irreducible ignorance or chance), events in the aggregate are subject to some stability and regularity—and thus to some predictability. Outcomes of events of a given type are observed over time. The relative frequency of a particular outcome is ascertained or estimates are made through statistical inference. Then, a prediction is made that a particular outcome will appear with the same relative frequency in the future period as in the past period. The prediction, of course, may be tempered with judgment as to ways in which the future may be different from the past. Still, the relative frequency or other estimate is the point of departure.

A very simple example will demonstrate the point. Suppose that the group of 10,000 houses referred to earlier in this chapter were such that each year five totally burned. The relative frequency (based on "a posteriori probability") would be $5/10{,}000$ or .0005. On the assumption

[9] Two particularly good compilations are found in the following works: Pfeffer, *op. cit.*, and Herbert S. Denenberg, "The Legal Definition of Insurance," *Journal of Insurance*, Vol. XXX (Sept., 1963), pp. 319–43.

that there were no partial losses and that this loss pattern would persist into the future, the "expectation of loss" would be .0005 times the total value exposed. If each house were valued at $15,000, the total exposure would be $150,000,000 (10,000 × $15,000). The expectation of loss would be .0005 × $150,000,000 or $75,000. On the further assumption that each house is equally susceptible to loss the annual loss cost per unit is $7.50. This amount "loaded" for whatever pro rata sum is required to operate the insurance mechanism would constitute the premium. This example of course is grossly oversimplified. Still, it suggests the essence of insurance.

Refinements

Insurance theory is complicated by (1) the necessity to provide multiple coverages; (2) partial losses; (3) dissimilar objects of insurance; (4) legal requirements that rates be "adequate, not excessive, and not unfairly discriminatory"; (5) taxes; (6) dividends; (7) changing technology; (8) changing customs; and (9) numerous other variables. In spite of all of these complexities, the basic idea remains the same, namely, to anticipate losses through prediction and to effect a redistribution of the burden of such losses.

The larger the number of homogeneous units under observation, other things being the same, the greater is the reliability of the prediction. This reliability involves the familiar "law of large numbers." In layman's terms, one practical effect is that as the number of observations increases, the disparity between actual outcome and probable outcome becomes smaller relative to the number of observations. This law is highly important to insurance and is one good reason why loss data are pooled for purposes of ratemaking.

SUGGESTED READINGS

DENENBERG, HERBERT S., *et al.* *Risk and Insurance*. Englewood Cliffs, N.J.: Prentice-Hall, Inc., 1964. Chaps. 1–13.

GREENE, MARK R. "Attitudes toward Risk and a Theory toward Insurance Consumption," *Journal of Insurance*, Vol. XXX (June, 1963), pp. 165–82.

MAGEE, JOHN H., AND BICKELHAUPT, DAVID L. *General Insurance*. 7th ed. Homewood, Ill.: Richard D. Irwin, Inc., 1964. Chap. 8.

MOWBRAY, ALBERT H., AND BLANCHARD, RALPH H. *Insurance: Its Theory and Practice in the United States*. 5th ed. New York: McGraw-Hill Book Co., Inc., 1961. Part I.

PFEFFER, IRVING. *Insurance and Economic Theory*. Homewood, Ill.: Richard D. Irwin, Inc., 1956. Part I, Chap. 8 of Part II, and the Appendix.

SNIDER, H. WAYNE (ed.). *Readings in Property and Casualty Insurance*. Homewood, Ill.: Richard D. Irwin, Inc., 1959. Chaps. 1–3.

WILLETT, ALLAN H. *The Economic Theory of Insurance*. Philadelphia: University of Pennsylvania Press, 1951. Chaps. i, ii, and vi.

WILLIAMS, C. ARTHUR, JR., AND HEINS, RICHARD M. *Risk Management and Insurance*. New York: McGraw-Hill Book Co., Inc., 1964. Part One.

Chapter 3

THE MECHANISM OF INSURANCE*

BY JOHN D. LONG

In the preceding chapter attention is given to some theoretical aspects of risk and insurance. In this chapter attention is given to some fundamentals of insurance practice. The mechanism of insurance is examined. In the process the point is recognized that practice is merely theory at work.

A preview in a general sort of way of the operation of the insurance mechanism is provided first. Next, the conditions necessary for this mechanism to operate are briefly described. Third, an introductory and general treatment of the principal types of ratemaking systems is presented. Fourth, a few comments are offered about the public control of this mechanism. The chapter is concluded with a contrast and comparison of the insured's and insurer's respective points of view. Almost in its entirety this chapter—like most of the others in this *Handbook*—is descriptive rather than analytical.

OPERATION OF THE INSURANCE MECHANISM

The existence of insurance rests on these circumstances: (1) individuals and organizations are subject to the possibility but not the certainty of losses which they may not be able to bear; (2) such losses, if anticipated and averaged over large groups, are often found to be bearable by individuals or organizations; (3) the process of anticipating and averaging is possible through insurers; (4) these insurers promise to pay for all or part of these stipulated losses suffered normally by the relatively few; and (5) they make such promise in return for payments from relatively many whose payments are expected to enable them to cover the losses, absorb the expenses of the mechanism, and leave a modest excess for contingencies and in some instances for reward to the owners of the equity in the insurer.

* The author gratefully acknowledges that some of the material in this chapter is based on ideas—published and unpublished—of Dr. Ralph H. Blanchard, Professor Emeritus of the Graduate School of Business of Columbia University.

Functions

A good way to understand the insurance mechanism and its operations is to consider the functions of an insurer. While authorities do not always agree among themselves on precisely what these functions are, the following ones are normally included: marketing, underwriting, rate-making or pricing, and loss adjustment. Other activities such as investing and loss prevention are almost always carried on by insurers. There is some question, however, whether or not these are a part of insurance, per se. The insurance mechanism, as it were, might be able to function without insurers doing either of these things. In addition, there are other activities in which insurers generally engage such as hiring, firing, paying taxes, and so forth. These activities are not considered here because they are not unique to the insurance mechanism.

The order in which the functions are previewed in this chapter does not suggest relative importance or sequence. All of the functions are discharged simultaneously; all are essential to the operation of the insurance mechanism.

Marketing. Treatment of risk by insurance involves anticipation of losses through prediction. Reasonably accurate prediction, in turn, depends on the stability which generally comes from dealing with large numbers of homogeneous "units of exposure" such as houses, automobiles, boilers, or whatever. Without large numbers the predictions are much more likely to go awry. Large numbers for prediction can almost never be obtained unless large numbers of people participate in the insurance venture. Successful operation of the insurance mechanism, then, depends on the insurer stimulating a sufficiently large number of prospective insureds to participate. This stimulation—including all of the "servicing" which goes with it—is the essence of marketing.

A characteristic which seems to attach itself to the sale of many goods and services but to do so with particular tenacity in respect to insurance is that of the need for persuasion. Experience demonstrates that "insurance has to be sold." Because losses are not certain and because long-run time preferences are involved, many people doubtless feel a natural reluctance to buy insurance. Of course, financial responsibility laws and strong customs temper this reluctance, especially in other-than-life insurance purchases. Still, there remains a reluctance to be overcome. This reluctance is both the principal reason for being and the principal challenge of marketing. Many of the resources of the insurance mechanism necessarily are addressed to attracting prospective insureds so as to provide the large numbers essential to reliable prediction.

Underwriting. In most interpretations of insurance contracts the prospective insureds are regarded as making offers which are then accepted or rejected by the insurers. In spite of the fact that much insurer energy has to be expended in persuading prospects to apply for insurance, by no means all of such applications can safely be accepted. Blanket acceptance could in itself easily upset the predictions because a disproportionate number of prospects with reason to expect earlier and/or larger losses than ordinary would apply. (In insurance terminology this process is called adverse selection.) The exercise of decisions as to which applications (offers) to accept and which to reject is the function of underwriting.

So often people not generally familiar with the insurance mechanism view the underwriting function as a distinctly negative one. Underwriters are pictured as saying "no." Such a conception is not in accord with the true nature of this function. Underwriting in respect to a successful insurer—and "success" here means the ability to stay in business over the long run—is essentially positive. It involves (1) attention to types of offers which can be accepted; (2) guidelines for identifying desirable prospective insureds; and (3) efforts to design coverage suitable for applicants with particularly high or low loss potential. Much of the material in the chapters on underwriting which appear in this *Handbook* shows the approaches used by various practicing experts to achieve this positiveness.

One additional point of confusion about this function is whether or not it includes the pricing aspect. As material in subsequent chapters clearly demonstrates, the answer in a broad sense is "yes." A decision as to whether or not an insurer is to accept a given offer cannot be made independently of the price which will be charged for the contract. In many lines of insurance which are not "controlled" by public authority, for example, insurance on bridges and tunnels, the decision to accept or reject and the decision to set a given price are inextricable. For most lines of insurance, however, rates generally are "filed" with the proper state official and rate changes have to be approved by such official. For all intents and purposes prices in these lines in the short run are fixed and the underwriting function has to be discharged in a manner largely divorced from ratemaking. For this reason underwriting and ratemaking are often regarded as constituting distinct functions and are so regarded here.

Ratemaking. As already indicated, the insurer makes conditional promises to pay those who suffer loss and exacts premiums from all those who are insured. Unless the insurer can collect at least enough to pay losses and expenses, including taxes, it cannot survive. Since the bulk of property-liability insurance nowadays is on an advanced, fixed premium basis, determination of how much premium to require is crucial.

The function of ratemaking is to some extent objective but to a large extent intuitive. It is often said that insurance demands possession by the insurer (or by a bureau in which it is a member) of data which indicate exactly what the losses will be in each of several different categories. As a fact, the insurance business is conducted on the basis of reasonable approximations and provision of safety margins. Were exact data required, there might be no new types of insurance introduced and, because of change, little if any existing kinds of insurance. Also, the question would arise as to how existing insurance ever could have been developed in the first place. The aim of insurance, rather, is to have predictions which are sufficiently safe and reliable for the long run. Thus, insurance is not an exact science but rather a practical service.

Loss Adjustment. Without losses and claims the incentive to buy insurance would soon wither. Moreover, losses are a fact of life. Virtually all insurance contracts are drafted in terms of a stipulated or determinable number of dollars or other monetary units. When a loss occurs or a claim is filed, the problem becomes one of ascertaining the monetary equivalent. Such process basically is the insurance loss adjustment function.

In some instances the conversion into monetary terms is quite simple. An example is a business interruption insurance loss where the contract provides that so many dollars are payable per day for so many days up to the maximum number of days of total suspension of operations. Even here, however, partial losses may prove troublesome.

In other cases the conversion is difficult indeed, as for example in the total or partial destruction of an old but costly bridge on a nearly abandoned highway route. Value as a concept in economics is exceedingly intricate. When applied to a structure or object of personal property which has been destroyed, to pain and suffering, or to mental anguish, it is all the more nebulous. Nevertheless, it is a phenomenon which has to be and is dealt with daily in insurance.

Premiums and Investments

Apart from what has been said about premiums in the description of insurance functions, additional comments are in order as to collection and investment of money by an insurer.

The basic idea of insurance does not require that premiums be payable as of the inception of the insurance contract. In fact, some "assessment mutuals" still operate today by calling for premiums only after a loss occurs. The idea is similar to that followed in a burial society except that in the latter losses are certain in the long run. It is an easy step from assessment after a loss to assessment whether or not loss occurs. Such regularizing of assessment permits the building up of a fund out of which losses are payable as they occur. From this manner of operation it is another easy step to levying an advance premium which is expected to be sufficient or more than sufficient to cover losses.

With premiums being collected in advance of the occurrence of losses, it is obvious that insurers have funds in their custody. The amounts depend on numerous variables including the pattern of loss occurrence, general level of rates, and size and incidence of expenses (and taxes). A major portion of these funds in the custody of insurers is normally invested. The investment yield provides additional funds which such insurers would not otherwise possess. Occasionally, the funds are buttressed even more with capital gains from disposal of securities or other assets in favorable markets.

Differences of opinion exist as to whether or not such investment income should be recognized expressly in ratemaking calculations. Whatever one's position, the fact is that such recognition is given implicitly even if not given explicitly.

While generalizations are dangerous, the following comments may be helpful. In a stock company the investment income is used—among other purposes—to reward stockholders. Were the stockholders not rewarded from this source, the reward would have to come from premiums. In one way or another the capital has to be rewarded for it to remain attracted to the insurance business. In a mutual insurer the investment income is used—at least in part—as a refund to policyholders and is thus in an obvious way reflected in the rate levels.

Loss Prevention

As indicated, loss prevention is not necessarily a part of the insurance mechanism. In fact, if loss prevention were 100 percent effective, insurance would not be needed at all. As a fact, however, most insurers do engage directly in loss prevention activities. Some insurers do so extensively. In addition, various insurance-sponsored organizations such as the National Safety Council and Underwriters' Laboratories, Inc., are leaders in loss prevention.

Aside from all humanitarian considerations, which are decidedly important in themselves, the rationale for insurer support of loss prevention must be somewhat along the following line: money spent in an effort to prevent losses will reduce insurance claims by an amount larger than the loss prevention expenditure—at least up to some point. There does not seem to be any clear-cut way, however, of determining such point. Perhaps insurers as a whole stop far short of it. Moreover, a particular insurer has no guarantee that its expenditures for loss prevention will result in reduction of its *own* claims as opposed to claims against competing insurers. Such a consideration is one strong reason why cooperative "broadside" prevention efforts receive support from individual insurance companies.

Closely allied to loss prevention is loss protection. While the two concepts undoubtedly overlap, prevention as the name implies has to do with taking steps to see that a loss does not occur. Protection, as used in this sense, has to do with minimizing losses which do occur. Other things being the same, prevention is preferred to protection and deserves a priority which it does not always receive.

Under this heading one final point should be noticed. While loss prevention is not a part of the insurance mechanism, loss prevention is introduced collaterally into many insurance contracts. A classic example is the boiler and machinery insurance contract in which inspection is of paramount importance. Workmen's compensation insurance also demonstrates this point.

REQUISITES OF INSURANCE

For the insurance mechanism as described in this chapter to operate, certain conditions are necessary. These are spelled out briefly in this section.

Insurable Interest

Insurance is associated with pure risk. The insured must be in a position where he faces an uncertain loss, that is, where he may lose or may not lose but where he does not know which outcome will occur. This condition of facing a possible loss upon the occurrence of a particular contingency is said to give such person an "insurable interest" in respect to the property which he stands to lose.

The nature—and, indeed, the complexity—of this matter of insurable interest is discussed and illustrated in Chapter 4. The important consideration in this immediate context is not so much the fine point of what constitutes an insurable interest as the mere recognition that such insurable interest must exist. Without an insurable interest an insured might not be sufficiently zealous in attempting to ward off the insured contingency. His lack of zeal could in turn frustrate the prediction process. Moreover, he might collect a sum of money when he had not suffered any loss and speculation would be introduced into the transaction.

Ability to Predict

From the heavy emphasis in earlier sections put on the ability to predict, one can see that this condition is a requisite of insurance. Furthermore, the predictions in the long run have to be reliable enough to permit insurer income to exceed insurer outgo.

This requirement involves several subconditions. First, there must be a sufficiently large number of insureds to permit the law of large numbers to operate. In this way the relative inaccuracy of the predictions can be kept within tolerable bounds. Second, individual insureds must be reasonably similar in terms of what they have exposed and in terms of the likelihood of suffering a loss. If they are not all reasonably similar, at least they must be divisible into broadly similar classes. Otherwise there will not be a close enough approach to equity to motivate individuals whose records or outlooks are better than the average to participate in the insurance undertaking. In other words, insurance is an averaging affair but the averaging must take place within a relatively narrow range. Third, there must be some stability in the pattern of the events being predicted. In the absence of finding some pattern or "curve" along which the outcomes of the events are expected to distribute themselves, the predictions will not be worth acting upon.

Measurability

Most insurance contracts carry promises of the insurer to pay an expressed or determinable amount of money to or on behalf of the insured. Most insured losses and claims, as already mentioned, have to be expressed sooner or later in monetary terms. For the insurance mechanism to be effective, therefore, insurable *values* must be reducible to monetary units. Insurance is to no avail in replacing the unique, such as an object of art, a family heirloom, a human life, or even a peculiarly lovable puppy dog. This limitation on insurance is quite a serious one which many people overlook.

To be subject to insurance, a given loss potential, then, has to be expressible in a money amount. Sometimes as in the case of certain "valued" policies (see Chapter 4) the amount is arbitrary. Nevertheless, it embodies an agreement as to what is expected from the insurer in case of a total loss. The point should also be made that to some extent virtually all loss adjustment is arbitrary. For example, there is nothing precise about the value of a partially burned apartment building or about the claims value of an injured back. The key point is that for insurance to be applicable the loss potential must lend itself to negotiation between reasonable parties who have some sort of precedent to guide them.

Fortuity

For the insurance mechanism to work the losses must be fortuitous. In view of the discussion about determinism and chance in Chapter 2, perhaps "fortuity" is a poor word here. The thought is merely that the losses must not occur at the discretion of the insured. Even if such events are technically in his control (as in the case of fire losses under the personal property floater), he must not intentionally *cause* them to happen.

This condition is closely related to the condition of an insurable interest. In fact, all of the conditions enumerated here are closely related. The general idea behind fortuity is that the insured must be positively interested in the loss-producing event *not* occurring. This is not to say that when one insured ceases to be interested in preventing such event from occurring the whole insurance mechanism will collapse. The point is, rather, that insureds generally must have this interest or the mechanism will collapse in a hurry.

Enforceability

Another condition necessary to insurance is that agreements involving insurer promises to pay losses must be enforceable by law. Without enforceability promises might not be carried out.

Enforceability requires not only that there be contract law but also that insurance contracts have the sanction of such a system of law. The legal system, in other words, must be permissive of the insurance mechanism.

Other

This matter of the requisites of insurance can be approached in numerous ways. Some readers might like to add conditions to the list presented. Others might like to break one or more of those presented into parts. There is room for considerable argument about what constitutes the perfect list. The description as presented here, however, should convey the fundamental points.

SOME FUNDAMENTALS OF RATEMAKING SYSTEMS

Setting a price on insurance is a critically important part of the insuring process. For this reason the present chapter includes a very brief preview of some of the principal systems used in arriving at price.

Judgment

One type of ratemaking is intuitive and is based on the knowledge, wisdom, and general "feel" of the ratemaker. It is the judgment system. Judgment is used to some extent in virtually every line of ratemaking and is used almost exclusively in a few, particularly in the "uncontrolled lines" (mentioned earlier) where mass statistics are not available.

Laymen probably underestimate the role of judgment in ratemaking. They may be prone to think in terms of an actuarial perfection which does not exist. Conditions change too fast for data to be that well suited to prediction.

Loss Ratio

A general system for adjusting rate levels is the "loss ratio" technique. As a ratemaking device this technique merely involves comparing actual losses with expected losses and adjusting the general rate level accordingly. Instead of using raw loss dollars, the losses—actual and expected—are expressed as percentages of the full premium dollar. (Since expenses as well as losses have to be paid out of premiums, the loss portion is expected to be substantially less than 100 percent.)

To take a simple example suppose that for a given line of insurance last year the actual loss portion of the premium dollar was 60 percent whereas the expected loss portion was only 55 percent. The indication is that rates are too low. The loss ratio technique would call for division of the actual loss portion by the expected loss portion to arrive at the indicated rate change ($^{60}/_{55} = +1.0909\%$). Whether or not the ratemaker would decide to make this much of a change in the rate level is an open question. The answer would depend in part on how credible he felt the data were—that is, their "believability" as indicators of the future.

Pure Premium

The general idea behind the pure premium system is that rates are set on the basis of a loss portion determined in the following way. For some appropriate time period of the past, figures are collected on losses and on units of exposure. Dollars of loss are divided by units of exposure to arrive at an indicated loss portion in dollars and/or cents per unit of exposure. This figure may be altered by judgment or may be used without alteration. To it is added expense, contingency, and perhaps profit portions. The pure premium system finds application, for example, in automobile insurance.

Schedule

The three systems which have been briefly described are systems to produce "class rates." A class rate is one which applies to each of many homogeneous insureds in the class. All members of the class are charged the same rate. Schedule ratemaking involves a different approach. Starting with some base figure, a rate is built to reflect the particular good and bad qualities of the object being insured. Charges and credits are based primarily on physical or "engineering" features of the building or whatever else is being rated. Under a system of schedule ratemaking no two insureds necessarily pay the same rate. Schedule rates are used extensively in fire insurance.

Experience—Prospective

Another approach which involves departures from class rates is experience ratemaking. Under this system the individual rates reflect the loss experience of the insured rather than the physical features of the object covered. Experience better than that anticipated for the class means that the insured pays a rate lower than the class rate. Experience worse than that for the class means that he pays a higher rate. Under a "prospective" experience system of ratemaking the rate for the current period is influenced by experience of some precisely defined period in the near-term past. The word "prospective" indicates that the rate is established in advance of the inception of the policy and is not influenced by the experience of the current period. This system is used, for example, in workmen's compensation insurance.

Experience—Retrospective

A variation of the above system is one in which the rate paid by an insured for a particular policy period depends in large part on his loss experience during that period. Since the rate is not determined until after the end of the period, the label "retrospective" is used. This system is applied to some large workmen's compensation and general liability insurance lines. Normally, the rate is allowed to fall between some minimum and some maximum and within that range is strictly a function of losses suffered.

REGULATION OF THE INSURANCE MECHANISM

Since the insurance mechanism does not function in a free market, a brief comment about public control is needed in this chapter. Insurance is said to be a business "affected with the public interest." Regulation takes several directions. Most of it—for reasons explained in Chapter 65—is at the state level. It involves among other things licensing, wording of contracts, rates, investments, accounting, and reporting.

Laws of the several states require that insurers be licensed by a state for the purpose of conducting business in that state. Licensing usually involves maintenance of certain minimum capitalization and sometimes deposits of guaranty funds. Some insurers are "admitted" into all the states; others operate in only one or a few states.

Licensing requirements also extend to agents, solicitors, and brokers. This licensing normally comes after successful completion of an examination. (These examinations in the opinion of many experts are not as rigorous as they should be.)

State laws spell out the formality involved in obtaining state approval of insurance contracts offered for sale in the state. The usual procedure is for policies, forms, and other contract supplements to be "filed" with the insurance commissioner or other official whose sanction is necessary to make the documents legitimate. In some areas of insurance, for example some types of inland marine insurance, such formality is not required.

One of the very sensitive areas of public control of insurance is pricing. Statutes of most states require that rates of at least some lines be approved by the insurance commissioner or his delegate. Petitions for changes in rates usually have to be supported by statistical evidence. In most instances the approval is required prior to the rate change. In other instances the filings become effective upon submission and remain so unless disapproved within a stipulated time by the rating authority. In many lines most of the filings of rates and forms are made by rating bureaus on behalf of member companies.

Another area of public control is investments of insurers. Control ordinarily has to do with how much can be invested in various media and with the procedure for evaluating investments for accounting purposes. The primary objective of such control seems to be the maintenance of solvency of insurers. Laws vary in stringency from state to state.

The laws also reflect an effort to secure adequate disclosure in financial statements and resonable consistency in accounting practices, especially as to expenses. Annual statements are required in extreme detail from all companies licensed in a given state. States cooperate, however, to minimize overlap by using a common format for annual statements and by establishing reciprocal agreements for the examination of insurance company records.

Regulation takes numerous other directions. These, however, are the principal ones.

VIEWPOINTS OF INSURED AND INSURER

The insured is interested primarily in buying protection against catastrophic losses. Unless the probability of such loss is so extremely remote as to be ignored, he usually wants the protection no matter what the probability of loss. He is concerned with the *possibility*. He has an incentive to buy which intensifies as he reflects upon the possibility. If the probability of loss is so high as to make the premiums out of reach, he may have to do without the coverage. Otherwise, he has an interest in buying it.

In respect to losses of less severity but greater expected frequency the insured usually has another rationale. If he feels that his loss experience will be worse than the average experience on which the rate is predicated, he will have a particularly strong incentive to insure. On the other hand, if he feels that his experience will be superior to that of the average, he will be less excited about insuring these relatively low-level loss potentials.

The viewpoint of the insurer may be that of encouraging, through its price structure and its underwriting, the prospects with superior loss records to seek insurance. In certain respects its guidelines and desiderata may be just the reciprocal in the short run of those of the insured. As a generalization, it may want most those insureds who want least to insure—especially in regard to moderate- and high-frequency type losses.

The matching of these interests within the mechanism of insurance takes place in a competitive market where each party to the prospective contract has to compromise and settle for something less than what to him would be perfection. This negotiation is also tempered on both sides by recognition that in the long run the interests of both parties coincide. Both are generally interested in a strong and competitive institution of insurance in the private sector of the economy. Both want coverages to match changing exposures. Both want a ready market. Both want rates high enough to make the insurance industry healthy and low enough to permit insureds to use insurance generously.

SUGGESTED READINGS

DENENBERG, HERBERT S., *et al.* *Risk and Insurance.* Englewood Cliffs, N.J.: Prentice-Hall, Inc., 1964. Part Three.

MAYERSON, ALLEN L. *Introduction to Insurance.* New York: Macmillan Co., 1962. Chap. 1.

MEHR, ROBERT I., AND CAMMACK, EMERSON. *Principles of Insurance.* 3rd ed. Homewood, Ill.: Richard D. Irwin, Inc., 1961. Part I.

MOWBRAY, ALBERT H., AND BLANCHARD, RALPH H. *Insurance: Its Theory and Practice in the United States.* 5th ed. New York: McGraw-Hill Book Co., Inc., 1961. Part I.

WILLIAMS, C. ARTHUR, JR., AND HEINS, RICHARD M. *Risk Management and Insurance.* New York: McGraw-Hill Book Co., Inc., 1964. Part One.

PART II

Fire and Allied Lines Insurance

Chapter 4

CONCEPTS ASSOCIATED WITH FIRE INSURANCE

BY GEORGE V. WHITFORD

Most of the basic concepts of insurance—at least insurance other than life and health—were created, developed, and refined in one way or another in the conduct of the fire insurance business. These concepts are now used not only in fire insurance but also in the newer forms of insurance being marketed today. This chapter is devoted to a recognition and review of some of these basic concepts. For convenience these concepts are classified under two main headings: Contractual Concepts and Financial Concepts.

The point should be recognized at the outset that, although the volume of fire insurance as measured by premiums is declining relative to the volume of several other types of insurance, careful attention to these concepts is as important now as at any time in the past. On this historical note it is interesting to observe that from Revolutionary times to very recently fire insurance was the principal activity of stock, mutual, and reciprocal carriers alike. As recently as 1939 automobile bodily injury premiums were only about one half the dollar amount of fire insurance premiums. Between 1939 and 1962 fire insurance premiums increased nearly threefold, while automobile premiums increased about tenfold. Workmen's compensation premiums currently are about equal to fire insurance premiums. The trend toward package policies (see Part VI) doubtless will accelerate the relative decline of fire insurance premiums in the national aggregates. Nevertheless, the concepts "born" in the fire insurance tradition are fundamental across the insurance spectrum.

CONTRACTUAL CONCEPTS

The nature of the insurance contract itself has a distinct bearing on numerous basic concepts. Hence, consideration of a few of the characteristics of this type of contract is in order.

Contracts in general must have certain legal ingredients to be valid. There must be a valid consideration; the parties must be competent to contract; the object must be legal; and there must be an offer and acceptance. Insurance contracts have additional characteristics which differentiate them from other legal agreements. While most contracts involve the exchange of equal values such as money for a building, an exchange of property for property, or future services for wages, an insurance contract depends in part upon an uncertain event. The premium paid by the insured may be grossly unequal to the amount which the insurer may have to pay if the untoward event comes to pass. This condition where performance of one party is so substantial but contingent upon some event which may not happen renders the insurance contract "aleatory."

The wording of fire insurance policies in large part is circumscribed by law. If a property owner wants insurance, he usually has to accept the wording of the contract as specified by the law of the state in which the property is located. Since this is true, courts generally construe obscure or uncertain conditions rigorously in favor of the insured who had no opportunity to bargain for his own wording.

Finally, a much higher degree of good faith is required in an insurance contract than in many other types of legal agreements. A person of poor moral fiber could sell his building without his character having any bearing on the transaction. A similar person entering into a fire insurance agreement could jeopardize such a contract by a future act of planned carelessness or arson.

Declarations: Warranties or Representations

Under common law an insurance contract—as indicated in the preceding paragraph—is a document generally based on utmost good faith between the parties. This degree of good faith may be relaxed somewhat by statute for certain types of insurance. In any case, the insurer is in the position of having to depend upon the truthfulness of the buyer of insurance in presenting the facts surrounding the application for insurance. These statements of the applicant, generally called "declarations," usually fall into one of two classes: warranties or representations.

A warranty, in effect, is a statement made by the applicant for the benefit of the insurance carrier that some condition exists as of the time of submitting the application or that some condition will exist at some instant or during some period in the future. Warranties are thus "affirmative" or "promissory." If the condition specified by the warranty does not exist, its absence is sufficient grounds to excuse the insurer from performing under the contract—even though the absence of the specified condition in no way contributed to a loss under the policy. For example, an insured who owns a pulpwood yard might have obtained a special rate for his fire insurance by warranting that a 30-foot clear space would be maintained between piles of wood in his storage yard. If at the time of a fire the wood were piled indiscriminately in the yard, the insurance company might be excused from making payment for the loss because of the breach of warranty. Readers can easily see that the concept of a warranty is a rather stringent and harsh one. For this reason courts are quick to look for exceptions to the application of warranty doctrines and are generally ready to give insureds all benefit of doubt. As a practical matter warranties are not routinely found in many types of insurance contracts except those pertaining to ocean marine transportation.

Declarations are more likely to be representations than warranties. A representation is a weaker type of statement usually made by the applicant to induce the insurer to enter the contract upon the terms stipulated. It may be oral or in writing. If written, it may or may not become a part of the written contract. A false representation does not necessarily excuse the insurer from performing under the contract. Only a "material" misrepresentation will render the contract of insurance voidable. A misrepresentation is "material" in the case where the insurer, had it known the facts, would not have entered the contract. A misrepresentation can be "material" even though made innocently. Here again, declarations in the absence of fraud are generally construed favorably to the insured. The warranty and representation doctrines are realities, however, and should therefore be familiar to all serious students of insurance.

Indemnity

A basic concept of long standing in fire insurance is that the insured is entitled to be compensated or made whole for the damage which has occurred but that he is not entitled to have a financial gain over and above his actual loss. A properly adjusted loss of property correctly insured simply places the insured in the same financial position he enjoyed immediately before the loss. He is not to gain because he bought, say, $18,000 of insurance on a $16,000 building. He is not to collect twice because he has two or more insurance policies for $5,000 each to protect a single piece of property worth $5,000. If he owns only one half of a $50,000 building, he is not to be reimbursed as if all of the property belonged to him. Without adherence to this concept, a serious moral hazard (see Chapters 14 and 29) could be created. If it were possible, for example, after fire damage to an old building routinely to recover twice the value of the building, an insured might well be tempted to provide the circumstances that could cause a fire to start. On the other hand, if the contract is based on the concept of indemnity, there is little incentive to encourage an insured to let down his safeguards or actually encourage ignition.

Two departures from strict indemnity are found in some fire and other insurance contracts. First, laws in some 20 states stipulate that the amount of insurance provided by a policy covering real estate must be paid in case of a total loss. Such policies are called "valued policies" and states with such laws are referred to as "valued policy states." This device is not a complete departure from indemnity because the amount of insurance in the first place is set with an eye toward the value of the property insured.

The second departure from indemnity is in the use of "replacement cost insurance" for dwellings and some other buildings. Assuming enough insurance is bought, the insurance company promises to repair or replace the damaged building without making any allowance for depreciation. Thus, the maximum recovery is the replacement cost new of the insured property. As will be brought out in subsequent chapters, the insured—in order to collect on this basis—is usually required to buy a relatively large amount of insurance and actually to repair or replace the damaged or destroyed structure.

Actual Cash Value

Closely allied to indemnity is the concept of "actual cash value." In fact, indemnity is carried into the fire insurance contract by a provision limiting recovery to the *actual cash value* of the loss as of the date of its occurrence. Actual cash value has generally been defined as the cost to replace the damaged property less depreciation, however it might be caused. For example, if an insured owned a 10-year-old building which would cost $100,000 to replace new, he would be entitled to that sum less depreciation. Depreciation would be determined by a consideration of the age of the building, its condition at the time of fire, obsolescence, and any other factor causing deterioration. Readers can see that "depreciation" in this sense is different from depreciation in the accounting sense. The latter, of course, involves simply a write-off of the cost (usually historical cost) of an item of property over its estimated useful life. One purpose of depreciation in accounting is to match costs against revenues in particular accounting periods. Another, assuming the firm does not operate at a loss, is to enable the firm to replace assets as they are worn out. The purpose of "depreciation" in the insurance sense is in ascertainment of the "true" value of a piece of insurable property and the "true" extent of a total or partial loss. The general idea of actual cash value is that the insurance company by using this concept is able to determine what payment is required to indemnify the insured who suffers a loss.

Insurable Interest

The concept of indemnity is also carried into the insurance contract by the requirement that the insured must have an "insurable interest" in the property on which he buys insurance. Generally, an insurable interest is such that the insured is distinctly more interested in the preservation than in the destruction of the property. This requirement usually means in practice that one who buys insurance on property must have some pecuniary relationship to the property and, thus, must be in a position to suffer monetary loss if the property is damaged or destroyed.

Determination of whether or not an insurable interest exists can grow quite involved in some instances. Usually, however, the matter is fairly obvious. A clear-cut example of an insurable interest arises from legal ownership of real or personal property. Another example is the insurable interest which a secured creditor has in the property serving as security for the debt. Thus, a savings and loan association has an insurable interest in the home on which it holds a mortgage. The owner of the home also has an insurable interest in it. A pawnshop owner has an insurable interest in the jewelry which has been pledged for a loan.

There are many more subtle—but nonetheless legitimate—examples of insurable interests. A manufacturers' agent has an insurable interest in a distant factory in which the goods he sells are manufactured. A cold-storage company has an insurable interest in the cheese and fresh vegetables of others which are in the refrigerator. In each case, a fire that would destroy or damage the property *could* cause a monetary loss. If the factory is destroyed, the commissions of the manufacturers' agent will stop until production starts again. After the fire in the cold-storage plant, the bailee may have to pay for the vegetables belonging to others which have been damaged and also may lose the storage charges he had anticipated collecting.

Without the requirement that anyone buying insurance on property must suffer a financial loss in case of damage to or destruction of the insured property, the chances of creating a moral hazard and even encouraging arson are obvious. Unless there is a chance of the insured's suffering financial loss at the time of, say, a fire, no court of law would enforce such an agreement. Such a contract would be a gambling agreement and against public policy.

Subrogation

The concept of indemnity is also related to subrogation. Subrogation has been referred to as the "stepping into the legal shoes of another." The term arises many times in succeeding chapters. If Smith owes money to the First National Bank, he will not be excused because that bank is sold and merged with the Second National Bank. The surviving bank will automatically succeed to the rights of the original creditor. In a similar way, if Jones through gross negligence causes a fire to Smith's property, Jones is not excused from his liability because Smith collects from an insurance company. The rights of Smith to make a claim against Jones are transferred to the insurance company after the loss to the extent Smith receives payment for the loss from the insurance company. This transfer is subrogation. In a sense the legal doctrine of subrogation, which exists whether written in the contract or not, performs two functions. First, it protects the concept of indemnity. Without subrogation, an insured might actually recover his loss twice and have a financial gain after the fire. Second, it prevents absolving from responsibility a guilty third party whose negligence or other wrong caused the loss in the first place. To excuse a tort-feasor in this fashion would not be in the public interest. Our legal system rests on the premise that the wrongdoer should bear the consequences of his wrongful act. While insurance companies do not often actually exercise the rights they acquire under subrogation, at least they can.

Proration

Still another concept running through fire and other insurance contracts is that of "prorating." Insurance in a particular company may be prorated among items of property insured in a particular policy. Liability for a particular loss may be prorated among companies "on the risk." Other types of proration also may occur.

Examining the concept in more detail, one can note that the fire insurance policy contains a "pro rata liability" clause which in effect divides the liability for a loss proportionately between the insurance policies when more than one policy is involved. This concept, of course, is also a backstop for the indemnity idea. Without proration nothing would prevent an insured from buying several policies and collecting fully under each one for a loss. The proration device is also used to allocate blanket insurance to specific items of property. The allocation is usually made so the insurance is spread among items of property in the same pattern that the total property value is spread among the same items.

Blanket Coverage

Insurance can be made to extend over more than one unit or one type of property in one location. A single contract can cover: two or more types of property in one location, one type of property in two or more locations, two or more types of property in two or more locations. Such insurance is referred to as blanket coverage and is in contrast to "specific" insurance which applies to one type of property in one location. For example, insurance on a dwelling is specific insurance. Coverage of the contents of three warehouses with one amount of insurance embodies the blanket approach. Students of insurance find the distinction between specific and blanket coverage very useful. For example, in the personal property floater (see Chapter 27), part of the coverage may be blanket and part may be specific.

The advantages of blanket insurance may be quite apparent. Suppose that an insured operates several retail stores where the total value of stock stays almost constant but where frequent variations of stock among stores occur. With blanket insurance he need give concern only to making certain that the total insurance is adequate. Without such an arrangement, he would continuously have to adjust the amount of insurance upwards or downwards at each individual location.

Direct Loss

Another fundamental concept reflected in the fire insurance contract is that of "direct" loss. A direct loss, say, by fire is one where fire is the proximate cause of the damage to or destruction of the insured property. Normally, this means that the property is consumed in whole or in part by the fire or that its physical appearance is changed by the fire, the resulting heat, or the efforts made to extinguish the fire (see more on this point in Chapter 5). Opposed to a "direct" loss is a "consequential" loss which stems only indirectly from the fire or other disaster. The basic fire policy covers only direct losses.

Consequential Loss

Direct losses as described above may in turn lead to other types of losses. The most common perhaps is the loss of income which may result from the necessary suspension of business activities normally conducted in premises damaged by fire. Another example is the spoiling of meat in a refrigerator which grew warm because of fire damage to a compressor on another floor of the building. These consequential losses are not covered in the Standard Fire Policy but may be the subject of extra coverages which can be provided as endorsements to the policy or as separate insurance.

Consequential losses, in turn, are normally classified in two categories. The first is referred to as "time element" and grows out of the passage of time between the occurrence of the direct loss and the completion of the repair or replacement of the damaged or destroyed property. The amount of the time element loss is not determined or determinable until after the passage of the time. In the second type of consequential loss the amount of the loss is determinable immediately after the direct loss and is not a function of time. This type has no convenient name comparable to time element but the meat spoilage loss cited above is an example. Another example is found in the case where a clothing manufacturer suffers a loss because jackets of a supply of children's suits are destroyed in a warehouse fire which left the trousers undamaged. The consequential loss stems from the fact that, when sold separately, the trousers lose most of their value.

Insurance to Value

A concept which spills over into many facets of insurance and into many insurance contracts is "insurance to value." This expression refers simply to the ratio in which the numerator is the amount of insurance and the denominator is the value of the insured property. In the ensuing pages of this *Handbook* many references will be made to this ratio and to the matter of adequate amounts of insurance generally. The importance of this concept lies in the fact that the amount of losses paid by insurance companies is not strictly a function of the amount of insurance in force. In fire insurance, most losses are much less than the total value of the damaged property. Total payments for fire losses made by a particular insurance company, then, could be almost as much in a given year when properties were insured relatively low to value as if those properties had been insured to their full value. Carrying the analysis one step further, in order to provide enough premiums to pay the losses the fire insurance rates would have to be higher, other things being the same, when insurance to value is low than when insurance to value is high. Fire insurance rates, incidentally, are usually stated as so much per $100 of insurance. Readers will find an understanding of this concept crucial to an understanding of the pricing of insurance as described, for example, in Chapters 13 and 28.

Coinsurance

A discussion of insurance to value leads to consideration of an extremely important concept in fire insurance and several other types of insurance. This concept is "coinsurance," and it has been associated with fire insurance since its very early days. The term is a particularly troublesome one for many persons. As manifested by the usual "coinsurance clause" in an insurance policy, coinsurance is a device through which the insurance company limits its liability for a loss to no greater proportion of the loss than the insurance which the insured is carrying on the property at the time of the loss bears to the insurance which the company specified (via the coinsurance clause) should be carried. The effect may be that, if the insured does not have as much insurance as he is required by the terms of the policy to have, he may not recover fully even for a loss which is less than the amount of insurance he is carrying.

The name "coinsurance" probably came about when someone said that the insured in such a case was a "co-insurer" with the insurance company because he did not buy enough insurance in the first place. In a sense the term does not fit because the person who is underinsured cannot normally be an insurer of his own property at all. The requisites of insurance are not present. Anyway, the term has stuck and insureds are loosely—and erroneously—thought of in these cases as being "co-insurers."

Harking back to the discussion of insurance to value, the reason for coinsurance can perhaps be best understood by first recognizing that most fire losses are partial losses. Actually, only about 2 percent of all fires result in a total loss. Assume that Jones and Smith own similar buildings each worth $100,000 and that the fire insurance rate on each building is 10 cents per $100 of insurance. If Jones carries, say, $80,000 of insurance on his property, he pays a premium of $80. If Smith, realizing that most fire losses are relatively small, buys only $20,000, he pays a premium of only $20. If the further assumption is made that each suffers a $20,000 loss, Jones has paid four times as much premium as Smith for reimbursement of a $20,000 loss. If an 80 percent coinsurance clause had been operative, Smith would have recovered only $5,000 (see illustration below). It becomes obvious that there is no equity where one man insures his property for 20 percent of its value and another insures his for 80 percent yet both receive the same payment for a given partial loss, even though one paid four times as much as did the other. In other words, a given set of rates applied to all insureds of a given class will not be fair if the insurance to value varies among the insureds.

While it would be theoretically possible to set a different rate for each different ratio of insurance to value, such a plan has many practical objections. A more feasible alternative for distributing the premium burden equitably among policyholders is available through the coinsurance clause.

The coinsurance clause, in effect, requires that the insured, in order to be able to buy the insurance at a particular rate, agree to carry at least a specified percentage (for example, 80) of insurance to the value of the property at the time of a loss. To the extent the insured fails to carry this much insurance, he will not collect fully for partial losses. Referring to the Jones-Smith example above, suppose that in consideration of being able to obtain the insurance at the rate of 10 cents per $100, each one of them was forced to accept a contract containing an 80 percent coinsurance clause. This would mean that the recovery after a loss would be limited by the following formula:

$$\frac{\text{Insurance Carried}}{\text{Insurance Required}} \times \text{Amount of Loss} = \text{Limit of Recovery}$$

The "Insurance Required" (the denominator of the fraction) is found by multiplying the value of the property at the time of the loss by the stipulated coinsurance percentage.

Assuming a loss of $20,000 and using this formula to determine how much money Jones could recover from the insurance company, the figures are:

$$\frac{\$80{,}000}{\$100{,}000 \times 80\%} \times \$20{,}000 = \frac{\$80{,}000}{\$80{,}000} \times \$20{,}000 = \$20{,}000$$

Jones recovers in full for the partial loss because he bought as much insurance as he covenanted to buy.

Turning now to Smith and applying the same formula to his $20,000 loss, the figures are:

$$\frac{\$20,000}{\$100,000 \times 80\%} \times \$20,000 = \frac{\$20,000}{\$80,000} \times \$20,000 = \$5,000$$

Smith collects only one fourth of his partial loss because he bought only one fourth as much insurance as he covenanted to buy in consideration of the lower rate (10 cents per $100) than would otherwise have been applied. Some readers might be interested in experimenting with other figures. In doing so, they should remember these additional points: (1) Recovery can never exceed the amount of the loss, (2) recovery can never exceed the amount of insurance, (3) recovery can never exceed the figure resulting from the use of the coinsurance formula, and (4) the *smallest* of these three limitations applies. If two or all are equally small, they limit the recovery to that amount.

The concept of coinsurance is fundamental to the rating, underwriting, and loss adjustment of property insurance. Readers who are not confident of their understanding of this topic are urged to restudy the above numerical illustrations.

FINANCIAL CONCEPTS

Numerous basic concepts of insurance are more closely related to insurance company finance than to insurance contracts. These concepts are discussed at length in Chapters 60 and 61 and are referred to frequently throughout the *Handbook*. Because of their particular importance to the proper understanding of Part II, three of them are described briefly in this chapter.

Unearned Premium Reserve

Premiums are normally collected by insurance companies in advance. A company at any given time in its operations, therefore, has collected premiums which it has not earned in the sense of providing protection over the full period of the policy's life. The amount of this unearned premium is in effect a debt of the company to the policyholder. Because of "short rate" cancellation provisions in most policies, the company may not have to refund the full unearned amount in case the policyholder cancels the policy; nevertheless, the full unearned premium is generally considered as a liability of the company.

The establishment of unearned premium reserves began in the fire insurance business. The early forms of marine insurance protected cargo while on board ship from one port to another. These trips were of relatively short duration. Whether the voyage was successful or not, the entire premium—once the voyage was undertaken—was immediately earned by the underwriter. As fire insurance developed, contracts were written at first for annual terms and later extended to three and five year terms. Two of the earliest fire insurance companies even wrote "perpetual" insurance contracts providing policies without limit of time except that a payment of a total loss terminated the contract. Premiums were generally collected in advance and policies contained cancellation provisions which permitted either party to terminate the contractual relationship at will.

In order to reflect accurately the earned premium income of a fire insurance company, it became necessary to establish a liability account (called a "reserve" in insurance accounting terminology—see Chapter 61) to show the portion of the premium not yet "belonging" to the company. In a sense this reserve became a fiduciary or trust account. For example, if a one-year policy carrying a premium of $120 were written on January 1, at the end of that month the company would have earned only $10. The remaining $110 of unearned premium would be offset by a reserve (or debt) of $110. Month by month, the remaining reserve would be decreased and assets freed for general use. Today, the sales income of all property and casualty insurance companies is determined not by the amount of premium dollars collected, but by the amount of premium dollars earned.

Loss Ratio

In order to measure the degree of success of operations and to make comparisons with operations in other companies, an insurance company needs some convenient measuring instruments. One such instrument is the loss ratio which is customarily set up as follows:

$$\frac{\text{Earned Premiums}}{\text{Incurred Losses}}$$

Since earned premiums for a given period—and not premiums written during that period—are the sales income of an insurance company (see preceding section), the earned premiums seem to be the proper figure for use in the numerator. Similarly, losses incurred during a given period as opposed to losses paid during that period seem to be the proper comparable figure for the denominator. As premiums must be earned to have financial validity, they must be related not to the losses paid during the period but instead to losses incurred. Because of the lag between the occurrence of a loss and the reporting of it there is sometimes added to the known incurred losses an amount reflecting an estimate of the losses incurred but not reported as of the date of computing the ratio. This refinement, however, does not alter the basic concept.

When the ratio is computed and used from period to period in a consistent manner, it gives company officials and others some idea of the relative success in covering current losses out of current premium income.

Readers can find more discussion of this subject in Chapter 60 and use of it in numerous chapters, for example, Chapter 13.

Expense Ratio

Another tool for use in evaluating insurance company performance is the expense ratio. A common way of expressing this ratio is as follows:

$$\frac{\text{Expenses Incurred}}{\text{Premiums Earned}}$$

The expenses and premiums, of course, are those related to a given period, such as a year. This ratio, when computed and used consistently from period to period, gives an indication of the relative efficiency of the company in operating the insurance mechanism. One important point in interpreting this ratio ties in with the preceding discussion of unearned premiums. A major portion of the expense in connection with the issuance of a policy is incurred when the policy is issued. Much fire insurance and other insurance is written on a three-year basis. Hence, for new insurance written, the expense during the first year is quite heavy, but relatively light in the succeeding years of the policy's life. On the other hand, premiums are considered as being earned strictly as a straight-line function of time. Thus, one third of the three-year premium is considered as being earned during the first policy year. One can see that the expense ratio may not necessarily indicate the actual state of affairs in the operation of an insurance company. This peculiarity is usually troublesome, however, only for companies where the volume of business and/or the average policy life is changing rapidly. Readers can find an elaboration of this rather abstruse point in Chapters 60 and 61.

APPLICATION OF CONCEPTS TO OTHER COVERAGES

Many of the basic concepts of the fire insurance business have been carried into newer forms of coverage and have the same application today as they did some 200 years ago. For example, a modern court may rule on representations concerning a homeowners policy, as an earlier court ruled on representations concerning a fire insurance policy. Many of the modern package policies contain the Standard Fire Policy provisions as an integral part of the new contract. The idea of indemnity is as alive today as ever, although some of the force of its earlier application has been modified by valued policy and replacement costs provisions.

Automobile insurance, which developed long after fire insurance, embraces the concept of actual cash value in the determination of the amount of physical damage claims. The same is true for burglary and several types of inland marine insurance. Insurable interest has precisely the same application this year as it did when the first insurance policy was written. The use of coinsurance has been extended to certain burglary contracts and many inland marine forms. Commercial package policies include provisions for time element coverages.

All of these concepts and numerous others not reviewed in this chapter have passed the test of time. An understanding of them is a prerequisite to comprehension of the many different forms of insurance which have been developed.

SUGGESTED READINGS

ANGELL, FRANK J. *Insurance: Principles and Practices.* New York: Ronald Press Co., 1959. Chaps. 3, 33.

ATHEARN, JAMES L. *Risk and Insurance.* New York: Appleton-Century-Crofts, 1962. Chap. 5.

GREENE, MARK R. *Risk and Insurance.* Cincinnati: South-Western Publishing Co., 1962. Chaps. 8, 9.

MAGEE, JOHN H., AND BICKELHAUPT, DAVID L. *General Insurance.* 7th ed. Homewood, Ill.: Richard D. Irwin, Inc., 1964. Chaps. 3, 9.

MOWBRAY, ALBERT H., AND BLANCHARD, RALPH H. *Insurance: Its Theory and Practice in the United States.* 5th ed. New York: McGraw-Hill Book Co., Inc., 1961. Chaps. 6, 26, 27.

Chapter 5

THE STANDARD FIRE POLICY

BY H. M. MOUNTAIN

The Standard Fire Policy is only a part of a complete insurance contract. In this chapter, however, attention is focused on the policy itself. The policy contains the basic general provisions applicable to any fire insurance transaction. It conveniently serves as a vehicle for the attachment of forms prescribed for insuring buildings, contents, or both, of various types of risks such as mercantile concerns, manufacturing concerns, dwellings, churches, schools, banks, and hotels, to name only a few of the many types of property to which it may be adapted. In addition to its being basic for insurance contracts covering direct physical damage to property, it also may be adapted to cover consequential loss due to interruption of business, loss of rents or rental value, and extra expense resulting from fire or other insured direct damage to, or destruction of, buildings and/or contents. The Standard Fire Policy's great flexibility is further demonstrated by its incorporation as the basic property insurance provisions in the recently developed Special Multi-Peril Package Policies.

STANDARDIZATION

The wording of the fire insurance policy is generally prescribed by state law. All companies insuring risks within a state must use the prescribed wording that is standard for that state. Before the adoption of a Standard Fire Policy, each insurance company issued policies worded according to its own ideas. The provisions of policies issued by different companies on the same property were often very different. Standardization of the policy was desirable for a number of reasons.

First, standardization of the basic provisions of all fire insurance policies on the same property greatly reduces confusion on the part of insureds as to the coverage obtained. Furthermore, the producer's problem of explaining the coverages is simplified. Since most states have adopted the 1943 New York Standard Fire Policy, insureds having locations in two or more states find uniformity of basic provisions very advantageous.

Second, standardization simplifies the adjustment of losses thus reducing time and expense for both the insured and insurer and promoting better relations between them.

Third, court decisions are more generally applicable throughout the nation. Such interpretation of standard phraseology reduces the need for litigation in the event of disagreement.

Fourth, as a result of standard basic provisions, the statistical data on losses and premiums are more valid and meaningful for ratemaking purposes.

The first Standard Fire Policy law was enacted in Massachusetts in 1873. New York enacted its first legislation on the subject in 1886, followed by the 1918 policy and the current 1943 policy. Between 1873 and 1943, many different Standard Fire Policies were used in the several states.

The Standard Fire Policy adopted by law in New York State in 1943 has been approved by the majority of the states, in some instances with minor modifications. Thus, the New York Standard Fire Policy has become virtually a nationwide standard. Minor variations from the 1943 New York Standard Fire Policy are required in California, Florida, Georgia, Hawaii, Indiana, Kansas, Maine, Missouri, New Mexico, North Dakota, South Carolina, and Vermont. More significant variations occur in the statutory policies of Massachusetts and Minnesota. The Texas Optional Coverage Policy contains a number of coverages with the option to select those desired given to the one seeking insurance. It also contains many of the conditions provided in the policies used in other states, but the basic provisions are generally similar to those in the 1943 New York Standard Fire Policy.

Frequent changes in the physical arrangement of the Standard Fire Policies have been made independently of changes in policy provisions. The objective has been to reduce clerical time and expense in policy writing. The Open Top, One-Write, and Optional Coverage arrangements are noteworthy examples of the efforts to simplify the mechanical execution of a complete contract.

Physically, the Standard Fire Policy is divided into two parts. The first page or face of the policy contains the insuring agreement. The provisions and stipulations appear on the second page. (See Appendix A.)

The agreement specifies the parties to the contract, the term of the policy, the amount of insurance, the property insured and its location, the consideration, the perils insured against, and conditions for assignment. The provisions and stipulations relate to concealment and fraud, property excluded, perils excluded, increase in hazard, vacancy and unoccupancy, requirements in the event of loss, other insurance, subrogation, cancellation, and suit. These provisions of the 1943 New York Standard Fire Policy are treated in this chapter under convenient headings rather than in the sequence in which they appear in the policy.

MAJOR COMPONENTS OF POLICY

Parties to the Contract

Obviously, the insurance company is one of the parties. The other is the individual(s), partnership, association, or corporation whose name is typed in the space provided for the insured's name. "This Company . . . does insure (the insured is named in the declarations) and legal representatives . . ." is policy language directly relating to the parties to the contract. A party who is not specified as an insured may not recover directly under the policy even though he has an interest in the property at time of loss. Court decisions seem to uphold the long-standing property insurance doctrine that an insurance contract is personal and does not follow the property.[1] This doctrine is further substantiated by the policy provision that assignment of the policy by the insured shall not be valid except with the consent of the insurer. The company has the right to know the party or parties whom it is insuring. For certainty of protection, all parties having an interest in the covered property should be named in the policy.

The inclusion of "legal representatives" of the named insured in the insuring clause automatically provides protection to the administrator of the named insured's estate or executor of his will in the event the named insured dies during the policy period. The same feature applies to other legal representatives such as guardians and receivers.

Policy Term and Premium

The inception and expiration dates agreed upon are inserted in the policy declarations in such a fashion as to delimit the period of time to which the insurance applies. Terms of one or three years are commonly used, but two- or four-year periods may be more appropriate on occasion. The trend is now away from five-year contracts. The insurance becomes effective at noon standard time at the location of the insured's property on the inception date and expires similarly on expiration date.

The premium for the fire, lightning, and removal coverage is specified. If other perils are insured against, the corresponding premiums are separately shown. Premiums are due and collectible on the inception date of the policy term, regardless of its length. It is common practice in most states, however, to provide for annual payments of term premiums under a deferred payment plan with the amount of each such payment and its due date specified.

---

[1] See, for example, *Michigan Fire and Marine Insurance Company* v. Magee *et al.* [218 S. W. 2nd 151 (Missouri, 1949)]: "It was the burden of the defendants in the instant case to prove that the policy was meant to insure any person other than Julia E. Magee individually, the only party named. . . ."

Description of Property

Space is provided in the policy for a description of the property insured, such as building(s), contents, improvements and betterments, and other items. Space is also provided for an indication of location(s) of the property, and the type of construction of the building insured and/or containing the property insured. This information is essential for identification purposes. Definitions describing in more detail the type(s) of property covered appear in the forms attached to the policy.

Property Excluded

The Standard Fire Policy does not cover accounts, bills, currency, deeds, evidences of debt, money, or securities. Unless specifically added by a form attached to the policy, the policy does not cover bullion or manuscripts. This list of personal property contains articles the principal value of which flows from use of the property as a medium of exchange, as legal claim against others, as an evidence of ownership, or, in respect to manuscripts, as a type of property virtually defying evaluation. The form attached to the Standard Fire Policy usually extends the coverage to records of account to the extent of the cost of blank paper and the actual expense of transcribing. The loss or destruction of money and securities and loss due to uncollectibility of accounts because the records are destroyed may be covered by other types of insurance.

Consideration

The "consideration," an essential element of a valid contract, consists, on the one hand, of the promises made by the insurer and, on the other, by the payment of premium by the insured plus his acceptance of the provisions and stipulations in the policy and perhaps in endorsements. The insured must comply with the provisions and stipulations to secure the benefits of the contract. The company's promises to pay indemnity in the event of a loss are conditional upon the fulfillment of the agreements of the insured.

Meaning of "Fire"

The word "fire" is not defined in the Standard Fire Policy but its meaning has long been established by court decisions and insurance practices to be *accidental* and *hostile* or *unfriendly*.[2] Intentional damage or destruction of property by the insured or at his direction is not accidental so far as the insured is concerned and therefore is not covered. Incendiarism by others than the insured is an accidental event to the insured and therefore is covered.

[2] See, for example, *Wasserman* v. *Caledonian American Insurance Co. et al.* [95 N. E. 2nd 547 (Mass., 1950)].

The fire policy covers damage by "hostile" or "unfriendly" fire, that is, one in a place where the insured did not intend it to be. A "friendly" fire is one confined to the place or receptacle intended for it. A fire kindled in a stove and fed an excessive amount of fuel may heat the stove to an extent that the finish on nearby furniture is blistered, but the fire is still within the confines of the stove and still a friendly fire. The damage to the furniture is not covered. If the heat from the fire in the stove ignited a newspaper on the furniture, the fire thus ignited would be unfriendly or hostile and the damage to the furniture caused by such hostile fire would be covered.

Fire is rapid oxidation accompanied by a flame or at least a glow.[3] Although fire is a form of combustion, there is a definite distinction between fire and combustion. The oxidation of decomposing organic matter may be so slow that the heat produced is dissipated without being noticed. Spontaneous combustion of grain, hay, or oil-saturated cloth may be so rapid that sufficient heat occurs to damage but not ignite the material. Those are instances of combustion but not fire.

Meaning of "Lightning"

Lightning is the second peril named in the Standard Fire Policy. Lightning frequently strikes building structures without fire ensuing. The lightning damage is covered and, if fire ensues, the fire damage is, of course, likewise covered. Lightning is electricity atmospherically produced by nature. Damage by electric currents *artifically* generated is not covered but, again, damage by fire ensuing from such electrical malfunction is.

Meaning of "Damage by Removal from Premises"

Damage by "removal from premises" endangered by a peril insured against is also covered. Damage by removal may result from breakage, exposure to the elements, or virtually any other cause. It is an obligation of the insured to make reasonable effort to protect his property from impending damage or destruction. If he has done so, any loss occurring as a result of removal under such circumstances can support a valid claim. Even though theft of insured property is specifically excluded, courts have interpreted theft loss concomitant with removal of property from a burning building as covered on the grounds that fire was the proximate cause.[4]

Closely associated with removal is the extension of the coverage pro rata for five days at each proper place to which any of the insured property has necessarily been removed for preservation from an insured peril. This allows the insured time to effect insurance at the new location.

---

[3] *Western Woolen Mill Co.* v. *Northern Assurance Co. of London* [193 F 637 (1905)].

[4] *Queen Insurance Co.* v. *Patterson Drug Co.* [74 So. 807 (Fla. 1917)].

Direct Loss

The Standard Fire Policy covers "direct loss." As brought out in Chapter 4, "direct loss" constitutes actual physical damage to or destruction of the covered property from fire or another insured peril. Direct loss extends to include damage when the insured peril is the *proximate* cause of the loss. For example, damage by smoke from a hostile fire or by water or chemicals used in attempting to extinguish the fire, constitutes direct loss. If fire damages the roof of an insured building and rain enters through the opening in the damaged roof before the insured can reasonably be expected to make temporary repairs, the rain damage to the interior of the building is direct loss because the original and proximate cause is fire. For the proximate cause rule to apply, there must be no intervening new and independent cause of damage between the fire and the loss.

Perils Excluded

The Standard Fire Policy specifically excludes loss by fire or other perils insured against caused directly or indirectly by (*a*) enemy attack by armed forces, including action taken by military, naval or air forces, in resisting an actual or impending enemy attack; (*b*) invasion; (*c*) insurrection; (*d*) rebellion; (*e*) revolution; (*f*) civil war; and (*g*) usurped power. Such damage being catastrophic is considered outside the province of private insurance. Destruction of insured property by civil authorities to prevent the spread of a conflagration is covered if the fire did not originate from a peril excluded by the policy.

Also excluded is loss resulting from the neglect of the insured to use all reasonable means to save and preserve the property at and after a loss or when the property is endangered by fire in a neighboring premises. The insured's obligation to protect covered property from further damage is as specific as his obligation to protect property from impending damage. For example, the fire department may have flooded a basement in extinguishing a fire on the first floor. Pumping the water out of the basement and drying off any insured property would be considered reasonable means of preventing further damage.

The policy also specifically excludes loss as a result of explosion or riot unless fire ensues, but even then provides coverage for the fire loss only. If the explosion or riot is caused by fire, the company is liable for the entire loss because fire is the proximate cause. Determining whether the fire caused the explosion or the reverse is essential unless explosion is a peril added by extension of the Standard Fire Policy.

The perils of nuclear reaction were unknown in 1943 when the current New York Standard Fire Policy was adopted. In 1957, nuclear reaction, radiation, and contamination were expressly declared *not* to be fire or other insured peril and a mandatory endorsement excluding such loss was adopted for nationwide use. Insurance coverage for losses of that nature will be treated in a later chapter. (See Chapter 64.)

EXTENT OF INSURER'S LIABILITY

Limitations

The company's liability in the Standard Fire Policy is the smallest of the following: (*a*) amount of insurance specified on the face of the policy, (*b*) the actual cash value of the covered property at time of loss, (*c*) the cost to repair or replace with material of like kind and quality, (*d*) the insured's interest, and (*e*) that proportion that the amount of the policy bears to the total amount of all applicable insurance whether collectible or not.

These limitations on the amount of the company's liability are supported by the concept of indemnity, discussed in Chapter 4. To indemnify an insured for actual loss sustained is to restore him to the same financial condition which existed immediately prior to the loss. To do more creates a financial incentive to cause a loss or exaggerate its extent. The amount of insurance applicable to the insured property is the *maximum* amount collectible. The company's actual liability is often less because, in the majority of instances, damage is only partial or one of the other limitations applies. It is the insured's responsibility to determine the amount of insurance he needs. He frequently has records of costs and other guides to assist him in estimating the value of his property. Also, he may consult competent appraisal experts for advice on value. Since property values fluctuate (for example, inventories), the problem of maintaining the optimum ratio of insurance to value is a continuing one. (See Chapter 7 for a discussion of reporting forms.) Any assistance given the insured by the company or its agent in estimating insurable value is a service that does not affect the insured's responsibility to determine insurable value and the appropriate amount of insurance needed.

Actual Cash Value

The Standard Fire Policy insures "to the extent of the actual cash value of the property at the time of loss." This amount theoretically is the cost of repairing or replacing the damaged property with other of like kind and quality in the same physical condition. Actually, parts for repairs or replacement in the same condition as that of the damaged property can seldom be obtained. Consequently, repairs and replacements are made with new materials. Generally, actual cash value means the cost of new materials at time of loss plus labor and other charges less depreciation for wear and tear, use, and obsolescence. In the insurance business, actual cash value is commonly defined briefly as replacement cost less depreciation. The objective is to determine the sound value of the property at time of destruction or, in the event of a partial loss, the value damaged. A few illustrations will indicate the application of the "actual cash value" concept to the Standard Fire Policy:

A manufacturer purchased a machine for $10,000 five years ago and its estimated productive life is 10 years. Assume that the same machine would cost $12,000 today when it is destroyed by fire. If the straight-line method of determining depreciation is used, its loss of value through use is one tenth annually and five tenths in five years. Its actual cash value at time of destruction on this basis is five tenths of $12,000 (present cost new) or $6,000.

Next, assume that finished products of the manufacturer were also destroyed. Their actual cash value is the cost of manufacturing the products, not the price at which he offers them for sale. Selling price includes profit. If goods in process of manufacture were destroyed, the cost of the raw materials, cost of labor, and other allocable costs incurred up to time of destruction constitute the actual cash value.

As a third example, consider the inventory of a merchant. The actual cash value of a stock of merchandise owned by a retailer is what it would cost to replace at time of loss. However, allowance for depreciation would be made in case the goods are shopworn or their value is reduced by style changes.

Fourth, the actual cash value of buildings covered in the Standard Fire Policy is generally the cost of constructing the same building at the time of damage, less depreciation which takes into account the condition of the building. The extent of depreciation would depend to a large degree upon the owner's practices in repairing and maintaining the building.

Determining actual cash value in every case is a special problem in applying the concept of indemnity. Valued policies or replacement cost provisions in fire insurance may influence the amounts payable—particularly for total losses.

The increase in the use of replacement cost provisions, by the way, doubtless can be attributed to the following:

1. Small fire insurance losses generally have been settled on a replacement cost basis, the actual cash value provision notwithstanding.
2. Inflation has created a serious problem for many insureds—especially churches, schools, and other public buildings.
3. Competition among insurers gave companies a strong incentive to provide this coverage.

The amount payable may also be influenced by use of "selling price" endorsements to cover finished stock of a manufacturer and goods sold but not delivered by a retailer or wholesaler at selling price rather than cost. (See Chapter 7.)

Cost to Repair or Replace

The policy further limits the loss to "not exceeding the amount which it would cost to repair or replace the property with material of like kind and quality within a reasonable time after the loss." This is not an obligation on either the insured or company to repair or replace the property but another approach to determining the amount of the loss.

Extent of Insured's Interest

Another limitation on the extent of the company's liability is "the interest of the insured." If two individuals jointly own property share and share alike, and if only one of them is the named insured in a policy covering the full value of the property, he could collect only one half in the event of damage by fire. Furthermore, the interest must exist at the time of loss and be of a nature that financial injury results from the loss. All interests should be named in all policies covering the particular property. Such an arrangement extends the protection to all interests and helps to avoid complications in loss settlement.

Pro Rata Liability

This provision limits the company's liability under the policy to no greater proportion of any loss than the amount of the policy bears to the total of all applicable insurance, whether collectible or not. For example, Company A's policy for $20,000 and Company B's for $10,000 would contribute two thirds and one third respectively in the payment of a $6,000 loss. In the absence of such a provision, the insured could collect the entire loss from either company or both—a violation of the concept of indemnity.

CONDITIONS SUSPENDING INSURANCE

Unless otherwise provided in writing added to the policy, the company is not liable for loss occurring

a) while the hazard is increased by any means within the control or knowledge of the insured, or

b) while a described building, whether intended for occupancy by owner or tenant, is vacant or unoccupied beyond a period of sixty consecutive days.

The insurance is suspended only while those conditions exist. Normal changes in hazard common to the type of occupancy are not an increase within the intent of the policy provision. The form attached to the policy usually grants permission for repairs, alterations, and construction of additions.

An increase in hazard not within the knowledge and control of the insured does not suspend the insurance. For instance, the hazard may be increased by other tenants or by the owner of a building in which the insured is one of several tenants.

An increase in hazard resulting from a change of occupancy, for example from private dwelling to restaurant or mercantile to manufacturing, suspends the coverage. The reason is that the rate at which the policy was issued may no longer be adequate for the risk.

"Vacancy" means the absence of both persons and furnishings or contents of a building. "Unoccupancy" refers only to the absence of persons. Fires are not promptly discovered in vacant or unoccupied buildings. Likewise, the probability of fires caused by irresponsible persons forcing entry into the building is greater. The form attached to the policy may extend permissible vacancy and unoccupancy up to an unlimited time, depending upon the public fire protection available to the insured and the part of the country in which the property is located.

REQUIREMENTS IN CASE LOSS OCCURS

Duties of Insured

The Standard Fire Policy sets forth in detail the following obligations of the insured in the event of a loss:

1. "The insured shall give immediate written notice to the company." "Immediate" has been interpreted by the courts as giving notice as soon as the insured can reasonably do so.[5] He should show due diligence in acting as soon as he can under the circumstances.

In practice, the insured usually notifies the authorized agent of the company, who in turn notifies the company. In general, knowledge on the part of an agent is knowledge by the company. From the company's standpoint, it is important to receive prompt notice in order to investigate the cause of loss and take such other action as circumstances merit.

2. "Protect the property from further damage." Even though loss due to the insured's failure to protect the property from further damage is specifically excluded, loss preventive action is made a definite obligation following a fire loss. This obligation emphasizes the fact that the policy insures against direct loss by fire or other specified peril and not loss from the insured's failure to protect the property from further damage. He is expected to take such steps as are reasonable to prevent any aggravation of the loss due to exposure to the elements and other conditions. The cost of protecting against further damage is a part of the loss payable under the policy.

3. "Forthwith separate the damaged and undamaged property, put it in best possible order." The fulfillment of this requirement not only prevents further damage but also makes it feasible for the insured and the company to ascertain the actual loss sustained. Some insureds erroneously think that the property should not be disturbed until a representative of the insurance company arrives.

[5] *Solomon* v. *Continental Fire Insurance Co. of City of New York* [55 N. E. 279 (N.Y., 1899)].

4. "Furnish a complete inventory of the destroyed, damaged and undamaged property." The inventory requirement makes an estimate of the loss and is in the nature of a preliminary statement of loss. The policy requires inventory information in detail as to quantities, costs, actual cash value, and amount of loss claimed. An inventory of *undamaged* personal property is customarily waived by the form attached to the policy when the amount of the loss is less than $10,000 and less than 5 percent of the total amount of insurance applicable. When the value of the property insured is substantial and only a small percentage is damaged, an inventory of the undamaged property would entail expense and time for the insured out of proportion to the amount of the loss.

5. Within 60 days after the loss, unless such time is extended in writing by the company, the insured shall render a proof of loss, signed and sworn to by the insured. The information required is more specific and detailed than that of the inventory. The fact that it is a sworn statement relates it to the policy provision regarding false swearing and fraud. The company must have substantial proof that a loss occurred in the amount claimed.

In case the insured fails to file proof of loss, the mortgagee upon notice is obligated to do so within 60 days thereafter.

6. Submit to examination. The insured is required to exhibit to any person designated by the company all that remains of the described property, submit to examination under oath, and produce for examination all books of account, bills, invoices, and other vouchers. This provision emphasizes the right of the company to full information about the loss, its amount, the insured's interest, and other pertinent facts in verification of the proof of loss and, if necessary, the right to develop additional information.

Appraisal

The policy provides, upon written demand of either party upon the other, for an appraisal when the insured and the company disagree as to the actual cash value of the property or the amount of the loss. Each shall select a competent and disinterested appraiser and notify the other of the appraiser selected within 20 days. The appraisers then select a competent and disinterested umpire. Should they fail to do so, the umpire is selected by a judge of a court of record within the state in which the property is located. The two appraisers submit only their differences to the umpire. In the vast majority of cases, the insured and the company reach an amicable agreement but, in case of disagreement as to the amount of loss, the appraisal procedure is specified and its use avoids some litigation. In the event of an appraisal the award is binding upon both the insured and insurer unless there is evidence of prejudice or bad faith on the part of the appraisers or umpire.

Company's Options

Insurance companies make cash settlement of practically all losses. The policy, however, gives the company the option to take all or any part of the property at the agreed value and to repair, rebuild, or replace the property destroyed or damaged with other of like kind and quality within a reasonable time. To repair or rebuild presents the problem of satisfying the insured that the repairs or replacement fully restore the property to its condition prior to damage and may involve entering into a construction contract separate and distinct from the policy contract.

The policy provides that there shall be no abandonment of any property by the insured to the company. The insured therefore cannot claim full payment of the actual cash value of the property and turn the property over to the company, but the company may offer to settle the loss on that basis.

When Loss Is Payable

The amount of the loss for which the company is liable shall be payable 60 days after proof of loss is received by the company and ascertainment of the loss is made either by agreement between the insured and company or by award according to the appraisal provision. In most instances, payment is made upon receipt of satisfactory proof of loss well within the 60-day period.

Suit

No suit or action on the policy for the recovery of any claim shall be sustainable in any court of law or equity unless all the requirements of the policy have been complied with and unless commenced within 12 months after inception of the loss.[6] If a company denies liability, suit may be instituted immediately by the insured.

Subrogation

The Standard Fire Policy contains a subrogation clause which provides that the company may require from the insured an assignment of all rights of recovery against any party for loss to the extent that payment is made by the company. For example, the insured property is damaged by fire caused by a negligent act of a third party. The company, after paying the loss, may require the insured to assign his right to proceed against the party responsible for the loss. This prevents the insured from collecting from the insurance company the amount for which it is liable and recovering also from the person legally liable for the damage.

---

[6] Statutes of some states lengthen the time for bringing suit.

OTHER POLICY PROVISIONS

Concealment and Fraud

"The entire policy is void if, whether before or after a loss, the insured has willfully concealed or misrepresented any material fact or circumstance" concerning the insurance, its subject, or his interest in the property, "or in case of false swearing by the insured, relating thereto."

The concealment or misrepresentation must be willful to void a policy. Intent to deceive the other party by willfully concealing material facts or misrepresenting them is essential.[7] In some jurisdictions even an unintentional misrepresentation due to mistake or inadvertence voids the policy provided it is material and misrepresents a matter which the insured is bound to represent truthfully. A misrepresentation, to be material, must be one of such importance that, had the company known the facts, it would customarily decline the risk or would have written it with entirely different conditions from those under which the policy was issued.[8]

Concealment and misrepresentation pertain not only to misleading the company into accepting the risk but also into making a loss payment. Utmost good faith of both parties is essential to a valid contract.

Cancellation

The policy contains a provision for the cancellation of the contract by either the insured or the company. The insured may request cancellation at any time. In that event, upon demand and surrender of the policy, the company must refund the excess of the paid premium above the customary short rates for the expired term. The insured receives as refund less than the pro rata premium for the unexpired term. This is considered proper and reasonable because the company has incurred all or at least the larger part of its expense for writing and processing the policy at its inception. There is no opportunity to distribute that expense over the entire policy period when an insured requests cancellation during its term.

The company may cancel at any time by giving the insured five days' written notice. In that case, the refund is the pro rata premium for the unexpired term. The provisions of the cancellation clause are clear but their application to specific cases may be complex. Many states have enacted statutes which modify the cancellation procedure. The insured's receipt of written notice in some cases may be open to question.

Mortgage Interests

The Standard Fire Policy provides that if loss is made payable in whole or in part to a designated mortgagee who is not a named insured, 10 days'

[7] *Hartford Fire Insurance Co.* v. *Clark* [61 So. 2nd 19 (Ala., 1952)].

[8] *Hartford Fire Insurance Co.* v. *Golden* [224 S. W. 177 (Ky., 1920)].

written notice of cancellation must be given to such mortgagee. It further provides that, if the insured does not file proof of loss, the mortgagee may do so within 60 days after being notified. If the company claims that no liability exists as to the mortgagor or owner, it shall be subrogated to all the mortgagee's rights of recovery or pay off the mortgage debt and require an assignment thereof and of the mortgage. Mortgagee interests usually require that the Standard Mortgage Clause be attached to the policy. That clause defines further the interest and obligations of the mortgagee beyond those recited in the Standard Fire Policy.

SUGGESTED READINGS

Fire, Casualty, and Surety Bulletins. Cincinnati: National Underwriter Co. Fire and Marine Volume, Fire Section.

LUCAS, JULIAN. *The Standard Fire Policy of the State of New York.* New York: Davis, Dorland & Co., 1943.

RIEGEL, ROBERT, AND MILLER, JEROME S. *Insurance Principles and Practices.* 4th ed. Englewood Cliffs, N.J.: Prentice-Hall, Inc., 1959. Chap. 22.

RODDA, WILLIAM H. *Fire and Property Insurance.* Englewood Cliffs, N.J.: Prentice-Hall, Inc., 1956. Chap. 3.

SCHULTZ, ROBERT E., AND BARDWELL, EDWARD C. *Property Insurance.* New York: Rinehart & Co., 1959. Chap. iii.

Chapter 6

FORMS TO ACCOMPANY THE FIRE POLICY—PERSONAL

BY EDWIN N. SEARL

Much has been said in the preceding chapter with respect to the policy itself. As previously discussed, the policy provisions serve the purpose of (1) identifying the parties to the contract, (2) specifying the period of time to be covered, the premium consideration, and the description of property covered and its location, and (3) setting forth the basic provisions of the contract, such as the amount of the company's liability, provisions for cancellation, and requirements in case loss occurs.

PURPOSE OF A "FORM"

A "form" is attached to the policy so as to:

1. Define the coverage under each item of the policy.
2. Describe any extensions or limitations in coverage.
3. Describe any additional perils insured against.
4. Modify, in some instances, the conditions of the policy to which the form is attached.
5. Clarify situations which are not provided for in the policy itself.

In essence, the form amends and clarifies the policy conditions so as to complete an "insurance contract." A form usually contains standard provisions which may be further modified by endorsement in order to meet the specific needs of the insured or the underwriting requirements of the company.

Some caution must be exercised in any study of insurance coverages. Forms are periodically revised, based upon changing conditions, and are not uniform in all geographical areas nor necessarily identical for all companies. This discussion is based primarily upon the *dwelling* coverages offered by most companies. These forms follow essentially a countrywide pattern but recognize territorial differences.

Common Dwelling Forms[1]

Usual dwelling forms include a fire form (with or without the Extended Coverage Endorsement), a named peril Broad Form for either building or contents, an "All Risk" Special Form for buildings only, and the various Homeowners Forms. The Homeowners Forms include personal liability, medical payments, and physical damage to property of others in addition to coverage of the insured's own property against physical damage. These Homeowners Forms are described separately in detail in Chapter 49.

Property Covered

A dwelling insurance contract, made up of the basic policy and a form, together with endorsements, if any, may be so written as to cover:

1. The dwelling structure itself.
2. The contents therein.
3. A garage or other outbuilding.
4. The rental value of the dwelling.
5. Necessary increase in living expense as a result of damage or destruction.
6. Trees, shrubs or plants on the premises.
7. Any combination of such properties or contingencies.

The form is usually so written as to be suitable for coverage on any or all of these properties. Coverage is made applicable by simply listing the amount and the nature of the coverage on the face of the policy.

Perils Insured Against

The perils insured against under the conditions of the Standard Fire Policy are "direct loss by fire, lightning and by removal from premises endangered. . . ." The coverage can then be expanded to include the "extended coverage" perils of windstorm, hail, explosion, riot, riot attending a strike, civil commotion, aircraft, vehicles, and smoke, and may be further extended by choice of form or endorsement to include a number of additional perils such as vandalism and malicious mischief, earthquake, or the various "Broad Form" or "All Risk" perils.

FIRE FORM WITH EXTENDED COVERAGE ENDORSEMENT

The usual Dwelling and Contents Form normally completes the contract with respect to coverage against fire, lightning, and removal and may also extend the contract to include the usual extended coverage perils.

[1] For the sake of emphasis all names of forms and endorsements will be capitalized. The "form" may be sufficient to complete the contract by attachment to the policy in those instances where no further modifications are desired. In other instances, one or more "endorsements" may also be necessary to modify the form, or possibly the policy itself, so as to provide the coverage which the parties are seeking.

Description of Property Covered

The first page of the policy is filled in to show a specific amount applicable to the dwelling building; to the contents; to trees, shrubs, and plants; or to other property for which coverage is desired. The form expands this brief reference on the policy face to indicate that insurance on the building will include building equipment and fixtures, and outdoor equipment pertaining to the service of the premises. Similarly, the form explains that insurance on the contents will include household or personal property usual or incidental to the occupancy of the premises as a dwelling, while contained in the dwelling, in the outbuildings, or anywhere on the premises.

The description of the property covered in the form has no meaning unless an amount is inserted on the face of the policy. The policy may be selective and cover the building only. In such a case any references in the form to contents coverage would be meaningless even though the printed words do remain in the contract. Similarly, the policy may be written for a specific amount to be applicable, for example, to outside radio and television antennae, lead-in wiring, masts, and towers. If this were done, all references to other property described in the form would have no significance inasmuch as the face of the policy would have no amount listed for dwelling, contents, rental value, or any other item.

This form can be used for specific coverage on trees, shrubs or plants by inserting a specific amount on the face of the policy. However, such contracts usually include specific limits of liability. For example, the coverage may be limited to not more than $100.00 on any one tree, $10.00 on any one shrub, and $1.00 on any one plant.

Extensions of Coverage

An attempt is made to meet the usual needs of the average insured, even under this most simple dwelling contract, by including certain extensions of coverage. The intent is to provide the insurance most *generally* needed for dwelling, contents, or other properties which can be covered under the form. The intent, further, is to help the insured avoid undue hardship from inadvertently failing to ask for coverage he might need. Finally, the intent is also to minimize the amount of investigating and individual tailoring of contracts used to provide this household insurance.

Routine coverage on dwelling outbuildings is simplified by automatically providing an additional amount of insurance up to 10 percent of the dwelling amount to be applicable to private appurtenant structures on the same premises. Additional insurance may also be written to cover specifically on such outbuildings. In the usual instance, however, this 10 percent extension of coverage is ample for most private outbuildings and no specific mention need be made in the contract in order to have the benefit of this basic coverage.

Another important simplification is a provision that up to 10 percent of the contents coverage is available off-premises, covering such property of the insured while away from the insured's premises but within the United States (including Alaska and Hawaii) or Canada. This off-premises extension applies also to personal property of other members of the insured's family residing in his own household.

Another extension, and one of particular interest to a tenant who would not normally purchase coverage on the building structure itself, is a provision that up to 10 percent of his contents coverage may be used to cover improvements, alterations, or additions which he may have made to the dwelling structure or to private outbuildings. This provision plugs a gap in coverage which might not be recognized by one unfamiliar with the individual circumstances and which could be easily overlooked by the policyholder himself.

The usual dwelling form automatically includes an extension of coverage to apply against the fair rental value of the dwelling for the time required to restore it to a tenantable condition. This is usually included automatically as an additional amount of insurance up to 10 percent of the dwelling coverage amount, but is prorated not to exceed $1/12$ of the total coverage in any one month.

If the dwelling coverage amount were $12,000, this extension would permit up to $1,200 as an additional rental value coverage which would be available up to $100 in any one month. If additional specific rental value coverage is desired, it can be purchased by listing a specific amount of rental value coverage on the first page of the policy and paying the appropriate premium.

Exclusions or Limitations[2]

A fire form usually carries a Nuclear Clause to clarify the intent that nuclear reaction or radiation is not to be considered in any sense as a fire phenomenon. Similarly, an Electrical Apparatus Clause customarily excludes coverage as a result of electrical injury or disturbance unless fire actually ensues. Dwelling forms in some areas carry a $50 deductible applicable to lightning losses to electrical devices. The purpose of this provision is to avoid controversy with respect to those losses under $50 where it is difficult to distinguish between actual lightning damage as contrasted with normal deterioration and short circuiting resulting from age or poor maintenance. In most areas, outdoor radio and television antennae and equipment are excluded from windstorm or hail coverage and in many areas cloth awnings and metal smokestacks are similarly

[2] All names of clauses are capitalized for the sake of emphasis.

excluded. Specific coverage, if desired, may be purchased by means of a separate item in the same policy.

Additional Coverages

Provisions are included in the form to accommodate the removal of household and personal effects to a new residence, with prorata coverage at both locations during the actual moving period. It is important to notice, however, that this coverage does not apply while the property is in transit between the two locations. When a dwelling is newly purchased and the previous dwelling is sold, the insurance on the dwelling building can usually be transferred to the newly purchased dwelling by specific endorsement.

The expense incurred in the removal of debris after the property has been damaged or destroyed is not strictly a part of the loss itself. For this reason, a separate provision is included in the form which picks up these expenses to be covered as a part of the fire or other loss. The coverage against the expense of removal of debris is not a separate amount but is included with the basic amount for the dwelling item. This expense, together with a total property damage loss, may then exceed the actual cash value (or replacement cost) of the property. A prudent purchaser may wish to carry sufficient insurance, by increasing the basic amount of coverage, to be in a position to be reimbursed for any maximum loss possibility.

The fire form also includes a definition of inherent explosion coverage, which is included as a part of the basic fire coverage. These provisions have no meaning—except in those increasingly rare instances where the Extended Coverage Endorsement is not purchased—inasmuch as the explosion provisions of the broader Extended Coverage Endorsement supersede the inherent explosion provisions.

Mortgage Clause

Interests and obligations of a mortgagee are described in lines 68–85 of the Standard Fire Policy which also authorize the attachment of additional provisions in writing. These additonal provisions are contained in a Standard Mortgage Clause customarily included in forms which apply to dwelling property or to commercial or industrial properties. Here again, the mortgage clause provisions are not applicable unless they are made a part of the contract by the insertion of the name of the mortgagee or trustee in the appropriate space on the face of the policy.

Extended Coverage Endorsement

The provisions of the Extended Coverage Endorsement are not peculiar to coverage on dwelling and household goods. They are essentially identical to the Extended Coverage Endorsement used so widely with practically all commercial and industrial coverages.

This endorsement extends coverage beyond that of fire, lightning, and removal, to include the perils of windstorm, hail, explosion, riot, riot attending a strike, civil commotion, aircraft, vehicles, and smoke. Perils which are so "everyday" as windstorm and explosion are nevertheless subject to widespread misinterpretation and confusion. For this reason, the Extended Coverage Endorsement clarifies the intent with respect to exclusion of other meteorological phenomena such as frost, ice, snow, or sleet. The endorsement also clarifies intent as to exclusion of interior damage unless the structure itself is opened by wind or hail and exclusion of phenomena such as sonic boom, electrical arcing, water hammer, and rupture of water pipes, which are often confused with explosion. Other provisions specifically applicable to the perils are enumerated in the endorsement and should be studied directly from the endorsement itself.

Most dwelling forms include a $50 deductible applicable to windstorm or hail losses to building structures. In some areas, the first $50 of coverage can be "bought back"; however, in many states, no coverage is available for the first $50 of windstorm or hail damage. This mandatory exclusion recognizes that these small losses are essentially maintenance losses which, if insured, would impose an unreasonable adjustment and investigational burden which ultimately would be reflected as an expense to the policyholder.

Other provisions, such as the Nuclear Exclusion Clause, the War Risk Exclusion Clause, and the Apportionment Clause are included in the endorsement as necessary extensions of similar provisions which appear in other parts of the fire insurance contract.

Liberalization Clause

This clause acts to keep the coverage up to date with respect to those items which have been revised to the advantage of the insured. It also benefits the agent and the company by avoiding the labor and expense involved if thousands of existing policies had to be physically endorsed to give the advantage of liberalized filings. This clause—which is employed widely in commercial and industrial policies also—provides that, if any change in form is subsequently approved for use and if existing insurance can be extended or broadened by substitution or endorsement without increased premium charge, such broadened coverage shall be considered in effect for the policyholder even though the physical endorsement or substitution has not taken place. On the other hand, restrictions in coverage are not written into the contract in this way. Restrictions must be actually endorsed into the contract by mutual agreement or be deferred until expiration (or cancellation) and renewal.

DWELLING BUILDING(S) AND CONTENTS—BROAD FORM

This form is the product of an evolution in coverage. It consists fundamentally of the "named peril" coverages normally provided in a dwelling and contents fire and extended coverage contract together with the so-called "Additional E.C.E. Perils" (which were available separately for

UNIFORM STANDARD

FORM NO. 49D
(Edition March '62)

DWELLING BUILDING(S) AND CONTENTS—BROAD FORM

($50.00 DEDUCTIBLE APPLICABLE TO CERTAIN SPECIFIED PERILS)

Insurance attaches only to those items specifically described in this policy for which a specific amount is shown and, unless otherwise provided, all conditions of this form and the provisions of the policy to which it is attached shall apply separately to each item covered.

No insurance shall apply hereunder if the described dwelling is SEASONAL, unless it is so described in this policy.

Any loss hereunder shall not reduce the amount of this policy.

SECTION I—COVERAGE
PERILS INSURED AGAINST

(THE ITALICIZED LETTERS FOLLOWING EACH PERIL REFER TO APPLICABLE PARAGRAPHS OF SECTION II "EXCLUSIONS")

This policy insures against direct loss to the property covered caused by:

1. **Fire and lightning** as provided in this form and in the policy to which it is attached. *(A)*

*2. **Windstorm.** *(A, B)*

*3. **Hail.** *(A, B)*

4. **Explosion.** *(A)*

5. **Sudden and accidental tearing asunder, cracking, burning or bulging (not by wear and tear, deterioration or rust) of a steam or hot water heating system,** except appliances for heating water for domestic consumption. (See also Peril 16). *(A, C)*

*6. **Vandalism and malicious mischief.** *(A, D, E)*

*7. **Burglars,** except with respect to property taken by burglars. *(A, E)*

8. **Riot, riot attending a strike, and civil commotion,** including direct loss from pillage and looting occurring during and at the immediate place of a riot, riot attending a strike or civil commotion. *(A)*

9. **Aircraft.** *(A)*

*10. **Vehicles.** *(A, F)*

11. **Sudden and accidental damage from smoke,** other than smoke from agricultural smudging or industrial operations. *(A)*

*12. **Falling objects.** *(A, G, H)*

*13. **Weight of ice, snow, or sleet** which results in physical injury to the building(s) covered or containing the property covered. *(A, H, I)*

*14. **Collapse (not settling, cracking, shrinkage, bulging or exp-nsion) of building(s) or any part thereof.** *(A, H, I)*

*15. **Accidental discharge, leakage or overflow of water or steam** from within a plumbing, heating, or air conditioning system or domestic appliance, as well as the cost of tearing out and replacing any part of the building(s) covered required to effect repairs to the system or appliance from which the water or steam escapes. *(A, C, E, J)*

*16. **Sudden and accidental tearing asunder, cracking, burning, or bulging (not by wear and tear, deterioration or rust) of appliances for heating water for domestic consumption.** *(A, C)*

*17. **Breakage of glass** constituting a part of the building(s) covered hereunder, including glass in storm doors and storm windows. *(A, E)*

*18. **Freezing of plumbing, heating and air conditioning systems and domestic appliances.** *(A, C)*

*19. **Sudden and accidental injury from artificially generated electrical currents to electrical appliances, devices, fixtures and wiring,** except tubes, transistors and similar electronic components. *(A)*

***NOTE: See Section III ($50) Deductibles.**

SECTION II—EXCLUSIONS
THIS POLICY DOES NOT INSURE AGAINST LOSS—

A. As respects Perils 1 to 19 inclusive: (1) Occasioned directly or indirectly by enforcement of any local or state ordinance or law regulating the construction, repair, or demolition of building(s) or structure(s).

(2) Caused by, resulting from, contributed to or aggravated by earthquake, volcanic eruption, landslide or any other earth movement; unless loss by fire or explosion ensues, and then this Company shall be liable for only such ensuing loss.

SECTION II—EXCLUSIONS *Contd.*

roof or walls by the direct action of wind or hail and then shall be liable for loss to the interior of the building(s) or the property covered therein as may be caused by rain, snow, sand, or dust entering the building(s) through openings in the roof or walls made by direct action of wind or hail.

Unless specifically covered under a separate item to outdoor radio and television antennas including their lead-in wiring, masts or towers, nor to lawns, trees, shrubs or plants.

C. As respects Perils 5, 15, 16 and 18: Caused by or resulting from freezing while the building(s) covered is vacant or unoccupied unless the Insured shall have exercised due diligence with respect to maintaining heat in the building(s) or unless the plumbing, heating and air conditioning systems and domestic appliances had been drained and the water supply shut off during such vacancy or unoccupancy.

D. As respects Peril 6: To glass (other than glass building blocks) constituting a part of the building(s); nor by pilferage, theft, burglary or larceny.

E. As respects Perils 6, 7, 15 and 17: If the described building(s) had been vacant beyond a period of 30 consecutive days immediately preceding the loss.

F. As respects Peril 10: To driveways, walks, lawns, trees, shrubs or plants caused by any vehicle owned or operated by an Insured or any tenant of the described premises.

G. As respects Peril 12: To the interior of the building(s) or the property covered therein, caused by falling objects unless the building(s) covered or containing the property covered shall first sustain an actual damage to the exterior of the roof or walls by the falling objects; nor to lawns, trees, shrubs or plants.

H. As respects Perils 12, 13 and 14: To outdoor radio and television antennas including their lead-in wiring, masts or towers, outdoor equipment, gutters and down-spouts, cloth awnings, fences, lawns, trees, shrubs, or plants; all except as the direct result of the collapse of a building.

I. As respects Perils 13 and 14: To fences, pavements, patios, swimming pools, foundations, retaining walls, bulkheads, piers, wharves or docks when such loss is caused by freezing, thawing, or by the pressure or weight of ice or water whether driven by wind or not; all except as the direct result of the collapse of a building.

J. As respects Peril 15: To the system or appliance from which the water or steam escapes.

War Risk Exclusion Clause (This clause applies to all perils insured against hereunder except the perils of fire and lightning, which are otherwise provided for in this policy): This Company shall not be liable for loss caused directly or indirectly by (a) hostile or warlike action in time of peace or war, including action in hindering, combating or defending against an actual, impending or expected attack, (1) by any government or sovereign power, (de jure or de facto), or by any authority maintaining or using military, naval or air forces; or (2) by military, naval or air forces; or (3) by an agent of any such government, power, authority or forces, it being understood that any discharge, explosion or use of any weapon of war employing nuclear fission or fusion shall be conclusively presumed to be such a hostile or warlike action by such a government, power, authority or forces; (b) insurrection, rebellion, revolution, civil war, usurped power, or action taken by governmental authority in hindering, combating or defending against such an occurrence.

Nuclear Clause: The word "fire" in this policy or endorsements attached hereto is not intended to and does not embrace nuclear reaction or nuclear radiation or radio-

FIG. 6–1. Dwelling Building(s) and Contents—Broad Form.

(3) Caused by, resulting from, contributed to or aggravated by any of the following—
(a) flood, surface water, waves, tidal water or tidal wave, overflow of streams or other bodies of water, or spray from any of the foregoing, all whether driven by wind or not;
(b) water which backs up through sewers or drains;
(c) water below the surface of the ground including that which exerts pressure on or flows, seeps or leaks through sidewalks, driveways, foundations, walls, basement or other floors, or through doors, windows or any other openings in such sidewalks, driveways, foundations, walls or floors;

unless loss by fire or explosion ensues, and then this Company shall be liable for only such ensuing loss.

B. As respects Perils 2 and 3: Caused directly or indirectly by frost or cold weather, or ice (other than hail), snow or sleet, whether driven by wind or not.

To the interior of the building(s) or the property covered therein caused by rain, snow, sand, or dust, whether driven by wind or not, unless the building(s) covered or containing the property covered shall first sustain an actual damage to

(Continued in next column)

active contamination, all whether controlled or uncontrolled, and loss by nuclear reaction or nuclear radiation or radioactive contamination is not intended to be and is not insured against by this policy or said endorsements, whether such loss be direct or indirect, proximate or remote, or be in whole or in part caused by, contributed to, or aggravated by "fire" or any other perils insured against by this policy or said endorsements; however, subject to the foregoing and all provisions of this policy, direct loss by "fire" resulting from nuclear reaction or nuclear radiation or radioactive contamination is insured against by this policy.

Nuclear Exclusion (This clause applies to all perils insured against hereunder except the perils of fire and lightning, which are otherwise provided for in the Nuclear Clause attached to this policy): Loss by nuclear reaction or nuclear radiation or radioactive contamination, all whether controlled or uncontrolled, or due to any act or condition incident to any of the foregoing, is not insured against by this policy, whether such loss be direct or indirect, proximate or remote, or be in whole or in part caused by, contributed to, or aggravated by any of the perils insured against by this policy; and nuclear reaction or nuclear radiation or radioactive contamination, all whether controlled or uncontrolled, is not "explosion" or "smoke".

SECTION III—$50 DEDUCTIBLES

A. As respects Perils 2 and 3: The sum of $50 shall be deducted from the amount of loss resulting from each windstorm or hailstorm. This deductible shall apply separately to each building or structure and separately to all personal property in the open. This deductible does not apply to contents in any building, nor to outdoor radio and television antennas when specifically covered under a separate item.

B. As respects Perils 6 and 7: With respect only to seasonal dwelling property this Company shall be liable only when such loss to all property covered hereunder exceeds $50 in any one occurrence and then for only such excess.

C. As respects Peril 10: With respect only to loss caused by vehicles owned or operated by an Insured or any tenant of the described premises, this Company shall be liable only when such loss exceeds $50 in any one occurrence and then for only such excess.

D. As respects Perils 12 to 19 inclusive: This Company shall be liable only when such loss to all property covered hereunder exceeds $50 in any one occurrence and then for only such excess. This $50 deductible is not applicable if the loss is also covered under any one of the Perils 1 to 11, inclusive.

Rental Value and Additional Living Expense are not subject to the application of these deductibles

SECTION IV—DEFINITIONS

A. **Dwelling:** This term shall mean any building, including additions in contact therewith, occupied principally for dwelling purposes by not more than 2 families; also, if the property of the owner of the described dwelling and when not otherwise covered, building equipment, fixtures and outdoor equipment, all pertaining to the service of the described premises and while located thereon or temporarily elsewhere; also, materials and supplies located on the described premises or adjacent thereto, intended for use in construction, alteration or repair of structures covered hereunder.

B. **Private Structures:** This term shall mean private structures (other than the described dwelling and additions in contact therewith) appertaining to the described premises and located thereon, but not structures used in whole or in part for commercial, manufacturing or farming purposes, nor any structures (except structures used principally for private garage purposes) which are wholly rented or leased to other than a tenant of the principal dwelling, covered hereunder.

C. **Contents:** This term shall mean household and personal property usual or incidental to the occupancy of the premises as a dwelling (except animals, birds, aircraft, motor vehicles other than motorized equipment used for maintenance of the premises, and boats other than rowboats and canoes); belonging to the Insured or members of the Insured's family of the same household, or for which the Insured may be liable, or at the option of the Insured belonging to a servant or guest of the Insured; all while on the described premises.

As to "Contents" —

(1) If, during the term of this policy such property is removed to another location within the limits of this State and occupied in whole or in part as the Insured's residence, this policy shall cover such property while at such new location up to the amount applicable and shall cease to cover at the former location, except that during the period of removal this policy shall cover at each location in the proportion that the value of such property at each location bears to the aggregate value at both locations.

(2) Loss due to change of temperature shall be limited to such loss resulting from physical damage to the building(s) or to equipment therein or to equipment on the described premises caused by any peril insured against.

(3) Loss shall be adjusted with and made payable to the named Insured unless other payee is specifically named.

Definitions Continued on Back of Form

THE PROVISIONS PRINTED ON THE BACK OF THIS FORM ARE HEREBY REFERRED TO AND MADE A PART HEREOF.

Form No. 49D (3-62)

CAUTION

WHEN THIS FORM IS ATTACHED TO ONE FIRE POLICY, THE INSURED SHOULD SECURE LIKE COVERAGE ON ALL FIRE POLICIES COVERING THE SAME PROPERTY.

NOTES TO AGENTS: 1. NO CHANGE OR ALTERATION IN THIS FORM WILL BE PERMITTED EXCEPT BY ENDORSEMENT, COPY OF WHICH MUST BE SENT TO COMPANY.

2. This form to be used only for covering buildings or contents of the following classes (except Farm Property):
Dwellings containing 2 families or less;
Private Boarding and Rooming Houses with not more than 20 rooms for lodging and (or) with not more than 20 boarders;
Nurses' and Sisters' Homes with not more than 10 sleeping rooms;
Private outbuildings in connection with the foregoing;
Household and personal property in buildings rated under Dwelling or Apartment House schedules.

FIG. 6–1 (*Continued*).

Definitions continued

D. **Rental Value:** This term shall mean the fair rental value of the building(s) or parts thereof, as furnished and equipped by the owner whether rented or not. Loss of Rental Value shall be computed for the period of time, following loss to the building(s) or to equipment therein or to equipment on the described premises by any peril insured against, which would be required with the exercise of due diligence and dispatch, and not limited by the expiration date of this policy, to restore the property to a tenantable condition, less such charges and expenses as do not continue.

As to "Rental Value" this Company shall be liable during the period of time, not exceeding two weeks, while access to the described premises is prohibited by order of civil authority, but only when such order is given as a direct result of damage to neighboring premises by any peril insured against.

E. **Additional Living Expense:** This term shall mean the necessary increase in living expense incurred by the Insured in order to continue as nearly as practicable the normal standard of living of the Insured's household for the applicable period described in (1) or (2), whichever is the lesser, and not limited by the expiration date of this policy: (1) the time required, with the exercise of due diligence and dispatch, to repair or replace the damaged or destroyed property; (2) the time required for the Insured's household to become settled in any permanent quarters.

As to "Additional Living Expense" —

(1) This Company shall be liable during the period of time, not exceeding two weeks, while access to the described premises is prohibited by order of civil authority, but only when such order is given as a direct result of damage to neighboring premises by any peril insured against.

(2) This Company shall not be liable for loss due to the cancellation of any lease, or any written or oral agreement.

F. **Trees, Shrubs or Plants:** This term shall mean trees, shrubs or plants on the described premises, except when grown for commercial purposes, but this Company shall not be liable for more than Two Hundred Fifty Dollars ($250) on any one tree, shrub or plant.

SECTION V—EXTENSIONS OF COVERAGE

A. **Private Structures:** The Insured may apply up to 10% of the amount of insurance applicable to the principal dwelling item under this policy as an additional amount of insurance to cover loss to Private Structures as defined in paragraph B of Section IV by any peril insured against.

B. **Trees, Shrubs, Plants and Lawns:** The Insured may apply up to 5% of the amount of insurance applicable to the principal dwelling item under this policy to cover loss to trees, shrubs, plants and lawns on the described premises (except those grown for commercial purposes) by Perils 1, 4, 6, 7, 8, 9, 10, 11 and 14 as provided in Section I, but this Company shall not be liable for more than its proportion of $250 on any one tree, shrub or plant including expense incurred for removing debris thereof. In no event shall the coverage under this extension apply to the perils of wind and hail nor any peril except those specifically set forth in this paragraph.

C. **Rental Value and Additional Living Expense:** The Insured may apply up to 10% of the amount of insurance applicable to the principal dwelling item under this policy as an additional amount of insurance to cover loss by any peril insured against of both (1) Rental Value of the described building(s) with respect to any portion thereof not occupied by the Insured, and (2) Additional Living Expense with respect to any portion of the described building(s) occupied by the Insured, but not to exceed said 10% for both (1) and (2) in the aggregate.

D. **Replacement Cost Coverage**—This extension of coverage shall be applicable only to a building structure covered hereunder, but excluding carpeting, cloth awnings, domestic appliances and outdoor equipment, all whether permanently attached to the building structure or not:

(1) If at the time of loss the whole amount of insurance applicable to said building structure for the peril causing the loss is 80% or more of the full replacement cost of such building structure, the coverage of this policy applicable to such building structure is extended to include the full cost of repair or replacement (without deduction for depreciation).

(2) If at the time of loss the whole amount of insurance applicable to said building structure for the peril causing the loss is less than 80% of the full replacement cost of such building structure, this Company's liability for loss under this policy shall not exceed the larger of the following amounts (a) or (b) —

(a) The actual cash value of that part of the building structure damaged or destroyed;

(b) That proportion of the full cost of repair or replacement (without deduction for depreciation) of that part of the building structure damaged or destroyed, which the whole amount of insurance applicable to said building structure for the peril causing the loss bears to 80% of the full replacement cost of such building structure.

(3) This Company's liability for loss under this policy including this extension of coverage shall not exceed the smallest of the following amounts (a), (b) or (c) —

(a) The amount of this policy applicable to the damaged or destroyed building structure;

(b) The replacement cost of the building structure or any part thereof identical with such building structure on the same premises and intended for the same occupancy and use;

(c) The amount actually and necessarily expended in repairing or replacing said building structure or any part thereof intended for the same occupancy and use.

When the full cost of repair or replacement is more than $1,000. or more than 5% of the whole amount of insurance applicable to said building structure for the peril causing the loss, this Company shall not be liable for any loss under paragraph (1) or sub-paragraph (b) of paragraph (2) of this extension of coverage unless and until actual repair or replacement is completed.

(4) In determining if the whole amount of insurance applicable to said building structure is 80% or more of the full replacement cost of such building structure, the cost of excavations, underground flues and pipes, underground wiring and drains, and brick, stone and concrete foundations, piers and other supports which are below the under surface of the lowest basement floor, or where there is no basement, which are below the surface of the ground inside the foundation walls, shall be disregarded.

(5) The Insured may elect to disregard this extension of coverage in making claim hereunder, but such election shall not prejudice the Insured's right to make further claim within 180 days after loss for any additional liability brought about by this extension of coverage.

E. **Off Premises Contents:** The Insured may apply up to 10% of the amount of insurance applicable to the contents item under this policy to cover loss to property so defined (except rowboats and canoes) belonging to the Insured or members of the Insured's family of the same household, while elsewhere than on the described premises but within the limits of that part of Continental North America included within the United States of America and Canada, and the State of Hawaii, by any peril insured against. This extension of coverage shall in nowise inure directly or indirectly to the benefit of any carrier or other bailee.

F. **Improvements, Alterations and Additions:** The Insured may apply up to 10% of the amount of insurance applicable to the contents item under this policy (if the Insured is not the owner of the described premises) to cover loss to improvements, alterations or additions to the described dwelling and private structures appertaining thereto by any peril insured against.

G. **Debris Removal:** This insurance covers expenses incurred in the removal of debris of the property covered hereunder which may be occasioned by loss caused by any peril insured against. However, the liability under this policy for both loss to property and removal of debris shall not exceed the amount of insurance applicable to the property damaged or destroyed.

H. **Property Removal:** This policy is extended to cover pro rata for 30 days at each proper place to which any of the property covered hereunder shall necessarily be removed for preservation from or for repair of damage caused by any peril insured against.

As respects Extensions of Coverage A, B, C, D, E and F—It is a condition of this policy that in the event the Insured

FIG. 6–1 (*Continued*).

elects to apply the optional extensions of coverage herein, this Company shall not be liable for a greater proportion of any loss than would have been the case if all policies covering the described property had contained identical optional provisions and the same election were made under all policies.

SECTION VI—OTHER PROVISIONS

A. **Control of Property:** This insurance shall not be prejudiced by any act or neglect of any person (other than the named Insured), when such act or neglect is not within the control of the named Insured.

B. **Increased Hazards:** The policy condition suspending this insurance while the hazard is increased is waived.

C. **Vacancy and Unoccupancy:** Permission granted for vacancy or unoccupancy without limit of time, except as respects Perils 5, 6, 7, 15, 16, 17 and 18 as provided in paragraphs C and E of Section II, and except as provided in any endorsement attached to this policy. A building in process of construction shall not be deemed vacant.

D. **Description of Property:** This insurance shall not be prejudiced if any error is made in describing the location of the property covered.

E. **Subrogation:** This insurance shall not be invalidated should the Insured waive in writing prior to a loss any or all right of recovery against any party for loss occurring to the described property.

F. **Alterations and Repairs:** Permission granted to make alterations, additions and repairs, and to complete structures in course of construction. In the event of loss hereunder, the Insured is permitted to make reasonable repairs, temporary or permanent, provided such repairs are confined solely to the protection of the property from further damage and provided further that the Insured shall keep an accurate record of such repair expenditures. The cost of any such repairs directly attributable to damage by any peril insured against shall be included in determining the amount of loss hereunder. Nothing herein contained is intended to modify the policy requirements applicable in case loss occurs, and in particular the requirement that the Insured shall protect the property from further damage.

G. **Liberalization Clause:** If during the period that insurance is in force under this policy, or within 45 days prior to the inception date therof, on behalf of this Company there be adopted, or filed with and approved or accepted by the insurance supervisory authorities, all in conformity with law, any changes in the form attached to this policy by which this form of insurance could be extended or broadened without increased premium charge by endorsement or substitution of form, then such extended or broadened insurance shall inure to the benefit of the Insured hereunder as though such endorsement or substitution of form had been made.

H. **Pro Rata Clause:** If this policy covers on two or more items for which specific amounts are shown, the amount of this policy applies to each item in the proportion that the specific amount shown for each item bears to the sum of all items.

I. **Apportionment:** This Company shall not be liable for a greater proportion of any loss less the amount of deductible, if any, from any peril or perils included in this form than (1) the amount of insurance under this policy bears to the whole amount of fire insurance covering the property, or which would have covered the property except for the existence of this insurance, whether collectible or not, and whether or not such other fire insurance covers against the additional peril or perils insured hereunder, nor (2) for a greater proportion of any loss less the amount of the deductible, if any, than the amount hereby insured bears to all insurance whether collectible or not, covering in any manner such loss, or which would have covered such loss except for the existence of this insurance; except if any type of insurance other than fire extended to cover additional perils or windstorm insurance applies to any loss to which this insurance also applies, or would have applied to any such loss except for the existence of this insurance, the limit of liability of each type of insurance for such loss, hereby designated as "joint loss", shall first be determined as if it were the only insurance, and this type of insurance shall be liable for no greater proportion of joint loss than the limit of its liability for such loss bears to the sum of all such limits. The liability of this Company (under this form) for such joint loss shall be limited to its proportionate part of the aggregate limit of this and all other insurance of the same type. The words "joint loss", as used in the foregoing, mean that portion of the loss in excess of the highest deductible, if any, to which this form and other types of insurance above referred to both apply.

J. **Occupancy Clause:** In consideration of the rate at which this policy is written, it is a condition of this policy that if the described dwelling is associated with and in proximity to farming operations (1) the agricultural products produced on the land are incidental to the occupancy of the dwelling and are principally for home consumption, or (2) that the occupants of the dwelling and buildings appurtenant thereto are not engaged in the operation of the farm and said buildings are in addition to a complete set of farm buildings on the farm and are not exposed within 200 feet by any farm building.

K. **Standard Mortgage Clause (Applies to Building Items only, but this entire clause is void unless name of mortgagee or trustee is inserted on the first page of this policy in space provided therefor):**

Loss or damage, if any, under this policy, shall be payable to the mortgagee [or trustee], named on the first page of this policy, as interest may appear, and this insurance as to the interest of the mortgagee [or trustee] only therein, shall not be invalidated by any act or neglect of the mortgagor or owner of the within described property, nor by any foreclosure or other proceedings or notice of sale relating to the property, nor by any change in the title or ownership of the property, nor by the occupation of the premises for purposes more hazardous than are permitted by this policy; provided, that in case the mortgagor or owner shall neglect to pay any premium due under this policy, the mortgagee [or trustee] shall, on demand, pay the same.

Provided also, that the mortgagee [or trustee] shall notify this Company of any change of ownership or occupancy or increase of hazard which shall come to the knowledge of said mortgagee [or trustee] and, unless permitted by this policy, it shall be noted thereon and the mortgagee [or trustee] shall, on demand, pay the premium for such increased hazard for the term of the use thereof; otherwise this policy shall be null and void.

This Company reserves the right to cancel this policy at any time as provided by its terms, but in such case this policy shall continue in force for the benefit only of the mortgagee [or trustee] for ten days after notice to the mortgagee [or trustee] of such cancellation and shall then cease, and this Company shall have the right, on like notice, to cancel this agreement.

Whenever this Company shall pay the mortgagee [or trustee] any sum for loss or damage under this policy, and shall claim that, as to the mortgagor or owner, no liability therefor existed, this Company shall, to the extent of such payment, be thereupon legally subrogated to all the rights of the party to whom such payment shall be made, under all securities held as collateral to the mortgage debt, or may at its option pay to the mortgagee [or trustee] the whole principal due or to grow due on the mortgage, with interest accrued thereon to the date of such payment, and shall thereupon receive a full assignment and transfer of the mortgage and of all such other securities; but no subrogation shall impair the right of the mortgagee [or trustee] to recover the full amount of his, her or their claim.

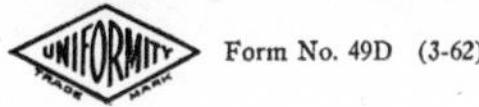

Form No. 49D (3-62)

FIG. 6–1 (*Concluded*).

several years) plus the provisions of "Replacement Cost" and "Additional Living Expense" coverages.

While some of the form provisions vary among territories and even among adjoining states, nevertheless the form reproduced herein illustrates the format, the usual coverages, the manner in which the exclusions are identified with the coverages affected, and other typical provisions.

As illustrated, the form includes six sections, namely *Coverage, Exclu-*

sions, Deductibles, Definitions, Extensions of Coverage, and *Other Provisions.*

Coverage, Exclusions and Deductibles

The perils which are insured against are clearly enumerated in Section I with exclusions applicable to specific perils tabulated and identified in Section II of the form.

A $50 deductible is applicable to specified perils as identified in Section III of the form. The principal application is (1) to windstorm or hail losses to buildings, structures, and personal property in the open and (2) generally to most of the broad coverages, that is, to those beyond the basic fire and extended coverage perils.

Definitions and Extensions

Definitions are essentially similar to those in the remainder of the fire insurance contract. The various extensions of coverage are continued and, in some instances, liberalized. Additional living expense insurance is provided to protect against the necessary increase in living expense in order to continue as nearly as practicable the normal standard of living of the household. Rental value insurance is provided with respect to any portion not occupied by the insured and is no longer limited to 1⁄12 of the coverage per month. These extensions of coverage, however, are limited in the aggregate for "one loss" to 10 percent of the amount of insurance on the dwelling.

Coverage of trees, shrubs, and plants is provided as an extension subject to a more liberal limit of liability than formerly. Such coverage, however, does not apply to damage by wind, hail, weight of ice or sleet, nor other peril not enumerated, unless specific insurance is purchased.

Replacement Cost Coverage

The principal extension of coverage under the Dwelling Building(s) and Contents—Broad Form is coverage of the dwelling structure for replacement cost as opposed to actual cash value. This extension provides payment by the insurer of "new for old" without deduction for depreciation. In order to have the benefit of this more liberal loss settlement, the insured must (1) carry insurance to at least 80 percent of the replacement cost and (2) actually replace the damaged building on the same premises.

In other words, there is no intent to adjust a loss on a replacement cost basis unless the insured has purchased his insurance on a replacement cost basis. Also, there is no intent to pay for an older dwelling on a replacement cost basis unless the insured desires to (and actually does) rebuild at the same location. The company does not intend to finance a move to a more desirable neighborhood nor to provide funds for a family to give up suburban living for a return to an apartment.

The replacement cost provisions do not apply to those items with a limited life expectancy such as carpets, cloth awnings, or domestic appliances. There is also some question as to whether replacement cost coverage can continue to be available for highly susceptible roof surfacing materials, particularly in geographical areas subject to recurring hailstorms.

Other Provisions

The provisions in Section VI of the form are essentially similar to those included in the Dwelling and Contents Form, although some of these have been liberalized in one manner or another.

DWELLING BUILDING(S) SPECIAL FORM

The Dwelling Building(s) Special Form differs in two important particulars from the Broad Form previously described, namely (1) coverage is applicable to buildings only and is not available for household goods and other contents and, even more importantly (2) the building coverage is against "all risks of direct physical loss, except as hereinafter provided . . . ." Thus, this form is frequently referred to as the "All Risk Form" or as the "Special Form."

In other respects the Dwelling Building(s) Special Form follows the same format as the "Broad Form." The $50 deductible provision is applicable under essentially the same situations. The "Definitions," "Extensions of Coverage," and "Other Provisions" are similar except that no coverage under this form is afforded to contents.

Exclusions

Any analysis of coverage under the "All Risk" form resolves itself into a study of exclusions. Under this form, any dwelling loss not excluded is considered to be covered.

It is the intent to exclude those losses which may be anticipated as essentially inherent in the ownership of property or which are not considered by the underwriter to arise out of insurable perils. This intent is stated in the following language:[3]

This policy does not insure against loss by wear and tear, deterioration, rust, mould, wet or dry rot; contamination, smog, smoke from agricultural smudging or industrial operations; mechanical breakdown; settling, cracking, shrinkage, bulging or expansion of pavements, patios, foundations, walls, floors, roofs or ceilings; birds, vermin, insects or domestic animals; unless loss from a peril not

[3] This exclusion is quoted from the form as recommended generally countrywide by the Inter-Regional Insurance Conference in March, 1962.

excluded in this policy ensues, and then this Company shall be liable for only such ensuing loss.

There is a minor difference in theft coverage inasmuch as the Special Form "excludes loss by theft of any property which at the time of loss is not an integral part of any dwelling building or private structure. . ." whereas the "Broad Form" totally excludes "property taken by burglary." Otherwise, the exclusions in the "All Risk Form" parallel in effect the provisions in the "Broad Form" which, of course, embodies the "named-perils" approach.

Advantage of "All Risk" Coverage

Any advantage to the insured under the Special Form is inherently in connection with those unanticipated or exceptional circumstances which may not even be visualized by the insured nor by the underwriter until after the event.

In many areas of the country, possibly because of its somewhat higher cost, the Special Form is purchased so infrequently there is some question as to whether it will continue to be available. Another reason for its infrequent use may be that those insureds who might be attracted to the "all risk" feature are apt to prefer the choices available to them under the Homeowners Program.

ADDITIONAL COVERAGES BY ENDORSEMENT

Coverage against certain additional perils may be desired and is available in most territories by endorsement. For example, earthquake coverage may be provided for dwelling buildings or contents by attachment of an Earthquake or Volcanic Eruption Endorsement and by payment of an appropriate premium.

The Radioactive Contamination Assumption Endorsement may be used to protect against loss by sudden and accidental contamination arising out of materials on the insured's premises. However, no direct loss coverage is presently available with respect to contamination from an off-premises source.

A Sonic Boom Endorsement is available in most parts of the country. The necessity for this endorsement is reduced by the fact that such losses are not excluded under either the "Broad Form" or the "Special Form" and are also included in several of the Homeowners Forms.

A coverage which is commonly purchased, particularly in suburban areas, is in connection with agreements for fire department response to a property which is beyond the city or district limits. A property owner so situated may request a Fire Department Service Clause providing reimbursement for those charges for fire department response which have been contracted for prior to the event.

It is still possible to purchase separate windstorm and hail coverage or explosion coverage by endorsement to a fire policy. However, there is practically no interest in such limited coverages now because of the widespread use of the Extended Coverage Endorsement or broader forms of coverage.

FARM FORMS

Insurance coverages for farm properties combine a need for personal coverage on a farm dwelling and household contents with commercial needs in connection with diverse business operations of a modern farm. Farm insurance is discussed in detail in Chapter 11.

As present-day farms become larger in size, though fewer in number, the operations usually become more mechanized. Operations may include processing of farm products on the farm premises themselves. The farm buildings may be greater in number, more specialized in design, and higher in cost. Equipment will definitely represent an even greater investment than in earlier years.

The insurance needs of owners of farm properties are increasingly important and also somewhat complex. These needs are reflected in a great variation of farm forms in different geographical areas, tailored to the farming needs in each area, and requiring rather a local analysis than a generalized countrywide review.

The farm coverages for the personal lines themselves follow the general pattern of other dwelling coverages. Available farm forms in most areas include a fire and extended coverage form, a "named peril" Broad Form, and several choices of a Farmowners coverage. (Farmowners Policies are discussed in Chapter 49.) However, each of these contracts should be studied. Only in that way can one become familiar with the coverages available to provide protection against insurable losses arising out of modern farming operations.

TRENDS

The public has several choices in purchasing personal lines insurance, that is, in obtaining coverage against property damage to dwelling and household belongings. Even the simple fire and extended coverage contract is a type of packaging of some necessary property damage coverages.

The "Broad Form" coverage includes protection against a number of additional perils, on a "named-perils" basis, plus a more elaborate packaging of other extensions of coverage, such as "Additional Living Expense" and "Replacement Cost" insurance. The "Special Form" provides a means of offering similar coverage for buildings only but on an "all risk" basis. This form has the advantage of protection against unanticipated contingencies not specifically excluded in the form.

The Homeowners Forms provide a choice for owner-occupants of eligible dwellings (and even for tenants) and provide rather extensive packaging which includes among other coverages personal liability and physical damage to property of others.

A recent study made by the author covering a two-week period and 18 midwestern states, shows that of the policies currently being written on dwelling properties:

54 percent utilized one of the "Homeowners Policies."
11 percent were written under the "Broad Form."
Less than 1 percent fell under the "Special Form."
34 percent continued to use the basic fire form (almost invariably with extended coverage).

An even more interesting tabulation (Table 6–1) shows the trend of selection according to amount of principal insured coverage for the policies issued during this two-week period.

TABLE 6–1

PERCENTAGE BREAKDOWN OF DWELLING CONTRACTS ISSUED DURING A TWO-WEEK PERIOD IN AN 18-STATE AREA IN MIDWEST
1964

Insured Amount	Percentage of Total Policies				
	Dwelling and Contents Form (With or Without E.C.E.)	Broad (Named-Peril) Form	Special (All-Risk) Form	Homeowners	Total
$10,000 or less	48%	12%	Less than 1%	40%	100%
$10,001–$15,000	14	9	Less than 1%	76	100
Over $15,000	13	13	2%	72	100
Composite	34%	11%	Less than 1%	54%	100%

This tabulation is based simply upon a count of the number of policies in each grouping. If policies for smaller amounts were disregarded, the "Broad Form" or "Special Form" appear to have nearly equal popularity with the Dwelling and Contents Form, even in the so-called "residual" dwelling business remaining after the general transfer of the bulk of dwelling insurance to the Homeowners Program. Considering also the increased premium per policy for these additional perils, the percentage of premium (not number of policies) would show an even higher figure for the broader forms.

These data suggest a definite corroboration as to increased acceptance by the insuring public of the broader coverages now available. The data, in the opinion of many observers, foretell an even more pronounced movement in this direction in the foreseeable future.

SUGGESTED READINGS

Fire, Casualty, and Surety Bulletins. Cincinnati: National Underwriter Co. Fire and Marine Volume, Fire Forms Section.

Gordis, Philip. *Property and Casualty Insurance.* 8th ed. Indianapolis: Rough Notes Co., 1961. Chaps. 3, 4.

Mowbray, Albert H., and Blanchard, Ralph H. *Insurance: Its Theory and Practice in the United States.* 5th ed. New York: McGraw-Hill Book Co., Inc., 1961. Chap. 9.

Policy, Form, and Manual Analysis Service. Indianapolis: Rough Notes Co. Fire Forms Section.

Schultz, Robert E., and Bardwell, Edward C. *Property Insurance.* New York: Rinehart & Co., 1959. Chaps. iv, v.

Chapter 7

FORMS TO ACCOMPANY THE FIRE POLICY—COMMERCIAL AND INDUSTRIAL

BY AMBROSE B. KELLY

When an order for insurance is given to an agent, a broker, or a salaried employee of an insurance company, it is often stated in such simple terms as: "Bind $2 million on my plant for Fire and Extended Coverage Insurance, effective at noon on April 1." The written evidence of the contract, when it is finally delivered to the insured to implement this terse order, is a bundle of paper with thousands of words. It consists of the Standard Fire Insurance Policy for the state in which the risk is located and one or more forms or endorsements. The purpose of the forms and endorsements is to adapt the comparatively simple Standard Fire Policy to the protection needs of the specific policyholder.

This chapter is devoted to a discussion of some of the forms commonly used in the insuring of commercial and industrial properties. Whereas Chapter 6 is structured in terms of several commonly used residential forms, this chapter is organized on the basis of types of provisions found in numerous commercial and industrial forms. The diversity of forms and practices in the insuring of commercial and industrial properties would render awkward any effort to select and discuss in detail any few "typical" forms. Because adaptation of the insurance contract to specific needs can become quite a task, the form may, and often does, contain more words than are found in the basic policy itself. The purpose of the form was described succinctly by Prentiss B. Reed many years ago when he said:

> The form, or written portion of the policy, describes the property, states how it is contained and where it is located, and also describes the interest of the insured if it is not that of unconditional and sole ownership. The form may also modify the printed portion of the policy. . . . A form may also add to the policy an agreement fixing the extent of the application of insurance under the policy and of the contribution to be made by the company in case of loss or damage and any other agreement not inconsistent with nor a waiver of the conditions or provisions of the policy. The warranties, clauses, and permits neces-

sary to fit the policy to the risk at the rate to be charged are incorporated in the form.

In its legal aspect the form, whether written, typed, or printed, is the written portion of the contract, and its terms override those of the printed portion in case of conflict.

In some cases a form will include provisions that increase the liability of the insurer as stated in the printed portion of the policy; in others, provisions that decrease it.[1]

The rating bureaus have prepared forms and endorsements covering most normal situations for use with the Standard Fire Policy of the respective states. These forms and endorsements are sometimes not adequate for the specialized problems of an insured, and a special form may be prepared for the particular risk by the agent or broker handling the insurance. Since there is a direct relationship between form and rate, any special form must be submitted to and approved by the rating bureau which has jurisdiction over the transaction. Forms for special classes of risk which are on a special rate basis, such as Highly Protected Risks or Public and Institutional Property, are promulgated by the appropriate rating bureau which also approves the rating schedules and perhaps specifies certain underwriting restrictions for such risks.

IDENTIFICATION OF THE INSURED/S

The first task of the person preparing the form is to identify the insured/s and his (their) interest in the property. It is possible that the situation may be a comparatively simple one in that the particular property to be insured is wholly-owned by one individual and that there are no other interests to be protected.

Characteristically, use of the personal forms as described in Chapter 6 involves relatively simple identification of insureds. Use of commercial and industrial forms, however, may lead to difficult identification problems. For example, the insured may be a large corporation which wishes to have a single policy covering not only its own interest in property but also the interests of subsidiaries and related corporations. As another example, the insured may be the mortgagee rather than the owner; again, the insured, rather than being the owner, may be simply the bailee.

From the standpoint of both the insured and the insurer, it is essential that the insured be clearly identified. If there is more than one insured, the form should state the degree to which their respective interests are to be covered. For example, if a building under construction is to be insured, the owner of the building may wish to include within the coverage of his policy the contractor's tools and equipment on the site which are used in

[1] Prentiss B. Reed, *Fire Insurance Underwriting* (New York: McGraw-Hill Book Co., Inc., 1940), p. 262.

the work of construction. Because this situation either exists or may arise, many forms will include the statement: "The policy shall also cover all contractors' interest in such property to the extent that the insured has agreed, prior to loss, to keep such interests insured or for which the insured is liable."[2]

DESCRIPTION AND LOCATION OF PROPERTY

The description and location of the property insured is just as important as the identification of the insured.

Description

Reviewing the standard forms issued by various rating organizations, one cannot escape the feeling that the primary purpose of many of the forms is to describe accurately and with as much detail as possible the property insured under the policy. For example, the Building and Contents Form used for commercial and industrial risks specifies that the "building" includes:

> . . . foundations, machinery used for the service of the building only, plumbing, electric wiring, electric sound, communication, stationary heating, lighting, ventilating, refrigerating, air conditioning and vacuum cleaning apparatus and fixtures, boilers, all only while in the building; ovens, kilns, furnaces, retorts, lehrs, forges, cupolas and driers, of brick construction or brick encases, resting on independent foundations built from the ground, all only while in the building; awnings, signs and metal smokestacks, screens, storm doors and windows if the property of the owner of the building and belonging to the building, while attached to or stored in it or other buildings on the premises; signs that are the property of the building owner and are in the open within 100 feet of the building; also all permanent fixtures, stationary scales and elevators, belonging to and constituting a permanent part of the building.[3]

On the other hand, the building coverage in this form does not apply to:

> Architects fees.
> Cost of excavations.
> Brick, stone, or concrete building foundations, which are below the under surface of the lowest basement floor or, if there is no basement, which are below the surface of the ground inside the foundation walls of the building.
> Brick, stone, or concrete foundations of machinery or boilers and engines, which are below the surface of the ground.
> Underground flues, pipes, underground wiring, and drains.[4]

One reason for these exclusions is that the property involved has comparatively little exposure to loss. If these items were included within

[2] Factory Mutual Rating Bureau, Form D–1 (1–61), p. 1.

[3] *Monthly Policy Form & Manual Analysis* (Indianapolis: Rough Notes Co.), p. Fire 132.B.

[4] *Ibid.* On an optional basis some of the items may be insured.

the building coverage, it would be necessary to take them into account in determining the applicable coinsurance limit. The insured would have the unhappy choice of (1) paying a premium for insurance which he does not need or want, or (2) being subject to a coinsurance penalty.

Much the same approach has been used in the commercial and industrial forms with reference to personal property. This property has traditionally been described in some such fashion as follows:

> . . . all contents and personal property of every description not belonging to and constituting a permanent part of the described building and only while contained in or attached to the building or on attached platforms, or while located in the open or in or on vehicles or railway cars in the open within 100 feet. It includes:
>
> Awnings, signs, and metal smokestacks only when the property of the tenant or lessee and not otherwise specifically covered. . . .
>
> Personal property (provided the insured is legally liable) while held in trust, on commission or consignment, for alteration or repair. Insurance applies to the value of labor or materials expended on the property of others and also to such property leased or sold but not delivered or removed. . . .
>
> The interest or liability under contract of the insured in articles covered under the policy that are purchased on the installment plan. . . .
>
> Books of account, drawings, card index systems, and other records, not to exceed the cost of blank books, blank pages, or other materials, plus the actual cost of labor in transcribing or copying the records.[5]

The modern trend, however, is toward very broad general statements of the property insured without any attempt to itemize. For example, the Highly Protected Risk Form used by the Factory Insurance Association, when applied to a policyholder who owns both building and contents, merely states:

> On real and personal property of the insured, subject to all provisions of this Policy including endorsements, while located on premises situated.

When such a simple statement is used, it is still necessary to specify that the policy covers the personal property of others while it is on the described premises; the personal property of the insured when it is in the open on land within 500 feet of the premises; the personal property of officers and employees of the insured and property of the insured while away from the premises for certain purposes.

Location

The allocation of part of the insurance to property away from the premises has become an important factor in forms written to cover all commercial and industrial property as well as in forms intended for residential property. For example, the Inter-Regional Insurance Conference (no longer in existence) recommended an Off Premises Extension to

---

[5] *Ibid.*

be used when the 80 percent or higher coinsurance clause applies. This extension permits the insured to apply up to 2 percent of the amount of each item of insurance under the policy (but not exceeding $5,000 under each item) to cover the described property, other than merchandise or stock, while temporarily removed from the described premises for purposes of cleaning, repairing, reconstruction, or restoration.

Provision of coverage on newly acquired locations for a short period of time is also becoming common. This arrangement allows the insured to have some insurance protection during the time he is arranging for long-run insurance for his new location. For example, under the Standard Property Form of the Factory Mutual Rating Bureau, coverage is afforded up to a limit of $50,000, or 1 percent of the face amount of the policy, whichever is smaller, for a period of 60 days from date of acquisition, at any location in the United States or Canada, rented or purchased by the insured after the inception of the policy. No coverage is provided under this clause on property in transit. Similar protection is given under the Highly Protected Risk Forms used by the Factory Insurance Association.

If the insured wishes the insurance to apply at only a single location, it is comparatively easy to give an accurate description of the location. This description may be a street address or other specification sufficient to identify and bound the property. (On occasion this description may be quite vague, such as "10 miles west of Oklahoma City on Route 66.")

When property of a large corporation is insured, there are often scores of different locations to be listed. Schedules are used for this purpose, particularly when it is necessary to group properties of a particular type together for rating or underwriting purposes. The form or the policy in that case will merely contain a reference to the schedules attached thereto, giving the location of the property insured.

Blanket coverage on both real and personal property and on all property owned by the insured within the United States has come to be the rule on commercial and industrial risks. This blanket treatment gives the policyholder protection against inadequate coverage at any location in the event of a total loss at that location, since the entire amount of insurance under the policy is applicable to any location. Sometimes a specific limit will be inserted in the form applicable to a particular location or locations despite the fact that the policy as a whole is written on a blanket basis. Complications ensue whenever there is blanket insurance on property which is also covered on a specific basis by other insurers. These complications are the reasons for the common exclusion in forms written on a blanket basis of property specifically or otherwise insured. More common is a special Other Insurance Clause made a part of the form under which the blanket coverage is excess over any specific insurance which may be in effect covering the interest of the insured in the property which is damaged or destroyed.

OTHER PROVISIONS

The Standard Fire Policy has a number of provisions suspending or restricting insurance—see lines 28 to 37, inclusive. There is also a statement in lines 9 and 10 that bullion and manuscripts will not be covered unless specifically named thereon. Because of these provisions in the policy, most of the commercial and industrial forms include permits which for certain activities supercede the suspending or restricting conditions in the policy.

For example, the Work and Materials Clause found in the Building and Contents Form grants the insured permission to use the premises in the way consistent with the occupancy described in the declarations in the insurance contract. As another example, the same form permits the insured to make "alterations, improvements and repairs" without causing the insurance to be suspended. Some forms also specify that bullion and manuscripts are "put back" into the coverage. For most insureds, however, bullion and manuscripts do not pose much of an insurance problem.

Readers can see that the general purpose of a permit is to afford some coverage to the insured which he would not have otherwise. Often, the permit is a device for restoring to the insured something which has been "taken away" in the policy itself. Use of permits varies considerably in the commercial and industrial forms.

Mortgage Clause

If a mortgagee or some other creditor is to receive the proceeds of the insurance, it is necessary to have a Mortgagee Clause or a Loss Payable Clause in the contract. The wording of the Mortgagee Clause is standard. Under it the courts have held that for practical purposes there is a separate insurance contract between the insurer and the mortgagee with the insurer agreeing to protect the interests of the mortgagee and to pay to him up to the amount of insurance available for loss or measured by destruction of or damage to the property.[6] In the event that no liability for the loss exists as to the mortgagor or owner because of a violation of policy conditions, the insurer becomes subrogated to all of the rights of the party to whom payment was made. The mortgagee on his part agrees to advise the insurer of any change of ownership or occupancy or increase of hazard which comes to his knowledge and to pay any increased premium for such additional hazard. The mortgagee also agrees to pay the premium if the owner does not do so.

This clause with virtually the same wording is used in most of the personal forms as well as in most of the commercial and industrial forms.

[6] *St. Louis Fire and Marine Insurance Company* v. *Witney, et al.* [96 F. Supp 555 (Pa., 1951)].

Clauses Establishing the Basis of Valuation

As brought out in Chapter 4, "actual cash value" is an important—and sometimes troublesome—concept in fire insurance. For many commercial and industrial properties the wording of the insuring agreement in the Standard Fire Policy may leave unanswered questions. In many instances this language is supplemented in the form with the aim of avoiding a dispute between the parties at the time of loss.

This supplementing may consist of a schedule assigning a value to certain property on a unit basis. This basis is often used when insuring a library, where a specific limit may be established per volume. If the library contains a rare book collection, the policy may contain a schedule listing these books and assigning a value to each one. Certain other types of property to which the normal basis of valuation is not applicable may also receive special treatment. For example, an arbitrary value may be assigned to material in files or to certain other types of property.

In some instances where the property to be covered includes finished products the policy may be written to include such finished products at either their sales price or at cost of replacement. If they are written on a sales price basis the recovery under the fire insurance contract will, of course, include the profit of the insured in such merchandise. It is quite common practice to include a Value of Stock Clause of which the following is a typical example:

(1) on stock in process, the value of raw materials and labor expended plus the proper proportion of overhead charges;
(2) on finished goods manufactured by the Insured, the regular cash selling price at the location where the loss occurs, less all discounts and charges to which the merchandise would have been subject had no loss occurred;
(3) on raw materials, supplies and other merchandise not manufactured by the Insured, the replacement cost.[7]

If there is a coinsurance clause in the form, all property is valued on the same basis for the application of the coinsurance clause as for the adjustment of a loss.

Replacement Cost

One of the significant changes in recent years in the insuring of certain commercial and industrial properties has been the increasing use of the replacement cost concept. (See Chapter 4 for a discussion of this concept.) The same general provisions usually prevail as when the replacement cost coverage is included in dwelling insurance contracts. One significant departure is that for churches, schools, and certain other public buildings the forms extend replacement cost to *contents*. Also, a few in-

---

[7] Factory Mutual Rating Bureau, Form D-1, p. 5.

surers will write as a separate amount of insurance the "depreciation" on such contents as furniture, fixtures, tools, appliances, machinery (if appraised), and other similar properties. With contracts written in this fashion, virtually all property covered under the policy (except inventories, supplies, drawings, records, manuscripts, and a few other types) is insured for the cost of replacement in new condition with materials of like size, kind, and quality.

The usual requirements of (1) an actual expenditure for repair or rebuilding and (2) maintenance of at least 80 percent of insurance to replacement value (for settlement on a replacement cost basis) are included in the commercial and industrial forms. If the property is not repaired or replaced, the settlement, of course, is on an actual cash value basis—in just the same way as in the Dwelling and Contents Forms and the Homeowners Policies.

In a few states special restrictions are imposed on insurance written on a replacement cost basis. Some forms require the replacement within the state; others specify within two years rather than merely within a "reasonable time." In the state of Washington replacement coverage can be written only on buildings, machinery, and equipment. In the state of Massachusetts furniture and furnishings and dwelling houses *must* be excluded.

When the replacement basis was first proposed, many insurance experts felt that it might lead to a substantial increase in moral hazard. However, experience with insurance written on this basis has disclosed that these fears so far appear to have been without justification. Apparently, the person who wishes to arrange a fire in order to collect insurance is not willing to wait until the property has been rebuilt in order to collect the full amount. This author feels that arson is never committed for the sake of securing a new building for an old one but, rather, that the arsonist wants cash.

SPECIAL RISKS

Over the years the fire insurance business has developed special forms each of which is intended to meet the needs of a particular type of business. The various rating bureaus, which promulgate most of the standard forms, recognize the problems of their respective territories and include among their approved forms several designed to make proper provision for the peculiarities of regional business. For example, the Fire Insurance Rating Bureau of North Carolina has two separate forms for tobacco warehouses, and two forms for tobacco curing barns, together with their contents. In those states in which cotton represents a major product separate forms are available for cotton gins, for cotton in bales, and for cottonseed oil mills.

Brokers or agents who specialize in a particular type of risk will often develop a form to provide tailor-made protection for such risks. As examples there are special forms for theatres, printing plants, and lumber yards. The grain business has its own group of forms, including those which provide coverage for grain charges. In all of these cases, the principal point of difference from the more commonly used forms is a more precise and detailed description of the various kinds of property to be insured. The tailor-made forms often include special permits or warranties that may be required for such risks. Anyone interested in such specialized forms can secure copies either from the rating bureau with jurisdiction in the territory or perhaps from brokers, agents, or insurance advisers who specialize in the type of insurance in question.

Highly Protected Risks

Insurance on industrial and commercial risks which meet the standards established by such organizations as the Factory Insurance Association, the Improved Risk Mutuals, and the Factory Mutuals is written on special forms developed by these organizations. Since risks of this kind are almost always protected by sprinklers as required for the hazards of construction or occupancy, these forms include sprinkler leakage protection. They normally omit the coinsurance clause, which is usual in forms for commercial and industrial property, since insurance on these risks is written for an agreed amount. Very broad clauses will be found covering new buildings and additions, the property of employees and property of others for which the insured may be liable. Because of the complexity of these risks, special schedules are normally used to list the locations insured and coverage is provided on a blanket basis.

Public and Institutional Property

One of the most interesting new developments has been the Public and Institutional Property Form. As is true with the forms used for Highly Protected Risks, insurance on this form is furnished by the insurers only when the insured has agreed to an inspection program. The program is for optional use in insuring hospitals, churches, schools, colleges, and municipal, county, and state installations. The most important features of the Public and Institutional Property Form are as follows:

1. Blanket coverage is given on all property, subject to certain exclusions. Scheduled coverage can be provided at the option of the insured by adding P.I.P. Form No. 2.

2. The mandatory deductible in the amount of $100 is applicable to loss by any peril other than fire or lightening. It applies separately to each building or structure with an aggregate of $1,000 per occurrence.

3. A sworn statement of values is required from the insured and an optional Amount of Insurance Clause is included in the form instead of a coinsurance clause.

4. The scope of the insurance, particularly with reference to personal property away from the premises and to newly acquired property, is broader than is usually the case.

5. At the option of the insured the insurance may be written on a replacement cost basis applicable to both personal and real property.

This form brings to the type of property which qualifies for it many of the features which in the past have been available only in the forms written for Highly Protected Risks. It was created to meet the competition of the Factory Mutuals, which were using their broad forms for large risks in this class.

REPORTING FORMS

The difficult problem of determining the correct amount of insurance on stock and finished goods for business establishments, particularly where inventory is subject to wide fluctuations, has been recognized by insurers. In order to provide an answer for the problem, they have provided a range of Reporting Forms. The basic idea is that the insured who reports his values at stated periods and maintains a limit of insurance sufficient to cover the maximum value at any time will pay a premium on the average value at risk during the year and still have adequate coverage during peak periods. When the insurance is written on a reporting basis, the insured avoids the danger of both underinsurance and overinsurance. He is spared the vexing necessity of adjusting the amount of his insurance as his values change. Rating bureaus in all jurisdictions promulgate Reporting Forms, with some restrictions on the type of property which may be insured under them. Except for those provisions which deal with the amount of insurance, the limit of liability, the adjustment of premium, the reporting requirements, and penalties for failure to report, these forms are similar to those used on other commercial and industrial risks.

A Reporting Form is written with a provisional amount of insurance. The proper rate is applied to the provisional amount of insurance to determine the provisional or deposit premium. The rating bureau, through its rules, tells how the provisional amount shall be determined and sets the highest limit of liability to apply at any one location. The limit of liability is almost always higher than the provisional amount of insurance on which the deposit premium is based. If more than one location is involved there may be a separate limit of liability at each location.

The insured makes reports at whatever interval of time is called for under the form, often monthly. An adjustment is made in the provisional premium based upon the full value of the insured property, less permitted specific insurance. This adjustment is made even though the amount on which premium is paid is greater than the limit of liability.

If specific insurance is available at any location where property is covered under a Reporting Form, the Reporting Form, under its terms, is always excess. If a loss occurs which involves both reporting and specific insurance, it is adjusted under the specific policies as though the Reporting Form did not exist. The difference between the amount recovered under the specific insurance and the full amount of loss is then paid by the reporting cover.

This whole procedure is, of course, dependent upon prompt and accurate reports of values by the insured. If the insured fails to submit a report when it is due, he is bound by his latest report. Under some of the forms, if the insured has made no reports at the time of loss he may collect only 90 percent of the amount for which the insurer would otherwise be liable. Under other forms, if the first report is not made, there is no automatic coverage on newly acquired locations and coverage is provided for not more than 75 percent of the limit of liability. There are also penalties in the event of errors in the report. Under the Full Reporting Clause, if the last value report filed prior to a loss is less than the actual value as of the time of the report, the insured's recovery is reduced in the same proportion that the reported value bears to the actual value.

The Reporting Forms are a great convenience to the insured and provide adequate coverage without requiring him to pay premium for unnecessary protection. However, they should never be used unless the policyholder has its accounting function so organized that accurate reports can be made on time. If there is any question as to whether or not reports can be filed when due, the insured is better advised to buy the coverage on a nonreporting basis.

ADAPTION TO NEED

The Standard Fire Policy is a statutory document which might be said to correspond to a bolt of cloth. What the insured must have is "the stuff" of the contract tailored to his own insurance needs. This is the purpose of the form. Through it the Standard Fire Policy becomes a flexible document which, in the hands of an expert, provides adequate protection against most of the perils to which the commercial or industrial property is exposed. A form can be drawn only by someone thoroughly familiar with the particular problems of the insured for whom it is prepared. If the insured has an Insurance Department or an Insurance Manager, one of the major responsibilities of such department or manager is the review of proposed forms. Any modifications in standard language necessary to indicate accurately and clearly the scope of the contract and the property to which it is to be applied should be sought. The time to argue over the application of the policy is when the form is being written, not after the loss.

SUGGESTED READINGS

Ackerman, S. B. *Insurance.* 3d. ed. New York: Ronald Press Co., 1951. Chap. 4.

Barbour, Robert P. *The Agent's Key to Fire Insurance.* 6th ed. New York: Spectator Co., 1949.

Fire, Casualty, and Surety Bulletins. Cincinnati: National Underwriter Co. Fire and Marine Volume, Fire Forms Section.

Gordis, Philip. *Property and Casualty Insurance.* 9th ed. Indianapolis: Rough Notes Co., 1962. Chap. 3.

Magee, John H. *Property Insurance.* 3rd ed. Homewood, Ill.: Richard D. Irwin, Inc., 1955. Chaps. 6, 10, 12.

Policy Form and Manual Analysis Service. Indianapolis: Rough Notes Co.

Reed, Prentiss B. *Fire Insurance Underwriting.* New York: McGraw-Hill Book Co., Inc., 1940. Chap. xii.

Chapter 8

ALLIED LINES INSURANCE

MARK R. GREENE

There is no generally accepted definition of what constitutes "allied lines insurance." This term is applied when it is desired to describe coverages closely associated and usually sold with fire insurance. For purposes of this *Handbook*, allied lines insurance will include the following:

1. Sprinkler Leakage Insurance.
2. Water Damage Insurance.
3. Earthquake Insurance.
4. Radioactive Contamination Insurance.
5. Vandalism and Malicious Mischief Insurance.
6. Standing Timber Insurance.
7. Optional Perils Insurance.
8. Demolition Insurance.
9. Increased Cost of Construction Insurance.
10. Data Processing Policy.

SPRINKLER LEAKAGE INSURANCE

To encourage loss prevention activities, property-liability insurers have generally granted sizeable discounts in fire insurance rates for the installation of automatic sprinkler systems. It is often possible for the insured to recover within five years the entire cost of installing a sprinkler system because of the savings in fire insurance premiums. Unfortunately, installation of an automatic sprinkler system introduces a new peril namely, the danger of damage to building and contents because of accidental discharge of water from the sprinkler system. Water damage losses of this type are excluded from extended coverage forms, but insurers offer an endorsement to the Standard Fire Policy which provides coverage. In some jurisdictions a separate policy against sprinkler leakage damage must be purchased. Sprinkler leakage protection is also offered under special multiple peril policies.

Need

Any merchant or manufacturer with an automatic sprinkler system is exposed to loss from sprinkler leakage. Even if the insured does not have a sprinkler system installed on his individual premises, he may still be subject to loss from sprinkler leakage because of the existence of systems in adjoining premises in the same building (especially on upper floors), or even from sprinkler systems in nearby buildings. For example, collapse of a roof-top tank containing water to supply sprinkler systems sometimes occurs, causing a deluge of thousands of gallons of water over the insured's property.

Coverage

Sprinkler leakage insurance covers loss resulting from direct damage by leakage or discharge of water or other substance from within any automatic sprinkler system or caused by fall or collapse of tanks which are part of such systems. The policy does not limit in any way the reasons for the discharge of water except that accidental leakage must be the proximate cause of loss (see exclusions below). Such discharge might be caused by heat radiation from the sun, other heat, mechanical injury, freezing, or defects in the equipment. For example, mechanical failure led to a $200,000 loss in a large Chicago department store when a six-inch pipe on the fourth floor of the store broke, due to a faulty casting in the pipe. In this loss a ¾-inch separation of the pipe, which was at the time under 160 pounds of pressure, allowed water to escape at a very rapid rate. By the time the water was turned off six to eight minutes later, the floor near the break was under five to six inches of water. The break occurred on the fourth floor of the building and water seeped downward to the third-floor lingerie shop, causing very large amounts of damage. Water leaked down to lower floors all the way to the basement, causing additional loss.

It is emphasized that the loss need not stem from a sprinkler system under the insured's control. Furthermore, losses from such sources as sprinkler heads, pipes, valves, fittings, tanks, pumps, and private fire protection mains are part of the automatic sprinkler system and losses from any of these sources are covered. For example, if the supporting members of a reservoir tank collapsed, the resulting damage would be covered.

Varying arrangements are possible as to which type of property is to be covered. If only losses to the building are insured, coverage includes the losses to permanent fixtures, machinery, and equipment, including the cost of repairs and replacements to the sprinkler system made necessary directly by breakage due to sprinkler leakage or freezing. There is no coverage for such parts of the building as excavations, foundations, grading, filling, underground pipes, wires, flues, pilings, or piers. Coverage on personal property can be all-inclusive or may be limited to stock only, furniture and fixtures, machinery, or some combination of these items. Property of others, such as employees' apparel or goods of customers held in trust, may be insured.

Exclusions

The standard sprinkler leakage endorsement excludes certain perils. For example, water damage from sources other than an automatic sprinkler system are excluded. Loss which can be traced directly to perils such as fire, lightning, windstorm, earthquake, riot and civil commotion, explosion, rupture of steam boilers or flywheels, and blasting are excluded. These perils would then be considered as the proximate cause of the loss. For example, if a fire occurs causing the discharge of water from the sprinkler system, the proximate cause of the loss is the fire and not water from the sprinkler system. Consequently, the fire policy would cover the entire loss. Similarly, if a windstorm blows the support tank over, windstorm insurance is necessary for coverage of the loss since the windstorm would be the proximate cause of the loss.

The sprinkler leakage endorsement also excludes losses stemming from order of civil authority, war, atomic fission, and nuclear reactions. If the insured is contemplating repairs, alterations or extensions of his building which will take longer than 15 days to complete, a special endorsement to the sprinkler leakage policy is required, for which extra premium is charged. Losses occurring while the building is vacant or unoccupied are excluded, but the insurer will grant permission for vacancy or unoccupancy without charge. It is necessary that a separate endorsement be added as evidence of such permission.

Coinsurance

Sprinkler leakage insurance is written with coinsurance which operates in its manner similar to the coinsurance clause commonly written with commercial fire insurance. Substantial savings in rates are made possible by the use of coinsurance. For example, it is possible to increase the limit of coverage fivefold for an increase in the premium of less than twofold if coinsurance is accepted.

Rating

Rates for sprinkler leakage are based upon the fire insurance rates in the territory in which the premises are located. Charges and credits are applied to a basic rate to reflect: use of protective devices and services as alarms; the susceptibility of the contents to water damage; the location of the contents within the building; and the type, condition, and construction of the building and equipment. Rate classifications include manufacturing, nonmanufacturing, and multiple occupancy. Rates also depend upon the type of sprinkler system. Adjustments in the rates for sprinkler leakage insurance are made if the supply pipe or tank of the sprinkler system is in another building, or if the insured's building contains no automatic sprinkler system.

Sprinkler Leakage Liability

Because water damage losses from leaking sprinkler systems may well include damage to property of more than one occupant of a building, it is generally very desirable for certain insureds to carry sprinkler leakage liability insurance. This coverage is also purchased by operators of storage warehouses in which the property of others is stored. It is well established that an insured is legally liable for loss to others' property caused by defective sprinkler systems for which he is responsible. The liability form is generally written to cover liability for damage to property similar to that which is owned by the insured in the described buildings.

Sprinkler leakage liability coverage includes liability assumed under contract for goods under the insured's control. For property not under the insured's control, separate contractual liability insurance is needed. For example, if the insured has signed an agreement with another tenant to be responsible for any type of losses resulting from the insured's sprinkler system, a contractual liability would result and would require separate insurance.

Consequential Loss Coverage

It is possible to attach consequential loss forms to the sprinkler leakage endorsement. Thus if the business is wholly or partially interrupted by sprinkler leakage damage, a business interruption form will make it possible for the insured to recover resulting loss of profits and fixed charges. Similarly tuition fees insurance, extra expenses, and other time element coverage may be attached.

WATER DAMAGE INSURANCE

It is well known that water can cause extensive damage to property. Unfortunately it has not been possible for the insurance industry to insure all types of water damage, but an attempt has been made to offer a somewhat limited protection through certain standard and widely used forms, of which sprinkler leakage insurance, discussed in the preceding section, is one. Illustrating some types of losses from water damage are the following, reported by the National Underwriter Company in the *Fire, Casualty, and Surety Bulletins:*

1. A janitor arranged the valves of a water heater in an apartment building in such a way that the water tank became overheated and broke, allowing a steady stream of water to emit from the boiler. Water came into the basement faster than the drain could remove it and overflowed into the hallway and into several basement apartments.
2. A heavy downpour of rain overloaded the sewage system for a large warehouse. Backup water exerted pressure on a drainage-pipe cap which was supposed to prevent such back-flow. The cap gave way and water was sprayed onto the walls of the basement causing damage of $72,604.

3. A rubber hose connection on an air-conditioning system permitted water to flow into a building and caused $22,665 of damage to the building and $4,208 of damage to the stock.

4. A venetian blind blew against a water faucet turning it on in the owner's absence. Water covered the floor of the home to a depth of several inches causing $5,000 damage.

5. The insured's daughter turned on the water in the bathtub and then left to watch television. The water overflowed causing severe damage.

6. A truck sheared off a fire hydrant near a factory, causing two tons of water per minute to fall on the roof until it collapsed under the weight. The loss was $180,000.

Coverage

Water damage insurance would have covered the losses cited above. Specifically, the basic insuring clause of the water damage policy insures

> . . . direct loss or damage caused by accidental discharge, leakage or overflow of water or steam from plumbing systems, tanks, heating systems, elevator tanks and cylinders, standpipes for fire hose, industrial and domestic appliances, refrigerating systems, air-conditioning systems, and rain or snow admitted directly to the interior of the building through defective roofs, leaders, or spouting, or open or defective windows, show windows, doors, transoms, ventilators or skylights.[1]

Exclusions

Basic exclusions under the water damage policy include the following:

1. Damage to systems, appliances, tanks, and parts of building which are a source of the water damage loss.
2. Damage caused by sprinkler systems or parts thereof (covered under sprinkler leakage policy).
3. Loss from flood, tides, rising or surface waters, or other similar inundation.
4. Backing up of sewers or drains.
5. Seepage, leakage, or influx of water through building walls, foundations, basement floor, sidewalks, or sidewalk lights.
6. Losses from gases, fumes, or vapor leakage.
7. Losses which can be traced to other common insurable perils such as fire, lightning, windstorm, etc.
8. Water loss the proximate cause of which is invasion, insurrection, riot, civil war, commotion, civil authority, or usurped power.
9. Loss caused by the neglect of the insured to use reasonable means to protect the property after damage.
10. Loss caused by rising temperatures (this loss may be covered by endorsement).
11. Water loss from breakage or leakage from underground supply mains or from fire hydrants.
12. Loss caused by aircraft, aircraft equipment, or objects falling from aircraft (this loss may be covered by endorsement).

---

[1] *Fire, Casualty, and Surety Bulletins* (Cincinnati: National Underwriter Co.), Fire and Marine Volume, Multiple Line, p. Wd–1 (June, 1951).

Loss or damage from interruption or leakage from street water supply, mains, or fire hydrants, or the leakage of refrigerants from refrigerating or air-conditioning systems may be added by endorsement for extra charge.

Rating

Water damage insurance is sufficiently complex to require the preparation of separate rating manuals. Rates vary with coinsurance requirements, protective devices, the destructibility and location of property, and the use of deductibles. For example, a 10 percent premium reduction is allowed with the use of a $50 deductible and a 15 percent for a $100 deductible.

Consequential Losses

Consequential loss coverage can be written in connection with water damage insurance. Business interruption insurance, profits and commissions, and other consequential coverages can be endorsed to the water damage policy.

Residence Coverage

Water damage insurance is written as a part of residence insurance under broad forms now being offered to the public. When offered in this way, the water damage insurance includes coverage for discharge of gas, oil, or chemicals from plumbing, heating, refrigerating, air-conditioning, cooking, or lighting appliances. In addition, such coverage usually includes the cost of repair or replacement of the apparatus which caused the loss but excludes water damage caused from freezing during the unoccupancy of the residence, unless the insured has taken certain precautions to prevent such loss.

EARTHQUAKE INSURANCE

Earthquakes have occurred in practically every part of the United States, although certain parts of the country (for example, the West Coast) are especially vulnerable to loss from this source.

Insurance against earthquake is written in different ways, depending upon geographical area. In the west coast states of Arizona, California, Idaho, Montana, Nevada, Oregon, Utah, and Washington, it is written as an endorsement to the Standard Fire Policy. In other parts of the United States earthquake insurance is written as a separate policy. In several areas, however, dwellings can be insured against earthquakes by an endorsement to the Standard Fire Policy.

The Hazard

Earthquakes, which arise out of the universal mobility of the earth's surface, occur almost continuously. Statistics suggest that each year the earth averages one great earthquake, 10 major earthquakes, 1,000 damage shocks, 10,000 minor strong shocks, and 100,000 shocks which are generally felt over a fairly wide area.[2] About 80 percent of the seismic energy of the world is released in the area surrounding the Pacific Ocean, and another 15 percent is released in a belt starting in the Mediterranean area and running easterly across Asia. However, very strong shocks have occurred in areas which seldom receive them, such as the one occurring in St. Louis, Missouri, in 1811 which was felt as far away as Boston, Massachusetts. Often the major damage from earthquakes is by resulting fire. In the great San Francisco earthquake of 1906, for example, the earthquake itself was estimated to have caused $20 million of loss and resulting fires to have caused $400 million of loss.

Coverage

When written as an extension to the Standard Fire Policy, earthquake insurance merely extends the basic coverage to include a new peril and does not add to the amount of insurance. Usually, a deductible of at least 5 percent of the value of the property is required, with premium reductions allowed for larger deductibles. The peril of earthquake is usually defined to include all losses from shocks that occur within any 72-hour period. The limits of the policy apply as though the series of shocks which may occur within this period come from a single earthquake.

Coinsurance applies to the earthquake peril in a manner generally similar to that which may be required in the basic fire insurance contract. One difference, however, is that damage to foundations and other underground portions of the building are not excluded even though they may have been excluded under the basic fire coverage. Such losses are, however, subject to the deductible amount. The earthquake endorsement may be added to business interruption and other consequential loss coverages.

When earthquake insurance is written as a separate policy (non–West Coast states), there generally is no required deductible or contribution clause. The separate policy, of course, has its own separate amount of insurance. Usually, at least 50 percent coinsurance is required and the policy covers damage from volcanic eruption in addition to the earthquake damage.

Exclusions

Generally, earthquake insurance excludes loss intended to be covered by other contracts such as loss from fire and lightning. Other basic provisions of the Standard Fire Policy apply to the earthquake endorsement such as the cancellation, apportionment, and suspension clauses. Wind, frost, cold weather, explosion, flood, tidal wave, high water, overflow, or

---

[2] L. Don Leet, "Earthquake," *Encyclopedia Americana* (New York: Americana Corp., 1957), Vol. 9, p. 495.

cloudburst are excluded whether or not caused by earthquake or volcanic eruption.

Any damage done to the land itself is also excluded. This latter exclusion may be important because earthquakes occasionally cause serious damage to the land by creating crevasses and displacement.

Rating

Because of its catastrophic nature, the price of earthquake insurance is high. Annual premiums vary from 2 to 25 percent of the value of the property depending upon susceptibility of a given area to loss. The usual term rules apply and there is a minimum premium.

When earthquake insurance is written on a residence, there is a 5 percent deductible applying only to earthquake loss. It is written only on policies that also insure extended coverage perils (see Chapter 6 for a discussion of residential forms which contain the Extended Coverage Endorsement).

RADIOACTIVE CONTAMINATION INSURANCE

Because of the increased use of radioactive substances in industry, a demand has arisen for coverage against possible loss to property arising out of their use in industry, research, and medicine. For example, radioactive substances used in medicine are found in hospitals, doctors' offices, nursing homes, and clinics. Use of radiography in the X-ray machine is well known. In industry, radioisotopes are used in gauging, radiography and inspection. Radioactive substances are used in electronic tubes, watch dials, batteries, Geiger counters, light meters, and so on. Radioactive substances are used for cold sterilization, pharmaceuticals, surgical dressings and instruments, food preservation, activating chemical reactions, and other purposes.

Although this coverage might be fittingly included in Part IV of the *Handbook*, it can also properly be considered as one of the "allied lines." Readers should be aware, however, that the subject is included in the inland marine manuals. There is, for example, an inland marine endorsement of this type for motor cargo policies.

Coverage

Insurance against loss from radioactive substances is provided by two different types of endorsements to the Standard Fire Policy. The limited form (Form A) insures against the loss caused by sudden and accidental radioactive contamination directly resulting *from* an insured peril, such as fire, windstorm, or explosion. The broad form (Form B) insures against the sudden and accidental radioactive contamination directly as an insured peril. In other words, coverage under Form A would apply only if an insured peril, such as fire or windstorm, released radioactive substances which in turn caused loss to other property, the proximate cause of loss being considered to be the fire or windstorm. Under Form B, however, no insured peril need precede the loss other than the unintended, sudden, and accidental release of radioactivity from some industrial, medicinal, or research use. In either case coverage is limited to contamination from materials used or stored on the insured premises.

It is important to note that insurance protection of nuclear reactor installations is not covered under the radioactive contamination endorsement. These installations are insured under special forms and are underwritten through the facilities of two different "pools," the Nuclear Energy Property Insurance Association (NEPIA) or the Mutual Atomic Energy Reinsurance Pool (MAERP). (See Chapter 64 for a discussion of the operation of these organizations.) On any premises in which there is a nuclear reactor or any new or used nuclear fuel elements, the radioactive contamination coverage provided in Forms A and B does not apply since it is assumed the insured will obtain coverage for the nuclear reactor itself and all consequences resulting from the use of these reactors.

The coverage provided under Forms A and B must have originated from contamination on the described premises. Any contamination which originated from off the premises is not covered. This limitation is an important one since it means the insured is unprotected against nuclear fallout or other nuclear hazards which might have originated from a nearby reactor.

Rating

Coverage under the two radioactive contamination assumption endorsements must be submitted for individual rating to a rating organization. The rates depend upon the hazards on the premises, there being presently six categories in which rates are promulgated. The least expensive rate applies to risks in which there are no known exposures to radioactive materials on the premises, but where coverage is desired to protect against the possibility of loss which might occur, for example, if radioactive substances were brought on the premises by unknown persons. In general, the rate increases as the quantity of radioactive material on the premises increases.

VANDALISM AND MALICIOUS MISCHIEF

Coverage

Insurance against the peril of vandalism and malicious mischief is generally written as an endorsement to the Standard Fire Policy in a manner similar to that in which extended coverage is written. It is also written on the Optional Perils Policy (see below). "Vandalism and malicious mischief" is referred to in the endorsement as "willful and malicious damage to or destruction of described property." In general the loss must have been caused intentionally by vandals. However, in court cases it has been decided that the insurance also covers damage by pranksters (usually children) who should have been aware of the natural consequences of their act, even though they may not have specifically intended to cause a loss.

Exclusions

Among the perils and losses excluded are damage to glass constituting part of the building (except glass building blocks), temperature or humidity change, depreciation, explosion of steam boilers or machinery, delay, deterioration or loss of market, and damage caused by burglars. (In some states damage to buildings caused by burglars is covered.) Coverage for these exclusions is generally available under other forms.

Rating

The rates for vandalism insurance are generally quite low with the exception of certain types of properties, such as golf courses. The rate is based upon the occupancy of the property in question and upon the coinsurance provisions. A minimum of 10 percent coinsurance is required.

STANDING TIMBER INSURANCE

This insurance technically is fire insurance. Its uniqueness lies not in the perils involved but rather in the nature of the property covered. Because of this uniqueness it is traditionally classified as one of the "allied lines" even though, strictly speaking, it is fire and lightning insurance.

Coverage

While standing timber insurance is written by most property and liability insurance companies, the underwriting hazards are particularly high. For this reason the coverage has many limitations. In general only the perils of fire and lightning are insured. Sometimes the requirement is imposed that the insured warrant the description and value of the trees to be correct. A limitation of liability of a given amount for each acre of standing timber customarily is imposed. Some policies exclude timber growing in such locations as to be "rendered impracticable or impossible to log at usual profit by ordinary customary methods."

Coverage is usually afforded on two classes of timber, merchantable timber and reforestation plantations (tree farms). Merchantable trees are usually defined in the policy as living trees, free of decay or other observable defects, and of a certain minimum size, such as six inches or greater in diameter, or four-and-a-half feet tall.

Underwriters will not usually accept softwood standing timber which is being logged except under certain conditions. Hardwood timber enjoys more ready acceptance for coverage. Coverage on plantations is limited to the actual outlay for trees and labor plus compound interest at a given rate from the date of planting.

Rating

Rates for standing timber insurance are developed from some base rate, say $1.00 or $1.25 per $100 of exposed value, to which certain charges are added depending upon the condition of the timber. For example, a charge might be added for slash which has been on the ground between five and seven years. If the standing timber is exposed by a steam railroad, by nearby portable sawmills, or by other roadways, other charges may be added. Credits are given for such features as approved lookout towers, equipped with telephones and manned by approved forestry personnel. Credit may be given also for the existence of a state fire patrol within the area or for erecting posters warning against carelessness with fire. Once the final rate has been determined, an additional charge known as the "dry season charge," equal usually to 80 percent of the annual premium, is added. No return premium is allowed if the policy has been in force during any part of the period from April through November, which months are considered to constitute the dry season. Coinsurance is usually required and a reduction in the rate is given upon the acceptance of higher coinsurance percentages.

OPTIONAL PERILS INSURANCE

Coverage

The Optional Perils Policy includes certain perils such as vandalism and malicious mischief, aircraft and vehicle damage, riot, civil commotion, and explosion. Most of these coverages may be written separately or in combination with each other. In general, however, riot insurance must accompany explosion coverage and vandalism coverage must accompany both explosion and riot coverage.

The Optional Perils Policy uses wording in the insuring agreement which is very similar to that in the Standard Fire Policy except that in the insuring clause, the words "direct loss by fire . . ." are replaced by the words "direct loss by the perils insured against and by removal from the premises endangered by the perils insured against in this policy except as hereinafter provided."

Conditions

The conditions of the policy follow fairly closely the wording of the Standard Fire Policy with certain exceptions. For example, provision is made for the apportionment of losses caused jointly by two or more perils. This clause is called joint loss provision and uses the limit-of-liability rule in settlement of the losses. Under this rule the limit of each insurer for joint losses is the proportion that the limit of liability of one type of insurance, considered separately, bears to the total aggregate limit of all applicable insurance. An example will make this clear. Let us assume that the insured has coverage under the Optional Perils Policy for explosion, riot and civil commotion, and vandalism and malicious mischief in the amounts of $10,000, $15,000, and $35,000, respectively. Assume further there is a loss of $5,000 which is considered to have been caused jointly by explosion and riot and civil commotion. Since the total limit of liability of *applicable* insurance is $25,000 and the limit for explosion coverage is $10,000, the explosion coverage is deemed to be responsible for $^{10}/_{25}$ of the loss ($2,000) and riot and civil commotion coverage is deemed to be responsible for $^{15}/_{25}$ of the loss ($3,000).

Exclusions

The Optional Perils Policy contains specific provisions defining each peril. For example, vandalism and malicious mischief coverage excludes loss to glass constituting part of the building, loss resulting from depreciation, delay, deterioration, or loss of market, change of temperature or humidity, and vacancy in excess of 30 days (except for builder's risks). In a similar manner various restrictions apply to the other insured perils.

DEMOLITION AND INCREASED COST OF CONSTRUCTION INSURANCE

The point has been made in earlier chapters of this *Handbook* that payment of merely the "actual cash value" of a loss to a policyholder may not cover all of his out-of-pocket costs—particularly if he rebuilds. (See Chapter 4 for a discussion of replacement cost.) The point should now be recognized that even replacement cost insurance may not be sufficient to cover all out-of-pocket costs. The policyholder who suffers a loss may face one or more of the following situations: (1) he may have to tear down some *undamaged* portion of a building because of a building ordinance; (2) he may incur expense in the demolition itself; and (3) upon rebuilding, he may have to adhere to minimum specifications superior to those which were used in the original construction of the building.

These possibilities of loss give rise to additional forms of insurance which are described in this section. The decision as to how these coverages should be classified is a bit arbitrary. By some criteria they are of consequential loss type and therefore should be included in Chapter 10 of this *Handbook* rather than in this chapter. Indeed, some insurance authorities do so classify them. Since a building ordinance, however, is in a sense an "additional peril" and since the discussion fits conveniently in this chapter, these forms of insurance will be taken up now. Because they are tied in closely with replacement cost insurance, it will be reviewed in this section also.

Replacement Cost Insurance

Replacement cost insurance, formerly known as depreciation insurance, is written to cover losses occasioned by the limitation of recovery under the Standard Fire Policy to the *actual cash value* of the loss—that is, the cost to put the insured in the same place he was before loss—no better and no worse. For example, assume that a building is destroyed to the extent of $50,000, which is 50 percent of its new replacement cost of $100,000. However, it is determined that $15,000 of depreciation is applicable since the building is not new. The insured is allowed under the Standard Fire Policy to recover only $35,000, the new replacement cost less depreciation. This manner of loss adjustment might put the insured under severe financial strain through no fault of his own. With replacement cost insurance, the insured could recover in full for his $50,000 loss, if certain conditions are met.

Conditions as to Commercial, Industrial, and Certain Other Buildings

There are certain conditions under the Replacement Cost Form which should be observed:

1. The building must actually be rebuilt, generally on the same site, within a reasonable time after the loss. (Some types of property, such as public or church buildings, need not be rebuilt on the same site.)
2. The insured is expected to purchase insurance equal or nearly equal to the full replacement cost of the building or be subject to coinsurance penalties (even if he settles on an actual cash value basis). The typical coinsurance requirement for use of the Replacement Cost Endorsement is 100 percent. The insured always has the option of settling on an actual cash value basis, if by this means he will collect more than he would under the replacement cost conditions (but the coinsurance provision still operates as to the actual cash value). If the insured does not wish to rebuild he will recover on an actual cash value basis with consideration given to coinsurance.
3. If the loss is both less than $10,000 and less than 5 percent of the amount of insurance, the requirement that an inventory be taken of damaged and undamaged property is waived.
4. Increased replacement costs occasioned by the operation of building codes are excluded.

Residential Property

Applied to residences, replacement cost insurance differs slightly in its coverage:

1. The inventory waiver clause, if any, applies to losses of both less than $1,000 and less than 5 percent of the amount of insurance.
2. Replacement cost coverage does not apply generally to carpeting, cloth awings, or similar equipment whether part of the building or not.

3. Repair or replacement of the property on the same site is not a requirement in residential property, although recovery is limited to what it would cost to rebuild on the original site.

4. Finally, while the insured is required to take insurance equal to 80 percent of replacement value, the clause does not operate as a coinsurance clause, penalizing recoveries made on an actual cash value basis, as is true with replacement cost coverage on commercial property.

Increased Cost of Construction and Demolition Insurance

Under many building codes a property owner, if he rebuilds at all, may be required to rebuild a partially destroyed building in a manner which costs him more than he can collect under the Standard Fire Policy, even with the Replacement Cost Endorsement added to it.

For example, the building code may require that a partially destroyed frame building be torn down and, if rebuilt at all, replaced with concrete or brick construction. The Standard Fire Policy only agrees to replace the damaged portion of a building with materials of *like kind and quality.* Even with replacement cost, the insured would not be able to collect for the added cost of the concrete or brick construction as opposed to the frame. Neither would he be able in case of a partial loss to collect for demolition or rebuilding of undamaged portions of a building. For these reasons an insured may suffer a loss which he can ill afford. Even though it might be argued that the added cost of construction occasioned by a building code actually represents a capital improvement which places the insured in a better position than he was formerly, it may be that the insured would have been fully satisfied with construction of the less costly type.

Demolition Insurance

This insurance goes by a variety of names including Demolition and Contingent Liability from Operation of Building Laws. It is added by endorsement to the Standard Fire Policy. The endorsement extends the policy and does not in itself change the amount of insurance.

By whatever name the endorsement goes, the general idea is that the insured may add coverage to his Standard Fire Policy for the loss occasioned by the enforcement of any building ordinance regulating the construction or repair of buildings which necessitates the demolition of any undamaged portion of a building which has suffered damage by the perils insured against. In other words, the policyholder can be paid for the actual cash value of the undamaged portion he had to tear down. In some forms (mainly in the Midwest and South) the expense of demolition is *not* covered; in other forms this cost of tearing down may be covered provided the insured has purchased enough insurance. The cost of this endorsement is related, of course, to the amount of insurance on the building and is also a function of the building rate.

Increased Cost of Construction Insurance

This insurance is also known as Excess of Replacement Cost and can be used only in conjunction with the replacement cost coverage. The form provides for an *additional amount of insurance*. This amount is to cover the increased costs of having to adhere (by virtue of a building code) to more rigid specifications in repairing or replacing the building than were required when the earlier construction of the building took place. With replacement cost coverage the policyholder could be paid for the cost of replacement new according to the "old" specifications. The *extra* cost incurred by having to use the "new" specifications, however, would be beyond the replacement cost benefits—hence the need for the Increased Cost of Construction Insurance Form.

The insurer's liability under this endorsement is limited to the smallest of three amounts: (1) the additional amount of insurance purchased; (2) the amount actually paid out for repair or replacement which would not otherwise have been recoverable under the Standard Fire Policy written without the added endorsement; or (3) the difference between the replacement cost of the existing building, without reduction for depreciation, and the replacement cost of a similar building conforming to the minimum requirements of the building code. In no case can the insured recover more than the cost of meeting minimum requirements of the building code. The insured must rebuild on the same premises in order to recover under the endorsement (educational or church properties excepted), and under forms used on the Pacific Coast he must rebuild within a two-year period. Such a provision reduces the moral hazard, for in some cases there might be a temptation for a dishonest insured to deliberately destroy his own property whose location had deteriorated, in the hopes of financing a new building at a more favorable location at the expense of the insurer.

The rates for this endorsement vary widely. A common rate is the 100 percent coinsurance building rate. The rate, however, may be twice the 100 percent coinsurance building rate.

Time Element Coverage

If a building code requires demolition of property and requires a more elaborate or costly construction, it is not unreasonable to suppose that this construction will take longer to complete than would be the case if the insured were rebuilding the old structure. This situation would increase the business interruption loss and other losses depending on the rebuilding time, such as extra expense or rental income losses. Accordingly an endorsement known as the Demolition and Increased Time to Rebuild Endorsement is available to permit the insured to recover consequential losses during the additional period of rebuilding caused by building code requirements. The insured must exercise due diligence and dispatch. Provisions of the endorsement are similar to the forms noted above.

Regional Differences

Readers are cautioned to notice that the type of "demolition" insurance varies widely by region of the country. In Eastern and Pacific states the demolition coverage can be combined with a "limited" increased cost of construction coverage to produce something more than provided by a Contingent Liability from Operation of Building Laws Endorsement—but something less than provided by the combination of (1) Contingent Liability from Operation of Building Laws Endorsement plus (2) Increased Cost of Construction (Excess of Replacement Cost) Endorsement.

An Example

Perhaps an example will help to clarify the coverages discussed in this section. Suppose an insured had a building the actual cash value of which was $100,000 and the replacement cost (new) of which was $125,000. Suppose that an actual cash value loss of $60,000 was suffered in a location where an ordinance dictated that the undamaged portion had to be torn down and that any rebuilding would have to conform to modern specifications. Suppose that these specifications meant, in effect, that $20,000 of extra cost would be incurred in meeting the new specifications —compared to rebuilding new according to the original specifications. Suppose that the expense of demolishing the undamaged portion of the old structure was $2,000. Suppose, finally, that the insured promptly rebuilt on the same site a structure intended for the same occupancy and spent $145,000 in doing so. If he had at the time of the loss a Standard Fire Policy in the amount of $125,000 endorsed to afford replacement cost coverage; if he had the Increased Cost of Construction Endorsement in the amount of at least $20,000; and if he had the Contingent Liability from Operation of Building Laws (or Demolition) Endorsement, he could collect $145,000. He could not collect the $2,000 he incurred as the expense of demolishing. In some parts of the country, he could have collected the $2,000 also if he had bought another $2,000 of insurance on the building item in the Standard Fire Policy.

DATA PROCESSING POLICY

One of the allied fire lines as yet quite new is the Data Processing Policy. Currently written on an all risk basis, the Data Processing Policy is actually a type of multiple line peril (see Part VI) but is discussed here because it illustrates the development of the application of fire insurance to specialized needs. To the author's knowledge currently only one group of insurers writes a specialized policy for data processing equipment and media. The company estimates that there were over 4,500 electronic data processing units in use in 1961 and that by 1968 there will be nearly 1,000 large computers, 7,800 medium computers and 43,500 small computers in operation.[3] Thus the market for this type of coverage should expand considerably in the future.

Examples of losses to data processing systems include the following: (1) a fire in the Pentagon building in Washington, D.C., destroyed large amounts of uninsured data processing media and equipment; (2) soot from a fire in another part of the building, carried into the air-conditioning system, resulted in a total loss of a memory drum in the Chase Manhattan Bank in New York; (3) sand was carried into a data processing system while the building next door was being sandblasted.

Risk of loss to data processing systems and media, together with the extra expense of restoring the system to normalcy following a loss, require special treatment. Insurance contracts such as the Standard Fire Policy, Boiler and Machinery Policy, and the Valuable Papers Policy have too limited coverage, unrealistic rating procedures, or certain rigidities in loss settlement methods. The data processing equipment and media risk is characterized by high susceptibility to loss, large concentration of values in small areas, and limited supply of skilled labor to restore the system to normal operation following a loss. These characteristics dictate the need for careful attention to the problem of insurance.

Three types of coverage are written:

1. *Insurance on the data processing equipment itself.* In general the policy is subject to 80, 90, or 100 percent coinsurance. The processing equipment is insured on an all risk basis. A schedule must be obtained of the units to be covered. All or part of an insured's equipment may be included. In case equipment is leased and the insured is responsible for only certain types of loss, the policy will insure the losses for which the insured only is subject. For example, the lessor may provide insurance on fire and extended coverage perils and the lessee is expected to be responsible for any other types of loss. The Data Processing Policy will cover this other exposure.

2. *Data processing media.* Before data processing equipment can operate the information must be in special forms called *media.* These media include magnetic tapes, punchcards, desks, drums, perforated paper tapes, and other materials. A substantial investment is made in media. Reproduction of them may be an expensive process. The Data Processing Policy can be written to cover media on a valued basis or on actual cash value on an all risk basis. No coinsurance applies to media coverage.

3. *Extra expense.* A very considerable cost might be involved in the extra expenses of resuming business in case the equipment of media of an electronic data processing system is damaged by an insured peril. The Data Processing Policy includes coverage for these expenses under a separate endorsement. No coinsurance applies to this section of the policy. In estimating the extent of loss

[3] St. Paul Fire and Marine Insurance Company, mimeographed release, 1961.

each insured is provided a worksheet on which he estimates the extra expenses of getting back into normal operation once a peril has occurred, that is, the extra cost of newspaper advertisements, rent of temporary facilities, trucking and moving expense, overtime, rental of temporary equipment, extra traveling expense, special protective services, and so on.

Rating

The Data Processing Policy is subject to a minimum deductible of $500. Higher deductibles are used with appropriate credits in the rate. In general, the rate for the Data Processing Policy is based upon the fire, extended coverage, and vandalism and malicious mischief rate with a loading to take care of the extra hazards involved in the all risk endorsement.

One requirement of media coverage is that a duplicate copy of each master program and/or instruction tape be contained in a fireproof safe or vault or combination-lock in another building which is rated as a separate risk by rating authorities. This requirement is common to valuable papers insurance and accounts receivable insurance, which are also offered in connection with the policy. In the application the insured is required to state the length of time necessary to reproduce the duplicate copies in case the originals were destroyed. The frequency with which the duplicate copies are brought up to date must be indicated. In this way accurate estimates of potential loss exposure can be provided.

Exclusions

Typical excluded perils under the data processing insurance forms include losses from mechanical breakdown and erasure, and electrical failure from lightning, blowout, short circuit, or other electrical disturbance unless fire or explosion ensues. These exclusions may be eliminated if the insured is willing to accept a substantial deductible amount, such as $25,000. The perils of corrosion, rust, dryness or dampness of atmosphere, and extremes of temperature are excluded. Other basic exclusions are delay, loss of market, war, and nuclear contamination. Since the final pattern of this insurance has not been in any sense standardized, undoubtedly an insured may obtain modifications in the terms and conditions described above to meet his individual needs.

SUGGESTED READINGS

ANGELL, FRANK J. *Insurance: Principles and Practices.* New York: Ronald Press Co., 1959. Chaps. 7, 8.

GREENE, MARK R. *Risk and Insurance.* Cincinnati: South-Western Publishing Co., 1962. Chap. 10.

MAGEE, JOHN H., AND BICKELHAUPT, DAVID L. *General Insurance.* 7th ed. Homewood, Ill.: Richard D. Irwin, Inc., 1964. Chap. 10.

MEHR, ROBERT I., AND CAMMACK, EMERSON. *Principles of Insurance*. 3d ed. Homewood, Ill.: Richard D. Irwin, Inc., 1961. Chap. 12.

MOWBRAY, ALBERT H., AND BLANCHARD, RALPH H. *Insurance: Its Theory and Practice in the United States*. 5th ed. New York: McGraw-Hill Book Co., Inc., 1961. Chap. 9.

RODDA, WILLIAM H. *Fire and Property Insurance*. Englewood Cliffs, N.J.: Prentice-Hall, Inc., 1956. Chaps. 8, 9, 10.

Chapter 9

BUSINESS INTERRUPTION INSURANCE

BY JOHN D. PHELAN

"Direct loss coverages" cover immediate losses to physical property. "Consequential loss coverages" cover secondary losses—losses which result from or are the consequences of direct losses.

The destruction by fire of an apartment building is a "direct loss"—the resultant loss of rental income to the owner is a "consequential loss." Destruction of a warehouse full of goods is a direct loss—loss of profits on those goods is a consequential loss.

Obviously, consequential losses involve somewhat more imagination than do direct losses but money is involved in both cases—and the consequential loss money is just as important as the direct loss money.

TIME ELEMENT COVERAGES

A broad segment of the consequential loss insurance field is labeled "time element coverages." These are the insurances covering consequential losses in which the element of time required to "repair, rebuild, or replace" the productive property is of particular importance in the size of the consequential loss.

Time is a vital element when a direct loss interrupts a flow of dollars. The destruction of the apartment building interrupts the flow of rental income dollars. Thus Rental Value Insurance is one of the time element coverages and the time (in months) required to rebuild or repair the apartment building is one of two factors used in determining loss, the second being the amount of monthly net rental income. Multiply one by the other and the result is the amount of gross rental income loss.

The loss of profits on a warehouse full of goods is a "single-shot" consequential loss in which there is no element of time—no flow of money being interrupted. As far as the first owner is concerned, there can be but one sale and one profit made on these particular goods. Hence, "profits insurance" as written today is a consequential coverage but is not in the time element group.

The principal time element coverages are:

1. *Rent or Rental Value*—insuring consequential loss of rents.
2. *Extra Expense*—insuring extra expenses paid in consequence of a direct loss to continue as nearly normally as possible the operation of a service business like a newspaper, dairy, and so on. (See next chapter for a discussion of No. 1 and No. 2.)
3. *Business Interruption*—insuring the consequential loss resulting when the flow of earnings from a business is interrupted by direct loss to the business.

The nature of time element consequential losses is the same regardless of the peril causing the direct damage. Thus the differences between fire business interruption and steam boiler business interruption are technical as to policy provisions rather than fundamental as to basic principle.

HISTORICAL DEVELOPMENT

The consequential loss concept is a fairly recent development in insurance coverages. While the losses insured are indeed real, they apparently seemed to nineteenth century underwriters to present greater moral hazard than did direct physical loss.

The French created *chomage* insurance in the 1860's to cover loss of profits on merchandise in connection with a direct loss (on an agreed percentage basis). A few years later, there were American developments of special forms to cover business interruption losses in the New England textile industry. In England, a form of profits coverage based on reduction in "turnover" was devised in the late 1800's with Cuthbert Heath, one of the great chairmen of Lloyd's, contributing to its growth.

Very early in the American development of business interruption coverage, the words "Use and Occupancy" made their appearance. Early forms described the values insured as those arising from the "use and occupancy" of the described buildings. This phrase—which is most illustrative of the consequential loss concept—persisted for years and undoubtedly had an influence on the U.S. development of business interruption insurance. Even today, the phrase "U. & O." is a common part of our insurance jargon.

Basic Business Interruption Purposes

In a capitalistic system, businesses are operated to make money. Business interruption insurance, in any of its forms, insures the money that a business makes.

Business interruption insurance is like accident insurance for a business since it keeps regular earnings flowing after the business has been wholly or partially disabled by a disaster caused by an insured peril.

Per Diem, Weekly, Monthly Forms

Earliest U.S. business interruption policies were Per Diem Forms for manufacturers written on a valued basis without "partial suspension" or "actual loss sustained" provisions. The insured was entitled to recover a specified amount per day of *total* interruption of manufacture regardless of his actual loss, which might exceed or be less than his insurance recovery. Partial suspensions of operations were not insured.

These defects were quickly remedied as the Per Diem Form became standardized as an "actual loss sustained" form. The loss insured was:

> . . . *the actual loss sustained* . . . for not exceeding such length of time as would be required with the exercise of due diligence and dispatch, to rebuild, repair, or replace such part of the property described as covered by this policy as has been destroyed or damaged, commencing with the date of the fire and not limited by the expiration of this policy, to wit:
>
> I. Net profits on the business which is thereby prevented.
>
> II. Such charges and other expenses as must necessarily continue during a total or partial suspension of business, to the extent only that such charges and expenses would have been earned had no fire occurred.
>
> III. Such expenses as are necessarily incurred for the purpose of reducing the loss under this policy; for not exceeding, however, the amount by which the loss covered is thereby reduced.[1]

This definition was followed by a clause limited recovery, in case of total suspension of business to $1/250$, $1/300$, or $1/365$ of the face of the policy for any single day's total suspension of business (depending upon whether operations were on a five, six, or seven days per week basis).

Partial Suspension under Per Diem

Per Diem Forms also provided that, in case of partial suspension of business, the recovery per day was limited to the same percentage of the per diem limit that the percent of suspension bore to total suspension. This obviously had an effect similar to 100 percent coinsurance.

Weekly, Monthly, and Seasonal Forms

The Per Diem Forms were quickly supplemented by forms with weekly and monthly limits of liability which reduced some of the inflexibility of the Per Diem Form. With the same purposes, seasonal forms appeared in which differing daily or weekly limits were set for different seasons of the production year. The Per Diem and Weekly Forms had the advantage of being reasonably easy to explain and the great disadvantage of inflexibility. In order to get full coverage, a daily or weekly limit had to be based on peak earnings, and few businesses run at capacity a full year.

[1] From a standard Per Diem Form.

Two-Item Contribution Forms

To solve these problems, there evolved the Two-Item Contribution Forms, which insured the "actual loss sustained" on a coinsurance basis without daily, weekly, or monthly limits. Two items of insurance were provided. Item I covered net profits, continuing expenses, and salaries of key employees; and Item II (optional) covered ordinary payroll for a 90-day basic period with extensions possible. Eighty percent or 100 percent contribution (coinsurance) clauses were used. In Item I, the coinsurance clause applied to a value determined by formula which amounted to annual "gross earnings" less heat, light, and power and less ordinary payroll. These forms gave the insured—if insurance was properly written—full coverage of his business interruption loss.

CURRENT BUSINESS INTERRUPTION FORMS

These Two-Item Forms have at last been superceded in recent years by single item Gross Earnings Forms, the present ultimate in the "actual loss sustained" concept. For those less sophisticated buyers and sellers, there is the no-coinsurance Earnings Form which is something between the Monthly Form and Gross Earnings. Currently there are these two modern forms of basic U.S. business interruption coverage:

1. The no-coinsurance Earnings Form for mercantile risks of the simpler type and the risk where the formula of "gross earnings" does not properly fit the risk situation.
2. The Gross Earnings Form for all other situations.

Each is discussed in its own area of importance.

Earnings Form

The no-coinsurance Earnings Form provides a total amount of insurance with recovery in any one month limited to a stated percentage of this total. Earnings insurance (still called Gross Earnings—Short Form on the West Coast) covers all "earnings . . . less operating expenses which do not necessarily continue during the necessary interruption of business" caused by an insured peril. The limit on recovery in any one month is usually 33⅓ percent on the West Coast or 25 percent elsewhere. Thus it can be seen that the Earnings Form is usually sold as covering three or four months' earnings. Except for this monthly limit, no coinsurance features are involved.

The rating of the Earnings Form is equally simplified, being, in the Midwest for example, the 80 percent coinsurance building rate. This rate is somewhat higher than the Gross Earnings rate for the reason that there is no coinsurance aspect of the form as respects partial interruptions. Hence, as the amount of insurance carried approaches that which would satisfy the coinsurance features of the Gross Earnings Form, the premium for Earnings insurance becomes higher than the Gross Earnings premium.

Earnings insurance was originally developed in an attempt to expand business interruption insurance sales in the smaller mercantile field and in the service risk area where Gross Earnings still is a very poor fit to the true exposure to loss. The small businessman has an objection to opening his books to an agent or broker and has difficulties with the coinsurance concepts of Gross Earnings. Agents serving these smaller accounts have not been enthusiastic salesmen of Gross Earnings.

The Earnings Form has not been a big seller—but neither has any other "U. & O." form in the small risk market. It has been adapted in modified form in a number of independent mercantile multiple-peril "packages" and in these is selling in modest volume.

Gross Earnings Form

The industry seems to have settled upon the Gross Earnings Form to provide the best business interruption coverage for substantial businesses as far as normal hazards are concerned. Here is a basically simple form complete in coverage concept. The measure of loss is the:

> . . . ACTUAL LOSS SUSTAINED by the Insured resulting directly from such interruption of business, but not exceeding the reduction in Gross Earnings less charges and expenses which do not necessarily continue during the interruption of business, for only such length of time as would be required with the exercise of due diligence and dispatch to rebuild, repair or replace such part of the property herein described as has been damaged or destroyed, commencing with the date of such damage or destruction and not limited by the date of expiration of this policy.[2]

Since all business financial blessings flow from gross earnings, a form which measures loss recovery in terms of reduction of gross earnings is the most complete as to coverage. Everything is included in gross earnings—profits, continuing expenses, management payroll, ordinary payroll. The forms specifically provide that "due consideration shall be given to the continuation of normal charges and expenses, including payroll expense, to the extent necessary to resume operations of the Insured with the same quality of service which existed immediately preceding the loss."[3]

Ordinary Payroll Exclusion or Limitation

Despite the somewhat obscure wording of the forms referred to above, the general interpretation is that there is a presumption of full ordinary payroll coverage under an unrestricted Gross Earnings Form.

To add flexibility, rules now generally permit the complete exclusion of ordinary payroll coverage or its limitation to coverage for 90, 120, or 180

[2] From paragraph 2 of Gross Earnings Form 3 (Mercantile) and Gross Earnings Form 4 (Manufacturing). This paragraph is the same in both.

[3] *Ibid.*

days. As a general practice, however, exclusion of ordinary payroll coverage is dangerous. In case of exclusion or limitation, use of the 80 percent Contribution (coinsurance) Clause is commonly required and rates are slightly higher.

Coinsurance Requirements and Rates

Each Gross Earnings Form requires that a coinsurance clause be used. In both the mercantile and the manufacturing form the name Contribution Clause is used. For single locations where full ordinary payroll is being insured, however, a wide choice of coinsurance percentages is offered. Furthermore, each different coinsurance percentage, of course, requires a different rate. Gross Earnings Form rates are generally based on the 80 percent coinsurance building rate and are supplied by the bureau

TABLE 9–1

TYPICAL RELATIONSHIP OF GROSS EARNINGS BUSINESS INTERRUPTION RATES TO FIRE BUILDING RATES—1964

Contribution Clause Percent	Percent of the 80 Percent Coinsurance Building Rate for Gross Earnings Form	
	For Manufacturing Risks	For Mercantile Risks
80	70	60
70	75	65
60	80	70
50	90	80

or other source supplying the fire rates. A typical relationship is shown in Table 9–1.

In practice, heavy use is made of either the 50 percent or the 80 percent Contribution Clause. Experts recommend use of the 80 percent clause in virtually all cases where there are substantial seasonal fluctuations in business earnings. The reasoning is that, with marked seasonal variations in the level of activity, a shutdown could occur at a time when even a short interruption of business would mean the loss of a very high proportion of annual earnings. Hence, a relatively large amount of business interruption insurance is needed to cover such a contingency. If a large amount of insurance is needed anyway, the insured might as well take advantage of the significantly lower rate available by using the 80 percent Contribution Clause.

Mercantile versus Manufacturing

The basic difference between mercantile and manufacturing businesses is recognized by a difference in the definitions of gross earnings in the mercantile and manufacturing forms.

A merchant is engaged in the business of selling things. When his business is interrupted, he loses *sales*. Hence, gross earnings in a mercantile form are basically defined as "total net sales" less "cost of merchandise sold."

A manufacturer's business is making things. When his business is interrupted, he loses *production*. This loss of production may not cause an immediate loss of sales since sales could go on from undamaged inventories of finished goods, but ultimately there is a resultant loss of sales.

Manufacturing forms basically define gross earnings as "sales value of production" less "cost of raw stock from which such production is derived." These business interruption forms for manufacturers consider goods "sold" when finished and do not cover loss of profits on finished goods. Rules usually require that a business be classed as manufacturing if it uses any machinery, except that necessary for building services or for auxiliary mercantile purposes.

"Other earnings of the business" are included in both forms and the manufacturing form recognizes that there may be a mercantile operation combined with manufacturing.

Service Risks

Service risks, such as hotels, restaurants, theatres, bowling alleys, repair garages, and so on, are those where principally service rather than merchandise is for sale and in which payroll is proportionately high. Service risks are the most difficult to handle properly under business interruption forms. To attempt to cope with the problem, the mercantile forms include "other earnings" of the business, and permit deduction of material and supplies concerned and of services purchased from outsiders which do not continue under contract.

It is in service risks that the use of an Ordinary Payroll limitation is most common. Here also there is an application of the Earnings Form which has only a monthly limit of recovery and no other coinsurance aspect forcing excessive insurance.

Problems of Fluctuating Values

In ascertaining the amount of business interruption insurance to buy, one has to estimate the amount of gross earnings for the 12-month period immediately following a loss. The loss may occur well toward the end of the policy period. Thus, estimates have to be made for 24 months in advance in order to arrive at the amount of insurance for a single year. It is easy to see how changing levels of business activity can play havoc with the estimates. If the estimates of gross earnings should be too low, the insured can easily find himself in trouble in meeting the coinsurance requirements. Moreover, the common practice of writing property insurance for a 3-year term aggravates this problem.

Happily, there are several solutions. The simplest one is the common recommendation that a 10 percent or similar safety factor be provided, that is, that insurance be at least 60 percent to value if the 50 percent clause is used. This precaution, coupled with annual vigilance on the part of the insured and agent or broker, may suffice in the smaller risk.

Another precautionary device is the use of an Agreed Amount Plan. The idea here is that the insurer agrees to accept a figure filed by the insured as to the amount of gross earnings for the insurance period. The insurer agrees to suspend the application of the Contribution Clause by accepting insurance based upon this amount. Thus, there is an agreed amount determined which is considered to satisfy the contribution clause requirement. The wording of this endorsement and the practices in its use vary slightly from one region to another. Only mercantile and nonmanufacturing risks are eligible for this arrangement. Rates for use when the Agreed Amount Plan is in force are specifically published and in some parts of the country are 5 percent higher than those which would otherwise apply. In some parts of the country the plan is limited to sprinklered risks, in other parts it is not. In some instances the insured's own unaudited figures may be accepted as the base for the rate publication. In the latter situation, the policy may contain still another endorsement penalizing the insured who suffers a loss after having submitted a substantially incorrect figure.

A third precautionary technique for avoiding a coinsurance penalty is the Premium Adjustment Endorsement. This endorsement permits the insured to receive a refund of the premium on the insurance which he bought which was in excess of the coinsurance requirements. The endorsement is not a reporting form (as described in Chapter 7), although it does have certain similarities. The insured buys a specific amount of business interruption insurance, pays a provisional premium, and then receives a refund in the event he has bought more than enough insurance to satisfy the coinsurance limit. The determination of how much insurance he actually needed is made on the basis of a statement of gross earnings he submits at the end of the period. The refund is subject to the insurer's retaining a minimum premium. The endorsement affects the coverage in only one important respect. The endorsement limits the insurer's liability to the same percentage of gross earnings for one year as the percentage appearing in the Contribution Clause. The reason for this restriction may not be obvious to readers. The point is, however, that business interruption forms do not limit recovery to a 12-month period following a loss but rather to the time required to resume operations with due diligence and dispatch. (The insurable value of estimated gross earnings is on a 12-month basis, of course.) A shutdown might last, for example, 16 months. Without the restriction described above an insured might buy a very large amount of business interruption insurance with this endorsement attached, enjoy protection for a long shutdown should it occur, but ask for a refund of premium in case the large loss did not occur.

In summary, the problem of fluctuating values is perhaps the most serious one in the business interruption field—far more so than in direct loss property insurance. Business interruption policies cannot be written or renewed without concern for this problem. Annual attention is a "must" no matter which solution is adopted.

Blanket Business Interruption

Business Interruption can be written blanket—covering more than one location. Contribution Clause requirements are a minimum 70 percent and an average rate applies.

When there are several locations in a mercantile business, the insured and the agent face a decision as to whether or not the insurance should be written blanket. The answer generally lies in the further question of whether there is an interdependence between the locations.

For instance, a warehouse and the retail store which it serves should be written blanket since loss at either location will affect earnings. However, there may be no reason to blanket retail stores at widely separated locations—different cities for example—and the insured's cost accounting may be simplified by writing them separately.

In the manufacturing field, it is generally desirable to blanket the various plants which are under a single financial control. Manufacturing operations are so often interrelated and the interrelationship changes so often that there are serious risks in not following the blanket route.

Extension of Period of Indemnity

Without modification, standard forms limit the period of indemnity to the "time required to rebuild." However, businesses often cannot resume operations at a full level immediately. To pick up this slack, it is now possible to extend the period of indemnity so that coverage extends to the time required to "restore" operations to a normal level.

Less Common Forms of Business Interruption

Contingent business interruption provides for coverage of loss caused by damage to an insured's suppliers or customers. If a manufacturer's production is heavily dependent upon parts manufactured by someone else, he may be shut down by an interruption at the other's plant. He is similarly involved in risk if he supplies only a few customers with his product. Also in the general area of contingent business interruption is the provision for covering loss resulting from damage to "leader properties" that attract customers to the insured. Thus, a small merchant in a shopping center is adversely affected if the major department store in the center is shut down.

Also close to the contingent forms in concept are those for insuring loss of commission by selling agents as a result of interruption damage at the factory and loss of income (or bonuses) by a store manager if his store is destroyed. Standard forms can be extended to cover liability for interruption caused by off-premises damage to public utility services. The special features of schools require a business interruption form called Tuition Fees. (See Chapter 10 for a discussion of the forms mentioned in this paragraph.)

A nonstandard form of coverage is a "valued" per diem or weekly form of Use and Occupancy which has enjoyed some popularity because a tax case held that the involuntary conversion rule applies and permitted special tax treatment of loss payments. The reasoning was that the specific benefit, unrelated to an earnings test, made the payment a property value, not an earnings value.

Valued Use and Occupancy is not provided in bureau filings and is available, therefore, only in the special markets. Moreover, to most businesses, its value is somewhat overrated. It requires more experienced selling and underwriting than do the orthodox forms.

UNDERWRITING AND ADJUSTING BUSINESS INTERRUPTION

The underwriter of business interruption looks for bottlenecks of any kind in which a small property loss may create a large business interruption loss. A specialized machine, a hard-to-replace component—these are his concern. He must attempt to engineer his risk so that the risk of loss to the bottleneck unit is reduced as far as possible.

Examples of the impact these bottlenecks have upon underwriting exposures are quite numerous. In a wire manufacturing plant, the specialized machine which draws the wire is the underwriter's risk. The rest of the plant has much the nature of warehousing. This situation is likely to be found in any operation where the product is highly specialized. Since business interruption is a line that is freely written, this search for bottlenecks additionally involves the fire underwriter's attempt to estimate his "probable maximum loss" for net line and reinsurance purposes.

Adjusting business interruption gives less trouble than might be expected provided qualified accounting people are used. The job is really more an accountant's than an adjuster's except as to the question of time required to rebuild where competent repair contractors must be involved. As in all loss areas, an attitude of reasonable compromise is sometimes necessary, but values can be about as precisely determined as in the direct loss areas.

In direct losses, depreciation, obsolescence, and betterment are the traditional bugaboos. In business interruption the problem is projection of probable earnings. Disputes on "time required to rebuild" can be settled, if necessary, by waiting for the job to be finished.

SUGGESTED READINGS

KLEIN, HENRY C. *Business Interruption Insurance.* 4th ed. Indianapolis: Rough Notes Co., 1960.

PHELAN, JOHN D. *Business Interruption Insurance Primer.* 5th ed. Indianapolis: Rough Notes Co., 1960.

RIEGEL, ROBERT, AND MILLER, JEROME S. *Insurance Principles and Practices.* 4th ed. Englewood Cliffs, N.J.: Prentice-Hall, Inc., 1959. Chap. 25.

Chapter 10

OTHER CONSEQUENTIAL LOSS INSURANCE

BY SIDNEY G. BEHLMER

This chapter is devoted to a description of the principal types of consequential loss insurance other than business interruption. Some are "time element" coverages; some are not.

The Contingent Liability from Operation of Building Laws Endorsement (in some parts of the country a similar endorsement is known as Demolition Endorsement) and the Increased Cost of Construction (Excess of Replacement Cost) Endorsement could very well be included in this discussion. The editors of the *Handbook*, however, have chosen to classify them in the "allied lines" category and treat them in Chapter 8.

There are wide differences from one part of the country to another in the forms, rates, and rules for many of the consequential loss coverages. In recent years an encouraging degree of uniformity has been attained throughout the United States in the forms, rates, and rules for business interruption and certain other coverages. Nevertheless, there are still so many variations in some of the consequential coverages that the particular policy, form, endorsement, or clause in a given state must be referred to specifically for definite information. The comments in this chapter, therefore, necessarily are limited to basic concepts plus salient features of a few coverages. Readers should keep in mind the fact that there are regional differences and that there are also other consequential coverages for more limited use than those described.

TIME ELEMENT COVERAGES OTHER THAN BUSINESS INTERRUPTION

Commissions of Selling Agents

A selling agent may handle, on a commission basis, the sale of a portion or all of the products of a manufacturing plant or of several manufacturing plants. His commission earnings may be impaired by damage to or destruction of either a certain lot of finished stock, which cannot be replaced to complete the sale, or a manufacturing facility which prevents the production of goods for future delivery. The Commissions of Selling Agents Form which has been recommended by all fire insurance rating organizations is similar to the Contingent Business Interruption Form for contributing properties.

The anticipated commissions of a selling agent which will be earned when a given lot of finished stock is delivered may be covered under a Profits and Commissions Form (see later section in this chapter). When a *series* of sales transactions by the selling agent are to be covered (sales from either finished goods in storage or from future production), the business interruption approach is employed, with gross selling commissions for the ensuing 12 months as the basis for a 50, 60, 70, or 80 percent Contribution Clause.

The Commissions of Selling Agents Form does not contain an exclusion of loss to finished stock such as is in the business interruption forms for manufacturing risks. (Neither do the Contingent Business Interruption Forms, by the way.) The commissions of the selling agent are based upon delivery of products of the manufacturing properties to customers whether those deliveries be from a finished stock inventory or from future production.

The primary reason for use of the Commissions of Selling Agents Form rather than the Contingent Business Interruption Form is the difference in rating treatment for the two forms. The customary rate for the latter is inadequate for the former. Consider the probability of a selling agent being able to substitute products from another source in the event of damage to or destruction of a manufacuring plant for which he regularly acts as selling agent. This probability is usually much less than the probability that the average manufacturer will be able to substitute supplies from sources other than the contributing properties named in his Contingent Business Interruption Form. The rules in a number of states, therefore, prohibit coverage on loss of commissions of selling agents under a Contingent Business Interruption Form.

The Commissions of Selling Agents Form calls for a separate amount of insurance for each manufacturing plant listed. The rate for each such item is the same as the rate for the Gross Earnings Business Interruption Form which would apply to the described property, considering the contribution clause percentage chosen.

Rent or Rental Value Insurance

Rent or Rental Value Insurance is probably the most commonly used of the consequential loss coverages. It may be provided by a separate policy, by endorsement to a policy covering one or more buildings, or by an item or extension of coverage in a direct loss policy. There are several variations of the coverage in each territory and many differences between territories in the wording of the coverage, rules, and rates. Basically, however, the coverage is against loss of rental income or loss of use as measured by rental value, caused by fire or other peril insured against which renders a building untenantable.

In owner-occupied property, one measure of the owner's-use interest is its rental value, that is, the amount he would necessarily pay as rent if the property were owned by another or the amount of rent he would have to pay for comparable space elsewhere. Suppose that an owner leases or rents a building, or a part of it, to a tenant and that the premises are rendered untenantable by fire or other peril for, let us say, six months. The owner will lose the rental income, less any expenses which he can discontinue during that period, unless the lease requires the tenant to continue to pay rent during such period even though the premises are untenantable. However, relatively few leases have such provisions because of the hardship they place on the lessee.

In providing coverage, no distinction is made between a loss of rents and a loss of rental value—either or both are covered. Therefore, in the case of an owner occupying part of a building and renting the remainder to a tenant, the rental value and the rental income are treated in the same manner. If a tenant is required by the terms of his lease to continue to pay rent even though the premises are untenantable, he can buy Rent Insurance. This insurance will provide protection against loss of the rent he would have to pay during the time the building is untenantable as the result of fire or other peril insured against.

Recovery is limited to the amount of the reduction of rent or rental value during the period of untenantability, "less charges and expenses which do not necessarily continue during the period of untenantability"; for example, the cost of janitor service, elevator service, heat, light, and so on, may be reduced or discontinued. The period of untenantability is "such length of time as would be required with exercise of due diligence and dispatch to restore the premises to a tenantable condition." While only some of the forms in use specifically limit recovery to the actual loss sustained by the insured, all contain provisions to accomplish the same purpose. Therefore, even though the form in referring to the described building contains the phrase "whether rented at the time or not" (meaning at the time of the destruction of or damage to the building), it is necessary for an insured to prove that the building would have been rented or would have been occupied for his own use had no fire occurred.

Some forms make specific reference to the premises as furnished and equipped by the owner, thus calling attention to the higher rent or rental value involved and the additional time that may be required to restore the premises, including the furnishings and equipment, to a tenantable condition.

A form containing a Contribution Clause is available in all territories, with a choice of percentages—for example, 50, 75, or 100 percent—applying to the rents or rental value that would have accrued to the insured (had no loss occurred) during the 12 months immediately following the date of damage or destruction. In some territories a Premium Adjustment Endorsement may be used with that form, or a Premium Adjustment Rent Form is available, with provisions for the submission of reports specifying the rents received during each year and an adjustment of the premium at expiration of the policy.

In many states a monthly limitation form is also available. Under such forms, the recovery for loss during any one month is limited, for example, to 1/6 or 1/9 or 1/12 of the amount of the Rent Insurance. Almost all dwelling policies contain either an extension providing rent insurance, a separate item, or both. The Dwelling Building(s) and Contents—Broad Form, the Dwelling Building(s) Special Form (see Chapter 6) and the Homeowners Forms (see Chapter 49) in most states provide an extension of coverage which is a combination of Rent Insurance and Additional Living Expense Insurance. The former is applicable to portions of the property rented to others.

In view of the multiplicity of forms, the only comment which can be made on the rates applying is that they are computed by taking a percentage of the rate applying to the building.

Additional Living Expense Insurance

If premises occupied for residential purposes by an owner or a tenant are rendered untenantable by fire or other peril, it becomes necessary for the displaced occupants to establish temporary living quarters elsewhere. The additional expense involved may be substantial. If the period of untenantability is of short duration, the members of the household may go to a hotel; if of longer duration, to a furnished apartment or other temporary quarters. Whatever arrangements are made, however, it is quite likely that the cost of shelter, food, laundry, and other attendant expenses of maintaining the household during such period will exceed normal expenses. Additional Living Expense Insurance is designed to cover such expenses which are in excess of normal.

A brief quotation from a dwelling form is a good way to convey some of the details of the coverage. The following pertinent sections appear in both the Dwelling Building(s) and Contents—Broad Form and in the Dwelling Building(s) Special Form which are available in most states:

> Additional Living Expense: This term shall mean the necessary increase in living expense incurred by the Insured in order to continue as nearly as practicable the normal standard of living of the Insured's household for the applicable period described in (1) or (2), whichever is the lesser, and not limited by the expiration date of this policy: (1) the time required, with the exercise of due diligence and dispatch, to repair or replace the damaged or destroyed

property; (2) the time required for the Insured's household to become settled in any permanent quarters.

As to "Additional Living Expense"—

(1) This Company shall be liable during the period of time, not exceeding two weeks, while access to the described premises is prohibited by order of civil authority, but only when such order is given as a direct result of damage to neighboring premises by any peril insured against.

(2) This Company shall not be liable for loss due to the cancellation of any lease, or any written or oral agreement.

Rental Value and Additional Living Expense: The Insured may apply up to 10 percent of the amount of insurance applicable to the principal dwelling item under this policy as an additional amount of insurance to cover loss by any peril insured against of both (1) Rental Value of the described building(s) with respect to any portion thereof not occupied by the Insured, and (2) Additional Living Expense with respect to any portion of the described building(s) occupied by the Insured, but not to exceed said 10 percent for both (1) and (2) in the aggregate.

The Homeowners Forms, available in most states, contain similar provisions. Form 1 contains the same 10 percent limitation but in Forms 2, 3, and 5 the limitation is 20 percent. Form 4, for a tenant, contains a limit of 40 percent of the amount of insurance on personal property.

When this coverage was made available a number of years ago, it was written under a separate form but such forms have generally been withdrawn in view of the extensions referred to above.

Extra Expense Insurance

The uninterrupted operation of some business enterprises is of vital importance. This continuance is crucial, even at a cost greatly in excess of normal, during the period required to repair, rebuild, or replace property which has been damaged or destroyed. Newspapers, banks, and milk distributors are examples of businesses in which uninterrupted operation is essential. Usually, either before or after a direct loss, such firms make arrangements for continuation of printing, processing, or other operations in alternate establishments which make it possible for them to continue to serve their customers. In that event, income will be maintained at about its normal level but expenses may greatly exceed the normal level.

The purpose of Extra Expense Insurance is to reimburse an insured for such extra expenses necessarily incurred during the period of restoration following damage to or destruction of the described property by fire or other perils insured against. Extra Expense Insurance does not provide protection against an interruption of business, that is, it does not cover loss of income nor profits, nor does it cover continuing normal business expenses. If an interruption of business with a diminution of income is anticipated, the insured needs business interruption insurance. If extra expense only is anticipated, Extra Expense Insurance will provide protection. If both a diminution of business and the incurrence of extra expense may occur, there is need for both.

There is some variation in forms used in various territories but the one used in the Middle West will serve for these general comments. Two sections of that form quoted below contain the basic concept of the coverage:

If the above described building(s) or contents thereof are destroyed or damaged by the perils insured against occurring during the term of this policy so as to necessitate the incurrence of Extra Expense (as defined in this form), this Company shall be liable for the Extra Expense so incurred, not exceeding the actual loss sustained, for not exceeding such length of time, hereinafter referred to as the "period of restoration," commencing with the date of damage or destruction and not limited by the date of expiration of this policy, as shall be required with the exercise of due diligence and dispatch to repair, rebuild, or replace such part of said building(s) or contents as may be destroyed or damaged.

The term "Extra Expense," wherever employed in this form, is defined as the excess (if any) of the total cost during the period of restoration of the operation of the business, either at the insured location or on other premises, or both, over and above the total cost of such operation that would normally have been incurred during the same period had no loss occurred; the cost in each case to include expense of using other property or facilities of other concerns or other necessary emergency expenses. In no event, however, shall this Company be liable for loss of profits or earnings resulting from diminution of business, nor for any direct or indirect property damage loss insurable under Property Damage policies, or for expeditures incurred in the purchase, construction, repair or replacement of any physical property unless incurred for the purpose of reducing any loss under this policy, not exceeding, however, the amount in which the loss is so reduced. Any salvage value of property so acquired which may be sold or utilized by the Insured upon resumption of normal operations, shall be taken into consideration in the adjustment of any loss hereunder.[1]

The section which provides for the insertion of limits of liability is as follows for the first three limits. There must be at least three, but the rules provide for spreading the percentages over a period as long as 12 months:

The limits of liability hereunder shall in no event exceed that percentage of the amount of this policy (at the time of a loss) which is stated below for the determined "period of restoration":

_______% when the "period of restoration" is not in excess of one month;

_______% when the "period of restoration" is in excess of one month but not in excess of two months;

_______% when the "period of restoration" is in excess of two months but not in excess of three months.

In the event that Extra Expense incurred by the insured during the longest period of restoration for which provision is above made does not exhaust the insurance hereby provided, then such unexhausted insurance shall apply for the remainder of the period of restoration.[2]

The percentage limits are cumulative and the highest percentage which may be allocated to any one month is 40; therefore, the maximum percent-

---

[1] Form 62 for Ohio (September, 1958 Edition).

[2] *Ibid.*

ages permitted are 40, 80, and 100. A month is defined as 30 consecutive days. With those percentage limits and a "period of restoration" of 25 days, recovery would be limited to 40 percent of the amount of the policy. On the other hand, if the "period of restoration" was 35 days, 80 percent of the amount of the policy would be the applicable limit of liability.

Using six months as an example of the period over which the limits of liability are distributed, the percentages might be 25, 40, 55, 70, 85, and 100.

The rate diminishes as the percentages are spread over a greater number of months. However, it is often difficult to estimate accurately the amount of Extra Expense Insurance which may be required and what the "period of restoration" is likely to be. Therefore, the first consideration should be adequacy of limits. The selection of limits should not be unduly influenced by a desire for a lower rate.

In addition to the three sections referred to, the form contains other provisions under 13 additional sections. It does not contain a Contribution or Coinsurance Clause. The rate is based upon the 80 percent coinsurance building rate but also depends upon the percentages in the limits of liability section. For example, the rate with 40, 80, and 100 percent is 2.06 times the 80 percent coinsurance building rate; but, with the percentages allocated over a six-month period, as shown above, the rate would be 1.61 times the 80 percent coinsurance building rate. There are, however, some territorial variations in rating treatment as well as in forms used.

Tuition Fees Insurance

The Tuition Fees Insurance Form for schools and colleges, which has been recommended to all fire insurance rating organizations and has generally supplanted older forms, is patterned after the Gross Earnings Business Interruption Form for mercantile or nonmanufacturing risks. In a sense it is a type of business interruption coverage and might have been included in Chapter 9. Since it is so specialized, however, it seems to fit better in this chapter.

The most important characteristic of Tuition Fees Insurance is based upon recognition that schools and colleges may need a "time element" which extends beyond the date of completion of the repair, reconstruction, or replacement of property which has been damaged or destroyed. "Tuition fees," as defined in the form, include not only tuition itself but also other income from students, for example, income from living quarters and meals provided. To illustrate, assume one or more buildings of a school are damaged by fire in December and cannot be occupied until repairs are completed on April 1. The school's income may be substantially reduced for the entire school year even though restoration of the facilities is completed by April 1. The Tuition Fees Form provides coverage to the beginning of the following school year, for example, September

10. If the end of the time required for restoration of the damaged or destroyed property should fall within the 30-day period preceding that opening date of September 10, the coverage would extend to the beginning of the next school year.

The form contains a Contribution Clause based upon either 80 or 100 percent of the tuition fees that would have been earned (had no loss occurred) during the 12 months immediately following the date of damage or destruction of the described property. Provision is made for listing the building(s) or structure(s) to which the coverage applies. If a single building or structure is listed, the recommended rates are 90 percent of the 80 percent coinsurance building rate when the 80 percent Contribution Clause applies, and 80 percent of the 80 percent coinsurance building rate when the 100 percent Contribution Clause applies. If the coverage applies to more than one fire division, blanket average rates will be published by the fire insurance rating organization.

When it is desired to include income other than tuition fees as defined in the form, such as income from athletic events, testing laboratories, or others, the form may be appropriately modified, in some territories, subject to approval of the rating organization. The four sections of the form containing its salient features are as follows:

2. If the above described building(s), structure(s), or contents thereof are damaged or destroyed by the peril(s) insured against during the term of this policy, this Company shall be liable for the ACTUAL LOSS OF TUITION FEES SUSTAINED by the Insured less charges and expenses which do not necessarily continue during the period of time, not limited by the date of expiration of this policy, commencing with the date of such damage or destruction and ending (except as provided in paragraph 3) on the date preceding the beginning of the first school year following the date that the damaged or destroyed building(s), structure(s), and contents thereof could, with the exercise of due diligence and dispatch, be rebuilt, repaired or replaced.

3. If the period of time (as provided under paragraph 2) for rebuilding, repairing or replacing the damaged or destroyed building(s), structure(s), and contents thereof shall end on a date within 30 days immediately preceding the beginning of the first school year specified above, the period of liability for loss under this policy is hereby extended to end on the day preceding the beginning of the second school year.

4. The words "beginning of school year," however modified, wherever used in this policy, shall mean the opening date of school in the Fall as prescribed, or as would be prescribed, in the school catalogue. . . .

7. Definition of Tuition Fees: For the purposes of this insurance, "Tuition Fees" are defined as the sum of tuition, fees and other income from students, less the cost of merchandise sold and materials and supplies consumed in services sold to such students. In determining Tuition Fees due consideration shall be given to the experience of the Insured before the date of damage or destruction and the probable experience thereafter had no loss occurred.

The remaining sections in the Tuition Fees Insurance Form are similar to those in the Gross Earnings Business Interruption Forms.

Leasehold Interest Insurance

Leasehold Interest Insurance is considered by many to be the most complex and least understood coverage of those dealt with in this chapter. The necessity for brevity precludes more than a bare outlining of the subject here. A leasehold interest may arise as a result of, or be created by, any one or more of the following situations:

a) Lessee occupying premises under an advantageous lease. The leasehold interest is the difference, for the unexpired term of the lease, between the actual rental value of the premises and the rent payable.
b) Lessee has a valuable lease and sublets the premises at a higher rental. The leasehold interest is the profit derived through subleasing for the unexpired term of the sublease(s).
c) Lessee has paid a cash bonus to acquire a valuable lease. The leasehold interest in such cash bonus is the unamortized amount of the bonus.
d) Lessee has made improvements and betterments to the building. The leasehold interest in such improvements and betterments is (1) the unamortized value of the improvements and betterments or (2) the increased rental value resulting from their installation.
e) Lessee has paid an advance rental, not recoverable in the event of cancellation of the lease. The leasehold interest in such advance rental is the unamortized portion of the advance rental.

There are territorial variations in the forms used to protect an insured against loss of his leasehold interest as a result of fire or other peril insured against but typical forms are the two used in the Middle West known as Leasehold Interest Form No. 105 and Leasehold Interest Special Form No. 105A.

Leasehold Interest Form No. 105 is designed primarily to cover the situations described in Paragraphs *a* or *b* above or when the situation described in Paragraph *d*(2) contributes to the leasehold interest described in either Paragraphs *a* or *b*.

Leasehold Interest Special Form No. 105A is designed to cover the specific leasehold interests described in Paragraphs *c*, *d*(1) or *e*.

Form No. 105 covers the leasehold interest as reflected by the difference between the rental value of the premises and the rent payable, without consideration of the various factors which are responsible for the creation of that leasehold interest, whereas Form No. 105A is limited to the particular kind of leasehold interest defined in that form.

The basic elements of the coverage provided by Form No. 105 are contained in the following sections of that form:

2. The term "interest of the insured as lessee" is hereby defined as the excess of the rental value of such premises over the actual rental payable (including any maintenance or operating charges paid by the insured) during the unexpired term of the insured's lease, whether the premises be occupied in whole or in part by the insured, or whether they be sub-let to other tenants, and is estimated at the date of this policy at $______ per month.

3. The term "net leasehold interest" as used herein is defined as that sum which placed at 4% interest compounded annually will be equivalent to the interest of the insured as lessee for each separate month of the lease unexpired.

4. It is a condition of this insurance that the following is a full and true copy of all the conditions of said lease relating to damage to the building by fire, and that no change shall be made in said condition unless consented to by this Company in writing endorsed on this policy: . . . [Conditions of lease are set forth here—Eds.]

5. It is a condition of this insurance that in the event the lease contains no conditions relating to damage to the premises by fire, the statutory requirements of the State in which the property is situated shall govern.

6. It is a condition of this insurance that the amount of this policy shall be automatically reduced from month to month as set forth opposite each respective month in the net leasehold interest table which accompanies this policy form, and a pro rata proportion for less than one month.

7. In the event of cancellation of the lease by the lessor after loss by fire in accordance with the Fire Clause hereinbefore quoted (or by statutory requirements in the absence of a Fire Clause) this Company shall be liable to the insured for the actual loss sustained not exceeding whatever amount of insurance remains in force at the date of the fire to be computed as follows: The interest of the insured as lessee as determined by adjustment shall be paid for the first three months succeeding the fire, and the net leasehold interest shall be paid for the remaining months of the unexpired lease (see table on the reverse side of this form).

8. It is a condition of this insurance that if the premises be rendered wholly untenantable by fire and the lease not cancelled, this Company shall be liable for its pro rata proportion of the actual loss sustained at a rate of not exceeding $________ per month, and pro rata proportion thereof for less than one month, and a pro rata proportion thereof for partial untenantability, for the length of time, not limited by expiration of this policy, as shall be required with the exercise of reasonable diligence and dispatch to render the premises again tenantable, but not extending beyond the expiration of the lease.

The policy is written for an amount representing the discounted value of the lease, in accordance with a table, on the effective date of the policy. The premium is computed on the average of the amount for which the policy is issued and the amount which will remain at its expiration as a result of the reductions in amount as provided in Section 6 quoted above. The rate is based upon the gross building rate and the "Fire Clause" in the lease.

Form No. 105A contains a blank space for the insertion of one of three specific wordings for the definition of "leasehold interest," depending upon whether that interest stems from a bonus payment, improvements and betterments, or advance rental. The form also provides for insertion of the "Fire Clause," if any, contained in the lease. The unamortized amount of: (1) the bonus paid, (2) the value of improvements and betterments, or (3) the advance rental at the inception of the policy becomes the amount of the policy. The basis of recovery is actual loss sustained by the insured without reference to a table as in Form No. 105.

This brief discussion of such an involved topic may leave readers somewhat confused as to details. The author suggests that for additional information they go directly to the manual or rule book of the appropriate fire insurance rating organization. Normally, several pages in such sources are devoted to the specifications of this coverage. One point of frequent confusion, however, should be eliminated by this treatment here. Leasehold insurance covers the insurable interest of the lessee—not the insurable interest of the lessor. The lessor's interest, even in a lease which is unusually favorably to him, can be covered by Rent or Rental Value Insurance.

NON–TIME ELEMENT COVERAGES

Consequential Loss Clauses

From the standpoint of terminology, Consequential Loss Clauses may appear to be a term which should have been avoided as a heading for this section since this entire chapter deals with "Other Consequential Loss Insurance." However, as commonly used in the insurance business, "consequential loss" in this case is used in a special sense to describe certain clauses which may be contained in or added to policy forms which cover contents. For example, a change in temperature due to damage to or destruction of refrigerating equipment, by a peril insured against, may cause spoilage of food or other merchandise requiring refrigeration. One type of those special clauses provides for a specific assumption of liability for the consequential loss caused by such change in temperature.

Consequential loss clauses of a different type, not related to a change in temperature, are designed for use on policies covering clothing while in process of being manufactured.

The following is the consequential loss assumption provision included without additional charge in the contents coverage section of a typical dwelling form:

> This policy also covers loss to personal property covered herein, while contained in the building(s) described, due to change of temperature as a result of physical damage to said building(s) or equipment therein, caused by a peril insured against.

Forms which cover mercantile or manufacturers' stocks of merchandise usually contain the following or a similar provision:

> In consideration of the premium at which this policy is written, and subject to its provisions and stipulations and those of forms and endorsements attached thereto, this policy is hereby extended to cover also Consequential Loss, except as excluded below, to stock (raw, in process, or finished) or merchandise covered hereunder, caused by change in temperature or humidity resulting from damage by the perils insured against to equipment used for refrigerating, cooling, humidifying, dehumidifying, air conditioning, heating, generating or

converting power (including their connections and supply or transmission lines and pipes) only when situated on the described premises or on the premises of the plant of which the building(s) described herein form a part.

It is important to note that most provisions of this kind restrict the coverage to loss resulting from damage to or destruction of equipment contained in the building or on the same premises. If the equipment or connections to the equipment are located "off premises," coverage can be obtained in most states by payment of an additional premium and the addition of a clause known as Consequential Loss Assumption Clause B (Off-Premises) or a similar clause.

These Consequential Loss Assumption Clauses also provide that the company shall not be liable for loss specifically excluded under (*a*) the riot provisions of the Extended Coverage Endorsement, or (*b*) the Vandalism and Malicious Mischief Endorsement. However, in many states a Consequential Riot and Vandalism Loss Assumption Endorsement is available. An additional premium is charged for each of the perils of "riot, riot attending a strike, and civil commotion" and "vandalism and malicious mischief," but the latter peril is not includible unless insurance against the former is also purchased. Under both Riot and Vandalism, physical damage to the equipment must occur. The mere turning off of a valve by a rioter or vandal, for example, would not make the company liable for a loss.

Clothing in process of manufacture is subject to a reduction in value if parts of the garments–trousers of suits, for example—in different buildings or at different locations than the remainder of the garments are damaged or destroyed. Consequential loss clauses and rules and rates for policies covering clothing manufacturers are contained in the rule books of most of the fire insurance rating organizations and in the rules of the Inland Marine Insurance Bureau applying to Garment Contractors Floater Policies.

Profits and Commissions Insurance

Indemnity provided by the Standard Fire Policy is "to the extent of the actual cash value of the property at the time of loss. . . ." The actual cash value of finished stock in the hands of its manufacturer, disregarding unusual circumstances, is the cost of reproducing the stock and does not include the profit which the manufacturer will realize when the stock is sold. That potential profit, which is subject to loss as the result of damage to or destruction of the finished stock, may be covered by use of a Profits or Commissions Form available in a number of states. In recent years, however, the separate form of that kind covering such profits, attached to a separate policy, has been almost entirely supplanted by use of a Market Value or Selling Price Clause included in the basic contract that covers the finished stock either specifically or blanket with other property.

It is important to distinguish between profits insurance, which is designed to cover the anticipated profit which a manufacturer expects to realize when his finished stock is sold, and business interruption insurance. The commonly used business interruption forms for manufacturing risks exclude "any loss resulting from damage to or destruction of finished stock." That exclusion is based on the premise that the manufacturer's profit is earned when goods are produced even though that profit is not realized until the finished stock is sold. The profit on finished stock, which was produced by past operations, is treated as an increment to the actual cash value of the finished stock whereas loss of profit from future operations which are curtailed or prevented as a result of damage to or destruction of the manufacturing facilities may be insured against by business interruption insurance. For example, consider the destruction of finished stock in a warehouse well-separated from the buildings of a plant containing the manufacturing operations, or at another location, which could occur without any effect upon production operations and without a business interruption insurance loss. Even so, the profit on that finished stock as well as its actual cash value would be lost.

The forms commonly in use are designed to cover a loss of commissions as well as a loss of profits. A broker or selling agent may be compensated by a commission for selling a stock of finished goods. If such stock, while in a warehouse awaiting delivery, were destroyed, his commission could be subject to a total loss.

With the increased use of Market Value and Selling Price Clauses, the forms and rules for profits and commissions insurance have been withdrawn in some states. Where they remain, the forms and rules vary from state to state. A typical form used in most Midwest states is designated as Profits and/or Commissions Form (to be used only for finished stock in the hands of its manufacturer or special or consigned stock in storage). The essential characteristics of the coverage are set forth in the following two paragraphs quoted from that form:

> If during the term of this policy the described merchandise is damaged or destroyed by the peril(s) insured against, this Company shall be liable under this policy for its proportion of the actual loss of profits and (or) commissions sustained by the Insured, but if the Insured is able to continue sales by the use or acquirement of other merchandise, this Company shall not be liable for more than its proportion of the actual loss of profits and (or) commissions resulting from an actual loss of sales and (or) a reduction in the amount of profits and (or) commissions derived from actual sales.
>
> It is a condition of this insurance that as soon as practicable after any loss, the Insured shall make use of or acquire other merchandise, if obtainable, for the purpose of continuing sales, if by so doing the amount of loss hereunder will be reduced and in the event of loss being so reduced, such reduction shall be taken into account in arriving at the amount of loss hereunder.

The rate applying to this form is the same as the rate applicable to the stock and a coinsurance clause may be used in the same manner as in covering the stock.

UNIFORMITY IN THE FUTURE

The consequential coverages dealt with in this chapter, and others of a similar nature, have, for the most part, been developed over the years as products of the various state and regional organizations in the fire insurance business. While some progress has been made in the direction of greater countrywide uniformity, their limited use as contrasted with many other coverages and a reluctance to make changes unless they appear to be imperative have been factors in perpetuating the territorial differences.

It appears, however, that current trends in the business, including package policy and special rating and coverage plans developed for use countrywide, will necessitate a reappraisal of territorial variations in some of the consequential coverages and will result in a greater degree of uniformity in any given coverage throughout the United States.

SUGGESTED READINGS

Fire, Casualty, and Surety Bulletins. Cincinnati: National Underwriter Co. Fire and Marine Volume, Consequential Section.

GORDIS, PHILIP. *Property and Casualty Insurance.* 9th ed. Indianapolis: Rough Notes Co. 1962. Chap. 7.

MAGEE, JOHN H., AND BICKELHAUPT, DAVID L. *General Insurance.* 7th ed. Homewood, Ill.: Richard D. Irwin Company, Inc., 1964. Chap. 11.

MEHR, ROBERT I., AND CAMMACK, EMERSON. *Principles of Insurance.* 3d ed. Homewood, Ill.: Richard D. Irwin, Inc., 1961. Chap. 12.

RIEGEL, ROBERT, AND MILLER, JEROME S. *Insurance Principles and Practices.* 4th ed. Englewood Cliffs, N.J.: Prentice-Hall, Inc., 1959. Chap. 25.

RODDA, WILLIAM H. *Fire and Property Insurance.* Englewood Cliffs, N.J.: Prentice-Hall, Inc., 1955. Chap. 11.

Chapter 11

FARM AND CROP INSURANCE

BY GEORGE F. RUTLEDGE

Despite the fundamental role of agriculture in the development of this country, the insurance needs of those engaged in agriculture have not been adequately met until recently. This somewhat paradoxical situation can be explained partly by the realization that insurance began in this country primarily as an urban institution and that farmers were separated both from the cities where insurance was prevalent and from each other. They were, for many years, almost out of touch with "city life" and in the main quite isolated from the industry of insurance. In this chapter attention is given to the changing insurance needs of farmers, to the insuring of farm properties—including crops and livestock—and to recognition of a few of the current problems associated with farm insurance.

CHANGING INSURANCE NEEDS OF THE FARMER

In some respects the insurance needs of farmers are little different today than they were many years ago. Property is subject now to the ravages of fire, windstorm, hail, and other perils. It was subject to these same perils then. Despite the similarities in the basic types of property then and now and the continuing threats of fire, wind, and hail, substantial differences in insurance needs do exist.

One difference, of course, is that, with the inflation of real and personal property values, many farmers have much larger absolute exposures of value than for comparable operations previously. Disasters or even moderate losses can be much more serious in terms of monetary values involved than was the case earlier.

Another difference between then and now is that, in the aggregate and on a per farm basis, there is so much more of such property today. This statement is true even giving consideration to changes in price levels. The successful farmer today operates a big business. Modern farm buildings are expensive. Today's farming methods require such buildings. The machinery and equipment necessary to the successful operation of a modern farm have increased dramatically compared to the requirements of even a few decades ago. Feed, seed, and fertilizer are used in much different proportions than in the early days.

Still another difference is that in modern society the public's general consciousness of the possibility of establishing legal claims against others extends to those who do business with farmers. In rural, as well as urban, business and personal life the liability hazard looms as an increasingly serious one. This condition is an element in a farmer's insurance needs which is not simply a difference in degree compared with the remote past. Rather, it is more a difference in kind.

Another difference is that modern farming machinery, facilities, and equipment have created a number of possibilities of loss to property and/or person which simply did not exist before. Automotive and other gasoline- or diesel-powered equipment is a case in point. Electrical equipment including motors for pumps, fans, and generators; electrical heating and cooling equipment; electrical milking equipment; and other such property have created new hazards. Increased use of pressure vessels such as boilers is another example. While all of these types of property increase the liability hazard referred to in the preceding paragraph, they also add considerably to the direct damage insurance needs of the farm itself.

For these and other reasons, farm insurance has become a growing part of the nation's insurance activity both in the size of the premiums involved and in the difficulties in matching coverages to exposures. Fortunately, the insurance industry has responded. Farmers today can take advantage of intelligently devised, reasonably priced insurance programs available to them through various marketing channels.

FIRE AND ALLIED LINES INSURANCE AND THE FARM

Many differences exist between farm insurance practices and nonfarm insurance practices. Some of these differences stem from the uniqueness of farm hazards; other differences are understandable only in the light of the history of farm insurance.

No Standard Policy

Perhaps the first item of major significance to be noted is that the "Standard Fire Policy" (as discussed in Chapter 5) does not necessarily extend to cover the farm. While stock companies have adopted a "basic policy" under which they provide farm insurance, there is no such thing as a "standard" mutual farm fire policy. A relatively large number of small farm mutual insurance companies write farm insurance. Most of these small farm mutuals do not fall under the aegis of state regulation—at least not under the usual provisions of state statutes which pertain to insurance generally. Consequentially, there is no precise legal wording to which fire policies of these companies must adhere.

The National Association of Mutual Insurance Companies has approved a "uniform" farm mutual policy. Because of the exemption of small farm mutuals from the insurance codes in most states, however, relatively few such companies have adopted this approved wording. This "uniform" policy follows exactly the 165 lines of the Standard Fire Policy as discussed in Chapter 5. Beyond this point, however, even the "uniform" policy may be subject to many variations from standard. One encouraging development is that traditionally worded clauses are coming increasingly into use in the forms and endorsements accompanying this policy. There are still many differences, however, between farm forms and those used in insuring nonfarm personal and commercial properties.

The overriding fact to bear in mind is that no standard contract is used in farm insurance. Since many readers who are familiar with the Standard Fire Policy may be tempted to carry over—even unconsciously—the wording of the Standard Fire Policy to farm insurance, this attention to possible discrepancies is well advised. Some policies are one-page simple statements. Others are large documents of the multipage type with declaration sheets, "snap-out" forms, endorsements, and other special provisions.

Extended Coverage Varies

Another point for emphasis is that the extended provisions, which readers have come to accept as standard, may not fit this mold in farm insurance. Some farm mutuals offer no coverage at all beyond fire and lightning. Others provide a limited "five point" extended coverage endorsement of explosion, riot (including riot attending a strike and civil commotion), aircraft and vehicle damage, and smoke damage. Some companies use the "seven point" extended coverage endorsement which adds windstorm and hail to the "five points" listed above. The "uniform" contract of the National Association of Mutual Insurance Companies is of the "seven point" type. A "multiple-peril endorsement" is often added to it to provide protection against losses from theft, vandalism, overturn, water damage and smothering, and freezing and electrocution of livestock. An "additional-peril endorsement," as used by many companies, is only slightly narrower. The basic policy of the stock companies is similarly based on the "seven point" extended coverage endorsement plus similar multiple peril extensions.

Insurance to Value

Another aspect of farm insurance has to do with the problems of insurance to value. These problems have provoked action in two principal directions.

First, the usual problems of small losses and low ratios of insurance to value are found in farm insurance. These arise particularly in connection with personal property which can be removed from burning buildings. To handle such situations the normal coinsurance device is relied upon; for example, in the Blanket Farm Personal Property Form as used by numerous companies. (This form will be described in more detail later in this section.)

Second, some unusual problems arise in the insuring of farm real property and the insurance-to-value problems take quite a different turn. Farm insurers are concerned over the relative inaccessibility of farm properties to efficient fire-fighting equipment and trained personnel. They are also apprehensive over the temptation which a farmer may have to be careless about protecting his buildings—particularly his old ones—from the ravages of fire. Hence, several devices have been created to encourage insureds to take care of their properties.

Deferred Loss Payment Clause. A number of insurance companies use the Deferred Loss Payment Clause for buildings (not contents) against the hazard of fire. The clause provides that the fire premium shall be decreased—or at least not set as high as it would be otherwise—and that the insurer shall withhold from initial payment any portion of a loss which shall be in excess of 60 percent of the amount of insurance on such building. (Buildings are not written in a blanket form.) The remainder of the actual cash value of the loss is payable when the insured repairs or replaces the building provided he does so within 12 months of the loss, within 300 feet of the site of the original building, and for the same use and occupancy; and provided also that he expends an amount which at least equals the actual cash value of loss of or to the original building. If the insured does not so repair or replace within 12 months, the initial payment constitutes his full recovery for the loss.

Percent to Value Provisions. Some companies, including a number of mutuals, provide that an amount, which at the most is only some percentage (such as 80) of the actual cash value of the insured property, is payable in case of a fire loss to such property. Such provisions undoubtedly reflect a continuation of the traditional mutual idea that a person should suffer a loss himself whenever his insurer is called upon to pay a loss on his behalf. Of course, the insured in such a case does not necessarily suffer if the loss is less than 80 percent of the value of the property. Still, the idea is there. The policy of one farm mutual company on this point reads as follows:

> . . . does insure . . . and legal representatives, to the extent of 80 percent of the actual cash value (ascertained with proper deductions for depreciation) of the property at the time of loss or damage, but not exceeding the amount which it would cost to repair or replace the same with material of like kind and quality within a reasonable time after such loss or damage, without allowance for any increased cost of repair or reconstruction by reason of any

ordinance or law regulating construction or repair and without compensation for loss resulting from interruption of business or manufacture. . . .

Policies of some other companies provide that no building or other item of property (usually excluding livestock) shall be insured for more than three fourths or less than one half of its actual cash value.

Other Limiting Provisions. Still other provisions are used by farm insurers to limit liability in case of total (or other relatively large) losses. Some companies resort to "loss clauses" where no more than some proportion, such as two thirds, of any loss is payable. Most companies set a limit as to the total amount payable for any head of livestock or any one fowl.

Forms Applicable to Fire and Allied Lines Farm Insurance

A wide variety of forms is used in farm insurance; hence, generalizations are difficult and dangerous. Attention will be called here, however, to a few of the more widely used forms.

Form 64. The Farm Property—Fire and Extended Coverage Form (Form 64) is filed in most of the states and is used by a large number of stock companies writing farm insurance. Under this form coverage can be provided for the dwelling, household and personal effects, buildings, silos, grain, hay, machinery and certain vehicles, private power and light poles plus outdoor wiring, poultry, livestock, and certain other properties. This form incorporates the regular "seven point" extended coverage endorsement and is designed to be used with the Standard Fire Policy. It prohibits other insurance on buildings in the absence of special permission and it contains the usual clauses in respect to liberalization, loss, nuclear contamination, electrical apparatus, work and materials, and construction, alterations, and repairs. It provides limited automatic coverage of newly acquired farm equipment, machinery, and vehicles or equipment, machinery, and vehicles acquired as replacement; it affords a limited off-premises coverage on grain, hay, machinery and vehicles, and livestock. The form contains no coinsurance or standard mortgage clause.

Blanket Farm Personal Property Form. For coverage of farm personal property, this form, in slightly more than a decade of use, has become the most popular and most frequently sold farm insurance form. Aside from the excluded items, it covers most farm personal property usual and incidental to the operation of a farm and even includes farm personal property purchased on the installment plan. Blanket Form No. F.P. 434 as used by numerous stock companies has two "items." The first is farm personal property except "Household and Personal Effects"; the second is "Household and Personal Effects." Some types of property are excluded. Not less than $10,000 may be written in "Item 1." The form includes the perils of fire, extended coverage, theft, and overturn, with theft and overturn being subject to a mandatory deductible of $50. The Blanket Farm Personal Property Endorsement used with the "uniform" policy of the

National Association of Mutual Insurance Companies has only one "item" but excludes "Household and Personal Effects" along with several other classes of property. It lists no perils but is tied in with the "uniform" policy and other supporting endorsements.

Unlike Form 64, the Blanket Farm Personal Property Form carries a coinsurance provision. (In Form No. F.P. 434 coinsurance applies only to "Item 1.") The stipulated percentage of insurance is 80. In the event of an aggregate claim which is less than 2 percent of the total amount of insurance the insured is not required to furnish an inventory of undamaged property. Nevertheless, the coinsurance clause may still be operative in such cases.

Aside from the specifically excluded personal property, the Blanket Farm Personal Property Form covers "just about everything" from the most minute spare part to the highest priced item of machinery or livestock. Among the excluded property besides household and personal effects are tobacco, cotton, money, securities, turkeys, livestock in transit by common carrier, windmills, crop driers, and so on. Several of these types can be included by endorsement and payment of additional premium.

Other. Various other forms are used rather widely for covering various parts of farm properties. For example, a form providing fire, lightning, and windstorm coverage as opposed to the regular fire, lightning, and extended coverage is used by numerous stock companies as Form 66. These companies also have a "Farm Dwelling(s) and Household and Personal Effects—Broad Form" which is used with the Standard Fire Policy.

Commonly Used Endorsements

Several endorsements in farm insurance are of wide enough use to warrant brief reference in this chapter.

Additional Living Expenses. This endorsement (which in some companies may be written alternatively as a separate policy) covers, up to certain limits, excess expenses of operating a household in temporary quarters because of untenantability of the regular dwelling due to damage or destruction by an insured peril.

Farm Dwelling Unoccupancy Permit. This endorsement may be attached to policies when a farm dwelling is unoccupied in excess of the 60 days allowed by most policies. Attached without charge at the request of the insured, it defines "unoccupied" as a dwelling completely furnished but with its habitants temporarily absent. The dwelling must be under supervision and care of a competent person and all doors and windows are to be closed and locked. It applies for 60 days only after which time a Farm Vacancy or Unoccupancy Permit becomes necessary. One type of the latter endorsement is issued for a specific time only, during which time the insurance is reduced one third. A second type provides for a charge for each 60 days of vacancy or unoccupancy in lieu of the reduction in the insurance. Both types stipulate that vacancy of the dwelling constitutes vacancy of the entire premises.

Improvements and Betterments. This endorsement provides for insuring of improvements and betterments to farm property as made by a tenant. Any fixtures, alterations, installations, or additions to an insured building which have been made at the expense of the insured tenant and which cannot be legally removed by him may be covered under this form. The form further provides that, if the damage is repaired or the building is replaced within 12 months, the insurance company will be liable for the actual cash value of the improvements. The endorsement provides, in case repairs or replacement should not be made as prescribed, for payment of that portion of the original cost which the unexpired term of the tenant's lease bears to the period from the date such improvements were made to the expiration date of the lease.

Other. Additional important farm insurance endorsements not yet mentioned in this chapter include: a brooder permit, an extended coverage exclusion endorsement, a grain extension endorsement, a grain on farm-acreage plan, a fire department service clause, a rural fire department protection clause, a theft of grain on farm endorsement, a rent or rental value endorsement, and various livestock endorsements. Also available are a vandalism and malicious mischief endorsement and a windstorm and hail deductible clause. Several of these coverages are treated in earlier chapters.

Miscellaneous Comments

Farm insurance is characteristically written on a five- or three-year term basis under an arrangement where the coverage is suspended in the event other insurance on the property is procured—unless special permission is granted in writing. Many mutual companies, however, still provide perpetual policies continuing in force as long as premiums or assessments are paid.

The packaging idea has encompassed farm insurance. Most of the coverages described in this section can also be incorporated into the Farmowners Policy. It, of course, includes liability features as well. (See Chapter 49.)

Underwriting Farm Insurance

Virtually all of the principles of underwriting described in Chapter 14 apply fully to farm business. In addition, farm underwriting has its own peculiarities, a few of which will be treated briefly in this section.

Threat of Total Loss. One such peculiarity—as already suggested—is the threat of total loss, particularly to real property. A farm underwriter must recognize that, in fact, many farm fire losses are total because of isolation and inadequate fire protection. About the most that can be hoped is that a fire, once started, will not spread. Farm electrical systems contribute materially to the fire hazard but, of course, permit the elimination of various other lighting and heating devices which might be even more hazardous. Lightning also continues to be the source of many farm fires; hence, lightning rods in adequate number and with proper connections are still of major importance to an underwriter.

Obsolescence. Another major underwriting problem in farm insurance is the fact that buildings and equipment may lose their utility. Mechanization of the farming industry has aggravated this problem. Outmoded and unusable buildings cease to be assets and become liabilities to farmers. Undoubtedly, obsolescence has been the prime cause of many a substantial farm fire. Thus underwriters must be especially careful about the type, age, and use of farm buildings and must be especially alert to appraise the quality of housekeeping in respect to such properties. A good farm underwriter may not be worth his salt until he realizes that the number of risks he should reject may greatly exceed the number he should accept.

Underwriting in Mutual Companies. Farm insurance is further characterized by some farm mutual insurance practices which warrant attention. In this country there are many relatively small farm mutuals whose members and policyholders are the farmers in the vicinity. Many of these companies have issued and/or still issue assessable policies. The small geographic area and the assessable feature make for a close relationship among the policyholders. Further, the company secretary or the director responsible for business in that area probably knows every insured personally and is familiar with his properties. Underwriting devices such as credit reports are virtually unheard of in the farm mutual field. Yet, inspection of the risk by the secretary or director usually provides far more accurate underwriting data than larger insurers can hope to obtain. Periodic calls at the farm—for any one of a dozen reasons—may keep the underwriter quite well informed as to the status of the risk. Moreover, the insured, because of his closeness to his neighbors, may have a peculiar incentive not to be the one to cause the loss.

Farm Insurance Ratemaking

Readers are referred to Chapter 13 for a discussion of fire insurance ratemaking generally. In this section brief mention will be made of a few ratemaking points of particular significance to farm insurance.

Assessment. The issuing of policies containing the assessment feature perhaps has been and still is more prominent in farm insurance than in any other type. While the number of companies using the "pure assessment" feature is declining, many small farm mutuals continue to operate on this concept. The most common device in use today is the "post assessment." It works like this: Once each year losses and expenses of the insurer are totaled. An assessment based on insurance per policyholder is then levied. Occasionally this "post assessment" feature is modified and the assessment is determined, levied, and collected in advance. If the assessment levied is larger than needs require, the excess may be refunded in the form of dividends. If the amount of money derived from this "advance premium" is insufficient to cover losses and expenses, the policyholder can still be asked to pay an additional assessment. This latter charge, however, is usually limited by the company's bylaws to one assessment per year and a maximum is also usually established.

Many large farm mutuals have qualified by law to issue nonassessable policies. A rate is established and a premium charged. The policyholder cannot become liable for an assessment but may be eligible for dividends if experience is favorable.

Classification. Up until about 1950 farm properties were generally not broken down into classes for purposes of ratemaking. Prior to the advent of the "Minnesota Plan" (so named because it was first filed and approved in Minnesota), farm risks for many companies were either "insurable" or "uninsurable" and one rate applied to a given type of property. Subsequently the stock companies making up the Farm Underwriters Association (of the middle western states) adopted a Special Farm Survey and Rating Plan which provides credits for superior features of risks. The plan has spread to other states where farm properties are classified as "superior," "average," or "poor." To date such plans have been used mainly by stock companies but increasingly the larger mutuals are adopting similar methods of "risk-rating."

Rate Levels. Until fairly recently farm mutual rates had been generally below comparable stock company rates. Lower acquisition costs, conservative loss adjustments, and a rather pronounced policyholder loyalty perhaps accounted for this disparity. The absence of any requirement for most small farm mutuals to file rates allowed them considerably more freedom. The assessment feature reduced the pressure to accumulate safety funds. In recent years, however, stock companies have offered farmowners policies and other multiple peril contracts to farmers at rates which are impressively low.

Loss Prevention

Fire prevention is uniquely important to owners of farm properties. Fire is a deadly threat to farmers and often results in total loss of the property. Lack of alarm systems, inadequate water supplies, long distances from fire departments, and perhaps poor road systems aggravate the situation.

Changes in technology, farming methods, and living standards have produced numerous new hazards. Today's farm may have a paint shop, gasoline pumps, gasoline storage facilities, full-fledged machine shops equipped for welding, and intricate electrical wiring systems. In addition, tons of inflammable hay, grain, and feed as well as unprotected frame buildings add to the danger.

The insurance industry has demonstrated a real dedication to loss prevention in farm life. In several states farm mutuals have been able to sustain rural fire departments by supplying them with trucks and equipment. Many such companies have supplied lightning arrestors and fire extinguishers for farm risks. A program of rural fire inspection by 4–H Club members has been an annual project of the National Association of Mutual Insurance Companies. The National Board of Fire Underwriters,[1] an organization serving capital stock insurance companies since 1886, has distributed large quantities of literature, films, and other types of information on loss prevention. Recently the National Fire Protection Association has become active in certain rural areas.

In spite of all of this effort, farm fire losses are still staggering. According to recent estimates, annual farm fire losses approximate $90 million. Some 3,500 persons are believed to lose their lives in farm fires each year.

LIVESTOCK INSURANCE

The preceding section on fire and allied lines farm insurance has brought out the fact that fire and extended coverage farm contracts provide insurance on livestock. Specifically, horses, cattle, sheep, and swine may be insured against the enumerated perils which, as has been noted, may include electrocution, theft, and other coverages supplemental to the usual fire and extended coverage perils. Virtually all farm insurance companies provide some sort of coverage on livestock. Livestock inland marine floaters are also issued.

Mortality insurance on livestock (as opposed to fire and extended coverage insurance) is provided by specialty companies. A full mortality policy covers most of the frequent reasons for loss. This type of insurance which pays in the event of death due to accident or sickness, is nearly "all risk." It is the policy most commonly used by the purebred breeder. It covers the actual cash value of each animal up to but not exceeding the amount scheduled.

Group plans covering cattle and horses are also available from specialty writers. An initial premium of approximately one half the regular mortality policy rate is charged. If no loss is suffered during the policy term, no further payment is made. If one animal dies, a deductible equal in percentage to the rate differential (approximately 50 percent) applies.

[1] See Footnote 5, Chap. 1.

Future losses are paid in full because the policy, by virtue of the first loss and application of the deductible, is converted to normal full premium. Ten animals or more are necessary for the group rate. Specific values must be indicated for each animal. No animal may be valued in excess of the total value of the other animals insured in the group.

Livestock insurance may be written to cover a certain period or event. It is then similar to the "trip insurance" which a person may buy prior to a journey by plane.

An inland marine form, the livestock floater, is also available and will provide protection against named perils resulting in death or necessary destruction of horses, cattle, hogs, or sheep. The basis for loss adjustment in this floater is actual cash value or, in the case of specifically scheduled higher-priced animals, the actual sales price (or, when no actual sales transaction has taken place, fair and conservative appraisal by competent judges). In all such cases, of course, these values are subject to acceptance by the insuring company.

CROP INSURANCE

One of the most devastating perils faced by the farmer is that of hail damage to his growing crops. In 1963 more than $110 million in premiums on crop hail insurance was written in the continental United States. Conservative estimates indicate, however, that not more than 10 percent of the total acreage of growing crops in this country is represented in crop insurance.

More companies apparently have been organized and have then become insolvent in the crop hail line than in any other line in the insurance business. Many persons have failed to realize that the hail peril to growing crops is one of violent cyclical fluctuation. One year may be almost loss free; the next may be catastrophic. Of prime importance are (1) the accumulation of adequate funds with which to pay future losses and (2) a spread of business over a large geographical area. Lack of knowledge of the pitfalls of producing crop hail business and adjusting crop hail losses has caused bankruptcy of many companies attempting to provide this type of insurance.

Indicative of the unpredictable aspects of this peril is the fact that, while no section of the country is immune from hailstorms, there is a tremendous regional variation in its incidence. The bulk of this insurance is written in the Great Plains area and the Middle West. The fact that rates go from less than 2 percent to more than 20 percent in this area indicates the great fluctuation in frequency and severity of hailstorms. North Carolina, Texas, Kansas, Nebraska, North Dakota, and Minnesota in recent years have been leaders in crop hail losses.

Specialized crop hail companies have been organized to protect the farmer against hail damage to his growing crops. Most of these are mutual companies, formed by the farmers themselves. Many general writing companies also offer crop hail insurance. Most of these are stock companies. Hail is the basic hazard of all crop insurance policies. However, it is not necessarily the only peril covered. The specialty companies have added fire and lightning to standing crops and crops in transit to the first place of storage. Most stock company policies provide crop insurance protection against the perils of fire, lightning, livestock, wind, aircraft, and vehicles in addition to hail.

Crop Hail Insurance Actuarial Association

Crop hail insurance written by the majority of stock companies is rated by the Crop Hail Insurance Actuarial Association. This nonprofit research and ratemaking organization came into existence in the fall of 1947. It is supported by more than 100 insurance companies—mostly stock fire carriers. It actually replaced a number of regional hail insurance organizations whose activities extended back for some 30 years. CHIAA files rates for its member companies and subscribers in many states. In addition, CHIAA conducts a threefold research program:

1. It seeks to improve the present crop hail insurance rate structure by determining the average geographical distribution of the hail hazard.
2. It keeps abreast of developments in weather modification and hail suppression.
3. It investigates other perils to growing crops.

Incidentally, each of the mutual crop hail insurers, for all practicable purposes, files hail rates independently, calculated upon its own experience. Although some have expanded to other areas, most of these companies are writing in one state only. Some have become subscribers to the Crop Hail Insurance Actuarial Association, following its rates and policy forms in certain states.

Percentage Plan

Most of the crop hail insurance in the United States is written on the percentage plan. Under this type of policy the proportion of insurance recovered by the insured is the same as the proportion of the crop destroyed. The companies have established amounts per acre for which they will ordinarily insure various crops. Within the maximum limit per acre established by the company, the farmer may purchase his insurance. The amount of insurance per acre purchased, of course, is dependent upon the estimated value of the crop per acre. In Iowa, for example, crop hail insurance on corn will probably average $60 per acre. In the event of loss, damage is figured on a percentage basis per acre and the loss is paid by applying that percentage to the amount of insurance per acre set out in the policy.

A minimum loss clause of 5 percent is mandatory in some states. Endorsements are also available which will materially reduce the policy rate. These are Excess Over Loss Endorsements by which the insured assumes the first 10 or 20 percent of loss. Under such an endorsement the premium may be reduced as much as one third and the farmer may buy a larger amount of insurance than otherwise for the same dollar outlay.

Bushel Plan

A small number of crop hail companies have followed a plan of a guaranteed price per bushel. This policy (available in only 10 states in 1963) pays the farmer for the number of bushels of crops destroyed, up to some maximum number of bushels stipulated in the policy. The higher this maximum, of course, the higher the premium. This maximum can be set at any figure, providing it is not more than the value of the crop stated in the policy.

This plan is comparable to the percentage plan in respect to total losses. On partial losses, however, a complicated procedure of determining the maximum yield by increasing the number of bushels insured is used.

Federal Crop Insurance Corporation

Federal "All Risk" Crop Insurance has been available to America's farmers since 1948. It allegedly does not replace the insurance carried on growing crops by private companies. It guarantees a set amount of bushel production from a farmer's total acreage, regardless of percent of damage by hail, drought, frost, freeze, or any unavoidable cause. Benefits can be collected from both FCIC and private insurance on the same crop.

This program is administered by one of the agencies in the United States Department of Agriculture. It is designed to provide financial stability where crop disaster strikes. Its proponents insist that it has been a successful operation and point out that FCIC insurance has paid $450 million to farmer-policyholders. The FCIC has paid claims to hundreds of thousands who have lost all or a part of their crop investment from one cause or another. A serious point of contention, however, is the extent to which administration costs and even loss payments are subsidized out of revenues produced by federal taxes.

SUGGESTED READINGS

ATHEARN, JAMES L., AND TOOLE, CAMERON S. *Questions and Answers on Insurance.* 2d ed. Englewood Cliffs, N.J.: Prentice-Hall, Inc., 1960.

BAINBRIDGE, JOHN. *Biography of an Idea.* Garden City, N.Y.: Doubleday & Co., Inc., 1952.

GEISE, HENRY. *Of Mutuals and Men.* Des Moines, Ia.: Iowa Association of Mutual Insurance Associations, 1955.

Roth, Richard J. "Crop Hail—A Growing Coverage," *The Spec*
1955), p. 34.

Schultz, Robert E., and Bardwell, Edward C. *Property Insu*
York: Rinehart & Co., Inc., 1959. Chap. v.

———"Crop Hail Insurance Actuarial Association," *Bulletin of th*
Meteorological Society, Vol. 36 (October, 1955), pp. 409–11.

Smith, Dennis. *Farm Fire Insurance Primer.* Indianapolis: Rough Notes Co., Inc., 1954.

"Tomorrow's Insurance Today," *Federal Crop Insurance.* Des Moines, Ia.: Iowa State Office, Federal Crop Insurance Corporation, 1960.

Chapter 12

LOSS PREVENTION IN FIRE INSURANCE

BY GERALD L. MAATMAN

The development of our modern civilization would have been impossible without the utilization of fire. Yet mankind has also found fire to be a formidable foe which, when unleashed, has the capacity to destroy his material wealth and being. The present-day technological explosion, which is producing countless benefits for man through new materials, machines, and energy sources, is also creating complex potential loss control problems. The continuing task of controlling fire and its associated hazards in our modern society represents a formidable challenge which cannot be ignored.

In this chapter attention will be given to the importance of loss prevention activities, to some of the techniques of loss prevention, to some of the organizations active in loss prevention, to development of loss prevention concepts, and to a brief recognition of some continuing loss prevention problems.

IMPORTANCE OF LOSS PREVENTION ACTIVITIES

Annual Property Losses By Fire

Statistics compiled by the National Fire Protection Association on total annual *direct* fire losses in the United States, which include damage to buildings, contents, motor vehicles, aircraft, and forests, indicate that the total dollar loss has been steadily climbing. For instance, there has been a fourfold increase from $320 million in 1942 to about $1,600 million in 1961 and the estimated 1962 annual loss is some 8 percent higher than that of the previous year.

The entire loss to society, however, is probably as much as three times the direct loss amounts. Indirect losses resulting from fire are just as tangible and in many instances more serious than the direct loss. Examples include loss of profits, customers, wages to employees, and rents; cost of replacing depreciated buildings and equipment with new; increased burden on welfare funds, and so on.

Effects of Inflation and Growth

It would appear on the surface that the constant sharp upward trend of direct annual fire losses indicates that loss prevention efforts to date have been of little or no value. However, there are two important factors which must be taken into account in evaluating these data. First, inflationary trends in the economy have substantially cheapened the value of the dollar. According to the Average Building—Commodity Cost Index which uses 1942 as a base year, the value of a 1942 dollar in 1961 was only 46 cents.[1] Therefore, if the 1961 annual loss is expressed in terms of 1942 dollar value, it would be approximately $750 million and thus represent only a 135 perecnt increase rather than the apparent 400 percent.

The other important influence which must be taken into account is the sharp increase in total burnable values which has occurred concurrently with the continuing growth of our economy and the growth in population. Studies made by the National Board of Fire Underwriters indicate that when total annual fire losses are compared with total annual gross national wealth (value of land, buildings, equipment, contents, and other reproducible assets), the results show that the proportion of gross national wealth destroyed by fire each year has been declining since 1900. In the 1896–1914 period, an annual average of 0.3 percent was destroyed. This figure was reduced to a 0.2 percent annual average from 1915 to 1934 and to a 0.1 percent annual average since that time. Thus, if loss prevention efforts in recent years had been confined to their 1896–1914 levels, it can be readily seen that the total annual fire loss in 1961 could conceivably have been as high as $4,800 million—assuming stable and proportional results from each loss prevention dollar. Therefore, it is readily apparent a good case exists that loss prevention activities are making a tangible contribution toward reducing total annual fire losses. However, the fact that the number of buildings and the number and character of fire hazards are increasing each year makes it imperative that loss prevention activities be continued and expanded on all levels.

TECHNIQUES OF LOSS PREVENTION

The Concept

Fire is usually described as being a chemical reaction consisting of rapid oxidation accompanied by the evolution of heat and light energy. It is a well-established fact that three basic elements must be present in order for a fire to take place. There must be (1) a combustible fuel available to burn, (2) oxygen to sustain the combustion, and (3) a source of ignition to heat all or a part of the fuel to a temperature at which it will

[1] See *NFPA Fire Protection Handbook* (12th ed.; New York: National Fire Protection Association, 1962), p. 23.

combine rapidly enough with oxygen to sustain its own reaction by the liberation of heat when the ignition source is removed. In recent years, a new theory has been developed to supplement the thinking about the traditional fire traingle. This new theory, which has obtained considerable support as a result of the development of new halogenated chemical extinguishing agents, holds that the development and propagation of fire through a fuel depends upon sustaining a complex chemical chain reaction in which intermediate reaction products are formed in several steps before the final combustion products are evolved. The very effective action of several of the new chemical extinguishing agents is credited to their ability to interfere with the formation of large amounts of these intermediate combustion products, breaking the combustion chain reaction.[2]

All loss prevention or loss control techniques are based in some manner upon removing or limiting one or more of the three basic elements of fire within any given situation.

Basic Methods of Approach

Construction of Buildings. It is desirable to use noncombustible materials wherever possible in the construction of buildings so as to reduce the total available fuel. Where this is not entirely practical, it is still possible to reduce somewhat the combustibility of some structural components or finish materials through the use of chemical impregnation treatments or fire-retardant surface coatings. Impregnation treatments have been proved effective in certain situations. The former is necessarily restricted to new buildings under construction while the latter method has its greatest application in the case of existing structures.

The use of noncombustible building materials does not necessarily guarantee that a structure will not suffer extensive or total damage as the result of a fire. Therefore, it is highly desirable to use building materials or assemblies which are fire-resistive to the extent that they will withstand a complete burnout of the contents and yet remain structurally stable.

Most large-loss building fires are due at least partly to the large interior areas which are open to fire spread. Therefore, a building should be divided horizontally at reasonable intervals with fire or division wall barriers, and vertically by the protection of all floor openings, so as to limit the area of a building which will be subject to any one fire. In addition, it is necessary to provide a sufficient clearance between buildings to eliminate the possibility of fire spreading between the structures. An alternative is to eliminate or protect exterior wall openings and roofs through which fire or heat could pass.

Where a potential explosion hazard exists due to the inherent nature of

[2] See A. B. Guise, "The Chemical Aspects of Fire Extinguishment," *National Fire Protection Association Quarterly* (April, 1960), pp. 330–36.

an occupancy, it is important to provide means of venting possible critical pressure buildup so as to minimize potential explosion damage to the structure. This venting is accomplished by providing windows or wall and roof panels which will fall outward or collapse at pressures considerably below that necessary to damage the basic structural supports.

The various service systems within a building such as electrical equipment, fuel, and heating devices must be designed and installed safely and arranged to shut off automatically in case of equipment failure. This shutting off avoids introducing sources of ignition or fuel for a fire or explosion.

Occupancy Features. The occupancy of a building introduces fire hazard problems which must be evaluated and handled in some manner.

1. *Use of Separate Areas.* First of all, combustible fuels of varying magnitude and character are normally used in connection with the occupancy. If any are of high combustibility, are easily damageable, and/or are of high value, consideration should be given to segregating such fuels in fire-resistive enclosures from the rest of the occupancy in order to reduce the amount of fuel or contents value subject to any one fire. This factor is especially important in industrial occupancies where separation of finished and raw stock areas from production is usually desirable in order to minimize the production interruption or loss of earnings potential from any one fire.

2. *Ways of Controlling Operations.* In many cases, materials used in manufacturing are subjected to abnormal temperatures and/or pressures which greatly increase their fire or explosion hazard potential. Examples include paint spraying or dipping, drying in ovens, mixing, baking, welding, heating, machining, pulverizing, and many other operations. These hazards must be evaluated and controlled in one or more of the following ways:

a) Eliminate Hazardous Materials. It is sometimes possible to substitute a safer material for a potentially hazardous one in a process or operation. For instance, a solvent having a high flash point can be used in dry cleaning or degreasing operations rather than a liquid with a low flash point.

b) Control Hazard within Safe Limits. For instance, in connection with an oven used to dry materials which give off flammable vapors, a continuous supply of incoming fresh air should be provided to keep these vapors diluted below their lowest flammable limit. In addition, safety interlocks must be provided to shut down the supply of heat and the conveyor line if the supply of diluting air is cut off for any reason.

c) Eliminate All Possible Sources of Ignition. In some instances, it is impossible or impractical to eliminate or significantly dilute dangerous quantities of flammable vapors or dusts from a particular room or section of a building. In such cases all possible sources of ignition must be eliminated from the area in question. This elimination involves among other things the use of explosion-proof electrical devices, fixtures, and equipment; the removal of all devices having open flames; and the bonding, grounding, and neutralization of any devices or materials capable of producing static electricity spark potential.

d) Segregate Hazardous Operations. Segregation of any hazardous process or operation from the remaining portions of the occupancy either with a fire-resistive separation or by removal to a separate detached building is another way to reduce the hazard. This segregation is frequently done, for example, in the case of auxiliary paint spraying operations.

e) Provide Local Automatic Protection. When hazardous processes cannot be segregated from other portions of the occupancy for operational reasons, some type of local fixed automatic extinguishing system may be used. In this manner the probability may be increased that a fire will not spread beyond the confines of the equipment. Carbon Dioxide and Dry Chemical Systems are two examples of this type of protection which is frequently provided for paint dipping tanks, drying ovens, and similar types of hazardous operations.

f) Educate Occupants. In addition to various possible physical hazards, the occupancy of a building introduces the all-important human hazard. Human carelessness is critical in fire and other losses. It is worthy of considerable emphasis in fire prevention efforts. Traditionally, organizations interested in fire prevention have attempted to approach this problem through the media of mass public education programs mainly concentrating their efforts on good housekeeping and on basic causes of fires. In recent years, increased emphasis has been placed on teaching school children good fire prevention habits with the hope that patterns of behavior can be developed which will carry over into adult life. Some success seems also to have been achieved, temporarily at least, in numerous cities through the use of mass building inspection programs by public fire departments.

Provision of Other Protection Facilities

Hand Fire Extinguisher. One of the basic fire protection concepts involves the provision of first aid fire extinguishing devices for use by building occupants on small incipient fires. These usually take the form of either portable fire extinguishers or building standpipe systems equipped with lightweight small capacity hose. Equipment of this type is normally dispersed throughout a building in such a manner that at least one unit can be readily available regardless of the location of a fire.

Sprinkler Systems. In those cases where the construction, size, and/or interior arrangement of a building is conducive to extensive fire spread or where the occupancy is of a hazardous nature or contains large amounts of combustibles, reliable automatic protection is much better than that offered by first aid extinguishing appliances. The most common means of providing such protection is by the use of an automatic sprinkler system. This equipment, of course, consists of a series of pipes extended throughout the building to which are attached numerous outlets called sprinkler heads. Individual heads are each maintained in a capped position, usually through the use of metal struts under compression, and arranged to open through the melting of a fusible link. The system is connected to one or more sources of water supply. In case of a fire, only the adjacent heads open to discharge water in a spray pattern over the fire.

The flow of water through piping can also be used to activate alarms, either locally or to a central station or fire department. Thus, a sprinkler system can perform the dual function of both an automatic extinguishing and alarm system. The automatic sprinkler system has achieved an enviable reputation. The records of the N.F.P.A. which cover some 100,000 fires occuring in sprinklered buildings over the past 65 years indicate that sprinklers controlled or extinguished the fires in 96 percent of the cases.

Other types of fixed extinguishing systems whose applications are normally limited mainly to local special hazard situations such as paint dip tanks include those utilizing carbon dioxide gas, dry chemical, foam, and water spray.

Automatic Fire Alarm. In addition to those types of protection which combine both fire detection and extinguishment features, there are several types of automatic systems whose function is merely to detect the presence of fire and sound an alarm. The more common types operate on the principle of either detecting an abnormal rate of temperature rise or the presence of smoke or visible flame in a given area. These systems can be arranged to sound only a building alarm or also to transmit a signal directly to fire department headquarters. In addition, where private central supervisory alarm service is available within a city, a signal can be sent to a central station which also maintains constant supervision over the operating condition of the system. Automatic fire alarm systems have their greatest application where conditions do not warrant the higher cost of a sprinkler system and where a principal concern is for life safety. The point should be noted, however, that while these systems turn in an alarm quickly, the fire usually continues until the fire fighters arrive.

ORGANIZATIONS ACTIVE IN LOSS PREVENTION

Within the Property Industry

Most insurance companies writing fire and allied lines coverages maintain some sort of fire engineering or inspection staff. The primary function of such staff is to evaluate mercantile, industrial, and public building risks on behalf of their underwriting departments prior to final selection. In addition, many companies provide a routine inspection service for their larger insureds and also provide technical consulting service on special fire hazard problems or fire insurance rating problems which arise.

Many insurance producing organizations operating mainly in major metropolitan areas also provide fire protection inspection and engineering services to their clients.

Major industrial concerns present complex fire hazard and underwriting problems. For this reason, various cooperative organizations have been formed to provide the large underwriting capacity, and engineering, inspection, and loss adjustment services necessary properly to handle such major properties. The two largest known organizations are the Factory Insurance Association, organized by a group of stock insurance companies and the Factory Mutual Engineering Division of the Associated Factory Mutual Fire Insurance Companies and the Improved Risk Mutuals. Both of those organizations also engage in extensive fire prevention public relations and information services. Comparable organizations, created to handle specific classes of property include the Oil Insurance Association, Cotton Insurance Association, Underwriters Grain Association, Associated Lumber Mutuals, Association of Mill and Elevator Mutuals, Simmonds, Lumbermen's Underwriting Alliance, and numerous others.

Other types of cooperative organizations have been organized purely for service functions. The most widely known of these is the National Board of Fire Underwriters organized in 1866 as an engineering, statistical, and educational organization by a large number of stock fire insurance companies. The N.B.F.U. maintains a staff of trained engineers which periodically surveys the public fire defense facilities of all cities over 25,000 population. In addition, the N.B.F.U. publishes various fire protection standards, including its National Building and Fire Prevention Codes which have been widely adopted by regulatory agencies. The N.B.F.U. also maintains an arson investigation staff, assists local officials, collects and tabulates fire loss statistics for member companies, and conducts an extensive nationwide public relations and educational program in fire prevention. Another similar but less extensive organization serves mutual insurance companies—the American Mutual Insurance Alliance. It also provides various fire protection educational services through its affiliated Federation of Mutual Fire Insurance Companies.

Another important group of service organizations includes various state and regional fire inspection and rating bureaus formed and supported by insurance companies whose primary function is to establish fire insurance rates on various classes of property. The bureaus also survey the public fire defenses of smaller cities within their respective jurisdictions and provide a wide range of fire protection service functions.

There are two important fire safety testing laboratories, the most widely known of which is Underwriters' Laboratories, Inc., organized in 1894 as a nonprofit organization and sponsored by the N.B.F.U. The primary function of U.L. is to test materials, equipment, and devices with reference to their life, fire, and casualty hazards and to publish lists of those which meet accepted standards of safety. In addition, technical standards are published by U.L. and investigations are conducted from time to time on specific fire safety problems. Underwriters' Laboratories is famous for its label on products whose design and construction have been checked and approved at the laboratories. The other important facility is Factory Mutual Laboratories, a part of the Factory Mutual Engineering Division, which also engages in testing, in investigating specific fire protection problems for its insureds, and in researching other problems.

Numerous organizations within the insurance industry engage in a wide variety of general fire prevention promotional efforts. These include the National Association of Insurance Agents, National Association of Mutual Insurance Agents, Association of Casualty and Surety Companies, the Insurance Information Institute, the National Association of Mutual Insurance Companies, various state fire prevention associations composed of insurance company field men, and various local or regional insurance agents' associations.

Outside of Insurance Industry

The most widely known fire prevention agency is the National Fire Protection Association, a nonprofit organization with over 20,000 members representing the fire service industry, insurance industry, equipment manufacturers industry, and general industry. The N.F.P.A. engages in a wide variety of both technical and promotional activities which include the publishing of some 180 technical standards. The most famous one is the National Electrical Code. N.F.P.A. also provides field engineering service to local regulatory agencies utilizing N.F.P.A. standards. It also maintains a fire record department for tabulating and classifying fire loss data. In addition, a week long meeting and a fall conference are held each year to revise technical standards and to provide a forum for discussion of fire protection topics. Also, various technical publications are periodically sent to members. In 1950, a professional section, known as the Society of Fire Protection Engineers, was formed to promote and maintain high professional engineering standards within the field. The S.F.P.E. now numbers some 1,200 members and has 16 local chapters located in various parts of the United States and Canada.

Other private organizations active in the fire prevention field include the American Gas Association, International Association of Fire Chiefs, U.S. Chamber of Commerce and its affiliates, National Safety Council, and various trade associations representing industries concerned in some manner with fire protection.

The federal government is also actively engaged in various areas of fire prevention. The National Bureau of Standards, Bureau of Mines, U.S. Forest Service, Federal Aviation Agency, Interstate Commerce Commission, General Services Administration, Office of Civil Defense, and the various military agencies are prominent in fire prevention problems. In addition, a committee on fire research was formed within the National Academy of Sciences—National Research Council in 1956 to study fire problems and encourage additional basic and applied fire research.

Private industry has become increasingly interested in fire prevention and protection from a self-preservation standpoint. Large corporations, in particular, now frequently employ full-time personnel to plan and administer their programs.

Private and university-affiliated research organizations are also showing increased interest in fire protection problems. Syracuse University, Illinois Institute of Technology Research Institute, Stanford University, and the Southwest Research Institute are engaging in various phases of fire research work.

DEVELOPMENT OF LOSS PREVENTION CONCEPTS

The applied science of fire prevention has had a long and colorful history. As with most other technical areas of endeavor, many of its early concepts and developments were slowly formulated from judgment and the painful experience of large-loss fires. Not until recent decades have loss prevention concepts been developed from basic scientific principles and research efforts. Therefore, to gain a proper appreciation of the present state of the science of fire prevention, it is necessary to trace some of its early development.

The first development which had a lasting effect on present day fire prevention methods was the invention of the Parmalee sprinkler head in 1878. This head proved to be the forerunner of modern automatic sprinkler design.

In the 1880's, heavy timber construction was developed for textile mills in New England. This type of building utilized wood columns, girders, and beams of relatively large cross section and thick plank floors and roof in an effort to produce a type of construction which would retain its structural integrity for a much longer period of time under severe fire conditions.

In 1902, A.F. Dean published the first edition of the *Analytic System for the Measurement of Relative Fire Hazard,* a fire insurance rating schedule which provided the first comprehensive qualitative analysis of the many physical factors bearing on the risk of fire.

The first two decades of the twentieth century saw (1) extensive fire testing of masonry, steel, and cast iron building components and (2) the development of standard fire resistance testing procedures for walls, floors, columns, and beams. During this period, Underwriters' Laboratories, Inc. began to develop into a major testing agency and also provided further impetus in the field of fire extinguishing equipment development.

The requirements of World War II accelerated the development of chemically impregnated fire-retardant lumber, mechanical foam, wetting agents to improve the fire fighting effectiveness of water, water spray nozzles, and a special dry chemical extinguisher for metal fires.

Some of the more important advances made during the past 15 years are (1) the development of several new types of extinguishing agents, (2) further refinement of various types of fire detection devices and safety controls, (3) development of several new types of fire-retardant coatings, (4) new methods of fireproofing steel structural supports, and (5) much more sophisticated methods of designing extinguishing systems. In addition, much greater emphasis has been placed on basic research of fire, its behavior, and its development.

CONTINUING PROBLEMS IN LOSS PREVENTION

Modern society is presently doubling its scientific knowledge about every 10 years. As this knowledge is being applied increasingly to the creation of new materials, products, and industries, loss prevention problems are being correspondingly multiplied.

The increased industrial and medical uses of radioactive isotopes for a multitude of applications is creating situations where the accidental release of certain types of these materials could cause contamination property damage and business interruption losses running into huge amounts. Such release could also delay access of fire fighters to the blaze.

The continued development of new processes and exotic materials in the chemical and petrochemical industries is creating new and more complex fire and explosion hazards, some of which are very difficult to foresee prior to the actual usage of the processes or materials. An example of this problem was illustrated in recent years with two explosions of bulk nitroparaffin stored in railroad tank cars.

The present building boom has brought with it demands for new building materials and faster and more efficient ways of constructing buildings. This situation has produced several disturbing potential fire damage problems. Plastic materials are being used in increasing amounts for insulation, interior finish, and structural purposes. The pressure of an extremely large number of different finished plastic products and the present confused state of fire hazard testing procedures makes it difficult for regulatory agencies properly to assess their fire and smoke hazard properties. Also, entirely new concepts, such as air-supported balloon-like structures, high strength prestressed concrete supports, and light-weight membrane type fireproofing for steel have been introduced. The fire damage potential of buildings embracing these concepts as compared with more conventional types of construction is significantly increased.

The use in commercial shopping centers and industrial properties of increasingly large open-area buildings is aggravating the problem of large-loss fires and creating difficult fire control problems for public fire fighting agencies. One frequent problem comes from the location of these properties at edges of municipalities where water supplies may be weak.

The extensive development and application of computer technology is accelerating the automation of processes and operations especially in the petroleum and chemical industries. The continued refinement of computer controlled operations is increasing the extent of automatic supervision of potential trouble such as changes in temperature, pressure, levels of liquids or solids, and so on. The character of loss prevention problems will be complicated still further with increasing dependence being placed on the proper operation of computers and their associated monitoring and detection equipment and circuits.

SUGGESTED READINGS

BAKER, W. J. "Automation—A Challenge to Fire Protection Engineers," *National Fire Protection Association Quarterly,* Vol. 55–2 (October, 1961), pp. 116–24.

FACTORY MUTUAL ENGINEERING DIVISION. *Handbook of Industrial Loss Prevention.* New York: McGraw-Hill Book Co., Inc., 1959.

FINNEGAN, J. H. "The Why of Growing U.S. Fire Losses," *National Fire Protection Association Quarterly,* Vol. 53–2 (October, 1959), pp. 158–61.

Fire Protection through Modern Building Codes. New York: American Iron & Steel Institute, 1961.

Fire Protection Handbook. 12th ed. Boston: National Fire Protection Association, 1962.

GUISE, A. B. "The Chemical Aspects of Fire Extinguishment," *National Fire Protection Association Quarterly,* Vol. 53–4 (April, 1960), pp. 330–36.

Inspection Manual. Boston: National Fire Protection Association, 1960.

Chapter 13

RATEMAKING IN FIRE INSURANCE

BY KENT H. PARKER

FACTORS INFLUENCING PROCEDURES IN FIRE RATEMAKING

The earliest examples of fire insurance rates embraced within their simple outline the essential elements found in fire ratemaking today: classification by hazard, recognition of loss cost or burning rate, and provision for expense and underwriting profit. The differences that characterize modern ratemaking lie in the degree of refinement of rating schedules, the adjustments to statistical data, and the demands of a more sophisticated and industrialized economy.

Historical Background

"The individual rate is the apex of a pyramid, whose base is bounded by continents, decades, and combined experience."[1] The first fire rates in this country were "flat rates" based on a very limited number of either construction or occupancy classifications. The fire underwriter in colonial days was largely concerned with residences and the small business establishments used for storage or sale of merchandise. Rates for dwellings might distinguish between brick and frame construction or between tile, shingle, or thatch roofs. Rates for other classes were differentiated by several hazard classifications assigned according to the stock of merchandise or the nature of the manufactory.

These methods continued for many years and well into the nineteenth century. Each newly formed fire insurance company established its rates and underwrote its business, based on its individual appraisal of the risk, and the knowledge or experience gained through its own resources.

Early Rate Development. Several influences were to affect these early practices in ratemaking. The country and its developing economy expanded from the seaboard. The companies followed and appointed agents who had authority to bind insurance and to establish the rate. Agents were

[1] A. F. Dean (ed. by W. R. Townley), *The Philosophy of Fire Insurance* (Chicago: Edward B. Hatch, 1925), Vol. I, p. 81.

expected to follow company tariffs or rating instructions. However, competition among agents led to rate cutting in an effort to secure a larger share of the insurance market. This competition produced the earliest form of rate war, in which companies found themselves committed to liability at inadequate rates.

The first collective effort to avoid destructive rate competition is found in the organization of "Local Boards of Underwriters." These were associations organized for the purpose of stabilizing conditions in their respective local areas whose members were local agents or underwriters operating in that area. Members agreed to charge minimum rates as established by the local board under schedules or tariffs which were considered to produce the needed rates for that particular city or area. Typical of such local boards were the New York Board of Fire Underwriters, founded in 1867, and the Chicago Board of Underwriters, incorporated in 1849. The local boards eventually lost their ratemaking function when company rating organizations assumed these responsibilities, but the local boards had a major position in fire insurance rating up to 1900, and in some cases even longer.[2]

The significance of the local boards in this historical summary is that they, more than any other factor, interjected the strong influence of local practices in fire ratemaking which continue to this day. Each local board developed tariffs or schedules for its own local area. The local board view was dominant, and fire rating practices developed from a local rather than national concept, contrary to later developments in casualty, fidelity, and other lines.

Another factor was the effect of repeated city and town conflagrations in the period from about 1835 to the early part of this century.[3] These conflagrations impressed on the public the necessity for organization of public fire departments, the installation of adequate water supplies, and the passage of proper building ordinances regulating construction and protection of hazards. But even before city or state legislative activity, the fire insurance underwriter realized that the simple form of tariff which had been in use in establishing rates was inadequate in dealing with the basic problem. If for no other reason than enlightened self-interest, rating methods were needed that would encourage better construction and protection, and the control or elimination of conflagration hazards.

Beginning about 1850, protection, construction, and exposure standards were adopted in the rating schedules. Provision was made for much more detailed analysis of the rate of the individual risk, depending on compliance with such standards.

---

[2] The Chicago Board of Underwriters continued to make rates for Chicago and Cook County, Illinois, until 1938, when such activity was assumed by the Cook County Inspection Bureau, a company rating organization.

[3] A. P. Rockwell, *Great Fires and Fire Extinction* (Boston: Little, Brown & Co., 1878). Also see *1958 Fact Book* (New York: National Board of Fire Underwriters).

Attempt at Centralization of Rating, 1866–1877. After each major city conflagration, many of the companies either were forced out of business through inability to meet claims, or found it necessary to replenish capital. The general inadequacy of rates as then established by the local boards to create reserves for payment of conflagration losses resulted in the attempt to achieve sounder rating practices through a national body.

The National Board of Fire Underwriters was organized in 1866, in a period when the business was suffering the demoralizing effects of extreme rate competition and excessive losses. The formation of the National Board had several objects but the one of interest was the intent to achieve a better rating result by centralizing control in a national body which would seek to secure adoption of adequate rates by each local board.

At that time there were about 460 local boards throughout the country. In the next several years some progress was made in the creation of tariffs or schedules, following a uniform pattern, for adoption by local boards, which produced a rate level keyed to countrywide experience. However, the tendency of competition to break down agreements to adhere to such rates ultimately defeated the attempt at centralization. The National Board abandoned all activity in ratemaking or control of rates in 1877.

State Compacts and Company Rating Associations. The subsequent period from 1877 to the early 1900's witnessed a great deal of activity at local and state levels to improve ratemaking methods. Some better answer was needed than the rate wars and demoralization that periodically affected even the soundest company.[4] In this period the prototypes of modern rating schedules were developed. Also, company-controlled rating organizations were formed. Rates produced by these schedules were adhered to through voluntary agreement in underwriting associations or through what became known as "state compacts."

The Western Union was the first of the regional underwriting associations. Its formation in the Middle West in 1879 was followed shortly by the Eastern Union, the South-Eastern Tariff Association and the Board of Fire Underwriters of the Pacific. These associations had many purposes, including control of agents' commissions; but their importance to an understanding of the development of fire rating is that their objectives either directly or indirectly fostered improvements in rating methods and finally led to the type of rating organization contemplated under current state laws.

In this period, rating was gradually taken over by company associations or state boards, although local boards were still active in the larger cities.

The schedules were developed by rating men in the company associations, and were applied by field men of the companies. In order to make

[4] From 1877 to 1908, over 900 fire insurance companies went out of business, largely because of insolvency.

the use of such rates mandatory by the local agents, the companies relied on adherence rules and enforcement procedures of the company trade associations. In some states, particularly in the Middle West, compacts or agreements were entered into for a given state or city. These attempts at correction of rating problems were to lead to public reaction and state legislation hostile to collective ratemaking.

The more important contribution of this period was the pressure for improved techniques in ratemaking and the first development of systematic ratemaking methods.

In 1876, after some seven years of study, C. T. Aubin, a civil engineer who was secretary of the St. Louis Board of Fire Underwriters, developed a rating schedule known as the Aubin Schedule. In its methods may be recognized not only provision for a system of hazard analysis but, more importantly, the first concept of the relativity of hazard. While the schedule did not survive, it undoubtedly had influence on other schedule theories and particularly on the later work of A. F. Dean.

In 1892, after undergoing extensive trials in various test editions, the Universal Mercantile Schedule was published. This schedule was the product of a committee of company underwriters assisted by technical people from various rating boards or associations in eastern and southeastern states. The chairman was F. C. Moore of the Continental Insurance Company, and it was largely through his effort that the schedule was published and ultimately adopted in a large number of states.

It was also in the 1880's and 1890's that A. F. Dean of the Springfield Fire and Marine Insurance Company, undertook the study of exposure formulas and other rating problems that became the *Analytic System for the Measurement of Relative Fire Hazard.* The first regular edition of this schedule was published in 1905 and this and subsequent editions were adopted gradually in midwestern states between 1905 and 1915. The 1921 edition is used today in 20 states and a separate eastern edition is in use in six New England states.

The theories of these two major schedules are referred to in a later section. Their importance is obvious, in that both were the first schedules or systems designed to provide universality of method in what previously had been purely a local development of rating practices.

Development of Modern Schedule Rating

To understand modern schedule rating in fire insurance, one must retrace briefly the situation as it existed in the period of 1880 to 1900.

Failure of Older Methods. The schedules then in effect were not much more than local tariffs, with some degree of analysis of hazard, primarily reflecting the collective judgment of underwriters as to proper rates for the conditions then existing. However, as soon as conditions changed, the rates were no longer a measure of the hazard. Agents and companies found it expedient to cut the rates; often the rates were abandoned almost as soon as they were established.

Anticompact Laws. The enforcement of these rates through trade associations or compacts was looked upon by the public as an attempt to combine to increase the cost of fire insurance. There was a strong public movement against trusts and combines in any business, and joint ratemaking was placed in this same category. As a result, many states passed antitrust or anticompact laws prohibiting concert of action in ratemaking.

After some years of experience with these laws, the states found that they did not accomplish the intended protection of the public. The extremes of competitive rates forced on the insurance companies not only harmed the public through frequent company insolvencies, but led to unfair discrimination in which one property owner was benefited at the expense of another.

Substitution of Antidiscrimination Laws. The first action of many states, following legislative investigation, was to adopt antidiscrimination laws, often in place of the previous antitrust or anticompact laws. Such antidiscrimination laws were intended to require a company to charge similar rates for risks of like hazard and under the same degree of protection. But the public interest in rating went further, and, commencing with Kansas in 1909, many of the states adopted full rate laws in which the states undertook affirmatively to regulate fire insurance rates.

Adoption of Rate Laws. A study of the reports of various legislative commission investigations will give a complete picture of the interest of the states in proper ratemaking methods.[5] In brief, the laws sought to protect the public against the harmful effects of either excessive, inadequate, or unfairly discriminatory rates. The laws recognized the necessity for development of rates based on the collective loss experience of the companies in order to achieve adequate and reasonable results. Therefore they contemplated ratemaking by rating organizations licensed by the state and responsible to state control.

It is perhaps an odd fact that the adoption of rate laws was not without opposition from the companies. In several states the laws were tested as to constitutionality, but upheld as a valid exercise of the police power of the state. While the rate laws produced rate litigation in some states, they had a marked influence in the character of ratemaking, and in achieving a degree of adequacy and stability in underwriting results that had been sought through the years prior to 1910.

Fire Rating Organizations Prior to S.E.U.A. Case. The fire rating organizations that evolved from this dual interest of the public and the companies in ratemaking, although privately operated except in Texas, were almost an adjunct of the regulating medium. Many of the laws

[5] Report of Merritt Committee Investigation, New York (1911). Reports made in Illinois, Ohio, and Wisconsin are also typical.

required every company except domestic mutuals or reciprocals to be a member or subscriber of a rating organization. As the associations formed by the stock fire companies were the only bureaus providing service on every class, the rates they established became a standard, subject to the right of companies to deviate, usually at a uniform deviation. The rating mechanism achieved almost an independent actuarial status, with the raters in the position of impartial administrators. The state was the watchdog against excessive rates and the rating system was the device by which property owners were treated uniformly and without unfair discrimination.

The decision of the United States Supreme Court in 1944 in the South-Eastern Underwriters Association case, holding that insurance was commerce and subject to the various federal laws applying to interstate commerce, reversed 75 years of legal precedent. It is not necessary to an understanding of ratemaking to cover all the problems created by this decision. However, subsequent passage of Public Law 15, exempting the insurance business from various federal antitrust and similar regulatory acts to the extent that the business is affirmatively regulated by the states, has materially affected fire ratemaking and the position of the rating organizations.

Rating Organizations after Passage of Public Law 15. The form of rate law adopted by most states as a result of Public Law 15 (based on the recommendations of the All-Industry Committee to the National Association of Insurance Commissioners) specifically disclaims any requirement for uniformity in rates, except to the extent necessary to conform to other provisions of the law. It places a rating bureau in a secondary position in that the law first requires a company to file its rates and then permits the company to satisfy this requirement by being a member of, or subscriber to, a licensed rating bureau which makes filings. Companies may file individually, or they may deviate from the filings of a bureau. Alternatively, a company may be a partial subscriber.

To assist in understanding the terms "member" and "subscriber," a member company of a rating organization is one which meets membership qualifications, adopts the constitution, and voluntarily accepts the obligations of membership, including responsibility for operation and financial support of the rating organization. A subscriber is a company which does not qualify for membership or may not wish to participate as a member, but which desires to receive the services of the rating organization. Under the rate laws, a rating organization must accept any licensed insurance company as a subscriber, and must provide its service without discrimination to both member and subscriber companies. If a subscriber company desires rating service on only one or more designated classes of risk or kinds of subdivisions of insurance, it is known as a "partial subscriber."

The new rate laws were intended to bring about a much greater degree of rate and form competition than had prevailed under previous fire rate laws. Elimination of adherence to bureau rates was a goal sought by those who were critical of the stabilization achieved under the previous system of bureau rating. The antitrust arguments that had existed at state level in the 1890's were given renewed prominence by power of federal interest and by the desire of certain companies to pursue an independent course in selected lines of business.

Later in the chapter this point is mentioned in connection with the effect of vigorous rate and form competition on statistical data. It is of importance in the present discussion to point out that the new laws have subordinated the status of bureau fire ratemaking, as developed in the period from 1910 to 1945.

Present Ratemaking Functions of Bureaus. The bureaus are still the principal source of fire rates, however, and readers should understand their present functions relating to ratemaking. These functions are performed for both member and subscribing companies. Due to the nature of property risk, practically all companies—whether stock, mutual, or reciprocal—underwriting a general class of business, find it desirable to secure the rating service.

Rating bureaus must maintain a complete set of filings with state insurance departments, covering not only rating schedules, basis or key rates, and charges or credits applicable, but also rules and clauses affecting the rates.

In fire insurance rating, the rates for other than class-rated risks (for example, dwellings and apartments are class-rated) are developed by inspection of each individual risk and the application of the rating schedule to the conditions found at inspection. This method of ratemaking is unique to the fire insurance field, and directs principal attention to the individuality of each risk. Obviously, it requires a large force of inspectors and rating personnel. The rates developed are published in rate tariffs or rate cards and distributed to member and subscribing companies and their agents. A copy of the rating survey is available on request of the property owner or his agent of record. Service is also provided by the bureau on recommendations for improvements which may eliminate hazards and permit a rate revision when improvements are completed.

In addition to the schedule rate, the bureaus adopt and file general rate adjustments following review of statistical results. Such reviews of experience are made annually, although general adjustments of rate levels may or may not result, depending on credibility and similar factors which will be discussed later. If a general rate adjustment is filed, the published schedule rate is subject to such adjustment.

Another important function of the bureaus that relates to ratemaking is the grading of the value of public fire protection. Each city, town, village, and public fire protection district is classified under a standard grading schedule that measures the relative value of its fire department, water distribution system, fire alarm system, and other factors in relation to the standard. (See Chapters 12 and 14.) There are 10 classes of public protection, depending on the points of deficiency. In cities over 25,000 population, the engineering surveys are made by the National Board of Fire Underwriters. The smaller cities, towns, and fire protection districts are graded by engineers of the rating bureaus. The surveys are made at intervals or when requested by city officials, and the classifications are published and used by the rating bureaus in establishing basis or key rates.

The rating bureaus also maintain stamping or auditing departments to assist companies in checking against errors and for compliance with filings. These departments examine the copies of policies issued and pass them on to the underwriting departments of the companies, with notice of any corrections that should be made. The rate laws generally provide that copies of uncorrected criticism slips be sent the insurance department of the state government after 60 days. The insurance department may then take action to insist on correction of the criticism.

At the time that a bureau audits the daily report, it also inserts the correct classification code under the statistical plan in effect in that state. The company then uses such code in reporting the premium or subsequent loss data to the statistical agency.

If these rating functions were not performed by rating bureaus, they would need to be duplicated to at least a partial degree by each of some two-to-three-hundred member and subscriber companies. The economies of rating bureau operation to the companies and public are obvious, even though deviation and independent filings are superimposed to a much greater degree than in the years prior to 1945.

MODERN RATING SCHEDULES AND RATING TECHNIQUES

The type of rating schedule will usually fall into one of the following several categories:

1. Minimum tariffs or flat rate schedules.

These are schedules used for rating classes of risks in which there are a great many units with only slight variations of hazard. The possible variation from the class or basis rate is minimal and reasonable rates can be made by broad groupings such as construction, protection, or occupancy, without requiring inspection and specific rating.

Typical examples are schedules for dwelling, apartment, and similar habitational risks; farm property; and the smaller stores in combination with dwellings and apartments.

2. General or comprehensive rating schedules.

These are schedules or rating systems designed to rate most classes of commercial, manufacturing, warehouse, and public occupancies, whether in single or multioccupancy structures. The degree to which such schedules lend themselves to comprehensive rating analysis, irrespective of construction or occupancy classification, will vary among rating jurisdictions. The more comprehensive schedules are usually referred to as "systems."

3. Class or special hazard schedules.

These are schedules designed for some particular class of occupancy and only used in rating such a class. If the risk involves hazards peculiar to a given industrial process or of an unusual underwriting nature, not commonly found in other classes, the schedule is referred to as a "special hazard" schedule. Examples are schedules for cotton gins, grain elevators, electric generating stations, and whiskey warehouses.

Purpose of Schedule Rating

Earlier in the chapter, it was pointed out that schedule rating had its genesis in the search of the underwriter for a rate that would match the hazard of the individual risk. The rating schedule is a device to measure hazard differences of construction, occupancy, private or public protection, and external exposure, which influence the degree of loss potential. These are the physical factors which underwriters also evaluate in the selection of their book of business, as hazard must be equated with rate.

Hazard Relations. The theory or method of constructing a schedule or rating system has varied. However, practically all schedules use charges for conditions or hazards that depart from standards, while credits are allowed for conditions better than standard or for installation of protective devices. There is no practical method of determining by statistical analysis of causes of loss, or similar data on actual fire claims, the exact weight which should be assigned to these parts of hazard. The interplay of hazards in typical risks results in an infinite combination of probabilities. The charges and credits are therefore based on engineering analysis and observation of fire hazard. The long-term result of application of the rating schedule can then be tested by examination of statistical data of fire experience.

The detailed degree of analysis of hazard in fire rating schedules has been criticized by the industry itself as constituting overrefinement, or as too costly a method. However, there is little question as to its value to and acceptance by the property owner or the state.

Encouragement of Compliance with Fire Standards. Schedule rating has had a marked effect in encouraging public compliance with sound fire prevention and protection standards. When the rate is correlated with the standards of building codes, building ordinances, national safety standards, and testing by national testing laboratories, the property owner's rate directly reflects his compliance with these standards. If he reduces or eliminates a hazard or installs protective devices, he receives prompt recognition in his individual rate. If the city expends his tax dollars in improvement of the grade of public protection, there is a definite reflection in insurance costs.

Avoidance of Unfair Discrimination. As to the state, the rating schedule has been the means by which it had evidence of avoidance of unfair discrimination in risk analysis, and uniformity of rate application to risks of like hazard. However, under the rate laws adopted since 1945, the prohibition of unfair discrimination is not tied to specific hazard analysis as in the older fire rate laws, and the effect of this on the present system of schedule rating will have to be observed in time.

Theories of Schedules Currently in Use

In this description of fire ratemaking the author can do no more than touch on the theories that underlie some of the principal schedules or systems that are in use today. The arguments of schedule makers as to superiority of one method over another can be found in published texts.[6]

Universal Mercantile. The Standard Universal Schedule for Rating Mercantile Risks (referred to as the Universal Mercantile Schedule) was conceived, as the name implies, as a rating instrument for all classes of property, to replace the hundreds of unrelated schedules in use prior to 1890 by local boards and tariff associations throughout the country. It starts with a base or key rate for a standard building in a standard city, and this base or key rate is modified to reflect the various grades of public protection. A system of uniform charges (in cents) was established for deficiencies from standards, with percentage credits for private protective features. A most important point was the recognition accorded in the rates between a building and its contents: the differential between building and contents rates increased as the rate of the building itself decreased.

No method was directly provided for adjusting the schedule results to sequential loss experience, for the schedule concept was that countrywide loss experience should govern the establishment of the rates, with modification only of the base or key rate to reflect the differences in local conditions. Also no system was set up for maintaining the schedule as originally conceived. The schedule has tended to be adapted and modified by individual rating organizations to fit the particular needs of each state, and no direct comparison can be made of one adaptation with another. However, variations of this schedule are the basis of schedules in use today in almost half the states.

Analytic System (Dean Schedule). Unquestionably the development of the Universal Mercantile had a marked influence on the thinking of A. F. Dean, in his studies leading to the *Analytic System for the Measure-*

[6] See, for example, Edward R. Hardy, *The Making of the Fire Insurance Rate* (Philadelphia: The Spectator Co., 1926).

ment of Relative Fire Hazard.[7] Dean likewise sought universality, but he believed there were relationships that had to be maintained if a rating system was to have permanence and be adaptable to differences in loss cost or burning rate, between one territory and another, or between one period of time and another. He termed this "relativity of hazard."

The Analytic System establishes a series of relationships. The Master Basis Tables are a mathematical device for recognizing the relative value of public protection and for maintaining relationships in adjusting the system to the required rate level. The actual or standard basis tables adopted in a particular territory are ratios of the Master Tables, and by adoption of differing ratios, the rate level may be increased or reduced by any desired percentage.

Charges and credits in the system are percentages applied to the basis rates, and are therefore directly proportional to the basis rate and the final rate level.

The net effect is in line with Dean's concept of relativity of hazard. Assuming a charge of 40 percent for a particular hazard, the effect in the final rate will be 40 cents if the basis rate is \$1.00, or 20 cents if the basis rate is 50 cents. The charge in each case is proportional to the rate level, that is,

$$\frac{.40}{1.00 + .40} = \frac{.20}{.50 + .20}$$

A change in rate level due to experience does not change the relation of the charge to the final rate. Also, the relation between two charges for different hazards is not changed by adoption of a different basis rate or rate level.

Two other features are worthy of mention. Combustibility of contents is treated as distinct from causative hazards, and the combustibility classification of the occupancy is used to modify charges for structural conditions or causative hazards. The exposure formula, a particularly important factor in achieving proper results in the earlier frame range towns of the Middle West, is most complete.

The Analytic System has been copyrighted since its earliest editions in order to maintain it as an identity. The system is maintained under supervision of the Western Actuarial Bureau and is revised periodically to recognize new developments in structural, occupancy, and protective features. The Middle West represents the largest area in the country with a comprehensive and homogeneous rating system, in use for over 50 years.

General Basic Schedule. Two other fire rating systems were developed subsequent to the Analytic System. The General Basic Schedule was

[7] J. S. Glidden, *The Analytic System for the Measurement of Relative Fire Hazard —An Explanation* (1916).

devised in 1929 by J. K. Woolley, then manager of the Washington Surveying and Rating Bureau.[8] It is a comprehensive system with many similarities to the Analytic System. In place of the basis tables, however, it uses a system of Divergency Factors and Divergency Charges to accomplish needed variation in rate level, for either classes or groupings of risk or for an entire rating territory. The transition of rate (rate curve) through various degrees of combustible to fire-resistive construction is accomplished more smoothly than in the older classification systems. Also it produces 80 percent coinsurance rates which are convertible to no-coinsurance rates or rates for other percentages of coinsurance under a formula which recognizes the reduced value of coinsurance as the rate (or hazard) increases.

The schedule is in use in Washington and has been through several editions, the latest edition being particularly designed to facilitate more rapid adjustment of rates by electronic data processing equipment in keeping with statistical indications.

Uniform Grading System. The Uniform Grading System was developed in the late 1940's by the Middle Department Association of Fire Underwriters, the rating organization for Pennsylvania and Delaware, to take the place of a number of schedules that were variations of the Universal Mercantile. The development of this system, under the direction of Carlyle H. Hill, Manager, was the result of several years of study and planning to improve rating methods in keeping with requirements of the new rate law.

The system produces a grading of hazard represented by grading points and the grading is made independently of rate or rate level. The rate is then produced by application of the final grading to one of a series of rate factors which can be selected to achieve the required rate level by classes or groupings of risks. The system is readily adaptable to rate level adjustments, and like the General Basic Schedule, the rates are 80 percent coinsurance rates convertible to other percentages of coinsurance.

The system has been successfully adopted in the state of Louisiana to replace a number of older schedules patterned after the Universal Mercantile.

Other Systems. The short summaries of these various schedules or rating systems do not do justice to the years of work and study given by underwriters and rating men to the subject of equity in fire ratemaking. In the course of this effort, many other systems were devised, tested, and debated but did not survive in actual use.

One such contribution was made by E. G. Richards of the North British and Mercantile Insurance Company, Ltd. He had been associated intimately with the establishment of the fire statistical plan adopted in 1914,

[8] J. K. Woolley, *The Principles and Mechanics of Fire Insurance Rating as Incorporated in General Basic Schedule* (1937).

and believed that rating methods relied too greatly on empirical evaluation of hazard and did not sufficiently reflect actual experience data. In 1915, he devised the Experience Grading and Rating System. The theory of the system utilized the principle of grading risks by quality grades which would then be related to the loss cost of each occupancy class to produce an experience rate. A later edition was published in 1921 but the system was never actually used for rating.

A fundamental problem confronting the system was the absence of a method actually to secure loss-cost data representing a pure classification result, for a major problem in fire classification is the composite building of mixed occupancy or mixed construction. However, certain of the rating systems developed since Richards' time have followed in some degree his theory of more directly relating hazard grade to experience rate level.

A National System? Those not familiar with the history of the fire insurance business will often question the diversity of rating schedules in use throughout the country. They wonder why a national fire rating system was never developed. In 1947 a great deal of work was done on the formulation of a modern system that could be so used. The attempt was not successful for a number of reasons. The cost involved and the obvious disruptions to current rating make renewal of such an attempt unlikely.

STATISTICAL PROCEDURES IN FIRE RATING

So far the fire rating schedule has been dealt with largely from the standpoint of hazard analysis. However, the final rate represents the sum of loss cost, expense cost, and underwriting profit. Consideration should be given next to the type of statistical data maintained and the method employed for reflecting loss and expense experience in the rate.

Before the adoption of rate laws, each company had its own method of keeping track of its classified underwriting experience, but guarded such data as privileged information for its own underwriting. The ratemaking organizations had little data except the total of fire premiums and losses for each company from the Annual Statements filed in each state. Adoption of the first rate laws gave impetus to collection of loss and premium data on a detailed and uniform classification plan.

Original Fire Statistical Plan

The forerunner of the present fire statistical plan was adopted by the National Board of Fire Underwriters in 1914. An Actuarial Bureau was set up to act as statistical agency and to prepare composite reports. The first plan was most detailed with over 600 occupancy classifications. This was simplified in later revisions when the number of classifications was found to produce unusable data.

Present Fire Statistical Plans

The new rate laws adopted following Public Law 15 uniformly gave each Commissioner authority to require statistical reports of classified underwriting experience. A new statistical plan entitled *Standard Classification of Occupancy Hazards* was devised and submitted for approval of the various states in 1946.[9] For fire property damage coverage, the plan provides for 115 occupancy classifications and six construction-protection classifications. Premiums and losses on each risk are reported annually for each state or rating territory in accordance with the requirements or "call" of the statistical agencies, of which there are three serving various groups of companies.

While most states require reports in the form of direct written premiums and paid losses, and this is the general form of report followed, the National Board Actuarial Bureau asks its members and subscribers to furnish a supplementary report under what is called the Earned-Incurred Statistical Plan. From the data the Actuarial Bureau prepares a composite report of direct earned premiums and incurred losses, in which earned premiums are calculated from the individual distribution of premium writings by term in each state. The Earned-Incurred Statistical Plan is the most accurate method available to the rating bureaus of determining classified direct earned premiums and incurred losses by state for use in rate level adjustment formulas.

Method of Review of Fire Experience

In fire insurance experience reviews or rate level adjustments, the almost universal procedure has been to use the "loss ratio" method (i.e., the relating of losses to premiums), rather than "loss cost" or what is termed in other lines the "pure premium" method. There are exceptions, such as the use of "loss cost" in the formula followed by the Factory Mutual Rating Bureau, in rating a specialized class of highly protected risks. But in the general fire business, data are not available as to actual amounts at risk to permit the calculation of "loss cost." The reason for the absence of such data is partly historical and partly the result of difficulty in handling the problems of varying term business or changes in amounts by endorsement or cancellation.

Underwriting Profit Formula. The rate laws recognize the use of both past and prospective loss and expense experience in determining rate level. Provision is also made for consideration of a reasonable margin for underwriting profit and contingencies. A few states have special references to underwriting profit allowances and others omit the specific reference to "underwriting."

---

[9] *Standard Classification of Occupancy Hazards* (New York: National Board of Fire Underwriters, 1947).

Review of the development of the Commissioners' 1921 Standard Profit Formula, or the 1949 amendment as adopted by the National Association of Insurance Commissioners, would be impossible in this summary.[10] The fire rating organizations in general follow the 1949 amendment in using a profit factor of 6 percent of earned premiums as a proper allowance for underwriting profit and contingencies. This allowance pertains to the future and is not a guarantee that an underwriting profit will be realized. As a matter of fact, because of the uncertainties in the business the actual fire underwriting profit in any cycle of years has been considerably under this allowance. In most recent years there has been no underwriting profit.

Expense Statistical Plan. Until recent years, there were very limited data available as to direct expense by state or line of business. The Annual Statement covered net countrywide expense for all lines written by the fire companies. Some few states such as New York had a special fire expense exhibit required of companies entered. It was the practice in many states to consider expense and profit as roughly 50 percent of premium. Rate level adjustments were made on an allocation of 50 percent of premium for pure loss.

An Insurance Expense Exhibit was adopted in 1948 by the N.A.I.C. as a supplement to the Annual Statement. This exhibit gives countrywide expense data separated as to major lines such as fire, extended coverage, and so on. In order to provide data on a direct basis which reflects individual state expense, the Actuarial Bureau of the N.B.F.U. in 1951 adopted a voluntary Statistical Plan for Expenses which allocates to each state those expenses specifically attributable to that state, such as commissions, taxes, fees, and bureau and allocated loss adjustment expense.

Review Formula. The sources of data have been described. Attention is now given to the review formula employed in current practices. The most common formula or method followed as a guide is that recommended by the Fire Insurance Research and Actuarial Association (formerly Inter-Regional Insurance Conference), a national fire advisory organization. First recommended in 1954, it has been revised several times, most recently in 1964.

The formula is prospective in that its purpose is to determine from experience, indexed to present costs and weighted for current trend, an indication of an adequate and reasonable rate level for the future.

The method is carefully detailed in the complete procedure but can be expressed as follows:

$$M = \frac{(L + A)}{[1 - (Ew + Ee + P)]}$$

---

[10] *Report of Special Subcommittee on Underwriting Profit or Loss,* Fire and Marine Committee, N.A.I.C., June 9, 1949.

where

M = Indicated modification in present rate level. For example, a 10 percent reduction in rate level is a 0.90 modification—and a 10 percent increase in rate level is a 1.10 modification.

L = Ratio of the actual incurred losses over a 6-year experience review period (indexed to current costs) to the corresponding earned premiums adjusted to the current rate level—with relative weightings of 30 percent to the latest year; 25 percent to the prior year; 15 percent to the second prior year; and 10 percent to each of the three earliest years.

A = Ratio of loss adjustment expense to actual earned premiums, for the latest available year.

Ew = Ratio of expenses from Schedules No. 1 and No. 3 of Expense Statistical Plan to written premiums, for latest available year.[11]

Ee = Ratio of other expenses (Expense Schedule No. 1, No. 2, No. 3) from Expense Statistical Plan to actual earned premiums, for latest available year.[12]

P = Allowance in rates for underwriting profit and contingencies.

The indicated change is then applied to the written premiums of the most recent year to determine the approximate dollar amount of premium increase or reduction necessary to adjust future rate level to the indication.

Adjustment of Class or Schedule Results

The actual adjustment in rates is accomplished by a review of the classified underwriting experience on an adjusted earned-incurred basis for the same experience period to determine the particular classifications or schedules which warrant modification. The individual class or schedule modifications are tempered through judgment or credibility modifiers. The net effect of increases or reductions in dollars is then balanced out to produce the approximate dollar effect of the overall rate level indication.

Credibility in Fire Statistics

Credibility of loss experience in fire insurance ratemaking is not measurable by statistical tests of the present loss data. The data do not give information as to number or size of exposures (i.e., units of risk and the amount subject) or loss frequency. Thus, credibility tables must be related only to premium volume and these cannot take into account the extreme range in chance probabilities between different classes of property. Except in the largest classes, such as dwellings, reliance on loss data for movement of rate level must be tempered by the knowledge of the rater and underwriter as to the risk. A large degree of judgment has prevailed in the method of adjustment of class- and schedule-rated

[11] For details of expense functions included under each Schedule see *Statistical Plan for Expenses,* National Board of Fire Underwriters, 1951 (revised December, 1961).

[12] *Ibid.*

groups, and no truly satisfactory substitute for informed judgment and knowledge of risk has yet been evolved.

The low frequency of fire loss and the need to establish reasonable averages is recognized in rate laws by requiring use of experience for not less than the most recent five-year period. The time factor cannot be extended indefinitely, however, as rate level in keeping with current trends is also a consideration.

In the case of some special hazard classes of risk rated under national schedules, the greatest degree of credibility can be achieved by reviewing countrywide loss experience for like classifications. In areas such as the Middle West where hazard analysis is uniform for like risks and the rating system maintains relativity between states, even though at different rate levels, it is feasible to review loss experience for the same classification over a large number of states in analyzing schedule relations.

Maintenance of Hazard Relations. Regardless of the method followed, the purpose is to make the adjustments in such manner as to maintain reasonable rate relativity in keeping with known hazard relations. As an example, the rate curve for risks identical except for class of construction or grade of public protection must be tested so there is no reversal which results in a higher rate for a better class of construction or the presence of public protection.

Other Factors to Be Considered in Statistics. Underwriting experience under the fire statistical plan is affected by many other factors that may need evaluation. Changes in the distribution of premium, year to year, between prepaid term and installment plans; changes in the term multiple; and cancellation and rewriting in anticipation of rate increases or following a rate reduction—all have an influence. Changes in forms or rules or increase in number or extent of deviations may likewise have a major effect on experience as a credible guide to rate level.

RATING OF ALLIED LINES

Until about 1938 the principal lines or perils directly allied to fire insurance were windstorm and explosion. Windstorm was usually written under a rider or combined fire and windstorm policy, while explosion was written either as full explosion under a specific peril policy or as inherent explosion by endorsement to the fire contract.

Extended Coverage

The merger of various specific perils into one supplemental contract ultimately became known as the Extended Coverage Endorsement. (See Chapter 6.) This endorsement extended the fire policy so that the amount of liability applied as a single amount against all perils. The desirability of this peril extension in place of the previous separate contracts, and the higher incidence of windstorm and hurricane catastrophes, particularly in eastern states, brought about a rapid buildup in volume. In 1942, the E.C.E. was made a major line on the Annual Statement.

Rating Method. The E.C.E. rates are usually "class" rates reflecting principal exposures, such as windstorm and hail, or inherent explosion, with small loadings for the other minor perils. The rates also are varied to reflect the difference between wind-resistive and ordinary construction, and among major class groupings such as dwellings, farm property, and commercial or manufacturing properties. The building rates generally contemplate a $50 windstorm and hail deductible to eliminate high frequency maintenance claims. The trend is toward mandatory deductibles because of the excessive claim costs on the full coverage contracts.

Catastrophe Problems. The major rating problem is found in windstorm and hail catastrophe exposure. The extent of the catastrophe problem can be understood in the light of about 160 catastrophe serial numbers assigned to specific storm occurences since 1949. The incidence of hurricanes on the heavily built-up eastern coast line has been particularly severe since 1938. No section of the country is immune to storm, however, and severe storms will cause thousands or even hundreds of thousands of claims over a number of adjoining states.

The 1921 Profit Formula was a fire formula and even in the 1949 amendment, there was no distinction made between fire and E.C.E. in the provision for catastrophe allowance. Because many of the single catastrophes have caused losses in the range of $10 million to $40 million and some as high as $200 million, it should be quite evident that proper recognition for contingency and catastrophe in the rates is most necessary.

Rate Level Review Procedure. Until very recently, the method for determining E.C.E. rate level was to use a 15-year loss experience base for each state, with the hope that by taking this longer period to encompass the wide fluctuations in storm losses, a reasonable average loss experience could be developed. However, the same profit factor of 6 percent was employed as in the case of fire insurance, as there was no separate formula for E.C.E. The underwriting experience has consistently produced a loss for the total E.C.E. business.

In 1962, after long study of the problem in an industry committee, the Committee on Rates and Rating Organizations of the N.A.I.C. approved a new method by which a catastrophe factor for each state can be determined and then can be held in the rate level, subject only to long-term review of catastrophe data. The catastrophe data available since 1949, and ultimately the review period, can be extended to a much longer period. The balance of the rate level is then based on what can be called "normal" loss experience for the latest six-year period, excluding that portion of losses that come within the catastrophe definition. Thus, provision is made not only for long term catastrophe recognition but also for variation of rate level by the trend of "normal" loss experience, using the same period as in the fire formula.

Other Allied Lines

Manual rates are provided for other allied lines such as sprinkler leakage, water damage, and earthquake insurance, together with rates for specific windstorm, explosion and riot, and aircraft and vehicle damage when not written under the E.C.E. Time element rates are factored from property damage rates, according to the nature of the coverage.

The principal development in other allied lines in recent years has been the broadening of peril extension endorsements to include collapse; interior water damage; rupture and bursting of heating appliances; weight of ice, snow and sleet; and falling objects. These extensions were first made available under named-peril forms, and subsequently under "all-risk" forms which cover against all risk of physical loss subject to specified exclusions. (See Chapter 6.) The rates are usually flat loadings for the additional perils, added to the basic E.C.E. rates, with provision for small deductible recognition.

CONTINUING PROBLEMS IN FIRE RATEMAKING

It is somewhat of a paradox that in this present day, when the theory and actuarial treatment of fire rating are approaching goals long sought by the underwriter and the state, influences that tend to modify or reverse many of the fundamentals of fire rating can be found.

Statistical Problems

The first such influence is reduction in the degree of homogeneity that formerly existed in statistical data from which the rate level must stem. Contrary to much that is being advanced by advocates of a return to open competition in coverage and rate, the state has an interest in uniformity of coverage. This uniformity is the only source of collective data producing a reasonable average fire experience ratio under the present system of relating loss to premium.

Effect on Statistics of Varying Coverage. Under present fire statistical plans, rates and coverages are inextricably bound, for coverage determines the amount of loss paid. If in a premium block of $100,000 the form employed by Company A results in $50,000 in claims but the form used by Company B has extensions or provisions that result in $75,000 in claims for identical loss occurrences, the combining of premiums and losses produces an average loss ratio of 62.5 percent. Obviously a rate level adjusted to this 62.5 percent loss ratio is excessive for Company A and inadequate for Company B.

Although a stylized example was cited for illustration, it represents a typical effect of the hundreds and thousands of deviations and independent filings throughout the country. An actuary cannot rely on data from such a heterogenous mixture, nor can rating organizations be wholly guided by indications of such collective experience. An increase in rate level may principally result in further deviation. The present statistical plans can be adjusted to reflect uniform deviations in rate, but cannot be adjusted in any practical manner to take into account the very large number of deviations in form or the effect of independent rating plans.

Possible Solutions to Statistical Problems. There are possible solutions short of abandoning the use of collective loss experience in fire ratemaking. One would be for the state to require experience under independently filed rates and forms to be separately reported, and experience under deviations to be identified and sufficient data submitted to permit resolving such experience to bureau level.

Another alternative that might ultimately have many other advantages, particularly in the light of current trends in multiple line coverages, fire deductible plans, and loss and expense modifiers, would be to supplement the present statistical method to permit development of pure premium or loss cost. If amounts of fire property damage liability and whole fire loss were kept on a classified basis, the rating organizations and the companies would have basic data from a single uniform source, for instance, the Standard Fire Policy or its equivalent. The data would then be available for computation of loss cost which underlies any fire contract, whether under bureau, deviation, or independent filing. This development of loss cost would also accommodate the growing need for rates which permit reflection of budgeted or varying expense components.

Rate Regulatory Problems

Fire rating has made considerable progress in recent years in utilizing loss and expense experience to adjust schedule measurement of hazard to actuarial standards. This sensitivity of rate level, however, in which there is but a small margin to the companies against adverse cycles of fire experience, must be balanced by a willingness on the part of regulatory authorities to consider and act on rate increases, when properly supported, just as promptly as in the case of rate decreases. The public interest is expressed by the language of the rate laws—that rates be "adequate, reasonable, and not unfairly discriminatory."

The degree of rate competition encouraged by revision of state rating laws, and by elimination of rate stabilization under former adherence rules, should have equal but counter influence in gaining quicker recognition of needed rate increases when filed by the rating organizations. As a practical matter, adequacy is achieved only through general filings adopted by the rating organizations. If the state delays action in approval of needed rate increases, because of political pressures or opposition, the result can be long periods of underwriting loss, in which the pressure mounts for withdrawal of companies and curtailment of a broad market.

Other Trends Having Influence on Fire Rating

Finally, the complexity of present day coverages is having a major impact on what was at one time a much simpler rating and coverage relationship.

Since its beginning in the early 1950's, the trend toward multiple line coverages and packaging of property and casualty lines in either indivisible or divisible premium contracts has gathered momentum. In the dwelling class, the growth of Homeowners Policies has been so rapid in a 10-year period that the largest segment of dwelling business is now covered in these multiple line contracts. (See Part VI.) Fire rating is confined to the residual dwelling risks, with attendant problems because of lower average values and amounts of insurance. In divisible premium multiple line coverages, the fire rate may be used in developing the property portion of the package, but the experience goes into a separate statistical plan for the commercial multiple line business and cannot be used directly for fire rate level review purposes.

Other influences of major impact are multiple location discount plans, fire deductible and excess of loss contracts, and the trend towards application of loss and expense modifiers to rating of an entire account, rather than the individual lines.

SUGGESTED READINGS

DEAN, A. F. *The Philosophy of Fire Insurance* (ed. W. R. Townley). Chicago: Edward B. Hatch, 1925.

*FINNEGAN, J. H. "Statistics of the National Board of Fire Underwriters," *Proceedings of the Casualty Actuarial Society,* Vol. 43 (1956), p. 82.

*GRAVES, C. H. "The Uniform Statistical Plan for Fire and Allied Lines," *PCAS,* Vol. 40 (1953), pp. 40–59.

HARDY, EDWARD R. *The Making of the Fire Insurance Rate.* Philadelphia: The Spectator Co., 1926.

*HURLEY, R. L. "A Credibility for Gauging Fire Classification Experience," *PCAS,* Vol. 41 (1954), pp. 161–75.

* LONGLEY-COOK, L. H. "Notes on Some Actuarial Problems of Property Insurance," *PCAS,* Vol. 46 (1959), p. 66.

________. "Problems of Fire Insurance Ratemaking," *PCAS,* Vol. 38 (1951), pp. 94–102.

________; HURLEY, R. L.; AND LANG, F. "Credibility of Statistics," *Proceedings of the Insurance Accounting and Statistical Association* (1962), pp. 362–65.

*MAGRATH, J. J. "Ratemaking for Fire Insurance," *PCAS,* Vol. 45 (1958), pp. 176–95.

*Also in *Fire Insurance Rate Making and Kindred Problems.* New York: Casualty Actuarial Society, 1960.

Chapter 14

UNDERWRITING IN FIRE INSURANCE

BY JOHN ADAM, JR.

The primary purpose of an insurance company is to accept risks. The man who decides which risks his company accepts or rejects is the underwriter. The word underwriter is, however, improperly used to describe many different positions in the property insurance industry. Some companies give the title of underwriter to map clerks, to rate checkers, or to those who pass on routinely acceptable risks. In this chapter the word "underwriter" will be used in terms of "desk underwriter" to mean the person who has the authority and responsibility to accept or reject risks applicable to a certain territory or class of business.

The nature of underwriting fire and allied lines insurance is described in this chapter. An attempt is made to emphasize some of the practical aspects of underwriting and to call attention to the essential characteristics of a good underwriter.

SELECTIVITY

The process of underwriting is inherently selective. It has been suggested that the fire underwriter's job is simply to select individual risks which he knows will not burn—a suggestion hardly correct because such selection is patently impossible. His job is rather to select a book of business which will have a desirable loss ratio. The underwriter is constantly striving to select certain types of risks and reject others in order to have a portfolio of risks which will produce the results desired by his company's management.

Occasionally the word "selectivity" is used in a critical manner. A company or type of company is said to be too selective and, therefore, not to be writing its share of the less desirable risks. The inference is that a company should accept risks "across the board." Such inference is out of order. If there is one characteristic which is the heart of underwriting, it is selectivity. Underwriting selectivity, however, is not simply accepting those risks which the underwriter's information shows to have all good qualities and no bad ones. Selectivity involves the class of risk to be accepted, the kind of risk within the class, and the amount of liability acceptable on that risk.

UNDERWRITING POLICY

Management must establish an underwriting policy as the first step in the selection process. While a desk underwriter may be consulted, rarely except in a small company does he have a decisive voice in the establishing of this policy. Before determining underwriting policy management must decide on its overall objective. Its objective may be a large volume and a minimum unit profit or even a minus underwriting profit (which means subsidizing its underwriting results from its investment results). In either case it will have a far different underwriting policy than will a company whose objective is a relatively small volume at a larger unit profit.

The determination of underwriting policy is closely woven into the total company fabric. For example, the underwriting policy of a direct writing company is subject to different pressures than is the underwriting policy of an agency company. The underwriting policy of a company using a lower-than-tariff rate structure involves different considerations than does the policy of a company operating on a tariff basis. A company paying a higher than standard commission must relate its underwriting policy to this practice. There are only 100 cents in a dollar. The number of those cents allocated to losses will heavily influence the overall underwriting policy.

After management determines its underwriting policy, it must define this policy in terms of a line sheet. This line sheet may define the classes of risks acceptable, prohibited, or borderline. For the acceptable or borderline classes there should be a limit of liability which may be either a strict limit or a series of guidelines to the desk underwriter. Both the classes acceptable and the limits are related to the company's reinsurance program. This line sheet, or guide, circumscribes the area within which the desk underwriter operates.

EFFECT OF RATE

In underwriting, generalities are dangerous. For example, one may look at a new concrete building in a well-protected area and say, "That's a beautiful fire insurance risk." The underwriter may check the rate and find it is 1½ cents per $100 (a gross premium of $15 for $100,000 at risk). His reaction may be that physically it is a good risk but at a rate of 1½ cents it is a poor risk. In short, from the underwriter's viewpoint, a relatively poor risk physically that is overrated may be more desirable than an excellent physical risk that is underrated.

As brought out in Chapter 13, fire insurance rating is a highly technical and precise occupation. As precise as it is, however, it has not yet become scientific enough so that the rate of each risk measures exactly all the hazards of that risk. One of the more dangerous generalizations for an underwriter to make is to assert that the rate measures the hazard. In truth, if all rates accurately measured all hazards of the risk, there would be little need for selectivity or for underwriting.

The relationship of the rate to the hazard has an even greater than normal importance to those companies charging substandard rates. Likewise, the so-called "surplus lines" company must give top priority to the rate in determining the acceptance of a risk. Thus fire insurance rates play an important part in the decisions of a skilled underwriter, and therefore any underwriter should have a familiarity at least with the general rate structure in his territory.

PRACTICAL UNDERWRITING

The underwriter can select only from risks which are offered to him. The source of these risks may be a local agent, a broker, a general agent, or a company salesman. For simplicity, in this chapter consider all of these as being included in the term "producer." If the producer has a basic understanding of his company's underwriting policy and keeps it in mind when prospecting, the desk underwriter's selectivity task is immeasurably lightened. If, on the other hand, the producer continually submits risks which do not meet the company's underwriting standards, the underwriter has little chance to build a satisfactory book of business. It is virtually impossible for an underwriter, however skilled he may be, to build a satisfactory underwriting portfolio from an unsatisfactory source.

Daily Report

The daily report is the record with which the underwriter starts his task. The daily report is usually a copy of the policy information other than the standard wording. Thus "the daily," so-called, tells:

1. The amount of liability.
2. The kind of coverage (as fire, fire and extended coverage, business interruption, or something else).
3. The name of the insured.
4. The location of the property.
5. The construction of the building insured or the building housing the insured property.
6. The occupancy (mercantile, manufacturing, office, or other).
7. The nature of the property if the insurance is on contents.
8. The coinsurance percentage (or similar condition) if any.
9. The encumbrances on the property.
10. The name of the producer.

When the daily arrives at the underwriter's desk, it should have with it any underwriting information already in the company files. Assuming the risk is new to the company and that there is no information in the file, the underwriter must decide whether he wishes to accept this risk without additional information or whether he needs additional information, and if so, what kind. This decision may be influenced by company policy, the underwriter's experience, his knowledge of the territory, and the producer.

If, for example, the daily showed the risk to be $7,500 on contents usual to a hardware store, subject to an 80 percent coinsurance clause, located in a one-story brick building with no encumbrances on the property, in a town familiar to the underwriter, and from a producer well and favorably known to the underwriter, he might approve the risk with no additional information. If he had the rate cards available, he might check to see what other occupants were in the building. He might also have the Sanborn map checked to determine the exposures. Possibly, he might have the Dun and Bradstreet credit rating checked.

On the other hand, if the risk were $200,000 on the contents of a multiple-occupancy metalworking plant, the underwriter certainly would want additional information. He would be interested in the financial condition of the insured and, depending on the credit rating, might well order a Dun and Bradstreet report to get more financial information. He would certainly want a physical inspection report to determine not only the hazards and how they were protected, but also such things as housekeeping, condition of building, management attitude, and exposures.

Once the underwriter has the financial and physical information he must decide whether he will accept the risk, reject it, accept it subject to certain recommendations, accept a portion of the risk, or perhaps defer the decision to his supervisor.

Moral Hazard

While one commonly talks about insuring a building or its contents, in reality the policy insures the interest of the insured in the insurable property. The individual or company, then, actually is insured rather than the property. If, for example, a $10,000 policy were written insuring a brick building at 109 Main Street in the name of John Jones, and if that building were subsequently destroyed by an insured peril, it would be contrary to public policy to allow John Jones to collect unless he had an insurable interest. To allow collection otherwise would turn insurance into a gambling device.

Nature of the Hazard. An insurable interest is at the heart of an insurance contract. The extent and intensity of that insurable interest is vital to the underwriting process. If the insured's interest in the property is such that he strongly wishes the property to remain in existence, then he and the underwriter have the same objective. If, however, for any reason the insured would wish the property not to be in existence, then his objective is opposite that of the underwriter. A moral hazard exists.

Moral hazard has been defined in many ways. In this chapter, moral hazard is considered to be any condition other than physical which may increase the likelihood of the insured property being destroyed. Moral hazard exists in all phases of the economic cycle. It exists during the most prosperous economic times and obviously increases in depressed periods. Moral hazard cannot be accurately measured; it cannot be rated; and sometimes it cannot be detected until after the loss, even if then. Yet if the destruction of property brought about by moral hazard could be measured, there is little doubt it would total many millions of dollars annually.

The skilled underwriter must be constantly on the alert for signs that moral hazard may exist. But the existence of moral hazard does not mean that the property will be destroyed. For example, an individually owned business may be constantly losing money and it may be obvious that the business will never again be a money-maker. It may be to the financial advantage of the owner to "sell the property" to the fire insurance company. Yet the moral fiber of the owner may be such that this will never happen.

Underwriting, however, is an occupation that depends on averages. If you have a thousand insured businesses which are consistently losing money and a thousand similar businesses which are consistently making money, the likelihood is that there will be more fire losses in the former group.

Situations Creating Moral Hazard. There are innumerable situations which can create a potential moral hazard. For example, two firms merge and the physical facilities of one become excessive. A new road will result in the taking of property. A business or industry becomes obsolete because of an invention. The population center changes, making the profit potential of a mercantile business precarious. In short, any time the insured would not be unhappy about the destruction of his property, the underwriter is confronted with danger signals.

All moral hazard does not originate with the insured. Arson is sometimes brought about by enemies of the insured. Property is sometimes destroyed as a result of revenge or hate or even competition. This factor becomes especially important when the insured property is in a class allied with or subject to the influence of unlawful elements.

Signs of Moral Hazard. The underwriter will find financial reports of great assistance in detecting moral hazard. He may also have at his disposal some loss information records which are kept by company organizations. Finally, he should carefully examine an insured's moral record.

One sound rule is always to look into any abnormal situation. If the insured has an abnormal number of claims, an apparent determination to collect overpayment on claims, an abnormal number of bankruptcies, an abnormal number of lawsuits, or abnormalities in his personal life, extra caution should be exercised by the underwriter.

Overinsurance is always a red flag to the underwriter. It is true that, if a policy is issued under an actual cash value clause, the insured cannot collect more than the actual cash value of the destroyed property regardless of the amount of insurance. Unfortunately, however, not every one knows this. Many an arsonist has overinsured his property thinking he could collect the full value of the policy. It is little solace to the underwriter of a suspected arson loss to know that the insured will collect only the actual cash value. Until a few years ago nearly all fire policies were issued on an actual cash basis. Subsequently there came into being the concept of replacement cost. Replacement cost coverage pays the cost of replacing property rather than actual cash value. Obviously, the potential moral hazard on a property insured for replacement value is increased as the difference between actual cash value and replacement value is increased. The greater the depreciation, the greater the potential moral hazard.

Moral hazard is one of the greatest unmeasured causes of loss, and many losses chalked up to poor housekeeping, spontaneous combustion, or electrical hazards actually result from moral hazard. A rate can compensate for an increase in physical hazard, but there is no rate adequate for moral hazard.

Physical Hazard

The three main classes of construction are: (1) frame, (2) brick or masonry, and (3) fire-resistive. While these terms are simple, their technical definitions are not. These terms may be defined somewhat differently by various rating organizations. In this chapter broad "working definitions" are used.

A frame building is one where the exterior walls as well as the interior walls, partitions, floors, and roof are of wood or other combustible material. A brick building differs from a frame building primarily in that the exterior walls are constructed of noncombustible building materials, such as brick or masonry, of a specified thickness, depending on the height of the building. Brick buildings, in turn, are ordinarily divided into two classes: (1) ordinary or brick-joist construction, and (2) mill or heavy timber construction. The difference between these two is in the internal construction of the building. The primary difference between the brick open joist and the heavy timber construction is in the dimensions of the wood used and in the pockets between the joists in the open joist construction compared to the relatively flat ceilings and floors in plank and timber construction. In the mill type of construction, the heavy timbers are ordinarily chamfered to reduce combustibility, and the general construction is of a type to resist both the spread of fire and the caving in of the building for longer periods than does ordinary joist construction. Of the two classes, the ordinary joist construction is far more common and the brick mill construction is becoming relatively rare in new buildings.

A fire-resistive building is one in which the walls, partitions, columns, floors, and roofs are of noncombustible materials which either by themselves or as a result of added protection will resist the standard time-temperature fire test for a certain number of hours varying from two to four. An inherent part of the concept of a fire-resistive building is that the floor openings are enclosed with fire-resistive partitions so that there are vertical as well as horizontal fire cutoffs formed by the partitions. There is also a minimum of combustible material used in the trim of such buildings.

Thus the definition of a fire-resistive building does not depend on the kind of material but rather on the resistance of the materials and construction to fire for a certain period of time. There are, of course, various gradations of construction within these classes, such as, for example, a semi-fire-resistive building and mixed construction, such as a frame and brick building. Also, there are considerations of building materials, such as cinder blocks, which do not fit into the brick, wood, or masonry type of construction. These blocks, while not combustible in themselves, have considerably less resistance to heat and water than do bricks.

Perhaps one of the most important points for an underwriter to consider in respect to a building is whether it is being used for the purpose for which it was built. One cannot speak, for example, of a frame or brick building being a satisfactory type of construction without knowing the use to which this building will be put. Thus the underwriter always has one additional area to investigate when a building has been converted to some use other than the one for which it was designed. Obviously, the construction and use of the building have much bearing on determining the amount of insurance that the underwriter will accept. A fire in a frame building could spread both more rapidly and more extensively than in a fire-resistive building. This rapid extension is possible not only because of combustibility, but also because the fire-resistive building by its nature has vertical and frequently horizontal fire cutoffs which the frame building does not. Hence, the larger a frame building, the greater the volume of combustible material exposed to a single fire area. On the other hand, a fully fire-resistive building ten stories high might have a probable maximum loss limited to a single story.

Then, too, the effect of the age, physical condition, and upkeep of a building must be weighed. For example, a new cinder block building with light interior framing would be far more damageable than a mill type, slow-burning building constructed 50 years ago but maintained in good condition.

Protection. The protection against fire may be roughly divided into two classes: public and private. Public protection involves all of the public facilities available to help prevent or extinguish a fire. The National Board of Fire Underwriters grades cities and towns into ten categories with the best protection being Class 1. These classes are used in rating the structures as well as in informing the underwriter what type of protection he may expect.

Charles F. Rupprecht in his work titled *The Modern Fire Underwriter* briefly outlines the character of protection usually found in these classes:

> *Class 1.* Excellent paid fire department, excellent water supply including high pressure system, telegraph fire alarm, and excellent structural conditions, building laws, and ordinances.
>
> *Classes 2 and 3.* Good paid fire department, good water supply and generally good conditions otherwise.
>
> *Class 4.* Fair paid or excellent volunteer (with paid drivers) fire department, good water supply. Generally a fair fire alarm system and fair laws and ordinances.
>
> *Class 5.* Poor paid or good volunteer (often with paid drivers) fire department, good water supply, not necessarily a telegraph fire alarm system, fair to poor laws and ordinances.
>
> *Classes 6 and 7.* Fair volunteer fire department, fair water supply, poor or no telegraph fire alarm system, generally poor laws and ordinances.
>
> *Classes 8 and 9.* Generally poor protection but sufficient to merit some recognition. Water supply usually for fire wells.[1]

Private protection encompasses all the devices an insured may use to help prevent or put out a fire, such as fire extinguishers, standpipe and hose, fire alarm, fire brigade, private hydrant system, or automatic sprinklers. While all of these may be of some help, underwriters usually give relatively little credit to any except automatic sprinklers. One reason is that the effectiveness of fire extinguishing devices depends primarily on their proper use. Too often, they are used improperly.

In Chapter 12 the point was made that the record of automatic sprinklers in extinguishing or confining fires is exceptionally good. Here, however, the underwriter must weigh (1) the effectiveness of the automatic sprinklers compared with the rate reduction allowed for these sprinklers and (2) whether the automatic sprinklers have a simple outside gong alarm or a connection to a central station. The damage caused by sprinklers left running for a considerable time after the fire is extinguished may be relatively large compared to the fire damage. The age of the sprinkler system and its upkeep must be considered along with the damageability of the property insured. Here, too, the alarm device which alerts someone to shut off the flow of water is of considerable importance.

[1] Charles F. Rupprecht, *The Modern Fire Underwriter* (Philadelphia: The Spectator Co., 1940), p. 34. (Rupprecht does not comment on Class 10.)

Exposures. Exposures may be looked at from two viewpoints, internal and external. The internal exposure is that of one tenant to another. Suppose, for example, a paper-specialty manufacturer is located in the basement of a three-story, fifty-year-old frame building. Suppose, further, that the three stories above are occupied by a metalworker who has welding equipment, spray painting equipment, and drying ovens. A small fire above the paper-specialty manufacturer could result in very heavy damage by water. On the other hand, the exposure would be somewhat less, though hardly desirable, if the paper-specialty manufacturer were located on the top floor. An internal exposure, then, is any hazard in the building that adds to the likelihood of a loss to the insured property. Internal exposure must be considered from both a physical and a moral standpoint.

The external exposures are buildings and/or occupancies of buildings located near enough to the insured property to increase the loss potential. Different underwriters use different rules of thumb to measure the seriousness of an exposure. Some rules are based on a set number of feet, some on a relationship between the size of the exposure and the distance from the exposing risk, and some on the charges that the rating organization makes for an exposing risk.

An underwriter is concerned primarily with the following possibilities: (1) that a fire originating in an exposing risk will spread to the insured property; (2) that heat, smoke, and/or water will result in damage to the insured property; or (3) both. Several factors must be considered in relation to each other. One is the construction of the insured risk. A fire-resistive factory building is far less likely to be damaged by an exposing fire than is a large frame apartment building. The second factor is the construction of the exposing risk. A fire-resistive building is certainly not as severe an exposure as a frame building of the same size. A third factor is the occupancy of the exposing risk. An exposing building occupied by a flammable plastics manufacturer would be a far more serious exposure than would an office building. Fourth, the distance between the insured risk and the exposing risk is important. Fifth, the exposure becomes more serious as the height of the exposing building exceeds the height of the insured building. The sixth factor is the extent and effectiveness of private and public protection available to confine a fire in the exposing risk. Finally, and most important of all, the interaction among these six factors is a compelling consideration.

Occupancy. In underwriting a building risk one must consider two kinds of occupancy hazard—common hazards and special hazards. Common hazards are those applicable to nearly all kinds of risks—for instance, heating and lighting. A special hazard is one peculiar to one or a few types of occupancy—for example, welding. Common hazards do not necessarily equate with inconsequential hazards. Many times the common hazards improperly handled can be worse than special hazards.

1. *Common hazards.* The type of heating equipment in a building depends in part, of course, upon the climate. In the North a large number of fires are caused by malfunctioning of heating equipment. This equipment may be pushed beyond its capacity, it may have been improperly installed, or it may have been inherently defective. Heating fires are also caused by the failure of safety devices or by human error and carelessness. There is little one can do about the first other than to be sure at the time of inspection that the devices have not been tampered with. The second may sometimes be avoided by observation, investigation, and control. Generally speaking, if heating equipment is of an approved type, the most important factor from an underwriting standpoint is that it be used as designed and that there be sufficient clear space between it and all combustible surroundings, including trash.

Special attention should be paid to heating equipment in buildings where the equipment is used infrequently. In the southern parts of the country where heaters are not regularly used, there is some tendency to be careless as to both the type of heater purchased and the installation. The thinking seems to be that the heating equipment is incidental to the building and will be seldom if ever used. Yet, when an unusually cold spell comes, the heating equipment and any adjacent combustible material are subjected to the same hazards they would be subjected to if used regularly. Buildings of light or substandard construction or of a converted use warrant careful examination. The chimney, and the vent or smoke pipes from the furnace through all combustible materials to the chimney, are particularly vulnerable areas. Underwriters should also attempt to visualize the extreme conditions in which the equipment may have to be used. They should not construe the fact that the building is still standing after last year's "coldest winter ever" as proof it will endure another winter.

Electricity is another of the common hazards which is often subject to only cursory interest. Electricity is taken so much for granted, it is easy to forget its inherent dangers. Electrical equipment properly installed, properly maintained, and properly used is one of man's safest servants. But electrical equipment improperly installed, improperly maintained, or improperly used is a frequent source of fires. The underwriter should be constantly on the lookout for "do-it-yourself" extensions of the original installation, for multiple extensions, for extension lines hung over nails or hooks, and for overfusing or underpowering.

Few laymen realize that there are limits to the size of wire through which electricity can safely travel; that wires come in different sizes for different purposes; that different types of equipment are required for damp as opposed to dry places; that special explosion type fixtures are necessary for explosive conditions; and that temporary equipment too often becomes "permanent" until destroyed by fire.

Perhaps the most talked about and least acted upon part of electrical systems is the fuse box. It is accepted practice for many people to correct a blown fuse by putting in a larger fuse, never realizing that the fuse is a safety device. The subject of fuses and wiring has become increasingly important since World War II because of the tremendous use of electrical appliances, many of which place a dangerous load on an outmoded electrical system. Overloading can occur anywhere—in dwellings, mercantile structures, offices, or apartment buildings.

If the general public could be persuaded to up-date heating and electrical equipment, the reduction in fires would be startling. It is the underwriter's job to be aware of any unusual electrical or heating hazard associated with a risk he accepts.

2. *Special hazards.* These can be touched upon only lightly. They encompass those hazards which might be peculiar to a particular risk such as welding, dip tanks, lacquer spraying, use of highly combustible materials, use of materials subject to spontaneous combustion, and so on. Adequately protected, these risks may not be as dangerous as they appear.

In the special hazard risk the underwriter faces several problems: (1) knowing exactly what the special hazard involves; (2) having management sold on the necessity of providing adequate protection; and (3) being aware of the change in a special hazard or the installation of a new special hazard. In respect to the first problem, the book entitled *Fire Insurance, Inspection and Underwriting* by Lincoln, Babcock, and Tisdale[2] can be of considerable help to an underwriter. In the second instance, if an underwriter is not convinced that management is aware of the degree of hazard or the necessity for adequate protection, he should approach the risk with great caution. Finally, there are some types of special hazard risks that an underwriter would be foolhardy to attempt to underwrite without a regular inspection service which will permit him to know immediately of changes or even of proposals for change.

Contents. In underwriting a contents line the underwriter, as noted above, must weigh the hazards created by the building, the external exposures to the building, and the internal exposures from the other tenants, if any. Having considered these factors as well as the ownership of the contents, the underwriter also must weigh the hazards of the particular contents. Contents risks, of course, are found in all kinds of occupancies from dwellings to heavy manufacturing. Because of space limitations, the discussion in this chapter is limited to mercantile risks. Similar thinking, of course, applies to other types of occupancies.

In underwriting contents risks there are three main considerations apart from the common or special hazards discussed above. They are: ignitability, combustibility, and damageability. Some contents have a

[2] Lincoln, Walter O., and others. *Fire Insurance, Inspection and Underwriting* (7th ed.; Philadelphia: Chilton Co., 1953).

high degree of ignitability, such as those subject to spontaneous combustion. Some products, though not subject to spontaneous combustion, have very fast combustibility, such as light paper or wood products. (It is important to distinguish between the combustibility of a given substance in its various forms. For example, a chamfered heavy wooden beam is not considered rapidly combustible, but wood shavings may be of such rapid combustibility as to be explosive. But both are the same substance, wood.) Some merchandise which is neither readily ignitable nor readily combustible is highly damageable. For example, jigs, tools, or tempered metal products can be easily damaged by heat or water. Then, too, the relative value of the property compared to the cost of salvaging it must be considered. The physical damage may appear small but the cost of salvaging may approach or even exceed the value of the article.

Thus, the underwriter must consider ignitability, combustibility, and damageability when determining both the acceptability and the amount of liability of a contents line. More important than each of these characteristics separately however, is their interaction. For example, a risk of relatively low damageability combined with a product of relatively high ignitability might be acceptable for a much higher line than a contents line of high damageability combined with low ignitability. The interaction of these factors sometimes multiplies the hazard geometrically rather than arithmetically.

Likewise, the nature of contents in relation to the construction of the building must be considered. The less combustible the building and the more limited the fire areas, the more acceptable becomes a contents line of high damageability or even of high ignitability. For example, a product of low combustibility but high damageability located in a frame building might be unacceptable to an underwriter who would write a substantial line on the same contents located in a fire-resistive building. Here again there is a relativity of increasing importance not only between the various contents factors but also between the contents and the building construction as well as the hazards inherent in the exposing tenants if the building is of multiple occupancy.

An encumbrance on contents may be a danger sign to the underwriter. It is not uncommon for machinery to be bought on the installment plan or subject to a conditional sale. It is uncommon in many areas for a merchant or manufacturer to place a chattel mortgage on his contents. In some cases a chattel mortgage is the last resort of a potential bankrupt and therefore should be carefully investigated by the underwriter. Here again any departure from the normal pattern by an insured is good reason for the underwriter to take a second look.

Coinsurance. In most territories there is for both contents and buildings (other than dwellings) a coinsurance clause or a clause of similar effect. The purpose of such a clause is to give a lower rate to the insured who carries a higher amount of insurance to value. The fact behind the coinsurance clause is that in protected areas most fires are relatively small or, to put it another way, are less than total. Therefore, the insured who carries insurance equal to 10 percent of his value would be far more likely to collect a loss equal to his total insurance than would the insured who carries 100 percent insurance to value.

As opposed to coinsurance, there is flat insurance where the insured does not agree to carry any particular amount of insurance. Flat insurance again raises the relationship between the rate and the hazard. A flat rate is the same whether the insured carries 5 or 50 percent of insurance to value. Obviously, the underwriter has selection working against him on a risk with 5 percent to value compared to one with 50 percent to value at an identical rate. Here again the underwriter must be concerned with the book of business he is developing and how each individual risk will affect this book.

Personal Hazard

There is one hazard which is neither entirely physical nor entirely moral, yet which often involves both. This is the personal hazard—sometimes called the management hazard or the insured's attitude. It is often more important than the apparent physical or moral hazard. If the owner or manager does not want a fire and applies intelligent measures toward prevention, there is a substantial reduction in the likelihood of a fire. This thought has been expressed in a number of ways. Because of its fundamental importance in underwriting it should be emphasized and reemphasized. The chief inspector of a self-insured national industrial company put it this way, "A clean risk never burns." Though he did not mean this statement literally, he did mean that the attitude of management evidenced by keeping the risk "clean" was effective throughout the operation of the risk so that the possibility of fire was greatly reduced.

Admittedly, differences of opinion can occur; but this writer's opinion is that the personal attitude of the owner or manager is one of the most important factors from an underwriting standpoint. This attitude must be deduced by the underwriter from the information he has at his disposal. At the risk of generalizing from the specific, a simple example can be studied. The risk is a brick apartment building which is 35 years old and located in a middle-class neighborhood. The inspector finds that a hole five inches in diameter has been punched in the front hall plaster and upon inquiry finds this condition has existed for six months. The additional physical hazard caused by this hole in the plaster could be considered relatively small compared to the hazard revealed by this evidence of management's lack of interest and pride in the property. It is also an indication of what is or what may become the attitude of the occupants of the property.

"A clean risk never burns." "Ownership is the crux of underwriting." "Rather a risk full of special hazards with good ownership than a 'riskless' property with poor ownership." These quotations give strong evidence of the importance skilled underwriters place on the personal hazard.

UNDERWRITING OTHER COVERAGES

There are many facets of underwriting which cannot be discussed in one chapter. Even in one chapter, however, the point must be made that, while fire is the principal hazard in a fire insurance contract, there are usually other perils such as extended coverage or vandalism and malicious mischief added by endorsement.

In the usual course of events the underwriter concentrates on underwriting the fire hazard and accepts the additional coverages with little or no underwriting. On some risks this practice can be disastrous. There are, for example, some types of risk (e.g., greenhouses) and some seacoast areas which are subject to severe windstorm damage. There are some manufacturing risks which have a high explosion hazard. In such cases the focus of the underwriting must, of course, center on these extreme hazards.

So, too, the underwriter must remember that the normal rates for additional perils are for normal conditions. A selection against the underwriter is apparent when the insured property is subject to more than a normal exposure. For example, vandalism is highly probable on a property owned by an insured who has a history of labor trouble, or a property owned by an ethnic group which has a history of unpopularity in the neighborhood. The underwriter must develop sensitivity to recognize the existence of conditions which create an unusual hazard.

The fire contract is also used to insure earnings from property. These coverages are usually referred to as time element coverages. The most important is business interruption insurance. (See Chapter 9.) In underwriting time element coverages, the underwriter is interested in the loss of property only to the extent that it will interfere with the operation of the insured's business. There might be a heavy property loss to a men's clothing store, but the business interruption loss could be relatively small if the men's store were able to reorder merchandise quickly and reopen in the building next door. On the other hand, there might be a relatively minor property loss in a factory using an imported hand-tooled machine, yet the whole factory operation could be held up for several weeks or months while this intricate, specialized piece of machinery was being replaced. Hence, while the time element underwriter must be interested in the likelihood of a fire (or other direct loss), the speed with which it will spread, and the damageability of the property, he must concentrate his greatest attention on the time it will take his insured to get back in business either at the same or a different location.

THE UNDERWRITER

A man can spend his lifetime in underwriting and still not know all the answers. Underwriting by its nature is neither a science nor an art though there are those who would like to treat it as one or the other. The competent underwriter must possess a body of systematized knowledge which he can call upon at will. Without this knowledge he is akin to a "seat-of-the-pants" pilot trying to fly a four-engined jet plane.

A wide body of knowledge, however, is not enough in itself. The skill or art with which the underwriter applies his knowledge will spell the difference between success and failure. There is no substitute for judgment and experience. Nor can the underwriter be given ironclad rules by which he selects his risks. Rules and policy there must be; but within these rules there must also be guidelines, and within the guidelines wide areas for the operation of judgment and for the skillful application of the underwriter's knowledge and experience.

From what has been said in this chapter it is apparent that the successful underwriter needs a broad knowledge of business and social conditions. Business and social conditions have a direct effect on the potential moral hazard. The underwriter not only must be aware of these conditions in his territory; he also must have a knowledge of the geographical and physical makeup of his territory, especially of those areas that are physically congested and pose a catastrophe hazard. The skilled underwriter as well must have considerable information about the physical operation of various kinds of risks so that he can envision their hazards, but he must know when to seek additional information. Good underwriters are frequently omnivorous readers with a well-developed sense of curiosity.

Imagination is another characteristic without which it is virtually impossible for anyone to become a skilled underwriter. Finally, a good measure of perspective and common sense will help the underwriter avoid the extremes of too great or too little selectivity. If an underwriter has these qualities and develops skill in their use, he may be successful. In some companies one additional ability is required, namely, the ability to communicate. While this ability may not be an inherent part of underwriting, it is an inherent part of many underwriters' duties.

It requires little ability to say "yes" when an acceptable risk is offered, but it sometimes requires considerable ability to say "no" to an unacceptable risk in such a way that the producer understands and accepts this decision without animosity. Every underwriter worth his salt will have to decline a multitude of risks in his lifetime. The greater his ability to do so and still maintain the good will of the producer, the greater will be his value to his company, the industry, and himself.

THE FUTURE

One of the considerations most significant to an underwriter is change. A risk underwritten a year ago may turn out to be drastically different on a reïnspection. A line of business that was highly prosperous may be eclipsed by another in a year's time.

So, too, the position of the underwriter in the property-liability insurance industry is subject to change. In days when there was less rigorous regulation of rates, when competition was mainly limited to companies operating within the American agency system, when property companies did not compete with casualty companies and vice versa, when life insurance companies were completely apart from the general insurance business, when the word "package" was foreign to the insurance vocabulary—in those days some companies could perhaps afford the concept of an underwriter as a "necessary evil."

That was yesterday. Underwriting has become one of the most highly skilled occupations in the entire industry. The success or lack of success of underwriting will determine the success or failure of many companies. This does not mean the old-time underwriter is coming into his own. It means that a new type of well-educated, knowledgeable, experienced, skillful underwriter will occupy a position of prestige.

SUGGESTED READINGS

Fire Protection Handbook. 12th ed. Boston: National Fire Protection Association, 1962.

KLEIN, HENRY C. *Business Interruption Insurance.* 4th ed. Indianapolis: Rough Notes Co., 1960.

LINCOLN, WALTER O., AND OTHERS. *Fire Insurance, Inspection and Underwriting.* 7th ed. Philadelphia: Chilton Co., 1953.

REED, PRENTISS B. *Fire Insurance Underwriting.* New York: McGraw-Hill Book Co., Inc., 1940.

RUPPRECHT, CHARLES F. *The Modern Fire Underwriter.* Philadelphia: The Spectator, 1940.

Chapter 15

UNDERWRITING LARGE RISKS

BY WILLIAM H. BERRY

The subject matter of this chapter is the handling of large risks. While the emphasis is on fire insurance, the chapter spills over into property damage insurance generally. It even has a few references to liability exposures and coverages. To the extent it goes beyond "fire and allied lines" it does not fit neatly in the organization of material here in Part II of the *Handbook*. On the other hand, this juncture seems as good as any for discussion of some of the difficult—but highly interesting—problems of insuring large risks. Many of the underwriting concepts developed in Chapter 14 apply here. As will be seen, however, large risks present some unique problems.

LARGE RISKS

As used in this chapter, the phrase "large risks" carries a dual meaning. One is that of high hazard or peril, as found in the catastrophic loss propensities of liquified petroleum gases, such as butane or propane. The other meaning is heavy concentration of values in property. For example, a structure such as the Mackinac, Michigan, bridge completed in 1957 at a cost of $80 million, is a "large risk." Another is an industrial installation with a single building and its contents involving $75 to $100 million of insurable value. Both of these types of "large risks" present very difficult and unique problems to the underwriter and engineer. They present problems of a type which will probably not diminish, because the development of the American economy, which creates such problems, is not likely to be reversed.

The high hazard type of large risk is prominent because of the trend toward greater use of more complicated materials, many with inherently dangerous characteristics. Never before have so many materials that are highly combustible, explosive, or toxic been used, transported, or stored on such a large scale. However, these materials are a necessary and useful part of our wealth of raw materials, on which our whole complex of chemical, plastics, synthetic textile, and other industries has been built.

The type of large risks involving a concentration of high-valued property is the result of the trend toward bigness. The growth of the American industrial plant, especially, is one of the marvels of our time. The very bigness, though, has presented major problems. There are enormous values subject to multiple perils. Also during the past 15 to 20 years a good part of American industry has moved into small towns or rural areas because of tax, labor, or other economic advantages. In numerous cases the fire ordinances and public protection and construction codes in the new locations left much to be desired in terms of safety and, generally, were not—and still are not—as stringent and efficient as are those in the cities from which the firms moved.

The skills required in the intelligent analysis of these risks are becoming more diversified and demanding than formerly. This requirement exists because science and industry continue moving forward in other fields, with more diversified use of our basic materials, nuclear energy, advanced power sources, improved electronic computers, and larger and faster means of transportation.

Upon first consideration, it is plain that the underwriting of these large complex types of risks requires great care and good judgment. The underwriters, engineers, and others associated in analyzing these risks must be experts of exceptional ability and experience. Readers should note carefully, however, that the experts use, at least at the outset, most of the same fundamental guideposts as are usable for any insurable risk with more commonplace characteristics. Extraordinary complications do arise, particularly in the determination of (1) an adequate rate to cover the probability of small as well as catastrophic losses and (2) the amount of liability which reasonably can be accepted by the individual insurer and perhaps by the group of insurers on the risk.

RESPONSIBILITIES OF THE COMPANIES

The companies are in business to make a profit; whether gains are for the benefit of the stockholders, policyholders, or both is not necessary to differentiate here. In any case, because its services are essential to the stability and growth of the economy, the individual company has an obligation to the public that must be met if it is to continue as a private enterprise.

As a matter of public service, the companies have a duty to provide underwriting facilities for the risks of great magnitude, consistent with their resources, capabilities, and ability to make a profit. The American insurance industry, in fact, has created quite an impressive record in keeping pace with technological advancements and with social practices of concentrating property values.

Extraordinary developments in science and industry make it incumbent upon the companies to continue to be concerned about fulfilling their responsibilities, whether through their individual facilities or through joint efforts of a group of companies. The problem of insuring the 1964 New York World's Fair Corporation was solved by the latter means. The Fair has been described as "the biggest and most fantastic showcase ever conceived and constructed by the minds and hands of men." In connection with handling the insurance and loss prevention services, companies were confronted with one of the greatest problems of capacity and facilities in the history of insurance in this country. Liability limits were exceedingly high. Property values have been estimated to aggregate something in the area of $600 million. It is to the credit of the American insurance industry that the solution to the problem of basic coverages was being provided as of the time of this writing through the use of only two basic markets. One was a package liability policy, issued as a joint venture by two leading companies. The other was a single fire insurance package provided through the facilities of the Factory Insurance Association. These programs were not only a convenience for the fair corporation; they also served as a means for establishing orderly procedures in underwriting this unusually large exposure and for providing efficient inspection and claims services.

Another outstanding example of how private insurance applied underwriting perception to a tremendously important problem involving large risks is the way it reacted to the revolutionary idea of the peaceful use of atomic energy. No risks ever considered by the insurance industry contained greater potential loss factors. Except for direct damage to "off-premises" property resulting from radioactive fallout, however, they are considered insurable. Progressive insurance company management accepted its obligations to provide insurance protection. This was achieved by forming, subsequent to the Atomic Energy Act of 1954, three industry associations, namely, the Nuclear Energy Liability Insurance Association, the Nuclear Energy Property Insurance Association, and the Mutual Atomic Energy Reinsurance Pool.

These associations, among others, illustrate the seriousness with which many companies have viewed their responsibilities in providing adequate insurance facilities to accommodate large risks which defy conventional insurance treatment. This business, by the way, is channeled through the usual production sources. This channeling underscores the fact that any success which the insurance business enjoys is interrelated with the incentive system inherent in the agent or broker relationship.

UNDERWRITING

Any serious attempt to deal with the problem of the large risk depends upon having some highly qualified person make a mature judgment about whether a risk is going to be declined or accepted, and if accepted, under what conditions. That person is the underwriter.

An unprecedented run of good luck or uneducated guessing cannot be depended upon to produce a profit for an insurer. To be successful over an extended period of time, an underwriter of large risks must possess a very high grade of intelligence and he must have experience in handling difficult exposure problems. He must approach every large risk with an open mind and a high degree of imaginative ingenuity while at the same time he must utilize every practical device available properly to analyze the risk factors.

A well-trained and experienced underwriting mind that can digest masses of technical detail for each risk, produce clear decisions, and over the years achieve a better than average degree of consistency, is the type of mind which companies value most. If a well-designed formula of sound principles is not used consistently as a background for underwriting, there always exists the danger of "good days" and "bad days." Inconsistent treatment of risks amounts simply to "plunging" in the case of the large risk. Temptation to make a quick profit by these means must be carefully guarded against, because—with large risks—millions of dollars of the company's assets may be involved.

Lack of Verifiable Data

The underwriter many times is not dealing with verifiable data. In fact, there may be no history of loss experience to guide him in his deliberations. Before the underwriter is in a position to determine the loss potential with even a reasonable approximation, he may need the results of certain research involving complicated engineering and testing work. Since some large risks are unique, he may be forced to depend substantially upon his broad experience as the only alternative to analyzing verifiable data which he wishes he had. Other risks may not be unique but may have a high degree of unpredictability. A unique risk may be one involving nuclear materials in a power plant reactor. Ultimately, such a risk may become commonplace as the nuclear fuels become competitive with the fossil fuels. An extreme example of what can happen in the reactor of a nuclear power plant is the great hazard of a "runaway" or "melt down" in the core. Even if this incident did not rupture the containment vessel and even if radioactivity were not released to its environment, property damage in the millions of dollars would certainly result at the site. Should all of the containment safeguards fail and radioactive material be released to the atmosphere, the third-party liability losses alone resulting from radioactive contamination would be incalculable.

Another aspect of the problem of estimating loss potential is found in the area of the "human element" and its unpredictability. When one deals with material things, he can engineer certain safeguards which can be expected to produce an extremely high degree of reliability—even when the most potent of nuclear devices or processes are involved. But when he attempts, by every refined method used in the most advanced disciplines of the behavioral sciences, to understand what goes on inside a human mind, he is compelled to admit slow progress—sometimes, even frustration. The problem is compounded when he is confronted with the direful prospects of what 12 minds on a jury can germinate in the way of a disastrous judgment.

It is understandable, then, why an underwriter may spend some restless nights when he has agreed to bind a nationwide fleet of long-haul trucks, continually on the move on cross-country highways. A liability case tried in Arizona in 1960 reminds him why he must be constantly aware of the latent danger of liability risks involving vehicles of this nature. A moving van was attempting to make a U-turn on a highway at night when a motorist collided with it. The record discloses most serious injury to the motorist. His guardian brought suit[1] against the van company and won a judgment reported to be the largest ever returned by a jury in the state of Arizona.

It is not intended to infer that all or even most large risks have preliminary data of so little evidential value as the extreme risks described above. The principal point, rather, is that the underwriter of the large risk many times must necessarily deal with a greater quantity of the unknown than his counterpart who underwrites ordinary risks. Accordingly, he must be more exacting than his counterpart in the development of a seasoned judgment before committing his company to what easily could be ruinous losses.

Rate Adequacy

The underwriter in considering acceptance of the large risk faces an urgent problem of rate adequacy. Because of the probable lack of loss experience, he will have to depend heavily upon fragmentary information and skillful approximation arrived at by analogy. Progressively greater refinement of the rate can be effected when loss experience, as it develops, provides the rating structure with greater credibility—assuming the risk lends itself to such experience treatment. Of course, some large risks may be free of losses altogether. The only safe ground for rate adequacy in this case is for the underwriter to have such a thorough knowledge of rate schedules applicable to analogous risks that he can stay at least within reasonable rating limits.

His basic rates for analogous risks are governed by such considerations as the plant's proximity to public and plant fire-fighting equipment and the nature of the product and its processes. The rate may be 5¢/$100

[1] *Johannessen* v. *Bekins Van & Storage Company* [No. 60831, Superior Court, Pima County, Arizona (1960)].

coverage or \$1/\$100 coverage. Complicating factors outside the characteristics of the large risk itself affect these rates disproportionately. Greatly influencing these simple yardsticks at this time is the accelerated pace of changes in the insurance business. Every conceivable type of policy is undergoing experimentation, which distorts even more any possible credibility toward which the underwriter may be building.

Another factor to be mentioned that adds further to his concern (and suggests a relevant matter for study by the reader) is that of "rate lag" affecting the basic rates. Some authorities hold that the business is changing so fast and that annual dollar losses are rising so quickly[2] that rate changes have not been responsive enough to provide commensurate relief for basic rate inadequacy.

Actuarial devices used in many rating plans of more commonplace risks enable the underwriter to gauge rather well the credibility of loss experience. The underwriter for the large risk is seldom so blessed! Many times he must work with the handicap of inadequate or even total absence of experience of an individual large risk. Still, he must determine whether or not he will accept it for the company. If he does accept the risk, he cannot depend upon using a standard rating procedure nor the usual means for keeping track of the risk after it is written to test for rate accuracy. More than likely, he will have to rely on his own perception and judgment from the inception of the coverage.

Custom-made Forms

He may accept coverage only after certain conditions have been agreed upon prior to acceptance, and he may also require that continuing conditions be met by the insured. Warranties are more common than in ordinary cases of insuring commercial or industrial properties. Working closely with the engineer, the experienced underwriter will fit existing protection to the particular conditions, depending upon whether he considers the risk one of heavy or light hazard. He is likely to request supplementary forms of protection and to require control of certain features of occupancy or operation. He may specify the arrangement or location of raw materials and finished stock. Such tailoring of insurance, of course, means that special forms are used with the Standard Fire Policy, if, indeed, this policy is used at all.

There is no formula for tailoring coverage to risks. A manufacturer of caustic chemicals, for example, has an insurance program differing greatly from that of a public service utility. Some few insureds feel that their financial position weighed against the chance of loss is so disproportionate that they wish no insurance at all on certain exposures. It has been

[2] Fire losses in the United States have more than doubled—from \$648,909,000 in 1950 to \$1,405,558,000 in 1963. Source: *Insurance Facts* (New York: Insurance Information Institute, 1964).

reported[3] that a very large and long-established steel company carries no fire insurance because it believes that it has such a strong cash position and its plants are so widely distributed, that it can absorb its own losses without impairing its capital structure.

Because of the high values on the large risks, the underwriter charges relatively few dollars of premium in return for risking many dollars on potential losses. Because of this dangerous relationship, companies accepting large risks must either (1) limit their liability or (2) insure a large enough number of properly underwritten risks to provide sufficient premium volume to average them out at a profit over a reasonable period of time, notwithstanding the occasional severe loss.

SELECTION CRITERIA

The underwriter is guided basically in his selection of large risks by the experience the company has had among the various classifications of business on which it has made commitments in the past. If it has had favorable experience with the large risk and has demonstrated an ability to make an underwriting profit, it probably can continue to do so only by unceasing surveillance of the variables affecting loss. It must have a continuous program of supervision of the risks already in its portfolio. On the basis of that experience it must continuously revise standards for selection of new risks.

As has been indicated elsewhere, such risks are valued as a source of income but require careful scrutiny because of the ever present chance of heavy loss. While volume is important, only proper selection of risks using rigidly enforced standards will help avoid serious loss.

Getting a "Picture" of the Risk

Upon being presented with specifications of coverage from a producer, the experienced underwriter will obtain the most detailed and accurate "picture" of the risk possible. The larger the risk or the more unusual, the greater the amount of additional data usually required. (This requirement in itself can be a very expensive part of the selection process.) Accurate information, based on the engineer's observations of favorable and unfavorable conditions, is essential to the underwriter before he makes a commitment. In fire and allied lines, unfavorable conditions may cause him to limit the line, or he may accept the risk only after certain improvements in the risk have been agreed upon and made.

Detailed information in an inspection report by a company engineer will greatly assist the underwriter in appraising the insurability of the risk, but other sources may be used also. Another excellent source of underwriting data which may be available consists of insurers formerly on the risk. Often, the carriers will make information readily available on a

[3] "What Price Insurance?", *Chemical Week* (March 16, 1963), p. 48.

reciprocal basis. This source is especially valuable when loss experience is available. Other sources used when specialized knowledge of the operations or conditions is desired are outside investigative agencies or laboratories.

Three Questions

After information is obtained from the various sources the underwriter may mentally subject the risk to certain criteria. Some of these are worth noting:

1. Is the risk so complicated or of such a nature that services such as continual extensive engineering, frequent audits of premium exposure, or special loss adjustment procedures are necessary? Special service beyond the normal service contemplated in a reasonable premium may have to be considered, with the view of making additional premium charges for required extra services.
2. Can an adequate rate be charged without making the premium prohibitive? When a schedule rate is not applicable and a special rate has to be developed, there may be a tendency to set it at a somewhat redundant level. This tendency is less pronounced as experience figures become available and have sufficient credibility to substantiate a proper rate adjustment.
3. In addition to being an individual risk of potentially catastrophic proportions itself, is the risk subject to multiple catastrophe losses? In fire and allied lines, for example, there may be an accumulation of exposure due to windstorm, earthquake, or other environmental perils to such a degree that the risk is not acceptable in a given geographical area.

The selection process continues upon renewal and affords an opportunity for reappraisal of the risk in the light of new experience developed by the risk itself or any similar risk. At renewal time, revision of coverages or rates may be made so as to "true-up" the risk. If the account has proven profitable, renewal may be effected with little or no change. If, on the other hand, the experience has proven unfavorable, the underwriter must determine the causes and request effective remedies.

It has been said that "any risk can be written at a price." This assertion is fallacious, however, because practicality is a basic consideration in the cost of insurance protection. Some unusual risks would require a premium approaching or perhaps even exceeding the amount of the anticipated total loss.

Under existing systems of insurance, selection of risks will continue to be not only important but essential to the company which makes a profit on its operations and maintains a normal growth pattern. Provisions in insurance laws allow a reasonable underwriting profit. Ordinarily, that profit should be judged in the same light as profit in other enterprises. A complication arises, however, in the fact that insurers sometimes face peculiar pressures. Because insurance is endowed with a large element of public interest, insurers can hardly allow a vacuum to exist in the market. Often, they provide coverages which considered on a strict profit basis doubtless would be withdrawn.

IMPORTANCE OF ENGINEERING

The engineering required in an intelligent analysis of hazards confronting the property-liability business today covers expanding fields of knowledge, particularly if the hazards involve an unusual type of risk. The engineer in carrying out his primary objectives of preventing and controlling the occurrence of loss is involved in civil, mechanical, electrical, chemical, metallurgical, and even aeronautical engineering.

In order for the underwriter to obtain important information for determining the insurability and rate basis of the large risk, he must often ask the engineer to undertake complicated and time-consuming surveys. However, he does not develop this information solely for the use of the underwriter. The information he produces may relate directly to loss-causing features of the risk and thus may be of vital interest to the insured. Accordingly, insureds often receive recommendations from the engineer, not only for the treatment of specific hazards in question but also for related ones as well.

The point should be mentioned here that the engineer is ready also to work hand in hand with and provide expert advice to the insured who is entering a new field of endeavor or constructing a new plant with unfamiliar hazards. An example is a machine-type parking garage, eight to ten stories high, that will accommodate 500 to 1,000 automobiles. This type of structure may pose a serious problem to the insurer with its automatic elevators carrying two or three million dollars worth of automobiles to designated parking spaces, each with a tank of gasoline. If it is possible to install protective features during construction, the insurer may advise on premium-saving measures and be able to consider the risk more favorably. The insured will gain by avoiding the greater expense of structural alterations after the building is completed. The larger the risk, the greater the cost of insurance. Minimizing hazards reduces the cost.

The secure maintenance of the economy is based on an effort to improve the measures by which prevention and protection are put into effect. Losses on the large risk are of such proportions that they attract and require national attention. The engineers should continue to keep abreast not only of economic and industrial growth trends but also of the research and development advances giving the companies newer and larger exposure problems.

LIMITING THE LOSS POTENTIAL

The insurer of a large risk faces the practical necessity of limiting its maximum possible loss. The insurer does not want any individual loss to assume such proportions that it might unduly affect the overall experience of more commonplace lines nor threaten its financial stability. Moreover, the insurer does not wish a dangerous accumulation of loss liability in a combination of various exposures. The very nature of most large risks suggests catastrophe, which is generally understood to mean a loss characterized by large size, suddenness, uniqueness, and infrequency.

A precise definition of what constitutes a catastrophe may vary among companies, syndicates, and pools. A common measuring stick is that one established by the Actuarial Bureau Committee of the National Board of Fire Underwriters. This committee considers any disaster involving stock fire insurance companies in losses estimated at $1 million or over as a catastrophe.[4]

Usual Ways

The usual ways for limiting large losses by the individual insurer, or a group of insurers, are three in number:

1. By establishing what management regards as a safe limit of retention of liability on the risk.
2. By transferring liability beyond the insurer's retention through the medium of reinsurance.
3. By sharing large amounts of liability through underwriting pools, syndicates, or associations.

This last approach allows a combination of insurers to underwrite large and unusual risks without putting an undue strain upon their individual resources from the standpoint of losses, engineering expense, inspection expense, or other administrative expenses. This approach has characteristics that date back to the early days of the English coffeehouse where individual underwriters, acting in the same capacity as insurers, combined into syndicates but remained severally liable to the extent of their respective participations in any contract.

Associations or pools have usually handled on an aggregate basis the large and unusual risks typified by concentrations of value involving many millions of dollars such as the ocean liner "Ile de France," the Golden Gate Bridge in San Francisco, a Boeing 707, or a DC–8. Associations or pools also provide protection for large manufacturing corporations, many operating on a nationwide or worldwide scale.

A Management Decision

The method selected for limiting loss requires a management decision based upon a number of factors such as: the insurer's financial resources, the field of insurance in which the company or group of companies has experience and growth, and the kind of business the company or group is best qualified to write. Naturally, the limit selected will reflect the in-

[4] *Catastrophe Loss Adjustment Procedure* (New York: National Board of Fire Underwriters, 1952), p. 2.

surer's underwriting policy be it liberal, conservative, or "middle of the road."

Readers should recognize that, ultimately, the size of the limit selected is a matter of judgment—a qualitative rather than a quantitative matter. The point has been emphasized in this chapter that averages may be meaningless in treatment of the large risk. In underwriting commonplace risks one can find some comfort in the functioning of the law of large numbers. This law is not necessarily of solace to an insurer on a large risk. Consequently, it seems reasonable to conclude that only the insurers that have the technical know-how and the financial resources can hope successfully to underwrite the large risks. Conversely, the unqualified insurers should approach the possibility of catastrophic loss on this type of risk with extreme caution and in some instances eliminate such possibilities by avoiding large risks altogether.

Quite often when a risk has large values or hazardous features at stake, the market for it is considered a challenge rather than an opportunity. Those carriers who have met the challenge have had to enlarge their capacity and show a willingness to venture into unfamiliar waters.

In appraising available markets for the large risk, particularly if it has unusual characteristics of exposure, one can classify them basically into three groups: (1) domestic carriers, (2) domestic pools, and (3) nonadmitted insurers including Lloyd's.

The business which has had to seek foreign markets has been largely that involving problems of capacity, and more particularly, breadth of coverage. In presenting risks to underwriters, professional brokers and agents have found at times that certain large and hazardous manufacturing operations, for example, were not adaptable to the Factory Insurance Association or the Factory Mutual's programs because coverage for certain unusual perils was not available. In attempting to place (1) all risk protection on buildings and contents, (2) umbrella liability on large comprehensive liability exposures, (3) difference in conditions on property lines, or (4) large fire deductibles or franchises, they have generally met with something less than a competitive spirit among many domestic carriers (see Chapter 40).

The domestic market is not static, however, and its already important position in the marketplace is increasing. The carriers most influential in the market at this time appear to be more willing than formerly to profit by the experimentation of the nonadmitted carriers and are adopting forms and practices which, in some cases, are tending to become standard.

It must be acknowledged that competition on a worldwide basis has had a salutary effect on this market. This effect was evidenced particularly during the past decade by the tendency of the more progressive carriers to consider proposals for coverage adjustable to the particular needs of the risk and to provide a market for certain areas of coverage that were previously available only through foreign sources.

The following example, quoted from an article by A. H. Criddle, shows how normally traditional markets are swinging toward practices that could be found formerly only in a less conservative nonadmitted market:

> A utility client had several machinery losses where the basis of indemnity was not satisfactory because the definition of accident required breaking into two or more parts. The prior definition had been considerably broader and one of the tests of a covered loss had been impairment of the function of the object without the concurrent requirement of demonstrating breakage into two or more parts. After the second such loss, the client demanded a contract that would contain the old definition of accident and, further, indicated that it considered the inspection services of the insurance company unnecessary, especially since its own engineers were competent and the utility was under no state code requirements of this nature. There was no admitted market that would meet these two conditions and it was necessary to look elsewhere. It was possible to tailor the policy terms and conditions to meet the needs of the client, as it is so often the case, in the London Market. Incidentally, it now is possible to obtain the broader definition of accident on a negotiated basis with certain domestic carriers and there are rumors that the broader definition again will be available generally in the not too distant future.[5]

Great strides also have been made in recent years in providing special coverages designed to insure certain general classes, such as the commercial property policy, the institutional property form, and the imaginative multi-peril package. In this last-mentioned area, there has recently been introduced by a leading domestic carrier a comprehensive tailor-made policy, an entirely new concept which provides in one package on a most competitive basis all of the property-liability coverages essential to the protection of any mercantile, manufacturing, processing, or service business. This type of policy would seem to be establishing a pattern as the ultimate in statisfying the buyer of insurance for the large risk.

TROUBLESOME RISKS

Some risks present difficult problems of insurability, even for the progressive underwriter. Others are generally regarded as being beyond private insurance. Those with localized characteristics, low frequency, and high loss potential seem to have attracted the most attention of underwriters in recent years.

Victims of the tidal waves in seacoast areas and victims of floods of inland rivers, with their devastating havoc, urge some form of reimbusement. The damage done by earthquakes and subsidence on the West

---

[5] A. Hawthorne Criddle, "The Agent-Producer Approach to Custom-Made Insurance," *C.P.C.U. Annals*, Vol. 14 (Fall, 1961), p. 261.

Coast has characteristics of a localized nature that require special consideration before such risks can be feasibly insured. These problems, although simple in character, are difficult for the underwriter because of extreme adverse selection. Only persons who are immediately exposed to such dangers of loss are interested in obtaining insurance or other means of reimbursement. Basically, unless a large number of persons are faced with a similar exposure to loss, it is highly questionable whether some form of contribution to the unfortunate few suffering loss would actually fall within the concept of "insurance."

Finally, many additional problems are anticipated with the expansion of the commercial uses of nuclear energy. Much, of course, has been done here already. One of the most difficult exposures with which to deal is that of off-premises contamination. This insuring problem is likely to increase in urgency and complexity. Also, continued serious study must be given to the newly created catastrophic loss potential associated with business interruption insurance on nuclear plants of one kind or another as they perhaps become commonplace in our economy.

SUGGESTED READINGS

Berry, William H. "The Challenge of Risks of Great Magnitude," *The Annals of the Society of Chartered Property and Casualty Underwriters,* Vol. 14 (Winter, 1961), pp. 317–30.

Catastrophe Loss Adjustment Procedure. New York: The National Board of Fire Underwriters, 1952.

Factory Mutual Engineering Division. *Handbook of Industrial Loss Prevention.* New York: McGraw-Hill Book Co., Inc., 1959.

Fire Hazards and Safeguards for Metalworking Industries. New York: The National Board of Fire Underwriters, Technical Survey No. 2, 1954.

Fire Protection Handbook. 12th ed. Boston: National Fire Protection Association, 1962.

McGill, Dan M., (ed.). *All Lines Insurance.* Homewood, Ill. Richard D. Irwin, Inc., 1960.

Michelbacher, G. F. *Multiple-Line Insurance.* New York: McGraw-Hill Book Co., Inc., 1957. Chap. 2.

Milne, William D. *Factors in Special Fire Risk Analysis.* Philadelphia: Chilton Co., 1959.

Scanlon, J. P.; Phelan, J. D.; and Dean, D. F. "Catastrophic Risks," *The Annals of the Society of Chartered Property and Casualty Underwriters,* Vol. 7 (March, 1955), pp. 26–44.

Chapter 16

LOSS ADJUSTMENT IN FIRE INSURANCE

BY BEN M. BUTLER

Insurance is purchased only because of the possibility of loss. The adjustment (including payment) of claims represents the final act in the insurance process. The payment of a claim by an insurance company brings the insurance contract "to life" in a fashion far more vivid than does any other single act in connection with the purchase, issuance, and maintenance of the contract. For this reason, the subject of loss adjustment, as developed in this chapter, assumes considerable importance.

While the title of this chapter emphasizes "Fire," the chapter extends to the adjustment of losses from various perils other than fire. In fact, the matters discussed in this chapter have general application to fire, allied lines, consequential loss, and many other kinds of insurance. Incidentally, the allied lines of insurance produce a larger number of losses than does fire insurance, per se.

HISTORY OF ADJUSTING

Adjusting of losses in fire and the allied lines has, in recent years, advanced to a state where it requires highly technical skills, extensive knowledge, and continuing education. In the early days of insurance in the United States, however, the payment of losses required no great skill or specialized ability. The number of insureds in any locality was small and losses were easily adjusted—often by an officer of the insurer. As insurance operations expanded and field offices were established, investigation and payment of losses became the responsibility of special agents or other company employees.

The continued growth of insurers soon made impossible demands on field men, requiring them to devote too much time to adjustments and taking them away from their production duties. As a result, company staff adjusters and self-employed adjusting representatives took over the adjusting activity. These men devoted their full time to adjustments on behalf of the insurers, the former as regular salaried employees and the latter on a fee basis.

Because of early practices, most insurance company officials naturally felt that a company's interests were best served by the attention of personal representatives to determine loss under its policies. Many properties in time, however, were covered by several policies, each written by a different insurer. When a loss occurred, frequently as many as 10 or 15 adjusters reported individually to the insured, seeking to determine the extent of loss and to arrange for payment. An attempt was made to overcome this extremely unsatisfactory and inefficient procedure by appointing one or two of the adjusters involved to act for all. While usually acceptable to the insured, this practice often was not acceptable to the insurers. It also remained an expensive procedure.

Adjusting Organizations

Sometime after the great Chicago fire of 1871, the concept of a specialized adjusting organization was developed. The Western Adjustment and Inspection Company was organized in Chicago in 1885 by 13 shareholders as the first venture in providing cooperative adjusting facilities. These shareholders were among those capital stock companies associated in the "Union" group of companies of that period. Soon identified as a "bureau" serving the insurance companies in the Midwest, it was followed in 1906 by the creation of the General Adjustment Bureau, Inc. to serve the northeastern states. This organization was followed by the Southern Adjustment Bureau (1909), the Pacific Coast Adjustment Bureau (1911), and the Texas Adjustment Company (1925), all of which were subsequently merged with General Adjustment Bureau, Inc. In 1959, the Western Adjustment and Inspection Company also became a part of General Adjustment Bureau, Inc., creating a nationwide adjusting facility for the insurance companies with 3,900 adjusters and 750 offices.

The Underwriters Adjusting Company was organized at Chicago in 1919 as an adjusting bureau to serve the Midwest. This adjusting group was formed by a small group of capital stock companies comprising the "Western Insurance Bureau," an association of companies dedicated to policies opposed to those of the "Union" group, noted above. This "bureau" originally was formed to adjust company losses in the same area served by the Western Adjustment and Inspection Company. It now has 117 offices and 410 adjusters in 14 states.

Although the adjustment bureaus are owned by certain of the capital stock companies, they hold out their services to all companies operating as stock organizations, writing business through the American agency system. Mutual, reciprocal, stock, "direct-writer," and similar organizations utilize the many independent adjusting groups or attorneys throughout the country, or their own staffs.

In addition to the two company-owned adjusting organizations, two company-sponsored organizations have been created to supervise adjusting activities. The Committee on Losses and Adjustments, created in New York City in 1902, and the Cook County Loss Adjustment Bureau, established in Chicago in 1926, supervise and assign adjusters to certain classes of losses. These organizations were set up by certain of the capital stock companies and represent member companies who support their operations by means of service charges. Other stock companies, not members, also avail themselves of this policing service, upon agreement.

Loss Service Organizations

Nationally, a number of organizations supervise and maintain standards of adjustments and adjusting procedures, either as a primary objective or in conjunction with other advisory or supervisory functions. The National Board of Fire Underwriters is the largest of these organizations and is supported by a large number of stock companies. The Mutual Loss Research Bureau and the Mutual Fire Association of New England serve in a somewhat similar capacity for certain mutual companies and reciprocals. Their activities with regard to loss adjustments include establishment of adjusting procedures, supervision and investigation of adjustment standards, creation of intercompany guiding principles, and supervision of catastrophe operations.

Salvaging operations and disposition of salvage are important in minimizing personal property losses. Two organizations have been established for this purpose and are sponsored by certain of the capital stock companies. They are the Underwriters Salvage Company of New York and the Underwriters Salvage Company (of Chicago). These organizations take over damaged merchandise from insureds, recondition it when possible, and dispose of it at auction or by private sale for the benefit of the insurer and the insured, as their interests exist. Where an adjustment may have been concluded on a constructive total loss basis, the net return from the sale of the damaged merchandise is applied by the insurer to reduce its loss. Where the insured is a coinsurer or sustains a portion of the loss because of underinsurance, the net proceeds from the disposition of salvage may be distributed to the insurer and the insured proportionately. Each of these salvage companies (and each of other small independent salvage organizations) has a number of warehouses and conditioning facilities throughout its operating area. The Underwriters Salvage Companies' combined operations extend nationwide.

Staff and Self-employed Adjusters

The activities of the company-sponsored bureaus have not eliminated the need for the company staff adjuster and the self-employed "independent" adjuster. While some companies rely fully on company-owned bureau adjusters, others rely in part or solely on "independent" adjusters. Some of the large insurers maintain their own staff of adjusters and also utilize the services of the company-owned bureau adjusting facilities, the "independent" adjusters, and the loss service organizations. Officials in these companies attempt to route the losses in the way which they feel will lead to the most expeditious processing.

THE ROLE OF THE ADJUSTER

Public Relations

The adjustment of losses is a complex business, requiring the highest degree of integrity and an extensive knowledge of insurance contracts. The adjuster—be he bureau, staff, or "independent"—must have a broad knowledge of policy coverages and conditions and their application to particular loss situations. But far more than this, the adjuster is the "spokesman" for the insurance policy, and the representative of the insurance industry in the eyes of insureds. The public relations aspect of loss work must not be overlooked.

Adjusters have contact with only a minority of the total number of insureds. Nevertheless, the work of the adjuster is conspicuous. Although insurance is taken for granted by most insureds as a necessary financial burden, the relatively infrequent loss adjustment is permanently noted. The result establishes the "face" of the insurance business and all companies are "tarred with the same brush." The reputation of the insurance business is not built on the promises to pay set forth in insurance policies. Nor is this reputation affected by the exceptions and limitations incorporated in those policies—that is, not until an adjuster brings them into action.

To the insured who has had no previous experience with an insurance adjustment, the meeting with an adjuster may be perplexing. The adjuster represents at once both the imminent prospect of financial reimbursement and a possible obstacle to that end. To the degree that the adjuster can convey the fact that he acts in behalf of the insured as well as the insurer, he will be able to reconcile these opposing reactions. The adjuster must demonstrate the character and reputation for honesty upon which the insurance business was built.

A task of the adjuster is to educate his claimants and ultimately the insuring public to the view that (1) insurance is a quasi-public trust; (2) insurance companies are custodians of public funds in that the insuring public as a whole pays for losses; and (3) equitable adjustments are not only desirable but essential to the well-being of the insurance business. Such education is difficult to accomplish. All of the skill and experience that an adjuster has may be called into play to allay the fears of an emotionally upset insured. His responsibilities include the exercise of sufficient skill in discussions with the insured to cause him to recognize that he has received prompt, considerate treatment and that he has been indemnified within the spirit of his insurance contract. The confidence which the public has in insurance, then, is dependent in large measure upon the adjuster.

Technical Knowledge

As the material in Chapter 5 through Chapter 11 attests, fire and allied insurance contracts are complex, indeed. A good adjuster must understand these contracts. New multi-peril contracts add further complexity. The staff adjuster, of course, works principally with his own company's contracts. Nevertheless, he must be able to understand and interpret the policies and forms of other insurers, when he finds other contracts also covering the interest of his insured. The company-sponsored bureau adjusters and self-employed adjusters of necessity work with policies and forms of many insurers and must acquire a thorough knowledge of all policies and forms. Fortunately, standard wording is very often used. This wording has been tested in the courts and is understood subject only to new court rulings brought about by changing economic and social conditions.

In addition to acquiring an understanding of the commonly used contracts, the adjuster also must learn to recognize the differences between standard contracts and those peculiar to individual companies or to specific types of property. Many such contracts have been developed in recent years.

Knowledge of another sort is essential to the successful adjustment of losses, namely, a knowledge of the characteristics of properties insured. There is, of course, a limit to any person's capacity to acquire and retain such information. Obviously, the range of insurable property precludes an adjuster being fully informed in all fields. Yet, to bring an adjustment to a proper conclusion, the adjuster must enter into a loss investigation with better than an average knowledge of the property involved—particularly as to repair or replacement costs. Much of this knowledge is acquired by experience; a great deal of it must result from continuing study. Many adjusters become expert in particular fields, while developing a general knowledge in others. Large mercantile building losses, for example, may be adjusted by the individuals who have an extensive knowledge of materials, labor, and architecture. A large merchandise loss requires the attention of adjusters thoroughly familiar with materials, design, pricing, and many other aspects of the manufacturing, wholesaling, and retailing of such products.

An adjuster may be able to utilize the advice and counsel of an expert who has devoted a lifetime to a relatively limited field. A building contractor, cotton broker, museum director, clothing buyer, lapidary, or other specialist may be of invaluable aid in certain cases in determining and obtaining agreement on value and loss to property within the expert's specialized knowledge.

A technical knowledge of still another nature is required of the loss adjuster. He must have a knowledge of business administration and of the legal system in which business is conducted. A good understanding of accounting is important to the successful adjustment of a stock loss. Familiarity with the law of contracts is requisite to determination of insurable interest, as, for instance, in the case of a leasehold or the sale and delivery of an item by a manufacturer. An understanding of the laws having to do with estates and the passing of title on the death of a property owner is likewise important. Equally necessary is a knowledge of general business practices and those practices peculiar to specific industries.

Adjusting Skills

First and last, an adjuster must be a *fact finder*. It matters not that the insured, the local agent, the company field man, or the neighbor has his own version of what the loss is, how it came to pass, or what should be done about it. These versions are very apt to be merely opinions. The adjuster is required to establish facts, uncolored by bias. Occasionally even excellent, experienced adjusters find themselves losing sight of this fundamental.

Human nature being what it is, a mere determination of value and loss is seldom sufficient to permit bringing an adjustment to a conclusion. Generally, the adjuster must "sell" the correctness and equity of the adjustment figure. He is able to gain acceptance only if he has developed a skill in persuasiveness stemming from knowledge, genuine interest, confidence, and diplomacy. The exercise of tact and consideration calls for a positive approach to each adjustment problem, tempered, however, by patience and flexibility. There is no place for the adjuster who is arrogant or rigid in his demeanor.

Part and parcel of the skill identified as selling is the particular skill of negotiating. As the word "adjustment" connotes, it is sometimes desirable to reach an agreement where differences exist. The ability of the adjuster to negotiate successfully under such conditions calls for highly developed techniques and a better than average knowledge of practical psychology. The successful result of negotiations, of course, is the acceptance by an insured of the fact that he has been fairly treated and that his insurer performed as it had promised.

The adjuster's job is only partly done when he reaches an agreement with the insured on the amount due under the contract. There still remains the descriptive presentation to the insurer's loss manager. This presentation normally consists of two parts: the written report and the accounting exhibit. The adjuster's written report requires not only grammatical construction but the use of words and phrases that portray precisely (1) the observations of the adjuster, (2) the activities of the insured, (3) the evaluation of the risk, and (4) the nature and extent of the loss. All of this information is important for, frequently, it is of value not only to the insurer's loss manager but to the insurer's underwriting department as well. The accounting exhibit or statement of loss, as it is commonly called, reflects (1) the determination of value and loss, and (2) the application of limiting clauses in the contract. This exhibit is supported by estimates, the adjuster's own computation, and/or in some cases bills for completed repairs.

Human Relations

Probably the least understood of an adjuster's skills is the one that stems from his personal awareness of his vulnerability to criticism and that enables him to take the proper steps to turn criticism into commendation. This skill is seldom successfully taught but comes from within himself and stems from all of the character and integrity developed through inheritance and environment. A successful loss adjuster must have the *desire* to be of service to insureds and to the insurance industry.

The adjuster must see clearly the dependence placed on him, individually, to carry out the obligations assumed by his principals. This recognition is evidenced in a sympathetic, understanding approach to insureds. It is evidenced in a willingness to assist an insured beyond the bare requirements of the adjuster's position. It becomes apparent in prompt inspection of losses and cooperative actions beyond normal expectations. These attitudes must prevail even though his principal is the insurer and the adjuster has the prime responsibility to adjust losses in accordance with the spirit, if not the letter, of the contract. In other words, the adjuster must guard carefully his responsibility to the insurer, while also carrying out, sincerely, his obligation to an insured.

A feeling for people and their problems produces many rewards for the man or woman who has chosen loss adjusting as a career. In any evaluation of the total knowledge and skills that make up the qualifications of a professional adjuster, a keen insight into human relations must rate quite high.

ADJUSTING PROCEDURES

The very nature of risk and underwriting places the adjuster in a framework of restrictive "rules" established to permit control of loss payments. Some of these are within the provisions of the contracts themselves. Others have been created as a part of the normal conduct of business by an insurer as regulated by the several states.

Losses normally are reported by the insured to his local agent or broker. In some cases, a report is made directly to the company. Although the policies provide for the manner in which losses are to be reported, the usual procedure is to accept virtually any method of notification, if such advices are timely and not fraudulent. In some situations, an insured may have specific authority to report a loss directly to an adjuster.

The actions required of an insured in the event of a fire or allied lines loss are set out in detail in the policies. This wording imposes upon the insured certain obligations and responsibilities. In actual practice, however, unless unusual or suspicious circumstances exist, the adjuster assists the insured in taking the necessary steps to perfect his claim. Where he must, of course, the adjuster follows the detailed procedures set out in the contract.

The activities of an adjuster encompass a multitude of details. Whether he is staff, bureau, or self-employed, once he receives an assignment, his task is to get the facts. From the inspection of an insured's policy, the agent's "daily" or the insurer's record, the adjuster must determine the term of the policy, identify the insured and the property location, and establish the coverage purchased and the limitations of such coverage. These fundamental facts will permit the adjuster to decide on the action he will take to "adjust" the loss.

The steps taken by an adjuster will vary with the size and type of loss, its location, the insured, local customs, and circumstances. Basically, however, all adjustments involve certain steps, once coverage, identification of insured, and location of the subject of insurance have been established. Through inspection and questioning of those familiar with the property and the circumstances of the loss, the adjuster must establish the cause of the loss, the value of the property, and the loss sustained. Although simply stated, this establishment may frequently tax the skills and resources of even the most capable adjuster.

Cause of Loss

Most losses in the fire and allied lines field are the result of natural causes or negligence, both within the general scope of "first-party" coverages. Frequently, however, the specific cause is difficult to determine. The insurers must learn the specific causes, however, in order to establish rates and meaningful loss figures. It is not sufficient for the insurer's statisticians that a fire resulted from an "undetermined cause." Accordingly, the adjuster has the responsibility of seeking the precise cause: lightning, short-circuit, spontaneous ignition, a carelessly discarded match or cigarette, or other identifiable happening. Reported causes are then analyzed by the Fire Insurance Research and Actuarial Association, the National Board of Fire Underwriters, the Mutual Advisory Association, the Transportation Insurance Rating Bureau, individual insurer's statistical departments, and perhaps other organizations. The results are interpreted as a guide to loss prevention, underwriting, and rate determination.

Value and Loss

The fire and allied lines adjuster, as has been noted, must develop a broad knowledge of values, reproduction costs, and repair costs. Values vary widely on both real and personal property, and are influenced by many factors. Materials, care, location, use, market, obsolescence—these are a few of the components that an adjuster must recognize in the determination of value. In some cases, an item of personal property may be in perfect condition yet possess virtually no value. In others, as is the case with antiques, the reverse may be true. With reference to buildings and structures, depreciation and reproduction costs may be the principal measurements of value.

The insured, under the terms of his policy, has the responsibility not only of preparing his claim but also of establishing the value of his property as a means of supporting his claim. In practice, he frequently arrives at the valuation with the help of the adjuster. Thus, the adjuster must be well versed in retail prices and building costs. In unusual cases, either the insured, the adjuster, or both may ask one of the experts mentioned earlier in this chapter to assist in the determination of values. The cost of this service is assumed by the party engaging the expert.

Frequently, value and loss are necessarily determined concurrently because the loss is total. In the case of a dwelling or mercantile building completely destroyed, figures would be prepared by the adjuster or by the insured, in effect "rebuilding the structure on paper." In the case of personalty, an inventory or listing of the items would suggest the "new" cost of each item, the total of which would serve as the foundation for the "actual" value as of the date of loss. In the case of either personal property or real property, the value to be determined is influenced by depreciation, except under those coverages that provide for payment on the basis of the cost to replace.

The procedures used to fix the amount of loss depend on the circumstances of the loss and the property involved. If competent repairmen are available to bid competitively on the job, the repair of a dwelling roof may be quite simple. Where repairmen are not available, as in a remote location, the *loss,* on the basis of cost to repair, may be quite a different figure. The normal repairs to a sound structure may be less expensive than similar repairs to a dilapidated structure. Similarly, 10 square yards of exterior painting at a third floor level is considerably more expensive than is a similar job requiring no scaffolding.

Determination of loss to personalty may be simple or may require "special handling." Where merchandise is invoiced currently, the question of repairing, reconditioning, repackaging, or discounting for special sale may be readily agreed upon by the insured and the adjuster. Shopworn or obsolete merchandise, on the other hand, may require disposition through a different retail outlet. Under such conditions, the loss is the difference between the already reduced value and the net return when disposed of as salvage.

Policy Conditions

An adjustment also involves the interpretation and application of the policy provisions. The determination of insurable interest is of first importance. If no interest exists, then no loss has been sustained by the insured. If no loss has been sustained, no claim can be maintained against the insurer. The practical test, simply put, is whether the damage or destruction may result in certain monetary loss to the insured, now or in the future. This determination, however, is not always a simple matter. Not infrequently, interests of legal representatives, vendors, remaindermen, tenants, and the like are involved. Care must be taken to determine that the insured has a valid interest in the subject of insurance and the amount or extent of that interest. It is entirely possible that a particular insured has sustained no loss, even though the property involved is damaged.

Of particular importance is the provision for the protection of a mortgagee. Under the Standard Mortgage Clause, used when real property is involved, a mortgagee actually may have greater rights than the named insured. In fact, occasions arise where the adjustment must be concluded with the mortgagee and the proceeds of the adjustment made payable to him. In other situations where a loss payee clause is used, it may only be necessary to include the mortgagee's name in the loss draft. The nature of a mortgagee's interest is always important and the adjuster must take pains to determine this interest before proceeding with an adjustment.

The responsibilities of an insured, after a loss, are carefully spelled out in the policy. The contract language may appear difficult but practical compliance is extremely simple. In fact, once the loss has been reported to the insurer, an insured will make no mistake by proceeding as he would if no policy of insurance existed. The insurer merely asks that it be given the opportunity to document or verify the loss.

Provision is made in the policy for the insurer to exercise certain options. One is that the insurance company may repair or replace damaged or destroyed property. Although this option is exercised only in unusual circumstances, it gives the company the opportunity to effect repairs or replacements when such procedure may be advantageous. Much more frequently used is the option to take all or any part of personalty involved in a claim, at an agreed or appraised figure. In losses involving merchandise, exercise of this option permits the insurer to attempt to minimize its loss by means of a salvaging operation. Also, this option is particularly useful to an insurer in case of an irresolvable disagreement as to the extent of a partial loss.

Salvaging procedures are not necessarily profitable, but may present the most expeditious and equitable means of bringing an adjustment to a conclusion. Even though the adjuster and the insured might have agreed on the value of damaged merchandise, they still might have trouble in arriving at an agreed loss figure. At the sole option of the insurer (there may be no *abandonment* to the insurance company), all or part of the merchandise or other personal property may be taken over by a salvaging organization and sold. The agreed value of this property then becomes the measure of the insured's claim and the net salvage proceeds are applied to determine the net loss to the insurer.

The disposition of personalty through salvaging operations may result in a return of part of the proceeds to the insured, as well. This situation will exist where a coinsurance, reduced rate contribution, or average clause is a part of the policy and the insured has not maintained an amount of insurance sufficient to comply with the provisions of the clause. The insured, then, will share in the net proceeds of the salvage disposition, reducing the portion of the loss assumed by him by means of reduction of the gross loss.

Limiting clauses in policies are frequently misunderstood by insureds and their application presents a problem for the adjuster. The coinsurance clause is the most frequently encountered limiting clause in building and contents coverages. Application of this clause obviously requires not only an accurate determination of value and loss but also effective communication with the insured. Similarly, the apportionment clauses of the basic fire form require careful application and explanation. Here the insured is on completely unfamiliar ground and must depend on the specialized knowledge of the adjuster or on legal advice.

Unlike some health and accident policies, provision is made in the fire policy for an apportionment of the loss among all policies covering the insured's interest. When all policies are written in the same manner, each policy assumes its proportion of the loss and proofs of loss are prepared for each policy, indicating the amount of the total due under each. Such apportionment is in keeping with the concept of indemnity to the insured and with the intention of the insurer to assume only its pro rata part of a loss. The apportionment provision in the extended coverage endorsement can create problems when two or more policies are not concurrent.

The task of the adjuster to effect a proper apportionment of a loss among several insurers also may be complicated, if two or more of several policies differ with regard to location, property, or interest covered. To provide for such nonconcurrencies, an agreement of "Guiding Principles" has been developed by the insurance business and most companies subscribe to these rules.[1] As a result, differences of opinion between companies as to the amount due under each policy virtually have been eliminated. Of even greater importance, insureds are paid promptly once the loss is determined.

An important provision of the Standard Fire Policy concerns subrogation to the insurer of the insured's right to proceed against a wrongdoer who may have been responsible for the damage paid for by the insurer. It is natural for an insured to look to the insurance company for indemnity under its contract of insurance, rather than to risk bickering or litigation in trying to recover from the responsible party. Although an insurer has no objection to paying for losses covered under its policy, it should be able to obtain reimbursement from a third-party wrongdoer. The adjuster must be certain that the insured does not waive this subrogation right after a loss. The normal procedure in subrogation matters is for the insured to execute a subrogation receipt or some similar authorization form at the time the proof of loss is signed or payment is made for the loss claimed. Although completion of the form is not necessary to support the subrogation right (for it is created in the policy), the form does assist the adjuster or an attorney representing the insurer to document the right to proceed toward collection.

Because differences of opinion do exist in the adjustment of insurance claims, provisions have been made in the fire policy for the formal handling of disputes between the insured and the insurer. In the event of a disagreement, either party to the insurance contract may request that an appraisal be conducted in accordance with the steps outlined in the policy. The appraisal procedure, or "reference" as it is called in some jurisdictions, was established in an effort to prevent litigation. Frequently, it is used successfully and differences are adjusted. In some instances, however, after appraisal procedures fail to achieve the end desired, the insured may institute legal action. Fortunately, the number of losses that eventually are brought into courts constitutes only a minute fraction of 1 percent of all claims handled.

ADJUSTMENT PROBLEMS

Problems in the adjustment of fire and allied lines losses can be numerous. These may stem from the circumstances surrounding the loss, the nature of the property involved, the character of the insured, or the limitations of the particular contract of insurance.

Inspection of Loss

One of the critical elements in the adjustment of fire losses is the ability of the adjuster to reach the insured and the scene of the loss quickly. An

[1] See Appendix B.

axiom in the insurance business is that "cold ashes reveal little of value." The sooner the adjuster arrives at the scene, the more information he is likely to obtain and the more favorable will be his reception by the insured.

Although intentional losses are relatively few in number, insurers do find themselves faced with the moral hazard. Adjusters must be constantly alert to identify improper claims. Arson is a favorite means of some insureds to liquidate indebtedness or to destroy evidence of criminal acts. The insured, himself, may be responsible for arson; on the other hand, it may be the act of someone not connected with the contract of insurance. When an adjuster has reason to doubt the legitimacy of fire, he may refer the case to local authorities or to a special agent of the National Board of Fire Underwriters. As far as the insurer is concerned, an investigation of arson is necessary only in the event that the arsonist chooses to present his claim under the insurance policy. However, civil and criminal authorities usually are very alert to arson, whether or not insurance is involved.

Allied Coverages

Fire, as suggested above, is not the only peril with which the adjuster and insurer must be concerned. Windstorm, explosion, riot, water damage, glass breakage, and numerous other specific perils have become a part of the ordinary direct damage contracts. Further, many policies today provide for coverage against "all risk of physical damage," excluding only certain perils felt to be uninsurable.

As more coverages have been added to the basic fire contract, the interpretation of each peril has become more difficult. In many cases, court interpretations are still not unanimous or complete. Also, the intentions of those who prepared the documents are subject to misunderstanding by insured and insurer, alike. Numerous as these problems are, their effect is minimized as the result of adjusters' interpretation of the spirit of the insurance contract.

Catastrophes

Major fires, such as the Chicago fire of 1871 and the San Francisco fire following the earthquake of 1906, demonstrated the need for a large number of skilled and experienced adjusters. Subsequently, the Texas City explosion of 1947 demonstrated the need for carefully trained adjusting staffs and a catastrophe plan for the insurance industry. Hurricanes and tornadoes have likewise demonstrated this need.

The bureau organizations, the National Association of Independent Insurance Adjusters, and some major companies have formal catastrophe plans. With large numbers of men at their command, they are able to move staffs quickly into catastrophe areas. Once on the scene, these adjusters operate under the general procedure established and supervised by the National Board of Fire Underwriters. Through this plan, thousands of claims can be processed efficiently from temporary offices, with the use of special forms, despite difficult and confused conditions. As an example, the adjusting bureaus have trained specialists in the supervisory and clerical operations involved in these situations. Special kits of forms and supplies are constantly available for shipment by air to distant points. Specialists in fire, windstorm, and hail losses are on constant alert to respond immediately to the call for assistance from the insurance industry.

SUGGESTED READINGS

MAGEE, JOHN H., AND BICKELHAUPT, DAVID L. *General Insurance.* 7th ed. Homewood, Ill.: Richard D. Irwin, Inc., 1964. Chap. 5.

MOWBRAY, ALBERT H., AND BLANCHARD, RALPH H. *Insurance: Its Theory and Practice in the United States.* 5th ed. New York: McGraw-Hill Book Co., Inc., 1961. Chap. 29.

REED, PRENTISS B. *Adjustment of Property Losses.* 2d ed. New York: McGraw-Hill Book Co., Inc., 1953.

PART III

Marine and Aviation Insurance

Chapter 17

DEVELOPMENT OF MARINE INSURANCE

BY CARL E. McDOWELL

Marine insurance is a form of indemnity and a function of maritime commerce. Its precise nature derives from the unique and awesome forces of the sea upon which that commerce is conducted. An oceangoing venture brings together a variety of individual economic interests and exposes them in common to largely uncontrollable and unpredictable perils. All these interests are bound together aboard a ship which, when separated from land and the haven of port, must become a self-sufficient thing. In this chapter the development of marine insurance is sketchily traced from its ancient beginnings to its modern refinement.

EARLY CONCEPTS

Modern marine insurance is basically a development of two concepts of maritime trade long in use around the Mediterranean—from at least the early Middle Ages and probably even before. These concepts are "general average" and "bottomry." There are references to general average in the code of maritime law of the Rhodians formulated in about the tenth century.

General Average

The more commerce grew in the old days, the more urgently the need was felt for some system of distributing marine losses. Total loss of ship and cargo, of course, presented no problem of distribution; everyone associated with the venture bore the loss of his interest. In other marine difficulties, however, certain parts of the cargo were lost (sometimes deliberately sacrificed), while the ship and the remainder of the cargo reached port safely. In such cases the question of who would bear the loss was of critical importance. The merchant whose share of the cargo had been jettisoned—at the discretion of the master—to save the ship and the rest of the cargo was naturally reluctant to bear all of the loss himself.

The doctrine of general average arose to bring about a workable balance in loss distribution. In marine terminology, the word "average" (from French *avarie* and meaning damage done in conveying goods by sea) traditionally has meant "loss less than total." A general average therefore is a loss less than total which benefits all interests in a particular venture in the proportion which their interests were preserved. This term is distinguished from "particular average," which refers to a loss less than total that does not benefit other interests in the venture. (Particular averages are discussed in the next chapter.)

The doctrine of general average provides that when there is a necessary, voluntary, and successful sacrifice of cargo or a vessel to protect all interests involved in the venture, that loss shall be borne on a pro rata basis by all those with an interest in either the cargo or the vessel. To put the thought another way: that part of the cargo and/or the vessel that completes the voyage shall be shared by all interested parties in the same proportion as they held of the original values before the loss was sustained.

Some who write on general average suggest that this doctrine is maritime custom and applies only to marine insurance. They are correct in the sense that, to the writer's knowledge, the doctrine is not enunciated as such in other than marine insurance contracts (and the marine insurance clauses of other types of insurance contract, such as the physical damage section of the automobile insurance contract). In another sense, however, general average is simply a specific example of an element of all insurance: distribution of loss. In any case, because of the custom in early maritime trade of heavily loading ships, and the frequent necessity of jettisoning some of the cargo in order to save the ship, general average developed explicitly in the marine community.

Bottomry

As maritime trade expanded and the size of ships and cargo increased, risk increased. Extension of trade routes, sending ships into strange waters, also increased risk. Financing long and hazardous voyages involved enormous costs and the discouraging possibility that the ship and the cargo could easily become a total loss.

To meet a pressing need for a system of treating at the outset of the venture the possibility of total loss, the practice of bottomry arose. It dates back at least to the Greek societies of Athens and Corinth. The practice of bottomry appears to have been fairly extensive also in Italy. Records suggest that it existed there at the beginning of the thirteenth century. Since Italy was active commercially from at least the fifth century A.D. up to the Crusades, bottomry was probably an important custom there long before the thirteenth century.

In essence, bottomry was (and still is) a contract—in the nature of a mortgage—by which the owner of a ship (or its master or his agent) borrowed money for financing a voyage and bound the ship as security for repayment of money advanced, when and if the ship returned from a successful voyage. If the voyage was successful, interest was also paid on the loan. If, however, the vessel was lost, the loan was not repaid. The money borrowed could be used to build the ship and/or to meet the expenses of the voyage. The distinctive feature of bottomry was its high rate of interest compared to the rate prevailing in simple moneylending—a difference accounted for by the risk of total loss through failure of the ship to make the trip safely. A similar contract covering cargo rather than hull is technically known as "respondentia"; but nowadays "bottomry" is used indiscriminately for both.

One can discern the germ of marine insurance in bottomry. While a given lender was probably unable to predict his losses within useful limits, at least the incidence of the loss was shifted. Actually, the bottomry concept manifested itself in several forms. For example, the contract might stipulate that the lender turn over money to the shipowner. The shipowner might merely act as if he had received the specified sum and promise to repay it within a certain time if the ship arrived safely at its destination. If the ship did return safely, restitution, in fact, was not made. If the ship was lost, the lender, by giving damages, pretended to restore the sum lent.

Another variation of the basic idea is found in the case where the "underwriter" would buy the ship and/or cargo and it/they became his risk and responsibility. Payment of the purchase price, however, would be deferred. If the ship arrived safely, the contract would be annulled and the "insured" would retain possession and regain ownership of his ship and/or cargo. If the ship was lost, the "underwriter" would pay the contract price for the ship within a stipulated time—a price that was in reality an indemnity for the loss of the ship and/or the cargo.

EARLY MARINE INSURANCE

With the rise of these more complicated business negotiations and contracts, there also arose problems of fitting such contract interpretation into the framework of traditional Roman law and of observing the stringent provisions for suppressing usury in the laws of the Church. In face of this, the first significant document about the theory of insurance was published in Lisbon about 1562. Its title is *Tractatus de assecurationibus et sponsionibus, nunc primum luce donatus, Petro Santerna lusitano, jureconsulto clarissimo authore*—"A Most Useful and Everyday Treatise on the Assurances and Promises of Merchants, Published by the Portuguese Jurist Dr. Pedro de Santarém." Santarém's definition of the insurance contract, though far from perfect, is still timely after 400 years of further development of the theory of insurance:

About this agreement of assurance, it is usual for great dissentions among merchants to arise and grow. For this reason, we must first see whether the agreement whereby one person, having agreed with another on the price of a risk, takes upon himself that other's misfortune, is licit in the manner in which it is normally practiced. (Part 1, paragraphs 1–2)

Santarém further established with some precision two fundamental concepts of the insurance contract:

1. It should be a contract made in complete good faith.
2. It should not be the means for the insured to get rich, but simply to avoid loss.

Although Santarém mentions the existence of other forms of insurance as well, he leads readers to the conclusion that they were few and relatively unimportant in comparison to the prevailing marine insurance with which he was mainly concerned. Santarém understood that, when the ship and the goods belonged to the same person, the insurance of the ship also covered the goods (Part IV, paragraphs 62 ff.). Insurance premiums for transport on land were as a rule 50 percent less than the corresponding rate for ocean marine insurance. At this time there was little reinsurance, though there is evidence of its limited use from about 1370.

The Lombards and the Hanseatic League

The early practice of sound marine insurance is clearly identified with the cities of Lombardy in what is now northern Italy, notably Florence and Genoa. Lombard merchants and bankers were early established in England. There, from the expulsion of the Jews in about 1290 until the Lombards were forced to abandon their business because of restrictive legislation under Elizabeth I, they were virtually in control of banking business in London. Lombards also settled and established business communities in Belgium, France, and other countries. Wherever they went they practiced marine insurance as well as banking and usury.

As the Lombards were conducting thriving business in Western Europe, the Hanseatic League was established among German seaports. The Lombards and the Hansa, perhaps by informal agreement, shared European trade—the Hansa generally north of Bruges in the Netherlands (now Belgium) and the Lombards to the south.

Merchants of Hamburg and Lübeck initiated the Hanseatic League by compact in 1241. Gradually the merchants of other free cities, including Bremen, Cologne, Brunswick, and Danzig, joined, until more than 80 cities were affiliated. Their purpose was primarily to gain greater safety and privileges in trading and stronger mutual defense against foreign aggression and restriction. The powerful city of Bruges joined the League as a means of mutual defense against the piracy of the Danes, the Swedes, "and other barbarous nations surrounding the Baltic." In the Hansa laws are specific references to bottomry, though not to marine insurance.

The Hansa was also represented in London, where its merchants had a virtual monopoly of trade with the Baltic and a statutory monopoly of the export of wool, in return for which they were responsible for suppressing piracy. They too continued to trade extensively in England until the reign of Elizabeth I, during which time Sir Thomas Gresham and the Company of Merchant Adventurers with patriotic jealousy contrived to have all Hanseatic merchants expelled from England by royal decree.

To the Hanseatic merchants is due credit for laying the foundation for Britain's subsequent preeminence in overseas trade, which from the expulsion forward remained in the hands of native Britons. To the Lombards is due credit for the origin of modern banking and hull and cargo "premium insurance," that is, coverage at a fixed price paid to the underwriter.

During the fifteenth century the rival republics of Venice and Genoa took the lead in commercial adventure and monopolized trade with India until they were largely displaced by the Portuguese, who found the sea route around the Cape of Good Hope in 1497. From the fourteenth to the sixteenth centuries the most important commercial center of the then-known world was probably the Adriatic Sea, with the maritime republics of Venice and Ragusa (Dubrovnik).

Subsequently, all the maritime city-states and countries of continental Europe followed the same general pattern of establishing commercial codes and insurance practices, each within the framework of its own juridical history but all with much in common. Some countries today are quite prescriptive; others leave more freedom of choice to the insurer. All, however, aim at adequate protection of the insured through promoting and maintaining sound business practices.

MARINE INSURANCE IN ENGLAND

In England, after the expulsion of the Hanseatics and the Lombards, the marine insurance business centered initially at the Royal Exchange (founded in 1568). Later it flourished in the popular coffeehouses that were centers for independent individual underwriters. In 1601 Parliament established a court of arbitration to settle insurance disputes, but it was not mandatory and was never as popular as the regular civil court facilities available to all. Somewhat earlier an Office of Assurances had been set up. This office is credited during its hundred and some years' existence with standardizing policies and clauses at an early date and reducing the volume of litigation.

Part-Time Underwriting

The London marine insurance market is made up today of the world-renowned Lloyd's underwriters and the British insurance companies. The two groups developed almost simultaneously. Lloyd's Coffee House, however, apparently was a meeting place for those whose common interest was various aspects of shipping a few decades before the first joint-stock companies were chartered early in the eighteenth century.

Then, and even earlier, the London market was made up, as it is today, of brokers and underwriters. The underwriters accepted risks and the brokers, as agents for merchants and shipowners, arranged terms with both parties and acted as go-betweens. The broker (known as office-keeper because he was the only one in the marine insurance transaction who actually had a place devoted to insurance business) was the only participant who gave his full time to insurance. Although there may have been a few full-time underwriters in the early days of Lloyd's, underwriting for most was a sideline carried on at odd moments of a merchant's —or journalist's or civil servant's—business day in the city. According to D. E. W. Gibbs' *Lloyd's of London:*

> Daniel Defoe, first of the great English journalists, ruined himself by dabbling in marine underwriting; and (Samuel) Pepys, the Admiralty clerk, at least once kicked himself for not writing a line as he could have done on a ship which was thought to be at sea but was actually (as Pepys knew) safe in port. Instead of using his inside information he "went like an asse to Alderman Bakewell and told him of it. Now what an opportunity had I to have concealed this and seemed to have made an insurance and got £100 with the least trouble and danger in the world. This troubles me to think that I should be so over-soon."
>
> But Pepys, nevertheless, did well enough at times out of insurance, usually with the help of a city merchant. . . .[1]

Although some underwriters did attend the Exchange, insurance was probably of secondary importance to the main business of the part-time underwriter. The broker's task, therefore, was to run about the city looking for businessmen known "to dabble" in underwriting. The underwriter in turn acted as a private speculator, not the member of a managed or controlled firm. Thus, as Gibbs suggests (page 21), the reputation of the London market and the protection of the insured depended entirely on the sound judgment of the broker, the go-between. Yet there is evidence that the reputation of the market did not suffer and that there was early confidence in and use of the London market by foreign shipping.

The Bubble Act

In the boom-and-bust cycle of the South Sea Bubble incident during the second decade of the eighteenth century, marine insurance met a crisis of depression, public disfavor, and official scrutiny which at first appeared to doom the old easy-going order of writing marine coverage. During the South Sea affair the mania to speculate in stock of heavily financed public corporations (much like that of the 1920's in the United States) made the

[1] D. E. W. Gibbs, *Lloyd's of London* (London: Macmillan & Co., Ltd., 1957), p. 20.

small-time individualist method of underwriting unpopular. Numerous unchartered combines, syndicates, partnerships, and other organizations sold shares on the open market and promised to eliminate the independents. The surprising result, after the climax of the speculation, a parliamentary investigation, and some finagling in high circles, was the so-called Bubble Act. This act forbade the existence of unchartered groups, gave two newly chartered companies a charter monopoly and at the same time protected the right of any private underwriter or particular person to underwrite any policies or to lend money on bottomry ". . . as if the Act had never been made."[2]

The two new charter companies, the Royal Exchange Assurance and the London Assurance, operating under the quasi-official aegis of King George I, fared badly at first. Although they survived, they soon left about 90 percent of marine insurance to the independents and turned their attention to fire insurance. The story of how this fluid, formless, independent market, now officially recognized but in no way regulated or controlled, developed into a self-regulated and safeguarded institution is in essence the story of Lloyd's underwriters.

Walpole's Premiership

Recalled to office in the troubled year of 1720, Robert Walpole undertook a 23-year premiership in the government (the longest in British history) and with sagacious common sense presided over a period of economic development and growth that saw the emergence of the provincial manufacturing towns and great enlargement of British port capacity. The importance of the period for marine insurance in England was pronounced in several respects: (1) Walpole gave great impetus to British foreign trade; (2) the volume of marine insurance increased disproportionately by comparison; and (3) the standing and importance of Lloyd's Coffee House noticeably increased. It is not definitely known when Lloyd's became indisputably first among the several favorite coffeehouses of the London marine insurance community. By 1740, however, Lloyd's provided the best available news about the world's shipping, messages from the Admiralty and from every British port, the latest gossip from just-arrived ships, and each casualty report the minute it reached London. Each year saw Lloyd's become more a market where brokers and underwriters sought one another out early each day. In the late 1730's Lloyd's was successful in its second attempt at periodical publication of shipping news, with the first appearance of *Lloyd's List,* which is still published today.

War

The following three quarters of a century were a time of war, most of it at sea. The War of Jenkins's Ear with Spain, which involved the War of

[2] Gibbs, *op. cit.,* p. 31.

the Austrian Succession and the Seven Years' War, the war with 13 of the American colonies, and the Napoleonic Wars marked Britain's history. During these years almost every policy signed at Lloyd's included war risks, which were predominantly of three classes: (1) capture by privateer (privateers were still widely used to supplement national navies), (2) capture in convoy, and (3) seizure of cargo in formerly neutral ports. Lloyd's underwriters suffered losses from all these, but war conditions generally brought temporary increase in premiums to marine insurers. Early in the period quick profits because of wartime rates brought the speculators back for a time.

The "New Lloyd's"

In 1769, as a direct or indirect result of this new outbreak of gambling fever, Lloyd's as we know the modern institution was born. Among the speculators at Lloyd's were gamblers betting on the survival chances of prominent people who were ill—newspaper reports of which are implied to have affected those chances in some cases. The other problem was that the quality of management of the old Lloyd's had declined during the generations since the death of the astute and ambitious founder, Edward Lloyd (1648–1713). In any case, the more serious-minded customers at Lloyd's decided to set up a rival Lloyd's of their own. This break marks the end of both the old Lloyd's and the long-out-of-date, haphazard system of uncontrolled underwriting practiced there. The "New Lloyd's" (as it called itself), after spending two years in cramped quarters operating as a coffeehouse, moved again and abolished the proprietary coffeehouse basis on which Lloyd's had always operated. A governing committee was elected and a subscription set up for members. The future of Lloyd's as a self-governing body of underwriters was assured and the first steps taken toward the arrangement familiar today.

As a self-governing organization with a home of its own, the New Lloyd's prospered. The underwriters were now masters of "the Room" and could exercise some influence over the behavior of those who attended (though many came regularly who did not pay a subscription).

Lloyd's approached the Napoleonic Wars in somewhat better condition than it had approached earlier wars. Also, it had the cooperation of a considerably better-organized and augmented navy to help reduce losses. The outcome of the investigation of the Parliamentary Committee of 1810 showed (1) that Great Britain was the most important country in the world for marine insurance, (2) that London easily came first in British marine insurance, and (3) that Lloyd's underwriters had at least 90 percent of the total marine business transacted in London.

The nineteenth century saw expansion and consolidation. A constitution was adopted for Lloyd's. Stricter membership rules were established to ensure that only solvent underwriters participated. Underwriting was restricted to the Room of Lloyd's itself. In the Act of 1871 Lloyd's was finally chartered and at last became a legal entity after a century and a half of underwriting the bulk of British marine insurance.

Fire was the first non-marine line entered by Lloyd's. Since then the underwriters have extended their activities to every underwriting area except life insurance.

Other New Companies

In the meantime other marine insurance companies had been established in London after the Marine Insurance Act of 1824 repealed the charter monopoly of the Royal Exchange and the London Assurances. In the ensuing 50 years at least 70 new companies entered the field in London and Liverpool. During the same half century, passage of the Joint Stock Companies Acts tended to transfer ownership of ships and merchandise from private hands to those of shareholders, for whose greater protection company directors sought wider cover (and smaller losses) than the great merchant princes of earlier times had considered satisfactory.

In face of these changes and in view of the fact that traditional policy clauses were not always applicable to the new steamships being insured and used to carry insured cargo, the London underwriting community met at Lloyd's in 1883. They met ". . . to consider the details and phraseology of certain Clauses usually inserted in the Policies of Marine Insurance with a view to the general adoption of an established wording for these clauses . . ." (as quoted in the Introduction to the 1963 edition of *Institute Time Clauses—Hulls*). A number of Lloyd's clauses were adopted for general use a few months later. These standard clauses, revised from time to time, are still in use as Institute Time Clauses—Hulls, the recommendation but not the requirement of the Institute of London Underwriters for its members.

Lloyd's underwriters and "the companies," most of which are members of either the Institute of London Underwriters or the Liverpool Underwriters' Association, are independent of one another but together form one market. Until the present century, except as concerns Lloyd's agents and shipping news, the two groups had little to do with each other. In recent years, however, they have come closer together, and they now cooperate in many matters of common concern (such as in joint committees on hull considerations, cargo, construction, atomic energy, and so on).

MARINE INSURANCE IN THE UNITED STATES

Although there was limited private underwriting in American colonial ports, there was no substantial marine insurance in what became the United States until the formation in Philadelphia of the first American company in 1792—the Insurance Company of North America. Before this time the upper limit that could be covered in the United States was about $25,000. Even that amount would have to be spread among most of the local underwriters. The history of early American marine insurance companies is of necessity closely interwoven with the early history of the Republic. During the early decades following achievement of independence, an undeclared war with France, and British harassment of American shipping that led to the War of 1812, threatened the freedom of the seas that was necessary to the life and prosperity of the new nation. The country to some extent was dependent on its merchant marine, which in turn relied on the new American marine insurance market. True independence therefore was not achieved until the end of the War of 1812.

With the advent of the clipper ships toward the middle of the nineteenth century, many insurance companies were formed, among them the Atlantic Mutual. Not all insurance enterprises in the nineteenth century were stock or mutual companies. Several Lloyd's-type associations existed for a while, but eventually new companies of this kind were prohibited by law.

Decline of the Merchant Marine

The story of marine insurance in the first century of American history, particularly the second half of that century, is one of struggle for recognition at home and of great competition from the British market. It was not always recognized in the government that marine insurance or, for that matter, a merchant marine, was necessary for national prosperity. British marine underwriters, by a series of arbitrary classifications for insuring purposes, made British vessels more attractive to shippers. These and other competitive measures were effective and contributed significantly to the decline of the American merchant marine from the ascendancy of clipper-ship days to the point reached in the 1890's at which time the United States had practically no merchant marine. In 1807 more than 90 percent of American foreign commerce was carried in American vessels; by 1910 less than 10 percent was so carried. The entire 1914 American tonnage, less than a million gross tons, would have been inadequate for the first wave of a single World War II amphibious landing. The Civil War tonnage of 2,296,894 gross tons was not again equaled until the war shipping program surpassed it toward the end of the First World War.

Slow Growth of Marine Insurance

From the end of the Spanish-American War to the First World War the American marine insurance industry increased slowly until there were about 30 American companies doing some marine business by 1914. With the advent of World War I, the need for American ships and marine insurance became apparent. Congress recognized the need for ships and encouraged extensive shipbuilding. American merchant marine tonnage doubled from 1914 to 1916, then soon redoubled. The increase from 1914 to 1920 was tenfold. The value of cargo also doubled and redoubled to more than $12 billion in 1920—an astronomical figure in that day. Bankers were generally unwilling to accept insurance certificates from belligerent countries. Although much of the new business went to Scandinavian, Spanish, and other neutral-country insurance companies, the increasing demand for marine coverage encouraged and necessitated marked expansion of the American marine insurance market. Many American fire insurance companies entered the field, often in association with established companies or in joint operation with an experienced independent underwriter. Some of these companies are participants in the American Hull Insurance Syndicate today.

Emergence of Syndicates

Various exchanges, syndicates, joint underwriting agreements, and other risk-treating arrangements were developed in the period of expansion immediately before and during World War I. The Cotton Exchange was formed in 1909 as a direct result of a single cotton-cargo loss of $1,250,000. Such associations were not merely the result of the fact that many inexperienced companies were entering the marine field or that increased capacity was necessary. These associations were required because of the demands of shipowners and shippers for new and increased coverage—demands that had to be satisfied by the American market if it was to meet foreign competition.

Congressional Encouragement

By 1916 Congress was aware of the pressing need for an adequate American marine insurance market. Indeed Congress at this time seemed to acquire a whole new concept of the position of the United States in world commerce and world affairs. It directed the United States Shipping Board to ascertain ". . . what steps may be necessary to develop an ample marine insurance system as an aid to the development of an American merchant marine" (Shipping Act of 1916, Section 12).

The 66th Congress studied the whole question of the expansion and strengthening of the American merchant marine. As part of this study, both the Senate Committee on Commerce and a subcommittee of the House Committee on Merchant Marine and Fisheries held very extensive hearings (400 pages in print) devoted exclusively to marine insurance. The express purpose was to find a way to encourage and build the American marine insurance market as an adjunct of the American merchant marine and as an aid to increased foreign trade. The House subcommittee also included with the record of the hearings certain "Recommendations of the Subcommittee" which were approved by the full committee on February 26, 1920.

As a result of these extensive studies and hearings, the Edmond Bill (H.R. 13839) was passed and became Section 29 of the Merchant Marine Act of 1920. The basic reason for the enactment of Section 29 was an affirmative one: a desire manifest in legislative history and economic development to create a strong American marine insurance market as an effective instrument for supporting an enlarged merchant marine and increased foreign trade. As stated in the House subcommittee "Recommendations":

> All evidence leads to the conclusion that a strong and independent national marine insurance institution is an absolute necessity to a nation's foreign trade equipment, that such an institution does not exist in the United States today, and that it is imperative to adopt ways and means to correct the present impossible situation if this country is to meet the strenuous international rivalry that the new era is certain to inaugurate. There can be no doubt . . . that marine insurance will be used, as probably never before, as a national commercial weapon for the acquisition and development of foreign markets. Failure to act now in strengthening our marine insurance facilities and placing them in an independent position free from foreign control, cannot be regarded otherwise than as the neglect of a duty and an opportunity.

The American Hull Insurance Syndicate

With Congressional encouragement, the American Hull Insurance Syndicate initiated operations on July 21, 1920, with an underwriting capacity for any one hull of about $2½ million, as compared with a maximum of about $500,000 per hull previously available in the American market. Since then the Syndicate has written the bulk of ocean-going hull insurance placed in the American market. There are at the time of this writing 84 participating companies. The total insurance written by the Syndicate rose from $50 million in 1921 to $200 million in 1939. By 1957 this total had increased to approximately $1¼ billion, some 25 times the 1921 amount. A recent statistical study indicates that in 1962 the total was in excess of $2 billion and has probably grown somewhat since that date.

What little hull insurance was written in the American market before the enactment of Section 29 was largely reinsured abroad. Today the risks assumed by the Hull Syndicate are retained by its subscribers. The underwriting capacity of the Syndicate has been increased to more than $10 million for any one vessel.

The capacity of the American market is substantially increased by the writings of American companies which operate independently of the Syndicate so that all but a handful of the world's largest ships can be wholly insured in the American market. By the outbreak of World

War II, the American marine insurance market was a healthy one, able to cope with the tremendous problems created by the war.

Continued Growth

In recent years Congress has not treated the marine insurance industry as a stepchild—as it did between the Civil War and World War II. The 79th Congress, in the Merchant Ship Sales Act of 1946, declared that an American marine insurance market was necessary for the national security and for the development and maintenance of the foreign commerce of the United States. Again, the House Committee on Merchant Marine and Fisheries of the 81st Congress said (H.R. 220): ". . . the Congress has several times in the past forcefully stated its position with regard to fostering the growth of the American marine insurance market."

Since the end of World War II, the American marine insurance industry has continued its gradual growth both in the absolute sense and relatively. The American market has made progress in the face of keen competition which has seen insurance rates on both hull and cargo gradually reduced to the lowest point in the history of commerce. One hundred and fifty years ago the rate of hull insurance on a single voyage to the West Indies was as high as 30 percent of the amount of insurance. Today the average rate on hull insurance written by the American Hull Syndicate on a one-year policy is approximately 1.6 percent. Based on an analysis of a number of risks selected at random by the Federal Trade Commission, the insurance rates on overseas cargo are on an average less than half what they were in 1947. One can conclude that American shipowners, exporters, and importers receive more insurance protection for lower cost than ever before.

NUCLEAR ENERGY

A major development in marine insurance in the twentieth century—as in almost every area of human existence and endeavor—is the ability to control the release of nuclear energy and the offering of radioisotopes and other radioactive products for transportation and insurance coverage. Shippers and insurers have been confronted with a distinctly new set of commodities and new risks. The market was at first hard-pressed to comprehend and cope with what has become known as "nuclear liability." It was able to handle with less difficulty the simpler problems of physical damage to nuclear cargo because former experience provided a more useful precedent for the physical damage than for liability. Scientific development in nucleonics temporarily outstripped the development of commercial capacity and readiness to transport, handle, insure, and otherwise service commerce in nuclear products.

In response to the needs of the private business concerns entering the nuclear-energy field under contract with the U.S. Atomic Energy Commission, and to the interest shown by the A.E.C., American companies joined in organizing the so-called nuclear insurance "pools." Since 1957 they have undertaken among themselves to insure the great new risks. This arrangement is simply an extension of the basic risk-reducing concept underlying all insurance. It is a further extension of the pattern illustrated by the association of private underwriters that became Lloyd's of London, and again illustrated in the association of American marine insurance companies as members of the American Hull Syndicate. Pool coverage, developed at first to meet the needs of inland transportation in the United States, has now been extended to provide adequate third-party liability coverage for ocean transport of nuclear materials. Many member companies of the American Institute of Marine Underwriters are in prominent participation in these new combines, to the extent that just before 1960 they provided 62 percent of the cover of the contributions of one of the two major nuclear pools. (The American Institute of Marine Underwriters is the national trade association of the industry, representing over 150 insurance companies. It engages in technical and promotional work in all areas of interest to its members, including forms, clauses, average adjustment, casualties, cargo loss, prevention, and legislation. These two pools together provide protection against legal liability of up to $60 million on any one policy.)

DEVELOPMENTS IN INTERNATIONAL MARINE INSURANCE

The accompanying graph (Figure 17–1) shows the increase in international marine insurance premiums for 25 years in three major marine insurance markets: (1) the British market, both Lloyd's and the British companies; (2) Switzerland; and (3) the United States. (The figures represent national currencies.) While the period during and after World War II in great part was characterized by inflation, in general the rising premium volume outstrips the rate of inflation and reflects the great expansion of world trade in the 1950's and the opening years of the 1960's.

The total ocean marine premium figure for 1963, hull and cargo combined, was $246 million—$15 million more than 1960 and more than twice as large as the 1941 volume of $118.7 million. The U.S. premium volume of inland marine insurance in 1963 was $425 million—more than $44 million greater than the 1960 total and close to seven times the 1949 figures of $64.4 million.

The U.S. merchant marine fleet as of July, 1963, totaled about 23,133,000 gross tons, excluding ships of less than 1,000 gross tons each. The world total at the same date was about 145,863,000 gross tons.

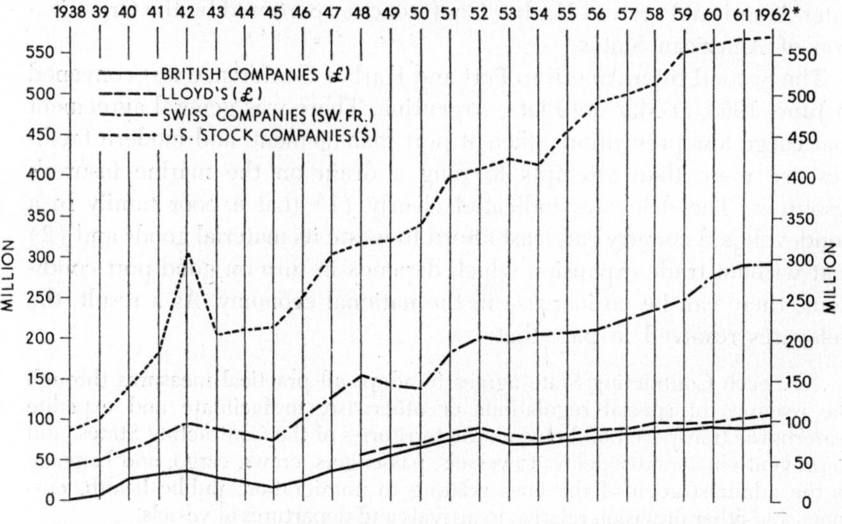

FIG. 17–1. International marine insurance premiums, 1938–1962 (in respective national currencies).

* The figures for 1962 are based on estimates.

SOURCE: Charles Zwonicek, "The Development of Marine Insurance During and After World War II," *International Insurance Monitor* (September, 1963), pp. 253–54.

NEW PROBLEMS

New problems which marine insurance must now meet and solve are numerous. Adequate hull and cargo insurance must be provided for shippers and carriers using nuclear-powered transports like the *N.S. Savannah.* Hydrofoil and "hovercraft" transports are on the drawing boards, and their nontransport counterparts are being successfully tested throughout the world. Handling of liquid cargo is rapidly being automated. New and strange liquid cargoes are being experimented with and transported, particularly flammable gases like liquefied natural gas and petroleum gas, which must be carried at their boiling points many degrees below zero. In fact, the whole area of technological change in the use of specialized ships—tankers and others—and the automation of the handling of dangerous cargo are of immediate concern to the marine insurer.

Probably even more important than nuclear and other technological advance is the narrowing gap between premiums permissible in face of today's intense international competition and the annual loss data of the various national markets. The marine insurer has of necessity had to concern himself more and more with (1) port improvement to facilitate both faster and safer handling of cargo and (2) the complicated field of cargo loss prevention so as to reduce preventable losses due to carelessness and/or willful pilferage. These have been primary areas of concern to the International Union of Marine Insurance and the (to date) two

Inter-American Port and Harbor Conferences, sponsored by the Organization of American States.

The Second Inter-American Port and Harbor Conference was convened in June, 1963, at Mar del Plata, Argentina. There was general agreement that cargo loss prevention, efficient port management, and modern facilities are more than attempts to plug a drain on the marine insurer's resources. The delegates indicated clearly (1) that a poor family in a nondeveloped country can least afford to waste its material goods and (2) that without trade expansion which depends in turn on good port conditions, there can be no increase in the national economy. As a result, the delegates resolved in part that:

> . . . each Contracting State agrees to adopt all practical measures through the issuance of special regulations or otherwise, to facilitate and expedite waterborne transportation between the territories of the Contracting States, and to prevent unnecessary delays to vessels, passengers, crews, cargo, and baggage in the administration of the laws relating to immigration, public health, customs, and other provision relative to arrivals and departures of vessels.

These measures include achieving some degree of uniformity of shipping and banking documents and standard port practices necessary to promote efficient international exchange of goods and services.

It is well known from experience that delays in clearing vessels by port authorities contribute as much to theft and pilferage as does poor law enforcement. And such practices as a punitive tax by Customs authorities on importers who wish to inspect their goods in the customs area must be corrected. Every marine insurance market is therefore intensely interested in combatting the rising crime rate throughout the world with responsible law enforcement, adequate port facilities and port management, and effective cargo loss prevention in general.

SUGGESTED READINGS

AMERICAN INSTITUTE OF MARINE UNDERWRITERS. *Exporter's Guide to Cargo Insurance.* New York: no date.

DOVER, VICTOR. *A Handbook to Marine Insurance.* 6th ed. London: H. F. & G. Witherby, Ltd., 1962.

GIBBS, D. E. W. *Lloyd's of London: Study in Individualism.* London: Macmillan & Co., Ltd., 1957.

INSURANCE INSTITUTE OF LONDON, HISTORIC RECORDS WORKING PARTY. *Institute Time Clauses—Hulls.* Report H. R. 3. London: 1963.

"Nuclear Risk in Ocean Transport and Its Insurability," *International Insurance Monitor* (1962). These were papers read at the Forum on Ocean Transport of Radioactive Materials, January 23, 1962.

SANTARÉM, PEDRO DE. *Tractatus de assecurationibus et sponsionibus.* Lisbon: Gremio dos Seguradores, 1961.

A photo reprint of an early edition, with Portuguese, English, and French translations.

STEFANI, GIUSEPPE, (ed.). *Insurance in Venice from the Origins to the End of the Serenissima.* Trieste: Assicurazioni Generali di Trieste e Venezia, 1958. Vols. I and II.

WINTER, WILLIAM D. *Marine Insurance.* 3d ed. New York: McGraw-Hill Book Co., Inc., 1952. Chap. 1.

ZWONICEK, CHARLES. "The Development of Marine Insurance During and After World War II," *International Insurance Monitor* (September, 1963), pp. 253–54.

Chapter 18

CONCEPTS ASSOCIATED WITH MARINE INSURANCE

BY ROBERT R. DWELLY

Certain concepts in marine insurance are fundamental to sound underwriting because of the nature of the hazards and the relationship among the parties. Many of these concepts are present in other types of insurance but have special significance in marine insurance. Others are peculiar to this type of insurance. Several of these concepts are described in detail in this chapter. They are: utmost good faith; warranties and related provisions; particular average; memorandum clauses, franchises, and deductibles; valuation; and double insurance.

UTMOST GOOD FAITH

Good faith is basic to all commercial contracts but in no other field has the doctrine of "uberrimae fidei" attained the degree of importance that it has in marine insurance. It is the very foundation of the business and the obligation of compliance rests equally on the three parties involved—the insured, the broker, and the insurer. The 1906 Marine Insurance Act of England is very precise in its provision. Section 17 of the Act reads as follows:

> A contract of marine insurance is a contract based upon the utmost good faith, and, if the utmost good faith be not observed by either party, the contract may be avoided by the other party.

The insured and his broker are obligated to disclose to the underwriter all of the facts concerning the risk being negotiated. Section 18(1) of the Act stipulates:

> Subject to the provisions of this Section, the assured must disclose to the insurer, before the contract is concluded, every material circumstance which is known to the assured, and the assured is deemed to know every circumstance which, in the ordinary course of business, ought to be known by him. If the assured fails to make such disclosure, the insurer *may*[1] avoid the contract.

[1] Emphasis provided.

Two important legal decisions (both English) are illustrative. Lord Mansfield in *Carter* v. *Boehm* (1765) said:

Insurance is a contract upon speculation. The special facts upon which the contingent change is to be computed lie most commonly in the knowledge of the assured only; the underwriter trusts to his representation, and proceeds upon confidence that he does not keep back any circumstance in his knowledge to mislead the underwriter into the belief that the circumstance does not exist, and to induce him to estimate the risk as if it did not exist. The keeping back such circumstance is a fraud, and therefore the policy is void. Although the suppression should happen through mistake without any fraudulent intention, yet still the underwriter has been deceived, and the policy is void because the risk run is really different from the risk understood and intended to be run at the time of the agreement. The policy would equally be void against the underwriter if he concealed anything within his own knowledge as, for example, if he insured a ship on a voyage, and he privately knew that she had already arrived, and in such circumstances he would be liable to return the premium paid. Good faith forbids either party, by concealing what he privately knows, to draw the other party into a bargain owing to his ignorance of that fact, and his believing the contrary.

Material circumstances or material facts, as they are more generally called, are such facts as will influence the insurer in his judgment of the risk that is being negotiated. The insurer's judgment may take various directions such as: determination of whether he will write the risk offered, determination of policy coverages and determination of the rate to be charged. In the event a denial of liability is made by the insurer on the grounds of nondisclosure it becomes a question of fact.

In the case of "The Bedouin," Lord Esher said:

The assured is not bound to tell the insurer what the law is. He is bound to tell him, not every fact, but every material fact. His obligation is this, that if he is asked a question—whether a material fact or not—by the underwriters, he must answer it truly. If he answers it falsely with intent to deceive, though it may not be a material fact, it will vitiate the policy.[2]

Not only is the insured bound to disclose every material fact known to him, he is also charged with the obligation of disclosing all material facts which in the course of his business ought to be known by him. If, through ignorance or neglect, he does not know any material fact, he will be assumed to have known it; and its nondisclosure will render the contract voidable. On the other hand, information concerning a fact (or facts) which does (do) not affect the risk need not be disclosed to the insurer. Neither need information which would diminish the risk be disclosed. In this latter regard, however, it is hard to imagine a situation when an insured or his broker would not disclose such information having in mind its possible beneficial effect on the rate to be quoted or the policy conditions to be named.

[2] 7 Aspinall, *Reports of Maritime Cases* 391.

As to the insurer, he is charged with knowing matters of general knowledge and being well informed about trade usages and customs, route, port conditions (for example, whether goods are loaded and/or discharged by lighters), stowage, packing, and the peculiarities of a particular cargo (for example, tea being susceptible to taint from other cargo of certain types). However, in this day and age of constant change and high degree of specialization, an insurer is well advised not only to keep himself as well informed as possible but also to be certain to ask for any and all information he may need to evaluate the risk. It must be kept in mind that the insured and his broker need not disclose every minute detail. As Frederick Templeman and C. T. Greenacre say in their authoritative work on marine insurance, "If sufficient is disclosed with regard to a material fact to enable an underwriter (insurer) to ask for futher information, if he wants, that is enough."[3] In the absence of the necessary degree of inquisitiveness on the part of the insurer he will be deemed to have waived the information insofar as that particular material fact is concerned.

WARRANTIES: IMPLIED AND EXPRESS

The subject of warranties is introduced in Chapter 4. Here it is applied specifically to marine insurance.

Implied

Certain implied warranties are an integral part of every marine insurance contract and have the force of law. They are as follows:

Legality. The adventure insured must be a lawful one. If the contracting parties are of the same nationality and subject to the same laws there is no question as to what is lawful. The insurer may not waive the implied warranty of legality for the obvious reason that granting insurance against the operation of a law of the land would be against public policy. Neither may an insurer waive the implied warranty of legality imposed by the laws of his country for the benefit of a foreign national. However, the insured and his insurer are not bound by the laws of a government foreign to each of them, and they may enter into a contract in respect to an adventure (risk) that may be in violation of the laws of such foreign government.

Seaworthiness. This is the most important of the implied warranties. The 1906 Marine Insurance Act of England, Section 39(4) states, "A ship is deemed to be seaworthy when she is reasonably fit in all respects to encounter the ordinary perils of the seas of the adventure insured." There is no implied warranty that the cargo be seaworthy but the Act does

[3] *Marine Insurance; Its Principles and Practices* (London: MacDonald and Evans, 1934) p. 20.

provide that at the commencement of the voyage the ship be not only seaworthy as a ship but also that she be reasonably fit to carry the cargo insured to the destination named in the policy.[4]

Should the voyage consist of different stages which require that she be further prepared or equipped for one or more of such stages, the implied warranty is applicable to each such stage and the ship must be "portworthy," "seaworthy," or "riverworthy" as necessary. As an example, a ship is insured for a voyage "at and from New York to Manaos, Brazil, and for 30 days after arrival." She must be "portworthy" at New York and after arrival at Manaos; "seaworthy" for the ocean voyage; and "riverworthy" for the Amazon.

There is no implied warranty of seaworthiness under English law in respect of vessels insured under "Time or Term" policies; but if, with the knowledge of the insured, the vessel be sent to sea in an unseaworthy condition, the insurer would not be liable for a loss due to unseaworthiness. Under American law, however, the weight of authority is to the effect that there is an implied warranty of seaworthiness in time-hull policies if the vessel is in port when the insurance attaches, and a continuing obligation on the part of the insured to use due diligence to maintain her in seaworthy condition during the term insured. Breach of warranty will void the insurance, but breach of the continuing obligation will merely excuse the underwriter from any loss arising therefrom.[5]

William D. Winter says:

> In England this principle (as to seaworthiness) is settled, but in this country there are exceptions to the general rule. However, it is generally required in this country that, when a vessel in an unseaworthy condition arrives at any point where repairs can be made or equipment or supplies obtained, the assured must there use diligence to make the vessel seaworthy. This exception to the general rule with respect to seaworthiness is made because in many cases, in the placing of hull insurance, especially when whole fleets are placed at one time from a named date, many of the vessels are at sea when the insurance attaches, so that, at that time, there would be no possibility of the owner's knowing the condition of his vessel. The facts upon which an implied warranty of seaworthiness would depend, in such cases, might not be provable.[6]

In the early days of overseas commerce it was not unusual for the owner of the carrying vessel and of the cargo carried to be the same. There was no justification for him to be relieved of the obligations imposed by the implied warranty of seaworthiness. As overseas trade be-

[4] The terms "hull," "cargo," and "freight" have technical meanings which are described in Chapters 19 and 20. Loosely, they mean respectively the ship, the goods carried, and the money paid for the transportation of the goods.

[5] For an excellent discussion of American authorities see Russell T. Mount, "SS Natalie Arbitration" (*American Maritime Cases,* 1959), pp. 2379–90.

[6] *Marine Insurance* (3rd ed.; New York: McGraw-Hill Book Co., Inc., 1952), pp. 217–18.

came more complex, however, and goods of numerous insureds were carried in a vessel the actual condition of which they knew practically nothing beyond the information contained in a Classification Register, it became the practice—it is now general—for insurers to include in cargo policies a Seaworthiness Admitted Clause. An example of such a clause reads:

> The seaworthiness of the vessel as between the Assured and these Assurers is hereby admitted.

This waiver on the part of the insurer results in his being precluded from raising the question of unseaworthiness with his insured insofar as a loss from a peril insured against under the cargo policy is concerned. Upon payment of the loss, however, he is subrogated to all rights of the insured against the ship and its owner(s).

The admission of seaworthiness in a cargo policy does not serve to relieve the vessel owner of his obligation to provide a seaworthy vessel nor of his liabilities under the Carriage of Goods by Sea Act or Harter Act. Hugh A. Mullins, in his *Marine Insurance Digest*, states in addition to other points:

> The seaworthiness demanded by the warranty is seaworthiness in fact and though the shipowner may have done all he thought was necessary to make his ship fully sound and in all respects well found for the voyage, the warranty would nonetheless be breached if he failed to discover some defect that impaired the vessel's seaworthiness.[7]

In the different jurisdictions of this country there is no unanimity of opinion as to the application of this implied warranty.

Additional Implied Warranties. These are (1) prompt attachment of risk and (2) no deviation from the voyage agreed upon.

1. *Prompt attachment of risk:* Unless advised to the contrary at the time the insurance is negotiated, the insurer expects that the risk will attach within a reasonable time. If the delay in attachment is unreasonable to the extent of changing the risk contemplated, the insurer is, by law, released from the contract. However, the insurer may not wish to stand on his legal rights and, in consideration of an additional premium, can agree to continue on the insurance. An example follows:

> An insurer—say in September—names terms and conditions (which are accepted) for insuring a vessel from Halifax to Liverpool. He is justified in expecting the vessel to sail in the immediate future. In fact, she does not sail until early December and therefore what was contemplated as a summer sailing becomes a winter one. The risk is substantially different and must needs be compensated for by an additional premium.

Necessarily, what is reasonable or unreasonable is in each case a question of fact.

---

[7] (Cambridge, Maryland: Cornell Maritime Press, 1951), p. 228.

2. *No deviation:* This implied warranty is applicable to voyage policies—both hull and cargo. There is a deviation when, after attachment of the risk, the customary and understood route for the voyage to the destination named in the policy is departed from. Should there be a *change* of destination from that named in the policy, there is then what is known as "change of voyage." This point is referred to later in this chapter. A voluntary deviation, without lawful excuse, gives the insurer the right to avoid the insurance from the time the deviation takes place. The reason is that a deviation changes the risk from that which was agreed upon and the insurer may no longer be bound under the contract. This avoidance is possible, even should the deviation reduce the risk from that agreed upon. There must be an actual deviation. A contemplated deviation does not void the insurance. As already mentioned, the deviation must be voluntary and is excusable in the following circumstances:

a) If necessary for the safety of the vessel or the subject matter insured.
b) To save life.
c) Where caused by circumstances beyond the control of the master and his employer.
d) To comply with a warranty, express or implied.
e) To obtain medical assistance for a person on board the vessel.
f) If caused by the barratrous conduct of the master or crew, if barratry be a peril insured against.

After the cause excusing the deviation is over, the vessel must resume her course and prosecute the voyage with reasonable dispatch. In present day cargo policies a deviation clause is always included and it is broad in the protection afforded the insured. A typical one reads as follows:

> This insurance shall not be vitiated by any unintentional error in description of vessel, voyage or interest, or by deviation, overcarriage, change of voyage, transhipment or any other interruption of the ordinary course of transit, from causes beyond the control of the Assured. It is agreed, however, that any such error, deviation or other occurrence mentioned above shall be reported to this Company as soon as known to the Assured, and additional premium paid if required.

It will be noticed that the clause makes reference to "change of voyage." There is a change of voyage when, after the attachment of the insurance, the destination of the vessel is voluntarily changed from the destination named in the policy. In the absence of the deviation clause the insurer is discharged from liability under the policy from the moment it was decided to change the destination of the ship and the fact that a loss occurs before the vessel may have left its original course has no bearing on the matter. Likewise, in the case of unjustifiable deviation and in the absence of the deviation clause, the fact that the vessel may have regained her route before any loss occurs is unimportant.

Express Warranties

Express warranties are embodied in the contract. They are included in the basic policy, included by endorsement to the policy, or incorporated into the policy by specific reference to some other document. The Marine Insurance Act (1906) of England, Section 33 stipulates that an express (sometimes called a promissory) warranty means:

> . . . a warranty by which the assured undertakes that some particular thing shall or shall not be done, or that some condition shall be fulfilled, or whereby he affirms or negatives the existence of a particular state of facts.

It is basic to the contract that a warranty (whether express or implied) must be exactly complied with and it is of no consequence whether it be material to the risk or not. In the absence of a "Breach of Warranty," "Deviation," or "Held Covered" clause the insurance is void from the date of the breach. Up to the time and date of the breach the policy is enforceable in respect of any loss covered thereunder. Express warranties must be literally complied with. It is not essential that the word "warranted" be used. A statement of fact past, present, or future, written or incorporated by reference in the policy, is equally binding. Examples of effective expressed warranties without the use of the word "warranted" include:

1. "Subject to survey and approval by the United States Salvage Association."
2. "American Ship Jupiter."
3. "Packed in wooden cases."
4. "No other insurance carried."
5. "To sail on or before 8/26/65."

In the author's opinion, however, in this day of liberal court decisions insurers should use the word "warranted" when their intent is that the statement be construed as a warranty. As for examples where the word "warranted" is used, the list is well nigh inexhaustible. "Trading Warranties" are the most general. It would be a rare instance in this day and age for an insurer to issue a time policy on a vessel without navigation limits which take the form of warranties. On oceangoing vessels the American Institute Trade Warranties are in common use.

There are other so-called expressed warranties in the basic contract which are not strictly "warranties." These are the "Free of Capture and Seizure Warranty"; the "Strikes, Riots and Civil Commotions Warranty"; the "Free of Particular Average Warranty." Mullins refers to them as "Exceptive Warranties" and describes them as warranties that exclude from the policy certain losses or causes of loss. It might be better draftsmanship if, instead of "warranted," the following wording were used:

> This policy does not cover any claim for loss, damage or expense caused by or resulting from . . .

whatever the perils or contingency may be that the insurer wishes to exclude.

PARTICULAR AVERAGE

The word "average"—whether it be related to "general" or "particular"—means partial loss. (See Chapter 17 for a discussion of general average.) A particular average is a partial loss (i.e., less than total) fortuitously caused by a maritime peril, which has to be borne by the party upon whom it falls. It is held by some authorities that the term "particular average loss" is redundant. However valid this assertion may be, this term is in common use today and applies only to damage by an insured peril to the subject matter insured. Expenses incurred for the purpose of preserving the subject matter insured (e.g., the vessel) are known as "particular charges" and are recoverable under the Sue and Labor Clause of the policy if incurred by the insured for the defense, safeguard, or recovery of the property in jeopardy as a result of a peril insured against. This recovery is in contradistinction to a general average expenditure.

Assume the case of a vessel carrying a cargo of sugar with freight payable at destination. Suppose that during the voyage she meets with heavy weather to such an extent that (1) her hull is badly damaged when a hatch cover is stove in, and (2) sea water enters the hold as a result of which (3) some of the sugar partially dissolves. Particular average damage thus is sustained by all three interests and under the customary insuring conditions applicable to each interest the respective insurers would have to respond. In the case of the ship the measure of indemnity is the cost of repairing the damage caused by the heavy weather—always, however, subject to the particular average conditions of the hull policy. (See later section on memorandum clauses, deductibles, and franchises.) Particular average losses under a hull policy are payable irrespective of whether or not the vessel is fully insured for her market value. There is no coinsurance aspect in a hull policy. The value given in the policy merely serves to establish the limit recoverable in respect to any one particular average loss.

Particular average losses on cargo (including freight) are usually paid as follows: There is on arrival at destination a comparison of the gross damaged value of the cargo—in this case sugar—as determined in the open market, with the gross sound value. The percentage difference represents the depreciation which is applied to the insured value of the cargo. Settlement is made for the amount so established except as affected by the franchise or deductible. There is added to this amount whatever expenses may have been incurred in the settlement of the loss. The same percentage of depreciation is applied to the insured value of freight payable at destination, if it has been insured by the same cargo owner. However, if the vessel owner has insured the freight, his claim would be for the actual amount of the freight lost, which might not be the same percentage of depreciation as for the cargo.

In a cargo policy there *is* the aspect of coinsurance. If the amount insured in the sugar example is less than the gross sound value of the sugar, the insured himself assumes the loss in proportion to the difference. On the other hand, in the absence of gross overvaluation amounting to fraud, if the insured value of the sugar is more than its gross sound value, he will collect proportionately more than his actual loss. An example of a valuation clause in a cargo policy is:

> Valued, premium included, at amount of invoice, including all charges in the invoice and including prepaid and/or advanced and/or guaranteed freight, if any, plus ______ percent. (The percentage on exports is usually 10 percent.)

In all valued policies—hull, cargo, and freight—short of an unwarrantably high value amounting to fraud, the insured and the insurer are bound by the value set forth in the policy.

MEMORANDUM CLAUSES, FRANCHISES, AND DEDUCTIBLES

Numerous devices have been used by marine insurers to relate the insurance to hazards of particular trades and to exclude payment for all or part of particular averages. These include memorandum clauses, franchises, and deductibles.

Memorandum Clauses

The memorandum clause—now largely outdated—became part of the Lloyd's S. G. Policy in 1749 and it is still a part of this contract. It reads as follows:

> N.B.—Corn, fish, salt, fruit, flour and seed are warranted free from average, unless general, or the ship be stranded—sugar, tobacco, hemp, flax, hides and skins are warranted free from average, under five pounds percent; and all other goods, also the ship and freight, are warranted free from average, under three pounds percent, unless general, or the ship be stranded.

Obviously, the adoption of the memorandum was an attempt on the part of insurers to express clearly their liabilities. It became evident, through the years, by reason of the numerous legal actions that followed, that the clause was not as clear as its drafters had intended.

The word "average" in the phrase "average unless general" refers, of course, to particular average. The word "stranded" has been interpreted by the courts so as to exclude a mere "touch and go." There must be a definite interruption of the vessel's progress. Two English cases illustrate this point. In one case a vessel remained aground for 90 seconds; in the other for 15 minutes. The first was not a stranding; the second was. Some of the commodities listed have also been subject to judicial interpretaion, the overall result being that they are to be understood in their ordinary commercial and mercantile sense.

With the development of marine insurance in America an extended memorandum came into use in this country. Winter quotes a typical memorandum clause as follows:

> Memorandum. It is also agreed that bar, bundle, rod, hoop and sheet iron, wire of all kinds, tin plates, steel, madder, sumac, wicker-ware and willow (manufactured or otherwise), salt, grain of all kinds, tobacco, Indian meal, fruits (whether preserved or otherwise), cheese, dry fish, hay, vegetables and roots, rags, hempen yarn, bags, cotton bagging, and other articles used for bags or bagging, pleasure carriages, household furniture, skins and hides, musical instruments, looking-glasses, and all other articles that are perishable in their own nature, are warranted by the assured free from average, unless general; hemp, tobacco stems, matting and cassia, except in boxes, free from average under twenty percent unless general; and sugar, flax, flaxseed and bread, are warranted by the assured free from average under seven percent unless general; and coffee in bags or bulk, pepper in bags or bulk, and rice, free from average under ten percent unless general.
>
> Warranted by the insured free from damage or injury, from dampness, change of flavor, or being spotted, discolored, musty or mouldy, except caused by actual contact of sea water with the articles damaged, occasioned by sea perils. In case of partial loss by sea damage to dry goods, cutlery or other hardware, the loss shall be ascertained by a separation and sale of the portion only of the contents of the packages so damaged, and not otherwise; and the same practice shall obtain as to all other merchandise as far as practicable. Not liable for leakage on molasses or other liquids, unless occasioned by stranding or collision with another vessel.[8]

Comparison of the American clause with the Lloyd's clause shows that the American clause excludes from particular average coverage many more commodities than does the Lloyd's clause. In the case of those commodities subject to a named percentage, there is no recovery under the terms of either memorandum quoted, unless the particular average damage amounts to, or exceeds, the named percentage of the insured value. When it does, the insurer pays the full amount and the percentages named do not operate as "deductibles."

F.P.A. Clauses. Coincident with the growth of overseas commerce and the need of merchants to obtain as broad a coverage as possible, the use of the memorandum, per se, has become outdated. The marine contract now contains some version of the F.P.A. (free of particular average) Clause. There are two basic clauses covering F.P.A. conditions. The one in more general use is known as the F.P.A.E.C. Clause. "E.C." stands for "English Conditions." The other is the F.P.A.A.C. Clause, "A.C." meaning "American Conditions." Basically, the former is the broader. Both cover general average losses but exclude particular average losses in the absence of certain contingencies.

---

[8] Winter, *op. cit.*, p. 218.

In the F.P.A.E.C. particular average losses are excluded ". . . *unless* the vessel or craft be stranded, sunk or burnt." It is sufficient to "open the warranty" if, at any time during the voyage (and this includes lighterage to and from the overseas vessel) there be a stranding or a sinking or the vessel be burnt. The opening of the warranty from the causes named renders the insurer liable for particular average damage to the cargo insured, irrespective of percentage, and there need not be any causal connection with the stranding, sinking, or burning.

The F.P.A.A.C. (American conditions) is more logical but, at the same time, more restrictive. To be covered, the particular average damage must be *caused by* the perils named. Strict interpretation of the perils "stranded, sunk or burnt" was somewhat limiting in effect, so that modern F.P.A. Clauses (other than A.C.) now contain additional wording which extends the coverage and which reads as follows:

> . . . but not withstanding this warranty these Assurers are to pay any loss of or damage to the interest insured which may reasonably be attributed to fire, collision, or contact of the vessel and/or craft and/or conveyance with any external substance (ice included) other than water, or to discharge of cargo at port of distress.

Under this extension, a fire damaging the cargo but *not* damaging (burning) the ship in any way would be recoverable. Such would not be the case in the absence of this added provision.

With Average Conditions. Another variation in limiting particular average coverage is found in "With Average Conditions" clauses. A typical one reads:

> Free of Average under 3% unless general or the vessel be stranded, sunk, burnt, on fire or in collision with any substance (ice included) other than water each package separately insured.

The difference between basic F.P.A. conditions and "with average" conditions should be kept in mind. With the former, there is no partial loss coverage afforded unless the warranty is "opened" by one of the named perils (E.C. Clause), or the partial loss is *caused* by one of the named perils (A.C. Clause); whereas under "with average" conditions coverage is afforded against the basic marine perils insured against in the policy if amounting to the specified percentage. For example, under F.P.A. conditions—either A.C. or E.C.—heavy weather damage would not be covered but under "with average" conditions it would be covered subject to its reaching the stipulated percentage.

Institute Cargo Clauses. With the development of overseas trade and the demand by importers and exporters for broader coverage than that provided by basic F.P.A. terms or "with average" terms, insurers—American and English—adopted "Institute Cargo Clauses." Such clauses are merely recommended, they are not mandatory. In England there are both "Institute Cargo Clauses (F.P.A.)" and "Institute Cargo Clauses (W.A.)."

Their adoption was an independent attempt on the part of the underwriters in the respective markets to compose clauses that would satisfy the requirements of importers and exporters and, at the same time, would bring about a certain degree of uniformity and do away with the many differing versions of clauses trying to accomplish the same purpose. The "Institute" in the title of the clause comes from "The Institute of London Underwriters" in England and "The American Institute of Marine Underwriters" in this country. In this country there is but one set of clauses, "American Institute Cargo Clauses." These are F.P.A. conditions but the clauses are readily adaptable to "with average" conditions as necessary.

The English Institute F.P.A. Clause reads:

> Warranted free from Particular Average unless the vessel or craft be stranded, sunk, or burnt, but notwithstanding this warranty the Underwriters are to pay the insured value of any package or packages which may be totally lost in loading, transhipment or discharge, also for any loss of or damage to the interest insured which may reasonably be attributed to fire, explosion, collision or contact of the vessel and/or craft and/or conveyance with any external substance (ice included) other than water, or to discharge of cargo at a port of distress, also to pay special charges for landing, warehousing, and forwarding if incurred at an intermediate port of call or refuge, for which Underwriters would be liable under the standard form of English Marine Policy with the Institute Cargo Clauses (W.A.) attached. This Clause shall operate during the whole period covered by the policy.

The American Institute Cargo Clauses (see Appendix C) read in part:

> Warranted free from Particular Average unless the vessel or craft be stranded, sunk, or burnt, but notwithstanding this warranty these Assurers are to pay any loss of or damage to the interest insured which may reasonably be attributed to fire, collision or contact of the vessel and/or craft and/or conveyance with any extermal substance (ice included) other than water, or to discharge of cargo at port of distress. The foregoing warranty, however, shall not apply where broader terms of Average are provided for hereon or in the certificate or policy to which these clauses are attached.
>
> Notwithstanding any average warranty contained herein, these Assurers agree to pay any landing, warehousing, forwarding and special charges for which this policy in the absence of such warranty would be liable. Also to pay the insured value of any package or packages which may be totally lost in loading, transhipment or discharge.
>
> Where this insurance by its terms covers while on docks, wharves or elsewhere on shore, and/or during land transportation, it shall include the risks of collision, derailment, overturning or other accident to the conveyance, fire, lightning, sprinkler leakage, cyclones, hurricanes, earthquakes, floods (meaning the rising of navigable waters), and/or collapse of subsidence of docks or warves, even though the insurance be otherwise F.P.A.

Franchise

In American and English marine insurance practice, "franchise" refers to a criterion, usually expressed as a percentage of the value of the subject matter insured, which, in terms of damage from a peril insured against, when reached, renders the insurer liable for the *full* amount of the damage. For example, if the loss is under 3 percent, none of it is payable. If it is 3 percent or more, all of it is payable.

In determining the percentage, before the days of "average irrespective of percentage," the insurer would name the percentage to be applied. He would base the percentage on his idea of the susceptibility of the goods to damage as well as their likelihood, at the end of the voyage, to show an inevitable deterioration or diminution quite apart from the intervention of a marine peril. This arrangement also had the effect of avoiding nuisance and petty claims.

As ships increased in size and goods increased in quantities, it became the practice to apply the franchise percentage to the insured value of a named portion of the whole, say, to each 10 cases, each 25 bales, or each 50 bundles. These arbitrary subdivisions are known as "series" and are on the basis of "running landing numbers." That is, the subdivision quantity is made up in the order the cases, bales, or whatever are discharged from the hold of the vessel. This numbering is to prevent selection against the insurer.

The adoption of the "series" concept is to benefit the insured. Should it work out that he could have recovered more of the damage sustained if he had not been on a "series" basis, then he is entitled to ignore the "series" and claim "on the whole." A precept of marine insurance is that a clause intended to benefit the insured may not work to his disadvantage.

The basic American Hull Form, that is, the American Institute Time (Hulls), is a "franchise" one, it being:

> . . . free from Particular Average under 3 percent, or unless amounting to $4850 but nevertheless when the vessel shall have been stranded, sunk, on fire, or in collision with any other Ship or Vessel, Underwriters shall pay the damage occasioned thereby, and the expense of sighting the bottom after stranding shall be paid, if reasonably incurred, even if no damage be found.

Should the application of the 3 percent result in a sum larger than $4,850, the latter figure applies. If the resultant 3 percent is less than $4,850, the lesser figure applies. It is the practice today to show separate values for the "Hull, tackle, apparel . . ." and the "Boilers, machinery, refrigerating machinery and insulation. . . ." The franchise may be applied to the hull value alone, insofar as claims for hull damage go; to the machinery value alone, in the case of machinery damage claims; or to the total value of hull and machinery, whichever is most advantageous to the insured. The application of the particular average franchise is "to each voyage as if separately insured," and the voyage clause in the American Hull Form defines several bases considered to be a voyage, thus allowing the insured some latitude in selecting the one suiting him best.

Deductibles

Deductible average conditions are seldom applied to cargo policies; they are more common in the field of hull insurance. The concept is simple: where damage is caused by a peril insured against, except in the case of a total loss and/or constructive total loss, which would be payable in full, there is no claim under the policy unless the damage exceeds a stated amount, in which event the excess of the amount is payable. The following is quoted from the American Institute Time (Hulls) Deductible Average Clause (July, 1960):

> Anything herein to the contrary notwithstanding, this insurance is warranted free from all claims of whatsoever nature (including claims under the sue and labor clause and claims under the collision clause) unless the accident results in a total loss and/or constructive total loss of the Vessel (in which case this clause shall not apply) or unless the aggregate of such claims arising out of each separate accident exceeds the sum of $________, in which case this insurance shall be liable only for the amount by which such aggregate exceeds said sum; but a recovery from other interests and/or parties shall not operate to exclude claims under this insurance provided the aggregate of such claims arising out of one separate accident if unreduced by such recovery amounts to said sum. For the purpose of this clause each accident shall be treated separately, but it is agreed (a) that a sequence of damages arising from the same accident shall be treated as due to that accident, and (b) that all heavy weather damage which occurs during a single sea passage between two ports shall be treated as though due to one accident.

This clause is added to the American Institute Time (Hulls) Form by endorsement. Certain amendments have to be made to that form to ensure there is no conflict with the average terms contained therein. These necessary amendments are automatically contained in the Institute endorsement embodying the Deductible Average Clause.

Deductible Franchise

As the term suggests, this provision is a combination of the "deductible" and "franchise" clauses. It is seldom, if ever, applied to cargo policies and only occasionally is it applied to hull policies and then generally to miscellaneous or small craft risks. Since there is no institute clause, whatever clause is used must be drafted to meet the requirements of the insurer. A simple wording might read:

> Notwithstanding anything contained to the contrary in the American Institute Time (Hulls) Clauses to which this endorsement is attached, this insurance is warranted free from Particular Average under 5 percent and from the aggregate amounts of any particular average claim payable hereunder there shall be deducted the sum of $2500.

VALUATION

A marine insurance policy is a contract of indemnity. A policy may be either valued or unvalued. The latter is seldom met with nowadays in marine insurance; but, as the term suggests, it is a policy where the value of the subject matter insured is not stated and is left to be subsequently determined. (Such unvalued or "actual cash value" settlement is routine in fire insurance.) Liability under the policy is, of course, subject to the limit of the sum insured.

A valued policy on the other hand is one that states the value as agreed between the insured and the insurer. A good guide or basis for ascertaining the measure of insurable value is clearly expressed in the English Marine Insurance Act (1906). Section 16 of the Act provides as follows:

> 16. Subject to any express provision or valuation in the policy, the insurable value of the subject-matter insured must be ascertained as follows:—
>
> (1) In insurance on ship, the insurable value is the value, at the commencement of the risk, of the ship, including her outfit, provisions and stores for the officers and crew, money advanced for seamen's wages, and other disbursements (if any) incurred to make the ship fit for the voyage or adventure contemplated by the policy, plus the charges of insurance upon the whole: The insurable value, in the case of a steamship, includes also the machinery, boilers, and coals and engine stores if owned by the assured, and, in the case of a ship engaged in a special trade, the ordinary fittings requisite for that trade;
>
> (2) In insurance on freight, whether paid in advance or otherwise, the insurable value is the gross amount of the freight at the risk of the assured, plus the charges of insurance:
>
> (3) In insurance on goods or merchandise, the insurable value is the prime cost of the property insured, plus the expenses of and incidental to shipping and the charges of insurance upon the whole:
>
> (4) In insurance on any other subject-matter, the insurable value is the amount at the risk of the assured when the policy attaches, plus the charges of insurance.

Of course, the foregoing may be varied by mutual agreement between the parties, hence the proviso: "Subject to any express provision or valuation in the policy."

In the case of freight it would seem that, should the vessel be a total loss very early on the voyage, the insured would be over-indemnified because of expenses at ports of call and destination which were not incurred due to the total loss of ship and cargo. Again, in the case of cargo, the legal basis of valuation as expressed in the Act does not seem adequate inasmuch as there is no provision for any anticipated profit. In present-day cargo policies it is the practice to make provision for anticipated profit.

If the valuation expressed in the policy, be it for hull, cargo, or freight, is one agreed by the parties in good faith, it cannot be questioned. It is binding, unless some portion of the value was not at the risk of the insured at the time of the loss. Mullins, in his *Marine Insurance Digest,* gives a good example of this point. He says:

> Suppose a shipment proceeding from the interior to New York and thence to Europe, with steamer freight to be payable on loading at New York and sup-

pose the shipment to be insured on a valuation made up of the invoice cost in the interior, the railroad charges and the steamer freight to Europe, with possibly an addition for profit. If the shipment became a total loss before it reached New York and so before the steamer freight was paid, the agreed valuation might be opened on the ground that the steamer freight was not at risk. If the agreed valuation contemplated a whole cargo (shipment) and the loss occurred when only part of the cargo (shipment) was at risk the agreed valuation might be opened.[9]

In the settlement of a particular average claim under a valued policy on cargo, after the measure (percentage) of loss has been determined in accordance with established practice, the percentage of loss is applied to the value insured and the insurer responds accordingly. Consequently, as in the "Particular Average" section, if the insured is somewhat over-insured he benefits and, conversely, if he is under-insured he is a coinsurer for the difference. This same basis applies to insurances on freight. It is incumbent upon the insurer to be sure that the insured value for hull, cargo, and freight is adequate and in line with current market conditions.

Apart from the measure of indemnity, the insured value is important in ascertaining a constructive total loss (C.T.L.). Under all three types of policy—hull, cargo, and freight—the insured value in present day practice is used in determining whether or not there is a constructive total loss. Consequently, if the insured value is too low, what would otherwise be a serious particular average claim may, through the mathematics of the situation become a claim for a "C.T.L." Such settlement, of course, is subject to proper tender of notice of abandonment by the insured to the insurer.

DOUBLE INSURANCE

When two or more insurances are (1) arranged on the same interest—hull, cargo, or freight—and (2) on behalf of the same insured and (3) the total of the insurances affected exceeds the insured value of the interest insured, there is said to be double insurance. Insurances on the same interest, or subject matter, by different persons having different insurable interests do not constitute double insurance. A mortgagor may insure the property for its full value and the mortgagee may insure for the amount of his mortgage. In the event of a loss there would necessarily have to be an adjustment between the parties so that there would not be an "over-indemnification" of either party.

American cargo policies today invariably contain clauses covering the situation in event there should be double insurance. They read as follows:

a) If an interest insured hereunder is covered by other insurance which attached prior to the coverage provided by this Policy, then this Company shall be liable only for the amount in excess of such prior insurance; the Com-

---

[9] Mullins, *op. cit.*, p. 264.

pany to return to the Assured premium equivalent to the cost of the prior insurance at this Company's rates.

b) If an interest insured hereunder is covered by other insurance which attached subsequent to the coverage provided by this Policy, then this Company shall nevertheless pay to the full extent of its liability under this insurance without right to claim contribution from the subsequent Insurors.

c) Other insurance upon the property of same attaching date as the coverage provided by this Policy shall be deemed simultaneous, and this Company will be liable only for a ratable contribution to the loss or damage in proportion to the amount for which this Company would otherwise be liable under this Policy, and will return to the Assured an amount of premium proportionate to such reduction of liability.

In the absence of any provision in the policy, where there is double insurance on the same interest, attaching at the same time and against the same risks, the insured may collect from either insurer for the full amount of the policy and the insurer who pays the loss will have a right against the other insurer for his proportion. The insured may not collect from both insurers for the full vlaue of each policy.

The English treatment of double insurance differs from the American. The English Marine Insurance Act (1906) sets forth their doctrine in Section 80, which reads:

80. (1) Where the assured is over-insured by double insurance, each insurer is bound, as between himself and the other insurers, to contribute rateably to the loss in proportion to the amount for which he is liable under his contract.

(2) If any insurer pays more than his proportion of the loss, he is entitled to maintain an action for contribution against the other insurers, and is entitled to the like remedies as a surety who has paid more than his proportion of the debt.

In practice, few cases of double insurance occur and, when one does, it is generally in connection with cargo. It is only when there is some misunderstanding for the responsibility of placing the insurance that it is likely to happen. Should both the buyer and the seller place insurance, a mutually satisfactory basis of cancellation will generally be reached between the party who did not have the responsibility and his insurer. Generally, the terms of the contract of sale will determine the responsibility. Necessarily, appropriate return of premium will be made.

SUGGESTED READINGS

MOUNT, RUSSELL T. "SS *Natalie Arbitration*" (A.M.C. 1959), pp. 2379–90.

MULLINS, HUGH A. *Marine Insurance Digest*. Cambridge, Md.: Cornell Maritime Press, 1951.

PHILLIPS, WILLARD. *Law of Insurance*. 5th ed. New York: Hurd and Houghton, 1867.

TEMPLEMAN, FREDERICK, AND GREENACRE, C. T. *Marine Insurance; Its Principles and Practice*. London: MacDonald and Evans, 1934.

WINTER, WILLIAM D. *Marine Insurance*. 3d ed. New York: McGraw-Hill Book Co., Inc., 1952.

Chapter 19

TYPES OF MARINE INSURANCE

BY GEORGE M. MARSHALL, JR.

A widely accepted definition of marine insurance incorporated in the English Marine Insurance Act of 1906 is as follows:

> A contract of marine insurance is a contract whereby the insurer undertakes to indemnify the assured, in manner and to the extent thereby agreed, against marine losses, that is to say, the losses incident to marine adventure.

The purpose of a marine insurance policy, therefore, is to indemnify for loss or damage sustained by an insured interested in a marine adventure. While no standardized marine policies are prescribed by law, there are "more or less" standard marine policies in general use in the principal marine insurance markets of the world. These are often modified by the incorporation of specially drawn clauses to meet the particular requirements of the individual insured. It is not difficult, however, to understand the strong tendency toward uniformity in the writing of marine insurance policies in light of the international character of the business and the need for underwriters to handle their risks through the medium of reinsurance.

CLASSIFICATIONS OF MARINE INSURANCE

In the early days of marine insurance both the cargo and the carrying vessel were frequently of the same ownership. Accordingly, the early types of marine insurance policies were written to provide insurance protection on these interests jointly. Subsequently, a separation of cargo-owning and ship-owning interests took place, giving rise to two broad classifications of marine insurance: cargo insurance and vessel insurance. Shipowners evolved into carriers of cargoes and passengers. Marine insurance contracts were developed and refined to provide specifically for shipowners' needs. Similarly, marine insurance contracts applicable to cargo were written to meet the specialized needs of merchants interested in the buying and selling of goods in foreign trade. (In a larger sense these contracts apply to the transportation of goods and/or merchandise by water in both foreign and domestic trades.) In the case of ship-owning interests, a further refinement of marine policies led to the classifications of hull, protection and indemnity, and freight insurances. Within these broad classifications, other types of policies were developed based upon the characteristics of status, type, use, and valuation of a vessel.

CARGO INSURANCE

The Insured

The owner who ships his goods by water for his own account, as in the case of interplant shipments, has an obvious insurable interest and no difficulty in obtaining protection under a valid marine insurance policy. Frequently, however, more than one party is interested in a shipment of goods while in transit from origin to destination. During this period of time, title (or the risk of loss or damage) often changes hands one or more times. The insured at any particular time may be the seller (consignor or exporter) or the buyer (consignee or importer) who may in turn, in some trades, sell the goods while still in transit to another buyer. The parties to a contract of sale of goods are usually free to arrange insurance protection directly with the underwriters using the services of an insurance agent or broker or indirectly by giving instructions to insure to freight forwarders, custom house brokers, combination export managers, or other specialized middlemen. These middlemen provide numerous other services in addition to the arrangement of insurance protection.

Assignment

One of the distinguishing features of a marine policy on goods is that the protection it affords is freely assignable without notice to the underwriter. Assignment is usually accomplished by endorsement of special policies of insurance issued by the seller-insured acting with authority of the underwriter. Assignment has the effect of transferring the rights to the insurance protection to the holder of the documents of title.

Types of Cargo Policies

Several types of cargo policies are in use. Common types are described in this section.

Open Policies. Most cargo insurance is arranged under the open or floating type of cargo policy which is designed to meet the requirements of an insured having a reasonable frequency of shipments year in and year out. It provides automatically, without special notice to the underwriter, insurance protection on all shipments made by or to the insured named in the open policy in which that insured has an insurable interest.

The open policy is customarily written to cover shipments made by iron or steel steamers or motor vessels, aircraft, mail and parcel post, including connecting conveyances such as railroad cars, trucks, lighters, and other types of harbor watercraft. It is occasionally extended to cover shipments by other types of vessels, for instance, ocean going barges. The geographical scope of the open policy varies considerably. It can be written to cover shipments made between ports throughout the world. It can be restricted to a specific trade such as between ports and/or places on the Atlantic coast of the United States of America or on the Great Lakes.

The open or floating policy is a continuous contract usually subject to a 30-day notice of cancellation by either the insured or insurer. No premium charge is made for the issuance of an open policy. Premiums are earned only as and when shipments coming within its terms are actually made. The insured is required to report such shipments to the underwriter as soon as practicable. These reports or declarations are used by the underwriters and insurance agents or brokers for various record purposes including the preparation of premium bills which are usually rendered monthly.

Special Policies. In the case of an exporter (an insured selling to an overseas customer) the usual open policy authorizes the insured to issue his own special policies of insurance covering individual shipments. These special policies of insurance are printed and supplied by the insurer and completed by typewritten wording by the insured. The special policies are usually issued in sets of original, duplicate, and as many copies as required. The pertinent details of the shipment are described in the special policy and include the amount of insurance, description of the voyage, description of the goods, the name and description of the conveyance, and the marks and numbers applicable to the shipment. The original and duplicate special policies are countersigned and endorsed by the insured to transfer the rights of the insurance protection to the holder of the documents of title. They become part of the commercial set of documents sent to the buyer. Two copies of each set of special policies are usually sent to the insurance agent or broker who in turn sends one copy to the underwriter as a "declaration" under the open policy.

The special policy is issued in accordance with the terms and conditions of the open policy. It is a complete insurance document in itself, however, containing all of the terms necessary to the transfer of insurance protection to the buyer of the shipment without reference to the open policy in the event of claim. This instrument makes it possible for an overseas settling agent of the insurer to provide on-the-spot claim-adjusting service.

Certificates. In many cases a self-contained instrument such as a special policy is not necessary to meet the requirements of the parties to a contract of sale of goods or a financing bank. Under these conditions it is sometimes the practice, particularly in certain import or domestic trades, for the open policy insured to issue certificates of insurance. This instrument certifies that insurance protection is provided under an existing open or floating policy covering for account of whom it may concern. (The special policies, themselves, are often referred to as certificates, but, technically they are not.)

Declarations. It is the general practice to include extra additional copies in the sets of special policies and certificates to be used as declarations (reports) of shipments (insured under the open policy) to the insurer. If an insured does not require special policies or certificates of insurance, it is customary to report shipments coming within the terms of the open policy on various types of declaration forms supplied by the insurer for this purpose.

Term Policies. Occasionally, cargo insurance is arranged under a term policy providing protection for a period of one year but this method of arranging cargo insurance is not common in the United States. A term policy sometimes provides highly specialized types of cargo insurance such as carriers' (vessel operators') legal liability to cargo where the policy may run concurrently with term policies insuring the vessels used to carry the cargo.

Trip Policies. A trip risk policy is used to cover an individual shipment for an insured who only occasionally requires marine insurance protection. Under these conditions, the volume of trade or frequency of shipments does not make it practical to arrange the open or floating type of policy. Coverage and rates applicable to each shipment insured under a trip risk policy are negotiated on a risk-by-risk basis.

Other Classifications. Numerous other types of cargo policies (and clauses within policies) have been developed to meet specific needs of sellers and buyers of certain commodities such as green coffee, rubber, flour, refrigerated cargoes, grain, coal, timber, various kinds of oils in bulk, and raw sugar. Space does not permit a review of these specialized types. Within the scope of this chapter it is sufficient merely to mention their existence.

Important Features of a Cargo Policy

In this section several features of cargo insurance policies are described.

Valuation. Cargo policies are invariably of the valued type. The insured and insurer agree on the value of the goods, usually by means of a valuation clause or formula. The application of the clause or formula develops an amount of insurance on which the premium charges are based and the losses adjusted. The purpose of the valuation clause is to develop a fair value for purposes of insurance, that is to say, to place the insured in more or less the same financial position as he would have been had no loss taken place on his goods.

The usual valuation formula includes the cost of the goods at point of manufacture, packing costs, inland and ocean transportation costs, a variety of shipping services, and documentation costs incurred prior to loading on board of the overseas vessel. The total of these items is frequently increased by a percentage of advance, usually 10 percent, to arrive at the amount to be insured which is roughly equivalent to the market value of the goods at destination.

In certain import commodity trades (such as green coffee beans, rubber, burlap, pepper, and others) it is customary to provide insurance on the basis of the highest market value attained during the voyage but usually for not less than a basic amount determined by a fixed value type of clause such as that described above. The changing value of goods due to expenses incurred and market fluctuations while in transit between origin and destination indicates the need for clarity in the wording of the valuation clause to meet the requirements of an individual assured.

Limits of Insurance. The open or floating type of cargo policy specifies maximum dollar limits of insurance on the basis of the type of conveyance or mode of transportation. Separate limits of insurance are named for "on deck" and "under deck" steamer shipments, aircraft shipments, and mail or parcel post, the latter often on a per package basis. The usual open policy contains an accumulation clause providing additional protection in the event there is an accumulation of values at risk in excess of the policy limits due to circumstances beyond the insured's control but for not more than twice the applicable policy limit of insurance.

Duty Insurance. Unless specially exempted, all goods imported into the United States are subject to payment of duty (an importation tax) by the importer. Machinery is available to obtain allowances or refunds of duty for shortages of or damage to imported goods. Unfortunately, the complicated duty allowance and refund rules and procedures do not afford complete protection to the importer. Furthermore, duty becomes fully at the risk of the importer when the goods enter the country. The importer insured can arrange a separate insurance under a standard endorsement designed to cover the increased value of the goods consequent upon payment of duty. The limits of insurance specified in an open policy are applied separately to amounts of duty.

Basic Marine Perils. The cargo policy contains a basic marine perils clause providing coverage against losses arising from "perils of the seas" and losses caused by certain named "perils on the seas" such as fire, barratry, jettison, and assailing thieves. The words "perils of the seas" have been interpreted by numerous court decisions to include losses caused by stranding of the carrying vessel, heavy weather, and collision of the carrying vessel with another vessel. The clause is broadened by the words ". . . and all other perils, losses and misfortunes. . . ." These words are interpreted as providing coverage against risks of the same nature as those specifically named in the preceding part of the clause.

Institute Cargo Clauses. Superimposed on the basic marine perils clause are the Standard American Institute Cargo Clauses adding the perils of explosion; total loss of a shipping package in loading, transhipment or discharge; bursting of boilers; breakage of shafts; latent defect in the machinery, hull, or appurtenances of the carrying vessel; and faults or errors in the navigation or management of the vessel by the master, mariners, mates, engineers, or pilots.[1] While the goods are in transit on shore, most cargo policies provide protection against the risks of collision, derailment, overturning, or other accident to the conveyance, fire, lightning, sprinkler leakage, cyclones, hurricanes, earthquakes, floods (meaning the rising of navigable waters), and/or collapse or subsidence of docks or wharves. (See Appendix C.)

Extended Perils. In addition to the foregoing perils incorporated in the printed part of the policy, certain named perils are sometimes added by additional clauses or endorsement. These include: theft, pilferage and/or nondelivery, loss or damage caused by actual contact of the insured goods with fresh water and/or water (commonly known as ship's sweat) condensed from atmospheric moisture upon the structure of the vessel and/or with other cargo and/or with fuel oil. The ultimate in protection is achieved by incorporating an "all risk" type of clause in the policy which provides protection against physical loss or damage from any external cause.

Perils Excluded. Losses arising from delay, loss of market, inherent vice, war, strikes, riots, and civil commotions are excluded from the usual marine cargo policies, including those issued on an "all risk" basis.

Strikes, Riots, and Civil Commotions. Coverage against the risks of strikes, riots, and civil commotions can be included in the open policy by a standard endorsement but is usually subject to a 48-hour notice of cancellation. It should be noted, however, that such cancellation does not apply to goods already at risk at the time cancellation becomes effective.

War Risks. Coverage against war risks can be obtained under a "war risk only" open policy subject to a 48-hour notice of cancellation and to certain other restrictions concerning the duration and continuance of coverage. These features distinguish it from the marine cargo policy. The

---

[1] These clauses were drafted by the Forms and Clauses Committee of the American Institute of Marine Underwriters and are generally accepted by members of the American Institute of Marine Underwriters as standard clauses for incorporation in ocean cargo policies. These clauses represent an effort to introduce some measure of uniformity in the cargo policy. Uniformity facilitates the conduct of business both with respect to underwriting and claim matters and is a great convenience to brokers, insureds, insurers, and reinsurers alike. Bankers readily accept the incorporation of institute clauses on policies by reference. This acceptance greatly simplifies policies and reduces their size. Incidentally, there are also London Institute Cargo Clauses drafted by the Technical and Clauses Committee of the London Institute of Marine Underwriters. They are widely used in the London market. Other markets also have their standard clauses for purposes of uniformity and convenience. See Chapter 18 for further discussion of these clauses.

war risk policy is a separate, independent, and standard policy. In the United States the contract generally used is that approved by the American Institute of Marine Underwriters. One of the more important distinguishing features is that war risk protection is provided only while the goods are waterborne with the exception of a brief period of time while goods are on shore at a port of transhipment. Shipments by air and/or mail, however, are insured against war risks on a "door to door" basis.

Losses Insured Against. After establishing that a loss has been proximately caused by a peril insured against, it is then necessary to determine the extent to which the loss is recoverable. With respect to physical loss of or damage to the insured goods, losses recoverable under the policy may be total (for the full amount insured) or partial (for an amount less than the total amount of insurance on a shipment). The range of protection extends from so-called "free of particular average" (excluding partial losses) or "with average" to "all risk" protection.

Under the "free of particular average" (F.P.A.) type of average clause, the underwriter responds for all total losses due to perils insured against but only those partial losses caused by perils specifically named in that clause, usually only those partial losses caused by stranding, sinking, burning, or collision of the carrying vessel.

Under the "with average" (W.A.) type of clause both total losses and partial losses are recoverable. The principal difference between the F.P.A. and W.A. clauses is that partial losses caused by heavy weather are recoverable under the latter type of clause. Partial loss protection, however, is often subject to a franchise or a percentage of the insured value which must be exceeded before the full amount of the claim as adjusted is recoverable.

Under the "all risk" type of clause partial and total losses are recoverable in full except in some few cases where deductibles are used to eliminate so-called trade or inevitable shortages or breakage losses. The amount of the deductible specified in the clause is deducted from the amount of the claim as adjusted to accomplish this result. This practice is in line with the primary purpose of insurance which is to provide protection against fortuitous or unexpected losses.

In addition to providing coverage against physical loss of or damage to the insured goods due to a peril insured against, the insurer also responds for certain types of expenses incurred to minimize loss or damage due to an insured peril. These expenses are discussed below under the headings of general average contributions, salvage awards, and sue and labor expenses.

General Average Contributions. When an insured ships goods by water he becomes a party to a maritime venture, hence subject to obligations imposed on him under general maritime law. Under the contract of carriage (bill of lading) he is required to contribute to losses sustained or expenses incurred for the benefit of all interests, namely hull, cargo, and freight. This type of loss or expense is known as general average. Specifically, a general average occurs when a voluntary sacrifice is made of a portion of ship or cargo or an expense is voluntarily and successfully incurred for the sole purpose of preserving both the ship and its cargo from an impending maritime danger. The expense of towing a ship to a port of refuge, for example, would be apportioned among the saved interests, namely ship, cargo, and freight. These interests would be required to contribute, in proportion to the values saved in each case, to the expense of towage. Goods damaged by water used to extinguish a fire at sea is an excellent example of a general average sacrifice. The owner of the water damaged cargo is reimbursed by contributions obtained from the saved interests as a result of the general average act. A contributing cargo owner can recover his share of the total general average contribution under his marine cargo policy, provided the contributory value of his cargo is not in excess of insured value. When this contributory value is in excess of the insured value, the insured recovers in the proportion which the insured value bears to the contributory value.

Salvage Awards. Under certain conditions, a cargo insured may be required to contribute to an award to a salvor of his cargo. Salvage charges, therefore, are rewards recoverable under the general maritime law by a salvor for saving property at sea such as removing a vessel and its cargo from a strand. An insured who owns cargo and who is required to contribute to the award can recover this expense under the terms of his marine cargo policy.

Most salvage situations are, however, a matter of contract between the salvor and the owners of the vessel acting in behalf of all interests in peril at sea. In such cases salvage awards come within the scope of general average, being treated as expenses voluntarily incurred for the benefit of all interests.

Sue and Labor Expenses. A marine policy contains a "sue and labor" clause which requires an insured to act in the preservation of his goods from loss or damage as if he had no insurance protection. Expenses incurred to lessen loss or damage due to an insured peril are recoverable under the policy up to the limit of insurance in addition to a claim for actual physical loss of or damage to the goods. The principal obligation of the insured under the "sue and labor" clause under present-day conditions is to preserve the underwriter's right of subrogation against third parties who may be held liable for the loss or damage.

Duration of Coverage. The actual points of attachment and termination of marine insurance coverage are usually determined by the contract of sale. The principal function of a marine cargo policy is to provide insurance protection while the goods are in the ordinary course of transit. Marine extension clauses, made a part of the open marine policy in most trades, have the effect of providing continuous insurance protection subject to the condition that there is no interruption or suspension of transit unless due to circumstances beyond the control of the insured. An interruption in transit at the direction of the insured terminates the insurance protection in the absence of a special agreement by the underwriter to continue the insurance in force during the detention or delay. A change in voyage, that is a change in the origin or destination of the shipment, is held covered subject to additional premium to be arranged.

In the American market it is currently the practice to impose a time limitation of 60 days (90 days on shipments via the Magdalena River) fixing the maximum period of coverage following completion of discharge of the insured goods from the overseas vessel at the final port of discharge on shipments to South America insured in terms of United States currency. The current London Institute clauses specify a maximum period of coverage on all shipments of 60 days after completion of discharge of the insured goods at the final port of discharge. In both cases insurance protection terminates upon delivery of the goods to the consignee, that is, delivery to the final warehouse at destination.

VESSEL INSURANCE

The Insured

Under the broad classification of vessel insurance fall insurance coverages of a wide range of loss exposures connected with the ownership and operation of a vessel. A change of ownership clause is frequently incorporated in the more common types of marine policies covering vessel interests. This clause makes it clear that the insurance is for the benefit of the insured named in the policy and that the protection afforded cannot be transferred to another party without the approval of the underwriter. The reason for this is simply that the underwriting is to a very large extent based on assessment of the reputation of the vessel owner or operator. Factors such as experience in vessel management, including maintenance of the vessel and selection of crews, must be taken into account. It is apparent, therefore, that a new insured might represent a new risk requiring different underwriting treatment.

Types of Vessel Policies

The subject matter of insurance is a vessel, which would include every description of watercraft used or capable of being used as a means of transportation on navigable waters and for commercial purposes as reviewed in this chapter. The description "watercraft" includes vessels in a great variety of sizes and uses, ranging from the largest oceangoing passenger liner navigating the seven seas to the smallest craft operated within the limits of a small harbor. Specific descriptions of the more common types of vessels are oceangoing passenger liners, tankers, dry cargo vessels, tugboats, barges, floating derricks, dredges, ferry boats, and fishing vessels. In addition to the hull itself, the subject matter of insurance includes tackle, passenger fittings, equipment, stores, boats, furniture, boilers, machinery, and appurtenances.

It is difficult to be definitive in the classification of marine policies written to cover loss exposures incidental to the ownership and operation of a vessel. There are numerous types of such policies subject to a variety of classifications based on a wide range of characteristics which can be considered separately or in combination. Classification is determined by characteristics such as risks insured against, the type of vessel, its use or status, waters navigated, the period and location of coverage, and the relationship between the insured and the vessel named in the policy. A description of "Hull," "Protection and Indemnity," and "Freight" types of vessel policies is undertaken in this chapter. Other types of policies are briefly mentioned with emphasis on their individual characteristics and principal functions.

Hull Policies

Perils Insured Against. The basic marine perils clause in the usual hull policy provides protection against loss or damage due to perils of the seas, fire, lightning, earthquake, assailing thieves, jettisons, barratry of the master or mariners, and ". . . all other like perils. . . ." The hull policy is considerably broadened by the Inchmaree[1] or Negligence Clause, a common wording of this clause reading as follows:

> This insurance also specially to cover (subject to the Average Warranty) loss of or damage to the subject matter insured directly caused by the following:
> Accidents in loading, discharging or handling cargo, or in bunkering;
> Accidents in going on or off, or while on drydocks, graving docks, ways, gridirons or pontoons;
> Explosions on shipboard or elsewhere;
> Breakdown of motor generators or other electrical machinery and electrical connections thereto, bursting of boilers, breakage of shafts, or any latent defect in the machinery or hull, (excluding the cost and expense of replacing or repairing the defective part);
> Breakdown of or accidents to nuclear installations or reactors not on board the insured Vessel;
> Contact with aircraft, rockets or similar missiles, or with any land conveyance;
> Negligence of Charterers and/or Repairers, provided such Charterers and/or Repairers are not Assured(s) hereunder;
> Negligence of Master, Mariners, Engineers or Pilots;
> provided such loss or damage has not resulted from want of due diligence by the Assured, the Owners or Managers of the Vessel, or any of them. Masters, Mates, Engineers, Pilots or Crew not to be considered as part owners within the meaning of this clause should they hold shares in the Vessel.

---

[1] So named for a ship which suffered an accident attributable to negligence of the crew. See Appendix C for a specimen policy of the American Hull Insurance Syndicate.

Expenses Insured Against. As in the case of cargo insurance, protection is also provided for certain losses sustained by the insured in the preservation of the venture, specifically losses or expenses classified as general average contributions, salvage awards, and sue and labor expenses.

Franchises and Deductibles. Coverages under hull policies are usually subject to a franchise clause stipulating that certain types of losses are recoverable in full only if they exceed a specified amount or percentage of the insured amount. A deductible average (loss) clause is frequently employed instead of a franchise. It is usually applicable to all losses except a total loss sustained under the policy, and in such cases the amount of the deductible is subtracted from the amount of the claim as adjusted. Franchises and deductibles eliminate small losses and the necessity to incur claim adjusting expenses which frequently exceed the amounts of the losses themselves. The use of franchises and deductibles often results in substantially reduced cost of vessel insurance.

Perils Excluded. The Inchmaree Clause quoted above excludes the cost and expense of replacing or repairing a defective part in the machinery or hull (because of a latent defect) which may have directly contributed to loss of or damage to the subject matter insured. Strikes, riots, and civil commotions risks are not covered in the usual hull policy but can be covered by a standard endorsement usually subject to payment of an additional premium. War risks are specifically excluded by an F.C. & S. Warranty (free of capture and seizure clause) but these risks can usually be insured against under a separate, standard form of war risk only policy.

Collision Liability. The usual hull policy includes a collision clause, often referred to as a "running down" clause, covering the insured's liability for collision loss or damage sustained by another vessel and its cargo arising out of negligent navigation of the insured's vessel. Liability for loss of life, personal injury, and/or wreck removal; for loss in respect of cargo, baggage and/or engagements of the insured vessel; and for loss or damage sustained by certain other classifications of property are specifically excluded. The usual practice is to insure against such risks under a separate protection and indemnity policy.

The collision clause is in the nature of a separate contract of insurance, providing collision liability protection up to the amount of insurance carried on the vessel named in the policy. Collision liability coverage is in addition to coverage provided against physical loss or damage sustained by the insured vessel.

Valuation. The hull policy is a valued contract and the insured valuation of a vessel is a matter of agreement at the time of attachment of the insurance. Normally, the insured value is predicated upon the market value of a vessel of similar type, age, and construction. In times of a shipping depression, when there is a surplus of ships and a lack of cargoes to carry, there may be a marked disparity between the insured and market values. It is common practice in certain ocean trades to show in the hull policy separate valuations for the hull of a vessel and its machinery when the coverage is subject to a franchise clause. In case of loss the insured is privileged to apply the policy franchise to each valuation separately. The beneficial effect to the insured is complete recovery of losses when they exceed a franchise amount lower than would be the case if hull and machinery were not separately valued.

Trading Warranties. All hull policies contain trading warranties or navigation limits, restricting the operation of the vessel to specified geographical limits. In some cases certain voyages or waters are specifically excluded either entirely or during stated periods of time. An extension of navigation privileges requires the approval of the insurer. It is not uncommon, however, to cover the operations of insured vessels on other than approved waters on a "held covered" basis subject to notification to the underwriter and payment of additional premium, if required.

Increased Value Policies. In addition to carrying insurance up to the amount of the agreed valuation in the hull policy, an insured customarily carries insurance on a vessel for an additional amount under a separate "increased value" policy. Under this policy the insurer responds for a total loss of the insured vessel and for certain other types of losses which exceed the amounts recoverable in the companion "full form" hull policy. Specifically, coverage is provided for: (1) losses sustained under the collision clause, (2) sue and labor expenses, (3) salvage awards, and (4) general average charges in the event that the vessel is assessed for such items on the basis of a higher valuation than that insured in the companion hull policy. This type of protection is occasionally referred to as "disbursements insurance" but more frequently as "increased value insurance."

The companion hull policy usually contains a so-called "disbursements warranty" stipulating that the amount of increased value insurance may not exceed a specified percentage of the agreed valuation in the hull policy, usually 25 percent. The increased value policy is written at a substantially lower rate than that charged under the "full form" companion hull policy. This practice often permits a vessel owner to obtain full coverage of losses up to the amount insured under the hull policy and coverage against a total loss and excess collision liability and expenses up to a higher amount under the increased value policy at a lower cost than would be the case if the entire amount of insurance were arranged under a "full form" hull policy. The disbursements warranty mentioned above prevents the abuse of this means of reducing insurance costs by limiting the amount of additional insurance that can be arranged under an increased value policy.

Protection and Indemnity Policies

Primary Protection and Indemnity Policies. As has been pointed out, the insured is protected under a hull policy against collision liability claims arising from damage sustained by another vessel and its cargo. Such insured is not fully protected, however, because he is subject to a wider range of maritime liability exposures associated with the operation of a vessel. The protection and indemnity insurance policy affords coverage against these risks. Broadly speaking, this policy provides for protection against practically all vessel maritime liability (other than that covered under the collision clause in the hull policy) incidental to the operation of a vessel. Specifically covered is liability with respect to persons, cargo, other property, and expenses incurred to comply with government regulations including fines and penalties incurred as a result of violation of law. It is customary practice to write the protection and indemnity policy in the same amount insured under the companion hull policy covering the same vessel.

Excess Protection and Indemnity Insurance. For centuries maritime nations have permitted a vessel owner to limit liability to the value of his vessel and pending freight as an encouragement to engage in overseas trades. In the United States this concept did not receive full support until the passage of the Limitation Act of 1851 which preserves the right of limitation to the vessel owner. This right is conditioned, however, on an absence of "privity or knowledge" of the vessel owner as to the cause of the loss. If he fails to meet this burden, he is personally liable. It should also be mentioned that the liability of a shipowner or operator in respect of cargo carried in his vessel is substantially reduced by the Harter Act in domestic waterborne trades and the Carriage of Goods by Sea Act in other trades. The vessel owner or operator is privileged to stipulate that contract of carriage (bill of lading) shall be subject to the Carriage of Goods by Sea Act in any trade. The vessel owner may also use the device of incorporating his vessel as a means of limiting his liability.

When all is said and done, however, the machinery available to a vessel owner for limiting his liability to the value of his vessel and pending freight is imperfect, and the phrase "privity or knowledge" is susceptible to many different interpretations by the courts. Under these conditions, it is not uncommon for vessel owners to arrange insurance protection against these additional risks under an excess protection and indemnity policy, usually for amounts substantially in excess of those insured against under the primary protection and indemnity policy described above.

Freight Policies

"Freight" policies, the third type of vessel policies reviewed here, pertain to charges for carrying cargo. The loss of a vessel involves the loss of her earning capacity because of the termination of freight contracts previously entered into. This circumstance gives the owner of an insured vessel an insurable interest in freight at risk or actually contracted for unless this risk is transferred to the cargo owner under the terms of the contract of affreightment. Freight refers to the money paid by a cargo owner to a vessel owner for carrying his goods from one port to another. In many trades freight is payable by the cargo owner whether the vessel is "lost or not lost." In such cases, freight is at the risk of the cargo owner and included in the amount of insurance under a cargo policy. In many other cases, however, the vessel operator does not earn the freight unless he delivers the cargo. In this event, he has an insurable interest in freight and can arrange insurance protection under a freight insurance policy which would protect him in the event that he is unable to earn the freight due to an intervening insured peril. In this sense freight insurance can be likened to "business interruption" coverage.

Other Classifications of Vessel Policies

Other types of vessel policies not fitting neatly into the classifications used above include the following:

Voyage and Time Policies. Until late in the nineteenth century, it was the general practice of vessel owners to cover their interests under "voyage" policies which provided protection during the current voyage of a vessel sometimes with an extension of coverage for periods of time up to 30 days after arrival at the final port of discharge.

The practice today, however, is to issue "time" policies which provide protection for a period of 12 months or occasionally shorter specified periods of time. Time policies have the obvious advantages of fixing the cost of insurance protection for a year in advance and eliminating the nuisance and expense of negotiating insurance protection at a much greater frequency. Apart from simplifying the arrangement of insurance protection, time policies make it possible for vessel owners to obtain substantial savings in premium charges.

Fleet Policies. It has also become common practice for the owner of a large number of vessels to arrange insurance protection under so-called fleet contracts in which each of the vessels is scheduled as to name and amount of insurance. The fleet policy makes clear that each vessel is deemed to be separately insured. An owner can often obtain more advantageous terms and lower costs under a fleet policy than if he were to buy protection under separate contracts written on individual vessels making up the fleet.

Port Risk Policies. Special policies, called port risk policies, have been devised to provide insurance protection on vessels while laid up and out of commission for various reasons including repair work, reconstruction, or simply because of adverse market conditions. It is a condition of the insurance that the vessel is laid up and will not be operated and further that it will be confined to a specified mooring or in some cases to the port described in the policy. Privilege is granted to move the vessel within the harbor limits for specified purposes not directly connected with the carriage of cargo although there may be cargo on board. The rate of premium on a port risk form is substantially lower than that which would be charged on the same vessel insured under a navigating form. The reason for this is simply the substantially reduced exposure to loss in the case of a vessel confined to the safety of a harbor.

Builder's Risk Policies. A specialized policy has been developed to cover a vessel while it is in the process of being built and often until delivery of the vessel has been made to the owner. This is called a builder's risk policy which provides practically "all risk" protection against physical loss of or damage to the subject matter of insurance. Coverage commences from the time of the laying of the keel and continues during the period of construction, launching, fitting out, and trials. Coverage is included against the risk of failure to launch, and expenses incurred to complete a successful launching. The risks of strikes, riots and civil commotions, and war are excluded.

The builder's risk policy covers materials used in the construction of the vessel while stored in buildings, workshops, yards, or docks where the vessel is being constructed, including coverage on such materials in transit to or from a shipyard or the vessel within the port of construction. One of the unusual features of a builder's risk policy is that it provides protection against collision liability and other types of vessel maritime liability usually insured against under a separate protection and indemnity type of policy. Liability is commonly excluded, however, for claims recoverable by employees under workman's compensation laws or similar legislation.

Miscellaneous Classifications. There are numerous variations in hull policies, and protection and indemnity policies, dependent upon the type of vessel insured. Ocean hulls such as passenger and cargo vessels employed in ocean trades, as distinguished from vessels operated on inland waters or in coastwise trades, are customarily insured under the American Institute Time (Hull) Policy or a similar policy in the case of foreign-flag vessels. Tug boats are customarily insured under a special tug policy, the distinctive feature of which is a collision clause extended to cover the liability of the owner of the tug for damage done by or to the vessels in the tow of his tug in addition to liability arising from collision of his tug and/or its tow with other vessels or objects. This coverage is commonly known as "tower's liability." Smaller vessels operating on inland or coastwise waters of the United States are insured under a variety of policies similar to the American Institute Time (Hull) Policy but modified to meet the special requirements of vessels operated in these trades. These are only some of the variations in policies based on type and operation of the vessel.

SUGGESTED READINGS

ARNOULD, SIR JOSEPH. *Law of Marine Insurance and Average.* 15th ed. 2 vols. London: Stevens & Sons, Ltd., 1961. (This edition edited by Lord Chorley of Kendal and C. T. Barlhache.)

DOVER, VICTOR. *A Handbook to Marine Insurance.* 6th ed. London: H. F. and G. Witherby, Ltd., 1962.

FLOCTON, K. J. *The Insurance of Ships.* London: Witherby & Co., Ltd., 1953.

GILMORE, GRANT, AND BLACK, CHARLES L., JR. *The Law of Admiralty.* Brooklyn, N.Y.: The Foundation Press, Inc., 1957.

MULLINS, HUGH A. *Marine Insurance Digest.* Cambridge, Md.: Cornell Maritime Press, 1951.

ROSE, C. L. *Insurance Notes for Shipbrokers.* London: Witherby & Co., Ltd., 1955.

TEMPLEMAN, FREDERICK, AND GREENACRE, C. T. *Marine Insurance; Its Principles and Practice.* 2d ed. London: MacDonald and Evans, 1951.

WINTER, WILLIAM D. *Marine Insurance.* 3d ed. New York: McGraw-Hill Book Co., Inc., 1952.

Chapter 20

RATEMAKING, UNDERWRITING, AND LOSS ADJUSTMENT IN MARINE INSURANCE

BY GILBERT B. OXFORD

Ocean marine insurance, being international in character, does not lend itself to either state or federal regulation. Determination of rates by any regulatory body would only present a target for international competitors and result in the loss of business to the regulated market. Moreover, many officials of the government of the United States are exceedingly suspicious of businessmen who, no matter how innocently, act in concert. Rating organizations are, therefore, the exception rather than the rule in marine insurance, although they are countenanced under some circumstances. Ratemaking and underwriting are largely matters of individual judgment, influenced by domestic and foreign competition. Since it is difficult to divorce the one from the other, *both subjects* (ratemaking and underwriting) will be dealt with jointly in this chapter. Brief attention is also given to loss adjustment in ocean marine insurance.

A school of thought among marine underwriters holds that in the absence of moral hazard there is a rate for any risk. With certain reservations the author subscribes to this theory. Marine underwriting has been said to be "the intelligent application of the experiences of the past to the expectations of the future." The same has been said of horseracing. Underwriters, however, lack the benefit of stud books when faced with a first-of-a-kind risk.

Marine insurance covers a wider field than most people realize. It is not surprising, then, that there is a tendency towards specialization. This tendency is possibly more noticeable in the American market than abroad, although even at Lloyd's certain underwriters become recognized as leaders in certain lines. Whether an underwriter specializes or not, he will find it convenient, and probably necessary, to separate his underwriting portfolio into a limited number of distinct categories. Traditional reinsurance arrangements dictate this. It seems logical, then, to follow this same pattern in this chapter.

Marine business falls into two general categories: "Hull"[1] and "Cargo"; premium is about evenly divided. Each of these classes could be split into numerous subdivisions, but such splitting will be kept to the minimum in this chapter. Legal liability coverages for ship repairers, stevedores, and others, when written under marine policies will fall in the hull category even though somewhat different underwriting principles are involved.

HULL RATEMAKING AND UNDERWRITING

Dealing with hull insurance first, perhaps the best advice to give an aspiring hull underwriter is to suggest he start with yachts. The number of pleasure craft today is so great that such craft now constitute almost a "mass market." Pleasure craft are either stock models or types which lend themselves to comparison with one another and hence to schedule rating. The business is largely agency produced. Since agents often need to indicate a rate on the spot, most companies writing the business have rate schedules and underwriting rules for the agents' use. These, incidentally, provide a ready starting point for the beginner. Also, because the policy is a comprehensive one, it exposes him at an early stage to many phases of the business. The next chapter is devoted exclusively to "Yacht and Small Boat Insurance."

Rates and Value

There is an underwriting axiom common to hull insurers which goes: "The lower the insured value is to replacement value, the higher the rate." Hull policies are usually written on a valued form, and partial losses are paid in full without regard to the value insured. Since the cost of repairs remains the same regardless of the value insured, the partial loss hazard remains a constant whereas total loss hazard varies with the value insured. It follows, then, that as the value insured on any given vessel decreases, the rate must increase. For example, a vessel valued at $100,000 and rated at 4 percent produces a premium of $4,000. Assuming that of the 4 percent, 3 percent or $3,000 represents the partial loss risk and 1 percent or $1,000 the total loss risk, then the same vessel insured for $60,000 would still require $3,000 for the partial loss risk but only $600 for total loss, making $3,600 in all or a rate of 6 percent on the lower value. Note that while the rate is higher the premium is actually $400 lower representing, of course, the decreased total loss risk. The reverse is also true: as values increase the rate should decrease. However,

[1] Readers are reminded that Mr. Marshall, Contributing Author for Chapter 19, discusses "vessel" insurance and within that term includes "hull," "protection and indemnity," and "freight."

underwriters are reluctant to reduce a rate for a small increase in value, figuring that the increase could be brought about by improvements, added equipment, or inflation, any of which would reflect in the partial loss hazard anyway. During the inflationary period of World War II the practice was to make no reduction in rate until the increase amounted to 30 percent.

Oceangoing Tonnage

The backbone of the hull business in any market is probably its oceangoing tonnage. Hull insurance is often thought of in respect to such vessels as the "United States," "Queen Elizabeth," and others of great size. The values involved in any of the big liners exceed the capacity of any individual national market. The business therefore must be spread over others either as direct placings or reinsurance. The "lion's share" internationally finds its way to the London market, although since World War II the American market has built up a significant and growing book of foreign business.

Different markets use different methods in rating business but all have the same objective of making a moderate underwriting profit. Also, all will try to make individual fleets stand on their own feet as far as possible. Fleets usually consist of vessels which are under the same management although they may be owned by separate corporations. Fleets may be split into categories either by age or type of vessel. Passenger vessels may form one category, dry cargo vessels another, and tankers a third. New tonnage may be treated separately from the old, as may vessels engaged in different trades. Of course, in all of these cases separate rates will most likely apply to the various segments of the fleet.

The underwriter must continually compare rates between fleets of a similar character or in the same trade. The broker's job is to see that the vessel or fleet he is placing bears a premium not out of line with that paid by competitors of his principals in the same trade. All such comparisons, however, must of necessity take into account the records of such fleets because rates must, of course, reflect record. Comparisons are not always easy to make. Earlier, the effect of valuation on rate was illustrated. The basis of insured values on oceangoing vessels follows no set pattern. In this respect underwriters pretty much follow the wishes of the owner. Many U.S. vessels in foreign trade are built with a government subsidy and in some cases with a government mortgage when delivered. No insurance is required on the subsidy although, naturally, the mortgage interest should be fully covered. Since the subsidy is not a fixed percentage but varies according to circumstances, insured values, presumably based on construction cost less subsidy, vary greatly. Then again, it is the practice to split the amount to be insured in a ratio of four to one, the value of the vessel for insurance purposes being stated as 80 percent of the total and the other 20 percent being written as "increased value" (an excess type of cover written at a lower rate and described briefly in Chapter 19). The term "disbursements" is also applied to this coverage.

Great Lakes Tonnage

In the U.S. and Canadian markets the class of hull business of next importance has to do with vessels plying the Great Lakes. In general the same principles apply except that the underwriter must adjust his thinking to the trade being strictly seasonal. The Lakes are icebound in the winter months. By custom, the recognized Lake season for steel vessels is from April 16 to November 30 inclusive, or a period of 229 days. If a vessel has already sailed on November 30 it is held covered at pro rata premium. Provision is also made for preseason and postseason sailings at varying multiples of the season rate—all of which multiples are part of the printed clauses—and consequently standard in all markets. Ice damage is a serious hazard on Lake business and one which is mostly avoidable by a careful operator. Underwriters are protected by a sizable deductible (3 percent or $20,000, whichever is less) to which all ice claims are subject. While Lake business differs in many ways from other wet marine insurance, the above discussion covers the more important differences.

Premium per Gross Ton

As a rough rule of thumb the economic life of an oceangoing vessel is 20 years, giving a depreciation rate of 5 percent per annum.[2] Theoretically, then, book value should be the depreciated value of the vessel but most insureds[3] want to insure for more than this amount. They prefer a figure which they feel is a fair market value as judged by the earning capacity of the boat. As it works out, any given vessel might be insured for a much higher or a much lower value with one owner than with another; therefore, a comparison of rates alone becomes meaningless. Consequently, underwriters in the U.S. market resort to translating the premium, loss costs, and valuations to a gross tonnage basis in an effort to find a common denominator.[4] For example, a vessel of 8,000 gross tons insured on a valuation of $2 million at a rate of 2 percent (or $40,000) would be valued at $250 per gross ton and classified as paying a premium of $5.00 per gross ton.

---

[2] Great Lakes vessels and others navigating on fresh water enjoy a much longer economic life. Incidentally, under a recent ruling the Treasury Department is now recognizing a rate of depreciation higher than 5 percent on ocean vessels.

[3] Editors' note: While the author much prefers—in the marine tradition—the use of the term "assured," he has graciously used "insured" in this chapter for sake of consistency in the *Handbook*.

[4] Gross tonnage is a measure of the internal volume of all enclosed spaces in the ship, and is equal to the tonnage below the tonnage deck, plus the tonnage of all *enclosed* spaces above that deck.

This premium can be further divided into premium for total loss and premium for partial losses. Assuming a rate of .6 percent for total loss, it would represent $1.50 per gross ton leaving $3.50 per gross ton for partial losses. In making comparisons, then, one should do so on the basis of the premium cost per gross ton after deducting the premium cost for the total loss risk. Except in unusual cases, total loss rates on comparable vessels do not vary greatly although values may vary. Translating the total loss cost per ton could be misleading and it is better to think of this portion of the risk on the basis of rates percent rather than cost per gross ton. Loss costs can be placed on a per gross ton basis also and shown separately for different types of risk as, for instance, total loss, particular average, general average or collision liability. If sufficient premium is not being obtained to take care of the partial losses, rates should be raised. The caliber of management is often more accurately reflected by the partial loss record than by that for total loss. Since the basic principle of insurance is the spreading of the loss "so that it lighteth lightly on the many rather than heavily on the few," underwriters do not expect to recover a total loss or, for that matter, a casualty of major proportions all in one year. While rating is based on the record of the past five years, major casualties are usually considered as spread over a 10-year period. It will be seen, then, that major casualties do not penalize an insured unduly.

Quality of Management

The quality of management is a prime consideration in hull underwriting. This quality is a reflection of the managers' attitude towards the upkeep and manning of the vessels and their ability in the selection of officers and crews. For example, whether or not masters are expected to push their vessels regardless of weather conditions in order to keep sailing schedules is a matter in point. The insured's attitude toward insurance also plays an important part in hull underwriting. Many damages to a vessel, particularly where the alleged cause is heavy weather, fall in a twilight zone between regular upkeep and fortuitous loss. Some insureds will be scrupulously fair in such cases, whereas others will claim everything possible as an insurance claim. Naturally, this attitude is reflected in the underwriting results and eventually in the insured's premium costs one way or the other. Wherever there is an abundance of small claims, underwriters are apt to suggest the inclusion of a deductible average. This deductible might be $5,000, $10,000, $25,000, or even $100,000. In all such cases underwriters are agreeable to an appropriate allowance in rate. This allowance is arrived at by reviewing the record over the past five years (or maybe longer), finding the savings that would have been made had the deductible been in effect, and translating them into a percentage of the insured value. Since every premium dollar contemplates a certain amount for commission and overhead, the underwriter can afford to be liberal and allow somewhat more than the equivalent loss saving. He can boost the figure for the commission he does not have to pay and for the expense of processing those claims that will be avoided because of the deductible. Then, again, there is a reasonable expectation that the insured will become more careful when losses directly affect his pocketbook, a reason, incidentally, why deductibles are of great importance when underwriting smaller types of vessels, such as dredges, tugs, barges, and the like.

Builder's Risks

The rating of builder's risks policies comes nearest to "rating according to the book." Here the larger portion of the risk represents fire hazards at locations with published fire rates. These rates, then, properly adjusted to reflect the fact that the exposure starts at nothing and builds up to the full insured value, should become a controlling factor in arriving at a proper rate. The Builder's Risk form is, however, an "all risk" form including launching and trial trips. It is necessary, therefore, to increase the fire rates appropriately. It is customary to add set percentages which vary with the value and construction material, whether wood or steel, for the launching, the trials, and the miscellaneous risks. A side launching, other things the same, will command a higher additional than an end launching. While builder's risks normally attach from the laying of the keel, it is not unusual for materials to be assembled prior to that time. In such cases the material may be covered by endorsement to the builder's risk policy from the time the material becomes at risk until the laying of the keel at the published fire rate loaded to reflect the "all risk" coverage.

Tugboats and Towboats

The underwriting of tugboats (also towboats of the pusher type used on the Mississippi/Ohio Rivers system) is something that should be left to the experts, which, however, is often not the case in actual practice. The class presents numerous problems. Only a few can be recognized in this chapter. There seems to be no logical relationship among the rates current in different local markets as, for instance, the Eastern Seaboard, the Gulf, and the West Coast. Differences in towing contracts may be part of the reason but competitive conditions probably are an even larger part. Rates for these vessels, including tower's liability, range all the way from less than 2 percent to more than 25 percent. The density of traffic in given areas has, of course, much to do with rates. It is easy to understand why there is such a wide variance of rates between such harbors as Boston and New York. Tugs are used for many purposes such as steamer docking, ocean towing, river towing, and towing of all kinds of nonpropelled craft such as carfloats, dredges, etc. Underwriters need to know, therefore, the particular hazards of the geographical area in which the tug operates as well as the use to which she is put. For example, tugs engaged in the sand and gravel trade may have to navigate creeks and inlets which are badly maintained and whose channel depths are not known. The same considerations must be taken into account with small oil or gasoline tankers whether towed or self-propelled.

Tower's Liability. The complicating factor in tug insurance is that the coverage usually goes far beyond that of physical loss of or damage to the tug and covers "Tower's Liability." This coverage is an extension of the Collision Clause and in its broadest form covers the tug owner's liability for practically anything untoward that happens growing out of the towing except claims for loss of life or bodily injury. The effect of valuation as discussed earlier plays a dual role. It is the measure against which premium must be assessed not only for losses to the vessel itself but also for liability claims. An old, low-valued tug engaged in a hazardous trade such as the New York State Barge Canal with its limited waters for passing other vessels and its numerous locks, must necessarily carry an unusually high rate in order to develop sufficient premium to cover these hazards. The accident frequency on tugs engaged in harbor towing (and to a lesser degree in steamer docking) is appreciably higher than on tugs engaged in outside towing.

Deductibles. Because there is a high loss frequency in this business, this insurance lends itself to the application of deductibles. In fact, very little business is written without them. In theory, the fact that the insured has a stake in his losses makes him a more careful operator. This care, however, is not always exercised. Deductibles vary considerably in amount and are influenced largely by the record of the risk. The deductible may apply to all claims resulting from an accident or may apply separately to damage to the tug and to any liability claim. Then, again, one amount may be deducted from damage claims and an entirely different one (probably higher) from liability claims. The size of these deductibles, of course, influences the rate. When an underwriter is asked to quote for several alternative deductibles, he must use a high degree of judgment.

Sistership Provision. Many tugs are owned by the same organization which owns the property being towed. Some are used exclusively in this manner. Since nobody can be legally liable to himself, it might be presumed that under such circumstances the tower's liability could not encompass the tow or its cargo if of the same ownership. This presumption would be correct except for the fact that the Collision and Tower's Liability Clause contains a "sistership provision" whereby the property commonly owned will be dealt with at arbitration as if of diverse ownership. Because of this peculiarity, the insurer of a tug might find itself paying for most of the losses occurring on the nonpropelled vessels of his insured or, for that matter, the owner's piers, wharves, and certain other properties. For this reason a prudent underwriter will exclude liability under the tug policy for losses to property of his insured or any subsidiary or affiliated corporation.

Protection and Indemnity

Protection and Indemnity Insurance is a package policy for shipowners. (See Chapter 19.) It covers third-party liability for property damage, death or bodily injury, carriers' liability, and employers' liability all in one. It originated with mutual clubs in England, which still insure a large portion of the world's ocean tonnage. Originally, premium was assessed on a valuation basis but this assessment was soon changed to a tonnage basis, the vessel's gross registered tonnage being used for the purpose. When underwriters in the United States started writing the business, they copied the English system as far as oceangoing tonnage was concerned.

Premium charges vary greatly, depending upon the type of vessel and trade. Passenger vessels, for instance, present a different underwriting problem than do dry cargo carriers. In the one case there is the possibility of passenger claims and a large crew with its personal injury potential but, generally speaking, a superior cargo risk. In the other case there is an average sized crew but the possibility of a poor cargo risk, especially when the ship carries a miscellaneous cargo and visits many ports for loading or discharging. Tankers have their own problems. Cargo claims are few but because of the explosive or flammable nature of the cargo an acute catastrophe hazard exists. Colliers on the other hand are less subject to either catastrophe or serious cargo claims.

Almost invariably "P. & I. policies" are subject to deductibles which are expressed separately for different categories of claims, such as cargo, loss of life, and others. The judicious application of the deductibles plays an all important part in successful underwriting. The cargo deductible on dry cargo vessels may be $5,000, $10,000, $25,000, or more per voyage, whereas for life and injury it may be as low as $500. While premium is charged on a tonnage basis, a limit of liability is shown in the policy which will usually be the valuation in the policies on hull or on hull and increased value combined.

On other types of vessels different rating methods are used. On miscellaneous craft, such as tugs, towboats, barges, ferries, harbor craft, and others the rate is usually charged on a percentage basis on the hull value. On fishboats, however (and the idea has spread somewhat to other classes), frequently the premium is charged at so much per man plus a percentum charge on the value insured to take care of such claims as damage to docks or for cargo, life, or injury claims in collision, and so on.

P. & I. as a class is a fertile field for loss or accident prevention and some leading underwriters maintain safety departments. Obviously, an insured will benefit from lower insurance costs if he institutes a good safety program.

CARGO RATEMAKING AND UNDERWRITING

Cargo underwriters think differently from hull underwriters and a different approach in underwriting is necessary. In the first place, valuation does not play such an important part and cargo is usually fully insured anyway. The customary basis of valuation is invoice value, plus freight and other charges, on top of which a percentage (usually, but not necessarily, 10 percent) is added.

"Cargo-hungry" Market

In theory, experience should influence rates even more in cargo than in hull but such practice is not always followed. The marine markets of the world are at the time of this writing what might be termed "cargo-hungry." Often a poor account will pass from one insurer to another or from one market to another, the process being repeated as each in turn finds out that the account is a losing proposition. Sometimes the insured is responsible for this process because of his insistence on "shopping around" rather than meeting the underwriter's demands for a fair rate. Sometimes the fault is the broker's who may feel that such action is in his client's best interests but who more likely is simply protecting himself against competing brokers. The careful underwriter, then, will want to know the record of the account. Information on this score is not always easy to develop as cargo claims are often paid abroad and the insured may be unaware of them unless the underwriter notifies him, which is not always done. Then, again, some underwriters do not advise their insureds of recoveries under subrogation and these can be a significant item in cargo results. Another item which might be overlooked is the matter of contributions in general average which the insurer will have guaranteed but may not be called upon to pay until two, three, or more years later. General average adjustments frequently take that long in preparation.

In the United States, cargo insurance falls into three broad categories, namely exports, imports, and domestic—the last including intercoastal, coastwise, Great Lakes, river, and other inland water shipments. Most exporters and importers (and to a lesser degree, domestic shippers) with any appreciable amount of business will have a Cargo Open Policy under which all shipments are automatically covered. As noted in Chapter 19, the custom is for insurers to provide an exporter with certificates and signing authority to enable him to make up and sign them himself. Naturally, copies of these are sent to the insurer and are the basis of his declarations. Importers usually declare by bordereau monthly or more often.

Influences on the Rate

On commodities such as cotton, rubber, coffee, cocoa, hides, wool, and so on which are traded on various exchanges in the world, rates must of necessity keep within a fairly narrow range. Information concerning rates is passed around quickly on these commodities. In these circumstances, the underwriter will be inclined to look at his experience with the commodity as a whole rather than the individual account. This does not mean, however, that a persistently bad account can ride on the good results of the average. Much depends upon the shipper who often controls the grade of packing and the choice of vessels on which the goods are shipped. A poor record must eventually be reflected in the insurance rates.

Even though certain commodities are traded on exchanges, they may also be imported directly by manufacturers, such as coffee roasters, leather tanners, or chocolate makers. These manufacturers normally buy insurance in these circumstances. In such cases the results are usually better than when the insured is a broker or middleman. The reason is that, when the goods are not too badly damaged, an end-user will very often process them and make a claim only after he has established his actual loss. Where a middleman is selling damaged goods, the purchaser will naturally want to play safe and consequently his bid for the goods will most likely reflect a discount for more than the actual damage.

Of the thousand and one other interests which enter into ocean trade, the one that most generally influences rates is the particular account's record of the ordinary run of claims. Underwriters expect and are glad to pay clean-cut total loss claims. Such claims are the reason for their being in business. They also readily pay claims for clean-cut perils of the sea such as storms, collisions, strandings, and the like. Such claims are not considered serious grounds for increasing rates unless they become so prevalent as to warrant a general increase applying to a whole trade. Under "all risk" conditions prevalent today many claims are presented for losses which in the old days a merchant would have absorbed himself. Pilferage, breakage, bending, twisting, denting, and rusting are examples. Naturally, the insurer can only allow so many cents in the dollar for this type of claim. If the claims exceed the permissible amount, rates should be adjusted accordingly. Of course, it is always possible to control the situation somewhat by inserting into the insuring conditions a reasonable franchise or, better still, a deductible.

Packing

Packing plays an important part in the safe transportation of most goods in export, import, and domestic trade. In the case of imports the underwriter must have a reasonable knowledge of the type of packing customarily used in various trades. However, if there is any doubt, he should make specific inquiry regarding packing. For instance, he would not want to grant "all risk" conditions on, say, canned tomatoes in cartons from Italy whereas he might be willing to do so if they were packed in wooden cases. On exports and domestic shipments the underwriter has an opportunity to offer suggestions on packing. A number of leading marine underwriters maintain a staff of surveyors who are well versed in packing problems and who can work out with an insured the best type of packing. Lacking a staff surveyor, an underwriter can always employ the services of an independent surveyor. Some packing experts work on an independent basis and make their services available for a fee to exporters or to underwriters.

Underwriting Knowledge

While packing is important, a host of other underwriting factors must be taken into consideration. First of all, there must be a meeting of the minds as to the proper insuring conditions, in which connection the broker plays a crucial part. In some cases this task is made easy by the existence of standard insuring conditions that have received acceptance in certain trades. Examples of these are the Bulk Oil Clauses, A.1 Meat Clauses, Timber Trade Clauses, and others. Underwriters do not wish to assume "trade losses" and should know in what commodities and to what extent they occur. For example, oil or grease will stick to the sides of tanks. Not as much can be taken out as was put in. The underwriter should specify that he will only be liable for losses in excess of a certain percentage—maybe one half of one percent. He is chargeable with whatever is common knowledge in a trade.

Because his endeavors touch upon many different trades he must store up a wide range of miscellaneous knowledge. In fact, he must become a "Jack of all trades." In addition to all this knowledge he must be a walking encyclopedia on geography, and an expert on the facilities, the labor conditions, and the probability of pilferage or exposure damage at each of the different ports around the world. He should know at what ports lighterage is probable and where it is the only means of delivery. He must also know the approximate time required for goods to go through customs at various places. In addition, knowledge of weather conditions around the world and at what seasons to expect what conditions is very necessary. All of these requirements may seem and, in fact, are "a tall order." Years of experience are necessary before one can underwrite cargo with confidence. However, underwriters have many sources at hand from which to obtain this knowledge.

The American Institute of Marine Underwriters is an organization which, in addition to doing other things, continually disseminates information of interest to the marine market. It has correspondents (and

Lloyd's has agents) at the principal ports of the world all of whom report regularly on conditions in their respective territories and particularly on any unusual developments.

Also, certain publications give information in concise form regarding ports, facilities, customs, and so on. There are books dealing with commodities, their characteristics and peculiarities. Any underwriter today would be lost without a chemical dictionary.

Even with these aids it still requires imagination and ingenuity to get a "true picture" of the risk being insured. An underwriter, for example, quickly learns it is almost impossible to make money insuring against theft and pilferage on automobile parts to lesser-developed countries. The same might be said of breakage of glass and fragile articles and of chipping of enamelware, porcelain bathtubs, and toilets. In all of these cases attention must be paid to packing and consideration given to deductibles. Household goods and personal effects can be particularly troublesome when the underwriter is dealing with someone unfamiliar with business terms or methods. Household goods expertly packed domestically can be acceptable risks, but too often these goods, when packed abroad, will arrive in a deplorable condition. The answer, of course, is to insure them only on limited conditions.

Freight Forwarders

A piece of good advice to the underwriter when he is offered an open policy for a freight forwarder is: "Stop, look, and listen!" Sometimes this business is desirable when the forwarder has a limited number of first class clients. Even here, the complexion of the account can change overnight by the addition of a new client shipping something with a high claim potential. Most freight forwarders, however, by the nature of their business do not have a restricted clientele. They may be called upon to act for beginners in the export trade who have no knowledge of the need for special export packing. Then, again, they will get their share of undesirable shipments such as household furniture or unboxed automobiles.

Duty and Freight

Duty and collect freight are items that may be covered by cargo policies. They take a lower rate than the cargo itself because they are items payable on arrival with no total loss risk on the voyage. On the other hand, "on deck" shipments, for obvious reasons, take a higher rate than shipments "under deck" and are usually insured on more restricted conditions. Perishable cargoes present their own problems. When carried in refrigeration, they are usually insured against the consequence of breakdown of the refrigerating machinery provided the duration of the breakdown is of 24 hours or longer. Meat is insured under special clauses which take into consideration the risks peculiar to the trade. Air shipments are usually written on the broadest conditions. It is interesting to note that the principal hazards are on the ground (such as theft, pilferage, and water damage) and not crash as might be expected.

What little is written here should serve at least to show the extensiveness of the subject. New ideas of cargo coverages crop up continually, presenting new problems. Despite his years of experience, the underwriter finds that the unpredictable always seems to happen. That is the charm of marine insurance!

Special Observation

When marine insurance was in its infancy, underwriting was on an intimate level (see Chapter 17). It was generally a local matter carried on by shipowners and merchants who were well acquainted with one another. A would-be underwriter could stroll down to the pier and size up the ship for himself. He probably broke bread with the owner or drank with the master at the local tavern. As business expanded and underwriting became a vocation rather than an avocation this intimacy became more difficult. The need for sound appraisal of the risk continued; it still exists and always will.

Out of this necessity grew the "classification societies" whose rules and regulations require any vessels classed by them to be built to certain minimum standards both as to hull and machinery and require inspections at specified intervals to see that the vessels are maintained up to the society's standards. Classification societies publish to subscribers various types of registers which are of invaluable aid to the underwriter whether he is considering a hull or a cargo risk. Vessel owners pay a fee for this service and naturally any subscriber wishing copies of the registers also pays a subscription fee.

The owners of some types of vessels—fishing boats, dredges, tugs, barges, and miscellaneous craft—frequently see no necessity for classification. In such cases the careful underwriter will require a survey by his staff or some competent independent surveyor. The services of such surveyors are highly useful in apprising the underwriter not only of the physical condition of the vessel, its upkeep, and its probable value but also of the degree of competency and success of the owner in his business. The underwriter in this way retains some sense of intimacy with the risk even if vicariously through his surveyor.

LOSS ADJUSTMENT

As the underwriting of hull risks is necessarily approached from a somewhat different viewpoint than is the underwriting of cargo risks, so it is necessary to adopt a different approach to the adjustment of hull claims than to adjustment of cargo claims. However, they have one thing in common. In case of a total loss the insurer pays the insured value which is agreed upon when the contract is negotiated and which in the absence of fraud cannot be questioned.

Documents

The documents to substantiate total loss claims vary between hull and cargo losses. On hull claims the following documents are required:

1. Insurance policy.
2. Affidavit of all the insurance on the vessel in effect at time of casualty.
3. Certificate of registry and enrollment.
4. Captain's protest.

For total loss cargo claims the following documents are required:

1. All negotiable copies of policies or certificates of insurance.
2. Original invoice.
3. All negotiable bills of lading, endorsed.
4. Statement from carrier certifying that goods were on board at the time of accident. In cases of total losses prior to shipment or after discharge covered under the Warehouse to Warehouse Clause, an appropriate statement from the trucker, railroad, warehouse, or other bailee having possession of the goods at the time of the loss.
5. Captain's protest.

In either case where a constructive rather than an actual total is claimed, evidence to that effect must be produced.

Contribution

Where either a hull or cargo policy is called upon for contribution in general average and the contributory value exceeds the insured value (reduced by any partial loss which may have been paid), the insurer is required to reimburse the insured only for such proportion of such amount as the latter value bears to the former.

For example:

Contributory value of hull	$1,000,000
Insured value of hull	800,000
General average contribution	10,000
Insurers pay 80 percent or	8,000

The same formula applies in case of cargo.

Work of Surveyors

In settling a hull claim the object is to reimburse the insured for the actual cost of repairing any damage attributable to the casualty subject, of course, to the policy terms as to franchise or deductible. Such amount is payable in full regardless of whether the insured value is less than the real value.

When an accident occurs, the insured through his broker notifies the underwriters who in turn appoint a surveyor to represent them and to agree with the insured or his representative upon the extent of the damage and the cost of repairs. In practice, the owner of an oceangoing vessel is usually on notice to call in the local representative of the U.S. Salvage Association to represent American underwriters. If English underwriters are involved, the London Salvage Association is notified. As both organizations have representatives located at convenient places abroad, much time is saved by direct action.

The surveyor's function is to ascertain the cause and nature of the damage in detail. Frequently, it is necessary to distinguish between damage of a general average nature and damage of a particular average nature. Naturally, the respective cost of repairs must be separated. The surveyor must also distinguish between damage due to the accident and damage due to ordinary wear and tear. There will always be borderline cases and the insured's attitude is frequently what separates a good risk from a bad one.

The cost of repairs, of course, includes the necessary cost of dry-docking. If the insured decides to take advantage of the occasion to effect repairs which would be solely for his account or for the periodical classification survey and if such owner's repairs are immediately necessary for the vessels's seaworthiness, as much of the dock dues as is common to both classes of work shall be divided equally between the owners and underwriters. Otherwise the owner would enjoy a free ride with all of the dry-docking costs charged to the underwriters.

Average Adjusters

On hulls where the value involved is such that the risk is divided among several or many underwriters, it is customary for losses to be adjusted by professionals known as "average adjusters." In most foreign markets average adjusters are individuals or firms independent of other activities. In the United States, however, independent adjusters are practically nonexistent and the profession is carried on by employees in separate departments in brokers' offices. It is customary for the heads or several members of these departments to be members of the Association of Average Adjusters of the United States. The requirements of membership are very strict and include a comprehensive written examination. The ethics of the profession and record of impartiality are jealously observed both here and abroad so that there can be no suspicion of their favoring the "hand that feeds them." The greater part of the adjuster's services is in the preparation of general average adjustments, including the taking of security from consignees. These services are necessary even if no insurance is involved.

Small Craft

The adjustment of losses on smaller craft where only one or a few insurers are involved does not necessarily require the service of the professional adjuster. They are normally handled by the loss departments of the insurers involved, acting on the findings of their surveyors. It is not unusual in these cases for the insurer to make settlement directly to a repair yard, with due regard to any deductible involved. In case of larger vessels, settlement of repair bills is usually between the owner and the repair yard. Frequently, however, when the owner has made large outlays, he will ask underwriters for a payment on account and such requests are usually granted where liability under the policy is clear.

Partial Losses on Cargo

Partial losses on cargo are settled on the basis of the percentage of damage as applied to the insured value. Where the loss involves the total loss of a part of the shipment (as, for instance, the theft of an entire case) it is a simple matter to determine from the packing list what goods have been lost. Comparison of the invoice value of such lost goods with the total invoice value establishes the percentage of loss. Obviously, if a slingload of 10 bags of raw sugar is lost overboard in loading or discharge out of a shipment of 500 bags, a 2 percent loss has been suffered and 2 percent of the insured value should be paid.

Where part or the whole of a shipment is partially damaged through an insured peril, a surveyor representing the underwriters, after making an examination to establish the cause and extent of the damage, tries to arrive at an agreed percentage of damage with the consignee. When such agreement has been reached, the insurer will pay that percentage of the insured value of the goods involved. Failing to reach any such agreement, the surveyor will suggest that the owner of the goods have them sold privately (usually to a salvage broker or someone accustomed to dealing in damaged merchandise) or at public auction. (It should be noted that the title to the goods always remains with the insured and is not taken over by the insurer.) In either of these circumstances, the surveyor must determine a fair market value for the goods from sales of similar goods of like kind and quality in sound condition. A comparison is then made between the sound value and the proceeds from the sale of the damaged goods. In this way the percentage of loss is established. This percentage applied to the insured value plus all charges for auction, carting, labor in segregating damaged goods from the sound, and so on makes up the claim against the underwriters. The surveyor's charges, if paid by the consignee or insured, will be reimbursed; otherwise they are paid directly by the underwriters (in the case of imports or domestic shipments this is nearly always the case).

At times an insured takes the attitude that, if his goods are damaged, it is up to the insurer to take them over and pay him the insured value as in the case of a total loss. This arrangement is known as settling the loss on a salvage loss basis and is the established practice in regard to goods which are so damaged they have to be sold short of destination to prevent them from becoming a total loss. However, it is not customary where goods arrive at destination in specie, because it could make the insurer liable for fluctuations in market values. Insurers are liable neither for loss of market nor for delay.

It is important to note that market value is after payment of duty. Sometimes duty is insured and sometimes not. If it is, the same percentage of loss will be paid on duty as on the goods themselves. The settlement of cargo losses is influenced considerably by the regulations concerning import duties in the country concerned. The scope of this chapter does not permit a detailed discussion of this intriguing subject other than to say that in some circumstances it might be more profitable to re-export the goods than to pay the duty.

SUGGESTED READING

WINTER, WILLIAM D. *Marine Insurance.* 3d ed. New York: McGraw-Hill Book Co., Inc., 1952. Chaps. 5, 6, 7, 9, 10, 11.

Chapter 21

YACHT AND SMALL BOAT INSURANCE

BY WALTER R. GHERARDI

According to Webster's Dictionary, a yacht is "any one of various types of relatively small vessels, characteristically with sharp prow and graceful lines, and ordinarily used for pleasure."[1] This description is interesting, but hardly gives a clear image of the extraordinary varieties of craft which are used for pleasure purposes. They range from canoes and outboard motorboats to large oceangoing steel vessels with values as high as $1 million.

The background of yacht insurance is not clear, but it presumably grew out of the forms of insurance granted on commercial vessels. The coverage on such vessels was on a "named peril" basis. Commercial marine insurance traces its origin to the beginnings of marine commerce and the terms and conditions used in marine policies are nearly as old as commerce itself. Many of these terms remain in today's yacht policies, primarily because they have been clearly defined by court decisions over the years.

Miscellaneous types of low-valued pleasure craft, which are legion in number, lend themselves to mass production methods of insurance. Aside from these craft, yacht and pleasure boats to a considerable extent require "tailor-made" methods of insurance. While the terms of coverage, generally speaking, are similar from one boat to another, each risk submitted to an underwriter is considered as an entity. Even two identical boats can differ materially from an insurance point of view because of maintenance, upkeep, waters to be navigated, navigation time, value requested, and experience of the owners.

PRINCIPAL COVERAGES

Generally speaking, yacht insurance is arranged so that a company issues one policy to cover all of an insured's requirements, that is, protec-

[1] *Webster's New International Dictionary of the English Language* (2d ed.; unabridged; Springfield, Mass: G. & C. Merriam Co., 1959).

tion for his yacht as well as liabilities arising through his ownership of it. These coverages are as follows:

Hull Coverage

Hull insurance covers the yacht itself, plus its spars, sails, tackle, apparel, machinery, boats, and furniture. The perils covered are illustrated in the following clauses, the wording of which may vary slightly among various policies used by underwriters today:

Touching the adventures and perils which the Company is content to bear and take upon itself, they are of the seas and waters as above named, fire, lightning, assailing thieves, jettison, barratry of the Masters and Mariners, and all other like perils, losses and misfortunes that shall come to the hurt, detriment or damage of the said yacht or any part thereof.

This insurance also specially to cover (subject to the deductible or other average clause, if any) loss of or damage to the property insured directly caused by the following:

> Accidents in loading, discharging or handling stores and fittings or in taking in fuel, or in hauling or launching or moving in shipyards or in going on or off drydocks, graving docks or slipways; While in shipyards or elsewhere on shore, windstorm, tornado, hurricane, earthquake, floods, collapse of buildings or other structures including collapse of shoring, blocking or staging; Explosions on shipboard or elsewhere; Bursting of boilers, breakage of shafts, or any latent defect in the machinery or hull, (excluding, however, the cost and expense of replacing or repairing the defective part); Contact with aircraft including articles falling therefrom, rockets or similar missiles; or with any land conveyance except while on public roads and highways; Negligence of Master, Mariners, Engineers or Pilots;

provided such loss or damage has not resulted from want of due diligence by the Assured, the Owners or Managers of the vessel or any of them.

Much of the foregoing is self-explanatory; however, some of the wording may not be clear to those who are not familiar with hull insurance. For example, the coverage provided by "perils of the sea" includes various marine perils such as heavy weather, stranding, and striking an underwater obstruction. It also covers damage to the insured yacht resulting from a collision.

Not specifically mentioned as a peril, but nonetheless covered, is loss due to sinking provided always that the sinking was as a result of an insured peril. Naturally sinking resulting from an uninsured peril such as unseaworthiness would not be covered.

The word "jettison" comes from the commercial form of hull policy and, though claims from this cause are infrequent, it still has application in the yacht policy. Basically, this is to provide coverage for loss resulting from the deliberate throwing overboard of equipment in order to save a yacht which might be in peril.

Barratry is a wrongful, unlawful act committed by the master or members of the crew without the knowledge or consent of the owner or charterer and resulting in loss of or to the yacht.

The insurance on a yacht is broad in scope. As a matter of fact, when a careful analysis is made of the coverage provided, it is evident that there are comparatively few accidents or losses which might occur which would not be covered by the policy.

Perhaps the greatest confusion which arises in connection with this coverage is that having to do with the disappearance of equipment of the yacht. As indicated in the clauses quoted above, mysterious disappearance is not a peril insured against. In this connection, it should be pointed out that, while the policy covers the yacht and all of its normal equipment such as furniture, cooking utensils, and navigation equipment, it does not provide coverage on the personal property such as clothing or fishing gear of the owner or his guests.

Exclusions. There are certain specific exclusions in respect to insurance on the hull. These are as follows:

1. Warranted free from loss of or damage to spars and/or sails and/or rigging while racing.

This exclusion can be removed by the payment of an additional premium or coverage may be granted at no additional premium by applying a deductible to spars and sails while racing. Coverage on spinnakers, while heretofore excluded from the racing coverage, is now available.

2. Warranted free of loss or damage in consequence of strikes, lockouts, political or labor disturbances, civil commotions, riots, martial law, military or usurped power or malicious act.

This exclusion may also be removed by additional premium.

3. Not liable for wages and/or provisions whether the average be particular or general.

The intent of this exclusion is that the insurance does not extend to any amounts expended by the insured on wages of the yacht's crew or on provisions.

Collision Clause. Included in the hull coverage, the Collision Clause provides insurance against liabilities of an insured for damage to another vessel in the event of a collision. The amount of such protection is the same as the insured value of the yacht. However, this insurance is additional to the basic coverage on the yacht itself. In other words, under the hull coverage, it is possible for an underwriter, as a result of a collision between two yachts, to pay twice the amount of the insurance on hull. This double payment would come about should there be a collision which destroyed the insured yacht and also damaged the other yacht at least to the extent of the insured value of the yacht, provided the owner of the yacht insured was held liable for the collision and could not limit his liability.

There is a Limitation of Liability Statute which provides that the liability of the owner of a vessel for any loss, damage or injury by collision, or for any loss or damage done, occasioned, or incurred without the privity or knowledge of such owner shall in no case exceed the amount or value of the interest of such owner in such vessel (and her freight then pending—if a commercial vessel is involved) after the accident. "Privity" has been defined as "some fault or neglect in which the owner personally participates."[2] "Knowledge" means "personal cognizance or means of knowledge of which the owner is bound to avail himself of contemplated loss or condition likely to produce or to contribute to loss, unless proper means are adopted to prevent it."[3] While this statute is of great importance to owners of commercial vessels manned by competent crews, and to a few large yachts operated by professional crews, it is of very doubtful value to the vast percentage of yacht and pleasure boat owners who operate their own boats.

Other Clauses. The policy has a clause known as "Sue and Labor." In yacht insurance this clause customarily reads as follows:

> In case of any loss or misfortune, it shall be lawful and necessary for the assured, his or their factors, servants and assigns to sue, labor and travel for, in about the defense, safeguard and recovery of the said yacht, or any part thereof, without prejudice to this insurance; the charges whereof this Company will contribute in the proportion which the amount herein insured bears to the valuation herein stated not exceeding the amount insured hereunder on hull. And it is especially declared and agreed that no acts of the Company or Assured in recovering, saving or preserving the property insured shall be considered as a waiver or acceptance of abandonment.

The meaning of this clause is clear, but attention is drawn to the fact that this is additional insurance up to the amount covered on the yacht. Under some very unusual situation involving a collision with heavy sue and labor expenses, it is possible that an insurance company would have to pay under the policy three times the amount insured.

As is customary in most marine insurance on vessels, the value which is to be insured is an agreed value between the insured and the company. In the event of a total loss, the full amount of the policy is paid, and in the event of a partial loss, the repairs are paid in full, but not exceeding the sum insured.

In order to outline the conditions under which an underwriter will respond for a constructive total loss on a damaged yacht, a clause appears in most yacht policies as follows:

---

[2] *The Carroll* [60F (2d) 985 (1932)].

[3] *Ibid.* p. 993.

No recovery for a constructive total loss shall be had hereunder unless the expense of recovering and repairing the yacht shall exceed the agreed valuation.

It is the custom for practically all yachts insured in the northeastern and certain other sections of the country to be laid up during the winter. In most cases an owner will remove a considerable amount of the equipment from the yacht for separate storage. The policy provides that this equipment is protected against the same perils as the yacht itself but only for an amount agreed upon in advance, usually 20 percent of the insured value. A higher amount can be agreed upon with the underwriters under special circumstances. The amount on the hull is reduced by the amount to be insured on the equipment, when the equipment is separated from the yacht. This reduction is made to prevent the total amount of insurance from exceeding the agreed value of the yacht and its equipment.

Protection and Indemnity Coverage

As a part of the same policy covering the yacht, an insured may protect himself against his liability arising out of his interest and operation. This section provides liability coverage for property damage and loss of life and bodily injury. The limits of liability for which an insured may protect himself are similar to those available for automobile insurance. Most yacht owners today carry limits considerably in excess of the value of their yacht.

The property damage liability coverage relates to liability for damage to the property of others such as docks, ways, cables, and other such items, as well as any collision damage to another yacht not covered under the Collision Clause of the hull section of the policy. This section also provides for expenses incurred, should the insured by required to remove or destroy the wreck of the insured yacht.

The bodily injury liability coverage relates to liability for loss of life, bodily injury, and payments made on account of life salvage. The policy usually will specify a limit of liability per person and a limit per accident.

An important provision of the Protection and Indemnity section of the policy is the water skiing limitation which is used in one form or another by most underwriters. The limitation either reduces Protection and Indemnity coverage or voids it entirely while the yacht is being used for water skiing or sports of similar nature, such as aquaplaning. This provision was necessary with the advent of high speed runabouts, used on crowded waters and piloted by someone whose attention might be divided between operation of the boat and observation of the skier being towed. Some insurers are willing to delete the limitation for an additional premium.

Longshoremen's & Harbor Workers' Compensation Insurance. Written separately, but only in conjunction with Protection and Indemnity, is Federal Longshoremen's & Harbor Workers' Compensation Insurance. This section provides coverage for the liability of the insured imposed by the Longshoremen's & Harbor Workers' Compensation Act of 1927 which requires a vessel owner to provide compensation coverage for casual workers employed aboard his yacht while upon the navigable waters of the U.S. The act does not cover crew members of the yacht. It is intended only to protect casual waterfront laborers such as carpenters, mechanics, and other workers.

Medical Payments. As a separate coverage, but written only in connection with Protection and Indemnity, is Medical Payments which is a voluntary coverage for payment of medical expenses incurred as a result of a person's injury aboard, boarding, or leaving the insured yacht. The insured need not be liable for the injury in order for this coverage to apply. The only persons not covered under this section are those under the Longshoremen's & Harbor Workers' Compensation Act or any other workmen's compensation act, trespassers, employees of the insured, and in some policies, the insured himself.

While this section does not cover an employee, crew members of the yacht have coverage similar to Medical Payments under the Protection and Indemnity section. Because federal law requires the owner of a vessel to provide maintenance and care for crew members who are injured or become ill in the course of their employment aboard the yacht, the Protection and Indemnity section will pick up this coverage as a liability of the insured.

GENERAL CONDITIONS

In addition, there are numerous important general provisions in a yacht policy. One of the most important of these reads as follows:

> The coverage under this Policy shall terminate upon the sale, assignment, transfer or pledge of the interest insured hereby or upon the use of the yacht for other than private pleasure purposes or upon the chartering or hiring of the yacht, unless previous written consent of the company has been obtained.

From the foregoing, it will be noted that any change in the original ownership or use for other than private pleasure purposes terminates the policy. Note also that this clause prohibits the chartering of the yacht unless previous written permission of the company is obtained. The reasoning behind this clause is that the underwriter examines a yacht risk from a point of view of not only the physical characteristics of the yacht itself but also the owner's knowledge and experience in its operation. Any change such as the use by persons other than the insured may change the degree of risk considerably.

Omnibus Clause

The Omnibus Clause or Definition of the Assured, as it is variously known, extends Protection and Indemnity and Collision Clause coverage to persons other than the insured who may be using the yacht with the permission of the insured. The result is that if a friend borrows an insured's yacht and, as a result of an accident, is held liable for either property damage or bodily injury, he receives the same protection under the policy as would be afforded the named insured. The policy does not extend, however, to a paid master or crew member of the yacht. Neither does it extend to any person or organization providing marine services such as marinas, yacht clubs, and shipyards.

The policy contains the information regarding a specific risk insured: the name of the insured and the agent or broker appear as well as the term of the policy. The agreed valuation of the hull is shown with rate and premium as well as the Protection and Indemnity coverages and their appropriate premium.

Lay Up Warranty

The Lay Up Warranty, found in most standard yacht policies requires that the yacht be laid up and out of commission between certain dates during the year. Usually a yacht owner may select this lay up period by considering the times he normally uses the boat. In some areas where the yachting season continues throughout the year the policy may be written so as to permit the full year in commission. The premium under such conditions naturally will be higher than for a yacht operating for only six months. While the definition of "laid up and out of commission" does not normally appear in yacht policies, it is understood to mean laid up in a safe berth for storage and not being used by the owner. These criteria are not applied by all underwriters. Some require that the yacht be laid up ashore. Others require that it be laid up in accordance with local custom, meaning ashore or afloat depending on the local practices.

It should be pointed out that while a yacht is warranted laid up and out of commission the full terms and conditions of the policy continue to apply during this period.

Lay Up Returns

The yacht policy contains a provision for the return of premium for periods during which the yacht is laid up during the navigating season permitted by the policy. Because of the fact that the degree of risk varies during the year, the rate is divided between port risk (or laid up coverage) and navigation coverage, with the greater portion of the rate being for navigation. Obviously, when a yacht is laid up while it is permitted to be in commission, the degree of risk is less than that contemplated by the underwriter in rating the policy. Therefore, a return of premium representing a differential in the port risk and navigating rates is allowed. The return is usually for minimum periods of 15 consecutive days and is paid at the policy expiration only if the yacht has not become a total loss.

Not all yachts are eligible for lay up returns. If the difference between port risk and navigating rates is small because of a low overall policy rate, lay up returns are not granted. Yachts insured for a low value may not be subject to lay up returns because the premium developed is small and must be considered minimum for such a risk. Some underwriters require a minimum value of $5,000, others, $10,000, before a yacht may be eligible for these returns.

Cancellation Returns

When a yacht policy is cancelled, it is usually necessary to refer to the policy to determine the proper return. Under the heading "Return Premium for Cancellation" appear several figures shown in "cents per cent" which indicate the amount of premium to be returned. Because of the differential in rate between navigating and lay up periods, the larger figure is for unused navigating time and the smaller for unused lay up time, each being for periods of 15 consecutive days. The rates of return are shown in the policy and usually they are on a net basis, that is, no return of commission is involved.

It should be noted that both lay up and cancellation returns are based on periods of 15 consecutive days. Returns are paid only on completed 15 day periods. Recently, some companies have revised cancellation provisions in yacht insurance to make them the same as cancellation provisions in the Standard Fire Policy, that is, simply short rate or pro rata. Lay up returns are usually not allowed on policies containing this type of cancellation provisions.

SPECIAL CONDITIONS AND COVERAGES

Certain conditions, exclusions, warranties, and coverages necessarily vary from policy to policy, depending on the type of yacht, where she is used, the equipment aboard, and, in respect to coverage, the wishes of the insured.

Cruising Limits

Every yacht is limited to cruising in a certain area and this area is clearly defined in the cruising warranty. Policy rates will vary according to the area in which the yacht is used, with more protected areas naturally having a lower rate level. The most common cruising limits on the east coast are from Eastport, Maine to Cedar Keys, Florida. This includes the entire U.S. Atlantic coast and the west coast of Florida. Others in general use are: The Great Lakes including the St. Lawrence River not below Quebec; and Chesapeake Bay. A west coast yacht would have a separate cruising limit for one of the following areas: Southern California; San Francisco Bay; Northern California; Columbia River; and Puget Sound.

Certain large oceangoing yachts may have limits of "Waters of the Western Hemisphere not North of 50° North Latitude."

Machinery Damage Exclusion

Underwriters in recent years were forced to take a rather hard look at their experience on runabouts and express cruisers. Lighter boats and larger engines have produced speeds in these craft formerly found only in racing boats with the result that losses due to striking submerged objects became more and more frequent. Obstructions and debris which can be easily avoided at 15 miles per hour, are a problem at 30 miles per hour because they are harder to spot and because reaction times are reduced. Engines operated at high speeds also are subject to mechanical damage. Because of this adverse experience, it is common for many policies on fast yachts to exclude damage to the rudder, propeller, shaft, or machinery unless the damage results from fire, collision, sinking from an insured peril, and in some cases stranding.

Additional Coverages

There are several special forms which may be written into a yacht insurance contract, depending upon the needs of the insured and the use of the yacht. These forms are as follows:

Port Risk. This is a coverage which provides full marine perils on a yacht, but requires that it be laid up and out of commission at a named location for the entire policy period. Should the insured require navigation coverage, an endorsement may be added at an additional premium to permit the yacht to go into commission.

Fire Only. This coverage, while written on a full yacht form, amends the policy perils to cover loss due to fire only, with the Collision Clause also deleted. Fire Only policies may be extended to cover explosion and theft of the entire boat, but in no case are they extended to cover full marine perils. There is usually no lay up warranty in a Fire Only policy, but the policy usually does contain a provision as to cruising limits.

Protection and Indemnity Only. For those yacht owners who do not wish to cover their yacht with hull insurance but still wish to cover their liability, there is available a Protection and Indemnity Only Policy. This policy provides the same liability coverages that are provided by the usual yacht policy, including collision liability. Premiums charged for Protection and Indemnity Only Policy are higher than those for Protection and Indemnity written in conjunction with hull coverage because the policy must provide full collision coverage rather than the excess over that coverage provided in the basic hull policy.

Increased Value. This form of coverage, available only on higher valued yachts, is written as a separate policy on a portion of the total insured value of the yacht, never more than 25 percent, and provides excess "total loss only" coverage on the hull as well as under the Collision Clause and Sue and Labor Clause. The rate for this coverage is usually half or less than half of that charged on the "full marine" policy covering the remaining insured value on the yacht. The purpose of the Increased Value Policy is to reduce the premium on the high valued yachts while providing substantially full coverage in amount. No recovery for a constructive total loss shall be had unless the expense of recovering and repairing the yachts shall exceed the insured value in the policy on the hull.

Builder's Risk. This is designed to cover a yacht from the time her keel is laid until she is turned over to her owner. While the policy is written for the completed value of the yacht, coverage is for the amount actually expended at the time of loss. The rates for Builder's Risk coverage depend largely on the fire rate at the builder's yard and on whether or not coverage is desired for launching and trial trips.

THE "ALL RISK" POLICY

The usual "full marine" type of policy and its variations have been discussed. Not yet mentioned in this chapter is a new policy which is finding wide acceptance among marine underwriters and yacht owners. There have been "all risk" policies available for the West Coast areas and certain inland waters, but only recently has an "all-risk" policy come into use in all parts of the country.

While the term "all risk" may indicate a considerable broadening of coverage over the "full marine" or "named peril" policy, in actuality the "full marine" form covers most of the frequent causes of loss to a yacht and the broadening is only in areas of *non-marine* perils.

To compare the "all risk" policy with the "full marine" policy, it is necessary to examine only the hull section of the policies. Neither the Protection and Indemnity nor General Conditions section varies much between the two approaches.

Where the "full marine" policy provides coverage only against the perils named, the "all risk" policy covers "all risks of physical loss or damage from any external cause" except as excluded in the policy. In addition, coverage formerly granted under the Latent Defect Clause is provided even though a loss of this type would not be due to an external cause. This policy further extends coverage while the yacht is being transported overland, but in some cases with the distance limited.

The exclusions, which are of prime importance in any "all risk" policy, are as follows:

Any loss or damage, resulting from wear and tear, or gradual deterioration.

Mysterious disappearance of equipment other than boats or launches and their outboard motors.

Marring, scratching, denting, and chipping while being transported by conveyance.

Any loss, damage or expense due to or caused by ice or freezing.

Wages and/or provisions whether the average be particular or general.

Any claim for loss, damage or expense caused by or resulting from capture, seizure, arrest, restraint or detainment, or the consequences thereof or of any attempt thereat, or any taking of the vessel, by requisition or otherwise, whether in time of peace or war and whether lawful or otherwise; also from all consequences of hostilities or warlike operations (whether there be a declaration of war or not), but the foregoing shall not exclude collision or contact with aircraft, rockets or similar missiles, or with any fixed or floating object (other than a mine or torpedo), stranding, heavy weather, fire or explosion unless caused directly (and independently of the nature of the voyage or service which the vessel concerned or, in case of a collision, any other vessel involved therein, is performing) by a hostile act by or against a belligerent power, and for the purpose of this warranty "power" includes any authority maintaining naval, military or air forces in association with a power; also warranted free, whether in time of peace or war, from all loss, damage or expense caused by any weapon of war employing atomic or nuclear fission and/or fusion or other reaction or radioactive force or matter.

Further warranted free from the consequences of civil war, revolution, rebellion, insurrection, or civil strife arising therefrom or piracy.

These exclusions are self-explanatory. Some readers might be interested to note that the old "Strikes and Riots and Vandalism" exclusion is not found in the "all risk" policy. Its absence, therefore, amounts to an extension of coverage. Some policies also exclude loss or damage to spars, sails, and rigging on sailboats while racing, while others exclude only spinnakers. These exclusions are not standard to all policies but are representative of most now in use.

A few losses which have been reported illustrate the broader coverage offered by the "all risk" policy. Such losses as equipment dropped overboard, damage caused by seagulls, and accidental damage caused to the yacht by the insured or his guests are payable under this contract.

UNDERWRITING

Underwriting a yacht policy is like underwriting any other form of insurance. It involves the collection of information which will permit a reasonable estimate on the part of the underwriter as to the desirability of the risk, although in the case of the classifications which are massed produced naturally such information is more limited in scope. In order properly to evaluate the risk offered, a yacht underwriter must know the condition of the yacht, the type, the intended use, the value, and finally the information regarding the owner.

Condition

Of prime concern to any yacht underwriter is condition. Many factors enter into its determination. Original construction is of course very important because good materials, design, and workmanship in a yacht can be expected to affect her durability and continued desirability as a risk. Maintenance is also important. A poorly cared for yacht will deteriorate rapidly. Pride of ownership in a yacht will show in the care she receives and the care with which she is handled. Age is of course also a factor but, because of construction and care, cannot be the sole indicator of condition.

On newer boats much of this information may be obtained easily but, for the sake of complete information, a survey should be made. An experienced yacht surveyor can tell quickly if the condition of a yacht meets the standards set by the underwriters, who rely heavily on his report. In addition, standards set by such agencies as the National Fire Protection Association and the Yacht Safety Bureau can be checked by the surveyor on any yacht. Should the yacht be in generally acceptable condition, but with some deficiencies, recommendations are usually submitted to the insured for corrective action.

Type

Certain types of yachts have proven to be better insurance risks than have other types. A small, high powered runabout or express cruiser can be expected to incur losses as a result of high operating speeds and obviously cannot be considered as good a risk as an auxiliary sailboat or a larger, slower cruiser. Sailboats with no auxiliary power have neither the speed hazard nor the fire and explosion hazard because there is no fuel aboard.

Intended Use

In order to determine the acceptability of a risk, the underwriter must ascertain the normal use to which the yacht will be put. Yachts which are frequently chartered are not always good risks because of their heavy use, frequently by people inexperienced in their operation. The suitability of a yacht for an owner's intended area of operation is also important. A small, lightly constructed boat to be operated offshore obviously would not be a satisfactory risk. Also, small runabouts used by young operators in crowded waters for waterskiing are considered most hazardous and producers often find such risks extremely difficult to place.

Value

The value to be placed on a yacht for insurance purposes is a very important factor. As previously mentioned, practically all policies issued on yachts are on a "valued form." This provides an owner with full protection for all losses covered by the policy, not exceeding, of course, the amount insured. Replacements of parts or repairs of damages are covered in full and are not generally subject to a deduction because of new materials replacing old materials. Accordingly, unless a yacht is insured for an amount that bears some reasonable relationship to its replacement value, the premium developed at normal rates will not be sufficient to take care of partial losses.

For example, if two identical yachts should suffer identical partial losses, the underwriters will respond for the same amount on each yacht always provided that the amounts involved do not exceed the insured values. If one of the yachts is 10 years old and because of several sales has depreciated in value to 50 percent of its replacement cost, the premium developed at normal rates would, of course, be very much lower than the premium developed on the other yacht if she were new and insured for her construction cost. Unless a very low value (as compared to replacement cost) is a reflection of the poor condition of a yacht, underwriters will increase the rate to produce a premium to take care of their full liabilities with respect to partial losses but to take into account their reduced liability in the event of a total loss.

The Yacht Owner

As in any form of insurance, it is most important to have full information about the yacht owner. He must be financially capable of owning and properly maintaining his yacht and his experience in its operation is obviously a factor to be taken into consideration in the assessment of the risk.

Moral hazard, as in all forms of insurance, is an important factor in assessing the desirability of a yacht risk. An acceptable insured must be a person of integrity and be financially able to own and maintain the yacht to be insured. A yacht of any size is expensive to own and operate and if an owner finds it more than he can afford, a moral hazard could arise.

RATING

The rating of a yacht policy depends on many factors. Basic rates are established for each of the cruising limits depending on experience and on the degree of risk in the area. These rates are subject to a 20 percent refund of premium in the event no claims occur during the year or they are subject to a 15 percent discount at the inception of the policy. The insured may elect which method he prefers. The established rates for yachts in northern waters are for six months in commission. Such rates must be adjusted for longer or shorter in-commission periods. The basic rates are for gasoline-powered yachts. Credits may be applied to these rates for yachts with no auxiliary power and for diesel power because of the reduction in fire and explosion hazards. Yachts equipped with approved fixed fire extinguishing systems also receive a rate credit.

A policy may also be written with a deductible clause at a reduced rate, the amount of reduction depending upon the size of deductible. The deductible applies to all partial loss claims under the hull coverage, and is not applied on a total loss. It does not apply to claims under Protection and Indemnity.

LOSS ADJUSTMENT

Close cooperation on the part of a yacht owner, his broker or agent, and the underwriters is of prime importance in the handling of losses and the adjusting of claims. Losses should be reported by an insured as promptly as possible in order that the insurer may take whatever steps he feels are warranted in the investigation of the matter. This report should be made before any repairs have been put in hand.

Minor damages generally do not necessitate the intervention by a surveyor on the underwriter's behalf, and quite frequently approval is immediately given by the company to an owner to authorize repairs for an amount considered fair and reasonable. In those instances where a question of the cause of the loss arises or the damages are more serious, underwriters assign a surveyor to attend on board. The surveyor, who is not an adjuster but a fact finder, endeavors to ascertain or confirm the reason for the loss or damage, to agree with the yard on proper repairs, and to come to an understanding regarding costs involved. He also holds himself in readiness to be of general assistance to the insured if any assistance is required. Papers usually required in support of a claim are a Marine Note of Protest or a statement signed by the yacht owner giving full particulars of the difficulty experienced and the bills which were received covering the repair of accidental damage.

Chapter 22

AVIATION INSURANCE

*BY WILLIAM W. WALTER**

Although the term "aviation insurance" properly applies to all of the many insurance coverages which are available against aviation perils, this chapter deals only with those which have to do specifically with the operation of aircraft themselves, namely, aircraft hull insurance and aircraft liability insurance. Other aviation policies such as Airport Liability, Hangarkeeper's Liability, and Aviation Products Liability Insurance will not be described in detail. The reason for the omission is that each is closely related to a familiar type of non-aviation insurance and is essentially an adaptation of that type for the purpose of covering some collateral aviation exposure.

With this discussion limited to the concepts and underwriting techniques peculiar to the insuring against the purest of aviation perils, namely, the operation of aircraft, perhaps the reader will gain a good understanding of aviation insurance. He will then be in a position to recognize and appreciate its basic concepts regardless of the particular policy in which they may be encountered.

While inclusion of this chapter in Part III of this *Handbook* is arbitrary, it does seem to fit quite well. Enough similarities exist between ocean marine insurance and aviation insurance to justify treatment of aviation insurance here.

THE NATURE OF AVIATION EXPOSURES

Attention is given in this section to a general description of aviation exposures. In subsequent sections evaluation of the risk, insuring techniques, aircraft hull insurance, and aircraft liability insurance are described.

* The author acknowledges the assistance of Mr. A. Kent Robinson and Mr. Robert A. Magrath, both of Associated Aviation Underwriters, in the preparation of this chapter.

Catastrophe Loss

Aircraft and the perils of flight present many unique problems for the aviation insurer but none is more fundamental than the constant exposure to catastrophe loss. The threat of this type of loss exists to some degree in every form of insurance but nowhere must it be given such positive consideration nor be more carefully underwritten than where aircraft are involved.

Of the many reasons for this condition the most significant is the physical properties of aircraft themselves. Because of the environment in which they operate they must be of relatively light construction and intricate design. Airplanes simply cannot be engineered in the same manner as trailer trucks or trains and made to accommodate the impacts of collision or the stresses and strains associated with other types of accidents to which they might become exposed. With specific design, weight, and speed requirements having to be met, aircraft must be accepted by insurers as being considerably more susceptible to substantial damage and total loss than is any other type of vehicle.

Substantial damage or total loss alone, of course, does not necessarily constitute catastrophe loss but with aircraft there always exists the possibility of personal injury, property damage, and loss of life. A review of some of the more recent aircraft accidents shows how quickly these factors can turn airplane accidents into major disasters. The problem is a growing one. As speeds, size of equipment, fuel load, and passenger capacities increase, the probability of this type of catastrophe will also increase.

Limited Spread

Complicating this exposure to catastrophe loss is a situation which provides the aviation insurer with a very limited spread of possible loss. The combined fleets of all the scheduled airlines in the world total at the time of this writing only about 3,700 aircraft. There are in fact fewer than 150,000 non-military aircraft of all types actively flying, of which well over one-half are registered in the United States. The significance of these figures is twofold. In the first place there are just not enough units at risk for the successful operation of the so called "Law of Large Numbers" upon which insurers traditionally rely for ability to predict losses. Secondly, numbers are too few to permit the development of credible statistics upon which actuarially sound rating formulae can be based. This absence of credible statistics places the underwriter in the position of having to rely solely upon his own judgment in selecting risks and determining rates.

Diversification

Though spread is limited and catastrophe loss a threatening possibility, the aviation insurer's task would not be nearly so difficult if each risk could be conveniently categorized, dealt with as a unit of a class and underwritten in a manner similar to automobiles. Unfortunately, this treatment is not possible. Even aircraft of identical make and model present insuring problems which make it impossible to rate them by class. Their values, for instance—and value is one factor which determines the size of possible loss and necessarily influences rate—can differ by tens of thousands or even hundreds of thousands of dollars depending upon the radios, navigational aids, or other types of equipment which might be installed.

Even more important to the underwriter than the varying factors which determine the amount of possible loss are those which have a bearing on the probability of loss. Factors such as prevailing weather conditions, the use for which an aircraft is flown and the experience and abilities of the pilots are as fundamental to this problem as are the number of hours flown and the quality of maintenance received. There exists so many variables vital to the proper analysis of every risk that the underwriter must treat each case in accordance with its own particular merits. He cannot rely on broad identification with a class to justify insurability or to act as anything but the most general basis for his rating.

Rapidity of Change

Having to shoulder the burden of prudent risk selection, the underwriter must be more than just an able insurance man. He must be technically versed in the structural and aerodynamic problems associated with flight as well as the operational and physiological problems encountered by the pilot. He must have an understanding and appreciation of aircraft power plants and, most importantly, he must be able to keep abreast of the developments and changes which take place almost daily within the industry. Aviation is a dynamic field and the underwriter cannot afford to find himself lagging behind. He must be constantly aware of new hazards which arise as speeds increase and the state of the art of flying becomes more sophisticated. He must be equally aware of the declining importance of hazards which may have been serious at one time but which are reduced or eliminated by advancing technology or other change.

EVALUATION OF RISK

Since so much depends upon the aviation underwriter's ability carefully and knowingly to select and rate his risks it will be helpful to discuss the factors upon which he makes his evaluation. He is concerned with four principal areas: (1) the type of airplane to be insured, (2) the abilities of the pilot, (3) geographical considerations, and (4) the purpose for which the aircraft is to be used.

Type of Aircraft and Equipment

The specific aircraft to be flown determines the insured value which will be placed upon it and the number of crew members and passengers it can accommodate. This information establishes for the underwriter the loss potential of his risk in terms of dollars by defining for him the top limit of loss to which he will be exposed with respect to physical damage to the aircraft and to some degree the maximum possible third party legal liability. He must consider this maximum loss potential before going on to the more important task of determining the probabilities of loss.

An aircraft's susceptibility to loss can be a function of any number of factors relative to its age, construction, and general configuration. The underwriter must evaluate each.

Age. The problem of age is largely one of gradual airframe deterioration and power plant weariness. After a period of time and after extensive exposure to the rigors of flight and the impact of numerous landings, all aircraft show signs of wear and tear. Often it is a decrease in performance by virtue of dents in the airfoils, corrosion of the skin, nicks in the propeller blades, or a dropping off of the rated horsepower of the engine. Most aircraft are designed with a sufficient margin built into their performance/weight ratio so that this decrease in performance has little effect on their airworthiness. With others, however, it is much more critical and any performance lag poses a serious problem.

Each type of airplane has its own effective life span ranging from a few years to several decades and many have inherent weaknesses which must be recognized. The underwriter must be acutely aware of all of these characteristics and give them full consideration in arriving at an underwriting decision. This consideration is especially needed in view of the fact that about half of all active U.S. civil aircraft were manufactured more than 10 years ago.

Construction. Though an airplane's construction undeniably has a bearing upon frequency of loss, it is far more meaningful to the underwriter as a guide to how expensive the aircraft is going to be to repair. They are not like automobiles where a dented fender is a dented fender regardless of make or model. With airplanes there is a considerable variety in the complexity of construction and in the types of materials used, with the result that each presents its own peculiar repair problems.

Aircraft made of tubular steel or wood frame covered by doped fabric are particularly susceptible to the hazards of hail, windstorm, and general deterioration; but they are relatively easy to repair. Many repair stations are available and rigged to recover or patch damaged skin and to repair or replace broken ribs and spars. These aircraft are quite different from aircraft of more traditional all metal construction. Here, even the most superficial damage requires the talents of an experienced metalsmith and the facilities of a specially equipped repair shop. With respect to aircraft of particularly complex construction, the underwriter must recognize that relatively minor damage can necessitate the replacement of an entire structural member at considerable expense. He must also give full consideration to the threat of a constructive total loss having to be declared in the face of inordinately high costs of repair.

Configuration. Aircraft configuration holds its own particular complications for the underwriter. For instance, those airplanes having so-called conventional landing gear (two main wheels mounted forward of the center of gravity with a balancing wheel in the rear) sit with a nose-high attitude on the ground which detracts from the pilot's forward visibility and increases the hazards associated with ground operations. On the other hand, the more common tricycle gear aircraft (two main wheels aft of the center of gravity and a third wheel up under the nose) promotes better visibility on the ground but is considerably less forgiving of landings on rough or soft terrain or taxiing collisions with low obstacles. Float planes and amphibians face the full range of marine hazards as well as those of flight. Multiengine aircraft, though they enjoy the added reliability of multiple power plants, present an asymmetrical thrust and drag problem when one engine fails which requires more advanced pilot skills to handle properly. Virtually every type of aircraft has some characteristic basic to its configuration which creates for it its own particular brand of potential problems.

One of the largest problems to be faced for some time in this area of aircraft configuration is the unique flight characteristics presented by the sweptwing airplane. To date this concern has been largely restricted to the airlines and their insurers; but, with more sweptwing jets being produced for private and corporate use, it is becoming a matter of general concern. The principal problem here is that of pilot retraining and the added exposure presented during the period of transition. The airplane with swept wings is no more difficult to fly than is its straight-winged sister. It is different, however, and its pilots do have to adjust their thinking and change some of their flying habits. Not all find this adjustment an easy thing.

Pilots

The old adage, "Aviation, like the sea, is not inherently dangerous, just mercilessly unforgiving of human error," is a truism which indicates the importance to the underwriter of pilot experience and ability in the evaluation of an aviation risk.

In this area the underwriter is fortunate to have operating in his behalf a rather intricate pilot licensing and rating system supervised by the Federal Aviation Agency. This system gives him at least some of the necessary assurances that the aircraft he is insuring is operated by a qualified aviator. This assurance alone, however, is not enough. The underwriter must investigate the pilot's background, experience, and accident record in order to make sure of the adequacy of his qualifications. Often, the underwriter will find it necessary to impose restrictions on the operation of an aircraft beyond those demanded by normal federal licensing regulations. Such restrictions may be imposed when a pilot first flies under the authority of a newly acquired rating or certificate or when he makes a transition from one type of aircraft to another. These restrictions are normally included in the wording of the policy itself and take the form of specific minimum flying hour requirements. Sometimes they are drafted to require that a pilot obtain so many additional hours of dual instruction before flying solo, or that he always be accompanied by a qualified copilot. Occasionally, they specify that flying be limited to fair weather and daylight hours and within so many miles of the home base.

The disturbing fact that over 60 percent of the non-airline accidents involve some degree of pilot error is evidence enough of the importance of the human factor in aviation. It justifies the utmost care taken by the underwriter in evaluating that aspect of each of his risks.

Geographic Considerations

The terrain, prevailing weather conditions, and other elements of the geography of airports used and areas of most concentrated flying also have a decided effect upon an underwriter's evaluation of a risk.

Airport location is of particular significance for it has an important bearing on the safe operation of the aircraft insured. Every airplane has minimum required runway lengths determined by the distance necessary for its takeoff and its landing roll-out. Each minimum is predicated upon the airfield being at sea level and its runway temperature being a constant 59 degrees Fahrenheit. As the elevation of the field and/or the temperature of the runway increases, the minimum also increases. An increase of 1,000 feet of elevation or 15 degrees Fahrenheit of temperature, for instance, increases the required minimum runway length by 10 percent. Clearly, one airport in the cool coastal areas of New England might be entirely adequate whereas its twin located 5,000 feet above sea level near Denver, Colorado, or on the Mojave Desert of California, where runway temperatures reach 120 degrees Fahrenheit, would be totally unacceptable from an underwriting standpoint.

There are other factors with which the underwriter must be concerned relative to airport location such as the probability of exposure to hail and severe windstorm. Another factor is susceptibility to fog, smoke, haze, duststorm, or other local conditions which result in unusually frequent periods of restricted visibility. These constitute a decided increase in the hazards associated with flight operations and cannot safely be ignored.

Purpose of Use

Every aviation risk is unique in its susceptibility to loss by virtue of the type of equipment flown, the attitude and aptitude of its pilots, and the geography of the particular part of the world in which it operates. Still, each risk must be classified relative to some denominator common to a number of others to permit the insurer to make comparisons. In aviation insurance the purpose for which the aircraft is to be flown is employed as that common denominator. It permits risks exposed to the same general types of perils to be compared with one another and provides the starting point from which the underwriter can proceed in exercising his underwriting judgment.

There are, generally speaking, five "Purpose of Use" categories used within the industry: (1) Airline, (2) Private Business and Pleasure, (3) Industrial Aid, (4) Commercial, and (5) Special Uses.

Airline. This term refers to that class of business involving the operation of large scheduled and non-scheduled air carriers. It is the most definitive of all of the use categories and the only one which provides the underwriter with fairly credible statistics upon which he can base a reasonable prediction of future losses. Many positive controls are imposed upon the operation of an airline which just do not exist in other aviation activities. These controls tend to standardize the quality of risks at a relatively high level by removing many of the exposure variables which distort the experience figures in other use classifications. Some of these exposure variables are: inexperienced pilots, poor maintenance, and inadequate airports. Although these controls provide the underwriter with a number of built-in protections against loss, they do not relieve him of any of his underwriting responsibilities. They effectively reduce the frequency of airline losses but they do not alter the fact that those losses which do occur have an extraordinarily high degree of catastrophe.

Private Business and Pleasure. This category applies to those risks which involve individually owned aircraft operated by the owner for his own personal use. There are a number of underwriting challenges common to risks within this category including those presented by pilots of limited experience, existence of flying clubs with multiple ownership of aircraft, aircraft which are of low value and marginally equipped, and the exposures associated with operation from airfields having limited facilities. The most important consideration of all, however, is the personality hazard. This hazard has to do with the pilot/owner's attitude towards his flying. Almost any pilot who takes his airplane and his flying seriously and who is interested in improving his aeronautical skills can be underwritten with some degree of success. Irresponsibility, immaturity, or "just plain boneheadedness" on the part of a pilot, on the other hand, introduces an element of exposure that makes him absolutely unacceptable regardless of his experience, the type of airplane he is flying, or any other factor relative to the account. The underwriter must be diligent in his efforts to detect the symptoms and to avoid risks of this kind.

Industrial Aid. This term is applied to corporate-owned aircraft which are used for the transportation of employees, business associates, and executives and which are flown by professional pilots hired on a full-time basis specifically for that purpose. These pilots normally are well qualified, commercially rated, and at the controls many hours every month. There is normally a considerable degree of control exercised over the nature and conduct of the flights by either the corporate owner or a chief pilot. Consequently, the rate structure for this use category is a bit lower than for Private Business and Pleasure. This use category is generally regarded as one of the most favorable in the aviation business. Its accident record compares favorably with that of the scheduled airlines.

Commercial Use. This term applies to charter operators, air taxi operators, and others who operate aircraft for general profit in transporting persons and cargo for hire, undertaking high altitude photography, and conducting similar operations not requiring a special waiver from the Federal Aviation Agency. This use category also includes the leasing of aircraft to renter pilots and the flight instruction of student pilots.

In underwriting and rating risks in this category the insurer must bear in mind two important facts. First, commercial aircraft are flown for many more hours a year than are private or industrial aid aircraft and these extra hours increase the exposure at least proportionately. Second, and more important, a very strong obligation exists on the part of the commercial operator to see to the safety and well-being of the members of the public he serves. This obligation is recognized by the courts as being considerably stronger than the obligation of a private owner to a guest and is reflected in the comparative size of awards granted in legal liability cases. For these two reasons rates for commercial exposures are generally much higher than are rates for other noncommercial categories.

Special Uses. This category is reserved for the many unusual uses to which aircraft are put, several of which require special waivers from the Federal Aviation Agency. Included within this class are crop dusting, low altitude photography, banner towing, pipeline patrol, flight testing, fire fighting, law enforcement, and many others. The only common denominator which exists between risks in this category is that each represents exposure to at least one of aviation's more serious perils. As a use classification it is of little assistance to the underwriter in terms of providing him with much of a framework within which to develop his rates, but it does serve to identify for him those risks to which very special and detailed underwriting attention must be given.

INSURING TECHNIQUES USED TO PROVIDE THE CAPACITY FOR AVIATION EXPOSURES

The great bulk of aircraft hull and aircraft liability premium is derived from risks which have a catastrophe potential far in excess of the retention capacity of any single prudent insurer.

The aviation insurance industry has not produced any particularly novel techniques in handling this problem. The only uniqueness is in the complexity of the permutations and combinations of those basic techniques traditionally used by the insurance community in general. A brief comment on the fundamental techniques of fragmentation, layering, syndicates and pools, and reinsurance illustrates the practices.

Fragmentation

Each of several independent underwriters accepts a proportionate part of an entire risk. Each severally and not jointly undertakes to share each and every dollar of loss from first to last. This method of operation is typical of the "London market" and is specifically the technique used by underwriters at Lloyd's of London.

It would be virtually impossible to find a sufficient number of these underwriters with enough experience to evaluate aviation risks for their own account or enough premium participation to justify the effort. Placement therefore requires that a portion of the risk be placed with an underwriter who has a reputation for sound aviation underwriting so that others may accept his judgment without having to make their own evaluations.

Layering

Each of several independent underwriters accepts a layer of the risk. That is, one underwriter pays the entire amount of the loss until the limits he has accepted are exhausted and then the next underwriter takes over payment of the loss until his limits are exhausted, and so on.

Since routine losses in aviation are comparatively high and would in fact run through a number of thin layers which would represent the capacity of a single underwriter, each layer usually represents the capacity of a number of underwriters. Generally, the combined capacities of those participants in any layer are made available through the facility of one underwriter among them who is skilled in aviation insurance.

The manner in which loss is spread within a layer can vary. Actually any one of the several basic techniques used to spread loss now being discussed can be utilized. Loss can be fragmented with each of several independent insurers assuming a proportionate share; it can be shared in accordance with the terms of agreement which bind participating insurers together in an underwriting syndicate or pool; or it can be spread by an underwriter independently insuring a layer through the placement of his reinsurance.

With each layer being led by a skilled underwriter in the field, there is not the true follow-the-lead situation between markets or layers which exists where risks are fragmented. There is, nonetheless, a requirement for a high degree of consistency among the terms of the contracts in the various layers. With entire market capacities being involved, it is not uncommon to find a reversal of the normal order of precedence. Often a company or group of participants providing one of the higher layers will actually dominate the placement.

Syndicates and Pools

A prearranged group of underwriters pools its capacities and establishes a common underwriting staff and plant. Risks accepted by the staff are shared according to a plan and the members of the syndicate or pool usually assume a joint responsibility to make good for a defaulting member.

This method provides for the aggregation of substantial retained capacity and makes possible the accumulation of substantial retained premium. Here large amounts of money are at stake on the basis of a single underwriting determination. The syndicate or pool enjoys a stability of capacity which enables it to keep rates from fluctuating from loss to loss. By virtue of the fact that underwriting and loss payment authority rests with a single agency, it has the added advantage of being able to respond rapidly with its full capacity to the needs of an insured as well as the ability to react promptly in the event of loss.

Reinsurance

In aviation, as in any other form of insurance where catastrophe exposure and capacity problems exist, reinsurance plays a most important role. It is utilized by the independent insurer writing aviation on his own account outside of a syndicate or pool to provide him with a capacity to compete. It is used by syndicates and pools and all nature of markets in order to spread the loss potential of risks they have assumed. It would be difficult to imagine any sizable aviation risk where reinsurance is not involved at every level of the insurance structure. This generalization holds whether that structure be fragmented, layered, written in whole or in part by a single underwriter, syndicate or pool, or a combination of all three.

Thus far in this chapter the nature of aviation risks and the problems and techniques involved in evaluating and insuring the exposures inherent to them have been described. The chapter is concluded with a description of the more salient features of the policies themselves.

AIRCRAFT HULL INSURANCE

Aircraft Hull is derived from the marine term "hull" and means insurance against physical damage to the aircraft itself.

Coverages

Although the usual perils of fire, theft, windstorm and land damage (collision while not in flight) can be and occasionally are written on a specified or "named" perils basis, coverage is normally provided on one of the following "all risk" bases:

All Risk Basis While Not in Motion. This coverage provides insurance for physical loss or damage while the aircraft is on the ground and not moving under its own power.

All Risk Basis Except While in Flight. This coverage provides insurance for physical loss or damage on the ground including such loss or damage occurring while the aircraft is taxiing.

All Risk Basis, Ground and Flight. This coverage includes all loss or damage occurring while the aircraft is on the ground, taxiing, or in flight.

The reason that "all risk" coverages are more desirable and more frequently written than named perils coverages is that the latter makes it incumbent upon the insured to show that the loss occurred as the result of one of the perils insured against; whereas under an "all risk" policy coverage is assumed unless the insurer can cite the application of a specific policy exclusion.

Limits of Liability

The insurer's limit of liability under an Aircraft Hull Policy is determined by the value of the aircraft insured as stated in the declarations of the policy subject to the application of deductibles and other modifying terms of the policy. In some instances the policy will be so written as to provide for payment of loss on an actual cash value or replacement cost basis with the stated value serving only to establish the insurer's maximum limit of liability. In other cases the policy will be written on a pure value basis with stated value, less deductibles, being the actual amount paid in the event of total loss. The tendency among underwriters in recent years has been to liberalize the terms of their contracts and so the valued basis has become more and more the accepted standard. It might be noted that, though risks are written on an actual cash value or replacement cost basis, similar to fire insurance, there rarely appears the imposition of a coinsurance clause.

The proper statement of value is vitally important, particularly where a valued contract is used. If the value is overstated, a possible moral hazard is created. If understated, the risk will develop inadequate premium, particularly with respect to partial losses. It is imperative that the underwriter look to proper market value of the aircraft and its accouterments at the time coverage is placed and to adhere to it as closely as possible. He must be constantly aware of the depreciation of values and adjust them as necessary whenever risks are presented for renewal. Many Aircraft Hull Policies provide for an automatic annual depreciation of approximately 12 percent. Where this provision appears, total losses are settled subject to the depreciation factor on a pro rata basis.

Rating

Rates are generally annual and expressed either as a percentage of the insured value or as a dollar amount applicable to each $100 of insured value.

For example:

Aircraft Insured Value	*Rate*	*Annual Premium*
$50,000	2% (or $2.00)	$1,000

Occasionally a loading factor will be applied to this rate in order to compensate for depreciated value. The philosophy here is that though values decrease and thus reduce the size of the premium available to pay losses, the cost of repairing the aircraft remains constant. Normally, this loading is in the vicinity of 25 percent of the basic policy rate and is applied to the difference between original list price and depreciated value.

For example:

Aircraft List Price	*Aircraft Insured Value*	*Rate*	*Annual Premium*
$70,000	$50,000	2% (or $2.00)	$1,000
	plus loading 20,000	.5% (or $.50)	100
			$1,100

Where a sizeable fleet of aircraft is insured, rates are sometimes geared to periodic reports of aircraft ownership and use. A common method is to apply a ground coverage rate to each aircraft for every day which it has been owned during the reporting period and then to apply a separate flight rate for each hour the aircraft is actually flown.

Deductibles

There is no established uniformity of deductibles among insurers. Almost any reasonable approach can be negotiated and incorporated within a contract. On better classes of business it is not uncommon to see deductibles eliminated altogether.

One of the more common schedules is the application of a flat deductible, say $50, to all not-in-motion losses and a percentage of the insured value as a deductible relative to all in-motion losses. Such percentages of insured value as 2½, 5, or 10, subject to certain minimums and maximums, are generally used in determining this in-motion deductible.

Reinstatement of Loss

In the event of loss or damage to an aircraft, its insured value is reduced by an amount equal to the loss until such time as repairs are completed. Since premium is fully earned on the amount of any loss arising under the Aviation Hull Policy, provision for the charging of an additional premium on this amount at the time of restoration of value normally appears. In risks involving better classes of business it is not uncommon to see this provision for additional premium waived. In such cases the insurer also usually agrees to the return of unearned premium in the event of total loss.

Loss Payable and Breach of Warranty

In recognition of the fact that so many aircraft are currently being financed, underwriters do make coverage available for the financial protection of lienholders. This coverage takes the form of an endorsement to the policy and is written for a modest additional premium ranging from 10 cents to 25 cents per $100 of outstanding loan. It provides that adjustment of loss shall be made with the named insured but that payment of such loss shall be to both the named insured and the lienholder as their respective interests may appear. It further provides that, with respect to the lienholder's interest only, the policy shall not be invalidated by any act or neglect of the named insured. This latter protection is particularly important to the lienholder since there are several warranties made by the named insured relative to the use of the aircraft, its proper licensing, and the experience and qualifications of its pilots which if violated does void coverage. (Note list of common exclusions which follow.)

Exclusions

Exclusions vary from insurer to insurer. Those usually found in this type of insurance specify that the insurance does not apply:

1. While the aircraft is being used for unlawful purpose with the consent of the insured.
2. While the aircraft is outside the geographical limits described in the policy.
3. While the aircraft is used for purposes other than those described in the policy.
4. While the aircraft, except for incidental taxiing, is being operated by other than the pilots specified.
5. When the aircraft is in flight, if:
   a) The Airworthiness or Pilot Certificates are being violated.
   b) With the consent of the insured, the aircraft is operated in violation of certain specific Civil Air Regulations.
6. To loss or damage caused by wear, tear, and deterioration including damage to tires unless as the result of loss otherwise covered.
7. To loss or damage due to conversion; war; strikes; riots; civil commotion.
8. To loss of use.

AIRCRAFT LIABILITY INSURANCE

Aircraft liability insurance provides the policyholder with protection against "third party" claims involving bodily injury or property damage arising out of his ownership, maintenance or use of aircraft.

Legal Liability Coverages

There are available to the insured three legal liability coverages each of which is generally written subject to its own specific limits of liability.

Bodily Injury Excluding Passenger Liability. This coverage protects the insured from the liabilities imposed upon him by law for damages for bodily injury, sickness, disease, or death suffered by any person or persons, other than passengers, due to an accident arising out of the ownership, maintenance, or use of any aircraft specifically described in the policy. Separate per person and per accident limits apply to this coverage.

Passenger Bodily Injury Liability. This insurance applies in the same manner as the coverage above but with respect only to passengers. Passengers are defined to include persons in, on, or boarding the aircraft for the purpose of flying therein or those alighting therefrom following a flight or an attempted flight. Again separate per person and per accident limits apply.

Property Damage Liability. This insures against the liability imposed upon the insured by law for damages because of injury to or destruction of property including the use thereof due to an accident arising out of the ownership, maintenance, or use of the aircraft insured. The limit for this coverage is a single limit expressed on a per accident basis.

The coverages noted above can be and are written on an occurrence basis as well as on an accident basis though normally the word "occurrence," when used, is defined within the policy terms as being an accident or a continuous or repeated exposure to conditions which result in damage or injury accidentally caused. Occasionally, Bodily Injury coverages are written on an undefined occurrence basis, though rarely is Property Damage coverage.

Limits of Legal Liability

The insurer's maximum limit of legal liability for bodily injury or damage arising out of any occurrence is dictated by the specific limits of liability indicated in the policy for each of the above coverages which might be provided.

In a typical policy these limits might appear as follows:

Liability Coverages	*Limits of Liability*
a) Bodily injury excluding passengers	$100,000 each person $300,000 each occurrence
b) Passenger bodily injury	$100,000 each person $300,000 each occurrence
c) Property damage	$100,000 each occurrence

As an alternative to the separate limits for each coverage, single limit legal liability insurance can be written. As the name implies, this policy provides only one limit which represents the insurer's maximum liability for one claim or for any combination of claims which might arise from one accident. Generally, all three coverages are included but occasionally single limit legal liability will be written for coverages *a* and *c* alone. This is true where for some reason the insured has no need for passenger bodily injury insurance or where, because of the character of his excess insurances, it is prudent to provide separate and distinct limits for that particular portion of his coverage.

It might be added at this point that because of the catastrophe exposures faced by many large corporate, commercial, and airline operators the acquisition of excess layers of liability coverage are a necessity in order to obtain the tens of millions of dollars worth of coverage needed. Often the arrangement of these excess layers has a decided influence on the limits of liability and the method of expressing these limits in either the primary policy or in any one given excess policy.

Limits might typically appear as follows:

	Liability Coverage	*Limit of Liability*
Either:	Single limit bodily injury and property damage	$500,000 each accident
Or:	Single limit bodily injury (excluding passengers) and property damage	$500,000 each accident

As is the case with the writing of separate limits for each coverage, single limit legal liability insurance can be written on either an occurrence basis or on an accident basis though generally where the word "occurrence" is used it is so defined as to limit recovery to damage or injury accidentally caused.

Medical Payments

This supporting coverage normally is available to selected non-commercial insureds where Passenger Bodily Injury Liability is written. This coverage provides payment for medical, surgical, ambulance, and related services and, in the event of death, reasonable funeral expense on behalf of injured passengers. Payment is made regardless of legal liability and is limited to the specific per person and per occurrence limits appearing in the policy for medical payments. (See Chapter 37 for a discussion of comparable coverage in the Family Automobile Policy.)

Guest Voluntary Settlement (Admitted Liability), Weekly Indemnity, and Permanent Total Disability Coverage

Guest Voluntary Settlement, or as it is more commonly known, "Admitted Liability," is a supporting coverage peculiar to aviation insurance and available to selected risks in conjunction with passenger bodily injury liability coverage. It provides that in the event a guest passenger suffers death or injury resulting in dismemberment, a sum up to but not exceeding a stated principal sum be offered the guest or his survivor provided that such an offer is requested by the named insured and that a full release for all bodily injury is obtained from the recipient. This insurance is designed to make it unnecessary for an insured's guest to resort to legal action to secure compensation for injury thus avoiding the embarrassment of a "friendly suit" and the necessarily high cost of litigation. The named insured always has the choice of either permitting the offer of voluntary settlement or of relying upon the protection of his passenger bodily injury liability coverage and the determination of his legal liability by a court of law. The written release is of course necessary in order to make any voluntary settlement binding upon the recipient.

Weekly Indemnity coverage can be included as part of Guest Voluntary Settlement. It provides that in the event a guest passenger is totally disabled from performing all duties pertaining to his occupation, the insurer will reimburse the named insured for payment made for loss of earnings up to a stated sum per week, not to exceed 80 percent of the recipient's average weekly wage, and for a period not to exceed a maximum stated number of weeks. Generally where Weekly Indemnity coverage is written for a period in excess of 52 weeks, coverage for that period extending beyond the 52nd week is contingent upon the party being totally disabled from performing the duties pertaining to *any* occupation.

Weekly Indemnity coverage can be written without the requirement that the disabled party sign a full release for bodily injury liability. When this is done coverage is usually limited to 80 percent of the average weekly wage, not to exceed $250, and is provided for a period not to exceed 52 weeks.

Permanent and Total Disability coverage can be provided in conjunction with Guest Voluntary Settlement whether Weekly Indemnity coverage is written or not. This coverage provides for the payment of a sum up to but not exceeding the stated principal sum (less any payment which might already have been made under Weekly Indemnity) in the event the injured party is determined to have been permanently and totally disabled. This coverage is contingent upon a full release being obtained from the recipient and again is offered only at the request of the named insured.

Rating

Each coverage provided under an Aircraft Liability Policy is rated separately according to the limits of liability provided. The premiums developed are normally annual. Occasionally, where large commercial fleets are concerned, rates are reduced to a per-passenger-revenue-miles-flown basis and premiums are paid periodically during the policy term under a reporting form.

Use of Other Aircraft

Although Aircraft Liability Policies are written with respect to specifically named aircraft, they do provide for the temporary use of substitute aircraft when the named aircraft is withdrawn from normal use for service or repair. With regard to individually owned aircraft used for private business and pleasure purposes only, coverage is further extended to include use of any other aircraft by or on behalf of the named insured or his spouse, provided such aircraft is not owned by or registered in the name of the named insured or his spouse or furnished for the frequent use of either.

Definition of Insured

Coverage under an Aircraft Liability Policy is provided not only for the named insured but also for any other person while using or riding in the aircraft described, and for any person or organization legally responsible for its use, provided such use is by or with the permission of the named insured. This extension of coverage does not apply, however, with respect to bodily injury or death suffered by any person who is a named insured, or to any employee of an insured with respect to bodily injury or death suffered by a fellow employee during the course of his employment. Further, in order to avoid covering those liabilities not normally contemplated by this type of insurance, the extension of coverage does not apply to persons or organizations engaged in the manufacture of aircraft or aircraft parts or in the operation of airports, aircraft repairs shops, aircraft sales agencies, flying schools, and others relative to accidents arising out of such manufacture or operation.

Aircraft Non-Ownership Liability

By virtue of the Definition of Insured (see preceding paragraph) the coverages provided an aircraft owner through his Aircraft Liability Policy are generally available to those who are permitted to use the aircraft or in whose interest the aircraft is used. These parties, however, may be reluctant to rely upon the owner's insurance and therefore prefer to purchase their own coverage. Such coverage is available to them through an Aircraft Non-Ownership Liability Policy. A policy of this type can be issued to cover the liabilities arising out of the use of a particular nonowned aircraft, or it may be issued to cover the liabilities arising out of the use of any nonowned aircraft by a specified pilot. An Aircraft Non-Ownership Liability Policy can similarly be written to cover any aircraft nonowned aircraft liability hazard to which an insured might be exposed during the term of the policy. This coverage is written as excess of any other valid and collectible insurance available to the insured and can be underwritten whether anticipated exposures are known or unknown.

Exclusions

As with the Aircraft Hull Policy, the Aircraft Liability Policy exclusions vary from contract to contract. Some of those more common to this type of insurance, however, specify that the insurance does not apply to:

1. Bodily injury sustained by the named insured.
2. Bodily injury sustained by an employee of an insured during the course of his employment.
3. Liabilities assumed under contract.
4. Damage to property in the care, custody, or control of the insured.
5. Liabilities of an insured, other than the named insured, for bodily injury or property damage arising out of his manufacture or sale of aircraft or aircraft parts and accessories or his operation of an aircraft service facility.
6. Liabilities of an insured who operates or permits the operation of the aircraft in violation of its Airworthiness Certificate or certain specific Civil Air Regulations.

PART IV

Inland Marine Insurance

Chapter 23

DEVELOPMENT OF INLAND MARINE INSURANCE

BY WILLIAM H. RODDA

Inland marine, the subject matter of Part IV of this *Handbook,* is a form of insurance against loss or damage to property. The phrase "inland marine" is not descriptive of the function of this kind of insurance but is more nearly descriptive of its growth out of ocean marine insurance. In this and the following seven chapters, a detailed description of this type of insurance is presented.

NATURE OF INLAND MARINE INSURANCE

Much of inland marine insurance pertains to the insuring of (1) property in transit over land, or (2) the insuring of property which is mobile by nature and for which there is no situs. There is a third area of inland marine insurance which has less relation to transportation. This area includes insurance on such property as bridges and tunnels, piers and wharves, and stocks of merchandise which are subject to a high probability of loss. A generation ago the marine underwriters were the only insurance people who were willing to insure broadly against loss of such property. By the time there was a need to define marine insurance, the covering of certain types of property had become so much a part of the marine insurance business that such insuring was continued as a part of inland marine.

Blurred Distinction

The distinction between ocean marine and inland marine is not sharply and uniformly drawn. By custom and general practice within the insurance business the covering of ships and goods on the oceans and on inland waters is considered ocean or "wet" marine, whereas the covering of property in transit over land is inland or "dry" marine. The insuring of small boats, and of imports and exports under some conditions, may be classified by an insurance company either way, depending upon the desires or practices of the particular insurance company.

State insurance laws set forth the kinds of insurance which may be written in each state. Most of these laws make no distinction between ocean marine and inland marine in their description of the underwriting powers which may be exercised by an insurance company. The rate regulatory laws of the states do make a distinction as to rate filing requirements for ocean and inland marine, but here also there is no clear line of demarcation between what constitutes one or the other.

The Floater Concept

An important feature of marine insurance is the willingness of underwriters to cover property wherever it may be without restricting coverage to a location. This feature is in contrast to the early principles of fire insurance under which property was covered only at locations stated in the insurance policy. One of the first applications of the floater idea to insurance of property on land was the development of the "warehouse to warehouse" clause under ocean marine policies. Originally, ocean marine insurance on cargoes was used to cover them while on shipboard, and until discharge at a port. Coverage of the goods until they were safely delivered to a warehouse in the port city was necessary. As cities grew and the distances from ship-side at the wharf to warehouse or factory became greater, there were increased chances of loss or damage to cargoes while they were being transported over land. Later, as land transportation developed, particularly with the advent of the railroads, it became customary for marine underwriters to issue policies that covered cargoes from the time they left the original point of shipment until delivered at final destination. Both the point of shipment and the destination might be many miles inland from the ocean or river port. Thus the ocean marine insurance policies, through "warehouse to warehouse" clauses, were extended to cover shipment over land as well as on water.

Development of "All Risk" Insurance

Another concept of marine insurance that is found in inland marine policies is the covering of property on an "all risk" as opposed to a named perils basis. Ocean marine policies from early years were written to cover against "perils of the seas." This approach is in contrast to that in early fire insurance policies which covered against loss from the specified peril of fire, or later from fire and lightning. Inland marine underwriters eventually came to insure against loss of property from "all risk" of loss and damage with certain exceptions. Thus, the exclusions in a policy came to delimit the breadth of the coverage. It should be noted that inland marine insurance policies presently may be issued on either an "all risk" or a specified perils basis, but that the idea of the "all risk" type of insurance was developed from the marine field.

EXPANSION OF INLAND MARINE

Much of the early expansion of inland marine insurance in the United States resulted from the willingness of marine underwriters to cover property on a broad basis. For example, the establishing of the Jewelers' Block Policy as an inland marine line came directly from the willingness to issue "all risk" policies. In the early years of the twentieth century jewelry store proprietors in the United States felt a need for insurance against loss by theft and other miscellaneous hazards. Fire insurance companies could not at that time insure against theft losses because state laws held this to be a "casualty" coverage. Casualty underwriters were generally unwilling to insure jewelers because they considered the theft hazard to be excessive. Underwriters at Lloyd's in London developed a "Jewelers' Block Policy" which provided a broad coverage of an "all risk" type. This insurance was written to a large extent initially as a non-admitted coverage, but eventually became recognized as an inland marine line. Underwriters at Lloyd's were not admitted to do business in most states, but they did (and still do) an extensive business in the handling of risks which other insurance companies do not want to insure or for which they do not have facilities. Lloyd's and other marine underwriters wrote (and still write) policies on such properties as bridges, tunnels, piers, and wharves. Later, coverage was issued on radio and television transmission towers.

Insurance on Goods in Transit by Rail

The growth of insurance on goods in transit over land was rapid during the first quarter of this century. It was influenced by World War I and subsequent developments. Early in their history the railroads in the United States generally were liberal in their handling of claims against them for goods lost or damaged in transit. Shippers did not feel a great need for insurance on their property being shipped by railroad because they were usually reimbursed by the railroad for losses in transit. Growth of the railroads plus governmental regulation brought about an end to the informality in the handling of claims by the railroads. In 1906 the Carmack Amendment to the Interstate Commerce Act required the issuing of a bill of lading as a receipt for each shipment. In 1913 the United States Supreme Court decided that a clause limiting the valuation of a shipment was binding upon both shippers and carriers. The result was that losses of property in transit came to be settled by the railroads in accordance with the terms of the bills of lading, which in many cases limited the recovery to less than the actual value.

Following the entry of the United States into World War I, the federal government took over the operation of the railroads. It was not clear at the time whether the government or the railroad was responsible to shippers for losses to goods in transit. This uncertainty, plus the interminable "red tape" in processing a claim where the government was involved, resulted in extreme delays in recovering for losses.

Shippers of goods by railroad were faced with increasing difficulty in collecting for loss of or damage to property in transit by railroad. A large proportion of rail shipments was under "released" bills of lading which limited recovery to the amount specified in the bill of lading. In many cases it was cheaper for the shipper to buy insurance from an insurance company than to pay the extra charges made by the railroad for a "straight" bill of lading which allowed recovery for the full value of the shipment. These facts, plus the uncertainty of making any collection whatever because of the confused situation under government operation of the railroads, encouraged the purchase of insurance on property in transit. When the shipper had an insurance policy covering his property, he could be assured of making immediate recovery for any losses. The insurance company took over the task of collecting from the railroad any amount for which it was liable.

Truck Transit

The increasing use of the motor truck also encouraged the insuring of goods in transit. During the 1920's the motor truck became an established part of cross-country transportation. Unfortunately for the shippers at that time, many of the truckers were operating with limited capital and equipment. In many cases claims for losses and damages were handled slowly or even ignored completely. If the trucker found himself in financial difficulty, he might drive his trucks to another part of the country to start business anew. Thus, the shipper who found it advantageous to use motor carriers also found it advisable to carry insurance against loss of his property while in transit.

The requirement imposed by some states and by the Interstate Commerce Commission that certain motor truck carriers have liability insurance (or post bond or securities) was also a factor in the inland marine business. This coverage, even though a third-party liability contract, was classified as inland marine insurance because it protected the trucker against loss from liability for cargo in his custody.

Chain Store Insurance Needs

There were other economic developments during the 1920's which influenced the insurance needs of business men. The chain store method of retailing was spreading rapidly. The operator of a chain of stores had some difficulty in keeping his stocks of merchandise covered with insurance under all circumstances. Existing insurance practices of fire and casualty companies required separate policies on property at various locations and on property in transit between locations. The chain store merchant needed insurance that would cover his stock wherever it might be: in factories, in warehouses, in transit, and in his retail stores. He also began to ask for a broad coverage comparable to that already available under transit policies. Again the marine underwriter showed himself willing to provide the facilities needed by business. Broad-coverage floater policies were written to cover the property wherever it might be, not only in transit but also in warehouses and stores.

CONFLICT WITH FIRE UNDERWRITERS

The 1920's were years of aggressive action by marine underwriters and of intense controversy within the insurance business. Marine departments of the insurance companies began to write insurance on goods which remained in stores, warehouses, or factories for many months at a time. Fire underwriters were prohibited by their charters or by state laws and rulings from issuing the broad coverage which the marine underwriters were providing. Fire underwriters also were restricted to the rates which were published by the fire insurance rating bureaus. The marine underwriters on the contrary were free of rate regulation, and could use whatever rate appeared to be satisfactory to them and their policyholders. The result was that many policies were written at rates below those which would be used for fire insurance. In fact, the charge was made and apparently generally supported that inland marine policies were written in many cases to cover broad perils of fire, wind, theft, and transportation hazards at rates lower than the fire underwriters were permitted to use in covering the single peril of fire.

The problem of the fire underwriters arose largely from three rules or practices of the business. First, the legal demarcation of the insurance business into fire, marine, and casualty lines prevented fire underwriters from writing in a single policy the broad coverage which was needed by general business. Second, fire insurance companies had by general custom restricted their coverage to apply only at locations and in amounts specified in the policies. Third, fire underwriters were bound by law or by rating bureau agreements to use only the rates which were promulgated by the bureaus.

A partial answer was found by fire underwriters in the formation of the Interstate Underwriters Board in 1929. The function of this board was to establish forms and rates for interstate multiple location properties. Fire underwriters started to cover property which was distributed among many locations and which had fluctuating values at different locations. However, marine underwriters continued to issue broad coverage policies which insured property not only in the course of transportation but also at fixed locations. With no standard marine policies and no bureau supervision, insurance coverages and rates varied markedly. This variation made exact determination of coverage difficult for policyholders. The rates which were charged for many inland marine policies were inadequate and, if continued, could have become a threat to insurance company solvency. Moreover, there was increasing pressure from fire and casualty underwriters for relief from unregulated competition. A widespread agreement was reached that some regulation of marine insurance was desirable.

REGULATION OF INLAND MARINE INSURANCE

During 1930, 1931, and 1932 efforts were made by the insurance business and by state authorities to bring some order to marine underwriting. Organization of the Inland Marine Underwriters Association by the principal stock companies in 1930 brought a degree of stability among the members of that organization. This association adopted standard forms and clauses and established rating methods for many of the inland marine lines. Insurance companies which did not join the I.M.U.A. were free to continue their highly competitive practices.

The Nation-Wide Definition

New York Insurance Superintendent Van Schaick was active in efforts to stabilize the marine operations within the United States. In 1932 he issued rulings which defined for New York State the conditions under which a marine insurance policy could be used to cover property. Further developments culminated in the adoption by the National Association of Insurance Commissioners on June 2, 1933, of the "Nation-Wide Definition and Interpretation of the Insuring Powers of Marine and Transportation Underwriters." This adoption by the N.A.I.C. was only a recommendation to the states and did not in itself have any legal effect. Its subsequent adoption as a ruling of the insurance commissioners in most states gave it the effect of state ruling or law in those states. Eventually it was adopted in 34 states.

This definition which was adopted in 1933 was not only a definition but was also an interpretation of the *underwriting powers* of the companies in the marine field. It was an effective restriction on what an insurance company could write under a marine policy. An interesting point to note is that the definition made no distinction between ocean and inland marine. This approach was reasonable because this definition was intended as an extension of the statutes of the states, and the statutes in most cases made no distinction between ocean and inland marine.

A principal purpose of the Nation-Wide Definition was to set up boundaries within which the marine underwriters could operate. The definition was intended to prevent their insuring property at fixed locations. The basic feature of the definition was that marine insurance should be used to cover property in transit and property which is of such a mobile nature that it has no regular location. There were compromises which extended the eligibility for marine insurance beyond this basic idea. Marine underwriters had been so active in the insuring of bridges and tunnels, and in writing Jewelers' Block Policies, for example, that these and similar coverages were included as permissible marine lines. The effect of the definition was to bring to an end the period of intense competition and to prevent marine underwriters from issuing broad policies for mercantile and manufacturing stocks. Fire and casualty underwriters were able to recover several millions of dollars of premiums which had been lost to the marine underwriters.

The restrictions imposed upon marine underwriters by the Nation-Wide Definition, plus the absence of multiple line underwriting authority, delayed for many years the ability of insurance companies to provide a broad coverage for merchants and manufacturers under a single policy. Until insurance laws of important states like New York were changed to permit multiple line underwriting, the policyholder who wanted complete insurance coverage was forced to follow the cumbersome practice of buying many different insurance policies.

The inland marine rating bureaus exercised a powerful influence for stabilization. From its organization in 1930 the Inland Marine Underwriters Association encouraged the use of uniform policies and forms to the extent consistent with providing the proper coverage. Three years after the adoption of the Nation-Wide Definition, in 1936, the mutual companies organized the Mutual Marine Conference to provide rate and form services to those companies. These two industry organizations established policies, forms, and rates for those lines of inland marine coverage that were susceptible to manual rating.

The South-Eastern Underwriters Association case was decided in 1944 by the United States Supreme Court (see Chapter 65 for a discussion of this decision). This decision subjected the insurance business to the federal antitrust laws and required the formalization of the ratemaking procedures of the inland marine rating bureaus. The stock companies organized the Inland Marine Insurance Bureau as their ratemaking organization and they converted the Inland Marine Underwriters Association into a trade association. The Mutual Marine Conference became the Transportation Insurance Rating Bureau. Both of these rating bureaus became licensed under the rate regulatory laws for the purpose of filing inland marine rates with the rate regulatory authorities of the states.

These rating bureaus continued to file rates only for those lines of inland marine insurance which are susceptible to manual rates or rating plans. Rating schedules or formulas have not been developed for those transit risks which vary so from one to another. The individual underwriter's judgment is the only feasible basis for premium computation in such cases.

Creeping Expansion of Inland Marine

Marine underwriters continued their efforts during the next 20 years to expand their scope of operation. The Nation-Wide Definition was amended in state after state to permit the writing of additional lines under marine policies. Whereas the 1920's had been an era of rapid expansion of marine underwriting, the period from 1933 to 1953 was an era of creeping expansion. By 1953 the definition had been amended in every one of the states which had adopted it. In many states the amendments were so extensive that marine underwriters again were insuring stocks of manufacturers and merchants on their own premises. A factor which hastened these developments was the breaking down of the traditional lines of demarcation between fire and casualty underwriting powers. In state after state it became permissible for an insurance company to write fire, marine, and casualty insurance, and to combine these coverages into a single policy. The underwriting powers of insurance companies broadened to permit such companies to write any combination of fire, marine, or casualty insurance. Thus, the "Nation-Wide Definition and *Interpretation of the Insuring Powers* of Marine and Transportation Underwriters" (italics added) was, in effect, outmoded by changes in the statutes of most states.

The Nation-Wide Definition was inconsistent with the multiple line statutes because the definition set forth what an insurance company could write under its policies. The new multiple line statutes, on the other hand, permitted an insurance company to write any kind of property and casualty insurance that (1) was permitted by its charter, and (2) for which it was qualified by reason of policyholders' surplus and other requirements of state law. In short, a multiple-line-qualified insurance company could not be restricted by any definition as to what kind of insurance it could write.

Many people in the insurance business felt that there was still a need for some definition of marine insurance to distinguish it from other kinds of insurance. They felt that, because of the somewhat nebulous area in which marine underwriters had operated, there was a particular need for a definition of marine insurance. Moreover, the statutory definitions generally were clear for fire, liability, and certain other types of insurance.

The 1953 Nation-wide Marine Definition[1]

The National Association of Insurance Commissioners adopted a re-

---

[1] See Appendix D.

vised "Nation-wide Marine Definition" in June of 1953. There were two important differences from the previous definition. First, it was broadened to include most of the expansion that gradually occurred in the 20 years since the adoption of the original definition. Second, it was clearly set forth as a document merely to determine whether a risk should be covered by a policy classified as an inland marine contract. It specifically stated, "This instrument shall not be construed to restrict or limit in any way the exercise of any insuring powers granted under charters and license whether used separately, in combination, or otherwise."

It might seem at first glance that the new definition would have little effect upon the operations of insurance companies. As long as it did not restrict the underwriting powers of an insurance company, one might wonder what difference classification of a particular policy as marine, fire, casualty, or a combination would make. The effect becomes apparent only when the definition is related to the rate regulatory laws. The rate regulatory laws of many states require that insurance companies, or rating bureaus on behalf of the companies, file and secure approval for insurance rates for most kinds of insurance. This approval is required under most state laws for fire insurance, for most casualty lines, and for inland marine insurance. An important exception applies to those inland marine risks which "by general custom of the business are not rated according to manual rates or rating plans." In practice there are many marine and inland marine lines such as motor truck cargo, installation floaters, installment sales floaters, bailees' customers risks, and transit risks, for which rates are calculated by the individual company underwriter. No filing of these rates is required. The result is that companies may use whatever coverage they consider desirable and may quote any rate that seems proper to them. Thus, it is advantageous to be able to classify a risk as inland marine. In such a case, the company may quote any rate it desires without making a filing with an insurance department, and without subjecting itself to any check on rate or coverage by any outside authority—except that, under the laws of most states, rates must be adequate, reasonable (not excessive), and not unfairly discriminatory.

The Committee on Interpretation

Even though the definitions were developed with great care and in considerable detail, it was evident that some machinery would be necessary to interpret borderline cases. In connection with the 1933 Nation-Wide Definition there was established a Committee on Interpretation. This committee has been continued for interpretation of the 1953 Definition. The Committee on Interpretation of the Nation-wide Marine Definition consists of 15 people: five represent fire insurance interests, five represent casualty, and five represent marine interests. There are representatives of stock, mutual, and reciprocal organizations. It is truly representative of the entire insurance business. The fact that marine interests have only a one-third vote in the decisions of the committee relating to their business probably reflects the original purpose, namely, to contain the marine underwriters within the areas which other segments of the business thought proper. However, the decisions of the committees, both under the 1933 definition and the current one, have been subject to little criticism.

Scores of interpretations have been issued by the Committee on Interpretation. Many of the interpretations relate to basic questions. For example, when the contents of a musical instruments store are insured under an inland marine policy, what proportion of stock unrelated to musical instruments can be considered as normal to the operation and thus also insurable under an inland marine policy? A related question is whether radios and television sets could be considered as musical instruments. Many of the questions which are brought before the committee are decided on the basis of whether or not the property is mobile. An asphalt plant which is used by a contractor for mixing road-surfacing material may be insured under a marine policy if it is truly a portable plant which is moved about from place to place.

Interpretations from the committee may be requested by insurance commissioners of the states or by insurance companies. When an interpretation is issued by the committee, it is sent to insurance commissioners or superintendents of all of the states which have adopted the definition. In most cases the interpretation is then adopted by each state. Occasionally a state will not adopt a particular interpretation as far as its application in that state is concerned.

The broadening of state insurance laws and regulations to permit multiple-line underwriting had a profound influence on inland marine insurance. One of the first efforts of insurance companies under their multiple-line powers was to furnish broad insurance on mercantile stocks. Many inland marine underwriters felt that this step could be accomplished best by expanding the operations of marine underwriters. Some of the broadening in the 1953 definition showed the results of this thinking. Included as insurable under marine policies were such risks as fur stores and dealers in farm machinery, cameras, and musical instruments. The justification for expanding inland marine insurance to cover such dealers was that fur coats, farm equipment, cameras, and musical instruments can be insured under marine policies when in the hands of the ultimate purchaser, and therefore they should be so insurable when in the hands of dealers.

Insurance for Retailers

As insurance companies acquired multiple line underwriting powers, marine underwriters felt that their facilities should be further expanded to include broad form coverage on practically all types of merchants. Several states amended the definition to permit the issuance of marine policies on such dealers as those in household appliances, office machinery and supplies, heating and air conditioning equipment, sporting goods, industrial machinery and tools, professional and scientific instruments, and marine supplies. For a time the inland marine rating bureaus had rate and form filings in effect for these policies in several states. The very broad Manufacturer's Output Policy which covered a manufacturer's stock under practically all situations was considered an inland marine coverage in some states.

There was a continuation of the struggle between the marine underwriters and the fire and casualty people in the insurance business. Many fire and casualty people felt that, with the newly acquired facility for issuing multiple-line coverages, broad insurance should be provided by combinations of coverage rather than by marine policies. The idea of issuing combination policies eventually prevailed. Expansion of the inland marine idea for dealers' policies was stopped. In time the permission to issue the several additional kinds of dealers' policies was revoked by most of the states that had expanded the Nation-wide Marine Definition beyond the 1953 version. The accepted method of covering dealers' stocks of merchandise was by means of the Commercial Property Coverage and later by the Special Multi-Peril Policy Program and similar programs.

INLAND MARINE INSURANCE IN A MULTIPLE LINE ERA

Multiple line developments and the rapid growth of the package insurance policies after World War II tended to submerge some of the inland marine coverages into the packages. All of the Homeowners Policies contain some floater coverage for personal effects, and Homeowners Form Number 5 includes the equivalent of the Personal Property Floater. (See Chapter 49.) For many years the Personal Property Floater had been a leading form of inland marine insurance to cover household and personal effects. With the advent of the Homeowners Policies, it rapidly dropped from its prominent position to that of a relatively unimportant line of inland marine coverage. The commercial packages began to absorb not only the insurance on dealers' stocks of merchandise but also a large portion of the insurance on goods in transit. For the first time in history, inland marine insurance was not only stopped from further expansion, but actually had a portion of its transit coverages absorbed into other forms of policies.

In spite of the growth of insurance packaging, however, certain economic developments are requiring increasing reliance on inland marine insurance. The increasing speed of transportation and the increasing volume of merchandise in the course of movement from factory to warehouse and from warehouse to store are characteristics of the economy. An efficient merchandising operation requires a rapid turnover of goods. This turnover means that a constant flow of goods through the channels of commerce must be maintained. Even though a portion of these goods in transit may be covered by the package insurance policies, the bulk of goods in transit must still be covered by insurance specifically designed for such a transit exposure.

Inland marine insurance constitutes a premium volume comparable in size to that of extended coverage, and about a quarter to a third of that for fire insurance. Practically all insurance companies writing property insurance of any kind also write inland marine insurance. The method of handling inland marine underwriting differs from company to company. Many insurance companies writing ocean marine insurance have a marine department that handles all forms of transit insurance. Others with substantial operations in both marine fields have separate ocean and inland marine departments. Among the larger insurance companies there tends to be an almost complete separation between fire underwriting and marine underwriting. The longtime rivalry between the fire underwriter and the marine underwriter continues within many insurance companies. Among insurance companies where fire insurance was the dominant business in the past, there tends to be a combination of fire and marine underwriting. This particular combination is most likely to be the case in a company which has not been in the ocean marine field. In such companies the property underwriting may be dominated by the thinking of the fire underwriter rather than by that of the marine underwriter.

The tendency toward the packaging of insurance has changed the organization of the underwriting function in many companies. Two principal methods are found among companies. First, some companies have developed what amounts to a committee type of underwriting for package policies. The group of underwriters which handles a policy consists of one or more property underwriters plus a casualty underwriter. The property underwriters may include a marine man if the company has done sufficient marine business in the past to have marine underwriters on its staff.

Second, some insurance companies have tended to develop multiple line underwriters rather than to use the committee approach. These companies have their package policy business examined by individuals who are trained to handle all phases of property and liability underwriting. If a particular risk has problems or exposures that are out of the ordinary for its class, then the underwriter is instructed to submit the line to specialists in the various fields of underwriting. Among the specialists usually is an inland marine underwriter who is familiar with the exposures in the transit portions of the risk.

SIGNIFICANCE

The social and economic significance of inland marine insurance is considerable. Commerce would be greatly hampered if it were not possible to insure property against loss in transit. Just as the origin of ocean marine insurance lay in the needs of merchants for protection of their ships and cargoes at sea, so the manufacturers and merchants of today find it necessary to protect their investment in their property in transit. The value of an individual piece of machinery or equipment may be in the many hundreds of thousands, or even in the millions of dollars. It is common practice for manufacturers to prepare a complete machine in the factory and then ship it to the purchaser for installation. A loss in transit would be a serious financial blow, and insurance protection is just as necessary then as later when the equipment is in use. The principal function of the inland marine business is the insuring against loss for the person who owns personal or commercial goods which are subject to loss away from home or in transit. Without such protection, commerce would be hampered and people would be discouraged from the purchase or use of many articles which are considered necessities in today's world.

SUGGESTED READINGS

Daynard, Harold S. *Paths and By-Paths in Inland Marine Insurance.* New York: Insurance Advocate, 1949.

Mowbray, Albert H., and Blanchard, Ralph H. *Insurance: Its Theory and Practice in the United States.* 5th ed. New York: McGraw-Hill Book Co., Inc., 1961. Chaps. 10, 11.

Rodda, William H. *Fire and Property Insurance.* Englewood Cliffs, N.J.: Prentice-Hall, Inc., 1956. Chap. 16.

———. *Inland Marine and Transportation Insurance.* 2d ed. Englewood Cliffs, N.J.: Prentice-Hall, Inc., 1958. Chaps. 1, 2, 3.

Chapter 24

INLAND MARINE INSURANCE—TRANSPORTATION

BY FRANCIS A. LEWIS

Inland transportation insurance in its classic form is today perhaps the least appreciated and most undersold form of protection essential to the manufacturer, merchant, and trader. This chapter is addressed to a description of this type of insurance. Attention is given specifically to background information, the Transportation Policy, certain allied contracts, and mail transportation insurance.

BACKGROUND

Perhaps the most straightforward way to develop the subject of inland transportation insurance is to define it. The following quotation is from the 1953 "Nation-wide Marine Definition." Part C of the 1953 definition refers to domestic shipments and provides that transportation policies may cover under the following conditions:

1. Domestic shipments on consignment, provided the coverage of the issuing companies includes hazards of transportation.
   a) Property shipped on consignment for sale or distribution, while in transit and not exceeding one hundred and twenty (120) days after arrival at consignee's premises or other place of storage or deposit; and
   b) Property shipped on consignment for exhibit, or trial, or approval or auction, while in transit, while in the custody of others and while being returned.

2. Domestic shipments not on consignment, provided the coverage of the issuing companies includes hazards of transportation, beginning and ending within the United States, provided that such shipments shall not be covered at manufacturing premises nor after arrival at premises owned, leased or operated by Assured or purchaser, nor for more than ninety (90) days at other place of storage or deposit, except in premises of transportation companies or freight forwarders, when such storage is incident to transportation.

From the above one can see that the intent is to set the insuring of domestic shipments completely aside from the traditional preserves of the fire and casualty underwriters.

Reasons for Insuring

Since the public interest is best served when public transporters and carriers are made responsible for the safety of the property of others in their custody, a question arises when an owner of goods considers the need for transportation insurance. It is: "Why insure goods in transit if the transporting carrier will pay for losses?" This question is a legitimate one but is one which can be answered simply and straightforwardly. The answer is that, while the carrier may pay some losses in full, it pays other losses only in part or not at all.

Among the reasons why buying transportation insurance may be better than relying on the uncertainty of a carrier to make good a loss are the following:

1. By law the carrier which takes reasonable care of cargo is not liable for losses caused by an Act of God such as flood or hurricane. Every year in the wake of flood or tornado, many people are surprised to learn that they cannot recover for this type of cargo damage from the trucking or railroad company. Transportation insurance is the only way a shipper can be sure of protection against losses of this type.

2. Insurance may reduce the total overall cost of making a shipment. In some instances the shipper can pay a lower freight rate by accepting a released or limited bill of lading which fixes the carrier's liability to some amount less than the full value. (See Chapter 23.) If he accepts such a bill of lading, and insures the full value under a transportation policy, his total outlay for freight and insurance premium may be less than the higher freight cost for a full value bill of lading without insurance.

3. After a loss, the amount of the carrier's liability may be a matter of dispute, or insufficient to satisfy the requirements of the shipper or the consignee. A properly written transportation policy eliminates this uncertainty entirely. The insured and the company agree at policy inception how the goods will be valued. Any one of several valuation bases which best meets his need may be chosen by the insured. For example, he may select the invoice cost plus freight, other charges, profit, and a percentage markup to take care of other increases in value. Other options are available.

4. Although there are many good carriers, certain others may be in a bad financial condition, which is not apparent to the innocent shipper, and may not have the money to pay claims. In other cases payments may be slow or the shipper even may have to sue. In the event a carrier becomes bankrupt, a judgment against him is little comfort to a shipper. On the other hand, transportation insurance will pay the shipper promptly and take over the burden of recovering from the carrier for its own account.

5. A merchant who ships F.O.B. (meaning "free on board") point of shipment can insure the goods (for the benefit of the buyer) through a transportation policy even though they are at the risk of the customer while in transit. Businessmen frequently use insurance in this way to preserve the good will of customers who may not have adequate protection of their own.

6. The function of a carrier is the prompt delivery of goods, and the payment of claims is an expense incidental to operation. The function of insurance is the prompt payment of claims, a paramount objective which is by no means incidental. Thus an insurance company, which by its very nature is equipped to give fast claims service, relieves the shipper of the time and effort spent in collecting claims from carriers. In some instances, too, an insurance company will have facilities to offer advice on the packing of cargo.

Types of Organizations and Persons Needing Coverage

Another question which arises in connection with the sale and use of transportation insurance is: "Who needs coverage?" The answer is: "Anyone with an insurable interest in goods in transit." This person or organization may be an owner shipping to himself (or itself) at another location, a seller, a buyer, an agent of the seller or buyer, a bailee, a borrower, a consignee, a consignor, a lessee, a lessor, or anyone else who may be liable for loss of or damage to such goods.

In this and the following paragraphs several common situations are described briefly. First, many firms ship their own goods from place to place for manufacturing, processing, temporary storage, or other purpose, and as owners they obviously need insurance.

Second, many other shipments are made under a contract between shipper and buyer or consignee. The contract usually specifies who will be responsible for loss or damage in transit. A very common agreement is the contract of sale which, besides describing the goods, price, delivery date, and so on, indicates where title and risk will pass from seller to buyer. There are many variations in these terms, a common one being F.O.B. at some identifiable point. For example, under the term of sale "F.O.B. rail carrier, Philadelphia," the selling price of the Philadelphia merchant includes all cost up to delivery into the custody of the rail carrier, with the merchant being responsible for loss up to this point. From this point on, the buyer must be responsible for loss, and pay all further costs including the freight. Thus, the risk is divided, the seller and buyer each having a part, and each may have his own transportation policy to cover his share. But when a buyer receives too few shipments to warrant having his own policy, the seller may agree to insure the goods for the entire trip under his policy. This arrangement is made to preserve customer good will and to promote business. Insurance costs may or may not be directly reflected in the sales price. If the merchant sells "F.O.B. destination" he quotes a delivered price and is responsible for loss until the goods are delivered. Most department stores and other retail outlets, in effect, sell on this basis. If the goods arrive damaged, the store replaces them and collects under its own policy. Coverage is also available for the merchant selling on credit to a new buyer who for some reason refuses to accept goods damaged while at his risk in transit.

A third common arrangement is that between principal and agent. The terms of an agreement between a manufacturer and his distributing agent will, for example, specify who will be liable for, or will insure, the goods in transit.

Finally, there is the contract of bailment. Under the law a bailee may be liable for goods of others in his care, custody, or control. For example, the dry cleaner who picks up and delivers may be responsible for customers' goods in transit as well as at his cleaning plant; but, because the transit risk in the majority of cases is minor compared to the location exposure, the transit coverage is usually included in specially developed bailee policies.

In summary, whenever property is in transit, somebody has a risk. The determination of the incidence of the risk and the resulting need to insure is a matter of importance.

TRANSPORTATION POLICIES[1]

The Nation-wide Marine Definition specifically authorizes coverage of transportation risks by an inland marine policy. It also permits up to four months coverage at location on domestic consignments and up to three months coverage at location on domestic shipments which are not on consignment. This class of business is unregulated to the extent that it is not subject to state laws requiring the filing of forms, rates, or rules. This absence of regulation is due to the fact that there are such infinite varieties of exposures with respect to commodities, length of haul, carriers involved, packing, and others, that a list of uniform exposures subject to class rates would be almost endless. Consequently a transportation insurance policy can be written, rated, and paid for in any reasonable manner which meets the needs of the individual insured. In fact, it is not uncommon for a policy to be individually typed from beginning to end.

Nature of Contract

Despite the varieties of risk, it is feasible to print a policy—sometimes called a "backer"—containing certain common terms and conditions. This Transportation Policy performs the same function as does the Standard Fire Policy, but it is not as highly standardized. Technically, it is not by itself a contract for it specifies neither the perils nor the types of transit covered. Like the fire policy, it requires that a form be attached to it to make the insurance contract complete. The large majority of transportation risks can be divided into a few categories which have in common such things as mode of conveyance, perils covered, and method of premium payment. Policy writing experience has led many companies to develop printed forms which will meet the insurance requirements of most insureds. The appropriate forms are then attached to the "backer." If

[1] See Appendix D.

a printed form fails in some minor detail, it can be amended by further endorsement. If the printed forms are substantially inadequate, a form to complete the policy can be completely tailored and typed to fit the risk.

Modes of conveyance should be specified in all cases, namely common carriage by truck, rail, air, or express; the insured's own conveyances; or any combination of them.

Carriage by water on inland lakes and rivers can be insured under the Transportation Policy. Such coverage is a part of inland marine insurance. Intercoastal shipments are customarily insured by ocean marine underwriters, but are frequently included in Transportation Policies, since they are "domestic shipments." If there is a waterborne risk, underwriters must provide "maritime" type protection such as coverage against assessments for general average and salvage charges.

The Transportation Policy, issued under a variety of names from company to company, may be on an annual basis or may run until cancelled. In subsequent paragraphs attention will be given to the manner of reporting shipments and paying premiums under such "open" contracts.

A Trip Transit Policy—as opposed to an annual or continuous contract—is also available. This policy is appropriate for an individual or business firm having no need for an open policy but occasionally requiring insurance on a single shipment. The Trip Transit Policy is usually complete, requiring no "backer." It calls for a description of the goods, the points of origin and destination, the name of the carrier, and the approximate shipping date.

Valuation Clause

Unlike most other physical damage policies, the open Transportation Policy does not call for specification of the insured value in dollars and cents. The reason is that the insured property shipped varies greatly in value with the kind and amount of goods a customer buys. One merchant may want $25 worth of one good; another $10,000 worth of something else. Under such circumstances it would be ridiculous to say every shipment shall be insured for $10,000 or some other fixed value. The policy is customarily subject to a negotiated limit of loss per type of conveyance and further subject to a catastrophe limit. Consequently, there is a need for some arrangement whereby the value of any shipment can be determined.

The valuation clause provides this arrangement by establishing a means of arriving at the value of the insured property. It is one of the most important clauses in the policy. Any one of several valuation bases may be used. The basis of valuation chosen determines the premium to be paid and the amount of the claim in case of loss or damage. For example, one manufacturer may want property not yet sold valued at "actual cost." This property could include in-bound shipments of raw materials as well as interplant shipments of goods-in-process and finished goods. The actual cost to the manufacturer for repair or replacement is the determining factor. Depreciation is not an element except to the extent that it already exists on used or "secondhand" property. The same manufacturer may want shipments that are sold and being delivered to be valued at the "selling price," including perhaps "incurred freight charges." This basis would cover not only his cost but profit as well.

In contrast, another manufacturer with similar operations may prefer to have all of his shipments valued at actual cost. In this case the premium will be lower, of course, than it would be if the valuation basis were selling price. Actual cost is normally a lower value than the selling price. The loss payments, in turn, also will be based on the actual cost.

There are other methods of valuation that an insured may designate at policy inception, or thereafter by endorsement. Whatever the terms may be, if they are clear and mutually understood, no difficulty should arise as to premium or loss payments while the contract is in force.

Other Provisions

Territory. The territorial scope of the policy should be well defined. It is to an insured's advantage to seek the broadest possible definition. A definition commonly includes the whole of the United States; definitions often include Canada.

Other Insurance Clause. An Other Insurance Clause makes the policy excess of other insurance. Where two or more Transportation Policies cover the same property, the custom is for the insurers to determine who bears the responsibility for insurance, make his policy primary, and make the other policy or policies excess. In cases involving other inland marine policies each containing conflicting other insurance clauses, most insurers abide by the "Guiding Principles," a voluntary agreement among casualty, fire, and marine underwriters which established procedures and obligations for settling such losses.

Benefit of Insurance Clause. A stipulation is found in the bill of lading of most carriers to the effect that the carrier shall have the full benefit of any insurance on the goods insofar as this provision shall not void the policy. Without some counteracting provision in the insurance policy, the insurer loses his right of subrogation against the carrier. The Benefit of Insurance Clause has been incorporated into the policy to preserve this right by saying the insurance shall not "inure to the benefit of any carrier or bailee," and that any breach of this agreement voids the policy. As an additional safety factor, insurers "advance" the amount of loss to the insured as a loan, repayable only to the extent of the recovery from the carrier through subrogation. This clause nullifies the carrier's contention that a loss payment has been made which should inure to his benefit.

Another clause gives the underwriter the right to sue the carrier in the insured's name with legal expenses being paid by the company.

Impairment of Carriers' Liability Clause. This clause voids the policy if any act or agreement by the insured prevents the insurer from recovering the full amount of loss from the carrier to the extent of the carrier's liability. The ordinary bill of lading issued by the trucker or railroad makes the carrier liable for the full value of the goods, but carriers in many instances are permitted to limit their liability to some amount less than the full value. There are many commodities for which liability may be limited under a bill of lading to so many dollars per pound, case, or other shipping unit, provided it is done with the consent of the shipper and a lower freight rate is charged. There are certain commodities on which carriers can limit their liability without consent of the shipper and without any accompanying reduction in freight rate. These involve commodities where the carrier's liability is limited by government regulation.

The ordinary express receipt of the Railway Express Agency limits liability to not more than \$50 on shipments of 100 pounds or less, and 50 cents a pound on shipments over 100 pounds. If the shipper wants the express company to be liable in excess of this amount, he must pay an additional charge. Thus, whenever an insured accepts a released value bill of lading or express receipt, he impairs the insurer's subrogation rights and violates the policy condition previously mentioned.

If the insured knows that some of his shipments will be under such documents, the policy can be endorsed to permit this arrangement. As a matter of fact, most policies are so endorsed because such shipments are very common. In some trades this arrangement has become customary and is understood as being routine. Underwriters should make it their business to determine in advance whether or not this arrangement exists. If it does, it calls for a higher rate. The importance of the Impairment of Carriers' Liability Clause is that it preserves subrogation recoveries, which reduce losses, which reduction, in turn, affects the policy rate.

Other Clauses. Other clauses in the basic policy set forth certain elementary conditions which hold unless modified by a superceding rider. Most clauses are self-explanatory but a few deserve some attention. A Labels Clause specifies in case of loss of labels that the contract will respond only for the cost of new labels, capsules, wrappers, and reconditioning of goods provided the loss was due to an insured peril. A machinery clause limits recovery for loss of a part of a machine to the insured value of the part and does not contemplate paying a total loss under such circumstances. This provision is important with older machinery, for the cost of replacing a part may exceed the insured value of the machine. In case of loss the Sue and Labor Clause obligates the insured or someone on his behalf to safeguard the property, with reasonable expenses incurred therefrom being paid by the insurer.

Rating

Ratemaking in inland marine insurance, including Transportation Policies, is covered in Chapter 28. A brief comment is appropriate in this chapter, however, to point out that there is nothing mysterious about determination of rates for transportation insurance. Although the insurance is not rated by means of formulas as in some areas of insurance, numerous factors are taken into account as a matter of judgment. Such things as the type of goods, the mode of conveyance, the type of packing, the type of bill of lading used, the experience of the shipper, part of the country involved, and so on are considered. After years of experience, an insurer can produce a rate which is adequate, reasonable, and not unfairly discriminatory.

In a typical case the insurer takes the above mentioned factors and others into account and devises a rate per $100 of values shipped. The policy requires periodic reports of shipments and periodic premium payments by the insured. An initial deposit of premium is usually made with an agreement to adjust it either way at the end of the term insured or at stated intervals in case the policy is a continuous one. Rates vary from as little as one or two mills per $100 to as much as 10 to 15 cents per $100. Flat premium policies are rare. In any event, transportation insurance contracts of any significant duration tend to become self-rating with the rates changing over a period of years to reflect upward or downward movements in the loss ratio for the account.

Movement by Owned Trucks

For the merchant who ships exclusively on trucks owned and operated by himself there is available a special variety of transportation insurance known as a Motor Truck Owner's Policy. It is customarily written for a term of one year and covers property as described in the policy while actually in transit on the trucks listed therein, subject to specified limits of liability per truck. Premium is determined by applying a rate to the limit for each truck and multiplying by the number of trucks. The goods are usually valued at "amount of invoice or cash market value if there be no invoice," and a 100 percent coinsurance clause sometimes applies in case of loss. The perils customarily covered are fire, lightning, explosion of conveyance, collision or overturn of conveying vehicle, bridge collapse, water perils while on ferries, tornado, and flood. Theft and numerous other perils can be added by endorsement.

With two exceptions the exclusions are similar to those of the Transportation Policy. First, the Motor Truck Owner's Policy excludes goods of others carried by the insured under a hauling agreement, but on occasion the policy is endorsed to cover the legal liability of the insured as a carrier. Second, the Motor Truck Owner's Policy also excludes goods, whether on or off trucks, while on the insured's premises or in any garage or other building where the vehicles are usually kept. The latter part of this exclusion pertaining to a garage is frequently deleted by endorsement. The remaining policy conditions are quite similar to those of the Transportation Policy.

An important underwriting consideration is the commodity carried. When theft coverage is requested on valuable goods that are susceptible to theft, a truck burglar alarm system is a highly desirable feature. As in the case of all transportation insurance, policies may be "tailor-made" with the underwriter's concurrence to fit the insured's needs. There are numerous concerns whose only risk is via their own trucks and many of these policies are issued. Where shipments involve other type of carriers, the Transportation Policy should be used.

Armored Car and Messenger Policy

Banks, large security brokers, and fiduciary institutions of all kinds can obtain transportation insurance on shipments by armored car or messenger of stocks, bonds, coupons, money, and other valuables by means of the Armored Car and Messenger Policy. Except for war perils and a few others, coverage is "all risk," attaches from the time of acceptance by the messenger or carrier, and continues until delivery. Rates vary with such factors as types of property, length of trip, and method of shipment. Separate limits of liability apply to the different types of property and methods of shipment, subject to an overall catastrophe limit. The policy is the open, reporting type. Excess of Loss Forms, which usually supplement other insurance carried, can be arranged on either a flat or reporting premium basis.

TRANSPORTATION BY MAIL

Insurance of goods moving in the United States mail channels can be considered under the headings of parcel post, registered mail, and first class mail insurance.

Parcel Post

When a business concern has a small volume of parcel post shipments consisting of very low-valued packages, it is possible that the time and expense to insure would outweigh the benefit derived. On the other hand, if the volume of mail shipments is relatively large, and if a good percentage of the packages have values of $25 or more, it is probable that insurance is worthwhile.

Insurance on parcels, of course, is available through the Post Office Department of the federal government. With this insurance being on an "all risk" basis and available at an apparently reasonable charge from the Post Office Department, the question arises as to how an insurance company is able to sell its policy. Here are a few reasons why private insurance on mail parcels can be sold:

(1) Private insurance also covers on an "all risk" basis and in most instances is cheaper than insurance through the government. (2) Private insurance also eliminates the necessity of the insured or his representative standing in line at a post office. (3) It does away with the need for filing postal receipts. (4) It provides a very useful record of mail shipments. (5) Government insurance is limited to $200 per parcel unless the insured "registers" the parcel. This "registration" is a comparatively expensive procedure. (6) The private insurance Parcel Post Policy covers up to $500 per package shipped by government insured parcel post and may go even higher on the open form. (The limit on ordinary parcel post is usually lower.)

There are two kinds of domestic parcel post insurance, the Coupon Form and the Open Form. The Coupon Form is used for merchants whose annual volume of mail shipments is under approximately $25,000, whereas the Open Form applies to larger shippers. Except for the rate and limits of liability under the Open Form, both policies are subject to filing requirements, and the coverage of each is essentially the same. The major distinction between them lies in the rate and collection of premium, but other minor differences exist.

Coupon Form. This form gets its name from the fact that it is part of a book containing 100 coupons or multiples thereof, the premium for each coupon being 5 cents. By reference to a premium charge or coupon table in the policy, the insured determines how many coupons are needed for a shipment of a given value. A stub record is prepared for each shipment specifying the consignee, address, date, class of mail, package contents, and value. Then the coupons are enclosed in the package or with the invoice sent to the consignee. The premium is earned as the coupons are used. Although the term of the contract is one year, it may be extended by endorsement if the coupons have not been used in that time.

Open Form. This form has no termination date and no coupons, but it does have a $50 annual minimum and deposit premium plus a judgment rate applicable per $100 of value mailed. It is printed with a monthly reporting clause which shows the rate and which requires the same information as that on the coupon stub with respect to each shipment. Each month the total values shipped are reported to the company with a check for the earned premium if the deposit premium has been exhausted. This form may be converted by endorsement to a quarterly reporting or an annual adjustment basis. It may also be endorsed to increase the limits of liability and to cover returned and incoming shipments.

Other Details. Like the Transportation Policy, each form calls for a description of the goods to be insured. Coverage is "all risk" on all shipments by ordinary parcel post or registered mail while in the custody of the Post Office Department. Property excluded is accounts, bills, currency, deeds, evidences of debt, money, notes, and securities; shipments sent on approval to strangers without an order; perishables, except against named perils; shipments improperly addressed, packed, or with postage due; shipments to persons at hotels other than the insured's salesmen, registered or en route thereto; packages with descriptive labels; and shipments not marked "Return Requested." The only perils excluded are those relating to war and nuclear contamination.

To insure fully a package over $100 in value, the shipper must insure the full value under the policy and also insure with the government for not less than $50. The requirement exists on these higher-valued shipments in order to obtain the better handling given to insured mail. On a total loss the insurer will pay the shipper in full and obtain reimbursement from the government for its share through subrogation.

Packages under $100 in value, which in most businesses represent a majority, do not have to be government insured. In case of loss either policy will pay the actual value not exceeding the amount insured as shown by the records, subject to limits of $100 per package shipped by ordinary mail and $500 per package shipped by registered or government insured mail. The Open Form may be endorsed for higher limits which suit the requirements of the insured. Ordinarily, both policies may be endorsed to cover government insured foreign shipments at judgment rates. If the foreign country does not have registered mail or government insurance facilities, insurers ordinarily do not wish to extend the policy. If the business firm has exports or imports covered by an ocean cargo policy, it is recommended that the foreign mail shipments also be covered under the ocean policy.

Registered Mail

Practically all policies discussed so far have excluded shipments of highly valuable property such as money, securities, and jewelry. The only exceptions are the Parcel Post Policy, which does not exclude jewelry, and the Armored Car and Messenger Policy, which is specifically designed to cover shipments of valuables by armored car or messenger. It should be noted also that the Parcel Post Policy's limits are too low where expensive jewelry is concerned.

Need for the Coverage. If a concern has no armored cars or messengers but has long distance shipments of valuables beyond the scope of armored cars, the practice is to ship by registered mail. This method of shipment is extremely safe as the result of very careful handling by the Post Office Department. Again the question arises as to why one should buy private insurance when the Post Office Department provides the "all risk" equivalent through registered mail. The major reason for private insurance is found in the maximum recoveries permitted by the government on registered shipments. These limits are as follows:

Type of Property	*Limit per Package*
Negotiable instruments, currency, jewelry, and merchandise	$10,000 when no commercial insurance applies to shipment; $1,000 when commercial insurance exists.
Non-negotiable instruments	Recovery limited to cost to replace or reissue property (not face value) provided declaration of this is made by sender.

Use by Fiduciaries. Actually, the Registered Mail and Express Policy is so necessary for certain types of insureds that little or no selling is required. It is of critical importance to many fiduciaries. A fiduciary is a person or organization holding a position of trust with respect to the funds or property of another. Banks, trust companies, insurance firms, brokerage houses dealing in securities, and investment corporations are examples of fiduciaries which make heavy use of this type of insurance. Even some large corporations whose business is not mainly of a fiduciary character but which have stock or investment departments need this type of insurance and may qualify for buying it on the same terms available to banks and other fiduciaries. Most of the following discussion applies to the insurance as available to fiduciaries.

Details of Coverage. The Registered Mail and Express Policy is open in term, covering continuously and worldwide, against "all risk" except for war and related perils. Registered mail insurance for fiduciaries is subject to state filing requirements. Property insured consists of bonds, coupons, stocks and other valuable papers, precious metals, currency, jewelry, and precious stones while being shipped by registered mail or express via land or air. "Land express" means only railroad express and does not include truck or bus carriers.

Coverage attaches when the property is accepted by a messenger or carrier and continues until delivered to the addressee. In contrast to parcel post insurance, this policy covers from premises to premises and covers theft from or by employees of the sender or addressee or from the post or express office.

In case of loss the insured may recover the value at either the time of dispatch or the time of loss or the cost of purchasing corresponding property, plus interest earnings, and shipping and insurance charges not exceeding in aggregate the amount declared. If securities are declared at market value or more on the shipping date, the insured also has the option of recovering replacement cost not exceeding 105 percent of the amount declared. Losses must be paid within seven days of receipt of proof. The policy also covers errors and omissions in declaring shipments and insures the amount that normally would have been declared, subject, of course, to premium thereon.

The Post Office Department requires that full value be declared by the sender on registered mail shipments of currency, jewelry, merchandise, and negotiables. Thus, the Registered Mail and Express Policy has no provision pertaining to the amount declared to the government as appears in the Parcel Post Policy on shipments over $100 in value. Incidentally, for certain types of registered mail, the Post Office Department also levies a surcharge based on the actual value of the property shipped.

Daily or Monthly Reporting Form. There are two forms of the policy. One is the Daily or Monthly Reporting Form which requires that the insured report to the company the details of each insured shipment and pay premiums at the rates specified in the policy rate schedule. Under this form the insured may elect the amount of insurance he requires on each shipment. If the value of all property shipped to any one addressee in any one day exceeds $5 million, such excess is covered only after notification to the company and confirmation of acceptance. A limit of $250,000 applies on any one shipping package containing currency, jewelry, and/or precious stones. The reporting form has two rate divisions: one for securities and one for all other property. It also contains an option whereby in case of loss to non-negotiable securities declared at less than market value, the insured may elect recovery of the cost of a lost instruments indemnity bond necessary for reissue of the securities.

For transfer agents, registrars, and trustees under bond indenture another reporting method exists. It is a flat premium endorsement to the Daily or Monthly Reporting Form which is available to cover shipments of securities only. The insured reports monthly the number of packages shipped and pays a premium per shipping package rather than a premium based on value shipped. This endorsement provides a registered mail limit of liability of $1 million on any one package of non-negotiable securities and $150 on any one package of certain negotiable securities. First-class mail limit of liability per package is $100,000. Losses are settled by the insurer's bearing the cost of an indemnity bond necessary for the reissue of the securities.

Annual Adjustment Form. This form is designed for the smaller shipper. A provisional premium is charged at the inception and on each anniversary with an annual adjustment of premium based upon the insured's report which is a single report of total shipments for the year. The insured must report full market value of all shipments and there is no division of rates between securities and other property. A lower limit of liability applies. Shipments to any one addressee in any one day exceeding $2.5 million are not covered unless reported to the company and confirmation is received.

Individuals or organizations such as attorneys; certified public accountants; building and loan associations; colleges; religious or charitable institutions; fraternal orders; or insurance agents or brokers are examples of insureds whose operations are not considered to be chiefly of a fiduciary nature, but who nevertheless have occasion to require insurance on valuable property shipped by registered mail or express. Registered mail insurance, rates, and forms for these persons or organizations are not required to be filed with state authorities. Hence the forms, rates, and rules are subject to company control. Moreover, since the fiduciary types of insureds constitute by far the greater market, the treatment of non-fiduciaries can be deferred to advance study. Suffice it to say that the coverage available is a bit more restricted than that granted the fiduciaries.

First-Class Mail

Expensive registered mail surcharges and accompanying detail in handling registered mail shipments have helped to create a demand for broad coverage on unregistered shipments sent by first-class mail. This demand is met by the First Class Mail Policy. The form, rates, and rules for the fiduciary class are subject to state filing requirements; but non-fiduciaries are written without such filing requirements and are subject only to company control.

First-Class versus Registered Mail. Registered mail is carefully watched and handled by the postal authorities. First-class mail does not receive such careful attention. Since the exposure of a valuable shipment sent unregistered is greater than that of a registered shipment, it follows that rates for a First Class Mail Policy, other things being the same, are higher than those for a Registered Mail Policy. But this difference is offset on highly valuable shipments by a lower mailing charge when the shipment is sent first-class unregistered.

The choice between a First Class Mail Policy and a Registered Mail Policy depends, among other things, upon the value per shipment. There is a point where it becomes more economical to use one policy instead of the other, depending on the difference in postage rates, the surcharge as discussed earlier, and the insurance costs involved. Therefore, there may be good reason for a shipper to have both a Registered Mail Policy and a First Class Mail Policy. There are other things which also have a bearing on the shipper's choice. The First Class Mail Policy does not cover all the property covered by a Registered Mail Policy. It covers only securities or certain other valuable papers but does not cover currency, jewelry, or precious stones. Likewise, the limits of liability under the First Class Mail Policy are considerably less than the limits available under the Registered Mail Policy.

Three Types of Policy. There are three separate policies covering first-class-mail shipments. All are continuous, covering "all risk," premises to premises, on shipments which the insured elects to insure via first-class mail and air mail within the continental United States. The only exclusion is against war risks. Each is subject to monthly reports although an optional annual adjustment endorsement is available.

Form A covers securities except those of the U.S. Government and detached coupons thereof. Negotiable securities are covered only between offices of the insured and in movement to other fiduciaries such as banks, investment firms, and trust companies. The insured must declare to the company at least the market value of the property insured and premium is computed according to a schedule of rates which vary according to whether negotiables, non-negotiables, or coupons are shipped.

Limits of liability are available up to $110,000 per shipping package not to exceed $1.1 million to any one addressee in any one day. In the event of loss the insured may recover replacement cost not exceeding 105 percent of the amount declared. Form A can be modified by use of a Flat Premium Per Package Endorsement which supplements the reporting provisions of the basic policy, changes the method of premium payment, and limits recovery to $25,000 on any shipment not reported under the basic policy.

Form B covers all securities plus other valuable papers such as revenue stamps and money orders. It is designed for low-valued shipments covering only for a limit of $500 per package or envelope. It further requires that the market value of property in any one package or envelope be $500 or less. The insured pays a flat premium per envelope or package and in the event of loss may recover replacement value.

The third type of policy, the Transfer Agents Mail Policy, is designed only for transfer agents, registrars, or trustees under bond indenture. It covers non-negotiable securities, excluding government bonds, and certain negotiables having a value per package of $150 or less. It differs from the other first-class-mail forms in that it also covers shipments via registered mail. Furthermore, its territorial range is broader since it includes some U.S. territories and Canada in the first-class-mail coverage and covers world-wide via registered mail. Premiums are paid at a flat premium per package. In the event of loss the company will pay the cost of an indemnity bond for the reissue of lost securities.

A feature of all three of the first-class-mail insurance contracts is that they may be endorsed to cover shipments by certified mail at premium costs less than that charged for first-class mail. Certified mail is a service of the Post Office Department similar to registered mail in that it provides the sender with a certificate of mailing and requires that the delivering carrier obtain a delivery receipt from the addressee. It does not, however, provide for indemnity by the government in the event of loss or damage. The postal charge for certified mail is less than the charge for registered mail.

SUGGESTED READINGS

Fire, Casualty, and Surety Bulletins. Cincinnati: National Underwriter Co. Fire and Marine Volume, Inland Marine Section.

RODDA, WILLIAM H. *Inland Marine and Transportation Insurance.* 2d ed. Englewood Cliffs, N.J.: Prentice-Hall, Inc., 1958. Chaps. 4, 6, 7, 11.

Chapter 25

INLAND MARINE INSURANCE—INSTRUMENTALITIES OF TRANSPORTATION AND COMMUNICATION

BY GEORGE W. NIXON

This chapter deals with the somewhat unusual subject of insurance on bridges, tunnels, dams, piers, wharves, docks, pipelines, power transmission lines, communication equipment, outdoor cranes, stevedores' gear, and other such equipment. Both physical damage and use and occupancy (business interruption) coverages are described. Readers will do well to keep in mind during their study of this chapter the tremendous values which are at risk in such properties and the uniqueness of the properties. Perhaps in no other area of insurance is individual underwriting consideration of the risk any more important than for properties discussed in this chapter.

THE NATION-WIDE MARINE DEFINITION

The classes of insurance generally falling within this chapter are specified under Section D of the "Nation-wide Marine Definition" adopted by the National Association of Insurance Commissioners on June 12, 1953, and later ratified by most of the states.

The specific language of Section D reads:

> Bridges, tunnels and other instrumentalities of transportation and communication (excluding buildings, their furniture and furnishings, fixed contents and supplies held in storage) unless fire, tornado, sprinkler leakage, hail, explosion, earthquake, riot and/or civil commotion are the only hazards to be covered. Piers, wharves, docks and slips, excluding the risks of fire, tornado, sprinkler leakage, hail, explosion, earthquake, riot and/or civil commotion. Other aids to navigation and transportation, including dry docks and marine railways, against all risks.

The foregoing includes:

1. Bridges, tunnels, other similar instrumentalities, unless fire, lightning, windstorm, sprinkler leakage, hail, explosion, earthquake, riot or civil commotion are the only perils to be covered.
2. Piers, wharves, docks and slips, but excluding the risks of fire, lightning, windstorm, sprinkler leakage, hail, explosion, earthquake, riot or civil commotion.
3. *a*) Pipelines, including on-line propulsion, regulating and other equipment appurtenant to such pipelines, but excluding all property at manufacturing, producing, refining, converting, treating or conditioning plants.
   b) Power transmission and Telephone and Telegraph lines, excluding all property at generating, converting or transforming stations, substations and exchanges.
4. Radio and Television Communication Equipment in commercial use as such including towers and antennae with auxiliary equipment, and appurtenant electrical operating and control apparatus but excluding buildings, their improvements and betterments, furniture and furnishings and supplies held in storage therein.
5. Outdoor cranes, loading bridges and similar equipment used to load, unload and transport.

The authority granted within the quoted words is affirmative, but there may be a degree of confusion as to what falls under which part of the definition when these words are read in conjunction with Section E2(m), "Mobile Articles, Machinery and Equipment Floaters" of this same definition. Section E2(m) reads as follows:

Mobile Articles, Machinery and Equipment Floaters (excluding motor vehicles designed for highway use and auto homes, trailers and semi-trailers except when hauled by tractors not designed for highway use and snow plows constructed exclusively for highway use), covering identified property of a mobile or floating nature, not on sale or consignment, or in course of manufacture, which has come into the custody or control of parties who intend to use such property for the purpose for which it was manufactured or created. Such policies shall not cover furniture and fixtures not customarily used away from premises where such property is usually kept.

Certainly, some of the property eligible under Section E2(m) can be considered as "aids to navigation and transportation" as stated in Section D. Relatively few conflicts in interpretation, however, have arisen. Section D deals essentially with fixed property, while Section E2(m) deals with mobile property. More important than the distinction between the sections is the fact that both are included in the Nation-wide Marine Definition. An interesting point is that the basic wording of Section D coincides precisely with Section 46:20(d) of the New York State Insurance Law but Paragraph 1 of the latter modernized the meaning of the word "tornado" by the substitution of "windstorm."

Many of the classes of business discussed in this chapter represent fantastic financial ventures. For example, the Verrazano-Narrows Bridge, crossing from Staten Island to Brooklyn, involves a total cost, including acquisition of land and condemnation values, in excess of $300 million. Obviously, the bondholders will require insurance to protect their investment. Even by using worldwide facilities, the insurance market is insufficient to protect the structure for the full amount represented by the physical value alone. To the physical value, of course, use and occupancy coverage must be added.

BRIDGES AND TUNNELS

In the inland marine area, insurance on bridges and tunnels is customarily classified as:

1. *Bridge Property Damage*—i.e., physical loss of or damage to the completed structure.
2. *Builder's Risk*—i.e., physical loss of or damage to the structure during the course of construction.
3. *Use and Occupancy*—i.e., loss of revenue resulting from physical loss of or damage to the structure.

Each risk must be individually underwritten and rated. Bridges and tunnels are insured under inland marine policies, unless fire, lightning, the extended coverage perils, and earthquake are the only perils to be covered. If these are the only ones, a properly endorsed Standard Fire Policy is used for the purpose.

All three types of coverage listed above are usually on an "all risk" basis, although a named perils Bridge Builder's Risk Policy is still available. Generally, the same types of insurance available for bridges are available for tunnels. The old term "U. & O." is still officially used instead of the modern term, "Business Interruption."

Bridge Property Damage Insurance

The Bridge Property Damage Policy covers direct physical loss of or damage to bridges and tunnels. Since this policy is normally issued to cover all risks of loss except those excluded, coverage is ascertainable only after study of the exclusions.

Exclusions. The usual exclusions are as follows (wording is not official):

1. Loss or damage or expense caused by or resulting from inherent defect, wear and tear, gradual deterioration, or expansion or contraction due to changes in temperature, unless resulting in collapse of the property or a material part thereof. However, under no circumstances shall the Company be liable for loss or damage caused by, or contributed to, by failure of the insured to keep and maintain the property in a thorough state of repair.

2. Loss or damage resulting from the negligence of the insured in not using all reasonable means to preserve the property at the time of or after any insured disaster.

3. Loss or damage from war and nuclear perils.
4. Loss or expense from labor disturbances, riot, civil commotion, sabotage, vandalism and malicious mischief, and numerous related activities.

The last-mentioned exclusion can be narrowed by payment of additional premium. These relatively narrow exclusions indicate that the physical damage insurance in an "all risk" policy is exceedingly broad.

Other Limitations on Coverage. Another provision, while technically not an exclusion, is a pertinent limitation of the coverage. It has to do with any material alteration in the design and construction of the structure during the policy period, with change in ownership, and with assignment. It may read as follows:

This policy shall be void unless otherwise provided by agreement in writing added hereto, if:

a) The character of the property or the design or construction thereof be materially altered or changed during the policy term; but this shall not apply to temporary alterations or changes which are incidental to the performance of necessary repairs and which are immediately reported to the Company in writing; or

b) Any change takes place in the interest, title, or possession of the subject of insurance; or

c) This policy be assigned or transferred.

Periodically some alteration or change will be made in a bridge structure requiring an analysis of the foregoing clause, particularly in reference to (*a*). Actually, there is no predetermined method which can be employed to know what constitutes a "material" alteration and what does not. The better part of wisdom seems to be to report all cases of doubt in order to secure agreement of the insurer if necessary. The problem of an additional premium is considered by the insurer after its determination of the facts.

In practical terms, the mere painting of a bridge would scarcely be considered as a "material change," but the addition of the second deck to the George Washington Bridge obviously was.

Valuation and Coinsurance. Losses arising out of bridge and tunnel insurance are generally settled on the basis of actual cash value. The insurer is accorded the option to rebuild, repair, or replace any damaged part, provided it gives sufficient notice of such intent to the insured. When losses are settled on an actual cash value basis, in no case can recovery exceed the cost of repairing or replacing the property with materials of like kind and quality.

Certain types of steel and concrete structures may be insured on a replacement-cost-new basis without any deduction for depreciation. When the insurance is so written, the coinsurance clause requirement (as discussed in the next paragraph) is based on the replacement cost figure.

Bridge and tunnel policies are written subject to a coinsurance clause (or "Average" clause) of 80 percent. The percentage may be amended to

90 or 100 by endorsement. The only exception is where the dollar coverage available in the worldwide market is insufficient to meet the conditions of the 80 percent coinsurance clause. In such cases the coinsurance percentage is adjusted to permit the insured to avoid a coinsurance penalty provided he buys whatever amount of insurance is available. The insuring of the Verrazano-Narrows Bridge—as mentioned earlier in this chapter—is a case in point. When the insurance is issued on an actual cash value basis—as is usually the case—the coinsurance percentage is applied against the actual cash value of the property at the time of the loss. When a replacement cost approach is used, the coinsurance percentage applies against the replacement cost of the structure. In the latter case, assuming the insured has complied with the coinsurance clause requirement, losses are settled in terms of replacement cost, but, of course, not to exceed the amount of insurance.

Deductibles. Because of the general nature of the property to be insured, it is customary in bridge and tunnel insurance to have a deductible of at least 1 percent of the 80 percent coinsurance amount. Varying deductibles are available, however, with a stop limit set at 5 percent.

In some cases of very large structures it is customary to limit the basic deductible percentage by a maximum dollar deductible. Furthermore, on risks located on the West Coast, separate deductibles are often used. For example, a 1 percent deductible may be used for all types of losses exclusive of earthquake and 5 percent deductible may be used for earthquake losses.

Debris Removal. The policy under discussion may be amended to provide debris removal and "demolition expense" coverage. (See Chapter 6 for a description of the debris removal clause in fire insurance forms and Chapter 8 for a discussion of demolition insurance as associated with fire and allied lines and called in some jurisdictions the "Contingent Liability from Operation of Building Laws Endorsement.")

The coverage is comparable to that provided under a fire policy so extended and reads:

> In consideration of an additional premium of $________, this policy is hereby extended, in the event of loss recoverable under this policy in the absence of this endorsement, to include ______% interest in cost of removal of material and debris formerly an insured part of the property, including cost of removal or demolition of any portion of the insured property no longer useful for the purposes for which it was intended, but only in the event the Assured is required by any valid law or ordinance in effect at the time of the property damage loss to effect such removal or demolition.
>
> In no event shall the Company be liable for a greater proportion of a loss payable under this endorsement than its proportion of the liability for property damage under the provisions of the average clause applicable thereto.
>
> This endorsement shall not increase the amount of insurance under this policy.

In addition, another form is available in about the same language with, however, a provision to increase the amount of the policy so that the coverage as provided by the endorsement would constitute a separate amount over and above the amount collectible under the basic policy.

In the case of both endorsements, and subject to an additional rate, it is possible to delete that portion of the endorsement reading: "But only in the event the Assured is required by any valid law or ordinance in effect at the time of the property damage loss to effect such removal or demolition." Perhaps it might be said that the use of this endorsement was created because of circumstances not comparable to the usual application of fire insurance.

In the event it is possible to repair or replace the bridge, most, if not all, of the expenses would be recoverable under the basic policy in the absence of the endorsement. However, most bridges cross water, and because it has been known that a part of a bridge has fallen into the waterway, the basic intent of the Debris Removal Endorsement is to provide for the removal of such property from the waterway, being definitely an additional expense not recoverable by the basic policy.

Bridge Builder's Risk Insurance

The builder's risk coverage is also a property damage type of insurance designed to cover bridges or tunnels in the process of construction. Two types of contract are available. The older one is a named perils policy; the other is "all risk." The named perils include "fire, lightning, flood, rising waters, ice, explosion, windstorm, earthquake, and collision." The "all risk" form includes direct loss or damage "however caused."

Exclusions. Certain exclusions are the same for both types of builder's risk contracts. For example, losses resulting from labor disturbances, riot and civil commotion, sabotage, vandalism and malicious mischief; neglect of the insured to act reasonably in protecting the property at and after a loss; delay in completion of the construction; business interruption; certain ordinances and court orders; war activities; and nuclear damage are excluded. This list is not a complete rundown of the exclusions common to both types of contracts—merely illustrative.

Each type of policy has additional exclusions which are peculiar to it. For example, the "all risk" contract excludes loss from "error, omission or deficiency in design, specifications or materials unless fire or explosion ensues and then only for the loss, damage or expense resulting from such fire or explosion." This form also, of course, contains a "wear and tear" exclusion as well as an exclusion for loss which results from expansion or contraction from changes in temperature unless such expansion or contraction results in collapse of all or part of the structure. The named perils contract, for example, excludes loss or damage from collision with construction material or equipment unless the collision results from one or a combination of the insured perils.

Property Covered. The Bridge Builder's Risk Policy applies rather broadly to the properties involved in the construction of the bridge or tunnel, all, however, at the site of operations. The structure itself; the materials, supplies, and equipment which in the normal course of events would become a part of the structure; the foundations and attachments; temporary structures used at the site in the construction of the bridge or the tunnel; and approaches and abutments are examples of properties which can be covered.

One of the important factors to consider in connection with this coverage is the range and value of insured property and the choices available as to what is to be considered as insured property. For example, coverage may be available in the Bridge Builder's Risk Policy (and the Bridge Property Damage Policy) with or without approaches or, in fact, covering solely one or more contracts. Commonly, policies are written to cover from abutment to abutment, including abutments. Differences in the definition of insured property from one contract to another exist, and policy coverage must be precisely delineated. The Use and Occupancy Policy, to be described in the next section, does not have to be limited in the same fashion as the direct damage contract. If differences in the definition of insured property from one contract to another do exist, however, they should be precisely delineated.

When—as is usual—the Bridge Builder's Risk Policy is limited to the "site of operations," considerable care must be exercised where movements are made by water. A special clause may be required to express by exact language the "time" of the attachment of the policy.

Other Features. The policy provides that the liability of the company increases as the property value grows but that the amount is never to be larger than the limit specified in the contract. The contract is a reporting form which calls for reports of value to be submitted as of the last day of each month. These reports are to be made within 15 days after the end of the month. Failure by the insured to submit such a report within 30 days after the end of the month terminates the insurance.

For insureds who prefer a flat premium arrangement there is an optional flat premium endorsement which calls for insurance in the full amount of the insured's completed contract price. In fact, the endorsement requires 100 percent coinsurance on this completed contract amount. The rate, of course, is altered accordingly. No monthly reports are called for.

The policy calls for a deductible usually of 1 percent of the values at risk as of the time of the loss subject many times to a minimum amount. When the flat premium endorsement is used, the deductible is usually stated as one half of 1 percent of the completed contract price.

Use and Occupancy

The purpose of this insurance is to provide for:

> Loss of revenue resulting from necessary interruption, total or partial, of the use of the property, resulting from direct physical loss or damage occurring during the term of this policy to the property, however caused, except as hereinafter provided.

Revenue is defined to be:

> . . . the income from tolls and other operating sources, less such maintenance and operating charges and expenses as do not necessarily continue during the period of total or partial suspension of use.

This policy, then, is really a type of business interruption coverage for toll bridges and tunnels.

The perils covered are generally the same as those in the "all risk" property damage policy. Also, the exclusions are roughly comparable except that several additional ones are specified. Two "suspension of use" exclusions are worded to exclude loss from:

> Suspension of use of the property by government or municipal authority, unless such suspension of use is occasioned by direct physical loss or damage to the property from an external cause which is not excluded elsewhere hereunder.
>
> Suspension of use of the property which may be occasioned by (or the extent that the same may be increased by) any ordinance or law, governmental or municipal order, regulating or prohibiting construction or repair of the property by suspension, lapse, cancellation of, refusal of, or delay in the granting of any license, lease, or permit or by any injunction or process of court.

The form also excludes loss from failure or breakdown of machinery or accessories unless resulting from an external cause not excluded elsewhere in the contract.

Per Diem. Such insurance is written on a per diem basis with no more than $1/365$ of the total amount of insurance recoverable in any one day. The contract can also be endorsed to specify a daily limit which may vary from one month to another—to take into account seasonal patterns in traffic. Finally, the contract may be endorsed to a basis much like the Premium Adjustment Plan for Business Interruption Gross Earnings Forms as described in Chapter 9. Under an Average and Adjusted Values Endorsement the insured pays a provisional premium based on 100 percent of revenue for the preceding year (or in cases of new structures the estimate for the next 12 months) but with an adjustment of premium annually. The maximum total premium is 125 percent of the provisional premium; the minimum is 75 percent. Further, the liability of the insurer is limited to 125 percent of the provisional limit on which the provisional premium is based. This arrangement is the most common one found in bridge and tunnel "U. & O."

Other Features. A deductible is used but is customarily expressed in number of days of a waiting period. The minimum number is seven. Alternative quotations are available for waiting periods of 14 days and 30 days.

As is common in most business interruption coverages, the contract does not cover any loss of revenue which occurs after the time the property could be restored to use with due diligence and dispatch. The following stipulation is also usually included:

It is a condition of this insurance that as soon as practicable after any loss or damage, the Assured shall resume complete or partial operation of the property and shall make use of other property, if obtainable, if by so doing the amount of loss hereunder will be reduced, and in the event the loss can so be reduced, such reduction shall be taken into account in arriving at the amount of loss hereunder.

It is not uncommon to base premium and losses on an 18-month or 24-month basis instead of a 12-month basis with all appropriate figures being increased proportionately.

DAMS

In many respects the insuring of dams is comparable to the insuring of bridges and tunnels. Underwriting views on dam insurance, however, vary materially.

Throughout the years dams of many types have been constructed. Consequently, each application must be examined very closely to determine the acceptability of the type of construction. One of the major problems is that the cost of excavation may not be recurrent. In such cases these costs should be excluded specifically when arriving at the proper amount of insurance.

Some of the dams erected in the United States have been so colossal in size that the worldwide market has been quite insufficient to provide insurance to value. As the result, most of the larger risks are written subject to a specific and agreed loss limit. "U. & O." insurance is seldom written on dams. An exception might be where a manufacturing plant uses the dam site as a source of its water supply.

Dam insurance definitely requires that complete information be submitted to the company for detailed consideration prior to issuance of any contract.

PIERS, WHARVES, AND DOCKS

Waterfront properties such as piers, wharves, and docks present difficult insuring problems. Fire, lightning, extended coverage, and sometimes other related perils are written on these properties by means of the

Standard Fire Policy and its accompanying forms. The Nation-wide Marine Definition excludes such coverage from inland marine. Additional hazards remain, however, to be covered by marine insurance contracts.

Some inland marine contracts for piers, wharves, and docks are written on a fairly narrow named perils basis which restricts coverage to action of the elements exclusive of the coverage provided by the Extended Coverage Endorsement. They cover, for example, physical loss as a result of tidal wave, high waters, and overflow. Other contracts are "all risk" and therefore include collapse and subsidence. A deductible is customary. Policies are individually tailored to such an extent that additional generalizations as to coverage are of no particular value.

Of crucial underwriting importance is the basic engineering design of the structure. Insurance companies usually use the services of professional engineering firms—or qualified engineers of their own—to examine the structure and assess the hazards. This examination includes attention to the current value of the property and the replacement value. The matter of the proper amount of insurance is always a difficult one, particularly in view of the fact that many of the structures are old.

PIPELINES

It is entirely practical to arrange coverage for pipelines following the general conditions of the Bridge Property Damage Policy and with an agreed deductible.

The major insuring problem involves river crossings. Where the pipeline is carried across the river by means of a pipeline suspension bridge, the problem is principally one of determining what the physical conditions are at the site of the particular crossing. When, however, coverage is needed on pipelines lying on the bottom of the waterway, an entirely different problem arises. Great care must be taken to determine not only the type of piping and the construction of the pipeline but also the method used to lay the pipe on the bed of the waterway.

Aside from problems of river crossings, consideration must be given to the possibility of a serious loss because of floods. The trench in which the pipe lies might be filled during a flood, or the overlay of the pipe might be washed away. Also, the method employed to repair or replace a pipeline in the event of a loss must be anticipated, including the facilities available at the site.

This insurance truly represents a classification of business which requires specific and detailed analysis of each risk. No two risks are the same. Insurance is written to cover not only the pipes, per se, but also "on-line" propulsion, regulating equipment, and other equipment appurtenant to such pipelines. Property at manufacturing, producing, refining, converting, treating, or conditioning plants, however, must not be included. The idea is that the property "on-line" used as an adjunct to the pipeline may be covered, but no producing, refining, or other such property used to extract or process the products flowing through the pipelines may be covered.

POWER TRANSMISSION LINES

Power transmission lines present such a hazard that they are not ordinarily insured. Normal annual losses are quite heavy. No insurer would favorably entertain propositions to cover these routine losses.

Beyond the point of normal losses, however, there is an insurable risk. Windstorm and other actions of the elements, particularly snow and ice resulting from a severe storm in a given area, could very well cause damage of great magnitude. In a few instances this catastrophic hazard is subject to insurance. A large deductible is used whenever insurance on transmission lines is sold.

RADIO AND TV COMMUNICATION EQUIPMENT

Still another class of business requiring careful individual underwriting is the insurance on radio and TV communication equipment. A single policy can be used to cover towers, transmitting operating equipment, studio operating equipment, miscellaneous studio equipment, and mobile or portable apparatus. A separate limit, however, is applied to each major item.

The policy is "all risk" but excludes (1) mechanical breakdown and (2) error, omission, or deficiency in design, specifications, work, or materials. Also, electrical disturbances except from lightning are normally excluded.

A business interruption coverage is also available. This time element coverage ordinarily follows the general pattern associated with business interruption insurance. In addition, coverage is available for physical loss or damage to the transmitting buildings resulting from collapse of the tower.

OUTDOOR CRANES AND LOADING BRIDGES

Insuring of outdoor cranes and loading bridges is an inland marine function. "Bridge" as used in this context is an entirely different type of structure than "bridge" as used earlier in this chapter where the reference is to a structure for vehicular traffic. A "loading bridge" is a mechanical structure used for the loading and unloading of cargo, such as ore, grain, and other bulk commodities.

Coverage is customarily "all risk" but is issued only after cautious underwriting of individual risks with much attention given to the engineering aspects of the property.

Experience with this insurance has demonstrated that unless a vigorous program of maintenance is constantly pursued, serious loss is always a possibility of major importance. The tremendous weights being lifted and the other daily stresses on the equipment cause maintenance and safety practices to be of prime importance to an acceptable loss ratio. Consequently frequent and rigid inspections are a necessary part of the insurance programs.

OTHER

Numerous other types of property may be subject to the insurance discussed in this chapter. For example, stevedores' gear and equipment may require specially tailored policies. This gear and equipment, certainly, are property of contractors and thus subject also to contractors floaters. Operations, however, are conducted at the waterfront. Thus, the question arises as to what coverage is required while the property is alongside, upon, or within a vessel.

As a practical matter the question of which insurance contract covers when in this and numerous other cases has to be answered by arbitrary guiding agreements. The subject of such agreements is beyond the scope of this chapter.

RECAPITULATION

Such a large number of insurance types has been included in this chapter that a few recapitulations might be helpful to the reader:

1. The point has been made often in this chapter that each risk requires individual underwriting and rating. Neither class nor schedule rating has a place in the pricing of these types of insurance. Rates are made almost entirely on judgment. A review of some of the types of losses which occur is sufficient to give the ratemaker pause:

a) Tacoma Narrows Bridge. This infamous collapse was probably due to aerodynamic instability and resulting fluttering.

b) Underwater Pipeline. Breakage of line was probably caused by severe underwater currents. In another instance, the anchor of a moving vessel dragged the pipeline, causing an extended break.

c) Dock. Severe damage was produced when a steamer collided with the dock. In another case a flood caused collapse of a dock.

d) TV Tower. A windstorm caused a tower to collapse.

e) Power Transmission Lines. Weight of snow resulted in collapse of lines and poles.

f) Outdoor Cranes. Overloading caused collapse of a boom.

g) Stevedores' Gear. Valuable gear was accidentally dropped overboard and lost.

The examples show that within the "all risk" feature of these policies the "unknown hazard" can be formidable and deserves a substantial premium.

2. Engineering and inspections represent an integral part of the underwriting of these risks. Insurers necessarily lean heavily on qualified people who are able to analyze the problems at the site and report their findings to the underwriters.

3. Understanding of local climatic and terrain conditions is an underwriting factor of major importance. These conditions can vary abruptly from one site to another even within a small geographic area and from one time to another for any one site.

4. Determination of insurable values and of acceptable amounts of insurance is more difficult than in respect to most other types of insurance.

SUGGESTED READINGS

Fire, Casualty, and Surety Bulletins. Cincinnati: National Underwriter Co. Fire and Marine Volume, Inland Marine Section (Bridges, Tunnels, etc.).

RODDA, WILLIAM H. *Inland Marine and Transportation Insurance.* 2d ed. Englewood Cliffs, N.J.: Prentice-Hall, Inc., 1958. Chap. 10.

Chapter 26

INLAND MARINE INSURANCE—BAILEE AND RELATED LIABILITY

BY MYRON DuBAIN

Each day millions of transactions occur in which one individual (or organization) leaves some of his (or its) property with another person (or organization) with the intention of repossessing it soon. The reasons for turning over the property are legion. The insurance aspects of such transactions grow quite involved. In this chapter some of these aspects—as they bear on inland marine—are discussed.

BAILMENT

Most of the transfers referred to above embody bailment. Bailment may be defined as the temporary transfer of personal property by one person, to the care, custody, and control of another, for some specific and lawful purpose—such as its repair, cleaning, storage, transportation, or other service.

There are three key phrases in the definition:

1. Bailment deals only with *personal property*.
2. *The care, custody, and control* of the property must be transferred to the bailee.
3. The transfer or delivery of the property must be *temporary*. It is of the essence of a contract of bailment, either express or implied, that after the purpose for which the property was transferred has been accomplished, it be redelivered to the bailor, or be otherwise dealt with according to his directions, or kept until he reclaims it.[1]

A *bailee,* then, is a person who has temporary possession of the personal property of others, while a *bailor* is a person who relinquishes control of the property for the purpose of some service being rendered.

A clear definition of bailment is important in order to distinguish it from two other situations, similar but not the same, in which property is

[1] *Corpus Juris Secundum:* 8 C.J.S. Bailment: 1.

transferred to another person. Each of these two situations lacks one of the essential ingredients necessary to a contract of bailment. The first occurs in a conditional sales contract. Here property is delivered to another person but in this case it is intended that legal title will also pass to the other party, and that the possession of the goods will be permanent. Even if this does not actually come to pass (repossessions are not unknown in the American economy!), the conditional sales contract still is not a contract of bailment since, by definition, the transfer must take place for the purpose of some service being rendered.[2]

The other case in which there is a transfer of property from one person to another, but in which there is no contract of bailment, occurs in a master-servant relationship. A laundress, for example, working in the home of her employer, is not a bailee since the employer is in a position to supervise or direct her work upon the "transferred" property. The missing ingredient necessary to the situation of bailment is that the *control* of the property has not been transferred, it still resides with the employer. If the laundress takes the clothes home, however, she becomes a bailee. The laundry is now in her care, custody, and control.[3]

Types of Bailment

There are several kinds of bailments and each involves different rights and duties on the part of the bailor and the bailee. Generally they are classified in accordance with the consideration involved and as such there are three types:

1. Bailment for the benefit of both parties.
2. Bailment for the sole benefit of the bailor.
3. Bailment for the sole benefit of the bailee.

The bailee, of course, has a legal obligation to exercise proper care of the property under his control. And although the technical terms of "care" and "negligence" are no longer used in some jurisdictions, the law often imposes on the bailee varying degrees of legal responsibility according to each of the three types of bailment.[4]

If the bailment is for the benefit of both parties, ordinary care is required of the bailee. If the bailment is for the sole benefit of the *bailor*, only slight care is normally required of the bailee. However, if it is the *bailee himself* who receives the sole benefit, then obviously his responsibility to the bailor is increased commensurately and the law frequently imposes great care upon him.

A precise interpretation of these terms would involve an excursion into the complex intricacies of the law far beyond the scope of this discussion.

---

[2] William H. Rodda, *Inland Marine and Transportation Insurance* (2d ed.; Englewood Cliffs, N.J.: Prentice-Hall, Inc., 1958), chap. 13.

[3] *Ibid.*

[4] 8 *C.J.S.* Bailment: 26.

In addition, there has been a recent trend in legal decisions to discard these distinctions between bailments with respect to the degree of care required of the bailee. They have simply made the bailee liable for *negligence* which, in turn, can be defined as failure to exercise a care appropriate to the hazard, that is, the degree and type of care which would be used by a normally prudent individual in the same or similar circumstances—or, that degree of diligence which the nature and type of his employment make it reasonable to expect of him. Negligence by the bailee in the performance of a required duty, or his failure to perform a required act, would render him legally liable for damages.

It is true, of course, that this legal liability can be increased as a result of contractual agreement and in like manner can be reduced. But, while a bailee may *diminish* his liability or limit the amount of his liability to an agreed valuation by contract in many jurisdictions, he cannot *exempt* himself from the consequences of his own fraud, willful acts, or negligence. However, the bailee generally may limit his liability for negligence to a stipulated amount. He may not, however, limit his liability for *gross* negligence.[5]

The Need for Insurance Coverage

This discussion points up an obvious and pressing need for insurance coverage to protect the bailee from suits for damages and resultant legal judgments. There are other and less apparent but equally important risks that a bailee faces by reason of his function as a bailee. It makes little difference monetarily to a bailee whether he goes out of business as a result of a legal judgment for damages or as a result of loss of customer goodwill! In either case he is out of business.

Consider, for example, the effect of a fire on a neighborhood dry cleaner, furrier, or jeweler. He might very well prove that the fire was not due to any negligence on his part and, consequently, have no legal responsibility for the loss of or damage to his customers' goods. That, however, would be little consolation to those upon whom his business and livelihood depend. It is for this reason that coverage is generally written to provide direct damage insurance—on either an "all risk" or specified peril basis—so that it pays for damage to the property of others in the hands of the bailee *whether or not there is legal liability*. The pure legal liability type of coverage, which affords limited protection only, is still written but is far less common. The broader coverage is more realistically attuned to the needs involved.

The Nation-Wide Marine Definition

Before reviewing the major policy forms available, it is important to understand how bailees' customers' insurance came to be written as

[5] *Ibid.*

inland marine at all since it would seem to fall more logically within the scope of the casualty coverages. Initially, the element of transportation to and from the bailees' premises probably attracted marine companies to the writing of this type of insurance. The attraction is not quite as illogical as it might seem to some readers. A significant portion of these risks arises during this time in transit. Further, marine policies and the accompanying underwriting flexibility made it possible to devise the kind of broad direct damage insurance coverage that these insureds needed for adequate business protection.

The original "Nation-Wide Marine Definition," however, limited the scope within which marine companies could legitimately write bailee coverage. The 1933 definition said simply that:

> Property in transit to, and/or from, and while waiting for, or undergoing processing in, bleacheries or fumigatories or on premises of dyesters, throwsters and other similar processors, until delivered to storage warehouses or final place of delivery contemplated at the time the shipment was made . . .

fell within the jurisdiction of marine underwriters.[6] Then the floodgates of interpretative bulletins were opened amending, redefining, and somewhat confusing the issue involved.[7] Fortunately, in 1953 the revised definition provided both greater clarity and a broader base from which marine underwriters could work. It authorized:

> Property in transit to, or from, and in the custody of
> (1) bleacheries, throwsters, fumigatories, dyers, cleaners, laundries *and similar bailees;*
> (2) needleworkers;
> (3) *other bailees* (not owned, controlled, or operated by the bailor) *for the purpose of performing work thereon* (as distinguished from the making of a complete article) *including the treatment of, or assemblage of property on the premises of bailees.*

Such policies shall not cover bailee's property at his premises.[8] Other sections of the definition permit the writing of Furriers' or Fur Storers' Customers Policies (Section *q*), Cold Storage Locker Plant Policies (Section *s*), and Furniture Shipment Policies (Section *y*).

Bailee Liability Covered in Other than Bailee Policies

In addition to the specific bailee policies discussed in detail in this chapter, coverage on customers' property is also built into such other inland marine contracts as the Jewelers' Block, Equipment Dealers Float-

[6] *Nation-Wide Definition and Interpretation of the Insuring Powers of Marine and Transportation Underwriters* (Chicago: National Association of Insurance Commissioners of the United States, June 2, 1933), Section (*p*).

[7] Bulletins #13, #26, #33, #37, #49, #102, #104, #106, #107.

[8] *Nation-wide Marine Definition* (The National Association of Insurance Commissioners, June 12, 1953), Section (*n*). Italics the author's.

ers, Camera and Musical Equipment Dealers Floaters, and the like. It is, therefore, impossible to determine accurately the overall premium volume represented by bailee coverages as such. Suffice it to say that they represent a significant portion of the total inland marine premiums written.

MAJOR INLAND MARINE BAILEE CONTRACTS

Textbooks generally list the following as the major bailee policies available:

1. Bailees' Customers Insurance (including Dyers, Cleaners and Laundries, Radio and T.V. Repair, and assorted miscellaneous contracts).
2. Furriers' Customers.
3. Motor Truck Cargo.
4. Furniture Warehouseman's Comprehensive Policy.

While this classification is useful, several other policies are also discussed in this section.

Bailees' Customers Policies

Bailees' Customers Policies are not standarized and vary somewhat by insurer. In general, however, they cover customers' goods but not the personal property of the insuring bailee and are written on either a named peril or "all risk" basis. As indicated earlier, they cover direct damage, regardless of any legal liability on the part of the bailee, to goods in his care, custody, and control for the purpose of rendering such services as cleaning, laundry, or repair. While the policy may be adapted to the several needs of various types of bailees who perform services on customers' property, three forms are quite common:

1. Dyers' and Cleaners' Form
2. Rug and Carpet Cleaning Form
3. Pressing and Tailor Shop Form

In each case an underwriter must consider several factors pertinent to his acceptance or rejection of a specific risk and these factors help to clarify the extent and kind of hazards involved. He must review:

1. The building in which the property to be covered is located, with particular reference to fire, theft, and water damage exposures.
2. The transit exposure.
3. The loss experience.
4. The nature of the property bailed.
5. The type of work to be performed.
6. The financial status and reputation (including ability) of the insured.
7. Peak and average values at risk and required limits of liability.

If the policy is to be written on an "all risk" basis, there are generally five exclusions. Usually no coverage is provided in the event of:

1. Loss or damage occasioned by moth, vermin, gradual deterioration or inherent vice or while the property is actually being worked upon (unless caused by fire or explosion).

2. Loss as a result of the infidelity of the insured's employees or of any person to whom the property is entrusted.

3. Loss from theft of goods left on a delivery truck overnight unless locked in the insured's private garage.

4. Loss or damage to property held in storage or to which a storage charge is made except where goods are held without instructions from the owner, and then only to a maximum of 45 days after processing is completed.

5. Loss or damage from the usual nuclear energy and war perils.

On a named peril basis, the Bailees' Customers Policy normally covers property:

1. *While in transit,* against direct loss or damage caused by: fire, lightning, explosion, windstorm, collision or overturning of vehicle, collapse of bridges and culvert, flood and perils of the seas; theft; robbery.

2. *Other than in transit,* against direct loss or damage caused by: fire, lightning, explosion, windstorm, hail, aircraft, vehicles and smoke; burglary, robbery; riot and civil commotion. (It would be well to recall the distinctions involved in the following three definitions: *theft* means any act of stealing, whether or not forcible entry or violence is involved, including larceny, robbery and burglary. *Burglary* means taking property from locked premises or safe by force. Most policies covering burglary require that there be visible signs of forcible entry. *Robbery* or holdup, means forcible taking of property from its custodian or messenger by violence or threat of violence. See Chapter 43.)

The most significant underwriting consideration with respect to the Dyers' and Cleaners' Form under this Bailees' Customers Policy is the hazard of a large loss by fire. Inspections are normally undertaken and usually the amount of liability accepted is determined in much the same way it would be in a comparable fire policy. The theft hazard, of course, is omnipresent and is primarily examined in relation to the probability of loss from delivery trucks.

Rating formulas vary widely as would be anticipated in a nonstandardized form. Generally, however, the basic factor is the fire rate for the average value in the bailee's plant. Loadings are then added to cover the other risks undertaken such as burglary, transportation, and so on.

Variations appear in the Rug and Carpet Cleaning Form and in the Pressing and Tailor Shop Form. The former is similar in most respects to the Dyers' and Cleaners' Form but limits of liability are sometimes set according to the type of rugs and carpets processed. On the other hand, many tailor shops do repairing and pressing and act as receiving stations for other laundries and cleaners. The nature of their operation is, however, less complex and consequently simplified bailees' customers policies are available to them.[9] Radio and TV shops, book binderies, and various other repair shops are further examples of the myriad types of risks that can be and are written under the Bailees' Customers Policy.

[9] Rodda, *op. cit.,* chap. 13.

Furriers' Customers Policy

The Furriers' Customers Policy is a highly specialized type of bailees' customers' coverage and is designed to meet the unique needs of furriers, fur storage concerns, department stores, cleaners, and similar bailees. The established customs in the fur business and the hazards involved in their operations differ substantially from those of dyers and laundries. For this reason, and because of the proportionately high premium volume Furriers' Customers Policies contribute to the bailee class generally, the subject warrants separate treatment.

The Furriers' Customers Policy covers furs and garments trimmed with fur accepted for storage by furriers, banks, stores, cleaners, general or fur warehousemen, cold storage concerns, and other bailees. It also covers other garments accepted by such bailees and other garments accepted for storage by laundries, cleaners, and similar bailees who accept furs or garments trimmed with fur for storage. Finally, it covers textiles and similar articles accepted in conjunction with their fur storage operations.

This business divides basically into three types and the Furriers' Customers Policy is so flexible and comprehensive that it can be drawn to fit each of the three or any combination of them as follows:

1. The storer who has his own vault and stores his customers' furs there.
2. The storer who accepts furs for storage but, having no vault, sends them to a wholesale storer.
3. The wholesale storer who has large storage facilities and accepts furs from stores, furriers, laundries, and cleaners. In most cases he also has facilities for repairing, remodeling, and cleaning furs and does this type of work for the stores and others who are not prepared to handle it.

The policy covers practically "all risk" of loss or damage from the time the insured takes custody of the property until redelivered to his customers. It provides coverage during pickup and delivery, while outside of vaults for cleaning, glazing, or remodeling and while in vaults during actual storage. It does not, of course, cover stock belonging to the insured or any subsidiaries or affiliates. The policy also specifically excludes loss or damage occasioned (*a*) by gradual deterioration, moth, vermin, or inherent vice; (*b*) by processing or any work upon the property unless caused by fire or explosion; (*c*) by war; or (*d*) by any liability assumed by the named insured under any agreement express or implied that would guarantee the results of any work to be performed upon the property or effect insurance in any amount other than that provided by the policy. There are the usual nuclear and war risk exclusions and a provision in the event of duplicated coverage as the result of any applicable fidelity bond or similar undertaking.

There are, as indicated earlier, two important ways in which the Furriers' Customers Policy differs from the Dyers' and Cleaners' Form as used in the Bailees' Customers Policy. The first is breadth of coverage (except, of course, in the case of "all risk" coverage in the Dyers' and Cleaners' Form). The second is in the matter of the receipt issued to customers. The very cornerstone of the fur storage business is the receipt issued by the storer. The policy recognizes the importance of this custom and requires that important conditions appear in the terminology of the receipt. It must be remembered in this regard that although it frequently has been considered to be against public policy to permit bailees to avoid completely the consequences of their own negligence, the courts have held that the bailor and the bailee may limit by contract *the amount* of the bailee's liability.

Whenever a furrier accepts a fur for storage, he ascertains the owner's valuation and issues a receipt for that amount. Even if the furrier is liable for loss because of negligence, it is likely that his liability will be limited to the amount stated in the receipt. The basic policy for the account of the bailor, then, only covers up to the amount specified in the insured's receipt.

Situations may arise where the furrier is unable to restrict his liability to the amount stated in the receipt as in the case of gross negligence, inadequate notice to the customer of the receipt provisions, or certain other irregularities. The policy may, therefore, be extended by endorsement to cover the insured's legal liability for excess values on either or both of two Excess Legal Liability Forms depending on the nature of the insured's operation. The policy on occasion may also be extended to cover monetary loss to the insured of accrued but unpaid charges rendered uncollectible on account of loss or damage to the insured property by perils insured against.

Underwriting fur storage risks is difficult, primarily because of the high unit value of each garment and also because of the possibility of catastrophe loss from fire or burglary. The in-transit hazard, discernible in all bailee's customers insurance, is present here, too, and intensified. Moreover, the insured's employees represent a significant fidelity risk. A careful inspection of each risk is warranted and a step-by-step analysis of procedures in handling merchandise seems prudent. The inherent possibility of catastrophic loss requires more than average concern and it is only by controlling the individual loss possibilities that a company can hope to turn a profit in this class of business.

Furniture Warehouseman's Comprehensive Policy

Since this policy deals with storage risks rather than with bailee risks which require work to be performed on the property bailed, it may appear inconsistent with the marine definition and therefore not a permissible inland marine coverage. As a matter of fact, prior to the 1953 revision of the marine definition it was *not* specifically permitted. But such risks are now specifically allowed under "Section *y*" of the "Nationwide Marine Definition." The necessary element of transportation is the factor that qualifies the risk:

> Furniture Shipment Policies, covering furniture, fixtures and equipment in bona fide course of shipment from one location to another location of the owner *including in place of deposit incident to such transportation while awaiting determination or availability of final destination*, in which event they must cover at time of issuance, transportation to or from such place of deposit but may not cover after delivery at destination. (The italics are the author's.)

The Furniture Warehouseman's Comprehensive Policy provides exceptionally broad coverage on the bailees' customers goods and is offered, if not by all companies, by the nation's major inland marine insurers. The policy is basically divided into three sections:

> *A*. Section *A* provides "all risk" coverage, with the normal exclusions and certain others which are peculiar to this classification (e.g., loss or damage occasioned by the breakage, marring, chipping, or scratching of such fragile articles as statuary, bric-a-brac, china, and glassware). Coverage applies only to such property as is specifically described in the basic policy to which Section A is attached and to such property which also belongs to the insured's customer. This coverage is for the account of the bailor and is purchased by him at his option.
>
> *B*. Section *B* covers the liability of the insured as a warehouseman or bailee (but not as a carrier) for direct physical loss or damage to property (as described in the basic policy) of customers of the insured while stored at specified locations. There are of course certain exclusions under Section B with respect to the liabilities of the insured which are peculiar to this class of business. There is also frequently a $50 deductible.
>
> *C*. Section *C* provides the insured's motor truck cargo carrier liability insurance, either on a schedule (flat annual) or a gross receipts (monthly reporting) basis.

Certain forms extending coverage to include Carrier's Liability under Released Rates Order No. MC362 of the I.C.C., Insured's Uncollectible Accrued Charges, Government Agency Contracts, and the like are also available.

Since the coverage provided the warehouseman under this policy is significantly broad, careful and selective underwriting is essential. The key qualifications looked for are:

1. Outstanding management in all phases of the furniture warehouse business.
2. Adequate finances.
3. Complete integrity.

In addition, the warehouse itself should be fully acceptable as respects physical exposures. The insured should have a good experience record, maintain first class equipment, employ qualified personnel, and cater to a clientele of a good class.

Bailee Cold Storage Locker Plant Floater

The Cold Storage Locker Plant Policy is similar to the Furniture Warehouseman's Comprehensive Policy in that the bailee coverage requirement of work being performed upon the property is not present. Specifically permitted as inland marine under Section *s* of the definition, the policy covers: merchandise of customers consisting principally of meats, game, fish, poultry, fruit, vegetables, and property of a similar nature. There are several variations in coverage provided, but generally the policy is written on a specified peril basis very similar to other bailee policies. There is, however, a coverage peculiar to the cold storage locker bailee. Protection is needed against consequential loss or damage caused by changes in temperature resulting from:

1. Total or partial destruction of refrigeration or cooling equipment, connections, or supply pipes by the perils enumerated.
2. Electrical interruption caused by breakdown of the electrical generating or transmission system, preventing the insured from maintaining operation of the cooling system.
3. Mechanical breakdown of the refrigeration or cooling equipment, connections, or supply pipes.

Some policies are written to cover consequential loss from any interruption of electrical power. An "all risk" form is also written.

As a class, Cold Storage Locker Bailee Policies do not develop a large amount of premium volume and their importance is on the decline. The advent of the home freezer and its wide consumer acceptance will doubtless force the trend to continue, with the consequent result that cold storage locker operations will be fewer and the market for this type of coverage proportionately smaller.

Motor Truck Cargo Insurance

A public motor carrier is, in effect, a bailee. The bailment, however, is a special type which is defined by common law and statute. The motor carrier is, in effect, an insurer of the shipper's property and, therefore, is generally responsible in full for any and all damages. In some instances liability may be limited to a specific amount.

It must be remembered first of all that under the definitions in the Motor Carrier Act of 1935, the trucker who hauls under contract is called a "contract carrier" while a "private carrier" is one who carries his own goods or goods for which he is the lessee or bailee. The liability imposed on a contract carrier ordinarily is less than the liability imposed upon a common carrier and is limited to the liability agreed to in the contract and to any loss resulting from negligence on the part of the carrier. The reason for this limitation is largely historical. It is a basic tenet of the common law that a person or corporate entity making a business of carrying property for a consideration is responsible for the safe delivery of the property. And consequently he or it is held responsible for any loss that might in any way be preventable by the exercise of caution or diligence on his part.

The breadth of the common carrier's liability gave rise to the development of insurance coverage protecting against judgments as a result of these legal obligations. Unlike the other bailee forms discussed, Motor Truckmen's Cargo Liability Insurance indemnifies the insured for loss or damage resulting from his legal liability as a carrier. It does not insure against losses unless he is legally liable for such loss.

The major "perils of the highways" are fire and theft. Collision and overturn contribute to loss but primarily as the proximate cause of the fire or theft. The basic policy is written on a "named peril" basis usually covering the trucker's liability for loss or damage caused by: fire, lightning; explosion; accidental collision, overturn, or upset; collapse of bridges, docks, and wharves; stranding, sinking, burning, and/or collision of any regular ferry; cyclone; tornado; windstorm; and flood.

Forms providing broader coverage for large motor carriers are available and are generally written with substantial deductibles. It should be noted in connection with Motor Truckmen's Cargo Liability Insurance that the Interstate Commerce Commission requires that all motor carriers participating in interstate commerce must have insurance of $1,000 covering their liability for cargo on each vehicle and a $2,000 casualty limit.

SIGNIFICANCE

Insurance protection designed to meet the needs of those who have temporary custody of the personal property of others has resulted in the development of various bailee liability coverages. The insurance needs of the bailee are actually twofold: (1) to protect him from judgments for losses or damages resulting from his legal liability, a liability imposed by law and not an outgrowth of contract; (2) to protect what might be called his "business reputation" and his customer goodwill in the event of loss of or damage to the property of others in his custody regardless of his legal liability for such loss or damage.

Inland marine insurers are permitted to write a wide variety of bailee coverage under Sections (*n*), (*q*), (*s*), and (*y*) of the 1953 "Nation-wide Marine Definition." This situation has come about largely as the result of the prevalent in-transit exposure and the traditional flexibility of inland marine insurance contracts. The major volume-producing classifications of the bailee coverages are the: (1) Bailees' Customers Insurance Policies, particularly the Dyers' and Cleaners' Form; (2) Furriers' Customers Policy; (3) Furniture Warehouseman's Comprehensive Policy; and (4) Motor Truck Cargo.

Bailee coverage is, however, built into any number of other broad inland marine policies. The total volume produced by this type of coverage is difficult to estimate because of the myriad ways it is written. There is no doubt, however, that it represents a significant proportion of the total inland marine writings. More importantly, it provides broad insurance protection to owners of property in the custody of others and gives them the right of recovery for loss in situations where otherwise they might have no such right.

SUGGESTED READINGS

CONKLIN, CLARENCE R. "Insurance of Warehousing and Other Bailment Risks," reprinted from University of Illinois *Law Forum,* Vol. 1957 (Winter, 1957), pp. 560–85.

Corpus Juris Secundum. Brooklyn, N.Y.: The American Law Book Company, 1945. Vol. 8. Bailments: 1–26.

MAGEE, JOHN H., AND BICKELHAUPT, DAVID L. *General Insurance.* 7th ed. Homewood, Ill.: Richard D. Irwin, Inc., 1964. Chap. 12.

RODDA, WILLIAM H. *Inland Marine and Transportation Insurance.* 2d ed. Englewood Cliffs, N.J.: Prentice-Hall, Inc., 1958. Chaps. 6, 8, 13, 14, 15.

Chapter 27

INLAND MARINE INSURANCE—FLOATERS

BY ROBERT F. DEGENER

The purpose of this chapter is to present a brief description of the concept of an inland marine insurance floater and to illustrate the use of floaters in the insuring of properties—both business and personal. Since the variety of floaters is so wide, no attempt is made to discuss each type or even to catalogue all of the types. Rather, the chapter is organized in the following way: the concept of a floater is first described; the distinction between scheduled and unscheduled floaters is reviewed; the Scheduled Property Floater Basic Policy is described; the Personal Articles Floater and the reason for its use are treated; and the insuring conditions, perils covered, property covered, and certain other features of several floaters are considered as illustrative of these types of insurance.

CONCEPT OF A FLOATER

The term "Floater" as used in inland marine insurance is not precisely defined. The general idea is that it is a type of marine insurance to cover certain property which is mobile and which usually "floats" from one location to another. An example is construction equipment. The 1933 "Nation-Wide Definition and Interpretation of the Insuring Powers of Marine and Transportation Underwriters" includes the word "floater" as does also the 1953 definition. Obviously, however, not all mobile property is eligible for floater treatment, for example, automobiles. Moreover, because of pressures, custom, and compromise certain properties which are characterized by long-run fixity of location, for example, fine art objects and household furniture, *can* be insured under floaters.

Section E of the 1953 "Nation-wide Marine Definition" is labeled "Personal Property Floater Risks" and includes a long list of floaters and other contracts which are deemed to be within the purview of marine insurance. The expression "personal property" as used in the name of the section of the definition means property other than realty. The list is divided into two parts. One pertains to floaters covering individuals; the other to floaters covering "Individuals and/or Generally." Most of the contracts listed cover items which in their normal course of use are moved from one place to another. Floaters can provide coverage not only at the several locations but also during the movement of the property from one location to another. Some of the contracts, however, can cover "stationary" personal property. The notable example is the Personal Property Floater. Interestingly enough, this contract was not included in the 1933 definition. The public pressure mentioned above caused most of the states adopting the 1933 definition to take the necessary action to allow the Personal Property Floater to be written as an inland marine insurance contract. The 1953 definition specifically includes the Personal Property Floater.

SCHEDULED VERSUS UNSCHEDULED FLOATERS

The concept of scheduling is quite important to an understanding of the nature and use of floaters. A "scheduled" floater is one in which certain property is described by individual items or perhaps by individual classes of items and where a specific amount of insurance applies to each item or each specifically defined class of items. A scheduled floater entails use of "specific" insurance.

An "unscheduled" floater is one in which individual items or classes of items are not specifically described and in which a single amount of insurance applies to any or all of the items or classes of items being insured. If, for example, there is $6,000 of insurance involved, it applies—barring any other limitations—to any one or more of the items in case of a loss; but no more than $6,000 is payable for any one loss. This type of coverage, of course, is "blanket" insurance.

In most inland marine floaters the preponderant amount of insurance is on scheduled properties. The Personal Property Floater may be one of the exceptions. Virtually all of the floaters provide an opportunity for the insured to buy some "blanket" protection on unscheduled properties.

SCHEDULED PROPERTY FLOATER[1]

For convenience and consistency a basic policy called the Scheduled Property Floater is used in insuring several types of the properties listed in Section E of the "Nation-wide Marine Definition." Actually, this policy is a collection of standard provisions plus a declarations section. The insuring clause and description of the property covered appear on a form attached to the policy. The provisions of this basic policy have to be included in the floaters issued to cover the specified properties. The floaters can include additional provisions. The point is simply that—under rating bureau and/or statutory authority—they must include these stand-

[1] See Appendix D.

ard provisions. There is no prescribed format for the standard and additional provisions. The Scheduled Property Floater is used as a basic policy in substantially similar wording by most companies.

A review, then, of the provisions of the Scheduled Property Policy is pertinent to an understanding of floaters in general. The Inland Marine Insurance Bureau requires the standard wording in the following:

- Bicycle Floater
- Camera Dealers' Floater
- Camera Floater
- Equipment Dealers' Floater
- Fine Arts Floater
- Furriers' Block Floater
- Golfers' Equipment Floater
- Horse and Wagon Floater
- Live Stock Floater
- Mobile Agricultural Equipment Floater
- Musical Instrument Dealers Floater
- Musical Instrument Floater
- Neon Signs Floater
- Personal Articles Floater
- Personal Property Floater
- Physicians' and Surgeons' Equipment Floater
- Radium Floater
- Silverware Floater
- Stamp and Coin Collection Floater
- Theatrical Floater
- Wedding Presents Floater

Misrepresentation and Fraud

This clause provides that any concealment or misrepresentation of any material fact or circumstance concerning the insurance or the subject thereof, or any fraud on the part of the insured or his agent, will void the policy. Any attempt by insurers to provide coverage in case of concealment, misrepresentation, or fraud of any sort would involve the moral hazard which is uninsurable. If insureds were permitted to conceal or misrepresent any material fact or circumstance having a bearing upon the issuance of the contract, the concept of fortuity of loss might be violated. Underwriters, however, should not labor under the impression that with a clause such as this in the policy, they are relieved of requesting the necessary information before issuance of the contract.

Notice of Loss

The insured is required to report to the company or its agent as soon as practicable any loss or damage which may become a claim under the policy and within 90 days of the date of such loss file a sworn proof of loss with the company or its agent. Failure by the insured to comply with this condition will invalidate any claim for the loss under the policy. While this clause places an obligation upon the insured, it is not a hardship upon him and his compliance assists the company in handling a claim. Very often, rights of the insured against other parties may be lost or prejudiced by a delay in reporting a loss to the company.

Examination under Oath

This clause clearly provides that the company has the right to examine all parties who may have an interest in the property involved in the loss

The clause is invoked only in those instances where the information furnished by the insured is not conclusive as to the nature and/or extent of a loss. In the absence of this clause, it would be necessary for the parties at interest to agree to such examination, or for the company to obtain such rights through court order.

Valuation

While this clause may be amended to fit peculiar individual circumstances, the customary valuation of a loss is based on the actual cash value of the property at the time the loss occurred. Consideration is given to depreciation "however caused." In most instances the valuation is limited to not more than the cost to repair or replace the property with material of like kind and quality. The intent of this valuation process is to place the insured in the same economic position as existed prior to the loss.

In some of the floater policies, however, valuation clauses are written to provide for settlement of losses on a "valued" basis. This term means that total losses will be paid on the basis of the values stipulated in the policy without consideration being given to depreciation, appreciation, or other factors. Partial losses are paid as proportions of this "valued" figure. Readers should be careful to note that the mere scheduling of property in a floater does not mean that—even as a practical matter—losses are adjusted on a "valued" basis. The "actual cash value" concept applies unless the "valued" wording is specifically included.

Settlement of Loss

This clause provides that loss shall be payable within a certain prescribed time (usually 60 days) after the acceptance by the company of satisfactory proof of interest and loss. Incidentally, the Collection from Others Clause provides that no loss is payable under the Scheduled Property Floater, if the insured "has collected the same from others." Thus, the idea is that other insurance is not allowed. In some floaters the "other insurance" provisions are expanded.

No Benefit of Insurance to Bailee

The policy contains a provision that the insurance shall not "inure directly or indirectly to the benefit of any carrier or other bailee." The controversy between insurers and carriers over the right of an insurer to subrogate against a carrier, such as a railroad, is discussed in Chapter 24. The discussion in that chapter brings out the point that the intent of this clause is to preserve for the insurer the right of subrogation against the carrier or other bailee liable for the loss.

Some floaters also have a related provision under which the insurer advances payment for a loss as a "loan" to the insured, pending the insurer's efforts to recover from the carrier. Repayment to the insurance company by the insured receiving such a "loan" is limited to the extent of the amount recoverable from other parties. The Impairment of Carriers' Liability Clause is not part of the standard provisions of the Scheduled Property Floater.

Reinstatement

Each claim reduces the amount of insurance by the sum paid, unless the sum be reinstated by payment of additional premium. It may be amended to provide that the policy will be automatically reinstated for an additional premium in the event of loss. On the other hand, it may be amended—as in case of the Personal Property Floater—to provide that the payment of certain types of claims does not reduce the amount of insurance.

Pair or Set

This clause is applicable when the rider attached provides coverage on items or articles which are made up of pairs or sets. The measure of loss or damage to a part of the pair or set in such instances is a reasonable and fair proportion of the total value of the pair or set, after giving consideration to the importance of the article or articles in the pair or set, but in no event is the loss to be construed as total. In spite of this provision, underwriters under certain conditions and upon surrender to the insurance company of the undamaged part of the pair or set will pay for the loss of the pair or set even though only one portion may be lost or damaged. A related "Machinery Clause" imposes a similar limitation on liability when the insured property consists of several "parts." The insurer is liable only for the lost or damaged part or parts.

Protection of Property

This clause provides that in the event of loss, it shall be lawful and *necessary* for the insured to do everything possible to safeguard and recover the property covered, all without prejudice to the insurance provided. Expenses so incurred shall be borne by the insured and the company proportionately to the extent of their respective interests. Actually, the clause merely provides that an insured will do what any prudent owner of property would do in the event of a loss if no insurance were in effect. This clause, commonly referred to as "Sue and Labor," is discussed also in Chapter 24.

Suit

"No suit, action or proceeding for the recovery of any claim shall be sustainable in any court of law or equity unless the same be commenced within twelve (12) months next after discovery by the Assured of the occurrence which gives rise to the claim"—so reads the standard provision.

It goes on to specify that, if the laws of the state within which the policy is issued provide a different limitation, then that limitation is applicable.

Appraisal

In instances where the insured and the company cannot agree as to the measure of loss, the method of arriving at the appraisal is specifically set forth in this clause. It is similar to the appraisal provision in the Standard Fire Policy and provides that the insured and the company each shall select a competent and disinterested appraiser and that the two so selected shall choose a competent and disinterested umpire. The clause further provides that in the event the appraisers cannot agree upon an umpire, such umpire shall then be selected by a judge. Differences between the appraisers as to actual cash value at time of loss and the amount of the loss shall be submitted to the umpire. An award by any two of the three shall determine the amount of loss, and the cost of the appraisers and umpire shall be borne equally by the company and the insured.

Cancellation

The basis on which the policy may be canceled is provided by this clause. The company is required to stipulate the number of days of notice required before cancellation by the company can become effective. This period is stated as the number of days after the mailing of the cancellation notice to the last-known address of the insured. The insured has the option to cancel the policy on any date desired.

Subrogation

The policy contains a subrogation clause which in addition to establishing the subrogation right specifies that the insured shall execute and deliver papers and do whatever else is necessary to secure this right and, after a loss occurs, save it from prejudice.

PERSONAL ARTICLES FLOATER

Another policy, which appeared in the early 1950's, has become quite popular for insuring on a scheduled basis personal articles of a relatively high value. The Personal Articles Floater, probably still unfamiliar to many persons in the insurance business, incorporates all of the standard provisions discussed above in respect to the Scheduled Property Floater and is, in effect, the Scheduled Property Floater in different garb.

The reason for using the Personal Articles Floater is that it can provide a "one-write" contract for covering one or more of numerous classes of scheduled personal property. Jewelry, furs, cameras, musical instruments, silverware, golfers' equipment, and stamp and coin collections, for example, can all be written in one contract. Except for personal jewelry and furs, each class of these properties can also be insured in a separate scheduled floater as well as in the Personal Property Floater. Most companies no longer issue separate jewelry or fur floaters. Jewelry and furs, of course, can be insured in the Personal Property Floater.

The Personal Articles Floater is a standard contract under Inland Marine Insurance Bureau filings and also under Transportation Insurance Rating Bureau filings. Only minor differences exist between the two bureau forms. With few exceptions the rates, rules, and special conditions pertaining to each class of business which may be insured under this policy are as applicable when the property is insured under this form as when it is written under a separate floater. The point is worth repeating that the Personal Articles Floater is a covenient and economical vehicle for bringing two or more classes of scheduled property into the same contract or scheduling any one of several classes of property.

An additional point is that the Personal Articles Floater is often appended as a supplement to a Homeowners Policy. (See Chapter 49.) Despite its use in this fashion, it, of course, remains a separate contract.

OTHER FLOATER COVERAGES

Many floater policies provide insurance on scheduled personal property of individuals such as bicycles, cameras, objects of fine art, golfers' equipment, musical instruments, physicians' and surgeons' equipment, silverware, stamps, coins, and wedding presents. Others cover scheduled business property such as contractors' equipment, agricultural equipment, livestock, morticians' equipment, theatrical equipment, neon signs, scientific instruments, samples, patterns, vending machines, stocks of goods which are moved about, and so on. As noted, some floaters also provide some blanket insurance on unscheduled property. By referring to the list presented earlier, readers can determine which of these contracts require use of the standard provisions and which do not.

It is impossible to give a detailed analysis of each floater in this chapter; accordingly, several important features which appear in some of the floaters will be dealt with in a general way.

Perils Covered

Floaters dealing with the property of individuals are generally written to insure "all risk" of loss of or damage to property covered, there being only few exceptions some of which will be explained later in this chapter. Some business floaters are usually written "all risk," as, for example, on neon and certain other signs. Other business floaters can be written either as "all risk" or named perils. An example is a salesman's sample floater. Most business floaters, however, are issued on a named perils basis.

Examples are theatrical equipment, contractors' equipment, and livestock floaters.

Some additional examples are cited now to illustrate the scope of the coverages provided:

Mobile Agricultural Equipment Floater. This coverage may be in either of two forms. Form A provides insurance on blanket items and insures against "all risk" of physical loss or damage from any external cause except as limited by the exclusions. Form B is similar but is used to insure scheduled items.

Livestock Floater. Insurance under the Livestock Floater is against death or destruction from named perils. Four separate forms (A, B, Monthly Reporting, and Winter Range) are available. The usual perils are against death or destruction directly resulting from or made necessary by: fire, lightning; windstorm, cyclone, tornado, hail, explosion, riot, riot attending a strike, civil commotion, aircraft and objects falling from aircraft, smoke; earthquake, collapse of bridges or culverts; flood, collision, derailment or overturn of a vehicle on which the property covered is being transported; stranding, sinking, burning or collision of vessels, including general average and salvage charges; and the risk of theft excluding escape or mysterious disappearance. Under the Livestock Floater full mortality insurance is not provided; death must be as the result of a peril named. (See Chapter 11 for additional treatment of livestock insurance.)

Theatrical Equipment Floater. As one additional detailed illustrative example, consider the Theatrical Equipment Floater. It provides insurance against direct physical loss or damage caused by fire, lightning or explosion; collapse of bridges or culverts; flood (meaning rising waters); windstorm, cyclone and tornado; aircraft or objects falling therefrom or other vehicles excluding however any vehicles owned or operated by the insured; smoke, meaning thereby smoke due to a sudden, unusual, and faulty operation of any heating or cooking unit connected to a chimney by a smoke pipe; theft, burglary and holdup; collision, derailment or overturning of land conveyances while the insured property is in transit thereon (but the coming together of railroad cars during coupling operations shall not be deemed a collision within the meaning of this policy); stranding, sinking, burning or collision of vessels, including general average and salvage charges; the crash or collision of a transporting aircraft. Additional coverages may be obtained for loss caused by water damage, sprinkler leakage, strike, riots, earthquake, and breakage.

Perils Excluded

As emphasized in this *Handbook*, coverage (especially "all risk") is not ascertainable until exclusions are examined. Among the perils commonly excluded are the following:

Wear, Tear, and Deterioration. This exclusion varies but refers to the general and ordinary deterioration, resulting from normal use of the insured property. Virtually every "all risk" floater has this exclusion.

Dampness of Atmosphere and Extremes of Temperature. In those instances where the property insured can be seriously affected as a result of dampness of atmosphere or extremes of temperature, this exclusion is necessary. Machinery and equipment come within the category of susceptibility to such damages. This exclusion will not be found in each of the floater policies discussed in this chapter but is found in those policies where the loss probability is acute. A good example is the Camera Dealers Floater.

Mechanical or Electrical Breakdown. There is no question but what anything of a mechanical nature, as a result of operation, will ultimately break down. Further, artificially generated electrical disturbances cause breakdowns which are outside the scope of insurance. "All risk" contracts normally have an exclusion of these maintenance-type losses.

Infidelity. Losses occurring as a result of infidelity on the part of an insured, the insured's employees, agents, or parties to whom the property is entrusted are excluded. For example, the Musical Instrument Dealers Floater excludes loss from infidelity, misappropriation, secretion, or conversion. This provision is of particular importance in dealer floaters. Fidelity coverage, of course, is obtainable under separate contracts for most risks.

Moths, Vermin, or Inherent Vice. Losses resulting from moths or vermin damage are excluded from practically every "all risk" coverage as are also any losses which can be attributed to "inherent vice." The terms are troublesome and have given rise to several disagreements. "Vermin" probably includes rodents. "Inherent vice" is an ambiguous expression but means generally the capacity of an object to destroy itself by rotting, spoiling, rusting, or some other comparable process—although, not all rotting, spoiling, or rusting is attributable to "inherent vice." One authority cites the deterioration of rubber automobile tires over time even when not in use as an example of a loss from "inherent vice."[2]

Other Perils Excluded. In addition to the exclusions referred to, others are often inserted in "all risk" policies because of the type of property insured. For example, in those policies where there may be an installation of equipment or erection of some structure, the policy may provide that the coverage will not attach for any loss or damage caused by faulty manufacture, installation, or erection. Another common exclusion is for loss or damage caused by processing or while the property sent out for processing is being worked upon.

---

[2] W. H. Rodda, *Inland Marine and Transportation Insurance* (2d ed.; Englewood Cliffs, N.J.: Prentice-Hall, Inc., 1958), p. 85.

Breakage is excluded from some of the floaters where the property insured involves glass or other fragile property of high value. Under the Stamp and Coin Floater, there is an exclusion for loss resulting from fading, creasing, denting, scratching, tearing, thinning, and transfer of colors.

In some policies there is an exclusion for losses resulting from mysterious disappearance or for unaccountable losses. The intent is to avoid the payment of claim under a policy where the insured has no prima facie evidence that a loss occurred. There is also a limitation in some policies with regard to the extent of the theft coverage while in unattended automobiles operated by the insured or his employees. In instances where the insured has no control over the operation of the vehicles the exclusion would not apply.

All policies—whether on a named peril or an "all risk" basis—exclude the risks of war, nuclear reaction, nuclear radiation, or radioactive contamination.

Property Covered

The customary procedure is to schedule most or all of the property to be covered. Each item so scheduled should be fully described and identified. Under certain conditions underwriters will provide some blanket coverage on nonscheduled items. Usually, this insurance is a small percentage of the total amount of insurance on the scheduled items. This blanketing usually applies when there are numerous small items involved. The name of the floater describes the kind of property insured, such as cameras, musical instruments, and so on. In the case of the Personal Property Floater, for example, the underwriters will blanket all of the insurance if the insured does not wish to schedule any property, but, of course, there are special limitations on any one loss to unscheduled items of certain types such as jewelry, watches, and furs.

Just about every one of the floaters has some exclusions in respect to property as well as perils. Properties of high susceptibility to loss, properties of such an unusual nature as to call for an additional premium, and properties normally insured in other contracts are excluded from floater coverage. Some illustrative floaters are listed below with some of their respective property exclusions:

1. *Golfers' Equipment Floater:* Golf balls, unless the loss results from fire or burglary.
2. *Mobile Agricultural Machinery Floater:* Automobiles, motor trucks, motorcycles, aircraft, and watercraft; feed, hay, grain and crops of any nature; and self-propelled harvester-thresher combines and certain other equipment used for custom work.
3. *Personal Property Floater:* Animals, automobiles, motorcycles, aircraft, watercraft or other conveyances except bicycles, tricycles, baby carriages, invalid chairs, and similar conveyances.

4. *Theatrical Equipment Floater:* Buildings and improvements and betterments thereto, furniture, fixtures, equipment or other property not actually used on the stage in the production or play, jewelry except costume jewelry, accounts, bills currency, deeds, evidence of debt, and animals.

5. *Wedding Presents Floater:* Realty, animals, automobiles, motorcycles, aircraft, watercraft or other conveyances or their appurtenances, monies, notes, securities, stamps, accounts, bills, deeds, and so on.

Deductible or Franchise Clause

Deductible or franchise clauses are used in some floater policies to eliminate small losses. The deductible clause provides that no loss is recoverable under the policy until the loss exceeds the amount of the stipulated deductible and that the company is then liable only for the amount in excess of such deductible. The franchise clause provides that no loss is recoverable until the amount of such loss exceeds the amount of the stipulated franchise, in which event the company then becomes liable for the entire loss. The franchise is not used nearly as often as the deductible.

SUGGESTED READINGS

DAYNARD, HAROLD S. *Paths and By-Paths in Inland Marine Insurance.* New York: Insurance Advocate, 1949.

HEDGES, J. EDWARD, AND WILLIAMS, WALTER. *Practical Fire and Casualty Insurance.* 7th ed. Cincinnati: The National Underwriter Co., 1961. Chap. vi.

MORTIMER, WILLIAM M. *Adjusting Practices, Inland Marine and Transportation Insurance.* New York: Transportation Service Co. 1951.

RODDA, WILLIAM H. *Inland Marine and Transportation Insurance.* 2d ed. Englewood Cliffs, N.J.: Prentice-Hall, Inc., 1958. Chaps. 12, 18, 19.

Chapter 28

RATEMAKING IN INLAND MARINE INSURANCE

BY HAROLD L. WAYNE

This chapter covers ratemaking in the inland marine insurance field. Inasmuch as such ratemaking is a combination of the classic and contemporary and of science and art, it will be helpful to consider some historical background and also to look at the myriad risks that make up the field of inland marine insurance.

Ratemaking in the inland marine field is a combination of all of the mores and rules pertaining to ratemaking as practiced in the other segments of property insurance and also to some extent as practiced in liability insurance.

The basic formula for both ratemaking and rate adjustment purposes is, of course, quite simple: Premium is to equal the sum total of losses incurred, plus actual expenses incurred, plus a reasonable margin for profit and contingencies. Were ratemaking an exact science and that formula practicable in all cases, this chapter could be concluded at this point. Such, however, is not at all the case. The formula sets forth for the reader the "classic" and the "scientific" but it does not cover the "contemporary" and the "art" in ratemaking in the inland marine insurance field.

FILED RATES

Inland marine insurance falls into two broad groupings: (1) those kinds or classes of risks which are subject to the rate filing requirements of state laws; and (2) those which are not. Discussion here deals primarily with the first category because only that segment of the business generally involves formalized ratemaking.

TABLE 28–1

CLASSES OF INLAND MARINE INSURANCE SUBJECT TO RATE FILING REQUIREMENTS—WITH ANNUAL PREMIUMS 1962 AND 1963

Class	*Earned Premiums*	
	1962	*1963*
Accounts Receivable	$ 1,961,209	$ 2,357,532
Bicycle Floaters	53,654	49,748
Bridges and Tunnels	3,129,002	3,132,529
Camera and Sound Equipment	3,698,049	3,758,550
Camera Dealers	775,870	765,216
Comprehensive Dwelling Policy	58,179	52,447
Cotton	636,231	499,321
Equipment Dealers	4,422,580	4,476,423
Films and Negatives	271,534	318,593
Fine Arts Private Collections	3,704,368	4,222,961
First Class Mail	2,037,908	1,871,330
Floor Plan Policies	338,276	354,072
Furriers' Block	1,206,971	1,255,586
Furriers' Customers	3,119,385	3,070,212
Garment Contractors	5,056,623	5,291,985
Golfers Equipment Floaters	188,549	187,263
Heating and Air Conditioning Dealers	95,568	56,799
Horse and Wagon	122,084	129,070
Household Appliance Dealers	62,477	65,325
Industrial Machinery & Tool Dealers	70,699	180,767
Jewelers' Block	6,102,559	6,354,385
Livestock Floaters	3,314,048	3,407,511
Manufacturers Output Policy	398,672	499,944
Marine Supply Dealers	101,825	100,220
Mobile Agricultural Machinery	8,055,706	8,441,146
Musical Instrument Floaters	2,512,028	2,614,277
Musical Instrument Dealers	451,115	479,094
Neon Signs	3,080,780	2,976,097
Office Machinery & Supply Dealers	31,882	33,223
Parcel Post	5,472,970	5,141,605
Personal Effects	4,166,195	5,850,324
Personal Furs	15,386,730	15,559,956
Personal Jewelry	60,109,208	66,399,832
Personal Property Floaters	19,553,350	16,181,909
Physicians' and Surgeons' Equipment	2,592,220	2,867,167
Professional or Scientific Instrument Dealers	73,666	21,186
Radioactive Contamination	7,985	9,400
Radium	58,603	47,753
Registered Mail	2,271,780	2,012,277
Rolling Stock Railroad	1,928,907	1,198,263
Silverware Floaters	247,726	251,137
Sporting Goods Dealers	50,268	36,390
Stamp and Coin Collections	671,231	752,932
Theatrical Floaters	286,532	301,034
Tourist Baggage	661,359	435,713
Travel Baggage	763,280	777,601
Valuable Papers and Records	1,444,277	1,760,113
Wedding Presents	130,755	123,621
Winter Range Livestock	99,472	30,442
Wool Growers Floaters	37,018	22,094

Historical Review

The most cursory review of the list of "rate-filed" classes shown in Table 28–1 brings forth several "whys" and "hows." Why, it could be asked, are rates filed for Bicycle Floaters which produced a nationwide premium volume in 1963 of only $49,748, when filings are not made for Motor Truck Cargo Policies which produced an almost seventyfold premium volume of $34,765,546? Why, it could be asked, are intricate processes of ratemaking used on many other relatively insignificant classes and not on other classes of so much more importance?

Historical background provides the answers. Before the decision of the Supreme Court in the South-Eastern Underwriters Association case and the subsequent enactment by the Congress of Public Law 15, no state required filings for inland marine insurance. (For a discussion of this decision and Public Law 15, see Chapter 65.) For many years prior to the S.E.U.A. decision, companies providing more than 90 percent of the market for inland marine insurance had cooperated to standardize forms and rates for a number of classes of risks which lent themselves to uniformity of treatment. This standardizing was done through what were called "conferences," such as the Jewelers' Block Conference, the Personal Effects Conference and others, all of which were integrated with the Inland Marine Underwriters Association in 1930.

Early Promulgations. As a voluntary association of stock companies, the IMUA prepared and promulgated uniform forms and rates for the following classes of inland marine insurance:

1. Personal Effects Floaters
2. Tourist Baggage Floaters
3. Personal Jewelry Floaters
4. Personal Furs Floaters
5. Parcel Post Policy (Coupon Form)
6. Jewelers' Block Policy

The Executive Committee of the IMUA was at the same time charged with the duty "at the earliest possible date":

1. To arrange by agreement to bring all lines susceptible to tariff rating by classes under the full jurisdiction of the Association (IMUA).
2. On lines not susceptible to tariff rating by classes but for the rating of which general formulas may be established, to arrange by agreement for the establishment of such formulas.
3. On lines not susceptible to tariff rating by classes or to the establishment of rating formulas, to arrange as far as possible for uniformity of contracts.

The purpose of the companies was to bring about uniformity in forms, rates, and rules for those classes of inland marine insurance for which uniformity would be advantageous to the insuring public and to insurance companies.

The S.E.U.A. decision had made it imperative that the industry either discontinue acting in concert or, alternatively, seek legislation which would give to the insurance companies the legal backing envisaged by the subsequently enacted Public Law 15. The companies concluded that the public and they alike would best be served by cooperative ratemaking on certain classes of insurance and not on others.

Thus, the Inland Marine Insurance Bureau was organized to serve as a licensed rating bureau for the purpose of prescribing uniform forms and rates for the rate-filed classes, that is, those involving cooperative ratemaking.

Mutual companies in 1936 organized the Mutual Marine Conference to perform for its members essentially the same services as those performed by the IMUA. With the enactment of rate regulatory laws applying to inland marine insurance, the Mutual Marine Conference became a licensed rating bureau, and the name was changed to Transportation Insurance Rating Bureau. In most respects TIRB performs for mutual companies the same functions as those subsequently described as performed by IMIB for its members and subscribers. Trade association functions are performed for mutual companies by other associations. Rates and ratemaking methods of TIRB for inland marine insurance are closely similar to those of IMIB.

"All Industry" Approach. Later, the IMUA joined in the cooperative "All Industry" endeavor that produced what ultimately became known as the "All Industry Rate Regulatory Bills." By the time the moratorium under Public Law 15 expired, the association had re-formed itself into a trade organization and had ceased all of its ratemaking activities.

A majority of the states adopted the proposed rate regulatory bills in substantially the form recommended by the industry and by the National Association of Insurance Commissioners. The Fire, Marine, and Inland Marine Rate Regulatory Bill made subject to rate filing requirements those classes of inland marine insurance which by general custom of the business had been written according to manual rates or rating plans.

Earlier drafts of the bill required the filing of only those classes of inland marine insurance for which rates were made by a rating bureau. This provision was a clear expression of the intent of the industry that rates made in concert be filed and, conversely, that filing was not to be required of rates not made in concert. The language finally agreed upon was intended to impart the same meaning.

Additional Classes. By 1945 when the newly formed IMIB began the takeover of the ratemaking functions of the IMUA, the list of classes had been expanded from the original six by the addition of the following, in the order set forth:

Bridges
Personal Property Floaters
Theatrical Floaters
Stamp Collections

Furriers' Customers
Fine Arts
Cameras
Wedding Presents
Horse and Wagon Floaters
Radium
Garment Contractors
Vehicular and Rail Tunnels
Musical Instruments

Since the activation of the IMIB, the list of classes falling within its ratemaking functions has been thusly expanded:

Accounts Receivable and Valuable Papers and Records
Agricultural Machinery and Livestock
Bicycle Floaters
Camera and Musical Instrument Dealers
Cotton Buyers' Transit Insurance
Dealers Insurance
Equipment Dealers
First Class Mail
Floor Plan Merchandise
Furriers' Block
Golfer's Equipment Floaters
Negative Film Floaters
Neon Signs
Parcel Post Open Form
Physicians' and Surgeons' Equipment Floater
Radioactive Contamination Insurance
Registered Mail
Rolling Stock
Silverware Floaters
Stamp and Coin Collections
Travel Baggage Insurance
Wool Growers

Five Rating Groups. The classes within the purview of the IMIB for its ratemaking purposes may be separated into five groups:

1. Those which lend themselves to class rates, e.g., Jewelry and Fur Floaters.
2. Those which are rated on a formula or schedule basis, e.g., Jewelers' Block Policy and Furriers' Customers Floaters.
3. Those for which rates are considered to be at the irreducible minimum, that is, at a level below which an adequate market would not be available, e.g., Registered Mail Policy.
4. Those which do not produce a credible volume, e.g., Bicycle Floaters and Radium Floaters.
5. Those which require individual risk rating, e.g., policies on bridges and tunnels.

The reader will have gleaned from the foregoing that the original ratemaking activities of the IMIB consisted of nothing more complicated or intricate than the adoption of the existing rates, schedules, and formulas of the IMUA. Indeed, the first filings of the bureau under the new rating laws so stated in just so many words.

Production of Statistics. Shortly after it became a going organization, the bureau began the preparation of a formal plan designed to produce the statistics necessary for ratemaking in the future. The statistical plan adopted following hearings by the New York Insurance Department required all companies licensed to do business in that state to report their figures to the IMIB as the statistical agent of the state. Mutual companies were required to report either to the IMIB or to the Transportation Insurance Rating Bureau which, in turn, sent its consolidated report to the IMIB for inclusion in an overall report covering the entire industry. Other states thereafter followed in adopting the same statistical plan and appointed the two organizations on a similar basis.

The statistical plans of the two bureaus called for the filing of premium and loss figures on a countrywide basis except for the Personal Property Floater. For the latter class, figures were to be reported state by state.

In adopting the plan of reporting statistics countrywide the New York Insurance Department, and subsequently the other state insurance departments, agreed with the bureau that no useful purpose would be served by a plan calling for figures on a state-by-state basis because such a plan could lead only to figures of little, if any, credibility. Under the newly adopted plan, separate premium and loss figures were called for not only on the classes of insurance then subject to rate filing but on a number of others as well. In an order dated November 28, 1945, the New York Insurance Department stated: "It is to be noted that no clear demarcation has been made between classes subject to rate filing and other groupings which are included only for purposes of information."

The statistical plan has been expanded materially over the years. Essentially, however, it still calls for figures on a countrywide basis except for those classes for which territorial rates are filed, e.g., Mobile Agricultural Equipment Floaters and those for which rates are no longer uniform countrywide, such as Jewelry and Fur Floaters.

Statistics compiled by the IMIB are reviewed annually and rate adjustments are made and filed when deemed necessary. Consideration is given: (1) to the actual figures for the five-year period under review; (2) to the weighted figures, that is, actual premiums adjusted to reflect all rate changes during the five-year period; (3) to trend, if any major change from the norm is indicated; and (4) to the credibility of the figures under review, considering, among other things, the premium volume of the class and nature of the risks involved from the standpoint of loss frequency and susceptibility. In order to avoid reversal of trends in future reviews, a single increase or decrease, with rare exceptions, is limited to no more than 25 percent.

Place of Judgment. Judgment is a vital but, obviously, an intangible element in determining inland marine insurance rates. While sound, knowledgeable judgment has an important place in insurance ratemaking generally, it is of unusual importance in the inland marine field. To illustrate:

A few years ago it became apparent that the industry would have to abandon the traditional uniform countrywide rating of jewelry and fur insurance if residents of certain metropolitan centers were to have a ready and sufficient market for the coverage. Losses in New York City, Chicago, and Los Angeles were running so high that the market for risks in those cities was becoming increasingly restricted. The influence of those losses on the countrywide picture was many faceted. To bring the countrywide rate to an acceptable level would have been unfair to insureds outside of "bad experience" cities, but also it would have failed to alleviate the situation within those cities to the point where risks could once again be freely placed.

Although there were no available premium and loss statistics, the insurance departments of the states involved were well aware of the tight market. Newspapers were, of course, constantly publicizing the burglaries and robberies. Consequently, significant increases were made in the rates in those large cities and premiums and losses for such cities were segregated from those in the remainder of the country. Since that time the statistical plan has been further expanded and it now requires the reporting of jewelry and fur statistics by states, and in a few instances cities or counties within a state.

Personal Jewelry Floater: An Example in Ratemaking

Personal jewelry insurance represents the largest single classification in the inland marine portfolio. Written premiums in 1963 amounted to $71,750,179 out of a total inland marine premium volume in the United States of $429,042,207.

It is an excellent class, therefore, to use in detailing what has occurred in the application of the ratemaking process to a class of inland marine insurance which lends itself more nearly to the "classic" treatment than does any other.

Rate History. When the IMIB took over from the IMUA, the countrywide rates for jewelry coverage were:

First $ 5,000 of insurance	$1.87 per $100
Next 5,000 of insurance	1.31 per $100
Next 40,000 of insurance	.75 per $100
Next 50,000 of insurance	.41 per $100
Policies in excess of $100,000	.66 per $100 on entire policy amount.

Thereafter the following revisions (with only an exception or two omitted) took place on the indicated dates:

September 1, 1949

First $ 5,000 of insurance	$1.60 per $100
Next 5,000 of insurance	1.10 per $100
Next 40,000 of insurance	.60 per $100
Next 50,000 of insurance	.35 per $100
Policies in excess of $100,000	.55 per $100 on entire policy amount.

December 1, 1955

New York City, Westchester, Nassau and Suffolk counties, New York; Cook and Lake counties, Illinois; Los Angeles County, California:

First	$ 5,000 of insurance	$1.60 per $100
Next	5,000 of insurance	1.10 per $100
Next	40,000 of insurance	.75 per $100
Excess of	50,000 of insurance	.50 per $100

All others:

First	$ 5,000 of insurance	$1.20 per $100
Next	5,000 of insurance	1.10 per $100
Next	40,000 of insurance	.75 per $100
Excess of	50,000 of insurance	.50 per $100

September 1, 1956

Bronx, Kings, New York and Queens counties, New York:

First	$ 5,000 of insurance	$2.00 per $100
Next	5,000 of insurance	1.40 per $100
Next	40,000 of insurance	.95 per $100
Excess of	50,000 of insurance	.60 per $100

Richmond, Nassau, Westchester and Suffolk counties, New York; Cook and Lake counties, Illinois; and Los Angeles County, California:

First	$ 5,000 of insurance	$1.60 per $100
Next	5,000 of insurance	1.10 per $100
Next	40,000 of insurance	.75 per $100
Excess of	50,000 of insurance	.50 per $100

All others:

First	$ 5,000 of insurance	$1.20 per $100
Next	5,000 of insurance	1.10 per $100
Next	40,000 of insurance	.75 per $100
Excess of	50,000 of insurance	.50 per $100

March 1, 1957

Cook and Lake counties, Illinois:

First	$ 5,000 of insurance	$2.00 per $100
Next	5,000 of insurance	1.40 per $100
Next	40,000 of insurance	.95 per $100
Excess of	50,000 of insurance	.60 per $100

No changes elsewhere.

January 1, 1960

Bronx, Kings, New York and Queens counties, New York; and Cook and Lake counties, Illinois:

First	$5,000 of insurance	$2.00 per $100
Excess of	5,000 of insurance	1.40 per $100

Richmond, Westchester, Nassau and Suffolk counties, New York:

First	$5,000 of insurance	$1.60 per $100
Excess of	5,000 of insurance	1.10 per $100

Los Angeles County, California:

First	$5,000 of insurance	$1.60 per $100
Excess of	5,000 of insurance	1.20 per $100

Elsewhere:

First	$5,000 of insurance	$1.20 per $100
Excess of	5,000 of insurance	1.10 per $100

January 18, 1961

Cook and Lake counties, Illinois:

First $5,000 of insurance.......................$2.00 per $100
Excess of 5,000 of insurance....................... 1.40 per $100

Bronx, Kings, New York and Queens counties, New York:

First $5,000 of insurance.......................$2.25 per $100
Excess of 5,000 of insurance....................... 1.75 per $100

Richmond, Westchester, Nassau and Suffolk counties, New York:

First $5,000 of insurance.......................$2.10 per $100
Excess of 5,000 of insurance....................... 1.45 per $100

Los Angeles County, California:

First $5,000 of insurance.......................$1.60 per $100
Excess of 5,000 of insurance....................... 1.20 per $100

Elsewhere:

First $5,000 of insurance.......................$1.20 per $100
Excess of 5,000 of insurance....................... 1.10 per $100

January 1, 1962

Los Angeles County, California:

First $5,000 of insurance.......................$1.75 per $100
Excess of 5,000 of insurance....................... 1.35 per $100

Cook and Lake counties, Illinois; Bronx, Kings, New York, Queens, Richmond, Westchester, Nassau and Suffolk counties, New York; and Los Angeles County, California:

No changes.

Elsewhere:

First $5,000 of insurance.......................$1.45 per $100
Excess of 5,000 of insurance....................... 1.30 per $100

March 15, 1962

New York State outside of designated counties:

First $5,000 of insurance.......................$1.35 per $100
Excess of 5,000 of insurance....................... 1.20 per $100

Cook and Lake counties, Illinois; Bronx, Kings, New York, Queens, Richmond, Westchester, Nassau and Suffolk counties, New York; Los Angeles County, California:

No changes.

Elsewhere, with two exceptions:

First $5,000 of insurance.......................$1.45 per $100
Excess of 5,000 of insurance....................... 1.30 per $100

January 1, 1963

New York State outside of designated counties:

First $5,000 of insurance.......................$1.45 per $100
Excess of 5,000 of insurance....................... 1.30 per $100

Los Angeles County, California:

First $5,000 of insurance.......................$1.90 per $100
Excess of 5,000 of insurance....................... 1.45 per $100

No other changes.

January 1, 1964

Territory			Rates Per $100
California			
Imperial, Orange, Riverside, San Bernardino, Santa Barbara, San Diego and Ventura counties.	First	$5,000	$1.23
	Excess of	5,000	1.11
Los Angeles County excluding Avalon, Beverly Hills, Culver City, county areas within Los Angeles, Los Angeles, San Fernando and Santa Monica.	First	$5,000	$1.62
	Excess of	5,000	1.23
Avalon, Beverly Hills, Culver City, county areas within Los Angeles, Los Angeles, San Fernando and Santa Monica.	First	$5,000	$1.90
	Excess of	5,000	1.45
Remainder of the state	First	$5,000	$1.45
	Excess of	5,000	1.30
Connecticut			$1.25
Florida	First	$5,000	$1.45
	Excess of	5,000	1.30
Illinois			
Cook & Lake counties	First	$5,000	$1.80
	Excess of	5,000	1.25
Remainder of the state	First	$5,000	$1.55
	Excess of	5,000	1.40
Massachusetts			$1.20
Michigan			$1.30
New Jersey	First	$5,000	$1.45
	Excess of	5,000	1.30
New York			
Bronx, Kings, New York and Queens counties.	First	$5,000	$2.40
	Excess of	5,000	1.95
Richmond, Westchester, Nassau and Suffolk counties.	First	$5,000	$2.00
	Excess of	5,000	1.50
Remainder of the state	First	$5,000	$1.80
	Excess of	5,000	1.45
Ohio			$1.20
Pennsylvania	First	$5,000	$1.45
	Excess of	5,000	1.30
Texas			$1.30
Zone 1—Maine, New Hampshire, Rhode Island and Vermont			$1.20
Zone 2—Delaware, District of Columbia, Maryland, North Carolina, South Carolina, Virginia and West Virginia			$1.20
Zone 3—Alabama, Georgia, Kentucky, Louisiana, Mississippi, Missouri, Tennessee and Puerto Rico			$1.20
Zone 4—Indiana, Iowa, Minnesota, North Dakota, South Dakota and Wisconsin			$1.10
Zone 5—Arkansas, Colorado, Kansas, Nebraska, New Mexico, Oklahoma, Wyoming			$1.20
Zone 6—Alaska, Arizona, Hawaii, Idaho, Montana, Nevada, Oregon, Utah, Washington			$1.25

Analysis of Change. The nationwide reduction in rates which became effective September 1, 1949, represented a compromise following hearings held by the New York Insurance Department. At that time, detailed statistics were available for the years 1946, 1947, and 1948 only. In the absence of figures for prior years, there was no basis upon which the bureau could calculate the ratio of losses incurred to premiums earned for that three-year period.[1] The only expense statistics available were those which had previously been filed with the New York Insurance Department by all companies licensed to do business in that state. It was the contention of the bureau that expense statistics had not been uniformly maintained and that those reported were therefore of doubtful accuracy or validity for ratemaking purposes. On the basis of the compromise, the rates were readjusted to reflect a profit and contingency factor of 6 percent, an expense factor of 39 percent, and a permissible loss ratio based on those factors of 55 percent.

The element of judgment so often essential in ratemaking was quite apparent in the rate changes which became effective December 1, 1955. For the first time there was a breakaway from uniform countrywide rates. Following analysis of all available figures, the bureau had this to say in a letter dated November 18, 1955, and addressed to the Insurance Departments in support of the filing:

> As respects Personal Jewelry insurance it is believed that the 25% reduction in the rate for policies under $5,000 will tend to make the coverage much more attractive to Assured owning a relatively small amount of jewelry and thus develop an increased volume of this desirable business. It is believed also that no change is warranted in the rate applicable to amounts between $5,000 and $10,000 although Assured in this bracket will benefit by the rate reduction for the first $5,000 of insurance. The rate for amounts from $10,000 to $50,000 is increased by 25% in view of the consistently high loss ratios for that bracket. The increase on amounts of insurance in excess of $50,000 is likewise warranted by the consistently high loss ratios. It is to be noted that there is a relatively small premium volume on policies of $50,000 or over.
>
> As respects the metropolitan areas of New York, Chicago and Los Angeles it is the belief and best judgment of the Bureau and its companies that the higher premium to be charged Assured whose principal residence is in such metropolitan centers is more than justified. There has been considerable curtailment of market in those metropolitan centers at present rates. It will be the purpose of the Bureau to require the maintenance of separate statistics therefor effective January 1, 1956.

The rate changes that became effective on September 1, 1956, and March 1, 1957, were also without statistical support in the strict sense. The market in New York City and in Cook and Lake counties, Illinois, had become tighter day by day to the point where companies were refusing to entertain any new lines. Wholesale cancellation of existing policies or rejection of renewals appeared imminent.

Newspapers in both New York and Chicago, under banner headlines,

---

[1] The formula for determining earned premiums on insurance written for a period of three years is based on one sixth of the current year's premiums, one third of the year immediately preceding, one third of the second preceding year, and one sixth of the third preceding year. Thus, premium figures would have been required from 1943 on to develop earned premiums for the years 1946, 1947, and 1948.

were daily publicizing the large jewelry and fur losses then taking place. The bureau obtained from a representative cross section of its members their 1955 and 1956 results in those two metropolitan centers. Based upon the market conditions, the well publicized losses, and the partial statistics the bureau was able to gather, the bureau sought and the insurance departments approved the rate changes effective September 1, 1956 and March 1, 1957.

The rate changes taking effect January 1, 1960, were based upon a combination of statistics and judgment. Once again they represented a material departure from long established custom.

Statistics for the five-year period from 1954 to 1958 inclusive showed earned premiums of $200,747,735, incurred losses of $111,698,269, and a loss ratio for the period of 55.64 percent. On the basis of an expense ratio of 47.09 percent (the figure actually used was 47 percent) and a 6 percent margin for profit and contingencies, the permissible (or "balance point") loss ratio for rate adjustment purposes was 47 percent. With no weighting of the figures to reflect the steady upward trend evidenced by the statistics, the 55.64 percent loss ratio for the five-year period indicated a needed increase of 18.38 percent in the rates.

A review of the statistics revealed that the loss ratios on policies covering on amounts in excess of $10,000 were consistently higher than those on policies of $10,000 and under. As against the overall loss ratio of 55.64 percent, the loss ratios for the several rating brackets were:

Bracket	*Ratio*
Policies of $5,000 and under	50.57
Policies from $5,001 to $10,000	54.16
Policies from $10,001 to $50,000	68.02
Policies from $50,001 to $100,000	80.03
Policies of $100,000 and over	69.86

In the judgment of those making the review it was fallacious to continue to provide lower rates for higher amounts of insurance and whatever advantage there might be in the spread was more than offset by other factors.

Although the bureau believed that the statistics justified the elimination of all rate differentials based upon amount of insurance, the relatively statisfactory ratios, particularly in the metropolitan centers, on policies of $10,000 and under influenced the retention of those two brackets. Accordingly, the rates were changed by the elimination of lower rates for policies in excess of $10,000. The overall effect of the increase could not be accurately determined but it was obvious that it would be well short of the indicated needed increase of 18.38 percent. Subsequently, detailed review, analysis, and calculations suggested that the changes produced an increase of 6.31 percent.

Later rate changes reflected to a lesser degree the element of judgment and to a greater degree the actual statistics for the class. The statistics for 1962, on the expanded basis, made possible a state-by-state review of results for two full years. Considering the high susceptibility of jewelry to large losses, it was concluded that an annual premium volume of $1 million was necessary for credibility for ratemaking purposes. Analysis of the figures for the two-year period indicated that in 10 of the 52 rating jurisdictions (the 50 states, the District of Columbia, and Puerto Rico), the average premium volume was in excess of $1 million. In the remainder it was obvious that results could be expected to vary sectionally. Seeking a logical way to establish rates on a sectional basis in keeping with the territorial differentials that might be expected, the IMIB found that the National Association of Insurance Commissioners' zonal grouping of states would produce the sought after homogeneity, provided each state within a given zone which itself produced a credible premium volume was rated on its own experience. This major change in rating philosophy also permitted the establishment in many of the states of a single rate for the class.

Judgment. This detailed review of jewelry rates illustrates the vital element of judgment even when dealing with a class which, on the surface, most readily lends itself to the application of the basic ratemaking formula. Had the companies, since the advent of rate regulation of inland marine insurance, been limited to rate changes for jewelry insurance only on the basis of the developed statistics, it would obviously have been impossible to place a jewelry line in the large metropolitan centers. By the same token, rates elsewhere would have become too high. Much the same could be said for the insurance of personal furs, the rating history of which differs not too much from that of personal jewelry.

Rating of Certain Commercial Classes

In addition to the personal lines classes, for which rate manuals are used, there are several commercial classes on which premiums are developed by the application of formulas. Some are relatively simple and others quite complicated.

Dealer Floaters. The simpler formulas are those applicable to the various dealers floaters, such as Camera and Musical Instrument Dealers Floaters. The formula for each of those classes is on file with the insurance departments and the rating of an individual risk is not difficult.

Bureau companies submit each individual risk to the bureau for rating. Basically, these formulas call for determination of the policy rate by adding to the specific fire contents rate certain specified loadings determined after the application of credits for burglar alarm systems, watchman service, debits or credits for size of population plus charges for each $100 of gross annual sales, and so on.

These formulas are designed to reflect, to the degree practicable, the rateable differences among the individual risks. Rate adjustments on these classes are made generally by the application of a fixed percentage increase or decrease to the overall premium determined in accordance with the formula.

To illustrate, statistics for the five-year period ending December 31, 1958, showed an improvement in the results on Camera Dealers Floaters and the then existing surcharge of 15 percent was reduced to 7½ percent.

Rating formulas for Furriers' Customers Floaters, Furriers' Block Policies, and Jewelers' Block Policies are far more complex. In each case detailed proposal or application forms designed to mesh with the rating schedule are obtained and transmitted to the bureau for rating. Most of the information called for in such forms must be furnished by the insured.

As in the case of the Camera and Musical Instrument Dealers Floater risks, Jewelers' Block Policy, Furriers' Block Policy, and Furriers' Customers Floater rates, generally speaking, are changed, as required, by a percentage increase or decrease applied to the final premium produced by the application of the schedule. Without presenting the filed schedules themselves, which are much too lengthy and complex to be set forth here (the Jewelers' Block schedule covers 15 closely set pages), there is no point in delving further into the ratemaking for such risks.

Bridges and Tunnels Insurance. Included within the inland marine classification as instrumentalities of transportation are bridge and tunnel risks. Such risks are individually rated by the bureau and involve ratemaking *entirely* on the basis of informed judgment. There are no "basic rates" or schedules or formulas. In rating these risks the bureau evaluates the detailed information contained in the required bridge inspection report, the plans, photographs, and other descriptive material. This information may be submitted in a given case or required by the bureau if deemed necessary.

Consideration is given (1) to the location of the risk; (2) to its general construction, such as the number of piers, the material of which they are constructed and how they are founded; (3) to the type, number, material, size, and kind of flooring of both moveable and fixed bridge spans; and (4) to the length and type of construction. Additional information is required covering date of construction; contract costs of substructure, superstructure, and approaches; and the estimated present values, if the bridge is not new. Detailed information is also called for which would permit evaluation of the perils of fire and lightning, floods and rising waters, ice, collision, explosion, strikes, riots and civil commotion, malicious damage, tornado and windstorm, earthquake, and collapse. Likewise in connection with construction, the inspection report must set forth in detail subsurface conditions as well as complete data with respect to the construction of the substructure, superstructure, and approaches. Also of importance in the consideration of each risk are its age; whether rebuilt, and if so when; the engineer on design; the contractors; the opinion of the engineer making the survey as to the design and present values; and his recommendations as to needed improvements, both those imperative and those merely desired.

With all of the foregoing information, a rate can be determined and filed for the individual risk. No two bridges are exactly alike, not excluding so-called twin structures. Moreover, values run from as little as a few hundred dollars on some privately owned bridges to well over $200 million. The insurable value on the Verrazano-Narrows bridge probably will be in excess of $300 million. The facts help explain the need for the application of sound judgment on an individual risk-rating basis. No one has yet been able to devise a workable schedule for the rating of bridge and tunnel risks.

Personal Property Floater

One of the early "all risk" package contracts was the Personal Property Floater. Originating some 40 years ago, the prototype of the present policy was an extension of a Personal Effects Floater to cover additionally the entire contents of the insured's home. In fact, the policy was designed to cover all personal possessions with such exceptions as automobiles, animals, jewelry and furs—items which generally were specifically insured. Thus, under the then new policy the underwriter replaced or covered the perils normally insured under specific fire and extended coverage contracts and residence burglary and theft contracts, to say nothing of the many other kinds of loss or damage which occur to such property.

Present Personal Property Floater rates evolved from the original schedules which were based upon: (1) the fire rate applicable on contents in the insured's residence; (2) a charge for $1,000 of residence burglary and theft coverage for each $6,000 of insurance at rates applicable for such coverage; (3) a charge for $1,000 of "Personal Effects" coverage at the applicable rate; and (4) the *sine qua non* for all other perils, that is, the appropriate loading over and above the other rate elements to cover the unknown and unanticipated.

The foregoing indicates why, of all inland marine risks, only Personal Property Floater rates varied state by state. During the early years of the IMUA, it became apparent that the then existing rates were insufficient in "windstorm states" and one of the very first changes called for the inclusion in the overall rate on risks in those states of a special charge for windstorm coverage.

As time went on, rates were adjusted, state by state, based upon the experience in the state. Traditionally, the adjustments were made in the "loadings" or the rate component for perils other than fire and, where applicable, windstorm. As a rule of thumb, the "loadings" were calculated as representing 80 percent of the full premium for the policy. Thus, an indicated increase of, say, 10 percent was translated to an increase of 12½ percent in the "loadings" (12½ percent of 80 percent of 100 percent = 10 percent).

The reader will have noted in this resume of the rating philosophy behind the Personal Property Floater another refutation of that old canard that all inland marine rates were simply "grabbed out of the air."

Other Classes

Just a sentence or two should suffice with respect to the few classes for which rates are at irreducible minima or which do not produce a credible volume for ratemaking purposes. The Registered Mail Policy is the outstanding example of the former and the Radium Floater of the latter.

For a recent five-year period, Registered Mail Policy premiums totaled $9,135,499. This insurance is highly important to banks, brokerage houses, and fiduciaries in general. There are several forms available, all at extremely low rates. For the two most popular forms the basic rates at the time of this writing were:

Daily or Monthly Reporting Policies—Securities, 4 cents per $1,000 of insurance. Currency, precious stones and bullion, 8 cents per $1,000 of insurance.

Annual Premium Adjustment Policy—All property, 6 cents per $1,000.

Using 6 cents per $1,000 as a conservative overall average, the liabilities assumed by the companies during the five year period amounted to something over $150 billion, or an average of some $85 million at risk each and every day. The protection provided is almost unfathomable. Substantial losses have been experienced and the potentialities are tremendous.

Radium Floater insurance at one time produced premiums of about $1 million per year. For the same recent five-year period as mentioned above, the premium totaled $324,710 and, because of the relatively small volume, single losses could produce wide fluctuations in loss ratio. For example, the loss ratio in 1961 was 19.80 percent but only four years earlier it was 72.14 percent. Hence the volume of premiums for this class of business is not credible for ratemaking purposes and, for that reason, rates are permitted to remain stationary.

NON-FILED CLASSES

For some of the most important classes of inland marine insurance the rates are not filed with insurance departments. Among the larger premium producing classes are:

Class	Written Premiums 1962	1963
Boats and Outboard Motors	$15,886,018	$15,692,043
Contractors Equipment Floaters	36,162,909	39,617,801
Installment Sales	12,278,530	12,978,546
Installation Floaters	8,180,000	8,588,372
Motor Truck Cargo	33,546,454	34,765,546
Transportation Risks	24,345,871	26,556,315

Much of this business is written on forms tailor-made to meet the requirements of the individul insured and at rates or premium which the company considers commensurate with the risk. This business requires careful and knowledgeable underwriting. As has so often been demonstrated over the years, woe to the underwriter who boldly plunges into the competitive market without the essential background and experience.

There is a wide divergence of rates and rating philosophies among companies just as there is a wide divergence of exposure to loss among risks. The latter must be weighed carefully in reviewing an offering by an agent or broker. With few exceptions risks must be submitted to the company for review, rate quotation, and acceptance. There is no discussion of the rating of a risk between companies nor can there be because of the prohibitions of federal antitrust laws.

It must be emphasized again that rates are not the product of imagination or culled from thin air. In a review of any risk, the inland marine underwriter must call upon vast and specific experience to assay and weigh the facts presented. He must evaluate the risk both as to acceptability with respect to loss potential and as to the rate level before committing the assets of his company to what might be an obligation of millions of dollars. The underwriter himself or the operating heads of his company no doubt have developed guideposts, but they are simply that, at best, and subject to various modifications by the individual responsible for setting the rates and assuming the risk.

Studious reading might make one wiser in the ways of rating inland marine insurance but it probably will not qualify him to evaluate and rate a risk in the non-filed category of inland marine insurance. To borrow a phrase from Sir Winston Churchill, only the "blood, sweat, and tears" of experience can do that.

SUGGESTED READINGS

Annual Statistical Reports. New York: Inland Marine Insurance Bureau.

Reports on Examination of the Inland Marine Insurance Bureau. New York Insurance Bureau, April 15, 1948; March 1, 1955; September 1, 1961.

Rodda, William H. *Inland Marine and Transportation Insurance.* 2d ed. Englewood Cliffs, N.J.: Prentice-Hall, Inc., 1958. Chaps. 2, 22.

Chapter 29

UNDERWRITING IN INLAND MARINE INSURANCE

BY ROBERT L. MAXWELL

In the early years the inland marine underwriter, like his ocean marine counterpart, performed all the functions of the transaction. He attracted the business; he appraised it; he set the price and specified the coverage; and, if satisfied, he wrote the risk. He also settled his own losses. The complexities of modern business, however, have brought about many changes as compared to the early days. Loss work in most companies has now been removed and placed with the general loss departments. Bureau controls of certain lines have brought about a difference in underwriting techniques and a somewhat higher degree of specialization in the ranks of the underwriter. There is still, however, a very large segment of the business remaining which is uncontrolled both as to form and rate, and the underwriting approach in this segment is very much the same as it was in the beginning.

NATURE OF THE UNDERWRITING FUNCTION

Organization

A review of the modern underwriting operations of a present-day company is useful at an early phase in this chapter. The executive in charge, of course, has the responsibility of deciding the underwriting policy and the type of organization he will have. Some companies will have the underwriters working under the chief underwriter, assuming responsibility for all classes of business but only for a given territory which may be a small portion of the country. Others will have their underwriters specializing on only a few classes but perhaps for the entire country or a relatively large entire territory within the country. In the first approach the underwriter for all classes needs a thorough knowledge of the territory he serves and a wide acquaintanceship with the individuals in that territory. In the second approach the underwriter, of course, covers a much wider territory. He cannot be expected to have as intensive an acquaintanceship within his territory. On the other hand, he will gain a greater knowledge of the specialized classes he is handling than "territory" underwriters are likely to have.

Either type of underwriter must effectively and thoroughly impart the underwriting policy to his field force or other sales representatives in the territory. The field representative must always be aware of the underwriting policy and not violate it. At the same time he must produce business within the framework of that underwriting policy. The field representative, therefore, soon learns that his work is twofold. First, he must know and carry out the underwriting policy of his company; second, he must sell the business in volume.

Some Basic Considerations

The inland marine underwriter was the first one to deal with multi-peril contracts. During an era when other branches of the business were thinking in terms of relatively narrow ranges of named perils, such as fire and allied lines or burglary and robbery, he had to consider a much broader range of named perils and even "all risk" coverages. In addition, the property he was insuring, for the most part, was constantly or intermittently on the move. When more and more policies were designed to cover in fixed locations, he had to acquaint himself with fire, tornado, burglary, and water damage underwriting, among many other types. The broad application of inland marine coverage under many different conditions requires the inland marine underwriter to possess qualities inherent in almost all first party underwriting. In addition, he has to be thoroughly acquainted with all types of transportation hazards, and also with the conditions of bills of lading, shipping receipts, and other transportation documents.

As in all other types of insurance, there are many physical hazards which must be taken into consideration in the underwriting of inland marine business. These must be determined and appraised on the basis of information obtained through inspection or other sources.

Perhaps the most important condition affecting practically all inland marine risks is what is termed in the business as a "moral hazard." (See Chapter 14 for a discussion of the "moral hazard" as it applies to fire and allied lines of insurance.) This term as used in marine underwriting goes beyond the question of honesty or dishonesty of the insured and encompasses generally the inability of an individual to perform his functions safely and carefully. The individual who *is* able to perform his job safely and carefully is the one the inland marine underwriter wants to insure. When investigating a risk the underwriter must be continually on the lookout as to whether or not his potential insured displays any habitual carelessness in the maintenance of his property or in the protection of his valuables, and whether or not there is excessive use of alcohol or association with persons of undesirable character.

Type and Size of Company

The broader the facilities to be offered by a company, the greater its necessity for bigger size and scope of services. If a company is going to write inland marine risks national in scope, that company must have underwriting and inspection services and loss facilities which also are national in scope. If a company decides to enter the inland marine field to write only personal lines it can, of course, operate with a much smaller force than that required for handling a full book of business. Loss adjustment facilities for personal lines can usually be contracted for through outside sources. Inspection services can likewise be purchased on this category of risk through outside services. To underwrite the larger commercial and industrial risks, however, underwriting facilities must be maintained on a par with those of the fire and casualty departments of the companies.

Another factor pertaining to the insurance company and having a bearing on the underwriting function is the size of the company's resources. With the exception of the bureau-controlled lines, there is little concurrence among companies in either forms and rates, so it is generally necessary for one company to write the entire line. This spread requires not only that the company retain a substantial portion itself but also that it be able to obtain adequate reinsurance treaties. Retention and reinsurance arrangements usually determine the size of the risk that a company can write. The company which can carry the largest line has the greatest advantage in obtaining business.

MAJOR ASPECTS OF THE UNDERWRITING FUNCTION

In the remainder of the chapter attention is given to several major aspects of the underwriting function in inland marine insurance.

Underwriting Policy

The general underwriting policy is usually established by the chief inland marine underwriting executive. He must, of course, take into consideration general company policy as set by the president or even by the board of directors. Many factors enter into formulation of this company policy.

Perhaps the first consideration in any insurance company is the nature and makeup of its production force. The practical choice is direct writing through employees or production through independent agents. While either type of operation may be successful, the underwriting technique varies considerably from one to the other.

Next to be decided is the line or lines of business to be written; for example, policies and forms to be used (and how filed) and personal lines, commercial lines, industrial lines, or some combination of them to be handled.

The general underwriting policy also must take into consideration the areas of the country in which risks will be accepted and the marketing effort to be devoted to each. The company may want to increase volume in some areas and avoid volume in another because of unusual hazards.

The underwriting policy, of course, must clearly define the size of line the underwriter will carry on any given risk or any given classification of risk. This line is usually determined by the amount the underwriter will carry net. The amount carried "net" means the total written and retained by the company. A company's capacity is increased by any additional amounts subject to "excess of loss" or other reinsurance contracts. As a rule, individual companies have automatic excess of loss contracts which enable them to write 100 percent of the line of which they would otherwise be able to take only a portion. A percentage of each premium dollar goes to pay the cost of the excess of loss contract. The larger the net line which the underwriter can carry himself, the lower the cost of the excess of loss contract, of course. Since the excess of loss contract is usually rated on an experience basis, the underwriter must set an underwriting policy which he hopes will make a profit for his reinsurers as well as for himself.

The Operating Framework

There are several hundred active classes of inland marine insurance. Some are bureau-controlled as to rate and form. On others both the rate and form are subject to the underwriter's judgment. To carry out properly the underwriting program, the company must thoroughly indoctrinate the field force as to policies, forms, rates, and rules on controlled business and see to it that the obligations that are legal in nature are met. On the uncontrolled classes the field force must know to what extent it can act on its own authority and when a problem must be referred to the home office. Every avenue of communication must be used to impart to the field force the elements of the underwriting policy.

Policies and Forms

In no other area of the business is the knowledge of contracts and their construction so important. The inland marine rating bureaus strive for uniformity by using the same clauses and forms wherever possible. (See, for example, the Chapter 27 discussion on the Basic Scheduled Property Floater.) Differences, however, do exist. The underwriter must be keenly aware of the impact of each clause and its application to a given risk. The underwriter does have the satisfaction of knowing that bureau-prepared forms for the most part have been reviewed by counsel or other highly trained specialists on the particular class involved.

The greatest challenge an inland marine underwriter faces, however, is the preparation of policies and forms on the so-called uncontrolled or tailor-made covers on many different and unusual types of risks. This task is a daily one with him. He must rely on his best judgment, as time and expense do not permit submitting forms to counsel for review except in very unusual situations. He will use, of course, as often as he can standard clauses in the makeup of the contract. Just as important as policy text is the preparation of binder forms which, until the policy is formally issued, are the sole basis of the coverage in the event of loss. Declaration forms and certificates are used to describe a specific risk under a master policy and must be carefully worded.

Of great importance to the inland marine underwriter is the preparation and use of various applications which when completed are the basis of his judgment as to whether he will or will not accept a given risk. The application must be so prepared and worded that it will develop for the underwriter all pertinent information and yet not be so extensive in detail as to be burdensome or irritating to his production force or to the insured. Most applications state that the information submitted is a condition of the insurance. In others, such as the Jewelers' Block Policy, the information is a warranty and is so stated in the policy.

Rating Systems

Chapter 28 recounts the developments leading to the formation of rating bureaus and to the filing of rates and forms for certain classes of business. Each member or subscriber of a bureau, of course, has its respective bureau file those rates and forms on its behalf.

Controlled Lines. The personal lines coverages are the principal homogeneous class of inland marine risks and make up the bulk of the business subject to rate filing. A second classification of inland marine business is subject to bureau rate control but the risks are individually rated by the bureau upon receipt of applications. As examples, the following risks are rated in that manner: Bridge (and Tunnel), Property Damage Policies, Jewelers' Block Policies, Furriers' Customers Floaters, and Railroad Rolling Stock Floaters.

As in any other rating systems, the publication of inland marine rates are on the basis of averages for the class. The inland marine underwriter must be thoroughly acquainted with the principal hazards involved in each particular line of business and be certain that the risk he writes is within the framework of the rating system. He must study the bureau's statistics closely and, more importantly, he must study his own. An adverse loss experience on any given class indicates the underwriting policy for the class is too broad and must be further restricted. If his experience is much better than the class, it could indicate the reverse. The underwriter also, if he chooses, can file a deviation and, upon approval, offer a rate lower than quoted by the bureau.

Uncontrolled Lines. On the balance of the inland marine lines—and this makes up the greater part of the premium income—there is such a variance in the nature of the risk and the conditions affecting the risk that it has been impractical to develop either a flat rate or a rating formula for these classes. Here the precepts of the original marine underwriter prevail. Underwriting and rating fuse into one process. The underwriter must appraise the conditions of each risk and then quote the coverage he is willing to write and the price he will charge for it.

In assessing uncontrolled risks the underwriter must be sure to consider the possible transit exposure as well as the location exposure, and extract proper premium for each. Broadly, in the case of the transportation exposure, he must ascertain whether or not the property is being hauled on the insured's own trucks in which case, even for the best-operated risk, he will have to obtain a substantial premium for the reason that virtually every such loss is absolute and without possibility of subrogation. On the other hand, if the property is in transit by a public truckman, a railroad, or an airline, he knows that under the normal bill of lading issued he can expect to recoup a substantial portion of his loss from the carrier. There are, of course, exceptions to this generalization. For instance, the carrier can issue a restricted or limited bill of lading which makes him liable for only a very small portion of a loss. (See Chapter 24.) This restriction is perfectly agreeable and acceptable to the inland marine underwriter, but naturally he will want to extract a greater premium for the greater probability of loss.

While the property is in a given location, the underwriter must first know what coverage he is giving and then figure a premium which is adequate. If the policy happens to cover only the risk of fire at location, he is in no different a position than the straight fire underwriter. If it covers the risk for burglary, robbery, or theft, then, of course, he must take into consideration the same hazards as would the burglary underwriter. If the coverage is "all risk," he must make charges for such additional perils as flood, water damage, collapse of building, and so on.

Because of the prohibitions in state and federal antitrust laws the inland marine underwriter is restrained from acting in concert with underwriters from other companies in pricing insurance in uncontrolled classes. He must not collaborate with other underwriters in this regard, except when it is only a matter of reducing the risk through reinsurance. This restriction requires, therefore, that elaborate experience records must be kept on each individual class of risks in the uncontrolled category as well as on the individual risk itself. If a given risk or given class develops an adverse loss experience, the underwriter can and must increase his rates, increase his deductibles, or greatly restrict his writings. Conversely, if his experience is exceptionally good, he must be constantly aware of the fact that his competitor may learn of this good experience, reduce the price, and take the business away. He must, therefore, protect his business, so to speak, by promptly rewarding the good-experience risk with a reduction in rate. Each company, for the most part, maintains statistical departments in order to produce continuously and promptly the information necessary to adjust rates of individual risks or classes of risk either upward or downward as experience suggests.

Underwriting Guides for Field

In order to attract business within the framework of the underwriting policy, the field force must know the company policy and be constantly updated on any additions, deletions, or other modifications in it. Many companies publish very attractive manuals for their field forces. Such a manual covers each segment of the business and describes the company's underwriting policy. The manual is usually supplemented by bulletins, letters, and other written media. Most important of all are the specialists from the home office who travel in the field, review with their field force the many problems and ramifications of the business, and explain the company's position and underwriting policy.

There are very few prohibited classes of inland marine business, that is, classes which insurers do not want at any price. On the other hand, however, in almost every class there are certain situations which make the business either prohibitive or restrictive. As an example, the writing of transportation risks on general merchandise is a common, everyday occurrence. But a single shipment of dynamite or other very highly volatile explosives would be sufficient grounds for the underwriter to decline the risk under any and all circumstances, or at least to require very restrictive underwriting conditions. Personal lines insurance is written by practically all companies in the inland marine field. Yet, with some companies, as an example, professional entertainers or other risks of high public exposure may not be written under any circumstances.

The underwriting guides referred to above will highlight, for the most part, those types of risks which the company wishes to avoid altogether. The guides will also outline certain conditions under which other risks may be written. The principal purpose, therefore, of all the underwriting guides to the field is twofold: first, to give to the field force as much underwriting latitude as the company possibly can on the reasonably normal risks, and, second, to give sufficient underwriting information to enable the field force to recognize the unusual or the more complex situation and refer that type of risk promptly to the home office for consideration.

Selection of Risks

Thus far in this chapter company organization, underwriting implementation, sales, and rating have been discussed. The success of the inland marine underwriter depends on bringing all of these factors into play for one purpose and that purpose is to select the risks from which he may expect a profit and decline those from which he does not. As there is a difference in the technique of underwriting the class-rated risk as compared to the individually-rated risk, each will be reviewed separately.

Class-Rated Risks. As previously mentioned, the personal lines business makes up the largest volume of the inland marine coverages which are class-rated without modification for individual risks. These risks are made up of policies covering all types of personal property. The premium for each of the lines in shown in the table in Chapter 28. There are some other classes of marine policies class-rated without modification which are not strictly in the personal lines category but for which the underwriting technique is not a great deal different. These classes are also listed in Chapter 28.

Personal lines underwriting requires such an unusual technique that many years ago certain companies developed specialist underwriters just for this class of business only and this practice has continued in today's highly competitive market. The class-rated underwriter must have a thorough knowledge of the various classes of business under his jurisdiction so that he may know how to select risks within the framework of the rating structure. While many factors will influence his judgment, there are certain basic considerations which almost automatically apply to each risk. In the case of a Jewelry or Fur Floater, the following must be considered:

1. Age, sex, and marital status.
2. Occupation.
3. Business and personal associates.
4. Neighborhood.
5. Financial status.
6. Personal habits.
7. Construction of premises and fire protection.
8. Loss history.

Adverse information on any one or more of the above points can be automatic grounds for rejection. The size of the risk that a company will write can be an important element. Jewelry and Fine Arts Floaters, and, in fact, many other schedules of personal property, can range from a few hundred to hundreds of thousands and, in some cases, to millions of dollars in value. The underwriting policy as to the size of line, therefore, can dictate whether size of risk alone could make a risk unacceptable.

Risks Individually Rated by the Bureau. The category of risks subject to this type of rating, as we have already noted, involves businesses whose values and exposures are substantial. The underwriter knows in general terms the most he can expect to obtain on a given risk insofar as the premium income is concerned. His selection of risks in this category, therefore, depends on the information concerning each risk. The rating applications, of course, describe quite thoroughly all the exposures and other factors which enter into the evaluation of the risk. In addition, the underwriter may also choose to obtain a separate inspection report either by his own company inspector or by outside professionals engaged in this type of work. (See, for example, the discussion on bridges in Chapter 25.) The underwriter likewise must be constantly aware of his experience on that particular class of risk over a period of time, as well as the experience of all companies which are members of his bureau and which also write this class of business. In fact, he takes into consideration all information which he can obtain and which is described in greater detail in the following paragraph on the uncontrolled rated class.

Risks Uncontrolled as to Rate and Form. In the case of personal lines business which is flat-rated by class, there exists great similarity and consistency from one risk to another. In the case of the bureau-rated classes, while there is a great similarity in the type of business, there are variables such as values, protection, and so forth, which require that each risk be individually rated. The uncontrolled classes of inland marine underwriting embody such a wide difference in so many conditions affecting the risk that no better way has as yet been devised than to let the inland marine underwriter, in a setting of competition, analyze the risk, specify the wording in the contract, and set the rate. While there are certain fundamentals to be considered in all risks, the variables in this segment of the business assume such importance that their treatment is totally dependent upon the ingenuity and the experience of the inland marine underwriter.

The underwriter is handicapped by the fact that no one individual can know everything about everything, or even something about everything. There are, of course, many areas where he can depend entirely on his knowledge and experience with respect to a given class of business and can accept or reject the risk based solely on that knowledge and experience. There are other areas where the risk is of a nature that it presents such technical problems that only a qualified engineer can analyze them and point out the hazards involved. In situations of this kind the underwriter must know where he can obtain that sort of technical advice. He has to secure an accurate appraisal of the risk in order to set an adequate premium or exclude in the policy certain perils or property he does not choose to cover.

Factors Affecting the Risk

The greatest single factor the inland marine underwriter takes into consideration is what he terms the "moral hazard" or, as discussed earlier in this chapter, the possibility that the insured is not able to do business safely and carefully. The following are the basic factors in this general category which automatically come to the inland marine underwriter's mind when he appraises any type of risk in this category:

1. *Pertaining to the insured:*
   a) What is his experience and reputation in his line of business?
   b) What is his financial position? Is it sufficient for him successfully to undertake the work he is doing?
   c) What is his loss record? This question may involve a submission of record to the underwriter and in many cases a sworn statement as to each loss sustained which would be covered under the policy in question and a complete, detailed analysis as to its cause.
   d) Is his equipment adequate and in proper condition? Is his help of proper depth and skill?
2. *Pertaining to the job:*
   a) If the job involves a risk at the location, is there any unusual condition as far as the location itself is concerned? Is the location in an area where there has been, is, or might be a flood? Is the area mountainous? Are there any adverse conditions brought about by the weather, such as extreme cold and snow in the northern states?
   b) What is the nature of the job itself? Does it involve a common and well-known type of venture, or is it unusual and perhaps experimental in nature? If the latter is the case, there is very little history for the underwriter to go on and, as a consequence, he will have to use greater caution in approving this type of risk.
   c) If the risk is exposed to or in buildings, what is their construction? What fire protection is maintained?
   d) If the risk is one of transportation, is the transportation of the usual type or types which characterize his book of business? Or is it a very unusual situation, such as the hauling of very valuable machines from one location to another and perhaps involving a hoisting risk to the top of a skyscraper?
   e) What volume of premium income does the underwriter have on the particular classification? If it is large and his experience is good, the possibilities suggested in *d* above will not be nearly as critical as if his volume were small and of the type where a single substantial loss could make the class unprofitable.

The underwriter normally finds that in respect to some of the above considerations the insured rates high, but in respect to other considerations he rates low. The underwriter is faced with balancing good points against bad ones. For example, certain risks can have very good physical exposures, such as a low fire rate and a superb construction. On the other hand, the contractor's ability or reputation may be unsatisfactory. In such a case the underwriter will reject the risk or else price it beyond the norm. In another case a contractor's reputation and experience can be of the best but some of the physical exposures of the job can be so severe as to warrant rejection or very cautious treatment of the risk. On those risks where the factors both as to the insured and the job are favorable the inland marine underwriter uses all the ingenuity he has to make his package attractive as to price and coverage.

The Underwriter's Relationships and Qualities

While the inland marine underwriter prides himself in being an individualist and in exercising a wide degree of judgment, his success is, of course, greatly dependent upon many other individuals and circumstances. First, he must rely to a great extent on the use of good judgment by his field representatives in developing proper underwriting information and in the selection and acceptance of risks at their source. Second, the underwriter must know wherein and to what degree he can trust others in the granting of broad authority. The expense of doing business is a critical factor. The fewer people required to handle a given risk from start to finish, the greater the benefit to the company. Third, because the development of technical information is very often necessary, he must rely on his engineering and inspection departments to obtain accurate data. Fourth, he is dependent on industry statistics. The statistics of the industry, as well as of his own writings, are the guiding beacon as to whether he is producing results that are average, above average, or below average. He must know how to interpret and use these statistics. At the same time, he must know those underwriting factors which no rate or statistical plan can take into consideration.

Although every day will bring a new challenge to the inland marine underwriter and thereby continually broaden his base of experience, he must nevertheless be alert to general business trends as well as to those which are social and political. Changes in business methods, such as automation, open up entirely new horizons, opportunities, and perhaps underwriting problems. He must be aggressive and approach underwriting problems not with the aim of avoiding them but rather with the aim of surmounting them, knowing full well that, whatever the problems, they call for judgment.

SUGGESTED READING

Rodda, William H. *Inland Marine and Transportation Insurance.* 2d ed. Englewood Cliffs, N.J.: Prentice-Hall, Inc., 1958. Chaps. 2, 3.

Chapter 30

LOSS ADJUSTMENT IN INLAND MARINE INSURANCE

BY HAROLD S. DAYNARD

The inland marine insurance loss adjuster is a "jack of all trades." He is a fire loss adjuster, a burglary loss adjuster, a cargo surveyor, and a liability claim investigator, all combined into one. This diversity of his calling is a result of the historical expansion of inland marine insurance to include an enormous assortment of mobile property coverages.

As a "jack of all trades," the inland marine adjuster cannot afford to be master of none. He is, so to speak, an across-the-board specialist. In this chapter the character of this extraordinary field of loss adjusting is described with specific emphasis placed on the following:

1. What special training is required of the inland marine adjuster?
2. What basic loss and investigation procedures are employed in his handling of losses?
3. What are the rules, customs, and practices which guide him?
4. How does he deal with specific types of losses?

These points, in substance, constitute a summary of materials spread over hundreds of pages in the works referred to in the bibliography at the end of this chapter.

TRAINING OF INLAND MARINE ADJUSTER

Because inland marine insurance is so broad and diverse, the training of an inland marine loss adjuster must be especially comprehensive. Fire and burglary loss men must be knowledgeable in building and contents loss problems relating to fire, windstorm, sprinkler leakage, other damage, and theft. The inland marine adjuster uses this know-how as a point of departure. He must also be familiar with the problems of loss of mobile property wherever the property may be, not only on location but also in transit. He must understand what to do when property is lost or damaged while it is in the custody of a carrier or other bailee. He must also be familiar with the special (block) comprehensive coverages in the jewelry, fur, laundry and dry cleaning, processing, garment manufacturing, warehousing, fine arts, stamp, camera, and other trades. He must understand the implications of the legal relationships among the first-party and third-party interests engaged in these trades.

Thus, to function effectively in his complex job, the inland marine adjuster needs training in the fundamentals of loss adjusting procedures; in evaluating personal and business properties including such diverse items as art objects, bridges, piers and dams, goods and wares in trade, medical and scientific instruments, mobile machinery, household goods, clothing, jewelry, furs and other personal effects. He requires schooling in the legal aspects of ownership and title, sales, and bailment; carriers', warehousemen's, and innkeepers' liability; negligence; and contract. He must become a seasoned insurance man and a thorough investigator, interrogator, and appraiser.

These demanding prerequisites for a competent inland marine adjuster command a feeling of respect, if not awe, on the part of many persons within and without the insurance industry. Although many inland marine insurance coverages are being absorbed into comprehensive package-type policies for homeowners and businessmen, the inland marine type of loss is still a matter for the specialist.

THE CLAIM REPORT

The basic procedures in inland marine loss adjusting, at least in their initial stages, are similar to those in other property loss adjusting fields such as fire, auto, and burglary (see Chapters 16 and 47). In every property loss assignment, the adjuster must furnish the insurer with a report of particulars to justify admission of liability and amount of payment under the terms of the policy. The report usually covers the items listed below:

1. *Insurable Interest:* Has the person who made the claim a right to do so under the policy? Is he a specified insured? If not, has he a right under the policy as a third party beneficiary?
2. *Property:* Is the property involved insured?
3. *Cause of Loss:* Is the cause of loss within the scope of the perils insured?
4. *Date of Loss:* Did the loss happen while the policy was in full force and effect?
5. *Location of Loss*: Did the loss happen within the insured location or territorial scope of the policy?
6. *Policy Conditions and Warranties:* Have all policy conditions and warranties been complied with?
7. *Exclusions:* Was the loss caused or affected by a peril which is specifically excluded from policy coverage?
8. *Claim and Recommendations:* What amount is being claimed and what, according to the valuation clause in the policy, is adjuster's determination as to the amount of loss?

9. *Salvage:* Is there any property involved that may be salvaged and how is this taken into account in the calculation of the amount of loss?
10. *Other Insurance:* Is there any other insurance carried by the claimant, insured, or anyone else which may be called upon to pay or to contribute to the loss?
11. *Subrogation:* Is there any third party who may be held responsible for the loss and what steps were taken to protect the rights of all concerned against such third party?
12. *General Remarks:* Does the adjuster have any criticism of the insured; was there any misrepresentation or concealment by the insured when the policy was first written or about any matter pertaining to the loss; are there any irregularities involved; is the loss bona fide?
13. *Enclosures:* Are photographs available? Can they show (*a*) a damaged property or undamaged property where damage is claimed; (*b*) points of forcible entry in burglaries; (*c*) scenes of serious thefts or other casualties? (Photographs surpass the best word pictures.)
14. *Documents:* Original signed statements, original shipping documents, and pertinent records kept by the insured in the regular course of his business (including receipts, invoices, appraisals, bills of sale, cancelled checks, and other evidential data) should accompany report to the insurer.

The foregoing data are usually obtained by the adjuster through any or all of the following means:

1. Interrogating the person making the claim, the insured, and all other interested parties and witnesses.
2. Checking with police and official authorities involved, if any, for corroboration of facts.
3. Auditing books and records; checking original purchase sources or appraisals to establish identification of property involved, quantities, and values claimed; and establishing ownership.
4. Inspecting and appraising property involved in cases of damage.

Need for Circumspection

When an inland marine adjuster becomes involved in developing basic information, he must be especially circumspect and resourceful. Inland marine insurances are broad, often covering "all risk." Under many inland marine policies the insured need proved nothing more to the insurer than the fact that the insured property is missing. Under the terms of a jewelry floater, for example, the policyholder need only convince the adjuster that the property is irretrievably gone or missing whereupon he will be indemnified whether or not he recalls what specifically happened to it. Thus the possible dishonesty of the insured—a part of the "moral hazard"—is more often a factor to be considered in inland marine adjusting than in other fields. The breadth of coverage calls for more painstaking interrogation and investigation than is required in other fields of adjusting.

Inland marine policies, moreover, are frequently "tailor-made" or improvised to fit the special needs of the policyholder without strict regard for standard forms or clauses. This point is brought out in earlier chapters, especially in regard to the "uncontrolled" classes of business. The result is that the contracts (often called "manuscript policies") are usually more intricate. When loss occurs, greater care is required on the part of the adjuster in determining coverage and amount of collectible loss than is required by conventional insurance contracts.

Non-Waiver Agreement

If a loss is suspicious, the adjuster may wish to investigate with extraordinary care, but he must avoid, at the outset, creating an impression that the insurer intends to admit liability. To protect all concerned he may ask the insured to sign a "non-waiver" agreement which, by its terms, permits the claim to be investigated and the amount of loss to be determined in the usual way, while the rights of all concerned are reserved.

Proof of Loss

The "Proof of Loss" is a sworn, formal document which, according to the terms of the policy, must be filed by the insured within a specified time. There are special forms for inland marine losses which differ from those forms used in the fire, burglary, and bonding fields. It is generally, though not uniformly, the practice for inland marine adjusters to issue the Proof of Loss Form to the insured for signature after the claim is adjusted, in which case the document serves only as a formal summation of the claim and adjustment. In suspicious cases, the adjuster, usually under insurer directions, may supply a blank form to the insured, without prejudice, and demand that it be filed. Here the document, when filed, serves as a sworn statement that sets forth the insured's specific claim, and it will be acted upon by the insurer according to its truth and technical sufficiency.

CUSTOMS, PRACTICES, AND LAW APPLICABLE TO INLAND MARINE LOSSES

Many important factors in inland marine loss adjusting arise out of traditional customs, practices, and the law. Some are peculiar to inland marine, some are not. They are just as important to the disposition of an insurance loss as are the printed terms of the policy. As a matter of convenience, this subject matter may be classified here in the following categories:

1. Definition of policy terms.
2. Rules of policy construction.
3. Basic law of insurance.
4. Burden of proof.

Definition of Policy Terms

In inland marine policies to a greater extent than in any other type of insurance, key terms are employed which govern the scope of coverage.

Yet the policy does not define them. Examples are: "all risk," "in transit," "while in the custody of," "personal property," and "members of insured's household." The question arises: "By whose definition of these terms is the policyholder bound?" The answer is, of course, *by legal definitions* and they in turn ordinarily are based in part upon the best dictionary definitions.

In some instances the court definitions have lacked clarity and have brought about considerable litigation. Here are generally accepted definitions of several common inland marine terms:

All Risk. A policy which insures "all risk" does not insure *all loss.* The term "all risk" implies the following conditions before the policy coverage attaches:

1. The loss or damage must be fortuitous (accidental). The term "risk" implies "chance." Thus, if a loss is not fortuitous, it is inevitable, like loss by wear and tear, or inherent vice. "All risk" by definition excludes this type of loss. The same thought is sometimes expressed by the authorities in the statement: "The loss or damage must happen to the subject matter from without," that is, the cause must be an extraneous one. If it is inherent to the subject matter, there is no "fortuity" or "risk" involved. For example, a precious stone such as opal sometimes develops an internal fissure. This is normal for opals. This damage is not insured by "all risk" insurance. The damage is not accidental. Some policies insure *"all risk"* by using the phrase "All risk of loss by an external cause," which clarifies the intent of "all risk" coverage.
2. The term "all risk" also implies that a loss will not be contributed to by insured's own willful act or fraud. The law does not permit one to insure against his willful or fraudulent acts.
3. The term also implies that the loss will be a lawful one. If the property insured is possessed or used illegally, the insurance, even if on an "all risk" basis, is void.

In Transit. This term is used in the Transportation Policy and various floaters but never defined in the policy. A suggested and simplified definition is:

Transit *begins* upon actual movement of the insured goods from the point of shipment bound for a specified destination; transit *continues* while the goods remain *en route* in the custody of authorized carriers, including temporary stoppages which are normal incidents to the trip; transit *ends* when carrier delivers the goods to the place authorized by the owner. Goods awaiting shipment, or resting at point of destination, are not in transit. (Loading and unloading may be covered by endorsement.)

Custody. This term is used in salesmen's and processors' floaters and various other inland marine policies in both insuring clauses and exclusions. Even the best definition of this term is too broad and awkward for precise application and its construction is troublesome. When applied to property, it means to have temporary charge of for safekeeping and it connotes control, although not necessarily physical possession. For instance, one has property in his "custody" when he has the key to a locker in which the property is located.

Personal Property. The term is used in the Personal Property Floater, Scheduled Property Floaters, and numerous commercial policies. The forms do not define the term. There are hundreds of legal decisions dealing with the definition and its myriad complexities. In its broadest legal sense, "personal property" is all property not connected to land and thus distinguished from "real" property. "Personal property" embraces movable objects, objects only temporarily attached to land (fixtures), and valuable papers. (Legally, "personal property" may include business or nonbusiness property. Laymen often refer to "personal" property as meaning "nonbusiness" property.)

Household. The term "member of insured's household" appears in a number of personal policies which insure a named person and "members of his household." The dictionary definition says a household includes all those who dwell under the same roof and compose a family. The difficulty with the terms "family" and "household" does not involve basic definition but rather application to given facts. Problems of interpretation arise when family members are *away from home.* How long can a member of the family stay away from home and still be regarded as a member of the household? The question is similar to defining one's "domicile." A "domicile" is one's permanent residence—the place where he always intends to return. Unmarried men in temporary military service are regarded still as members of their parents' household, if they have no residence outside of the army other than that of their parents. Children away at school are in a similar category. But children who have married and moved away, or who have otherwise "gone out on their own," have been "emancipated" and are no longer members of their parents' household.

Rules of Policy Construction

Legal rules of contract interpretation affect the rights of policyholders and insurers, sometimes making it easier for the insured to obtain indemnity for a loss and sometimes enabling the insurer to deny liability. For instance, there is an established rule that any "ambiguity" in the policy shall be resolved against the insurer. This rule is an extension of the law of contract which holds that a contract ambiguity shall be resolved against the party who drew the contract. Insurance law presumes that all policies were written by the company, hence the language shall be construed in favor of the policyholder.

Another rule of interpretation is *ejusdem generis,* which means that, when general words in a contract follow an enumeration of particular items, the general words are construed to be limited to items of the same kind as those specifically mentioned. For example, when a policy covered "furniture and other personal property," a court held that the only "other personal property" covered was property resembling furniture, and that the term did not extend to a portable pier on the property.[1] Therefore the

[1] See *Warshauer* v. *Employer's Fire Insurance Company* [247 Wisc. 469, (1945)].

ejusdem generis rule is a caution signal to adjusters. Catchall phrases like "all other property" are not as broad as they might seem to laymen.

Basic Law of Insurance

All insurance policies are subjected to the fundamental law of insurance and this fact is reflected in many standard policy clauses. But the law applies to the contract whether or not any reference is made to it. Inland marine loss adjusting necessarily takes into account numerous legal concepts, including indemnity, insurable interest, fraud and misrepresentation, breach of warranty, waiver estoppel, subrogation, and so on. Rather than review each of these concepts here, the author invites readers to review Chapter 4 and the earlier chapters in Part IV of this *Handbook* where these and other concepts are treated.

Basic legal concepts guide the inland marine adjuster at every turn during the course of his investigation and adjustment of a loss. For example, when he discusses the worth of an item of property, the "indemnity" concept should be paramount in his thinking. He should not offer an amount equal to the cost of new merchandise for lost or damaged used property, or tolerate fancy custom-shop prices on bargain basement articles. When speaking to a claimant, he should ask himself: "What is this person's interest in the matter?" (concept of insurable interest). When inspecting damaged property, he should inquire: "What has been done to mitigate the damage?" (concept of "sue and labor"). Throughout the entire investigation he should be wondering: "Are we being dealt with above board?" "Are all facts and records being disclosed?" "Is the insured telling the whole truth?" (concept of fraud and misrepresentation). Before proceeding beyond the initial stages of his investigation, he should study the policy from beginning to end and make sure he says or does nothing to give the insured grounds for a claim of waiver or estoppel. Finally, his ever-alert sixth sense should prompt him to find the third party responsible for the loss, if there is one, so that the insurer's subrogation rights will be protected.

Burden of Proof

This term involves legal procedure. Without going into its technical aspects, readers may note that it has to do with the requirement, as between the party who is suing and the party being sued, of producing proof that is more convincing than that adduced by the other party. The party who is said to have the "burden of proof" must produce a *preponderance of evidence* with respect to his side of the issue.

Generally, the party who seeks by suit to enforce a contract must show, in order to prevail, that he has performed all the conditions precedent to the contract, that is, his part of the bargain. The question as to whether or not he has done so is extremely technical.

When insurance contracts are involved, it is fairly well settled that:

1. The insured has the burden of proving that the loss falls within the terms of the contract, and that all policy conditions have been complied with on his part.
2. The company has the burden of proof with respect to any defense based upon a policy exclusion, or upon fraud or other misconduct on the insured's part.

The *extent* of an inland marine adjuster's investigation will be guided by these rules. He should ask himself whether or not evidence is required merely to resist a weak claim. If so, such evidence must meet, with equal force, that which is adduced by the insured. But if the insurer intends a defense based upon a policy exclusion or misconduct on the insured's part, then the adjuster must help the insurer prepare to defend with facts which are weightier than those to be offered by the insured—with facts which not only will neutralize those in opposition but also which will convince a judge or jury.

ADJUSTMENTS UNDER SPECIFIC COVERAGES

Inland marine loss departments are frequently organized into two divisions: *Personal* and *Commercial.* The reason, as will be seen, is that the two types of inland marine loss require different adjusting procedures—or at least differences in emphasis.

Personal Coverages

"Personal loss" refers to a loss under one of the "personal" as distinguished from the "business" coverages. Personal loss adjustments are generally regarded as less complicated, compared to commercial loss adjustments. This idea is a misconception arising from a tendency on the part of many adjusters to be more lax in the investigation of personal losses. The "personal loss" category includes loss under the Personal Property Floater, Personal Effects Floater, and Personal Articles Floater, including insurances on floating property such as cameras, sports equipment, jewelry, furs, silverware, and other personal property. Many of these are "all risk" policies which insure anywhere in the world and apply while the insured is traveling.

There are two major phases in adjustments of "personal" losses. First, the insured must be sufficiently interrogated and investigated to establish the bona fides of missing property claims. The insured's representations should be corroborated by the records of official authorities to whom reports should have been made. Second, insurable interest, ownership of the property, and true values should be established by verification of purchase or appraisal transactions and by application of proper depreciation. There is no area of loss investigation that requires greater care and skill than that involved in scrutinizing appraisals, ownership, and value. Experience establishes beyond any doubt that many "insurance" appraisals veil tax-free sales and usually state values exaggerated beyond actual cost. The "personal" lines adjuster must be sufficiently familiar with values to exercise independent judgment as to the accuracy of appraisals. Experts can help when the size of the loss warrants their employment.

The value of articles of utility, such as clothing, depreciate according to their use. The amount ordinarily payable for used personal property is replacement cost at time of loss less allowance for depreciation.[2] Deductions for depreciation on furs are usually from 10 percent or more for each year of use, depending on the durability and style of the furs. Depreciation on clothing varies. A tuxedo which is rarely worn may depreciate perhaps as little as 10 per cent per year, whereas men's and women's outerwear ordinarily depreciates in value from 20 to 40 percent per year and articles of clothing such as hats, lingerie, and shoes depreciate from 50 to as much as 100 percent per year. Poor quality or highly styled property depreciates faster than do well-made and conservative articles.

Property such as jewelry and fine arts can be insured at agreed values in which case, in the event of a bona fide loss, payment of the full amount of insurance is required.

Commercial Coverages

Goods, merchandise, and equipment coverages are known as "commercial" lines and include transportation, carrier liability, bailee, block, and various floaters covering salesmen's samples, contractor's equipment, goods at processors and at garment contractors, and so on.

Transportation Insurance. Insurance on shipments by rail or motor carriers, mail insurance, and carrier liability insurance constitute a vast subject matter as may be concluded from the bibliography at the end of this chapter.

To adjust transportation losses, the inland marine adjuster must have wide experience in the field and a thorough understanding of documents and technical language altogether different from those in every other field of insurance loss adjusting. These special areas are treated at length in the author's *Handbook on Transportation Insurance Claims.*[3] A summary of the captions in the outline of that publication is presented here as an expedient way to suggest what is necessarily involved in adjusting transportation losses:

---

[2] "Used Market Value" as a measure of loss in household goods cases has been disapproved. *Blanche Crisp* v. *National Security Insurance Company* [326 SW 2d 326 (Texas S.C. 1963)].

[3] Harold S. Daynard, *Handbook on Transportation Insurance Claims* (New York: Insurance Advocate, 1961).

Background of Federal Regulations. The Minute Regulation of the Transportation Industry. Interstate Commerce Act. Original Abuses Which Led to Regulation. How Remedies Were Attempted in the Carmack Amendment of 1906 and the First and Second Cummins Amendments.

Liability of Carriers. What Law Applies. Federal, State or Common Law. "Exempt Zones." Local Law. Common Law. Rule of Absolute Liability. Specific Responsibilities of Shipper. Of Carrier. Duty of Consignee. Packing. Waiver of Shippers; Default. The Common Carrier as a Warehouseman.

Limitation of Liability. How a Carrier May Reduce Its Liability. Types of Clauses. Released Rates Orders. Losses to Which Released Liability Apply.

Common versus Contract Carrier. Common and Contract Carrier Distinguished. Tests to Be Applied. ICC Rulings. Common Law Distinctions. Important Differences in Their Liability to Shipper.

Filing of Claims Against Carrier. Importance of Doing It Correctly. When to File Claim. With Whom—How? What Is Not a Claim. Suggestions for Avoiding Defective Filing of Claim.

Measure of Damages. General Rule of Carrier Liability. Cost versus Selling Price. Retail or Wholesale Price. Profits. Consequential Loss. Where There Is No Market Value. Damage Claims.

Transportation Policies. Loss Procedure Depends on Type of Policy. The Four Major Classes of Transportation Insurance. Shippers' or Consignees' Policies. Documents. What Are Their Purposes? The Bill of Lading. Freight Bill. Waybill. Standard Form of Presentation of Claim. Indemnity Agreement. Over, Short and Damage Report. Documents Necessary for Each Claim. Loss of Entire Carton. Pilferage. Concealed Losses. Damage Claims. Interview of Truckman. Procedure in Representing Carriers' Insurer. What Information to Get from Assured, Employees, Claimant. Trip Transit Claims.

The F.O.B. Rule. What Does It Mean? Its Relation to "Title." What Is Presumed in Absence of FOB Terms. Rules of Passage of Title. "Ascertained goods." "Unascertained Goods." Fungibles. "Appropriation." Buyers' and Sellers' Obligations under FOB Terms. FOB Shipping Point. Freight Prepaid. Freight Allowed. FOB Car at Seaboard. FOB Vessel. FAS Vessel. C.I.F. Variations of C.I.F.

Freight Forwarders, Carloading Companies and Packing Houses. Historical Need for the Freight Forwarders. Their Function. Their Status as a Current Mass Production Business. Method of Operations. Advantages Offered. Package Consolidating Companies. Their Function and Manner of Operation. Whom They Represent. Their Connection with Truckmen. How They Affect the Question of Risk of Loss. The "Packing House" Endorsement.

Imports and Exports. Their Place in Inland Marine Loss Adjusting. Imports. Appraisers Stores. Customs Clearance. Consumption, Warehouse and Other "Entry" Forms. Customs Bonds. Release of Goods from customs.

Exports. Shipping Permit. Dock Receipt. Documents. Export Declaration. Dutiable Value. Ad Valorem and Specific. Foreign Consular Invoices. Certificate of Origin.

Middlemen in Export. Import Trade. The Export Commission House. Manufacturer's Agent. Export Merchant. Broker. The Freight Forwarder. Ocean Bills of Lading. Straight and Order. "Received for Shipment." "On Board."

Liabilities of Shipowners. Harter Act. Carriage of Goods by Sea Act.

Marine Insurance. Perils of the Sea. Open Policies. Average (Particular and General). Warehouse to Warehouse Clause.

Packing and Marking. Protection of Goods against Strain, Moisture and Pilferage. Marks. Advertising Contents. Designating Weight and Numbers. Unwrapped Goods.

Air Freight. Its History in This Country. Air Carrier Liability. Domestic and International Carriers. Warsaw Convention.

What Is Transportation Loss Adjusting Really About? Does a Book Knowledge Make a Good Adjuster? Abilities Really Required. Desirability of Practical Experience. A Tour through the Garment Manufacturing District. The Incredible Realism of Transit Losses. Everyday Illustrations. Just What Do the Transportation Policies Intend to Underwrite?

Digest of Legal Decisions Relating to Transportation Policies. Introduction. How to Read and Understand a Legal Decision. Why Only One Legal Decision Cannot Be Relied upon to Answer a Question. Meaning of "Stare Decisis." "Holding" and "Obiter Dicta" Distinguished. Where to Find the Cases.

Carrier Liability. Bill of Lading. Its Three Functions. Legal Significance of Recital of Quantities Therein. Shipper's Load and Count. Must Bill of Lading Be Signed? Commencement of Carrier's Liability. Where Must Goods be Delivered by Shipper? Must a Bill of Lading Be Issued? Is a Contract in Writing Necessary? Duties of Carrier. Furnishing of Equipment. Improper Loading. Delay. Common versus Contract Carrier. Rule of Absolute Liability. Right to Limit Liability. Notice of Claim. When Must Documents Be Sent? Verbal Notice. Tracer. Waiver of Notice by Carrier. Pilferage. Packaged Goods. Bulk Goods. Damages. Damage Claims. Non-Deliveries. Loss of Profits. Owner's Duty to Minimize Damages.

Losses Arising under Transportation Insurance Contracts. Trust and Commission Clause. Owners' Discreet Right under Policy. Shippers' Policies. Misdescription of Goods. "In Transit"—What Does It Mean? Storage. Does Issuance of the Bill of Lading Start the "Transit"? Unsuccessful Delivery to Consignee. Delivery to Imposter. Where the Goods Have No Destination. Refused Goods. Deviation from Transit. Temporary Abandonment of Shipment. Overnight Stop at Driver's Home. Risks (Defined). Fire. Lightning. Cyclone. Hurricane. Flood. Collision. Derailment. Perils of the Sea. Particular Average. General Average. Theft. Mysterious Disappearance. All Risks. Riot. Civil Commotion. Neglect by Assured. General Clauses. Territorial Limits. Excess Insurance. Fraud and Concealment. Benefit of Insurance. Appraisal Clause. Sue and Labor. Subrogation.

This outline indicates, among other points, the importance of subrogation. The adjuster must understand the use of the "loan receipt," subrogation receipts, and trust agreements. He must be familiar with the background of the "Benefit to Bailee Clause" and "Impairment of Carrier's Liability Clause."

Bailee Coverage. A "bailee" is one to whom property has been entrusted by another (the bailor) usually for their mutual benefit, for instance, a garment sent by an owner to a cleaner for cleaning. Bailee insurance refers to coverage obtained by the custodian for the benefit of the owner of the property.

The initial adjusting procedures have been stated earlier in this chapter. Emphasis in bailee claims however, should be placed on the following:

1. The policy sometimes affords the insurer the option to adjust with the custodian or with the owner directly. Where property is destroyed or stolen, the owner should be contacted directly for verification of property, identification, value, and other applicable insurance. There are special customer's forms or affidavits in existence for the purpose of obtaining this information.
2. Customers' or owners' claims are usually documented with: (*a*) The customer's claim form (in which the owner supplies a description and itemization of the property and states the amount of his claim and the details of his own insurance, if any). (*b*) Original or copy of storage or cleaning or processing receipt or contract, to be checked against the custodian's (insured's) records.
3. The customer's property is usually directly insured under the bailee insurance whether or not the bailee is legally liable for the loss. But the bailee's liability may be limited to an amount declared by the owner or other person entrusting the property to the insured. The legal validity of such limits of liability is a complex question which has not been uniformly dealt with by the courts.
4. As a rule of law, bailees are usually liable to the owners of goods or merchandise, only if negligent, but as suggested above, the usual purpose of bailee insurance is to insure payment of loss to the customers irrespective of fault, and where bailee protection is sought.
5. Where the aggregate of customers' claims exceeds the policy limits, the adjuster may not pay some claims to the exclusion of others. Nor may he prorate without the consent of all claimants. Payment of the policy fund directly to the insured is an acceptable alternative, if the policy permits it and if underwriters can be held harmless against further claims. In some cases, a deposit of the policy fund in court by a procedure known as "Interpleader" may be desirable, in which event distribution of the insurance fund is made under court order.

Block Coverages. Jewelers' Block, Furriers' Block, and Camera and Musical Instrument Dealer Floaters are included in this category. In some instances written "proposals" are required from the prospective insured in advance of writing the policy. In the case of the Jewelers' Block Policy, the proposals are incorporated into the insurance policy and designated as warranties.

Other Commercial Coverages. Losses arising under the various salesmen and contractor floaters involve the same basic adjustment procedures as outlined earlier in this chapter. In addition, emphasis is placed on the following phases of investigation:

1. Loss frequently occurs while the property is in the hands of someone other than the insured, such as salesmen, processors, contractors, or other agents or independent contractors.
   a) Detailed statements as to cause of loss should be obtained from the custodian and witnesses; possible third party liability should be thoroughly investigated.
   b) Other applicable insurance should be looked for and checked.

c) Documents, such as receipts, consignment memos or charges, or invoices which pertain to the relationship between the custodian and insured should be obtained. They often reveal the true interests and liabilities involved.

d) The custodian of the insured property usually has records that may be checked against those of the insured as to identity and quantity and sometimes value, labor performed, or charges incurred in connection therewith. These documents may include shipping receipts, itemized bills for labor performed, cutting tickets, and production and consignment records.

2. In damage cases, the inland marine adjuster must be familiar with the specific commodity involved or get the help of an expert. Expert knowledge is necessary to determine answers to questions such as: "Can damaged parts be replaced?" "Can soiled or damaged goods be cleaned or reprocessed?" "Should damaged cut goods be completed?" "Should soiled piece goods be redyed or reprocessed?" "What are the most economic means of salvage?"

3. An audit may be required of all goods outstanding at all insured places, at insured value, for coinsurance purposes.

It is customary for the adjuster when investigating a block loss, to reexamine the representations made in the proposals. A material misrepresentation or a breach of warranty by the insured may constitute a defense to a claim.

General procedures in handling block losses are similar to those previously discussed. Block policies usually combine coverages on the insured's own property, the property of others held by him as custodian, and the insured's legal liability with respect to other classes of property. These policies also incorporate location and transportation features. Therefore, the various procedures discussed in the previous sections should be adapted to the handling of losses under block policies.

EXPERIENCE

The purpose of this chapter has been to supply a sketch of the inland marine adjusting field. Appendix A provides additional detail as to how losses covered in two or more policies eventually come to rest in one or more of the insurers. The reader, however, should regard any such reviews, attempted within the span of so few pages, at best as merely introductory.

No adjuster can earn his stripes by confining his researches to reviews of this type. Such outline can, perhaps, arouse his curiousity and lead him into this challenging field of insurance. In the course of his career, an adjuster must become familiar with the material referred to in the bibliography at the end of this chapter. He must spend months or years in a company claims department as a trainee and a similar period in the field. He encounters new problems and questions each day and he applies his education to these problems until he solves them. The writer knows of no shorter route, but he has found the long and hard one very rewarding.

SUGGESTED READINGS

BUGAN, THOMAS G. *When Does Title Pass.* Dubuque: Wm. C. Brown Co., 1951.

DAYNARD, HAROLD S. *Handbook on Transportation Insurance Claims.* New York: Insurance Advocate, 1961.

———. *Paths and By-Paths in Inland Marine Insurance.* New York: Insurance Advocate, 1949.

GWERTZMAN, MAX J. *Law of Transportation and Its Relation to Transportation Insurance.* Larchmont, N.Y.: Macade Press, 1950.

KAHN, FRITZ R. *Principles of Motor Carrier Regulation.* Dubuque: Wm. C. Brown Co., 1958.

MACLEAN, STUART O. *Inland Marine Insurance; Loss Principles and Practice.* Cincinnati: National Underwriter Co., 1952.

MILLER, JOHN M. *Law of Freight Loss and Damage Claims.* Dubuque: Wm. C. Brown Co., 1961.

MORTIMER, WILLIAM M. *Adjusting Practices, Inland Marine and Transportation Insurance.* New York: Transportation Service Co., 1951.

RODDA, WILLIAM H. *Inland Marine and Transportation Insurance,* 2d ed. Englewood Cliffs, N.J.: Prentice-Hall, Inc., 1958. Chap. 21.

PART V

Liability Insurance and Related Lines

Chapter 31

NATURE OF THE LIABILITY HAZARD

BY SPENCER L. KIMBALL

So far this book has treated mainly of hazards that are, in a sense, natural hazards. A building burns; a ship sinks or is damaged by storm or collision; a gem disappears in transit; hail destroys a crop. The owners, or those with security interests in the property, may purchase property insurance to indemnify themselves against the damage thus suffered from the destruction or diminution in value of the property. Such insurance might be termed "loss" insurance.

Liability is a hazard of quite another sort, for it is purely an artificial creation of the law. Insurance designed to protect against the liability hazard has characteristics which vary, depending on the way in which the legal system structures the liability. It is possible to conceive of a legal system that makes no provision at all for liability of one person to another; persons living under such a system would not need liability insurance. No civilized legal system has a doctrine so extreme, though some primitive peoples have no provision for liability. Even in the civilized world the range of variation is substantial.

The contrast of late nineteenth century rules respecting the employer's liability to his employee for injury suffered in the course of employment with the present rules under workmen's compensation laws illustrates the range of variation. Under the former there was no liability unless the employer himself was negligent. He was not vicariously responsible for the negligence of his employees; in addition courts were quick to find an "assumption" of any given risk by the employee, or to find that he was contributorily negligent and therefore disqualified from recovery. By contrast, under modern workmen's compensation legislation, an employer is liable for all personal injuries by accident "arising out of and in the course of the employment." The employer is liable no matter how careful he may be, and even if the injured employee is careless. Moreover he is liable not for a lump sum determined by a jury, as in the common law negligence action, but for a scheduled amount fixed by statute and payable in installments. Obviously, insurance policies designed to protect the employer against liability would be dissimilar in the two cases. Under the common law rules employers might even feel that they needed no insurance protection, so unlikely would be a successful suit against them.

In this chapter some of the doctrines of the legal system under which we live are explained. This is preliminary to a study in the succeeding chapters of the different kinds of liability insurance developed to meet the needs artificially created by the doctrines of the legal system.

INTRODUCTION TO TORT LAW

Basically the hazard to be insured against is the possibility that one may be held liable in a court of law, or by an administrative body such as an industrial commision administering a workmen's compensation law, to pay damages to another person for injury to the latter's person, property or other interests. In the main, this liability is the creation of the law of torts.[1] Attention here is restricted to tort law, as it exists in the United States at the present time.[2] In the Anglo-American legal system, the courts have developed most of tort law, though legislatures have occasionally made important contributions, as in the case of workmen's compensation. In our federal system, the law of torts is mainly determined by the states rather than by the federal government, and varies from one state to another. There are over 50 different systems of tort law in the United States, and this diversity will continue as long as the federal system lasts. Anyone who must handle practical problems in tort law or liability insurance must not forget the variation that exists. In dealing with a claim, the insurer must operate within the framework of a single state's law.

It is fortunate for present purposes that the differences are less important than the similarities, so that an introductory statement may legitimately describe these 50-odd systems as if they were one. In this chapter the discussion is at a level of generality that permits treatment of the systems as if they were uniform.

Classification of Torts

The person on whom a loss initially falls could protect himself by purchasing loss insurance, whether accident insurance for injury to his person, collision insurance for injury to his car, or fire insurance for the

[1] In some instances, potential liability may be assumed by contract and insurance then written to cover the assumed liability. See Chapters 32 and 34.

[2] The most convenient sources for study of the law of torts are William L. Prosser, *Handbook of the Law of Torts* (2d ed.; St. Paul: West Publishing Co., 1955); Fowler V. Harper and Fleming James, *The Law of Torts* (Boston: Little, Brown & Co., 1956); Clarence Morris, *Morris on Torts* (Brooklyn: Foundation Press, Inc., 1953); and Charles O. Gregory and Harry Kalven, Jr., *Cases and Materials on Torts* (Boston: Little, Brown & Co., 1959). This list by no means exhausts the important sources, others of which can be ascertained from the bibliographical references contained in the works listed here.

burning of his home. If he wants complete assurance of full compensation for his loss, he must purchase such insurance, for the starting principle of tort law is that a loss will be left to be borne by the person on whom it happens to fall unless there is some good reason for transferring it to another. The rules that determine when such a loss will be transferred are the rules of tort law.

Basically, there are three reasons for a transfer. The actor must pay the injured person for the damages caused by his action (1) if he intended to cause harm, or (2) if he acted in a way that negligently caused harm, or (3) if his activity is one of a small number of activities that are regarded by the law as so dangerous that anyone engaging in them must pay all damages caused, however careful he may have been not to cause harm. These three categories are sometimes referred to as (1) the intentional torts, (2) negligence, and (3) absolute or strict liability for extra-hazardous activity.

Illustrations of the intentional torts are assault, battery, trespass to land, and libel. Though there are cases in which these torts are, for certain purposes, included within the scope of coverage of an insurance policy,[3] no insurance written has as its main purpose the protection of the insured against liability resulting from his own intentional torts. Indeed, such coverage might be regarded as contrary to public policy. But there is no objection to insurance against the intentional torts of one's employees, and such coverage is obtainable. However, it is relatively of too little importance for extended treatment in this chapter.

NEGLIGENCE

The reason for transferring loss that is most important for liability insurance is that the defendant has been negligent. Negligence is conduct that is blameworthy; it produces liability because it creates a greater risk of causing damage than the actor may legitimately impose on another. It would be quite possible, of course, to have a legal requirement that any

[3] In *Wheeler* v. *O'Connell*, 297 Mass. 549, 9 N.E. 2d 544 (1937), plaintiff was a motor vehicle inspector who demanded that a truck driver show his license and the truck's certificate of registration. Instead of complying the driver started the truck forward and the plaintiff was injured. The court held that the injured inspector could recover against the insurance company on the automobile liability policy on the truck, especially in view of the purposes of the Massachusetts compulsory automobile law. The same result was reached in *Hartford Accident Indemnity Co.* v. *Wotbarst*, 95 N.H. 40, 57 A. 2d 151 (1948), giving similar effect to the New Hampshire Financial Responsibility Law. The case of *Robinson* v. *United States Fidelity and Guaranty Co.*, 159 Miss. 14, 131 So. 541 (1931) went even further. There the policyholder was held entitled to recover from the insurer for his liability and court costs in an action for assault and battery committed by his employee in his place of business. But see *Weis* v. *State Farm Mutual Auto Insurance Co.*, 242 Minn. 141, 64 N.W. 2d 366 (1954), holding an automobile policy did not cover an intentional tort, at least when the policyholder is seeking to recover.

person causing harm to another should pay for any damage caused by his conduct, irrespective of fault. Indeed, this is what the law has chosen to do for extra-hazardous activity, the third category. However, so to rule would undoubtedly have the consequence of making persons more reluctant to undertake activity that caused risk of harm to others. In the period of the industrial revolution it might have had disastrous results in discouraging enterprise, since business activity by its nature subjects people to risks, and automatic liability would have made entrepreneurs reluctant to create new business enterprises. Thus the law long ago decided to give its stamp of approval to most ordinary activity by declining to shift any loss resulting from it so long as the actor was exercising reasonable care. In the modern context, this means, for example, that a person driving a car is not liable for injuring or killing another, provided he was driving carefully, that is, with that standard of care that is ordinary and normal in society and that is required by the law. The loss remains where it falls initially unless there is some good reason to shift it and in this case the good reason would be negligent or careless driving. Similarly a doctor treating a patient is not liable if the patient dies as a result of the treatment, unless there was a failure to exercise appropriate care. Liability arises only if the conduct is not reasonable.

It is not possible within a few pages to do justice to the subject of negligence, on which volumes have been written. All that is attempted here is to sketch the main outlines of the doctrine, as a basis for understanding the nature of the liability insurance policy.

Nature of Negligence

Negligence is carelessness; it is the absence of that amount of care or standard of care that the law requires the actor to exercise. It is not a state of the actor's mind; it is conduct that does not meet the standards set by the law. The tests of the existence of negligence are objective, not subjective. Quite obviously the amount of care required by the law is not always the same. It varies depending on the relationship of the parties, on the foreseeability of the harm, on the seriousness of the risks, on the qualifications of the actor, and on other factors. But unless he suffers from a special incapacity such as is inherent in being a child, the actor must conform to a standard of care that would be exercised by a reasonable man under similar circumstances. Though the child will only be held to a standard consistent with his capacity, a grown man must, in general, meet the standard of the reasonable man whether he is capable of it or not. The law does not take account of the deficiences of the actor, though it will raise the standard if he holds himself out as having special qualifications, as in the case of a medical specialist. The standard of the reasonable man, or the reasonably prudent man, is the basic operating principle of negligence law, and pervades the whole. "This excellent but odious character stands like a monument in our Courts of Justice, vainly appealing to his fellow-citizens to order their lives after his own example."[4]

Standard of Care

There is a variety of ways of ascertaining the standard. First, in some cases there are statutes or ordinances prescribing certain clearly defined conduct. Failure to conform to the statutory requirement will be negligence, provided the statute was enacted to protect a class of people, of whom the plaintiff is one, against the very kind of harm inflicted. Thus when there is a train wreck caused by the absence of safety equipment required by statute, there is a clear case of negligence. But a person injured by a train which was operated without carelessness, but in violation of a Sunday blue law, would not be able to recover for negligence, since the statute was enacted for purposes other than to protect the plaintiff against accident.

Second, sometimes the courts will prescribe detailed and precise requirements, the violation of which will constitute negligence. In an earlier day, some courts held that when an automobile driver came to a railroad crossing, he had to stop, look, and listen, and if the view was obstructed, he even had to get out of his car and go look up and down the track. Failure to do so was negligence. Of course, the stop, look, and listen rule in this extreme and specific form would be anachronistic in the days of high-speed transportation, but there exist other illustrations of specific standards of conduct imposed by courts, violation of which is negligence.

On the whole, however, neither the court nor the legislature lays down explicit rules of conduct as a standard of required care. Instead the court simply instructs the jury in general terms about the principle of law and leaves it to the jury to decide what the reasonable man would do. The standard is a flexible standard applied by the jury. The infinite variety of circumstances under which people perform acts that may cause harm to others renders it absolutely impossible to define in advance precise rules of conduct adapted to the many diverse circumstances.[5] The law must be stated in general terms, leaving to some tribunal a considerable discretion in applying the standard to the specific facts of the case. Sometimes, the nature of the accident clearly suggests negligence. In such cases the court may say *res ipsa loquitur* (the thing speaks for itself), and place the

---

[4] A. P. Herbert, *Misleading Cases in the Common Law* (2d ed.; London: Methuen & Co., 1927), p. 12. Herbert remarks, further, that "in all the mass of authorities which bears upon this branch of the law *there is no single mention of a reasonable woman.* It was ably insisted before us . . . that no such reference is found, for the simple reason that no such being is contemplated by the law; that legally at least there *is* no reasonable woman." (p. 13). Quoted with permission of Sir Alan Herbert, Doubleday and Co., Inc., and Macmillan and Co., Inc. Extract comes from "*Fardell* v. *Potts:* The Reasonable Man."

[5] An elaboration of the considerations that bear upon the standard will be found in Prosser, *op. cit. supra,* pp. 124–46, or in any of the other standard works on torts.

burden on the defendant to show that the accident happened without negligence. The mere proof of the accident will get the plaintiff to the jury and support a jury finding for the plaintiff. Examples are sponges left in a surgical wound, or a barrel rolling out of a second story window. There are also occasions when reasonable men could not disagree, on the evidence presented, and then the court will take from the jury its power to find or deny negligence.

Elements of the Cause of Action

The separate elements or requirements that are said to be necessary to establish a cause of action in negligence are (1) a legal duty to conform to the standard of the reasonable man, (2) breach of that duty by failure to live up to the standard, (3) actual harm or damage to the plaintiff's interests, and (4) a causal connection between the breach of duty and the harm that is close enough to satisfy certain standards.

The "No-Duty" Rules

Thus far the nature of the reasonable man standard has been discussed. Everyone has been presumed to have a duty to use reasonable care all the time, but this is not completely accurate. Courts frequently deny recovery in actions for negligence on the ground that the defendant owed no duty of care to the plaintiff.

There are really two kinds of situations in which the court will say there is no duty. In one kind the statement is really only another way of saying that the defendant was acting in a reasonable way. Thus a court might decide that a doctor sued by an uninoculated patient who got rabies had no duty to inoculate against rabies because he had no knowledge that his patient was bitten by a rabies-susceptible animal. When the court says "no duty" in this situation, it means that the doctor was acting reasonably under the circumstances.

However, there are many cases in which conduct is not reasonable but in which there is no duty to act in a reasonable way. Thus, suppose a strong swimmer stands on a pier and watches a child drown a few feet away, making no effort to save him. The conduct is far below any reasonable man standard, but in this case the swimmer has in truth no duty to act.

There are many cases in which there is no duty in the latter sense. Thus, while a landowner has a duty to see that the condition of his premises is such that persons going by along a public way are not endangered, he has no duty of care to trespassers coming on his property. Even if the property is unsafe and likely to cause harm to a trespasser, he is not liable if he fails to use care to put it in safe condition.[6] As a matter of

[6] The "no-duty" rule does not prevent liability for affirmatively dangerous conduct, such as setting spring guns to catch trespassers.

fact, this particular "no-duty" rule can be carried even further, for the landowner has no duty of care even toward licensees and social guests coming onto the property with permission. It is only toward the so-called "invitee"—a person coming onto the property for a business purpose advantageous to the landowner—that there is a duty to use care to put the premises in reasonably safe condition. In other words, the reasonable man rule applies only with respect to the invitee. In the other cases there is no duty at all, except to refrain from affirmative acts intended to do harm, or from active negligence with respect to persons whose presence is known.

Sometimes the consequences of the no-duty rule with respect to trespassers appear inhumane, and this has led many courts to modify the rule. The "attractive nuisance" doctrine is one modification. Under it trespassing children are treated as if they were business invitees, to whom the landowner owes a duty to make the premises reasonably safe. The doctrine is applied when there is something on the land that attracts children to trespass in order to play. Examples are railroad turntables and pools of water. The attractive nuisance doctrine has not been adopted everywhere.

There are other "no-duty" rules. The seller of land and the lessor of land are held to have no liability for disrepair of the premises, after the new buyer or the lessee has had time to repair. Thereafter a person injured even on the public way cannot recover from the seller or the lessor.

Much more important to the insurance man, however, is the no-duty rule that in former times sheltered from liability the suppliers of chattels, who had no duty except to their immediate vendees. Thus the manufacturer and all wholesalers of commodities had no duty to the ultimate purchaser to make sure that the commodity was what it purported to be and that it was safe for human use. This inhumane doctrine has been softened in the past few decades, and manufacturers and suppliers of chattels have been made liable for injury resulting from the condition of the chattels. It has even become possible to argue that the trend is going too far in extending the liability of remote parties in the chain of supply. But whatever the merits of the rule, the gradual change in the law by extending the range of the duty of care has made products liability an important part of liability insurance.

Causation

It would not be appropriate here to deal at any length with problems of causation in the law of negligence. The requirement that there must be a reasonably close causal connection between the conduct that breaches a duty of the actor toward the injured party and the ensuing harm is a very difficult requirement to interpret and apply. There must of course be at least a causal connection *in fact*. This means that there is no liability, in general, if the harm would have happened anyway. But in addition, there must be what the courts call "proximate" cause. By this is meant that there must be an unbroken chain of events. If there are intervening acts or events, such as the subsequent negligence of a third person or an act of God, that make the causal connection between the negligent act and the harm seem too remote, then there will be no liability. Under what circumstances the connection will be regarded as too remote, or conversely, when it will be regarded as proximate, are questions of great subtlety.

Contributory Negligence

Even if a plaintiff who has an interest protected by law is able to show that the defendant has breached a duty, and that the breach of duty led proximately to harm or damage to the protected interest, he will still lose if the defendant can show that the plaintiff was also negligent with respect to his own interests, even to a small extent. This is the doctrine of contributory negligence. Some statutes replace it by a "comparative negligence" doctrine, under which the plaintiff's negligence, if relatively minor, merely reduces recovery and does not bar it altogether. But there are even more complications than this. If the plaintiff, by his contributory negligence, has gotten himself into a position of danger from which he cannot extricate himself, and thereafter the defendant is negligent, then in some jurisdictions a "last clear chance" doctrine will neutralize the contributory negligence defense.

The above brief sketch will suffice to describe the general outlines of the law of negligence. It is the field of liability most relevant to liability insurance, for most policies are designed to protect the policyholder against the consequences of a lawsuit for negligence. The automobile liability policy; the owners', landlords', and tenants' liability policy; and the general liability policy all have as their main thrust the protection of the policyholder's pecuniary interests against such attack.

SPECIAL NEGLIGENCE PROBLEMS

Malpractice

Contrary to the notion that prevails rather widely among laymen, there is no special doctrine of "malpractice." Doctors and other professionals are liable for negligence in accordance with the general principles already explained. But malpractice is currently receiving so much attention that a few special observations about it may be helpful.[7] The discussion will be directed specifically toward medical practice, though the principles are the same for all professionals.

The duty of the physician is only to use reasonable care in diagnosing and treating his patients. He has no duty to effect a cure or even to

---

[7] Malpractice liability for doctors is ably discussed in Burte Shartel and Marcus L. Plant, *The Law of Medical Practice* (Springfield, Ill.: Charles C. Thomas, 1959).

improve the patient's condition unless he has assumed such a duty by promising results. The duty of reasonable care exists whenever there is a relationship of doctor and patient; the fact that the patient is a charity patient does not diminish the doctor's duty at all. Even if he volunteers his services in an emergency case, he still has at common law the duty of reasonable care. Unreasonable claims against doctors who have volunteered their services in emergencies have led very recently to a rash of "Good Samaritan" statutes, relieving them of liability or at least lessening the standard of care required.

The degree of care required is that which other practitioners of the same kind usually exercise in the same or similar localities under similar circumstances. It will be noted from this statement that the level of care required: (1) varies with the size of the community; (2) varies with the level of the training of the doctor, so that a specialist is held to a higher standard than a general practitioner; and (3) varies with time, so that the doctor is under some obligation to keep reasonably abreast of new developments in his field. Moreover, the standard of care is that applicable to the school to which the doctor belongs, so that a homeopathic physician is judged by different standards than apply to the allopathic school.

Doctors may render themselves liable in a great variety of ways. A wrong diagnosis will not necessarily lead to liability, but a superficial diagnosis will. If the doctor does not follow generally accepted procedures in either diagnosis or treatment, he may be held guilty of negligence. If he fails to give proper instructions to the patient, or to a nurse, or to hospital attendants, he may be liable. If he fails to consult the patient's prior physician to get the full background of the case, he may be liable. If a general practitioner fails to refer the patient to a specialist, or one specialist to a different one, when such handling is indicated by the diagnosis, he may be liable. If he abandons the case without giving the patient time to get another doctor, or if he exposes the patient to contagious disease by carelessness, he may be liable. These only illustrate and do not exhaust the ways in which a doctor may fail to exercise reasonable care.

Ordinarily, the doctor cannot be adjudged negligent unless there is, in the record, testimony of medical experts on which such a finding can be based. Unsupported lay testimony is not enough. The only exception is in those cases where the nature of the event is such that an absence of negligence seems highly improbable—a so-called *res ipsa loquitur* (the thing speaks for itself) case. Medical testimony by one doctor against another is not easy to obtain, and this has led courts sometimes to extend the *res ipsa loquitur* doctrine beyond its normal limits. The most common application of the *res ipsa loquitur* doctrine is in the cases of a foreign object left in a surgical wound, of extraction of the wrong tooth, of X-ray burns, and the like.

The malpractice liability of lawyers, accountants, dentists, and even insurance agents, is based upon identical principles, though none of these other fields has been developed by as much litigation as malpractice of medical practitioners. But malpractice liability is receiving greater attention in these fields, too, and the need for malpractice, or errors and omissions, insurance has increased apace.

Product Liability

We have already seen that a broad "no-duty" rule formerly sheltered suppliers of chattels from liability to anyone except their immediate vendees. But the rule has been eroded over the last century by a series of exceptions that have at length made the rule itself obsolete. The exceptions to the no-duty rule were three: (1) cases in which the seller knew that the chattel was dangerous and failed to disclose the fact, (2) cases in which the chattel was furnished for use on the seller's premises, and (3) the most important exception, sale of an article imminently or inherently dangerous to human safety. The category of things "imminently" or "inherently" dangerous was long a vague and poorly defined category, but in this century it has expanded so that this third exception has virtually swallowed up the rule. The decisive case came in 1916, when the ultimate purchaser of an automobile was injured by the collapse of a defective wheel. The manufacturer was held liable. Superficially the case was merely a slight extension of the class of "inherently dangerous" articles, but in reality it pointed the way to a major extension of liability.

The foregoing development was an extension of negligence doctrine, by limiting or eliminating a "no-duty" rule. But another development also took place, in which a strict liability on a theory of "warranty" has been extended to the ultimate purchaser or user of a commodity. The seller's warranty is a term of the contract of sale, express or implied, making the seller an "insurer," to at least some extent, of the quality and safe condition of the goods. Though it has its origin in tort and is a hybrid, the warranty has more affinity now to a contractual obligation. Thus, if negligence cannot be proved, in at least some jurisdictions it is possible to impose a "products liability" on most persons in the supply chain without any showing of negligence at all. In any case, few manufacturers or sellers of articles that can possibly cause harm if defective can now afford to be without products liability insurance, to protect against the possibility of liability for bodily harm or property damage to the ultimate purchaser or user.

STRICT LIABILITY

Brief consideration is now given to strict or absolute liability, against which insurance is also possible and prevalent. The strict liability cases are a miscellany, and seem to be increasing in number, both as a result of case law development and of statutes. Strict liability is imposed whenever the hazards created by the conduct are such that it seems unsound social policy to permit the actor to impose any risk of such harm on the person injured.

The first illustration is workmen's compensation. After the human costs of the industrial revolution had become appreciated, and after industry had become well enough established that it could bear heavy adventitious costs more easily, workmen's compensation laws were enacted imposing on the employer the costs of the physical harm caused to the persons of his employees by the industrial process. This liability was imposed irrespective of fault. Except in the case of the employer large enough to self-insure, insurance of the risk was made virtually compulsory as well.

The use of explosives is another activity that results in strict liability for the user in some jurisdictions. Quite reasonably, the user is compelled to treat all damage caused by his activity as a cost of the enterprise in which he is engaged. Damage caused by trespassing cattle is an early common law illustration of strict liability. A more modern common law illustration is the collection on one's land of large quantities of substances likely to escape and to do damage if they escape, such as a reservoir of water. In all of these and in other cases some jurisdictions have created liability without fault. Although some of these risks are unusual and difficult to insure, there is nothing improper about them as a subject for insurance activity. Some are no doubt included in policies that are mainly directed at negligence. The underwriter, however, is likely to be concerned if there are possibilities for strict liability within the scope of the policy, for the problems and dangers of the two are quite different.

JURIDICAL RISK

So far the law of torts has been outlined as it appears in the opinions of the courts and in the enactments of legislatures, describing the theoretical framework of the law underlying the liability insurance policy. However, there is another dimension of risk that is of great importance in liability insurance. Intervening between the theoretical formulation of the legal doctrine and the decisions of actual cases is the process of judicial administration. Law must be applied, and it is applied by a system of courts and administrative agencies in which the human element is all too apparent. Some inadequacies are inevitable in any system of judicial administration. Among them are risks against which one must insure, if he seeks full protection against loss.

Cost of Defense

The first of these risks is the risk of incurring costs because one is defendant in a lawsuit. Lawsuits may be started whether there is negligence or not. One law professor used to make this point to an early class in torts by asking the question, "Can the injured person sue in this case?" As he expected, the answer frequently came back "no." He would then reply, "You are dead wrong. *Any* fool can *sue*. The real question is whether he can *win*." It is of the greatest importance to the development of liability insurance that any fool can always sue, for this means that no person, however careful he may be, can have real assurance that he will not be the defendant in a lawsuit alleging that he negligently injured the plaintiff's person or property. If the court eventually finds the policyholder negligent, the cost of defense increases the burden of the judgment, and the policyholder needs protection against both. But more important, even if the court eventually holds that he was not negligent, the costs of investigation, trial, and sometimes appeal may make the ultimate vindication a Pyrrhic victory. Lawyers are professionals whose services do not come cheaply, and quite aside from the legal fees, the costs of a trial in a personal injury case may be very substantial indeed. The stakes are high in these days of high verdicts, and in order to protect himself against liability by default, the defendant may have to employ not only one or more attorneys, but also photographers, doctors, private investigators, engineers, and other experts. Against these costs a man may insure, and it is important to insure. In our system this is a part of liability insurance, though theoretically the costs of defense could be separately insured.

Claims Consciousness

The risk of unjustified claims is probably becoming constantly higher, as the prevalence of liability insurance makes the public ever more claims conscious. The development of liability insurance teaches the public generally that there is a ready source of funds against which judgments can be collected and hence makes the public more conscious of the possibility of success in personal injury lawsuits and thus more ready to bring them. Liability insurance is plagued by a problem that is an inevitable result of its own successful development. An insurance buying public is a claims-conscious public.

Fact Distortion

Discussion of the cost of defending an unjustified lawsuit leads to another related risk—the risk that is inherent in the difficulties of the fact-finding process itself. There is no assurance that even extreme care will prevent the filing of unjustified lawsuits. Moreover, there is no assurance that a court will always decide that the claim is unjustified whenever the facts, if they were known, would dictate such a result. Often not the facts but rather distortions are presented to the jury (or to the court). Many factors distort the jury's perception. First, there are subjective factors in the jurymen themselves—a dislike for the defendant because on the witness stand he appears to be obnoxious, or has an objectionable lawyer; a liking for the plaintiff, or his lawyer; a feeling that somebody should pay whenever anyone is hurt, and the election of the defendant to be the payor simply because he is well able to pay, or because he is probably insured, or because he came out of the accident without injury and should be made to share the loss. These subjective factors are not under effective control by the judge or by the law for, though there can be reversal of a verdict for the plaintiff if the jury admits that it was influenced by extraneous considerations, there can be none if the jury's reasons remain unexpressed, provided its verdict is one that reasonable men *could* reach.

Some objective factors, too, distort the perceptions the jury forms of the event. Most important, a visual image must be coverted into words by witnesses. In their nature words are imprecise instruments. Moreover, many witnesses are inexpert in the use of language. Further, each witness saw only a portion of the event and saw it from a vantage point that provided some distortion. Moreover, delay in the process of litigation ensures that the testimony comes at a time when memory has begun to fade. Again, in the process of preparation for trial, the testimony may be distorted by the questioning of counsel, which has an influence on the way in which witnesses formulate their stories, even when there is no improper "coaching" of the witness. And of course testimony may be perjured. Finally, the testimony is subject to the distorting influences of the trial itself. It is presented in an artificial form and the witness may be subject to a severe cross-examination, designed to destroy the effectiveness of his testimony, and often successful in doing so even when the testimony is accurate.

When all these possibilities for distortion are considered, one wonders how so much truth manages to come through in the trial of a lawsuit. But even if one can rely on the system to produce a brand of justice that is right more often than it is wrong, it is clear that such justice is only a rough approximation, and that the system makes a good many errors. The risk of such error must be insured against even by the man who knows he is always careful.

Uncertainty in Legal Rules

Yet other risks are inherent in the nature of the judicial process, existing even when cases are tried by judges, but even more clearly when they are tried by juries. One risk is the uncertainty of the legal rules themselves. Even when a rule of law is seemingly formulated in a clear and precise way, it is often difficult to decide whether to apply it to a set of facts. Often more than one possible rule may be applicable, and the need to determine which rule to apply gives discretion to the tribunal.

Often the selection of the rule turns on the meaning given to a key word. For example, a defendant landowner has no duty of care to a trespasser on the land, but he has a duty to someone lawfully using the adjoining public way. A great deal depends on the point at which a person ceases to be a user of the public way and becomes a trespasser. This makes for doubt in the application of a set of legal rules; they have a deceptive appearance of certainty that does not hold up. This difficulty is seldom appreciated by the layman; even the lawyer is not always fully aware of the range of choice that is thus left to the tribunal.

Legislation by Juries

This is not the only way in which legal uncertainty may appear. A judge or jury may be free to decide a case without articulating reasons for the decision. In doing so, the law may be altered without perception of any change by outsiders. New doctrines are "bootlegged" into the law. For example, the doctrine of contributory negligence is in theory a part of the law of negligence where not changed by statute. Juries are instructed by the judges that if the plaintiff is negligent, even slightly, they must find for the defendants. This is a standard instruction. But if the jury sees that the plaintiff was only a little bit negligent, and thinks that while it would be fair to reduce the amount of his compensation, it would not be fair to deny him recovery altogether, it may find for the plaintiff, but in a lesser amount than it would have done had the plaintiff not been negligent. So long as the jury does not explain what it is doing, it has uncontrolled power so to act. In this way, the jury is applying in the common law action for negligence a *de facto* doctrine of comparative negligence. The doctrine reduces the amount of recovery because of the plaintiff's contributory negligence, without barring him completely.

All of these risks are inherent in the nature of the legal process, quite apart from the risk of liability created directly by the law. They are risks against which insurance is necessary. Fortunately, they do not require a separate type of insurance, for they are naturally assimilated within the liability insurance policy. But it is impossible to understand fully the nature and operation of liability insurance without understanding these peripheral risks.

SUGGESTED READINGS

Gregory, Charles O., and Kalven, Harry, Jr. *Cases and Materials on Torts.* Boston: Little, Brown & Co., 1959.

Harper, Fowler V., and James, Fleming. *The Law of Torts.* Boston: Little, Brown & Co., 1956.

Morris, Clarence. *Torts.* Brooklyn: Foundation Press, Inc., 1953.

Prosser, William L. *Handbook of the Law of Torts.* 2d ed. St. Paul: West Publishing Co., 1955.

Chapter 32

GENERAL LIABILITY INSURANCE

BY ROY C. McCULLOUGH

The term "general liability insurance" embraces liability insurance other than automobile, aviation, workmen's compensation, employer's liability, and the liability portion of boiler and machinery and marine coverages. By reference to the table of contents readers can see in which other chapters of this *Handbook* these subjects are covered.

A typical general liability policy provides for one or more of the following coverages, as selected by the insured:

1. Bodily injury liability.
2. Property damage liability.
3. Medical payments. (Sold only in connection with accidental bodily injury liability insurance.)

In this chapter the "Schedule" liability policy approach is treated. The "Comprehensive" policy approach is the subject of Chapter 34. Comprehensive liability coverages are also incorporated into various package policies described in Part VI. Professional liability coverages—a subject in themselves—are discussed in Chapter 33.

CONCEPT OF A SCHEDULE POLICY

In direct damage insurance the expression "peril" is used fairly consistently to refer to loss-causing phenomena such as fire, windstorm, hail, and so on. In liability insurance terminology there is no one expression uniformly used to refer to types of liability claims. In this chapter the expression "hazard group" is used for the purpose of identifying activities and areas of exposure.

The major general liability hazard groups include:

1. Premises and operations.
2. Elevator.
3. Construction and alteration.
4. Protective. (Independent contractors.)
5. Products–completed operations.

6. Contractual liability. (Separately available as to bodily injury liability and property damage liability.)

Originally the industry developed separate policies for each of the major hazard groups such as premises–operations, elevator, and products. An insured who wished coverage under several hazard groups needed just as many policies.

Separate policies still exist in some companies, but their use is infrequent. Instead, most now provide schedule type policies. Each such schedule policy provides insurance for such coverages and such hazard groups as the policyholder selects. Thus, he may purchase bodily injury (B.I.) and property damage (P.D.) liability for premises and operations only and decline to purchase elevator, products, or other hazard group coverage either because he has no exposure in such fields, because he desires to "self-insure" such exposures, or (more rarely) because he is purchasing such coverages from another insurer.

Each of the hazard group portions of a schedule policy provides the same coverage as would exist in a separate policy. Each of the listed hazard groups is designed to be mutually exclusive of the others, just as the separate policies were.

Most companies maintain two different schedule liability policies:

1. A policy for owners', landlords', and tenants' risks.
2. A policy for manufacturers' and contractors' risks.

"Owners, landlords, and tenants" is insurance argot for a wide group of risks whose primary (not sole) exposure is that arising out of occupancy of premises, including other exposures not strictly "premises" matters, but which have customarily been rated in the "O. L. & T." section of the "General Liability" rate manual. Such risks are rated on some basis other than payroll, such as area, frontage, admissions, sales, or receipts. Typical O. L. & T. risks include apartments, hotels, office buildings, theaters, retail stores, wholesalers, and storage warehouses.

The Manufacturers' and Contractors' (popularly known as "M. & C.") group of classifications is intended for risks such as those suggested by the phrase, whose activities might embrace not only premises exposure but also considerable exposure not directly related to any particular premises. These risks are rated in the M. & C. portion of the liability manual and are usually rated on the basis of payroll.

In order to save supplies, companies will often combine the two by using a single jacket which provides all provisions common to both policies. They will attach to the jacket appropriate supplements as may be necessary according to whether the risk falls in the O. L. & T. or the M. & C. classification, and according to what hazard groups are insured, for instance, premises and operations, elevator, product, and/or independent contractors.

Schedule policies provide only for such hazard groups and coverages as are specifically indicated, generally by showing a premium charge on the "schedule" or declarations page. Thus, there is insurance for stated hazard groups only, as contrasted with the concept—used in comprehensive policies—of embracing all liability hazards not specifically excluded.

INSURING AGREEMENTS

The insuring agreements in schedule liability policies are generally applicable to both O. L. & T. and M. & C. contracts. Some variations are pointed out in a subsequent section.

Bodily Injury Liability

The company promises:

> To pay on behalf of the insured all sums which the insured shall become legally obligated to pay as damages because of bodily injury, sickness or disease, including death at any time resulting therefrom, sustained by any person caused by accident and arising out of the hazards hereinafter defined.

The term "bodily injury" is not synonymous with "personal injury." It does not include such types of tort damage as defamation, libel and slander, false arrest or imprisonment, malicious prosecution, invasion of privacy, or withholding of civil rights.

Although the above clause limits payments to sums that the insured owes as a legal obligation, B.I. contracts include as a supplementary insuring agreement a promise by the company to pay first aid expenses incurred by the insured for imperative medical attention to others at the time of the accident.

Property Damage Liability

In almost the same language as in the B.I. insuring agreement the company promises to pay the insured's liability for damages because of damage to or destruction of property, including the loss of use thereof, caused by accident.

Medical Payments

The bodily injury coverage provides for only those damages for which the insured is legally liable. This liability may include the reasonable medical expenses of the claimant. Many insureds find it desirable, however, to provide for the payment of medical expenses of those injured upon their premises or in their business operations, regardless of the question of fault or legal liability. They may, if they desire, purchase medical payments coverage providing for reasonable and necessary medical expenses incurred within one year from the date of accident. The per person limit chosen is often $250 or $500 but can be much higher.

Medical payments coverage is like accident insurance, payable regardless of fault, and payable in addition to any sums the claimant may be entitled to recover by way of damages against the insured. Many claimants are content to accept the payment of medical expenses without pursuing any claim for damages.

Medical payments coverages under a general liability policy customarily exclude the named insured, his business associates, employees, or tenants. Otherwise, the coverage would provide a 24-hour accident coverage for those customarily on the premises.

Contractual Liability

The B.I. (bodily injury) and P.D. (property damage) insuring agreements quoted above cover the insured for sums he is "legally obligated to pay as damages." This wording would include liability assumed by contract in absence of any exclusion in another part of the contract.

Schedule liability policies customarily exclude all liability assumed by the insured "under any contract or agreement," except, in cases where products liability insurance is purchased, warranties of goods for products.

The reason for the contract liability exclusion is that underwriting of the policy is based on the concept that the risks assumed by the insurer will be those normally expected in a risk of the general class insured. If, however, the insured has expanded his own liability by voluntary agreement, then the attitude of the underwriter as to acceptance or rating may be somewhat different. Thus, if the owner of a store has assumed liability for injuries caused by independent concessionaires, he has expanded his own liability beyond that ordinarily contemplated.

Liability of others assumed by "hold harmless" or other contracts has become so customary in certain situations that coverage is ordinarily granted as part of the "premises" exposure by means of a separate insuring agreement covering "incidental written agreements." This insuring agreement operates to except from the contract liability exclusions the following written agreements relating to premises:

1. Easement agreements except railroad grade crossing agreements.
2. Agreements required by municipal ordinance, except in connection with work for the municipality. (Example: hold harmless agreement required by municipality as condition to permitting store to build vault under sidewalk.)
3. Elevator or escalator maintenance agreements.
4. Leases of insured premises.

It should be noted that the contract liability exclusions of a policy do not exclude liability that would exist against the insured in absence of the contract.

As to contract liability not falling within the listed exceptions to the exclusion, the insured may protect himself by purchasing the fourth coverage available under the schedule liability policy—that of contractual liability. This coverage provides for separate statement of B.I. and P.D. limits. It is thus possible to purchase contractual liability insurance for B.I. or P.D. alone, even though the other coverages embrace both.

This coverage, as printed in the policy, provides the insured with protection against the liability assumed by him under certain specific types of written agreements. Other contracts may be covered by specific endorsement.

Many insureds overlook liabilities they have assumed in contracts, particularly those in connection with leases, permits, or contracts to supply services, do construction, or make installations. While insurance companies, agents, and brokers should point out the possibility of contract exposures, they cannot be expected to be so familiar with the customer's affairs as to detect these exposures unless they are brought to their attention by the insured or the attorney who may have examined the contract on behalf of the insured.

Defense, Settlement, Supplementary Payments

In addition to agreeing to pay for the damages for which the insured is held liable, the company agrees, as to B.I. and P.D. coverages, that it will defend any lawsuits against the insured alleging injury covered by the policy and seeking damages, even if the suit is groundless, false, or fraudulent. The company agrees to pay the various expenses incidental to legal proceedings such as the cost of appeal bonds, bonds to release attachments, expenses of litigation and investigation, costs, interest accruing after entry of judgment (until the company has paid its portion of the liability), and reasonable expenses incurred by the insured at the company's request. These expenses are payable in addition to the policy limits.

Although the company is obligated to defend suits against the insured, the agreement specifically reserves to the company the right to make such investigation, negotiation, and settlement of any claim or suit as it deems expedient.

Definition of Insured

On the point of who is protected by the policy, the term "insured" is exceedingly broad. It includes the persons *named* as insured in the declarations and also includes any executive officer, director, or stockholder of the named insured while acting as such and any firm or organization acting as real estate manager for the named insured. Insurance in the name of a partnership protects the partners for their liability as such.

In absence of a specific endorsement to the contrary or in absence of their being included as named insureds, the policy does not protect anyone other than those described above. Thus, insurance in the sole name of a tenant does not protect the landlord. Insurance in the name of an employer does not automatically protect his employee. In most cases extensions in the contract may be made (sometimes without additional premiums and sometimes with an additional premium less than the cost of separate insurance) to provide such additional protection. Covering several interests under one policy, however, requires that the interests so grouped share the protection afforded by the applicable "per person," "per accident," or "aggregate" limit. It is not multiplied or accumulated by reason of several insureds being protected as to a single accident or occurrence.

ACCIDENT VERSUS OCCURRENCE

Each of the insuring agreements discussed thus far covers only injuries "caused by accident." Certain types of injuries for which an insured may be liable are not "caused by accident."

The term "accident" contemplates an undesigned, sudden, and unexpected event. It generally contemplates a single happening traceable to a definite time, place, and cause. The concept also generally negates a deliberately intended act, even though the act may have an unexpected result.

Construction of the terms "accident" and "caused by accident" has proven troublesome. Judicial precedents are by no means in accord. For example, liability was denied for disease of a tenant alleged to have arisen out of the landlord's failure to provide heat. There are cases on both sides of the question as to whether or not the gradual contracting of a disease or illness (such as radium poisoning or dust diseases) over a lengthy period constitutes an accident. Another difficult group of cases is that involving the natural and inevitable result (even though not intended) of acts deliberately and intentionally undertaken. For example, dribbling paint down the side of a house by an insured working on the house was held not to be "caused by accident." Erecting a building—an intentional act—inadvertently over the property line was held not to be an accident.

Damage resulting from an assault or deliberate trespass by an insured is, of course, not "caused by accident" from the standpoint of such insured. Even here the courts have sometimes found coverage on the grounds that the damage was sudden and accidental as viewed from the standpoint of the injured party.

In order to protect against an insured's vicarious liability for assault and battery committed by employees in the course of employment, liability policies usually state that assault and battery shall be deemed an accident unless committed by or at the direction of the insured.

Most companies provide optionally, and for an additional premium—usually specially rated—that the phrase "caused by accident" may be deleted and the word "occurrence" substituted. This substitution affects not only the coverage but also the limits of liability applicable to allied items of damage. Such endorsements often define "occurrence" as an event or continuous or repeated exposure to conditions, which unexpectedly causes injury during the policy period. Exposure emanating from a single source is deemed to be one occurrence and thus subject to the applicable liability limit.

While occurrence coverage is freely available for bodily injury, underwriters are less willing to grant (and charge substantially higher rates for) an "occurrence" endorsement when applied to property damage liability. Such endorsement is particularly dangerous from an underwriting standpoint in connection with property damage liability sold under the products–completed operations hazard group. Elimination of the "caused by accident" feature in such cases may have the unintended result of making the policy a sort of "manufacturers' malpractice" cover guaranteeing against usual and expected claims for re-execution of work or replacement of products because of faulty design or workmanship.

DIFFERENCE BETWEEN O. L. & T. AND M. & C.

The principal (not sole) difference in coverage between the O. L. & T. and the M. & C. policies is found in the hazard group dealing with premises–operations. In the O. L. & T. contract the premises–operations hazard is described as: "The ownership, maintenance or use of *the* premises and all operations *necessary or incidental thereto.*" The "Definitions" section of the O. L. & T. contract defines "premises" as the premises *designated in the declarations* and ways immediately adjoining. There is no coverage for undeclared premises except for a limited automatic coverage of newly acquired premises. The off-premises operations covered by the O. L. & T. contract are those necessary or incidental to the described premises.

The M. & C. description of the premises and operations hazard is the same except that it omits the words italicized in the definition above. The modified definition, therefore, is: "The ownership, maintenance or use of premises, and all operations." Under the M. & C. contract no definition of "premises" is required. The declaration customarily lists premises owned or occupied by the insured but the coverage is not limited to those listed.

Subsidiary O. L. & T. exposures of an M. & C. risk may be included under the M. & C. form. However, they take the rates and premium bases developed by the O. L. & T. portion of the liability manual.

RELATIONSHIP AMONG HAZARD GROUPS

If an insured bought all of the coverages available under the schedule liability policy and various optional endorsements, plus an automobile policy, and a malpractice contract for any professional liability, he would have fairly broad liability insurance protection. If that were his choice, however, he could probably accomplish the same object more simply by purchasing a Comprehensive General Liability Policy which would automatically embrace all of the indicated exposures except malpractice (see Chapter 34).

The principal present purpose of the schedule policy, therefore, is to permit picking and choosing—by agreement between insured and underwriter—just what exposures will be covered under this particular contract and what will be left to other contracts or to "self-insurance." Each of the different blocks or areas of insurance is designed to be mutually exclusive; overlapping (with one or two specific exceptions) is not intended. To produce the mosaic effect, each hazard group carries its own set of exclusions. The bulk of this language is not to eliminate risks considered uninsurable but simply to mark out the dividing lines between hazard groups and the dividing lines between this type of general liability insurance on the one hand and, say, automobile insurance or marine or other property insurance, on the other.

A look—as an example—at some (not all) of the premises–operations exclusions may help to illustrate the point. All liability arising out of the ownership, maintenance, or use of aircraft is excluded. Liability from automobiles and watercraft is similarly excluded if the accident occurs away from the premises. The premises–operations coverages also exclude the elevator hazard. The purpose here is to permit (or require) coverage under the elevator portion of the policy. Another exclusion typical of this compartmentalized approach excludes liability for damage to a building or to property within buildings caused by discharge, leakage, or overflow of water or steam from plumbing, heating, refrigerating or air conditioning systems, steam pipes, collapse of tanks, automatic sprinklers, or rain or snow coming through defective doors and windows, and so on. This exposure may be covered by removing the exclusion for an additional premium or by purchasing a separate policy covering water damage and sprinkler leakage liability. The premises–operations coverage also excludes liability arising from products, completed operations, and work of independent contractors.

Similarly, the other coverages carry comparable exclusions which rule out protection against legal claims which can be defended and/or paid under the premises–operations coverages.

ELEVATOR LIABILITY

Under a schedule liability policy there is no automatic coverage of elevators operated, maintained, or controlled by the insured. It must be specifically purchased. Liability of a tenant in a building, including contractual liability under the lease, for the operation of elevators used jointly with other occupants is included in the premises–operation hazard and no specific elevator coverage is required. The term "elevator" includes passenger escalators. The term "elevator" may or may not include a dumbwaiter, depending on size.

There is nothing that requires special comment in regard to bodily injury liability or medical payments coverage under the elevator hazard group. However, property damage liability coverage is somewhat different. It does not contain the usual exclusion of liability for damage to all property in the care, custody, or control of the insured. Instead, the exclusion is confined only to property owned, occupied, rented, or used by the insured. Thus, in the usual case, the liability of the insured for personal property of others, while being transported on the elevator, is covered. On the other hand, if the elevator controlled by the insured gets out of hand and damages a building rented to the insured, there would be no coverage.

Elevator collision insurance may also be purchased on an optional basis. It is effected by attaching an endorsement to the schedule policy. It does not cover any loss paid under the property damage portion of the policy. It is sold only on policies where property damage liability insurance is also included. It covers any damage by collision of the elevator with any other object and thus covers damage to the elevator itself and damage to the insured's own property regardless of whether the property involved was on or off the elevator.

LIABILITY CLAIMS ARISING OUT OF CONSTRUCTION AND ALTERATION

Special attention should be given to construction and alteration work planned by an insured. The treatment for all such hazards is not automatically provided under the O. L. & T. nor the M. & C. contract. Further, the method of handling such exposures differs in the two contracts.

First, there is a certain amount of automatic coverage without additional premium under the premises and operations section of both policies. This section covers normal maintenance and repairs where new construction or demolition is not involved and there are no structural alterations involving the changing of building size. In such a case, since the premises and operations insuring clause covers all operations necessary or incidental to the insured premises, coverage is automatically provided to the named insured. This statement is true whether the work is done by the employees of the insured or by independent contractors.

In the case of the O. L. & T. policy, it should be noted, however, that only described premises are covered. The M. & C. policy covers all premises of the insured.

Where the alterations go beyond routine maintenance or minor alterations not involving a change of size, and involve demolition, new construction, or change in size of building, there is no automatic coverage under the premises and operations hazard group of the O. L. & T. policy. Coverage of the named insured must be added at the described location by taking out insurance under division 3 of the policy—"structural alterations–independent contractor hazards." This requirement exists whether the work is done by independent contractors or by the insured's own employees.

As to the M. & C. contract, however, the liability of the named insured for such major work is automatically covered by the premises and operations hazard group *if* the work is done by employees of the insured. Additional premium, if any, is payable on audit. But if the work is done by independent contractors, there is an absence of coverage under the premises and operations hazard group and the exposure is covered only if coverage has been purchased under division 3 of the policy—"independent contractors' protective liability."

LIABILITY FROM ACTS OF INDEPENDENT CONTRACTORS

Ordinarily when one assigns a task to be completed by an independent contractor for a fixed or determinable price, there is no employer-employee relationship or principal-agent relationship such as to make the person for whom the work is being performed liable for the independent torts (negligent or intentional) of the contractor, his subcontractors or employees of either. The owner of land may contract for the erection of a building of a certain size and specifications; the contractor undertakes to erect it within a stated time; and the exact method is up to the contractor. He may do the work through his own employees. He may subcontract it. He establishes working hours and construction methods. The landowner retains limited, if any, supervision and no day-to-day control. It is even possible that the task of supervision may be entrusted to another independent contractor such as an architect or consulting engineer.

Liability for torts is, therefore, *primarily* a responsibility of the contractor or subcontractor whose negligence (or whose employees' negligence) caused the accident. This point may be further buttressed by contract provisions whereby the contractor and/or subcontractors assume the entire liability not only for their own negligence but also for acts of concurrent negligence on the part of the contractor and the owner, and, in some cases, even of the owner's sole negligence.

Under such circumstances some owners and principals feel that they have adequate protection by reason of the contractor's hold harmless agreement and, therefore, require no insurance. This feeling is, for the most part, wishful thinking.

The owner has not shed all of his exposures by a hold harmless clause. He still has risks remaining which cannot effectively be transferred and he will need insurance for these. First, as owner of land on which construction is being done, he may be liable for certain claims that arise simply because of the ownership of land and are not related to the contract. (He is automatically covered for such premises exposure under the premises–operations part of an M. & C. Liability Policy and he may be covered under an O. L. & T. Liability Policy if the premises is described in the declarations or by suitable endorsement.) Second, he is liable for his own acts of negligence. Such negligence may have been in failure to use due care in the selection of the contractor, or some action in the sphere of the owner's limited supervision. Courts are loath to construe "hold harmless" and other idemnification agreements as protecting a person against his own active negligence. Third, there may be non-delegable duties imposed upon an owner of real property either by statute (such as scaffolding acts) or by common law. (See, for example, the discussion in Chapter 31 on "strict liability.")

Presence of the independent contractor has reduced the exposure of the owner to ultimate liability for torts of the contractor and his "subs." Even, however, if he does succeed in transferring ultimate liability from himself to the general contractor, the owner is still open to being sued. He needs, at the least, protection against costs of litigation.

There are a number of ways of attempting to handle exposures inherent in the owner-principal–general contractor–subcontractor relationship. One method was to include the owner as an additional insured under the M. & C. coverage maintained by the general contractor with respect to the work in question. This method is seldom used now.

The usual arrangement currently is for the owner to protect himself by carrying owners' and contractors' protective liability coverage insuring against contingent liability for activities of independent contractors. Such coverages normally exclude any act or omission of the named insured or his own employees other than general supervision of the work performed. Such acts or omissions are covered under the premises–operation hazard.

Under the M. & C. Liability Policy liability for independent contractors may be covered on a blanket basis by purchase of insurance under the independent contractors hazard group. This coverage is not confined to construction or to structural alterations and it also gives protection for the insured's contingent liability arising out of the actions of an independent contractor used by the insured to do servicing or installation work.

Printed portions of the O. L. & T. Liability Policy make provision for optional coverage for major structural alterations, new construction, and demolition whether done by the named insured's own employees or by contractors. In the usual O. L. & T. risk this activity will be the type of independent contractor hazard encountered. If coverage is desired for other operations which are the subject of independent contracts, it may be included by endorsement. Premium is most often based on the contract price or other payments made to the independent contractor.

Several additional points worth noting are as follows:

1. In the M. & C. policy, the premises portion is rated on the basis of the insured's own payroll. Ordinarily no premium is collected on the payroll of independent contractors. In keeping with this feature, the premises–operations portion of the policy excludes liability properly covered under the "independent contractors" hazard group.

2. While the M. & C. Liability Policy does contain a specific hazard group to cover the insured's contingent liability for activities by independent contractors, the O. L. & T. Liability Policy, on the other hand, has no express exclusion or definition of the independent contractors' hazard. Remember, however, that the O. L. & T. premises coverage applies only to premises specifically described in the declarations and operations necessary or incidental thereto. Thus, unlike the M. & C. contract there would be no automatic permanent coverage of premises on which, for example, a new store or a new hotel was being built by independent contractors.

3. In the O. L. & T. policy, installation work done by independent contractors is automatically included in the premises–operations coverage, if the installation is an operation necessary and incidental to the activity at the insured premises. No separate insurance is ordinarily needed.

THE PRODUCTS–COMPLETED OPERATIONS HAZARD

The exposure of liability for products or workmanship in business is steadily increasing. The number of products claims arising out of alleged injury from products improperly made, improperly labeled, or improperly packaged is constantly increasing. The cases are virtually infinite in variety. They range from the traditional cigarette butt in a bottle of soda or piece of glass in the hamburger, all the way to multi-million-dollar suits alleging destruction of an aircraft and death of its occupants as a result of a defective part or component.

Products

Products liability may be purchased as an optional coverage under a schedule liability policy. As a general rule, it is desirable to purchase this coverage from the same insurer furnishing "premises–operations" cover. Some underwriters will refuse to accept products coverage without also insuring the premises–operations hazard. This refusal is a consequence of the difficulty in establishing a dividing line between products liability on the premises and that off the premises; between the operations hazard and the completed operations hazard. It is not uncommon, however, to find the products liability hazard carried in an insurer other than the insurer of the premises hazard. This situation is likely to occur in the case of products not freely underwritten. Thus, a manufacturer may wish to go to a special risk market, apart from his usual liability insurers, to obtain coverage on something such as a new and untried hair lotion or face cream. On occasion, distributors and retailers of a product are provided products protection under policies maintained by the manufacturer of the product.

Most products liability coverages also apply to injury from containers such as bottles or cartons in which the product is packaged. Vending machines are not considered a products exposure on the part of the company on whose premises they are placed. They are usually covered as part of the "premises," and rated under the O. L. & T. section of the manual.

The time element in products liability insurance is important. The policy applies only to accidents which occur during the policy period. The date of the accident is the time when the damage resulted. It is not the date of the incident or neglect which caused the product to be harmful. Neither is it the time when the claim is presented. Thus, on an automobile sold in 1962, which is defective because of some part omitted when manufactured in 1961, as a result of which someone is injured in 1963 and suit is brought in 1964, the 1963 policy applies. There is no liability under any of the policies applicable to 1961, 1962, or 1964, in absence of specific language to that effect. If an insured or insurer terminates products liability coverage, and the insured does not replace it, the insured has no protection against future accidents from goods already sold and in the hands of distributors or the public. Conversely, when a products liability risk is accepted by an underwriter, in absence of special exclusionary language he will automatically assume liability for future accidents on products sold and operations completed long before the risk was offered. Premium is generally charged on the basis of sales or units or other measure of current volume.

The premises–operations coverage, of course, excludes products liability. It is also intended to exclude any liability for accidents from completed or abandoned operations. In the usual case both of these are accidents occurring away from the insured's premises. The schedule liability policy excludes from the premises–operations hazard any liability arising from the products–completed operations hazard as defined in the policy.

Except for certain risks indicated in the rating manual classifications and in the policy declarations (principally food-handling risks such as restaurants, hotels, and certain food stores) product liability arising out of an accident occurring *on the premises* of the insured is covered under the premises–operations hazard. For example, if the customer in a hardware store is injured while examining a defective piece of lawn furniture, or his clothes are soiled while examining improperly packaged paint, or some similar event occurs, the premises–operations portion of the coverage responds regardless of whether or not the insured had purchased products liability insurance. But an accident occurring after possession of the goods has been relinquished and the goods have been taken from the insured's premises is covered only under the products–completed operations portion of the policy. In the case of restaurants and the food-handling risks noted there is no products coverage under the premises feature.

Completed Operations

Closely related to products liability is "completed operations" liability. The premises–operations portion of the policy is intended to cover accidents that occur while insured operations are going on. For example, suppose the manager of the hardware store mentioned above undertakes to install linoleum in a customer's kitchen. Suppose further that, while installing the linoleum, he negligently damages the house or injures a third person and a claim is made against the hardware store. The hardware store liability insurance applies as a part of the operations hazard included as incidental to use of the premises as a hardware store. On the other hand, the premises–operations hazard is designed to exclude such incidents as the one involved in a well-known case where an electrical contractor was hired to connect motors to fans in poultry incubators as a part of a general change in electrical current used in the area. Many months later the fans were turned on when the incubators were put in use. Because they had been improperly installed, a large number of eggs failed to hatch. This error was not covered since it came under the completed operation exclusion which provides that there will be no coverage arising out of the hazard of operations if the accident occurs after the operations have been completed or abandoned and the accident occurs away from the insured's premises. Operations are not to be deemed incomplete because of having been improperly or defectively performed, or because further operations may be required pursuant to any agreement, such as a service agreement. (The loss, of course, would have been covered were insurance purchased under the "products–completed operations" hazard group.)

By specific language it is made clear that completed operations are covered under the products–completed operations hazard group and *not* the premises–operations group even though the operations themselves, as contrasted to the accident, took place on the insured's premises.

Expressly excepted from the completed operation hazard (and hence covered under the premises–operations portion of the policy) are such activities as pickup and delivery, leaving of tools, uninstalled equipment, and abandoned or unused materials. Also excepted are certain specific classifications where the rating manual includes completed operations coverage as part of the premises and operations hazard.

LIMITS OF LIABILITY

Bodily injury liability insurance as covered in the schedule liability policy or separate O. L. & T. and M. & C. contracts provide separate limits of liability for each person and for each accident. Property damage liability insurance sets forth a limit applicable to each accident.

The term "standard limits" refers to the amount of coverage embraced in the premium quotation in the rate manual. These are usually $5,000 each person and $10,000 each accident for bodily injury and $5,000 each accident for property damage liability. Optional "Excess Limits" may be purchased increasing the sums insured.

Medical payments insurance premiums are quoted in terms of a limit for each person of $250, $500, or $1,000 subject to a total limit of $10,000, $25,000 or $50,000 for each accident. Per person and often total limits can be raised.

The "each person" limit is the maximum amount of the company's liability for all damages (including damages claimed by another person, such as a husband, for care and loss of services) arising out of injury, disease, or death sustained by one person as a result of any one accident. The "each accident" limit is subject to the each person limit and states the total limit of the company's liability for all damages sustained by two or more persons as a result of any one accident. It is important to know in connection with the "each accident limit" that under the products hazard, all damages arising out of one lot of goods or products prepared or acquired by the insured shall be considered as arising out of one accident regardless of the fact that injury may occur at such different places and times.

In property damage liability, the "each accident" limitation is the maximum amount payable for all damages to property and loss of its use as a result of one accident, regardless of the number of persons or owners involved. Where limits are stated only in terms of "each person" and "each accident," payment does not (as is sometimes the case in property insurance) reduce the policy as to future accidents. Thus, on an annual policy, it is possible to expend the limit in a single accident in one month and pay the same sum all over again in the future without having to "restore" the coverage by payment of an additional premium. However, there are some types of exposure where the possibility of multiple accident is such that, in order to avoid an undue accumulation within the policy period, and still permit a high limit per accident, it is necessary to place an "aggregate" limit on total payments for all accidents during the policy period. This situation exists in the case of products exposures. An aggregate limit is the total limit of the company's liability for the indicated hazard group during the policy period. In the case of three-year policies the aggregate limit, if any, is applied separately to each annual period.

Excepting contractual liability limits, there is no accumulation of limits of liability by reason of overlapping coverage of a specific accident among more than one hazard group. In such case the highest "each person" and "each accident" limit apply. Several insureds covered in the same policy share limits.

OTHER USUAL EXCLUSIONS IN ALL SCHEDULE LIABILITY POLICIES

While, as indicated above, most of the exclusion language is to determine the dividing line between elements of coverage, there are some exclusions which limit the policy as a whole.

War Exclusion

War risks are excluded from the medical payments coverage, "first aid," and contractual liability insurance.

Liquor Control Laws

Some states have laws imposing special liability upon operators of businesses in which liquor is sold, based on the concept of making owners or operators of such premises liable for accidents and injury which result from improvident sale of alcoholic beverages. B.I., P.D., and medical payments coverages of the schedule liability policy exclude liability imposed upon the insured as a person engaged in the business of manufacturing, selling, or distributing liquor (or as the owner or lessor of premises used for such purposes) by reason of any statute or ordinance dealing with alcoholic beverages. This exclusion is popularly known as the "dram shop law exclusion."

Workmen's Compensation and Employer's Liability Exclusions

The policy excludes any obligation under a workmen's compensation, unemployment compensation, or disability benefits law and any bodily injury, sickness, disease, or death of an employee of the insured arising out of and in the course of his employment.

Nuclear Risks

This exclusion is treated in Chapter 64. It applies to all liability coverages except those discussed in Chapter 64.

"Care, Custody, or Control" Exclusion

Liability insurance is intended as protection against "third party" exposures. It is not intended to take the place of fire, windstorm, or other property damage coverages on property of others in the insured's possession. Accordingly, property damage liability coverages customarily exclude damage to property owned, occupied by, or rented to the insured, property used by the insured, property in the "care, custody, or control" of the insured, or property over which the insured for any purpose is exercising physical control. Thus, a general liability policy maintained by a bailee does not cover his liability for damage to property he is holding for others. Considerable difficulty has been experienced in construing the exclusion where there is some question as to just what portion of the damaged property is under the "care, custody, or control" of the insured. In general, the exclusion operates to eliminate coverage on that part of a building or premises on which the insured was working but may still protect him as to damage to other portions of the building or premises not within his control.

On specific application underwriters will sometimes afford broader property damage liability insurance by eliminating or modifying the "care, custody, or control" exclusion as to certain types of property.

x, c, u Exclusions

Property damage liability coverages for certain classifications in the M. & C. section of the "General Liability" manual provide that the normal coverage for these risks—identified by symbols *x*, *c*, or *u* after the manual code number—excludes property damage from blasting, explosion, collapse of property, and damage to underground property. These exclusions are put into the policy by special endorsement when the policy is written for risks in the indicated classifications. Subject to individual underwriting, an insured may obtain removal of the exclusion.

SUGGESTED READINGS

Fire, Casualty, and Surety Bulletins. Cincinnati: National Underwriter Co. Public Liability Section.

GORDIS, PHILIP. *Property and Casualty Insurance.* 9th ed. Indianapolis: Rough Notes Co., 1962. Chaps. 24, 25.

KULP, CLARENCE A. *Casualty Insurance.* 3d ed. New York: Ronald Press Co., 1956. Chap. 10.

WERBEL, BERNARD G. *General Insurance Guide.* New York: Insurance Educational Publications. Public Liability Section.

Chapter 33

PROFESSIONAL LIABILITY INSURANCE

BY JOHN C. PARISH

To establish the precise "beginning" of professional liability insurance is difficult, but the following front page story from an issue of *The Boulder Tribune* in 1905 indicates that the exposure has existed for a long time.

SUING FOR DAMAGES—Dr. C. S. Elder of Denver Defendant in a Suit for Negligence in Practice of His Profession.

Mrs. Mary Flamboe is plaintiff in an action in the district court against Dr. C. S. Elder, at present treasurer of the city and county of Denver. It is a case for damages wherein malpractice is alleged in that, after performing an operation, the defendant is charged with negligently leaving in a sponge not discovered until eight weeks later by a Boulder physician, who was called in to relieve the lady from great pain. Milton Smith of Denver appears for the defendant and Norton Montgomery and A. C. Patton for the plaintiff.

University medics are enjoying the trial of the case of Mrs. Flamboe against Dr. C. S. Elder of Denver in the district court. It is a case for damages for alleged negligence by the doctor, the specification being failure to remove a piece of gauze inserted by him in the wound caused by a delicate operation. It is a question for experts to decide and many physicians are being called in as witnesses. It makes an interesting study for the medical boys.

Dr. C. S. Elder made a splendid witness for himself in the district court yesterday. He explained surgery as applied to the troubles of the gentler sex in a way so plain, so free from the usually involved, halting and uncertain manner of physicians on the stand as to make a great impression on the jury. And the court room was filled with doctors and lawyers who were charmed with the facile way in which he made intricate matters plain to the jury.

He stated positively that he inserted four pieces of gauze in the wound in Mrs. Flamboe and that he removed four. This is the crux of the case. Did he or did he not?

Doctors Craig and Perkins of Denver and Dr. Place of Boulder were appointed a committee to examine Mrs. Flamboe on the part of the defense and did so yesterday. Medical students and others still find the case an interesting one judging from their presence there. Dr. Farrington, Dr. Place and other doctors have been on the stand. Drs. Craig and Perkins are star witnesses for the defendant. The operation was performed about a year ago by Dr. Elder at University hospital, he being the professor of gynecology and abdominal surgery of the University.

By the early 1920's numerous suits had been filed against persons in various professional areas, principally medicine. Some professional liability has come into prominence only in recent years. The number of instances of litigation and the size of the judgments against professionals and quasi professionals have been fantastic. A claim-conscious public has unearthed causes of action which perhaps were not even imagined a few years ago.

The purpose of this chapter is to present a discussion of various types of insurance contracts which have been developed to meet the professional liability exposures of doctors, lawyers, architects, engineers, insurance agents (or brokers), accountants, and others. Individual and institutional insurance for those in or associated with the medical profession is treated under the section entitled "Medical Professional Liability Insurance." Coverages for other professionals are considered under the caption of "Errors and Omissions Insurance." The chapter concludes with a brief description of the markets, underwriting, and claims characteristics of professional liability insurance in general.

SOME GENERAL COMMENTS

A few general observations are in order before attention is turned specifically to medical professional liability insurance.

First, the usual schedule liability policies (such as those discussed in the preceding chapter) do not adequately cover professional or quasi-professional liability claims. Nor do the comprehensive policies (as described in Chapter 34) adequately cover such claims. The usual general liability policies insuring certain risks indicated in the standard rating manual classifications *exclude:*

1. Injury, sickness, disease, death, or destruction due to
   a) the rendering of or failure to render
      (i) medical, surgical, dental, X-ray or nursing service or treatment, or the furnishing of food or beverages in connecting therewith;
      (ii) any service or treatment conducive to health or of a professional nature; or
      (iii) any cosmetic or tonsorial service or treatment:
   b) the furnishing or dispensing of drugs or medical, dental, or surgical supplies or appliances; or
   c) the handling of or performing of autopsies on dead bodies.
2. Injury, sickness, disease, death or destruction due to the rendering of or failure to render any cosmetic, tonsorial, massage, physiotherapy, chiropody, hearing aid, optical or optometrical services or treatments.
3. Injury, sickness, disease, death or destruction due to the rendering of or failure to render any professional service.

Second, as brought out in the preceding chapter, general liability policies usually cover legal obligations for damages for bodily injury or loss of property arising out of accidents. Occasionally, as also brought out in the preceding chapter, such policies are endorsed to read "occurrence" instead of "caused by accident." Even so, they still may not cover certain processes which give rise to professional liability claims. Continued or repeated exposures to X-rays or contagious diseases, allegation of personal restraints, assault and battery, libel, slander, and improper design might be cases in point.

Third, generalizations in this chapter are dangerous. Professional liability insurance policies and endorsements are not standardized among the companies offering this coverage. A trend toward standardization is discernible in respect to professional liability insurance offered to doctors, dentists, hospitals, and lawyers.

Fourth, the insuring clauses in medical professional liability insurance generally include "malpractice, error, or mistake" in the performance of the medical speciality involved. The insuring clauses in "errors and omissions" coverages generally contain a "negligent act, error, or omission" provision covering professional or quasi-professional firms or individuals.

Fifth, these professional liability claims reflect not only upon the individual's reputation but also upon his standing among his colleagues and his own self-confidence when placed under attack by a plaintiff's attorney.

MEDICAL PROFESSIONAL LIABILITY INSURANCE

Medical professional liability classes can be grouped into three categories:

1. Hospital and related institutions such as convalescent or nursing homes, homes for the aged, homes for the mental-psychopathic, sanitoriums, and health institutions where regular bed and board facilities are maintained for the care of patients.
2. Clinics, dispensaries, and infirmaries usually incidental to industrial or commercial enterprises where there are no regular bed or board facilities. (This group should be distinguished from such institutions as are operated by dentists or medical doctors, as such risks are covered and rated under individual physicians' and surgeons' liability contracts.)
3. Individuals including (but not necessarily limited to) physicians, surgeons, dentists, nurses, osteopaths, chiropodists, chiropractors, various types of medical technicians, opticians, physiotherapists, optometrists, and veterinarians. (This category also includes medical laboratories, blood banks, and optical establishments.)

Not all medical professional liability policies are the same. They vary not only in exclusions and in broadness of insuring clauses but also in company interpretations of the policies. Within this chapter no attempt will be made to compare policies issued by various insurers. Rather, the comments will be directed toward those accepted as "standard" policies.

Hospital Professional Liability

The Hospital Professional Liability Policy is generally used for institutions in categories 1 and 2 above. The common insuring clause is:

1. Payment on behalf of the insured of all sums which the insured shall become legally obligated to pay as damages because of injury, including death, sustained by any person, arising out of
   a) malpractice, error, or mistake committed during the policy period
      (i) in rendering or failure to render to such person, or to the person inflicting the injury, medical, surgical, dental, or nursing treatment, including the furnishing of food or beverages in connection therewith, or
      (ii) in furnishing or dispensing drugs of medical, dental, or surgical supplies or appliances if the injury occurs after the named insured has relinquished possession thereof to others, or
      (iii) in handling or performing autopsies on deceased human bodies, or
   b) acts or omissions of any individual as a member of a formal accreditation or similar professional board or committee of the named insured, or as the person charged with the duty of executing directives of any such board or committee, committed during the policy period.
2. Coverage applies only to injury, including death, sustained by any person, arising out of malpractice, error, or mistake committed during the policy period.

It is significant that coverage includes but is not limited to bodily injury and property damage. For example, the various personal injuries, such as mental anguish, would be covered. Further, depending largely upon individual company interpretation, there may be coverage for such contingencies as false arrest, malicious prosecution, willful detention or imprisonment, libel, slander or defamation of character, invasion of privacy, and wrongful eviction or wrongful entry. The "injury" must arise, however, out of malpractice in the rendering of treatment. The word "treatment" is not used in the ordinary sense as pertaining to remedies but comprehends supervisory acts and administrative care in the use of facilities in the overall care of patients.

Coverage is afforded not only for injury to patients but also injury to third parties arising out of the actions of patients. An example of this is where a deranged patient escapes his confinement and causes injury to another, thereby imposing liability upon the institution for failure to maintain proper security. On and off the premises products coverage is afforded thereby making it unnecessary to purchase separate products liability. The policy applies to occurrences during the policy period. There is no time limit on the appearance or discovery of the injury. This feature is unusual to most public liability policies and is necessary because of the possible late development of losses. Considerable time may elapse between the act and the manifestation of the injury.

Definition of Insured. The definition of "insured" for nonprofit hospitals, institutions, and clinics is defined as the named institution and also each member of the named insured's board of trustees, directors, or governors while acting within the scope of his duties. For profit hospitals, institutions, and clinics, the "insured" includes any partner, executive officer, director, or stockholder while acting within the scope of his duties. "Executive officer" is deemed to mean such executives of corporations as president, vice president, secretary, or treasurer. The term does not include such officials as superintendents, administrators, or supervisors of various hospital departments. If coverage is desired beyond this definition, additional premiums are warranted under the additional interest rules of rating.

Supplementary Agreements. The defense, settlement, and supplementary payments clause provides that the insurer will:

a) Defend any suit against the insured alleging such injury and seeking damages on account thereof, even if such suit is groundless, false or fraudulent; but the company may make such investigation and negotiation and, with the written consent of the named insured, such settlement of any claim or suit as the company deems expedient.

b) Pay all premiums on bonds to release attachments for an amount not in excess of the applicable limit of liability of the policy, all premiums on appeal bonds required in any such defended suit, but without any obligation to apply for or furnish any such bonds.

c) Pay all expenses incurred by the company, all costs taxed against the insured in any such suit and all interest accruing after entry of judgment until the company has paid, tendered or deposited in court such judgment as does not exceed the limit of the company's liability thereon.

d) Reimburse the insured for all reasonable expenses, other than loss of earnings, incurred at the company's request.

The foregoing defense and supplementary payments coverage is much the same as found in other liability policies, with two exceptions which deserve comment. First, unlike most general liability policies, these contracts do not provide for the payment of "such immediate medical and surgical relief to others as shall be imperative at the time of the occurrence." Because of the type of services readily available in hospitals and related institutions, such payments are not reimbursable under hospital liability. Second, unlike most general liability policies, written consent of the insured is required in the settlement of any claim or suit.

Exclusions. The Hospital Professional Liability Policy insuring clauses are very broad from a coverage standpoint and must be defined or qualified by certain exclusions. These exclusions are not unduly restrictive in nature but, rather, are designed to eliminate exposures not contemplated within the purpose of the policy. Such exposures are embraced in other types of available insurance. The exclusions are as follows:

1. Liability because of bodily injury, or sickness, disease, or death of any employee in the course of his employment or obligations under any workmen's

compensation, unemployment compensation, disability benefits, any similar law.

2. Liability of an insured, if an individual, for his personal acts or omissions of a professional nature. (There are many individually owned hospitals, nursing homes, and related institutions operated by doctors, nurses, or other professionals. The hospital policy is not designed to cover individual professional liability arising from personal acts of such individuals. Such exposures are covered under individual professional liability policies as discussed later in this chapter.)

3. Liability arising out of the ownership, maintenance, use, or loading or unloading of any motor vehicle, trailer, semitrailer, watercraft, or aircraft. (These exposures are the proper subject of other liability policies.)

4. Liability from incidents involving nuclear energy. (This exclusion is the customary exclusion which appears in virtually every liability policy except those discussed in Chapter 64.)

Limits and Other Features. Unlike the limits under general liability policies, which usually apply on a "per person" and "per accident" basis, hospital professional coverage is on a "per claim" basis with an "aggregate" per policy per annum. Basic limits are $5,000 per claim and $15,000 aggregate.

The other conditions of the Hospital Professional Liability Policy are generally similar to those in other liability policies. The premium for all types of hospitals, mental institutions, sanitariums, nursing homes, and homes for the aged is based upon a "per bed" and a "per 100 outpatient visits" rate. Since, by definition, clinics, dispensaries, and infirmaries do not have inpatients, the rate is based on the number of outpatient visits. The "per bed" rate applies to the average occupancy of the institution in question subject to audit provisions contained in the policy. Beds are defined to include bassinets and cribs.

A classification has been adopted on a broad basis to include:

1. Clinics, dispensaries, and infirmaries.
2. Convalescent or nursing homes and homes for the aged.
3. Hospitals—not otherwise classified.
4. Mental-psychopathic institutions.
5. Sanitariums or health institutions.

Each of these classes is further divided to apply to private, charitable or eleemosynary, and governmental institutions. The purpose is to give further recognition of the varying degree of immunity, if any, that may exist within a particular state. When the subject of tort liability of charitable and governmental institutions is considered, there are few guides that could be generalized within this chapter, for, in fact, immunity is a most comprehensive study in and of itself. Where immunity exists by statute, little problem exists; however, only a limited number of states fall within this category. In the states where such statutes do not exist, search of court decisions must be made, and there is considerable variation and lack of uniformity from state to state. The subject is of vast importance to producers and underwriters, since established rates have a direct bearing on complete immunity, partial immunity, or complete liability. The trend is definitely in the direction of holding charitable and governmental hospitals liable for their negligence, and thus rate adjustment to meet this trend is most important to underwriters.

Endorsements extending basic hospital professional liability insurance to include additional interests are few in number. Because of the method of rating, the extension of coverage to include additional interests can substantially impair the immunity on which the company could rely as a defense. For this reason, the market for extension of coverage is limited and involves a matter of individual company underwriting judgment. The definition of "insured" in such policies already has been outlined. Some companies will extend such definitions to include the interest of superintendents, managers, or administrators. Another possible extension is to include the interest of all employees and volunteer workers. Premiums for such extensions vary widely and are quite substantial.

Physicians', Surgeons', and Dentists' Professional Liability Policy

In the individual medical professional categories, it will be found, as in the case of the Hospital Professional Liability Policy, that all contracts on the market are not the same. For this reason, the present resumé will be limited to an analysis of so-called "standard" policies. The Physicians', Surgeons', and Dentists' Professional Liability Policy is the basic instrument for insuring this class of individual professionals.

Insuring Clause. The common insuring clause is:

Payment on behalf of the insured because of injury arising out of:

a) malpractice, error, or mistake in rendering or failing to render professional services in the practice of the insured's profession committed during the policy period by the insured or any other person for whose acts or omissions the insured is legally liable;

b) acts or omissions committed by the insured during the policy period as a member of a formal accreditation or similar professional board or committee of a hospital or professional society.

Here again "injury" is not limited to bodily injury and property damage. The injury must, however, arise out of the rendering or failing to render professional services or the activities enumerated in (*b*) above. Coverage for personal injury claims is, undoubtedly, more important to individual medical professionals than to those engaged in any other occupation. Illustrations of exposures common in the medical professional's practice for which he should have protection are:

1. Assault or battery arising out of lack of consent to surgery or going beyond consent given.
2. Libel and slander arising from betrayal of professional confidence.
3. Personal restraint, false imprisonment, and malicious prosecution arising in the care of psychiatric patients.

4. Undue familiarity and alleged illegal abortion.
5. Counterclaims which arise when the doctor brings action to collect fees.

Through individual company interpretation, there can be a wide divergence of opinion as to whether or not such allegations are covered under the insuring clause.

Historically, many malpractice actions do not commence until years after the alleged error in professional services took place. For this reason, the coverage period in the policy is defined to cover acts committed during the policy period with no limitation on the discovery period.

Two mutually exclusive insuring clauses are contained in this policy. One pertains to individual coverage, the other to partnership coverage. The policy is so designed in the "Definition" section and in the policy schedule that individual coverage or partnership coverage can be written separately or in combination if appropriate charges are made.

Supplementary Agreements, Limits, and Rates. The defense, settlement, and supplementary payments section of the policy is identical to the hospital policy. No immediate medical coverage is provided. Written consent of the insured is required in the settlement of claims and suits.

The exclusions eliminate coverage for:

1. The use of X-ray for therapy. (This exclusion can be removed by payment of additional premium.)
2. Any insured as a proprietor, superintendent, or executive officer of any hospital, sanitarium, clinic with bed and board facilities, laboratory or business enterprise. (This exposure is the proper subject of the Hospital Professional Liability Insurance Policy.)

Basic limits of liability are $5,000 each claim, subject to a $15,000 annual aggregate. The policy limits apply separately to each individual named as insured in the policy, with the same policy limits applying separately to the partnership entity. The average limits are $100,000/$300,000 but protection for higher limits is common.

Rates are established for each state. Four classifications exist for rating purposes for physicians and surgeons and are designed to recognize the actuarial fact that as the degree of complexity of a doctor's surgery practice increases, his exposure to claims increases proportionately. Briefly, these classes are as follows:

Class 1. No surgery other than incision of boils, suturing of skin, or obstetrical procedures.

Class 2. Minor surgery or obstetrical procedures not constituting major surgery.

Class 3. Major surgery and surgery performed by proctologists and opthalmologists.

Class 4. Special surgery such as the practice of cardiac surgeons, urologists, neurosurgeons, obstetrician gynecologists, orthopedists, otolaryngologists, plastic surgeons, general surgeons, and thoracic and vascular surgeons.

Additional premiums apply for the use of shock and X-ray for therapy. Miscellaneous additional charges apply for the employment of other doctors and certain technicians. A partnership charge is made where such an exposure exists and is to be covered. Rates for professionals other than physicians and surgeons are on a "per person" basis, and in some instances additional charges apply to recognize specific exposures prevalent in the specialty involved.

ERRORS AND OMISSIONS INSURANCE

Classification

The second and relatively new category of professional liability insurance is referred to as errors and omissions. Because of the fact that new classes of this type of coverage are being created by ingenious underwriters, classification would be very difficult. Professionals who can now be covered by errors and omissions insurance include, but are not restricted to, lawyers, insurance agents and brokers, accountants, real estate agents, appraisers, abstracters, title insurance agents, architects and engineers, advertising agents, adjusters, directors and trustees, fiduciaries, travel agents, and data processing firms.

A variety of policies and rates are in existence for these specialty coverages. With the exception of lawyers' professional liability, there is no "standard" policy for these classes. Because of this lack of uniformity, an analysis of policies could not do justice to every company and, in fact, could be misleading. A description of the Lawyers' Professional Liability Policy is presented. Some of the characteristics which this policy has in common with other errors and omissions policies are pointed out with respect to the insuring clauses, exclusions, and conditions. The reader should be cautioned, however, to consult the particular policy involved when considering coverage questions.

Lawyers' Professional Liability Policy

The standard Lawyers' Professional Liability Policy follows the Physicians' and Surgeons' Professional Liability Policy to the extent that it is set up on the basis of two separate mutually exclusive insuring clauses: one for individual coverage and the other for partnership coverage. The primary purpose of these separate insuring clauses is to prevent a pyramiding of limits where there are many partners and a claim may be made against them jointly or severally. On the other hand, the designated policy limit will apply to each partner or lawyer named in the policy, and in addition, if a partnership exists, the said limit will also apply to the partnership entity. The insuring clause reads:

> . . . to pay damages because of any act or omission of the insured, or of any

other person for whose acts or omissions the insured is legally responsible, and arising out of the performance of professional services for others in the insured's capacity as a lawyer.

By definition, the insured's acts as an administrator, conservator, executor, guardian, trustee, or similar fiduciary are deemed to be professional services for others in the capacity as a lawyer to the extent that such acts are those for which, in the usual attorney-client relationship, the insured would be legally responsible as an attorney for a fiduciary.

Essentially, each other class within the field of errors and omissions insurance has a similar insuring clause. They are usually based upon "any act or omission" or "any negligent act, error, or omission" arising out of the insured's particular profession or specialty involved.

Supplementary Agreements and Definitions. The defense, settlement, and supplementary payments provisions of these policies follow most other liability contracts. For obvious reasons, no immediate medical coverage is provided in most of them. In addition, the majority stipulates that written consent of the insured is required in the settlement of any claim or suit. Some state that the amounts paid under the defense, settlement, and supplementary payments clause are in addition to the limit of liability stated in the "Declarations"; others do not.

Under the lawyers' policy, the insured is defined as each named lawyer in the "Declarations." Automatic coverage is provided for additional lawyers who become partners of the partnership insured under Coverage B. If coverage is provided for all employee lawyers at policy inception, any additional lawyers employed during the policy period are automatically covered. The "Definition of Insured" provisions in other errors and omissions policies contain many variations. These variations are largely dependent upon the nature of the profession or specialty and upon individual company practice designed to fit particular purposes or to gain competitive advantage. Some definitions are similar to that in the lawyers' policy; others include any partner, executive officer, director, or stockholder while acting within the scope of his duties as such. Some policies, in addition to the above, include all employees while acting within the scope of their duties as such.

An interesting aspect of the various errors and omissions contracts is the "Policy Period, Territory" which has been developed upon generally much broader lines than in most other liability policies. An example of such broad coverage is contained in the Lawyers' Professional Liability Policy. Actually, it is open on both ends. It covers acts or omissions during the policy period and has an unlimited discovery period. The insured's liability is covered regardless of when the claim is brought, if the act or omission occurred during the policy period. In addition, acts or omissions occurring prior to the policy period are covered if the claim is made or suit is brought during the policy period providing the insured had no knowledge or could not have reasonably foreseen any circumstance which might result in claim or suit. This policy period provision is the broadest found in these various contracts. Any individual working with these contracts, however, should be alert for variations in the discovery period provisions because many contracts are more restrictive. Some stipulate that the error and the claim must take place during the policy period; others stipulate that the claim or suit must take place during the policy period. In the latter case, there may be coverage for prior acts or omissions if the claim is brought during the policy period, but there is no discovery period for acts or omissions occurring during the policy period but undiscovered at the expiration, termination, or cancellation of the policy.

Exclusions, Limits, and Rates. In reference to exclusions, the reader should consult the particular policy under consideration because of the many variations and excluded exposures common to one profession and not to others. Generally, dishonest, fraudulent, criminal, or malicious acts or omissions of the insured are excluded. In connection with these exposures, some policies provide coverage to the employer for such acts of employees; others exclude these exposures across the board. Because of the broadness of the insuring clauses, these policies generally exclude bodily injury to, or sickness, disease, or death of, any persons; or damage to or destruction of property. The purpose of such exclusions is to eliminate ordinary premises and operational exposures, which are the proper subjects of public liability policies.

The conditions of the various errors and omissions policies are not unlike other liability contracts. However, there is considerable variation in the "Limits of Liability" and "Other Insurance" clauses because of the multitude of forms. Reference to these sections should be made for specific classes under consideration.

Under most errors and omissions policies, rating is generally on a staff or per capita basis. In others, such as Real Estate Errors and Omissions, receipts may be used where such unit of exposure more adequately measures risk variation. Much greater use is made of deductibles, and in fact, under several of these classes, full coverage is not available. Experience has shown that the deductible eliminates small nuisance claims and is psychologically desirable when dealing with individual professional protection. Deductibles also have an effect upon the rate and premium and recognize the fundamental purpose of such contracts, which is to insure against the catastrophe.

SPECIAL ASPECTS OF UNDERWRITING AND CLAIMS HANDLING

To this point the comments have been directed to the various professional liability coverages, divided for emphasis into two categories—

medical professional and errors and omissions. The remaining comments deal with markets, underwriting, and claims characteristics in the professional liability field in general.

The market for medical professional liability is not as extensive as that for general liability. There are may companies which offer complete facilities for the so-called standard liability coverages but have not entered the professional liability field. With the specialized nature of the class involved, the application of an entirely new set of underwriting rules and claims procedures is required with respect to hospitals and related institutions. Considerable importance is given to the location of the institution, staff qualifications, physical plant, whether operated for profit or charity, and manner of operation. Clinics, dispensaries, or infirmaries in connection with industrial or commercial enterprises are generally written in conjunction with and follow the underwriting of the principal operation of the insured. For individuals in the medical field, the professional background—including medical school, internship, and residency—as well as years of practice are important underwriting criteria. For all professionals, their educational background and affiliation with recognized professional societies should be taken into consideration as well as their professional integrity and loss record.

Geographic influences have been an important consideration in company underwriting practices. Generally speaking, the claims activity in certain of the large metropolitan centers has been much greater than in smaller urban and rural areas where the population is less migratory. Some classes of specially trained plaintiff attorneys in larger populated areas have stimulated claims and made professionals more susceptible to large payments and jury verdicts.

Not unlike other categories of insurance, the rates for professional liability classifications are promulgated by class and territory. Depending upon a credible volume, such rates are established on a state or national basis. Central statistical gathering agencies or bureaus perform ratemaking functions for their member companies. There are companies writing a substantial volume of this general class which are not members of these bureaus and which promulgate and use their own rates.

Another factor which undoubtedly contributes to the limited market for professional liability insurance is the highly specialized and technical skill required in the handling of claims. The conduct of the claims adjuster toward the professional who is facing a claim is much different than in other liability situations. The complete cooperation of the doctor, lawyer, accountant, dentist or other professional must be ever-present, and the insured must have confidence in his company's claim representative. The insured must be convinced from the outset that the company has a genuine and sincere desire to help him. With these characteristics evident, the insured must then be instructed in the procedures which are customarily followed in defending alleged malpractice cases, and he must accept the possibility that others must be brought into the preliminary discussions, such as other company local representatives and perhaps experts whose technical skill in the particular profession will be helpful in building a defense.

As in no other field, claims procedure requires that a thorough investigation be made of the insured's own qualifications, of his professional, social, and community background, for all of this material may be necessary in the event of a jury trial. With the facts of the particular occurrence clearly established, the company, the insured, and the attorneys must then determine the next course of action—disposal short of suit or resort to the courts. The claims personnel must be constantly alert to fraudulent claims and be ready to resist vigorously the sort of racketeering in this specialized field which so seriously affects the reputation and practice of the professional.

Unlike the liability situations discussed in other chapters, professional liability nuisance settlements are seldom made. Such action by the inexperienced only implies the guilt of the insured, and such indications must be avoided wherever possible. Where the claims circumstances have indicated that liability exists, much depends on the skill of the professional liability claims adjuster, who will endeavor to make the best possible settlement within the limits of the policy. Since it has been pointed out earlier in this chapter that no settlement can be made without the consent of the insured, it is necessary to keep him informed of the merits of the case at all times and to advise him of the recommended action. It takes a special talent as well as abundant experience for a claims adjuster adroitly to close a case without overpaying it. When liability is not clear or obviously does not exist, the adjuster must convince the insured that an energetic defense is wise, for capitulation to a claimant's demands just to avoid the notoriety of a court trial will often be regretted.

Bad or unfavorable results in the practice of medicine frequently give rise to demands by the claimant for restitution, but every bad result is not in and of itself proof of malpractice or negligence. In the past, the doctrine of *res ipsa loquitur* in malpractice cases was rarely, if ever, used. Medicine is not an exact science, and bad results can and do occur. Even with the greatest of care, the unexpected can happen in surgical or medical procedures. It has been said the human body is not susceptible to precise understanding, and the care and skill required of a medical man is the degree of learning and skill common in his profession and locality. These are considered paramount in determining whether or not the medical man in a given circumstance has been negligent.

In establishing the degree of professional negligence, three essential elements are generally considered.

1. A relationship must exist between the professional (insured) and the client. (This can also be obtained under the doctrine of *respondeat superior.*)
2. The professional failed in some duty he owed to the client.
3. The failure was the proximate cause of injury, loss, or damage.

Essentially, the same distinguishing traits are present in most professional liability claims, but it is also apparent that the same involved problems will not be faced in the lawyers', accountants', abstracters', adjusters' and other professional fields as those which exist in the practice of medicine. For example, much of the liability which might arise against a lawyer would be through the existence of a contractual relationship. Adjusters, real estate agents, insurance agents and brokers, title agents, architects, and engineers find themselves in many of the same claims situations as lawyers.

SUGGESTED READINGS

ADAMSON, O. C., II. "Medical Malpractice: Misuse of *Res Ipsa Loquitur,*" *Minnesota Law Review,* Vol. 46 (May, 1962), pp. 1043–59.

CURRAN, WILLIAM J. "Symposium on Professional Negligence," *Vanderbilt Law Review,* Vol. 12 (June, 1959), pp. 535–47.

DEAN, EUGENE M. "Professional Liability Claims," *The Independent Adjuster,* Vol. 28 (Fall, 1963), pp. 6–34.

MARKHAM, BURR B. "A Medical Legal Problem," *Minnesota Medicine,* Vol. 42 (March, 1959), pp. 251–58.

"Medicine and the Law," *Journal of the American Medical Association,* Vol. 170 (June 20, 1959), pp. 973–78.

MORRIS, R. CRAWFORD. "Medical Malpractice: A Changing Picture," *Insurance Counsel Journal,* Vol. XXIII (January, 1956), pp. 23–32.

SMITH, CARLTON. "Who Says Doctors Can't Police Themselves," *Medical Economics,* Vol. 40 (July 1, 1963), pp. 69–77.

Chapter 34

COMPREHENSIVE LIABILITY INSURANCE

BY EDGAR E. ISAACS

In the preceding chapters, the multitude of liability hazards is noted as is also the use of scheduled and specialized liability policies. This item-by-item enumeration of the early development of liability insurance strongly underscores the maxim that necessity is the mother of invention. Clearly, third party liability insurance, rather than being the product of orderly planning, grew as the need arose for each specific coverage. Thus, old records disclose that an Employer's Liability Policy was modified by endorsement to afford protection against claims that might be brought by the public and, similarly, a Team's Liability Policy was originally utilized to insure early model automobiles. Such improvisation is a far cry from the "comprehensive" liability policies as discussed in this chapter.

DEVELOPMENT OF BLANKET LIABILITY COVERAGE

Gradually, the single-hazard approach became increasingly awkward. The reasons include the following: (1) the unwieldiness of developing a separate policy to cover each newly recognized hazard, (2) the confusing variety of rating techniques and premium bases employed, and (3) the dangerous likelihood of either gaps or overlaps occurring in the intended protection. Thus arose the stimulus to search for a better system, that is, a blanket coverage concept for writing insurance on multi-liability hazards. The advent of the schedule liability policy was a step in an evolutionary process of improvement. The schedule policy is an improvement over the use of several single-hazard policies. The step was not a very inspired one, however, for it preserved the shortcomings of named peril insuring language. Moreover, the absence of a specific premium charge for a division of coverage meant that no insurance was extended under that section of the policy.

Undoubtedly, the growth and increased complexities of the business community in the immediate post-depression period supplied potent pressure for a more inclusive, yet streamlined, liability insurance arrangement. Thus in 1940 was born "The Comprehensive Liability Insurance Program"—a joint development effort of the National Bureau of Casualty and Surety Underwriters and the Mutual Casualty Insurance Rating Bureau. Individual companies had for some time been experimenting in selective situations with special combinations of liability covers, automatic pickup and deletion of exposures, and with individually negotiated premium bases. This treatment developed into a definite trend early in the 1930's in certain western states, but the first formalized attempt at a countrywide uniform coverage program was initiated in 1939 through the rating organizations mentioned above. Promulgation followed the next year.

A dictionary definition of the adjective "comprehensive" is:

> *Comprehensive*—1a: covering a matter under consideration completely or nearly completely: accounting for or comprehending all or virtually all pertinent considerations.
> b: *of insurance:* covering all hazards of a given type with the exception of individual hazards specifically excluded.
> 2: having the power to understand or grasp: of wide mental grasp.[1]

Clearly, therefore, adoption into insurance parlance of the label "comprehensive" liability coverage did not imply an all risk policy without conditions, limitations, or exclusions. The development of comprehensive liability insurance involved the substitution of blanket insuring agreements for the specified perils phraseology. It involved also the facility to cover under a single policy all of an insured's liability exposures, however numerous, varied, or widespread they might be and whenever they might arise during the policy period. In other words, the newly adopted comprehensive concept not only embraced insurance against specifically enumerated hazards, but also against unenumerated, unrecognized, or newly arising exposures. That the drafters planned soundly is shown by the fact that the original program continues to be employed, virtually unchanged, a quarter of a century later.

TYPES OF COMPREHENSIVE LIABILITY POLICIES

The following types of comprehensive liability contracts are in general use throughout the insurance industry:

1. Comprehensive General Liability Policy (CGL).
2. Comprehensive Automobile Liability Policy (CAL).
3. Comprehensive Liability Policy (CL) (being a combination of the CGL and CAL, hence the broadest policy offered insofar as scope of coverage is concerned).

[1] *Webster's Third New International Dictionary, Unabridged* (Springfield, Mass.: G. & C. Merriam Co., 1961), p. 467.

4. Comprehensive Personal Liability Policy (CPL).
5. Farmer's Comprehensive Personal Liability Policy (FCPL).
6. Storekeeper's Liability Policy (while denied the label "Comprehensive," it employs a single blanket insuring agreement, and hence seems properly to belong with the family of comprehensive covers).
7. Hybrid liability, miscellaneous casualty, and property covers, namely the various Homeowner's Policies, Special Manuscript Policies, the Composite Mercantile Policy (widely utilized in Canada), and recently a wide variety of new contracts combining or "packaging" liability and property exposures, but which preserve the form and substance of the several comprehensive liability covers.

Considerable differences of opinion may arise as to whether the varying combinations of liability and property covers now developing properly fit within the comprehensive liability category or, in fact, represent an entirely new family of insurance contracts. In this chapter it is sufficient to take cognizance of this highly important and continuing development and to be alert to the tremendous competitive pressures implicit in this experimentation. Scope of coverage, breadth of a company's underwriting powers, financial capacity, lowered premiums, and economies of packaging several insurable hazards together are all being vigorously brought to bear in keen sales battles aimed at capturing the commercial risk's favor.

COMPREHENSIVE GENERAL LIABILITY POLICY[2]

Insuring Clauses

The bodily injury liability insuring clause of this contract reads as follows:

> To pay on behalf of the insured all sums which the insured shall become legally obligated to pay as damages because of bodily injury, sickness or disease, including death at any time resulting therefrom, sustained by any person and caused by accident.

The property damage liability insuring clause reads:

> To pay on behalf of the insured all sums which the insured shall become legally obligated to pay as damages because of injury to or destruction of property, including the loss of use thereof, caused by accident.

Standing alone, these two insuring agreements are remarkable in the breadth and liberality of the protection they extend. Each and every one of the liability hazards treated in the two preceding chapters can be covered under the Comprehensive General Liability Policy (assuming necessary endorsements) and, additionally, any newly arising hazards which may cause bodily injury or property damage are automatically covered. Thus, the protection of this policy automatically tracks (1) changed or new business operations, (2) additional locations, (3) expan-

[2] See Appendix E.

sion of an enterprise into additional states, (4) development of new products, (5) alteration of premises, and (6) acquisition of other business entities (this point presumes the absorption of such additional business entities, for if the other legal entity continues, it would be necessary to endorse its name onto the policy in order to effect coverage in its behalf). In short, a blanket commitment is made to assume under a single policy all responsibility of a named insured for bodily injury or property damage caused by accident—limited only by the policy conditions and exclusions.

Exclusions

A truism within the insurance industry is that restrictions, limitations, and qualifying terms appear throughout the phraseology of every policy and that reference to the exclusions section alone is not sufficient to ascertain the precise boundaries of the intended coverage. While it therefore follows that a policy must be analyzed as an instrument of the whole, such note of caution does not prejudice the basic principle that the Comprehensive General Liability Policy covers all losses except those specifically excluded. Exclusions are sometimes classed either as premium exclusions or underwriting exclusions, although this distinction may seem meaningless to one who accepts the theory that every risk can be insured at some price.

Exclusions Applying Both to the Bodily Injury and Property Damage Coverages. The Comprehensive General Liability Policy does not apply:

1. To liability assumed by the insured under any contract or agreement other than (*a*) if in writing, a lease of premises, easement agreement, agreement required by municipal ordinance, sidetrack agreement, or elevator or escalator maintenance agreement; and (*b*) as respects the insurance which is afforded for the products liability hazard, a warranty of goods or products.

Excluded types of *written* contractual agreements may usually be covered upon special negotiation between insured and insurer to set a fair premium for such transfer of risk and the establishment of appropriate underwriting controls over the additional types of liabilities assumed. This is regarded as a combination premium and underwriting exclusion. However, some underwriters offer coverage for liability of others assumed under any contract or agreement if it is in writing, feeling that it is preferable to constrict the contract in selected situations, but being generally content to provide blanket contractual coverage.

2. To any obligation for which the insured may be held liable in an action on a contract or an agreement by a person not a party thereto.

This is known as the "third-party beneficiary exclusion" and was adopted in the fall of 1955 as an additional exclusion or underwriting limitation. It is of significance primarily in connection with insureds who do work for governmental bodies wherein by the terms of the work agreement a contractor may be required to assume full responsibility for all injury or damage sustained by the general public and without regard to negligence on his part. Where such agreements exist, a member of the public need only show that he was damaged by reason of the insured's operations and then claim as a third-party beneficiary under the agreement to which he himself is not even a named party. Various court decisions are on record awarding a third party recovery from the contractor, regardless of whether the injury or damage sustained was due to his negligence or other legal fault. Such a contractual commitment represents a positive extension of the ordinary concepts of legal liability insurance, and, accordingly, good underwriting practice dictates that the making of such agreements be discouraged—hence the exclusion. While its waiver might be obtained through negotiations with the underwriter and payment of an additional premium, it falls more into the category of an underwriting exclusion than a premium exclusion.

3. Except with respect to operations performed by independent contractors and except with respect to liability assumed by the insured under a contract of the type covered by the policy, to the ownership, maintenance, operation, use, loading or unloading of watercraft or automobiles away from the insured's premises, or of aircraft.

The exact wording of the watercraft exclusion is handled in such fashion that it may be overcome merely by framing the policy premium schedule, indicating that coverage is intended, describing the boating hazard, and entering the appropriate premium charge therefor. Hence it is purely a rating exclusion. Automobiles constitute a separate and major subject of insurance for which specific policies have been designed. Thus, only their use around the insured's premises is covered, except, of course, insofar as liability is assumed under a covered contract or in connection with work sublet. This portion then is essentially an underwriting exclusion. Similarly, insurance for the ownership and operation of aircraft is considered a field unto itself and one which is best covered under separate specialized policies. Only contingent liability and contractual liability arising out of the use of aircraft by independent contractors is contemplated herein.

4. To injury, sickness, disease, death or destruction due to war, whether or not declared, civil war, insurrection, rebellion or revolution, or to any act or condition incident to any of the foregoing, with respect to (*a*) liability assumed by the insured under any covered contract or agreement or (*b*) expenses for medical and surgical relief to others incurred by the insured.

The logic of this underwriting exclusion seems self-evident.

5. To liability imposed upon the insured or any indemnitee, as a person or organization engaged in the business of manufacturing, selling or distributing alcoholic beverages, or as an owner or lessor of premises used

for such purposes by reason of any statute or ordinance pertaining to the sale, gift, distribution or use of any alcoholic beverage.

This exclusion, like that of third-party beneficiary, was introduced into the basic policy in 1955. (See reference in Chapter 32 to the "dram shop law" exclusion.) A number of states impose by statutes varying degrees of responsibility upon persons engaged in the liquor business who might have perchance influenced or contributed towards the intoxication of an individual who in turn causes injury to another. It should be noted that this exclusion has application only to those people or firms *engaged in the liquor business* or *owning premises* in which such a business is carried on. It does not apply to an individual or firm who or which gives or serves spirituous liquors only coincidentally to his business of another nature. If the manufacture, sale, or distribution of alcoholic beverages is not the regular commercial activity of such individual or firm he or it would still be covered by the policy in the event of being enjoined in a claim growing out of someone becoming intoxicated as the result of having partaken of their hospitality and, while so affected, causing injury to another. This exclusion has comparatively limited application and can be eliminated by payment of proper additional premium. However, broader coverage may be available under a special Dram Shop Liability Policy.

Exclusions Applying Only to the Bodily Injury Insuring Agreement. Under the Comprehensive General Liability Policy further exclusions apply as follows:

6. Under bodily injury liability to any obligation for which the insured or any carrier as his insurer may be held liable under any workmen's compensation, unemployment compensation or disability benefits law or under any similar law.

Coverage for such liabilities may be readily obtained under other policies and the exclusion may not be eliminated.

7. Under bodily injury except with respect to liability assumed by the insured under a contract of a type covered by the policy, to bodily injury to or sickness, disease or death of any employee of the insured arising out of and in the course of his employment by the insured.

This language dovetails with Coverage B of the standard Workmen's Compensation and Employers' Liability Policy which is specifically drafted to fill this particular coverage need. Here again, a separate type of insurance is involved and the exclusion may not be eliminated. Notice, however, that this employee exclusion does not remove coverage for liability that the insured may have assumed under a written contract as insured in the policy.

Exclusions Applicable Only to Property Damage Insuring Agreement. The remaining four exclusions will not be set forth verbatim because they are lengthy and extremely difficult to follow without reference to other terms, conditions, and definitions within the policy contract. A brief explanation of their general intent will probably suffice, and in analyzing them (exclusions 8 through 11), it is important to bear in mind that the CGL is a legal liability contract and that some of the excluded exposures may be more logically and more adequately covered under a direct damage type of insurance.[3]

8. This exclusion is concerned with the elimination of coverage from damage to property owned; occupied by; rented to; or in the care, custody, or control of the insured or over which the insured for any purpose is exercising physical control.
9. This one involves the exclusion of damage to property of others caused by the discharge, leakage, or overflow of water; the blockage or backing up of sewers; flooding or seepage of water occurring on or from premises owned by or rented to the named insured and which damages or destroys buildings or property therein. It is purely a rating exclusion and was not contained in the first version of the Comprehensive General Liability Policy.

There are two distinct schools of thought on the proposition as to whether this particular limitation has any rightful place in the basic policy. Some underwriters reason that the degree of exposure is so varied or inconsistent as not to lend itself to any semblance of standardized rating. Others take the view that virtually every risk has an exposure to legal liability loss arising from damage caused by water, and therefore, in keeping with the concept of broadness of scope of coverage, the preferred mechanics of handling would seem to be that of including the coverage in the basic policy and making appropriate premium charge therefor. In those situations where the protection held no interest to a particular insured, the policy could be specifically endorsed eliminating the coverage. This endorsement would also serve as a visual and continuing reminder that he had chosen not to carry protection against this important exposure to loss.

10 and 11. The final two exclusions have limited application. They are significant only to those insureds performing blasting (certain explosions are also excluded) or who may cause the collapse of or structural damage to a building or may damage or destroy underground property in connection with their excavating, drilling, or similar operations.

The policy drafters contemplated that these two exclusions at the option of an individual company might be incorporated in the basic policy or omitted and handled by an exclusion endorsement unless, of course, it be the intent to afford the coverage. Like exclusion 9, they are purely rating exclusions.

[3] For a precise and complete explanation of the underwriting intent behind these exclusions see an address by Mr. Richard H. Elliott, Manager of the General Liability Division of the National Bureau of Casualty Underwriters before the Insurance Seminar in Eugene, Oregon, June 19, 1957 and entitled "How Comprehensive Is the Comprehensive General Liability Policy."

Minimum Policy Premiums and Comprehensive Coverage Charge

As initially conceived and introduced, the Comprehensive Liability Insurance Policy program contemplated minimum policy premiums of $100 for bodily injury and $50 for property damage. These amounts applied to standard limits in the CGL and also to the Comprehensive Automobile Liability Policy (CAL). The rules governing the Comprehensive Liability Policy (CL—the combination contract) logically stipulated the *sum* of the two separate policy minima, namely, $200 for bodily injury and $100 for property damage at standard limits.

The reasoning seems to have been that the writing of comprehensive liability insurance should be confined to those insureds whose exposures produced a sufficiently large policy premium to justify the expense both of a thorough initial risk survey and policy terminal audit. As might be expected, these minima, however logical the reason therefor, quickly underwent "surgery." Competitive practices of insurers and the popular demand for these most appealing covers on the part of proprietors of small businesses were responsible for the more lenient qualifications. Currently, an annual policy minimum of $25 is stipulated for Comprehensive General Liability insurance, which minimum is not subject to adjustment for (1) increased limits of liability, (2) any term discount for policies written for a term in excess of one year, or (3) modification under any rating plan. No minimum premium is applicable to the Comprehensive Automobile Liability Policy, or the Automobile section of the combined (CL) contract.

Also, in the beginning much sales fanfare was accorded to the so-called "unknown hazards" feature of this policy. Many people in the business presumed that the comprehensive coverage special premium charge was assessed for this feature. In actuality, it was generally felt that in order to avoid allegations of unfair discrimination, it was necessary to charge more for this broadened comprehensive coverage than an insurer would obtain for the sum of the various single covers. This premium surcharge was fixed at 1 percent of the aggregate premium of the policy, as otherwise developed, subject to a bodily injury minimum of $10.00 and $5.00 for property damage standard limits.

A second reason for the added premium was the realization among underwriters that irrespective of the conscientiousness with which surveys of exposures and audits of insureds' records were conducted, certain exposures would, from time-to-time, be overlooked. The additional premium of 1 percent was viewed as necessary additional income to enable an insurer to meet this type of loss. Here again, these minima gradually gave ground before competitive trade practices and were entirely discarded at the time of the latest manual revisions issued by the National Bureau of Casualty Underwriters and Mutual Insurance Rating Bureau.

Alluding further to the "unknown hazard," this term has largely proven to be a misnomer. Experience with the program has developed very few situations that can truly be categorized as stemming from an "unknown hazard." The more practical label would seem to be the unrecognized, undetected, overlooked, or forgotten hazard. The automatic coverage given by the policy is, of course, a very important and appealing feature, but even so current rating rules do not require the assessment of any special premium for it.

COMPREHENSIVE AUTOMOBILE LIABILITY POLICY

The broad field of automobile insurance will be dealt with in Chapters 37–39. Accordingly, only a reference is made here to the fact that all automotive insurable hazards of a particular risk can be insured under a Comprehensive Automobile Liability Policy—properly extended by endorsement to also include various physical damage perils. It is a fine and attractive contract worked out with the same meticulous care accorded the Comprehensive General Liability Policy.

COMPREHENSIVE LIABILITY POLICY

This insurance contract provides the broadest scope of protection against liability claims thus far devised. It has been matched only by certain manuscript type or individually tailored covers and it is steadily growing in popular appeal. The full range of coverage features contemplated by the separate Comprehensive General Liability Policy (CGL) and by the Comprehensive Automobile Liability Policy (CAL) are combined under this (CL) deluxe cover.

A single insuring clause for all bodily injury liability, and another for all property damage liability are feasible, although most policy drafters prefer to retain the coverage format followed in the two separate Comprehensive Automobile and General Liability Policies. It is not unusual, however, to find only one bodily injury insuring agreement employed. Understandably, the policy language can be considerably simplified where two rather than three or four coverage agreements are involved. Many insurers think this advantage is outweighed by the greater flexibility possible with separate insuring agreements applicable to automotive hazards and to miscellaneous liability hazards—albeit separate agreements do materially complicate the phrasing of the several tracking exclusions.

It is not unusual to find an insured purchasing the full complement of coverages, even though at time of policy issue he does not own any automobiles or, conversely, has no miscellaneous liability exposures. For example, a church body or the owner of real estate might choose to pay a nominal premium for non-owned automobile exposures plus the comprehensive feature charges. This choice is made against the possibility that some day it (or he) might be enjoined in a claim growing out of the use of an automobile in its (or his) behalf, although not specifically authorized, by a caretaker, refuse hauler, or someone else. Selection of the Comprehensive Liability Policy is accordingly highly recommended as always being in the best interest of the insuring public.

ADDITIONAL POINTS ABOUT THE POLICIES DISCUSSED

Before attention is turned to the Comprehensive Personal Liability Policy and related contracts, several observations can be made about the three policies already described.

Personal Injury versus Bodily Injury

The standard insuring phraseology of each of the three policies reviewed limits the coverage to *bodily injury* as distinguished from *personal injury*. The latter term is, of course, far broader in that it would encompass such additional torts as libel, slander, invasion of privacy, undue familiarity, mental anguish, alienation of affections, discrimination, false arrest or false imprisonment, or wrongful eviction. Understandably, underwriters have been hesitant to offer coverage widely on a full *personal injury* basis (and in some situations it might even contravene public policy to do so), preferring to determine what the potential exposure might be on a risk-to-risk basis and negotiating an appropriate additional premium for the broadened coverage.

Caused by Accident versus Occurrence

Both the bodily injury and property damage liability insuring clauses of comprehensive liability policies (except in the Comprehensive Personal Liability and Farmer's Comprehensive Personal Liability Policies) are framed on a *caused by accident* basis. As used for liability insurance purposes, *accident* is generally interpreted to mean a sudden, unexpected, and undesigned event identifiable both as to time and place. It has become rather commonplace for underwriters to expand the bodily injury insuring clause to an occurrence basis. (See Chapter 32 for a discussion of this point in respect to schedule liability policies.) In fact, some insurers have adopted it as their standard policy language for bodily injury. Claims growing out of sickness, disease, inhalation of noxious fumes, noise, radiation damage, exposure to contagious disease or harmful dusts, or professional misfeasance or nonfeasance are clearly considered as being covered under an *occurrence basis,* whereas considerable uncertainty might prevail under the *caused by accident* wording.

Occurrence Basis Property Damage Far-reaching

Substitution of *occurrence* for the three little words of *caused by accident* seems quite another matter, however, in respect to property damage liability. It may bring within the purview of the coverage a host of situations which have heretofore been viewed purely as business risks. Thus noxious fumes emitted from a manufacturing plant which gradually damage or deteriorate surrounding real or personal property would seem to be covered. Contamination, mistaken identity such as remodeling the wrong house or cutting down the wrong tree, and acts of omission such as failure to connect an alarm or sprinkler system or to provide sufficient heat are additional examples. Likewise, if machinery or equipment which an insured installs does not measure up to prescribed specifications and other costly work is involved incident to making the required modifications, it is likely that the property damage cover would be called upon to respond therefor. The standard property damage liability insuring clause does not limit coverage to tangible property. Therefore, the granting of undefined or unmodified *occurrence basis* property damage coverage might involve a carrier in such far-reaching things as patent or copyright infringements, erroneous or inaccurate investment advice, faulty structural design, or miscellaneous property loss due to error or omission. While such hazards are proper subjects for insurance protection, they lend themselves to specialized handling and a full understanding between the contracting parties as to precisely what is to be covered, rather than being swept in unwittingly under a legal liability instrument and quite likely without adequate premium recompense.

Worldwide Territorial Provision Timely

Present policies (except Personal or Farmer's Comprehensive Policies) customarily extend coverage only to accidents occurring in the United States, its territories, its possessions, or Canada. While this limitation was originally inserted in deference to the difficulty which companies might encounter in defending an insured in some remote corner of the world, it is highly unrealistic in the face of current business intercourse. Whether or not a business concern sells or distributes its products abroad, more than likely some items will find their way beyond the territorial scope contemplated under the policy. They may be components installed in another manufacturer's product which in turn is sold abroad; they may be transported abroad as supplies or equipment for our armed forces; or they may be carried along by world travelers. With the existing speed and efficiency of worldwide communications, it would seem that American insurance companies could readily arrange for proper investigation and adequate defense of claims growing out of an accident irrespective of where it happened. American underwriters have sometimes voiced fear of prejudice on the part of a foreign tribunal in assessing damages against their insureds, and therefore, when considering extension of coverage beyond the United States and Canada, have stipulated that they will only be obligated to defend cases brought in a court of U.S. jurisdiction. No such proof of excessive awards exists. In fact, those few United States insurers which do transact a worldwide business confirm what English and European companies have oft reported, namely, that the potential value of a liability claim is generally higher in this country than elsewhere in the free world.

The time seems past due for companies to establish prompt investigative facilities and competent defense and adjustment counsel in behalf of American insureds wherever they may become involved.

Company's Exclusive Right to Settle Claims Examined

An auxiliary insuring agreement contained in all three comprehensive liability policies obligates the insurer to defend any suit brought against the insured and also grants to it the right to "make such investigation, negotiation and settlement of any claim or suit as it deems expedient." This time-honored exclusive right reserved to the company to settle claims is viewed as being of the utmost importance to it, and is founded on the premise that since it is the carrier's funds which are at stake in a lawsuit, its opinions as to defense or settlement should govern.

However, this concept is being subjected to some challenging of late, particularly by large corporate buyers of insurance. Their dissatisfaction is twofold, centering first in the product's liability area, and secondarily, in concern over the impact that too liberal claims settlements will ultimately have on their insurance costs. Firms which spend large sums in creating a favorable corporate image and in establishing a reputation for the quality of their products might be entirely justified in objecting to disposal of a claim under circumstances which could impair their hard won prestige. As already suggested, this situation is most likely to arise in connection with the manufacture and sale of products. Since a favorable reputation for a firm's wares is as important to it as is a fine professional standing to a doctor or lawyer, it is argued that an insured's consent to settlement should be solicited. The premise perhaps becomes more controversial or strained when it revolves only around future premium costs, for a recalcitrant or unrealistic policyholder could severely prejudice an adjuster's handling of a claim if he had it within his power to block a settlement. On the other side of the coin, however, rests the acknowledged fact that for those insureds who buy their coverage subject to a retrospective rating plan, or whose premiums are sufficient to qualify them for largely *self–premium rating*, every claim's payment either pushes up their insurance cost or reduces the amount of return premium they might otherwise receive.

In recognition of the powerful considerations pro and con this proposition, certain students of the insurance process have suggested that the enlightened approach would be to amend the insuring clause so as to make it obligatory upon the carrier to obtain the written consent of its insured prior to compromising or settling a product's liability claim. If the parties cannot agree as to whether continued resistence or settlement of the claim is preferable, then they shall choose a mutually acceptable arbiter who after evaluating the facts will attempt to compose the two viewpoints; failing that, he must cast his vote on one side or the other. If he agrees with the insured, then the company must continue to defend. If he favors the insurer, then the insured must bear that portion of any resultant court verdict or subsequent settlement outlay which is in excess of the amount for which the case could have been settled at the time that the arbiter was engaged.

No such Solomon solution appears possible in establishing the impact which claims payments have on an insured's ultimate premium costs. In the instance of very large risks, their premiums are substantially and quite directly tied to the number of claims incurred and the aggregate cost of settlement thereof—loaded for company expenses, premium taxes, a small insurance charge, and a factor for contingencies and profit. Such an insured has a very real and immediate interest in the claims adjustment philosophy and practices of his carrier and in urging them to resist to the utmost. On the other side of this particular coin is the fact that a professional full-time adjuster is a far better judge of what is fair and practical in claims handling than is even the most conscientious insured.

Composite Rating

Despite the superiority of the blanket coverage concept employed in the several comprehensive liability contracts, no change is introduced into the rating bases utilized in the various separate liability policies discussed in Chapters 32 and 33. Thus area, frontage, admissions, number of elevators, gross sales, payroll, contract price, number of and use of motor vehicles, and hired car cost all play their appropriate part in developing the total premium for the comprehensive coverage. Utilization of these various rating bases normally produces the most accurate pairing of hazard insured with premium charged. Nevertheless, many persons become restive with the complexity of premium calculations and statistical effort which the rating entails. Also, they deplore the absence of uniformity in classifying the various underwriting exposures.

For risks which develop a worthwhile premium, the ultimate premium may be structured to a single rating base. The label given to this technique is "Composite Rating." It involves simply determining the actual exposures over a given 12-month period on the conventional underwriting bases and applying thereto the several manual rates and minimums to produce an indicated premium for the risk. All other rating considerations such as experience rating, fleet discount, and graded expense discount keyed to size of risk are taken into account to produce the final comprehensive policy premium. Once this is ascertained, the insured has a free choice of whatever single rating basis seems most appealing and logical to him. Gross sales, total payroll, or payrolls subject to social security tax withholding are often selected. The indicated total premium as computed on the standard rating bases is divided by sales or payroll to produce a composite rate.

THE "WRAP UP" UNDERWRITING CONCEPT

Recently, a concept—called "wrap up"—has received considerable attention. The term is used to indicate a broad and coordinated plan of insurance coverages and premiums applicable to a single large risk project. The term usually applies to multiple insurable interests. For example, the insurance coverages for a group of insureds involved in a large construction project will be "wrapped up" in one big package. The owner, the general contractor, and all subcontractors may be so covered for workmen's compensation, combination automobile and general liability, and even, in some cases, fidelity plus builder's risk and contractors' equipment. In some respects this concept embodies the very essence of the comprehensive approach.

Mixed and sometimes quite strong viewpoints both pro and con exist within the insurance community as to the propriety, or even legality, of combining under one set of policies protection for the diverse interests of a project owner, the general contractor, and various subcontractors. However, the weight of logic seems clearly to rest with those supporting the "wrap up" concept. It offers advantages of (1) centralized purchasing of the several insurances from a single insurer with the concomitant size of risk premium discount, (2) elimination of overlaps or avoidance of gaps in coverage or limits of liability, (3) a unified and effective approach to accident prevention and claims handling, and (4) premium savings due to the elimination of hold-harmless and contingent liability coverage requirements.

COMPREHENSIVE PERSONAL LIABILITY POLICY

The Comprehensive Personal Liability Policy does for the individual what the Comprehensive General Liability Policy does for the proprietor of a business. Every individual is faced with nonbusiness potential liability 24 hours a day and the Comprehensive Personal Liability Policy is specifically designed to insure all such risk. It is perhaps the ultimate, or very close to it, in legal liability covers. The bodily injury and property damage features are incorporated into one insuring clause and a single limit of liability applies to each occurrence. The full coverage of the policy extends not only to the named insured, but also, if a resident of his household, to his spouse, the relatives of either, and any other person under the age of 21 in the care of an insured. With respect to animals and watercraft owned by an insured, the policy also covers any person or organization having custody or possession thereof with the permission of the owner; likewise, with respect to farm tractors and equipment, either animal-drawn or self-propelled, employees are included as additional insureds.

For a flat premium not subject to audit, it covers what it was formerly necessary to insure under half a dozen separate policies. An individual's liability for personal acts, including sports activities; residence premises; premises in which an insured is temporarily residing; cemetery lots; vacant land; ownership of dogs or other animals on or off the premises; use of saddle animals on a highway or elsewhere; power lawn mowers; motorized golf carts; canoes, rowboats and power boats equipped with motors of small horsepower; employer's liability to caddies, fishing or hunting guides, and to residence employees—all these and more are covered at a nominal flat premium. Also, an insured's activities as a trustee member of a board or committee of a religious, charitable, or civic organization is protected. Pleasure boats utilizing relatively large horsepower and relatively large sailboats may be covered by special endorsement of the policy and the payment of an additional premium. Many owners of these larger boats, however, prefer to insure their risk under a special marine policy obtained from a knowledgeable marine underwriter. Such contracts normally provide the broadest possible coverage on the boat hull, as well as liability coverage (protection and indemnity) under the maritime laws.

The operation of automobiles away from the insured's premises; ownership or operation of the larger and more powerful boats; the insured's ownership of "business property," or accidents arising out of "business pursuits"—which is to say the practice of his occupation, profession, or trade—constitute the principal limitations on the scope of coverage of this policy.

Voluntary medical payments up to a limit of $250 per person are extended in connection with any bodily injury covered by the policy, and as the expression implies, this feature operates irrespective of the question of an insured's legal liability.

Physical damage to property is another important feature of the Comprehensive Personal Liability Policy. It was added in 1961 and covers damage or destruction of property *of others* up to $250 provided it is not caused intentionally by an insured over 12 years of age.

Recently the coverage has been further broadened without additional premium charge to include liability for fire, explosion, smoke or smudge damage to property of others while in the insured's care, custody, or control. This has significance particularly in connection with an insured who rents his home from someone else, and it also includes the renting of vacation quarters and temporary occupancy of hotel or motel rooms. Contractual liability now applies to liability of others assumed by the insured under written contract so that the policyholder has coverage if he signs a hold harmless agreement in connection with the renting of power tools, power equipment, self-powered golf carts, and such.

The coverage is framed on an *occurrence basis* and is applicable to losses occurring anywhere in the world. *Personal injury* as distinguished from *bodily injury* is not extended.

No one should be without this important, extremely broad and reasonably priced insurance contract. Many feel that it is the biggest bargain available in insurance protection today. The identical coverage may be obtained as a part of the several Homeowners Policy forms.

FARMER'S COMPREHENSIVE PERSONAL LIABILITY POLICY

The Farmer's Comprehensive Personal Liability Policy follows closely the coverage granted under the Comprehensive Personal Liability Policy with a few changes especially designed to meet the exposure of a farmer —including his business liability in connection with his occupation of farming.

Like the CPL Policy, it covers the named insured, his spouse, relatives of either, other residents of his household, and any other person under the age of 21 in the care of the insured. With respect to animals and watercraft owned by the insured, it covers the liability of any person or organization legally responsible therefor. With respect to farm tractors and trailers and self-propelled or animal-drawn farm implements, any employee is considered an additional insured while operating such equipment. Like the CPL Policy, it is a single limit policy covering both bodily injury and property damage under one insuring clause.

Products liability insurance is afforded on farm products, including coverage on farm stands for the sale of the farmer's produce, even though the stands may be away from the farm premises. Animal collision insurance can be included for a small charge. It covers loss of livestock caused by collision on public highways of such livestock with vehicles owned by others. It would not, however, apply to such animals while being transported.

Coverage for custom farming can be insured at an additional premium if the insured performs such work for others under contract and for a charge. If such activity is only incidental, such as neighborly exchange of work, it is covered without charge. Employer's liability insurance for farm labor is a very important and often substantial hazard for farmers and is not covered unless it is declared and the proper premium is paid thereon. However, the basic policy covers the employer's liability to casual employees such as fishing or hunting guides and residence or domestic type employees—the same as is done in the CPL Policy.

The Farmer's Comprehensive Personal Liability Policy, like the CPL Policy, may be issued for periods of one, three, or five years.

STOREKEEPER'S LIABILITY POLICY

The Storekeeper's Liability Policy is especially designed for retail merchants and may be issued for many types of retailers. It is a comprehensive policy in its concept, affording both bodily injury and property damage coverage via a single insuring agreement for accidents arising out of the operation of a retail store. The premium for the entire coverage—premises liability, products liability, and medical payments—is determined by the single factor of area of the premises. Parking areas used in connection with the store premises (if no charge is made for parking); booths or exhibits at fairs or expositions; and premises not owned by the insured, but which are used temporarily for meetings, employees' picnics, or other recreation activities all fall within the scope of the basic coverage. Newly acquired store premises are automatically covered subject to the requirement that notice thereof be given to the company within 30 days and appropriate additional premium charge be paid. Contractual liability is covered, as defined, and products liability and completed operations hazards are also insured in about the same manner as under the Comprehensive General Liability Policy with one important exception, namely, that it does not apply to gas or equipment operated by gas for heat or power or involving the installation and service of such. An exclusion which probably has broader import is that pertaining to elevators. No provision is made for insuring an elevator under the Storekeeper's Liability Policy even at additional premium. There are a number of retail enterprises which by either the nature or scope of their operations do not lend themselves to coverage under this specialized policy. Examples include auction stores, barber or beauty shops, department stores, drug stores, and supermarkets. Reference to the Storekeeper's Liability Policy manual should be made for the complete list and other qualifying rules.

COMPREHENSIVE LIABILITY AS A SECTION OF MULTI-PERIL POLICIES

A wide variety of multiple-peril policies designed for the commercial risk and combining several types of liability insurance with various property hazards coverage has recently made its appearance. In retrospect, one may conclude that this development was an inevitable one following the introduction of the Homeowners Policies a decade ago and their remarkable acceptance in the market place. These new commercial forms are thoroughly considered in subsequent chapters (see Part VI). It seems sufficient here merely to point up the fact that the several comprehensive liability covers are destined increasingly to be "packaged" with property and crime hazards. Harking back to the definition of "comprehensive," one must notice that the adjective does not relate exclusively to legal liability insurance. The concept is employed in connection with other broad forms of insurance protection, namely, comprehensive crime bonds and comprehensive material damage coverages. Recently several insurers have given the title "*Comprehensive Business Policy*" to their broadest and most flexible combination property-liability package contract. It would appear that in time this label will attain the same preeminence for insurances applicable to commercial enterprises as the Homeowners Policy enjoys in the personal insurance field.

SUGGESTED READINGS

Comprehensive General Liability Insurance Rules for Business Operations and Comprehensive Automobile Liability Insurance Rules (Supplement to the Automobile Casualty Manual and Manual of Liability Insurance). New York: National Bureau of Casualty Underwriters.

ELLIOTT, RICHARD H. "How Comprehensive Is the Comprehensive General Liability Policy?" A paper presented June 19, 1957, at Eugene, Oregon, before an Insurance Seminar sponsored by the Institute of Oregon Underwriters. Reprints through National Bureau of Casualty Underwriters.

Fire, Casualty, and Surety Bulletins. Cincinnati: National Underwriters Co. Public Liability Section.

KULP, CLARENCE A. *Casualty Insurance.* 3d ed. New York: Ronald Press Co., 1956. Chapter 10.

Series of articles in *Annals of Society of Chartered Property and Casualty Underwriters.* Vol. 10 (January, 1958):

COX, HERBERT C. "A New Look at the Comprehensive General Liability Policy," p. 61.

ADAMS, JOHN R. "Policy Exclusions," pp. 62–65.

LENTZ, ROBERT P., JR. "Additional Coverages," pp. 66–69.

RUBLEE, ROBERT M. AND SPITZMILLER, GEORGE E. "The Problem of Adequate Limits," pp. 70–73.

COX, HERBERT C. "Rating Considerations and Presentation of a Broadened Contract," pp. 74–79.

NORTHERN CALIFORNIA CHAPTER. "Improving the Comprehensive Liability Policy," pp. 80–92.

Chapter 35

WORKMEN'S COMPENSATION LEGISLATION

BY JOHN W. HALL

From the viewpoint of the individual worker, the possibility of his having to leave employment because of injury or illness generally presents the greatest risk to his well-being and that of his family. Even relatively nonserious injuries and diseases may result in medical care expense, and the more serious disabilities may cause a reduction in, or elimination of, the worker's income or his earning ability.

Injury, illness, and death may result from many causes. Very broadly, and perhaps illogically, in the light of present day thinking, these causes have been classified according to whether or not they emanate from the worker's employment. Workmen's compensation legislation provides for the payment of benefits determined according to law for covered *occupational* injuries or disease incurred by a covered employee *without regard to the fault* of the employer, as a matter of right, with the compensation remedy generally *the exclusive remedy* of the covered employee. The limitation of benefits to occupational injury or disease, and the exclusiveness of the remedy, distinguish compensation from other benefit systems (voluntary or social life and health insurance).[1] The reasons for the limited scope of workmen's compensation laws may be found in history.

DEVELOPMENT OF WORKMEN'S COMPENSATION LAWS

Early Economic and Social Factors

Occupational injury and disease resulting in medical care expense, loss of income, and death are frequent occurrences in an industrial economy.

[1] Even in jurisdictions with "elective" statutes, compensation is the exclusive remedy after the injury or disease has been incurred. Where the employee is not entitled to compensation benefits for his occupational injury or disease, he may have the right to pursue the common law remedies. Further, the statutes of some juris-

Despite rapid and real progress in the fields of prevention, occupational injuries may still account for nearly one half of all accidental injuries each year. Much progress must still be made.

The economic losses from occupational injury and disease became a real threat to the welfare of the individual worker in the eighteenth century as the place of work shifted from the farm and small village shop to the industrial complex.

Prior to the eighteenth century, agriculture, the trades, and the sea were the principal sources of employment. The status of agricultural labor was little better than serfdom. Trade and industry were conducted under the guild system. The master craftsman maintained and trained the apprentice; the guild controlled product prices, wages, hours of work, methods of work, and duties of the master craftsman towards the apprentice and journeyman. From early times, seamen worked under a separate class of rights and duties dependent upon maritime law under the jurisdiction of the courts of admiralty. An injured sailor was entitled to care, cure, maintenance, and wages to the end of his voyage. Thus, it may be seen that prior to the eighteenth century, social and economic factors affecting the worker presented a natural barrier against a suit for damages against a master. However, social justice of the time seemed to include a responsibility of the master for the welfare of his servants and employees.

The advent of the great industrial development in England (beginning in the eighteenth century) and the United States (beginning in the early nineteenth century) radically changed the conditions under which men worked, and raised social questions about the relationship between employer and employee. The "Industrial Revolution" gave birth to new industries and new manufacturing techniques. It brought together great numbers of employees—unskilled, undisciplined, and often selected without regard to character. These employees were exposed to new and unheard-of hazards. Work areas were poorly lighted and poorly ventilated. Workers became fatigued from long hours of work. There was child labor. Labor was plentiful; wages were low. Many managers seemed to consider labor in an economic sense—as a factor of production—ignoring the fact that a man is a human to whom an obligation is owed. Increasingly, the master became a corporate person acting through directors and officers, and the relationship of master and servant ceased to be personal in nature.

The Law of Employers' Liability

As work-incurrêd injuries became more frequent and severe, the question of who should bear the financial burden arose. Prior to the develop-

dictions expressly give the right to sue where the employer fails to insure or otherwise provide payment, or where the employer injures the employee intentionally or through gross negligence. Where the injury was caused by a third party outside the employer-employee relationship, the employee can sue the third party.

ment of workmen's compensation, the injured worker's legal right to obtain indemnification rested in case law.

Case law assumes that the financial burden of damages rests with the injured party unless he can prove that another's fault was the proximate cause of injury. In disputed cases, fault is ascertained in a court of law. If the negligence of the employer is the sole cause of an accident or disease, he is responsible for the resulting damage to the injured or ill worker. (See Chapter 31 for a discussion of negligence.)

Negligence itself involves questions of fact and thus can change as attitudes and standards change. As time passed the application of the negligence concept in employer's liability changed until the point was reached where many courts held that the master owed a legal duty to employees for the exercise of due care in providing: (1) a place of work reasonably safe for the purpose intended; (2) machinery, tools, materials, and appliances reasonably safe in relation to the work to be done; (3) fellow servants reasonably fit, competent, and sober; (4) adequate rules enforced for the safe conduct of the business; and (5) reasonably suitable and sufficient warning of dangers of which the employer is aware and of which the worker is excusably ignorant. A violation of any of these duties constituted negligence on the part of the employer.

The burden of proof of negligence rested with the injured employee. Jobs were scarce, and many workers doubtless felt that any action against the employer might result in unemployment. In many cases the facts of the accident were not easily obtainable; frequently fellow employees were reluctant to testify as witnesses. Most early juries were composed of the employer's peers—the property owners and industrialists. Further, the employer had only to defend himself successfully against the employee's accusations of negligence—a task often not difficult. Case law afforded the employer three defenses which blocked easy recovery by employees for occupational injury:

Defense of Contributory Negligence. If an injured employee contributed to his own injury by his own avoidable act, he could not recover damages from the employer. Even where an employee's injury was a consequence of a violation of an employer's duty, he was not entitled to recover damages if his own negligence (even though relatively minor) was a contributory cause of the injury. It was felt that an employee should not profit from his own lack of care.

Defense of Assumption of Risk. The employer was not held liable for injury to an employee who, knowing the facts with respect to an unsafe condition of the premises or work involved and understanding the risk likely to attend his employment, voluntarily entered into the employment. Stated differently, the employee could not claim damages for injuries arising from his voluntary assumption of the known and ordinary risks of his employment.

Defense of Fellow-Servant Fault. An employer might not be liable for an injury to an employee who, while acting within the scope of his employment or in connection therewith, was injured solely as a result of negligence of a fellow employee. This doctrine was an exception to the established rule of *respondeat superior* under which the employer or master was held responsible to third persons for injuries inflicted by his agents or employees.

Because a right of action on behalf of an employee was personal to him, traditional case law dictated that this right expired with his death. Traditional case law afforded no remedy for death caused by wrongful acts.

Employers' Liability Statutes

The tragic results produced by these case law rules during a period of rapidly rising occupational injury and death rates brought about public dissatisfaction. In too many cases, there was either a grossly inadequate award or no award at all. In a few cases awards were much too high. Even though juries tended gradually to be more sympathetic, the waste, uncertainty, delay, and high cost of law suits rendered the case law remedy of little value as a means of alleviating the financial burden of occupational injury or disease. Gradually, employers' defenses were modified—first by the lenient interpretation of a few courts and later by the incorporation of these court modifications into statutory law. The fellow-servant rule was modified by the courts in a few jurisdictions through the adoption of the *vice-principal rule*, the *superior-servant rule*, and the *con-association rule*.[2]

In a few jurisdictions it was ruled that the injured worker need not assume a hazard of an employer's violation of a safety statute, and the rule of *comparative negligence* was adopted.[3] (See Chapter 31; also see Chapter 37 for application of this concept to automobile liability claims.)

By the end of the nineteenth century employers' liability statutes began to appear. These statutes were designed to accomplish one or more of the following objectives: (1) codification of the case law duties of the employer to the employee; (2) prohibition against employers and employees

[2] *Vice-principal rule.* The duty of the employer to provide a safe place to work, etc., is considered a nondelegable duty or responsibility. The employer is responsible for injuries to workmen caused by the negligence of other employees when such other employee is vested with the responsibility of performing this duty.

Superior-servant rule. The employer is responsible for injuries to workmen caused by the negligence of another employee where such employee is vested with the authority of supervision or direction, that is, has the authority to exercise actual control over the work activities of the injured workmen.

Con-association rule. "Fellow servants are not in common employment unless their duties bring them in association to such a degree that they can exercise influence over each other." See Thomas D. Shurmon and A. A. Redfield, *A Treatise on the Law of Negligence* (6th ed.; New York: Baker, Vourhies, and Co., 1913), Vol. 1, p. 694.

[3] *Comparative negligence.* A modification of the defense of contributory negligence in which consideration was given to the extent to which the negligence of *each* party contributed to the injury: "Where there has been negligence in both the plaintiff and the defendant, still the plaintiff may recover (at least partially) if his negligence was slight and that of the defendant was gross in comparison." Melvin M. Bigelow, *Law of Torts* (8th ed.; Boston: Little, Brown & Co., 1907), p. 187.

entering into contracts relieving the employer of liability for occupational injury and disease as a condition precedent to employment; (3) permission for personal representatives of deceased employees to bring suit for damages where the employee's death was wrongfully caused by the employer; and (4) abrogation or modification of the case law employer defenses. By 1908 nearly all jurisdictions had statutes modifying one or more of the common law defenses, but these modifications were limited in their application. Most commonly, these modifications were aimed at the removal of the fellow-servant fault doctrine and were confined mainly to railroad workers and a few other extra-hazardous occupations.

The Federal Employers' Liability Act of 1908 was applicable to railroad employees engaged in interstate commerce. Hence, even in the most progressive jurisdictions, defects remained in the case law remedy even as modified by employers' liability statutes. In too many instances, it was still necessary for the injured employee to resort to the courts for redress. This situation necessitated a lengthy and involved legal procedure. Trials, re-trials, and appeals were costly and the outcome uncertain. Injured employees were inclined to resort to legal action only where the injuries were particularly serious and where their case seemed clear-cut. Thus, the difficulties which injured employees had in recovering damages placed the burden and cost of their misfortunes directly upon those injured, and these individuals were least able to suffer the burden of the costs involved. Moreover, the occasional spectacularly high judgments rendered many employers also wary of this litigation.

The cost, waste, and delays, as well as the employer-employee antagonisms of litigation, were still present under employers' liability, just as under case law. And, as with the case law, the emphasis still tended to be on the concealment of accidents rather than on attempts to reduce them.

While America was experimenting with legislation designed to modify the results of the case law rules of employers' liability, a far-reaching experiment was taking place in some European countries. Germany took the lead in the early 1880's, and by 1910 virtually all of the countries of Europe had adopted some system of workmen's compensation.

These events did not go unnoticed in the United States. The United States Department of Labor took official notice, in its 1893 publication, of a report on compulsory insurance in Germany. Shortly thereafter, bills following the European models were introduced in several states but failed to gain passage. It became apparent through the unsuccessful attempts of several states to enact workmen's compensation legislation that a thorough study was necessary to determine the needs for compensation systems, their requirements, their relation to the legal system, and, important to employers, their cost. Intensive commission investigation of the problem of occupational disability was the next step.

Some 31 investigatory commissions were established between 1909 and 1913. Nine others were in operation in the next six years. These investigating bodies, through joint conferences, hearings, and intense study, recommended unanimously that employers' liability be abolished. From these investigating committees emerged: (1) a severe indictment of the record of employers' liability legislation, and (2) the foundation for recommendations that later evolved into workmen's compensation laws.

Compensation Evolves

Workmen's compensation legislation involved an entirely new legal concept: *liability without regard to fault.* The cost of occupational injuries and disease was to be assessed against the employer even though he was not negligent or otherwise responsible under case law or employers' liability statutes. The various investigatory commissions developed a consensus that under modern industrial conditions the employment relationship was ample reason for assessing the employer for the cost of compensating workers for occupational injury or disease. Industrial accidents and disease were recognized as inevitable hazards of industry. They were not due to anyone's guilt, but rather to the nature of an industrial economy characterized by long hours, new and complex processes, mechanization, repetitive operations, speed, and the use of toxic materials. Their costs were legitimate costs of production. According to this theory of *occupational risk,* these costs should be shifted forward to the consumer in the price of the product in the same manner as are depreciation and obsolescence.[4] Under this concept of liability without fault both the employee and the employer sacrifice certain rights. The employee gives up his right generally to sue his employer because of covered occupational injury. The employer gives up his defense rights and his rights to resist paying specified benefits for covered occupational injuries suffered by the employee.

The specific objectives of workmen's compensation legislation included:

1. The prompt payment of adequate benefits according to a fixed and predetermined schedule to injured employees or their dependents.
2. The elimination of the costs of litigation to the employee and to society.
3. The establishment of a guarantee of benefit payment because benefits must be secured by a form of "insurance."
4. The promotion of safety and health activities because the employer would observe directly the relationship between loss prevention and loss reduction activities and the cost of workmen's compensation benefits.
5. Provision of medical and rehabilitation services.[5]

---

[4] The economic and social implications of this rationale were sharply criticized, and the principle of *least social cost* evolved as an alternate general justification, that is, compensation was desirable when compared with other remedies because the economic and social costs would be reduced to the minimum.

[5] Herman M. and Anne R. Somers, *Workmen's Compensation* (New York: John Wiley & Sons, Inc., 1954), pp. 27 and 28. Although the provision of medical services and rehabilitation did not arise until after World War I, these important services are now widely considered a part of the objectives of workmen's compensation.

Other by-products which were anticipated from workmen's compensation legislation included the reduction of friction between the employer and employee and the salutary effect upon the burden of public and private relief. Early laws were very limited in scope and failed to meet many of these objectives. The extent to which these objectives are even now achieved is the subject of much discussion today.

Although a few state legislatures enacted narrow compensation acts with low benefits prior to 1908, the Federal Employees' Compensation Act of 1908 providing benefits for civil employees of the federal government and public employees of the District of Columbia (reenacted in 1916 proved to be the turning point. In 1911, 10 states adopted workmen's compensation laws. By 1920 all but six jurisdictions had such laws. These jurisdictions passed laws prior to 1948 and the Longshoremen's and Harbor Workers' Compensation Act was adopted providing benefits for longshoremen and private employees of the District of Columbia.

Because of the exclusiveness of the remedy (after injury), workmen's compensation statutes supplant case law and employers' liability statutes for the great majority of occupational injuries. However, there are still wide areas where responsibility is fixed in the traditional manner:

1. Railroad employees in interstate commerce are covered by the Federal Employers' Liability Act. The Merchant Marine Act (1920) made the Federal Employers' Liability Act applicable to seamen. Under this act, if an employee has a right of action against the employer, the employer may not plead the common law defenses of fellow-servant fault and assumption of risk. Comparative negligence is substituted for contributory negligence.

2. There are many occupations and injury circumstances for which no specific employers' liability legislation exists, but in which a tort action under the case law may still be available. Depending upon the circumstances and jurisdictions, the following generalizations apply:

a) The particular employee is not subject to workmen's compensation coverage because:
   (1) His employment is exempt, or
   (2) The act is elective and has been effectively rejected, or
   (3) The injured worker is not legally defined as an employee, but rather as an independent contractor, partner, etc.

b) The injury sustained is not compensable because:
   (1) It was not caused by employment in the manner defined in the act, or
   (2) It is not a type generally covered.

c) The injury arose under circumstances where the controlling act expressly gives a right to sue, chiefly:
   (1) Where the employer fails to insure or otherwise secure payment, or
   (2) Where the employer injures the employee intentionally or, more commonly, through gross negligence.

d) The injury was caused by a third party outside the employer-employee relationship and the employee pursues his right against such third party.[6]

[6] *Ibid.*, p. 35.

Because of these limitations, many workers are still uncovered by workmen's compensation laws. It is estimated that about 80 percent of the workers in this country are covered.[7]

AN ANALYSIS OF WORKMEN'S COMPENSATION LAWS

One noted authority stated that the "striking feature of the laws of the various jurisdictions is their dissimilarity. . . . American compensation laws differ not only in detail but in every major feature."[8]

Ideally, an analysis of workmen's compensation laws would involve a detailed comparison of the laws of the various jurisdictions. Such a comparison is beyond the scope of this chapter. The following items are particularly important in the consideration of American compensation laws: (1) persons and employments covered, (2) injuries and diseases covered, (3) benefits provided, (4) administrative system, and (5) method of securing benefits.

Persons and Employments Covered

No workmen's compensation law covers all employees or employment. The law of each jurisdiction must be studied to determine which employees come within the act.

Almost without exception, compensation laws apply only to *employees*. Usually an employee is a person who is in the service of another under a contract of hire, express or implied, and who performs service for a valuable consideration. An employee is always an individual.

The law imposes liability upon the employer. An employer may be defined as a person, firm, partnership, association, or corporation. Many of the laws define the functions of an employer by including the terms "employing," "employs," "carrying on any employment," and "employing another in service or under a contract of hire." Generally, the term employment refers to all cases where there is the relationship of master and servant. Independent or subcontractors are not, in the absence of special provisions, considered employees. However, many states make the principal contractor responsible for the payment of compensation to employees of subcontractors unless the subcontractor furnishes satisfac-

[7] Alfred Skolnik, "Workmen's Compensation Payments and Costs," *Social Security Bulletin* (U.S. Department of Health, Education, and Welfare, Social Security Administration, December, 1959). The fact that 20 percent of the total workers are without workmen's compensation for occupational injury and disease does not mean that their losses will be uncompensated. There are many who argue that the case law rights, especially if bolstered by employer liability statutes, present a reasonable possibility of a much larger award than that obtainable under compensation, particularly in those areas where compensation benefits are considered inadequate. In fact, unless compensation laws are liberalized, there may be an increasing tendency to seek ways of utilizing traditional common law remedies.

[8] C. A. Kulp, *Casualty Insurance* (3rd ed.; New York: Ronald Press Co., 1956), p. 93.

tory evidence of workmen's compensation insurance. In numerous states the owner may also be liable.

Compulsory and Elective Laws. Workmen's compensation laws may be either elective, compulsory, or a combination of both. As regards private employment, the laws of 30 jurisdictions are compulsory in nature, that is, compensation is compulsory and is the exclusive remedy for private employment.[9] The remaining 24 laws are elective as regards private employment.[10] According to the 1962 U.S. Chamber of Commerce *Analysis of Workmen's Compensation Laws,* two jurisdictions, Kansas and Texas, have compulsory coverage for specified (and presumably hazardous) employments such as mining or motor bus operation. Under the elective law, the employer and/or employee have/has the right to elect or reject the compensation remedy. Generally, the employer who rejects compensation for his employees is deprived of his case law defenses—contributory negligence, assumption of risk, and fellow-servant fault where employee claims arise. The severity of this provision is such that these laws are virtually compulsory in actual practice. Generally, where the employee rejects compensation in favor of the case law remedy, the common law defenses are restored to the employer. Again, in practice, this option is seldom, if ever, exercised by the employee, since there is little chance he would be employed should he do so. Election is presumed unless the employer (or employee) gives specific notification to the contrary to the employee (employer) and to the proper authorities, prior to injury.

In 18 of the 24 jurisdictions having the elective type of law, compensation is compulsory, at least in part, for public employment.[11] Except for Delaware, Mississippi, and New Hampshire, all jurisdictions having compulsory laws for private employment also have compulsory laws for most public employment. The most frequent exclusions are of elective officials and policemen and firemen having benefits under a separate retirement system. Civilian employees of the federal government are covered on a compulsory basis by the Federal Employers' Compensation Act.

Coverage by Schedule Vis-à-Vis Coverage by Exclusion. Even in jurisdictions having compulsory laws, workmen's compensation statutes

---

[9] Alaska, Arizona, Arkansas, California, Connecticut, Delaware, District of Columbia, Hawaii, Idaho, Kansas, Maryland, Massachusetts, Michigan, Minnesota, Mississippi, Montana, Nevada, New Hampshire, New York, North Dakota, Ohio, Oklahoma, Rhode Island, Utah, Virginia, Washington, Wisconsin, Wyoming, Federal Employees' Compensation Act, and Longshoremen and Harbor Workers' Act.

[10] Alabama, Colorado, Florida, Georgia, Illinois, Indiana, Iowa, Kansas, Kentucky, Louisana, Maine, Missouri, Nebraska, New Jersey, New Mexico, North Carolina, Oregon, Pennsylvania, South Carolina, South Dakota, Tennessee, Texas, Vermont, and West Virginia.

[11] Colorado, Florida, Georgia, Illinois, Iowa, Kentucky, Louisiana, Maine, Nebraska, New Jersey, North Carolina, Oregon, Pennsylvania, South Carolina, South Dakota, Texas, Vermont, and West Virginia.

never apply to all workers in private enterprise. Some types of employment are excluded either because they are not included in a schedule of covered employment or because of a specific exclusion. Several points are made as follows:

1. *Coverage by Schedule.* In 11 states, covered employment, generally only hazardous occupations, is by list or schedule.[12] It was felt that compulsory coverage for hazardous occupations would be constitutional under the state police power since it was a necessary aid to the safety and welfare of the working population. Today, in many of these jurisdictions, this scheduling or listing of extra hazardous employments constitutes a stumbling block to the comprehensive coverage of employees. The situation is analogous to named peril insurance when compared with an "all risk" coverage. However, in some of these jurisdictions, the law refers only to hazardous employments, or to a specific list of hazardous employments, with a blanket reference to all other hazardous employments or all other employments. In such cases, depending upon interpretation, these laws may provide very broad coverage.

2. *Coverage by Exclusion.* The laws of most jurisdictions follow a more liberal approach and cover all private employment with certain exceptions or exclusions. Common exclusions are agricultural, domestic, and casual workers. Eighteen jurisdictions have some coverage of agricultural workers.[13] In most of these jurisdictions, coverage is compulsory. In nine of these jurisdictions, coverage is limited to agricultural workers engaged in power occupations only. The usual exclusion is that of domestic service. Seven jurisdictions provide some coverage.[14]

The laws of 11 jurisdictions exclude coverage for casual workers. The definition of "casual" varies. Some jurisdictions provide that casual employment includes employment that is not in the usual course of the employer's trade, business, profession, or occupation without reference to a period of work. Other jurisdictions exclude only "irregular," "spasmodic," or "non-periodic" employment. The usual exclusion embodies both definitions, that is, the work must be both irregular or nonreoccurring *and* not within the usual course of the employer's trade, business, or profession. Perhaps the most realistic definition of casual is found in Florida and Nevada where casual employment is work con-

---

[12] Illinois, Kansas, Louisiana, Maryland, Montana, New Mexico, New York, North Dakota, Oklahoma, Washington, and Wyoming.

[13] Alaska, Arizona, California, Connecticut, Hawaii, Kentucky, Louisiana, Massachusetts, Minnesota, New Jersey, New York, Ohio, Oklahoma, Puerto Rico, South Dakota, Vermont, Wisconsin, and Wyoming.

[14] California, Connecticut, Massachusetts, New Jersey, New York, Ohio, and Puerto Rico. The Massachusetts law is elective, and California provides coverage for domestic workers employed over 52 hours per week for one employer. New York has a similar division requiring coverage for domestics employed a minimum of 48 hours per week by the same employer in cities or villages of 40,000 or more.

templated to be completed in 10 or fewer days and involving a total labor cost not in excess of $100.

Less common exclusions are employees of public institutions, employees of common carriers engaged in intrastate commerce, and employees engaged in activities peculiar to local jurisdictions. Examples of the last category include part-time baby sitters, cleaning persons, harvest help, vendors or distributors of newspapers, volunteer workers at camps, gardeners, professional athletes, turpentine laborers, in-dwelling members of employer's family, out-workers, airmen, and such.

3. *Numerical Exemptions.* In approximately half of the jurisdictions, employers are exempt from the operations of the workmen's compensation law if they employ fewer than a stipulated number of workers.[15] The range varies from two to fifteen employees, the most common exemption being for employers employing fewer than three workers. In a few jurisdictions, a numerical exemption may not apply to particularly hazardous occupations. The numerical exclusion is found regardless of whether the law of the jurisdiction provides coverage by exclusion or by schedule.

4. *Voluntary Compensation.* Where an employee or employment does not come under the workmen's compensation law of the jurisdiction involved, the laws of many jurisdictions provide that the employer may provide protection voluntarily. Such a *voluntary decision where no previous coverage exists at law* should be distinguished from "elective" coverage in that the employer does *not* lose his case law defenses if he does *not* choose the voluntary coverage. On the other hand, where an employer does so volunteer to come under the terms of the law, the law applies as if it had been made mandatory.[16]

Injuries and Diseases Covered

Even where a worker is in covered employment, he is not eligible for benefits unless he has suffered a loss caused by an occupational injury or disease as defined within the terms of the law.

Occupational Injury. When first conceived, the most dramatic losses were caused by industrial accidents and hence, most early laws provided benefits only for occupational injuries. Even today, because not all occu-

[15] The 29 jurisdictions making no numerical exemption include: Alaska, California, District of Columbia, Hawaii, Idaho, Illinois, Indiana, Iowa, Louisiana, Maryland, Minnesota, Montana, Nebraska, New Jersey, North Dakota, Oregon, Pennsylvania, Puerto Rico, South Dakota, Utah, Washington, West Virginia, Wyoming, and Federal Employees' Compensation Act.

[16] In contrast to voluntarily placing himself under the act, an employer may purchase *voluntary compensation insurance*. Under this form of insurance, the employer secures compensation benefits for those employees not required to be covered under the law. This purchase is a purely voluntary service on the part of the employer and he may discontinue it at any time without formal procedure with the state authority. See the next chapter for more discussion of this point.

pational diseases are covered or because benefits may be less for disease than for injury, it is necessary to define an occupational injury.

Nearly all jurisdictions require that a compensable injury must be accidental. Thus a person who willfully injures himself is not entitled to compensation because the injury is not accidental in the sense indicated. Often, the law will further define accidental injury by stipulating that injuries arising from certain causes are not due to accidents, for instance, intent to injure self or another, intoxication, willful failure to use a safety appliance or observe safety regulations, or failure to perform a duty required by statute.

Few compensation statutes are specific in defining an accident. Originally, the term was intended and interpreted to be limited to injuries which were the result of chance, that is, something fortuitous and unforeseen as contrasted to something designed, planned, or occurring in the normal course of events. Accident was something that was unexpected either as to its happening or to its result, and which occurred with such suddenness as to have a definite and fixed time and place. Because a distinction between accident and disease may seem at times to be unclear or arbitrary, because the law is insufficiently specific, and because of a tendency on the part of the administrative agencies to expand the protection afforded by state compensation laws where the legislature refuses to do so, the definition of accident has received constant expansion and is taking in more and more occupational disabilities which were considered previously as disease.

To be compensable, the laws originally intended that accidental injuries should arise from employment. Most jurisdictions define an occupational injury as one "arising out of *and* in the course of employment." The intent of this provision is to be certain that there is a causal connection between the occupation and the injury. Theoretically, the injury must be related directly to the work of the employee and must occur while he is at work. The statutes of a few jurisdictions further define the intent by stating that injuries are not compensable if caused by third persons for reasons which are personal to such employee, or where the injury was due to willful misconduct. As with the definition of accident, the concept of occupational injury has been expanded by interpretation to include many events perhaps not contemplated originally by those who drafted the law.

Occupational Disease. Occupational disease may be defined as "an injury arising out of employment and due to causes and conditions characteristic of, and peculiar to, the particular trade, occupation, process, or employment, and excluding all ordinary diseases to which the general public is exposed."[17] Today, provision for some coverage of

[17] *State Compensation Laws Bulletin 161* (Washington, D.C.: U.S. Department of Labor, U.S. Government Printing Office, revised, 1960), p. 17.

occupational diseases is included in the laws of all jurisdictions, except Wyoming.[18] The laws of 19 jurisdictions schedule or specifically list diseases which are compensable.[19] Scheduled diseases range from one disease in Alabama and Mississippi to as many as 45 and 47 diseases in Texas and Colorado respectively. The 34 remaining jurisdictions provide substantially full coverage for all occupational diseases either directly in the statute or through interpretation. Under both the schedule and full coverage laws, jurisdictions vary regarding compulsory and elective application. The trend is towards full coverage, with its advantage of automatic extension to new diseases as they appear—such as those caused by radiation.

Benefits Provided

Compensation benefits are available as at least partial indemnification for the medical care expenditures and loss of income arising from occupational injury or disease. Because an injured worker may often be restored to a useful, active, and helpful life (physically and mentally), rehabilitation benefits are increasingly available.[20]

Medical Benefits. The laws of 40 jurisdictions, either by specific statutory requirement or administrative interpretation, provide for medical benefits without limit as to time or dollar amount.[21] The laws of the remaining jurisdictions establish either a maximum benefit duration or a dollar amount limitation, with nine of these jurisdictions providing limited additional benefits with the consent of the administrative agency.[22] Often these limited additional benefits are available in those instances where it is believed that the extra payment will result in a reduction in the period of disability, that is, materially hasten recovery. A few laws provide lower medical care expense benefits for occupational disease than for accidental injury.

---

[18] Mississippi provides protection only for injuries from exposure to ionizing radiation.

[19] Alabama, Arizona, Colorado, Georgia, Idaho, Iowa, Kansas, Louisiana, Maine, Mississippi, Montana, New Hampshire, New Mexico, North Carolina, Oklahoma, South Dakota, Tennessee, Texas, and Vermont.

[20] A few states provide special additional benefits such as: constant attendants, extra benefits for disfigurement, extra benefits to minors illegally employed, and prosthetic devices as needed.

[21] Alaska, Arizona, Arkansas, California, Connecticut, Delaware, District of Columbia, Florida, Hawaii, Idaho, Illinois, Indiana, Maine, Maryland, Massachusetts, Michigan, Minnesota, Mississippi, Missouri, Nebraska, New Jersey, New Mexico, New York, North Carolina, North Dakota, Ohio, Oklahoma, Oregon, Pennsylvania, Puerto Rico, Rhode Island, South Carolina, Texas, Utah, Vermont, Washington, Wisconsin, Wyoming, Federal Employees' Compensation Act, and Longshoremen's and Harbor Workers' Act. In a few of these jurisdictions, full benefits are not payable for certain occupational diseases.

[22] Alabama, Colorado, Georgia, Iowa, Kansas, Kentucky, Louisiana, Montana, Nevada, New Hampshire, New Jersey, South Dakota, Tennessee, Virginia, and West Virginia.

Disability Benefits. The term "disability" has been the subject of varying court interpretation. Depending upon jurisdiction, disability has been held to mean the (1) inability to earn full or part wages, at the work in which the employee was working at the time of injury; (2) inability to perform *any kind of work* which might be obtained; or (3) inability to secure work. The problem arises because the word "disability" is often undefined in the law. Disability is compensated by weekly periodic payments. Given the type of benefit (total or partial disability), the monetary benefit received by the disabled worker varies among the jurisdictions with (1) the compensation rate, usually a percentage of the average weekly wage; (2) the maximum weekly benefit; (3) the maximum term or duration of benefit payment; (4) the maximum aggregated dollar amount; and (5) the length of the waiting period and its retroactive features.

Total Disability. Disability is considered total where employment is rendered impossible. *Permanent* total disability involves the presumption that no future work will be possible. Numerous statutes list certain major injuries such as loss of both legs or feet, both arms or hands, both eyes, or any two important members of the body, as being both permanent and total. Nonspecified injuries or diseases which, in fact, result in total disability are entirely possible and hence are also subject to compensation. *Temporary* total disability, by its nature, permits the possibility of a cure, that is, the employee is unable to work while he is recovering from the injury, but he is expected to recover. Temporary total disability ends when the worker recovers sufficiently to be able to return to work (partial disability benefits may begin at this time). Often, the temporary nature of a disability is unknown and hence benefits for permanent and temporary total disability tend to be identical or very similar, with the benefits for temporary disability ceasing when total disability ceases to exist.

The rate of compensation is usually expressed as a percentage of the average weekly wage received by the disabled worker. This percentage ranges from a low of 50 to a high of 75 with the usual limitation being 66⅔. All jurisdictions impose a maximum payment per week which as of the time of this writing ranged from a low of \$28 per week to a high of \$121.15 per week for total disability. Most laws provide a limit upon the number of weeks that benefits will be paid, varying from 300 to 1,000 weeks for temporary total disability. Increasingly, however, the laws provide permanent total disability benefits for life and temporary total disability benefits for the period of total disability. Some laws provide an additional maximum limit in the form of an aggregate dollar payment, for instance, \$10,000 or \$20,000.

The waiting period, which applies only to disability income benefits, refers to the period of disability after injury which must elapse before compensation benefits begin. All laws but Oregon's provide for a waiting period ranging from two to seven days with the majority of the states requiring a seven-day period. Most laws require that benefits be retroactive to the date of injury if disability continues for a specified length of time ranging from five days to more than seven weeks. In these cases, the waiting period results in no penalty to the employee.

Partial Disability. Partial disability impairs earning capacity, but does not involve a total inability to work. Such partial disability may be preceded by a period of temporary total disability during the healing process. Although the worker cannot go back to his old job, he can often perform or be trained to perform other types of work. *Permanent* partial disability exists when a person has suffered a permanent injury. *Temporary* partial disability exists when a worker is temporarily incapacitated to the extent that he is unable to exercise his full earning capacity.

A schedule of benefits is often provided in the law for those partial disabilities which are presumed to be permanent. Such a schedule sets forth a specified number of weekly payments to be made for particular losses such as an arm, leg, hand, foot, eye, thumb, first finger, second finger, third finger, fourth finger, the sight of one eye, or the hearing of one or both ears. Generally, the payment is a product of the number of weekly payments specified for the specific disability multiplied by the weekly compensation benefit. Often the weekly compensation benefit is expressed as a percentage (66⅔) of the *weekly wage loss* because of partial disability. A maximum dollar benefit per week and an aggregate maximum payment may be expressed in the law. Often the partial disability benefit is paid in addition to the temporary-total disability benefit during the initial period of recovery. It is argued that, by receiving a known benefit, the injured worker can adjust better to his handicap and recover his proper place in industry. Nonscheduled partial disabilities may be either permanent or temporary in nature.

Disability benefit payments are frequently the same for occupational injury and disease as for accidental injury. However, some laws do not pay benefits for partial disability resulting from occupational disease or certain occupational diseases such as silicosis.

Even a brief discussion of disability benefits under workmen's compensation laws would not be adequate without mention of the fact that the laws of 15 jurisdictions make some provision for additional benefits for dependent children. Except where the dependent child is mentally or physically impaired, benefits generally cease at age 18. The amount and condition of benefit vary considerably among states, and in many instances these additional allowances are limited by the fact that the same weekly maximum dollar benefit or the same aggregate maximum dollar benefit is payable whether or not there are dependents.

Death Benefits. In addition to providing funds for the expenses attendant on death, death benefits may be designed to help compensate those who are dependent on the deceased workman. However, the method of determining these benefits does not stipulate that the deceased must previously have provided financial benefit to those entitled to the benefits under the law.

The laws vary considerably among jurisdictions. Benefits are available for widows and dependent children and in a few jurisdictions for dependent parents, brothers, and sisters.

Benefits are usually expressed in terms of a percentage of weekly wages of the deceased worker, subject to a maximum weekly benefit and often to a maximum benefit period. In some states a maximum aggregate dollar benefit is defined. Subject to these limits, the widow's weekly benefit ranges from 35 to 75 percent of the deceased's weekly wage. Although the maximum weekly dollar benefit may remain constant, the percentage of weekly wage may be increased where there are children. Children's benefits generally cease at age 18. In some cases they continue as long as the child is mentally or physically dependent. Often there is a provision under which benefits for the widow cease upon her remarriage.

The compensation laws of every jurisdiction except Oklahoma provide payment for burial expenses subject to a specified maximum amount which ranges from $100 to $1,000.

Rehabilitation. Rehabilitation has been defined as the "restoration of the handicapped workman to the fullest physical, mental, social, vocational, and economic usefulness of which he is capable."[23] This broad definition includes three essential elements: (1) physical-medical rehabilitation or the effort to restore the individual worker as nearly as possible to the state of health which existed prior to the industrial injury or disease; (2) vocational rehabilitation which involves the retraining of the injured worker to perform a new occupational function; and (3) psycho-social rehabilitation which involves, where necessary, the redirection of the individual's conscious and subconscious thought patterns so that he may become better adjusted and able again to perform a useful function for society. All three of these elements, so closely interrelated, involve the services of many competent professional persons.

As indicated previously, the earliest concept of workmen's compensation did not include rehabilitation. Gradually, rehabilitation has come to be considered an important feature of a complete workmen's compensation program. Increasingly, it is recognized that administrative agencies have an important role with respect to the rehabilitation of the injured worker. They are the first to learn of the work-incurred injury or disease and are thus in a position to study the case and make recommendations for rehabilitation. A successful program of rehabilitation, especially physical rehabilitation, must begin soon after the date of injury.

---

[23] Report of the Rehabilitation Committee, International Association of Industrial Accident Boards and Commission, U.S. Bureau of Labor Standards, Bulletin 142, p. 170. As quoted in Kulp, *op. cit.*, p. 113.

Progress in providing adequate rehabilitation services for occupational injury and disease has been slow. Today, the laws of 26 states, the District of Columbia, the Federal Employees' Compensation Act, and the Longshoremen's and Harbor Workers' Act make specific provision for some rehabilitation benefits.[24]

Security for Compensation Benefits. The workmen's compensation law of every jurisdiction requires that the employer must secure the payment of compensation benefits, either through the purchase of insurance in a private insurer or state fund, or by qualifying as a self-insurer, depending upon the jurisdictions in which he operates.

Subsequent Injury Funds. A subsequent injury may be defined as an injury sustained by an employee who has suffered a previous injury such that the disability resulting from the combined effect of both injuries is greater than if there had been no previous injury. In the absence of specific exceptions, the employer in whose employ the second injury is sustained is liable generally for the compensation benefits payable based upon the injured employee's current disability status. The assessment of the total cost of such compensation benefits upon the current employer creates an obstacle to the employment of handicapped persons.

The laws of the majority of the jurisdictions have provisions which limit the liability of the employer to payment for the disability resulting from the second injury considered by itself. "Subsequent injury funds," which provide payment for the additional compensation due because of the combined result of both injuries, have been established in 48 jurisdictions.[25] The laws of 17 jurisdictions have been broadened in order to apply to *any* previous disability rather than only to those disabilities that involve the loss of use of a specified member of the body.

Depending upon the jurisdiction, subsequent injury funds are financed by (1) special appropriation, (2) assessment upon all insurers providing the coverage, (3) specified payments by insurers in cases where a worker has died of occupational injuries without leaving dependents, and (4) a combination of (1) and (3).

Administration

The direct responsibility for administering the various compensation laws rests with either the courts (Alabama, Louisiana, New Mexico, Tennessee, and Wyoming) or an independent commission or board created for the purpose. The principal areas of administration involve the supervision of the election process (in those jurisdictions where compen-

---

[24] Alaska, Arizona, Connecticut, Delaware, Florida, Georgia, Hawaii, Maine, Massachusetts, Minnesota, Mississippi, Missouri, Montana, Nevada, New York, North Dakota, Ohio, Oregon, Pennsylvania, Rhode Island, South Dakota, Utah, Virginia, West Virginia, Wisconsin, Wyoming, and Washington.

[25] The jurisdictions not having such legislation include: Georgia, Louisiana, Nevada, New Mexico, and Virginia.

sation is elective), the continual evaluation of the law with a view toward legislative improvement, the supervision (direct or indirect) of the reports of occupational injury or disease and claim payments, the supervision (direct or indirect) of rehabilitation programs where applicable, and the investigation and decision of claims in dispute.

Generally, in order to sustain a valid claim, the employee must give notice of injury or disease to the employer within a stipulated period of time following the accident or exposure. The employer must then report the event to the proper agency.

Where claims are uncontested, payments are effected either directly or by agreement. Under the direct payment procedure, scheduled benefits are paid directly to the worker by the employer (or his insurer) even though the recipient of the payments has not agreed formally to the benefit. Should the injured worker or his dependents fail to receive their legal benefits, the administrative agency will investigate the claim.

Under the agreement system, the worker and employer (or his insurer) agree upon a settlement before payment is made. In a few jurisdictions this agreement must be approved by the administrative agency.

Where claims are contested, the administrative agency may appoint a referee or hearing officer who will hear the case and render a decision. The decision of the referee or hearing examiner may be reviewed on appeal by either party to the administrative commission or board, an appeals board, or the courts. The administrative commission or board usually has exclusive jurisdiction over the determination of facts with final appeal to the courts limited to questions of law.

SUGGESTED READINGS

CHEIT, EARL F. *Injury and Recovery in the Course of Employment.* New York: John Wiley & Sons, Inc., 1961.

———, AND GORDON, MARGARET S. (eds.). *Occupational Disability and Public Policy.* New York: John Wiley & Sons, Inc., 1963.

JACOBS, CARL N. "The Present Status and the Future of Workmen's Compensation Laws—The Viewpoint of Management." *Industrial Medicine and Surgery* (March, 1961), pp. 119–23.

JAFFEE, A. J. (ed.). *Workmen's Compensation and Vocational Rehabilitation.* New York: Bureau of Applied Social Research, Columbia University, 1961.

KULP, CLARENCE A. *Casualty Insurance.* 3d ed. New York: Ronald Press Co., 1956. Chaps. 5, 6.

LANG, FRANK. *Workmen's Compensation Insurance—Monopoly or Free Competition?* Homewood, Ill.: Richard D. Irwin, Inc., 1947.

SMEDLEY, LAWRENCE. "The Crisis in Workmen's Compensation," *Washington Insurance Newsletter, Inc.*, No. 716 (September 23, 1963).

SOMERS, HERMAN M. AND ANNE R. *Workmen's Compensation.* New York: John Wiley & Sons, Inc., 1954.

State Workmen's Compensation Laws. Washington, D.C.: U.S. Department of Labor, revised May, 1960.

Threat to Survival of the State Workmen's Compensation System. Chicago and New York: American Mutual Insurance Alliance and Association of Casualty and Surety Companies, 1962.

UNITED STATES CHAMBER OF COMMERCE. *Analysis of Workmen's Compensation Laws,* 1962 as amended.

UNITED STATES DEPARTMENT OF LABOR. *Proceedings, International Association, 66 Industrial Accident Boards and Commissions.* Washington, D.C.: U.S. Government Printing Office, 1913–1962.

Chapter 36

WORKMEN'S COMPENSATION AND EMPLOYERS' LIABILITY INSURANCE

BY GEORGE F. REALL

The subject of the Workmen's Compensation and Employers' Liability Insurance Policy is treated in this chapter so as to have as much practical value as possible. It will, of necessity, be limited as to detail and will be focused on fundamentals, leaving to the reader the task of inquiring into authoritative sources for answers to his particular questions. The source books of the basic rules and procedures applicable to the underwriting of a workmen's compensation risk are the workmen's compensation and employers' liability insurance manuals used by rating and statistical organizations having jurisdiction over this type of insurance. For the purposes of this chapter, the publication of the National Council on Compensation Insurance[1] will be used and will be referred to simply as "the manual."

Workmen's compensation and employers' liability insurance is reviewed in this chapter in three fundamental aspects: policy and coverage, classifying the risk and determining the premium, and experience rating.

POLICY AND COVERAGE

Workmen's compensation insurance is afforded by a standard "Workmen's Compensation and Employers' Liability Policy" the provisions of which are in general use by insurance companies throughout the United States. Two basic coverages are afforded: "Coverage A" provides work-

[1] The National Council on Compensation Insurance is a statistical and ratemaking organization for workmen's compensation and employers' liability insurance. Its membership is composed of both stock and mutual carriers, as well as reciprocal insurers and a small number of state funds. At present the Council is qualified in 24 states as a rating organization and is qualified in 13 states as an advisory organization. In some of the advisory states the Council assists independent rating bureaus. Such bureaus are found in 13 states, and perform essentially the same functions as the National Council, but their jurisdiction is confined to individual states.

men's compensation benefits, and "Coverage B" provides insurance for the employer's liability to his employees in circumstances where the latter are able to maintain actions at law. (See Appendix F.)

One of the basic concepts of the standard policy is that it provides statewide workmen's compensation and employers' liability coverage for all operations of the insured in the state designated in the policy. Coverage is made applicable in a given state by simply designating that state in Item 3 of the Declarations page. This entry automatically activates the coverage afforded by the policy, including (1) complete workmen's compensation coverage for all employees subject to the workmen's compensation law, and for all operations at all locations in the state or states listed, and (2) employers' liability coverage to take care of the occasional situation where the injury is not covered by the workmen's compensation law and the employer may be subject to common law liability. The combination of these two coverages is intended to provide the employer with virtually complete protection against all liability for occupational injury and disease arising out of the employment relationship.

Coverage A

Coverage A provides that the carrier agrees to pay promptly when due "all compensation and other benefits required of the insured by the workmen's compensation law." This is a sweeping engagement to meet the employer's workmen's compensation obligations to his employees throughout the state without regard to location or type of operation except as otherwise qualified in the exclusions.

The exclusions applicable to Coverage A are the following:

1. Exclusion (*a*), which provides that "the policy does not apply to any operations with respect to which the insured has qualified as a self-insurer."
2. Exclusion (*b*), which states that "this policy does not apply unless required by law or described in the Declarations, to domestic employment or to farm or agricultural employment." These occupations are commonly excluded from the coverage of workmen's compensation laws, and are the only two classes of employment not automatically covered under the policy.

Where permitted by law, other limitations may be made upon the broad workmen's compensation coverage afforded under Coverage A, but an endorsement is required in order to effect such limitations. The most common endorsement of this type is one which excludes certain locations of the employer from the coverage afforded by the policy. This type of endorsement, of course, can only be utilized in those states where it is permissible to insure by locations. At this point it should also be noted that the rules of the manual require that *with respect to any one location*, the policy must apply to all operations.

Many of the conditions contained in the workmen's compensation policy are typical of those appearing in a liability policy. There are two, however, which are peculiar to Coverage A. Condition 8 entitled "Statutory Provisions" sets forth some of the typical provisions in workmen's compensation laws which are required to be made a part of any workmen's compensation policy. For example, the first provision is that the company shall be directly and primarily liable to any person entitled to the benefits of the workmen's compensation law. Thus, a unique feature of the compensation policy is that the company is primarily liable to someone other than the insured. Another important provision in Condition 8 is the statement that all of the provisions of the workmen's compensation law shall remain a part of the policy as fully and completely as if written therein. This incorporates the statutory language of the workmen's compensation law into the policy by reference. Condition 16 states that terms of the policy which are in conflict with the provisions of the workmen's compensation law are amended to conform to such law. It is apparent, therefore, that the foregoing provisions are necessary in order to preserve the policy as an effective instrument for affording coverage throughout the country. This technique automatically takes into account differences in workmen's compensation laws of the several states.

Coverage B

Coverage B provides that the carrier agrees:

> To pay on behalf of the insured all sums which the insured shall become legally obligated to pay as damages because of bodily injury by accident or disease, including death at any time resulting therefrom, sustained in the United States of America, its territories or possessions, or Canada by any employee of the insured arising out of and in the course of his employment by the insured, either in a state designated in Item 3 of the Declarations or in operations necessary or incidental thereto.

Why is there any need for employers' liability insurance when the workmen's compensation laws are so broad in their scope of coverage? It is true that employers' liability claims are a relatively small percentage of the total losses incurred by the companies. Nevertheless, some such losses do occur and they can be costly. Furthermore, the fact that they are few in number means that the inclusion of this coverage in the workmen's compensation policy produces a very small impact on the cost of the policy.

There are two types of action under Coverage B. First, there are the cases where a direct action is brought by an employee against his employer. Second, there are cases where a third party, who has been held liable to the employee in an action at law on account of his injuries, in turn seeks indemnity from the employer. The direct action under Coverage B is most likely to occur in a situation (1) where the employee is within a class of employees excluded from or rejecting the compensation act, or (2) where the particular type of injury is not covered by the act. Injuries under the jurisdiction of another state or under federal jurisdiction, are also examples of a possibility of a direct employer's liability action.

Another instance of direct action under Coverage B is the case where a husband or wife sues the employer for loss of consortium. The purpose of Coverage B is to fill these occasional gaps in coverage.

The third-party "liability over actions" against the employer to which Coverage B applies are specifically described in that portion of Condition 9 which provides for the coverage of "damages for which the insured is liable by reason of suits or claims brought against the insured by others to recover the damages obtained from such others because of such bodily injuries sustained by employees of the insured arising out of and in the course of their employment." The type of case contemplated here has become of increasing importance, particularly in the field of maritime law.[2]

Exclusions (*a*) and (*b*) mentioned above apply to both Coverage A and Coverage B. In addition, four exclusions pertain to Coverage B alone. Exclusion (*c*) excludes contractual liability. Exclusion (*d*) excludes certain liabilities involving employment of persons in violation of law. Exclusion (*e*) is a limitation upon the time within which a disease claim may be made. Exclusion (*f*) prevents any overlap between Coverage A and Coverage B by excluding from the scope of Coverage B any workmen's compensation or similar obligations.

Workmen's compensation insurance is unusual in that it provides an "open-end" coverage, that is, without a dollar limit as in most insurance policies. In other words, a company underwriting this liability promises that it will pay all indemnity benefits, subject to the individual employee limits set forth in the statute, and all medical payments, which, for all practical purposes, are unlimited in most states. Furthermore, there is no limit to the number of employees who may be compensated by the company for injuries arising out of a single accident. An employer who purchases workmen's compensation insurance, therefore, has complete compensation coverage even for losses of a catastrophic nature.

Coverage B differs from Coverage A in this respect in that a limit of liability applies to the coverage afforded under Coverage B. The standard limit of liability is $25,000 but higher limits may be purchased. The application of the limits of liability is set forth in Condition 9 of the policy. With respect to bodily injury by accident, the limits of liability apply on a per accident basis, and with respect to bodily injury by disease, the limit is an aggregate limit per state for the policy term.

Supplementary Coverages

The needs of some employers are not adequately met by the basic coverages provided under the Workmen's Compensation and Employers'

[2] For example, see *Ryan Stevedoring Company* v. *Pan Atlantic SS Corp.* [U.S. 124, 76 Supreme Court 232 (1956)].

Liability Policy. For such insureds there are many supplementary coverages available by endorsement, some of the more important of which are:

Voluntary Compensation. The Voluntary Compensation Endorsement enables an employer to extend the benefits provided by the Workmen's Compensation Act to those of his employees who may not be entitled to such benefits under the terms of the Act. Hence, it serves as a means of closing some of the gaps that still exist in coverage provided under workmen's compensation laws. Under the terms of the endorsement, if such an employee is injured in the course of employment, he may elect to accept the scale of benefits provided by the designated workmen's compensation law or pursue his usual common law remedies.

All States Coverage. The All States Endorsement provides that if the insured undertakes operations in any state not specifically designated in the policy, and is required to pay a compensation loss under the law of such state, the company will reimburse him for such payment. Although the endorsement does not provide workmen's compensation insurance, it does have the value of protecting the insured in the event that he unexpectedly finds himself subject to a compensation liability before he has had an opportunity to purchase a policy in a new state. Of course, it also provides the employee with assurance that his rights to benefits will not go unsatisfied. It does not, however, cover fines or penalties imposed on the insured for failure to comply with the requirements of the workmen's compensation law. Voluntary compensation coverage is often afforded in conjunction with the All States Endorsement.

Additional Medical Coverage. This endorsement provides additional medical benefits to an injured workman over and above those provided by the compensation law in the small number of states where medical benefits are still subject to a statutory limit.

The United States Longshoremen's and Harbor Workers' Compensation Act Coverage. This endorsement is available to afford coverage to those employers who are subject to the provisions of this act.

Employers' Liability Coverage. The Employers' Liability Endorsement is attached to the workmen's compensation policy and affords employers' liability coverage, but not workmen's compensation coverage. It was created for use in states where private carriers are not permitted to write workmen's compensation insurance.[3]

With the foregoing coverages, both basic and supplementary, the complex insurance needs of the modern employer can be met effectively.

---

[3] Nevada, North Dakota, Ohio, Oregon, Washington, West Virginia, and Wyoming have so-called "monopolistic state funds," organizations which have exclusive right to insure within the respective states the employers' workmen's compensation liability.

CLASSIFYING THE RISK AND DETERMINING THE PREMIUM

Classifying the Risk

Workmen's compensation insurance is noted for the refinement of its pricing program. The manual contains a listing of over 650 classification codes with a description of the business operations contemplated under each code. The outstanding compliment to be paid to a program of this type is that it provides the ability to make the most equitable apportionment of compensation costs among the many employers in the state. It does have its difficulties, however, one being the problem it presents to the actuary of establishing rates for each such classification, since the availability of an adequate volume of experience for each is important to sound ratemaking.

The very detailed classification system also suggests that the determination of the rate to be charged an employer depends upon the simple process of finding the classification language which "fits" his activities. Actually, the process of assigning the proper classification rate to the employer is a bit more involved.

Single Enterprises. The fundamental basis of the classifying process in workmen's compensation may be found in the rule of the manual relating to so-called single enterprises. That rule states:

> Single Enterprises. If a risk consists of a single operation or a number of separate operations *which normally prevail in the business* (emphasis supplied) described by a single manual classification, that single classification which most accurately describes the entire enterprise shall be applied. . . .

In other words, the object in classifying the insured's operations is to invoke the classification which most nearly describes the business as a whole. This is in contrast to attempting a dissection of the operations within the business, and either by the use of analogy, or by an attempt to make a direct fit, having two or more classifications apply.

There are limitations on this rule, the most important of which relates to the construction trades where notwithstanding the predominance of a particular trade, employees are assigned to classifications according to the job they are actually doing. Thus, the total payroll involved in the construction of a building, for example, is divided among the steel erection workers, carpenters, plumbers, concrete workers, and so on.

Other important limitations to the rule are found in the so-called "Standard Exceptions"[4] and "General Exclusions"[5] referred to in the rule itself. Employments within these categories are separately classified and

[4] *Clerical Office Employees* (not subject to operative hazards of the business); *Draftsman* (no operative hazards); *Outside Salesmen, Collectors or Messengers* (no handling of merchandise); *Drivers, Chauffeurs and their Helpers.*

[5] *Members of Flying Crew; Maintenance and Repair* (by contractors); *New Construction; Stevedoring; Saw Mill Operations.*

rated unless the controlling classification specifically provides otherwise.

Multiple Enterprises. Where the insured's business includes a separate operation which does *not* normally prevail in the business otherwise described by one classification, such operation is to be separately classified. However, even this permission to segregate business operations is subject to several limitations. For example, operations known as "General Inclusions" may not be separately classified unless they have absolutely no relation to the operations described by any other classification applicable to the risk.[6] Also, some classifications carry the restriction "N.P.D." which means "no payroll division." The effect of this rule is that classifications carrying such a restriction may not be employed where there is another classification, within the scope of the restriction, which is otherwise applicable to operations covered by the policy. An exception is made where the operations described by the classification constitute a separate and distinct enterprise having no connection with the operations covered by any of the classifications encompassed by the restriction.

The most basic requirement of singleness with respect to the classification of the insured's operations is that found in the rule of the manual providing that the payroll *of any one employee* shall not be divided between two or more classifications. The entire payroll of each employee shall be assigned to the highest rated classification representing any part of his work. This rule applies in all cases except construction, erection, or stevedoring work where the rules of the manual permit division of payroll provided the original records of the employer disclose the proper allocation of the individual employee's time.[7]

Once the proper classification(s) are applied, the determination of the premium may be undertaken.

Determining the Premium

Payrolls and Manual Rates. Workmen's compensation premium is determined fundamentally by the application of a so-called manual rate to each $100 of employee payroll. This is done by classification of industries each of which has its own rate listed in the manual. Thus an employer having a payroll of $100,000 under classification code 8742—"Salesmen" which carries a manual rate, for example, of $.10, would pay a premium of $\frac{\$100{,}000}{\$100} \times \$.10$ or $100.[8]

---

[6] *Aircraft Travel by Employees* (not flying crew); *Commissaries and Restaurants* (except in connection with construction, erection, lumbering, or mining operations); *Plant Hospitals; Maintenance and Repair* (by employees); *Printing or Lithographing.*

[7] Manual, Section XIII, Rule 5.

[8] Space does not permit other than passing mention of special minimum charges such as minimum premiums and loss and expense constants to which the premium as otherwise calculated is subject.

The determination of payroll for each classification on the policy is actually made upon final audit. The amount of the payroll which is used for premium determination purposes has several limitations which are set forth in the manual.[9] One of the more important operates to exclude that part of all overtime earnings which is based upon a premium rate of pay. Another is the limitation (usually $300) of an employee's average weekly remuneration.

A per capita basis of premium is used for coverage of servants in connection with residences, estates, and farms.

Premium Discount Plan. A mandatory program is applicable in nearly all states where private workmen's compensation insurance is written. It operates to reduce the standard premium which is that calculated by the application of manual rates to payrolls, as described above, and further modified by the application of the Experience Rating Plan (described later in this chapter). The accompanying table summarizes the operation of the Premium Discount Plan:

TABLE 36–1
ILLUSTRATION OF PREMIUM DISCOUNT PLAN IN WORKMEN'S COMPENSATION AND EMPLOYERS' LIABILITY INSURANCE

Standard Premium	Discount	
	Stock* Companies	Nonstock Companies
First $ 1,000	0.0%	0.0%
Next 4,000	9.0	3.0
Next 95,000	14.0	6.0
Over 100,000	16.5	8.5

The premium reductions made possible by the above program arise out of substantial decreases in the allowance in the rate structure for acquisition and field supervision, and for general administration and payroll audit expense as the size of the risk increases. The lower discounts for nonstock companies allow for the fact that such companies pay dividends on the premium remaining after application of the discount. Premium discounts are calculated on an interstate basis so that the insured receives the benefit of the higher discount effect resulting from the consideration of his total premium.

The following is an example of the calculation of a workmen's compensation premium applying the stock schedule of premium discounts. A standard premium of $150,000 is assumed:

---

[9] Manual, Section VI, "Basis of Premium."

Standard Premium	*Amount of Reduction*
First $ 1,000	$ 000
Next 4,000	360
Next 95,000	13,300
Over 100,000	8,250
Total	$21,910

In other words a net premium of $128,090 will be paid by the insured.

In effect the workmen's compensation premium is further influenced by two types of plans both of which are based upon a measurement of the individual policyholder loss experience. The fundamentals of such plans are outlined in the following section.

EXPERIENCE RATING

The topic of ratemaking in liability insurance is treated generally in Chapter 45. Experience rating, however, is peculiarly important to workmen's compensation insurance. Hence, a brief discussion of prospective and retrospective rating is included in this chapter.

In workmen's compensation insurance, claims arise with a sufficient frequency so that, from an actuarial point of view, the presence or absence of losses over a period of time can be accorded significance in making price distinctions among insureds. Since the number of claims and, to a lesser extent, the cost thereof depend largely upon the safety-consciousness of the insured and his employees, and upon the claims prevention work of the insurance company, it is most desirable in the interest of sound public policy that there be a direct financial incentive to keep accidents to a minimum.

Experience Rating Plan

Although "experience rating" fairly describes any plan which uses the loss experience of the individual risk as a basis of making price distinctions, one such plan has come to be known as the "Experience Rating Plan." Like premium discounts, it is a mandatory plan for eligible insureds. In most states, eligibility is set at an average annual premium of $750. Simply expressed, the plan involves a comparison of actual losses incurred during the experience period (which is usually three years) with the losses to be expected, based upon the average of the indications of the particular classification or classifications under which the policy is written. The resulting ratio ("experience modification") is applied as a "credit" or a "debit" to the premium otherwise produced at manual rates. However, the application of the modification is *prospective,* that is, as of the next renewal date of the policy.

The Experience Rating Plan represents another contribution to the equity of the overall workmen's compensation pricing program by its recognition of individual risk loss characteristics. But it is also a most valuable bridge between the concepts of insurance as a business and as a stimulation of concern for human welfare, since it provides a real and immediate incentive for safety-mindedness.

The Experience Rating Plan[10] provides that in the rating process each claim is "split" into a primary and excess portion. The plan contains a table of primary values ranging from a low of $750 to a high of $3,750. All primary losses are considered in the rating process. The percentage of the excess loss which is included in the rating varies from 0 to 100, depending upon the size of the risk. These percentages are called "W Values" and are included in Table III of the Experience Rating Plan Manual. From the case of the smallest eligible insured where no excess loss enters into the calculation of the rate, to the largest insured where all of the loss is a factor in the rating, an increasing amount of the excess loss is considered.

The above procedure incorporates the principle of "credibility" where increasing effect is given to incurred losses as the size of the risk becomes larger. It also recognizes that, in general, an insured with a multitude of small losses is inherently a worse risk than one of the same size which involves a single claim or a smaller number of large claims, even though the dollar loss is the same.

As stated above, the Experience Rating Plan procedure contemplates a comparison of the insured's losses with those "expected" according to the average experience of all insureds in the same classification or classifications. Expected losses are derived by applying to payrolls for each classification that part of an "expected loss rate," found by reference to Table II of the Plan. Comparable to the primary and excess split with respect to actual losses, expected losses are cast in terms of primary expected loss and excess expected loss. A so-called "D Ratio" also included in Table II is applied to the expected losses for each classification to produce the primary expected losses.[11]

---

[10] Reference is to the Experience Rating Plan Manual (Workmen's Compensation and Employers' Liability Insurance) published by the National Council on Compensation Insurance and in common use throughout the country.

[11] Table III of the Experience Rating Plan also contains a list of "B Values" ranging from 7500 to 0 as the size of the risk increases. The B Value is applied equally to the numerator and denominator of the experience rating formula and its purpose is to dampen the swing in the experience rating modification for smaller insureds. Another value which is used for the same purpose along with the B Value is the expression (1 − W Value) × Expected Excess Losses. Thus the precise calculation of the experience rating modification is as follows:

$$\frac{\text{Actual Primary Losses} + [\text{W Value} \times \text{Actual Excess Losses}] + \text{B Value} + [(1 - \text{W Value}) \times \text{Exp. Excess Losses}]}{\text{Expected Primary Losses} + [\text{W Value} \times \text{Exp. Excess Losses}] + \text{B Value} + [(1 - \text{W Value}) \times \text{Exp. Excess Losses}]}$$

The Experience Rating Plan is applied on an interstate basis whereby the experience rating modification is derived from a consideration of the total losses and total expected losses for all states involved in the insured's operations. Most states have approved the plan on this basis. The use of manual rates, plus experience rating, plus the system of premium discounts is referred to as the "guaranteed cost" basis of premium in workmen's compensation insurance.

Retrospective Rating

Retrospective rating is the second fundamental type of experience rating.[12] It is superimposed upon the Experience Rating Plan and it provides the eligible insured a greater opportunity to have his own loss experience play a direct role in the determination of his premium. Retrospective rating is more responsive than the Experience Rating Plan to the latest experience of the insured. Instead of applying the modification of premium prospectively, retrospective rating modifies the premium for the policy period just expired based on the experience of that same period. Whether retrospective rating applies is a matter of contract between the insured and his carrier. There are several different plans which are available and they provide for varying degrees of emphasis on the loss experience of the insured. Generally speaking, they all give much greater and more immediate effect to the insured's own loss experience than does the Experience Rating Plan. This fact produces many important aspects to the underwriting of workmen's compensation risks. In the first place, for those insureds who, within a certain limit, desire to base their premium on their own individual loss experience, retrospective rating offers greater savings from better than average loss experience than are offered under the Experience Rating Plan. Thus, retrospective rating is very attractive to the larger type of insured who has a good safety program.

As mentioned in a previous section, workmen's compensation insureds are assigned to business classifications for statistical and premium determination purposes. As is to be expected, there will be instances where an insured feels that his classification is not quite suitable to his business and believes that his operations are not as productive of losses as are other businesses in the same classification. Naturally, a separate classification cannot be created for only one insured and, as mentioned earlier, the Experience Rating Plan is counted upon to adjust for such differences among risks. Nevertheless, in such case it is often possible for a Retrospective Rating Plan to be suggested as a means of giving the maximum and most immediate effect to the more favorable loss experience of such insured, if indeed such loss experience is forthcoming.

---

[12] Retrospective rating is discussed herein in the light of the rules of the Workmen's Compensation and Employers' Liability Insurance Manual published by the National Council on Compensation Insurance.

Retrospective rating operates as follows. First, a portion of the standard premium is set aside to cover all company expenses except claim expense and taxes. This amount is known as the "basic premium." Secondly, payments and reserves on losses which have been incurred during the term of the rating are increased for claim adjustment expenses. This is done by multiplying the losses by a "loss conversion factor." The sum of the two items is multiplied by a "tax multiplier" which is used to introduce the necessary provision for state premium taxes. The final result is the premium paid by the insured provided, however, that it is subject to a minimum and maximum in terms of a percentage of the standard premium. The ability of the policyholder to have his retrospective premium "stopped" at some maximum must naturally be the subject of a charge. Similarly, the imposition of a minimum premium, regardless of the retrospective premium calculated, should be the subject of a savings or a reduction in premium. The net effect of these two facts is the use of a so-called "insurance charge" which is also included in the basic premium previously referred to. It is obvious that, given the same minimum premium, as the maximum premium decreases the insurance charge contained in the basic premium increases.

It is possible to limit the amount of losses resulting from each accident which will enter into the calculation of the retrospective premium as described above, thus making the retrospective premium dependent more nearly upon the incidence of normal loss than the occurrence of one or more losses of a catastrophic nature. Where this is done, the amount of loss excluded from the retrospective premium calculation is replaced by a premium charge arrived at by multiplying the standard premium for the risk by a so-called "excess loss premium factor." Such charge depends upon the limitations selected.

Every retrospective rating plan has integrated into it the program of premium discounts, described earlier in this chapter. The expense allowances contained in the basic premium reflect the influence of such discounts.

Tabular Plans

There are four retrospective rating plans which have an established set of rating values according to the premium size of the insured. In other words, for each of these plans there are tables where, for a designated standard premium, there is a specific basic premium percentage,[13] a maximum premium percentage and, except with respect to Plan C, a minimum premium percentage. In each of these plans the loss conversion

[13] The basic premium percentages in the tabular retrospective rating plans reflect the premium discounts used by stock companies. Non-stock companies adjust back to the level of their own premium discounts by multiplying the final retrospective premium, including the minimum and maximum premiums, by the use of "non-stock adjustment factors" which appear in the tables.

factor is the same, the usual case being 1.14. Taxes, of course, will depend upon the individual state requirement. Risks producing $1,000 or more of standard premium are eligible for the following plans.

Plan A. Under this plan the standard premium is the maximum premium payable by the insured. Relative to the other plans, there is a very high minimum premium, and the basic premium percentage is high since a greater insurance charge is needed in view of the lower maximum premium. For example, according to the National Council Retrospective Rating Plans, at a $10,000 standard premium size, the basic premium is 28 percent. The minimum premium is 82 percent and the maximum premium, of course, is 100 percent.

Plan B. Here the range between minimum and maximum premium is broadened, the insured being subject to a lower miminum premium but on the other hand being subject to a premium payment which may run considerably in excess of standard premium if his loss experience is severe. At a $10,000 standard premium level the basic premium is 23.7 percent which reflects the lower insurance charge made possible by bringing the maximum premium well up over the standard premium. The minimum premium is much lower than Plan A, being 55 percent. The maximum premium is 165 percent.

Plan C. This plan differs from the previous plans in that it has no specified minimum premium. The maximum premium percentage is the same as Plan B. However, because the minimum premium is lower than, for example, Plan B, a higher basic (27.9 percent) is charged.

Plan J. This plan was the most recent introduction in retrospective rating and its purpose was to satisfy the needs of relatively smaller insureds who were unwilling to be subject to the maximum premium possible under Plans B and C, or the high minimum premium under Plan A. At the $10,000 standard premium level, the maximum premium is 125 percent which stands in contrast to the 165 percent under Plans B and C. The minimum premium is 63.5 percent as against the 82 percent for Plan A. However, as would be expected, the basic premium is 30.1 percent, which is the highest of all the tabular plans.

It will be noted that all of the values referred to above are those contained in the one-year retrospective rating plans. There are three-year tabular plans which at comparable premium intervals permit lower minimum and maximum premium percentages, and, of course, lower basic premium percentages, than the one-year plans. This is due to the fact that the larger the exposure to losses, the less violent the fluctuations in loss experience are likely to be.

Since the selection of a particular retrospective rating agreement depends on an expectancy of what the loss experience of the insured is going to be, underwriters generally will be interested in risks which have shown a reasonably consistent performance so far as the swing of the loss experience is concerned. Thus a logical approach in determining the suitability of retrospective rating for the risk and in determining the particular type of plan to be used, is to make an analysis of loss experience for several years past. It is generally true that the larger the risk the more suitable it is for retrospective rating, since the larger risks are generally more stable than are the smaller ones. On the other hand, eligible risks in the smaller sizes which have demonstrated a fair consistency in loss experience may be written on an appropriate rating plan. In this connection, three-year rating plans are becoming more popular in recent years. Since these plans consider the average loss experience of the insured over the three-year span, and in doing so "smooth out" the movements in loss ratios that can be expected with smaller insureds, they might be described as making a big risk out of a small one.

Of course there are many other specific considerations which may apply in the choice of retrospective rating and the selection of a particular plan. Thus, a significant change in the nature of the insured's business operations, or in his safety program, may be relevant. On the other hand, risks which are otherwise unattractive to the underwriter might be accepted on a retrospective rating basis.

Plan D. There is a fifth type of retrospective rating plan which is called Plan D. Unlike the tabular plans, Plan D permits a selection of rating values at any standard premium size, although the requirement of adequate expenses and insurance charge must be met. In effect, this fact makes Plan D of special value with large risks whose loss characteristics are reliable enough for more precise rating.

However, there are differences in Plan D as contrasted to the tabular plans other than the variety of rating value selections. In the first place, under Plan D rules the loss conversion factor (for stock companies) may vary from no set minimum to a maximum of 1.20. The loss conversion factor for non-stock companies may go as high as 1.40. The effect of a loss conversion factor in excess of 1.14 is to vary a part of expense, other than loss adjustment expense, according to the loss experience. On the other hand, a loss conversion factor of less than 1.14 would mean that only part of claim adjustment expense is being treated as a function of losses. Notwithstanding the treatment of the loss conversion factor, however, the total expense provided for by the insurance company must be precisely that which would be charged for the same size policy under a guaranteed cost program.

Another difference between Plan D and the tabular plans lies in the fact that Plan D permits the combination of workmen's compensation insurance with other lines of insurance such as automobile liability, general liability, automobile physical damage, burglarly, and glass. The plan is administered jointly by the appropriate rating organizations for the lines involved. In using Plan D under these circumstances the expenses charged to the insured are determined for each line individually. On the other hand, in determining the minimum premium, the maximum premium, and the insurance charge, the total premium and expected losses for all lines combined are used as table entries. In other words, the overall premium determination for the risk reflects the degree to which the aggregate loss experience for all subject lines of insurance is better or worse than the average. At the same time each line of insurance retains its separate identity for manual ratemaking purposes. Eligibility for Plan D is placed at $5,000 in terms of standard premium.

With a combination of lines, Plan D affords a better spread of losses than is otherwise possible. It also gives the insured a compact rating treatment of the various lines of insurance.

SUGGESTED READINGS

Hobbs, C. W. *Workmen's Compensation Insurance.* 2d ed. New York: McGraw-Hill Book Co., Inc., 1939.

Kulp, Clarence A. *Casualty Insurance.* 3d ed. New York: Ronald Press Co., 1956. Chaps. 6, 7, 17, 18.

Magee, John H., and Bickelhaupt, David L. *General Insurance.* 7th ed. Homewood, Ill.: Richard D. Irwin, Inc., 1964. Chap. 15.

Michelbacher, G. F. *Multiple-Line Insurance.* New York: McGraw-Hill Book Co., Inc., 1957. Chaps. 5, 6.

Mowbray, Albert H., and Blanchard, Ralph H. *Insurance: Its Theory and Practice in the United States.* 5th ed. New York: McGraw-Hill Book Co., Inc., 1961. Chap. 14.

Reall, G. F. "Liability Without Fault," *Proceedings, 1962 Section of Insurance, Negligence and Compensation Law of American Bar Association.* Chicago: Wallace Press, Inc., pp. 108–61.

Chapter 37

FAMILY AUTOMOBILE INSURANCE

BY CALVIN H. BRAINARD

A favored specimen of Duryea's "first marketable automobile in America" is near its 75th birthday in the Smithsonian Institution secure from the forces of destruction it helped to set in motion and which in a recent year caused 40,900 deaths, 1,500,000 disabling injuries, 10,000,000 property damage accidents and a financial loss estimated at $7,300,000,000.[1] To alleviate the burden of this loss, society utilizes various types of insurance made available by private enterprise and also by governmental sources. It is helpful for students of the subject to distinguish between insurance generally applicable to automobile accidents and the specific automobile insurance to which this and the next two chapters relate.

AUTOMOBILE INSURANCE

In Table 37–1 the consequences of automobile accidents have been divided into six categories. In respect to most of these categories, insurance purchasable in connection with the ownership, maintenance, or use of automobiles shares the burden of indemnity, in varying degrees, with other kinds of insurance. In two categories (5 and 6 in Table 37–1) this share approaches 100 percent. For all practical purposes it can be said that (1) the automobile itself, as a property item, can be covered only by *automobile physical damage insurance* and (2) *automobile liability insurance* offers the only comprehensive protection against third-party claims and suits arising out of automobile accidents. These are the two principal divisions of automobile insurance.[2]

[1] *Accident Facts* (Chicago: National Safety Council, 1963).

[2] Because insureds in automobile accidents are frequently involved with liability claims as well as physical damage to their own automobiles—a complementary relationship especially prominent in this field—liability and physical damage coverages are customarily made available in a single *combination* policy. However, this is not necessarily so. For example, garage liability, automobile comprehensive liability, and automobile dealers' physical damage policies are not combination contracts and automobile insurers affiliated with finance companies may not write liability coverage at all.

TABLE 37-1

INSURANCE AGAINST AUTOMOBILE ACCIDENTS AND LOSS

CATEGORIES OF LOSS INVOLVING AUTOMOBILES[1]	AVAILABLE AUTOMOBILE INSURANCE[2]	OTHER INSURANCE	
		Social	Private
1. Death	Accidental death benefit Medical payments (funeral costs) Uninsured motorists coverage	OASDI Workmen's compensation insurance[3]	Life insurance Health insurance
2. Injury and illness	Disability benefits Medical payments Uninsured motorists coverage	OASDI Workmen's compensation insurance Temporary disability insurance (in four states)[3]	Life insurance Health insurance
3. Damage to real property	....	....	Fire insurance Homeowners insurance
4. Loss of or damage to personal property (except automobiles)[4]	Limited personal effects coverage	....	Fire insurance Homeowners insurance Theft insurance Inland marine floaters Fidelity bonds
5. Loss of or damage to automobiles (and their equipment)	Physical damage insurance (collision and comprehensive)	....	(Fidelity bonds do not exclude automobiles; other property insurance forms may be applicable to automotive equipment in some instances.)
6. Legal liability (for losses listed above)	Automobile liability insurance	....	General liability and Bailee liability insurance (in certain situations)

[1] These categories involve automobiles either as a cause of loss or as the thing sustaining the loss.

[2] That is, available to the individual exposed to the indicated losses. In the first five loss categories, the victim of an automobile accident may also be able to look to the tortfeasor's automobile liability insurance as a source of recovery. But this is not "available" to him in the sense that he can buy it for his own protection against direct loss.

[3] Although not customarily thought of as insurance, the Unsatisfied Judgment Funds in Maryland, North Dakota, and New Jersey could also be mentioned here.

[4] Examples: A bicycle run over by an automobile, cargo stolen from or damaged in a truck, or dwelling contents damaged by collision or fire caused by an automobile.

On a market basis, automobile insurance can be divided in another important way: (1) insurance for the "family automobile" and (2) insurance for the business automobile—taxis, buses, trucks, dealers' automobiles, government vehicles, cars owned by corporations, etc. This chapter deals with the former; the latter will be considered in Chapter 38.

Identifying the Family Automobile

Nowhere in manuals or contracts is reference made to a "family automobile" as such although underwriters undoubtedly had the concept of it in mind when they named the most important contract in this field the Family Automobile Policy. To identify the "family automobile" in trade language it is necessary to begin with the *private passenger automobile,* a title given by manual definition to a large class of motor vehicles:

1. Of the private passenger, station wagon, or jeep type not used as a public automobile.
2. Of the pickup body, delivery sedan, or panel-truck type with load capacity of 1,500 pounds or less, owned by an individual or husband and wife (resident in the same household), and
   a) not customarily used in the insured's business other than for driving to and from work, or
   b) used in the business of the U.S. government by an employee thereof.

This classification must be restricted to exclude private passenger automobiles (*i*) not owned by an individual or husband and wife (that is, those owned by corporations or partnerships), and (*ii*) those not having four wheels. And it must be broadened to include (*iii*) private passenger automobiles hired by an individual or husband and wife under a long-term lease, (*iv*) farmers' trucks (of any body type) with a load capacity of 1,500 pounds or less, and (*v*) trailers designed for use with a private passenger automobile as, for example, utility, boat, and home trailers.

Policies for the Family Automobile

The history of automobile insurance dates from about 1898, when the Standard Fire Insurance Policy and the Teams' Liability Policy were adapted respectively to provide simple forms of physical damage and liability insurance on automobiles.

For many years thereafter policies differed somewhat from company to company until confusing comparisons and difficulties with statutory filings led the American Bar Association and state insurance departments to request a uniform phraseology. Accordingly, between 1933 and 1935, forms committees established by the National Bureau of Casualty (and Surety) Underwriters, the National Automobile Underwriters Association and the American Mutual Alliance worked on the development of a national standard provisions policy program which became effective on January 1, 1936. This program was adopted by all bureau members and subscribers and closely followed by independent insurers. It has since evolved dynamically with changing times and needs.[3]

Standard policies are available sometimes as separate liability and physical damage contracts but usually as combined liability–physical damage contracts. The latter, known as *combination* policies, provide in a single contract the essential coverages an automobile owner may need without necessarily requiring him to purchase all of them. If an insurer has multiple-line underwriting authority, it can and probably will offer its agents and customers the convenience and economy of a combination policy. Insurers without multiple-line charters can achieve the same result through an affiliated company empowered to write the coverage they themselves cannot issue.[4] This chapter deals with the combination policy, on which family automobiles are usually insured, unless the contrary is otherwise indicated.

The Basic Automobile Policy. The Basic Automobile Policy was the first standard provisions policy promulgated by the bureaus (January 1, 1936). Originally applicable to all classes of motor vehicles, it is now confined (*a*) to business automobiles and (*b*) to a small proportion of family automobiles which are ineligible for the Family Automobile Policy. The latter includes family automobiles (*i*) owned by insureds subject to an automobile assigned risk plan (in most states), (*ii*) owned jointly by individuals other than husband and wife resident in the same household, and (*iii*) written on a fleet plan basis in conjunction with business automobiles.[5] Also, in Massachusetts, the Basic (physical

[3] The following comments pertain to this paragraph: (1) The adoption of a statutory standard form in West Virginia in 1934 and plans for similar action in other states gave much impetus to the "Bureau" program. (2) The National Bureau of Casualty Underwriters and the American Mutual Alliance cooperated in writing the liability section while the National Automobile Underwriters Association wrote the physical damage section. In subsequent references to Bureaus it will be understood that the NAUA has jurisdiction over physical damage insurance whether the stock or mutual Bureau is involved in the liability section. (See Chapter 45 for a discussion of Bureaus.) (3) In the early 1940's, the work of the American Mutual Alliance in the field of policies and forms was taken over by the Mutual Insurance Rating Bureau. (4) In view of (*a*) the growth in numbers and importance of independent (non-bureau) insurers issuing nonstandard forms and (*b*) the swelling controversy over competition versus regulation in rates and forms, the reader may be interested in reviewing the late E. W. Sawyer's comments on standardization published in 1936 to accompany the introduction of the new bureau program. They are apposite at this time. [See E. W. Sawyer, *Automobile Liability Insurance* (New York: McGraw-Hill Book Co., Inc., 1936), Chapter 1.]

[4] In a multiple line organization the contract will be issued by a single company. In an affiliated group organization the contract will be issued jointly by two companies, the collision coverage being given in some instances to the casualty insurer and in others to its running mate, the fire insurer.

[5] It will be remembered that the concept of "family automobile" is restricted to motor vehicles having four wheels. Therefore, motorcycles and three-wheeled motor vehicles of the private passenger type, even though used for family purposes, are not insurable (as owned automobiles) on the Family Automobile Policy and must be written with a Basic Policy. (An analysis of the Basic Policy will be found in Chapter 38.)

damage form) must be used in all cases where physical damage insurance is desired in addition to the liability coverage provided mandatorily by the Massachusetts Motor Vehicle Policy.

The Family Automobile Policy (FAP). In 1956, recognizing the desirability of a policy designed especially for the needs of family car owners, the various bureaus jointly promulgated a new standard provisions contract called the *Family Automobile Policy*. This quickly became and still is (as revised subsequently) the most important contract in the family automobile field. Family automobiles owned by an individual or by husband and wife resident in the same household must be insured with this policy unless (*a*) they qualify for one of the newer Special contracts, (*b*) they are insured on a Basic policy (for reasons already stated), or (*c*) they are insured under certain other alternative or statutory policies mentioned below.

The Special Package Automobile Policy. By 1958 it was generally recognized that, despite the coverage advantages of the new FAP, bureau companies were still losing ground to independent direct-writing insurers in the family automobile insurance market. There was a serious need for an economy policy which could (*a*) provide broad packaged coverage for family risks, (*b*) be marketed through existing agency service systems, and (*c*) compete favorably on a price basis with the product of direct writers. Late in 1959 these objectives were substantially met when the National Bureau of Casualty Underwriters introduced the Special Automobile Policy and its companion Safe Driver Insurance Plan.[6] In the same year, to achieve similar objectives for its members, but using a somewhat different approach, the Mutual Insurance Rating Bureau brought out the Package Automobile Policy. Effective January 1, 1963, both bureaus revised their respective policies to issue a single Special Package Automobile Policy reflecting a compromise between the two earlier policies. The eligibility requirements for the Special Package Automobile Policy are essentially the same as those for the FAP but underwriting acceptability is usually more restricted. An appreciable part of the insurance formerly written on the FAP has now been transferred to the Special Package Policy.

Massachusetts Motor Vehicle Policy. According to the Massachusetts Compulsory Automobile Liability Security Act of 1927, all automobiles registered in that state (with certain exceptions) must be insured for compulsory bodily injury liability coverage on a Massachusetts Motor Vehicle Policy. Compulsory coverage does not apply off the "ways" of the Commonwealth or to "guest occupants" nor does it include property

[6] The Safe Driver Insurance Plan can be used without the Special but not vice versa (except in two states). The SDIP is currently available (1963) in all states and the District of Columbia except Indiana, Louisiana, Massachusetts, New Mexico and Texas. In Indiana and New Mexico, the Special is authorized for use even though the SDIP is not.

damage liability. However, these and other exposures may be optionally insured in the contract for an additional premium. Physical damage insurance for family cars registered in Massachusetts is available on a Basic "form" written either separately from or in combination with the Massachusetts Motor Vehicle Policy. (See Chapter 39 for a discussion of compulsory automobile liability insurance in Massachusetts, New York, and North Carolina.)

Garage Liability, Schedule Automobile Liability, and Comprehensive Automobile Liability Policies. These three standard provisions policies are designed for business risks and are described in Chapter 38. It should be noted here, however, that under certain circumstances it is possible for individuals to include their family automobiles under the coverage provided by these contracts on their business operations.

Nonbureau Policies. In addition to the Massachusetts Motor Vehicle Policy and the various standard policies used by bureau members and subscribers, there are other policies written on family automobiles by nonbureau (independent) companies, one of which is the insurer of some 5,000,000 vehicles. These contracts are sold under a distinctive company brand name and may differ in one or more particulars from the standard bureau policies. Essentially, however, they are quite similar in insuring agreements and conditions to the Family Automobile Policy which they have widely imitated.

THE FAMILY AUTOMOBILE POLICY[7]

General Description

The Family Automobile Policy (FAP) is a skillfully drafted document; nevertheless, it is necessarily lengthy and highly complex. Printed in a type size slightly smaller than that used by daily newspapers, it runs to twelve pages in booklet format and to six legal-size pages in the traditional format. It contains almost twice as many words as appear in the average chapter in this *Handbook* and a full commentary on their technical implications would require a work of textbook size.[8] (See Appendix G.)

This length and complexity are attributable to several causes:

1. The FAP is a schedule policy in which the declarations and insuring agreements may provide for as many as nine separate coverage items.[9]

[7] First revised edition, with amendatory endorsement issued effective January 1, 1963.

[8] For a comprehensive analysis of the FAP see Calvin H. Brainard, *Automobile Insurance* (Homewood, Ill.: Richard D. Irwin, Inc., 1961).

[9] Bodily injury liability, property damage liability, medical payments, total disability, death indemnity, uninsured motorists coverage (family protection), comprehensive (fire and theft, etc.), collision, and towing and labor costs. (Many companies make total disability and death indemnity coverages available only by endorsement to the FAP. Technically, they are not a part of the FAP as promulgated.)

2. These coverages involve three major insurance areas (property, liability, and personal) with differing principles, legal rules, and underwriting requirements necessitating a corresponding diversity in policy declarations, provisions, and conditions.

3. The FAP is designed specifically for the needs of typical family automobile owners, a risk classification to which it can be restricted only by means of exclusions and definitions.

4. Unlike the Homeowners Policies which are of comparable length but which are composed from distinct and well-known contracts, the major insuring elements of the FAP are quite dissimilar in format and substance to related traditional coverages. Uninsured Motorists Coverage, for example, is a unique type of insurance.

5. Statutory requirements pertaining to financial responsibility laws, cancellation clauses, uninsured motorists insurance, state amendments, etc., cause additional complexities.

The coverages scheduled in the FAP may be divided into three categories: personal insurance, property insurance, and liability insurance.

Personal Insurance

Injury, illness, or death sustained by an insured person as a result of an automobile accident may cause: (1) extra expense, (2) impaired earnings, and (3) psychic loss (pain, shock, anguish, etc., connected with an actual injury). As insurance against one or more of these adverse effects, the FAP offers the coverages described below.

Medical Payments. It is estimated that in most states, more than 80 percent of the FAP owners elect this coverage. It provides up to $5,000 per insured person for all reasonable expenses incurred within one year from the date of accident for necessary medical, surgical, X-ray, dental, ambulance, hospital, professional nursing and funeral services, and also for prosthetic devices. This is the same blanket medical expense insurance as provided in the Comprehensive Personal Liability Policy described in Chapter 34. Under both contracts it serves common underwriting objectives: (*a*) to stave off or reduce the seriousness of third-party actions and (*b*) to enable the insured to satisfy without subterfuge or collusion a moral obligation to social guests (under the CPL Policy) and to guest passengers (under the FAP) in jurisdictions where the law of torts imposes no duty of ordinary care toward them and hence no legal liability. However, the FAP and CPL Policy differ in that the former includes while the latter excludes the named insured and his relatives as beneficiaries under the contract.[10]

Under *Division 1,* the named insured and relatives are covered while occupying an owned automobile, a nonowned automobile (with the

[10] Throughout the FAP, the "named insured" includes not only the individual named in the declarations but also his spouse if a resident of the same household. And "relative" means a relative of the "named insured" who is a resident of the same household.

owner's permission), or if struck by an automobile or trailer of any type. Under *Division 2*, other persons are covered while occupying (1) an owned automobile (operated with consent of the named insured), or (2) a nonowned automobile driven by the named insured or by a relative, provided, in the latter instance, it is a private passenger automobile.[11] Thus, if the named insured (or a relative) took a guest for a ride in an owned or a nonowned automobile and they were injured, the medical expenses of both would be covered. But if the named insured (or a relative) took his guest for a walk and they were struck by an automobile, only the former would be covered. While the named insured and his relatives can obtain broad, nonrestricted medical expense coverage under various health insurance policies, only automobile medical payments coverage provides them with insurance for the benefit of guests who may be injured while occupying an automobile.

Total Disability. Approximately one and a half million disabling injuries result from automobile accidents each year. Much of this disability lasts only one or two days; some of it is permanent. The total disability benefit pays the named insured(s) up to $50 a week for one year if the insured is continuously prevented from working at *his own* occupation and for life thereafter if he is continuously prevented from engaging in *any* occupation or employment. To be eligible for this coverage the insured person must be engaged in a remunerative occupation the average weekly earnings from which exceed by a substantial margin the weekly benefit available to him under this and other personal accident insurance. Otherwise, moral hazard and overutilization might result.

Death Benefit. Approximately 40,000 deaths are caused by automobile accidents each year. Funeral expenses can be covered under medical payments. Against the risk of lost earning power and extra expense from loss of services, a death benefit is available providing up to $10,000 per insured person for death resulting from bodily injury caused by an automobile accident.

These three coverages are restricted types of personal accident insurance. They pay off simply upon "proof of loss," that is, proof of medical expense, disability, or death. It is not necessary for the insured to demonstrate that he actually sustained a net financial loss as a result of the

[11] In all of the FAP's various divisions "owned automobile" means a family automobile owned by the named insured and described in the policy, a temporary substitute for it, a replacement of it, and also additional family cars purchased subsequently if the company is notified during the policy period and insured all family automobiles owned by the named insured on the date of such acquisition. Family trailers are insured without description or premium charge unless physical damage insurance is wanted. "Nonowned" automobile means any automobile or trailer not owned by or furnished for the regular use of either the named insured or any relative except that under the physical damage section coverage is further restricted to "a private passenger automobile or trailer." "Occupying" also includes entering into and alighting from.

accident. That is, the contract is not one of indemnity; it contains no subrogation clause. It is entirely possible for the insured to collect even though the medical, disability, or death expenses are completely indemnified in other ways.[12]

Uninsured Motorists (Family Protection) Coverage. This insurance is classified with the personal coverages because it is direct first-party insurance purchased by the named insured and for the exclusive benefit of insured persons against the financial consequences of their own bodily injury. (Only in a few states is property damage included.) However, it differs from the preceding coverages in making recovery contingent not only on proof of loss but also upon (1) an accident involving an uninsured motorist (or hit-and-run driver) and (2) a right to damages in accordance with the substantive law of negligence as interpreted by mutual agreement between the insured and his insurance company or, in the event of disagreement, by arbitration. It is also dissimilar in being affected by the indemnity principle. That is: (1) insured persons may not collect under uninsured motorists coverage and also from the uninsured motorist; (2) the benefit otherwise payable is reduced by the amount collected for the same injury under (*a*) the policy's medical payments or bodily injury liability coverages, or (*b*) workmen's compensation, disability benefits, and similar laws.

Uninsured motorists coverage provides reimbursement for all extra expenses, lost earnings, and psychic loss for which the insured would be awarded damages in an actual action at law against the uninsured motorist. The maximum benefit is determined by the bodily injury liability limits stipulated in the applicable state financial responsibility laws. As with other coverage divisions of the FAP, insured persons under a given policy include not only the named insured and relatives (the family group) but also other persons. The family group is protected in nearly all situations against accidental injury caused by an uninsured motorist—either as pedestrians or as occupants of automobiles. Other persons are covered only while occupying (*a*) owned automobiles (for which the coverage has been purchased), (*b*) replacements thereof, and (*c*) certain nonowned automobiles while being operated by the named insured.

Property Insurance

The *personal coverages* of the FAP bear on bodily injury suffered by insured persons in automobile accidents. The property or *physical dam-*

[12] This frequently causes an undesirable coverage redundancy which forms committees have sought to overcome in the Special Package Automobile Policy. (One prominent automobile insurer has experimented with a kind of limited absolute liability arrangement in accordance with which a schedule of benefits similar to but more restricted than the three personal coverages described above is offered without regard to fault to *any* third party injured by the insured's automobile on condition that he release the insured from liability for bodily injury under the law of negligence.)

age coverages are concerned with the loss suffered by insured persons because of damage to or loss of their automobiles. In the former category, the operative words are "bodily injury" and "automobile accident"; in the latter, they are "automobiles" and "damage." In both, the insured persons are the direct beneficiaries of the contract and payment is made upon proof of loss and without need for legal processes. Because bodily injury can be much more serious than automobile damage, the personal coverages might be considered more important than the property coverages. However, bodily injury is insurable under alternative programs of life and health insurance whereas automobile insurance is the only direct coverage against physical damage to automobiles. Furthermore, it is frequently required insurance when automobiles are being financed.

Probably the most serious and frequent cause of automobile physical damage is collision loss. Against this peril the FAP offers deductible collision insurance to pay for loss (1) in excess of the deductible amount (which may be as low as $25 or as high as $250), (2) to owned automobiles driven by anyone (with permission) and also to nonowned private passenger automobiles while operated by or in the custody of an insured person, (3) caused by the collision of the automobile with another object or with a vehicle to which it is attached or by its upset.

Against other perils, the FAP offers comprehensive physical damage insurance with or without a deductible of $50 for each loss. This coverage pays "for loss caused *other than by collision* to the owned automobile or to a nonowned automobile."[13] Such loss cause could range from fire, explosion, windstorm, theft, flood, and other well-known perils, down to the most bizarre incidents. If the insured buys both collision and comprehensive, his FAP provides well-nigh perfect protection against insurable automobile physical damage, and aside from deductibles, it makes little difference to the insured under which coverage his loss is paid. However, if the insured purchases comprehensive only, the cheaper of the two coverages, his protection would be seriously affected by the way in which the insurer interpreted the meaning of "collision." For example, would comprehensive apply if thieves stole the car and wrecked it in a collision; if the gas tank ruptured because of a collision, and fire or explosion destroyed the car; if a windstorm upset the car and damaged it? In answer to these questions the contract provides that:

> For the purpose of this coverage (Comprehensive), breakage of glass and loss caused by missiles, falling objects, fire, theft or larceny, explosion, earthquake, windstorm, hail, water, flood, malicious mischief or vandalism, riot or civil commotions, or colliding with a bird or animal, shall not be deemed to be loss caused by collision.

[13] As concerns physical damage insurance, "nonowned automobile" refers only to private passenger automobiles and utility type trailers. (It should be noted that the definition of trailer under physical damage excludes home trailers. However, home trailers owned by the insured may be added to the FAP by endorsement.)

That is, comprehensive will cover these losses even though a collision might technically be included in the chain of causation leading up to them. This is not to say that if an insured had only collision coverage, these same loss causes would in every case be excluded.

Two incidental benefits automatically granted with comprehensive coverage are: (1) fire and lightning insurance on personal effects of the named insured and relatives while such effects are upon or contained in the owned automobile (subject to a $100 limit per occurrence) and (2) transportation expense indemnity up to $10 a day (but not more than $300 total) in the event of the theft of a covered automobile.[14]

It has been noted that when collision and comprehensive coverages have been purchased on an owned automobile (or trailer) they also apply to nonowned private passenger automobiles (or trailers)[15] operated by or in the possession of the insured with the owner's permission. This feature is important because it is about the only way a family car owner can insure his bailee liability with respect to borrowed automobiles. However, in order to collect under the policy it is not necessary that any liability actually be incurred. All physical damage insurance payments under the FAP are made upon proof of loss and without regard to fault.

Collision coverage is written on an actual cash value basis, that is, without a stated dollar amount of insurance. Comprehensive coverage is written either way depending on the insurer's preference. Of insurers using the stated amount basis, some regard it as an agreed value in the event of a total loss while others (the majority) consider the stated amount merely as an upper limit on the company's obligation which cannot in any case exceed the actual cash value. In the event of loss, the insured must protect the automobile, notify the insurer promptly (and the police also in event of theft), file proof of loss within 91 days, submit for appraisal any dispute as to the amount of loss, cooperate with the insurer in all matters, and inasmuch as property insurance is subject to the principle of indemnity, do nothing to prejudice the insurer's right of subrogation. The company can pay for the loss in money or repair or replace the damaged or stolen property.

A third coverage available under physical damage insurance:

> . . . pays for *towing and labor costs* necessitated by the disablement of the owned automobile or of any nonowned automobile, provided the labor is performed at the place of disablement.

The limit per disablement is usually $25.

---

[14] The company will also pay the expense of returning the stolen car to the insured (or to his policy address) from the point where it is recovered.

[15] Subject to a maximum of $500 on nonowned trailers.

Liability Insurance

Even if all persons and property owners had sufficient protection under personal and property insurance to meet the financial consequences of automobile accidents (and unfortunately most do not), there would still be under existing laws a distinct need for automobile liability insurance because (1) the property insurer, after paying a loss, is subrogated to the insured's right of action against responsible parties and (2) under most personal coverages the indemnified insured is not prevented from exercising that right in his own name. The nature of legal liability has been described in Chapter 31 and the benefits and services provided by the liability insurer in Chapters 32, 33, and 34. Therefore, discussion will be limited here to aspects of both topics which are peculiar to automobile liability and to the liability coverage of the FAP.

Automobile Liability. Rules of law frequently encountered in the handling of automobile third-party cases are as follows:

1. *Negligence Per Se:* This concept is discussed in Chapter 31.
2. *Gross Negligence:* In the operation of an automobile, negligence may be ordinary (mere carelessness) or gross (recklessness—shocking indifference to safe driving). Under *guest statutes* (enacted in 27 states) this difference is important because in the absence of proof of gross negligence a guest has no cause of action against the host owner or operator.
3. *Comparative Negligence:* In Arkansas, Georgia, South Dakota, Mississippi, Nebraska, and Wisconsin, the contributory negligence of the plaintiff does not bar an action for damages if his negligence is less than that of the defendant. However, his damages are diminished in proportion to his contributory negligence.
4. *Last Clear Chance:* The defense of contributory negligence is withheld from defendants who had, but failed to seize, a last clear chance of avoiding an accident.
5. *Vicarious Liability Laws:* The negligence of *minor operators* is imputable to the parent (or guardian) in many states and to the person furnishing the automobile in several states. In about 17 states, some of which are also included in the preceding categories, the negligence of *any driver* is imputed to the owner of the vehicle.
6. *Family-Purpose Doctrine:* In some jurisdictions, by statute or judicial application, the owner of a family-purpose automobile will have imputed to him the negligence of members of his family who have an accident while driving it.
7. *Long-Arm Laws:* By driving into a different state from the one in which they are licensed, motorists automatically appoint an official of that state—its secretary or commissioner of motor vehicles—their agent to accept service of summons. Accordingly, an injured person can force a nonresident motorist to return from a distant home state to face a lawsuit in the state in which the accident occurred.
8. *Contractual Liability:* Automobile liability can arise from contract as well as from tort. For example, if the insured rented a trailer under an agreement in which he assumed the lessor's liability for accidents caused by defects

in the trailer, he would be contractually liable for third-party claims. (Contractual liability of this kind is not excluded in the FAP when it involves an automobile or trailer otherwise covered by the contract.)

Extensions. The benefits provided by the FAP under this coverage are similar to those of other liability policies: (1) professional services in the investigation of accidents, negotiation of settlement, rendering of legal defenses, and so on; and (2) the payment of damages and certain supplementary costs.[16] In view of the widespread territorial usage and potential destructiveness of the family automobile, the encompassing sweep of the long-arm laws, the claims consciousness of third parties, the frequency of accidents, the size of jury awards, and the possible loss of driving privileges, these two benefits, important enough in other liability areas, are indispensable in the field of automobile liability. They are available to *insured persons* whenever "bodily injury" or "property damage" arises out of the ownership, maintenance, or use of an "owned automobile" or a "nonowned automobile."

The meaning of owned and nonowned automobiles has already been described. The definition of insured persons requires comment; it differs from corresponding definitions in the general liability policies described in earlier chapters.

1. *Owned automobiles.* With respect to owned automobiles the insured persons include (*a*) the named insured and residents of the same household; (*b*) any other person using such automobile within the scope of the named insured's permission; (*c*) any other person or organization legally liable because of the acts or omissions of an insured under (*a*) or (*b*) above.

2. *Nonowned automobiles.* With respect to nonowned automobiles insured persons are (*a*) the named insured, (*b*) any relative, but only with respect to a private passenger automobile or trailer, (*c*) any other person or organization (not owning or hiring the automobile) legally responsible because of the acts or omissions of an insured under (*a*) or (*b*) above.[17]

Each insured person is covered up to the policy's limits of liability which basically are $5,000/$10,000 for bodily injury and $5,000 for property damage.[18] However, the applicable limits are not increased by the

[16] In addition to the usual bodily injury and property damage liability coverages and supplementary payments clause, all of which are described in Chapter 34 in reference to the Comprehensive Personal Liability Policy, the FAP agrees to pay the premiums on bail bonds up to $100 a bond. Also, FAP liability coverage is on an "occurrence" basis.

[17] The named insured is covered while using a nonowned automobile of any body type unless such use is for business purposes, in which event coverage is restricted to a private passenger automobile. Both named insured and relatives are covered only if using nonowned automobiles within the scope of the owner's permission as that is reasonably believed to be granted.

[18] This method of expressing limits of liability is common to all dual-limits liability policies and has been explained in Chapter 32. In the FAP the limits are on an *occurrence* basis and can be increased for an additional premium. $100,000/$300,000 limits for B.I. and $25,000 for P.D. can be obtained for premium increases of 62 per-

inclusion of more than one insured person in a claim or suit. For example, if an injured third party brought suit against both owner and driver (e.g., parent *and* child, or principal *and* agent), the insurer's liability for damages on a basic limits policy would not exceed $5,000 even though both defendants were insured persons. As with other liability policies, the insurer assumes the cost of its professional services and all supplementary payments in addition to the limits of its liability for damages.

Other Aspects of Coverage

Restrictions. Probably the most important restrictions of coverage are those implicit in the policy's definitions. For example, a "nonowned automobile," as previously noted, does not include an automobile owned by a relative or furnished for the regular use of either the named insured or a relative.[19] However, there are many express *exclusions* where: (1) public policy is involved (e.g., injury intentionally caused by the insured); (2) other contracts and rate structures apply (e.g., public livery use, occupational injuries to employees, exposures involving automobile businesses, nuclear energy liability risks); (3) the loss is not fortuitous (e.g., wear and tear, mechanical breakdown); (4) perils could cause catastrophic loss (e.g., war and radioactive contamination); (5) there is damage (under liability coverage) to property owned or transported by the insured or rented to him or in his charge (other than a residence or private garage).

Other Insurance. Under all sections the FAP covers nonowned as well as owned automobiles and "other persons" as well as members of the insured's family. For this reason, and also because of the high proportion of family automobiles which are insured, overlapping insurance is likely to exist in many claims situations. The general rule on such cases is that the insurance on the owned automobile is primary while that on the nonowned automobile is excess.

Conditions. The conditions provide: (1) that the FAP applies while the automobile is within the United States, its territories or possessions, or Canada, or is being transported between ports thereof; (2) that in the event of loss the insured must give prompt notice of the occurrence and of all claims resulting from it, and must assist, cooperate with, and secure subrogation rights for the insurer; (3) that the usual clauses apply as to changes, assignment, declarations, and action against the company;

cent and 20 percent in the respective basic limits premiums. In states where financial responsibility laws require more than basic limits, the manual rates are for limits of $10,000/$20,000 B.I. and $5,000 P.D.

[19] Relatives' automobiles should be separately insured. Liability coverage for the regular use of nonowned automobiles can be obtained in accordance with the Non-Owned Automobile section of the Manual Rules. (See *Automobile Casualty Manual*, National Bureau of Casualty Underwriters, 125 Maiden Lane, New York 38, N.Y. This manual is applicable in all states except Massachusetts and Texas.)

(4) that the policy may be cancelled short rate by the insured and pro rata by the company upon giving the insured 10 days' notice except that with respect to liability insurance, and after the policy has been in effect for 60 days or effective immediately on renewals thereof, the company shall not exercise its right to cancel except for stated causes.[20]

The Special Package Automobile Policy[21]

The reasons for the development of this contract have already been given. They center around competitive economies which are sought in various ways.

1. *Packaging.* In conformity with the trend to package all essential coverages in one contract, the SPAP in Part I includes for a basic undivided premium all the coverages individually scheduled in the FAP as liability, medical expense, accidental death benefit and uninsured motorists (family protection). The usual physical damage coverages are separately available in Part II except that the premium for comprehensive includes towing and labor costs.[22]

2. *Single Limit.* Part I provides a single limit for bodily injury and property damage liability thus granting broader protection and reducing—in combination with the package approach—the number of operations performed in the rating and issuance of new and renewal policies.[23]

3. *Handling.* From a signed application submitted by the agent and made a part of the declarations, the company obtains all information needed to issue the new policy and to determine the rates under the Safe Driver Insurance Plan. Thereafter, renewals (semiannual or quarterly) are automatically machine processed upon premium payment very much as with life insurance. This eliminates policy returns and free insurance, cuts handling costs, and allows agents more time for sales activity.

4. *Elimination of Nonessentials.* Payments made under medical expense coverage as well as under uninsured motorists coverage operate to "offset" liability settlements negotiated with the same claimant. And medical expense coverage is made (*a*) excess over other forms of health insurance (e.g., Blue

[20] These concern (*a*) failure to pay premiums, (*b*) fraudulent misrepresentations, (*c*) epilepsy and heart disease, (*d*) revocations of licenses, (*e*) criminal activities, (*f*) serious instances of traffic violations (e.g., drunken driving), (*g*) successive instances of less serious violations (e.g., speeding), and (*h*) violation of the policy's conditions. It will be noted that accident frequency is not a grounds for cancellation. However, the company is under no obligation to renew the policy. Continued experimentation with limited cancellation clauses can be expected.

[21] For a detailed comparison of Special and Family Automobile Policies, see Brainard, *op. cit.*, chap. 15. It is estimated by one of the largest bureau members that about 10 percent of its family automobile insurance is now written on the SPAP. Although a standard provisions policy, it is usually given a distinctive brand name by individual companies.

[22] The insured may buy Part I without Part II, and, if he purchases both comprehensive and collision, Part II without Part I. However, if only comprehensive or collision is purchased, Part II is not available without Part I.

[23] For example, one rate entry can provide for a combination of $25,000 single liability limit, $1,000 medical payments, $1,000 accidental death benefit and $20,000 uninsured motorists coverage. With the FAP, for comparable coverage, it would be necessary to determine and enter five separate rates.

Cross–Blue Shield) and statutory benefits (e.g., workmen's compensation) and (*b*) subject to the subrogation condition. Intrafamily claims and suits are excluded; trailer, temporary substitute, and nonowned automobile coverage is somewhat restricted; physical damage to nonowned automobiles is covered only if the insured is legally liable for such loss; relatives are covered only if they do not have private passenger automobiles of their own; automatic coverage on additional cars is granted for only 30 days.

Rates

Liability rates for family automobiles vary by:

1. State.
2. Territory (in which the automobile is principally garaged).
3. Classification.
4. Driving record sub-classification (where Safe Driver Insurance Plan applies).

The highest-rated classification (2*C*) applies where there is an unmarried male owner or principal operator under 25 years old; the lowest (1*A*) applies where there is no male operator under 25, no business use, and no driving to and from work. Between the lowest and highest there are four other principal classes reflecting intermediate gradations of hazard by driver and usage. Safe Driver Insurance Plans vary somewhat by states but the essential idea in all is to increase or decrease manual class rates in accordance with the hazards implicit in the driver's traffic and accident record during an experience period of usually three years prior to policy issuance or renewal.[24] The liability rates resulting from the application of these four factors may be further modified as follows.

5. If the policy insures two or more automobiles owned by an individual or husband and wife and there is no male operator under 25, the rates are reduced 20 percent on any of such automobiles as are not used for business purposes.
6. Where there are male operators under 25, the applicable rates may be reduced 10 percent if evidence is presented that all such operators have successfully completed an approved driver education course.
7. Compact automobiles (such as Corvair, Falcon, Comet, Valiant, etc.), excluding vehicles of the "sports car" variety, receive a 10 percent credit from the rates otherwise applicable.
8. If the policy is certified under a state financial responsibility law, a surcharge applies.[25]

For policies effective on and after January 1, 1965, the basic rate structure described above has been still further refined (1) by providing

[24] Points are assigned for traffic violations in accordance with their seriousness and also for certain accidents. In one state the basic class rate is increased 150 percent for a four-point score (the maximum) and reduced 15 percent by a zero-point score.

[25] See Chapter 39 for a discussion of financial responsibility laws. For Safe Driver Plan risks the surcharge is 10 percent, for others it is 5, 25, or 50 percent depending on the seriousness of the offense for which certification is required.

a new and higher rate class for youthful unmarried female operators, and (2) by differentiating among risks in all youthful driver classes on the basis of attained ages from 17 (and under) through 24 (age 29 in one class), the rates decreasing as the age increases. For each of the resulting 5,200 classifications a factor is provided (ranging from .40 to 5.60), and the applicable rate is found by multiplying a territorial base premium by the appropriate factor.[26]

Assigned Risks

Applicants who are unable to obtain automobile liability insurance through normal channels because of age, driving record, or other unfavorable underwriting factors, may make application to their state Motor Vehicle Assigned Risk Plan.[27] If eligible for assignment, they will be distributed equitably among individual insurers which must accept them during a three-year assignment period. The insurance is usually provided on a Basic Automobile Liability Policy for the liability limits required by the applicable financial responsibility law.[28] Eligibility for assignment is contingent on freedom from: (*a*) certain serious physical and mental disabilities, (*b*) convictions of felonies and high misdemeanors, (*c*) repeated convictions for serious traffic violations, and (*d*) other enumerated offenses.[29]

SUGGESTED READINGS

Accident Facts. Chicago: National Safety Council, Annual.

Automobile Insurance Plans. Cincinnati: The National Underwriter Co., 1961.

Best's Aggregates and Averages. New York: Alfred M. Best Co., Inc., Annual.

[26] A convenient key provided by the bureaus readily produces the factor needed. This new system also applies to physical damage rates but, in addition, deductibles, and age and make of automobile are also taken into account. (See *Manual of Rules and Rates,* National Automobile Underwriters Association, 125 Maiden Lane, New York 38, N.Y.)

[27] The reader should consult the Assigned Risk Plan in his state for individual variations.

[28] In 1963 the National Bureau of Casualty Underwriters promulgated the Automobile Excess Indemnity Policy for private passenger automobiles. With higher rates and certain coverage restrictions, this new standard policy may induce more insurers to provide excess liability insurance limits on assigned risks. Limited Medical Payments coverage and Uninsured Motorists coverage are also available with this policy. This new program should be of special interest to parents of youthful assigned risks because (1) under vicarious liability laws, parents may be held liable for the negligent driving of their children and (2) under their own automobile policy (Family or Special Package) coverage on "nonowned automobiles" does not include automobiles owned by relatives.

[29] To cite one of many possible examples, an applicant losing his license for drunken driving and later arrested for driving without a license, would not be eligible for assignment if both offenses occurred during the 36 months immediately preceding his application for assignment.

BRAINARD, CALVIN H. *Automobile Insurance.* Homewood, Ill.: Richard D. Irwin, Inc., 1961.

CRANE, FREDERICK G. *Automobile Insurance Rate Regulation.* Columbus: Bureau of Business Research, The Ohio State University, 1962.

EHRENZWEIG, ALBERT A. *"Full-Aid" Insurance for the Traffic Victim.* Berkeley: University of California Press, 1954.

GREEN, LEON. *Traffic Victims.* Evanston, Ill.: Northwestern University Press, 1958.

PIERCE, JOHN E. *Development of Comprehensive Insurance for the Household.* Homewood, Ill.: Richard D. Irwin, Inc., 1958.

SNIDER, H. WAYNE (ed.). *Readings in Property and Casualty Insurance.* Homewood, Ill.: Richard D. Irwin, Inc., 1959. Chaps. 51, 52.

ZOFFER, H. JEROME. *The History of Automobile Liability Insurance Rating.* Pittsburgh, Pa.: University of Pittsburgh Press, 1959.

Chapter 38

COMMERCIAL AND GARAGE AUTOMOBILE INSURANCE

BY JOHN K. DEEKS

In contrast to the owner of the "family automobile," the average business insured engages in a greater variety of operations and consequently faces an increased complexity in his insurance needs. These needs in turn require more elaborate coverage and rating programs even though the basic insurance and supplementary benefits available to the business insured are essentially the same as those applying to the individual owner of a private passenger automobile.

GENERAL COMMENTS

At the outset, recognition should be given to the fact that "business" uses of automobiles involve numerous types of vehicles and ownership. As brought out in the previous chapter, much business use of automobiles—particularly use of private passenger automobiles owned by individuals—is subject to the Family Automobile Policy. Many other business uses, however, require other policies.

The increasingly frequent practice of using leased automobiles poses another general point. In any one of the uses described below the insured may be the owner or lessee of the automobiles. An owner may also be a lessor. The primary insurance on leased automobiles may be bought by either the lessor or the lessee.

Types of Business Risks

Business risks are generally divided into categories on the basis of the type of automotive equipment they use.

Commercial Risks. The commercial automobile is ordinarily associated with the business risk, although business firms frequently use private passenger automobiles as well. The commercial "automobiles" may be regular trucks, tank trucks, truck-trailer units, or tractor-semitrailer units. Such equipment may be used to transport property of the insured or of others. Insureds hauling property of others are commonly referred to as "truckmen" or "movers." Also, among the business risks is the large miscellaneous group of owners of ambulances, police automobiles, fire trucks, and other vehicles involving special uses. Road and building construction contractors and municipalities use special forms of automotive equipment such as power shovels, cranes, and graders. Such special equipment is usually insurable in whole or in part as automobiles although the insured often has the option of insuring his liability in connection with the equipment under his general liability policy and physical damage under an inland marine policy.

Public Automobile Risks. This group includes all operators of automobiles used to transport people for a charge. Examples are taxicabs, public and private livery vehicles, general passenger buses, school buses, and special purpose buses.

Garage Risks. In terms of frequency and size the garage is one of the more important business risks. Insureds under this heading include dealerships in new and/or used automobiles, certain dealerships in automotive equipment or automobile implements, repair shops, service stations, storage garages, and other public parking facilities.

Automobile Insurance Needs of the Business Risk

All such insureds are concerned primarily with liability resulting from bodily injury to others or damage to the property of others caused by automobiles, whether they be owned or nonowned. In the case of public automobiles the liability is increased by the responsibility for the safe transportation of passengers. Many garage insureds have an additional liability resulting from possible damage to automobiles in their custody for repair or safekeeping.

It is not unusual to find that an insured in the course of business (1) will assume the liability of others through a contract or agreement, (2) will assume responsibility for damage to equipment of others when leased to him, or, in the case of truckmen, (3) will assume responsibility for damage to equipment of others when received from other truckmen in interchange operations. A more direct need of the business risk arises from the possibility of loss or damage to owned equipment caused by fire, theft, collision, or other perils.

Insurance Contracts Available

Several automobile insurance policies and endorsements are available to members of the business community. These include the Basic Policy, the Comprehensive Automobile Liability Policy, and the Garage Liability Policy. In Massachusetts, where bodily injury coverage is compulsory, a special policy is utilized, which, except for the statutory coverage, is equivalent to the Basic Policy. Since the liability coverage on garage-owned automobiles is also subject to the compulsory insurance requirement, there is also a special Massachusetts Garage Liability Policy.

THE BASIC POLICY

General Discussion

The Basic Policy is the most common instrument for insuring commercial operations. It is the oldest of the policies in common use and is generally a combination form, affording third-party liability coverage, medical payments coverage, and physical damage coverage. The coverages of the Basic Policy apply to automobiles described in the policy and to replacements of such automobiles. The policy will also cover additionally acquired automobiles, provided (1) all owned automobiles are originally insured under the policy and (2) the insured notifies the insuring company within 30 days of the acquisition of the additional automobiles. Characteristically, the policy also protects any other person, firm, or organization (other than a garage) using or responsible for the use of the insured owned automobile, provided the automobile is being used with the permission of the named insured. However, the physical damage insurance of the policy does not carry an additional interest provision such as is found in the Family Automobile Policy. Commercial automobiles are not so freely and informally loaned as are individually owned private passenger automobiles. Consequently, it is not assumed that the owner intends to extend the benefit of his physical damage insurance to the lessee or borrower. If he does, a simple provision in the lease or other agreement under which the automobile is used will foreclose subrogation by the insurer for damage that may be the fault of the user. If such a provision is absent, the insurer may exercise its subrogation rights against the user as well as any other third party legally responsible for damage to the vehicle.

Exclusions of the Basic Policy

In order more clearly to understand the Basic Policy, it may be viewed as though three separate contracts were involved: (1) liability, (2) medical payments, and (3) physical damage. The insuring agreements, definitions, exclusions, and conditions applicable to each form of coverage may be read independently of the others.

The exclusions of the Basic Policy are standard automobile exclusions, most of which are discussed in Chapter 37. In addition to those applying under the Family Automobile Policy the following exclusions appear in the Basic Policy: (1) contractual liability, (2) workmen's compensation obligations, and (3) the "cross trailer" exclusion. The last mentioned exclusion voids coverage when the automobile is used for the towing of any trailer owned or hired by the insured and *not* covered by like insurance in the company, or while any trailer covered by the policy is used with any automobile owned or hired by the insured and *not* covered by like insurance in the company. The purpose of the exclusion is not so much to force the insuring of trailers as to force coverage for both auto and trailer into the same company. One of the most fruitful sources of inter-insurer disputes prior to the general adoption of the "cross trailer" exclusion was the accident involving a tractor-trailer unit insured in different companies. It is difficult enough to identify the cause of an accident with the tractor alone or the trailer alone (for the obvious reason that the real instrumentality of fault is human, not mechanical). Arguments are prevented by the general practice of insuring both tractor and trailer—or neither. Further evidence of the treatment of automobile and trailer as a unit of liability exposure may be found in the "Two or More Automobiles" statement in the policy which provides for the application of the insurer's limits of liability singly to the unit.

Uses of the Basic Policy

The Basic Policy is designed to provide insurance primarily on described automobiles and has only limited automatic coverage for additional or replacement automobiles. Hence, its use in the commercial field is usually limited to risks with only a few automobiles where reporting is not a burden. Through the use of endorsements, however, the policy lends itself to a multitude of coverage extensions and combinations to make it the most versatile and popular of the commercial automobile policies. In this way the policy may be adapted to accommodate the insurance needs of all types of business insureds except the liability exposure of a garage.

Use of Other Automobiles; Uninsured Motorist; Death and Disability. In the case of certain smaller risks including proprietorships the Basic Policy is frequently expanded to include use-of-other-automobile coverage, uninsured motorist coverage, and death and disability coverage. (Death and disability coverage may be afforded *only* if a private passenger automobile is insured in the policy.)

Combined Additional Coverage. In lieu of comprehensive physical damage coverage, the insured may elect to buy coverage on a stated perils basis, such as fire or theft. (Certain vehicles such as dealers' automobiles, motorcycles, and motor glides are not eligible for the comprehensive coverage.) These stated perils will often be supplemented by the so called "combined additional" coverage, protecting against loss caused by windstorm, hail, earthquake, explosion, and so on, including malicious mischief and vandalism which are on a deductible basis.

Public Automobile Coverage. The various types of public automobile risks may be written through the use of appropriate endorsements primarily designed to offset the livery exclusion of automobile policies. The property damage coverage for public automobile insureds offers one of the few exceptions to the exclusion of damage to property transported by or in charge of the insured. The insured is protected for liability resulting from loss of or damage to property of passengers.

Occurrence Basis. "Occurrence basis" of coverage is occasionally substituted for the "accident basis" at a small additional premium. This substitution is not as important an extension of coverage on automobiles as it is on certain types of general liability exposures since it is not common for the average automobile user to become liable for injury that could not be said to be "caused by accident." (See Chapters 32, 33, and 34 for discussion of "accident versus occurrence.") A typical situation calling for the extension of occurrence coverage is that of the gravel-hauling contractor gradually weakening a bridge as a result of repeated crossings.

Contractual Liability Coverage. Contractual liability coverage is not commonly written under an automobile policy since it is essentially a general liability matter. Insureds do not usually contract in advance to be liable for injury caused by the use of automobiles. There is generally a broader base for assumed liability, although the use of automobiles may be a part of the hazard. Where, however, the liability assumed relates only to the use of automobiles, the coverage may be afforded by endorsement to the automobile policy at premiums determined in accordance with the general liability rating procedure. (See Chapters 32 and 34 for treatment of contractual liability insurance.)

Risks Subject to Interstate Commerce Commission or Public Utility Commission Requirements. Interstate bus and truck operators are subject to ICC regulations which, except for certain exemptions, require that liability insurance be carried in specified limits. Intrastate operators are similarly regulated in most states by the respective Public Utility Commissions or their equivalents. Evidence of insurance must be filed with the appropriate regulatory authorities and this filing is usually accomplished by the use of certificates. Increasingly, the filings are on a continuous basis, that is, they remain in effect until terminated. In every case the policy must be endorsed with prescribed forms, the effect of which generally is to obligate the insuring company to cover all automobiles—owned, hired, and nonowned—used by the insured in his transportation operations. The required endorsements usually contain a reimbursement provision permitting the insurance company to seek restitution from the insured in the event of having to pay a claim that would not have been covered except for the filing. Cases where the reimbursement agreement is invoked are extremely rare primarily because underwriters are aware of the importance of affording the necessary broad coverage and obtaining appropriate premium.

Fellow Employee Coverage. Automobile insurance basically does not cover the liability of an employee for injury to a fellow employee arising in the course of business. At the request of the insured, however, insurers may delete the exclusion from the automobile policy. While admitting the possible exposure to an employee, insurers are generally reluctant to extend coverage in this area. Injuries of this type are properly insurable under workmen's compensation coverage or employers' liability coverage. Direct action by the injured employee against the offending employee is unlikely, and as a matter of fact, by statute or court decision, suits against fellow employees are barred in some 21 states. (It is interesting to note that the fellow employee limitation does not apply to the named insured.)

Fleet Automatic Coverage. If the insured owns five or more automobiles, the Basic Policy may be amended by endorsement to afford fleet automatic coverage. Under the terms of the endorsement the insurance applies to all licensed owned automobiles and trailers, including all those acquired during the policy period. The earned premium is determined by adjustment at the expiration of the policy. Fleet automatic coverage may be applied to the physical damage as well as to the liability coverage. An attractive feature of the fleet automatic coverage is the fact that a discount is applied to the liability and collision coverages based on the number of automobiles in the fleet. In the case of collision, trailers and semitrailers are used in addition to the automobiles to determine the discount.

Hired Automobiles and Employer's Nonownership Liability Coverage

Several types of insurance may be added to the Basic Policy by endorsement. They are usually bought as a package and are subject to a single minimum premium. If only one type is bought, the same minimum applies.

Hired Automobiles. Hired automobiles are defined very broadly as automobiles used under contract in the behalf of the named insured or loaned to the named insured provided they are not owned by an executive officer, partner, or an employee who is given an operating allowance for the use of the automobile. Note that the definition includes borrowed automobiles, automobiles hired without drivers—the named insured assigning his own employees to drive the automobiles—and automobiles hired from independent contractors such as public truckmen (who also furnish drivers) where it is more a service that is being hired than specific equipment. It is also important to note that, while the definition of hired automobiles is broad in scope, the same definition would also apply where the term "hired automobile" is used in the "cross trailer" exclusion, thereby having the important effect of modifying the limitation of coverage in that exclusion.

The additional interest coverage afforded on hired automobiles is just as extensive as on owned automobiles except that there is no coverage to the owner of the hired automobile or his employee, unless the coverage is on a specified car basis. Also, if the automobile is hired from an intermediate lessee of the owner, there would be no coverage for such lessee. Hired car coverage is excess over any other available insurance when the premium basis for the insurance is cost of hire. If otherwise, the insurance is primary and participates with any insurance that may be carried by the owner of the hired automobile.

Hired automobile coverage is usually rated on a cost of hire basis at a rate per $100. However, expenditures to public carriers who are performing services pursuant to their franchise and subject to statutory insurance requirements are exempted. In other situations the owner of the hired automobile may provide evidence that he carries insurance (not self-insurance) that protects the hirer on a direct and primary basis, in which event the hired car rates are reduced to 5 percent of the otherwise applicable rate. Where automobiles are hired without drivers, the cost of hire used in rating is increased to reflect the remuneration of the driver, subject to a maximum of $100 a week. If such hiring is on a long-term basis, that is, leased automobiles, the agreement of hire frequently provides that the hirer will be responsible for the insurance. In such cases the automobiles are rated as though they were owned by the hirer and coverage is modified to protect the owner of the hired automobile while it is being used in the business of the hirer or by or on behalf of the hirer for personal or pleasure purposes. As stated above, the insurance would be no longer excess.

Employer's Nonownership Liability Insurance. By definition, nonowned automobiles are any automobiles other than those owned or hired. For coverage purposes under the endorsement, the nonowned automobile is:

1. A private passenger automobile used by any person in the business of the named insured, or
2. A commercial automobile used in the business of the named insured but only if used by an employee and such use is occasional and infrequent.

The coverage does not apply with respect to an automobile owned by a partner if the named insured is a partnership. It is important, therefore, that the individually owned automobiles of partners be separately insured and at adequate limits. Only under the partner's policy can the partnership be protected—as an additional insured—against liability arising out of a partner's use of his own car on partnership business. In contrast to the broad additional interest coverage afforded on owned and hired automobiles, the nonownership coverage is limited to the named insured and any executive officers of the named insured. However, it does not protect the executive officer with respect to an automobile owned by him or a member of his household. Nonownership coverage is always excess.

The rating basis for employer's nonownership insurance utilizes definitions of Class 1 persons and Class 2 employees. The former includes direct agents or representatives as well as employees whose usual duties in the business of the named insured include the use of automobiles. Class 2 employees are all other employees. The rates for Class 1 persons vary by state and territory. They are usually about 7 percent of the private passenger business use rate. For Class 2 employees there is a low countrywide rate which in turn is subject to a "size of risk" reduction. Where the operations are not subject to any great fluctuations, risks are usually flat rated and the adjustment waived.

Truckmen. Truckmen require special attention because of a modification of the additional interest feature in connection with both owned and hired automobiles. It is intended that the insurance conform with the obligation the truckman assumes under his filings—ICC and PUC. If the truckman uses automobiles or trailers hired from others or if other truckers operate their equipment under his franchise rights, the insurance inures to the benefit of the owner of the hired equipment or the operating truckmen (1) provided such owner or truckman, if subject to ICC or PUC obligations, is not a self-insurer and (2) provided further that, if he carries hired car insurance, he carries it with a company which would give reciprocal coverage to the owner of equipment which he in turn may hire or to franchise truckmen operating over his route. When his equipment is being operated under another truckman's franchise, the truckman's insurance then operates as excess and only with respect to his own liability. Under the coverage afforded the owned automobiles of a truckman there would be no coverage to another truckman if the equipment is used in the business of such other truckman.

Heavy and Specialized Carriers. Certain truckmen are engaged in the transportation of heavy or oversized machinery or equipment requiring the use of specially constructed automobiles or special handling. Under the owned car insurance of such a carrier, coverage applies on a primary basis with standard additional interest protection. This exception to the general trucking coverage program is due to the fact that this special equipment is expected to be operated to destination by the insured's own employees and not be subject to interchange arrangements.

Movers of Household Goods and Office Furniture. These insureds involve another exception to the standard trucking additional interest coverage. The owner's automobile insurance covers on a primary basis at all times and normal additional interest coverage applies. The hired car insurance is standard, which means that there is no protection to the owner of a hired automobile or his employees.

COMPREHENSIVE AUTOMOBILE LIABILITY POLICY

General Discussion

Agents and underwriters look upon the Comprehensive Automobile Liability Policy as one of the most advanced and saleable contracts on the market. In contrast to previously mentioned policies where insuring agreements apply to specific hazards, the Comprehensive Automobile Liability Policy insurer agrees to protect the insured's liability arising out of accidents caused by the ownership, maintenance, or use of *any* automobile.

The policy should be studied from the standpoint of the two general categories of insured: (1) the named insured and (2) the additional insureds. The named insured receives the broadest possible automobile coverage and is subject only to (1) the necessary common exclusions and (2) limitations that may be imposed by endorsements. (The policy may be endorsed, by the way, to afford 30 days' automatic coverage for excluded uses.)

An important restriction has recently been introduced with respect to additional insureds in the area of loading and unloading—a limitation that applies to any automobile policy except those where eligibility is limited to individually owned private passenger automobiles. Its purpose is not to eliminate an exposure but to contain it within the policy where it belongs from an economic standpoint and where coverage now may be found, that is, a general liability policy. The endorsement is limited both as to scope and as to interests affected. The limitation applies only to accidents occurring on or adjacent to premises owned, rented, or controlled by the person against whom the claim is made or by his employer. Further, it is only the interest of the owner, renter, or controller of the premises or his employee that is eliminated. The interest of the automobile operator or owner remains unaffected.

The policy exclusions are minimal. Generally, the excluded exposures are those which are normally insured under other contracts of insurance. Examples are: (1) liability assumed under any contract or agreement, (2) liability for damage to property transported by or in charge of the insured, and (3) liability for injury to employees including workmen's compensation obligations. In addition to the foregoing there is the usual nuclear exclusion and the remainder of the standard property damage exclusion relating to owned or rented property. Note that there is no "cross trailer" exclusion with respect to the named insured. The policy affords complete owned, hired, and nonowned automobile coverage which would make the exclusion meaningless as respects the named insured. Similarly, since it is expected that the entire exposure of the risk will be underwritten, there is no livery exclusion.

Automobiles are defined the same as in the extended Basic Policy—owned, hired, and nonowned. These definitions are used for two purposes: (1) to limit coverage afforded additional insureds and (2) to facilitate rating. With respect to the owned, hired, and nonowned automobiles the additional interests are covered to the same extent as they are under the Basic Policy.

The rating of the Comprehensive Policy is the same as for the extended Basic Policy. While formerly a small additional flat premium was charged, this charge has been discontinued and only normal rating bases apply, the hired and nonowned automobile coverages being subject to the prescribed minimum premiums. The Comprehensive Policy should be used for any risk where complete automobile coverage is sought.

The Comprehensive Automobile Liability Policy is usually (but not necessarily) written jointly with general liability insurance under the same policy—the contract being known as the Comprehensive Liability Policy. (See Chapter 34.) This manner of insuring is to be highly recommended since many accidents involve fringe areas, such as loading or unloading of the automobile, where the distinction between automobile and general liability insurance may result in a question of jurisdiction if separate insurers are involved. Automobiles are specifically defined in the Comprehensive Liability Policy, paralleling the definitions in the extended Basic Policy. The definition includes all types of self-propelled equipment such as contractor's equipment. Some types are unqualifiedly stated to be automobiles—others are defined to be automobiles only when being operated solely for locomotion. Still other types of such equipment are defined not to be automobiles, thereby allocating them to the general liability category.[1] Thus when the Comprehensive Liability Policy is used, the definition of automobile serves a dual purpose. It defines the extent of the positive grant of coverage under the automobile portion of the policy; and, since the same definition of automobile applies to the general liability coverage, it defines the limit of the latter coverage as respects automobiles. There can be no dispute about protection when both types of insurance are carried in the same company.

Use of the Comprehensive Liability Policy

The Comprehensive Liability Policy may be extended by endorsement to afford all of the supplementary coverages available under the Basic Policy endorsement program. In addition to including medical payments coverage, which is not afforded by the Comprehensive Liability Policy, per se, the policy may be endorsed to include physical damage coverage

---

[1] A revision of the Comprehensive Liability Policy is under consideration at the time of this writing. One of the more important changes contemplated is the substitution of the General Liability Policy as the base for insuring against liability for the use and operation of practically all contractor's equipment.

on owned automobiles, garage liability coverage, dealers' physical damage coverage, and garagekeepers' legal liability coverage.

It is not generally recommended that the Comprehensive Liability Policy be used as a vehicle for affording garage liability coverage since the Garage Liability Policy (see below) has been especially prepared for the garage risk. To insure a garage under a Comprehensive Liability Policy it is necessary to use a lengthy endorsement which in effect restates the Garage Liability Policy coverage and rating provisions with respect to the garage hazard. However, some garages will operate equipment, such as tank trucks or haulaways, which is excluded from the Garage Liability Policy. In such cases it is practical to use the Comprehensive Liability Policy. The insured then has standard garage liability coverage plus comprehensive coverage on his other exposures. There is one exception. Where the garage operation is included in a Comprehensive Liability Policy, it is still not intended that there will be any protection under the policy for the use of any garage automobile in any prearranged or organized racing or speed contest.

GARAGE LIABILITY POLICY

Since automobiles are the product with which the garage operator deals, it is impractical to apply normal owned and nonowned automobile coverage on the conventional basis or to use normal rating procedures. The garage operator may sell automobiles, repair them, or provide facilities for their safekeeping. His use of his premises is intimately related to his business of handling automobiles. He needs protection for liability arising out of the use of his own automobiles, whether they are being operated in the course of sales or otherwise. He needs coverage for his operation of customers' automobiles and for any work he does on such automobiles. Lastly, he needs coverage for his use of his premises in the garage business.

A special policy was devised at an early date to fulfill the insurance needs of the garage owner. It was probably the earliest of the package policies, being a composite of automobile and general liability insurance. Recently, the policy was revised and, with updated policy language and arrangement, is now in three parts: liability, medical expense, and garagekeepers' legal liability.

Part I—Bodily Injury and Property Damage

Under Part I, coverage is afforded for the use of the premises for garage purposes and also for the use of automobiles. The premises liability coverage is equal in scope to that of the Comprehensive General Liability Policy subject to the limitation that injury arise out of garage operations. There is no "products exclusion" and the insured is protected for liability arising from accidents resulting from work done on automobiles or from the sale of automobiles or parts. Further, employees are covered basically as additional insureds for garage operations on premises as well as while operating automobiles.

The products liability coverage is subject to standard products property damage exclusions. If the insured supplies a defective part or does a faulty repair job on an automobile belonging to a customer and this in turn is the cause of an accident after the automobile has been returned to the customer, the garage would not be covered for any damage to the part supplied nor for the price of its faulty work. Damage to the rest of the automobile would be covered, except that such damage as results from faulty workmanship is subject to a deductible of $100. The insured is fully covered for any bodily injury or other property damage liability that may result.

The new policy clarifies another important area of the products coverage. If an automobile is sold by the garage and is subsequently damaged or destroyed because of some defect or improper presale servicing, there is no coverage for any liability the garage operator may have for such damage. The policy excludes all damage to automobiles sold, if the damage results from a condition existing at the time the automobile is transferred to the purchaser.

Coverage Option. At the option of the insured the automobile coverage may be limited to apply only to automobiles that are neither owned nor hired. This option is not available to dealers but is often attractive to repair shops and service stations because of the reduced premium. In such cases, any owned or hired automobiles must be insured separately.

Additional Interests—Automobile. Additional interests are covered practically to the same extent as the named insured. In contrast to other policies the named insured is covered for the use of partner-owned automobiles in the business, but no additional insured is covered with respect to his own automobile nor does the policy cover any partner or employee for damage to property owned by or in charge of the named insured—a feature characteristic of any policy that affords general liability coverage extended to protect employees as additional insureds.

Option–Limited Coverage for Certain Insureds. Because of the broad additional interest coverage, customers and other nongarage personnel are protected for their use of garage automobiles. Such a person is covered while he is driving a demonstrator or an automobile lent to him for his personal convenience while his own automobile is undergoing repair.

Many garage insureds have expressed concern about having any resulting losses charged to the garage policy, often impairing the experience of the garage and increasing the premium under rating plans. At the option of the garage, the policy may be endorsed in most states with a corresponding rate reduction, whereby coverage for the customer is voided if he has his own insurance. If he has no insurance or carries lower limits than required under the financial responsibility law of the state, the garage policy would protect him up to such required limits. The foregoing option is available only to franchised and nonfranchised dealers, and to repair shops if the policy is on an "all automobiles hazard" basis.

Exclusions. In addition to the standard policy exclusions there are several other exclusions that have an important bearing on the coverage. The property damage exclusion, newly expressed in "care, custody, or control" terminology, carries an important exception. The exclusion does not apply to damage to property of others caused by servicing hoists. (Under the previous policy this coverage was excluded although it could be added by endorsement at an additional premium.)

The average garage does not use automobiles in racing or speed contests, although occasionally a garage will do so for advertising purposes. Since underwriters did not feel that such infrequent but often excessive exposure should be reflected in the rate level for all garages, it was concluded that the exposure should be eliminated from the standard policy coverage. Many garages conduct an automobile or trailer rental business as a sideline. Such vehicles are excluded and must be separately insured. Haulaways, tank trucks, and trailers, if being operated other than in the course of delivery, demonstrating, or testing, are also excluded. These, too, should be separately insured.

Part II–Expense for Medical Services

The revised policy now makes provision for writing premises medical payments coverage without having to resort to the use of an endorsement. The coverage may only be written if automobile medical payments is also afforded. The automobile medical payments coverage tracks the bodily injury coverage, that is, it applies only if the use of the automobile is covered under bodily injury.

If medical payments coverage is bought under a policy carrying the "Limited Coverage for Certain Insureds" Endorsement, the medical payments coverage is not affected, that is, the customer would be protected for medical payments even though he was not covered for bodily injury liability.

Part III—Garagekeepers' Legal Liability

This coverage is a partial buy-back of the property damage exclusion on property of others in charge of the insured. It is important to storage garages, parking lots, and body and repair shops as a means of covering their liability as bailees with respect to automobiles left in their custody for safekeeping or repair. Coverage is contingent upon establishing liability on the part of the insured. At the same time coverage is on a stated perils basis—usually fire, theft, collision, and riot and civil commotion coverage including malicious mischief and vandalism. The collision coverage protects the insured for damage not only to automobiles but also to other property of a kind customarily left in charge of garages. Damage to such other property is subject to a limit of $5,000. Garagekeepers' legal liability insurance is also available by endorsement to the Basic Policy.

Extensions of the Garage Liability Policy

The policy is commonly endorsed to provide coverage for elevators, liability of owners of the premises, and contractual liability, other than that basically afforded by the policy. These extensions are made in accordance with general liability rules and rates. Uninsured motorist coverage and death and disability coverage are also frequently added to the policy.

Dealers' Physical Damage Supplement

One of the more important developments in connection with the revised policy is the availability of the Dealers' Physical Damage Supplement. Previously it was customary to use the Basic Policy with an endorsement to afford this coverage. Dealers' physical damage coverage is on a stated perils basis. Comprehensive physical damage coverage is not available. Coverage applies to automobiles held for sale or used in his garage business. It is a blanket form with no description of the automobiles necessary. There are two rating options: (1) Monthly Reporting Form "A" which requires the reporting of values monthly and (2) Blanket Form "B" where the premium is based on a selected limit of insurance with no reports necessary. In either case the rating basis for all coverages except driveway collision is a rate per $100. Driveway collision is rated on a per automobile basis, depending upon the distance traveled and the value of the automobile. With the availability of this Dealers' Physical Damage Supplement, the automobile or equipment dealer may include practically all of his automobile and general liability insurance protection under a single policy.

SUGGESTED READINGS

APPLEMAN, JOHN A. *Automobile Liability Insurance.* Chicago: Callaghan & Co., 1938.

BRAINARD, CALVIN H. *Automobile Insurance.* Homewood, Ill.: Richard D. Irwin, Inc., 1961.

KULP, CLARENCE A. *Casualty Insurance.* 3d ed. New York: Ronald Press Co., 1956. Chap. 8.

MAGEE, JOHN H., AND BICKELHAUPT, DAVID L. *General Insurance.* 7th ed. Homewood, Ill.: Richard D. Irwin, Inc., 1964. Chap. 16.

RIEGEL, ROBERT, AND MILLER, JEROME S. *Insurance Principles and Practices.* 4th ed. Englewood Cliffs, N.J.: Prentice-Hall, Inc., 1959. Chap. 33.

Chapter 39

MOTORISTS' FINANCIAL RESPONSIBILITY LAWS

BY THOMAS C. MORRILL

An airlines executive once said that crashes are the price civilization pays for speed. Automobile deaths, injuries, and property damage are part of the price that is paid for mobility. The subject of this chapter is the problem of financial responsibility for automobile liability claims.

BACKGROUND

In 1963, 43,600 deaths were caused by automobile accidents in the United States. Injury totals, never as precise as fatality figures, were projected from insurance data as 1,605,000, and property damage accidents as 5,329,000. These represented a frequency of 2.34 bodily injury and 7.78 property damage claims paid per 100 insured passenger cars. Both rates—as presented in Table 39–1—show declines during the five-year period for which the figures were available at the time of this writing.

TABLE 39–1

U.S. Automobile Accidents Frequency Rates
(Number of paid claims per 100 insured passenger cars)

Type	1959	1960	1961	1962	1963
Bodily injury	2.71	2.77	2.76	2.39	2.34
Property damage	8.43	8.41	8.37	7.99	7.78

Source: Insurance Institute for Highway Safety as reproduced in *Traffic Safety* for July, 1964, p. 11.

Despite the 60 million vehicles now operating in America and the increasing concentration of population in congested urban areas, the automobile accident problem has been held in check. The large numbers needed to express the death and injury figures obscure the fact that, at least in relation to the increasing numbers and usage of cars, there has been no significant increase in the *rate* of accidents for many years. In fact, the death rate dropped year after year from an average of 18.2 per 100 million vehicle miles in 1923–27 to less than half that figure by 1947. It has held below six deaths per 100 million miles since 1957.[1] In 1963 it was 5.5.[2]

The containment of the incidence of accidents satisfies no one, least of all the traffic safety professionals, in view of the size of the problem that remains, but the expertise which has been developed suggests the means by which future gains may be made. These include improved street and highway systems, better regulation of drivers, and the upgrading of laws and of their enforcement by the police and the courts. Through the Insurance Institute for Highway Safety, the major trade associations of the automobile insurance business fill a significant role in the traffic safety field, with a budget (1963) of about $1¾ millions annually.

In its early days the automobile was a much more vicious, ill-controlled death dealer than it is today. Within a short span of years, after the motorcar began to appear in significant numbers, public inquiries were launched into the means for reducing accidents and compensating the victims. A 1921 state commission in Massachusetts, investigating "the expediency and necessity of requiring the owners of motor vehicles to carry liability insurance," found, among other data, that there were 582 automobile fatalities in Massachusetts in 1919.[3] By contrast, there were 575 motor vehicle deaths in that state in 1961.[4] In that time the number of passenger cars registered in the state grew from about 241,000 in 1919 to about 1,712,000 in 1962.

Society's concern over the consequences of millions of high-speed vehicles, operated by millions of amateur drivers, whizzing over the streets and highways, was expressed in demands for measures that would check the rate of accidents and that would provide financial redress for those injured. The two separate objectives were mingled in legislative proposals. For example, both the Massachusetts compulsory law and the modern "safety responsibility" bill were offered by their drafters as both safety and financial responsibility measures.

The sanctions of these laws against drivers who had accidents or committed serious violations of traffic laws, or who proved to be financially irresponsible, were urged as steps toward removing the accident-prone from the highway.[5] Early financial responsibility proposals were linked with recommendations for improved driver licensing laws.

---

[1] *Accident Facts* (Chicago: National Safety Council, 1963), p. 59.

[2] *Ibid.*

[3] Morris Pike, "Some Aspects of the Compulsory Automobile Insurance Movement," *Proceedings of the Casualty Actuarial Society*, Vol. IX, Part I (1922), p. 29.

[4] *Accident Facts, op. cit.*, p. 64.

[5] William J. Constable, "Compulsory Automobile Insurance," *Proceedings of the Casualty Actuarial Society*, Vol. XIII, Part II (1927), p. 201; also Ralph H. Blanchard, "Compulsory Motor Vehicle Liability Insurance in Massachusetts," *Law and Contemporary Problems*, Vol. III (1936), pp. 537–53.

The ability of the injured to collect damages is affected both by the financial resources against which a claim may be asserted and by the legal considerations surrounding the claim itself. The burden to exercise some degree of care rests upon all. When one's own negligence causes the accident, or contributes to it, or exceeds that of the other party, depending upon the law of the state, he is usually barred from recovery. In the few states using the comparative negligence doctrine (see Chapter 37 for a list), a party whose negligence contributes to an accident may still recover, but his award is diminished by the extent that his fault was responsible for the injury.[6]

The reasonableness of the negligence system of law has been endlessly explored by lawyers, professors, students, and legislatures. The points made include the observation (1) that the chance of accident is inherent in the operation of the motorcar; (2) that the need for medical care and other assistance is as great for the guilty as for the innocent; (3) that testimony and evidence as to the facts of an accident are notoriously inaccurate and difficult to reconstruct; and (4) that the courts in their decisions have steadily eroded the fault doctrine. Many have urged that the negligence approach be replaced by a compensation system, analogous to workmen's compensation, under which all who are injured would receive an award based on the extent of their injury rather than upon the absence (or extent) of fault.[7]

Except for a later discussion of these compensation proposals, this chapter does not concern itself with the merits or demerits of the existing negligence system, but only with the various means by which the states have dealt with the problem of financial redress for those entitled to recovery under the existing law. The problem to be discussed is not who shall recover, but rather how the innocent victim who has suffered injury and survived the issue of fault may not then fail to obtain his allotted compensation because of the financial incompetence of the guilty party.

PUBLIC VEHICLE FINANCIAL RESPONSIBILITY

The principle that public vehicles carrying passengers for hire should be compelled to establish financial responsibility has long been accepted.[8] Surety bonds or policies of insurance with prescribed limits are required.

In 1907 the Georgia Public Service Commission declared that its juris-

---

[6] See Richard M. Nixon, "Changing Rules of Liability in Automobile Accident Litigation," *Law and Contemporary Problems,* Vol. III (1936), pp. 476–90.

[7] For an excellent bibliography on this subject, see "A Selective, Annotated Bibliography" prepared by Orval Etter, Analyst, Bureau of Public Administration, University of California, in "Appendix C" of *Preliminary Report, Plans for Inquiry Into the Wisdom of a California Automobile Accident Commission* (California State Printing Office, 1959), p. 22.

[8] See Morris Pike, *op. cit.*, pp. 23–27.

diction extended over common carriers by motor. In 1914 Pennsylvania enacted a statute regulating common carriers.[9]

A New Jersey compulsory insurance law for public vehicles was enacted in 1916. By 1922 ten states had such laws, and municipalities were establishing mandatory liability limits for taxicabs.

The requirements were soon extended in most states to freight-carrying vehicles. In 1935 the Federal Motor Carrier Act was enacted by Congress, with mandatory insurance provisions covering interstate commercial trucking.

The negligence laws of the states lay an extra burden of care and responsibility on the operators of public passenger vehicles. The licensing and regulation of such vehicles by federal, state, and municipal authorities facilitated the addition of mandatory insurance requirements. Prudent business practice dictated the purchase of insurance protection against the claims of passengers and others, so that there was little incentive for the responsible operators of public vehicles to oppose such laws. The question of required limits of liability has, however, been a continuing subject of concern both to the legislatures and the operators.[10]

FINANCIAL RESPONSIBILITY LAWS

Forty-seven states and the District of Columbia have elected to enact laws of the financial responsibility type to meet the problem of motorists' ability to respond in damages for their fault in automobile accidents. Three states have elected to adopt compulsory insurance laws. Several states have supplemented these laws with other laws designed to close all or part of the gaps in protection left by both financial responsibility and compulsory statutes.

The financial responsibility laws of the states vary considerably in detail, but are alike in principle. A motorist who is involved in an accident causing bodily injury, or more than minor property damage, or who is convicted of a serious traffic law violation, is required to provide security for the damages inflicted or file proof of his future responsibility, or both. These requirements do not apply if the motorist carries an automobile liability insurance policy at least equal to the minimum limits prescribed by statute. Failure to provide security or proof of responsibility, or to satisfy a judgment arising out of an automobile accident, triggers the suspension of driving privileges until the requirements of the law have been met.

---

[9] See "Compulsory Liability Insurance for Commercial Motor Vehicles," *Law and Contemporary Problems,* Vol. III (1936), pp. 571–78.

[10] See "Are $2,500–$5,000 Insurance Limits Adequate for Taxicabs Today?" *A Report of the State of New York Insurance Department* by Superintendent of Insurance Robert E. Dineen, 1950.

The most common criticism of financial responsibility laws is that they give the uninsured motorist a "first bite." No one is required to be financially responsible until there is an occurrence which proves the need. Many of the "first bites" may go uncompensated.

Advocates of this approach respond that laws which attempt to eliminate the "first bite" contain far greater defects, that the cure is worse than the disease, and that the "first bite" charge applies equally to compulsory laws. The essential purpose of financial responsibility laws, they point out, is to exert a strong suasion on all to be insured without taking on the vices of compulsory insurance.

Early Laws

The first financial responsibility law, that of Connecticut, was described by its drafter, Robbins B. Stoeckel, as follows: "Its purpose was, and is, to secure a larger percentage of responsible autoists on the highways."[11] Stoeckel was state commissioner of motor vehicles in Connecticut from 1917–33.

The Connecticut law was enacted by its general assembly of 1925, to become effective January 1, 1926. It required the operator to provide proof of ability to respond in damages for those convicted of reckless driving, operation while intoxicated, or evasion of responsibility, or held responsible for an accident resulting in death or injury to any person or property damage of $100 or more. Proof might also be required of the owner of the vehicle, if he were not the operator.

A similar law was enacted in Vermont effective June 1, 1927, and in Maine effective January 1, 1928. Rhode Island and Minnesota also enacted financial responsibility laws in 1927.

New Hampshire in 1927 passed a law with a somewhat different thrust. It provided that a plaintiff in a civil action arising out of an automobile accident could make a preliminary motion asking the court to find the defendant "probably liable." If the motion were granted, the court must require the defendant to deposit security, within limits, for the judgment that might be rendered against him. Failure to make the deposit was punished by forfeiture of the driver's license and registration.

Model Bill

In December, 1928, the National Committee of Seventeen of the American Automobile Association proposed a model "Safety-Responsibility" bill. The committee had been appointed to study compulsory liability insurance, but decided that the type of law recommended was a preferable solution to the uninsured motorist problem.

The "safety" character of the AAA bill was drawn from a provision

[11] See "Administrative Problems of Financial Responsibility Laws," *Law and Contemporary Problems,* Vol. III (1936), pp. 531–36.

calling for the enactment of a Uniform Motor Vehicle Operators' and Chauffeurs' License Act. In addition, the model bill called for mandatory suspension of the driving permits of those found guilty of serious violations of the motor vehicle laws. Besides the established penalties for these violations, the bill barred convicted drivers from the road until they had established proof of financial responsibility against future injuries to persons or property.

Provision was also made for suspension of driving privileges as long as a judgment remained unsatisfied, and for proof of responsibility thereafter. A reciprocal provision forbade the issuance of a driver's license to any person whose right to drive was suspended in any other state because of failure to respond in damages or because of serious traffic law violations.

The "model" financial responsibility bill has undergone numerous revisions over the years. Beginning with New Hampshire in 1937, all of the states with such laws now require the deposit of security for damages resulting from an accident, unless the operator or owner has liability insurance or the equivalent. This form of strengthening these laws has proved to be a most effective feature, and the laws are often referred to as the "security-responsibility" type.

Writing in the fall of 1951, Henry S. Moser[12] divided the then 44 state laws, plus that of the District of Columbia, into three categories of "mild," "medium strength," and "strong." The "mild" laws of nine states and the District of Columbia suspended operating privileges of persons who were convicted of certain offenses or failed to satisfy judgments until future proof of responsibility was given. Thirty-five states also provided for suspension of driving privileges after an accident, or for failure to deposit security for the damages. Of these 35, six, Moser said, were of "medium strength" because the sanctions following an accident applied only if the driver were at fault, and in one of these, conviction was required. In the remaining 29 states, "strong" laws called for the suspension of drivers' licenses and, frequently, revocation of registration plates, regardless of fault, if the test of financial responsibility was not met.

Table 39–2, a chart compiled by the Law Department of the Association of Casualty and Surety Companies, shows the major provisions of state financial responsibility and related laws as of October, 1962. It reflects both the general agreement of these laws on the principles of financial responsibility and their diversity as to many details.

These laws are an endless target for legislative amendment, and bills for that purpose are introduced in virtually every legislative session. Mostly, the changes that are enacted tend to strengthen the laws, although instances of weakening the sanctions of the laws also occur. The

[12] An address by Henry S. Moser entitled "The Road for the Uninsured Motorist" delivered at Insurance Law Section, American Bar Association, September 17, 1951.

TABLE 39-2

ANALYSIS OF AUTOMOBILE FINANCIAL RESPONSIBILITY AND RELATED LAWS
October, 1963
(Compiled by the Law Department, Association of Casualty and Surety Companies)

State	Liability limits	Compulsory insurance?	FINANCIAL RESPONSIBILITY LAWS — Scope (P—Proof; S—Security; Sat.—Satisfaction. Figures indicate number of years proof required)			Minimum property damage	Requires security (S), proof (P); from driver (D), owner (O)
			Accidents	Convictions	Judgments		
Alabama	5/10/1		S	P - 3	Sat. & P - 3	$50	S - D & O
Alaska	10/20/5		S & P - 3	P - 3	Sat. & P - 3	$200	S & P - D
Arizona	10/20/5		S & P - 3	P - 3	Sat. & P - 3	$100	S & P - D & O
Arkansas	10/20/5		S	P - 3	Sat. & P - 3	$100	S - D & O
California	10/20/5		S (y)	P - 3	Sat. & P - 3	$100	S - D & O (y)
Colorado	5/10/1		S	P - 3	Sat. & P - 3	$50	S - D & O
Connecticut	20/20/1	(b)	S	P - 3	Sat.	$100	S - D & O
Delaware	10/20/5		S	P - 3	Sat. & P - 3	$100	S - D & O
Dist. of Col.	10/20/5		S	P - 3	Sat. & P - 3	$100	S - D & O
Florida	10/20/5		S & P - 3	P - 3	Sat. & P - 3	$50	S & P - D & O
Georgia (dd)	10/20/5		S & P - 3	P - 3 (tt)	Sat.	$50 (f)	S & P - D & O
Hawaii	10/20/5		S	P - 3	Sat. & P - 3	$100	S - D & O
Idaho	10/20/5		S (y)	P - 3	Sat. & P - 3	$100	S - D & O (y)
Illinois	10/20/5		S & P - 3	P - 3	Sat. & P - 3	$100	S & P - D & O
Indiana	10/20/5		S & P - 1 (d)	P - 3	Sat. & P - 3	$50	S & P - D & O (x)
Iowa	10/20/5		S	P - 3	Sat. & P - 3	$100	S - D & O
Kansas	5/10/1		S	P - 2	Sat. & P - 2	$100	S - D & O
Kentucky	10/20/5		S	P - 3	Sat. & P - 3	$100	S - D & O
Louisiana	5/10/1		S	P - 3	Sat. & P - 3	$50	S - D & O (n)
Maine	10/20/5		S & P - 3	P - 3	Sat. & P - 3	$100	S & P - D & O
Maryland	10/20/5	(a)	S & P - 3	P - 3	Sat. & P (ii)	$75	S & P - D & O
Massachusetts	5/10	Yes	(ee)		Sat. (P. D.)		(ee)
Michigan	10/20/5		S & P (g)	P - 3	Sat. & P - 3	$100	S & P - D & O (g)
Minnesota	10/20/5		S	P - 5	Sat. & P - 5	$100	S - D & O
Mississippi	5/10/5		S & P - 5	P - 5	Sat. & P - 5	$50	S - D & O
Missouri	5/10/2		S	P - 3	Sat. & P - 3	$100	S - D & O
Montana	5/10/1		S	P - 3	Sat. & P - 3	$100	S - D & O
Nebraska	10/20/5		S & P - 3	P - 3	Sat. & P - 3	$100	S & P - D & O
Nevada	10/20/5		S (y)	P - 3	Sat. & P - 3	$100	S - D & O (y)
New Hamp.	10/20/5		S & P - 7	P - 7 (d)	Sat. & P - 7	$50	S & P - D & O
New Jersey	10/20/5		S	P - 3	Sat. & P - 3	$100	S - D & O
New Mexico	5/10/1		S & P - 3	P - 3	Sat. & P - 3	$100	S & P - D & O
New York	10/20/5	Yes	S		Sat.	$100	S - D & O
North Carolina	5/10/5	Yes	S (e)	P - 2	Sat. & P - 2	$100	S - D & O
North Dakota	10/20/5		S	P - 5	Sat. & P - 5	$100	S - D
Ohio	10/20/5		S	P - 3	Sat. & P - 3	$100	S - D & O
Oklahoma	5/10/5		S (t)	P - 3	Sat. & P - 3	$100	S - D & O (t)
Oregon	5/10/5		S & P - 5	P - 5	Sat. & P - 5	No min.	S & P - D & O
Pennsylvania	10/20/5		S	P - 3	Sat. & P - 3	$100	S - D & O
Rhode Island	5/10/1	(c)	S	P - 1	Sat. & P - 1	$100	S - D & O
South Carolina	10/20/5		S & P - 5	P - 5	Sat. & P - 5	$50	S & P - D & O
South Dakota	10/20/5		S	P - 3	Sat. & P - 3	$100	S - D & O
Tennessee	10/20/5†		S & P - 5	P - 5	Sat. & P - 5	$100	S & P - D & O
Texas	10/20/5		S & P - 5	P - 5	Sat. & P - 5	$100	S & P - D & O
Utah	10/20/5		S	P - 3	Sat. & P - 3	$100	S - D (v)
Vermont	10/20/2		S & P - 3 (j)	P - 3	Sat. & P - 3	$35	S & P - D
Virginia	15/30/5		S	P - 5	Sat. & P - 5	$50	S - D
Washington	10/20/5		S	P - 3	Sat. & P - 3	$100	S - D & O
West Virginia	10/20/5		S	P - 3	Sat. & P - 3	$100	S - D & O
Wisconsin	10/20/5		S	P - 3	Sat. & P - 3	$100	S - D & O
Wyoming	10/20/5		S	P - 3	Sat. & P - 3	$100	S - D & O

ACCIDENTS						
		INSURANCE IN EFFECT				
Regardless of fault?	Applicable by reciprocity to accidents in other states?	Information required in accident report?	Notice or verification required from insurer? (* - Only if policy not in effect)	OTHER EXEMPTIONS 1. Parked car; 2. Car stopped, standing or parked; 3. Certain motor carriers; 4. Certain publicly owned vehicles.	Unusual provisions	Supplementary laws
Yes	Yes	Yes	Verif.	1,3,4		
Yes	Yes	Yes	Verif.*	1,4	(gg)	
Yes	Yes	Yes	Verif.*	2,3,4(r) (s)		
Yes	Yes	Yes	Notice (o)	1,3,4(r)		
Yes	Yes	Yes	Verif.*	1,4(r)	(aa)	IMP UMR
No	No	Yes	Verif.*	4	(oo)	
Yes	Yes	Yes	Verif.*	1,3,4(p) (r)		
Yes	No	No	Notice	2,3,4	(ff)	
Yes	Yes	Yes	Verif.*	1,3,4 (r)		
Yes	Yes	No (m)	Verif.*	1,4		UMR
No	Yes	No	Notice	1,3,4	(l) (hh)	UMR
Yes	No	No	Notice	1,3,4	(gg)	
Yes	Yes	Yes	No	1,4		
Yes	Yes	Yes	Verif.*	1,3,4	(pp)	UMR
Yes	No	Yes	No	3		
Yes	No	Yes	Verif.*	2,3,4		
Yes	No	Yes	Verif.*	1,3,4	(qq)	
Yes	No	Yes	Verif.*	1,4		
Yes	Yes	Yes	Verif.*	1,3,4 (mm)	(hh)	UMR
No	Yes	Yes	Verif.*	3,4		
Yes	Yes	Yes	Verif.*	1(r)		UJ3
Yes	No	Yes	No	1,4(jj)	(cc)	
No	Yes	Yes	Verif.*	2,4(r)	(gg)	
Yes	Yes	Yes	Verif.*	1,4		
Yes	Yes	Yes	Verif.*	1,3,4		
Yes	Yes	Yes	No	1,3,4		
Yes	Yes	Yes	Verif.*	1,4	(l) (qq)	UMR
Yes	Yes	Yes	Verif.	1,4		
No	Yes	Yes	Verif.*	4		UM
Yes	Yes	Yes	Verif.*	1,3,4(s)	(z)	UJ2
Yes	Yes	Yes	Verif.*	1,4	(hh)	
Yes	Yes	Yes	No	3,4	(gg)	IC UM
No (e)	Yes	Yes	Verif.*	1,3,4(rr)	(gg)	UMR
Yes	No	No	Notice	2,4	(gg) (h)	UJ1
Yes	Yes	Yes	Verif.*	1,4	(l)	
Yes	Yes	Yes	Verif.*	1,3,4		
Yes	Yes	Yes	Verif.*	1,3,4(r) (bb)	(ss)	UM
Yes	Yes	Yes	Verif.*	1,4		UMR
Yes	Yes	Yes	Verif.*	2,4		UMR
Yes	Yes	Yes	Verif.*	1,3,4	(nn)	UMF
Yes	Yes	Yes	Verif.*	1,3,4		
Yes	Yes	Yes	Verif.*	1,3,4	(l) (qq)	
Yes	Yes	Yes	Verif.*	1,3,4	(pp) (hh)	
Yes	Yes	Yes	No	1,4(r)(s)		
No (j)	No	No	Verif.*	1	(gg) (j)	
No	No	No	Notice	1,3,4(i)	(f)	UMF
Yes	Yes	Yes	Verif.*	1,4	(gg)	
Yes	No	Yes	Verif.*	1,4	(aa)	
Yes	Yes	Yes	Verif.*(kk)	1,3,4		
Yes	Yes	No	Notice	1,4		

TABLE 39-2—*Continued*

NOTES FOR TABLE 39-2

†—Effective July 1, 1964.

a—Application of minor for driving license to be accompanied by proof, same to be maintained until minor reaches 21.

b—Vehicles owned by minors cannot be registered unless proof filed; minors under 18 may operate only insured vehicles.

c—Minors owning motor vehicles must furnish proof before registration.

d—Requirement of proof discretionary.

e—Appeal to court automatically stays suspension, and court may exempt motorist not at fault.

f—Where damage is less than $300, security not required in behalf of non-resident except on request.

g—Proof not required if claims settled or security filed BEFORE suspension.

h—Commissioner may stay suspension for not exceeding four months in case of hardship or doubt as to liability.

i—Person whose proof furnished by employer.

j—Security required only if operator is convicted as a result of accident.

k—In case of undue hardship Commissioner may dispense with release.

l—Minimum security $500.

m—Motorist completes and returns SR-21 form mailed by F.R. Division.

n—Registration of owner not suspended where under law owner is not legally liable.

o—Insurer must pay $5 filing fee if SR-21 not filed within 50 days after accident.

p—Car stopped at stop sign or light, or where other person convicted.

q—Inapplicable to person who was unable to procure insurance because of race or color.

r—Person who has received payment for his damages.

s—Operator employed by owner.

t—In hardship cases court may modify extent of compliance with security requirement, and in that event proof is required.

u—If insurer of any operator settles, all operators deemed released.

v—Owner subject to law if employer of driver. In that event registration of employer suspended.

w—Privilege to drive as chauffeur in course of employment not suspended.

x—Discretionary as to owner.

y—When license restored after lapse of 1 year without suit, proof must be given for 3 years.

z—Non-owner subject to requirements may operate vehicle when owner has furnished proof.

aa—Applicable only to accidents on streets and highways.

bb—Owner exempt if vehicle operated by bailee for hire or by person not his agent, employee or member of his family. Driver exempt if employer's vehicle was operated.

cc—Court has discretion to restore license where needed for occupation.

dd—Amendments effective 3/15/64, contingent on appropriation.

ee—In action against nonresident, plaintiff may move for security.

ff—Commissioner may issue limited license or registration when necessary for occupation or livelihood.

gg—Law affects driving licenses only, not registrations.

hh—$10 fee on reinstatement of license.

ii—Period proof required not specified in law.

jj—Car stopped at traffic signal.

kk—As respects permission, insurer may correct report only by filing affidavit within 30 days after receipt.

mm—Where operator of other vehicle is convicted of drunk driving, negligent injury or negligent homicide.

nn—Minimum security $250.

oo—Request for hearing stays suspension.

pp—Minimum security $200.

qq—$25 fee on filing proof.

rr—Commissioner may exempt person where another person involved has been convicted.

ss—Minimum security $100.

tt—Also requires showing of insurance after minor violations.

UM—All policies must include uninsured motorist coverage.

UMF—All policies must include uninsured motorist coverage. Fee imposed on uninsured registrant.

UMR—All policies must include uninsured motorist coverage unless rejected.

UJ1—Unsatisfied Judgment Fund, state operated, effective 7/1/47; assessment on all motorists (maximum $1); applies to b.i. judgments, including hit-and-run cases, obtained by residents; $300 deductible.

UJ2—Unsatisfied Claim and Judgment Fund, insurance company operated, effective 4/1/55; assessment on uninsured motorists (maximum $15) and on insurers (maximum ½ of 1% of premium); applies to b.i. and p.d. claims, including b.i. in hit-and-run cases, of residents (and nonresidents, subject to reciprocity): $100 deductible from p.d. claims.

UJ3—Unsatisfied Claim and Judgment Fund, insurance company operated, effective 6/1/59; assessments on insurers (10% of deficiency, maximum ½ of 1% of premium) and remainder on uninsured motorists; applies to b.i. and p.d. claims, including b.i. in hit-and-run cases, of residents (and non-residents, subject to reciprocity); $100 deductible

IC—Motor Vehicle Indemnification Corporation, insurance company operated and supported, pays to limits of 10/20 b.i. claims resulting from accidents caused by financially irresponsible motorists, including hit-and-run and disclaimer cases. Effective 1/1/59. Also provides that where owner or operator of motor vehicle involved in b.i. accident fails to produce proof of financial security within 48 hours any peace officer may impound vehicle
or owner shall cause vehicle to b
until final disposition of claim. Pr
not affected.

IMP—Vehicle involved in accident must b
until owner or operator complies wi
cial responsibility law.

Compulsory Laws

Massachusetts. Applicable to all owr
motor vehicles registered in the state
owners of motor vehicles operated
state for more than 30 days in any yea
erage prescribed by statute; territory:
ways of Massachusetts only; guest co
excluded; all policies coterminous with
tration; owner must file certificate of
ance; 20 days' notice of cancellation
reasons, required—to other party and
trar; notice of intent not to renew
given by insurer before November 16
cellation or refusal to renew reviewab
Board of Appeal; operation without re
proof punishable by fine of $100 to $
imprisonment for one year; rates ma
Insurance Commissioner.

New York. Applicable to all owners
tor vehicles registered in the state, and
owners and operators of motor vehicle
in the state, resident or non-resident; co
prescribed by regulation; territory: U.S
Canada; policy need not be coterminou
registration; owner must file certificate
surance, but after first year, upon rene
registration, statement by applicant that
is in effect is acceptable; 20 days' noti
days' in case of non-payment of premiu
named insured required upon cancellat
failure to renew by insurer; upon termi
by cancellation or failure to renew,
shall be filed by insurer with Commis
within 30 days after effective date; de
penalty provisions relating to operation
out proof in effect, applicable to
vehicles registered in New York or else
violation results in revocation and is p
able, in case of resident, as misdemear
fine of $100 to $1000 and/or imprisonme
one year; rates made by insurers, subj
prior approval of Superintendent.

North Carolina. Applicable to all owr
motor vehicles registered in the state
erage: financial responsibility as defin
financial responsibility law; territory: U.S
Canada; policy need not be coterminou
registration; owner must file his certific
insurance; 15 days' notice to named insur
quired upon cancellation or failure to ren
insurer; no termination by cancellatio
otherwise by insurer without 15 days'
notice to Department; owner of motor v
registered in state who operates or p
operation without financial responsibil
effect guilty of misdemeanor; rates ma
company-operated bureau created by la
quires merit rating.

—o—

most clear-cut long-range trend has been away from the early limits of liability of $5,000/$10,000 for bodily injury and $1,000 for property damage to $10,000/$20,000/$5,000. The latter set of limits applied in 30 states and the District of Columbia as of October, 1962. Connecticut had a $20,000/$20,000/$1,000 limit and Virginia $15,000/$30,000/$5,000.

A complete text of a model financial responsibility law is contained in the Uniform Vehicle Code, as revised in 1962.[13]

The Industry Program

The automobile insurance business, through its three major trade associations, supports a total program for dealing with motorists' responsi-

[13] National Committee on Uniform Traffic Laws and Ordinances, *Uniform Vehicle Code* (rev. 1962), pp. 75 et seq.

bility problems,[14] which is discussed later in this chapter. One of the facets of the program calls for "new concepts" in the application of the financial responsibility principle. These proposals for "toughening up" the financial responsibility laws are summarized by the automobile insurers as follows:

> This part of the program will encourage all motorists to become financially responsible and will remove from the road irresponsible motorists.
>
> The program provides protection to the public by assuring that those motorists who have been involved in accidents or in traffic violations and who have demonstrated their need for financial responsibility will either provide financial responsibility or be removed from the highways.
>
> The specific proposals provide for broadening the scope of the Financial Responsibility Law by:
>
> 1. Making it applicable to all accidents resulting in property damage of $50 or more (as well as to all accidents resulting in bodily injury or death).
> 2. Providing for suspension of *both* the license and registrations of *both* the owner and operator of an uninsured vehicle involved in an accident or in a serious traffic violation if the requirements of the law are not met.
> 3. Making it applicable to convictions of all moving traffic violations.
> 4. Making it applicable in other states on a reciprocal basis.
>
> The proposals would increase the sanctions against irresponsible motorists by:
>
> 1. Providing for impoundment of uninsured motor vehicles involved in accidents and where security is not deposited.
> 2. Requiring uninsured motorists involved in accidents to deposit a minimum of $500 as security.
> 3. Requiring security to remain on deposit for a minimum of two years, and providing for suspension for at least two years where security is not deposited and claims are not settled.
> 4. Requiring an uninsured motorist convicted of any moving traffic offense to obtain insurance, and, upon a second conviction, to maintain insurance (or other proof of financial responsibility) for five years.
> 5. Requiring the owner and operator of an uninsured vehicle involved in an accident to carry insurance for five years.
> 6. Requiring the owner of an uninsured vehicle involved in a serious violation to carry insurance for five years even though the vehicle was at the time operated by someone else. The five year insurance requirement would of course also be applicable to the convicted driver.
> 7. Imposing a $25 fee for reinstatement of a license suspended under the law.

Certain of the financial responsibility provisions of the Industry Program for Responsibility on Our Highways have met with considerable resistance from motor vehicle law administrators and legislatures.

Only Nebraska and Tennessee enacted the provision requiring (1) a showing of insurance (or its equivalent) upon the first conviction of a mov-

[14] *A Program for Responsibility on our Highways*, prepared by American Mutual Insurance Alliance, Association of Casualty and Surety Companies, and National Association of Independent Insurers.

ing traffic violation and (2) proof of financial responsibility for the future upon a second such conviction within one year of the first conviction if the motorist was without insurance (or its equivalent) at the time of the first violation and is again without insurance (or its equivalent) at the time of the second violation.

In 1961, two years after the enactment, Nebraska repealed this provision in its entirety, and Tennessee severely limited its applicability to "drag racing, reckless driving, and speeding." A bill based on the industry program's provision passed both Houses of the Colorado Legislature in 1961 but was vetoed by the governor.

South Carolina enacted a provision which went even further than the provision called for under the industry program. Applicable to persons convicted of a violation for which four or more points were chargeable under that state's point system, it required proof of financial responsibility for the future even of motorists who were insured at the time of the violation. In 1961, two years later, because of the public outcry about the unfairness in penalizing even insured motorists by requiring them to purchase the higher cost future proof coverage, a coverage for which the market, even at the somewhat higher price, was quite limited in South Carolina, the legislature repealed this provision in its entirety.

In Tennessee only, the impoundment provision of the industry program was enacted in modified form, applicable only to accidents involving a death or personal injury requiring hospitalization and where suspension of the operator's license was required. It was repealed in 1961, two years later.[15]

Difficulty has also been encountered in keeping the dollar amount of property damage involved in an accident which determines whether the accident is subject to the FR Law down at the $50 level called for under the industry program. In both Nebraska and Tennessee this amount has been increased to $100.

Objections to particular features of the industry program have been generated by motor vehicle law administrators' complaints about the undue administrative burdens they placed, or would place, upon them and their departments. The harsher features of the program have drawn fire from legislators as well. All things considered, the financial responsibility provisions of the industry program must remain, in concept, as a set of tools which are available to improve the effectiveness of existing financial responsibility laws. In some states, existing laws have been highly successful in obtaining very high percentages of insured motor vehicles. In other states, these same, or similar, laws have proven less successful. Perhaps the issue most significant is the efficiency and effectiveness of the administration of the law. Good administration can undoubtedly wring more out of existing laws than poor administration could

[15] Impoundment provisions predating the industry program remain in effect in such states as California and New York.

obtain with the full measure of the industry program. There is much that can be done in this area to maximize the effectiveness of existing laws, and certainly the improvement of these laws along the lines indicated by the industry program will require the full enthusiasm, cooperation, and assistance of the motor vehicle administrator in selecting or adapting the particular tool, or tools, most likely to do the job in his state.

EFFECT ON PROPORTION INSURED

The purpose of the financial responsibility laws is to increase the proportion of insured cars through strong suasion, short of compulsion, to establish financial responsibility.

Figures as to the share of registered vehicles which are covered by automobile liability insurance have always been difficult to obtain. At best, it has been necessary to rely on estimates, often based upon the proportions of insured and uninsured vehicles shown in accident reports made to the states under financial responsibility laws. These figures tend to be overstated to the extent that the uninsured evade the reporting requirement through private settlements with other parties to accidents, or otherwise. The degree of overstatement can only be estimated.

Nevertheless, it is clear that all of the forces which have played on the public mind since the advent of the motorcar have produced an overwhelming recognition of the desirability of carrying automobile insurance. The most significant of these forces surely have been the financial responsibility laws, the enforcement activities, and the public educational efforts surrounding them. Today it is possible to say that automobile insurance has "an intense social sanction."[16]

When the Massachusetts compulsory law was enacted in 1925, it was said that only one fourth of the owners of the state's 750,000 motor vehicles were covered by insurance.[17] The strengthening of the New Hampshire law in 1937 is reported to have increased the percentage of insured cars from 36 to 75.[18] A private study is said to have revealed that only 27 percent of the cars in Manitoba were insured in 1945, after 15 years under a financial responsibility law, but the enactment of the strengthened variety in 1946, with impoundment and unsatisfied judgment fund features brought the share of insured to 87 percent in one year and to 95 percent by 1951.[19]

---

[16] Joseph W. Newman, *Motivation Research and Marketing Management* (Norwood, Mass.: Plimpton Press, 1957), p. 148.

[17] G. F. Michelbacher, "On Some Insurance Problems Incidental to Compulsory Automobile Insurance," *Proceedings of the Casualty Actuarial Society,* Vol. XII, Part II (1926), p. 212.

[18] Harold M. Jones, "The New York Motor Vehicle Safety Responsibility Act," *Proceedings of the Caualty Actuarial Society,* Vol. XXVII, Part II (1941), p. 331.

[19] A report by George H. Kline and Carl O. Pearson, "The Problem of the Uninsured Motorist" (New York Insurance Department, 1951), p. 40.

It is a fair generalization (1) that, countrywide, fewer than 25 percent of the owners of motorcars were buying automobile insurance by the mid 1920's, but (2) that this proportion has increased state by state according to the stringency of its particular law and the efficiency of law enforcement. Where the sanctions turn on the reporting of accidents or conviction of traffic law violations, obviously the effectiveness of accident reporting, the police, the prosecutors, and the courts determines how far the law

TABLE 39–3

PERCENTAGE OF MOTOR VEHICLES INSURED IN STATES HAVING FINANCIAL RESPONSIBILITY LAWS

April, 1963

State	*Percent*	*State*	*Percent*
Alabama	*	Missouri	75
Alaska	91.4	Montana	71
Arizona	75–80	Nebraska	92
Arkansas	71.9	Nevada	*
California	89.2	New Hampshire	92
Colorado	80	New Jersey	95.06
Connecticut	84.8	New Mexico	65
Delaware	83	North Dakota	91.1
Dist. of Col.	80	Ohio	88.6
Florida	80	Oklahoma	66
Georgia	60–65	Oregon	91.1
Hawaii	80	Pennsylvania	*
Idaho	90	Rhode Island	88
Illinois	92.46	South Carolina	96.61
Indiana	*	South Dakota	87
Iowa	96	Tennessee	90
Kansas	85	Texas	75
Kentucky	65	Utah	91
Louisiana	73.5	Vermont	91.8
Maine	82	Virginia	94.5
Maryland	*	Washington	*
Michigan	90	West Virginia	80
Minnesota	93	Wisconsin	90.3
Mississippi	67	Wyoming	*

* Figure not available to compilers.

SOURCE: Based on Accident Report Information or Estimate of Administrators and compiled by Association of Casualty and Surety Companies.

reaches to those to whom it should apply. In 1963, the figure of 85 percent represents an "educated guess" as to the proportion now insured in the United States. The growth of that figure, multiplied by the vast growth in the numbers of cars in use, has been responsible for the great expansion of the automobile insurance business.

Table 39–3 presents the state-by-state estimates of the percentage of motor vehicles insured, compiled as of April, 1963, by the Association of Casualty and Surety Companies. The table omits Massachusetts, New York, and North Carolina, which have compulsory insurance laws.

COMPULSORY INSURANCE LAWS

Public vehicles, as described earlier in this chapter, have in most states long been subject to compulsory insurance laws. The first application of compulsory insurance to private vehicles was in Massachusetts. A bill for that purpose first appeared in the Massachusetts legislature in 1918. A series of inquiries followed, under legislative sponsorship, and the Massachusetts law was finally enacted in 1925, effective January 1, 1927.

The law requires (now as then) that the owner of a motor vehicle or trailer required to be registered must provide security for his liability to pay damages to others for bodily injury including death of at least $5,000 on account of injury or death of one person and of at least $10,000 for injury or death of more than one person. The security may be provided by an insurance policy in an authorized company, by a surety bond, or by the deposit of $5,000 with the Division of Highways. No registration plates may be issued unless the registration application is accompanied by a certificate which gives evidence that the requisite insurance or other security is in effect.

The Massachusetts law is two-edged in its compulsory feature. It compels the car owner to insure and it also compels the insurance companies to provide insurance to all comers, subject to the right of appeal to an administrative-level board.

The Massachusetts statute is limited in its application to bodily injury liability only, and does not require property damage liability coverage. It does not apply to accidents occurring on private ways, or to guest occupants of a motor vehicle. It does not require coverage for travel outside of Massachusetts, and it does not apply to out-of-state cars traveling in Massachusetts.

Many Massachusetts motorists nevertheless protect themselves against claims not covered under the compulsory law through the purchase of voluntary additions to the statutory requirements. These are known as "B" coverages. A special commission which inquired in the late 1950's into the operation of the Massachusetts law concluded that 90 percent of all Massachusetts car owners carried property damage insurance, 96.5 percent had extra-territorial and 94 percent had guest coverage.[20]

For more than 30 years Massachusetts was the only state with a compulsory law of general application. Then the state of New York adopted its Motor Vehicle Financial Security Act, effective February 1, 1957. North Carolina enacted a compulsory law effective January 1, 1958. Although compulsory insurance bills are introduced in virtually every session of every legislature, these three states stand alone as of 1965 in

[20] Commonwealth of Massachusetts, *Report of Special Commission Relative to the Motor Vehicle Laws and the Insurance Laws as They Relate to Motor Vehicles and Certain Related Matters* (Boston: The Causeway Print, 1959), p. 114.

adopting this means of dealing with motorists' financial responsibility.

The New York law provides that no motor vehicle shall be registered unless the application for registration is accompanied by proof of financial security which must be continuously maintained during the registration period. If insurance lapses, the license plates must be surrendered. Financial security may be proved by a bond, deposit, or an insurance policy which provides automobile bodily injury liability coverage of at least \$10,000/\$20,000 and property damage liability coverage of at least \$5,000. The North Carolina law corresponds to the New York law, except that the minimum limits of coverage required are \$5,000/\$10,000/\$5,000.

Unlike Massachusetts, New York first relied upon the financial responsibility approach. Its original financial responsibility act was effective September 1, 1929. A strengthened law adding security provisions was effective January 1, 1942.

In 1951, when compulsory insurance proposals were being hotly debated in New York, estimates of the proportion of insured cars in the state ranged from 90 to 95 percent. The New York Safety Responsibility 1950 annual report fixed the figure at 94 percent.

The *New York Daily News,* in a series of articles which appeared in April, 1963, charged that there were "twice as many non-insured drivers on the roads now as there were before the (compulsory) law was passed."[21]

The article states:

> Before the law was passed, 3 percent of the cars in this state were being operated without insurance. Last year 6 percent were without insurance coverage.
>
> The 6 percent figure represents 373,708 vehicles driven by delinquent motorists evading the law through all kinds of chiseling practices. Of these cars, 74,714 are in the New York metropolitan area alone, operated by deadbeats who don't have a dime in insurance to offer any victim of an accident in which they are involved.

Rhode Island requires proof of financial responsibility before it will register a motor vehicle for a person between 16 and 21 years of age. The provision was effective in 1955. New York passed a similar law in 1951. Connecticut requires proof of responsibility before it will register a vehicle owned by a minor, and persons under 18 may operate only insured vehicles. Maryland requires minors to furnish proof with applications for drivers' licenses, proof to be maintained until the driver is 21 years of age.

THE GAP CLOSERS

The endless studies of motorists' financial responsibility that have been made are virtually unanimous in emphasizing the gaps that remain under

[21] *New York Daily News,* April 23, 1963, p. 2.

both financial responsibility and compulsory insurance laws, even though they differ as to the size and importance of the gaps. Financial responsibility laws are criticized because the accidents to which sanctions apply may produce valid claims against financially irresponsible drivers. Compulsory laws are criticized because valid but uncollectible claims may arise against drivers and/or owners of out-of-state cars, hit-and-run vehicles, and stolen cars, and against drivers who are successfully evading the insurance requirements.

Possible "gap closers" include unsatisfied judgment funds; uninsured motorists coverage; medical payment coverage; group and individual accident, medical, and hospitalization insurance; and the Motor Vehicle Accident Indemnification Corporation in New York state.

Unsatisfied Judgment Funds

Maryland, New Jersey, and North Dakota have unsatisfied judgment funds as supplements to financial responsibility laws. Their purpose is to meet valid claims, subject to differing criteria, arising against the uninsured. Proponents have urged their enactment in lieu of compulsory insurance laws, and the legislatures have treated them as such.

Those who operate automobiles without financial responsibility—the uninsured—are barred from recovery from the funds. Proponents declare that the funds provide a means of recovery for all who have a rightful claim against an irresponsible motorist.[22] Opponents challenge the equity of putting the costs of these funds in whole or in part on the insured, either through direct fees or charges against insurers.

The first of these was the North Dakota Act, effective July 1, 1947. It is financed by an extra $1.00 registration fee on each motor vehicle. Claims are limited to uncollectible judgments for bodily injury or death arising out of a motor vehicle accident in the state, up to $10,000/$20,000, subject to a $300 deductible, including hit-and-run accidents. Limits were $5,000/$10,000 until 1963. The fund is operated by the state.

The New Jersey Act, which took effect April 1, 1955, is financed by funds collected from motorists and from insurers. Uninsured motorists are to pay at least $3.00 but not more than $15.00 at the time of registering a vehicle, the amount to be set by the Director of the Division of Motor Vehicles. All other motor vehicle registrants pay a fee of $1.00. Any additional amount needed is assessed against automobile insurers, subject

---

[22] For a discussion of the pros and cons of unsatisfied judgment funds, see "The Road for the Uninsured Motorist," an address by Henry S. Moser before American Bar Association, Sept. 17, 1951; "The Problem of the Uninsured Motorist," a report by George H. Kline and Carl O. Pearson, (New York Insurance Department, 1951); "Which Road for the Uninsured Motorist?," an address by Alfred J. Bohlinger, New York, May 7, 1951; and "The Uninsured Motorist," a report by Richard M. Heins, Paul S. Wise, R. Newell Lusby and Arthur C. Mertz, *Journal of Insurance,* Volume XXIV (September, 1957), pp. 114–22.

to a limit of ½ of 1 percent of aggregate net direct written premiums for the preceding calendar year. Claims and judgments against uninsured motorists may be settled by the fund for both bodily injury and property damage, the latter subject to a $100 deductible. Hit-and-run cases are limited to bodily injury only. This fund is operated by insurance company representatives.

The Maryland Unsatisfied Claim and Judgment Fund is effective as to accidents occurring on or after June 1, 1959. The fund was raised initially by a $1.00 registration fee on insured motorists, an $8.00 fee on the uninsured, and a charge against automobile insurance companies of ½ of 1 percent. It is maintained by fees against the uninsured and insurance companies only, the latter limited to 10 percent of the fund's previous year's deficiency or ½ of 1 percent of automobile premiums, whichever is smaller.

The Maryland Fund was in serious financial condition in 1963. Its manager reported a deficit of $2 million in November, 1962. By April, 1963, the deficit had grown to over $3 million. To increase the income of the fund, the annual charge to uninsured registrants, originally $8.00, was raised to $26 in 1961, to $32 in 1962 and to $70 in 1963. When the fee was $26, over 40,000 motorists paid it; at $32 the figure dropped to 20,000. As of April, 1963, only 1,184 had paid the $70 charge.

At the November, 1962, meeting of the fund's board, the manager described the fund's predicament in part as follows:

> It is operating in the red, with a current deficit of more than $2,000,000. The problem cannot be solved merely by increasing the fee on the uninsured motorist. As this fee had increased, total receipts have decreased. In other words, fewer people pay the fee. This does not mean that more motorists take out insurance . . . the reports of accidents caused by uninsured motorists do not decrease . . . we are getting down to a hard core of uninsureds . . . who will not buy insurance or keep it in force. . . . The Board is striving for stricter enforcement of the law, more teeth in the law. It wants this law to work, to get the uninsured to pay the fee or to get off the road.

The Maryland fund applies to bodily injury and ($100 deductible) property damage, plus bodily injury only for hit-and-run accidents. It is operated by insurance company representatives.

New York found it necessary to superimpose an unsatisfied claim fund on top of its compulsory law. When Governor Averill Harriman signed the compulsory law, he said:

> I approve this bill with regret that the innocent victim of the hit-and-run and the stolen car and the out-of-state automobile will be unable to receive the benefits afforded to others. This gap in the law will continue to demand remedial amendment and I will continue to press for legislation to fill the void.

The legislature created the Motor Vehicle Accident Indemnification Corporation in 1958, to begin January 1, 1959. As of March 31, 1963, it had paid $8,636,200 on 6,375 bodily injury claims, had closed 10,533 claims without payment, and had 9,608 open claims reserved at $23,333,478. The fund is operated and supported by automobile insurers. From 1961 to 1963 the annual assessment against insurers was $11 million.

The MVAIC manager reported in May of 1963 that claims were running at a rate of almost 800 a month, reflecting a steady increase, year by year, since inception. He observed:

The ultimate average reporting cannot be ascertained at this time. The number of uninsured cars in the state with outstanding violations against them has also been increasing, perhaps not percentagewise as our figures have shown, but at least numerically. Experience indicates that there are large numbers of persons driving in New York State against whom orders to pick up their plates are outstanding, and these orders emanate from the Department of Motor Vehicles to the respective police departments.

At least one official from the New York Police Department has indicated that the task of retrieving license plates of uninsured persons is so great that due to limited manpower, 100 percent enforcement of orders from the Motor Vehicle Department is virtually impossible. However, I have been informed that as of January, 1962, the task of picking up license plates has been assigned to precinct patrolmen, whereas previously this chore was assigned to the Detective Bureau. What the net result of this change will be cannot be predicted at this time.

The bulk of claims against this Corporation stems from the Metropolitan area. Principally, the highest incidence of claims reported to us develop from accidents caused by persons driving without insurance (45 percent New York state uninsured; 20 percent out of state uninsured), rather than "hit and run" situations (16 percent).

The average cost per claim paid excluding allocated claim expense was $1,355 since the inception of the organization.

Your Board of Directors believes that the present rate of assessment will probably suffice for 1963. Looking to the future, however, it is still too early to predict the number of claims that will be received or the total amount of incurred losses for 1962.[23]

Uninsured Motorists Coverage

For some years a coverage has been available to car owners which, as a part of their own automobile insurance policy, puts them in effect in the same position, if injured by an uninsured motorist, as they would have been had the uninsured carried the limits of liability prescribed by the state's financial responsibility law. It permits the innocent victim to make claim against his own insurance company for damages to which his injuries may entitle him.

In 1956 major segments of the industry made this coverage available virtually nationwide (not sold in Massachusetts). Its appeal as a solution to the uninsured motorists problem has led several states to require that it be a part of every automobile insurance policy, usually subject to rejec-

[23] Thomas F. O'Boyle, *Report of Secretary and Manager* (New York: Motor Vehicle Accident Indemnification Corporation, 1963), pp. 7–8.

tion by the insured. California, Florida, Georgia, Illinois, Louisiana, Nebraska, North Carolina, and Rhode Island have mandatory uninsured motorist coverage laws with right of rejection. New Hampshire, New York, and Oregon laws are mandatory with no right of rejection. In all of these states, the insured pays a premium for the coverage, as set by his insurer, ranging generally from $3 to $10 a year. South Carolina and Virginia have mandatory uninsured motorist coverage laws which impose the costs on the uninsured. (See Chapter 37 for a treatment of some of the details of this insurance.)

Medical Payments Coverage

A common automobile insurance coverage of long standing is medical payments. It can be purchased usually for limits from $500 to $5,000, and the benefits are payable to occupants of the insured car for bodily injuries whether caused by an insured or uninsured motorist, or otherwise, and regardless of fault. The coverage follows the insured, his spouse, and relatives of his household into other vehicles or as pedestrians.

Many automobile insurance policies also offer death, dismemberment, and disability coverages for injuries arising out of automobile accidents. These are schedule-type accident coverages, and again do not depend upon the responsibility of the car involved or upon the absence of fault. (See Chapters 37 and 38.)

COMPENSATION PROPOSALS

The fact that many who are injured as a result of automobile accidents are unable to obtain any financial help, either because the guilty party is financially irresponsible, or because the victim cannot establish his own innocence or the guilt of another, has led some students of the problem to urge the adoption of a system which would deal with automobile accidents in the same manner as workmen's compensation insurance deals with injuries arising out of occupational accidents. No such proposal has been adopted in the United States. The Province of Saskatchewan, Canada, has a limited statutory program of the compensation type, which operates through a state fund in conjunction with voluntary, private insurance.[24]

---

[24] For an exposition of this subject, see "Report by the Committee to Study Compensation for Automobile Accidents 299 (Columbia University Council for Research in Social Sciences, February, 1932); also Albert A. Ehrenzweig, *"Full Aid" Insurance for the Traffic Victim* (Berkeley: University of California Press, 1954); also Frank P. Grad, "Recent Developments in Automobile Accident Compensation," *Columbia Law Review,* Volume 50 (March, 1950), and *Law and Contemporary Problems,* Vol. III (1936), pp. 583–97 and pp. 598–608.

THE PROBLEMS WHICH REMAIN

Although the broad base of motorists' responsibility in this country rests upon the security-type financial responsibility law, the three compulsory statutes, and the welter of appendages in the form of unsatisfied judgment funds and mandatory uninsured motorist coverage make a confusing picture. It is clear that no single solution acceptable to all has emerged. Differences among the states may be expected as far ahead as anyone dares to peer.

Some observers would argue that the negligence or fault concept prevents most of the uncompensated victims of automobile accidents from obtaining financial redress. But the literature of the subject leaves the impression that this point is of far greater concern to students of the problem than it is to the legislatures or the public. In any event, the immediate problem of the insurance business seems to be one of living with the existing legal system and the existing responsibility laws.

No discussion of this subject would be complete that did not consider the human nature aspects, the greed, connivance, perjury, and fraud which have worked their way into the automobile accident picture. To many students, the problem is one of pure theory, in a world peopled by mangled, innocent, and uncompensated victims. It seems important to recognize that, however shocking that aspect of the matter may be, the practical man, and surely the practical insurance executive, must live and work in a world which is also peopled in part by those who look upon the automobile accident as a prime opportunity for personal enrichment.

What it called the "phony claim problem" was examined by the Special Commission appointed in 1956 by the Massachusetts legislature. It found that claims based on outright fraud were small in number, but that a substantial number of claims were based on injuries that were either exaggerated or imaginary. One official witness presented evidence that a large percentage of bodily injury claims in Massachusetts are "nuisance" in nature, that is, are pressed not for their merit but for what insurers will pay to avoid litigation. He said that the high rate of bodily injuries in the Massachusetts statistics was due to reports filed to support a claim.[25]

The unearthing of a phony accident ring in a major community is a regular event. In 1960, *The Oregonian*, Portland, Oregon, revealed that an investigation was before a federal grand jury dealing with rackets which "allegedly involve nearly 200 persons in a complex of criminal activity and

---

[25] Commonwealth of Massachusetts, *Report of Special Commission Relative to the Motor Vehicle Laws and the Insurance Laws as They Relate to Motor Vehicles and Certain Related Matters, op. cit.*, p. 48 *et seq.* See also "The Liability Claim Racket," *Law and Contemporary Problems,* Vol. III (1936), pp. 491–504 *et seq.*; "Phoney Accidents Are Costing You," *Family Weekly* (May 13, 1962), p. 4.

unethical conduct involving members of the bar, and, it is believed, ultimately, licensed physicians."[26]

In 1961, the *Houston Post* ran an extensive series[27] under the caption of "The Unscrupulous." In one of these articles, the reporter said:

> Only a few of Harris County's approximately 2500 attorneys and 1500 doctors can be listed among The Unscrupulous who are forcing higher personal injury insurance rates, excessive settlements and verdicts against insurers.
>
> But these few—with a network of "runners," ambulance-chasers, wrecker and ambulance drivers, hospital attendants, police officers, friendly insurance adjusters, garagemen, and photographers—have a business so thriving that it is spreading to neighboring cities, towns and counties.

In Dade County, Florida, the Miami newspapers conducted two exposés of fraud, collusion, and exaggeration in automobile claims.[28]

The moral, if any, is simply that these outcroppings of less than admirable human traits must be taken into account in measuring the practicality of legal schemes for protecting the innocent. The cost of fraud and exaggeration is an important part of every automobile insurance premium today. The practices which exist corrupt the fringes of the professions and the public character. Remedies for financial irresponsibility which ignore the facts of human nature will do the public no real service.

Political Aspects

The first time that rates were reviewed in Massachusetts on the basis of the initial year's experience under its compulsory law, the political foment caused by the rate increase which the statistics called for led to the resignation of the insurance commissioner. An observer at the time[29] said that the commissioner was "vilified, threatened and cajoled," and finally resigned without setting rates for the coming year, 1929. His letter of resignation contained these paragraphs:

> The result is that no memorandum revising these rates will be filed by me, and the rates established for the year 1928 will stand. This relieves you and his honor, the Lieutenant-Governor, of any necessity of fighting me in the courts, and the Attorney-General of the necessity of defending me against his will.
>
> As I view the whole matter now, this unusual situation of an under-executive having to contest with his superiors in authority is the result of an attempt to solve a mathematical problem by the introduction of a factor of political expediency. This is neither right nor proper.

Thirty-five years later, in 1963, insurance regulatory officials in two states were summarily dismissed by their governors for the sole reason

[26] *The Oregonian,* Portland, Oregon (October 28, 1960), p. 1.

[27] *Houston Post,* beginning April 26, 1961.

[28] *Miami Herald* and *Miami News,* January 1, 1960 and subsequent issues; *Miami News,* November 26, 1962.

[29] William J. Constable "Massachusetts Compulsory Automobile Liability Insurance," *Proceedings of the Casualty Actuarial Society,* Vol. XV, Part II (1929), p. 171.

that they had approved increases in automobile insurance rates. Political influences on rates have been a growing source of concern to many insurance managers. These influences have been greater under compulsory laws than under other financial responsibility provisions, and greater in states where the rating laws require the insurance commissioner publicly to approve rates in advance of their use.

Adequate rates for the hazard assumed are a basic requirement of private insurance enterprise. Politics is an uncomfortable factor in the pricing of insurance, but it must be reckoned with and not ignored in measuring the practicality of legislative proposals.

Enforcement

The *sine qua non* of all types of financial responsibility laws is enforcement. We have seen how the proportion of insured cars varies widely under comparable security-responsibility laws. The police must catch violators and process accident reports. The courts must convict the guilty, and the records must be forwarded to state administrators. The central authority regulating drivers' licenses and registrations must receive and process the reports, keep master records, and apply the sanctions of the law, which include suspension and revocation of the licenses and registrations. Any weakness in any link of the enforcement chain reduces the effect of the financial responsibility law.

The enforcement problems under compulsory law were described in connection with the New York law. Depending on the source, the proportion of cars insured was no higher in 1965 under compulsory than it was under the responsibility law, and may be less. The *New York Daily News* series of April, 1963, revealed that the preponderance of license revocations issued against insurance violators was never served by the enforcement officers.

Both New York and North Carolina have capped their compulsory laws with a mandate that insured drivers also protect themselves from the uninsured through the uninsured motorists coverage. New York has also added an unsatisfied claim fund to take up the rest of the slack.

The Maryland experience under a financial responsibility law plus an unsatisfied judgment fund is obviously at a near-crisis level. Only one explanation is plausible: that the financial responsibility law is poorly enforced, or else the number of uninsured claims would be far less and the number paying the fee on uninsured registrants would be far greater. The situation in that state already calls for emergency treatment.

One distinction in the enforcement problem stands out: under financial responsibility laws, while enforcement can apparently range from bad to excellent, the size of the problem is manageable, since the law must be applied *only to those who have had an accident or violation and are financially irresponsible.* Under compulsory laws, enforcement must be applied continuously to the operator of every registered vehicle. The magnitude of the difference is shown in the much higher, measurable cost of administering the compulsory laws, and the unmeasurable but material difference in burdens on the police, the prosecutors, and the courts.

A hard, realistic appraisal of the enforcement problem is an inescapable element in judging the merit of particular legislative approaches. There is little evidence that this aspect of the matter has had serious legislative attention in many states.

THE INDUSTRY PROGRAM

Earlier, it was noted that the three major trade associations of the automobile insurance business have an agreed program for dealing with financial responsibility legislation. These are the American Mutual Insurance Alliance, the Association of Casualty and Surety Companies, and the National Association of Independent Insurers. Together, they represent more than 500 separate insurers which transact about four fifths of the automobile insurance business in the United States.

The legislative platform published by this group calls, first, for "better traffic safety," second, for "more financial responsibility," and, third, for "improved insurance coverages."

The traffic safety objectives of the program are implemented at the legislative level by the experienced staffs of the three associations and at the professional safety level by the Insurance Institute for Highway Safety, which is also a joint enterprise of these three groups.

The financial responsibility proposals of the industry are set forth earlier in this chapter. In essence, they call for a strong security-type financial responsibility law, broad in its reach and stringent in its application.

The improved insurance coverages refer principally to uninsured motorist protection, secondarily, to pedestrian accident policies.

The essence of the industry program is reliance upon well-enforced security-type financial responsibility laws to reduce the uninsured segment of the driving population to a minimum, and to provide those who are themselves responsible with protection against the irresponsible through coverages which they may purchase for themselves at modest cost.

The enforcement of the financial responsibility laws, varied in effectiveness as it may be, is nevertheless functioning in an established pattern in all but a few states. The means for improving this enforcement pattern are known and being implemented by the insurance industry wherever possible.

The industry, while not basically sympathetic to laws which compel the purchase of its services, has supported mandatory uninsured motorist coverage bills which include the right of rejection, but only in states which have appreciably narrowed the uninsured segment of car owners. The ability of the uninsured motorist coverage to reach to situations where compulsory cannot recommends this approach.

The industry's brochure[30] which outlines this program concludes with this pronouncement:

> The proposals contained herein provide a basis for a satisfactory solution to the problem of the irresponsible motorist. They seek to achieve a proper balance between social needs and individual freedom. We know that they will succeed only if all interested groups—legislatures, vehicle administrators, the judiciary, law enforcement officials, the press, safety groups, automobile clubs, and insurance carriers and agents—all cooperate in leadership and support.

SUGGESTED READINGS

Commonwealth of Massachusetts, *Report of Special Commission Relative to the Motor Vehicle Laws and the Insurance Laws as they Relate to Motor Vehicles and Certain Related Matters.* Boston: The Causeway Print, 1959.

Conard, Alfred F.; Morgan, James N.; Pratt, Robert W., Jr.; Voltz, Charles E.; and Bombaugh, Robert L. *Automobile Accident Costs and Payments: Studies in the Economics of Injury Reparation.* Ann Arbor: University of Michigan Press, 1964.

Ehrenzweig, Albert A. *"Full Aid" Insurance for the Traffic Victim.* Berkeley: University of California Press, 1954.

Heins, Richard M.; Wise, Paul S.; Lusby, R. Newell; and Mertz, Arthur C. "The Uninsured Motorist," *Journal of Insurance,* Vol. XXIV (Sept., 1957), pp. 114–22.

Law and Contemporary Problems, Vol. III (1936).

Report by the Committee to Study Compensation for Automobile Accidents. New York: Columbia University Council for Research in Social Sciences, 1932.

[30] *A Program for Responsibility on our Highways,* prepared by American Mutual Insurance Alliance, Association of Casualty and Surety Companies, and National Association of Independent Insurers.

Chapter 40

EXCESS LIABILITY, UMBRELLA, AGGREGATES, AND DEDUCTIBLES

BY BERNARD J. DAENZER

The matter of obtaining insurance above the conventional liability limits, the technique of removing gaps in liability insurance protection, the use of deductibles, and the emergence of contracts which provide both liability and physical damage insurance are treated in this chapter.

THE TREND TOWARD SEPARATE EXCESSES

Since World War II there has been a growing tendency toward the purchase of separate "excess liability insurance contracts." This term is industry jargon for a liability insurance contract which pays, up to a maximum, liability claims against an insured but only to the extent each claim exceeds some specified limit of primary insurance or "self-insured" retention. Prior to the war, there was a complacency about limits with very few demands from the public or from producers beyond $100,000 per person and $300,000 per accident for bodily injury and $50,000 per accident for property damage. Rarely was the treaty capacity of the insurance carrier exceeded. Few Lloyd's excesses were placed. The change beginning in the early 1940's arose for several reasons explained below.

Size of Verdicts

An insured cannot pick his claimants. The injured party may turn out to be a professional golfer, entertainer, or rising young executive with an annual income of $50,000 or more. Nor can the insured pick the kind of injury which will develop. There may be serious injury to the brain; the spine may be damaged beyond repair. Medical bills alone may run into hundreds of thousands of dollars. The insured cannot predict the size of his property damage exposure. His vehicle may hit a train and cause derailment. The vehicle may hit the side of a building on stilts and cause the entire structure to sag. A negligent fire may spread to 20 buildings. Widespread catastrophic liability may result from the sale of a simple toy which is toxic.

Furthermore, the insured cannot anticipate what a jury is going to do. The size of verdicts has been leapfrogging during the last two decades. The *Fire, Casualty, and Surety Bulletins* of the National Underwriter Company present an up-to-date record of the highest judgments recorded for personal injury to one person in each state. Some of the currently high verdicts are:

New Jersey	$1,215,140
New York	1,100,000
Illinois	750,000
California	650,000
Oklahoma	650,000
Ohio	625,000
Florida	550,000
Michigan	526,000
Minnesota	500,000
Delaware	470,000

The limit required for all the settlements in a single accident can be astronomical. Consider an explosion in Oregon which involved only one truck but which killed 12 persons, injured over 100 others, and caused estimated property damage of $9,300,000. Consider the protection needed when an oil truck hit the Santa Fe Chief near Bakersfield. Fourteen persons were killed and the train was derailed. As another example, how high is "up" really becomes a problem for the manufacturer of a component for a missile. If a missile were to go off course and hit an American city and if the defective component were to be traced to one manufacturer, his need for liability insurance would be astronomically large. Expansion in manufacturing, contracting operations, aviation, utilities, and electronics opens up a vista of many times the maximum of 20, 30, or even 40 million now pyramided into a large liability program.

Claims in Excess of Policy Limits

With the rise of verdicts at all levels in all states, plaintiffs' attorneys have become accustomed to demanding enormous dollar figures for damages. When the damage clause in a complaint exceeds the policy limits, it is necessary for the insurance company to notify the insured that any excess eventually needed will have to be paid by him. To say the least, this notification creates a very uncomfortable feeling in the insured, his producer, and his professional counselor.

Actual settlements can be very embarrassing as in the case of the millionaire who, with limits of only $5,000/$10,000, was involved in a very serious accident in which the driver of the other vehicle was killed.

Another example was a successful and wealthy contractor with only $25,000 per person and $50,000 per accident in his bodily injury coverage who faced a verdict of $250,000. In many business cases the contribution needed from the insured firm was the death knell of the business; many other insureds have had to do very costly financing in order to avoid bankruptcy and stay in business.

Liability Treaty Limitations

In seeking higher limits, brokers and agents found that many insurance carriers had insufficient liability capacity. In many cases the insurer had to be persuaded to place facultative reinsurance for a very high limit, which placement was costly to the company. In addition, unless such an insurer had a large volume of high-limit business, it could not get a spread of such business and participate in the premium for the excess. Some company officials felt that they should not be involved at the primary level with frequency of loss and also be involved in high limits for catastrophe. It is interesting that Lloyd's underwriters are divided, with individual syndicates having preferences for different levels of liability. The frequency underwriters choose one layer; catastrophe underwriters choose other layers.

Broader Coverage with Low Limits

A company underwriter will have more courage to take on difficult classes (such as products liability with a "batch" exposure; completed operations liability for contractors; premises-operations liability for hotels, rooming houses, theaters, skating rinks, or swimming pools; or liability for trucking risks) if he knows that he is only involved to the extent of $10,000/$20,000 for B.I. and $20,000 P.D. or perhaps $25,000/$50,000 and $25,000 respectively. It may also be possible for the producer to negotiate a broader wording with respect to (1) care, custody, or control, (2) blanket contractual, or (3) occurrence type property damage, if the underwriter knows that he has only a low limit. (See Chapter 32 for discussion of 1 and 3.) This broader wording may be easier to obtain if the entire first layer of coverage is on a retrospective rating plan. The producer of the business or the buyer may then find it easier to buy his excess separately. The excess contract can follow the same conditions as in the primary contract.

Agency Experience and Individual Risk Experience

Insurance company officials have a tendency to look at their entire book of business from a producer and not distinguish clearly between severity of loss and frequency of loss. They often make statistical studies which will simply show the overall loss ratio of each agency involved. Moreover, many insurers use a contingent commission system under which the agent may get from the insurance carrier an additional commission in case the business he has produced proves profitable. If very large limits are written and a fortuitious loss occurs, this loss may prejudice the record of the agency and the possibility of the collection of contingent commissions. With respect to the buyer, there is also the problem of individual risk experience. If the experience under the primary contract is bad because of frequency of loss, it will affect the cost of the excess insurance in the same carrier, since the excess will normally be calculated as a percentage of the primary cover. If the excess is purchased separately and rated independently, its price may not be affected by the experience of the insured under his primary policy.

Convenience of Handling

An insured may have separate liability contracts in various states. He may have different contracts for different subsidiaries. He may have uneven limits for automobile, comprehensive general liability, aviation, malpractice, and perhaps the section of a package policy which includes premises liability. The insured can bulk-buy one combined single limit for bodily injury and property damage which will be excess over all of the individual policies and bring his limit up to one amount commensurate with his needs. There is often a price advantage to a combined single limit and there may be additional savings in "layering" (this concept is also discussed in Chapter 22) if the insured needs many millions of coverage.

EXCESS LIABILITY

Excess liability insurance provides coverage above some specified figure up to some specified limit. For example, such a contract may provide payment to the extent that a bodily injury claim exceeds $20,000/$40,000 up to $100,000/$300,000.

A straightforward excess liability policy must be distinguished from umbrella liability and from excess aggregate liability policies. Umbrella liability is a broad blanket excess legal liability contract which "picks up" over a self-insured portion the gaps in the liability program of an insured. Excess aggregate is available for self-insurers and provides a liability cover for all losses in one policy year up to an aggregate amount over an aggregate deductible for the year. (See section in this chapter on "Nature of Excess Aggregate Contracts.")

Excess Never Wider than Primary

Excess liability as such is never wider than the basic coverage. It is only excess "as covered by and defined in the primary policies." In fact, the excess cover may be more narrow than the primary. For example, standard policies developed at Lloyd's and in domestic companies make it quite clear in the exclusions that if the primary policy has been extended in any way to cover care, custody, or control (other than that picked up in sidetrack agreements or in the elevator coverage) or has been extended in any way to cover workmen's compensation and employers' liability exposures, the excess does not cover unless a proper endorsement is issued. Excess liability wordings vary by company. It is necessary that the producer or the buyer make certain that there are no exclusions in the excess cover which would curtail the breadth of coverage desired for full limits.

One or Several Excess Contracts

A separate excess may be written over each policy. The most frequent type of excess is an ordinary automobile excess liability cover. The wide use of assigned risk plans, where only minimum amounts of primary insurance are granted, make necessary a market for higher limits at adequate rates. Amounts up to $100,000/$300,000 may be purchased rather readily at fairly standardized rates. Excesses are available not only for assigned risks, but also for youngsters, military personnel, those with physical impairments, the over-age, those with poor driving record, those with actual loss experience, the immigrants, and the difficult occupational groups. These groups include bartenders, actors, actresses, gamblers, musicians, waterfront workers, circus and carnival people, migratory workers, and others.

It is usually better to arrange the excess policy for a commercial client so that it does go over *all* of the policies he holds, even though these policies may cover different types of hazards and may have different limits. Originally, limits were shown as a dollar amount excess of a dollar amount, for example, bodily injury $75,000/$250,000 excess of $25,000/$50,000 and property damage $75,000 excess of $25,000. Misunderstandings arose. It was found better to show the total limits and indicate that the company is covering the difference between those total limits and the primary limits. Standard wordings at Lloyd's have been drawn in this way so that the total limits in the excess contract are the summation of the primary, the underlying layers, and the excess being written in the contract. Continuing the example, the limits in the excess contract would be "100/300/100" in all over (primary of "5/10/5" and a second layer of "20/40/20").

There is no problem in having a combined single limit for both bodily injury and property damage instead of separate limits as expressed above. Even though the primary policies have split limits for bodily injury and property damage and split limits per person and per accident in the individual policies, the excess may be expressed as a single combined limit for both bodily injury and property damage. For example, $1 million, $2 million, or $5 million, with the difference between that limit and any of the primary covers protected. Ordinarily, savings will result from the use of a combined single limit. Moreover, the insured then knows his top dollar limit for any one incident.

Pricing of Excess Liability

For all of the difficult classes, excess limits both at Lloyd's and in domestic companies will cost more than the cost as figured by use of ordinary excess tables contained in the bureau manuals. The biggest difference in price is in the area between $10,000/$20,000/$10,000 and $25,000/$50,000/$25,000. The spread in pricing decreases as the limits go up. At higher limits the cost per $1,000 may go down from a dollar per $1,000 to as little as 30 cents per $1,000. Malpractice excess limits are separately priced and are extremely costly because of the trend in the last few years in malpractice verdicts. (See Chapter 33 for a discussion of malpractice liability insurance.)

The cost of excess layers may be subject to adjustment and, if so, the adjustment will always relate to the primary limits. The final factor which is quoted on each excess layer is not related back to the premium for a primary of $5,000/$10,000 for bodily injury but always to the full premium for the first primary layer whether it is $10,000/$20,000, $25,000/$50,000, $50,000/$100,000, $100,000/$300,000, and so on.

Wherever the primary limit is written as an aggregate (as for example in products-completed operations), the excess is also written as an aggregate. (See Chapters 32 and 34 for discussion of aggregate limits.) This practice may also be followed in coverages for errors and omissions or malpractice.

It is necessary to notify the underwriters on the excess layers if there is any change in the primary premium or in the underlying excess layers, if any. Notice should be given of any incident which is likely to give rise to a claim to the excess underwriters. They must give consent to costs which might affect them. If the total claim involves the excess layers, all of the costs are split proportionately and the underwriters on the upper layers have a right to be in on the handling of the case if it is going to affect them.

UMBRELLA LIABILITY

Development of the Contract

The appearance of the "umbrella" was an outstanding, unique event in the brief history of excess liability insurance.

According to a research study project of the Northern California Chapter of the Society of Chartered Property and Casualty Underwriters, umbrella liability was introduced in the United States in 1947.[1] The wording reflected a considerable amount of imagination and courage on the part of Lloyd's underwriters. The contract was aimed at large buyers of insurance with the idea of providing broader protection with the new concept of picking up all of the gaps in other coverages—over a self-insured retention by the insured.

The new contract served almost as an errors and omissions policy for any exposure which may have been overlooked. The umbrella "back-stopped" all of the individual policies. Thus, if there were a gap resulting from a policy exclusion or a missing policy, the capital and surplus of the insured had at least catastrophe protection over the self-insured amount —which was usually pegged at $25,000. The insurer often required that the primary coverages be brought up to date and properly broadened before the umbrella was added. Thus, the umbrella program had the effect of forcing the insured or his advisor to scrutinize every liability contract—automobile, comprehensive general, aviation, watercraft, advertiser's liability, errors and omissions, malpractice, bailee liability coverages, and others.

In 1959 the Lloyd's program ran into trouble. Two things had gone wrong. First, in the sale of the umbrella the technique had been used of reducing the primary bodily injury limits to $25,000 per person and $50,000 per accident, or even less. The idea was to reduce the primary limits sufficiently so that the savings in the reduction of limits would largely pay for the umbrella. The premium level became too thin and the reduction in limits put the coverage in the working area of frequency of loss instead of the area of catastrophe. Second, the wording was made so broad that it picked up many exposures which were not contemplated. It was even found that some large suits for patent infringement developed where the insured might have known of the possibility of patent infringement at the time the insurance was placed. Tort actions for willful perpetuation of nuisances, trespass, and unfair business practices were included. Contractual guarantees on a number of risks of "just doing business" were interpreted as covered.

In June, 1960, Lloyd's consulted with many brokers and developed a new contract. Some domestic carriers followed the new Lloyd's pattern; others created contracts of their own which followed the American wordings in other liability policies and further tightened certain areas. With no standard contract in the United States, each company's policy must be examined to make sure that it is truly broad-form umbrella insurance and not merely an ordinary excess liability contract. Permission was granted for a dropping down of the self-insured retention in the gaps area to

[1] For an excellent report of this study group, see "Umbrella Liability Coverage," *Annals, Society of CPCU*, Vol. 13 (Winter, 1960), pp. 243–74.

$10,000. Defense protection was granted in these areas under the deductible without charge to the insured. A separate contract was devised for the liabilities of executives in business and for professionals.

A Few Basic Points about the Umbrella

Some basic points apply to all umbrellas. First, the umbrella is not "level at the top." A few companies have written "difference between" contracts similar to the wording mentioned under excess liability, but the vast majority of umbrellas follows the underlying coverages in their peaks and valleys. There is always one million, or five million, or ten million more than each specific basic limit. If there is an aggregate in the primary liability such as in the products liability section, the umbrella becomes primary when the aggregate is exhausted.

Second, a common misunderstanding is that there is a $25,000 or $10,000 gap or space between the primary and the umbrella insurance. No such corridor exists. In those areas where the insured has purchased a primary cover, the protection applies right up to the top dollar of the umbrella. Most umbrellas have very few absolute exclusions. The usual ones are: war, product guarantees, performance guarantees, faulty workmanship, and certain things with respect to advertising such as a mistake in the advertised price, an incorrect description, a failure to perform the contract resulting from an ad, or a trademark infringement. The statutory part of workmen's compensation is excluded unless excess workmen's compensation coverage over a self-insured portion is endorsed onto the contract.

The third important feature of the umbrella is that it drops down to $25,000 or $10,000 in those areas which are not covered in the primary. This feature means that (1) coverage which would otherwise have required separate policies is picked up and (2) that exclusions in primary coverage are in effect eliminated for losses above $10,000 or $25,000. Most umbrella insurers safeguard themselves by having certain exclusions which will apply if the underlying insurances are missing, for example, assault and battery at the direction of the insured, owned aircraft, owned watercraft, and suits by one employee against another employee. If the primary policies pick up these exposures, however, they are also covered in the umbrella.

Fourth, as a general rule most excess insurers insist on a full Comprehensive General Liability Policy on the bottom before writing the umbrella. There are cases, however, where there may be difficult products exposures, difficult completed operations, or difficulties with respect to blanket contractual or occurrence P.D. where the carrier will purposely write the umbrella with the insured retaining the first layer. Such a carrier may require a retention of $50,000 or $100,000 on very large lines.

An Example

One can appreciate the breadth of the contract only if he comprehends the entire risk. Figure 40–1 shows a sample program for a commercial client. It is presumed that this client is carrying $100,000/$300,000 on automobile, $100,000/$300,000/$300,000 aggregate on products for bodily injury in the Comprehensive General, and $100,000 property damage with the various aggregates in the normal contract. It is further presumed that the client has insurance of $200,000 for a bailee exposure where property of others is in its custody. Finally, in its workmen's compensation policy, which is unlimited on the statutory part, a limit of $25,000 on section B is presumed. The umbrella is represented in the chart by the gray shaded area which provides excess over the primaries and then picks up excess over the self-insured (S.I.) portion which is shown in white at the bottom as possible exclusions or missing policies. In the list on the left-hand side of the chart are simply examples of the gaps covered above the self-insured plateau which in this instance has been pegged at $25,000.

Examples of Uses of the Umbrella Contract

Since uses of the umbrella may be unfamiliar to numerous readers, some examples of the need for this type of insurance are cited.

World Wide Cover. Even modest size commercial firms today set up sales offices in Europe, the Far East, or Africa. They may send employees abroad to check on installations or the performance of their product. They definitely have products liability exposures when their products go, say, to the Philippines, Japan, or central Europe. Unfortunately, many insureds fail to advise their broker, agent, or company when they start trading abroad. The umbrella does provide a catastrophe protection over the self-insured amount for the firm. The ordinary Comprehensive General or Comprehensive Automobile Liability Policies do not follow them abroad. The products exposure can be dangerously large with different climates and different types of employees or agents.

Personal Injury. Legal liability for *bodily* injury from negligence is only one type of tort. The term "personal injury" opens up the whole book of torts. (See Chapters 31, 32, 33, and 34 for information pertinent to this point.) It includes mental injury, mental anguish, shock, sickness, disease, disability, false arrest, false imprisonment, wrongful eviction, detention, malicious prosecution, discrimination, humiliation, libel, slander, defamation of character, invasion of privacy, and so on. False arrest and wrongful detention are especially important for department stores, discount houses, supermarkets, hotels, and municipalities. There have even been suits for wrongful detention where someone has been locked in a warehouse in error. Discrimination, humiliation, and invasion of privacy can be ex-

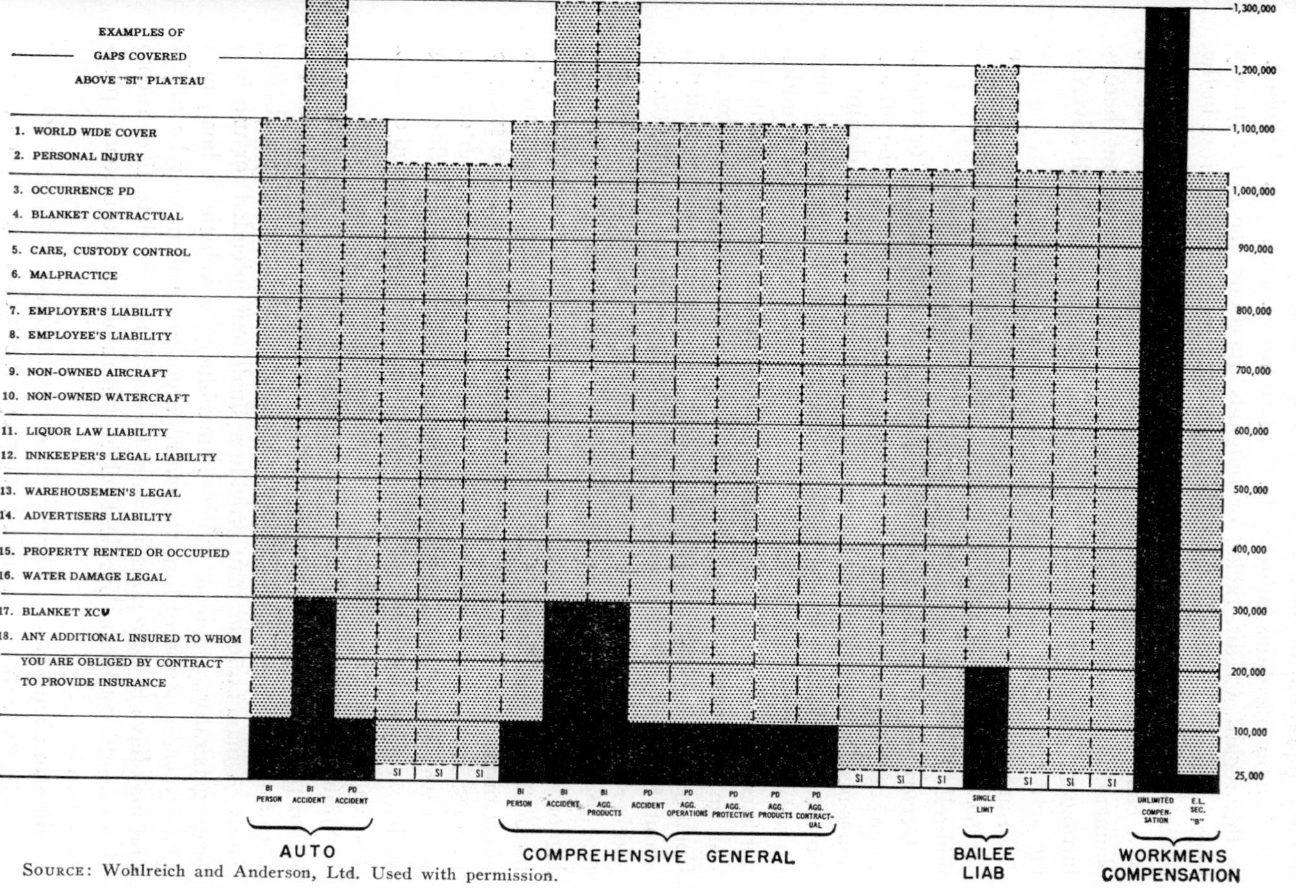

SOURCE: Wohlreich and Anderson, Ltd. Used with permission.

FIG. 40–1. Umbrella Liability.

tremely important for theaters, hotels, restaurants, supermarkets, and the entire communications industry. Real estate firms have a special problem in this regard. Credit, racial, or religious questions may arise in any business. A good example of a defamation of character claim arose in the milling business where an insured wrote a dismissal letter which resulted in a claim for $30,000 because of the employment difficulties of the claimant. Infringement of patents is no longer in the umbrella but there is infringement of copyright, title, or slogan in connection with all advertising activities.

Insurers now so define personal injury in their contracts that they do not get involved in the willful torts mentioned earlier which beset the first umbrella contracts.

Occurrence PD. Occurrence PD claims, and care, custody, or control claims are the two big gaps covered by the umbrella. Catastrophe protection is needed in each area. For example, a metallurgical firm had sulphur-dioxide gas emitting from its stacks. The smoke over a period of time caused damage to growing crops in the area. This damage was not sudden nor fixed in time or place; therefore it did not arise from an *accident* but was an *occurrence* within the definition. It was not covered by the Comprehensive General Liability Policy, but the case was settled for about $100,000 in excess of the self-insured retention of $25,000. As another example, a contractor started pumping out water in the construction of a hotel near a lagoon. He thought the water was coming from the lagoon. In fact, he was changing the water table. Other structures along a main street began to sag. Claims for the change in water level and its effect on neighboring lands ran into eight figures. This example suggests that a $25 million limit may be advisable in some cases. In another case tar paper was sold to a chain of supermarkets. Felt and coal tarpitch emitted such a strong order that foodstuffs were condemned over a period of time. The condemnation resulted in a claim for $500,000.

Mining companies and chemical companies which have to pile huge waste products have had tremendous losses when heavy rains over a period of time have washed down chemicals or debris into neighboring farms. A manufacturer may provide a small unit intended for use in a large generator, a delicate piece of machinery, a vehicle, a boat, or a plane. Over a period of time the entire larger mechanism may be ruined and may have to be replaced should the small unit be defective. Such a claim would not be an "accident" claim but rather an "occurrence" products liability claim.

Blanket Contractual. The general counsel of a company may not clear all contracts with the insurance company, the broker, or the consultant. Even if the general counsel agrees to do so, the sales department or the manufacturing department may not clear all contracts with the general counsel. Primary carriers most frequently restrict contractual liability because of the very wide exposure possible. A contract can pick up the liability of others, workmen's compensation exposures, and tremendous property damage exposures. A contractor in one large city ended up by holding the entire city harmless from all accidents on streets and sidewalks. Under the umbrella the coverage is there, whether the contract is oral or written.

Care, Custody, or Control. Courts are not dependable in what they construe as being in the care, custody, or control of an insured. A firm may discover that it has in its custody an entire building, expensive data processing machinery, leased machinery and equipment, property sent on consignment, property stored under a bailment, or property under construction. Even property under installation at far distances may be under its custody.

A careful review of the underlying insurance is made by the umbrella underwriter, but one can never anticipate what will develop. On one occasion the upper section of a catalytic cracking tower partially collapsed and deflected some 15 degrees after which fire ensued. While there was builder's risk coverage, it did not include testing. It was held that the accident did occur during testing and a loss was paid for about $400,000 over $25,000. Unusual lease wordings and unusual lease-back arrangements are danger points in every commercial concern. There is an interesting question as to whether or not a real estate firm has custody of the houses to which it has keys. Many firms are very casual in their arrangements with sub-contractors. It may be very difficult to determine who has the custody of the property until actual litigation. Companies today have a tendency to switch from owned equipment to leased equipment without full analysis of their exposures.

Malpractice. A large insured may operate a hospital and buy specific coverage for malpractice. A small insured may just have a first aid facility, simply hire a doctor or a nurse, or refer patients to a doctor or a nurse outside the premises, and not think about having malpractice coverage. The umbrella contract applies above the self-insured limit.

Moreover, insurers may have professional liability exposures which they least suspect. Courts today are holding many types of insureds responsible for their errors or omissions. Personal injury or property damage resulting from improper or inadequate performance, design, faults, or specification inadequacy is covered.

Employer's Liability. Many large insureds carry only $25,000 on Section B of their workmen's compensation policy. Many others increase it only to $100,000. There may still be gaps with respect to foreign operations, or to employees in certain monopolistic state fund states. Although claims are rare, catastrophe limits may be necessary for (1) casual employees excluded from statutory coverage in certain states, (2) occupational diseases not listed in some states, (3) loss of hearing,

(4) loss of consortium, and (5) the "third-party-over" situation where a third party sued by a firm's employee brings the insured in as the employer. Substantial recoveries may be gained by changing the nature of the claim from workmen's compensation to third party liability through this device. Courts have upheld the right of the third party to sue and recover from the employer of the injured person the amount of damages the third party sustained in the action brought by the injured person.[2]

Employee's Liability. An employee becomes a named insured in the unbrella policy. He may be sued individually. If he has no other protection for his business pursuits as an extension to a Comprehensive Personal Liability Policy, he at least has the coverage excess of the self-insured deductible. This feature is extremely important where the umbrella provides defense for such claims. The insurer automatically covers all of the costs of litigation, which sums can be substantial. For example, the operator of a large crane can punch a hole in a ship or the side of a building. A nurse employed may be sued for malpractice. Some umbrellas even pick up the coverage for fellow-employee suits, but even where done this has been limited to claims other than those in respect to automobiles and aircraft. There is a great danger that any coverage in this area will start a trend toward suits by one employee against another, and militate against the injured employee's taking compensation in a case where there has been the careless act of some other employee on the job. Many claims men feel that compensation should be the exclusive remedy and that an injured employee should not be encouraged to bring an action against a fellow employee.

Nonowned Aircraft. If companies do not own aircraft, officials usually forget about the nonownership aspect of aircraft liability. It is not picked up in the normal Comprehensive General Liability Policy. Management may even decide to send a memo around advising everyone not to fly a plane nor to rent a plane and take the responsibility for the craft. Even the best memo, however, does not stop a new salesman who knows how to fly from, say, renting a plane and covering West Virginia out of Washington, D.C. He can destroy a school, a theater, a church, or other property. As the result, a substantial amount of the capital and surplus of the corporation can be wiped out. It has been found that employees in contracting, financing, manufacturing, retailing, wholesaling, and certain other firms do on occasion rent private planes. If such renting is an activity in the course of normal employment, the company can be held responsible.

Nonowned Watercraft. Again, because watercraft is not owned, the exposure from rental of watercraft may be forgotten. The sales manager

[2] See: *Westchester Lighting Co.* v. *Westchester County Small Estates Corp.*, 278 NY 175 (1938); *American District Telegraph Company* v. *Kittleson*, 179 Fed. 2d 946 (1950); *Ryan Stevedoring Company* v. *Pan Atlantic SS Corp.*, 350 U.S. 124, (1956); *General Electric Company* v. *Moretz*, 270 Fed. 2d 780 (1959).

may charter a boat and take a number of customers on a fishing trip. If they drown and it is shown that the salesman was negligent in either the selection or operation of the vessel, there may be a substantial invasion of capital and surplus through satisfaction of the resulting judgment. If these costs of using such watercraft are usually put through as business expenses, it would be hard to show that the activities were not in the course of business.

Liquor Law Liability. "Dram shop" liability may be excluded from primary insurance such as treated in Chapters 32 and 34. In certain states, if a person who has been served on the premises injures someone while intoxicated, the owner or operator of the premises may be brought into the suit as a defendant. The premises need not be a hotel, restaurant, or tavern operation. Various other types of premises used for such purposes come under the exclusion of the basic policy.

Innkeeper's Legal Liability. Exposures under this heading actually are in the area of care, custody, or control but have a special importance because of statutory and common law. This liability is particularly important to hotels, restaurants, public halls, catering places, theaters, galleries, motels, apartment hotels, churches, clubs, exhibitions, and amusement places. Such liability is, of course, picked up (above the self-insured limit) in the umbrella.

Warehousemen's Legal Liability. This exposure is also in the area of care, custody, or control but likewise has a special legal aspect where the insured has been construed to be a warehouseman in respect to the property of others. Warehousemen are being held by the courts to a degree of duty which makes them almost guarantors of the property on their premises. Catastrophe liability can result from a negligent fire. In one example such a fire was started by the watchman himself with a carelessly tossed cigarette. In another situation a fire resulted from explosion where paints and chemicals were in proximity to heat. In one case the warehouse and its contents gently subsided into the filled ground of mud. The umbrella can cover this liability regardless of the cause of the property damage—except for the few exclusions cited early in this discussion.

Advertiser's Liability. The mere fact that a concern uses neither radio nor TV does not mean that it is immune from suits for serious exposures in advertising. Even if the firm uses only a simple system of advertising in newspapers, magazine, handbills, or pamphlets, there can be suits for libel; slander; defamation; infringement of copyright, title, or slogan; unfair competition; idea misappropriation; or invasion of the right of privacy. The cost of defense can be enormous. With radio or TV, separate acts can be committed simultaneously throughout the country and a firm may be suddenly faced with 25 or 30 suits in separate jurisdictions at the same time. This exposure can be handled with an umbrella contract.

Property Rented or Occupied. The basic CGL Policy excludes property owned by, occupied by, or rented to the insured. While the property owned is not covered under the umbrella (since the insured cannot sue himself) legal claims for loss of or damage to the property occupied or rented are covered by the umbrella and can be very important. Unless the counsel for the company has taken care of all of the premises which are occupied by the insured, the company may be exposed to substantial claim when a building is destroyed and the company is responsible.

Water Damage Legal Liability and Sprinkler Leakage Legal Liability. The normal CGL Policy has an exclusion with reference to water pipes, steam pipes, air-conditioning systems, industrial appliances, sprinkler systems, tanks, rain, or snow. If separate water damage legal liability and sprinkler leakage legal liability are not purchased, the umbrella will pick up the exposure which is in excess of the self-insured amount. A sales office in a huge multi-tenanted building may have 10 stories below it. If there is negligence and a burst pipe results in water flowing down over a long holiday weekend, a million dollar loss can occur. The exact amount of one water damage legal liability loss was $962,000.

Blanket "XC&U." Unless specifically endorsed, the Comprehensive General Liability Policy does not cover a contractor for blasting, collapse, or underground damage. If a new job is taken on which involves any of these exposures, the only protection the contractor would have would be the umbrella excess.

Additional Insureds. If the named insured is obligated by contract to provide insurance to any additional insured, the umbrella policy "backstops" the insured since any person or organization enjoying a contract right to have insurance provided for him (or it) is granted coverage by the policy with respect to the operations of the insured and the facilities used by the insured.

Special Extension of Umbrella Liability

Umbrellas have sometimes been broadened to cover extensive protection and indemnity liabilities arising from shipping fleets and other marine operations. In the London market it has been called a "bumbershoot" instead of an umbrella and picks up both the nonmarine and marine liabilities with a single limit. A frequent extension is to include excess fidelity. Again, the matter is one of bulk buying since the same capacity can be used as catastrophe protection over a blanket position bond or a commercial blanket bond. It has also been done over a banker's blanket bond.

A further refinement of umbrella extension is to have the same combined, single catastrophe limit apply (1) to a direct damage insuring clause as "balance of perils" for "all risk" including flood, earthquake, collapse, subsidence, sonic boom, wave wash, rain, and snow—all subject to a reasonable deductible—but excluding the named perils of the ordinary coverages carried by the insured and (2) to an umbrella insuring clause as described in this chapter.

Several companies provide an umbrella for the individual so that the executive, physician, surgeon, dentist, lawyer, accountant, architect, or engineer can buy a "broad-form" over his normal personal contracts. This policy does more than give prestige with its limit of a million or more in protection. Juries can hand down tremendous verdicts against individuals as well as corporations. People in the public limelight, those in any phase of entertainment business, and those who might be guilty of malpractice may need as much as a $5 million limit. There is usually a $10,000 deductible for the nonprimary coverages. Expense of defense is covered.

Rating

There is no standard rating for the umbrella. The commercial umbrella with a primary of $100,000/$300,000 and $100,000 will normally be rated for the first million at approximately 10 percent of the primary Automobile Policy premium and 20 percent of the Comprehensive General Liability Policy premium. To this may be added judgment factors according to the individual risk. There was a time when there was a minimum premium per annum of about a thousand dollars; but small commercial risks are now written with $500 as the minimum three-year premium. The personal coverage for executives and professionals for the normal risk runs $270 for three years for a million; $540 for three years for five million.

EXCESS AGGREGATES AND DEDUCTIBLES

The risk-bearing capacity of an insured is hard to determine. The minimum certainly should be 1 percent of the "free surplus" of the concern plus 1 percent of its average annual net earnings during the last five years. If the cost of standard insurance is high in relation to gross income, it may make good business sense to take a substantial deductible in relation to free surplus and earnings. Too many insureds pay enormous sums for first dollar coverage and leave themselves exposed for catastrophe. It would be better for them to have a self-insured portion on the bottom and use their money to protect themselves on the top across-the-board for all perils. With respect to third-party liability and workmen's compensation, there has been a reluctance on the part of American underwriters and insureds to have a deductible. The underwriter fears lack of control and possible failure of the insured to report a claim since he might feel that the claim would not exceed the deductible. The insured is concerned that, if the deductible includes not only the amount to be paid the third party but also the cost of adjustment he (the insured) will not be able to control the handling by the carrier and will end up with a lot of his own money spent on small claims and adjusting expenses.

Use of Deductibles

The bulk of liability business is written without a deductible. Only when there has been an underwriting problem of frequency has a deductible been used for smaller and medium size risks. Even in these cases the business has been placed largely in the foreign market or in specialty American companies. These deductibles usually are small, for example, $100, $250, or $500. Only in respect to the very large risk is a serious approach usually taken on the part of the insured in using a "self-insurance" program. Such insureds clearly need "excess aggregate insurance" for public liability, automobile liability, and workmen's compensation exposures. These insureds may be faced with the possibility of frequency of loss. They need a stop-loss cover over an aggregate deductible. This need is over and above the catastrophe protection which ordinarily is needed for any one accident or occurrence.

Nature of Excess Aggregate Contracts

In "excess aggregate" all of the settlements, the judgments, the legal costs, the weekly payments for compensation, the medical bills, the surgical bills, the hospital nursing, the funeral expenses, and the reserves set up by some servicing company are aggregated. As soon as these aggregate claims exceed the aggregate deductible during one policy year, the excess is paid to the insured by the "excess aggregate" insurer on a monthly or quarterly basis as reported.

For automobile and comprehensive general liability, the actual loss record for the last three to five years is studied meticulously by the insured and insurer; trends and sales are noted; a safety margin is determined; and then an aggregate amount is purchased to serve as excess over the self-insured aggregate deductible determined. The underwriter for the excess aggregate will normally then require that excess liability for any one accident or occurrence be purchased since two or more lives may be involved in one incident, and there may be a very substantial single claim. If, for example, there is a specific excess liability policy for $1 million over $25,000 self-insured for each and every loss, the excess aggregate will then apply only to the first $25,000 for each incident.

In workmen's compensation the excess aggregate may be excess of a dollar amount. Normally, however, the plan is one whereby the ordinary premium is calculated for the risk by applying regular classification rates to the insured's payroll and then modifying the result by any experience credit or debit. About 10 to 15 percent of the premium is used for the purchase of an excess aggregate coverage over an aggregate retention by the insured of 75 percent of the normal premium for loss and loss expenses.

An underwriter will require as a condition to an excess aggregate contract that a servicing company be appointed. There must be a supervision of all the legal obligations of the insured; accurate records kept; adequate inspection and safety work performed; monthly or quarterly reports made to the employer and the carrier; a tabulation made of payments and reserves; a procedure set up for making all statutory reports and presenting required legal notices; and an overall guidance established as to the work performed by the employees of the insured in the self-insurance program. During the last 40 years there have been a great number of servicing companies created with about a dozen very large ones in the field.

With regard to automobile and workmen's compensation liability, it is necessary that the insured qualify as a self-insurer under the laws of the various states. Bonds or deposits may be required. This cost as well as the cost of the servicing company have to be borne by the insured.

Building Excess Aggregate into Umbrella

An excess aggregate may be built into the umbrella. There is a danger very often in the purchase of inadequate limits for excess aggregate. Without the umbrella, the usual figure of $250,000 may be purchased, but any claims department supervisor can tell a large insured of instances where unusual frequency suddenly developed in a risk and produced a long series of bad injuries. The umbrella, therefore, not only can protect the insured against a big catastrophe—such as an explosion, a fire, or a poisoning—but also can provide a large limit for an aggregate of many losses.

There are serious problems for the insured in self-insurance arrangements. First, the geographic area of exposures may be large. Handling losses can be costly without the service of numerous branch offices of an insurance carrier. Each case must be carefully analyzed to make sure that the firm's expenses are going to be less than the normal insurance carrier's expense loading. Second, the reserves set up by the insured and the servicing agent and unpaid at the end of the year are not subject to any tax credit. There is a deferring of tax credit until payment is actually made. There is also a problem in that the normal excess aggregate contract will have a commutation clause whereby the underwriters may have an actuary fix a lump-sum settlement two years after the expiration of the excess aggregate to take care of workmen's compensation payments due over a long period of time. It then becomes the duty of the employer to invest the sum to provide the weekly amount needed for the workmen's compensation cases each week.

A cover which has a special kinship to excess aggregate is retrospective penalty insurance. If an insured has purchased a retrospective plan (see Chapter 36), he is usually interested in the largest possible savings, but he may be apprehensive about the maximum possible loss to be borne under the retrospective plan. With a retrospective penalty arrangement, he can stop his retrospective premium charge at 110 percent of standard.

SUGGESTED READINGS

BEAM, MAX W. "Domestic Excess and Surplus Markets," *Annals, Society of Chartered Property and Casualty Underwriters,* Vol. 14 (Fall, 1961), pp. 265–71.

GRAHAM, JOSEPH J. "Large Line Packages in Casualty Insurance," *Annals, Society of Chartered Property and Casualty Underwriters,* Vol. 15 (Spring, 1962), pp. 67–78.

NORTHERN CALIFORNIA CHAPTER. "Umbrella Liability Coverage," *Annals, Society of Chartered Property and Casualty Underwriters,* Vol. 13 (Winter, 1960), pp. 243–74.

Chapter 41

BOILER AND MACHINERY INSURANCE

BY LYMAN B. BRAINERD

When a boiler or other piece of power equipment explodes or suffers a serious failure, the owner may be faced with many kinds of losses. In addition to damage to the unit itself, his building and its contents may be destroyed; he may be held liable for damage to property of others; bodily injury liabilities may be involved; loss of income due to business shutdown is likely; and goods in process or storage may spoil from lack of heat or refrigeration. All of these exposures can be covered under a single Boiler and Machinery Policy which is, in a sense, a package policy—one of the earliest to be developed in America. This chapter deals with this policy and its commonly used endorsements.

Although one of the smallest casualty lines (annual premiums approximately $85 million), boiler and machinery insurance (sometimes referred to as power plant insurance) is notable for its strong emphasis on loss prevention, for unusual flexibility in selection of coverages, and for refinement of its rate structure.

The kinds of equipment and many of the hazards insured under boiler and machinery policies differ in a number of ways from those in other lines of insurance. These features and the origin of the line will be treated briefly before the insurance coverages and provisions are described.

ORIGIN AND BASIC CONCEPTS

Boiler and machinery insurance first appeared in the United States in 1867 and grew out of the necessity for finding a way to curb the alarming and increasing number of boiler explosions occurring at the time. The first company was organized by a group of engineers whose objective was prevention of boiler explosions—insurance was a corollary in this effort.

The new company was founded on the principle that a boiler, correctly designed and constructed, would be safe if operated properly. Control of the design and construction factors could be obtained through cooperation with boiler manufacturers. Control of operating conditions in plants where boilers were used posed a more difficult problem but offered the greatest rewards, since operating errors were then a leading cause of failure, as they are today. The founding engineers concluded that a reasonable degree of safety could be obtained by employing a corps of specially trained men to examine operating practices periodically and inspect the physical condition of boilers in the plants of their clients. It was not possible, of course, to guarantee that these inspections would eliminate all possibility of explosion; therefore insurance coverage was added to provide indemnity in the event of such an occurrence. A somewhat similar arrangement had been employed in England and this fact was probably known to the founders of the line in this country.

Success of the venture soon led to application of the same principles to the explosion hazard of unfired pressure vessels and later to "explosions" of flywheels on steam engines. The latter step introduced machinery insurance.

From that point, the line grew to encompass other vessels and a great variety of machines, both mechanical and electrical. The insured hazards were broadened far beyond the original explosion concept and the broadening process still continues.

INSURABLE EQUIPMENT

Any piece of insured equipment (boiler, vessel, or machine) is referred to in the Boiler and Machinery Policy by the generic term "object." As used in this chapter the word "object" will have the same connotation.

Insurable objects are to be found in practically every kind of factory and commercial or public building. Although a few classes of objects are used only in large power stations or manufacturing plants, others are to be found in smaller business concerns, such as dairies, laundries, dry-cleaning plants, cold storage warehouses, and the like. Insurable objects will also be found in buildings requiring heat, hot water supply, or air conditioning; thousands of policies are written to cover apartment houses, schools, churches, hospitals, hotels, restaurants, theaters, stores, garages, and similar properties.

Every policy covers at least one object; most policies cover several; and many cover hundreds of objects. There are so many different kinds and types of objects that a complete listing here would be impractical. However, they are grouped into 13 general classes as follows:

Boilers and Vessels	*Machinery*
Boilers, Fired vessels, and Electric steam generators	Turbines
Unfired vessels	Wheels and Shafting
Auxiliary piping	Engines, Pumps, Compressors, Fans, and Blowers

Systems of refrigerating and air-conditioning vessels and piping
Residence boilers and vessels
Miscellaneous machines, Gear wheels, and Enclosed gear sets
Deep well pump units
Small compressing and refrigerating units and Air-conditioning units—cabinet type
Rotating electrical machines, Transformers, and Induction feeder regulators
Miscellaneous electrical apparatus

There is no requirement that all of the objects in the insured's plant be covered in the policy; any one or more can be singled out for insurance. Therefore, it is necessary that the policy clearly identify the insured objects so that they may be distinguished from those not covered. This identification is accomplished, in some cases, by specifically describing each piece of insured equipment. The following are typical policy descriptions:

No. 1 Fire Tube Boiler, Class 2, 72″ Diameter.
No. 5 Air Tank, 2′ × 6′.
No. 654321 General Electric Steam Turbine, 2500 kw.

The plan of specific descriptions is giving way to the optional blanket group plan, preferred by a growing number of insurance buyers. Under this plan insured objects are designated by groups. A policy can be written, for example, to cover all boilers, all air tanks, and all steam turbines.[1] The blanket group plan simplifies policy handling, shortens policy wordings, and provides for automatic coverage when new objects are installed or old ones are removed.

In addition to naming the objects, the policy *defines* them. It is not sufficient, of course, to state that certain vessels or machines are insured; the policy must also establish what shall constitute the insured object and what parts, attachments, or connections are excluded. For this purpose a definition of object is provided for each of the above 13 classifications of objects. These definitions appear in a definitions endorsement attached to each policy or in the schedules which list the insured objects, depending upon the policy format used by the insurer.

HAZARDS

It is common knowledge, to be sure, that boilers and other pressure containers do explode. And it is generally known that some machines have heavy parts, rotating at high speed, which can fly apart due to centrifugal force and cause widespread damage. These obvious hazards produce

[1] Actual policy wordings used to describe insured groups are tailored to fit the individual buyer's needs.

most of the property damage losses of catastrophe proportions under boiler and machinery insurance.[2] The total amount involved in such occurrences, including business interruption losses, occasionally exceeds $1 million and in one instance (explosion of a paper machine roll) exceeded $3 million.

Violent explosions, however, constitute only a small proportion of the total number of boiler and machinery accidents. In fact, the explosion hazard is not present in the operation of some types of machines.

In the majority of accidents the damage is confined to the insured object, or affects surrounding property in a relatively minor way. Boilers "burn," bulge, crack, and rupture (as distinguished from violent explosions) due to scale, low water, corrosion, failure of protective devices, and/or human error. Unfired vessels fail from some of the same causes. Machines break, and their bearings and other parts that rotate or slide in contact with each other overheat, "burn out," or score due to improper lubrication, faulty adjustment, overload, loosening, failure of controls, or mishandling. Machines that have electrical parts are exposed to the additional hazards of short circuit and electrical burnout due to many causes including mechanical failure, moisture, lightning, and line surges. Fire within electrical machines sometimes follows such occurrences.

Depending upon the size and value of a vessel or machine, damage confined to the unit itself can involve substantial loss as illustrated by the following case histories:

1. In a public utility plant, replacement of boiler tubes, burned as the result of a low water condition, cost $55,000.
2. When a large paper machine roll (unfired vessel) cracked, damage to the roll exceeded $65,000.
3. Breaking of a connecting rod in a 3300 hp diesel engine caused damage to the machine in excess of $100,000.
4. When a blade broke in a 22,000 kw steam turbine, internal damage to the unit that followed involved repair costs of almost $200,000.
5. A short circuit in a 4000 hp steel mill motor resulted in a $95,000 repair.
6. Burnout of a 30,000 kw transformer produced a claim of $75,000.

Equipment in average-sized plants rarely involves values indicated by the above cases, but loss of a vessel or machine worth $5,000 or $10,000 can be an equally serious matter to the owner of a small business.

DEFINITIONS OF ACCIDENT

Hazards insured under a Boiler and Machinery Policy are referred to as "accidents." Thus the policy covers loss from "accidents" to "objects."

The first policy covered boiler explosion only, and the insured "acci-

[2] Furnace explosions, optionally insurable under boiler policies and covered by the extended feature of fire policies, can also cause widespread damage. These are combustion explosions, or detonations, of gases in the fuel burning spaces of a boiler unit, as distinguished from bursting of boilers due to pressure of steam or water.

dent" was defined as: "a sudden and substantial rupture of the shell only caused by the action of steam." This concept of specifically naming the kind of failure which would constitute an insured accident was followed in succeeding policy editions. But as new classes of insurable objects were added to the line, separate definitions were needed to describe their peculiar hazards. And as coverages were broadened far beyond the original explosion concept, these definitions increased in length and complexity.

In 1961 an important step was taken with the introduction of a new, single definition of accident which could be applied to all classes of objects. This replaced over a dozen definitions formerly in use, greatly reducing the number of engineering terms in the policy. This definition of accident reads as follows:

"Accident" shall mean a sudden and accidental breakdown of the Object, or a part thereof, which manifests itself at the time of its occurrence by physical damage to the Object that necessitates repair or replacement of the Object or part thereof; but Accident shall not mean (a) depletion, deterioration, corrosion, or erosion of material; (b) wear and tear; (c) leakage at any valve, fitting, shaft seal, gland packing, joint or connection; (d) the breakdown of any vacuum tube, gas tube or brush; (e) the breakdown of any structure or foundation supporting the Object or any part thereof; nor (f) the functioning of any safety device or protective device.

In summary, it can be said that, in general, boiler and machinery policies cover loss from breakdown of an insured object subject, of course, to the qualifications of the accident definition and other policy provisions.[3]

BASIC COVERAGES

A package of four principal coverages is provided under the standard Boiler and Machinery Policy, only one of these being optional. These coverages can be classified as follows:

1. Loss on property of the insured.
2. Expediting expenses.
3. Liability for damage to property of others.
4. Liability for bodily injuries (optional).

A single limit per accident applies to these coverages collectively and it is important therefore that the selected limit be adequate to cover the sum of exposures to the first three types of loss, plus bodily injury liability exposures, if that option is exercised. The policy limit applies to each

[3] Optional accident definitions are available for boilers and turbines. These provide restrictive coverages at reduced premium charges. The boiler option, called "limited coverage," insures only a tearing asunder caused by pressure of steam or water. There are three turbine options: "limited," "explosion," and "combined" which afford various degrees of restrictive coverage. Too lengthy for discussion here, these definitions can be found in policies.

accident, being automatically reinstated after a loss. The amount of insurance as reflected by this single limit is available to pay the losses in the order as listed above. The insurance is applied first to property loss of the insured; second to expediting expenses, assuming the limit was not exhausted in the settlement of the property loss; and so on as long as the limit is adequate. Defense and other legal costs, of course, are in addition to the limit.

Loss on Property of the Insured

All property owned by the insured is covered against loss from direct damage due to an accident to an insured object; the policy does not specify buildings, contents, etc., as do most other forms of property insurance.

Several exclusions apply to loss on property of the insured. Loss from fire (or from use of water or other means to extinguish fire), loss from accidents caused by fire, and loss from combustion explosion outside an insured object are specifically excluded. Thus, overlapping with fire and extended coverages is avoided insofar as possible.[4]

The exception made in respect to fire damage to certain objects which have electrical parts applies to: motors, generators, transformers, miscellaneous electrical apparatus, and others. Electrical breakdown in such machines is sometimes followed by fire and it is not always practicable to make a clear distinction between the electrical damage and the fire damage. For that reason, a special provision, applicable only to such objects, alters the fire exclusion in such a way that damage to the object by fire is covered if it originates therein. This special provision does not appear in the policy itself but is found in the definitions endorsement or schedule applicable to the object in question.

Loss from flood is excluded but an accident to an insured object caused by flood is covered. Other exclusions concern indirect losses, such as business interruption and spoilage of property due to lack of power, light, heat, steam, or refrigeration. In respect to the insured's property, no indirect loss is covered under the basic policy but coverage for business interruption and consequential (spoilage) damage insurance can be added by endorsement.

[4] Overlapping with fire and extended insurance occurs principally with respect to fire in electrical machines; explosions of unfired vessels and hot water boilers under certain circumstances; and furnace explosion losses, when that optional coverage is included in the boiler policy. However, overlapping with other types of insurance may also be involved in connection with business interruption and consequential damage losses and property damage liability, but not bodily injury liability. When overlapping occurs in a loss situation, that portion of the insured's loss which is covered by both policies is, of course, divided between insurers in accordance with the provisions of their respective policies. In the majority of cases, however, policy provisions, limits, and other conditions are such that the overlapping loss is divided equally. See Appendix *B* for further treatment of this point and for a general discussion of "guiding principles" used in settlement of overlapping losses.

Expediting Expenses

This coverage provides payment for extra expenses incurred in expediting repairs, or making temporary repairs, to the property of the insured directly damaged in an accident. The amount payable under this coverage is limited to the amount paid for direct damage loss on the insured's property but not in excess of $1,000. Expediting expense coverage is a fixed provision of the policy. No premium credit is allowed for its deletion.

Liability for Damage to Property of Others

In the event that property of a third party, wherever located, is directly damaged by an insured accident, the policyholder is indemnified for such amounts as he is obligated to pay by reason of his liability for such damage, including loss of use of such damaged property of others. No "care, custody, or control" exclusion, such as discussed in Chapters 32 and 34, appears in this provision.

Liability for Bodily Injuries

This optional coverage provides indemnity for such amounts as the insured is obligated to pay by reason of his liability for bodily injuries or death, caused by an insured accident. However it does not apply to liability under any workmen's compensation, unemployment compensation or disability benefits law, or any similar law. Furthermore, the coverage is excess insurance with respect to any other insurance or agreement to indemnify the insured for such liabilities.

General

In connection with the liability coverages, the policy contains the usual agreement found in liability policies with reference to expenses incurred in connection with legal proceedings.

The policy also contains war damage and nuclear energy exclusions, but coverage is provided for accidents arising out of strike, riot, civil commotion, acts of sabotage, vandalism, or malicious mischief.

All coverages in the policy or endorsements thereto apply only to loss resulting from accidents which occur while the object is in use or connected ready for use at the location specified for it in the policy. This provision relates to the general intent of the policy to insure accidents arising from causes connected with functional operation of objects but not, for example, damage incurred during transportation, installation, or repair work. A condition of the policy provides that the insurance company shall be permitted at all reasonable times during the policy period to inspect insured objects and the premises where they are located. The policy also contains a unique provision which permits the company, upon discovery of a dangerous condition with respect to any insured object, to suspend insurance with regard to that object. It is seldom necessary for a company to invoke this clause for insureds usually recognize the importance of shutting down objects which are in imminent danger of accident. This right to suspend insurance applies only with respect to the object subject to the dangerous condition.

The policy limits indemnity for loss on property of the insured to its actual cash value. However, the cost of repair or replacement in excess of actual cash value can be insured by endorsement.

Newly acquired objects at existing or newly acquired locations are automatically insured for 90 days provided that the new objects are of the same general character as others already insured under the contract.

USE AND OCCUPANCY INSURANCE

Use and occupancy coverage, in the boiler line, or "U. & O." as it is generally called, is similar in purpose to business interruption insurance in other lines. This purpose is to indemnify at least partially for loss of income which results from an insured property damage peril. The U. & O. is afforded by endorsement to the standard Boiler and Machinery Policy but under a separate insuring agreement and separate limit of loss.

Several variations in forms of U. & O. are available but they can be divided into two general classifications: valued forms and actual loss sustained forms.

Valued Forms

Valued business interruption forms, seldom used in other lines of insurance, are applied to the majority of U. & O. risks in the boiler line, and to smaller risks in particular. They are less detailed than actual loss sustained forms. They do not require reports of profits and expenses from the policyholder for underwriting or loss adjustment purposes, and they call for considerably less data and fewer computations in the adjustment of losses. These factors make for easier handling of the comparatively frequent, short-term, business interruption losses encountered with boiler and machinery risks but at some sacrifice of accuracy in the measurement of loss.

In addition to a limit of loss, valued U. & O. forms place a limit, known as the maximum daily indemnity, on the amount payable for any one 24-hour day. The daily limit is paid for each full day that the insured's business is totally shut down due to an accident. If a maximum daily indemnity of $1,000 has been purchased, for example, and business operations are totally suspended for a full day, the insured receives $1,000, irrespective of his actual loss of income.

Partial prevention of business is adjusted on a pro rata basis. If a manufacturer's output of finished products is reduced by 50 percent, or if the sales in a restaurant are reduced by 50 percent, for one day, the valued form pays 50 percent of the maximum daily indemnity without inquiry into the actual loss of profits and unearned expenses. The form provides a formula for measuring the percentage reduction of business when partial shutdown is involved.

Because of this method of loss adjustment it will be noted that the daily limit purchased should approximate the insured's average daily value of profits and overhead. This limit will provide a reasonably accurate relation between loss and indemnity if the business is one that operates at a fairly steady pace. However, if wide fluctuations occur, a loss payment may fall considerably short of, or exceed, the actual loss, depending upon the rate of business operations at the time of interruption.

Provision can be made under valued forms for varying the daily limit for predictable periods of business fluctuation, as in a seasonal business; but if fluctuations are sizeable and difficult to forecast, an actual loss form should be considered.

Actual Loss Sustained U. & O.

The form most frequently used for this type of U. & O. more nearly resembles business interruption insurance in other lines. No separate limit is placed on the amount payable per day. The insured is required to provide an income statement prior to issuance of the coverage and at certain times during term. In making a claim a detailed proof of actual loss of profits and unearned expenses is required.

Coinsurance is applicable under actual loss U. & O. forms but may be suspended for an additional premium charge if annual reports of U. & O. values are furnished. At inception of the coverage, the premium charge must of necessity be based upon the insured's estimates of the profits and fixed expenses he expects to earn. But profits and expenses actually earned may differ from his estimates to a greater or lesser degree and, for that reason, provisions are made for recomputing the premium annually to bring it in line with realities. Thus, there is a return premium if the true values are less than the original estimates. But if actual values exceed the original estimates, the situation is reversed and may be handled in one of two ways. If coinsurance were suspended during the policy period, full coverage would have been provided for all losses up to the limit and an additional premium is justified to bring the charge in line with actual values which turned out to be greater than the original estimates. If, on the other hand, coinsurance was in effect throughout the policy period, no additional premium is charged. Such a charge would not be justified because, in the event of loss, the insured would not have recovered in full because of operation of the coinsurance clause.

General

Underwriting methods and rates for the Boiler and Machinery U. & O. Endorsement provide a high degree of flexibility for tailoring coverage to fit exposures. It is not necessary, for example, to place the same amount of U. & O. coverage on all objects. In fact, it frequently happens that some of the objects insured for direct damage are also insured for U. & O., while others are not.

High U. & O. limits are needed for vessels or machines exposed to catastrophic explosions and consequent long periods of business interruption. On the other hand, even the most severe accident to some objects, such as an electric motor of ordinary design, will cause a relatively short interruption and may affect only a portion of the insured's operations. In such cases lower U. & O. limits are indicated.

In recognition of these and other variations of exposure, the underwriting scheme for the Boiler and Machinery U. & O. Endorsement permits different limits for different classes of objects insured under the same policy and it is not unusual to find four or five separate limits in the same contract.

Deductibles are also available for U. & O. coverage. These are usually applied under the "delayed midnight" plan. Indemnity does not commence until a specified midnight (first, second, third, etc.) following the time that the insurer receives notice of the occurrence. Deductibles can also be provided in the customary manner whereby the insured absorbs a specified number of the first dollars of every loss.

Premium charges for valued U. & O. are based on the type and size of objects insured for this coverage, the daily limit, the total limit, and delayed midnight or deductible insurance, if any. Actual loss sustained U. & O. premiums take the same factors into account but are judgment rated. Estimates of the percentage of business that will be affected by an accident and the expected length of interruption enter the premium computation.

When a U. & O. loss occurs, the insurer brings its inspection and engineering facilities to bear on the problem of restoring business operations. Wide experience with such problems often enables the insurer to shorten very materially the period of interruption. Many policyholders consider this feature a leading consideration in the purchase of U. & O. coverage.

CONSEQUENTIAL DAMAGE

In the boiler line, consequential damage refers to spoilage of property due to lack of power, light, heat, steam, or refrigeration caused by an accident to an insured object.

This coverage is provided by an endorsement having a separate insuring agreement and a separate limit. Unlike direct damage insurance, only property specifically named in the endorsement is insured, usually being goods in process or in cold storage. If the described property is owned by a third party, the policyholder is protected for his liability for spoilage of such specified property of others.

Consequential damage insurance can be furnished on a coinsurance, or no-coinsurance, basis. Premium charges depend upon the amount of insurance, the coinsurance basis, if any, and the kinds of objects insured for this kind of loss.

OTHER INDIRECT COVERAGES

Power Interruption

Premium volume for power interruption insurance amounts to a negligible fraction of the total boiler and machinery premium volume. It provides payment of a selected amount per hour (subject to a limit per day and a limit per occurrence) for deprivation of usable electric current, steam, water, gas, or refrigeration, furnished to the insured by a public utility. The deprivation must be caused by an accidental occurrence to physical equipment of the public utility. It can also be written to cover spoilage of specified property (or liability for spoilage) arising from the same cause.

Rates are not listed in the manual but are furnished upon application to the insurance company.

Power interruption insurance bears little resemblance to other boiler and machinery coverages. No indemnity for direct damage loss is included and inspection service for prevention of accidents is not offered.

Outage

Outage insurance is rarely written today as modern U. & O. coverage provides more suitable protection. A "valued" insurance, it provides for payment of an hourly indemnity for each working hour that an object, insured for this coverage, is out of service due to an accident. The test of loss is the extent to which the object cannot perform its function, not loss of revenues or production as is the case with various other types of insurance. Substitution of other equipment to perform the functions of the damaged object relieves the insurer of liability.

Rates for outage do not appear in the manual but can be furnished upon application.

RATE STRUCTURE

The boiler and machinery rate structure is complex due to its refinement and flexibility. For direct damage coverage, a separate premium charge is made for each insured object. With few exceptions, the object charge is dependent upon its size, capacity, pressure, or some similar determinant, and not upon its dollar value. For example, over 50 separate rates are listed for electric motors according to capacity as measured by horsepower; over 350 rates are possible for a steam turbine depending upon its capacity, use, and the degree of coverage desired.

This refinement of rates is due to the extremely wide range of sizes of some equipment. Steam turbine units, for example, are built in sizes ranging from under 10 kw up to hundreds of thousands of kw capacity. Values of individual units run from less than $1,000 to many millions of dollars. This spread produces a corresponding spread of loss potentials and inspection costs that enter the makeup of premium charges. Under the circumstances, an "average rate" would not be practical.

Flexibility of the rate structure is illustrated by the fact that the policyholder who owns 100 electric motors, for example, may insure all of them, only one, or any desired number. Flexibility is also indicated by the arrangement that permits him to buy indirect coverages for one or more classes of objects selected from many otherwise insured in the same policy.

The rate structure offers a wide choice of deductible amounts for both direct and indirect coverages. If a policy premium exceeds $4,500, the insured can elect to have it written under a premium adjustment plan which is similar in principle to retrospective rating plans in some other lines.

The premium charge for direct damage insurance on any kind of boiler or machinery object includes a factor for inspection expense. The size of this factor in relation to the total object charge is not uniform for the different types of objects, but generally speaking it is much greater than similar charges in any other line except elevator insurance. The loss portion of the premium dollar also varies as respects different classes of objects; and, from the ratemaking standpoint, each class of object has some of the characteristics of a separate line of insurance. It has its own typical hazards, its distinctive accident frequency pattern, an individual scale of loss factors, and a separate percentage of inspection expenses. Thus, for rating variations based on loss factors, such as deductible insurance and retrospective rating plans, a single percentage discount is not applicable. When such rating is applied to a policy, discounts must be determined separately for each class of object to be insured, including separate credits for U. & O. and consequential damage exposures.

The foregoing factors, and others, provide latitude in shaping coverage to fit the needs of the risk but require detailed surveys and an understanding of hazards and exposures as respects both direct and indirect loss potentials for best employment of the premium expenditure.

INSPECTION SERVICES

Several references have been made in this chapter to the importance of inspection service provided by boiler and machinery insurers. The underlying principles of this service have remained unchanged since its founding: prevention of accidents to insured equipment in plants of insureds, and cooperation with manufacturers of boilers and pressure vessels in the production of equipment that meets accepted safety standards.

The latter service is conducted on a fee basis and the expense involved does not enter insurance premium charges. The cost of inspections in plants of insureds is part of the premium charge and, in fact, constitutes one of the largest single items in charges for the direct damage insurance. It can be said then that a part of the premium is returned to the policyholder in the form of a service directed primarily toward reducing the probability of failure but, as a concomitant, often resulting in added life for the equipment and reduced operating and repair costs.

One of the most important factors in the success of this service is the "clearing house" operations of the insurance company's engineering organization. The findings of field inspectors in thousands of plants are reported to the company. The data thus collected are correlated and developed into safety standards and procedures for detecting accident-producing conditions in their incipient stages. This information, circulated to all field inspectors, enhances each man's knowledge far beyond his personal experience and observations.

Although inspection service is considered by many policyholders to be one of the more important factors in the purchase of such policies, it is interesting to note that the policy does not obligate the insurer to make inspections. Nevertheless, the benefits of the service to the insured, and to the insurance company, are evident and it is obvious that such inspections will generally be made.

The importance of this safety work is also attested by the fact that approximately 75 percent of the states and over 30 cities require at least some degree of safety inspection in connection with boilers, pressure vessels, or both. Inspections are provided on a fee basis by these states or cities, but in most cases inspections by insurance companies are accepted in lieu of those provided by the governmental organization.

In short, the insured has three obligations: (1) a moral obligation to prevent loss of life and limb, (2) a legal obligation to comply with state and/or municipal laws, and (3) a financial obligation to protect the business from loss. Purchase of a Boiler and Machinery Policy can be helpful in respect to all three.

SUGGESTED READINGS

ACKERMAN, S. B. *Insurance.* 3d ed. New York: Ronald Press Co., 1951. Chap. 7.

JETER, A. G. *The Boiler and Machinery Line of Insurance.* Hartford: The Hartford Steam Boiler Inspection and Insurance Company, 1962.

KULP, CLARENCE A. *Casualty Insurance.* 3d ed. New York: Ronald Press Co., 1956. Chap. 13.

RODDA, WILLIAM H. *Fire and Property Insurance.* Englewood Cliffs, N.J.: Prentice-Hall, Inc., 1956. Chap. 22.

STEPHENS, W. L. *A Producer's Boiler and Machinery Notebook.* Cincinnati: National Underwriter Company, 1963.

Chapter 42

TITLE, PLATE GLASS, CREDIT, AND EXPORT CREDIT INSURANCE

BY ROBB B. KELLEY

This chapter is the vehicle for treatment of the following miscellaneous lines: title insurance, plate glass insurance, credit insurance, and export credit insurance.

TITLE INSURANCE

Title insurance, as "invented" in the United States, is a business that develops over $100 million in annual premiums. One description of the title insurance industry offered in 1957 went in part as follows:

> (There are) . . . 147 companies, of which 77 have more than one outlet in their home state, 31 operate in more than one state, and 11 in 5 or more states . . . representing, at an average premium rate of 3½ dollars a thousand, 28½ billion dollars of Title insurance coverage.[1]

Title insurance has been defined as

> . . . a contract of indemnity relating to land described in the policy, protecting the Insured against loss or damage by reason of defects, liens or encumbrances in the insured title existing at the date of the policy and not expressly excepted from its terms.[2]

Title insurance definitely is a contract of insurance and not of suretyship. Hence, companies issuing title insurance contracts are in the insurance business and come under the control of state insurance regulation.

Purchasers of land and mortgagees of real property have come to rely on the title insurance company for protection against loss growing out of undiscovered defects in existence at the time the policy is issued. While the usual insurance contract looks to the future, title insurance looks

[1] Quintin Johnstone, "Title Insurance," *Insurance Counsel Journal*, Vol. XXVI (July, 1959), p. 373.

[2] Charles F. Grimes, "The Lawyer, His Client and Title Insurance," *Student Lawyer Journal* (April, 1958), reprint, n.d.

backward. Defects and encumbrances arising after the date of issue of the Title Insurance Policy are not covered.

Need for Title Insurance

Even though a purchaser of real property retains an attorney and a professional searcher of titles such as an abstracter, there is no financial guarantee that no defect exists. Furthermore, an abstracter's liability may be barred by a statute of limitations which begins to run from the date the mistake was made rather than from the time of discovery of the error. In the event of negligence of the searcher, recovery is dependent upon his financial responsibility. Many possibilities for hidden defects exist where there would be no negligence on the part of the searcher. The following are some of the more serious hidden risks not revealed by the public records:

1. Erroneous recital of marital status of the titleholder, including all titleholders in the chain of title.
2. Undisclosed heirs.
3. Mistaken interpretations of wills and other documents.
4. Mental incompetence.
5. Deeds executed by minors.
6. Fraud and forgery.
7. Deeds defective for want of proper delivery or executed under an expired or revoked power of attorney.
8. Mistaken identity due to similar or identical names.
9. Errors in the public records.

Members of professional and trade groups who are primary customers for title services are lawyers, real estate brokers, home building companies, and mortgage lending institutions. The most significant demand for title insurance has come from many life insurance companies which demand mortgagee coverage. They require use of a title insurance company which carefully searches the title as well as provides a Title Insurance Policy.

This requirement discourages companies from using an approach of insuring the title but making no search of the public records. Some title insurance companies collapsed during the depression of the thirties.

Types of Title Insurance

A title insurance company generally maintains its own private indexes and records, called title plants, in the locality where its home office is located. Title insurance companies generally write no other type of insurance. These plants, usually located in large cities, are so organized and maintained that they are a source of ready information regarding title to real estate, such as recorded deeds and mortgages, confirmed special assessments, and rates of general taxes and special assessments. The plant also contains up-to-the-minute information on pending suits and judgments in various state, municipal, and federal courts which affect titles to land. As a result, buyers can get prompt and accurate information necessary to their decision making. In many contracts of sale the buyer agrees to the transaction only if the seller's title is one that a specified title insurance company would insure subject to no more than the standard exceptions. In many instances the buyer's requirement of marketability is tied to the title insurance examination report.

Currently the American Title Association policies are in widespread use. There are two general types of title insurance policies: (1) owner's policies or fee policies and (2) mortgage policies, mortgagee policies, or loan policies.

Owner's Policies. The owner's policy is designed to meet the normal title insurance needs and requirements of owners of real estate. An excerpt from such a policy is as follows:

AMERICAN TITLE ASSOCIATION OWNER'S POLICY
STANDARD FORM A—CENTRAL REGION—1960

BLANK TITLE INSURANCE COMPANY

a corporation of ________, herein called the Company, for a valuable consideration, hereby insures the party named in Schedule A, hereinafter called the Insured, the heirs, devisees, personal representatives of such Insured, or, if a corporation, its successors by dissolution, merger or consolidation, against loss or damage not exceeding the amount stated in Schedule A, together with costs, attorneys' fees and expenses which the Company may become obligated to pay as provided in the Conditions and Stipulations hereof, which the Insured shall sustain by reason of:

Any defect in or lien or encumbrance on the title to the estate or interest covered hereby in the land described or referred to in Schedule A, existing at the date hereof, not shown or referred to in Schedule B or excluded from coverage in Schedule B or in the Conditions and Stipulations.

(The following additional line is found in Standard Form B: . . . or unmarketability of such title.)

Owner's title insurance is usually interminable, the protection extending to the heirs at law or devisees of the property owner in the event of death and to the corporate successors of corporate owners. A mortgagee policy, however, is usually terminable upon the discharge of the debt except in case of foreclosure or deed in lieu of foreclosure. In some areas where title insurance is used extensively in land title transfers, owner's policies may insure against unmarketability of title. This is the case in ATA Standard Homeowner's Policy, Form B above—not to be confused with Homeowner's Policies as discussed in Part VI. In those areas where the abstract and attorney's opinion method still is dominant, title insurance companies tend to refuse to insure marketability.

The owner's policies vary by region (for example, one region is the

Northeast) regarding general exceptions applicable to the region. The exceptions are printed as items in Schedule B. Following such printed exceptions are the typed specific exceptions applicable to the estate or interest covered by the policy.

Mortgage Policies. The Mortgage Title Insurance Policy provides that the person to whom the mortgagee is making the loan has title to the real estate pledged as security or that the trust deed or mortgage evidences a valid lien on the real estate. An example of particular policy wording follows:

American Title Association Standard Loan Policy
Revised Coverage—1960

BLANK TITLE INSURANCE COMPANY

a corporation of ________, herein called the Company, for a valuable consideration, hereby insures those designated herein as Insured against loss or damage not exceeding the amount stated in Schedule A, together with costs, attorneys' fees and expenses which the Company may become obligated to pay as provided in the Conditions and Stipulations hereof, which the Insured shall sustain by reason of:

1. Any defect in the execution of the mortgage described in Schedule A, but only insofar as such defect affects the lien or charge of said mortgage upon the estate referred to in this policy; or
2. The invalidity or unenforceability of the lien of the mortgage upon said estate; or
3. The title to the said estate being vested at the date hereof otherwise than as herein stated; or
4. The unmarketability of the title of the mortgagor; or
5. Any defect in or lien or encumbrance on said title at the date hereof not shown or referred to in Schedule B or excluded from coverage in the Conditions and Stipulations; or
6. The priority over the mortgage at the date hereof of any lien or encumbrance not shown or referred to in Schedule B or excluded from coverage in the Conditions and Stipulations; or
7. The priority over the mortgage of any statutory lien, or right thereto, for labor or materials which lien or right exists at the date hereof, whether recorded or not, or arises from construction which is to become security for and is to be paid for in whole or in part from proceeds of the indebtedness secured by the mortgage which the Insured has advanced or is presently obligated to advance; and

   (The use of the following clause changes this policy into American Title Association Loan Policy—Additional Coverage—1960:

   any assessments for street improvements under construction or completed at the date hereof which now have gained or hereafter may gain priority over said mortgage; and)
8. Subject to the provisions of Schedule B, the Company further insures that the assignments shown in Schedule A, whether recorded or not, are valid and enforceable and vest title to the mortgage in the Insured free and clear of all liens.

Two outstanding differences that usually exist between the owner's type of policy and the mortgage type are:

1. The liability in a mortgage policy decreases as the mortgage payments are paid to reduce principal and terminates on final payment.
2. There is a possible salvage value in the equity between the amount of the mortgage debt and the market value of the property.

General Provisions

Title policies specify in Schedule A the date of the policy, the amount, name of insured, the property, and the deed or instrument by which title is vested. Schedule B lists exceptions and limitations involving estates, interest, defects, objections to title, liens, charges, or encumbrances which the policy does not cover.

The company agrees to defend at its expense—in addition to the limit of the policy—all litigation against the insured based upon a title defect covered in the policy. This agreement holds whether the claim asserted proves valid or not.

Exclusions

There are certain risks not covered in Title Insurance Policies. They are:

1. Defects disclosed by title examination. When found, they are listed in Schedule B.
2. Defects that physical inspection and survey of the premises would disclose are not covered in owner's policies but are covered in mortgagee's policies. These include adverse possession, unrecorded leases, and easements that would be disclosed by an inspection of the premises.
3. Defects created subsequent to the date of the policy.
4. Defects of which the insured was aware or which he assumed prior to the date of the policy.
5. Restrictions of any governmental regulation on the use and enjoyment of the premises.
6. Title to personal property, even when affixed to the realty.
7. Some hidden defects not disclosed by a competent examination of public records or physical inspection of the premises or survey. This last exclusion deals with risks which are considered beyond the ordinary by the underwriters. For example, mechanics' or materialmen's liens or other statutory liens for labor or material not shown of record are excepted. Some companies cover, under a mortgagee's policy, such liens (*a*) if a physical inspection of the premises shows no sign of recent construction, or—when there has been recent construction—(*b*) if there is satisfactory evidence of payment, (*c*) if lien waivers or releases are secured, or (*d*) if security is posted for payment of any unpaid construction costs.[3]

Reserves, Claims, and Rates

Paid losses to written premiums in title insurance run about 2 percent. This generalization, however, is complicated by the fact that no uniform accounting system is followed. For example, most companies, in reporting

[3] Johnstone, *op. cit.*, p. 376.

losses paid, do not appear to include unallocated claim expense. Some companies apparently include in their premium income the charge for the entire cost of the policy to the customer, including the charge for search, examination, and, in some instances, escrow or closing costs.

Title insurance has a characteristic found in boiler and machinery insurance and in elevator public liability insurance where inspection costs take a larger proportion of the premium than is the case with most types of insurance.

One title insurance executive has indicated his company's losses, expenses of litigation, salaries, and expenses of the claim department average between 2 and 3 percent of the total premium. About 25 percent of the premium goes for acquisition, and about 60 percent for searching the records and passing on the title. About one half the losses result from the title company's own errors of omission or judgment. The other half comes from the so-called hidden losses.[4]

Two types of reserves will be mentioned: (1) the unearned premium reserve and (2) the loss reserve. The unearned premium reserve in title insurance is typically figured by assigning 10 percent of the premium to a reserve, and 5 percent of this credit is taken down from the reserve each year until the entire credit has been recovered in 20 years. This figure coincides with the average period that risks stay in force. Experience has demonstrated that this 10 percent is generally adequate. The loss reserve is an evaluation of a reported loss, including any prospective litigation expenses.

It should be kept in mind that the title insurance premiums are paid only once, and are not annual as is the case in most kinds of insurance. The term is not annual, but runs indefinitely. Some statistical studies indicate that with the increasing use of title insurance, the amount of the average claim has risen substantially.

The premium is developed from allowances for (1) the cost of services, (2) reserves required by law, (3) the risk, and (4) profit. Moreover, the rate structure for title insurance is complicated by local usages and forms. It starts with a basic rate for original insurance, and then gives the customer a reduced cost consistent with (1) reduced exposure, and (2) cost of processing. One system sets forth a schedule of prices based upon applications for individual policies. Three basic schedules are used in the following circumstances.

Schedule I —Where the title insurance company has never insured the property.
Schedule II —Where a prior owner's policy is outstanding.
Schedule III—Where increased amounts of insurance or broadened insurance is written at charges over and above the basic rates shown on Schedules I and II.

---

[4] William H. Deatly, address to The Advertising Club of Baltimore on the occasion of the 75th Anniversary of the Title Guaranty Company of Baltimore, date unknown.

These schedules do not include cases where the title insurance company is asked to perform unusual services or assume some extraordinary risks. These schedules are of a package nature, for they include all charges for a preliminary report and policy. Each schedule is illustrated in Table

TABLE 42–1
ILLUSTRATIVE SCHEDULE OF TITLE INSURANCE RATES
1964

SCHEDULE I

INITIAL COVERAGE INSURANCE

Basic Consideration	*$1,000 Owner's Policy*	*$1,000 Mortgage Policy (No owner's)*
A. A complete merchantable abstract is not produced	$85.00	$80.00
B. A complete merchantable abstract is left, which is dated more than 10 years ago	60.00	55.00
C. A complete merchantable abstract is left, which is dated within the last 10 years	40.00	35.00

Owner's policies are issued only for the full value of the property. For insurance in excess of $1,000, see Schedule III.

A mortgage policy becomes void upon the discharge of the debt secured by the trust deed or mortgage in respect to which the policy is issued (except in case of foreclosure or deed in lieu of foreclosure), and, because it is terminable, it is issued at a smaller premium than an owner's policy.

SCHEDULE II

CONTINUATION OR REISSUE—RATE PER THOUSAND OR FRACTION THEREOF

A. Prior owner's policy issued more than 2 years ago.

Policy Amount	*Owner's*	*Mortgage*
First thousand	$28.00	$22.00
Over $1,000 to include $20,000	2.00	1.50
Over $20,000 to include $50,000	.75	.75
Over $50,000	.25	.25

B. Prior owner's policy issued within the last 2 years.

Policy Amount	*Owner's*	*Mortgage*
First thousand	$23.00	$18.00
Over $1,000 to include $20,000	1.50	1.25
Over $20,000 to include $50,000	.75	.75
Over $50,000	.25	.25

SCHEDULE III

INCREASED OR ADDITIONAL INSURANCE—RATE PER THOUSAND OR FRACTION THEREOF

	Owner's	*Mortgage*
Over $1,000 to include $20,000	$5.00	$3.50
Over $20,000 to include $100,000	4.00	3.00
Over $100,000 to include $1,000,000	3.00	2.50
Over $1,000,000 to include $5,000,000	2.00	2.00
Over $5,000,000	1.50	1.50

42–1. (The material was obtained from the Chicago Title and Trust Company and is used by the author with permission.)

Transfer of title insurance policies is usually not permitted. A policy held by a mortgagee or one who holds some other type of encumbrance may be transferred to the owner at a foreclosure sale where the property is bought by or for the insured. Other transfers may be permitted by the company by special agreement.

The insured must (1) notify the company within 10 days, in writing, of action questioning the validity of the title; (2) allow the company to use the insured's name in the defense; and (3) give reasonable cooperation in the defense of the action.

Torrens System

The "Torrens System" exists on a voluntary or optional basis in 19 states in the United States. The system works as follows: An owner of real property can obtain through court procedure a certificate of title. He applies to the courts to register his title. At a hearing he proves his title by submitting an abstract, survey, and other relevant information. The title is then "registered" and he is given a certificate. Subsequent transfers of title may then be recorded on the same page.

Advantages of this system are:

1. The registrant gets an unquestionable title, while he gets only an indemnity under the title insurance.
2. Many titles can be improved under the Torrens System, while under title insurance the insured gets only indemnity. Moreover, title insurance is not available in many rural territories.
3. Much legal controversy and expense can perhaps be eliminated.
4. Title transfers are speeded up and simplified.

The Torrens System has not "caught on" in this country. Several reasons can be suggested. No organized promotion effort has been made. There are questions of constitutionality and law in some jurisdictions which prevent the conferring of a clear and final title. Some insurance companies do not lend on Torrens certificates unless a Title Insurance Policy is obtained. Others will not take an uninsured certificate during the period following the initial registration when the registration is open to attack.

Under this system one finds the usual troubles of a government operation compared to private enterprise. Service too often has been slow.[5] The judicial proceedings required under the first registration are slow and expensive;[6] the seller is generally reluctant to go into court; and the buyer is satisfied with a reasonable proof of title. Only subsequent buyers reap the benefit under the Torrens System.[7] Such a system could be made to

[5] Johnstone, *op. cit.*, pp. 378–88.

[6] *Ibid.*

[7] *Ibid.*

work only if it were made mandatory. This system does not possess the benefits of free enterprise and competition inherent in the institution of title insurance.

PLATE GLASS INSURANCE

Plate glass insurance is one of the oldest forms of casualty insurance. An English glass insurance company began operations in 1862, and the first plate glass insurance policy in the United States was written by a domestic specialty writer in 1867. The early insurers were, with one exception, monoline companies. Today almost all plate glass insurers are multiple-line companies. The annual volume of business written is modest—somewhere around $50 million. Many retail stores carry no plate glass insurance policy. Probably only a fourth or a third of the readily insurable plate glass in the United States is covered by plate glass insurance.

The reason for the relatively low volume written in relation to the market may be found in the fact that chance for serious loss is not great. This fact, coupled with the long-followed rule-of-thumb average ratio of one loss in four years, encourages the plate glass owner to "self-insure." As one writer has observed, "Probably in no other line of insurance is the selection so manifestly against the company."[8] This fact keeps rates higher than they would be otherwise.

Insurance surveys of business risks increasingly tend to show plate glass insurance as an example of a coverage which can be eliminated in favor of coverages where the amount of a single loss could be much more serious. Only a survey of the glass exposure can fairly answer the question of relative seriousness of loss.

Some ground floor fronts have plates of such size that $3,000 to $4,000 may be required to replace a single plate. In other cases, of course, the largest possible loss is much smaller. Modern architects tend to use plates of unusual size, shape, and type of glass.

Comprehensive Plate Glass Policy

Glass insurance is a simple form of insurance. The Comprehensive Plate Glass Policy is a broad contract filed and rated by the National Bureau of Casualty Underwriters and the Mutual Insurance Rating Bureau.

The insuring agreement covers damage to glass (and lettering, and/or ornamentation, if insured) caused by breakage or by chemicals accidentally or maliciously applied. The coverage also includes without additional charge:

---

[8] F. S. Garrison as quoted from C. A. Kulp, *Casualty Insurance* (3d ed.; New York: Ronald Press Co., 1956), p. 296. Mr. Garrison's statement appears in PCAS, Vol. XIII, 1926, p. 341.

a) Repairing or replacing frames immediately encasing and continguous to such glass when necessary because of such damage.

b) Installing temporary plates in or boarding up openings containing such glass when necessary because of unavoidable delay in repairing or replacing such damaged glass.

c) Removing and replacing any obstructions (other than window displays) when necessary in replacing such damaged glass, lettering, or ornamentation.

The limit of liability under (*a*), (*b*), and (*c*) is $75 each, which amounts to an aggregate limit of $225. These limits apply separately to each occurrence of loss at each location separately occupied or designed for separate occupancy.

The declarations must describe the glass, and the lettering and ornamentation if the insured wants them covered. Breakage is not defined in the policy but adjusters generally consider a fracture through the entire thickness, regardless of where located on the plate, to be a breakage. The smallest break in a plate is a total loss.

The limit of the company's liability is based on actual cash value or replacement with glass of like kind or quality. Some coverage is on a stated amount basis, one example being lettering. In practice for most losses this policy is a replacement contract. Some buyers attach importance to the fact that an insurance company may more speedily obtain replacements because it is a substantial customer for plate glass. When numerous losses occur simultaneously in an area, priority would tend to go to the larger buyer of glass. A show window is highly regarded in many types of businesses and the speed of glass replacement is an important consideration.

The policy is not reduced by payment of any loss or replacement of broken glass, lettering, or ornamentation. The insurance company has the usual salvage and subrogation rights. Neither right is of much value. Smaller pieces of broken glass are much less than proportionately valuable. According to one text, for example, ". . . 16 square feet is 1/9 the area of 144 square feet, but is worth only about 1/50 as much."[9] Only in about 15 cases out of 100 is the cause of the breakage known, and many individuals responsible for breakage offer poor collection possibilities.

The insured has the usual duty of reporting the loss as soon as practicable and the company has the right to require a proof of loss. In practice, formal proof of loss is seldom requested.

The Comprehensive Plate Glass Policy is practically an "all risk" contract, there being but two exclusions: (1) loss by fire—at the insured premises or elsewhere and (2) loss due to war, whether or not declared, civil war, insurrection, rebellion or revolution, or to any act or condition in connection with such happening.

[9] Robert Riegel and Jerome S. Miller, *Insurance Principles and Practices* (4th ed.; Englewood Cliffs, N.J.: Prentice-Hall, Inc., 1959), p. 613.

The Other Insurance Clause provides that the insurer participates on a pro rata basis with other applicable insurance in paying a covered loss. Where there is nonconcurrent insurance such as the Comprehensive Plate Glass Policy and the Standard Fire Policy with the Extended Coverage Endorsement and glass breakage caused by a windstorm, the casualty and fire insurers generally follow the "Agreement of Guiding Principles." This agreement is a statement of loss settlement practices followed by most fire and casualty insurers in situations involving an apportionment of loss property covered by nonconcurrent policies of both types of carriers. (See Appendix *A.*)

Premium Computation

The premium computation allows most premiums to be developed off a single rate table of basic premiums and modified by appropriate multipliers and discounts. In the "Rate Tables" section of the manual the basic premium is determined by the *size* of the glass. The *class* is next determined from the "Directory of Glass." Reference is then made to the Classification and Rate Chart for the variables to ascertain the Class-Position multipliers which are the class or kind of glass and the *use and position* of glass in the building. Then any discounts are applied based upon *occupancy* and some other miscellaneous considerations. Next, the *territory* is checked for the appropriate territorial multiplier. Each state contains at least one territory.

Special types of objects such as lettering, designs, ornamentation, memorial windows, stained glass windows, and glass valued in excess of $5 per square foot require slightly different treatment. Rating of structural glass also requires a different procedure.

The policy term is one year in all states except those which allow a three-year term with the premium (2.7 times annual premium) paid in advance or equal annual installments (3 times annual premiums).

Other Contracts

Residence glass may be insured under a Comprehensive Plate Glass Policy by endorsement on either a specific item basis, a blanket basis, or a combination of the two. When residence glass is endorsed on a blanket basis, there is a $50 limit on any one pane or plate of glass. The $50 limit is removed from any items of glass specifically insured. Except for the $50 limitation, the residence glass endorsement contains the same coverage, exclusions, and limitations as the Comprehensive Plate Glass Policy. Residence glass coverage may also be added by endorsement to a Homeowners Policy as an option. When endorsed to a Homeowners Policy the residence glass coverage is identical to the Comprehensive Glass Policy Residence Endorsement.

"All risk" coverage may be written on stained glass set in leaded sections (including glass in memorial windows), neon and flourescent signs, halftone screens and lenses, and rotogravure screens (fire is excluded in the rotogravure screens).

The "50–50" coverage calls for 50 percent of the regular premium and provides that the insured must stand all losses up to the amount of saving or retention. He then has full coverage on all losses over this amount. This coverage has been withdrawn by the National Bureau of Casualty Underwriters in all states except Texas, but is written in a number of states by independents and Mutual Insurance Rating Bureau filers.

The Vandalism and Malicious Mischief Endorsement attached to the Standard Fire Policy excludes damage to glass on business property which forms a part of a building except glass building blocks. A Comprehensive Plate Glass Policy is the only answer for coverage against malicious breakage of store fronts and show windows. The special multi-peril forms introduced in 1962 will tend to reduce the need for separate plate glass policies because coverage is incorporated in the multi-peril program. However, at present the special multi-peril policies may include plate glass insurance but the rating is accomplished by using the Glass Manual and then allowing the package discount. It remains to be seen whether the plate glass line as a separate type of insurance will be a victim of the multiple line revolution.

CREDIT INSURANCE[10]

Difficulties with receivables are said to contribute to about one out of every nine failures among manufacturers and one out of every six failures among wholesalers.[11] Dun & Bradstreet report that about 99 percent of all commercial transactions in the United States and Canada are on credit terms. Only two insurance companies, one a monoline and the other a multiple line carrier, write credit insurance (as the term is used in this section) in the United States and one of these also writes in Canada. The total premium volume in both countries runs about $10 million annually. These premiums protect more than $10 billion worth of sales. Some firms have used credit insurance continuously for over 40 years.

Nature of Coverage

Credit insurance indemnifies for abnormal credit losses arising from failure by business debtors to pay because of insolvencies or protracted default. It is sometimes known as commercial credit insurance to distin-

[10] For a more detailed discussion see Clyde William Phelps, *Commercial Credit Insurance as a Management Tool* as cited in the readings at the end of this chapter. The author gratefully acknowledges this source of information.

[11] *Ibid.*, p. 9.

guish private credit insurance from various government insurance programs such as the Home Mortgage Insurance Program of the Federal Housing Administration. Credit insurance should not be confused with credit life insurance and credit health insurance.

Credit insurance is written for manufacturers, wholesalers, advertising agencies, or other service organizations dealing with business firms. It is not written for retailers or consumer lending institutions.

Auxiliary Services. In addition to the indemnity under the coverage, the insured also receives the benefit of auxiliary services such as assistance in preventing bad debt losses; collection aids; reduction of interest costs, collection expenses, and other extra costs caused by small accounts; and salvaging of insolvent accounts for the insured, including cases where the indebtedness on the account exceeds the insurance coverage carried on it.

Normal Losses Excluded. The policies do not usually cover normal credit losses. They cover losses in excess of what the insured may be expected to sustain in the normal course of business. The policies refer to the primary loss which is an agreed percentage of the insured's annual net sales. In turn, the net sales are the gross sales less allowances and invoice price of goods returned and accepted. The primary loss is figured initially on the experience of the average business firms in the insured's business classification. For renewal policies consideration is also given to the individual experience of the insured. The minimum amount of primary loss is set forth in the policy, and the primary loss is shown also as a percentage of net covered sales. The insured is responsible for the primary loss in any year before the credit insurance company becomes liable for any payment. In effect, the primary loss is a deductible. It helps reduce premiums and promotes carefulness on the part of the insured. The primary loss could be insured but it would only amount to a trading of dollars between the company and the insured.

Coinsurance. Coinsurance can be applied in credit insurance. Unlike the coinsurance in fire coverages where there is a relation to the amount of insurance to be carried, coinsurance in credit insurance works as a deductible. Accounts with first, second, and third credit ratings may take a 10 percent coinsurance which means the policyholder is reimbursed on the basis of 90 percent of the insured loss. A 20 percent coinsurance figure would amount to 80 percent reimbursement of the covered invoice price and would be applied on accounts with less acceptable credit ratings.

The largest writer of credit insurance reports that most policies since January 1, 1960, have been issued to cover each account for 100 percent, which means the elimination of the coinsurance feature. This company still uses the primary loss deduction which is usually a fraction of one percent of the annual sales volume.

Collections

Most policies are written on what is known as an optional collection basis. The policy usually provides that an account which is past due, but not by more than three months, under the original terms of sale, may be filed with the credit insurer for collection. These accounts are accepted as claims the day they are filed. Of course, no claims are accepted until the insured has absorbed the primary loss. The company makes a collection charge based upon a schedule of fees shown in the policy. The insured, however, has the option of handling his own insolvent accounts. In such a case he must use "due diligence" in making collections.

Insolvency

The policy states that a debtor shall be considered insolvent and his account become a claim under any one or more of the following conditions (which do not necessarily include his being adjudged a bankrupt):

1. A debtor shall have absconded.
2. A sole debtor shall have died.
3. A sole debtor shall have been adjudged insane.
4. A receiver shall have been appointed for a debtor.
5. The stock in trade of a debtor shall have been sold under the Bulk Sales Act.
6. A writ of attachment or execution shall have been levied on a debtor's stock in trade and said stock sold thereunder, or the writ returned unsatisfied.
7. A debtor shall have made a general offer of compromise to his creditors for less than his indebtedness.
8. Possession shall have been taken under a chattel mortgage given by a debtor on his stock in trade.
9. A debtor's assets shall have been assigned to, or taken over by, a committee for the sole purpose of liquidation.
10. Possession shall have been taken of a debtor's assets under an assignment or deed of trust executed by the debtor for the benefit of his creditors.
11. A voluntary or involuntary proceeding shall have been instituted to adjudge a debtor bankrupt.
12. A proceeding for an arrangement of the debts of a debtor shall have been instituted in a court of bankruptcy.

Credit insurance policies cannot be cancelled by the insurance company during the term of the policy. There is an exception to this rule, however, in the case of the extraordinary coverage rider. Such a rider pertains to specifically named debtors of the larger marginal and unrated accounts. The policy may be cancelled only as it affects future shipments. The insurer is liable for any shipments made within the limits of coverage prior to the date of cancellation notice.

EXPORT CREDIT INSURANCE

A few companies in this country have written credit insurance protecting exporters to an agreed percentage of approved accounts against losses caused by the insolvency of foreign buyers. This coverage generally has not been competitive with insurance available to foreign exporters with whom U.S. exporters compete.

Foreign Credit Insurance Association

During 1962, 72 insurance companies formed a voluntary unincorporated group known as the Foreign Credit Insurance Association to write "Export Credit Insurance." This insurance amounts to a guarantee to an exporter that in the event a foreign buyer fails to meet his payment obligations due to insolvency, other commercial reasons, currency inconvertibility, war, expropriation, or certain other political contingencies, the FCIA policy will protect the exporter in accordance with its terms and conditions.

This insurance is written with the Export-Import Bank of Washington, an agency of the United States government which is called the Ex-Im Bank throughout the policies.

Types of Coverage

Two general types of policies are written. One is a comprehensive policy which includes Coverage A—commercial credit risks, and Coverage B—political risks only. Examples of political risks are inconvertibility of foreign currency to dollars, expropriation, confiscation, war, civil commotion, and restriction of export or import licenses.

Under Coverage A the insured is indemnified up to 85 percent of his loss. This percentage is shared equally between the FCIA and Ex-Im Bank. Under Coverage B the Ex-Im Bank indemnifies the insured up to 85 or 95 percent of his loss, depending upon the duration of the policy. This is a combination policy but the FCIA does not underwrite any of Coverage B.

The second general type of policy covers political risks only. This coverage is written by the Ex-Im Bank in response to the exporters' demand for it. Ex-Im Bank officials recommend the comprehensive rather than only the political coverage because the dividing line is sometimes very thin between political and commercial risks. The policy indemnifies the insured up to 85 or 90 percent of the loss depending upon the duration of the policy.

There are two durations of coverage: (1) the short-term, which is any agreed period up to 180 days, and (2) the medium-term which runs from

181 days to five years. Under the medium-term policy, installment payments, including interest on outstanding balances, are insured rather than accounts receivable. Heavy goods such as equipment parts, engines, and other durable products requiring longer credit terms are insured under the medium-term. The insurance may be obtained on a case-to-case basis, on a revolving line of credit (repetitive sales) to one buyer, or on a "whole turnover" basis. "Whole turnover" encompasses all credit export sales and applies generally to the short-term policy—as opposed to the medium-term policy. Political risk coverage in the medium-term policies is 85 percent.

Information with regard to applications and coverages can be obtained from insurance agents and brokers or from FCIA. This insurance is an example of private enterprise and the federal government attempting to spur exports by making credit conditions more competitive.

SUGGESTED READINGS

American Title Association. *Public Regulation of Title Insurance Companies and Abstracters.* Philadelphia: Villanova University Press, 1961.

Gueble, A. F. "Credit Insurance—Its Role in Modern Insurance Merchandising," *Rough Notes,* Vol. 103 (September, 1960), pp. 27, 86–92.

Johnstone, Quintin. "Title Insurance," *Insurance Counsel Journal* (July, 1959), pp. 374–96.

Kulp, Clarence A. *Casualty Insurance.* 3d ed. New York: Ronald Press Co., 1956. Chap. 12.

Magee, John H., and Bickelhaupt, David L. *General Insurance.* 7th ed. Homewood, Ill.: Richard D. Irwin, Inc., 1964. Chap. 18.

Oppenheimer, Robert H. "Credit Insurance and Foreign Trade." Unpublished thesis, Graduate School of Business, New York University, 1961.

Phelps, Clyde William. *Commercial Credit Insurance as a Management Tool.* Baltimore: Commercial Credit Company, 1961.

Riegel, Robert, and Miller, Jerome S. *Insurance Principles and Practices.* 4th ed. Englewood Cliffs, N.J.: Prentice-Hall, Inc., 1959. Chaps. 38, 39.

Chapter 43

DISHONESTY INSURANCE

BY HAROLD G. EVANS

The subject of this chapter is insurance for loss arising from burglary, robbery, or theft. Though the generic term "Dishonesty Insurance" is used to label this chapter, there is no implication here that this term is uniformly used to delineate this area of insurance; there is simply the implication that the term is useful and descriptive in this regard. Since it might, and sometimes does, also embrace fidelity coverages, readers are cautioned that fidelity bonds are treated in Part VII of this *Handbook*.

The coverages described in this chapter, while relating to various types of loss, do all have the common quality of providing indemnity for loss of money, securities, merchandise, or other personal property caused by the dishonest acts of the public. They do not normally overlap with any burglary, robbery, or theft coverage discussed in Part III (Marine and Aviation Insurance), in Part IV (Inland Marine Insurance), or in Chapter 37 in respect to automobile theft insurance.

EARLY HISTORY IN EUROPE AND THE UNITED STATES

The exact beginning of burglary-robbery-theft insurance is probably not recorded. However, as early as 1161 A.D. an insurance fund for such type of loss was set up in southern France and received special license by edict of Pope Alexander III (1159–81). His order set forth premium calculations, assessments, and administration by the clergy as well as other operating details.[1]

In 1788 Englishman William Weller advertised to insure against "loss of Property by Burglaries, Highway and Footpad Robberies, and Public and Private Theft. . . ."[2] However, his business venture met an early doom when his request for a royal charter was refused. Approximately

[1] Alfred Manes, *Versichergswesen: Güeterversicherung* (Property Insurance) (5th ed.; Berlin: Teubner, 1931), Vol. 11, p. 168.

[2] *Times* (London) March 18, 1788.

100 years later in 1889, the Mercantile Accident and Guarantee Insurance Company was persuaded to write burglary insurance by P. C. Allan, a retired constable. Subsequently, this company became recognized as the first English underwriter of burglary insurance.[3]

In the United States the very early burglary, robbery, and theft coverages were written in marine policies. Although one company was incorporated to write burglary and fire insurance in the early 1800's and several more were incorporated to write burglary insurance in the late 1800's, it was not until the turn of the century that burglary insurance was written in volume as a separate class. By 1940 the premiums written had climbed to $28,340,000. In 1959 they peaked at $116,500,000 and then started to recede. In 1962 the written premium was $112,000,000.[4] The decrease could be traced directly to the growth of the personal and commercial multiple peril contracts which include the perils of burglary, robbery, and theft.

NEED FOR BURGLARY, ROBBERY, AND THEFT INSURANCE

The growth of crime was the big influence on the premium increase. In 1930 the Federal Bureau of Investigation published a booklet entitled *Uniform Crime Report for the United States,* the first of many annual editions. These annual reports have indicated an alarming increase in crime.[5] In its report for 1940 the FBI tabulated 53,435 robberies, 316,369 burglaries, and 902,113 thefts.[6] In its report for 1962 the count was 95,260 robberies, 892,800 burglaries, and 539,900 thefts $50 and over.[7] Recently, the FBI reported the growth of crime in the period 1958–62 outstripped population growth about five to one. Figure 43–1 depicts this relative growth.

In 1900, burglaries, robberies, and thefts were recognized as being concentrated more in large cities than in small towns or villages. By 1961 the picture had changed somewhat with crime still strong in large cities but rapidly spreading and increasing in small towns and rural areas. Nearly two thirds of the U.S. population now reside in cities of over 50,000 and in their suburbs. The crime rate (incidence of crime in proportion to size of population) in such cities in nearly three times as high as

[3] Author unknown, "Jubilee of Burglary Insurance," *The Policy* (Sept. 15, 1938), pp. 1186–87.

[4] *Insurance Statistics* (New York: Insurance Information Institute, 1963), p. 17.

[5] The total number of criminal acts is unknown. The FBI figures are based on crime reports received from policing bodies throughout the country.

[6] This figure does not include auto thefts. Thefts are defined to include but not be limited to burglaries and robberies. See later section on definitions.

[7] In 1957 the reported number of thefts had climbed to 1,721,170. To make the statistics more meaningful and manageable, subsequent theft counts were reported on a $50 or more basis.

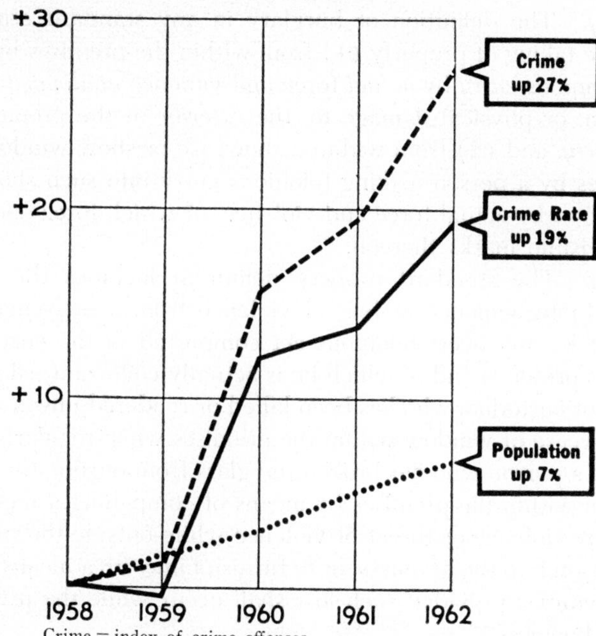

Crime = index of crime offenses.
Crime rate = number of offenses per 100,000 population.
SOURCE: Uniform Crime Reports (Washington: Federal Bureau of Investigation, 1962). Used with permission.

FIG. 43–1. Crime and population—United States, 1958–1962. Percent change over 1958.

that of rural areas and twice as high as that of cities below 50,000 population.[8]

The targets of this type of crime are items that can be readily used or disposed of. Money heads the list; it is followed by clothing, food, and other necessities of life. Other targets which are not as frequently stolen but which by their nature promote attention when taken are liquor, furs, jewelry, and tobacco.

DEFINITIONS, EXCLUSIONS, AND CONDITIONS

Before any analysis of policies used to insure against loss of money, securities, merchandise, and other property can be properly assimilated, an understanding of basic definitions, exclusions, and conditions common to standard contracts is essential.

Definitions

Burglary and robbery have distinct and different meanings and are usually defined in a policy to give countrywide uniformity and to avoid conflict with statutory definitions that vary slightly by jurisdiction.

[8] Federal Bureau of Investigation Uniform Crime Reports, 1961, p. 3.

Burglary. The definition of burglary in any standard crime policy includes the taking of property (1) from within the premises by a person making felonious *entry* by *actual* force and violence *evidenced* by *visible marks* upon, or physical damage to, the *exterior* of the premises *at the place of entry,* and (2) from within a showcase or show window outside the premises by a person making felonious entry into such showcases or show windows by actual force and violence, of which force and violence there are visible marks thereon.

Robbery. The standard robbery definition includes the taking of property (1) by violence or fear of violence from a messenger or custodian, (2) by any overt felonious act committed in the custodian's or messenger's presence and of which he is actually cognizant, (3) from the messenger or custodian who has been killed or rendered unconscious, (4) from a showcase or window within the premises when regularly open for business by a person who has broken the glass from outside the premises, or (5) from within the premises by means of compelling a messenger or custodian by violence or threat of violence while outside the premises to admit a person into the premises, or to furnish him with a means of ingress into the premises, provided such loss shall occur while the premises are closed for business.

Theft. Theft is defined in the personal policies as "any act of stealing" but is not defined in commercial policies. *Webster's Seventh New Collegiate Dictionary* (Springfield, Mass.: G. & C. Merriam Co., 1963) defines theft on page 915 as the "act of stealing" or "an unlawful taking (as by embezzlement or burglary) of property." It is the broadest crime term and includes all forms of burglary and robbery losses.

Exclusions

Each coverage may have its own particular exclusions but there are some exclusions common to almost all crime policies. These are loss due (1) to war, insurrection, rebellion, or revolution; (2) to any fraudulent, dishonest, or criminal act by any insured, partner, officer, employee (sometimes deleted or amended), director, trustee, or authorized representative; (3) to nuclear reaction, nuclear radiation, or radioactive contamination; and (4) loss of manuscripts, records, or books of account.

Conditions

Many conditions of the crime policies are similar to those of liability, fire, and marine policies. However, there are some conditions that should be highlighted.

Interests. Burglary, robbery, or theft policies cover property in which the insured has an insurable interest. The Ownership of Property—Interests Covered Clause states (1) that insured property may be (*a*) owned by the insured, (*b*) held by him in any capacity, or (*c*) property for which the insured is legally liable but (2) that payments are limited to the amount of insured's interest in such property including the extent of the insured's liability to others.

Books and Records. Every business keeps some kind of records. The 24 words of the Books and Records Clause (found in commercial policies) merely state that records shall be kept in such a manner that the insurer can accurately determine from them the amount of the loss. The clause does not require any particular accounting or record-keeping system and indirectly recognizes that the record-keeping system will vary by business and product. The only requirement is that the records be sufficient to confirm accurately the amount of the loss claimed.

Other Insurance. The words of the Other Insurance Clause place any burglary, robbery, or theft insurance as excess insurance over any other valid and collectible insurance. In many policies it is further stated that the insurance does not apply to (1) property which is separately described and specifically insured in whole or in part by other insurance or (2) property otherwise insured unless such property is owned by the insured.

Duties. Most policies, under the Insured's Duties When a Loss Occurs Clause, require notice of loss to the company or its authorized agent as soon as practicable and a proof of loss filed within 60 to 120 days after loss. Burglary, robbery, or theft policies require in addition that the police be notified if the type of loss is a violation of law. This extra duty is important to the insurer because it serves as a possible deterrent against fraudulant claims, and it occasionally reduces the amount of loss by the recovery of stolen property by police.

DESCRIPTION

The numerous types of policies can be divided into two groups: personal and commercial. The personal is made up mainly of the Broad Form Personal Theft and the Personal Theft Policies. The commercial is composed of (1) various named peril and broad-form money and merchandise policies for general business, (2) specialized named peril and broad-form policies for banks and financial institutions, and (3) other miscellaneous crime policies.

Personal Policies

Broad Form Personal Theft Policy. This contract covers (1) theft or mysterious disappearance[9] of personal property, (2) damage by theft to

[9] "A policy insuring against 'mysterious disappearance' provides coverage against the loss of property which has vanished under circumstances which cannot be explained. It does *not* cover property which is lost to the assured from *any known cause*." There is general agreement "that losses occasioned by the simple losing of

premises and property within, and (3) vandalism and malicious mischief to the interior of the premises and to other insured property in or away from the premises.

Coverage is divided into two sections: (1) loss from the premises and (2) loss away from the premises. A separate limit is indicated for each, but insuring for loss away from the premises is optional. The insurance can be written to cover all property or be scheduled between (1) jewelry and furs, and (2) all other property. Most coverage is sold on a blanket basis unless values to be insured are unusually large and easily segregated.

A sub-limit is provided on certain types of property: money loss is limited to $100; securities to $500; and boats away from the premises to $500. Additional limits can be secured on money and securities.

Personal Theft Policy. This policy parallels in many ways the coverage for the Broad Form Personal Theft Policy but does not include "mysterious disappearance" as a separate insured peril. A single limit of insurance covers personal property on and away from the premises. There is no coverage for loss from unattended vehicles off the premises; loss of boats on or off the premises; and loss from a dormitory, fraternity, or sorority house.

Despite the fact that the Personal Theft Policy is broad and suitable to the needs of most people, and though the premium is approximately 50 percent less than the Broad Form Personal Theft Policy, it is not sold frequently. For every dollar of Personal Theft premium written, there is approximately $21 of Broad Form Personal Theft premium written.[10]

General Business Coverages

A large number of commercial policies are in use. The number and variety are so great as to be easily confusing to the layman. One development which is somewhat simplifying is the use in recent years of the Special Coverage Policy. This policy serves somewhat the same function as does the Scheduled Property Floater as discussed in Chapter 27 in relation to inland marine floaters. Thus, the Special Coverage Policy is a skeleton to which is endorsed the provisions necessary to adapt the basic agreements, conditions, and exclusions to the specific need for coverage. The Special Coverage Policy is not a contract without the endorsement(s). Its use, however, is a convenience. Unfortunately for a beginning student, the need still remains to consider the particular coverages

---

property, misplacement, mislaying or the mysterious inability to find lost property are not covered." Both statements from a report by a joint committee of Pacific Coast Fire Loss Association and Inland Marine Claims Association of the Pacific reprinted in the *Insurance Advocate*, Vol. 73 (July 28, 1962), pp. 6, 7 and 17. The title is "An Adjusting Guide for Mysterious Disappearance."

[10] *1961 Compilation of Burglary Insurance Experience* (New York: National Bureau of Casualty Underwriters), Exhibit A, Sheet 1.

individually. Moreover, the skeleton is not used for some coverages. Hence, in the following discussion attention is given to the individual coverages. In case an individual policy (as opposed to the Special) is ordinarily used, the policy is specified.

Mercantile Open Stock Burglary Policy. This contract protects the businessman for loss or damage to merchandise, furniture, fixtures, and equipment within the premises and damage to the building (if he is the owner or is liable for such damage) by burglary or by robbery of a watchman while the premises are not open for business. The definition of premises is important because it determines the area where the marks of forced entry must be found to comply with the definition of burglary. The standard policy defines premises as the interior of that portion of the building at the designated location which is occupied by the insured for the type of business stated in the policy declarations but does not include showcases or show windows not opening directly into the interior of the premises or public entrances, halls or stairways.

The policy limits the insurer's liability to $50 for loss or damage to any one article of jewelry (including watches or gems), and to $100 for loss of or damage to property from a showcase or show window located outside the building but within the building line. These limits may be increased for additional premiums.

In addition to the regular exclusions, there is no coverage for loss (1) of furs, or articles containing fur which represents their principal value, by removal from within a showcase or show window by a person who has broken the glass from the outside or by an accomplice of any such person; (2) occurring while there is any change in the condition of the risk; (3) during a fire; and (4) due to damage by vandalism and malicious mischief.

Most buyers of the Mercantile Open Stock Burglary Policy do not desire to secure insurance to value because they do not anticipate a total loss of stock and other personal property. To guard against low limit buying that would produce insufficient funds to cover losses and expenses, a coinsurance provision is written into the policy. Under such a coinsurance provision the insured is required to carry a limit of insurance at least equal to the smaller of either the coinsurance limit or coinsurance percentage or be subject to a possible penalty in the event of loss. The coinsurance limit is set forth in the "Burglary Manual" (of the National Bureau of Casualty Underwriters) for each class of merchandise varying from $2,000 to $40,000. The coinsurance percentage is indicated in the manual for each territory and varies from 40 percent to 80 percent.[11]

[11] For example, an insured with a stock exposure of $30,000 situated in a territory with a 40 percent coinsurance percentage would need a limit of $12,000 (.40 × $30,000 = $12,000) to meet the requirement of the coinsurance percentage. If he maintains at least this much insurance, he will not suffer a coinsurance penalty.

This coverage has several possible extensions. The most frequently used is the endorsement including thefts other than burglary and robbery of a watchman, with a mandatory $50 deductible. Since "theft" is the broadest crime term, the extension of the coverage is great and eliminates the forced entry requirement of burglary for indemnity; however, mere disappearance of property is excluded. (See footnote 9.) Other optional extensions include forcible exit and the deletion of certain exclusions such as damage by vandalism and malicious mischief.

Mercantile Robbery. This policy contains two optional insuring clauses. One is to cover robbery inside the premises. (It was formerly called the "Interior Robbery" section.) It provides reimbursement for loss of money and securities and *other property* by robbery or attempted robbery within the premises and also for damage to the premises provided the insured is the owner or is liable for such damage. Whether or not the premises are open for business, the insured needs robbery protection while he or any one of his employees is in the premises. The second optional insuring clause covers robbery outside the premises. The old name, "Messenger Robbery," is still widely used. This clause provides reimbursement for loss of money, securities, and other property by robbery or attempted robbery outside the premises while such property is being conveyed by messenger. The word "messenger" includes the insured, a partner thereof, or an officer, or any employee thereof who is in the regular service and has been duly authorized by the insured to have care and custody of the insured property while outside the premises. For an additional premium this coverage may be extended to cover loss by burglary or theft from the home of the messenger.

Paymaster Robbery. This coverage (often written in the Special Coverage Policy) provides reimbursement for loss by robbery of payroll funds from a messenger while away from the premises and also of payroll funds on the premises. It is designed for firms, especially manufacturers, having little money exposure other than a weekly cash payroll. The policy extends coverage for property other than payroll funds up to 10 percent of the limit of insurance away from the premises, but not on the premises.

Safe Burglary. The general term is "mercantile safe burglary." The insurance may be written in a separate policy, in a Scheduled Robbery and Safe Burglary Policy, or in the Special Coverage Policy. Indemnity is provided for loss of money, securities, and other property from within a safe (a vault) by safe burglary or attempted safe burglary. "Safe Burglary" is defined in the policy to include (1) the taking of money, securities, or other property from within a safe located within the premises by a person making felonious entry into the safe, when all doors of the safe are duly closed and locked by at least one combination or time lock, provided that entry into the safe shall be made by actual force and violence, of which force and violence there are visible marks made by tools, explosives, electricity or chemicals upon the exterior of (*a*) all doors of the safe if entry is made through such doors, or (*b*) the top, bottom or walls of such safe through which entry is made; or (2) the taking of the safe from within the premises.

The Broad Form Money and Securities Policy. This coverage was first marketed in the early 1940's to go beyond the scope of robbery and safe burglary insurance. It can replace several individual contracts such as the Safe Burglary, Interior Robbery, and Messenger Robbery Policies. Merchants have long recognized that not all money losses are limited to the perils of safe burglary and robbery. The Broad Form Money and Securities Policy, written either separately or in the Special Coverage Policy, has a very broad insuring clause providing coverage for wrongful abstraction, disappearance, and destruction (all undefined in the contract).

The contract has two insuring agreements usually captioned "Loss Inside the Premises" and "Loss Outside the Premises." The former covers loss of money and securities from anywhere within the premises; the latter covers loss outside the premises while being conveyed by messenger or while within the living quarters in the home of the messenger.

While the main function of this policy is to provide reimbursement for loss of money and securities, it parallels the other property coverage of the policies which it replaces by extending to loss of other property (1) by robbery inside the premises, (2) by safe burglary, (3) by robbery while being conveyed by messenger outside the premises, and (4) by theft while within the living quarters of the home of the messenger.[12] However, despite these extensions, the Broad Form Money and Securities Policy does not eliminate the need for open stock burglary (or theft) insurance.

The Paymaster Broad Form. This coverage provides payment for loss of payroll funds by actual destruction, disappearance, or wrongful abstraction. This contract can be written to cover losses occurring (1) both on and off the premises or (2) only on the premises. Unless an additional premium is paid, there is no premises cover when no custodian is on duty. Outside coverage applies while money and securities are being conveyed by a messenger or armored car or within the living quarters in the home of the messenger. It is intended for firms which desire broader coverage than contained in the Paymaster Robbery Policy. In effect it is an "all risk" coverage (actual destruction, disappearance, or wrongful abstraction) of payroll funds.

Comprehensive Dishonesty, Disappearance, and Destruction Policy. This contract, commonly called the "3–D," was developed shortly after the introduction of the Broad Form Money and Securities Policy and combines burglary and bond coverages. It has five basic insuring agree-

[12] Number 4 is provided by an endorsement to the messenger robbery coverage.

ments. Insuring agreements II and III of the 3–D Policy duplicate the two insuring agreements of the Broad Form Money and Securities Policy—both inside and outside the premises. The definition of premises is broader and applies to any location in which the insured is doing business. Insuring agreement IV insures for loss due to acceptance of money orders and counterfeit paper currency. The bond insuring agreements are I ("Employee Blanket Fidelity") and V ("Depositors Forgery").[13] Other crime coverages that can be added to the 3–D (or DDD) include open stock burglary (or theft), and paymaster broad form.

There is one other major benefit which the 3–D has over individual policies providing the same coverages but in different companies. It is sometimes difficult to determine whether a money loss results from a dishonest employee or is merely a disappearance. If the money and securities coverage is carried by one company and the employee dishonesty coverage by another, the insured may have a problem in getting one or the other company to accept the loss. However, with these coverages in the same company in the same policy, this problem does not occur. Other benefits to the insured in having all the small crime insurance in one contract are the advantages from one premium due date and a continuous policy.

The 3–D is very appealing to big, medium, and small businesses for many reasons. (The manager of a very small business or the business with very few employees or very little cash and merchandise may find the Broad Form Storekeeper Policy and sometimes the Blanket Crime Policy more suited to his needs and budget.) The initial 3–D solicitation step of surveying the entire crime exposure may reveal the need for some or all of the coverages found in the insuring agreements and often highlights gaps in the existing program, overlapping of separate policies, underinsurance, and overinsurance. Since all 3–D insuring agreements are rated separately and are optional, the insured is not forced to buy all insuring agreements just to get what he actually needs but can elect the coverages he wants. With no ceiling on the limits of protection that may be purchased, the insured is able to secure a policy tailored in terms of coverage, limits, and cost. As a result, the insured, instead of having three or four policies with different expiration dates and separate bookkeeping transactions, winds up with one policy, one premium bill, one premium due date, and one bookkeeping transaction. Since the policy is continuous, he has no expirations to miss or renewal dates to watch. As for cancellation, either the insured or the insurer must take affirmative action to sever this continuous contract.

Blanket Crime Policy. The Blanket Crime Policy parallels the 3–D Policy in types of coverages, but instead of having individual limits for each of five insuring agreements of the contract, there is a single limit of

[13] See Chapter 54.

insurance applicable to all. A single limit as low as $1,000 can be written. Whatever the size of the limit, it is blanket.

Such a contract is bought, just as the 3–D, to provide reimbursement for many types of large and small crime losses. If the businessman could predict what type of crime might cause him a loss, and also the amount of such loss, his selection from the several crime coverages would be simplified. But he cannot. Nevertheless, he can normally determine his maximum exposures to any particular type of crime. If he makes his maximum exposure the limit for this package crime policy, he has solved the knotty problem of choice of coverages and limits sometimes encountered under the 3–D.

The cost of the Blanket Crime Policy will be lower in some cases than the cost of similar coverages under the 3–D and higher in other cases. (It is a frequent practice to get a quotation under each type of policy.) In addition, it is important to realize that the part of the premium computed for insuring agreements II and III (Broad Form Money and Securities) is based on the actual money and securities exposure subject to small minimum premiums or the single limit of the policy, whichever is lower.

Theft coverage on office equipment is optional. Open stock burglary coverage on merchandise is not available in the Blanket Crime Policy and, if desired, must be purchased separately.

Storekeeper's Burglary and Robbery Policy. The Storekeeper's Burglary and Robbery Policy was designed in the early 1930's for the small merchant to provide named peril coverage for burglary and robbery exposures at a cost commensurate with the limits. In brief its seven insuring agreements are: (1) robbery inside the premises of money, securities, and other property; (2) robbery outside the premises of money, securities, and other property, including the wallet or bag containing such property, while such property is being conveyed by a messenger; (3) kidnapping; (4) safe burglary and loss not exceeding $50 of money and securities within the premises by burglary; (5) theft of money and securities within a night depository in a bank or from within the home of the messenger or custodian; (6) burglary or robbery of a watchman of merchandise, furniture, fixtures, and equipment within the premises while the premises are not open for business; and (7) damage to the premises and to property within the premises by robbery, kidnapping, burglary, safe burglary, robbery of a watchman, or attempt thereat. The minimum amount of insurance that may be purchased is $250 for each agreement and the maximum amount is $1,000.

Broad Form Storekeeper's Policy. Developed in the late 1950's, the Broad Form Storekeeper's Policy is for the small merchant who desires broader crime coverage under one policy than provided by the named peril Storekeeper's Burglary and Robbery Policy, yet who does not need limits of insurance which would enable the use of the 3–D or Blanket Crime

Policy. The policy can be purchased in units of $250 up to $1,000. Its nine insuring agreements are as follows: (1) "Employee Dishonesty," (2) "Money and Securities Loss Inside the Premises," (3) "Money and Securities Loss Outside the Premises," (4) "Merchandise Burglary," (5) "Money Orders and Counterfeit Paper Currency," (6) "Theft From Home of Messenger," (7) "Depositor's Forgery," (8) "Damage by Vandalism and Malicious Mischief," and (9) "Damage By Burglary and Robbery." This policy, except for relatively low limits, is somewhat similar to the 3–D Policy discussed above.

Office Burglary and Robbery Policy. Another package policy, the Office Burglary and Robbery Policy, accomplishes the same purpose for business and professional offices as the Storekeeper's Burglary and Robbery Policy does for general business. Its insuring agreements are similar but in some respects broader. The differences are as follows: (1) theft of office equipment is provided in lieu of burglary of merchandise, furniture, fixtures, and equipment, and (2) loss of money and securities is covered up to $100 by burglary instead of only $50. It can be written with a limit per insuring agreement as low as $250, and in as many additional multiples of $250 as needed. Certain classes of offices are ineligible for this contract.

Bank and Financial Institutions Coverages

Bank Burglary[14] and Robbery Policy. The coverage is for loss of money and securities. While available in a separate policy, the coverage is most frequently written on an excess-of-loss-basis (over a Bankers Blanket Bond) rather than on a primary basis and can be secured for burglary, robbery, or both. The coverage may be written at reduced rates to cover only securities. This arrangement usually occurs when the Bankers Blanket Bond limit is sufficient to cover all probable money losses but not losses of securities.

Combination Safe Depository Policy. Banks which have safe deposit boxes for use of their customers can be held liable for loss of the contents from such safe deposit boxes. The Combination Safe Depository Policy has been designed to protect the banks, trust companies, and safe deposit companies against such losses. Coverage A provides the vital legal liability protection, and Coverage B provides the goodwill burglary and robbery coverage for loss of customers' property.

Other Bank Coverages. Numerous other bank or financial institution coverages are available. Such policies include—but are now limited to—the following:

1. Securities in Custody of Correspondent and Depository Bank.
2. Securities in Custody of Federal Reserve Bank and Treasury Department.

[14] Burglary is defined in this policy as safe burglary.

3. Lessees of Safe Deposit Boxes.
4. Securities of Lessees of Safe Deposit Boxes Coverage.
5. Securities Deposited with Bank or Trust Company Coverage.

In the main, the contracts provide burglary and robbery insurance. Some include vandalism and malicious mischief coverage. Some are written to cover "actual destruction, disappearance, or wrongful abstraction."

Church Crime Coverage

Church coverage pays for loss of money and securities and other property by theft or attempted theft from within the premises, from within a night depository provided by a bank or trust company, or from the care or custody of a person duly authorized by the insured to have custody of the property. Although churches are eligible for many of the individual burglary or robbery policies, a special church coverage was developed for their needs. One incorporated change was the amendment of the Books and Records Clause permitting payment for unrecorded plate collections. The insurance is customarily written by attachment of the Church Coverage Form to the Special Coverage Policy.

Accounts Receivable and Valuable Papers

Somewhat of an anomoly in the insurance business is the fact that accounts receivable and valuable papers policies can be either "Inland Marine" or "Burglary." Almost identical policies are filed through the Inland Marine Insurance Bureau (see Chapter 28 for references to the work of this bureau), the National Bureau of Casualty Underwriters, and also the Mutual Insurance Rating Bureau. The fact is that the coverages are in many ways unlike other inland marine or other burglary coverages. Since both policies are dealt with, however, in the "Burglary Manual," they will be treated in this chapter.

Accounts Receivable Policy. This contract protects the businessman for his inability to collect his accounts receivable because the supporting records were either lost or damaged. This coverage is distinctly different from credit insurance as discussed in Chapter 42. Its insuring agreement is very broad, stating that it pays *all sums* due from customers but not collected as the direct result of loss of or damage to the accounts receivable records. With such a broad insuring agreement there are many recognizable perils covered, but the most important is fire.

This policy is written with a limit sufficient to take care of the catastrophe loss, but its real value comes from its other services. The policy provides for (1) the expense incurred by the insured in reestablishing records of accounts receivable following loss or damage; (2) any collection expense in excess of normal, made necessary because of such loss; and (3) all interest charges on any loan to offset collections pending repayment of such sums made uncollectible by such loss or damage.

There are two forms available, the Reporting Form and Non-Reporting Form. The Reporting Form is used most often, requiring monthly reports from the insured of his total accounts receivable. The Non-Reporting Form has been on the market for several years, but its use has not yet been greatly developed. It is limited to insureds with accounts receivable totalling $50,000 or less.

Valuable Papers and Records Policy. Direct physical loss of valuable papers and records is insured in this policy. The definition of "valuable papers" is broad and includes written, printed, or otherwise inscribed documents and records including books, maps, films, drawings, abstracts, deeds, mortgages, and manuscripts, but does not mean money and securities. The insurance can be written either on a specified or blanket basis. The specified basis carries the lower rate but requires the insured and insurer to be able to set an agreed value on each specified item. The blanket coverage is the most popular but has the major limitation that there is no coverage if the property cannot be reproduced. Incidentally, a combination contract called the Valuable Papers, Records, and Accounts Receivable Policy is also on the market.

Additional Contracts

Innkeeper's Liability Policy. Under the Innkeeper's Liability Policy the insurer agrees to pay all sums which the innkeeper shall be legally obligated to pay by reason of liability for damages because of damage to, destruction of, or loss of property belonging to a guest at the hotel. Under common law an innkeeper is an insurer of a guest's property against all loss or damage except loss which occurs as a result of an act of God, an act of public enemy, or loss caused by negligence of the guest himself. The policy limit of liability is $1,000 per guest, subject to an aggregate limit of $25,000 for all losses per policy period, but these limits can be adjusted upwards for an additional premium. In most contracts there is a deductible provision.

For innkeepers providing safe deposit boxes, additional legal liability protection may be desired. The limits provided under the standard innkeeper's contract may not be sufficient for the individual sizeable losses that can occur from the safe deposit boxes. To cover this large loss possibility, a Hotel Safe Deposit Box Coverage with limits from $25,000 to $1,000,000 can be purchased at very nominal rates to back up the Innkeeper's Liability Policy. It is endorsed onto the Special Coverage Policy.

Other. Many other miscellaneous coverages are listed in the Burglary Manual. The usual procedure is to use the Special Coverage Policy with appropriate endorsements. Some of these coverages are: Money and Securities Destruction, Warehouseman's Liability, Camp Burglary or Theft, Property in Public Entrances or Hallways, Money Orders and Counterfeit Paper Currency, Grave Stones in Cemeteries Theft, Outdoor Signs and Bulletin Boards Theft, and Vending Machine Theft.

Another group of coverages intended to discharge the social obliations of the individual who (or of the corporation which) desires that the injured party be indemnified consists of theft coverages for Personal Property of Customers, Clients, Other Business Guests, and Visitors; Tools Belonging to Employees; Personal Property of Employees or Students; and Storeroom and Baggage Room. Here again, the Special Coverage Policy is used.

POLICY AND RATEMAKING BODIES

The Burglary Division of the National Bureau of Casualty Underwriters was established November 1, 1923. Prior to that time a group of burglary underwriters from leading companies met regularly to determine rules, rates, and coverages. Since its formation, the Burglary Division of the National Bureau of Casualty Underwriters has guided bureau members, subscribers, and others along burglary insurance lines. The Mutual Insuring Rating Bureau, NBCU's counterpart, was organized January 1, 1940, to provide similar services for mutual companies.

UNDERWRITING QUALIFICATIONS

To qualify for burglary, robbery, or theft insurance the individual or firm must maintain high moral standards, adequate safeguards, and financial stability. Failure to meet all three qualifications would normally disqualify the individual or firm for crime insurance.

The moral hazard is the greatest single factor in crime underwriting because it is so easy to make a fraudulent claim and remain undetected. When William Weller, in the late 1700's, applied for a Royal Charter to write burglary insurance in England, he was refused. The reasons given were that the company would be subject to so much *fraud* and *imposition,* that it would ". . . parent as great frauds as those which it was instituted to combat . . . ," and ". . . conduce to slackness on the part of the policyholders in preventing, resisting, detecting, and apprehending thieves."[15] Even though history has clearly proved this early pronouncement to be greatly exaggerated and too severe, it is still the cornerstone of crime underwriting.

Adequate safeguards for personal theft insurance are usually assumed to exist and are seldom investigated except in the largest group of cities. However, safeguards for commercial crime insurance are regularly investigated and may take many forms. Some firms need only minimum security—that is, a firm may have a totally enclosed building, satisfactorily locked where felonious entry cannot be made without force and violence

[15] See footnote 1.

TYPES OF STRUCTURES	PERCENT	DOOR	WINDOW	ROOF	OTHER
RESIDENCE (Anywhere on premise)	100.0	61.4	33.7	.2	4.7
RETAIL STORE	100.0	49.2	39.3	4.6	7.0
WAREHOUSE OR PLANT	100.0	45.1	41.7	4.0	9.2
PUBLIC BUILDING (School, Library, etc.)	100.0	38.8	52.9	.9	7.4
GAS STATION, GARAGE, ETC.	100.0	39.7	53.6	.9	5.7
BUSINESS OR PROFESSIONAL OFFICE	100.0	53.1	37.6	1.6	7.7
BANK (Savings and Loan, etc.)	100.0	56.1	34.1	2.4	7.3
OTHER (Boxcar, Private Clubs, etc.)	100.0	60.0	27.2	1.6	11.2
TOTAL BURGLARIES	100.0	53.6	38.3	1.7	6.4

(Due to Rounding May Not Add to 100 Percent)

SOURCE: Uniform Crime Reports (Washington: Federal Bureau of Investigation, 1961). Used with permission.

FIG. 43–2. Burglary by place of entry.

upon the exterior of the premises. Other firms demand average security. Such a firm may have a building totally enclosed, satisfactorily locked, with all accessible openings protected with bars and ironwork. For businesses requiring maximum security, all of the foregoing is needed plus a burglar alarm system or central station watchman service. However, at best, thorough and complete protection is not an absolute deterrent and simply postpones or hinders entry for a time and increases the chance of a successful alarm.

Figure 43–2 indicates the usual places of entry for burglary by type of risk as set forth by the FBI. The chart indicates that doors and windows are the most vulnerable places of entry and require the most attention from an engineering viewpoint. Attack through front doors and windows is less frequent than through rear or side openings.

There are firms which make themselves more subject to loss than others by poor money handling. When a business is known to keep excess funds on the premises, it becomes a target. Any large or excessive accumulation invites loss by robbery, safe burglary, and disappearance. More frequent use of banking facilities reduces this loss attraction. If quantities of money must be kept on the premises, then a money chest is needed. Money chests are designed to prevent safe burglaries and are constructed of solid or laminated steel at least an inch thick. Since steel is a good conductor of heat, the combination of a chest within a safe can lessen burglary and fire worries for most valuables.

When money and securities are conveyed by a messenger outside the premises, guards may be necessary. The number of guards and the time when used will vary based on the amount of money and securities carried, the area through which the travel will take place, and the time of day. If the trip is too hazardous, police or armored car service may be necessary.

Financial stability is a barometer on both moral standards and adequate safeguards. An individual or firm with a good financial standing is thought to be less prone to create a fraudulent claim and more inclined and able to spend sufficient funds for adequate safeguards. Individuals or firms in bad financial standing are thought to be just the opposite.

LARGE OR UNUSUAL RISK HANDLING

Large or unusual risks frequently require special handling of policy, form, or rate. The coverages, exclusions, or conditions of standard policies can be changed to meet specific situations. Occasionally, the case may demand a complete departure from standard policies and the creation of a manuscript policy. The rate (and premium) may be adjusted through the use of experience rating, retrospective rating, deductibles, and franchise clauses. Firms developing annual premiums of $100,000 or more make their own rates.

TREND TO PACKAGES

A new method of marketing burglary, robbery, and theft insurance was created with the advent of the personal and commercial multiple peril and multiple line packages. In the field of personal insurance the Homeowners and Comprehensive Dwelling Policies grouped several coverages, including theft, and became overnight successes. The Homeowners Policies are now the leading means of providing personal theft insurance. In commercial insurance the Special Multi-Peril Policy Program, Commercial Property Coverage Program, and other packaging efforts[16] are becoming important vehicles for burglary, robbery, and theft insurance. Some provide an "all risk" coverage; others are on a named peril basis. The future is expected to bring many more packages that include theft for all segments of business.

Nevertheless, the entry of the package policies does not imply an abrupt end to individual burglary, robbery, and theft policies, particularly for businesses. For many years to come there will be a need for individual policies, regardless of package programs. Firms which do not desire the packages, which are ineligible for the packages, which need

[16] See Chapters 49 and 50 for a discussion of these personal and commercial packages.

supplemental crime insurance in addition to package theft coverages, or which require tailored coverages will demand individual burglary, robbery, and theft policies for quite some time.

SUGGESTED READINGS

FEDERAL BUREAU OF INVESTIGATION. *Uniform Crime Reports for the United States.* Washington, D.C.: U.S. Government Printing Office. (Annual)

FIRE, CASUALTY, AND SURETY BULLETINS. Cincinnati: National Underwriter Co. Burglary Section.

GEE, HAROLD F. *Broad Form Crime Insurance Primer.* 2d ed. Indianapolis: Rough Notes Co., 1957, 1958.

MEHR, ROBERT I., AND CAMMACK, EMERSON. *Principles of Insurance.* 3d ed. Homewood, Ill.: Richard D. Irwin, Inc., 1961. Chap. 15.

PACIFIC COAST FIRE LOSS ASSOCIATION AND THE INLAND MARINE CLAIMS ASSOCIATION. "An Adjusting Guide for Mysterious Disappearance," *Insurance Advocate,* Vol. 73 (July 28, 1962), pp. 6–7, 17.

VANCE, WILLIAM R. (BUIST M. ANDERSON [ed.]) *Handbook on the Law of Insurance.* 3d ed. St. Paul: West Publishing Company, 1951. (Hornbook Series.) Section 199.

WERBEL, BERNARD G. (ed.) *General Insurance Guide.* 5th rev. ed. 1958 (with revisions through August, 1963). Greenlawn, N.Y.: Werbel, 1958. Pp. 2001–2671.

Chapter 44

LOSS PREVENTION IN LIABILITY INSURANCE AND RELATED LINES

BY DWIGHT M. McCRACKEN

The emergence of workmen's compensation legislation marked a change of considerable importance in social thinking. This transition did not mark the beginning of loss prevention activities in this country, because many enlightened employers had already taken the initiative in promoting safe plant conditions and safe practices. However, it did give a powerful impetus to the movement and can be considered the prime mover in promoting organized safety efforts on a broad scale. It also focused the attention of insurance companies on safety services as a means for reducing the number of accidents and thereby insurance premiums.

In this chapter attention is given to loss prevention organization and functions generally; to specific activities in respect to workmen's compensation, automobile fleet coverages, and general liability; and to some new or rejuvenated concepts in loss prevention.

LOSS PREVENTION ORGANIZATION

Most insurers have loss prevention departments staffed by college-trained or other technically oriented persons. The larger the insurance carrier, generally speaking, the more complex is the organization of loss prevention activities. A large carrier writing business nationwide and organized into geographical divisions and subdivisions typically organizes its loss prevention department along the same geographical pattern. In each subdivision a loss prevention manager may head up a staff of men and report directly to the division manager of his own department who, in turn, may report to the home office manager of loss prevention. Staff specialists may assist at the several levels.

Such an organizational structure accomplishes a dual purpose. It places the man responsible for direct service to a group of policyholders as close as possible to the locations he services. It also gives the direct service representative a depth of technical backup.

LOSS PREVENTION FUNCTIONS

The loss prevention department carries out two major functions: (1) inspection and evaluation of prospective business to provide the underwriting department with information it needs in deciding whether or not the prospect should be underwritten and, in some cases, what rates to charge; (2) education of policyholders in avoidance of losses. The latter is, by far, the function demanding the greater time and effort.

An additional function is the relaying to the underwriting department of information about changes in operations at the various policyholder locations so that proper classifications can be applied. Since this function is fairly routine, little further mention need be made of it in this chapter. Moreover, many of the points which could be covered under function (1) above are treated in Chapters 14, 15, 29, and 46.

The principal attention in this chapter is given to the matter of servicing policyholders (function number 2 above). The varieties of coverage and the problems encountered under the various coverages render this subject exceedingly broad and complex. Some policyholders, for example those using the Family Automobile Policy, obviously are not serviceable on an individual basis. In other instances, however, policyholders should be and are serviced on an individual basis. In this chapter policyholder loss prevention service in (1) workmen's compensation insurance, (2) automobile fleet insurance, and (3) general liability insurance are discussed. While other coverages could be added to the list, *Handbook* space will not permit. Before these particular coverages are treated, a general description is presented of the activity of insurance company loss prevention specialists.

The activity of the property-liability insurance carrier's loss prevention department is basically the same under every coverage. Essentially, it is to advise the policyholder regarding any condition that might cause injury to persons or property for which the policyholder might be held financially liable. To advise implies to point out the problem and to suggest an adequate solution and then to cooperate with the policyholder in putting the solution into effect. The loss prevention specialist studies the policyholder's procedures, organization accident records, and types of facilities used. He then presents a detailed safety program to management. The program is tailor-made to suit the needs of the policyholder and involves specific steps for putting the recommendations into operation. The loss prevention specialist provides safety literature on specific problems, safety posters, and handout material and in most cases attends accident review committee meetings at regular intervals. Finally, he keeps management informed on the progress of the program by providing charts showing accident rates and accident cost, as well as furnishing reports that pinpoint trouble spots and show where greater effort should be expended. In brief, his responsibility is to advise management of the best program to adopt, to assist in launching the program, and then to follow the progress and keep management informed, participating in the meantime in those parts of the program where he can benefit it the most.

WORKMEN'S COMPENSATION AND EMPLOYERS' LIABILITY INSURANCE

Of the three major types of coverage mentioned above, workmen's compensation presents, by far, the most varied and difficult safety problems. The reason is the immense variety of operations to be found in industrial, commercial, construction, and other businesses. Particularly in industrial plants, there are literally thousands of different operations encountered by loss prevention service experts. In a single day, a service representative may visit a steel mill, a mattress manufacturer, and a tannery for rare skins (such as those from lizards, snakes, and alligators). The next day, his itinerary may include a rendering plant, a furniture manufacturer, and a textile finishing plant. To be effective, loss prevention experts must know production and distribution processes, types and characteristics of machinery and equipment involved, kinds of accident which are prevalent, prevailing management philosophies, the terminology common to each type of business, and many related matters.

In approaching loss prevention in the workmen's compensation area, numerous carriers use checklists or other guides to call attention to fundamentals. One such list—the eight-point "Basic Plan" shown below—has been used successfully by one carrier for a number of years. This "Basic Plan" serves as a convenient vehicle for presenting the material in this section; it also is a good general guide for activities of loss prevention specialists of insurance carriers. Many of these points are applicable to other exposures as, for example, those embodied in automobile fleet coverages and commercial and industrial liability coverages.

Point 1: Sustained Management Support and Direction

Sustained management support and direction heads the list because it is first in importance. In fact, it is absolutely essential to the success of the loss prevention program. For an accident control program to be effective, top management must *believe* in the program and back up its belief with concrete actions on a continuing basis.

Conversely, if management believes in and actively supports the accident control program it *will* be an effective one. Success in accident control requires companywide, coordinated cooperation at all levels. Only top management can assure this cooperation. It requires the delegation of responsibility and authority of a high order. Again, only top management can do such delegating. Finally, it needs periodic stimulus *from above,* which can come only from top management.

There are several activities that indicate whether or not top management is giving sustained support and direction.

Cooperation. Because accidents can occur anywhere and to anybody, accident control is a companywide problem requiring cooperation at all company levels. The top executive should require active cooperation from all his assistants, department heads, and supervisors. Every department must be included, and every employee of every department should be made aware that his cooperation is required.

Responsibility for Control of Accidents. Management should make clear that there is an important difference between *responsibility for the functioning of the accident control organization* and *responsibility for the control of accidents.* The former responsibility is carried by a single individual who has been assigned the duty of heading up the accident control program. His responsibility lies in seeing to it that the program functions effectively. The latter responsibility, that for the control of accidents, rests primarily upon the department heads and supervisors. Of course, everyone shares this responsibility to a degree, but the bulk of it lies upon the supervisors because they are *closest to the problem.*

It is important for management to emphasize this distinction. Otherwise, supervisors are prone to assume that since a safety program has been put into operation to control accidents they are thereby relieved of accident control responsibility.

Responsibility for the Functioning of an Accident Control Program. For best results and for reasons of good organization, every establishment should have one person charged with the responsibility for the effective functioning of the accident control organization.

In the small locations the owner or manager is often the active leader and director of accident control activities. In the larger locations, one person should be specifically charged with responsibility for the effective functioning of the accident control program. This responsibility may be full-time or part-time. In either case, he should function in his accident control activities as a *staff* employee. He is a specialized advisor to management, supervisors, and employees, as well as a prime mover and coordinator of accident control activities. His objective is to induce maximum program participation at all three of these levels.

Personal Participation by Top Executives. In every organization, regardless of size, the top executive, or one of his immediate assistants, should frequently manifest interest in the accident control program. He can do this by discussing the program, writing about it, attending meetings, providing budgets, asking for reports, and so on. This participation should be such as clearly to imply that the program is important and that results are expected.

Point 2: Adequate Loss Prevention Organization

A loss prevention organization is absolutely essential to the success of any loss prevention program. "Organization" does not mean just a safety committee that meets regularly; it means a *planned* set of *safety activities.* An organization requires a structure, assigned personnel, and delegated responsibility.

The makeup of the safety organization, its size, and complexity will vary in accordance with the size of the establishment, the type of company organization, and the kind of company operations. Many business firms are organized into "line" and "staff" activities. The "line" can be looked upon as the fundamental pattern in which operating authority is distributed. The "staff" is composed of specialists whose contribution to the good or service being produced is only indirect. Staff activities assume greater importance in the larger and more complex business organizations in which the need for specialized knowledge of many types arises.

Responsibility for the functioning of the accident control or loss prevention organization is normally a *staff function,* even though it might, in some instances, be assigned as a staff duty to a member of the line organization. There is a sound reason why safety should be a staff function. For, if it were a line function, it would necessarily have to be assigned to the top man in the line organization. If it were assigned to a line supervisor, as a line function, his influence would extend only to the employees directly under him.

Point 3: Active Participation by Supervisors

Every member in the organization is responsible for employee accidents. However, the heaviest burden falls upon the first-line supervisor. He is in direct contact with his employees and is responsible for their training, performance, and job conduct. He is held accountable for the production of his people, for the work methods, and for the machines and equipment. In short, he supervises his group. Since safety is an essential element of efficient production practice, it is the supervisor's responsibility to see that his work area is free of accident hazards and that his men are trained in safe work methods. The supervisor is just as responsible for a poor accident record as he is for a poor production record. It is imperative, therefore, that every supervisor participate actively and continuously in the company's accident control program. This participation must go far beyond merely attending meetings of safety committees. It must include investigation of accidents, safety inspections, employee counseling, indoctrination, and personal example.

It is sometimes possible for top management to be misled into accepting as satisfactory a supervisory participation program which is one in form only. Companies sometimes "hold" supervisory safety committee meetings and "require" supervisors to investigate accidents and serve on plant inspection committees. Too often, however, this participation is a routine, uninspired matter of "going through the motions." Participation is not *active* unless the results show in terms of effective committee meetings, thorough and productive accident investigations, and plant inspections which produce sound recommendations. In addition, the degree of active participation can be measured by the condition of the individual work areas, the housekeeping, the machine safeguarding, the physical hazards, and the attitude of the employees.

Point 4: Effective Employee Safety Education

Unless an accident control program carries its safety messages to the individual employee, it misses its chief purpose. This fact means that management must have a companywide safety education program. It is obviously impossible, except in very small establishments, to bring all employees into safety committee meetings, accident investigations, and safety inspections. However, it is essential that all employees profit from these activities, and it is for this reason that supervisors are urged to participate actively, on the assumption that they will pass along to their employees the lessons learned. Unless the supervisors do pass along this knowledge, however, the program will be choked off at the higher levels without ever reaching the bulk of the employees.

The detailed methods used to educate employees in safety will vary considerably but they will usually be adaptations of one or more of the following: new employee orientation, job training, committee membership, departmental meetings, safety films, safety demonstrations, and similar activities.

Point 5: Control of Accident Hazards

Safeguarding of Machines and Equipment. Machine accidents are often serious. As a type they are not as prevalent as many others but, because of their usual severity, they demand serious attention. The heaviest machine exposure is quite naturally found in industrial plants, although it is an important consideration in construction operations and increasingly even in certain areas of mercantile and commercial establishments.

An adequate machine guard must give the maximum of protection with the minimum of interference with production. There is no doubt that in certain individual cases the placing of a guard on a machine will slow down production. There is no support for the position taken by some safety men that adequate machine safeguarding will in every case speed up, or at least not impede, production. What can be argued, with good evidence, is that adequate guarding will *in the long run* improve the production rate by preventing loss of time and all the other direct and indirect losses which stem from employee injuries.

These machine guards not only should be installed; they should be used. Proper use requires supervisory control. Temporarily removing guards, or rendering them inoperative, should be strictly forbidden except when maintenance requirements necessitate temporary removal.

Equipment other than machines, for example, electrical equipment and pressure vessels, should be safeguarded. In evaluating the adequacy of protection it is usually necessary to be *guided* by state and federal, and sometimes municipal codes and standards—as brought out in Chapter 41. It is unwise, however, to be *limited* by these codes and standards when more rigorous measures appear in order. These codes frequently embody *minimum* requirements, whereas loss prevention thinking should be geared to *adequate* requirements.

Finally, to evaluate an establishment's efforts in regard to safeguarding of machines and equipment, one must consider (1) the proportion of the total exposure which has been guarded, (2) the effectiveness of the individual guards, and (3) the degree of supervisory control operative to insure the continuous use of the guards. High ratings in these three accident control measures are the results of careful planning and active follow-up.

Establishment of Safe Work Methods. By *work methods* is meant the way in which workers do their jobs, the manner in which each step in the job is performed, and also the sequence in which the successive steps are taken.

Analysis of any group of accidents shows how prominently unsafe work methods stand out as principal and contributing causes. Even the safest piece of equipment becomes a hazardous agent if unsafely used. The elimination of physical hazards and the maintenance of good housekeeping are necessary and important elements of an accident control program; but, unless supplemented by safe work methods, they lose much of their effectiveness.

In large establishments, it is common to have a department devoted exclusively to setting work methods. At the other end of the scale are the very small establishments with no methods control aside from that informally dictated by the owner or manager or automatically built into the skill of the individual workmen.

Loss prevention specialists in insurance companies and elsewhere generally hold that safety thinking should enter into methods planning. This view follows logically from the belief that accident prevention has, in addition to its humanitarian aspects, a direct effect upon efficiency of production. The person responsible, therefore, for setting up work methods, whether formally or informally, should sincerely believe that accident prevention is an important production factor and should be guided by this belief at each step in his methods planning. Further, it is necessary that the line organization responsible for supervising work methods be similarly convinced of the importance of safe work methods and that this conviction be passed along to the first-line workers.

Control of Occupational Health Hazards. For the purpose of this discussion, the expression "occupational health hazards" is defined as (1) the presence of harmful air contaminants in the form of dusts, fumes, mists, vapors, and gases; (2) exposure to excessive intensities of temperature, pressure, humidity, light, radiation, and noise; (3) the possibility of skin contact with harmful chemicals; and (4) the presence in the working environment of infectious pathogens.

A comprehensive loss prevention program must include an *awareness* of occupational health hazards and, where such exposures exist, a planned set of measures for keeping them under *control.* Awareness is stressed because these hazards are frequently overlooked either through ignorance of their potentialities or because their effects commonly accumulate silently and almost imperceptibly over a considerable period of time. Unlike other hazards, therefore, the very recognition of an occupational health exposure often presents a problem in itself.

Where such exposures exist or may occur, even temporarily, the loss prevention program is not adequate unless planned measures are adopted to (1) recognize the hazards, (2) measure their severity, and (3) keep them under control. These planned measures may, of course, vary within wide limits according to the size of the establishment and the nature of its operations. Judgment as to the adequacy of existing control measures in any given case is governed accordingly.

Provision of Personal Protective Devices. Even with optimum safeguarding of methods, machines, and equipment and with control of occupational health hazards, a certain degree of hazard to the person of the worker often remains. Recourse, therefore, to personal protective devices such as safety glasses and shoes, rubber gloves, asbestos leggings, hard hats, and respirators is often appropriate. Persuading employees to use such safety devices consistently is, of course, a continuing problem.

Point 6: Adequate Medical Program

One of the most significant developments in the loss prevention field over the past 20 years is the recognition of *industrial medicine* as an important factor not only in the prevention of accidents but in economical and effective case handling after the accident. Also, it has been found that a good medical unit contributes a number of beneficial side-effects, all of which bear either directly or indirectly upon increased worker efficiency and hence lead to reduced production costs.

Now the term "loss prevention" means more than simply "accident prevention." It is no longer possible or desirable to confine loss prevention efforts solely to those factors *directly* related to accident prevention. Present thinking is becoming increasingly geared to the concept of the *whole man,* to the worker as a complex physical, mental, and emotional human being. And, in a sense, the industrial medical staff serves the primary function of helping loss prevention people deal with the so-called "human factors" which are rapidly gaining recognition as having such an overwhelming role in accident causation.

Although industrial medical programs vary widely, ranging from a small first-aid kit to what amounts to a fully equipped and staffed company hospital, the fundamental function remains the same, namely, to provide local treatment for injuries and to attempt to maintain physical and mental health of the workers to such a degree that accidents do not occur. At the minimum, an industrial medical program should furnish prompt and effective first-aid treatment for injuries and illnesses, should follow up on the more serious cases in order to hasten convalescence and assure maximum rehabilitation, should maintain records of treatments, and should provide for pre-employment medical examinations.

In small establishments, where paid, in-company medical personnel cannot be financially justified, everything beyond simple first-aid treatment will necessarily be handled by referral to outside medical practitioners. But these outside medical practitioners can be advised by management regarding job requirements, type of physical examinations desired, and so on, as well as helped by the loss prevention medical advisory services of the insurance carrier.

In larger establishments, in which either part-time or full-time medical personnel can feasibly be employed, a really adequate program should go even further. The medical personnel should be familiar with company working conditions in order to make realistic pre-employment appraisals. They should maintain medical records adapted not only to good case follow-up but also to the furtherance of accident prevention efforts. Ideally, they should also be trained in health counseling in regard not only to physical health but to mental and emotional conditions as well.

Point 7: Regular Inspections to Detect Unsafe Conditions and Practices

A comprehensive loss prevention program must include inspections to detect unsafe conditions and practices. Except in the very small establishments where the owner or manager is in constant or very frequent association with all workers, it is essential that inspections be scheduled to take place regularly at frequent intervals.

Scope of Inspections. No operations area should be exempt from inspection. Accidents can happen anywhere, even where least anticipated. Although obviously more time should be devoted to the more hazardous areas, less hazardous areas should be inspected thoroughly and regularly.

Who Should Make Them? In very small establishments the question of who should make inspections is not of great importance. But, in establishments large enough to require divided supervision, but not large enough to warrant a safety engineering staff, supervisors should participate in inspection activities. A supervisor should be assigned to inspect other work areas in addition to his own.

How They Should be Made? The purpose of an inspection is to detect physical hazards and unsafe work practices. The question of how an inspection should be made can be answered in each case in terms of the nature and size of the establishment's operations, and also in terms of the training and experience of the inspectors. Sometimes hazard checklists can be used. Too often, however, the items on the checklist blind inspectors to dangers not listed.

The observance of a physical hazard or unsafe practice is of no value unless it leads to corrective action. Elaborate records are not essential. The record is only a means to an end, and this end is attained by any method which provides a permanent record of the inspection findings. In the final evaluation, the adequacy of a given inspection procedure is measured not by the methods, records, or checklists, but by the concrete results in terms of sound, practical recommendations brought to the attention of those able to follow through on them.

Point 8: Investigation of Accidents to Determine Corrective Measures

As a working definition, an accident is an unexpected event, frequently but not necessarily resulting in bodily injury or damage to equipment or material. While something could be gained from investigating every accident, such thoroughness is seldom found. At the minimum, every "serious" accident should be investigated.

The foremost purpose of an accident investigation is to discover the principal cause and the important contributing causes of the accident. Once this purpose is accomplished, specific corrective measures can be recommended. The worth of these recommended corrective measures depends directly upon how carefully and intelligently the investigation is conducted.

Five guides for the investigation of accidents are:

1. An accident should be investigated as soon after it occurs as possible, while the details are still fresh in the minds of witnesses and the physical surroundings remain substantially unchanged.

2. The investigation should never be allowed to degenerate into a search for the person responsible. This approach creates mistrust, hard feelings, and noncooperation. Instead, an impersonal factfinding attitude should prevail. The facts themselves will often automatically reveal who was responsible, but the fixing of blame, in itself, should never be allowed to enter in as a purpose of the

investigation. The ultimate goal is a corrective one, not a disciplinary one; it is constructive, not destructive.

3. The immediate supervisor of the injured employee should assist in the investigation because (*a*) he is responsible for the safety of his workers, (*b*) he usually must follow through on the resulting corrective measures, and (*c*) he is in a favored position to contribute to the investigation by virtue of his more intimate knowledge of employee operations.

4. A careful and intelligently conducted investigation has educational value at all levels: top management, supervisory, and employee. Hence, it is important to take full advantage of this by getting management participation and by making sure that the constructive lessons gained from the investigation are brought home to the employees.

5. Accident investigations should be an established part of every company's policy. The policy should specify what accidents are to be investigated, who is to make the investigation, and what disposition is to be made of the findings and recommended corrective measures.

AUTOMOBILE INSURANCE

Providing loss prevention service to firms using fleets of trucks, buses, and passenger cars is much simpler than providing the same service to workmen's compensation policyholders. The types of vehicle in use and the operations performed are few in number when contrasted with the almost infinite variety of machines and operations found in industry. This statement is not to imply, however, that it is easier to reduce the frequency of accidents of a fleet. In fact, accidents with fleets may produce a higher frequency than, say, in-plant accidents. The reasons are three: (1) the driver is unsupervised during his working hours; (2) he is operating a moving vehicle over a public way on which other machines are also moving; and (3) his safety is more dependent upon the actions of others than is that of a machine operator in an industrial plant. Insurance company loss prevention personnel are concerned with three factors in connection with prevention of vehicle accidents: the driver, the vehicle, and the highway.

For insurance purposes fleets are often divided into "Common," "Contract," and "Private Carriers." The first two transport property or passengers for compensation, while the third transports property or products of the owner. From a loss prevention viewpoint, in regard to setting up an accident prevention program, it is essential to know what types of vehicle are operated (bus, tractor-trailer, straight-body, panel delivery, or others) and what garaging arrangements obtain. For example, there may be a central terminal operation or a scattered fleet in which each operator garages his vehicle at a small branch terminal or even at his home. Actually, the specific loss prevention service techniques are determined largely by the fleet garaging arrangements.

The eight-point "Basic Plan" for a comprehensive loss prevention program, described in the previous section on workmen's compensation, applies also to fleet policyholders if some obvious minor changes in terminology are made. Hence, to avoid repetition, it can be assumed that all eight points are applicable, and discussion can be restricted to those points where greatest emphasis should be placed.

Four minimum requirements for every fleet, regardless of type, size, or number of vehicles, are: (*a*) a vehicle maintenance program, (*b*) an accident reporting and reviewing procedure, (*c*) a driver training program, and (*d*) a driver selection procedure. It must be stressed that these four requirements should constitute the *minimum program.* In fact, unless a fleet policyholder complies with these, it would seem advisable for the underwriting department to take a long second look at the risk's desirability.

Vehicle Maintenance Program

It is generally conceded by loss prevention specialists that a rather low percentage of total vehicle accidents is due to mechanical failure; estimates run from about 10 percent to 20 percent. Of course, the causes of vehicle accidents are often very difficult to determine, particularly when there are no witnesses and the driver is killed. Even when two or more vehicles are involved and there are witnesses, determination of cause is difficult. Nevertheless, it is definitely known that *some* accidents are caused by mechanical failure. It therefore makes good sense to set up a maintenance program that will insure that all vehicles are kept in good repair and that certain essential items, such as tires, headlights, directional signals, brakes, steering mechanism, and windshield wipers receive regular and frequent inspection and immediate attention when necessary.

Fleets garaged at sizeable terminals are usually serviced by company mechanics, and the control over a maintenance program is relatively easy to achieve. Scattered fleets, however, present some problems. The company may set up truck servicing standards, but it is incumbent on the individual driver to follow these standards on his own initiative. It is necessary, therefore, that a strict follow-up procedure be developed and rigidly enforced.

Accident Reporting and Reviewing Procedure

In spite of the maximum of precautions, accidents will happen. When they do, it is most important (1) that the driver know exactly how to handle the situation at the scene and (2) that subsequently the accident be thoroughly reviewed with the driver to determine if he did everything reasonably possible to avoid the accident, and, if he did not, just what more he should have done.

Records should be kept of the accident history, accident costs, and motor vehicle violation history of each driver. The value of a careful review of the entire accident sequence cannot be too highly stressed. Review may be by a member of management heading up an accident review committee, preferably a committee of fellow-drivers. The educational benefits derivable from these reviews should extend to as many drivers as possible. Surprisingly enough, a committee of fellow-drivers often is more successful in getting at the facts in an accident review than is a management committee. The fellow-drivers are less likely to accept excuses and rationalizations, in the bad sense of the term. In the author's experience as consultant for accident review committees, there is seldom any attempt on the part of fellow-drivers to protect, or cover up for, the driver who is under examination. Committees of this type are particularly effective if the management member creates an atmosphere of impartial inquiry bent upon getting the facts primarily to prevent future accidents rather than to ferret out guilt for the current one.

Committees of the above type are most easily workable with fleets having a single garaging terminal or several sizeable terminals. For scattered fleets, a different approach is generally more practical. In the latter case, a detailed accident report should be routed by the driver through his supervisor to the head office accident judging committee. The committee arrives at its opinion by reviewing the report and then sends its decision back to the supervisor and driver. Any differences of opinion or need for further clarification usually can be handled by correspondence. In the event of very serious and costly accidents, however, it is customary to call the driver in to the head office for a personal report.

There are many other types of accident review committees. The two described are typical, but procedural and other differences between fleet operators dictate that the loss prevention representative of the insurance carrier tailor-make the type of accident reporting and reviewing procedures best adaptable to and most practical for each policyholder.

Driver Training

There is no question about the fact that driver training, together with driver selection described below, is the most important facet in a fleet loss prevention program. The driver controls an expensive vehicle, which can also be lethal, and his training largely determines how safely he drives it. He can avoid many accidents which the layman would consider unavoidable.

This brings up the important distinction between legal driving and defensive driving. Many drivers know their legal rights and too often feel that if they stay within them they are good drivers. On the other hand, the defensive driver feels the responsibility not only to observe legal obligations but also to be on the watch continuously for other drivers who may disobey laws or make mistakes. He drives defensively and, by so doing, makes it difficult for the other drivers to involve him in accidents.

This concept of *defensive driving*, developed by loss prevention specialists as that around which all driver training should revolve, is also the concept upon which accident review judgments are based. It is not enough that the driver can show that he was *legally* in the right; he must show that he took *every reasonable precaution* to prevent the accident. Unavoidable accidents under this type of judgment become quite rare.

Driver simulators have come into prominence in recent years. Many hope that these devices may serve training purposes much as similar devices have aided in pilot training. There are differences, however, between piloting a plane and driving a car which some feel may limit the usefulness of driving simulators in their present stage of development. With so much exploratory work going on in this field, it is quite possible that a simulator may be developed that will do an effective training job.

The insurance carriers have specialists on their loss prevention staffs to advise and assist policyholders in setting up effective training programs. Some insurance carriers are conducting valuable research in car and truck safety, are holding training courses for the driver-trainers of policyholders, and are performing a public service by promoting driver skill contests. Because they are convinced that highway safety is everybody's business, and that it is a problem that will grow more acute year by year as the number of vehicles increase, they are attacking the problem from every conceivable angle.

Driver Selection

Driver selection is the most difficult part of the program. Certain factual material can be obtained, such as the history of the applicant's violations and reported accidents, references from previous employers, a medical examination record, and verification of his possession of a driver's license for the type of vehicle he is to drive. However, the accuracy and usefulness of some of these data are questionable.

Driver attitude has emerged in recent years as perhaps the one characteristic of overriding importance. Hence, many investigators have devoted their efforts to the development of a quick and easy way to determine this attitude. Psychological tests, biographical questionnaires, and depth interviews have been advanced, either singly or in combination, as capable of revealing an applicant's fundamental attitude. To the best of the author's information, none of these has gained a very wide circle of convinced adherents. General opinion seems to be that much more research is needed. Perhaps the most fertile field to be explored in this connection is the depth interview, or projective techniques, similar to those now widely used in motivation research.

GENERAL LIABILITY INSURANCE

Many of the points made earlier in this chapter apply with equal force to loss prevention activities in the realm of general liability insurance. Four types of business will be examined from the standpoint of loss prevention. Perhaps these examples will indicate some of the general problems, techniques, and opportunities.

Industrial Plants

General liability exposures in industrial plants in most instances are similar to those discussed in the workmen's compensation section. Visitors to the plant are exposed to similar dangers, albeit to a lesser extent because they do not usually operate any of the equipment. On the other hand, lack of familiarity with plant layout adds to the hazard for visitors. A general liability safety program, therefore, often supplements the existing workmen's compensation program, and when performed concurrently with it, may require only slight additional effort.

Nonemployees who might be affected adversely by plant operations, products, and hazardous conditions are (1) visitors to the plant, such as salesmen, service men, contractor's men, concessionaires, and employees' friends; (2) persons living in, working in, or passing through the vicinity of the plant; (3) persons exposed to operations conducted by the policyholder at locations away from the plant; and (4) persons who buy the policyholder's products.

The loss prevention approach is to explore the hazards to each of these four categories of exposed persons and recommend necessary corrective action. Hazards to category 1 have been mentioned above. Hazards to category 2 include fires, explosions, and emission of toxic materials from the plant into the neighborhood. Hazards to category 3 depend upon the type of operations being conducted at locations away from the plant. Hazards to category 4 include bodily injury or property damage growing out of use of the policyholder's product, when the fault can be traced back to the manufacturer.

Service-Mercantile

Many types of business cater directly to the public, such as places of assembly for entertainment or other purposes and structures for institutional, residential, office, mercantile, and storage occupancies. Operations may include the provision of meals, lodging, entertainment, nursing, medical care, and other personal services, plus all mercantile operations.

The general liability exposure of these policyholders, as contrasted with industrial plant policyholders, is usually limited to members of the public on the premises. These members of the public, known variously as guests, customers, patrons, patients, and the like, are *invitees* (see Chapter 31). The policyholder owes them the maximum of obligation in regard to their safety. In further contrast between these *invitees* and industrial workers, the policyholder can exercise only a limited control over the unsafe acts of invitees. Loss prevention activity is accordingly limited rather exclusively to the physical hazards of the premises.

Construction Operations

Construction operations present the greatest variety of general liability hazards, as well as the most severe. For example, in road building jobs, the prevalent types of accidents arise from improper and insufficient warning signs and barricades, vibration damage due to blasting and pile driving, inadequate lighting of parked equipment, contact with overhead utilities, breakage of underground utilities, and equipment striking vehicles. Building construction, particularly in thickly populated areas, presents such hazards as: vibration damage to adjacent buildings from blasting or pile driving; settlement of adjacent buildings due to disturbing the foundation and underpinning; materials blowing or falling off the building and striking pedestrians, vehicles, or adjacent buildings; pedestrians tripping over poorly lighted and uneven temporary boardwalks; and contact with overhead or underground utilities. Prevention is mainly a matter of maintenance, cautions, warnings, and good engineering.

Stevedoring Operations

Stevedoring creates the danger of bodily injury to: (1) clerks, checkers, and other incidental help, not employed by the policyholder in question; (2) truckers bringing cargo to, or taking it from, the pier; (3) contractor's men working on the pier or vessel; (4) incidental business callers, such as inspectors, engineers, cargo surveyors, shippers, salesmen, and contractors; (5) social callers, such as guests of the line, and friends and relatives of crew members; and (6) ship's passengers, where a cargo ship is carrying passengers or where the ship is a passenger vessel.

Studies have shown that about half of the accidents involving bodily injury arise from the operation of vehicles such as lift trucks, tractors, and trucks. Lift trucks are the cause of about two thirds of all the accidents. Most of the remainder result from cargo falling either from a vehicle or from a pile on the pier.

The principal exposures to property damage are: (1) contractor's equipment on pier or shipboard, (2) trucks, (3) pier structures, (4) cars parked on pier, (5) neighboring vessels, and (6) lighters. Studies have shown that over 90 percent of these property damage claims arise from the property being struck by vehicles.

Prevention depends on attitudes, inspections, maintenance, good work methods, warnings to outsiders, and numerous other points discussed earlier in this chapter. In summary, in general liability loss prevention one tries to make it difficult for members of the public to hurt themselves, regardless of how unsafe their behavior. The property damage element allows for greater control because the damage is inflicted in most cases by acts of the policyholder's employees, who are under direct supervision.

CHANGING EMPHASIS

Throughout the history of the safety movement, as in every development, emphasis has shifted from one aspect to another. Also, new concepts have been developed, such as the quite recent emergence of industrial medicine.

Accident Proneness

The concept of accident proneness has a history almost as long as the organized safety movement itself, but it is only in recent years that it has become a lively issue. In brief, the concept is that everyone is accident-prone to some degree, naturally, because everyone has accidents, but that certain people are much more accident-prone than others and hence, over a period of time, have more accidents. Individuals in this latter group are the "accident-prones." This issue is very controversial at present and is one that needs some soundly based research.

Personal Causes of Accidents

Personal causes of accidents, especially as to their incidence in relation to the whole accident-causation picture, is also an old concept that has only recently begun to receive serious attention. Many years ago, the loss prevention profession was almost unanimously convinced that about 85 percent of all accidents were caused predominantly by "personal actions." Conventional methods of education and training were utilized to try to reduce this biggest of problems facing the loss prevention experts. Results of this intellectual approach had a measure of success but a quite meager measure in view of the enormity of the problem. This relative lack of success has been largely due to a confusion that still exists over the *definition of accident causes* and, also, to a lack of understanding of human motivation and how it can be redirected.

Accident Cause

A "redefinition of accident cause" in scientific terms, rather than popular, has been made by one large insurer. This redefining has cleared up a number of the obscurities of accident proneness and personal causes of accidents. In brief, the prevalent definition today is that accidents are caused by unsafe acts of persons and unsafe conditions. A little reflection, however, quickly shows that a condition can never be a cause for the simple reason that a cause is always an action. By the same reasoning, a failure to act cannot be an accident cause. Therefore, *a cause, newly and logically defined, is either an unsafe action of a person or an impersonal action of something else, or a combination of both.* The use of this definition facilitates the pinpointing of essential accident causes and frequently suggests the remedies simultaneously.

Motivation

Motivation as applied to humans is another concept which is receiving increasing attention, as the emotional side of human nature appears to assume greater importance than the intellectual—so far as human attitudes and actions are concerned. It is felt that conventional safety education which leans largely on the intellectual approach must be supplemented by emotional reeducation to attain really solid and substantial results.

These concepts could, by further development, create one of the greatest steps forward yet seen in the safety movement, because they could provide the technique for attacking successfully the 85 percent, or more, of accidents now attributed principally to personal causes.

SUGGESTED READINGS

BLAKE, ROLAND P. (ed.). *Industrial Safety.* 2d ed. Englewood Cliffs, N.J.: Prentice-Hall, Inc., 1953.

DEREAMER, RUSSELL. *Modern Safety Practice.* New York: John Wiley & Sons, Inc., 1958.

HEINRICH, H. W. *Industrial Accident Prevention.* 4th ed. New York: McGraw-Hill Book Co., Inc., 1959.

SIMONDS, ROLLIN H., AND GRIMALDI, JOHN V. *Safety Management.* Homewood, Ill.: Richard D. Irwin, Inc., 1956.

Chapter 45

RATEMAKING IN LIABILITY INSURANCE AND RELATED LINES

BY JAMES M. CAHILL

There are two misconceptions about insurance rates. Many purchasers of insurance believe that companies are free to charge whatever they choose. Others, however, believe that uniform rates are charged by all companies and that these are determined by a rigid formula. Neither concept is correct. Only in rare cases is there complete uniformity of rates or rules on the part of all companies writing a given type of insurance in a given state. But in all cases the rates used must comply with the provisions of the rate regulatory laws in effect in all of the states, including the requirement that rates shall not be excessive, inadequate, or unfairly discriminatory. (See also Chapter 13.)

Individual companies may function independently in determining the particular rates and rating procedures they propose to use, or companies may elect to affiliate with a rating bureau for the pooling of experience data, actuarial knowledge, and ideas as to how rates should be established. Even in the case of companies affiliated with a rating bureau, there is still not complete uniformity of rates and rating procedures. Deviations and other departures from bureau filings are generally permissible under the provisions of the rate regulatory laws and through the practical manner in which rating bureaus operate in the competitive field of liability insurance and related lines.[1] Most of the companies which are independent of a bureau do not actually determine their rate structures "from scratch" but instead use the published manuals of rates and rules of a rating bureau as their base from which to introduce changes of one kind or another. Similarly, bureaus cannot ignore what "independents" do. Rating structures, therefore, represent an interplay of the ideas of competing ratemakers. There are two or more liability rating bureaus

[1] With the growth of multiple line underwriting, use of the word "casualty" seems to be declining.

functioning in most states. In view of the variety of ratemaking methods thus possible, it will be necessary to confine this chapter to basic principles with specific reference to the methods currently used by national rating organizations.

UNIQUE PRICING PROBLEM

In most other industries, wholesale or retail price structures can be derived from the known cost of manufacturing the product or providing the service, with proper allowance for overhead and profit, and with due recognition of the competitive situation. The insurance business is different in that the ultimate cost to the insurance company of its product—insurance protection—will not be known for several years. The insurance rate charged today involves an intelligent prediction of the number and cost of loss events expected to arise from the risk covered by the insurance. In establishing an insurance rate, reliance must be placed to a large extent upon what has happened in the past as a basis for predicting what will happen in the future. To obtain such data, statistical plans are employed under which detailed experience by classification and territory, generally within states, is compiled.

Recognition of Trend

While these data serve as a reliable starting point in ratemaking, it would be unrealistic in all instances to establish a rate structure therefrom on the assumption that the experience results of one or more years in the past would be exactly duplicated in the future. In order to establish accurate rates for the future period, it usually is necessary to adjust the experience to reflect trends in claim costs, accident frequency, or other changes which are known to have occurred. The ratemaker employs informed judgment in deciding to what extent and by what methods these influences should be reflected in a rate structure. While trend factors of some type are commonly used in insurance ratemaking, their purpose has largely been to update experience to reflect known changes in conditions. Seldom has any attempt been made to project such trend factors into the future when the rates will be in use. While the idea of such a projection clearly has merit in principle, practical problems and considerations have obstructed its use to date.

Evolution of Statistics

Until high-speed data processing equipment became available, the experience for workmen's compensation and for the various liability lines was compiled on a *policy year* basis, that is, the losses incurred under all policies issued within a particular year were matched with the exposures and premiums under the same policies. Since a policy year spans two *calendar* years in which insurance is afforded under annual policies issued in the particular policy year, there was an inevitable time lag in compiling the experience of a completed policy year.

Now, however, for the major liability lines the experience is compiled on an *accident year* basis. This experience matches the losses with date of accident within a 12-month period with the exposures and premiums earned within the same period regardless of the effective date of the policy. The accident year period usually is January 1 through December 31, but experience may be compiled for any other 12-month period such as July 1 through June 30. This produces not only a more homogeneous group of experience from a time standpoint but also makes possible the compilation of up-to-date statistics at an early date after the completion of the accident year period.

Development of Experience

At each annual statistical reporting, it is the established practice in liability insurance ratemaking to trace the development of the experience for each policy or accident year for the lines that evidence significant changes as the experience matures. Such development reflects mainly whether the loss reserves established for outstanding claims tend on the average to be too high, accurate, or too low. By the time the final statistical report for a policy or accident year is made, virtually all claims are closed and the remaining loss reserves constitute only a small percentage of the total incurred losses, so any subsequent changes would have little, if any, effect on the results. From a review of the data for prior years, development factors are determined to apply to the experience of the particular year or years being used for rate level determination purposes to bring such experience to the equivalent of a fully developed basis. The development factors may have a plus or minus effect.

Expense Provisions

The provisions for expenses are determined from an annual review of the countrywide expense data reported by the companies to the state supervisory authorities in the Insurance Expense Exhibit. (This exhibit is filed as a Supplement to the Annual Statement to show primarily the incurred loss and expense results by major lines of insurance. The expenses are reported on an item basis such as general expenses, commissions, and other. See Chapter 61.) Since expense data are not subject to frequent or sharp fluctuations, the provisions for expenses included in the manual rates often remain unchanged for several years. The provision for loss adjustment expense is determined as a function of the incurred losses because it is in fact a part of the cost of the loss and it is almost universally included with the loss provision in ratemaking. Company administrative, inspection, and bureau expenses are generally provided for as a function of premium. Budgetary provisions are commonly included for total production cost allowance, including commissions to agents or brokers, and for premium taxes. In addition, there is a 5 percent provision for underwriting profit and contingencies in the rates for most lines in almost all states. This is no guarantee of profit; a 5 percent margin can be realized only if the total losses and expenses do not exceed 95 percent of the total premium.

The words "losses" or "loss ratio" as used hereafter shall be understood to be inclusive of all loss adjustment expense.

THUMBNAIL SKETCH OF RATEMAKING PROCEDURE

Usually the indicated statewide rate level change from present rates is determined first by analyzing the basic limits experience or comparable data, exclusive of catastrophes for the policy or accident years under review. The proposed statewide rate level is then distributed by territory and classification by methods which will be explained later in this chapter. Also the subject of the credibility assignable will be explained. The statewide rate level change may be determined by the pure premium method or by the loss ratio method, both of which produce identical results.

The first step in the *pure premium method* is the determination of the average amount of incurred losses per unit of exposure. Thus, this method may be used only for lines for which the exposure is compiled. Both development factors and trend factors when applicable are reflected in the average incurred losses per unit of exposure. In the next step the corresponding average pure premium underlying the present rate structure is determined by multiplying the present average rate by the expected loss ratio, which is the percentage of each premium dollar provided for losses and loss adjustment. Finally, dividing the indicated pure premium by the present pure premium determines the indicated rate level change—as illustrated by the following example:

Incurred Losses Including Loss Adjustment Expenses ÷ Earned Exposure = Pure Premium Indicated

$$\$3,500,000 \div 100,000 = \$35$$

Present Average Rate × Expected Loss and Loss Adjustment Ratio = Present Pure Premium

$$\$50 \times .655 = \$32.75$$

$\$35.00 \div \$32.75 = 1.069$ or $+6.9\%$ indicated change in the statewide rate level

Indicated Average Rate = $\$50.00 \times 1.069 = \$53.45$

In the *loss ratio method,* the incurred losses including development and trend factors are divided by the corresponding earned premium at present rates for the experience period under review. When this loss ratio is divided by the expected loss ratio, the indicated rate level change results. This process is illustrated by the following example:

Incurred Losses Including Loss Adjustment Expenses ÷ Earned Premium at Present Rates = Loss and Loss Adjustment Ratio

$3,500,000 ÷ $5,000,000 = .700

Expected Loss and Loss Adjustment Ratio = .655

.700 ÷ .655 = 1.069 or +6.9% indicated change in the statewide rate level

CREDIBILITY

In determining either the statewide rate level or its distribution by territory and classification, there is always the problem of the degree to which the indications can be considered reliable. Seldom are the data available in sufficient volume for all categories to warrant 100 percent credibility or belief in the indications.

By limiting the size of the maximum loss used in ratemaking, the number of claims needed for complete or unbiased loss statistics for ratemaking purposes is reduced. In liability insurance, for example, this reduction is accomplished by limiting the losses used in manual ratemaking to the basic limits of liability. But even then there is still the question of whether the available data are of sufficient volume to assure a representative sample of losses. Actuaries have used mathematical tools from probability theory to investigate and solve this problem for the various lines of insurance. The conclusions of their studies as published in the *Proceedings of the Casualty Actuarial Society* have taken the form that, for any particular line of insurance with a known overall claim pattern and maximum single loss, a sample of loss experience will be credible if it contains at least a certain minimum number of claims. In automobile liability insurance, for example, at least 1,084 claims are currently considered necessary for 100 percent credibility by territory, and where there are fewer claims the credibility assignable is reduced appropriately.

Credibility may also be assigned on the basis of the volume of expected losses rather than on the number of claims. This method is used for workmen's compensation insurance.

THE RATEMAKING PROCESS

The experience used in ratemaking is analyzed separately by line, the provisions for expenses differ by line, and the units of exposure vary by line. Even within one line of insurance the ratemaking process develops not one rate but many rates, each applicable to a different group of risks. A line of insurance may have several sublines; automobile liability, for instance, encompasses such sublines as private passenger cars and garages, which vary as to units of exposure, accident frequency, and size of claim cost.

Units of Exposure

Private passenger cars are rated on the basis of an exposure unit of one car-year, whereas for garages the exposure basis is payroll. Where the exposure units differ, there must be separate computations to derive the rate. But even where the exposure unit is the same throughout a subline such as private passenger cars, it does not necessarily follow that each unit measures exactly the same degree of hazard. The hazard of a car-year of exposure for drivers who work in an office is not the same as for salesmen who are on the road almost every day of each week. Thus, while exposure units are chosen to reflect the hazard so that doubling the number of exposures means doubling the hazard, exposure units by themselves are inadequate for measuring much of the variation in hazard from one risk to another within a single line or subline.

Accident Frequency

One of the two components making up the average loss cost per unit of exposure is the frequency of loss. Inasmuch as the rate includes provision for the expected loss cost, variation in the claim frequency from one type of risk to another requires different rates. To illustrate, private passenger cars driven mainly in a congested metropolitan area can be expected to have a higher accident frequency than cars driven chiefly in rural areas. Thus, the location of the car affects the loss cost and hence the rate. On the other hand, cars from the same neighborhood can have significantly different accident records in the case of those driven by male teenagers versus those used in mature families with no young drivers. In this second example the locality is the same, but differences in the kind of drivers indicate the need for different rates.

Size of Claim Cost

The second component making up the average loss cost per unit of exposure is the size of loss. The amounts of damage for claims are in many cases established by juries which vary significantly in their judgment of proper reparation. Thus, two similar accidents in separate localities can result in a higher award on one than the other. Out-of-court settlements are influenced by the size of jury awards in the particular locality. Also, even within the same locality there are variations in the potential magnitude of loss which need to be taken into account when establishing the rates. To take an example from boiler insurance: explosion of a high-pressure boiler will generally tend to result in a larger loss than explosion of a low-pressure boiler. Thus, significant differences in size of claim cost from one group of risks to another suggest the need for separate rates for each such group.

Rate Groups

The variations within one line of insurance call for the establishment of rate groupings which will reflect the often sizeable differences inherent in one group as contrasted to another. Ratemaking would be much simpler if it were practicable to have only a few very broad groupings of risks for rating purposes. But consistent pressure for the fragmentation of a line of insurance into more and smaller rate groups is created by the competition in rates among insurance companies. In any rate group the worse-than-average risks are in fact paying less than their loss-potential would indicate, and the better-than-average risks are paying more. The alert competitor can offer the better-than-average risks a lower rate by setting them apart in a new grouping based on criteria designed to effect such differentiation.

The pressure for more and smaller rate groups is balanced by both theoretical and practical reasons which oppose this pressure. The smaller the group, the less experience is available for ratemaking and hence the lower the credibility of that experience. The more groups there are, the more difficult it is to define these groups clearly. This difficulty adds to the chance of error in the assignment of a risk to the proper group.

Variations due to the differences in locality are taken into account by establishing rate territories. Variations due to other causes are taken into account by the establishment of rate classes. This process results in a two-way grouping system; a particular rate group consists of a particular rate class in a particular rate territory.

The Rate Territory

For product liability, where the product may be sold in areas far from the point of manufacture and where, therefore, the exposure hazard cannot be assigned to a particular locality, the rates are usually countrywide rates, that is to say, there is only one rate territory. Some lines set up each state as a rate territory, but the most common situation is to have more than one rate territory within each state. The obvious separation is between the big cities and the rural areas. Ordinarily, territory boundaries follow political boundaries such as county or township lines for ease of definition. When two rate territories which are contiguous in the same state become nearly alike with the passing of time, it becomes desirable to combine them into one rate territory. Conversely, knowledge of changing conditions within one rate territory leads to subdividing it so that accurate rates may be established reflecting the different results to be expected in the newly defined areas.

The Rate Class

Variations other than territorial are identified on the basis of criteria that should be clear and objective; these define the rate class. Thus the car used for business is in one class; that used for pleasure is in another.

Producing the Manual Rates

The rate manuals set forth a rate for each class by territory. In any one year, the experience for many of these rate groups is not sufficient for the purpose of making valid estimates of indicated changes in these rates. Primarily for this reason, rates are not made directly from a rate group's own experience but rather are made through a multistep process which has the advantage of introducing greater stability in the rates from year to year as a result of using more credible experience. One standard approach is the three step process that first produces a statewide change, then distributes this change to each territory in the state, and finally distributes the territory change to each class in the territory. In all three steps, limitations may be imposed on the percentage change in either direction. The justification for such limitations is to prevent too wide fluctuations in rates from year to year.

AN EXAMPLE

Statewide Rate Level Change

As an example of the process of changing the statewide rate level, consider the subline of private passenger cars. The experience for all the classes and all the territories in a particular state is accumulated to get the total private passenger car experience for the state. The indicated change, referred to as the statewide rate level change, is then computed either by the pure premium or the loss ratio method. For purposes of discussion assume the latter. Because rates made from experience are to apply in the future, it is essential to use the latest experience consistent with the need for credibility. The latest two years are usually used for private passenger cars with the most recent year getting a heavier weight; in fact, if the state's volume is large enough, the latest year alone is sufficient. Because of the time interval required to collect and compile the statistics, use of the latest possible experience, however, does not always result in a proper rate for future needs. For this reason, where the need for adjustment is demonstrable, the experience is adjusted to reflect subsequent trends.

Territory Differentials

The statewide rate level change is distributed among the territories in the state to get the indicated change for each territory. The one year or two years of experience used for the statewide indicated change is not sufficient for the separate territories because of the resulting low credibility that would be assignable in many instances. For this reason three to five years of experience are used for the territories, thereby adding credibility to the data and producing greater consistency in the rates. The loss ratio is computed for each territory; it is then compared with the same expected loss ratio used throughout, and an indicated change is derived. Because of the different experience periods used, it is unlikely that the total effect of the territorial changes will exactly equal the statewide rate level change previously computed. The statewide change is the most current, however, and hence the territorial indications are adjusted so that their overall effect conforms to the statewide change. Use of a simple arithmetic adjustment proportionately corrects each territory change in the desired direction.

Class Differentials

Because of the multiplicity of classes, experience for most classes by territory or even by state lacks sufficient credibility for ratemaking. Fortunately, it has been shown that, whatever the level of rates may be, the relationship between classes is fairly consistent from one territory to another. Thus countrywide experience can often be used to develop class differentials related to a base classification such as pleasure car Class 1A for private passenger liability.

The process of calculating the new rates consists of first multiplying the present average rate for the territory by the appropriate territory rate level change and then dividing this result by the average differential for the exposures by classification in the territory to obtain the indicated rate for the base classification. For private passenger cars, the new rates for the other classifications are obtained by multiplying the new Class 1A rate by the class differential for each of the other classifications.

Additional refinements to the rate group structure, such as the well-known safe driver insurance plan, are essentially extensions of the classification system.

The process of determining the statewide rate level change, its distribution by territory, and the revised rates for the base classification are illustrated by Table 45–1.

Minimum Premiums and Expense Constants

For some risks the rate is so low or the number of exposures so few that the resulting premium would be too low to cover even the administrative expense of handling the policy if a minimum premium did not apply. The minimum premiums are usually established by a formula which varies by line. In workmen's compensation insurance, loss and expense constants are included in the minimum premium formula but also apply to other risks up to a specified premium size. These have been determined to be

TABLE 45-1

ILLUSTRATION OF CALCULATION OF REVISED PRIVATE PASSENGER CAR RATES

Statewide Rate Level Change—Bodily Injury

(1) Accident Year	(2) Premium at Present 10/20 Rates	(3) 10/20 Incurred Losses* Developed to a Final Reporting Basis	(4) Number of Claims	(5) Loss Ratio* (3) ÷ (2)	(6) Weighting Factors
1961	$4,795,613	$3,136,331	3,485	.654	15%
1962	5,217,184	3,662,463	3,938	.702	85%

(7) Weighted Average Loss Ratio* (.654 × 15% + .702 × 85%)....	.695
(8) Trend Factor....................	1.032
(9) Product (7) × (8)....................	.717
(10) Expected Loss Ratio*....................	.655
(11) Credibility Based on (4)....................	1.000
(12) Rate Level Change $\left[\frac{(9)}{(10)} - 1.00\right] \times (11)$....................	+9.5%

Territory Rate Level Change

(13) Territory	(14) Present Average 10/20 Rate	(15) 1960–62 10/20 Pure Premium	(16) 1960–62 10/20 Loss Ratio*	(17) 1960–62 Number of Claims	(18) Credibility Based on (17)	(19) Formula Loss Ratio* (16) × (18) + .691 × [1.0 − (18)]	(20) Index (19) ÷ .692	(21) Indicated Territorial Rate Level Change [(20) × 1.095] − 1.0
1	$36.06	$25.53	.708	4,910	1.00	.708	1.023	+12.0%
2	30.02	17.89	.596	769	.80	.615	.889	− 2.7
3	27.50	16.67	.606	402	.60	.640	.925	+ 1.3
4	22.06	14.71	.667	3,606	1.00	.671	.970	+ 6.2
Statewide	30.47	21.05	.691	9,687		.692		

Calculation of Class 1A Rates

(22) Territory	(23) Indicated Average 10/20 Rate (14) × [1.0 + (21)]	(24) Average Differential to Class 1A Rate	(25) Indicated Class 1A Rate (23) ÷ (24)
1	$40.39	1.211	$33
2	29.21	1.167	25
3	27.86	1.171	24
4	23.43	1.065	22

* Including all loss adjustment.
Note: All data are hypothetical.

necessary in order to produce a proper and adequate provision for losses and expenses on the risk sizes to which they apply. There has been only limited use of constants for this purpose in other insurance lines.

RATEMAKING BY LINE

A brief outline follows of the specific ratemaking procedure for the major lines of liability and related lines of insurance. (A few comments about ratemaking can be found also in the respective chapters where the several lines are discussed.)

Liability Insurance

The term "liability" as used here includes private passenger and the several commercial lines of automobile liability insurance as well as the numerous sublines of general liability insurance.

While there are many minor variations in procedure by line, the overall methods are similar. Rates are usually reviewed on a state basis and overall rate levels are customarily determined by the loss ratio approach utilizing the experience for all classes within the subline. Premiums at present basic limits rates are compared with the basic limits incurred losses. Statistics are collected on an accident-year basis for some major lines, while for other lines the policy-year basis is still in use.

Usually the experience of the latest one or two years on a weighted basis adjusted for development and any trend in average paid claim cost is used to determine the statewide rate level change, which is distributed among the territories on the basis of three to five years of experience. The experience of each territory is compared with the average experience statewide to determine the degree to which each individual territory is different from the average. The index of territory experience to the statewide average is then multiplied by the statewide rate level change to obtain territory rate level change factors. For automobile insurance, the territory rate level change is then used with countrywide class differentials to obtain rates by class. To obtain rates by class for certain general liability sublines, a similar countrywide class differential approach is used; however, class rates for other general liability sublines reflect either territory class experience to the extent credible or some combination of territory class experience and countrywide class differentials.

Automobile Physical Damage Insurance

The rate level indications for automobile physical damage insurance are determined from calendar-year experience. The indicated statewide premium is derived from a two-year weighted average of incurred losses, adjusted to current costs, plus average incurred company expenses and provision for acquisition, taxes, and underwriting profit and contingencies. This indicated premium is compared with the two-year weighted average of earned premiums adjusted to current rate level to derive the overall rate level change for the state. Catastrophe losses are limited according to formula, and are compensated by a factor applicable countrywide to the premium for coverages subject to catastrophe loss. The statewide rate level change is distributed to class and coverage on the basis of adjusted loss ratios and to territory on the basis of loss costs. Periodic review of countrywide data determines the premium relationships as to age and value and also other rate differentials which are maintained in standard premium schedules.

Workmen's Compensation Insurance

In workmen's compensation insurance, rates are determined by state without any territorial subdivisions. (See Chapter 36.) The mean of the indicated rate level change is based on the mean of the loss ratio for the latest 24 months of policy year data (ending with any month, not necessarily December) and the more current loss ratio for the latest 12 months of calendar year experience (ending with June or December). The rate level change is distributed among three broad industry groups: manufacturing, contracting and all other. In the calculations, the premium is adjusted to present rate level with appropriate adjustments for the premium derived from loss and expense constants and for the "off-balance" of the experience rating plan. (Application of the experience rating plan results in a preponderance of credits versus debits, hence an "off balance.") The incurred losses are limited to exclude catastrophe losses (for which a \$.01 rate increment applies), are adjusted by loss development factors, and are brought to the level reflecting the latest compensation law amendments. Rate level changes by class are determined using a formula pure premium process which consists essentially of a credibility weighting of the class pure premiums indicated by the experience data and the present pure premiums on rate level.

Boiler and Machinery Insurance

As brought out in Chapter 41, boiler and machinery insurance provides coverage separately for direct and indirect damage. For direct damage, country-wide rates are determined from basic limits experience on the current rate level. Moreover, inspection expense is such an important element in the ratemaking process that the combined loss and inspection ratio is compared with the expected provision in the rates for these items. The overall rate level change is distributed among the classes by means of the pure premium approach. For indirect damage, a countrywide rate level change is calculated on the basis of overall experience, with total collected premium adjusted to current rate level. The overall rate level change is then distributed by class on the basis of class loss ratios.

Burglary Insurance

In burglary insurance, ratemaking is based on a review of the latest five calendar accident-year loss ratios for each type of insurance by statistical territory for each state. The premium used is total collected premium adjusted to the current level of rates. The loss ratios are reviewed as to magnitude and trend to determine the rate level changes judged necessary to reproduce the expected loss ratio in the future. The indicated change is translated into a rate change by assigning the statistical territory to the rate schedule that most nearly approximates the indicated rate level. The rates are set forth by schedule as for automobile physical damage, based on countrywide differentials which are reviewed and adjusted periodically.

Glass Insurance

Ratemaking in glass insurance is based on a review of the latest two and five calendar accident-year loss ratios by state. The statewide rate level change results from the middle value of three loss ratios: the expected, the statewide two-year, and the statewide five-year. The premium is total collected premium at current level of rates. The incurred losses are adjusted to eliminate abnormal losses in the state's experience (for which program a countrywide provision equal to 2 percent of the rate level losses applies) and for changes in the price of glass and installation costs. Full credibility is given the statewide experience. The indicated change is distributed to territory on the basis of the five-year loss ratios with credibility weighting. The indicated change is translated into the rate change by amending the multiplier for the territory.

RATES FOR INDIVIDUAL RISKS

Manual rates, as average rates, are appropriate for risks of small premium size. It would be inequitable, however, to apply manual rates without modification to risks of large premium size because the diversity of hazard which such risks present can usually be measured and differences of consequence should be reflected in their rates. Thus individual risk rating plans, customarily on an interstate basis, are established to provide a means for properly rating risks of large premium size.

Experience Rating

The experience of the risk during a recent period is utilized to measure whether it is better or worse than the average represented by the manual rates for the classifications applicable to the risk. In general, a comparison is made between the actual losses of the risk and the corresponding expected losses. Credibility is assigned according to the volume of experience data for the risk, varying from a small percentage in the case of risks barely qualifying for rating, to a high percentage, or even self-rating, in the case of the large risks. In this way, the resulting modifications applicable prospectively to the current manual rates are tempered in a scientific manner, and unjustifiably high credits or debits are avoided in the case of risks whose size is such as not to entitle their indications to full credibility. A limitation is imposed on the maximum effect that a single loss or accident may have on the modification so that risks will not be unduly penalized by infrequent and fortuitous large claims.

Under the retrospective form of experience rating, the premium of the risk is adjusted after expiration of the policy in accordance with the actual losses incurred under that policy, subject to prescribed minimum and maximum premium limits. Thus, within limits acceptable to both the insured and the carrier, the premium for the risk is determined by its own experience; yet, at the same time, the element of insurance is retained. Whereas prospective experience rating produces scientific estimates of what the rates should be for a risk in accordance with the extent to which it appears to be better or worse than average on the basis of actual experience, retrospective rating goes further and adjusts the premium for the policy term in accordance with the actual losses incurred during that term so as to come as close as possible to the premium actually needed to cover the true cost of the insurance afforded. Retrospective rating plans are available on an optional basis. One of the retrospective rating plans, namely, Plan D, permits the combination of the workmen's compensation, third party liability, automobile physical damage, burglary, and glass coverages of a risk for overall retrospective rating purposes.

Schedule Rating

The schedule type of rating plan has some application to liability insurance in most states. (Also, see Chapter 13 for a discussion of scheduled rating as applied to fire insurance.) Under it, the physical conditions of the risk and other aspects which may be expected to have an effect on its experience, such as an active safety organization, may be taken into account. Debits as well as credits result under this responsive plan which can be used to give immediate reflection to items that are recognized by both insureds and underwriters as having a bearing on the probability or severity of losses.

Composite Rating

Under this plan, composite rates on a common underwriting basis for a number of lines of insurance are determined in lieu of having separate rates applicable to the different exposure bases, such as payroll, sales, area, and so on, which would normally be applicable to the risk.

Premium Discount

In several states for liability insurance, and countrywide for boiler and machinery insurance and for workmen's compensation, "Premium Discount Plans" are in effect, reflecting standardized downward gradation of expenses by size of risk. The initial starting point for the reflection of such expense gradation is usually at the $1,000 premium point. Elsewhere, the various rating plans generally permit the reflection of expense savings based on an analysis of the individual risk situation.

COMPETITION

The objective of insurance ratemaking is to establish rates that will furnish proper provisions for losses and expenses during the period when such rates apply. To this end, actuaries have made significant progress in advancing the science of ratemaking. At the same time, the vigorous competition in the insurance business has engendered a high degree of flexibility in rating methods together with a willingness to experiment and to develop new coverages to meet the needs of the insurance-buying public. While rate regulation is in effect in all states, aggressive competition nevertheless has its place with the result that great freedom of choice as to rates, policy coverage, and degree of service afforded remains available to the purchaser of insurance.

SUGGESTED READINGS

LONGLEY-COOK, L. H. *An Introduction to Credibility Theory.* New York: Casualty Actuarial Society, 1962.

MARSHALL, RALPH M. *Workmen's Compensation Insurance Ratemaking.* Rev. ed. New York: Casualty Actuarial Society, 1961.

Studies by Members of the Casualty Actuarial Society: Automobile Insurance Rate Making. New York: Casualty Actuarial Society, 1961.

Chapter 46

UNDERWRITING IN LIABILITY INSURANCE AND RELATED LINES

BY HAROLD J. GINSBURGH

NATURE OF THE UNDERWRITING FUNCTION

At one time the "underwriting" function embraced all the functions connected with the insurance transaction. The underwriter appraised the risk, accepted (or rejected) it, set and collected the premium, and settled losses. While insurance was not "sold" in the present sense, the "underwriter" performed the sales function by being present with others like himself at a place where it was known they could be met by those seeking insurance.

With the great changes that have taken place in the economic and social structure of society, the institution of insurance has taken on enormously increased scope and complexity. Many different types of insurance now deal with a great variety of hazards. The insurer, instead of being a single individual familiar with and carrying out all phases of the insurance transaction, has become an organization predominantly of corporate form—in other words, an insurance company—in which the several elements of the insurance transaction are separate activities conducted by persons who specialize in them. Thus the person today designated an underwriter performs the specialized function of appraising the risk, deciding whether or not to accept it for his company (selection), and setting the price or premium for the insurance (rating). Dealing with the applicant for insurance and collecting the premiums (sales), physical investigation (engineering and inspection), dealing with claimants (loss settlement), and keeping the necessary records of the entire transaction (accounting and statistical), are the responsibilities of other specialized segments of the insurance organization or company.

In a modern multiple line insurance organization, all these necessary functions are of very great importance. They must be coordinated closely with each other and with the underwriting function; but upon the underwriting function, the selection and pricing of risks, must fall the major responsibility for the ultimate results of the insurance operation, in the form of profit or loss from "underwriting" (in the broad sense of the term).

The underwriting activities for liability and other types of insurance treated in Part V of this *Handbook* are variously organized, depending on the size and nature of the company's business, the geographic scope of its operations, the sales methods it uses, and the management principles it follows. Within the underwriting function as a whole underwriters fill a variety of roles. These depend on their knowledge and experience, and on their competence to devise and apply underwriting techniques or to direct others in their application. Underwriting responsibility ranges widely. At one extreme, a "desk" or operating underwriter, perhaps located in a branch or field office of his company, may deal entirely and immediately with individual risks in accordance with company general policy and rules of practice. At the other extreme, the underwriting executive may be concerned with the establishment and maintenance of company general underwriting policies, with the overall results achieved, and only occasionally with a particularly large or unusual risk. Whatever the level at which he works, and the aspect with which he is primarily concerned, the underwriter's function is fundamentally that of the selection and pricing of risks to be insured.

CONDITIONS AFFECTING RISKS AND THEIR UNDERWRITING

The conditions to be considered by the underwriter, whether he is underwriting an individual risk or formulating underwriting policy, include: (1) those pertaining to the risk itself and its environment and (2) those pertaining to the insuring company in relation to the risk.

Conditions Pertaining to the Risk and Its Environment

In this category of conditions are: first, those of legal or political character; second, those which are objective in nature, being physical or observable; and third, those which are subjective in nature, being psychological or moral.

Included in the group of legal conditions are those imposed by the common law, by statutory law, by judicial decisions, by decisions of governmental administrative or quasi-judicial bodies, and by decisions or orders of regulatory authorities. Thus, the legal environment becomes of paramount importance to the underwriter of so-called "third party" coverages, whether in the area of underwriting policy or in the area of individual risk underwriting.

A few examples will illustrate the situation. In some states the statutes make the user of certain materials, known to be highly poisonous or otherwise injurious, liable for injuries to others therefrom without regard to negligence—a condition referred to as "absolute liability." (See Chapter 31.) Some states impose absolute liability on the user of explosives, as in blasting. The underwriter considering liability coverage for prospective insureds will want to know, as part of the risk hazards, whether a manufacturer is using certain substances or materials, or whether a contractor will be doing blasting. He will also be concerned with the existence of an absolute (or strict) liability statute in the state of location, for this may heighten greatly the chance of loss arising from the hazards. An outstanding example of the influence of legal conditions is, of course, that of workmen's compensation insurance. Here the insurance given must be coextensive with the provisions of the state's workmen's compensation act, however amended while the policy is in effect, and subject further to continuing interpretation through quasi-judicial decisions of administrative bodies such as industrial accident boards and commissions. Finally, an example of another type of condition in this general group is the existence of a state regulatory policy, sometimes political in origin, which keeps rates well below their required level.

Another group of conditions pertaining to the risk and its environment, which always must be considered in underwriting insurance risks, are those which are objective in nature. They are of physical character and are either directly observable or manifested by records or other documents. The existence (or absence) of these conditions can be determined by inspection or similar means. Thus, for workmen's compensation insurance for a manufacturer the underwriter would want to know (1) the physical condition of the premises and immediate surroundings, (2) the physical conditions and quality of maintenance inside the plant, (3) the type of machines used, (4) the evidence of safe practice in the form of physical safeguards as well as safety rules and their enforcement, (5) the nature of the product, (6) the nature of the materials and the process used, (7) the record of accidents and losses, and so on. A complete list would include all facts bearing on the chance of loss which are obtainable by direct observation or perusal of records. These conditions of an objective and physical nature pertaining to the risk will vary in importance and significance between risks and certainly as between different types of insurance. For instance, the construction of a safe has the utmost materiality to burglary insurance, but has no bearing on liability insurance for the premises. It must be remembered that these objective factors are not necessarily physical constructions; they include such things as records of events or present procedures.

Conditions of a subjective nature constitute a third group of those pertaining to the risk and its environment. Though collectively usually called the "moral hazard" (see Chapter 14), they include psychological factors as well as those normally thought of as moral. Since they arise from human mental characteristics and attitudes, they are not easy to determine. Often they can be detected only through experienced interpretation of a variety of information and the correlation of given circumstances with related human attitudes. Nevertheless, they are of great importance in insurance underwriting. The honesty and integrity of the insured (or officers and other agents of an insured corporation) may be involved in claims under the policy, or in the payment of the proper premium. Often it is not dishonesty per se but general attitude which is significant. Habitual carelessness evidenced in the maintenance of property or in display and protection of insured valuables, excessive use of alcohol, or frequent association with persons known to be of criminal or bad moral character are indicators of moral hazard. These are examples of only a few of the elements of moral hazard, which can arise not only from the insured himself but also from those relatives and associates who may be involved with him in the subject matter of the insurance. Moral hazard may exist also in the general environment. An example is found in the kind of community attitude toward insurance companies and other corporations which in some localities produces inordinately large jury verdicts in liability cases.

Conditions Pertaining to the Insuring Company in Relation to the Risk

Distinguished from the conditions pertaining to the risk itself, and its environment, are those pertaining to the insuring company in relation to the risk. Among these an important condition is the character and extent of company service facilities, especially in the areas of inspection, safety engineering, and claim handling. The underwriter's decision to accept or to reject a risk may sometimes turn on his company's ability to bring to bear, at a reasonable cost, service facilities to modify or control conditions pertaining to the risk and its environment which otherwise might make the risk unacceptable. Generally speaking, a company undertaking to write a given line of insurance will have set up the service facilities required for it. However, the location of a particular risk or the nature of the services required may make the cost of providing these services, in relation to the other elements of the transaction, a matter of concern to the underwriter.

Another condition pertaining to the insuring company which affects the underwriting function is the size of the company's financial resources. This condition, in combination with the nature and extent of the reinsurance arrangements it makes, will govern the amount of liability the company can assume on any single risk. The relationship is not only a matter of underwriting prudence but is also in many cases the result of statutory or regulatory requirement.

MAJOR ASPECTS OF THE UNDERWRITING FUNCTION

General Underwriting Policy

Against the background of the conditions which affect the underwriting function, its major aspects can now be examined. The first of these here considered is the establishment of general underwriting policy for the company in which the function is operating. This policy is usually the responsibility of the company's chief underwriting officers, whose jurisdiction extends over its entire underwriting operation.

The total underwriting function in a given company may be split up among several departments, each dealing with a particular line or group of related lines of insurance (e.g., workmen's compensation and liability, automobile, burglary, glass, etc.). With the growth of package policies and multiple line operations, however, there is a tendency toward less segmentation. The development of underwriting policy will involve information and advice from the company's operating underwriters. It will also involve information and advice from the sales, claim, engineering, legal, and other departments of the company. It will take into account all pertinent conditions such as have been outlined in previous sections of this discussion.

The adopted statement of underwriting policy should govern the entire underwriting function, however this function may be organized departmentally in the company. It should delimit the geographical areas in which the company will operate to accept risks, and the lines of insurance (or classes within them) the company will or will not write. It should indicate whether in certain localities the company's business should be increased or should be restricted, and in what lines the increase or restriction should be emphasized. Furthermore, it should specify whether certain proportions should be sought and maintained among various classes of business written by the company.

Establishment of general underwriting policy may extend to reinsurance matters, such as the type, amount, and sources of reinsurance the company will employ in the several lines of insurance. Having regard to reinsurance and the company's own financial resources, general underwriting policy will limit the amount of liability the company should assume on a single risk in a given line of insurance. A statement of underwriting policy should be essentially one of objectives, principles, and basic structure—analogous to a constitutional document and not to a manual of operating procedure. Nevertheless, it is subject to change as experience of the company under it shows change to be warranted.

The Operating Framework

In order to implement general policy with consistent practice, officials in the company's underwriting department must proceed to erect the framework within which the underwriters will select and price individual risks. This important aspect of the underwriting function involves: first, preparation of insurance contracts and related forms as well as the many forms necessary for recording, organizing, and transmitting information for underwriting activities; second, choice of a rating system in existence or development of one of its own for each of the various lines of insurance; and third, the preparation of written material to guide the company's sales forces, whether agents or employees, in the submission of business.

The Insurance Contracts. The contract is a statement in specific terms of the insurance coverages and related services the insuring company is providing to its policyholder in return for the premium and various agreements from the policyholder. The underwriter is responsible for determining the substance of the contract—the nature and occasion of the loss insured against, the hazards or classes of hazards to be covered, specific hazards or classes of hazards to be excluded, and conditions under which the insurance will apply or not apply. For expression of this "underwriting intent" in language which will meet legal requirements, the underwriter turns for assistance to the legal department. He may also consult the claims department, whose function it is to apply the terms of the contract in actual situations.

In some instances, though not to the degree present in fire insurance, the scope of coverage and even the language of some liability and other insurance contracts will be specified, in whole or in part, in state statutes or regulations. The company may be a member of a rating organization which has adopted for a given insurance coverage "standard" language or "standard provisions" for contracts. In such cases the company then follows this standard wording.

Closely related to the policy are the endorsements and binder forms. The policy itself generally contains a section referred to as declarations or, less frequently, as warranties. The declarations include the name and address of the policyholder, information about the location of the risk, and perhaps information on previous insurance and losses, as well as information for the classification and rating of the risk. The underwriting department will prepare an application form for use by the policyholder or agent from which the declarations can be copied. Sometimes the underwriter will prepare an application or survey form of considerably broader scope than the declarations themselves, in order to obtain more information for risk appraisal.

Rating Systems. The establishment of rating systems for the various lines of insurance the company will write is an extremely important element in the underwriting department's responsibilities. It involves setting up the price structure which will determine the company's premium income for the risks it assumes. A rating system for a given line of insurance will include, with respect to defined coverages, (1) a set of classifications of risks, (2) classification rates, (3) rating plans for modification of classification rates to the requirements of individual risks where warranted, and (4) underwriting rules to govern the application of the classifications, the rates, and the rating plans.

Rating systems may be developed by individual companies, or by intercompany cooperative rating organizations which function through committees of company underwriters. The federal antitrust laws do not apply to such cooperative activities under certain conditions as specified in Public Law 15. Even as a member of a rating bureau, a company may deviate from the bureau's rating system, or may eventually decide to leave the organization in order to develop its own system.

Whether the underwriter participates directly in developing his company's own rating system, participates as a representative of his company within a rating organization, or is simply called upon to evaluate the efficacy of a rating system for his own company's use, he must understand the principles on which a rating system is based as well as the nature and structure of its several components. For example, it is important (1) that classification criteria be properly chosen, (2) that they be closely related to the loss potential, (3) that they be objective in character and not matters of individual subjective opinion, and (4) that they be readily and economically ascertainable by the company and its agents. These matters are particularly important in lines of insurance where the risk unit is small and numerous, as in private passenger automobile insurance, and where the classification is therefore the primary rating tool. Furthermore, such classifications should be as nearly homogeneous as is practicable with respect to the significant characteristics of the individual risks placed within them. From a practical viewpoint, the choice of a classification structure must strike a balance between the high administrative cost incident to a large number of relatively narrow classifications and the competitive vulnerability resulting from only a few very broad classifications.

In the development of rating systems, the underwriter can call upon the company's statistical department for experience records and upon the actuarial department for advice and assistance in both the theoretical and practical structure of rates and rating plans. The rating system as such is still an underwriting responsibility. Rating systems are an element of insurance which is subject to an especially high degree of state regulation. Once filed with a state authority, whether or not subject to formal approval or acceptance, a rating system must be adhered to in all particulars, until changed by a new filing.

Underwriting Guides for Field. A third element in the underwriting department's task of constructing the framework for selection and rating of risks is the preparation of guides for the sales function. The underwriting policy governing the company's operation must be made clear to the agents and salesmen, through whom the risks making up the company's business are submitted for the underwriter's consideration. The information should be given in statements which interpret underwriting policy in specific terms, so that neither producer nor underwriter will spend time unproductively on unwanted business. Thus these statements or guides usually list classes of risks in several categories. "Prohibited" risks are those the company does not wish to write. Those called "restricted," "questionable," or "conditional" are risks the company is willing to consider, but which the agent or salesman has no authority to bind without the specific consent of the company's underwriter in each case. Usually all other risks are in the third category, which the company will write freely and which the agent or salesman has authority to bind. Often this last category is not listed in detail, but is referred to as "all other risks." Sometimes, however, a company wishing to extend its business in certain directions will establish a list of "preferred" or "desirable" classes.

A class of risks may be placed on the "prohibited" list for various reasons. The class may present an extraordinary hazard or a catastrophe hazard the company does not wish to assume; the class may not be covered by the company's normal reinsurance arrangements; or the class may require specialized service facilities the company does not have and does not wish to set up. Examples of classes found on prohibited lists are coal mining and explosives manufacturing for workmen's compensation insurance, tent circuses for liability insurance, transportation of explosives for automobile insurance, loan companies and check-cashing services for robbery insurance. Not only classes of risks, but an entire coverage encountered within a general line of insurance otherwise written may be placed on a prohibited list. For example, some companies prohibit professional liability or directors' liability within the general liability line.

The designation "prohibited" is often interpreted to mean (1) that when the specified class or operation constitutes an important portion of the substance of the entire risk, the company will not accept the risk; but (2) that if the prohibited class or operation is found to exist only as a minor and incidental part of a sizeable risk otherwise highly desirable to the company, the underwriter may accept the entire risk, including the "prohibited" portion, rather than lose it to a competing company. This decision is indeed a matter of underwriting judgment involving a nice summing up of opposing factors. In some cases the underwriter finds a way to proceed by making special reinsurance or special service arrangements. The nature of "prohibited" lists is such that their scope will vary from company to company—though underwriting consensus produces a considerable degree of correspondence.

"Restricted," "questionable," or "conditional" lists will usually include classes and coverages in which inherent hazard, and consequently the probability of losses, is generally serious but varies to a considerable degree from risk to risk. Thus, a careful underwriting analysis is required, and the producer may not bind the insurance until the underwriter's approval has been obtained. An example of a "restricted" or "conditional" coverage, because of the variety of conditions encountered, might be contractual liability. A company might place machinery or engine manufacturing on its workmen's compensation "restricted" list, since one risk in such classes might present a serious occupational disease hazard in an incidental foundry, while another might buy all its castings from an outside source. In contradistinction to "prohibited" business, however, business in the "restricted" category is generally found acceptable in sufficient amounts to warrant submission of the classes for underwriting. Here, too, the relative weight of a questionable element in the whole of an otherwise desirable risk may bear on the underwriter's decision.

Selection of Risks

It is within the guidelines of policy and practice previously discussed that the operating underwriter carries on his primary task of analyzing, appraising, selecting, and rating risks for his company. The scope and complexity of the task, the nature of the technique applied, though not the nature of the responsibility, differ between two general categories—class rated business and individually rated business.

Class Rated. Class rated business consists of risks to which are applied the rates for the classifications in which they fall, without modification for individual risks. It should be mentioned that so-called rating plans for such risks, as in private passenger automobile insurance, are in reality methods of subclassification, producing smaller *categories* the components of which still carry the *average* rate for their group.

For the most part, class rated risks are found in personal lines, though certainly not entirely so. Generally speaking, class rated risks are risks the size of whose exposure to loss is small regardless of the nature or seriousness of the hazard involved. Examples are: the activities of a single individual for liability insurance; the existence of a single private residence or small retail store for liability insurance; and the operation of a single private passenger automobile. Usually the unit premium per risk is small, and so is the unit amount available for underwriting expense. The underwriter will plan his approach to risk selection accordingly. He will determine in advance certain specific conditions or characteristics, which are not already a part of classification criteria, which are indicators of physical or moral hazards (related to the line of insurance), and which are likely to produce large adverse variation from the class average. Information on these will be obtained from the application for insurance and from the risk inspection report ordered from independent investigating companies. The presence of certain of these conditions or some combination of them will constitute a basis for immediate rejection of the risk, or make acceptance conditional upon direct connection with other desirable business written by the company.

The underwriter's task is first to make certain the risk has been properly classified, and therefore properly rated, and second to review the specified factors beyond the class criteria which will determine the risk's acceptability. The underwriting policy of the company will, of course, influence the approach taken to class rated business, particularly in the nature and scope of conditions considered to make risks unacceptable.

Private passenger automobile insurance can be taken as an example of class rated business. An underwriting department might settle on the following items of information, concerning the applicant and the vehicle, to be reviewed in each case (detailed descriptions or qualifications of the items are not here given):

- Age, sex, and marital status
- Other occupants of household (drivers)
- Length of licensed driving experience
- Occupation and stability of employment
- Stability of residence
- Physical impairment
- Accident record
- Conviction record
- Insurance record (cancellation, refusal, nonrenewal)
- Use of alcohol or drugs
- Use of vehicle—purpose and extent
- Age, condition, and maintenance of vehicle
- Place vehicle kept when not in use

The list is illustrative, not necessarily exhaustive. Some specific degree of the condition disclosed by each item may be selected in advance for general application as the criterion for acceptance or rejection, either by itself or in relation to other criteria.

Individually Rated. The second general category of business for application of underwriting techniques is individually rated business. This business consists of risks, generally industrial and commercial enterprises, for which classification rates are modified by rating plans to produce rates applicable to the individual risk.

Individually rated risks are generally those whose exposure to loss is relatively large and usually complex. For automobile insurance, for example, instead of a single vehicle, the risk will be operating a fleet of vehicles. For liability insurance, instead of a single residence or small store, the risk will be operating a considerable industrial or commercial enterprise, with manifold activities, relationships, and obligations. Whether risks be small or large, class rated or individually rated, the underwriter's basic responsibility remains the same—so to select and rate risks as to produce an underwriting profit for his company. However, between the two categories, the scope and complexity of the underwriting problem differ and so will the underwriter's approach. Contrasted with class rated risks, individually rated risks usually present, and are affected by, a greater diversity of the legal, objective, and subjective conditions of the type outlined earlier in this discussion. Thus, a broader and more diversified experience is required of the underwriter. Though there may be a number of broad general areas to be analyzed in all cases, the underwriter must call on his experience to tell him what to look for specifically within these areas in each separate case presented to him.

The larger individually rated risk often involves the simultaneous consideration of several related lines of insurance, especially as respects the "third party" lines (workmen's compensation, the various forms of nonautomobile liability, and automobile liability). Sometimes other lines are included as well. Regardless of such a situation, however, for each line of insurance the underwriter's problem involves an analysis of the risk's operations and hazards, and an appraisal of the probable efficacy and cost of application of the company's service facilities—in control of hazards, management of claims, audit of exposure, and so on.

This analysis includes initial classification and the determination of rates and premium within the company's filed rating system and embraces consideration of relationships that may exist between the risk and the company in other lines of insurance. The underwriter will base his analysis, his rating, and his ultimate decision for acceptance or rejection primarily upon information from and about the risk, obtained by the agent, broker, or salesman, often under guidance by the underwriter. If the case warrants, inspections or surveys will be made by the company's service departments. The underwriter may also obtain information from business or financial reporting agencies. The insured's loss experience on the risk may be available through a rating organization of which the company is a member. The underwriter will consult his own company's experience in the insurance of the type of risk under consideration, as well as the experience of other companies, if available.

Obviously, the breadth and depth of information sought will vary greatly with the size and complexity of the risk under consideration. What must be kept in mind is that the underwriter needs much more information properly to select and rate individually rated risks than is required merely to classify them, and information in greater variety than is needed to select class rated business.

As has been mentioned, individually rated business usually is concerned with industrial and commercial enterprises. In the scope and direction of his appraisal, the underwriter will, of course, be influenced by the specific lines of insurance under consideration, as well as by the size and complexity of the risk. Having in mind the coverages to be given, the amount of liability to be assumed and the approximate magnitude of the premium applicable, he will consider the nature of the risk's business, its operations, and the products in which it deals—whether commodities or services. He will be interested in the risk's financial strength and stability, its credit standing, and in the reputation of its management for integrity and competence in its field. Physical and moral factors related to the coverages under consideration will be reviewed, as well as the claim and loss history of the risk.

The underwriter must be watchful of adverse selection, that is, an effort by a prospective insured to insure only those elements of his total risk within a general line of insurance which he believes present a high probability of loss, or to obtain more insurance on these elements than on other elements. In liability insurance, for example, such a situation may be evidenced by a request for much higher limits of liability on one element than on another—a particular type of coverage, a location, an operation, a product. These requests sometimes alert the underwriter to conditions otherwise not apparent. He responds on the theory that where there is smoke there is probably fire, and if the insured is concerned, the underwriter probably should be also.

The nature of underwriting analyses and determinations on individually rated risks of substantial size may be illustrated by a list of some of the matters that would be of concern to a hypothetical underwriter dealing with a submission of workmen's compensation and general liability insurance for a contractor in connection with a road building project:

The contractor:

Record of successful undertakings.
Financial position, working capital, and credit standing.
Practice in maintaining permanent supervisory group.
Record showing attitude toward safe practice (employees and public); co-operation with insurer.
Equipment; owned or rented.
Insurance loss experience record in lines considered.

The job:

Amount of contract price (as indication of size of project); beginning and termination dates.
Route of projected road and nature of terrain.
Density and character of population and structures adjacent to roadway.
Probability of blasting; nature of state law governing liability.
Use of existing or new right-of-way.
Requirements for maintenance of traffic.
Crossings of existing highways.
Crossings of railway lines; maintenance of rail traffic.
Type of road construction; number, type, and size of bridges.

The insurance:

Existence, extent, and insurance of subcontracting.
Coverages required; need for completed operations, contractual and railroad protective liability coverages.
Limits of liability requested.
Accessibility for company services in control of accidents and claims.
Appropriate rating plans and procedures within the company's filed rating systems; resulting rates and probable premium.

Not all of the foregoing might be applicable in some cases, while in others additional matters might arise for consideration. Furthermore, for the underwriter the question of acceptability is not divorced from the question of rate and premium. He may be willing to assume a risk for a given premium which he would not accept for a lesser amount. Thus, the flexibility of approach permitted by the company's filed rating systems is of considerable importance. For example, in the third party lines, retrospective rating has been a growing method of premium determination for the larger risks. It has its greatest utility on risks characterized by high loss frequency with low to moderate severity. It is not suited to risks at the other extreme—with low frequency and high catastrophe potential. An underwriter might be willing to accept a given risk only on the basis of retrospective rating, while he would refuse to accept another if retrospective rating were insisted upon by the prospective insured.

UNDERWRITER'S RELATIONSHIPS AND QUALITIES

From much of what has been said in this discussion of the underwriting function in a modern insurance company, it should be apparent that the operating underwriter does not carry on his work in a walled-off compartment. The information he must have to fulfill his responsibility comes to him through his company's sales and service functions. In fact, the agent or other salesman is at the first point of screening risks to be written by the company. Quite often, a practical aspect of the operating underwriter's exercise of his responsibility lies in his appraisal of a given agent's care in picking risks for submission to the company, as evidenced by the record on a substantial volume of business placed by him. For example, in the case of risk submitted by an agent who provides a large volume of business to the company, the extent of the underwriter's probing and his final decision on the risk may be influenced to a considerable degree by the company's overall record on the total business produced by the agent. The competent underwriter learns to work with his service departments. On occasion his willingness to accept a given risk may be influenced by his reliance on these departments to improve and control conditions which otherwise would give him pause.

After a risk has been put on the books of a company, the underwriter's task is not over. He will constantly check on his judgments by keeping under surveillance the business he has accepted. Arrangements usually will be made in a company for the service departments to alert the underwriter to any adverse developments in a risk or other change in conditions. In any event, before the end of the policy term, each risk will be reviewed for renewal, when the company's own record on the coverage can aid the decision to renew or not.

Statistics can constitute an important tool for the operating underwriter. He should understand their use and abuse, whether they be statistics for an individual risk, a class, a territory, or a whole line of insurance. If he is to use statistical material as an aid in risk appraisal or as a means of checking on the results of past activity he must understand, to some extent at least, its interpretation—the credibility that can be attached to its indications, the pitfalls of averages and their comparison, and the like.

The competent and successful casualty underwriter can never "stand still" in knowledge of the subject matter with which he deals. His education is a continuing and broad process. To do his job well he should keep abreast of social, political, and legal changes; of the movement of population; of developments in the materials and methods of industry and commerce; of scientific developments; and of the interaction of all of these with developments in insurance, its coverages, and its rating processes. Seeking and maintaining knowledge of these things and bringing it to bear on a tremendous variety of situations are the bases of the fascination and absorbing interest of casualty insurance underwriting.

POSITIVE FUNCTION

Too often underwriting is looked upon as a negative activity. It is thought that the underwriter's first impulse is to reject. But the competent, knowledgeable underwriter understands that the acceptance of risks at a profit is the aim of the insurance enterprise. He views his function as fundamentally a positive one, namely, to select the risks to produce a profitable and growing business for his company. His knowledge, experience, powers of analysis, and judgment may sometimes enable him to accept risks to the benefit of his company which a less informed, less experienced underwriter might be fearful to consider. Nevertheless, it is the mark of the competent underwriter that he does not hesitate to reject a risk when there is valid reason to do so. The key to competent, productive underwriting is the application of *informed* and *reasoned* judgment.

SUGGESTED READINGS

MEHR, ROBERT I., AND CAMMACK, EMERSON. *Principles of Insurance.* 3d ed. Homewood, Ill.: Richard D. Irwin, Inc., 1961. Chap. 25.

MICHELBACHER, G. F. *Multiple-Line Insurance.* New York: McGraw-Hill Book Co., Inc., 1957. Chaps. 9, 11.

SNIDER, H. WAYNE (ed.). *Readings in Property and Casualty Insurance.* Homewood, Ill.: Richard D. Irwin, Inc., 1959. Part III.

Chapter 47

LOSS ADJUSTMENT IN LIABILITY INSURANCE AND RELATED LINES

BY BENJAMIN HORTON

Many of the points discussed in earlier chapters on loss adjustment in other lines are equally valid in respect to the several types of insurance treated in Part V of this *Handbook*. (See Chapters 16, 22, and 30.) In this chapter numerous matters peculiar to liability and related insurance claims are treated.

Liability insurance losses arise from situations where the person asserting the claim is not a party to the insurance contract. For example, an automobile owner who is insured for public liability is involved in an accident in which a pedestrian is injured. The pedestrian claimant seeks recovery called "damages." Since he is not named in the policy, he is called a "third party." This type of action is referred to as a "third-party claim."

Some Part V insurance claims are paid directly to the insured, for example, dishonesty insurance claims. Most claims, however, are paid "on behalf" of an insured. Both types will be discussed in this chapter, but initial and principal attention will be given to third-party claims such as arise in public liability and workmen's compensation and employers' liability insurance.

THE ADJUSTER

The adjusting function begins with the man in the field who actually conducts the necessary investigation and deals with the people involved in the claim. He is commonly called an "adjuster." He may be a salaried employee of the insurance company involved or be an individual who works on a fee basis.

Salaried employees of insurance companies who handle claims are usually referred to as "staff adjusters." Fee adjusters include practicing lawyers who handle claims along with their law practice, company-owned adjustment bureaus, and "independent" adjusters. The company staffs, the bureaus, and the independents include many men who are law graduates—but many more who are not. It is essential, however, that any third-party adjuster become familiar with numerous basic concepts of the law which are embodied in the adjusting process. Contrasted to the general practices in fire and allied insurance, relatively fewer liability and "miscellaneous" insurance claims are handled by large company-owned bureaus.

Third-party claim adjusting calls for an extraordinarily wide variety of activities which necessarily involves more than one person. There is first the interpretation of one or more insurance policies which may be quite technical in phraseology. This interpretation spills over into several important and complicated branches of the law, including contracts, torts, evidence, and damages. Next, there is the evaluation of the results of injuries (including their cost in dollars), the temporary and permanent effects on the individual, and the extent of pain and suffering. Third, claims involve just about every type of property known to man, with the problems of determination of replacement cost, extent of depreciation, possibility and cost of repair, and the concurrent problem of loss of use. Fourth, since all claims involve people, the problem of dealing with other humans is ever-present.

To become as self-reliant as possible, an aspiring adjuster should learn as much as he can about the several categories of the subjects mentioned above. Such education necessarily goes beyond any formal schooling which the individual may have undertaken. Some of it comes only with experience.

In earlier chapters where characteristics of successful adjusters are discussed, a knack for fact-finding is stressed. This ability is likewise of crucial importance in effective liability claims work. This point is easily seen when one remembers, for example, (1) that negligence is the basis for many liability insurance claims, and (2) that negligence involves questions of fact.

Third-party claim adjusting has at least one dimension not generally found in adjusting in other lines of insurance. A significant percentage of third-party claims involves litigation. The liability of the insurance company is determined either by agreement between the adjuster and the claimant or by the courts. Where agreement fails, litigation is required. The American system of justice as it applies to claims for damage by one party against another is based on the ancient legal concept of adversaries. Regardless of the facts of any individual claim, the law presumes a dispute. The insurance carrier in effect takes over the defense of one of those parties. Thus the adjuster, as the servant of the carrier, becomes a party to that dispute. He is not and cannot be an impartial observer. At all times he must remember that he is responsible to a principal, and that, until there is final disposition of a claim, his principal is an adversary in the finest traditions of justice of the English-speaking peoples. In this role the adjuster must remember that the basic insuring clause in most liability policies provides for payment on behalf of the insured of all sums which the insured shall become *legally obligated* to pay as *damages* for bodily injury or property damage. The adjuster must of necessity understand what is meant by the words "legally obligated" and "damages." Every action he takes is, in the final analysis, pointed toward those words.

THIRD-PARTY CLAIMS

Adjustment Function Generally

In previous chapters the content and structure of third-party policies have been described. The point is worth repeating that the intent of those coverages is (1) to provide a defense against third-party claims, (2) to pay the expense connected with the defense, and (3) to indemnify the insured up to the policy limits for his loss arising from a verdict by the courts in the event they determine him to be liable for damages arising from an activity or situation covered in the policy. No claim for damages by a third party matures until there is a verdict from a court. Settlement of such claims by agreement prior to final verdict is the result of purely voluntary actions of the insurance carrier and the claimant. The initiative for such settlement rests solely with the carrier.

Generally speaking, third-party claims involve alleged bodily injury, death, or property damage produced by negligent action on the part of an insured. There are special areas, of course, such as malpractice, personal injury rather than bodily injury, special liability under certain federal statutes, and workmen's compensation, where actions not involving negligence are insured. In all cases, the adjuster attempts to determine whether or not the insured would probably be found by the courts to be legally liable to the claimant.

In cases involving legal liability, the courts award monetary judgments to the claimant called "damages." Such judgments are either compensatory, being a recognition of his actual monetary loss plus his general damage, or punitive, being designed to punish the defendant. The awards for pure monetary loss are usually referred to as "special damages."

Most jurisdictions recognize the ancient rule of contributory negligence as being a bar to recovery on the part of the claimant. However, some states have the comparative negligence rule which authorizes the courts to apportion the degrees of negligence and contributory negligence and base their awards accordingly. For a more extended treatment of this topic see Chapter 31.

In approaching a claim, the adjuster must appraise the probabilities involved, both as to liability and damage. With the aid of his probability estimate, he should use a combination of experience and judgment to discount the value of the claim to the claimant. The figure at which he arrives becomes the amount the adjuster should be willing to recommend as voluntary payment for disposition of the claim. This figure must be realistic. If too high, the company's loss experience will be adversely affected. If too low, the company will be exposed to the needless expense of litigation plus the possibility of an award for damages in excess of the amount for which the claim could have been settled.

Third-party claims other than in special situations such as workmen's compensation are disposed of by the payment of money to the claimant and the execution by the claimant of a binding release. In some situations, such as claims for wrongful death or injuries to infants, a court order authorizing a settlement is required. Litigated claims require satisfaction of the judgment, including payment of interest and court costs. All payments for damages, of course, are controlled by the limits of liability as contained in the declarations of the policy. (For an occasional exception to this statement see the subsection in this chapter entitled "Judgments in Excess of Policy Limits.")

Investigation

Third-party claims require specific investigation of the basic problems of coverage, liability, and damage. This investigation is reported by the adjuster to the company. Outlines of the reporting procedures recommended for automobile and general liability claims by the National Association of Independent Insurance Adjusters are included in Appendix H of this *Handbook*. It is essential that the adjuster conduct this investigation with an open mind and that he obtain and report the facts.

While there are certain basic principles of law involved, the vast majority of cases turns on the facts. If negligence is defined in brief as the failure to use due care under the circumstances, two questions become important: Just what were the circumstances? What actions were taken by either party involved in the accident or occurrence which might be held to be failure to use due care? The adjuster normally starts his investigation with a report from some individual. He also examines the scene and the instrumentalities involved. Physical evidence at times may be most revealing. In many cases such evidence is preserved through such means as photographs, diagrams, or actual retention. In any case the adjuster must have an adequate mental image of the scene and the physical details so as to be able to interview the participants and the witnesses properly.

The adjuster normally takes either written or oral statements from various individuals. He should use extreme care so as to be certain that each statement represents the actual version of the person interviewed. An unskilled adjuster can easily and unwittingly color the interview. In interviewing participants and witnesses, the adjuster's aim should be to obtain and preserve their recollection of an accident or other occurrence as they saw it. For each individual interviewed the adjuster should obtain the name, age, address, occupation, marital status, and such other information as will identify him currently and in the future. The interviewee's position in or relationship to the actual chain of the events should be specified and his description obtained of pertinent events which transpired before, during, and after the occurrence. If the claim involves an accident arising out of moving objects, vehicles, or persons, the chain begins before motion is observed, carries through the accident itself, and continues until all motion has ceased. The interview should also cover the results of the occurrence insofar as they are known to the individual being interviewed.

There are various ways of recording interviews. One of the most popular is a simple narrative form statement prepared by the adjuster and signed by the witness, in which the substance of the interview is set forth. In other situations a stenographer is present and the entire interview is transcribed and certified. In still other cases an electronic device is used to record the entire conversation.

In addition to his interview the adjuster should meticulously examine the physical evidence, including all pertinent documentary evidence available. The investigation as to liability is completed by obtaining and preserving such documentary evidence as he can locate. Examples include public records, deeds, leases, contracts, or other pertinent papers.

Coverage

The handling of all insurance claims is based ultimately on the insurance contract. The adjuster must take it as he finds it; he has no authority to extend or otherwise modify the contract. He must determine whether or not the person against whom the claim is made is an insured protected by the policy. He must ascertain whether or not the claim arose from an activity or operation embraced within the insurance contract. In regard to both the insured and the activity, he must doublecheck to make sure that no exclusion is applicable. Each one of his actions must be in accordance with the policy conditions and his duties must include advice and counsel to the insured as to the insured's duties as prescribed by the insurance contract. Generally speaking, the adjuster can accept coverage but does not deny or disclaim it. In the event a coverage question arises, the question itself is reported along with whatever investigation was required to the company for consideration and decision.

Adjusters must remain aware at all times of the legal doctrines of waiver and estoppel. An adjuster can and sometimes does inadvertently undertake actions or make statements which can amount to a legal waiver of a valid right on the part of the company to disclaim coverage. The concept of estoppel is quite similar. It applies when the actions or statements are such that the company is legally estopped from asserting some defense which in the absence of such actions or statements would have been available to it. When coverage questions arise, the alert adjuster, therefore, will deliver to the insured a letter setting forth the coverage problem and stating that any actions in proceeding further do not constitute a waiver of any of the provisions of the insurance contract. This statement is known as a "Reservation of Rights." It is also common practice to obtain the insured's signature on a document called a "Non-Waiver Agreement" which contains about the same information as the reservation of rights letter.

Legal Liability

The law operates in such a manner as to create many forms of legal liability. One example of liability is taxes. However, liability contracts are so drawn that, through the wording of the insuring agreement and the exclusions, the principal coverage involved is a legal claim made by one person against another because of bodily injury or property damage. It is the adjuster's problem to determine the degrees of negligence on the part of all concerned and to estimate the probabilities in the event of litigation.

Damages

Since a third-party claim hinges on legal liability for damage, it is essential to know what can be anticipated if there is a jury verdict. Special damage or actual monetary loss can be estimated. Attempts can be made to verify a property loss; property has a value, known or unknown. The property damaged either is or is not repairable for a figure within that value. If there is a claim for loss of use of property, the value of such loss of use is normally not too difficult to measure. Thus, the determination of special damage on property claims is usually subject to reasonably precise evaluation.

The item of special damage for bodily injury claims is likewise susceptible of measurement. The adjuster simply verifies the actual expense for medical treatment, hospitalization, drugs, nurses, prosthetic devices, and such. Loss of income is also an item of special damage, although frequently not as easy to determine. Thus, by means of hard work the adjuster usually can determine the amount of special damage within a reasonable degree of accuracy, even in situations where he is receiving little or no cooperation from the claimant.

The estimation of general damage, however, is another matter. This category is what the jury may award for other than actual monetary loss. The prime examples are "pain and suffering" and permanent disability. The adjuster uses a combination of medical testimony, experience, simple judgment, and other elements to determine within a rather wide range a typical jury's award for general damage. The wide fluctuations from area to area and from time to time within given areas complicate these estimates.

Special problems arise in claims for wrongful death. Not only does the legal measure of damage vary from one state to another, but also different interests may present the claim in various states. In some jurisdictions the claim adheres to the widow or other dependents, while in other jurisdictions it is presented by the representative of the estate of the deceased. One simplification is found in the statutory limitations as to amount of recovery for wrongful death which exist in a number of states.

Contribution

The doctrine of subrogation sometimes is a factor in public liability claims. A more important factor, however, is that of "contribution." This problem arises when the facts are such that possibly two or more defendants not insured under the same policy may be held liable to the claimant.

Investigation of the facts should always be pointed towards discovery of all parties potentially liable. When two or more adjusters representing different companies are working on a case, they often cooperate. When they complete their respective investigations as to the facts of the accident, they quite frequently agree as to percentage of liability to be assumed by each company and arrange for only one adjuster to handle the actual negotiations for settlement.

The matter of contribution also spills over in some instances to insurance other than liability which may be available to an insured or claimant. Sometimes the availability of more than one medical expense coverage, for example, may influence—at least indirectly—the nature or size of third-party claims.

Appraisal

An adjuster seldom, if ever, knows all the facts. Certainly, he does not in the initial stages of a liability claim. However, it is necessary that the appraisal or evaluation of a liability claim be undertaken at the time of the initial report or knowledge of it and be reviewed continuingly throughout the duration of the claim.

One reason for initial appraisal and continuing reevaluation concerns the problem of reserves. The accuracy of the financial statement of the company depends to a considerable extent upon the accuracy of the individual reserves set up for its unresolved claims. These figures are frequently revised as more information is obtained.

It is also necessary to evaluate claims from the standpoint of out-of-court settlement possibilities. Generally speaking, amicable and just settlements benefit both claimant and insurance carrier. However, if the proposed settlements are in excess of a reasonable figure, litigation is much the better recourse. Consequently, the point should be noted once again that the determination of what is a proper figure is a critically important claim function.

There are no final rules for claim evaluation. The approach necessarily is one of study of the facts and the applicable law. Beyond the facts and the law, the adjuster has to make assumptions concerning the unknown. In this process he usually has to speculate about negligence, contributory negligence, liability or the lack of it, property damage, loss of use, general damages, permanent injury, pain and suffering, and numerous other factors which can influence a verdict. He then makes a decision which ultimately is arbitrary as to what amount, if any, he is willing to recommend as payment to avoid or dispose of litigation.

Claims Larger than Liability Limits

One special problem is worthy of comment. Many third-party claims and even many judgments are in excess of policy limits. In numerous cases insurance companies have been ordered to pay judgments beyond the policy limits. In the face of these cases, any threat of a judgment in excess of the policy limits produces rather ominous overtones. Most claims, in fact, are of such nature that there is little reason to anticipate an excess judgment.

Experienced adjusters, however, learn to be wary and are never casual about any claim until it is settled. The excess judgment claims which do arise stem generally from three types of situations.

First, some cases involve policies with limits so modest and obvious negligence so gross and serious that it is only reasonable to anticipate a verdict in excess of policy limits. These cases seldom involve adjusting difficulties. It is customary for the adjuster to disclose and tender the policy limit of liability. If this disclosure and tender are handled in a timely and proper manner, there should be no danger to the company.

The second type of excess cases comes from a small but important minority of claims which turn sour and which leave the company vulnerable to charges of negligence or even bad faith in claims handling. Often, there is some question as to an "opportunity" the adjuster had but did not accept to settle out of court for a much smaller figure than the resulting judgment. In other situations there may be facts which make it doubtful that an adverse verdict for any amount will come forth but which suggest that, should the jury decide against the insured, it might do so on a grand scale.

Finally, there is the freak type of case which, by all odds, should lead to small judgments but which, for reasons known only to the juries, produces surprisingly large judgments. Of the three types, this one is perhaps the most frustrating to the adjuster.

There are two different rules of law in the various jurisdictions as to insurer liability for amounts in excess of policy limits. In a minority of states, the courts take a "negligence" approach. In short, this approach provides that the company can be held liable for the excess judgment because of negligence in reaching its decisions as to how to defend the claim. This rule can be a very harsh one because it seems that there is almost a presumption of negligence on the part of the company in handling the case. It can be most difficult for the insurance company to prove it was not negligent in making its various decisions which basically involve a substantial degree of judgment and even occasionally some "guesswork."

The majority rule in the excess judgment situation is that the company is presumed to use due care and good faith in arriving at its decision. Any refutation of this presumption requires solid proof by the claimant as to company negligence or bad faith. The effect of this rule is that policy limits virtually should be ignored in arriving at claim decisions. The adjusters, in effect, should arrive at the claims decisions and act on them as though coverage were far in excess of the potential verdict involved in the claim. The only rub is that the adjuster cannot be certain that this approach will be taken in a given case by a given court.

One additional aspect of judgments in excess of policy limits involves the duality or even multiplicity of claims, some of which may be quite trivial, arising out of the same accident or occurrence. Frequently, the situation arises where no single claim has a discernible potential of exceeding the per person limit, but the aggregate of liability has a very strong potential of a total of verdicts in excess of the per accident limit. This sort of situation can present a question as to how much of each claim will be paid out of the insurance proceeds. When the judgments arise chronologically out of different suits, the insurance proceeds are usually dispersed on a "first-come-first-served" basis until the policy accident or occurrence limit is exhausted. When multiple judgments arise simultaneously out of one suit, the insurance funds may be rationed to the claimants in the ratio of total funds over total claims. Where the application of this ratio would cause the per person limit to be exceeded in respect to a given claim, the excess is prorated in comparable fashion among other eligible claimants. As a practical matter, when there is doubt as to how a policy limit should be distributed (but no doubt that the limit would be exhausted), the money is tendered by the company to the court under a "bill of interpleader." Furthermore, there are few instances in multiple-claim judgments where insurers have been held liable beyond policy limits.

There can be no easy or simple solution to the problem of judgments in excess of policy limits. Adjusters would probably be wise to expect the courts to hold the insurance carriers to an increasing degree of accountability to the insureds and to the public. It is most important for every person involved in third-party claim handling to use extreme care and to proceed in total good faith. Anything less might render the carrier liable for a judgment in excess of policy limits. It is always advisable for the insured to be consulted and to approve in advance the plan of action followed.

WORKMEN'S COMPENSATION CLAIMS

Nature

Claims for workmen's compensation are actually for third-party liability (employee versus employer) but the legal liability is of a very special nature. It arises under statute and not from tortious acts. The various workmen's compensation laws are designed to compensate the injured workman regardless of fault. (See Chapter 35.) The laws substitute specified awards for such injuries in place of the damages discussed earlier in this chapter. Thus, the problems of determination of negligence and contributory negligence do not affect claims.

Coverage

While the policy insures the liability of the employer to the employee under the workmen's compensation law, the company may be liable directly to the injured employee or his beneficiary. (See Condition 8 of the policy.) With only very few exclusions and the minimum of simple policy conditions, coverage determination is usually not difficult. However, it is still necessary for the adjuster to verify that coverage is in order and that the claim is one which is proper under the policy.

The typical workmen's compensation statute applies to a workman whose injury is one "arising out of and in the course of his employment." Liability by the employer (and thus the insurer) can be denied to the workman only if his injury does not meet this "double-barrelled" text. It is necessary for the adjuster to know and understand the application of this statutory rule in his particular state. Even when statutes are identical in wording, interpretation by administrative bodies can vary from one jurisdiction to another. It is the adjuster's duty to investigate and determine whether or not the claimant is entitled to compensation benefits.

The various acts generally provide for payment of (1) medical expense, including prosthetic devices, (2) disability or "loss of time" payments, and (3) in respect to fatal injuries, death benefits.

Medical Expenses. Some acts give the employee free choice of physicians, while others state that the employer shall provide reasonable medical care. In either case, the adjuster closely watches the medical treatment. The adjuster's goal is for the claimant to recover as quickly as possible. He attempts to see to it that the physician is competent and qualified to treat the injury. He normally has a great deal to say about the use of specialists. He normally participates in decisions relating to surgical procedures or other special treatments. His responsibility includes the verification of proper medical expense and the payment therefor.

Disability. Disability may be partial or total. The acts provide for payment during disability and set forth a method for determination of the rate to be paid. This rate is based on earnings, with maximum and minimum amounts set forth. Loss of time payments in fact are often at the statutory maximum. The adjuster is responsible for computation of the rate, and for recommendation of payment of the benefit provided.

Disability is also either temporary or permanent. Payments for temporary disability are made weekly and terminate when the claimant recovers or returns to work. Disputes can and do arise as to termination of temporary disability, but such cases constitute a small minority of total claims.

Statutes containing schedules for permanent injuries (total disability or partial) apply in many cases. Some injuries, such as blindness in both eyes or double limb amputations, are by definition permanent and total. In some states the adjuster and claimant agree as to the extent of permanent injury. In others, certain designated officials either examine and pass on the agreement or make their own award to the claimant. In all situations the adjuster investigates and appraises the claim from the standpoint of permanent disability.

Death. Claims for death benefits usually are reasonably simple to handle as far as determination of amounts is concerned. The matter of whether or not the death was accidental and whether or not it arose out of and in the course of employment may become awkward to establish. Also, questions frequently arise as to the identity of proper beneficiaries or disposition of the funds when no claiming beneficiaries can be located.

Subrogation

The typical compensation act provides that if the claimant is injured through the negligence of a third party other than his employer he may collect compensation benefits and also pursue his remedy against the wrongdoer. In such cases, the employer, and through him the insurance carrier, may be entitled to reimbursement from collections from the third party. Such reimbursement is for amounts up to the workmen's compensation benefits. When such a situation exists and the employee recovers from a third party, the adjuster takes steps to recover for the carrier the benefits paid and to do so in a manner consistent with the laws of the particular jurisdiction. If necessary, counsel is retained and suit is filed.

Administration

Disputes can and do arise. The typical statute calls for a state compensation board to hear the disputes through referees appointed by the board. The findings of the board usually are final as to the facts of the case. It issues awards based on its findings. Either party may appeal to the courts if there is a question of law. Depending on the laws of the state involved, the adjuster will either appear before the board or engage counsel to represent the company.

The processing of compensation claims also presents administrative problems in the claims office. Medical expense is paid as bills are received unless there is indication that they will exceed the statutory limit (sometimes stated in terms of number of days of medical care) found in some state acts. Disability payments, both temporary and permanent, usually are made on a weekly basis. Thus, workmen's compensation insurance involves much more office detail than do most other types of insurance claims.

Employers' Common Law Liability

The Workmen's Compensation and Employers' Liability Policy, of course, provides coverage to the employer to protect him against actions by employees at common law rather than under the compensation statutes. When such claims are presented, the adjuster works along the same general lines discussed earlier for third-party liability claims.

OTHER COVERAGES

Automobile Physical Damage

This coverage is pure property insurance. This coverage normally is written in a combination policy with public liability cover. However, the adjustments are handled in the same general manner as for personal property involved in fire or inland marine losses. The services of the National Automobile Theft Bureau and various law enforcement agencies are an integral part of the settlement of theft claims.

Medical Payments Insurance

Many liability insurance contracts provide for reimbursement of medical expense incurred by an insured or others as a result of certain types of accidents. In such cases the adjuster examines the coverage and determines to whom it applies. He investigates and verifies the amount of the claim. He doublechecks the policy limit and recommends the appropriate payments.

Dishonesty

There are many insurance contracts dealing with and providing coverage against loss from dishonesty. Only a very general survey of the adjustment function can be presented as the contracts themselves differ so greatly.

As with all other claims, the adjuster must first investigate from the standpoint of coverage. He must examine his policy closely so that he can apply its provisions as to the type of crime, where and how it occurred, and the person who perpetrated it. Definitions of dishonest acts—such as burglary—are critically important in this type of adjusting. Before he begins to adjust the claim, the adjuster should seek all the facts of all phases of the crime and try to identify the criminals.

Dishonesty claims quite frequently are overstated, due basically to the "very human" tendency to include various shortages of money or goods arising from unknown causes in the claim for known dishonesty. It is the obligation of the insured to prove the claim to be a proper one under the policy or bond. Normally, he is called on to support the claim with records. The adjuster must verify all phases of the claim, including particularly the correctness of the amount.

Dishonesty loss payments always involve the possibility of recovery, even though the probability may be remote. This restoration comes not only with physical recovery of the property involved but also through subrogation proceedings against the thief, if he is known. The adjuster examines every claim for recovery possibilities and takes appropriate steps to obtain it if indicated.

A FIDUCIARY

The adjuster has many and varied responsibilities. However, no matter what action he is taking at a particular time, he must always keep in mind that he is acting on behalf of a principal, the insurance company. In litigated third-party claims he is a participant in the adversary system of justice. He cannot possibly function properly unless he recognizes that he owes complete fidelity to his principal for whom he acts in a fiduciary capacity.

The very word "fiduciary" connotes integrity. Integrity includes, but involves a great deal more than, "honesty" as the term is normally used. It includes faithful performance, diligent investigations, complete and accurate reporting, realistic appraisals of possibilities and probabilities, and properly conducted negotiations. The adjuster should always be a person of complete integrity. The now classic words of the late Justice Cardozo, applying to fiduciaries in general, apply to adjusters. The Justice said: "Not honesty alone but the punctilio of an honor the most sensitive is then the standard of behavior."[1]

The adjuster's daily contacts are with the public, and particularly with persons involved in or with spectators to unfortunate occurrences. The

[1] When this opinion was given Mr. Cardozo was speaking as a judge of the New York Court of Appeals. See *Meinhard* v. *Salmon*, 164 N.E. 545 (1928) for the full statement.

adjuster is the visible image of insurance at work. While recognizing his obligations to his principal, he must approach each person with courtesy, consideration, and attention. He must attempt to create respect for himself and his principal, even though his decisions must of necessity be disappointing at times to those with whom he deals.

SUGGESTED READINGS

Adjusters Reference Guide. Published quarterly by the Insurance Field Company, Louisville, Kentucky, in cooperation with the National Association of Independent Insurance Adjusters.

DONALDSON, JAMES H. *Casualty Claim Practice.* Homewood, Ill.: Richard D. Irwin, Inc., 1964.

MAGARICK, PATRICK. *Successful Handling of Casualty Claims.* Englewood Cliffs, N.J.: Parker Publishing Co., 1955.

PART VI

Multiple Line Insurance

Chapter 48

EVOLUTION OF MULTIPLE LINE INSURANCE

BY DAVID L. BICKELHAUPT

Had an insurance expert in the United States gone to sleep a few years ago and not awakened until today, he would have a tremendous adjustment to make in reorientation to current insurance ideas and practices. One of the most significant changes observable as he reviewed the interim would be the trend toward multiple line insurance.

The essence of *multiple line* insurance is the combination of the two traditional lines, or general types, of insurance known as *fire* insurance and *casualty* insurance. These lines were, for a long time in the history of American insurance, separated by law and custom, unlike European insurance which had few such restrictions. Today all the states permit fire and casualty insurance to be written in one contract by an insurance company or group. Multiple line company groups, multiple line companies, and multiple line contracts are all part of the trend, with the combination of fire and casualty insurance in a single contract being the most important recent development.

The reasons why the multiple line trend has occurred and the methods by which the change has been achieved are the subject of this chapter.

PURPOSES AND SIGNIFICANCE OF MULTIPLE LINE INSURANCE

The underlying basic motives influencing company management decisions in entering multiple line operations are desires for (1) profits, (2) power, (3) prestige, and (4) benefits to policyholders.[1] The relative strength of each of these motives depends on the circumstances involved in the decision-making process of the individual companies.

Perhaps a better way of classifying such basic objectives is to identify as goals the improvements which multiple line insurance may achieve in

[1] David L. Bickelhaupt, *Transition to Multiple-Line Insurance Companies* (Homewood, Ill.: Richard D. Irwin, Inc., 1961), p. 45.

(1) costs (lower), (2) coverage (more and better), and (3) convenience (greater). These goals are logical ones for companies, agents, and policyholders alike. For the insurance company, they may be attained by economies of size, reduction of overlapping or duplicate services, stability of loss ratios through diversification among many perils, greater satisfaction and ease of loss adjustment under broader policies, larger insurance amounts in relation to values exposed to loss, less adverse selection against the company, fewer contracts and records, and simplified billing systems.

Specific motives for writing multiple line insurance may also exist. Examples of these more detailed motives are the hopes for maintaining or improving the industry position of a company, future increased capacity for writing more and larger risks because of better spread of loss, broader multiple line services on a wider geographic basis, and the unification of company departments into integrated operational units.

Multiple line underwriting is an accomplished fact in many facets of insurance. Most of the major insurance companies are now operating on a multiple line basis. Certainly, however, not all companies have thrown aside the "American System" of limiting and compartmenting insurance. Mono-line insurance *companies* can still be identified, operating successfully in one or a few closely related parts of the insurance business. Many companies that are licensed for multiple line operations are and shall be for many years, practically speaking, single line insurers with a decided emphasis on either property or liability insurance.

Insurance *contracts,* too, are often multiple line in nature. The best example of a multiple line insurance contract is perhaps the Homeowners Policy. This contract, combining fire, theft, and liability insurance in one "package" contract, accounted for only $30,000 in premiums in 1950. Homeowners contract sales dramatically increased to $179 million in 1956 and $770 million in 1960.[2] Additional examples include the rapid introduction of forms for office contents, industrial and commercial property, public and institutional property, and farmowners as well as special multi-peril contracts for many specific businesses. In 1962 commercial multiple-peril net written premiums were $157 million and Homeowners premiums were over $1 billion.[3] Multiple line contracts thus have grown in a decade from almost nothing to well over $1 *billion* in sales!

WHAT MULTIPLE LINE INSURANCE INCLUDES

If the whole field of insurance today were divided into logical parts, the divisions would include: (1) property, (2) liability, (3) life, and

[2] Frederic J. Hunt, Jr., "Homeowners—The First Decade," *Proceedings of the Casualty Actuarial Society,* Vol. 49 (1962), pp. 12–36.

[3] *Best's Fire and Casualty Aggregates and Averages* (New York: A. M. Best Co., 1963), pp. 118–19, and pp. 196–97.

(4) health insurance. Unfortunately for the student of insurance, the growth of insurance has not always followed the logic of theory. History, tradition, and legal requirements have played important parts in developing insurance in separate compartments, or lines of insurance. For many years, marine, fire, and life insurance were the titles for the major lines in the United States. Companies specialized in providing separate financial protection against such perils.

Casualty insurance did not appear until the latter part of the nineteenth century, its most rapid growth occurring in the present century. Liability, theft, automobile, workmen's compensation, and health insurance as well as miscellaneous categories of coverage such as glass, boiler and machinery, and fidelity and surety bonds often were thrown together under definitions in the state laws as casualty insurance. A company would write one, a few, or all of these kinds of casualty insurance by meeting the capital and surplus requirements of the states in which it did business.

In recent years a somewhat different classification is more meaningful, even though laws of the states may still use the traditional groupings. Briefly, marine, fire, and allied lines of insurance are referred to as *property* insurance; casualty insurance has become primarily *liability* insurance as public liability, automobile, and workmen's compensation insurance have grown in importance; and *life and health*[4] insurance have become more closely related.

Although multiple line developed historically as a term combining fire and casualty insurance, one might argue today for a redefinition of its use to mean property plus liability insurance.[5] Most of the legal barriers between these major kinds of insurance have been removed.

All lines insurance is a newer, but in many ways parallel development in insurance. The term includes property, liability *and* life and health insurance written together by one company, company group, or contract.

---

[4] Note the inconsistency of *health* insurance, which developed both within casualty insurance companies and life insurance companies. Today it appears that the life companies predominate, writing about two thirds of the total health insurance. Together, life and health perils are often combined as "personal" insurance based on the insured himself, as opposed to losses involving "property" of the policyholder.

[5] Although far from universally used, the terms are gradually appearing. The American Risk and Insurance Association has formed several committees on terminology in recent years. One of these, the Committee on Property and Liability Terminology, had the unusual and difficult task of deciding first what the committee's title should be! After many meetings of some of the best insurance minds in the U.S., the indicated title was chosen [see *The Journal of Insurance*, Vol. XXIV (December, 1962), p. 558]. Obviously, fire, marine, and casualty will not disappear from the language of insurance immediately. Logic may suggest consistency in future use of the term property and liability, but the "drag of custom," as C. A. Kulp called it, will undoubtedly cause the terms fire and casualty to be used for many years. Doubters need only look to the widespread continued use of the older terms in the names of major insurance companies today.

Evidence of this trend abounded during the last decade, too, as "probably three-fourths of the larger property-and-casualty companies or groups now own a life affiliate."[6] Many companies have added life insurance facilities in the past few years. The development of "package companies" writing all kinds of insurance, perhaps in the future in a single contract of protection, deserves its own special analysis. However, multiple line insurance and its growth will point out many of the objectives, benefits, problems, and pitfalls of the broader all-lines movement.

GROWTH OF THE MULTIPLE LINE CONCEPT

Early Mono-Line Specialization

As one learns about multiple line insurance, he might easily question why the combination of fire and casualty insurance has been so belated in arriving on the American scene. The answer is not obvious, especially for a business which has built its growth and stability on the concept of proper spreading of losses.

Diversification has long been a major goal of insurance. The fallacy of too great a geographical concentration of property risks has been dramatized in stories about the Chicago and San Francisco fires, and in such modern examples as the Texas City or Hurricane Donna disasters. How is it, then, that insurance companies who practiced the old adage of "not putting all their eggs in one basket" were apparently tardy in adapting the same idea to product diversification by lines of insurance?

The full answer lies somewhat buried in history. Research about the first American insurance companies brings forth evidence that almost all insurance in the late eighteenth and early nineteenth centuries was written by mono-line companies. Although often not limited by statute or charter to doing business in one line, these early pioneers voluntarily limited themselves to specialized parts of the insurance field. The reasons are partially conjecture, but the small size of many of the early insurance companies, the lack of capital for expansion, and other factors undoubtedly were important. It seemed part of the philosophy of the times to "stick to one's own business," and not venture needlessly into more uncertain kinds of insurance as the needs for other coverages grew.

The idea persisted past the middle of the nineteenth century, when the first insurance departments in the states appeared to provide supervision

[6] Benjamin N. Woodson, "All-Lines Underwriting: Five Years Later." *Journal of the American Society of Chartered Life Underwriters*, Vol. XVI (Summer, 1962), p. 239. Note the use of the words *property and casualty* in this quote, an example of inconsistency which will also probably continue for many years. The author of this article is a close observer of the all-lines trend, and his earlier article "All-Lines Underwriting: New Fashion or New Era?", in Vol. XII (Winter, 1957) of the *Journal of the American Society of Chartered Life Underwriters* should be required reading for students of this phenomenon in insurance.

for the by then well-established business of insurance. The legislatures of the states and the administrators in the insurance departments decided that limiting insurance companies to one or a few closely related kinds of business was good regulation as well as good business. It was easier to provide laws for insurance "by line," with specific licensing and taxation laws applied separately to most kinds of insurance. So the concept of mono-line insurance changed from what had been merely business practice to the laws of the states, and the "American" system of compartmenting insurance was firmly established.

This development occurred in spite of common use of the multiple line idea for many years in Europe. In Lloyd's of London and other English insurers, all kinds of insurance had been combined successfully for centuries.[7] The other European nations also did not usually restrict insurance companies to specific kinds of insurance, and then as now most laws and regulations applied to insurance in general rather than to individual lines of insurance. In the United States the trend almost from the start was toward specialization rather than diversification by lines of insurance. Thus it remained until the twentieth century.

Contrasting Trends of the Early 1900's

The legal obstacles to multiple line insurance were quite simple and effective. In order to do business in most states, a company had to obtain a charter and a license which specified the kinds of insurance contracts it could write. Under the licensing laws a fire company could not write insurance on casualty perils, and a casualty company could not write insurance on fire perils.

A few states had laws which permitted multiple line insurance, but the "Appleton Rule" of New York State was a deterrent to any insurance companies using the broader powers. This rule, first set forth about 1900, said that out-of-state companies must follow all domestic company laws. Thus a Wisconsin insurance company, even if Wisconsin statutes permitted multiple line insurance, could not write such contracts in New York, in Wisconsin, *or in any other state* if it wanted to do business in New York. Since many of the companies wanted to be admitted to New York State (for prestige, market, or other reasons) the Appleton Rule effectively discouraged multiple line insurance companies outside of New York. The extraterritorial effect of this important rule continued its restrictions on underwriting powers of companies until 1949 when New York permitted full multiple line companies.

Legal barriers against multiple line insurance were not complete. A

---

[7] See William D. Winter, "The Multiple-Line Concept," *Examination of Insurance Companies* (New York Insurance Department, Volume I, 1954); and A. J. Bohlinger and T. C. Morrill, *Insurance Supervision and Practice in England* (New York Insurance Department, 1948).

single company could not write both fire and casualty insurance in the early 1900's (a few exceptions existed by special charters), and in general that situation continued until mid-century. However, beginning in the 1920's, the laws of many states did permit several companies to conduct a multiple line business as a *group* of companies. A fire company could own a casualty company, or a casualty company own a fire company, and circumvent the restrictive nature of the state laws. Such company groups or "fleets" became common in the 1920's and were especially significant in the rising automobile insurance market of that decade. By 1940 almost 100 company groups were in operation.[8]

Much of the early history of multiple line insurance centers around these groups of companies. They combined fire and casualty insurance in operating their business, even though legally such perils could not yet be combined in one company or one contract. One must be careful in studying the multiple line trend to differentiate between the growth of multiple line groups in the 1920's and 1930's, as opposed to the later development of single multiple line companies and multiple line policy contracts in the 1940's and 1950's.

Another fast-growing part of the insurance market was inland marine insurance. As railroad and motor truck transportation risks grew, inland marine insurance coverages expanded to provide broad protection. Oftentimes such contracts were exempt from the restrictive laws preventing fire and casualty companies from writing multiple line insurance. Many of the early marine insurance "block" contracts were multiple line in nature, combining fire, theft, and a wide variety of other perils. "Floater" policies on movable goods often were written on an "all risk" basis.

The trend was confined in its scope by the Nation-Wide Definition and Interpretation of the Insuring Powers of Marine and Transportation Underwriters in 1933. (See Chapter 23.) An industry agreement, this method of permitting multiple line contracts for certain purposes and types of inland marine risks was codified into the laws of most states. Insurers were put back into their "compartments," and the traditional American system of mono-line insurance was strengthened again. The inland marine contracts were specifically limited to insurance on goods in shipment, instrumentalities of transportation such as bridges and tunnels, and certain definite categories of personal property floater risks.

Modern Multiple Line Legislation

Although the tide was subdued until the 1940's, it could not be stemmed. Increasing agitation for broader multiple line powers by fire and casualty insurance companies appeared. The most significant landmark in this growing urge to permit multiple line insurance was the work of the Diemand Committee of the National Association of Insurance Commissioners. The report of the Diemand Committee in 1944 strongly

---

[8] *Best's Fire and Casualty Aggregates and Averages, op. cit.*, 1960, p. 15.

advocated immediate but limited multiple line powers. It recommended that the state laws be changed as soon as enabling legislation could be passed to permit any fire or casualty company to write multiple line insurance of five specific kinds: (1) outside the U.S., (2) reinsurance, (3) automobile insurance, (4) aircraft insurance, and (5) personal property floaters.

The logic of modern needs prevailed. The result was "partial" multiple line laws, which appeared in most of the states between 1944 and 1947. By 1947, these five kinds of multiple line insurance usually could be written by a single insurance company, licensed either as a fire company or a casualty company. These statutes did not permit complete or "full" multiple line insurance by a company, but they were indicative of the, by then, strong trend toward multiple line operations.

"Full" multiple line insurance laws permitting a single fire or casualty company to write almost any kinds of perils except life insurance were the final step. A few states already had such laws, and in fact over 20 states had such legislation in the statutes before other states passed the "partial" laws. The trends overlapped, although the significant turning point was action by the state of New York. The Appleton Rule referred to above was the brake applied to out-of-state companies which might otherwise have "gone multiple line" sooner.

From a legal standpoint the year 1949 was the culmination of the trend toward multiple line insurance laws. New York's "full" multiple line law[9] was passed, and the new era of fire-casualty insurance began in earnest. By 1951 all but four states, and by 1955 the last state (Ohio), permitted multiple line insurance companies.

RECENT CHANGES TO MULTIPLE LINE INSURANCE

With an understanding of the background of multiple line insurance, one can appreciate the fact that progress has been slow and that a trend has not been consistently apparent. During the last two decades, however, this trend has been almost overwhelming in its rapidity and widespread effects.

Methods of Change

The changes to multiple line companies have been accomplished primarily in three ways: (1) multiple line company groups (often used as an intermediate legal step), (2) new company charters or charter amend-

[9] Chapter 667, Laws of 1949, New York State. The title of the act, "To Amend the Insurance Law, in Relation to the Organization, Licensing and Financial Requirements of Insurance Companies," is interesting. Apparently the title of "Multiple Line" did not always receive legislative favor, for the idea of fire-casualty combinations was still not wholeheartedly accepted. Evidence of the difficulties encountered in securing legislative approval also included the fact that many states took a decade to pass the "partial" and then "full" multiple line laws, and that five states still permit multiple line companies only by departmental ruling rather than specific laws.

ments, and (3) company mergers. The changes made by the vast majority of insurance companies were gradual. Legal and operational changes often involved a series of steps over a period of years. However, looking at the insurance business as a whole causes one to be amazed at the extent of the trend within one generation.

Groups of companies operating more or less as multiple line entities have been an important method of combining fire and casualty insurance. Legislation since the 1920's has permitted companies in a given fleet to do business together, the techniques involving combination of operations through either stock ownership, common management personnel, or reinsurance arrangements. The growth of multiple line company groups has been steady since the 1940's, and today over 140 major groups including almost 400 insurance companies are in business. One might imagine a declining role for these group operations since 1950 when the multiple line laws of most states permitted a single company to write all fire and casualty kinds of insurance. However, the number of groups continues to rise, as mono-line insurance companies purchase other companies or begin new affiliates. Although mergers may reduce the number of company groups eventually, market growth and expansion into multiple line business still continue to increase the number of groups. Such insurance company groups account for almost two thirds of the total fire and casualty business today.[10]

Individual insurance companies, as separate corporate entities or as members of company groups, are now also a major part of multiple line insurance. Through new charters or amendments to old charters many companies have achieved multiple line status during recent decades. Variations in the state laws prevent generalization from being accurate without exceptions, but it is fair to state that most of these changes have occurred since 1940. The trend has been most pronounced since 1949, and today it is rare to find a major insurance company that does not do business in both fire and casualty fields. The increased number of charter amendments[11] in the early 1950's indicates that the normal method for an established single line insurer to embark on multiple line operations was to expand the charter powers through amendments permitting the company to write additional kinds of insurance. Even new companies formed in the past decade have often been established as single line insurers, then later expanded to new lines as their surplus growth permitted them to meet financial requirements for multiple line licensing.

---

[10] *Best's Fire and Casualty Aggregates and Averages, op. cit.*, 1963, p. 15. About $10.5 billion of $16.5 billion premiums in 1962 were accounted for by some 435 companies organized into 156 company groups.

[11] Bickelhaupt, *op. cit.*, p. 79. Amendments increased from 183 in 1940–45 to 327 in 1950–55 in New York State.

Company mergers, in which one company is absorbed into another, are an increasing phenomenon of the 1960's. Mergers often have multiple line diversification as a major objective.[12] While formation of company groups and expansion of charters and licensing powers prevailed in the two decades immediately preceding 1950, mergers of existing companies have been a major trend since the late 1950's. One rarely reads an insurance periodical today without noting some proposed, in process, or completed merger.[13] Many of these mergers involve not only a change to a multiple line company, but often are a combination of two or more multiple line companies into a larger multiple line insurer.[14]

Requirements for Multiple Line Operations

In order to become a multiple line insurer, a single company or a company group must meet certain legal requirements in each of the states in which insurance is to be sold. Some of these requirements are classified as general legal procedures, others are primarily financial, and a third category includes a wide variety of operational changes necessitated by the broadened product diversification of multiple line insurance.

The legal and financial requirements start with the first steps which must be taken to obtain *multiple line* authority. This process is more inclusive than just legal sanction under the new multiple line laws to combine fire and casualty insurance. It means the whole series of procedures to achieve proper incorporation, charter powers, and licensing under the various state laws. Written proposals, public advertisements, stockholder or policyholder approval, hearings, and filing of charter and bylaws are required in most states to attain or change legal incorporation. Then application is made for a license, or certificate of *authority,* to write insurance of specified kinds.

Before a company acquires a license and attains multiple line authority, the most important requirement which must be met is the minimum capital and surplus standard. The insurance codes of the states vary greatly in setting these minimums. In several states a multiple line insurer needs only surplus of $100,000 to obtain a license. Other states, such as California, Connecticut, New Jersey, and New York, require over $2,000,000 of policyholders' surplus (capital plus surplus) before a full multiple line license will be issued. The range of financial requirements is amazing, the strictest state requiring 35 times as much policyholders' surplus as

---

[12] John D. Brundage, "The Urge to Merge," *The Annals of the Society of Chartered Property Casualty Underwriters,* Vol. 12 (January, 1960), p. 80.

[13] As an example, see *The National Underwriter,* Vol. 67 (January 25, 1963), pp. 1 and 17.

[14] K. R. Rathert, C.P.C.U., "Insurance Mergers—What Next?" *The Annals of the Society of Chartered Property and Casualty Underwriters,* Vol. 13 (Winter, 1960), p. 221.

does the most lenient state. The average state sets the minimum policyholders' surplus required at between $500,000 and $750,000.

The financial requirements are obviously for the purpose of assuring basic financial solvency of the companies. The state laws specify that surplus requirements by the companies must be met before beginning business. Many states also require the amounts to be maintained as the company operates its multiple line business.

The wide scope of operational changes required by multiple line insurance is significant. The major functions of insurance companies have all been responsive to the multiple line trend. These changes may not be required in a legal sense, but they have occurred on a widespread basis. Perhaps some of them are not essential requirements for multiple line action; instead, they are labeled as results for the majority of the insurance companies.

Marketing of insurance is one such area tremendously affected by multiple line ideas. Broader contracts combining fire and allied lines, theft, and liability are present in almost all insurance markets today. Account selling, embracing all kinds of insurance, is advocated for both personal and business policyholders. The advantages of one contract, one bill, and one agent are extolled in the insurance advertisements. The changes which such a new system has brought to the insurance business within a few years are spectacular! They pervade almost every phase of agent and company marketing techniques, from recruiting and training agents to prospecting for policyholders. Contracts have been redesigned, manuals and rates changed, commissions combined, bills consolidated in premium financing plans, and sales departments reorganized. The adjustments are still continuing.

Nor have other major insurance functions escaped the effects of multiple line changes. Underwriting, rating, and loss payment in the multiple line era are separately discussed in Chapters 51 and 52. Administrative services within insurance companies have been realigned to meet new multiple line needs. Records, filing systems, statistics, and research activities have been reappraised to accomplish objectives more efficiently. Insurance supervision by the state has changed to include multiple line examinations and licenses for agents. Executives have broadened their knowledge to include new fields of insurance. Legal departments have studied new cases as they have occurred under changed wording in new contracts. In all, few areas of the insurance business have escaped the requirements and results of the multiple line trend.

THE FUTURE OF MULTIPLE LINE INSURANCE

No ordinary crystal ball can be used to forecast the future for multiple line insurance. The task is too complex. The continuing effects of the trend have been so diverse that it would take a hundred soothsayers with mystic globes of cinemascope proportions to make the necessary predictions.

One might argue that the multiple line trend is complete. A case can be made for such an assertion; loopholes in the argument readily appear, however, as the nature of the insurance business is analyzed. For example, suppose that multiple line insurance is glossed over with the remark that all-lines (property, liability, *life, and health*) insurance is the major trend of the present decade. Such a general statement, though undoubtedly true to some extent, is misleading in its implication that the change to multiple line has been completed.

As a new billion-dollar-a-year business, multiple line insurance is well established. A sizeable proportion of the property and liability insurance business is now written in multiple line contracts. The domination of the market is more clearly seen when multiple line insurance companies are analyzed. One hundred and seventy-two stock and mutual multiple line companies wrote over $7.4 billion of the total $16.5 billion property-liability premiums in 1962.[15] The point was made earlier that two thirds of the sales are now made by some 160 multiple line company groups.

Consider, however, the incompleteness of the changes. Hundreds of the 3,500 or more property and liability insurance companies still are mono-line, and many of those firms have no immediate plans for expansion into other kinds of insurance. (For example, see Chapter 11.) Specialty companies in automobile, fire, glass, boiler and machinery, title, credit, bonds, and professional liability insurance still exist. Some of these have deep roots in the business and have succeeded in single lines of insurance through the advantages of specialization. Hundreds of companies write only fire and allied lines business on farm properties. Diversification of business by lines is not yet a panacea for all these companies, and may not be for many years in the future, if ever.

Special note could be made of the incomplete changes which exist in insurance regulation under which multiple line insurance companies operate. Most rating bureaus are presently organized on a mono-line basis, one primary exception being the Multi-Line Insurance Rating Bureau. Capital and surplus requirements for insurance companies do little to encourage multiple line insurance, for the majority of the states merely total the individual requirements of single lines to establish the multiple line requirements. Standard insurance contract wording, as in the Standard Fire Policy, must be used in the new multiple line contracts.

Multiple line insurance is not all laws and contracts, either. It is *people,* and a sizeable portion of the 600,000 persons[16] employed in property and liability insurance is trained in and dedicated to specific kinds of insur-

---

[15] *Best's Fire and Casualty Aggregates and Averages, op. cit.,* 1963, pp. 42 and 148.

[16] *Insurance Facts,* 1964 (New York: Insurance Information Institute), p. 7.

ance. At least two of the three generations of persons now employed in insurance grew up under and gained their primary knowledge and experience on a mono-line basis. Such a situation cannot change completely in a few years. Adjustments can and will be made, but they will be gradual in many respects. Retraining, rehiring, and rethinking are all part of evolution toward multiple line insurance which is still occurring.

The rapid progress has been amazing in the perspective of history. It is continuing, and it is merging in some aspects of growth with the newer and broader all-lines trend. The factors which slow the changes are many. They include general reluctance to change, the costs of change, the normal conservatism of most financial institutions including insurance, the manpower shortages, the regulatory requirements, tradition, the advantages of alternative methods, and many others.

It is reasonable to predict continued and significant growth in multiple line insurance. In succeeding chapters in Part VI the personal and commercial multiple line insurance contracts, and the underwriting and loss payment problems of the new era of multiple line insurance are discussed.

SUGGESTED READINGS

BICKELHAUPT, DAVID L. *Transition to Multiple-Line Insurance Companies.* Homewood, Ill.: Richard D. Irwin, Inc., 1961.

BLANCHARD, R. H. "Insularity in Insurance," *Proceedings of the Casualty Actuarial Society,* Vol. XXVIII (1941–42), pp. 279–82.

BOHLINGER, A. J., AND MORRILL, T. C. *Insurance Supervision and Practice in England.* New York Insurance Department, 1948.

BRUNDAGE, JOHN D. "The Urge to Merge," *The Annals of the Society of Chartered Property Casualty Underwriters,* Vol. 12 (January, 1960), p. 80.

CAHILL, J. "Multiple-line Underwriting," *Proceedings of the Casualty Actuarial Society,* Vol. XXXVI (November, 1949), pp. 1–8.

DAVIS, S. C. "Impact of Multiple-line Underwriting on the Capital Structure of Insurance Companies," address given at the American Association of University Teachers of Insurance, December 27, 1957.

DIEMAND, J. A. "Developments in Comprehensive Property-Casualty Insurance," *Journal of the American Association of University Teachers of Insurance,* Vol. XIII (March, 1946), p. 60.

HUNT, FREDERIC J., JR. "Homeowners—The First Decade," *Proceedings of the Casualty Actuarial Society,* Vol. 49 (1962), pp. 12–36.

MAGEE, JOHN H., AND BICKELHAUPT, DAVID L. *General Insurance.* 7th ed. Homewood, Ill.: Richard D. Irwin, Inc., 1964.

MCGILL, DAN M. (ed.). *All Lines Insurance.* Homewood, Ill.: Richard D. Irwin, Inc., 1960.

MICHELBACHER, G. F. *Multiple-Line Insurance.* New York: McGraw-Hill Book Co., Inc., 1957. Chap. 1.

PERLET, HARRY F. "Multi-Peril Trends," *Proceedings of the Thirteenth Annual Insurance Conference.* Columbus: Ohio State University Publications, College of Commerce Conference Series Number C-148, March, 1962, p. 141.

PIERCE, JOHN E. *Development of Comprehensive Insurance for the Household.* Homewood, Ill.: Richard D. Irwin, Inc., 1958.

WINTER, W. D. "The Multiple-Line Concept," *Examination of Insurance Companies.* New York Insurance Department, Vol. I (1954).

WOODSON, B. N. "All-lines Underwriting: New Fashion or New Era," *The Journal of the American Society of Chartered Life Underwriters,* Vol. XII (Winter, 1957), p. 69, and "All-lines Underwriting: Five Years Later," Vol. XVI (Summer, 1962), p. 239.

Chapter 49

HOMEOWNERS AND OTHER PERSONAL PACKAGES

BY H. R. HEILMAN

The Homeowners Policy may be defined as a contract which combines on an indivisible basis property and liability insurance required to protect an individual's investment in his home. Many different Homeowners Policies are available providing different degrees of protection in a variety of ways. All of them have three common characteristics. They have high minimum requirements of coverage and amounts of insurance; they contain both first-party and third-party insurance; and the premium is indivisible. This chapter is given over to a discussion of the Homeowners and other personal packages.

EARLY VERSIONS

In the previous chapter the developments in the multiple line field which made the Homeowners Policy possible are described. At the time of this writing the Homeowners contract is the most significant product of that development, important not only in its own right but because the decisions which made it possible opened the way for other multiple line contracts.

Like all important insurance developments the Homeowners Policy has deep roots and was influenced by earlier types of coverage. One of these, the Householders Comprehensive Policy had been written in England for many years and some version was provided by Lloyd's before 1914. While it borrowed from older plans, the Homeowners Policy introduced important new ideas and represented an advance over any previous contract.

When the Diemand Committee (see Chapter 48) was undertaking its multiple line studies in 1943 and 1944, its members decided at the outset to aim for a unanimous report. A majority favored legislation which would permit a Householders Comprehensive Policy but this recommendation was not included because some members did not agree. There was a view that such a policy would be so expensive that only the rich could afford it. On this point John Diemand observed:

> I am not thinking of it from the standpoint of the rich man. In my own territory I am thinking of the 400,000 individually owned homes around Philadelphia. . . . I think that form can be made to appeal to that particular fellow.[1]

First Homeowners Policy

Multiple line legislation was passed in Pennsylvania in 1949 making it possible to provide comprehensive coverage for "that fellow" and he was particularly eligible for such coverage. At that moment in history, the middle-class American family was enjoying an unprecedented increase in prosperity. Following World War II millions of these families were acquiring homes of their own and equipping them with expensive furniture and laborsaving devices.

This great mass market was not being serviced adequately by the insurance industry. A survey made in 1949 showed that many families had never been solicited for insurance beyond that which their mortgagee required. Fire insurance on homes was usually written for the amount of the mortgage and was not increased to follow the inflationary upsweep of values. Personal property was even less adequately covered and relatively few individuals bought personal liability or theft protection. These essential coverages were not bought because the insurance agent could not afford to sell them. The small premium which each separate contract would develop was inadequate to justify the expense of soliciting, policywriting, and premium collecting. The obvious need was for a simple package policy combining all these coverages with a convenient installment payment plan.

In the fall of 1950 the Insurance Company of North America introduced the first Homeowners Policies which did all these things. One of these contracts, the Homeowners Comprehensive Policy, contained all the distinctive features which today set Homeowners Policies and rating plans apart from other kinds of insurance.

Multiple Peril Insurance Rating Organization

The development of such multiple line contracts presented a very difficult problem to most insurers. Companies generally relied on rating bureaus to design and rate their contracts and each existing rating bureau was limited to one of the several compartmentalized sections of the business.

As an answer to this problem, a group of stock companies organized a national multiple line rating bureau in the spring of 1951. The bureau was

[1] From "Proceedings of Multiple Line Underwriting Committee of the Committee on Laws and Legislation of the N.A.I.C." at a meeting on January 5, 1944.

named the Multiple Peril Insurance Rating Organization—in the alphabetical parlance of the trade "MPIRO." Its purpose was to deal with "all risk," multiple-peril, and other policies written for an indivisible premium.

By the fall of 1952 MPIRO had filed Homeowners Policies for its members in four states and a year later this number had increased to 19 states. In that year, 1953, Homeowners premiums totalled $2,900,000. (See Chapter 50 for additional comments about MPIRO.)

Interbureau Insurance Advisory Group

While MPIRO and Insurance Company of North America officials were working hard to gain acceptance of the indivisible premium concept which defined the Homeowners Policy as a new kind of insurance, officials in a strong segment of the stock insurance industry were working equally hard to upset this concept. (See Chapter 50 for more discussion of this point.) These individuals considered it essential to require these policies to be treated as collections of separate coverages. Under this view the Homeowners Policy was a fire policy to which had been added a liability policy, a theft policy, and certain extensions in coverage. They insisted that each premium and loss must be separated into these components and added to the statistics of those classes.

In many states these interests attempted to persuade regulatory officials and state legislatures that the indivisible premium approach should be prohibited by law. In at least one state this same effort is being made as of this writing.

At the same time, these companies were losing dwelling premiums to the Homeowners Policy and accordingly formed an organization to develop a competitive divisible policy. The organization was named Interbureau Insurance Advisory Group and acted as an advisory organization rather than a rating bureau. In the fall of 1954 Interbureau had its policy ready which was filed jointly by the fire and casualty rating bureaus.

This policy was called the Comprehensive Dwelling Policy or "CDP." It was designed to have a high degree of flexibility with no percentage or mandatory relationship between the various coverages, leaving the insured relatively free to purchase amounts of insurance in any one coverage group to fit his personal needs. With this emphasis on divisible premiums, optional coverages, and optional amounts, the CDP was in many ways an approach to packaging exactly opposite to the Homeowners approach.

Conflicts and Developments

From 1954 to 1956 competition was keen among companies selling the MPIRO Homeowners Policies, independent companies selling their own Homeowners Policies, and Interbureau companies pushing the CDP.

While the CDP was introduced as an alternative to the Homeowners Policy, it soon became apparent that the latter was more popular because of its simplicity and economy. By 1955 Interbureau had set up its own Homeowners statistical plan and companies serviced by that organization were writing Homeowners business using filings made by the various state rating bureaus. At the same time, many MPIRO companies were writing the CDP. The result was that by 1956 most companies were writing both policies with Homeowners gaining steadily.

In the spring of 1956 representatives of the two organizations, MPIRO and Interbureau, began to discuss consolidation which was finally accomplished in May of 1957. The successor organization was the Multi-Peril Insurance Conference, known as "MIC." A year later MIC produced its residential program designed to be a compromise between the Homeowners and CDP plans.

The contracts so developed were called "New Homeowners" Policies. (Later as rate and form changes took place, the changed policies were called "New New Homeowners" and "New New New Homeowners.") The program for these contracts was a compromise. On the one hand, MIC served as an advisory organization, following the Interbureau precedent. On the other, the contract followed closely the older MPIRO Homeowners program with an indivisible premium policy. The principal differences in the newer policies were the reduced rates and changed terminology.[2]

CURRENT HOMEOWNERS FORMS

Basic Features

Separate Kind of Insurance. Throughout its introductory period nearly all the conflicts and misunderstandings were caused by failure to grasp the most important characteristic of all true package policies. The Homeowners Policy is not a fire policy with extensions of coverage, nor is it a collection of contracts which can be bought separately. It is instead a separate kind of insurance different from the sum of its parts. This difference is produced by the other important basic features listed below.

Integrated Coverage. All Homeowners Policies include protection on

[2] Curtis M. Elliott, Professor of Insurance at the University of Nebraska, made the statement: "The so-called New Homeowners is not really a combination of the old Homeowners and the Comprehensive Dwelling policy as it is so advertised. . . . It is nothing more than a slightly changed Homeowners." [Panel on "Packages Policies" at a meeting of the Kansas Association of Independent Insurance Agents in Wichita as reported in the *National Underwriter,* Vol. 62 (Oct. 3, 1958), p. 30.] Similarly, Newell G. Alford, Jr., Deputy Superintendent of Insurance of New York, found in a formal opinion that the New York Fire Insurance Rating Organization's "New New Homeowners" program was not fundamentally different from the older Homeowners plan. [See Opinion in the matter of NYFIRO, NBCU, and IMIB Hearing Pursuant to Section 186 of the Insurance Law (of New York) relating to Homeowners Policies, Aug. 28, 1963.]

the dwelling and its contents, protection against loss by theft, and personal liability coverage. The insured is not permitted to select only those coverages where he may consider his exposure greatest.

Fixed Relationships. Minimum amounts are required for various coverages and the amount of coverage on household contents bears a fixed relationship to the amount of insurance on the dwelling building. While the contents amount may be increased, it cannot be reduced below the standard percentage. In addition, theft insurance is provided in the full amount of this contents coverage.

Indivisible Premium. A single indivisible premium applies to the whole policy and no share of this premium can be identified as applying to any portion of the coverage. This feature is one of the key reasons for the expense saving which the policy provides. One item is booked for accounting and statistical purposes instead of many.

Forms Available. Broad personal liability insurance is provided in all forms used with Homeowners and Tenants Policies. The differences among the forms apply to property insurance, and are discussed in detail under Coverages and Perils. The forms are as follows:

Homeowners Standard Form (A or 1)—Named peril coverage on buildings and personal property.

Homeowners Broad Form (B or 2)—Broader named peril coverage on buildings and personal property.

Homeowners Broad Form with Special Building Endorsement (B+ or 3 + 4)—"All risk" coverage on buildings, broad named perils on personal property.

Homeowners Comprehensive Form (C or 5)—"All risk" coverage on buildings and personal property.

Tenants Broad Form (Tenants B or Form 4)—Broad named peril coverage on personal property.

Tenants C—"All risk" coverage on personal property.

Eligibility Requirements. There are five requirements the insured must meet to be eligible for a Homeowners contract. Since Tenants forms are designed for the insured who rents an apartment or house, some of these will not apply:

1. He must own the described dwelling.
2. He must occupy it as his permanent (not seasonal) residence.
3. The dwelling must be used exclusively for residential purposes (but professional office use is permitted).
4. Not more than one additional family nor more than two roomers may have residence in the dwelling.
5. The insured must not engage in farming as his principal occupation. (Such insured might be eligible for the Farmowners Policy. See later discussion in this chapter.)

Coverages

Property Insurance—Section I. Property insurance is provided in Section I of the policy and four separate coverages are always included.

1. *Coverage A—Dwelling.* This coverage is similar to that provided for a dwelling under regular fire insurance forms. (See Chapter 6.) This coverage also includes a 5 percent extension to cover trees and plants against certain of the named perils, but not windstorm or hail. The minimum amount of Coverage A permitted on the Homeowners Standard Form (A or 1) and Broad Form (B or 2) is $8,000. On the Comprehensive Form (C or 5), the minimum is $15,000.

Like the Dwelling Broad Form and Special Forms, replacement cost coverage (see Chapter 4) applies automatically if the amount of insurance under Coverage A equals at least 80 percent of the replacement cost of the dwelling, or if the loss is less than $1,000 and also less than 5 percent of the insurance under that coverage.

2. *Coverage B—Private Structures.* A separate amount equal to 10 percent of the amount of Coverage A applies to private structures such as storage sheds or garages located on the premises and appertaining to the premises. Replacement cost coverage applies as in Coverage A.

3. *Coverage C—Unscheduled Personal Property.* Coverage C applies to all personal property, except that which is specifically described and insured by endorsement to the Homeowners Policy or on a separate scheduled Personal Articles Floater. Personal property covered under Coverage C includes all personal property on the premises owned, worn, or used by the named insured, family members of his household, or at his option, owned by others so long as the property is on the premises. A minimum amount of insurance on Coverage C is built into the contract. This minimum is one of the important features of the policy and tends to offset the too prevalent custom of buying inadequate amounts of insurance to protect personal property. These minimum amounts of insurance on Forms A and 1 and Forms B and 2 vary materially between companies. Many companies provide a standard limit of 40 percent of the amount of Coverage A which can be reduced to 30 percent. Other companies provide a standard limit of 50 percent which cannot be reduced. On these forms all companies provide, as additional insurance, 10 percent of the limit for Coverage C (but not less than $1,000) to property away from the premises.

On the Homeowners Comprehensive Form (C or 5) a minimum amount of 50 percent of Coverage A applies. Like the Personal Property Floater, this limit applies worldwide, subject to a limit of 10 percent in secondary dwellings unless increased.

4. *Coverage D—Additional Living Expense.* A separate amount of insurance will pay the necessary additional living expense (and rental value when applicable) which the insured incurs as the result of loss under Coverages A, B, or C. This is a most important benefit, payable when the insured needs it most. Most companies provide 10 percent of Coverage A for Additional Living Expense on the Standard Form (A or 1) and 20 percent on the Broad Form (B or 2) and Comprehensive Form

(C or 5). Some companies in the interest of simplicity, provide 20 percent on all forms.

Liability Insurance—Section II. Section II of the policy provides liability insurance and three coverages are always included for the basic premium. In general, Homeowners Policies tend to be broader than separate CPL contracts. The principal broadened provisions are fire legal liability coverage on residences in the care, custody, and control of the insured and, in some companies, business pursuits coverage for clerical employees. Some companies also provide broader coverages on outboard motors without endorsement or additional premium. A few companies provide coverage on all outboard motors without charge. These are the three coverages included for the basic premium:

1. *Coverage E—Personal Liability.* This coverage is like the personal liability insurance provided in the Comprehensive Personal Liability Policy discussed in Chapter 34. Most companies build in a basic limit of $25,000 in most states. The basic limit can be increased for an extra premium.

2. *Coverage F—Personal Medical Payments.* This coverage, similar to that available in a CPL Policy, covers medical or funeral expenses without regard to legal liability if arising out of the use of the premises or the insured's personal activities. A limit of $500 per person and $25,000 per accident is generally built in.

3. *Coverage G—Physical Damage to Property.* Physical damage to the property of others caused by the insured without regard to liability is provided by this coverage. Loss arising out of the use of automobiles, aircraft, boats, or farm equipment is excluded, as is intentional damage by an insured over 12 years of age. A limit of $250 is provided automatically.

Perils Insured Against—Section I

Through the years, the coverages in the various Homeowners Policies have become increasingly uniform regardless of type, the major remaining differences now being the perils covered in Section I.

Homeowners Standard Form (A or 1). This contract protects against loss under Coverages A to D caused by fire, extended cover perils, vandalism, theft, and limited glass breakage. These perils may be listed:

Fire and Lightning—As covered under the fire policy.

Removal—Essentially "all risk" direct loss protection for property removed from premises endangered by any insured peril.

Windstorm and Hail—As covered under the regular Extended Coverage Endorsement. In most areas a $50 deductible applies. To distinguish this deductible from one applying to other perils, it is designated "Loss Deductible Clause No. 1." See the discussion on deductibles which follows.

Explosion—In some forms this protection is somewhat broader than afforded in the Extended Coverage Endorsement in that steam boiler explosions are not excluded.

Riot and Civil Commotion—As covered in the Extended Coverage Endorsement.

Vandalism and Malicious Mischief—As covered under a separate Vandalism and Malicious Mischief Endorsement.

Aircraft and Vehicles—As covered in Extended Coverage.

Smoke—As covered in Extended Coverage.

Glass Breakage—Up to $50 on building glass.

Theft—Theft insurance applies in the full amount of the coverage involved and thus gives much more protection than the insured would normally buy under a theft policy. Theft includes loss by burglary, robbery, or larceny, but the words "mysterious disappearance" are not included. It is important to note that a $1,000 limit is imposed on any single item of jewelry or fur.

Bureau forms exclude steam boiler explosion and sonic boom in Form 1, although they are covered in Forms 2, 3, and 5. Most independent companies cover these hazards in all forms.

Homeowners Broad Form (B or 2). This policy adds the following perils: falling objects; weight of ice, snow or sleet; collapse of building; water escape; rupture of hot water heaters; freezing of plumbing, heating, or air-conditioning systems or domestic appliances; injury to electrical appliances, devices, fixtures, or wiring by artificial electricity; and full building glass breakage. (See Appendix I.)

The Broad Form theft coverage is the same as that in the Standard Form but it can be broadened by attachment of the Extended Theft Endorsement, for an additional premium, which adds to the theft peril the words "mysterious disappearance" and gives unlocked unattended automobile coverage. Some independent companies include one or both of these extensions in the basic Broad Form without charge.

The Broad Form may also be broadened still further by extending the building coverage to an "all risk" basis, creating what is known as the "B plus form," or in Bureau parlance, Forms 3 and 4.

Homeowners Comprehensive Form (Form C or 5). Use of this form results in the broadest Homeowners Policy available. It provides "all risk" insurance on all the Coverages in Section I, except on trees, plants and shrubs, and boats. Like all "all risk" types of insurance, the contract cannot be sold successfully to a claims-conscious insured who is intent on recovering his premium for a succession of small events. It is invaluable, however, for the policyholder who desires protection for serious losses however caused.

Probably the most significant difference in coverage between the Standard and Broad Forms and the Comprehensive Form is that the Comprehensive provides a $1,000 limit per loss rather than per item on jewelry and furs. The reason for this is obvious. As this is an "all risk" form, it would be impossible to include the equivalent of a Personal Articles Floater for $1,000 on each item owned by the insured.

Tenants Form B (Form A). This one is the most common tenants form, sold by all insurers. It is the equivalent of Homeowners Broad Form with Coverages A and B eliminated, and with certain modifications to meet a tenant's needs.

Tenants Form B sold separately lacks the mechanism in other Homeowners contracts which requires the amount of insurance on personal property to be at least 30, 40, or 50 percent of the amount carried on the dwelling. It is particularly important, therefore, to investigate carefully the values involved where these forms are sold. A minimum amount of $3,000 or $4,000 is required for Coverage C. Personal property off-premises is protected worldwide in an amount equalling 10 percent of Coverage C, but not less than $1,000.

Improvements and betterments coverage is important to the tenant. It is generally provided for 10 percent of the amount of Coverage C. There is no provision for replacement cost coverage on improvements.

Tenants Form C. Some independent companies, and all companies in Texas, provide an "all risk" tenants form roughly the equivalent of a Personal Property Floater plus a Comprehensive Personal Liability Policy. At least one company has discontinued the writing of P.P.F. contracts as such and instead sells only a Tenants Policy C.

The minimum amount of coverage on unscheduled personal property is $5,000 and conditions follow closely those of Homeowners Comprehensive Form with Coverages A and B deleted.

Deductibles

There is great similarity among companies in the treatment given deductibles. In the Standard Form (A or 1) and Broad Form (B or 2) a $50 windstorm deductible (Loss Deductible Clause No. 1) applies either on a mandatory or optional basis, depending on state custom. On the Broad Form (B or 2), a second deductible is available either applying to just the "Broad Form" perils or to all other perils except fire, lightning, windstorm, and hail. In the Comprehensive Form (C or 5), a different approach is used in that an "across-the-board" deductible, except for fire and lightning, of $100 or $500 applies.

There is an interesting difference in the treatment of deductibles between bureau and independent forms. Until 1956, deductibles applied regardless of the size of loss. Then an independent company, believing that the purpose of a deductible was to eliminate the small loss, and not to penalize the insured on a large loss, introduced a provision that the deductible did not apply when the loss, including the deductible, was $500 (now $250) or more. As a counter move to this, the bureau introduced the "disappearing deductible" which operates in such a way that the larger the loss the smaller the deductible until it becomes zero when the loss equals $500.

Limitations in Coverage

There are relatively few limitations in the Homeowners Policies and in some cases they represent actual broadening rather than restrictions from other conventional forms. They came into being largely through attempts to find a common meeting ground between fire and theft practices. Except for the limitation on jewelry and furs discussed earlier, they are basically as follows:

Money. A $100 limitation on money comes from a theft policy while money is excluded under the Standard Fire Policy. The amount can be increased to $500.

Securities. Securities, tickets, notes, and similar property are also excluded in the Standard Fire Policy but included in a Homeowners Policy subject to a $500 limit which may be increased to $1,000. Manuscripts are covered up to $1,000 in most forms.

Boats. Again there is a compromise between fire and theft practices. Theft policies cover $500 on boats. Fire forms have no specific limit on-premises but off-premises cover rowboats and canoes only. Homeowners Policies cover all boats on- and off-premises on a named peril basis for $500, but for obvious reasons exclude windstorm off-premises outside of fully enclosed buildings.

Stamp and Coin Collections. Stamp collections are limited in bureau forms to $500 and coin collections to $100, although some companies provide $1,000 on both. As with jewelry and furs, the intent is to provide reasonable protection to insureds with modest values and to require those with large values to insure them specifically at proper premiums.

Rating and Modifying Homeowners Forms

Basic Rate Tables. Every means of simplifying the task of computing the final Homeowners premium has been adopted. Tables listing the various amounts of coverage available show directly the final three-year premium for the entire policy. If separate policies were provided, many manuals and arithmetical computations would be required.

Factors influencing the basic premium are: construction of dwelling building, fire protection classification, theft zone classification, and in some areas windstorm zone. When the appropriate class has been determined for these factors, the policy premium is shown on the table for all amounts in common use.

Optional Coverages. One of the basic Homeowners Policies will fill the needs of most insureds without alteration. However, many options are available to meet special needs. In addition to the Extended Theft Endorsement referred to earlier, the most common ones are:

Increased Amounts. The amount of insurance on Coverage B (outbuildings) and Coverage C (personal property) may be increased. Bureau rules also permit the increase of Coverage D (additional living expense). In addition increased limits are available for liability and medical payments.

Secondary Dwellings. If an insured owns and occupies a secondary dwelling in the same state or has personal property at a secondary location, this property can be added to the Homeowners Policy by endorsement, giving him the equivalent of a second Homeowners or Tenants Policy. If he owns a secondary dwelling in another state, the same coverage can be afforded by use of a second and supplementary Homeowners Policy.

Office Occupancy. Policies may also be extended to cover professional and office occupancy under both Sections I and II.

Business Pursuits. Under Section II business pursuits and farmers comprehensive personal liability coverage can be added when needed.

Floaters. A Personal Articles Floater or Valuable Personal Articles Endorsement may be added to schedule items of large values such as jewelry, furs, fine arts, cameras, musical instruments, and stamp and coin collections. Some companies also add "all risk" insurance on outboard motors and boats by endorsement.

Merit Rating. Some companies give rate credits ranging up to 20 percent to insureds who have enjoyed a loss-free record under contracts issued by those companies.

Policy Term. Homeowners Policies are written for one of two terms: three years or continuous (a few companies also provide a five-year version). Premium tables and charges are usually expressed on a three-year basis, and annual payment of three-year premiums is permitted with the level annual premium equalling 35 percent of the three-year figure. Continuous policies permit premium payment on a monthly, quarterly, semi-annual, or yearly basis at appropriately modified premiums.

FARMOWNERS POLICIES

A Farmowners Policy is an integrated multiple line contract. It resembles the Homeowners Policy and is described on the basis of comparison with Homeowners characteristics previously discussed in this chapter. Paragraphs dealing with perils, limitations, and rating are omitted since Farmowners Policies are identical with Homeowners in these respects.

Eligibility Requirements

Subject to certain occupancy requirements, Farmowners Policies may be issued to:

1. A farm owner who occupies the farm.
2. A farm owner who manages, directly or by contract, a tenant-operated farm.
3. A tenant farmer.

Forms Available

Three named peril forms are available, each following closely the comparable Homeowners forms. No "all risk" Farmowners forms are generally available. The three are:

1. *Standard Form (Form A or 1)*
2. *Broad Form (Form B or 2)*
3. *Broad Form Tenants (Tenants B or Form 4)*

Coverages

Property Insurance—Section I. *Coverages A—Dwelling; B—Private Structures; C—Unscheduled Personal Property;* and *D—Additional Living Expense,* follow very closely their counterparts in Homeowners Policies. In addition, minimum limits are the same apart from Coverage C. Here the minimum limit is almost universally 40 per cent for Coverage A, while there is some variation among companies in this relationship in the case of Homeowners Policies.

Coverage E—Farm Personal Property. An important feature of the Farmowners Policy not found in Homeowners Policies, this coverage is provided on a scheduled basis or alternatively on a blanket basis with 75 percent or 80 percent coinsurance. Minimum amounts are required in some cases to qualify for Farmowners coverage; in others to qualify for discounted rates. Bureau forms insure against loss by fire, extended coverage perils, vandalism, theft, and overturn. Some independent companies give broader protection under their blanket coverage with "all risk" protection on mobile equipment and broader named perils protection on the balance.

Coverage F—Farm Barns, Buildings and Structures. Another unique feature calling for more detailed discussion, this coverage enables the insured to protect these important values against loss by the same perils applying to Coverages A, B, C, and D, under Form A or 1, but not Form B or 2. If minimum amounts of insurance are met, preferred rates are available. In the case of Tenants Policies, coverage applies to the insured's interest in improvements and betterments made to these outbuildings.

Liability Insurance—Section II. Section II provides three coverages.

1. *Coverage G—Farmer's Personal Liability.* This coverage takes the place of the personal liability insurance found in the Homeowners Policy. It provides liability protection against bodily injury or property damage arising out of the farm operation or personal activities, including fire and explosion legal liability. A minimum limit of $25,000 is built into the package premium.

2. *Coverage H—Personal Medical Payments.* This coverage follows Homeowners Coverage F. A minimum limit of $500 is built into the basic premium.

3. *Coverage I—Physical Damage to Property of Others.* This one is identical with Homeowners Coverage G and a minimum limit of $250 is built into the basic premium.

Optional Coverages

The optional coverages available under Homeowners Policies may also be added to Farmowners Policies. In addition, employers liability coverage may be added to Section II. (See Chapter 11 for additional discussion of farm insurance.)

SIGNIFICANCE OF HOMEOWNERS POLICIES

Since its introduction in 1950 Homeowners insurance has grown at a meteoric pace. Premiums written by U.S. companies have grown from $30,000 in 1950 to approximately $1 billion in 1962. From this growth it is possible to forecast with reasonable accuracy some most important future developments.

First, from the viewpoint of premium alone it seems clear that Homeowners writings will outstrip those for fire insurance itself in the not too distant future. Expressed differently, this statement means that a policy giving multiple line protection to one group of buyers will develop more premium from them than fire insurance will develop from all the groups combined.

This fact points up the revolutionary change which is transforming the entire insurance structure. The broad divisions into which property and casualty insurance is divided developed along the paths they did, partly because the laws required some separation, but also because there was "natural" development along these lines not only in this country but in England and elsewhere. Experts were trained in divisions of the insurance business which were devised to fit the convenience of the insurers, putting like problems together. Thus, specialists were developed to handle fire insurance, marine insurance, liability insurance, and so on. The most important aspect of the Homeowners development is the discovery that the buyer very much prefers classification based on his desires rather than those of the insurance company.

The Homeowners success has led to similar equally dramatic growth in the commercial multiple line field. Commercial packages are discussed in Chapter 50. It now seems probable the future classifications and development of expertise will tend to be made from the viewpoint of occupancy rather than peril or coverage. If these changes occur, they will have profound effect on the structure of insurance companies, and on the nature of insurance statistics, ratemaking, and rate regulation.

SUGGESTED READINGS

GEE, HAROLD F. *Personal Lines Insurance*. 4th ed. Indianapolis: Rough Notes Co., 1960.

HUNT, FREDERIC J., JR. "Homeowners—The First Decade," *Proceedings of the Casualty Actuarial Society*, Vol. 49 (1962), pp. 12–36.

MEHR, ROBERT I., AND CAMMACK, EMERSON. *Principles of Insurance*. 3d ed. Homewood, Ill.: Richard D. Irwin, Inc., 1959. Chap. 16.

MOWBRAY, ALBERT H., AND BLANCHARD, RALPH H. *Insurance: Its Theory and Practice in the United States.* 5th ed. New York: McGraw-Hill Book Co., 1961. Chap. 17.

SCHULTZ, ROBERT E., AND BARDWELL, EDWARD C. *Property Insurance.* New York: Rinehart & Co., Inc., 1959. Chap. xiii.

Chapter 50

COMMERCIAL INSURANCE PACKAGES

BY JACK E. LARSON

On the heels of the developments in Homeowners and other personal package insurances, with their tremendous impact on the dwelling class came a revolution in commercial insurance. While package innovations for business risks appeared about the same time as did the Homeowners, the initial changes were not as extensive. But changes begun in 1952 accumulated, expanded, and "spilled over" into numerous kinds of insurance. Today property-liability companies find themselves in the midst of an upheaval, with a large block of commercial insurance being converted to the new packages. This mass movement and redistribution of premium dollars between insurance companies and their agents have created an intensely competitive market in commercial insurance without precedent in the past half-century, the full effect of which it is still too early to judge.

This development of commercial package insurance is reviewed briefly in this chapter. The description is broken down into three periods of development: early, middle, and recent. The early period covers from about 1950 to 1957; the middle period from 1957 to 1963; and the recent from 1963 to the present.

EARLY PERIOD OF DEVELOPMENT

A commercial package policy may be defined for practical purposes as a combination of at least two of the following types of coverages: fire, inland marine, and liability insurance. The coverages and premium may be divisible or indivisible, the insuring provision "named peril" or "all risk."

Most package policies developed in the early 1950's tend to share four common characteristics. First, they represent a combination of two or all of the following kinds of insurance: fire and allied perils, burglary, and inland marine (but not third-party liability insurance). Second, they do not provide a package discount of the fire rate for packaging, although other rates are discounted. Third, they contain an "all risk" insuring provision. Fourth, they cover personal property but not real property.

From these common characteristics there were, of course, significant exceptions, which will be mentioned in the description of the individual coverages. Furthermore, the periodization of developments does not imply that coverages originating in the early period are no longer available. At the time of this writing all are in effect; some are still widely sold, while others have languished. Collectively, they exerted an important influence on the later packages. Seldom in the insurance business does one come up with an entirely new idea. Often a new development involves transplanting a concept from one kind of insurance to another, or otherwise refining or giving a "new twist" to an existing concept. Thus, the package policies with "all risk" insuring provisions, which began during the early period, are modeled after inland marine policies covering at fixed locations, such as the Jewelers' Block Policy. Conversely, inland marine during its period of rapid expansion had borrowed heavily from fire and casualty practices.

"All Risk" Coverages

In retrospect, it appears the tendency toward "all risk" coverage grew out of the feeling that multiple-line insurance was synonymous with "all risk" coverage. Then, too—as mentioned above—many of the contracts were modeled after inland marine "all risk" prototypes. At this time the "package discount" had not yet come into vogue for business insurance, and the sales presentations emphasized coverage. The pattern of "all risk" insurance for personal property was carried forward into the later contracts. The "all risk" insuring provisions for personal property are quite similar from one contract to another. Hence, the following explanation applies generally to all programs in which such coverage is afforded, whether of the early or later periods. Some significant departures from the general pattern are pointed out in the description of individual programs.

Under an "all risk" insuring provision, the insurer is liable for any loss from a fortuitous happening unless the loss is excluded. Thus, the extent of coverage is determined largely from what is not insured, as itemized in the exclusions and limitations. In the commercial package policies the exclusions with respect to personal property fall into four groups.

In the first group specified types of property are excluded. Usually, such property poses a materially different exposure requiring another approach for rating or specifying conditions. Furthermore, it is contemplated that the property can be insured under another policy. In this group the commercial package policies may exclude automobiles, motor trucks, trailers, similar vehicles, watercraft, aircraft, money, and securities. Also excluded is loss to steam boilers by explosion.

In a second group the policy excludes property while in certain situations with exposures not contemplated by the policy conditions and rate levels. The more important exclusions pertain to property during shipment by mail or property sold on a deferred payment basis. If an overlap is likely, it will exclude property insured under an ocean marine contract.

A third group relates to excluded perils which account for most exclusions found in a policy. Because of the variety, this group may be divided into subgroups:

First, some perils are not covered because of a catastrophe potential. Such are the perils of war, earthquake (which may be insured under a separate policy, nuclear fission (see Chapter 64), flood (which is insured in some inland marine policies), and water damage from seepage through walls and floors or backup of sewers or drains.

Second, other losses are not covered because they are natural and expected occurences, or intrinsic to the property. Such are changes in flavor, shrinkage, wear and tear, deterioration, or inherent vice.

Third, certain limitations apply to causes not contemplated by the rate level because of possible frequency or inevitability of loss in the normal course of handling the property, or because a materially different exposure is represented. For example, inventory losses are excluded; also mysterious disappearance; infidelity of the insured, his associates, or employees; and theft of property from a motor vehicle, unless the vehicle is fully enclosed and locked and unless the theft results from forcible entry. Similarly, the policy excludes breakage of glass or articles of a fragile nature, marring, scratching, and similar types of losses. Also excluded are losses by mechanical or electrical breakdown and faulty workmanship.

Fourth, the insuring provisions of the basic coverage contemplate only direct losses. Thus, there are excluded indirect losses arising from delay in shipment, loss of market, or business interruption.

Manufacturer's Output Policy

The Manufacturer's Output Policy was the first generally known commercial package. Its forerunner was a coverage tailored for an automobile manufacturer's account during World War II. Later with the S.E.U.A. decision and enactment of new rating laws in the states, it was necessary to bring the coverage in line with state filing requirements. The coverage ended up under the jurisdiction of the Multiple Peril Insurance Rating Organization (MPIRO) after the founding of that body by a group of companies. At MPIRO the coverage underwent a major revision, became known as the Manufacturer's Output Policy, was first filed in 1952, and is now in effect in the majority of states.

A landmark of commercial package development, the Manufacturer's Output Policy at the time of its introduction represented new concepts in coverage, rating, and method of filing, which established a precedent for later developments. The policy contains coverage the equivalent of that contained in separate fire, inland marine, automobile physical damage, water damage, and burglary policies; and its combination of coverages is subject to a rating plan tailored for larger manufacturing risks.

In 1952, such a combination of insurance overlapped and extended beyond the borders of any single traditional rating organization. At that time, if the various coverages embraced in the Manufacturer's Output Policy had been rated countrywide by the traditional rating organizations, it would have required collective action of no fewer than 34 fire bureaus, one inland marine bureau, one automobile bureau, and one casualty bureau. To be sure, an alternative existed for solving the problems arising out of the diversity of bureau jurisdictions through a program of cooperative action, which is described subsequently.

As to product specifications, the Output Policy (its popular name) is designed for practically all kinds of manufacturing risks. It covers the insured's personal property in most situations, while in warehouses, at processors, at retail premises, in transit, in custody of salesmen, or away from the premises for other reasons. Included in the property covered are (1) improvements and betterments, (2) property of others in the custody of the insured and for which he is liable, and—significantly—(3) motor vehicles, a type of property excluded from other commercial packages.

The insuring provisions, while similar to those of other "all risk" commercial packages in most respects, also contain a few interesting variations. There is a liberalized flood exclusion, which does not apply to certain named property, property in course of transit, or property while on processors' premises. There is no exclusion with respect to water damage from seepage through floors and walls or due to backup of sewers or drains. It excludes loss to motor vehicles by collision or overturning.

The term of the policy is continuous. The premium is provisional subject to the annual minimum of $1,000, with the insured reporting values at risk and paying premium monthly. In format, it represents an integrated multiple-peril contract, complete in itself without inclusion of the Standard Fire Policy provisions.

It is also interesting to note that the policy may be endorsed to insure against flood or earthquake. The rating structure is significant because of its flexibility, which allows the discounting of the fire and extended coverage rates. The policy may be written for deductible amounts of $5,000 or less.

Industrial Property Policy

The next program made available to the manufacturers was the Industrial Property Policy. It differs from the Manufacturer's Output Policy in major respects. It was introduced in 1957 under the auspices of the Interbureau Insurance Advisory Group (referred to as I.I.A.G.—see Chapter 49).

Differences in multiple line philosophy and method, as represented in the contrast between the Homeowners and Comprehensive Dwelling Policies, were carried forward in equally distinct patterns in the commercial packages. While I.I.A.G. viewed the commercial package as a fire policy to which other coverages have been added, MPIRO treated it as a new kind of insurance. In the I.I.A.G. programs the premium and losses were separately maintained by the companies for each kind of insurance, while under an MPIRO program the premiums and losses were allocated to the entire policy. I.I.A.G. was an advisory organization, and recommended its programs to the various bureaus involved; MPIRO was a countrywide rating organization and made its filings directly with the states.

To qualify for the Industrial Property Policy, a manufacturing risk must have at least two locations. The minimum premium is $2,500 for the basic coverage. In format, the design is conventional with the coverage form attached to the Standard Fire Policy.

The Industrial Property Policy was the first major commercial package to make building coverage available. In addition, the policy covers personal property usual to the business, including property for which the insured may be liable; fixed and movable machinery and equipment; and improvements and betterments if the insured is not owner of the building.

In another respect the Industrial Property Policy constitutes a "first." At the time it was introduced, the policy was the only one providing the two coverage tracks—named peril as well as "all risk." This approach was a forerunner of alternate coverage tracks used in later programs. It was also indicative that underwriters were beginning to have reservations about surfeiting the market exclusively with "all risk" insurance for all kinds of businesses.

In the named perils version, applying both to building and personal property and called the Industrial Property Form, insurance is provided against direct loss by fire; extended coverage perils; falling objects; vandalism and malicious mischief; weight of snow, ice, and sleet; sprinkler leakage; burglary; and robbery. The Industrial Property Form comes in two editions: nonreporting and reporting. The nonreporting edition insures personal property at specified locations, while the reporting edition also insures at newly acquired locations but only if reported by the insured.

The "all risk" version, applicable only to personal property, is accomplished by attaching the Special Personal Property Endorsement to the Industrial Property Form. In addition to converting the insuring provisions to "all risk," the endorsement extends the policy to apply also to property in transit or away from the premises for other reasons, subject to certain exclusions. While the endorsements contain the usual exclusions customary to "all risk" contracts, it should be noted that the endorsement applies only to finished goods. It excludes property at locations used for manufacturing or processing and property away from a scheduled location and in the custody of salesmen. There is also a limited $100 deductible clause, which does not apply to loss by fire, extended coverage perils, vandalism and malicious mischief, burglary, robbery, and to property in transit.

In rating treatment, the Industrial Property Policy contributed another significant innovation. For the first time under a package policy, not only was the building coverage included but also the premium for such coverage was subject to a credit for the criteria of dispersion of property, fire loss ratio, number of fire losses, and premium size, subject to a maximum credit of 15 percent.

Dealers' Policies

At its convention in June 1953, the National Association of Insurance Commissioners adopted a revised Nation-wide Marine Definition. (See Chapter 23 and Part IV generally.) This document delineates the jurisdiction of inland marine insurance. While this action at the convention had no official effect, it encouraged state insurance departments to adopt the revised definition as an insurance department ruling.

The revised definition expanded inland marine insurance in several areas, but most important was the provision for new policies for dealers in merchandise. These were for dealers in agricultural and construction equipment, cameras and musical instruments, and furs. (See Chapter 27.) The Inland Marine Insurance Bureau (I.M.I.B.) promulgated rules, rates, and coverage for the added dealer classifications. The insuring provision is "all risk" subject to customary exclusions. As in MPIRO's policies, the premium is treated as indivisible for statistical purposes without separation into fire and other traditional components.

As the market drift to broad insurance for mercantile risks gained momentum, some persons thought that the I.M.I.B. would become the bureau to assume jurisdiction over mercantile multiple line insurance. Subsequently, however, the "fire people" in the industry acted, resolved temporarily the question of bureau jurisdiction, and authorized the introduction of a single multiple line plan for all mercantile risks, which events are discussed in subsequent sections of this chapter.

Commercial Property Coverage

Concurrent with the development of the individual dealers' policies in the I.M.I.B., several insurance companies in California, acting independently outside the bureau system, introduced mercantile block type policies with "all risk" coverage. These policies could be used for most retailers and wholesalers. Subsequently, the Pacific Fire Rating Bureau promulgated a similar type of policy in California for its members and subscribers.

The I.M.I.B. dealers' policies, the Mercantile Block Policy in California, the restiveness of officials in some companies, and other factors combined to compel the industry to agree on an organization to serve as an agency to develop a package program for mercantile risks on a countrywide basis. A possible solution would have been to extend inland marine insurance to embrace not only the dealers' policies it then had but all kinds of merchants. This solution, however, could have meant stretching the inland marine concept very far. There were, of course, in the middle 1950's two bodies already constituted to handle multiple line insurance: MPIRO and I.I.A.G. Each embodied a different multiple line philosophy. Officials of their member companies hesitated to embark on another program which would widen the schism when the industry was seeking uniformity. Since liability and theft insurance represented a small proportion of premium in the package at that time, the possibility of naming a casualty bureau was not seriously considered. Ultimately, the authority to proceed with the formulation of a countrywide, multiple line program for merchants was accorded to the Inter-Regional Insurance Conference (I.R.I.C.) by a vote of its Executive Committee. That body was an advisory organization established to coordinate the activities of regional fire advisory bodies and fire rating organizations. As an advisory organization, I.R.I.C. sponsored the development work of a program, which in turn was recommended to its participating advisory bodies for submission to rating bureaus for filing—a procedure similar to that followed by I.I.A.G.

A preliminary version of the new mercantile package was unveiled in 1955, then revised, and reintroduced in 1956 as the Commercial Property Coverage. The coverage is composed of a form attached to the Standard Fire Policy. It is designed for practically all mercantile risks, that is, firms engaged principally in the sale of merchandise whether retail or wholesale. It was the first policy to bring package insurance to "Main Street" on a large scale.

Coverage is afforded on stocks of goods, wares, and merchandise of almost every description relating to the business, and also includes—at the insured's option—furniture, fixtures, equipment, and tenants' improvements. Coverage is provided in a wide variety of situations not only at the specified locations but also at locations not regularly used or controlled by the insured. It covers property while it is in transit and while it is in the custody of salesmen or away from the premises for other reasons.

The insuring provision is "all risk," subject to the customary exclusions and limitations. The coverage is subject to a limited $50 deductible clause which does not apply to loss by fire, extended coverage perils, vandalism and malicious mischief, sprinkler leakage, burglary or robbery, nor to property in most transit situations.

The coverage may be written on a nonreporting or reporting basis. If reporting, the premium is provisional. The values are reported monthly, and at the end of the policy term the actual premium is computed, with the difference between the provisional and earned premiums being adjusted between the insured and the insurance company.

While Commercial Property Coverage constituted a major step forward in multiple line developments, many insurance company officials did not greet it enthusiastically because of underwriting problems it entailed.

Office Contents Special Form

Brought out under auspices of the Inter-Regional Insurance Conference, this form may be used for practically any office occupancy except those in the same fire division with a mercantile or manufacturing occupancy of the insured. The coverage is composed of the form attached to the Standard Fire Policy. Broad in scope, the form covers office contents such as furniture, fixtures, equipment and supplies usual to an office occupancy, and includes the insured's interest in improvements and betterments. Subject to a limit of 10 percent of the amount insured or $10,000, whichever is less, the coverage also applies to the property covered while it is away from the insured premises, including property in transit. It also covers money and securities against loss by burglary or robbery, subject to a limit of $250. The insuring provisions are "all risk" with the customary exclusions and limitations.

MIDDLE PERIOD OF DEVELOPMENT

Bureau Reorganization

Functioning in commercial package insurance in 1957 were two rating organizations (MPIRO and the I.M.I.B.) and two advisory organizations (I.I.A.G. and I.R.I.C.). Since these bodies sometimes worked at cross purposes, industry officials (representing most of the stock companies) considered it advisable to concentrate multiple line responsibility in one place. They began negotiations that subsequently culminated in two reorganizations. In 1957, the Multi-Peril Insurance Conference (MIC) emerged from a combination of the old rivals in the personal package business—MPIRO and I.I.A.G. (See Chapter 49.) This new body was awarded "advisory" jurisdiction over all then existing multiple line programs except the miscellaneous dealers' policies that remained in the I.M.I.B. MIC, an advisory organization along the lines of I.I.A.G, developed programs which were then recommended for filing to bureaus having rating jurisdiction over the components. In 1960, the Multi-Peril Insurance Conference lost its identity and became a division of the Inter-Regional Insurance Conference, which until that time had been a countrywide advisory body for fire insurance.

First Commercial Package Policy of the Middle Period

While the stock-bureau companies were tidying up organizational loose ends and laboring to compromise the old Homeowners–Comprehensive Dwelling schism, a new development popped into the market. It set off a whole new chain of events. In 1958, an independent insurer announced its Funeral Director's Policy, a package policy including third-party general liability and a package discount which applies to the premium for all components, including fire and extended coverage. The same insurer soon announced additional packages—for motels and apartments. This trio of new products, influenced by the Homeowners prototype and possessing simplicity, convenience, and price advantage, soon proved to have sales appeal.

There was nothing particularly startling about this development since the precedent had been established by the Homeowners Policy. But it flew in the face of the then prevailing climate of fire-casualty opinion that viewed with alarm any further extension of the package discount to fire insurance and further inclusion of third-party liability insurance in package policies.

Growth of Independent Filings

In the years 1959 to 1961, many fire-casualty managements did some serious "stock-taking." By then, the competitive effects from companies operating outside the bureau system had become obvious. The stock-bureau companies not only represented a progressively smaller share of the market for private passenger automobiles but also incurred worsening loss ratios in this contracting spiral, despite rate increases. In the Homeowners development many such companies were slow starters. The lion's share of growth and profit went to an independent. Against this background the new commercial packages came on the scene. Some companies, previously dedicated bureau adherents, took a new tack. Changes in management evaluations of the commercial package market became apparent with a trickle of independent filings. Such filings subsequently flooded the market.

Similarly, this quickening prompted the remaining bureau companies to utilize the bureau machinery not only to respond more promptly to competition but also to create competition.

Characteristics of the Commercial Package Policy during the Middle Period

Most policies initiated in this period tend to share three common characteristics. First, they are composed of mandatory or optional coverages representing the following kinds of insurance: fire, water damage, burglary or theft, glass, boiler and machinery, general liability, inland marine, and fidelity. In this period all major kinds of property-liability insurance except automobile and compensation were included in the package. Second, a package discount applies to the entire premium for the policy, including fire and extended coverage. Third, property damage coverage usually features three tracks: basic named perils, broad named perils, and "all risk."

Bureau's Special Multi-Peril Program

The number and types of commercial package programs in today's competitive market are so varied, it is not possible to discuss all of them in this chapter. To illustrate the scope of recent multiple line plans, the "program" used by the bureau companies is described. It is the Special Multi-Peril Program, formulated by the Inter-Regional Insurance Conference. It embraces separate programs for motels; apartments; offices; mercantile risks, retail and wholesale; and institutional property, meaning property of educational, religious, sanatory, charitable, governmental, and nonprofit organizations.

The manual of the Special Multi-Peril Program contains general rules for all programs and special provisions which apply separately to each program. The policy term is three years for all programs. The premium may be prepaid or paid in annual installments. In most states, when the premium is payable annually, an installment charge of 5 percent applies. Credit may be granted for existing specific insurance.

As to format, the basic policy (called the Special Multi-Peril Policy) contains the declarations, provisions of the Standard Fire Policy, and certain conditions for Sections I and II. The contract is completed by attaching the appropriate form for the section. Section I, applying to property damage coverages, usually consists of Coverage A for the building and Coverage B for personal property. Section II consists of Coverage C (general liability) and Coverage D (medical payments). In most cases, both building and personal property coverages are required if the insured owns such property. In Section II, Coverage C is required, except that the hazard of products-completed operations may be deleted in most cases. Coverage D is optional. Section I coverages may be written optionally under two or three coverage tracks—named peril, broad named peril, and "all risk." Such Section I coverages and the Section II coverages are summarized below.

Basic Named Perils Coverage—Section I. All forms used for this coverage are designated "Special." In the Office Program, for example, the form is captioned "Special Office Form." While the insuring provisions vary among the programs, all of them apply at least to loss by fire and the extended coverage perils. In the Office Program, the form also covers loss by vandalism and malicious mischief. In the Apartment Program, the form also includes burglary, sprinkler leakage, and vandalism and malicious mischief. In the Motel Program, additional perils insured against are water damage from plumbing, heating, or air-conditioning systems; sprinkler leakage; vandalism and malicious mischief; and breakage of building glass subject to a limit of $50 per pane and $250 in any one occurrence.

A number of "fringe" coverages are contained in the "Extensions of Coverage" subsection of each form. Most are borrowed from customary provisions in fire, liability, dishonesty, and inland marine contracts; some are innovations. In most cases, the extensions are subject to nominal special limits of liability. All the forms which contain building coverage have a replacement cost clause.

There are two deductible clauses, each for an amount of $50. As a result of a "disappearing" feature (such as in the Homeowners—see Chapter 49), the deductible becomes smaller as the size of loss increases. The deductible finally disappears altogether. Clause No. 1 applies to loss by windstorm or hail to buildings or personal property in the open. It is mandatory if the extended coverage rate contemplates a deductible. Loss Deductible Clause No. 2, which is optional, applies to losses other than by the perils of windstorm, hail, fire, or lightning. When the loss under either clause is between $50 or $500, the insurer is liable for 111 percent of the loss in excess of $50. The deductible does not apply if the loss is $500 or more.

Definitions of the perils insured against and the policy's exclusions and limitations are, for the most part, the same as those applying to a fire policy, a fire form for the same kind of property, the Extended Coverage Endorsement, and the Vandalism and Malicious Mischief Endorsement.

Broad Named Perils—Section I. In the Office and Apartment Programs, there may be attached to the Special Form the Optional Perils Endorsement, which adds the perils of breakage of building glass, subject to a limit of $50 per pane and $250 per occurrence; falling objects; weight of snow, ice, or sleet; water damage from plumbing, heating, or air-conditioning systems; and collapse of building. In the Mercantile Program the Additional Coverage Endorsement, which may be attached for personal property only, adds the perils of falling objects; weight of snow, ice, or sleet; sprinkler leakage; and vandalism and malicious mischief. Broad named perils coverage is not provided in the Motel and Institutional Programs.

"All Risk" Coverage—Section I. Under all programs "all risk" insurance on the building may be afforded by the Special Building Endorsement. While its limitations and exclusions generally are those customary for such broad coverage, a few should be noted. Steam boiler explosion is excluded. Building glass coverage is subject to special limits of $50 per pane and $250 per occurrence except for loss by certain named perils. Likewise, buildings under construction are covered only for loss by certain named perils. Loss by theft is limited to property which at the time of loss is an integral part of the building. Deductible treatment is similar to that described for the Special forms except the amount of the deductible for perils other than fire, lightning, wind, or hail is $100 (instead of $50) and such deductible cannot be waived.

"All risk" coverage in respect to personal property may be afforded for: (1) the Office Program by the Special Office Personal Property Form which has provisions similar to those of the Office Contents Special Form; (2) the Mercantile Program by the Special Commercial Property Form which has provisions similar to those of Commercial Property Coverage; and (3) the Institutional Program by the Special Institutional Personal Property Form, which, however, excludes theft coverage.

Section II. Coverage C applies to bodily injury and property damage liability. It covers the insured's legal liability to members of the public arising out of the ownership, maintenance, or use of the premises and operations necessary or incidental thereto. Insurance is provided on an occurrence basis for the hazards of premises operations, elevators, and structural alterations. It also applies to the products-completed operations hazard except in the Office Program in which the coverage may be added by endorsement. A single limit of liability applies to bodily injury and property damage.

Coverage D (medical payments) provides for payment of medical expenses incurred by members of the public who sustain bodily injury as a result of accidents arising out of the ownership, maintenance, or use of the premises and all operations necessary or incidental thereto.

In the Mercantile and Institutional Programs, Section II applies not only to the premises designated in the policy declarations but also to similar premises acquired by the insured during the policy term if the insured reports such acquisition to the insurer within 30 days. It should be noted, however, that other premises and operations to which Section II does not apply may be picked up by the Comprehensive General Liability Endorsement.

Optional Coverages. The foregoing was a description of the more important coverages under the Special Multi-Peril Program. No attempt will be made to itemize the myriad of optional coverages that may also be used for the individual programs except to note (1) that all the programs provide time element coverages; (2) that steam boilers and machinery may be insured by the Boiler and Machinery Supplement, and (3) that crime exposures may be insured by the Comprehensive Crime Coverage Endorsement (the equivalent of the Comprehensive Dishonesty, Disappearance and Destruction Policy).

RECENT PERIOD OF DEVELOPMENT

By late 1963 the growth of the independents caused further bureau reorganization. The Inter-Regional Insurance Conference had exercised countrywide advisory functions for the bureau pattern of fire insurance to which the vast majority of companies still adhere, and for multiple-line insurance, an area where an increasing number of companies operate independently. Because of the cleavage, Inter-Regional was replaced by two new organizations. These are (1) the Fire Insurance Research and Actuarial Association, conducting, on an advisory basis, research and technical activity for fire and allied lines, and (2) the Multi-Line Insurance Rating Bureau, which assumed rating jurisdiction over multiple-line insurance.

In product development, the most significant recent event is the inclusion, in the package, of automobile liability and automobile physical damage insurance. The movement to include such insurance, begun simultaneously by several companies, gained impetus from the "Comprehensive Business Policy" introduced by one of the large company groups. This policy also is notable for its overall approach to multiple-line insurance, which resembles that of the Comprehensive Dwelling Policy. It is expected that in due time the package expansion will spread over the last major jurisdictional barrier and embrace compensation insurance. The package version that began in the middle period as a combination of fire and general liability insurance is becoming a self-contained vehicle to accommodate an entire fire-casualty account.

SIGNIFICANCE FOR THE FUTURE

While the growth percentagewise of commercial package insurance has been dramatic, the real significance lies in its potential. The premium writings by U.S. companies grew from $28 million in 1956 to $151 million in 1962.[1] Premium figures alone, however, may never completely measure its importance, since the premium for such components as automobile probably will not be recorded as multiple line.

The commercial packages have promoted and intensified competition, causing a vast redistribution of premium dollars among companies in the business market, just as the Homeowners Policy has been doing in personal insurance. A property-liability company's market standing a few years hence will to a large degree reflect its success today in coping with the many problems brought about by packaging.

As did the Homeowners Policy, the commercial packages are causing revolutionary changes in companies' internal structures. Underwriting and other departments which have been divided according to the traditional kinds of insurance are being regrouped to process integrated coverages that cut across the old boundaries. In other cases separate multiple-

---

[1] Countrywide net written premiums compiled by New York Insurance Department for all companies licensed in New York.

line departments have been established and superimposed on, or dovetailed into, the existing organization.

The beneficiary from this turmoil is the buyer of commercial insurance. He is receiving more value for his premium dollar, reflecting a reduced cost for a unit of insurance. There is now available to him a wider selection of insurance products. Also, he may buy insurance not generally offered previously. Now he has the convenience of one policy instead of several, and may pay his insurance bills in evenly spaced installments.

SUGGESTED READINGS

HINES, HAROLD H., SR. "The Future of Package Policies for Larger Commercial Risks." *The Annals of the Society of Chartered Property and Casualty Underwriters,* Vol. 15 (Fall, 1962), pp. 259–67.

KENNEY, ROGER. "These Eventful Days." *The Journal of Insurance Information* (January–February, 1964), pp. 19–24.

———. "Time for Great Decisions by Smaller and Medium-Sized Property and Casualty Companies," *United States Investor,* Vol. LXXV (March 2, 1964), pp. 29, 30, 35–36.

MAGEE, JOHN H., AND BICKELHAUPT, DAVID L. *General Insurance.* 7th ed. Homewood, Ill.: Richard D. Irwin, Inc., 1964. Chap. 19.

MCGILL, DAN M. (ed.). *All Lines Insurance.* Homewood, Ill.: Richard D. Irwin, Inc., 1960.

MEHR, ROBERT I., AND CAMMACK, EMERSON. *Principles of Insurance.* 3d ed. Homewood, Ill.: Richard D. Irwin, Inc., 1959. Chap. 16.

RODDA, WILLIAM H. "The Multi-Peril Program." *Best's Insurance News* (Fire and Casualty Edition), Vol. LXIV (October, 1963), pp. 25, 102–3.

STODOLKA, JAMES P. "The Impact of Packaging," *The Annals of the Society of Chartered Property and Casualty Underwriters,* Vol. 15 (Fall, 1962), pp. 253–57.

Chapter 51

RATEMAKING IN MULTIPLE LINE INSURANCE

BY HARRY F. PERLET

GENERAL OBSERVATIONS

The rating of multiple line policies involves many problems which are not present in the rating of the individual or specific lines. In this chapter several of these problems are recognized and some general rating practices described. With multiple line insurance itself so new, there is considerable difference within the industry as to preferred rating methods and directions which refinements should take. Insofar as preferences are expressed or implied in this chapter, they are naturally those of the author.

Multiple line policies embrace several coverages, which when rated alone involve dissimilar rating methods. Rates for most property damage coverages, such as fire and extended coverage, are on a straight dollars and cents per $100 basis and the premium for any given amount is merely the amount times the constant rate. Rates for some coverages, such as burglary and theft, and also many "all risk" coverages, are on a so-called step basis in which the rate for the first increment of value is relatively high and progressively decreases as the amount increases. Thus, the rate per $1,000 for the first $5,000 of coverage may be $1.00; for the second $5,000 it may be $.50; and so on. In liability coverage, the rate may be a flat amount, such as $10 for a $10,000 CPL policy, or it may be a rate per square foot, per $100 of sales, or per some other unit of exposure. It is self-evident that attempting to merge these diverse ratemaking practices into a single workable procedure for a multiple line policy presents problems.

Some Definitions

A "multiple line policy," as used herein, and as generally accepted by the industry, is a policy in which are included property and liability lines of insurance. Any policy with two or more major lines, that is fire (and allied perils), inland marine, liability, dishonesty, or certain other, can be thought of as "multiple line." In common usage, however, the term currently includes at least fire (or inland marine) and liability coverages. Further, the term "multiple peril" is often equated with the term "multiple line" and the two terms are used interchangeably. In this chapter the term "package policy" will also be used to refer to multiple line or multiple peril coverages.

Other terms that need defining are "indivisible premium" and its converse, "divisible premium." An indivisible premium is one which can not be broken down into component parts such as a fire portion, windstorm portion, and liability portion, as to the policyholder. It may be divisible as to the insurer and still remain an indivisible premium. However, if it is apportioned on the face of the policy among the various coverages afforded, then it is a divisible premium.

Perspective

Because of the historical development of the business in the United States, the custom has been to issue individual policies for individual perils, each with its own rate or premium. Thus, it was customary to issue a separate fire policy, a separate windstorm policy, a separate vandalism policy, a separate explosion policy, and so on. Not until the advent of the Extended Coverage Endorsement in the early 1930's did a trend start towards incorporating several perils into one policy for a single rate.

Most of the "package" contracts, such as some of the inland marine coverages, embody the straight fire rate (or fire plus extended coverage rates) as a base, to which is added some type of loading to recognize the additional coverage provided. The requirements are not uniform from state to state. In these packages, and there are contemporary contracts of this type, the fire rate is usually kept inviolate and used as the foundation upon which the total premium is erected. This approach probably was and still is correct for this type of package contract where there are no restrictive eligibility rules, minimum coverages, minimum premiums, or other features to justify modification of the fire rate. However, experience has demonstrated conclusively that it is neither necessary nor proper to use an unadjusted fire rate in a true package policy.

BASIC PACKAGE RATEMAKING PROCEDURES

The usual procedure in making a rate for a new package policy is (1) to start with the rates for the specific coverages being incorporated into the package; (2) to adjust these rates for the differing conditions existing under the package, if necessary; and then (3) to apply a package discount to recognize the overall package conditions. To a certain extent, the specific application depends upon whether the final premium is to be divisible or indivisible. The following will illustrate package ratemaking methods for each of these types of premiums:

1. The Homeowners Policy, which is a truly indivisible premium package.
2. The Commercial Property Coverage Policy, which is indivisible as to the insured, but divisible as to the insurer.
3. The Special Multi-Peril Policy, which is on a divisible premium basis.

Indivisible Premium Rating Procedure

The rating of the Homeowners Policy is a good illustration of erecting an indivisible package premium. Even though the Homeowners embraces many coverages, it is relatively simple. This simplicity is due primarily to the fact that few variables or options are contained in the basic policy. Thus, if an insured purchasing a Form 1 or Form 2 contract (see Chapter 49) desires $15,000 of building coverage, he automatically gets $6,000 contents coverage (insured against the perils specified in the contract, including theft), some additional living expense coverage, $25,000 comprehensive personal liability, and $500 medical payments coverage. (The liability and medical payments in these forms were $10,000 and $250 respectively in most states until recently.) With fixed amounts of coverage, it is relatively easy to construct a premium table which will give the total premium for a policy based on the amount of insurance on the dwelling building.

In erecting this premium for Homeowners Policies, ratemakers used the fire and extended coverage rates as a basis. Over the years, these rates have tended toward stability in most states and appeared to reflect properly the differentials between classes of construction and classes of protection. There are occasional revisions. Residence theft and comprehensive personal liability rates likewise have become stabilized.

Next comes the adjustment of the specific rates to reflect differing package policy conditions. For example, in many states refinements of dwelling classifications have produced a multitude of fire rates with many of the rates only one cent apart. These slight variations perhaps are proper for a straight fire and extended coverage policy carrying a relatively low total premium. The one cent differential may produce a difference of several percentage points in the final premium. However, when carried over into the package policy, such differential may produce only a $3 to $5 differential for a three-year policy and be only 1 percent of the total premium. Hence, to keep the number of premium groups within reasonable limits, certain consolidations are made in pricing Homeowners Policies. Table 51–1 illustrates part of a typical so-called array for erecting the fire and extended coverage component of the Homeowners premium.

Most of the headings in Table 51–1 are self-explanatory. The one heading which might be confusing is that entitled "Rates after Multiplication by Modification Factor." The original Homeowners used much the same rating methods outlined above, except that standard term factors of 2.5 or 2.7 were used together with a package discount of 20 percent which was soon revised to 25 percent. The combination of these two factors produced a so-called modification factor of 1.875 or 2.025 depending upon the term factor employed. $[(1.00 \times 2.5) - .25(1.00 \times 2.5) = 1.875]$. The modification factor was later changed to 1.8, which is the figure used at the time of this writing. With a 40 percent combined discount on a three-year basis, the arithmetic is: $[(1.00 \times 3) - .40(1.00 \times 3) = 1.80]$. Therefore, multiplying the annual fire and extended coverage premium by 1.8

TABLE 51–1

ILLUSTRATION OF DEVELOPMENT OF HOMEOWNERS PREMIUM COMPONENT

1	2	3	4	5	6**	7***	8	9
Protection* and Construction	Annual Fire Rate		Annual Fire and E.C. Rate		Rates after Multiplication by Modification Factor		Total	Grouping (Average of Column 8)
	Buildings	Contents	Buildings	Contents	Buildings	Contents		
7 Class Brick	30	32	46	48	.828	.346	1.174	
6 Class Frame	31	33	47	49	.846	.353	1.199	1.197
8 Class Brick	32	33	48	49	.864	.353	1.217	
9 Class Brick	34	34	50	50	.900	.360	1.260	
7 Class Frame	34	36	50	52	.900	.374	1.274	1.283
8 Class Frame	36	37	52	53	.936	.382	1.318	
9 Class Frame	38	38	54	54	.972	.389	1.362	
10 Class Brick	38	38	54	54	.972	.389	1.362	1.361

* See Chapter 13 for a discussion of classes of municipal fire protection.
** 3 times Column 4 less 40%.
*** (3 times Column 5 less 40%) times 40%.

provides the three-year Homeowners fire and extended coverage component of the formula rate for the building. As the contents are 40 percent of the building amount, multiplying the contents rate by 1.8 and then by 40 percent gives the rate needed for the contents components. Adding the building and contents components together gives the formula rate which, when applied to a given amount of insurance on the building, produces the fire and extended coverage component of the premium, not only for the building but also for the contents.

One further point should be made with respect to the table, namely, the grouping. As indicated above, it is desirable to group rates within certain ranges where the grouping will produce little or no distortion. As a matter of practice such grouping is usually limited to a maximum tolerance of 5 percent. This average or group rate is shown in the last column entitled "Grouping."

The next step is to build in the theft and liability premiums. The theft rate is adjusted because standard theft rates are based on policies whose average size is about $1,200 and which were purchased on a selective basis. When theft is to be written in the same amount as the fire coverage, use of unadjusted rates produces an excessive theft component. The usual practice is to use a loading equivalent to the theft premium for 20 percent of the contents amount subject to the minimum of $1,000 of coverage and the maximum of $4,000. These premiums can be easily converted into dollar loadings and added to the dollar rate for the comprehensive personal liability coverage and multiplied by 1.8 to produce the three-year loading for theft and liability. These combined loadings can then be added to the fire and extended coverage premium to

TABLE 51–2

Illustration of Premium Groups

Protection and Construction	Premium Group	Protection and Construction	Premium Group
6 Class Frame	1	7 Class Brick	1
7 Class Frame	2	8 Class Brick	1
8 Class Frame	2	9 Class Brick	2
9 Class Frame	3	10 Class Brick	3
10 Class Frame	4		

produce the total formula premium for the package by size of policy and by premium group. The premium group reflects the variations in construction and protection used in creating the rate table. Using Table 51–1 above as an example, the assignment of premium groups might be as shown in Table 51–2.

Readers can see that, according to the illustrative table, 7 Class Brick, 6 Class Frame, and 8 Class Brick all take the same rate after grouping and that they are all assigned to Premium Group 1. Similarly, the other protection and construction classes with like premiums are grouped together and given the same premium group number. In actual practice, because of different available deductible options, there will be many more premium groups but the foregoing illustrates the concept. Once these calculations are made, it is relatively simple to construct a premium table somewhat along the lines of Table 51–3.

The procedure outlined in Table 51–3 produces what might be termed the formula premiums for the Homeowners program. The formula premiums are computed merely to establish a relativity of rates between risks

TABLE 51–3

ILLUSTRATIVE PREMIUM TABLE—HOMEOWNERS

Size of Policy	Premium Group			
	1	2	3	4
$ 8,000	$131	$138	$144	$158
$ 9,000	143	150	158	173
$10,000	155	163	171	189

and the rate levels are then adjusted, based to a great extent on experience, to produce the proper level within a given state. The method of making such adjustments is discussed in a subsequent section.

A variation of the Homeowners ratemaking approach, which should be mentioned because it is also used extensively in the Farmowners Program, is found in the rates for the Tenants Policies. This approach has possibilities for other multiple-peril programs and is particularly adaptable to those situations involving a wide range of specific rates. It contemplates the establishment of a premium table giving premiums for various policy amounts according to an index number, which is usually the annual fire and extended coverage rate. Thus, given an annual fire and extended coverage rate, it is possible to "pre-compute" a premium by policy size which includes not only the fire and allied perils premium, but the theft and liability premiums as well. This method can also be developed to employ the grouping techniques described above. A typical rate page for this type of rating procedure appears in Table 51–4.

To use this table it is only necessary to determine what the specific annual fire and extended coverage rate of the risk may be. Thus, if the risk is located in a building with a 25¢ fire rate and 10¢ E.C. rate and the insured desires $7,500 of coverage, the net premium is readily determined from the table to be $55. This premium already has been adjusted for package discounts and may be applied directly to the policy.

As pointed out above, this method is more adaptable to situations where there is a wide range of specific rates, and certain companies have

TABLE 51–4

ILLUSTRATIVE PREMIUM TABLE—TENANTS POLICY

Index Rate*	Amount of Insurance			
	$4,000	$5,000	$7,500	$10,000
Up to .33	$28	$35	$52	$70
.331 to .35	30	37	55	74
.351 to .37	32	39	59	79
.371 to .39	34	42	62	84

* Usually the annual fire and extended coverage rate.

adapted it in a limited way to some commercial programs. It is very flexible and can be made to fit a variety of situations as long as the number of variables, other than rates, is kept small.

Premium Indivisible as to the Insured Only

The foregoing illustrates the usual procedures involved in producing totally indivisible rates or premiums for a package policy. In this instance, once the items have been merged, the premiums become truly indivisible. When these premiums are subsequently adjusted on their own experience, this indivisibility precludes the precise allocation of any portion of the premium to any given peril or coverage. Contrasted to this completely indivisible premium is a second group of package policies which employ a premium that is indivisible as to the insured but which is still divisible as to the insurer. A typical example of this is the Commercial Property Coverage (CPC). (See Chapter 50.) An analysis of this rating procedure is not of great technical interest other than illustrating how specific rates may have to be adjusted to fit the package conditions, irrespective of whether a true package discount is employed.

In the CPC Program the base for the rate is the specific fire and extended coverage rate for the risk. To this base is added a loading to recognize the additional perils included under the "all risk" approach. These rates are totalled and shown on the face of the policy as a single rate or premium. So far as the policyholder is concerned, the premium is truly indivisible, but it is possible for the insurer to break out the premium for statistical reporting and comparison purposes.

The fire and extended coverage rates are on a manual basis (non-discounted). The important concept in the erection of the CPC rate was the development of the "all risk" loading for the policy. An analysis of the type of risk to be covered indicated that the major exposures were theft (or burglary) and water damage. Rates were already available for specific theft and water damage policies, but it was not believed that they fully reflected package policy conditions. For example, most burglary coverages are sold only to target risks with a definite burglary exposure. For many reasons very little theft coverage had been sold. It was found also that, generally, burglary coverage had been sold only in larger cities where the experience naturally would be worse. Further, there was a tendency to purchase only the minimum amount permitted under the rules, which varied from $2,000 to $20,000. As the coverage under CPC is now sold to insureds (1) with quite dissimilar amounts of exposure, (2) who are located in various size towns, and (3) who carry the coverage in an amount equal to the fire coverage rather than to modest sums of $2,000–$3,000, it was apparent that these basic rates had to be adjusted considerably.

It was believed that the territorial relativities used for specific burglary coverage did not properly reflect the conditions which would obtain when the coverage was written under the "all risk" package. For example, adjacent to many large cities are suburban areas which, due to modern transportation, are as readily accessible as the city itself. Apparently, these areas should be grouped together with the adjacent city. Thus, territories in the CPC were established on a county or larger area basis. Next, the larger towns in each state were grouped and analyzed by using crime frequency rates developed from F.B.I. crime reports, loss experience from the burglary statistics, and company underwriting information. From this analysis there evolved a new set of territories and a somewhat different set of rate differentials between territories. Territories were then reviewed according to their water damage propensities and this review in turn resulted in some slightly different relationships. The net result was a refinement to establish 15 territories—rather than the seven in the burglary manual—which permitted the isolation from the remainder of the state of "hot spots" of differing but greater exposure.

The list of occupancies was then reviewed in the light of both water damage and theft possibilities. In burglary treatment there are nine so-called trade groups; under CPC this classification was refined to 19 groups. While this refinement increased both the number of trade groups and the territories, it provided a more accurate appraisal of the exposures which the "all risk" approach demanded.

The premiums and rate levels produced by this analysis were then properly adjusted to reflect the fact that they were originally pitched to relatively small policy amounts, whereas under the CPC they would be applied against the full value of the insured property. This adjustment also recognized the fact that these rates would not only be applied against merchandise values, but also against the value of furniture and fixtures.

The foregoing detailed discussion has been included because it provides a good example of the adjustments that are frequently required in specific rates to recognize the differing conditions between specific policies and package policies, even though each might contain the same perils.

Divisible Premium Computation

The Special Multi-Peril Policy (see Chapter 50) rating procedure is analyzed because it represents a group of policies which has premiums that are divisible in respect both to the insured and to the insurer. While the fire, extended coverage, and other premiums may be combined on the face of the policy, this combination is not mandatory, as it is under CPC. Therefore, the Special Multi-Peril Policy can be said to give rise to a truly divisible premium.

The total SMP premium is made up of a fire premium, extended coverage premium, loadings for additional perils and coverages, and a liability premium. With respect to the fire and extended coverage premium, there is no initial adjustment, prior to application of the package discount. However, in the area of the additional perils loadings, several adjustments have been required. In establishing these loadings, it was necessary to make a series of comparisons between the rates for specific coverages in order to maintain some relationship to these rates and yet come out with a logical rate for the package. Thus, for example, there are specific loadings available for the Office Contents Special Form ("all risk" office contents form) and for the Special Extended Coverage Endorsement ("all risk" building form). There also are specific rates for vandalism, sprinkler leakage, and several other named perils. These rates were usually devised for specific coverages or policies and also frequently reflected the judgment of different groups of underwriters. This arrangement presents no real problem when written in separate contracts. Many problems of rate relativity are created, however, when these diverse elements are brought together in a package policy where gradations of coverage are provided from straight fire and extended coverage, up through the addition of single specific perils, to an additional perils coverage combining several perils, and finally to "all risk." Thus, the loading for \$100,000 of "all risk" coverage on buildings presumably should not be larger than \$100,000 on contents. On the other hand, it should be larger than the sum of the specific rates for the major perils included in the "all risk" coverage, unless there is some good reason why this should not be so, as shown above under the CPC. Similarly, the rates for an additional perils endorsement should be somewhat lower than the sum of the rates of its components, but it cannot be more than the "all risk" loading.

Accommodating these various rate levels and keeping precise relativity is practically impossible when the diverse origins of the specific rates are considered. As an example, rates were available for "all risk" building coverage and the rates for the additional perils coverage on a named perils basis were established at a given percentage of the "all risk" rate. As these rates were on a step basis, this procedure produced rates for the additional perils coverage that in some cases were higher than the comparable specific rates for the same perils, at least in smaller amounts. Therefore, occasionally, there are instances when the component rate for the package before discount may be either unaccountably higher or lower than its companion specific rate.

The liability coverage under the SMP Program has generally been on a combined single limit basis, that is, the same limit applicable to both property damage liability and bodily injury liability. The liability rates are the manual rates converted to a combined single limit basis and with no adjustment other than the package discount and the term "multiple." The rates and premium produced under the foregoing are then subjected to the prescribed package discount to produce the final SMP premiums.

Package Discounts

This discussion leads to the general subject of package discounts. The general factors and the justifications therefor are set forth in the next chapter on "Underwriting and Loss Adjustment in Multiple-Line Insurance."

All packages, even those with indivisible premiums, usually start with a package discount applied to the specific rates. This discount originally was based on underwriting judgment and the actual amount of the initial discount in a program that is going "self-rating," such as the Homeowners, is usually of minor importance. By "self-rating" is meant the establishment of a rate based on the group of risks written under the package and not a rate based on the entire risk classification which would include those risks written under the package and similar risks written under specific policies. As long as it is somewhere in the proper area, experience over time will tend to bring about any needed correction. Once the program does go self-rating, as will be discussed in the next section, the rate actually is based on the experience of this new "class" and there is no longer a discount involved. The matter then becomes purely a rate adjustment problem and is handled in much the same manner that other rate adjustments are handled.

ADJUSTMENT OF PACKAGE RATES OR DISCOUNTS

The methods of adjusting package rate levels, either by means of adjusting the discount or by means of adjusting the actual rate in the case of self-rated policies, as a practical matter present little difference.

The foregoing procedures are not mutually exclusive in that there may be intermediate steps in going from the use of specific rates plus discount to full self-rating. There is usually a period, even for packages with such tremendous growth as the Homeowners, where the package experience is not fully credible and yet the specific rates underlying the package rate may be adjusted, presenting the question as to what extent the changes in specific rates should affect the package.

To determine when a policy is eligible to full self-rating, as well as to determine the extent to which changes in specific rates should be reflected in package rates, it becomes necessary to apply some type of credibility formula. This formula permits the weighing of the package experience and changes in the specific rate to determine a final rate level that reflects both the package experience and the specific rate experience.

The adjustment of the rate level of an indivisible premium policy such as Homeowners is quite similar to the rate adjustment of any specific policy. The following will show the development of a package rate through to full self-rating.

When the first Homeowners was devised, the rate treatment consisted in using the specific rates together with the modifications previously mentioned and with the resultant figure subjected to a 20 percent discount. At this stage, the only adjustment, other than possible change in the specific rates, was by means of changing the discount, and in fact such adjustment was made a few years later when the discount was increased to 25 percent. When the "new" Homeowners was devised in 1958, it was recognized that sufficient experience was accumulating to permit the program to go on a self-rating basis. This metamorphosis occurred in a very short time. In fact, by 1959 or 1960 the volume of Homeowners premium in most states exceeded the premium of specific dwelling policies.

After a detailed study of the matter and consideration of many factors, the underwriters concerned with the problem adopted a "balance point loss ratio" method of adjustment and arbitrarily established the ratio at 54 percent. "Balance point loss ratio" (also called "permissible loss ratio") adjustment contemplates the adjustment of rate levels, based on experience, to a level, which, if it had been in effect for the experience period, would have produced the expected or permissible loss ratio. Thus, if the balance point loss ratio is 50 percent and the actual loss ratio is 60 percent, the disparity indicates that rates should be increased 20 points, that is, to a 120 percent level ($50 \times 1.2 = 60$) so that the losses will then be 50 percent of the premiums. This figure was used for most filings in the early 1960's. The application of the 54 percent balance point loss ratio to the Homeowners rate level adjustment is relatively simple from a mechanical standpoint but the other factors entering into the final establishment of the rate level are far from simple.

Earned Premiums

It is generally accepted that earned premiums are the proper figures to use in ratemaking, particularly when premium writings are increasing rapidly. When written premiums get to the point where they are practically the same from year to year, use of written as opposed to earned premiums makes little difference. With a rapidly rising premium volume, such as for the Homeowners, the ratio of earned to written will vary by year and from state to state. Hence, use of written rather than earned premiums in ratemaking can produce tremendous differences.

The necessity for obtaining as accurate an earned premium as possible is demonstrated by the fact that a 2 percent difference in earned premiums is equivalent to approximately a one point difference in loss ratio. It is not difficult to have an error of 5 to 10 percent in earned premium calculations for an individual state, particularly if countrywide ratios are used.

The Homeowners statistical plan has been designed to produce relatively accurate earned premiums on a form by form and a state by state basis. There are other methods which might produce even more accurate results, but the slight increase in accuracy would be more than offset by the increased cost.

Incurred Losses

The use of incurred losses rather than paid losses is also accepted as more accurate and proper, particularly for a contract which involves third-party coverage where loss settlements might be delayed. Incurred but not reported losses are important in a growing class.

The conversion of paid losses to incurred losses follows standard practices. It is necessary to make proper provision for the treatment of catastrophe losses, such as windstorms, fires, explosions, and others. At

TABLE 51–5

ILLUSTRATION OF WEIGHTING OF EXPERIENCE

Experience	Fire Weighting Factor	Homeowners Percent of Total 6-Year Premium
1957	10%	1
1958	10%	4
1959	10%	5
1960	15%	10
1961	25%	23
1962	30%	57

the present time in respect to Homeowners rates this is done principally on a judgment basis; but studies are being made and eventually a proper method of treating these occurrences will be developed.

Trends

Because of the rapidly changing tempo of the times which affects all business, including insurance, it has become fairly common to introduce trend factors of one type or another into the rate formulas.

Consideration has been given to this matter but no definite set of factors for Homeowners has been introduced. A trend factor is primarily used to give greater weight to the experience of later years. In a sense the Homeowners program actually has a built-in trend factor in the form of its rapidly expanding premium volume. Table 51–5 illustrates this point when the weighting factors as commonly used in fire ratemaking are compared with the actual Homeowners percentage of total premium volume by year in a sample state for a period in the late 1950's and early 1960's.

This table illustrates that the latest year of Homeowners experience had 57 percent weight as compared to 30 percent for the fire experience.

However, as Homeowners premium writings tend to level off some type of trend factor may have to be introduced.

Credibility

The credibility tables employed for the Homeowners program are relatively not as important as they were sometime ago because most states now have sufficient experience for the program to be fully credible. However, the tables illustrate several principles that are of general application.

The basic credibility table employs the commonly used square root formula with $5 million of earned premium as a fully credible premium volume. The square root credibility formula is used in several lines of insurance and appears to produce reasonably accurate results. The formula is: $Z = \frac{\sqrt{P_1}}{\sqrt{P}}$ where Z = the credibility factor; P_1 = premium volume for which credibility is desired; and P = premium volume estimated to be fully credible.

The novel feature which the Homeowners credibility treatment introduced was the so-called seasoning factor. In most cases where credibility factors have been used, they were introduced after the line had been in existence for many years, or for a line of insurance where exposure, as measured by units, was sufficient, and no measure of exposure by time was required. However, the Homeowners was a relatively new line of insurance with definite low-frequency catastrophe exposures. The "seasoning factor," therefore, was introduced to recognize this fact. The factor was constructed so as not to give full credibility until five years of experience had been accumulated, regardless of premium volume. The seasoning factor table was as follows:

Experience Period	*Factor*
a) Less than two years	20%
b) Two years but less than three	40
c) Three years but less than four	60
d) Four years but less than five	80
e) Five years or more	100

The method of application is to multiply the credibility factor as obtained from the credibility table by the seasoning factor to obtain the final credibility modification. Thus, if the credibility factor is .80 and the program has been in for four years, the credibility modifier would be $.80 \times .80 = .64$.

There has been criticism of the seasoning factor.[1] This criticism rests primarily on the point that, if premium volume is the proper method of

[1] See, for example, Dudley M. Pruitt, "The Seat of Wisdom," *Proceedings of the Casualty Actuarial Society*, Volume XLV (1958), pp. 11, 13–15.

measuring exposure, the length of time is unimportant. For an occurrence of a high-frequency low-severity type, such criticism may be valid. However, for the perils of fire, windstorm, and so on, it appears that no matter how large might be the exposure, as measured by premium volume, it could not correctly measure these low frequency occurrences. These can only be measured, at least roughly, by a time factor.

Once all of the foregoing factors have been properly established, it is relatively simple to apply a formula and produce the final premium modification. The procedure is as follows:

1. The net credibility factor is computed by multiplying the factor from the credibility table by the factor from the seasoning table.
2. The gross indicated rate change is calculated by the formula $\frac{LR_a}{LR_f}$ (where LR_a equals the actual loss ration and LR_f is the formula loss ratio, in this case 54%).
3. The net indicated rate change is calculated as follows:
   Indicated change $= Z(R) + (1 - Z)$
   $Z =$ net credibility factor from 1 above
   $R =$ gross indicated rate change from 2 above.
4. To assess the possible effect of rate changes for specific coverage components the foregoing formula may be modified to substitute the Homeowners rate level for R and multiply the component rate level by $(1 - Z)$.

The foregoing illustrates the method of adjusting Homeowners rates, which in turn illustrates the general concepts which can be used in connection with any indivisible premium policy on a self-rating basis.

At the time of this writing there is no extensive experience with respect to the adjustment of package discounts in the case of policies, such as the SMP Program, which employ specific rates as a base. In actual practice, adjustment is not expected to differ too much in result from that obtained above for the Homeowners Policy. It will be necessary to obtain loss ratios based on a credible volume of premium. Eventually, a balance point loss ratio will have to be established and the package discount will be adjusted to bring the actual results as close as possible to the established balance point loss ratio. This area is only beginning to be explored as respectable volumes of premium are being produced. The data will not be available in useful statistical displays until one or two years from the time of this writing. There is reason to believe that the adjustment procedures as finally evolved will closely parallel the Homeowners procedures, except that the end result will be an adjusted package discount rather than an adjusted package rate.

STATISTICS

Closely tied in with all ratemaking is the matter of statistics. The term "statistics" was once defined as "a bunch of numbers looking for an argument." This definition seems especially appropriate in the case of insurance statistics. The statistical plans for the various packages differ greatly, not only because they have been subject to considerable experimentation, but also because the methods of rating employed by the various packages differ significantly. The following comments will deal with the major programs separately.

Homeowners

The Homeowners statistical plan is designed to accommodate data on total premiums and total losses. Premiums are reported, as stated previously, so that they can be converted to an earned basis. Losses are reported on an incurred basis and also by cause of loss. Cause of loss figures are developed, not to be used specifically in ratemaking, but to indicate any unusual trend as well as to explain any unusual loss situation, such as a catastrophe. Premiums and losses are also reported by policy size, by construction and protection, by state (and territory in several states), by deductible, and by form. This information is sufficient to adjust Homeowners rates on the basis of their own experience and, where credible premium volumes are present, with no reference to the rates or premiums for specific policies. The entire industry—stock, mutual, bureau, and independents—uses the same statistical plan, which is a unique fact in itself. Thus the statistics can be readily merged for ratemaking purposes.

Special Multi-Peril Policies

The SMP policies, being on a divisible premium basis and embodying different rating techniques, have required a somewhat more detailed statistical plan. The first major breakout in the SMP program is by line of insurance. The premiums and losses for the property insurance section (Section I) and the liability section (Section II) are reported separately as are the premiums for the boiler and machinery coverage and the comprehensive crime section.

So far as the property section is concerned, the latest plan calls for a breakout of the fire premium and the extended coverage premium, and the placing of all other premiums into either an "all risk" or a named peril code as the case may be. The premium is further broken down by type of occupancy—for instance, motel, office, and so on—and by construction and protection. This breakdown permits a comparison of SMP statistics with experience developed under specific policies. Furthermore, this statistical plan will develop information to permit the program to go self-rating, at least in certain areas, if credible premium volumes are developed in the future. The statistical plan for SMP policies is under review at the time of this writing.

There are several general observations that should be made with respect to package policy statistical plans. First of all, experience with contracts such as the Comprehensive Dwelling Policy (see Chapter 49) has demonstrated the necessity of a single integrated statistical plan to provide for the collection of all experience in connection with a given policy. It is impossible to report statistics for these policies under several plans to several different agencies and obtain any meaningful figures.

Second, it is not proper to merge the statistics produced for package policies with statistics for specific policies. There are two rate problems involved here. First, there is the problem of whether or not withdrawing of premiums and losses from the specific classes would result in a decrease in credibility of statistics for the specific class. Second, there is the problem of whether or not the merging of the package figures and the specific class figures would produce improper results.

With respect to the first question, it is of course possible that withdrawing the premium from the specific classification will result in (*a*) splitting total premiums to the point where neither the specific nor the package experience is credible, or (*b*) a small and, therefore, noncredible premium volume either under the specific program or the package program.

While the possibility of (*a*) above exists, the point is not reached in the case of large volume classes, such as dwellings and apartments. With respect to (*b*), no insuperable problem is presented from a ratemaking standpoint. First of all, many rates are made based on figures that are not credible. To a great extent judgment enters into all ratemaking and becomes relatively more important in the absence of credible statistics. If the premium volume withdrawn by the package is small, it would affect credibility of the specific figures very little, and these rates would continue to be used for the package. On the other hand, if the package premium gets large, it will become credible in and of itself, and the rates for the residue in the specific field, if too small to be credible, will be made on judgment, as many rates are made today where credible figures are lacking.

With respect to the second question as to whether the merging of these figures would produce improper levels, it is believed that any inaccuracy produced by a possible lack of credibility would be much less than the distortion introduced if the discounted premiums of the package were reported back into the normal classes on a collected basis. Such reporting would introduce a considerable distortion into the basic figures rather than produce a broad rating base. The inclusion of discounted premiums in the total (1) might very well improperly inflate loss ratios, thus producing too high a rate for other risks in the class which do not have the discount available to produce the necessary adjustments and (2) might also distort the indicated package discount for those eligible for packaging.

SUGGESTED READINGS

Fire Insurance Rate Making and Kindred Problems. New York: Casualty Actuarial Society, 1960.

HUNT, FREDERIC J., JR. "Homeowners—The First Decade," *Proceedings of the Casualty Actuarial Society,* Vol. 49 (1962), pp. 12–36.

LONGLEY-COOK, L. H. "An Introduction to Credibility Theory," *Proceedings of the Casualty Actuarial Society,* Vol. 49 (1962), pp. 194–221.

PERLET, HARRY F. "Commercial Multiple Peril Rules," *Annals of the Society of Chartered Property and Casualty Underwriters,* Vol. 16 (Winter, 1963), pp. 361–68.

———. "Multiple Peril Trends," *Proceedings of the 13th Annual Insurance Conference.* Columbus: The Ohio State University, 1962.

SIMON, LEROY J. "Rate Making For Package Policies," *Proceedings of the Casualty Actuarial Society,* Vol. 48 (1961), pp. 204–8.

Chapter 52

UNDERWRITING AND LOSS ADJUSTMENT IN MULTIPLE LINE INSURANCE

BY HARRY F. PERLET

Proper underwriting is essential to permit insurers to make a profit in multiple-line insurance. It stands to reason that if rates, which on an overall basis are barely adequate, are discounted from 15 percent to 25 percent or more, there must be some offsetting factors if a profit is to be made. Cautious underwriting is necessary. The bulk of this chapter deals with this subject. Reinsurance of multiple line coverages is treated very briefly. In several paragraphs toward the end of the chapter a few loss adjustment matters peculiar to multiple line insurance are discussed.

RULES

The usual package policy program has certain built-in features which are intended to provide some underwriting safeguards. The following are generally recognized as the basic factors which have an effect on underwriting and on the size of the package discount.

Better Selectivity

Generally speaking, most true package programs have an eligibility rule which is designed to isolate the better-than-average risk from a broader general class. It has been demonstrated conclusively that package programs and particularly the required aspects of packaging, including restricted eligibility rules, higher minimum premiums, and the like, tend to break out from the major class or group a better subclass or group. In addition, packaging also creates a more subtle subclassification because it seems that the persons who purchase package policies generally are a better type of insured than those who do not. They take pride in their possessions and want to be "fully protected." They generally are unlike those of the marginal type who purchase only a small amount of coverage for only selected catastrophe-type exposures.

A classic example of this selectivity in operation is the Homeowners program. By restricting the writing of policies to owner-occupied dwellings only, with $8,000 or more of coverage, a superior subclass has been established. This point is demonstrated by the fact that, while Homeowners Policies are written at substantial discounts below specific rates, the loss ratio is better than that for straight dwelling fire and extended coverage business.

Generally speaking, the bureau-sponsored package programs tend to have more restrictive eligibility rules than those of the independent filers. This condition is brought about by the fact that, as long as the independent company is the only one with a given product, it can control its underwriting and pick and choose its risks without any particular eligibility rule. However, when a program is made generally available to all companies and agents, it becomes practically impossible, in a competitive market, to exercise any great underwriting control. Therefore, more restrictions must be put in the eligibility rules of bureau programs if the experience of those programs is to reflect only the better class of risk.

Reduction of Risk

Reduction of risk is accomplished under package programs in three ways. First, there is the requirement with respect to certain mandatory coverages; second, there is the tying in of one or more additional perils to the fire contract; and third, there is the ready availability of many optional coverages.

Since each insured carries the mandatory coverages, he has difficulty selecting against the company. Of course, to a certain extent this requirement can react against the insurer. Liability insurance must also be provided for an insured who may be an excellent fire risk but a poor liability risk, or vice versa. However, an overall reduction of risk generally obtains and benefits the insurer.

Tying in coverages such as burglary and comprehensive personal liability to a universally required coverage, such as fire, resulted in a tremendous increase in the volume of premium for these collateral coverages. In 1953, residence theft premiums were about $22 million and CPL premiums were about $40 million. In 1960, residence theft premiums had dropped to $14 million and CPL to about $32 million. Applying a rough rule of thumb based upon the relationship of the components in the original premium computation, the theft premium portion of the Homeowners premium for 1960 was about $192 million and the CPL portion about $77 million. Of course, additional exposures bring with them additional losses, but nowhere near in direct proportion to the indicated premium volume increase.

With respect to optional coverages, generally speaking, the exposure to loss is less than under fire and extended coverage, in that the included perils do not produce catastrophes. Moreover, the loss frequency produced by these perils is usually low. Therefore, if they are made readily available as part of the package, there is incentive to purchase them. This incentive, in turn, develops a better spread. As an example, sample surveys conducted in 1962 by the Inter-Regional Insurance Conference show that over 40 percent of the insureds who purchase a mercantile package also purchase some type of business interruption coverage under the package program. It is estimated that only about 10 percent of the insureds who buy mercantile insurance under separate policies buy business interruption insurance.[1] Many other similar instances have been observed which indicate the effect of packaging—even on optional coverages.

Expense Savings

There is a definite savings in packaging coverages which is difficult to equate to a precise percentage of the premium. Expense savings are realized in three major areas: first, in processing of larger premium policies; second, in reducing the number of transactions involved in processing; and third, in permitting a single inspection to cover both property and liability. To some extent these areas overlap, but in many aspects they are different.

With respect to the first point, it is obvious that many expenses are constant and do not vary with the size of the premium; or, if they do vary, it is not in direct relationship to the size of the premium. It costs just as much to type a $100 premium policy as it does a $1,000 premium policy. If the dollar cost is $5.00, it is 5 percent of the $100 policy, but only half a percent of the $1,000 policy. If ten $100 policies have to be written to equal the one $1,000 policy, the total cost would be $50 rather than $5.00. By combining several coverages into one policy, the size of the premium is increased and the savings illustrated by the foregoing examples are brought into play. Thus, the writing of a Standard Fire Policy with the Extended Coverage Endorsement, a CPL Policy, and a theft policy would cost approximately three times as much as the writing of one Homeowners, which includes all three coverages. Similarly, there are other items, such as travel, salaries, and so on, which may be somewhat larger for a larger premium policy than for a smaller premium policy, but not in direct proportion. In the commercial realm, it is customary to have a risk inspected and this procedure can be combined so that a single inspection can serve both property and liability purposes, thus eliminating a duplication that on larger risks can run into considerable amounts.

The same reasoning applies to the divisible premium policies, and

---

[1] Mark R. Greene, *Insurance Management of Small Retailers* (Eugene: Bureau of Business Research, University of Oregon, 1962), p. 30.

particularly commercial risk policies, such as the SMP Policy. Perhaps they do not apply to the same degree because factors such as coinsurance and insurance education have tended to produce the proper insurance to value and the greatest combinations of coverages possible under specific policies. However, the principle is still applicable because of the incorporation of liability coverages, business interruption coverages, and others, into the single policy.

An additional point in the commercial field is the fact that for business reasons, it has been fairly common to split up a line among many producers, each with a separate policy and usually for a small premium. The package rules are designed to discourage this as much as possible. Also, the incorporation of liability coverage into the package and the use of indivisible premiums tends to prevent splitting as it is not customary to divide liability coverage. Therefore, packaging does tend to create larger premium policies even in the commercial area.

From the foregoing, it is evident that the overall value of packaging as reflected by the package discount is not necessarily, and in fact should not be, identical for all packages. It will vary depending upon the classification of the particular risks under consideration, the number of mandatory coverages required, the minimum premium, and many other facts—each of which contributes to the overall discount. It is difficult, if not impossible, to determine the extent to which each contributes and because of the varying effects, it is evident that the total package credit at the outset must be established to a large extent on informed underwriting judgment and should not necessarily be the same for all packages. For example, the original Homeowners discount was 20 percent which was alleged to consist of 10 percent for the better class of risks and 10 percent for expense savings. This discount was soon increased to 25 percent and now, if it could be established, probably would be found close to 30 percent or even 40 percent.

The following example outlines the variables that are present in the various coverages under the SMP program and suggests why discounts should not necessarily be identical.

1. *Mandatory Coverages—Perils* (*By Program*)

Motel........................Fire; E.C.; V. & M.M.; sprinkler leakage; weight of ice, snow, or sleet; collapse; limited glass breakage; limited water damage; and liability coverages.

Apartment....................Fire, E.C., V. & M.M., sprinkler leakage, burglary, and liability coverages.

Office.........................Fire, E.C., V. & M.M. sprinkler leakage, and liability coverages.

Mercantile....................Fire, E.C., and liability coverages.

2. *Minimum Premiums*

	Section I	*Section II*
Motel	$250	$135
Apartment	50	50
Office	50	50 per policy
Mercantile	$ 50 to $650—Varies, see manual	

3. *Size of Premium.* In addition to a higher minimum premium requirement, the actual premium developed for the average motel policy appears to be higher than for the average apartment policy. This differential seems to have the effect of developing lower expenses in relation to premium and seems to justify a higher credit.

4. *Nature of Properties Covered.* Mercantile properties are generally found in multiple occupancy buildings while motels, apartments, and offices are usually operated by a single insured. This circumstance reinforces the factor of a better class of insured by allowing such an insured to exercise sole control of his premises as opposed to a multiple-occupancy situation. It is obvious that the effect of this subclassification on a fairly uniform group of risks such as motels, for example, could be considerably different than for such a heterogeneous class as mercantiles or intermediate groups, such as apartments or offices.

5. *Mandatory Coverages—Property.* It is mandatory to cover both buildings and business personal property under the Motel, Apartment House, and Office Programs while building coverage is optional under the Mercantile Program.

Some have advocated the establishment of a single uniform package discount based apparently upon the belief that the only advantage in packaging is expense savings and that this should be uniform for all packages. As shown above, the expense savings is only one, and not necessarily in all cases the major, element in the package discount. Further, the savings in expense itself can vary among policies.

Probably the most important single factor of all the foregoing is the restricted eligibility rule of the various packages as set forth under "Better Selectivity" above. Expense savings may partially offset the discount, but the better loss experience of the refined risk classification is the major area in which the offset can be realized. As pointed out above, it has been conclusively demonstrated that package policies do tend to break out the better class of insured. The main reasons were set forth above and will not be repeated—other than in the form of an admonition that weakening these rules can only lead to trouble. There is constant pressure to relax the restrictions in favor of broadened eligibility rules, lower minimum amounts, and fewer mandatory coverages. If these pressures are allowed to alter the underwriting requirements for the package approach to the point where they are similar to those for specific policies, the package loss experience can be expected to deteriorate.

FORMS

In addition to the premium savings, another feature which makes packaging attractive is the granting of more protection without the gaps or overlaps which exist between separate specific policies. A homeowner who purchases a fire policy with a vandalism endorsement on it and also purchases a theft policy has certain overlapping coverages. Similarly, an insured who purchases an Owners', Landlords', and Tenants' Liability Policy and also a Boiler and Machinery Policy may very well have duplicate coverage in certain areas. The true package embodies an attempt to eliminate these overlaps.

Conversely, there are certain gaps in coverage which can be overcome in the package. For example, many small retail risks have a nominal transit exposure which is hardly worth a separate policy. This coverage can be provided under the package at little cost. Also, most packages now have nominal extensions of coverage, such as for extra expense, personal effects, valuable papers, and so on, which will take care of the minor incidental exposures, but at the same time encourage the insured to note his possible exposure and take out additional insurance if he needs it. In effect, the manual, the applications, and the worksheets all provide a ready check list of optional coverages to eliminate gaps in coverage.

Every effort is made to keep the forms as close to the specific coverage as possible. Certain clauses, such as the nuclear exclusion and the war risk exclusion are retained verbatim so as not to upset existing reinsurance treaties. Most package policies do require the use of forms and endorsements which are specifically tailored to their use.

This requirement is due to several reasons, of which two are particularly important. First, when several coverages are brought together in a single policy, the differences naturally stand out. Thus, an examination of the various time element coverages (such as rents or gross earnings) available as specific policies will disclose a variation in language, placement, and other treatment of provisions. When the coverages are separately available, these differences are not apparent and there is little compulsion to change them. However, when the coverages are brought together in the same program, the differences immediately stand out and lead to pressure to make them uniform. A second reason for the special forms and endorsements is the fact that the basic package policy and forms contain provisions which are usually contained in endorsements under specific policies. For example, the Extended Coverage Endorsement is actually an endorsement to the Standard Fire Policy. On the other hand, the multiple peril form is attached to a multiple peril policy and the form enumerates the perils of fire, wind, etc., all as one coverage, rather than as "extended coverage." This arrangement in turn eliminates the need for "substitution of terms" provisions and other similar provisions contained in the specific forms.

Another basic concept of most package programs is the mandatory coverages. Therefore, it is customary to combine into a single form all of the provisions for the property section, for example, including those applicable to fire, extended coverage, and other perils. In specific policies each coverage is treated separately. The general conclusion is that most packages require special forms and special endorsements tailored to the package. This requirement permits editing to eliminate overlapping and contradiction which in turn leads to a clearer, more integrated coverage.

As a corollary to this matter of mandatory coverage, it sometimes happens that a risk has certain exposures which the insurer does not wish to assume, even though it might come within the purview of the mandatory coverage. An example in point is the mandatory comprehensive personal liability coverage under the Homeowners written for an insured with a particularly vicious dog. Another Homeowners example involves the 10 percent outbuilding extension where a given outbuilding might be in extremely poor repair. Under such conditions, it is permissible to attach a so-called "restrictive" endorsement to eliminate these undesirable exposures, in those cases where they are not contemplated by the rate.

By and large, the form differences do not affect the underwriter quite as much as they do the adjusters, as will be pointed out later. An example is the possibility of extending coverage available under the package, some of which extensions also entail additional amounts of insurance. Certain extensions, such as the additional amount on outbuildings, may result in an unexpected large loss under certain conditions. For example, the outbuilding extension is automatically 10 percent of the building amount but is established as an actual dollar amount of coverage. In the case of a total loss of, say, a $200 outbuilding in a valued policy state, there is a definite possibility that the company might be liable for the full amount, which might be several times $200.

The forms may also contain some cutbacks in coverage as well as broadened coverage due to the process of merging several diverse coverages into one program and the consequent compromising of the differences between forms. For example, the Homeowners Forms 1–4 contain a limitation of $1,000 on single articles of jewelry, furs, and such, whereas the standard theft coverage does not. This limitation exists for two reasons. First, because it is permissible to provide scheduled "all risk" coverage under the Homeowners and the underwriters want to encourage such method of writing. Second, Form 5, which is an "all risk" coverage, is patterned after the Personal Property Floater and has a $250 limit on unscheduled jewelry and furs. It is not deemed proper for the restrictive Forms (1–4) to be too much broader, if at all, than Form 5. The $1,000 limit was introduced as a compromise.

The foregoing illustrations demonstrate some of the instances in which the underwriting of package policies has been improved by form language and provisions.

SPECIFIC UNDERWRITING PROBLEMS

Account Underwriting

The first underwriting problem encountered with package policies is the necessity to think in terms of account underwriting rather than peril underwriting. An often used example to demonstrate this problem is the sprinklered fireproof warehouse in the middle of a large city. From a fire standpoint it may be an excellent risk, but from a vandalism or theft standpoint it may be the poorest kind of risk. This illustration is an extreme case, but similar problems in varying degrees are present in all risks. The underwriter must then determine, on balance, whether the account taken as a whole is or is not acceptable. He must look to the whole account and not to just one or more of the peril coverages.

Another facet of this same problem is the fact that liability rates in the package are "frozen" for a period of three years, following the property concept. With high frequency type occurrences, such as are encountered in the liability field, this rigidity may detract from the underwriting attractiveness of many risks as far as the package is concerned.

The development of packages has created a need for multiple line underwriters. There is disagreement as to whether it is possible to make any one person into a competent multiple line underwriter because of the complexities of the various coverages. Such development may be possible in the dwelling field. In the commercial area, however, most companies find it better to have a department staffed by competent underwriters, each familiar with his own particular line but working with others as a single team.

Pyramiding Limits

Another problem with packages is the possibility of pyramiding limits. For example, a $25,000 Homeowners Policy does not present the possibility of a mere $25,000 total loss but rather one which may run as high as $42,500 ($25,000 for the building, $10,000 on the contents, $5,000 additional living expense, plus $2,500 on outbuildings). In addition, there could be at least $25,000 of liability loss if a fireman were injured through the negligence of the insured. It must be remembered that the additional living expense and outbuilding coverage are now additional amounts of insurance for which actually no premium is collected, whereas, under prior coverages, they were merely optional methods of distributing the $25,000 of building coverage (but are now also additional in these separate coverages). It might be well to note also that there is a growing tendency to make these optional extensions additional amounts of insurance under many of the commercial package policies. Underwriters must be very careful in establishing lines to accommodate this possibility.

Package policies have tended to induce companies to take a larger proportion of the total risk. In fact, one of the underlying purposes of the package is to put as much coverage as possible in one policy and one insurer in order to reduce the expense of several small premium policies. The rules are specifically written to encourage this larger participation or, conversely, to discourage line splitting. The one exception to this is the SMP program where a percentage participation is permitted on Section I (property coverage) only. This exception was made in the belief that some risks otherwise eligible for an SMP program would be so large that no one company could write the entire Section I coverage.

REINSURANCE

Packaging has created some problems in reinsurance, particularly so far as indivisible premium policies are concerned. It is customary for many companies to reinsure only certain catastrophe coverages, such as windstorm. Such custom raises the question as to what portion of the package premium is allocated to windstorm. The general practice is to estimate a percentage of the premium for fire, windstorm, and so on, with the estimate based on the relationship of the components as they were originally included in the premium. These percentages are accurate enough for reinsurance or taxation purposes and are generally accepted by reinsurers and insurance departments. Because of the widespread acceptance of the package concept, some reinsurers now accept reinsurance on a single treaty–single retention base.

Reinsurance under the commercial packages does not present the same problem because commercial packages usually are on a divisible premium basis. However, in the cases where premiums may be on at least a partially indivisible basis, a reliable percentage breakdown can be estimated. Since losses may exceed the "face" amount of insurance (for instance, on the dwelling in a Homeowners), retentions and/or pro rata cessions may have to be increased.

LOSS ADJUSTMENT

Adjustment of losses under the package policy usually poses no different or more unusual problems than those encountered in connection with the counterpart coverage under specific policies. The few differences are actually more apparent than real as the following comments will illustrate.

Language of the Contract

Although an effort is made to have the language of the package policy track as closely as possible the language of the specific policies, identity in some cases is not possible. In most cases the language is identical or very similar. A given provision may be contained in the policy rather than the form or vice versa. It, therefore, becomes necessary for the adjuster to read and become acquainted with the entire contract and not assume that merely because a given provision is not in the familiar place where he has been used to seeing it in a specific policy, that it is not in the package contract at all.

First- and Third-Party Adjusting

Another aspect of loss adjustment under package policies is the trend in some cases to have the same adjuster be both a first- and third-party adjuster. The expense saving which this combination provides has offsetting disadvantages. Adjusters trained for third-party claims have a much different outlook in that they generally are not dealing directly with the insured, that is, the customer, but usually are dealing with a third-party claimant who is a stranger to the contract. (See Chapter 47.) Adjusters trained for first-party claims on the other hand are dealing directly with the insured and they are interested in keeping him reasonably happy. (See Chapters 16, 20, and 30.)

Furthermore, usually a given loss involves only a first-party or a third-party claim, and only infrequently do both types occur to the same insured at the same time. If there is sufficient adjustment work to keep an adjuster busy in each line, there really is then no reason for trying to make any one person a multiple line adjuster.

Psychological Factor

One area in which loss adjustment under packages may be said to differ from that under specific coverages is not lingual but rather is psychological. When a person receives a package policy, he may be inclined to read it or at least parts of it. For the first time people—including agents, insureds, loss adjusters, and others—discover coverages or exclusions that may have been in specific policies for 15 or 20 years but of which they were unaware.

In this same vein, it is found that there is a tendency to treat any package—from the simplest to the most complex—as being an "all coverage" policy. They are sometimes sold in this manner, or conversely, the insured frequently is not fully advised that his particular package only has certain coverages. It is somewhat natural to assume that a dwelling package policy covers the usual exposures of a dwelling, and if the limitations are not pointed out to the insured, there is a tendency to make a claim for any and all losses. This point does seem to be at variance with that in the preceding paragraph. Paradoxically, both seem to be in order. Further, some of the pictorial and other advertising has also contributed to this condition.

Claims Consciousness

Still another claims factor is operating. Many coverages are being sold for the first time on a mass market basis. Examples are residence theft and

TABLE 52–1

NUMBER OF LOSSES PER MILLION DOLLARS OF HOMEOWNERS EARNED PREMIUM 1955–1961

Year	All Losses	All Losses except Wind
1955	4030	2400
1956	5150	2500
1957	4280	2800
1958	4270	2840
1959	3800	2370
1960	3850	2470
1961	4085	2675

SOURCE: Derived from Homeowners Policy statistics compiled by the National Board of Fire Underwriters.

liability coverages which formerly were sold to only a few. As components of the Homeowners, they are now being sold in great quantity. It is natural, therefore, that the total number of losses should increase. Additional losses, however, do not mean that these contracts are the loss breeders they are sometimes alleged to be. There is no doubt that insureds are tending to become more claims conscious. The package policy probably has contributed to this consciousness. However, an analysis of package policy loss experience does not indicate any sharp trends in this direction. Table 52–1, a frequency study made to determine the Homeowners losses per $1 million of earned premiums, is of interest.

It can be seen that while the frequency did increase in 1961, it has fluctuated up and down by year with no decided trend yet indicated. With respect to severity of loss, the picture is slightly different but not alarmingly so. Using the same years, the dollar size of loss is estimated to be as shown in Table 52–2.

It will be noted that except for the year 1961, the upward trend was less than 10 percent in six years which no more than equals the effect of inflationary trends. It is too early to tell whether the jump in 1961 is

TABLE 52–2

AVERAGE SIZE OF HOMEOWNERS LOSSES IN DOLLARS 1955–1961

Year	All Losses	Wind Losses Only	All Losses except Wind
1955	$ 92	$72	$106
1956	88	62	105
1957	61	55	109
1958	95	60	112
1959	89	49	113
1960	105	86	115
1961	121	87	140

SOURCE: Derived from Homeowners Policy statistics compiled by the National Board of Fire Underwriters.

merely a fluctuation or an indication of the beginning of a rising trend in loss severity.

In summary, the adjustment of losses under package policies from a technical standpoint usually presents little difference from the adjustment of a similar loss under a specific policy. In some respects, it may be simpler because usually there is only one insured involved and only one policy rather than several with overlapping coverage. As a consequence usually only one adjuster handles the entire loss. Losses are increasing, but not too far out of proportion with the premium volume increase.

SUGGESTED READINGS

See references at end of Chapter 51.

PART VII

Suretyship

Chapter 53

HISTORY, NATURE, AND USES OF SURETYSHIP

BY HERBERT S. DENENBERG

Suretyship and insurance, two words which are used to describe devices for converting uncertainty to certainty, can both be traced etymologically to the same Latin word, "*securus,*" which means free from care or secure. Thus insurance and suretyship, claiming a common linguistic heritage, are related to such words as "security," "sure," "secure," and "assure."

This link between two words and two great institutions is far more than a matter of language. It is a matter of function and purpose as well as a matter of marketing and regulation. Indeed, to the consumer seeking the security which is the essence of both insurance and suretyship, the two are parts of the larger process of insurance programming. That is, the economics of insurance and suretyship are identical. By injecting certainty into economic activity, both of these institutions lessen the inhibiting effect of risk on the decision-making process and make for a more productive, rational, and effective allocation of resources.

There are, however, some useful distinctions that can be drawn between insurance and suretyship. These distinctions have justified the separate treatment customarily accorded suretyship, and they are examined in detail later. The general nature of suretyship is explored in this chapter. This exploration is accomplished by a look at the history and development of suretyship and an examination of real and alleged differences between insurance and suretyship. Finally, the purpose and methods of suretyship are further elaborated.

HISTORY OF SURETYSHIP

Suretyship comprises arrangements involving the assumption of liability for the obligation of another. The surety agrees to protect the obligee (or beneficiary) against the default of the principal (or obligor).

The development of suretyship can be divided into two broad periods: The era of personal suretyship and the era of corporate suretyship. Perhaps a punster would prefer to describe the former period as the error of personal suretyship. If nothing else, an account of personal suretyship is the classic and compelling proof of the need for corporate suretyship.

Personal Suretyship

The personal surety[1] was an individual who acted either gratuitously or for a consideration. On the other hand, a corporate surety enters into surety contracts as a business, and is commonly referred to in current legal discussions as a "compensated surety."

The era of personal suretyship is the history of a form of contract; in fact, the oldest recorded contracts are those of sureties. The era of corporate suretyship is the history of a business, that is, the entering into of surety contracts as a business rather than as a mere incidental relationship. Thus like insurance, suretyship may be viewed as a contract and as a business. And like insurance, as later discussion demonstrates, it may also be viewed as a technique or device as well as an instrument of business planning.

Perhaps the most famous, but not the earliest historical references to personal suretyship are in the Bible, which is replete with warnings against becoming a surety. The Biblical warnings dramatically reflect the fear of personal suretyship. Commentary on these Biblical references in the literature of suretyship also reflects in a striking fashion some of the ingrained attitudes and insights of the surety underwriter.

In Proverbs, this grim statement appears: "My son, if thy be surety for thy friend, if thou hast stricken thy hand with a stranger, thou art snared with the words of thy mouth, thou art taken with the words of thy mouth."[2] Job laments: "Who is he that will strike hands with me?"[3] Crist, a noted writer on corporate suretyship, explains that "striking hands" was an early method of sealing the surety contract, and then observes that Job "obviously was unable to avail himself of the services of a resourceful and persuasive broker."[4] From Proverbs there is a further caveat: "Take his garment that is surety for a stranger";[5] Crist comments that this is probably "the earliest reference to the modern expression of "losing one's shirt."[6]

---

[1] Sometimes referred to as a private surety, an accommodation surety, or a nonvocational surety.

[2] Proverbs 6:1–2.

[3] Job 17:3.

[4] G. W. Crist, Jr., *Corporate Suretyship* (2d ed.; New York: McGraw-Hill Book Co., Inc., 1950), p. 3.

[5] Proverbs 20:16 and 27:13.

[6] Crist, *op. cit.*, p. 3.

Of course, all Biblical references to suretyship are not warnings. In Genesis, Judah becomes surety to his father for his brother, Benjamin.[7]

There are records of surety contracts made approximately 5,000 years ago, but which have a striking resemblance to the modern bond. The Library of Sargon I (circa 2750 B.C.) contains a record of a surety contract in which a lessee's performance was secured by a local merchant, while the lessor served his military obligation.

The great Code of Hammurabi, at once primitive and advanced, containing the barbarous *lex talionis* (the law of retaliation) and at the same time allowing women to engage in business and giving them as many business rights as men, also contained a provision for state fidelity bonding. Each city and its governor were made "sureties" to the victim of any bandit, unless the bandit was captured and executed. This system, closely related to the English frankpledge, is perhaps beyond the bounds of what is technically suretyship. But the historians of suretyship, like the historians of insurance, frequently broaden the gauge of their definitions to include much that is within the spirit if not within the letter of their interest.

Another early expression of suretyship was hostageship. Here the debtor secured his obligation by delivering to his creditor a hostage who would be freed upon the payment of his debt. However, in the event of default, the hostage would be put to death, mutilated, or perhaps merely enslaved, depending upon the agreement. Of course, as time passed the system was refined; for instance, the hostage would not be imprisoned, but would be under obligation to report to the creditor in the event of default, for execution or other appropriate disposition. This refinement eliminated the expense of pre-execution room and board bills.

Happily, all ancient surety arrangements were not of such a harsh nature. According to Herodotus, the Babylonians annually auctioned off women of marriageable age. When all of the beautiful women were disposed of to the highest bidder, and no further bids were forthcoming for the left-overs, another approach was resorted to. The ugly women were disposed of to the men who demanded the smallest dowries. But to assure performance under such unpromising conditions, each prospective husband was required to furnish a surety who guaranteed that the marriage ceremony would in fact be performed. Perhaps this is the earliest forerunner of the modern performance and contract bond, although the more cynically inclined would be apt to describe it as a form of bail bond.

This historical development could be elaborated in detail and there is an ample record of suretyship among the Greeks, the Romans, in the civil law, and in English common law, based in turn on the prior Anglo-

---

[7] Genesis 43:9. Other Biblical references to suretyship are as follows: Genesis, Chapters 42 and 44:32; Proverbs 11:15, 17:18, 22:26; Ecclesiastes 29:18.

Saxon legal development. Even the *Magna Carta* contained provisions for suretyship to assure the performance of the King's promises. Some of this development is familiar to us from English literature. Perhaps the best known literary excursion into suretyship is Shakespeare's "Merchant of Venice."

Corporate Suretyship

Defects of Personal Suretyship Gave Impetus to the Development of Corporate Suretyship. The defects of personal suretyship, boldly announced by "almost every reference now extant to early suretyship" touched all the parties to the contract. In the overly mild words of one early proponent of corporate suretyship, there was the possibility of "mutual injury" to all three parties to the contract.

1. *Surety's View.* The personal surety faced disasters ranging from death in the ancient world to financial suicide in modern times. Even the wisest man was faced with the alternative of exposing himself to ruin, or refusing the request of a friend or relative who needed a bond and often had no other alternative.

2. *Principal's View.* The principal faced the converse of the dilemma of the would-be surety. He could either give up the opportunity which required the bond or impose on his friends, relatives, or associates to go surety for him. If he was lucky enough to obtain a friendly surety, he would then be under a moral obligation to reciprocate. A final alternative was to seek a surety for a price, but it is easy to see why the price of a personal surety would soar far beyond normal values, and in many cases even such an arrangement was not forthcoming.

3. *Obligee's View.* Even the obligee, the person the contract was designed only to benefit, found many disadvantages in personal suretyship. The obligee might find it difficult to determine the status and reliability of the private surety at the inception of the contract. Subject to no regulation such as is now used to guard the corporate surety, the private surety, even if initially dependable, might at any future moment become unwilling or unable to perform. The surety would ordinarily make no preparation for a loss, and unlike the corporate surety, was bound by the laws of mortality. Finally, when it became necessary to enforce the contract against the surety, the obligee had to expect that the surety would receive favored treatment in the courts. It was frequently said that the personal surety was a favorite of the law and his contract *strictissimi juris.* In other words, the courts sought to impose on the surety the "least burdensome obligation that was consistent with any meaning that his words might bear."[8]

---

[8] Herschel W. Arant, *Handbook of the Law of Suretyship and Guaranty* (St. Paul: West Publishing Co., 1931), p. 140. See also Laurence P. Simpson, *Handbook on the Law of Suretyship* (St. Paul: West Publishing Co., 1950), pp. 94–100.

Early Proposals. The defects of personal suretyship were always obvious, but they were further compounded by the industrial revolution and the subsequently and continually increasing complexity of governmental and economic activity. As early as 1720, an advertisement appeared in the *London Daily Post* announcing the formation of a company to carry on a surety business, the bonding of the fidelity of servants, clerks, and others who held a position of trust and confidence. The advertisment indicated inauspiciously that stock would be offered for subscription at the Devil's Tavern. The company was seemingly one century too early, and was not equipped to operate on any "scientific" basis. It apparently collapsed shortly after its organization.

An American, William L. Haskins, is frequently given credit for having conceived the modern notion of the corporate surety in a pamphlet published in 1837. Haskins mentioned contract bonds, fiduciary bonds, and credit guarantees, but not fidelity bonds. In 1840, Professor De Morgan of London University, proposed a fidelity business based on the law of large numbers. He correctly predicted the formation of a fidelity company. The very year the article was published, two such companies were formed in London. The first was the British Guarantee of Trust Company and the second, the Guarantee Society of London. These events marked the birth of the fidelity phase of corporate suretyship, but in America much of the rest of corporate suretyship was yet to be born.

American Development. The first American surety company was the Fidelity Insurance Company (1865), formed to carry on a fidelity business like its English counterparts. This formation was followed by a succession of new companies and new forms of contracts. The Fidelity and Casualty Company was formed in 1876 and was the first company to write court bonds and license and permit bonds. This company was also authorized to write other lines of insurance, and so are most modern companies. The American Surety Company was organized in 1884 and was the first company to write contract bonds. Two companies now no longer in existence are credited with first writing fiduciary bonds. The Fidelity and Deposit Company, organized in 1890, first wrote public official bonds.

All of this development was not as smooth and continuous as this brief description might indicate. There were difficulties in raising capital and in winning public acceptance. There were those who doubted that the fidelity risk was even insurable. Principles and precedents had to be developed. As suretyship continued to increase in importance, some companies developed unsound practices relating to rates, reserves, and underwriting. For example, some companies would execute bonds in amounts greater than their total capital and surplus.

As competition mounted, so did many of the abuses. The business was in need of regulation, and the situation—prior to 1906—was described by a report to the predecessor of the National Association of Insurance Commissioners as regulatory chaos.

Early Regulatory Development. One of the turning points in the regulation of corporate suretyship was the organization in 1908 of the Surety Association of America, by a group of corporate sureties. This association sought to impose a regimen of self-regulation. One of its most important steps was the creation of the Towner Rating Bureau, which operated from 1909 to 1947 when it was merged with the Surety Association of America. The latter organization has continued to operate since its formation and now sets rates, establishes forms, secures and analyzes data, makes filings with regulatory authorities, provides a forum of discussion, and performs any other function incident to its objectives.

Modern Development. During the balance of the twentieth century, corporate suretyship continued to grow in importance and efficiency to the point where it has been aptly described as "The Balance Wheel of American Business." It continues to offer many of the basic contracts developed in the last century, and many new contracts to meet almost every conceivable need.

Premium volume increased, especially in the last several decades, and is now approximately one third of a billion dollars annually. A recent government circular, listing companies holding certificates of authority as acceptable sureties on federal bonds, lists 209 companies, with individual underwriting capacity ranging from $45,000 to over $100 million, and with a total qualifying power of nearly $1 billion.

The surety business is now considered a form of casualty insurance and is regulated as such, although one observer has noted that "there is at least as wide a gulf between casualty insurance and bonding as between fire and liability."[9] With the advent of the multiple line laws, the importance of the separation of lines of insurance is of less moment. Today, most surety business is carried on by multiple line companies but there are important bonding specialists. The stock company dominates suretyship, with a much smaller portion of premiums going to mutuals, and a near infinitesimal fraction going to reciprocals and state funds.

Lines and Particular Types of Bonds. Suretyship is ordinarily divided into two major classes—surety bonding and fidelity bonding. This breakdown is not totally satisfactory, as the term "surety bond" is used to describe all surety bonds as well as one subclass.

Fidelity bonding, sometimes referred to as dishonesty insurance, responds for losses caused by the dishonesty of employees, within the terms of the bond. Fidelity premiums now account for about one third of the total bonding premium. Surety bonds (as a subclass standing alongside of fidelity bonds) may be divided into the following categories: (1) contract

[9] C. A. Kulp, *Casualty Insurance* (3d ed.; New York: Ronald Press, 1956), p. 17.

bonds, (2) court bonds, (3) fiduciary bonds, (4) public official bonds, (5) license and permit bonds, and (6) miscellaneous bonds.[10] Contract bonds secure the performance of contracts. Court bonds secure the performance of litigants, when they desire to take some action that will affect the rights of others. For example, before a plaintiff can replevin property he will have to post a bond to protect the rights of the person from whom the property is to be taken. Fiduciary bonds secure the performance of certain persons who are appointed to a position of trust, for instance, administrators, guardians, and such. Public official bonds secure the performance of public officials. License and permit bonds secure the performance of certain licensees such as liquor store owners, auctioneers, and others. Miscellaneous bonds secure performance of a variety of agreements.

INSURANCE VERSUS SURETYSHIP

A considerable amount of discussion in the literature of suretyship turns on the differences between suretyship and insurance, and on whether suretyship is in fact insurance. This discussion, surprisingly enough, has generated a considerable amount of heat and some sharp differences of opinion. Few would deny that there may be important differences between insurance and suretyship, but many of the alleged differences may in part reflect, in Kulp's words, "an oversimplification and overstatement of bonding peculiarities." A review of these real or alleged differences is useful, as it throws some light on the nature of bonding.

Any such review should be tempered at the outset by recognition of differences between major surety lines as well as between particular bonds within each major category. Generalizations valid for one line or one type of bond may have no relevance elsewhere. Contracts combining insurance and surety contracts in one package—for instance, the Comprehensive 3–D Policy, Blanket Crime Policy, or the Bankers' Blanket Bond —may further confuse the issue, but they should be analyzed in terms of their underlying building blocks.

The distinction between suretyship and insurance can be examined from the viewpoint of the respective parties to the contract.

Surety's Viewpoint

Surety Expects No Losses. Many bonds are underwritten on the theory that the corporate sureties involved "take no risk whatever and that the premiums they receive are merely 'service fees' for the lending of credit."[11] In this sense they operate like bankers. Suretyship is in fact very

[10] For Annual Statement purposes, premiums for public official bonds are classified as fidelity. (See Chapter 54.)

[11] Crist, *op. cit.*, p. 7.

close to banking in many ways and similarity is most obvious in contract and court bonds.

In the lines which most nearly resemble banking, several interesting analogies between banking and suretyship can be made. The loss ratio of the surety may be compared to the charge-off of the banker. Both suretyship and banking may experience great losses during a major depression and virtually none during times of prosperity. Charge-offs reached a peak of 75 percent in the early 1930's while the surety's loss ratio soared to 106 percent. It is also interesting to note that the banker and surety underwriter frequently may raise the same questions about an applicant, summarized in the so-called three "C's": character, capacity, and capital. Like the banker, the surety may also require full or partial collateral. In such cases it may truly be said that the surety (as well as the obligee) takes virtually no risk.

In view of the lack of substantial risk in some bonding lines, and since the surety may also provide various investigative and advisory functions, the service element looms large. There are also several insurance lines where the service element is important: boiler and machinery, title, credit, and glass insurance.

Significance of Salvage. There are two important sources of funds for loss payments in suretyship: (1) the premium dollar and (2) salvage. Salvage is the amount recovered by the surety from the defaulting principal indemnitor, and others after the loss has been paid. The ratio of salvage to gross losses frequently runs higher than in most lines of insurance. However, "salvage" (in the form of subrogation recoveries) may also be important in insurance (for instance, automobile physical damage lines).

Predictability of Experience. Most insurers are able to predict future experience within a reasonable range by reliance on the law of large numbers. Corporate sureties, at least in some lines, may not be able to rely on the law of large numbers and may not be able to obtain the degree of predictability of some insurers. Surety classifications may be too small to develop sufficient statistical credibility. This situation may of course be found in some insurance classifications as well. Many types of bonds are subject to cyclical swings, are sensitive to the business cycle, and are at the mercy of a heavy catastrophe hazard. These factors seriously impair any attempt to predict future losses. There is one further difference which has been described as maturity of experience:

> In insurance rate making, that maturity contemplates a cycle long enough to include fat years as well as lean years. Because insurance losses are largely self-revealing, that cycle need not be excessively long. In surety rate making that cycle must be almost indeterminate, for it must include not only an adequate number of years to measure known losses but also sufficient time to discover losses skillfully concealed and losses indefinitely deferred.[12]

---

[12] *Ibid.*, p. 181.

To complicate the picture further, the recovery from salvage may extend over decades and these recoveries may be extremely irregular in the short run. For many reasons, therefore, the judgment factor in surety rating may be more important than in many insurance lines.

Noncancellability and Indeterminate Nature of Contract. Many surety bonds are written for long terms without the right of cancellation. Of course, in life and health insurance there may be no right of cancellation, but in property and liability insurance both the insurer and insured usually have the right to cancel. Another peculiarity of suretyship is the indeterminate nature of some bonds in which termination is conditioned on some future performance of an obligation. This indeterminateness may be compounded in bonds where the obligee may submit a claim long after the premium-paying period is over.

Contracts Prepared by Others. The corporate surety may have to deal in many contracts prepared by others. On the other hand, the insurance contract is usually described as a contract of adhesion—it is prepared by the insurer and the insured must take it or leave it. The surety contract may also be a contract of adhesion but with the "adhesive" on the other side. Again, there are also insurance contracts which are not prepared by the insurer, the Standard Fire Policy being the most notable example. In this connection, it is interesting to note that the contract of the corporate surety is ordinarily construed like an insurance policy, that is, it will be construed in favor of the insured or obligee. But a contrary rule may obtain when the bond or policy is not drafted by the insurer or surety:

> There are exceptions to the rule that the wording of an insurance policy will be construed most strongly in favor of the insured. The rule does not apply when the wording is not that of the insurer, but is taken from a statute or from some source that the assured is responsible for.[13]

Dual Underwriting. The surety must underwrite both the principal and the obligee. In fact, Lunt's book on surety bonding contains a slightly more extensive discussion of underwriting of fidelity bonds from the viewpoint of the obligee than from that of the principal. Lunt cautions:

> It seems clear that a surety company is taking undue chances when it bonds even a presumably honest man in favor of a dishonest employer.[14]

The relationship is too delicate to draw in a dishonest obligee, and the obligee and his methods of operation will influence the possibility of loss.

Other Underwriting Considerations. Suretyship may be distinguished from insurance on the claim that adverse selection is more evident in suretyship and that fraud is more damaging in suretyship. These underwriting problems are important in all lines of insurance and may be as

---

[13] *Sturgis National Bank* v. *Maryland Casualty Co.*, 252 Mich. 426 (1930).

[14] Edward C. Lunt, *Surety Bonds* (rev. ed.; New York: Ronald Press Co., 1930), p. 40.

difficult in some lines of insurance as they are in suretyship. It has been noted that the surety may be required to pay even when the bond has been obtained by the fraud of the principal. In answer, it could be pointed out that under the Standard Mortgage Clause and the Family Automobile Policy, an insurer may be forced to pay a third party even if the insured committed fraud in obtaining the policy.

Principal's View

Primary Responsibility of Principal. The principal always stands between the surety and his liability. That is, in suretyship, the usual expectation is that even if the surety must pay the loss, the principal will still be liable to the surety. (Of course, default of the principal renders the surety immediately liable to the obligee.) There is always a basic underlying obligation resting on the principal which in no way is diminished by the surety's payment. On the other hand, in insurance, the company promises to pay for the loss irrespective of the liability of a third party. Even here there are exceptions. In theft insurance, the insurer always has recourse, in practice or theory, against the thief. This similarity is only one of many between crime insurance and fidelity bonding. It also explains in part the relationship between forgery insurance and suretyship. Credit insurance is also, in this broad sense, related to suretyship, even though it remains a speciality line which is rarely written by companies transacting a corporate bonding business. In fact, credit insurance is only one line that could easily be cast in the form of either insurance or suretyship.

Premium Payor for Benefit for Another. The principal may pay the premium, but the bond benefits the obligee. In some situations, the obligee may pay the premium. Usually, the insured pays the premium and receives the benefit in the event of loss, but this is not a rule without exception. For example, the mortgagor may pay a premium for the Standard Fire Policy, with the benefit accruing to the mortgagee.

Premium Payment Not Consideration. In insurance, the premium is ordinarily the consideration for the contract. In suretyship, when the bond is obtained by the principal, the consideration is the undertaking, the performance of which the bond is to secure. For example, if an employer requires a bond on an employee, the hiring of the employee would be the consideration for the bond. Therefore, the employee's failure to pay the premium will not in itself invalidate the protection.

Principal the Third Party to the Contract. Some authorities argue that insurance is a two-party contract whereas suretyship is a three-party contract. Most of the discussants of this matter do not bother to define the term "party" although it is not an unambiguous term. If the term "party" is used to mean those with whom the "contract is actually made or entered into"[15] the bond may sometimes be a two- or three-party contract. Many

[15] Black's Law Dictionary (St. Paul: West Publishing Co., 1914), p. 1329.

fidelity bonds, for example, are made without even the knowledge of the principals. Of course, the surety would still have rights against the defaulting principal, but they would be equitable rather than contractual in nature. In any event, an insurance contract may involve three or more parties,[16] although it ordinarily involves two. The distinction based on the number of parties may be generally true, even if subject to notable exceptions, but it certainly is not of the essence.

Obligee's View

The obligee is sometimes called the "insured" and/or "beneficiary" by analogy to the insurance contract. These labels are entirely logical. From the viewpoint of the obligee the surety contract operates like insurance and provides benefits upon specified contingencies. To the obligee the bonding–insurance distinctions are of little concern. There is, however, one interesting legal difference between bonding and insurance which may be of special interest to the obligee. The Statute of Frauds requires that any contract to answer for the debt, default, or miscarriage of another must be in writing and signed by the party to be charged therewith or his agent. There is authority for the view that because of this rule, an oral surety contract is not enforceable. Some of the decisions in point are to the contrary, holding that the surety contract, like the insurance contract, may be enforceable even if oral. As a practical matter, of course, corporate surety contracts are almost always written instruments.

Spectrum of Suretyship

From this discussion the conclusion is drawn that the distinctions between bonding and insurance can best be arranged in a spectrum made up of the various surety lines. At one extreme is fidelity bonding which most autorities consider to be very close to, if not in fact, insurance. At the other extreme is contract bonding involving mainly a credit risk. Somewhere in between, moving generally from the pure surety side toward the insurance side of the spectrum, would be court bonds, fiduciary bonds, public official bonds and license and permit bonds. This arrangement represents a very rough lineup of classes of bonds subject to change over time, as the historian looks backward, or as the business itself moves forward. The distinctions represent useful concepts but they should not be used as mere molds into which the complexities and nuances of bonding can be stuffed.

---

[16] William R. Vance, *Handbook of the Law of Insurance* (3d ed.; St. Paul: West Publishing Co., 1951), p. 117. In a technical-legal sense even a two-party insurance contract may become a surety contract. For example, under an automobile physical damage policy, a third party tort-feasor may be responsible for the damage to the insured's auto. In such a case, the insurer has become a surety because "between the insurer and the one who causes the harm, the latter should bear the ultimate loss." American Law Institute, *Restatement of the Law of Security* (St. Paul: American Law Institute, 1941), pp. 236–37.

USES OF SURETYSHIP

Whether suretyship emphasizes pooling or merely extends credit, it has already been noted that it creates certainty in place of uncertainty in the transactions it touches. Its major premise is that "promises are fragile" and it is a device to make them dependable. It operates in all phases of the economy in countless and everchanging ways.

Accounting for the full impact of corporate suretyship would require an extensive cataloguing far beyond the scope of this chapter. To mention only one of many uses, the contract bond has become an integral part of the construction industry. The surety stands ready to guarantee the successful transition of any contract from the blueprint stage to the completed project. It thus protects the owner and the architect—laborers and vendors. This certainty redounds to the benefit of others in ever-widening circles, and to the economy at large.

To fulfill its fundamental purpose, the corporate surety, like the insurer not only offers its guarantees, but also indulges in extensive services to eliminate and minimize losses. For example, in fidelity bonding, the surety may conduct an extensive investigation of the principal and advise the obligee as to sound practices to prevent loss. The mere issuance of the bond may be a service; it is, in effect, a certification of ability to perform. At the same time the surety stands ready to take appropriate action against any defaulting principal, a fact which minimizes and prevents loss at the same time. It may also take appropriate action, *with* a defaulting principal, as when it assists the principal in properly completing a construction project.

All of this has been made possible by the growth of corporate suretyship. In a little more than a century, it has grown from a mere idea, through a feeble and uncertain beginning, to a position of virtually unquestioned strength and capacity. And it stands ready to impart that great strength and capacity to any promise that can be backed by a corporate surety.

SUGGESTED READINGS

BACKMAN, JULES. *Surety Rate-Making.* New York: Surety Association of America, 1948.

CRIST, G. W., JR. *Corporate Suretyship.* 2d ed. New York: McGraw-Hill Book Co., Inc., 1950.

DENENBERG, HERBERT S., *et al. Risk and Insurance.* Englewood Cliffs, N.J.: Prentice-Hall, Inc., 1964. Chap. 13.

HUEBNER, S. S., AND BLACK, KENNETH, JR. *Property Insurance.* 4th ed. New York: Appleton-Century-Crofts, Inc., 1957. Chap. 13.

LUNT, EDWARD C. *Surety Bonds.* Rev. ed. New York: Ronald Press Co., 1930.

MACKALL, LUTHER E. *The Principles of Surety Underwriting.* 6th ed. Philadelphia: The Spectator, 1951.

MORGAN, WILLIS D. "The History and Economics of Suretyship," *Cornell Law Quarterly,* Vol. 12 (1926–1927), pp. 153–71; 487–99.

MOWBRAY, ALBERT H., AND BLANCHARD, RALPH H. *Insurance: Its Theory and Practice in the United States.* 5th ed. New York: McGraw-Hill Book Co., Inc., 1961. Chap. 16.

STURGES, WESLEY A. "Suretyship and Guarantee," *Encyclopedia of the Social Sciences,* Vol. 7 (1934), pp. 482–87.

Chapter 54

FIDELITY BONDS AND UNDERWRITING

BY JOHN F. BEARDSLEY

Fidelity bonds embrace many aspects of both suretyship and insurance (see Chapter 43), despite the fact that in its basic and simplest nature, the individual fidelity bond is the prototype of the typical three-party surety obligation.

The individual fidelity bond is evidence of an undertaking wherein the surety agrees, subject to stated conditions, to indemnify the obligee (the employer) against loss resulting from the dishonesty or default of the principal (the employee) occupying a position of trust in the service of the obligee. Such bond thus typifies the true surety relationship with two parties (principal-employee and surety) joining to guarantee the third party (obligee-employer) to the specific obligation that the employee will handle with fidelity the property entrusted to him by his employer.

There is also a further identity with suretyship in the inherent concept of no loss ultimately accruing to the surety, because the principal is required under an extensive body of law to repay the surety for whatever loss the latter might have sustained by reason of the principal's default. This requirement, although thoroughly grounded in the common law, is generally brought directly to bear through the use of a signed application which contains a specific agreement of indemnity whereunder the employee obligates himself to repay and hold harmless the surety if loss occurs.

As the economy expanded and as corporate surety practices kept pace with it, fidelity bonds became increasingly broader in their terms. Simultaneously, underwriting procedures took a course steadily away from the historic surety basis on which these bonds were founded and towards insurance-type underwriting of them. Today, fidelity bonds are often referred to as "dishonesty insurance," with good reason and with the active encouragement of most underwriters. Dishonesty, being an inherent peril in human relationships, can be insured against in the same way that losses due to other common perils are insurable. A loss caused by the dishonesty of an employee differs little, in the last analysis, from that caused by a burglar or holdup man. While employee dishonesty losses may not be discovered as rapidly, they still mean loss of money or valuable property. Employee dishonesty thus has become but one peril in the overall crime exposure which business institutions have to face, and "dishonesty insurance," as in the case of other types of insurance, is therefore written with an expectancy of loss. (See also Chapter 43.)

None of the foregoing, however, is intended to infer that fidelity bonds may successfully be—or in fact are—underwritten wholly on the law of large numbers. The underwriting principles of suretyship which embrace the investigation, evaluation, and selection of risks still apply in important degree; and with the steady rise in the crime rate so evident throughout the nation since World War II, these principles have even greater application now than previously.

FIDELITY CONTRACT

Individual and Schedule Bonds

The foundation and keystone of the many broader types of fidelity coverage now available is the Individual Bond, issued to cover a named employee in favor of the insured employer for a specified dollar amount, this amount often being referred to by underwriters as the "bond penalty." If the named employee leaves the service of the insured, it is necessary to cancel the bond and write another on his replacement should similar coverage be desired. This sometimes burdensome necessity led to development of the Schedule Bond as a logical outgrowth of the expanding practice of bonding employees. This development enables an employer to purchase a single instrument to cover two or more designated employees. The Insuring Clause and most other clauses of the Schedule Bond remain identical to those in the Individual Bond, but a schedule is attached which names the individuals covered and the amount of coverage applicable to each. Changes in amounts or in personnel are accomplished by use of "Change Notices," which effect the desired addition or elimination of name, and increase or decrease in amount, with such premium adjustment as is resultant from the change.

Some employers, however, are subject to frequent turnover in personnel in certain departments or positions, and the Name Schedule Bonds, with the reporting entailed in the use of Change Notices, may create a clerical problem in such situations. This problem was readily solved with the innovation of the Position Schedule Bond, coverage under which applies in the amount designated for the occupant of any position listed in the schedule, and Change Notices are thus much reduced because only new or additional positions and changes in amounts occasion a need for their use. Despite their general similarity, however, the two schedule bonds differ in an important respect. While the Name Schedule

Bond covers listed employees when occupying *any* position in the service of the insured, it is essential under a Position Schedule Bond to prove that a loss-causing employee actually was occupying a bonded position at the time he caused the loss. Most sureties also limit their liability, under a special condition in the bond, to the portion of any loss that the number of employees stated as holding a bonded position bears to the number of employees in fact employed in such position. Generally speaking, the Position Schedule Bond is underwritten with more caution than is the Name Schedule Bond.

Blanket Bonds

Individual Bonds and Schedule Bonds, restricted as they are to designated employees and positions, have virtually disappeared from the present business scene, except in such specialized cases as treasurers of clubs, fraternal orders, church groups, and the like, where the sole exposure rests with one or two readily identifiable people. The manager or proprietor of the usual business establishment has to measure an exposure involving many people, and he can no more guess which of these employees will succumb to embezzlement than he can guess the exact prices of common stocks two years hence. Recognition of this fact, along with others involved in the changing patterns of an expanding economy, led the surety companies to the development of true "blanket" types of bonds. (See Chapter 4 for a discussion of the "blanket" concept.) With their introduction, underwriting procedures were revolutionized, with corresponding benefits to employers. The term "blanket" in insurance parlance has been loosely defined as meaning a policy which covers several different exposures under one item instead of as separate items. The blanket bonds, originating with the Bankers' Blanket Bond in about 1915 and later the modern Commerical Blanket Bond and Blanket Position Bond for mercantile risks, meet this definition as squarely as any other insurance contract, and probably represent the first truly "blanket" coverage devised. (See Appendix J.)

Commercial Blanket Bond versus Blanket Position Bond. The Commercial Blanket Bond and the Blanket Position Bond are standard contracts used by all member companies of the Surety Association of America, and may be issued to any employer other than a financial institution or a public official. The insuring agreement of each is perhaps more simple than that encountered in any other type of insurance contract. Under its terms, the surety agrees to indemnify the employer against loss of money or other property sustained through any fraudulent or dishonest act committed by an employee during the period the bond is in force—subject to the continuity of coverage provision, General Agreement C. This agreement merely means (1) that there has to be *loss* to the insured, (2) that such loss be due to *dishonesty*, and (3) that such dishonesty was on the part of an *employee;* and even if the insured cannot directly identify the employee or employees who caused the loss, coverage applies to the extent of the penalty of the bond as long as he can furnish affirmative proof of the loss and of dishonesty by some employee or employees.

The bonds cover each and every employee on the insured's payroll, without selection and without designation beyond the definition of "employees" as contained in the contract. New employees are automatically included under the bond without premium adjustment, except in the event of merger or consolidation, and thus there can be no possible failure, through oversight, to include specific employees. There is, nevertheless, a necessary and important reservation to the benefit of the surety. It is a provision in the bond that coverage will not apply to any employee from and after the time the insured acquires knowledge or information that such employee had committed any fraudulent or dishonest act in the service of the insured or otherwise, whether before or after employment with the insured.

Fidelity coverage, as represented by these two blanket bonds in their latest forms, has taken on the format of insurance in addition to the many other similarities described earlier in this chapter. While the contracts have become essentially two-party agreements, with the obligee now referred to as "insured" and the surety referred to as "underwriter," an important distinction remains in the fact that the bonds are continuous and stay in full force and effect until formally cancelled by either the insured or the company. Lacking an expiration date, there is thus no renewal involved as in other types of coverages, and premium anniversaries have no direct relationship to the term of the bond, since that period is, in fact, indefinite and automatically continuous until a formal termination.

Blanket bonds for the commercial field (as contrasted with most Bankers' Blanket Bonds) are written on the so-called "loss sustained" basis, which indemnifies for loss sustained by the insured during the bond period—subject to the continuity of coverage provision, General Agreement C. Time for discovery of losses which occurred during the life of the bond is necessarily extended after termination of the bond, because fidelity losses by their nature tend to remain hidden over long periods. In the case of the Commercial Blanket Bond, the extension is accomplished through a provision which gives the insured a period of 12 months after termination in which to discover losses sustained during the life of the bond. In the Blanket Position Bond, the discovery period is two years.

The most prominent difference between the Commercial Blanket Bond and the Blanket Position Bond rests in the application of the bond penalty to loss, particularly the collusive type of loss involving more than one employee. The Commercial Blanket Bond may be issued from a minimum penalty of $10,000 upwards, without ceiling, with the penalty of the bond being aggregate as to any one loss regardless of the number of employees involved in such loss. The Blanket Position Bond, on the other hand, is a multiple-penalty contract, and its amount, which may range from a minimum of $2,500 to a maximum of $100,000, applies separately to each employee identified as a defaulter. Thus, if five identifiable employees, acting in collusion, steal $50,000, a $10,000 Blanket Position Bond would cover the loss in full. Under a Commercial Blanket Bond, coverage in the amount of $50,000 would have had to be purchased to reimburse the insured for this same loss.

The author confesses a personal preference for the Commercial Blanket Bond so long as it is carried in an amount sufficiently large to cover not only the collusive type of loss, but, more importantly, to provide ample coverage against the business-destroying catastrophic losses engineered by one person. This opinion ties in, of course, with a strong feeling that fidelity coverage should essentially be treated as catastrophe insurance and purchased in amounts truly commensurate with exposure. Nevertheless, many insureds have a real and well-founded preference for the Blanket Position Bond, and in such cases that contract is often written as primary cover, supplemented by a Commercial Blanket Bond in considerably larger amount as excess, with the combination providing proper coverage for the risk under the "catastrophe approach."

Package Contracts. Recent years have seen the development and widespread acceptance of "Combined Crime Coverages" in a package policy to provide fidelity, forgery, and broad-form disappearance and destruction insurance in a single policy for mercantile risks. (See Chapter 43.) The most commonly used and best known of these packages are the Comprehensive 3–D (Dishonesty, Disappearance and Destruction) and the newer Blanket Crime Policy. The former is the more flexible since it may be written optionally to cover one or more of the basic insuring agreements in varying amounts and endorsed to provide a wide variety of burglary and/or theft coverages. The Blanket Crime Policy, on the other hand, is a "single limit" contract, written in uniform amount for the basic insuring agreements which are mandatory. Thus, one advantage of the Blanket Crime Policy is that its single penalty covers all insured perils, thereby minimizing chances of underinsurance as to any such peril. The fidelity coverage under the 3–D may take the nature of either the Commercial Blanket Bond or the Blanket Position Bond, at the insured's option. Under the Blanket Crime Policy, it is available only in the aggregate penalty form of the Commercial Blanket Bond.

Bankers Blanket Bonds

Commercial Blanket Bonds and Blanket Position Bonds, although "blanket" in the sense of providing automatic coverage on all of the employees of the insured mercantile risk, indemnify solely against loss resultant from employee dishonesty. Bankers' Blanket Bonds, on the other hand, are "blanket" not only in the fidelity coverage provided under their terms, but are also "blanket" as to other exposures, in that they provide indemnity against other types of crime losses in addition to employee dishonesty. They are "blanket," too, as to the *amount* which applies to the several exposures insured; but they are not intended to provide coverage against all losses. They contain important exclusions. Issued in a number of different patterns with each designed specifically for the kind of institution to be insured, Bankers' Blanket Bonds are written for commercial banks, savings banks, stockbrokers, savings and loan associations, and other types of financial institutions. Most of them provide in a single contract indemnity for loss occasioned by employee dishonesty, burglary, robbery, theft, disappearance or destruction of property on the insured premises and while in transit, and with optional coverage for check forgery and securities forgery at additional premium.

The great majority of these bonds are now issued on the "discovery basis," under which coverage applies for losses discovered during the currency of the bond, regardless of when they might actually have taken place. Bankers' Blanket Bonds afford extremely broad protection on money, securities, and certain other personal property. They have been subjected to steady revisions over the years to bring them to this point. Continuing efforts have been exerted by bonding companies to provide coverage needed by the banking fraternity as the result of new and greater exposures created by the rapid economic growth of this country.

Public Official Bonds

Public Official Bonds over the past several years have been treated generally as belonging to the fidelity class, and for statistical purposes the premiums and losses accruing therefrom are reported in the fidelity experience of most surety companies. Since the essential hazard is the dishonesty of the principal and since the risk involved in bonding a public official is basically the same as that in bonding employees under a fidelity bond, this practice is a logical one.

Required by Law. There are compelling reasons, however, to regard Public Official Statutory Bonds as surety contracts. Such bonds are founded in law and are given under a statute or ordinance which requires the public officer to "faithfully perform" the duties of his office and "account for and pay over" all monies belonging to the public body to which his bond runs. Most bond forms (the word "form" is used in various statutes and has a special meaning in respect to Public Official Bonds) are prescribed in the law, as a result of which the obligee is guaranteed all the remedies and processes granted by statute—that is, that the bonded official will do exactly what the law says he must do in his capacity as holder of the office. If appropriate statutes do not prescribe the form of bond for a given office, a "common law" type may be executed and conditioned similarly for faithful performance of duty. As a general rule, both forms are coextensive with the term of office, and the bond remains in force until a successor to the principal is elected or appointed and qualifies as required.

The laws and the courts have clearly placed a heavy weight of responsibility and liability upon the holder of a public office. Under the oath which he takes upon assuming office, he becomes responsible for all phases of the administration of that office, and he becomes liable for the loss of public funds, whether occurring with or without neglect or default on his own part. This liability, therefore, extends to losses caused by deputies and employees, by burglary and robbery, and by bank failure, unless the official has used depositories and made deposits in strictest accord with the letter of the statute pertaining to keeping of public funds.

Underwriting. The underwriting of Public Official Bonds, consequently, differs from ordinary fidelity bond underwriting procedures to the degree that these elements of liability inject additional hazards for the principal and the surety. The depository feature is particularly important and is customarily covered by requiring copies of the official resolutions of the appropriate governing unit designating the banks to be used by its money-handling officers. In those states where the law does not exonerate an official from loss by such resolution, the bank deposits must be protected by depository collateral placed in escrow. Most sureties endeavor to make sure that adequate burglary and robbery insurance is carried, and practically all sureties urge, and frequently insist, that subordinates be bonded in favor of the principal official.

Public Employees Blanket Bonds. These bonds are of comparatively recent development, and have won widespread acceptance in recognition of the exposure of the larger governmental units to loss because of the dishonesty of or breach of faithful performance by employees not required by law to give an individual bond. Patterned after the two types of blanket fidelity bonds discussed above, the Public Employees Blanket Bond provides coverage similar to that given in the Commercial Blanket Bond or Blanket Position Bond and also provides such coverage on a dishonesty or faithful discharge of duty basis. Each is available with the insuring clause conditioned upon dishonesty or extended to faithful performance. Consistent with the concept of blanket coverage, each provides the fullest possible protection to the insured public official whose subordinate employees are so bonded, and therefore to the public at large.

UNDERWRITING

Applications

The underwriting of all Individual Bonds and Schedule Bonds, whether pure fidelity or public official, customarily commences with an application completed and signed by the principal.

Application from Principal. The application, in addition to requiring general information on the nature of and duties of the position or office which the principal will occupy, contains important questions on his background and financial status. In the case of Public Official Bonds, a financial statement is emphasized, while the straight fidelity application requires a chronological record of prior employment. Both contain an agreement of indemnity, as commented upon in an earlier section of this chapter. In the case of blanket bonds, however, the application is required of the insured since the underwriter's scrutiny will be directed to the nature of the overall risk rather than to the individual employees to be blanketed under the bond in question. The application contains the details of employee classifications and their total number which are essential for computing the premium, and while there is of course no indemnity agreement involved, there is a general affirmation to the effect that all employees, to the insured's best knowledge and belief, have no history of dishonesty.

Individual Employee Applications. The use of individual employee applications, although not usually an underwriting requirement, is strongly urged by underwriters to support the insured's own application when a fidelity blanket bond is carried, unless a prior carrier has already received them. Most bonding companies maintain investigation departments as an adjunct of their fidelity operations. Insureds are entitled to use these facilities. The surety checks with former employers and personal references for any facts which suggest prior dishonesty on the part of the employee. The surety on a fidelity bond is not interested in job performance or qualifications, but directs its inquiries almost entirely to the matter of the honesty or dishonesty of the employee. (On the other hand, the surety is interested in performance in respect to Public Official Bonds.) With some frequency bonding companies are able to secure reports on this aspect from former employers who might have proved reluctant to give it directly to the new employer. Another important advantage in the use of individual applications is the moral effect created when the employee completes application for bond and thereby receives notice that he is subject to dealing with a bonding company in case of any lapse in honesty during his employment with the insured.

Nature of the Risk

Despite the fact that the surety may conduct extensive investigation of individual employees and do its underwriting cautiously, the nature of the risk remains a matter of basic importance. This consideration applies with special emphasis in any era of steady and appalling increases in the crime rate throughout the nation. If the employer (1) does not follow sound personnel policies, (2) does not maintain internal and external management and accounting controls of a quality commensurate with the size and nature of his business, (3) does not thereby make every effort to eliminate the opportunity for employees to become dishonest, and above all (4) does not follow strictly ethical and honest business practices on his own part, the risk can never be a good one. Moreover, some risks will be undesirable from an underwriting standpoint even though the insured makes every effort to keep the possibilities of loss to the minimum. An example of such a risk might be one whose business involved a very high proportion of outside collectors in ratio to the head office people. The bonding companies usually reject not only the "isolated" offering involving only such undesirable occupations individually or in schedule, but also the blanket bond under which there is not a sufficient number of inside management and clerical-type employees. Experience proves some kinds of business operations to be more susceptible to employee dishonesty than others, and the rate manual is responsive through variations of the premiums to be charged, thereby indicating the general desirability of classes of risks by the kind of business in which they engage.

Finally, the experience of the risk itself is probably the major underwriting test. Bankers' Blanket Bonds issued to commercial banks are subject to mandatory experience rating whereby the premium for a given bank is debited or credited, dependent upon that bank's own experience during a designated period immediately preceding the normal anniversary date of the bank's coverage. Likewise, most blanket bonds for mercantile establishments, and most Public Employees Blanket Bonds, are subject to experience rating.

Special Underwriting Devices

In addition to experience rating, other special underwriting devices are available to make the individual risk more attractive to the surety. Two of the more commonly used involve the exclusion of certain types of employees as a class, and/or deductibles in the amount of coverage. Both are based on the point that, if the insured necessarily engages in practices or in a kind of business which tends to produce a high and regular frequency of nominal losses, then he should bear the cost of such losses as a normal operating charge to his total cost of doing business. Thus, the mercantile establishment of a kind having a large number of outside collectors, with a limited or measurable dollar exposure on each, may exclude all such collectors from its blanket coverage while still receiving protection on all other employees who might subject it to a loss of catastrophic proportions. Similarly, the bank which customarily runs a high percentage of small forgery or mysterious disappearance losses may absorb such losses itself through use of an underwriting deductible on its bond. In both examples the insured may well benefit through increased experience credits in its premium development in addition to creating a far more receptive market for its bond coverage in the future.

Dishonesty insurance, like other types of insurance, involves the inherent concept of certainty of loss—that is, some losses are inevitable. Human nature being what it is and frailties of mortals being the hazard insured against, even the most careful and prudently managed business can have a fidelity loss. In "blanket" bonding, the insurer assumes this certainty of loss before it even commences investigation of the employees covered. In fact, it may not investigate at all. With the assumption that loss will occur as the starting point, fidelity underwriting is being based increasingly on examination of the nature of the overall risk. To the extent that the normal expected hazard is increased by procedures or ways of doing business peculiar to a given insured, the risk becomes subaverage. In such a case the underwriter will want correcting elements injected through devices such as premium surcharges for class of business, underwriting deductibles, or exclusions of loss-productive classes of employees in their entirety.

ADEQUACY OF COVERAGE

Increasing Need for Protection

Embezzlement has reached the proportions of a national scandal, with thievery by employees estimated as totaling over $1 billion annually. Since many employers have not availed themselves of bonding coverage, only about 6 percent is recoverable under dishonesty insurance. It has been said that the only *sure* way to prevent employee dishonesty is not to have any employees, because embezzlement is not preventable even by use of all the audit and accounting controls available to the most alert and conscientious management. Unfortunately, recent claim records of bonding companies substantiate a radical upward curve in the amounts of individual losses. Only insurance in adequate amounts can guarantee that a business will not suffer a loss through employee dishonesty.

The assets and sales income of a business enterprise are usually described as the heart of that enterprise. If the heart is irreparably damaged by employee defalcation, with no insurance or with insufficient insurance, there will be no business left to operate, or, at best, the firm will face a long period of financial difficulty. The upward trend of employee dishonesty has served to impress management increasingly with the vital necessity of an adequate amount of fidelity bond protection. This type of insurance is now commonly thought of as a catastrophe line rather than as a source of reimbursement for the petty and trivial theft.

Determination of Size of Bond Penalties

The question of adequacy of amount has long been a difficult one for purchasers and underwriters. Any estimate as to the loss potential in a given individual business is a very unsatisfactory yardstick, because management cannot possibly know at what rate—or of more importance perhaps—for how long a trusted employee will steal its funds. Fidelity losses by their nature remain hidden for considerable periods of time and often may not be discovered until after the bond is terminated. Such loss is likely, therefore, to have reached a magnitude sufficient to jeopardize the future operations of the employer, if not, in fact, to force him to close his doors, as has been the case in an alarming number of instances in the recent past.

Surety Association of America Study. The measure of fidelity exposure cannot be gauged to the specifics of property values which are readily determinable amounts for fire insurance or burglary insurance. In an effort to provide a realistic answer to the problem, a committee comprised of member companies of the Surety Association of America made a long and careful survey of losses of $10,000 or more actually sustained by insureds over a period of 10 years. This committee attempted to relate to the study various factors governing exposure, such as total assets, goods on hand, annual gross sales or income, nature of the business, its size, and the number of its employees. From this study of hundreds of cases, it was apparent that, while there is no gauge whereby *maximum* potential loss could be measured, it is possible to relate certain of these factors to the amount of loss in a large number of actual instances.

This relativity produced a formula (entitled "How Much Honesty Insurance"). Published in 1956, it has been in widespread use since then. It gauges the *minimum* coverage appropriate for a commercial risk of any size and employs an "Exposure Index" as a weighted base. The index is derived from the two principal elements of exposure: (1) current assets which measure values subject to loss at all times and (2) gross sales (or income), which reflect the turnover in such values. Briefly stated, it is the dollar sum of: (1) 5 percent of the value of goods on hand; (2) 20 percent of the total current assets less goods on hand; and (3) 10 percent of annual gross sales (or income). When applied to a table of values, this dollar sum produces the *minimum* amounts of coverage recommended for the particular insured under examination. Tests of the formula against the actual losses surveyed showed that the formula would have provided full protection in 95 percent of the cases.

The aspects of underinsurance revealed by the study were significant —in fact, startling. The losses which fell into the first two brackets of the Exposure Index ($125,000 or less) were fully covered by the bond carried in only 15 percent of the cases. In other words, 85 percent of the smaller risks were underinsured. Equally significant were the figures relating to loss amounts, which showed that of the total number of losses reported in the amount of $50,000 or more, 22.2 percent were fully covered by the bond, while 77.8 percent were underinsured.

Underinsurance in Financial Institutions. The effect of underinsurance has been felt also in the financial institutions field, despite two prominent influences. First, for many years the American Bankers Association has distributed to its membership a table of recommended amounts of coverage related to the size of commercial banks. Second, the New York Stock Exchange since 1960 has required minimum amounts of coverage to be carried by all its members, related to the size of the stockbroker firm or corporation.

From 1901 through 1958, total employee defalcations in commercial banks in the United States ranged annually between $3.6 million and $9.5 million. In 1960 for the first time, such defalcations in commercial banks exceeded 100 in number and $10 million in amount. In 1961, 113 cases involving almost $13 million were reported, of which 12 were underinsured to the aggregate extent of $3,286,730. One loss exceeded the coverage in force by over $200,000, and in the most widely publicized case the loss exceeded coverage by $1,075,000. Five of the 12 underinsured banks were forced to close, and all of this deficiency occurred despite the repeated and urgent recommendations of the American Bankers Association, federal and state bank supervisory authorities, and state bankers associations for insurance adequate to meet the potential catastrophic embezzlement loss.

Catastrophe Loss Approach

The concept of primary and excess layers of coverage has always had a prominent position in the techniques of fidelity bonding. With exposures being subjected to more careful and scientific examination, excess coverage has been brought into even more widespread use. In the financial institutions area, particularly, coverage in the form of separate primary and excess bonds is the almost universal practice.

The newest such contract in use in the commercial bank field, in fact, is the Excess Bank Employee Dishonesty Blanket Bond, designed especially to provide coverage against only one peril of catastrophic potential, namely, employee dishonesty. It may only be written as excess cover over an underlying amount related to the bank's size and, under present rules, in units of $1 million.

Specific excess indemnity is available with the mercantile blanket bonds. Use of an Excess Indemnity Endorsement enables an insured to purchase additional coverage on selected key people on a name or position basis and thereby to retain the benefits of blanket coverage as underlying, while getting higher than normal coverage to meet the exposure among those officers and employees occupying important or especially vulnerable positions.

Complete blanket coverage is generally preferred by the larger risks which gauge their insurance programs to indemnity against catastrophes.

In such cases, the Blanket Position Bond is often written as primary insurance up to its maximum permissible limit of $100,000 (or perhaps a Comprehensive DDD or Blanket Crime Policy in amounts commensurate with the easily measured burglary exposure) with a Commercial Blanket Bond written in an important amount as excess over it.

MAGNITUDE OF PROBLEM

As commented upon earlier, gross losses to American business, due to embezzlement, are estimated variously at between $1 billion and $1½ billion each year, of which amount 3 percent to 6 percent is insured. Annual losses to American business, due to fire, are about the same but are about 90 percent insured. In Table 54–1 some data from the early 1960's show the amounts of insured fire and fidelity losses.

TABLE 54–1

FIRE AND FIDELITY LOSSES INCURRED BY STOCK AND MUTUAL INSURERS 1960–1963

Year	Fire	Fidelity
1960	1,107,824,000	$52,759,000
1961	1,209,042,000	58,640,000
1962	1,265,002,000	43,206,000
1963	1,405,558,000	44,115,000

SOURCE: *The Spectator and Argus Charts* for respective years and *Insurance Facts.*

Loss prevention is a responsibility of all employers and is fostered by establishing and maintaining proper controls and audits so as to minimize the opportunity for embezzlement by employees and by establishing and maintaining personnel policies of quality so as to minimize the temptation to embezzle. It is the concurrent responsibility of the fidelity bond underwriter to afford advice and encouragement to the employer in these matters, as well as to drive home the point that fidelity coverage is truly catastrophe insurance.

SUGGESTED READINGS

BACKMAN, JULES. *Surety Rate-Making.* New York: Surety Association of America, 1948.

Fidelity Bonds. New York: Surety Association of America, 1960.

GEE, HAROLD F. *Agents Bonding Guide.* Indianapolis: Rough Notes Co., 1963.

How Much Honesty Insurance. New York: Surety Association of America, 1956.

The Public Official and His Surety Bond. New York: Surety Association of America, 1958.

Chapter 55

SURETY BONDS AND UNDERWRITING

BY NORMAN A. BURGOON, JR.

Whereas an insurance policy is a two-party agreement between the insured and the company, a surety bond involves three parties. It is an agreement by the surety to be responsible to the obligee for the obligation or conduct of the principal. A surety bond guarantees performance by the principal of (1) the terms of another agreement, such as a contract, (2) a fiduciary relationship, or (3) obligations imposed by law. In this chapter surety bonds are considered in the narrow sense to exclude fidelity bonds and to include such major classes as contract bonds, license and permit bonds, and judicial bonds.

MAJOR CLASSES OF SURETY BONDS

Contract Bonds

Construction Contract Bonds. Construction of public and private improvements has become the largest single industry in our economy. It accounts for about 15 percent of our gross national product and in annual awards for construction work is about $100 billion. Bonds, with rare exceptions, are required by law to guarantee performance of every contract for public improvements. Many private owners and institutions likewise insist on such bonds before awarding construction contracts. Consequently, construction contract bonds comprise the largest group in the surety field. (See Appendix J for specimens.)

While the provisions of contract bonds vary somewhat with different owners, they follow similar lines. First, when an owner advertises a project for bidding, he normally requires all bidders to accompany their proposals with a guarantee, usually in the form of a Bid Bond or certified check. The bid bond generally guarantees that, if awarded the contract, the principal will (1) enter into the contract and furnish the required performance and payment bonds or (2) pay the owner (up to the limit of the bid bond penalty) the difference between the principal's price and the cost of awarding the contract to the next higher bidder.

The Performance Bond guarantees to the owner that the contractor will complete the project within the scheduled time, for the agreed upon price, and in strict accordance with the plans, specifications, and contract. If the contractor fails to perform, the surety on the performance bond may undertake to finish the work or pay the owner the excess cost (up to the bond penalty) of having the work completed by another contractor.

Ordinarily, a separate Payment Bond is also given to guarantee that the contractor will discharge his bills—and often those of his subcontractors—for labor and material used in the project, although this obligation is sometimes included in the performance bond.

Construction contracts occasionally require the builder to guarantee the project, or certain portions thereof, against defective workmanship and materials for stated periods of time. Although this protection is normally afforded under the performance bond, some owners ask for a separate Maintenance Bond for the purpose. The underwriting of construction contract bonds will be discussed later.

Miscellaneous Contract and Indemnity Bonds. Public bodies often require bonds to guarantee contracts of a miscellaneous nature such as collecting garbage, removing snow, furnishing supplies, wrecking buildings, and so on. In general, underwriting involves much the same elements as for a construction contract bond.

Performance of almost any agreement, however, can be guaranteed by a bond. In matters that affect the public interest, many types of bonds of a miscellaneous nature are required. Examples would be bonds covering the payment of income and other taxes, those guaranteeing that a real estate developer will with his own funds construct streets, sewers, etc. in a subdivision, and bonds providing for direct payment by an employer of workmen's compensation claims.

Instances of bonds covering private agreements are as varied as the number of business transactions where suretyship is appropriate. Only a few examples can be given. Railroads, upon the filing of a proper bond, will permit shippers or consignees to defer payment of freight charges or to order the railroad to divert shipments in transit or to deliver them without presenting bills of lading. Corporations or their transfer agents will reissue securities claimed to be lost or destroyed with a satisfactory bond of indemnity. Many lessors require bonds guaranteeing the terms of lease agreements involving the payment of rent, and/or covenants to build, alter, or return property to its original condition. The underwriter in this varied field must always very closely examine the nature and terms of each particular risk. The financial responsibility of the principal usually is of utmost importance as many of these miscellaneous bonds, directly or indirectly, involve ability to pay or finance in addition to ability to perform certain work or other obligations.

License and Permit Bonds

Bonds required by the federal government or by any state, county, or municipality as a condition to the issuance of a license to engage in a certain business or activity or to the granting of a permit to exercise a particular privilege are referred to as License and Permit Bonds. With the growing trend of government regulation of an increasingly complex urban life, this type of bond is growing steadily.

The occupations and privileges for which license or permit bonds are required are too numerous to list completely, but the following is a representative group:

- Plumbers
- Electricians
- Bricklayers
- Boxing promoters
- Canneries
- Business schools
- Sign permits
- Street obstructions
- Vault permits
- Franchise
- Itinerant merchants
- Billiard hall operators
- Used car dealers
- Insurance agents
- Real estate brokers
- Money lenders
- Oil & gas permits
- Ticket agencies
- Securities dealers
- Wreckers

Some License and Permit Bonds—often called Compliance Bonds—guarantee only that the business will be conducted or the privilege exercised in conformity with the governing laws. Others protect the public against loss from physical damage in instances where persons or property are endangered. Still others guard against fraud, misrepresentation, and unfair dealings and occasionally indemnify against failure to perform under contractual agreements.

Generally, the compliance type of License and Permit Bonds indemnifies only the governmental body named as obligee against direct loss or legal liability claims for damage sustained by a third party. The other types of License and Permit Bonds described herein often extend to any aggrieved person the right to sue for recovery directly against the principal and surety for damages sustained.

In amounts up to $5,000 License and Permit Bonds covering relatively nonhazardous occupations or privileges and not guaranteeing contractual agreements or the payment of money are usually accepted by the surety company upon the agent's representation that the applicant is honest and dependable and knows his business. Larger bonds, those involving hazardous operations (such as franchises, wrecking, or use of explosives), and those covering agreements or payment of money, require a close examination and evaluation (1) of the applicant's reputation, (2) of his experience in his field, and (3) of his financial responsibility.

Judicial Bonds

The term "Judicial Bond" may be applied in a general sense to any bond or undertaking filed in connection with court proceedings. It embraces two main categories: Fiduciary Bonds and Court Bonds.

Fiduciary Bonds. A court fiduciary is one appointed by a court to manage and distribute property in accordance with a will, a deed of trust, or a statute. He frequently is required by law to give bond guaranteeing the faithful performance of his duty. Some of the more common types of fiduciary are:

ADMINISTRATOR (ADMINISTRATRIX)—A person appointed by the court to collect and distribute the estate of a decedent who dies without a will. The principal duties of an administrator are to collect the assets, file an inventory, give notice to creditors, pay the debts in proper order, distribute the balance to the persons entitled under the law, and account to the court.

EXECUTOR (EXECUTRIX)—A person named in a will to execute its terms. The duties of an executor are identical to those of an administrator except that the assets remaining after payment of debts are distributed pursuant to the provisions of the will.

ADMINISTRATOR CUM TESTAMENTO ANNEXO (C.T.A.)—A person not named in a will but appointed to carry out its provisions.

ADMINISTRATOR DE BONIS NON (D.B.N.)—A person appointed to succeed an administrator who has died, resigned, or been removed.

ADMINISTRATOR CUM TESTAMENTO ANNEXO DE BONIS NON (C.T.A.D.B.N.)—A person appointed to succeed an executor or administrator cum testamento annexo who has died, resigned, or been removed.

RECEIVER IN EQUITY; RECEIVER OR TRUSTEE IN BANKRUPTCY—A person appointed to take possession of property pending litigation, or in insolvency, or bankruptcy proceedings. His duties are generally prescribed by statute and performed under close supervision of the court.

GUARDIAN, CURATOR, OR TUTOR OF A MINOR—A person appointed to manage the property of a minor. He must keep the estate properly invested, make appropriate expenditures for maintenance and education of the minor, file accountings as required, and deliver the remaining property to the minor when he becomes of age.

GUARDIAN, COMMITTEE, CURATOR OR CONSERVATOR OF AN INCOMPETENT—A person appointed to manage the property of one who has been adjudicated incompetent. His duties are similar to a guardian of a minor except that the delivery of the property to the ward may only follow an adjudication of competency, in the absence of which the remaining property is turned over to the ward's executor or administrator when he dies.

TRUSTEE—A person appointed to carry out the terms of a trust created by a will or other instrument. The trustee must keep the estate invested in accordance with the provisions of the instrument under which he is acting or as provided by law, disburse the income and principal to carry out the intent of the trust, and file accountings, if required.

Court Bonds. A court bond is required of a party in litigation by statute or rule of court. Its purpose is to indemnify the opposite party against a wrongful procedure or to guarantee payment of a judgment.

The form of bond is prescribed by statute or rule of court. Liability can be terminated only by (1) voluntary settlement of the issue or (2) prosecution of principal's action to final judgment and satisfaction of the judgment if he loses.

The law makes certain remedies available to parties involved in disputes. Some of these remedies involve the seizure of another person's property by a sheriff or bailiff, the release of property already in legal custody, or the granting by the court of a stay in the enforcement of another person's legal rights. The enforcement of these remedies may result in loss or damage to the opposing party. For this reason, statutes frequently require the giving of a bond to indemnify the injured party in the event the court finally decides in his favor.

Court bonds fall into two general categories, namely, "plaintiffs" bonds and "defendants" bonds. Generally, plaintiffs' bonds are regarded as the less hazardous of the two because they are usually executed on behalf of a party who is a creditor, voluntarily pursuing what he considers to be a valid cause of action against the other party. Defendants' bonds are ordinarily required by an alleged debtor who has been sued or whose property has been seized. Some of the more common types of court bonds are:

1. *Attachment*—Under certain circumstances, property of a defendant may, at the request of the plaintiff and upon his furnishing of an attachment bond, be seized and held. The property is usually held by the sheriff or marshal until the suit is decided. Then, depending on the outcome, it will be used either to satisfy a judgment for the plaintiff or returned to the defendant. If the decision is in favor of the defendant, the attachment bond is liable for any damages he sustained by having his property seized and held.

2. *Garnishment*—Similar to attachment except that here the property attached is in hands of a third party rather than the defendant.

3. *Replevin*—A replevin bond is given by a plaintiff who claims the right to possession of personal property. Upon granting of the writ, the property is seized by the sheriff and delivered to the plaintiff. The bond guarantees the property, or its value, will be returned to the defendant if the litigation is decided in his favor, and that he will be indemnified for damages sustained.

4. *Injunction or Restraining Order*—When a court, on petition of a plaintiff, issues an injunction or restraining order requiring a defendant to perform, or refrain from performing some act, a bond is required of the plaintiff to indemnify the defendant against any damages he may suffer as a result of the action, should the decision of the court be in his favor. These bonds are often quite hazardous.

5. *Cost*—These bonds are usually required of nonresident plaintiffs and guarantee payment of any court cost assessed against the principal.

6. *Release Attachment, Garnishment*—Normally a defendant whose property has been attached or garnished may obtain its release by giving bond. This bond guarantees that the property or its value will be available to satisfy the final judgment if rendered in favor of the plaintiff. It may guarantee payment of the judgment regardless of the value of the property.

7. *Counter Replevin*—A defendant from whose possession property has

been taken under a writ of replevin may have it returned by giving bond. This bond guarantees the property or its value will be available to satisfy the judgment of the court, if in favor of the plaintiff.

8. *Dissolve Injunction or Restraining Order*—A defendant against whom an injunction or restraining order has been issued may have the operation of the writ suspended by giving bond indemnifying the plaintiff against any damages he may suffer as a result of such suspension. As in the case of an injunction bond, these bonds may be required under a wide variety of circumstances and can be very hazardous.

9. *Appeal and Supersedeas*—In most situations, an unsuccessful party to litigation is given the right to appeal. When the appeal is from a judgment or decree requiring the payment of a sum of money, or performance of certain acts, the appeal does not defer compliance unless a bond is given guaranteeing the appellant will satisfy the judgment or decree, if affirmed, with interest, costs, and damages.

UNDERWRITING

Construction Contract Bonds

Contract bonds are really credit guarantees, and the contractor's ability to qualify for bonding is one of the major keystones of his operations. They prompt suppliers to extend liberal credit for materials to be furnished; they encourage banks to lend money for needed working funds and for a bidder's certified check; and they permit the owner to make partial payments to the contractor with safety while the job is in progress.

The successful completion of a construction contract depends upon many factors. Some—like bad weather, strikes, and death of the contractor—cannot be foreseen. Others—like experience, background, and financial ability—are determinable. Hence, in order successfully to handle bonds guaranteeing these undertakings, the underwriter must carefully investigate and evaluate all those factors.

Contract Documents. From the contract, specifications, and the bonds, the underwriter will glean many items of importance to the underwriting picture. He will learn the size and type of the project to determine whether it is in the contractor's line of work and within the scope of his experience. He is interested in determining that the completion date is not unrealistically short or so unusually long as to create an extra hazard to the surety in guaranteeing the contractor's solvency. The underwriter will want to find, too, that the penalties for failure of the contractor to complete on schedule are not unreasonable.

These documents will show, also, how the contractor is to be paid as the work progresses, how much is to be retained from each monthly estimate, and whether or not payments are to be made completely in cash. Generally speaking, monthly payments of less than 90 percent of the value of work performed and materials furnished create an undue strain on the contractor's working funds. On the other hand, payments of 100 percent add to the surety's risk because upon default there remains in the hands of the owner less money to reimburse the surety for unpaid bills and excess costs of completion. Occasionally, an advance payment is made by the owner to the contractor before the work has started and in those cases the surety charges an additional premium to compensate for the additional hazard.

It is important to develop the fact that the contractor is carrying complete insurance coverages to protect against not only his *legal* liability but also any *contractual* liability imposed by the contract documents.

On private work, the underwriter will seek to determine that the owner has the funds available to pay the contractor as the work progresses. The bonds themselves will be checked for provisions that may be unduly onerous on the contractor and the surety, and the scope and time limit of maintenance guarantee will be investigated.

Character, Experience, and Equipment. Among the many considerations of contract bond underwriting, none is more important than good character. Unless the applicant's reputation for integrity and honorable dealings is good, the risk is great that (1) underwriting details, including financial information, may be erroneous; (2) improper shortcuts may be taken in complying with the specifications; and (3) the moral fiber needed to cope successfully with the situation when unforeseen troubles develop is likely to be missing.

In judging whether a contractor is qualified by experience to undertake a particular project, the underwriter is interested in determining that the contractor previously has successfully performed similar projects of the same relative size and nature. While a switch from one line of contracting business to another can successfully be made under appropriate conditions, a plain building contractor would not normally be considered a good risk on a large, heavy engineering project. Similarly, a contractor who regularly is performing contracts in amounts up to $100,000 would likely be a poor risk on one of $1,000,000.

The underwriter must also be satisfied that the contractor owns the necessary amount and type of equipment required to perform the project under consideration or that he has arranged to secure it. In the latter case, part of the cost of rental or purchase of additional equipment may adversely affect the contractor's working capital.

Other Work on Hand. In order to evaluate whether the contractor has sufficient capital and/or organization, the underwriter is vitally interested in a complete disclosure of the contractor's other work currently under way. In this area, it is important to know how much work remains to be done, whether the jobs were secured at favorable prices, whether the work is on schedule, and whether the jobs are profitable.

Subcontracts. The amount and nature of work to be performed under subcontracts and the quality of the subcontractor is often of importance in handling contract bonds. If a subcontractor defaults or fails to pay his bills for labor or material, the general contractor can be ruined by having to pay more to complete the subcontracted work and to discharge the unpaid bills even though he may already have paid the subcontractor. More and more, general contractors make it a habit to require Performance and Payment Bonds of all but the very strongest subcontractors and the presence of such bonds on close cases sometimes means the difference between acceptance and rejection of the general contractor's application.

Adequacy of Price (Bids). After the proposals have been received, the underwriter will review a complete list of the bids before passing on the execution of the final bonds in order to determine that the low bidder's price is in line with that submitted by other qualified contractors, experienced on the type and size of the particular job. Generally speaking, the low bidder's price is "well in line" and quite satisfactory if within 5 percent of the second responsible bidder and within 10 percent of the first three or four bidders.

While the low bid may be quite satisfactory even though the spread is greater, further investigation in this area may be necessary unless the other underwriting factors are superior and outweigh the apparent bid deficiency.

Financial Information. The furnishing of reliably prepared, detailed, and reasonably current financial information is vital. While contractors' failures are caused by a variety of factors, the prime reason for sureties' losses is the reliance upon misleading and inaccurate financial reports. Financial statements should never be more than a year old, and in the case of smaller contractors should be obtained at six-month intervals. Unless the statement has been fully audited by a CPA conversant with contractor accounting procedures, and unless the auditor gives his unqualified opinion that the balance sheet correctly reflects the financial condition, the underwriter will often require a substantial verification of the assets and the liabilities.

The purpose of reviewing the financial statement, of course, is to determine that the contractor has sufficient assets, liquid and otherwise, properly (1) to finance the contract under consideration, as well as the remaining portion of his other work; (2) to pay fully his bills for labor and material between monthly payments and while retainage builds up; and finally (3) to cushion any losses caused by increased labor and material costs, strikes, bad weather, uninsured mishaps, failure of subcontractors, death, and so on. With some variation, the underwriter will look for the contractors' excess of current assets over current liabilities, that is, "net quicks" or working capital, to approximate 10 percent of the total uncompleted work, including the contract under consideration. The working capital requirement may be considerably higher for a relatively new contracting firm or if other underwriting factors are slightly deficient; and it often is lower where the contractor is an old, well-established concern abundantly experienced or possessed of a large amount of valuable noncurrent assets.

Also of importance is the ratio of current assets to current liabilities. Two to one is ideal; four to three or worse may indicate the contractor is overtrading on his invested capital and it can spell trouble if even a small portion of the so-called current assets becomes slow or impossible of collection.

Current assets are normally limited to the following:

1. Cash and readily marketable securities, unrestricted and under the sole control of the principal.
2. Accounts receivable—retainage and those currently due from financially responsible debtors and not in dispute.
3. Notes receivable—only those payable within one year and adequately secured.
4. Cash value life insurance—only that where the insurance is payable to a corporate applicant or to the estate of an individual or partnership applicant.
5. Inventory—the fair value of that portion of materials usable on current contracts.

Fixed assets, too, are often important to the overall underwriting picture. Unencumbered construction equipment and income-producing real estate or other valuable improved property often provide borrowing capacity to supplement working capital and add to the contractor's loss-paying power. If any weight is to be given to real estate, the underwriter must be assured that the applicant holds title in its name alone or the indemnity of co-owners must be secured.

In reviewing the liability side of a contractor's financial statement, the underwriter wants to know the terms of any bank debt, whether and how it is secured, how much bank credit is available and on what terms, and, finally, the bank's opinion of the contractor as a credit risk. Generally speaking, all bank debt payable on demand or within one year even though secured by equipment or other assets is viewed as a current liability. All taxes, accrued wages and expenses, accounts payable of all types, including retainages due to subcontractors, and amounts due for material purchased or work done by subcontractors even though the bills have not been received, are also current liabilities; so, likewise are loans due to officers or other individuals unless the payment of these latter items is subordinated to the surety or the indemnity of such creditors is obtained.

Vitally important, too, are a statement of profit and loss and a careful review of comparative statements for three or four years to evaluate progress or lack of it. Any unusually large improvement casts doubt on the accuracy of the current statement.

Indemnity, Subordination, and Collateral. Sometimes, a case that is marginal from an underwriting standpoint is made acceptable by the surety's obtaining indemnity from officers, wives or other co-owners of assets belonging to the applicant contractor, or other persons possessed of financial responsibility. In like manner, the surety sometimes obtains from certain "friendly" creditors a subordination of their right to collect the amounts due them during the progress of a contract sought to be bonded. Infrequently, collateral in the form of cash or marketable securities will be deposited with the surety to lend additional support to the risk.

Whenever indemnity, subordination, or collateral is to be taken, it is important that it be obtained in proper form *before* the bond is executed in order to provide "consideration" and to assure its legality. When the offeror is a corporation, the underwriter must determine that the concern has the legal power to provide this security.

Joint Ventures. A joint venture, in effect, is a copartnership arrangement formed by two or more concerns to perform a specific contract. Joint ventures may be formed to provide contractors a satisfactory method of spreading the loss on very large projects, or for the purpose of pooling sufficient capital, experience, and equipment to permit two or more capable contractors to qualify for a larger program or job than any one of them could undertake alone.

In some instances, several contractors will submit a joint venture proposal in which all of the interested parties are named, and all are directly bound to the owner for the performance of the contract. In other cases the bid may be submitted in the names of one or more of the joint venturers acting for the whole group. Another plan employed infrequently is for the joint venturers to form a new corporation to undertake the contract, with each contractor contributing his share of the cash capital necessary to equip the job and carry on the work and perhaps giving his indemnity in addition to that of the new corporation.

In every case, however, the parties enter into a joint venture agreement defining as between themselves the extent of each participant's interest in the profits or losses accruing on the contract and outlining the details of how the actual work will be managed and carried forward. In most instances, the joint venture agreement will provide for the establishment of a segregated cash fund for the purpose of financing the construction, into which all estimates are deposited and from which all bills are paid.

Debt Paying Record. Of great importance in the consideration of any contract bond risk is an evaluation of the contractor's debt-paying record. This information is generally provided by Dun & Bradstreet reports or credit associations, and is sometimes supplemented by direct inquiry forms addressed by the surety company to the contractor's principal suppliers. A contractor who pays his bills in a prompt manner and takes advantage of discounts usually has adequate capital of his own to finance properly the volume of work he is performing, or at least has sufficient bank credit to supplement his own capital for this purpose. A prompt and discount-pay record also demonstrates that the contractor is a good collector and probably means that his accounts receivable, in the main, are due from solvent debtors.

Conversely, a contractor with a slow or past due record for paying his obligations is quite often undercapitalized for the scope of his operations, has a poor internal system for collecting his receivables, or has too many accounts due from people who are unable to pay promptly or who, perhaps, are disputing the debt. In any event, a slow debt-paying record is always a cause for alarm and quite often means that the contractor is a poor risk for the surety.

Fiduciary Bonds

The surety must first assure itself that the applicant and his attorney are persons of integrity. Next, their ability, as measured against the duties they will have to perform, must be considered. In cases where the estate is likely to remain open for a long time, or where the principal is operating without assistance from an attorney, the surety may take joint control of the estate funds under an arrangement whereby all withdrawals must be countersigned by the surety's representative and access to the estate's safe deposit box permitted only when he is present.

Going Business. An executor, administrator, or trustee of a decedent's estate or a guardian or committee of an incompetent's estate may come into control of a going business, either owned or controlled by the decedent or incompetent. In these cases the risk of the surety is enlarged by the responsibility the fiduciary will have for seeing that the business is properly operated or liquidated. If the business is to be continued, care must be taken to see that the fiduciary obtains proper authorization, including a decree of a court of appropriate jurisdiction, if necessary.

Indebtedness to the Estate. When the proposed fiduciary is indebted to the estate, it is necessary to find out how he proposes to discharge his obligation. The law, in most states, takes note of a conflict of interest represented by the merger of the obligation to collect and the obligation to pay in the same person. It either charges the fiduciary with the amount of the indebtedness as if it were money on hand or requires him to prove he is insolvent and unable to pay. The surety will, in most cases, insist upon prompt payment of the indebtedness, unless it can assure itself the fiduciary's distributive share will exceed the amount of his debt.

Prior Custody of Assets. When the proposed fiduciary has had possession or control of any of the assets prior to application for the bond, the surety must assure itself he is in a position to account. Prior possession or control of the assets could arise under a previous court appointment in the same or another capacity or by virtue of a power of attorney given by a decedent or ward prior to death or incompetency. There will be a merger of the duty to pay and the duty to collect in the same person. This merger results in a possible conflict of interest which could make the surety liable for a default occurring before the effective date of its bond.

Court Bonds

All court bonds are financial guarantees, and because it is usually impossible to forecast how long the litigation will last before final judgment is rendered, the surety considers them as long-term risks. As such, the underwriter must be satisfied that the principal is, and will in all likelihood remain, abundantly able to satisfy the obligation. Usually the surety must be furnished a detailed current financial statement of the applicant. If he is an individual, the underwriter will want to know his age, occupation, approximate income, and, if employed, how long he has been with his present employer. Also, the underwriter will usually want to review a Dun & Bradstreet or other mercantile report and to consider the recommendation of the agent, the attorney in the case, and local bankers or other businessmen.

While the underwriter will not attempt to anticipate the final outcome of the court action, the furnishing of an accurate summary of the pending litigation is important to his consideration of the bond.

If in the judgment of the underwriter, the financial worth of the applicant is not sufficient, the bond may be made acceptable to the surety by taking the indemnity of third parties or by depositing collateral with the surety in the form of cash or negotiable securities.

SUGGESTED READINGS

Contract Bonds—Underwriting Principles and Practices. Baltimore: Fidelity and Deposit Company of Maryland Press, 1949.

Crist, G. W., Jr. *Corporate Suretyship.* 2d ed. New York: McGraw-Hill Book Co., 1950.

Judicial Bonds—Underwriting Principles and Practices. Baltimore: Fidelity and Deposit Company of Maryland Press, 1949.

Lunt, Edward C. *Surety Bonds.* New York: Ronald Press Co., 1930.

Mackall, Luther E. *The Principles of Surety Underwriting.* Philadelphia: The Spectator, 1951.

———. *Surety Underwriting Manual.* Indianapolis: Rough Notes Co., Inc., 1963.

Wentz, George R. *Fidelity and Surety Bonding.* Wellesley Hills, Mass.: Lee Publishing Co., 1939.

Chapter 56

FIDELITY AND SURETY RATEMAKING

BY WARREN N. GAFFNEY

A thumbnail treatment of the philosophy and techniques of ratemaking for the fidelity and surety lines and a smattering of specifics and historical background are presented in this chapter.

EARLY HISTORY OF RATES

Individual Rates

Ratemaking for fidelity and surety bonds in the early days of American corporate suretyship was an individual company matter, for, prior to 1908, there were no rating bureaus to classify and establish rates or to assemble industrywide statistics. No reliable information exists as to just how surety risks were priced but it is reasonable to assume that company executives and underwriters negotiated the premium for the different kinds of bonds, appraising the risk in each case on the basis of their own judgment. Eventually company manuals were printed but most of them contained instructions for the producer to contact the home office for rates whenever in doubt. One of the few reports that has come down through the years relates to the Fidelity Insurance Company, a New York corporation, which was among the first companies to write bonds on a commercial basis. It remained in business for one year only, 1867, during which it wrote 33 bonds for aggregate premiums of $619. This figure is an average premium of about $18 per bond and indicates how humble was the origin of a business which in 1963 generated premium volume in excess of $300 million annually.

Rate Competition

After its feeble beginning, the business became profitable over a period of years and rates for fidelity and surety bonds proved to be high, thus encouraging the incorporation of many new companies. By 1900 competition had become vigorous. Indiscriminate and shortsighted rate-cutting was the order of the day. In a few years conditions throughout the industry deteriorated to such an extent that company executives urged that a limitation be put upon any one risk which a company could assume and that steps be taken to compel the accumulation of proper reserves for fidelity and surety claims.

NAIC Examination Committee

A committee appointed by the National Association of Insurance Commissioners in 1907 to examine all surety companies found that carriers had been writing risks for premiums so small and inadequate that it was virtually impossible for any of them to set up claim reserves. The classic illustration referred to by the committee was the bond of the Treasurer of Cook County, Illinois, which one surety company admitted having written without charge because it was a "target risk." The same company, on another piece of business, had taken one thousand cases of canned tomatoes as collateral security for a bond. The record does not reveal what credit or discount was allowed for such a liquid deposit but the incident shows what some underwriters did in those days in an effort to protect against loss. A number of insolvencies occurred in the wake of this investigation. Commissioners as well as leaders of the industry realized that if corporate suretyship were to endure and command public confidence, regulation by the industry itself or the commissioners would be necessary.

Surety Association of America and Towner Rating Bureau

Consequently, on October 29, 1908, with the approval of the National Association of Insurance Commissioners and the Treasury Department of the United States, the Surety Association of America was created to institute corrective measures, including the formulation of rules and guidelines regarding rates, reserves, forms, and underwriting practices. The new association approached its program through a number of committees. A subcommittee prepared a classification code which was adopted on December 3, 1909, with the recommendation that all member companies record their business in compliance therewith. It was subsequently amended many times and not until 1926, when report of premiums was changed from a net to a gross premium-written basis, was the predecessor of the present-day classification code finally approved.

With respect to rates, the new association soon found that it could not properly complete this phase of its work without the help of an independent organization which would devote full time to such a task. The Towner Rating Bureau was therefore established on October 1, 1909, and began immediately to review existing rates—retaining those deemed to be reasonable and adequate and making the necessary changes in others. During the preparation of the first manual, the bureau was called upon to promulgate rates for many new risks. Bulletin No. 1 was issued on September 27, 1909, and announced a scale of rates for "shipbuilding contracts in excess of $1 million." About one year later the first rate scale for federal official bonds was released in Bulletin No. 31. The separate rates for bonded federal positions set forth in this schedule represented existing rates plus increases as allowed by the act of August 5, 1909. That act prohibited acceptance by the government of any official bond costing "more than 35% in excess of the rate of premium charged for a like bond during the calendar year 1908." Many rates adopted around that time for Public Official Bonds, Court Bonds, Fiduciary Bonds, and other bonds were predicated (1) upon statutory limitations which placed maximums on the premium which a public body could pay for an official's bond; (2) on what a successful litigant could charge his opponent for the expenses of procuring an attachment, a costs bond, or an appeal bond; and (3) on the amount which a fiduciary could charge his estate for his qualifying bond. Several of these statutes are in force today and surety companies continue to charge the rates set up thereunder.

The earliest Towner Rating Bureau Manual of which any record exists is dated March 31, 1910. By agreement, members of the Surety Association of America were obliged to use the standard bonds promulgated by the association and to charge the rates contained in the bureau manual. That manual consisted of 30 pages of fidelity bond rates; 15 pages of court, fiduciary, and insolvency bond rates; 22 pages of contract bond rates; 12 pages of miscellaneous bond rates; 16 pages of license and permit bond rates; 14 pages of federal official and federal license bond rates; 3 pages of general public official bond rates; and a general index. The bureau also issued a separate public official manual which set forth the rates for specified positions and titles in the several states. Thereafter, the manual pages were revised and expanded from time to time to include new rates or modifications of existing rates.

Aftermath of SEUA Decision and Public Law 15

After the SEUA decision in 1944 and the enactment of Public Law 15 in 1945 (see Chapter 65), rate regulatory laws were passed in the several states. In order to comply more effectively with these laws, the Surety Association of America and the Towner Rating Bureau merged in October, 1947, retaining the name The Surety Association of America for all subsequent operations. In compliance with such laws, the association was licensed as a rating organization in the District of Columbia, the Commonwealth of Puerto Rico, and all states except Louisiana and Hawaii. It acts as an advisory organization in the two states mentioned. It has also been designated by all states, the District of Columbia, and the Commonwealth of Puerto Rico as their statistical agent to perform the statutory duty of gathering for them all classification loss experience relating to fidelity, surety, guaranty, and forgery bonds and to make compilations thereof in accordance with law.

Most rate regulatory laws provide generally that rates shall not be excessive, inadequate, or unfairly discriminatory. They also require in substance that in making rates due consideration shall be given (1) to loss experience within and outside the state; (2) to conflagration or catastrophe hazards; (3) to a reasonable margin for underwriting profit and contingencies; (4) to dividends; (5) to savings or unabsorbed premium deposits allowed or returned by insurers to their policyholders or members or subscribers; (6) to past and prospective expenses, both countrywide and those especially applicable to the state; and (5) to all relevant factors within and outside the state.

SURETY ASSOCIATION OF AMERICA'S INFORMED JUDGMENT BASIS OF RATEMAKING

Changes to a formula guide method of rating large classes of fidelity were accomplished quite recently and are discussed later in this chapter. Neither before nor since the rate regulatory laws became effective, however, has the Surety Association in the making and reviewing of rates for fidelity, surety, and forgery applied an automatic formula or adhered strictly to statistics. Nevertheless, the composite result reached by the staff after counseling with member companies has constituted an evaluation of losses, expenses, such additional statistics as may be available, and various other relevant factors listed in the rating statutes. This process has long been known as the exercise of informed judgment in the making and reviewing of fidelity, surety, and forgery rates. The "other relevant factors" which receive due consideration in this process are not the same for all coverages but are very important in the ratemaking procedures. They are many and include economic conditions generally or those applicable to a class of business, changes in law or legal effect, competition, potential volume, size of risk, adequacy of bond penalty, nature of the hazards, analogy to known hazards, statutory limitations, the value of the credit extended, the extent of the credit risk, and the nature of the service required.

It is noteworthy that, while informed judgment has been dominant in the rate review and ratemaking programs of the Surety Association, such judgment has included consideration of quite comprehensive loss experience and other statistics compiled by the association.

There is, for example, the Insurance Expense Exhibit for Member Companies which is prepared annually by the Surety Association and sets forth important information by Annual Statement line of business. Table 56–1 shows the percentages of net gain or net loss from underwriting prior to federal and foreign income and real estate taxes. These marked variations in underwriting experience are rather characteristic of the fidelity and surety business.

"Classification Experience"

Another detailed compilation of statistics important to rate review and ratemaking is the "Classification Experience." It is prepared from the reports of experience filed by all reporting companies in accordance with instructions contained in the Surety Association Uniform Statistical Plan. It sets forth the premiums and loss experience by separate code and by class of business. Such classification experience data are compiled on a countrywide basis for all coverages as well as on a statewide basis for the

TABLE 56–1

FIDELITY AND SURETY GAINS AND LOSSES(–)

(Percentages of Earned Premiums)

1957–1962

	1957	1958	1959	1960	1961	1962	Total
Fidelity	–5.9	0.3	6.2	– 3.2	–0.8	14.5	2.0
Surety	5.8	9.0	12.9	–10.7	5.3	9.2	5.2

so-called "state-rated" Public Official and License and Permit Bond business. Individual state experience data have very limited value. This fact applies particularly with respect to coverages that are subject to countrywide rating plans, for the reason that the small volume of such business in a state permits wide fluctuations in loss statistics making it difficult, if not impossible, to draw reasonable conclusions therefrom.

"Cost Study"

A further statistical aid is the Report on 1954 Fidelity and Surety Expense Costs (generally referred to as the "Cost Study") prepared by Wolfe, Corcoran and Linder, independent casualty actuaries. A compilation of expense data for 1954, it relates the data to direct premiums earned that year for the 10 broad divisions of the business, and was based upon statistics for the nine largest member writers in the fidelity and surety field. While the study was a pilot effort in a sense and subject to some qualifications, it has been helpful when used in conjunction with other available statistical information. This cost study was considered in the last Report on Examination of the Surety Association, which was conducted by the New York Insurance Department and participated in by the Insurance Departments of the states of Florida and California, dated July 1, 1957, and filed as of March 12, 1958, where at page 35 the following interesting comments appear:

The Cost Study made is a good beginning in the direction towards the desired goal of producing an acceptable method of rate making. It is admitted that the attainment of this objective is a tremendous and difficult task requiring extensive research and representing many problems. This is especially so in the field of fidelity and surety where rate making is based more on underwriting judgment and historical precedent, rather than statistical data analysis.

One of the goals of the Surety Association is to obtain another such cost study covering the most recent complete year.

That substantial consideration of loss statistics has long been included in the deliberations of surety ratemakers is evidenced by a letter written on November 17, 1919, by R. H. Towner, founder of the Towner Rating Bureau, to the Honorable Louis F. Hart, Governor of Washington, where he stated, in part:

> One company had a loss ratio on surety bonds of thirty-six hundred percent, another of eight hundred and ninety-eight percent, and a third of two hundred and eighty-three percent. Until we get figures for the present year, these 1918 figures are the latest available, and they indicate that in some manner you must have been misinformed, both as to the amount of contract premiums paid in Washington and as to the results to surety companies.

NEW RATING APPROACH FOR FIDELITY CLASSES

The similarities that mark fidelity and insurance and the differences that distinguish surety from insurance are ably and exhaustively discussed in *Surety Rate-Making* by Jules Backman (New York: The Surety Association of America, 1949). See also Chapter 53 of this *Handbook*. Generally, in the rating of insurance lines a formula or formula guide has been used. This technique has afforded insurance commissioners a ready barometer by which to test the validity of rate filings and has also enabled the insurance industry to reach decisions more speedily in a business that has grown enormously in volume and increased incredibly in its complexities. There has been an ever-growing school of thought in the industry and in the ranks of state supervisors that fidelity is so like conventional types of insurance that it should be treated as such even to the point of having the applicable ratemaking and rate reviewing processes placed on a formula guide basis. Convictions to this effect have been expressed strongly by many state insurance commissioners and executives of member companies of the Surety Association.

Subcommittee to Develop Formula

Accordingly, a subcommittee of the Executive Committee of the Surety Association was appointed several years ago (1) to work with the staff to produce formulas and ratemaking procedures for all fidelity sublines, divisions, and classes; and (2) to develop the recoding and reporting procedures and to achieve the reclassification, recoding, and reporting necessary to implement such an approach. This movement toward formula rating is a landmark of such significance in the history of the Surety Association, that, if the patriarchs who in their era contributed so substantially to the philosophy, growth, and success of corporate suretyship were alive today, they would be nothing less than incredulous.

Formula Guide for Bankers' Blanket Bonds

Through the joint and very considerable efforts of the subcommittee and the staff, a formula guide (shown in Table 56–2) was developed for Bankers' Blanket Bonds, the largest subdivision of the financial institutions subline of fidelity. On November 22, 1960, this formula guide was

TABLE 56–2

FORMULA GUIDE FOR FIDELITY FINANCIAL INSTITUTIONS (BLANKET)
BANKERS BLANKET BONDS FOR COMMERCIAL BANKS
(Ratios Are Expressed as Percentages of Estimated Direct Premiums Earned)

Item	First $1,000 of 3-Year Pure Premium*	Excess over $1,000 of 3-Year Pure Premium*	Average
*Expense other than Operating & Adjustment Expense	23.00%	23.00%	23.0%
**Operating Expense (Other Acquisition & General)	29.55	11.82	17.7
(Expense other than Adjustment Expense)	32.55%	34.82%	40.7%
Permissible Loss & Adjustment Expense	47.45%	65.18%	59.3%
I.B.N.R. Loss Reserve	1.00	1.00	1.0
***Permissible Loss & Adjustment Expense	46.45%	64.18%	58.3%
Unallocated Adjustment Expense	10.50	10.50	10.5
***Permissible Loss & Allocated Adjustment Expense	35.95%	53.68%	47.8%

* Including 5% for underwriting profit and contingencies.

** The *average* Operating Expense ratio of 17.70% is graduated so that the ratio applicable to the excess over the first $1,000 of 3-year pure premiums is reduced to 40% of the ratio applicable to the first $1,000 of 3-year pure premium.

*** Excluding (changes in the) I.B.N.R. (Incurred But Not Reported) Loss Reserve (for which there is a minimum statutory requirement for Fidelity classifications of 10% of Net Premiums in Force).

sent to all state insurance supervisors for their advanced information. The proposed rating basis was tested on more than 1,500 bank cases. This project involved a staggering number of man-hours of the staff of the Surety Association and the underwriters of the subcommittee. Thereafter, the rates and rating procedures relating to the formula guide became effective in 49 of the 50 states.

Underwriting Profit. It is to be noted that a factor of 5 percent for underwriting profit and contingencies was provided in the item "Expense Other than Operating and Adjustment Expense." Many students of the business thought at the time that in a line which traditionally had been rated on the basis of informed judgment and which is admittedly volatile and responsive to changes in our economy, a larger factor for underwriting profit and contingencies, at least for the transition period, should be used. However, in the last Report on Examination of the Surety Association referred to previously, the following appears on page 29:

> In the absence of any determination as to a reasonable allowance for underwriting profit and contingencies, a tentative factor of 5% has been used in this report. Such a provision of 5% is similar to the allowance for underwriting profit and contingencies for other lines of insurance used in most of the states. It may be noted that Fidelity and Surety rates with some exceptions are countrywide rates.

Because it was believed that the foregoing quotation was generally representative of supervisory thinking or, at least, would have a strong influence thereon, the factor of 5 percent for underwriting profit and contingencies was used on the assumption that it would be based upon appropriate experience periods.

Difficulties of Transition. In changing from informed judgment rating for commercial banks to a formula guide basis, extreme care was required to avoid excessive dislocations of business on the books of member and subscriber companies of the Surety Association. The difficulties were further accentuated by the necessity to produce rates and rating procedures which would gain the approval of all or almost all state insurance departments. As stated above, Surety Association rates for commercial banks as well as for most of the fidelity line have been applied countrywide.

An interesting sidelight occurred during the transition. During the period when the new rates and rating procedures were on file pending approval, the state insurance supervisors generally were highly satisfied with the changes in the method of rating fidelity. In addition, some of them were curious to learn the probable effects of the new rates on banks by size. They were advised that generally under the new rates and rating procedures the premiums charged to many small banks would be reduced somewhat, especially if they carried adequate coverage, and the premiums charged to many large banks would be increased. These results were dictated partly by informed judgment but also by an analysis of certain data contained in the annual reports of countrywide classification experience for the nine year period from 1951 to 1959.

"Basic Rate Table"

It is fitting, at this point, to consider briefly some of the rating procedures for financial institutions, particularly commercial banks. The cornerstone for the rating procedures for practically all blanket forms of financial institutions was originally established on December 6, 1915, and developed into a "Basic Rate Table." The "Basic Rate Table" contained minimum premiums according to bond amount for penalties of $25,000 or more. An additional per capita charge was made for employees in excess of 25, figured on a graduated scale and subject to a percentage increase for bond amounts greater than $25,000.

Originally, the premiums computed on the basic rates were subject to surcharge for class of insured. This surcharge eventually became identified as the "surcharge for form" as specific bonds were drafted to fit the needs of various financial institutions eligible for Bankers' and Brokers' Blanket Bonds.

With the introduction of specific contracts for particular classes, it was appropriate in some cases to depart from the traditional basic rate and to design a rating procedure that was deemed more suitable to the class for the exposure under the new form.

Commercial banks consistently have been, and still are, the major subdivision in the financial institution field. The table of "Basic Annual Premiums or Rates" for commercial banks, under the recent revision, provides for a coverage charge according to bond amount, plus an employee charge on a graduated scale subject to percentage increase according to bond amount. The entire table of "Basic Annual Premiums or Rates" for commercial banks cannot be reproduced here but partial sections are set forth to illustrate the application of this rating procedure for bond penalties up to $500,000 and for employees up to 500. The rating procedure set forth produces the basic premium which is subject to modification for form of coverage.

Modification for Form Selected

The specific forms for commercial banks are the Bankers' Blanket Bond Standard Form No. 2 and Form No. 24. Standard Form No. 24 is the more widely accepted. It provides broader coverage. Form No. 2 provides the essential coverages and is generally utilized to provide additional or "excess" coverage. Standard Form No. 24 is rated at 95 percent of the "Basic Annual Premium." The Standard Form No. 2 is rated at 87½ percent of the "Basic Annual Premium."

Where the Standard Form No. 24 is modified to delete the Teller's Shortage Exclusion Clause, the first $25,000 of coverage is rated at 125 percent of such "Basic Annual Premium" with the remaining "Basic Annual Premium" for coverage in excess of $25,000 subject to the standard rate of 95 percent.

The rating procedures also provide for the deletion of misplacement coverage above $25,000 of coverage. Where coverage is so modified, the "Basic Annual Premium" for coverage above $25,000 is rated at 90 percent of such "Basic Annual Premium" for Form No. 24 and at 83⅓ percent thereof for Form No. 2.

Coverage on additional locations operated by commercial banks is included in the standard forms. There is an additional charge for each such location calculated at a flat rate of $5.00 per employee, subject to a minimum charge of $100 or $250 depending upon the extent of the banking operation conducted at the location. The $100 minimum applies to locations that afford only limited banking facilities as distinguished from a general banking business.

Various optional coverages are available to commercial banks, the

TABLE 56–3

EXCERPTS FROM "BASIC ANNUAL PREMIUMS OR RATES" FOR COMMERCIAL BANKS

1963

Coverage Charge

The following coverage charges are applicable to bonds of $25,000 or more regardless of the number of Employees.

Bond Amount	*Coverage Charges*
$ 25,000	$175.00
50,000	250.00
75,000	325.00
100,000	375.00

Thereafter, for each additional $25,000, add $25.00 up to a bond amount of $500,000.

Employee Charge

Add to the coverage charge an annual charge for each Employee according to the following table for $25,000 bonds (minimum 3 Employees):

First	50 (0– 50)	Employees	@	$25.00	each
Next	50 (51–100)	"	"	20.00	"
"	50 (101–150)	"	"	15.00	"
"	50 (151–200)	"	"	10.00	"
"	100 (201–300)	"	"	8.00	"
"	200 (301–500)	"	"	6.00	"

Increase the Employee charge given above according to the following percentages for bond penalties in excess of $25,000.

Bond of	$	50,000	– 30%
"	"	75,000	– 50%
"	"	100,000	– 60%
"	"	125,000	– 65%
"	"	150,000	– 70%

Thereafter, for each additional $25,000, add 2½% up to a bond amount of $500,000.

more important of which provide forgery protection on checks and securities. The check forgery protection is provided by Insuring Clause D and the securities forgery coverage by Insuring Clause E.

For Insuring Clause D a charge is developed on the first $25,000 of coverage for each regular and special checking account depending upon the average amounts of deposits of the bank, ranging from 14¢ per regular account to 50¢ per regular account, while special accounts are charged for at a flat rate of 7¢ per account. There is a charge for coverage in excess of $25,000 on a graduated scale at a rate per thousand of coverage.

The charge for Insuring Clause E coverage is developed on a graduated premium table depending upon the average amount of loans and discounts, and for banks with average loans and discounts of $5 million or less the premiums charged in the tables represent the annual manual premium for Insuring Clause E. For banks with average loans and discounts of over $5 million there is an additional charge based upon such loans and discounts which is added to the basic premium developed from the tables for the amount of coverage.

The foregoing review illustrates the essential elements of the revised rating procedures for commercial banks but not those applicable where deductibles are employed or in the allocation of certain added premium charges for branch or location charges where coverage is written on a "primary" and "excess" basis.

New "Experience Rating Plan"

With few exceptions the premiums developed for financial institutions have been subject to an "Experience Rating Plan" for many years. From time to time changes and modifications were made in this procedure which, until recently, applied to all financial institutions coming within the scope of the plan. Insureds under this procedure were able to obtain a reduction in premium of up to 40 percent for favorable experience, the maximum premium for unfavorable experience being the manual rate. This arrangement still applies for all financial institutions which are now subject to experience rating other than commercial banks. The "Experience Rating Plan" for commercial banks, however, has been completely revised. It is based upon sounder actuarial concepts in that it relates actual experience to "Size of Premium" and "Expected Losses" within primary limits and excess limits. A table of values has been developed for premiums subject to experience rating with related expected loss ratios, credibility factors, and single loss limitations. Under this "Experience Rating Plan" the "Experience Modification" is restricted to the range of from .500 to 1.500.

Formula Guide for Rating Mercantile Establishments

The development of a formula guide basis for rating mercantile establishments was recently accomplished by the subcommittee and the staff after years of intensive work and after reviewing and analyzing more than 2,000 mercantile establishments cases. Among the difficulties was the fact that in place of the homogeneity that characterized the bank risks, here there was a marked heterogeneity and also a pressing and general demand for a greater degree of flexibility.

General Approval. The Formula Guide for Blanket Bonds for Mercantile Establishments was submitted to all insurance departments for their advanced information on March 28, 1963, and the Revision of Rates for such Blanket Bonds, relating to this formula guide, was filed for approval with all insurance departments on May 4, 1963, with an effective date of June 5, 1963. (See Table 56–4 for this formula guide.) Approvals of this rate filing were obtained from the several insurance departments with gratifying regularity. At the time of this writing approvals had been received from 49 of the 50 states plus Puerto Rico and the District of Columbia. It should be stated, however, that a number of states required

TABLE 56–4

FORMULA GUIDE FOR FIDELITY–MERCANTILE ESTABLISHMENTS (BLANKET)
BLANKET BONDS FOR MERCANTILE ESTABLISHMENTS
(Ratios Are Expressed as Percentages of Estimated Direct Premiums Earned)

Item	*First $750.00 of 3-Year Pure Premium**	*Excess over $750.00 of 3-Year Pure Premium**	*Average*
*Expense other than Operating & Adjustment Expense	28.00%	28.00%	28.00%
**Operating Expense (Other Acquisition & General)	39.13	15.65	23.10
(Expense other than Adjustment Expense)	67.13%	43.65%	51.10%
Permissible Loss & Adjustment Expense	32.87%	56.35%	48.90%
I.B.N.R. Loss Reserve	1.00	1.00	1.00
***Permissible Loss & Adjustment Expense	31.87%	55.35%	47.90%
Unallocated Adjustment Expense	10.50	10.50	10.50
***Permissible Loss & Allocated Adjustment Expense	21.37%	44.85%	37.40%

* Including 5% for Underwriting Profit & Contingencies.

** The *average* Operating Expense ratio of 23.10% is graduated so that the ratio applicable to the excess over the first $750.00 of 3-year pure premiums is reduced to 40% of the ratio applicable to the first $750.00 of 3-year pure premium.

*** Excluding (changes in the) I.B.N.R. (Incurred But Not Reported) Loss Reserve (for which there is a minimum statutory requirement for Fidelity classifications of 10% of Net Premiums In Force).

some modifications in the Experience Rating Plan which accompanied the new rates.

As was the case with respect to the Formula Guide for Commercial Banks, here again a factor of 5 percent for profit and contingencies was used.

Differences in Old and New Rating Systems. Dishonesty coverage on employees of mercantile establishments was originally provided by means of Individual Fidelity Bonds each covering a named employee. An early improvement consisted of Fidelity Schedule Bonds listing either the positions or the names of the individuals to be bonded and the amount for which covered. Thereafter, and since the introduction of Blanket Fidelity Bonds in 1926, there has been a decided change from such specific bonding of employees to the blanket forms of coverage. (See Chapter 54.) As in the financial institution field, the development through the years of the blanket bonds necessitated the adoption of a table of rates which became the "Basic Rate Table" for all insureds for the blanket form selected. Unlike in financial institutions where the form number was synonymous with a designated class of insured, the mercantile establishment rating procedures included a "Basic Rate Table" for each particular form of coverage which was in turn subject to surcharge or discount for the class of business of the insured.

The prior classifications for mercantile establishments had been developed to meet the needs of the business requirements of the market and reflected to a large extent the types of businesses covered. On the other hand, the new Fidelity Industrial Classification Code was predicated on the Industrial Classification Manual published by the executive department of the United States government which in turn had been prepared with the assistance of well-known economists.

Under the new classifications there is a greater degree of classification refinement and the new classifications may be logically grouped and consolidated into ever-expanding useful pools of experience as contrasted with the former catchall known as "Unclassified Codes" which contained about one half of the classification experience.

The determination of the "Class Rate Modifications," under the new refined classification system, necessarily required the exercise of informed judgment. There are reductions in rate for certain major groups and increases for others.

Another aspect of rating mercantile risks until the recent revision was the classification of employees based upon occupations and positions, designated Class A, Class Special A, Class B, and Class C. The Class A group comprised substantially all those employees who, as a part of their regular duties, handled, or had custody of money, securities, or merchandise. Class B employees were those who did not, as a part of their regular duties, handle or have custody of money, securities, or merchandise. Class C wage earners were those who did not, as a part of their regular duties, handle money. Under this employee classification, the developed premium was predominantly influenced by the number of Class A employees. Special Class A employees embraced such positions as canvassers, chauffeurs, collectors, demonstrators, and the like.

The revised rating procedure provides that Class 1 employees consist of those heretofore known as Class A (except Special Class A) employees plus 5 percent of the first 100 of those employees who were formerly Class B and C plus 1 percent of all such employees in excess of 100, disregarding fractions. Separate "Basic Premium Tables" provide the charges for Class 2 (formerly known as Special Class A) employees, and are graduated according to bond amounts between $10,000 and $25,000. The charges for Class 2 employees for a $10,000 bond apply to bond amounts of $10,000 or less, and the charges for a $25,000 bond apply to bond amounts of $25,000 or more.

Another difficulty encountered by underwriters in applying the previous rate structure was centered on the special underwriting and rating considerations for "additional retail locations," particularly in the "chain store" classification. This classification was defined as "6 or more retail stores," in which event there was a "classified line" surcharge of 100 percent applicable to the basic premium for Class A employees.

The increased exposure, the spread of hazard, the difficulty of control, and such were not adequately measured by the charge for increased personnel nor the surcharge associated with numerous retail locations. The most reasonable course, and the one followed in this revision, is to compensate for the increased exposure and other conditions listed in the previous sentence by instituting an appropriate charge for each such additional retail location. The charge is calculated as a proportion of the coverage charge inherent in the Class 1 employee rate tables. Thus, recognition is made of the difference between risks as represented by the number of such locations.

New "Experience Rating Plan." The flexibility sought by the industry is found in the new "Experience Rating Plan" which was filed with the rate revision. Space does not allow a full treatment of this plan. Among other things, the plan requires an experience modification based on premiums and losses for the first $10,000 (or less) of coverage during a three-year or six-year experience period and allows up to a maximum credit of 50 percent or a maximum debit of 50 percent according to the size of premium used in experience rating and the amount of losses incurred. It also provides for expense flexibility by incorporating into the promulgation of the risk modification a reduction in "Production Cost Allowance." This provision has been disallowed in some states. The plan also contains an element of schedule rating in that it permits the underwriter to adjust the modification in accordance with an "Underwriting Table," subject to a maximum additional charge equal to the "credibility value" used in determining the experience modification, or 30 percentage points, whichever is lower. The credibility value increases with the size of the risk. "Tables of Values," one based on a three-year experience period and the other on a six-year experience period, are attached to the plan. These tables set forth "Premiums Used in Experience Rating," "Premium Modifier," "Adjusted Loss Multiplier," and "Single Loss Limitation." The factors contained in the "Underwriting Table" and the range of modification in percentage points applicable to them are as follows:

	Range of Modification (Percentage Points)		
	(Decrease)		*(Increase)*
1. Audit Procedures	−15	to	+15
2. Internal Controls	−15	to	+15
3. Management & Personnel—(Qualifications & Procedures)	−10	to	+10
4. Classification Peculiarities (unique or unusual conditions of exposure or hazard)	−10	to	+10

It should be stated that amendments in this "Underwriting Table" have been required in several states. Furthermore, studies and collaboration between companies and their producers, and consideration by state supervisors of the overall problem, may require further modification in the expense modification and schedule rating sections of the Mercantile Establishment Experience Rating Plan.

Efforts of the Surety Association to develop formula guide bases of ratemaking for the remaining sublines, divisions, and classes of fidelity are continuing.

RATING SURETY CLASSES

Brief attention is now given to ratemaking for surety bonds. One of the elements often overlooked in the charge made for a surety bond is the value of the service which the bond renders to the one who purchases it. This is well stated by G. W. Crist, Jr., in *Corporate Suretyship:*[1]

> The principal who pays a premium for a bond simultaneously receives something of substantial value and benefit to him, a value separate and apart from the ultimate liability of the surety to the obligee. . . . he is thus enabled to qualify for a position of trust or for public office or on a desirable construction contract.

Use of a Formula

The question of formula ratemaking for surety has been considered exhaustively by Dr. Backman in *Surety Rate-Making* earlier in this chapter. On pages 355 and 356 he makes these sage remarks on the subject:

> In the light of the lack of data concerning demand, the inadequacy of formulas at turning points in the economic cycle, the changing relationships in the economy, etc., it is clear that surety rates cannot and should not be set by formula alone. Such a procedure would be too inflexible to meet the needs of a widely fluctuating surety business. It would establish a strait-jacket where fluidity is required. That such a formula might be useful as one of the guides in rate-making is probable. But to expect that surety rates, with their extreme fluctuations in experience, can be set and maintained at the proper level by this device, is to expect a high degree of coincidence between a theoretical formula and the economic facts of life. It may be doubted that such a coincidence would occur very frequently.
>
> The desire on the part of regulating authorities for simple, quantitative automatic formulas or yardsticks is understandable. However, unless the conditions are appropriate for the establishment and application of such yardsticks, they would create more problems than they solve. There is nothing about formula pricing which assures that its use will result in rates which are reasonable, adequate, and non-discriminatory. On the contrary, the creation and use of a

---

[1] G. W. Crist, Jr., *Corporate Suretyship* (2d ed.; New York: McGraw-Hill Book Co., Inc., 1950), p. 172.

formula which cannot be supported by the economics of the industry inevitably must result in a situation where the statutory standards are not met.

This does not mean that criteria are not available to carry out the mandate of the law. Standards or bench-marks are available, as has been indicated earlier. But they are more difficult to apply than simple mathematical formulas.

The challenge to devise a formula for surety is fraught with difficulties. The relevant factors of volume, credibility, economic conditions, volatility, statutory limitations, changes in law, the credit risk, the nature and value of the services, and the problems with respect to the surety classifications are unique and extremely complex.

General Rate Revision for Construction Contract Bonds

The most important rate revision in the surety line in a great many years was the "Construction Contract Bond General Rate Revision," effective July 20, 1955. Among other changes, that revision accomplished the following: Previously, the rate scale for Class A bonds was $7.50 per thousand on contract price until a contract price of $2,500,000 was reached and at that point it dropped to $6.00 per thousand. Under the scale provided for in the revision, the rate on contract price of $7.50 per thousand up to a contract price of $100,000 is continued; but for contract prices over $100,000 the rate is set at $5.00 per thousand on contract price until a contract price of $2,500,000 is reached. Thereafter, in the succeeding brackets of contract price, the comparison between the previous and the revised rate scales is as follows:

Class A Bonds

Contract Price	*Previous Rates Per M*	*Revised Rates Per M*
Next $2,500,000	$5.75	$4.00
Next $2,500,000	5.50	3.90
Over $7,500,000	5.00	3.60

The previous rate for Class B bonds remained at $10.00 per thousand of contract price until a contract price of $2,500,000 was reached when it dropped to $8.00 per thousand. The revised rate scale remains at $10.00 per thousand up to a contract price of $100,000 but is reduced to $6.50 per thousand on contract price over $100,000 until a contract price of $2,500,000 is reached. In the succeeding brackets of contract price, the comparison between the previous and the revised rate scales is as follows:

Class B Bonds

Contract Price	*Previous Rates Per M*	*Revised Rates Per M*
Next $2,500,000	$7.67	$5.25
Next $2,500,000	7.33	5.00
Over $7,500,000	6.67	4.70

The following extract from the rate filing letter on that general rate revision is a good example of the exercise of informed judgment in a difficult class of business and it is noteworthy that this occurred in a rate revision relating to approximately 80 percent of the contract bond premium volume and constituted a reduction of approximately 18 percent with no rate increase involved:

The foregoing reduced rates represent our judgment in the light of all factors relevant to this type of surety credit including, among other things, the economic trends with respect to costs and competition in our industry and in the construction industry since the last general contract rate revision in 1945. Since that time new construction activity has increased from somewhat less than $6 billion annually to over $37 billion as reported for the year 1954 by the U.S. Department of Commerce. In the same period, public construction (included in the foregoing) has increased from about $2.4 billion to about $11.5 billion. Each successive year has shown an increase in the amount of new construction and each year has resulted in a greater volume of contract bond premiums. It is of particular interest to note that the prophesied new construction volume for the year 1955 is in the neighborhood of $41.8 billion.

Our studies indicate that construction capacity has more than kept pace with the increase in volume and the capacity for providing corporate surety credit has also increased. Material advances have been made in the techniques of construction, in supervision, in cost analysis, in other technical facilities and in the extension of surety credit. It is, therefore, our belief that the proposed new rates will prove to be adequate, as well as reasonable and not unfairly discriminatory.

Construction contract bond premiums comprise what is by far the most important subline of surety premiums since over two-thirds of all surety premiums are contract bond writings. Even though total contract bond writings are not large, nevertheless we estimate that these new reduced rates will result in nationwide annual savings in excess of $9 million based on the most recently available data at hand.

TRANSITION

Procedures in ratemaking for fidelity bonds will often be in a state of flux because, as old contracts become obsolete and new contracts of indemnity are created, new rates and rating rules become necessary. As this chapter is being written, fidelity lines are beginning to feel the impact of package policies which include many property and liability covers along with fidelity and forgery protection. It is too early to make predictions with respect to this trend.

The above discussion indicates that formula guide ratemaking is an accomplished fact for commercial banks and mercantile establishments; and that it is expected to be used in the entire fidelity line in the near future. However, it also reiterates some of the manifold and oft-expressed reasons why the quest for the formula rating of surety lines is so complex and difficult a problem.

SUGGESTED READINGS

BACKMAN, JULES. *Surety Rate-Making*. New York: Surety Association of America, 1949.

BUTTON, COL. JOSEPH. *Reminiscences*. New York: Towner Rating Bureau. Address delivered at joint annual meeting of International Association of Casualty and Surety Underwriters and National Association of Casualty and Surety Agents, White Sulphur Springs, W.Va., October, 1926.

CRIST, G. W., JR. *Corporate Suretyship*. 2d ed. New York: McGraw-Hill Book Co., Inc., 1950.

LUNT, EDWARD C. *Surety Bonds*. New York: Ronald Press Co., 1930.

———. "Surety Rate-Making, An Approach to the Subject," *Proceedings of the Casualty Actuarial Society*, Vol. XXV, Part I (November, 1938).

Report on Examination of The Surety Association of America, 1957, by New York Insurance Department, participated in by Insurance Departments of California and Florida.

WOLFE, CORCORAN & LINDER. *Report on 1954 Fidelity and Surety Expense Costs to Fidelity and Surety Cost Study Committee of The Surety Association of America*. New York, October, 1955.

Chapter 57

DEFAULTS IN SURETYSHIP*

BY ALANSON R. FREDERICKS

The ideal expert to handle defaults in suretyship is a man with years of practical experience. He is an admitted attorney, a graduate engineer, and a certified public accountant. He has the patience of a Job, the inquisitiveness of a ferret, the tenacity of a bulldog, and the judgment of a Solomon. To find such a man still young enough to be employable is akin to a "task of Hercules." Since such paragons are rare indeed upon this green earth, this chapter is written for lesser men and women who aspire to know some of the fundamentals of the subject.

"KNOWS OF SURETYSHIP"

The handling of a claim on a surety bond calls for the application of knowledge and practical experience, tempered by good common sense. Numerous points developed in Chapters 16, 20, 30, 47, and 52 also apply to suretyship. In addition, there are basic ground rules which can be termed the three fundamental "Knows of Suretyship."

"Know Your Bond"

Although the condition clause is especially important, the entire bond should be meticulously read. The bond specifies, of course, *what* the principal and surety are obligated to do; it also specifies *when, to whom,* or *for whom* such obligations are owed. While there are "standard" provisions, there are nevertheless many variations which depend in part upon the requirements of the pertinent statute, ordinance, or regulation. Moreover, bonds also vary with the whims and vagaries of architects, individual owners, prime contractors, and surety companies. In short, there is a myriad of bonds, each with its own peculiarities.

---

* This chapter is confined to defaults on bonds other than fidelity. Treatment of fidelity bond defaults is closer akin to adjustment of dishonesty insurance claims.

"Know Your Files"

The bond claims officials should examine not only the underwriting file for the bond in question, but also *all* files for the same principal, particularly the credit file. Thus, it should be possible at the outset to approximate the maximum potential liability for claims which could and usually do result by chain reaction. In addition, it should be possible to spell out sources of salvage by a careful examination of the financial statements of the principal and the indemnitors, even though the dollar valuations placed on individual assets may be somewhat fanciful. These files should be retained with, and even incorporated into, the claim jackets.

"Know Your Business"

The person responsible for taking action in case of a default must remember that the contract in default is a surety bond and not an insurance policy. He must remember that a surety, in effect, agrees to perform, if its principal cannot, but that it can look to its principal for recoupment and reimbursement for all monies advanced, either for loss or expense. Salvage is a heavily weighted factor in treatment of surety defaults. This right of recoupment is predicated upon several bases and the surety can pursue this right without being required to elect one basis to the exclusion of the others.

Generally, an agreement of indemnity is obtained from the principal prior to the execution of the bond. Such agreements differ among companies as to content and format, yet invariably there is a specific provision that the principal will hold harmless and indemnify the surety against any loss or expense. When a surety pays a claim on its bond, it can, and in the majority of instances will, obtain from the claimant an assignment, particularly when a contract payment bond is involved.

The surety also has the right of equitable subrogation, falling heir to all the rights and privileges of the person to whom payment is made. While a surety on court bonds, in most instances, is primarily liable, it is considered secondarily liable on contract and fiduciary bonds. The condition clause in these bonds reads in substance: "If the principal does what he is supposed to do, then this bond is of no effect; otherwise it remains in full force."

Last but not least, no surety should set itself up as a final arbiter between a bond claimant and a solvent principal. Sometimes it may be advisable, in order to achieve an ultimately greater benefit, to pay a disputed claim. Yet, in such instances, a surety can resign itself to the fact that it probably will have to prove this claim in order to recoup from its principal or indemnitor. Although generally the indemnity agreement provides that the surety has the right to settle, the evidence of such payment is but prima facie proof of the propriety thereof and of the indemnitor's liability therefor.

FIDUCIARY BOND CLAIMS

Fiduciary bonds fall into four general classifications insofar as the activities of the principals go:

A. Collecting and distributing
   1. Administrators
   2. Executors
   3. Guardian *ad litem* or Special Guardian
   4. Trustees and Receivers in Bankruptcy
   5. Assignees for Creditors
   6. Receivers
B. Preserving and investing
   1. Guardians and Committees
   2. Trustees
C. Holding for refund or as life tenant
D. Selling, mortgaging, and leasing of realty

Class A

Class A bonds are theoretically short-term and the fiduciary's main function is to collect assets, pay creditors, and then distribute the balance remaining to the distributee/s in accordance with the laws of descent and distribution (where an Administrator's Bond applies) or in accordance with the provisions of the will (where an Executor's Bond applies). Such distribution should not be made until the statutory period for the filing of claims has expired. In some jurisdictions, a decree barring creditors after a day certain can be obtained. In other jurisdictions, such as New York, no distribution may be made to heirs, distributees, or legatees before the end of a statutory period, except at the risk of the fiduciary. Thereafter distribution is proper, and the rights of creditors who file subsequently are limited to the assets remaining in the fiduciary's hands.

A guardian *ad litem* or special guardian collects the assets, generally a sum recovered as a result of litigation, and makes payment over to a permanent guardian appointed to preserve the assets.

A receiver, trustee, or assignee in federal bankruptcy or state insolvency proceedings collects the assets, pays the administration costs and expenses, and then distributes to the creditors, as directed by the court. If any balance remains (and such balances are rare, indeed), it is returned to the bankrupt.

Claims on Class A bonds arise through the failure of the fiduciary to perform his statutory duties. He may fail to obtain all of the collectible assets; make distribution without satisfying all just debts; prefer some creditors; or operate a business of his decedent without authority, either from the court or by the terms of the will. Obviously, there is also the possibility of outright embezzlement.

Class B

On Class B bonds there are usually all of the hazards associated with Class A bonds plus the potential liability of loss through investing funds in securities not approved or permitted, either by will or by statute. The investment hazard is not as great today as in the past. Many states have adopted the "prudent man" criterion. This rule is that when a reasonable and prudent business man would make such an investment, the trustee likewise is permitted to make the investment, there being no extenuating circumstances. Some danger exists in the retention of nonlegal securities, comprising part of the original assets received. Generally, however, the courts allow a reasonable time in which to dispose of them.

Class C

A Refunding Bond presents a somewhat different problem since it guarantees the refund of a distributive share in an estate in the event that there be an adjudication adverse to the recipient. The financial inability of the distributee to repay is the sole cause of loss.

A Life Tenant's Bond is particularly hazardous in those states which require that there be assets of the same monetary value as originally received in the life tenant's estate for distribution to the remaindermen in accordance with the terms of the original will. Fortunately, such laws are definitely in the minority and such bonds are rarely written under them. In the majority of states a life tenant is required to hold the corpus which he receives intact but is not a guarantor of its value. While there may be an investment danger, it is generally held that even though the value of the corpus depreciates, there is no liability if the investments are in securities approved by statute or permitted by the terms of the will. However, if realty is part of the assets received, the risk is more hazardous. In such instances, the estate of the life tenant may be faced with a claim by the remainderman based on the common law action of "waste"—to permit or allow a lasting damage to the realty, thus destroying or lessening the value of the inheritance.

Class D

A bond to permit the sale, mortgage, or lease of realty in an estate is in many states a type of License Bond, good only for a definite period. If nothing is done, there is no liability on the bond. In other jurisdictions, the license is not limited as to time, and the liability continues until the property is (1) mortgaged, leased, or sold; (2) an accounting made; and (3) the net proceeds paid over to the general fiduciary.

Claim Procedure

The handling of claims arising in connection with these bonds is much the same from one class to another. Immediately upon notice (1) the claim should be acknowledged; (2) the fiduciary and his attorney should be asked for their version of the matter; and (3) a formal request, in writing, should be made upon the fiduciary and indemnitors, if any, to indemnify and hold harmless the surety for any loss, claim, or expense which may be incurred.

Claimants can be either creditors or beneficiaries. No matter who the claimant may be, any default means that the original assets in the custody of the fiduciary, as well as the assets remaining on hand, must be listed in detail. Theoretically, the original assets should have been set forth in the application for the bond; but, as a practical matter, such listing usually is of little help in the event of a default. The fiduciary and his attorney should be in a position to give complete information. An examination of the court records may reveal an original inventory or appraisal and will show if the fiduciary has filed any accountings. If there has been a transfer tax proceeding, the schedules should contain information about assets being handled by the fiduciary.

If the claimant is a creditor, the settlement procedure should involve a listing of all other creditors who have claimed or will claim against the assets. The list should specify the amounts involved and to what extent payment has been made.

If the claimant is an heir or beneficiary, a copy of any will which may be involved should be obtained. If there is no will, the names and ages (if minors) of the possible distributees and their degree of kinship to the decedent or grantor should be learned. Court records should be examined and a synopsis made of the petitions and orders contained in them. Copies of any accounts filed and allowed by court orders should be obtained, if they are available. If such copies cannot be obtained, at least the data in the summary statement of the account should be secured. It is well to note, in cases of court orders, which parties were given notice of the proceedings and the method used. Also, if any releases or refunding bonds were filed, detailed information about them should be compiled. All copies of receipts from creditors, including anything from the local, state, or federal tax authorities, of course should be added to the file being established on the defaulting principal. If the assets of the trust or estate have been subject to the surety's control, the joint control and counter-signature records should be examined and any pertinent information noted.

It may be well, particularly in small communities, to discuss the situation with the producing insurance agent. Quite often he knows the family background, the relationship between the various interested parties, as well as the financial condition of the principal. It is well to remember that a bond does not have to respond for any financial interest, including commissions, which the principal may have in a particular trust or estate.

If objections are filed in an accounting proceeding, it is important to keep in mind that only to the extent of the objections filed, and only to those objectors, is there any obligation on the part of the surety. As to all others who might have the same rights but fail to file, such rights are waived. There cannot be tacit objections, but there can be a tacit consent to the actions of the fiduciary. Probably in no other branch of suretyship does waiver and estoppel play such an important part.

COURT BOND CLAIMS

Court bonds, required in connection with litigation, are frequently divided into two classes—plaintiffs' and defendants' bonds. (See Chapter 55 for a description of court bonds.)

The nature of the surety's obligation differs somewhat in each case. The requirements for such bonds, and, to a great extent, the provisions thereof and the liability thereunder are governed by statute and their judicial interpretations. In this type of suretyship the surety, in practically all cases, is the sole signatory and is, therefore, primarily liable. Liability comes into being as a result of a judicial decision adverse to the person bonded. In addition, there is a separate determination by the court as to the bond liability. The exceptions to this generalization are, first, Bail Bonds, where the liability is the penal sum of the bond itself and, second, Appeal or Supersedeas Bonds, where the liability is the amount of monetary damages awarded to the successful litigant on the merits of the case by the appellate court. In all other cases, actual damages must be proved in court by the successful litigant. In most jurisdictions, such damages include actual loss resulting from the use of the bond, as well as attorneys' fees directly related to the bond, as differentiated from services rendered in connection with the litigation proper.

It is necessary to obtain a copy of the court order entered in favor of the successful litigant, together with any order assessing damages on the bond. Notice of claim should be given to the principal and the indemnitors, if any, and a demand made to furnish funds to pay the claim or to settle the matter directly with the claimant. If collateral has been obtained at the time the bond was written, the surety should advise the principal and the collateral owner, if the collateral owner is not the principal, that the surety will use the collateral to pay the claim.

If there is any possibility of appeal from the judgment, it is extremely important that the individual responsible for handling default satisfy himself that the statutory period has expired before payment is made.

CONSTRUCTION CONTRACT BOND CLAIMS

Proper treatment of claims on fiduciary and court bonds may require some knowledge of law and of basic mathematics blended with common sense. However, a claim on a contract bond is a "horse of a different hue." There are no arbitrary rules which can be generally applied. Every facility of the surety should be utilized fully. Each case is unique unto itself. Experienced bondsmen may agree on the method to be used in a particular default but seldom agree on all the details of application of that method and of the decisions which must be made. Handling of defaults in suretyship is truly a second-guesser's paradise.

Defaults are seldom restricted to a single contract or a single bond. Too often the principal has additional jobs, each in a different stage of completion. Some may be unbonded; others may be bonded but with different sureties. The job sites may be far afield and widely separated but all or some may involve some of the same subcontractors and material suppliers.

Review of Types of Contract Bonds

While construction contract bonds are described at length in Chapter 55, a brief review is presented here of a few features particularly salient to treatment of defaults.

Performance Bonds. Performance bonds secure to the owner the performance of the contractor's obligations under the contract covered. (Supply or bid bonds—among others—fall into this category.) The owner is generally the sole named obligee and the only person to whom the surety owes an obligation. Under the third-party beneficiary theory, however, third parties frequently have a right of action on performance bonds. In many instances a separate performance bond and a separate payment bond are given in connection with one job. The Miller Act[1] contains a requirement of separate payment and performance bonds with respect to U.S. government contracts.

Payment Bonds. The function of payment bonds is to secure the payment of all labor and material suppliers and subcontractors in connection with the contract covered even though the owner is the sole named obligee. Such claimants may have a direct cause of action on the bond, either by statute or by bond language. In most jurisdictions the claimant must protect his rights by compliance with the pertinent state laws or with the terms of the bond. In connection with a payment bond filed

---

[1] *Miller Act,* 40 U.S.C.A. Secs. 270a and 270b, Aug. 24, 1935, c. 42; Sec. 1, 49 Stat. 793; Sec. 2, 49 Stat. 794; Sec. 270b amended Aug. 4, 1959, Pub. L. 86–135, Sec. 1, 73 Stat. 279.

under provisions of the Miller Act mentioned above a claimant contracting directly with the principal may sue the principal and the surety *after* 90 days *after* furnishing the last item of labor and material. A claimant having no such direct relationship, but having furnished labor or materials to a subcontractor, must give notice of nonpayment to the principal *within* 90 days *after* furnishing the last item of labor and material. If no notice be given, the claimant is barred from suit on the bond. In any event, all suits on the bond must be commenced *within* one year *after* furnishing the last material or performing the last work on the contract. Prior to August 4, 1959, the cutoff date for bringing suits on bonds filed pursuant to the Miller Act was one year after the date of final settlement of the contract as determined by the Comptroller General of the United States.

Performance and Payment Bonds. Both performance and payment may be bound in a single document. Use of these combination bonds was permitted for U.S. government contracts under the federal Heard Act,[2] the predecessor of the Miller Act. However, in this single bond, the claims of labor and materialmen are subordinated to the owner's primary right of recourse to the bond to secure the performance of the contract. Fortunately, from the viewpoint of those who work with defaults, the use of this combined bond is not as prevalent now as it once was. Increasingly, even state and local governments' bodies are requiring separate bonds. This right of priority produces numerous "headaches" in handling defaults. The reason is that it is extremely difficult to effect performance without paying outstanding labor and material bills. In the event of an ultimate default of the contract itself, there is the risk that such payments, plus the cost of performing the contract, will exceed the bond penalty.

Indemnity Bonds. Indemnity bonds run in favor of the owner alone, and protect him against all damages caused by the default of the principal. No person, other than the obligee, has any direct right of action thereon. However, the lien law and related laws of the state in which the contract is to be performed are extremely important. While payment of claim is usually made only to the obligee, a laborer or a materialman could be paid directly, if he has perfected his lien rights.

Types of Claims

When difficulty arises, the surety learns of it in one or more of the following ways: (1) notice from unpaid bond creditors; (2) notice from owner of default or possibility of default; and (3) notice from principal of financial difficulty.

Notice from Unpaid Bond Creditors. The notice should be acknowl-

[2] *Heard Act*—Aug. 13, 1894, c. 280, 28 Stat. 278.

edged and an itemized statement of account, with invoices in duplicate, showing dates of delivery on the job, should be requested. Moreover, inquiry should be made of the principal about his reason for nonpayment. While the notice is not necessarily an omen of serious difficulty, it is a "red flag" of warning—especially when complaints of creditors are numerous, when amounts involved are substantial, or when the claimant is either furnishing material vital to the completion of the contract (for instance, steel for a bridge) or is an unpaid laborer. A surety can then be almost certain it is faced with a serious situation which requires immediate and careful attention. The chances are better than even that there is now not only a payment problem but also a mushrooming performance bond crisis.

Notice from Owner of Possible Default. Upon receipt of such notice, the surety should ascertain from the owner and verify with the principal the reason for the difficulty. The cause could be any one or any combination of the following:

1. Failure to perform in accordance with work-flow schedule.
2. Inadequate work force on the job.
3. Complaints of delinquent accounts from laborers, materialmen, or subcontractors.
4. Shortage of material and equipment available for the job.
5. Lack of competent management on the job site or in principal's organization.
6. Lack of cooperation between the principal and the owner or their respective representatives.
7. Difficulties with subcontractors.

It may be possible to adjust the situation by tact and persuasion, but if the cause is based upon financial difficulties of the principal, any such adjustment is usually but a lull in a storm. An initial engineering survey may be helpful. Yet regular and frequent periodic inspections likely will be necessary to prevent default.

Notice from Principal of Financial Difficulty. This type of notice usually is presented on the morning of the day the payroll is due. In such cases time is of the essence. Unless the payroll is met, the job will shut down. The subcontractors may seize upon such event as an excuse upon which to terminate their contracts and assert whatever rights they may have for payment on a *quantum meruit* basis. (This basis involves the question of how much is the work done actually worth without being limited to contract prices.) It is ordinarily advisable to meet the current payroll, obtaining the immediate consent of any reinsurers. These funds are "look money" well spent to buy time to obtain the necessary information upon which to predicate a considered solution to the problem.

The principal's predicament may have been the direct result of:

1. Too low a bid.
2. Overextension.

3. Lack of experience in the type of contract involved.
4. Excessive costs due to improper supervision or to unforeseen circumstances.
5. Pressure from noncontract creditors.

Procedure

The normal procedure for the surety in handling contract bond claims is as follows:

1. Examine copies of all contracts, plans, and specifications, as well as all subcontracts, noting particularly completion dates, as well as any per diem rate for liquidated damages as a result of delay.
2. Examine copies of all bonds and applications.
3. List all uncompleted contracts, the percentage of completion (measured both by dollars and by work done), noting whether they be bonded or not (if so, by whom), as well as the nature of the work involved.
4. List all outstanding accounts for labor, materials, and subcontractors on each project.
5. List all amounts due to other creditors.
6. Inventory all materials and equipment owned by principal on the job sites or elsewhere, the value and location thereof, noting any encumbrances thereon.
7. List all rental equipment on the job sites, showing the amount due and the rate, noting particularly if it be an outright lease or a rental purchase agreement. (Usually the surety is liable for rental of the equipment, but not for monthly payments due for purchase.)
8. Check principal's original bid sheets as well as the bid record of the contract itself.
9. Survey the job and estimate the cost of completion. (It is better practice, in addition, to obtain an estimate from various sources for the purpose of comparison—from the principal, from an independent or staff engineer, as well as from other contractors, particularly the second and third original bidders who may be interested in taking over.)
10. Check the principal's books and records. (Look particularly to see whether or not they are up-to-date, with bills properly allocated to each project, and with detailed records broken down by job.)
11. Obtain a copy of the last financial statement of the principal—preferably one prepared by a C.P.A.
12. Obtain from the principal a list of key personnel, with an outline of duties and with a statement of the principal's opinion of the capabilities of each key person.
13. Ask the owner's architect or supervising engineer whether the principal's supervision of the job is satisfactory, capable, and whether the principal has sufficient equipment to perform the contract.
14. Check for any assignments of contract monies, verifying whether or not notice was given to surety.
15. Check the status of the principal's existing or pending liability for federal and state taxes.
16. Examine the last approved payment requisitions or estimates, not only for the particular contract, but for all others in which the principal is involved. (These should show the status of the work of the subcontractors.)

If the claim concerns a payment bond only, not all of the foregoing steps need be taken. Still, it is always necessary to verify the amount owed and to be assured that it is a bond obligation. Payment can be made with the principal's concurrence, after the surety makes certain that the aggregate amounts paid, plus the possible future payments, will not exceed the bond penalty. If the aggregate amounts requiring payment look as though they might exceed the penalty, then the surety should make no payments but rather institute an interpleader action if no voluntary arrangements can be made with creditors to accept pro rata payments.[3]

The above outline sets forth the preliminary workload for contract bond claims where both performance and payment coverages are involved. Although considerable time may be required to amass, correlate, and evaluate this basic information, the facts obtained are the raw material for good decisions.

Protective and Preventive Measures. At the same time certain protective and preventive measures should be taken. A word of warning should be injected at this point in the chapter. Optimism is a disease to which contractors are particularly susceptible, and, without fail, it will be in its most virulent and contagious stage when a surety is brought into the picture. The surety, therefore, should take every precaution. A grain of salt may help, but stark realism is the most effective antidote.

At the outset, the principal will insist that his difficulty is but a temporary interlude which can be handled quite easily with the assistance of the surety. He will iterate and reiterate that he intends to continue in the contracting business and, therefore, that the surety can rely on his full and complete cooperation. At such a point the surety should remind the contractor of the surety's obligation to indemnify and should emphasize that the surety's objective is to minimize any and all loss. The surety should point out that it takes time to garner all the necessary facts, but that, in the meantime, the surety will do its utmost to keep the bonded jobs operating. However, it is imperative that the principal sign certain papers:

1. A letter to the surety and to the obligee on each bond, admitting the principal's inability to continue the contracts and requesting the surety to take over in each instance. (This letter is vitally important, since it can be construed as an admission of voluntary default. It will be used in the event that it is necessary and more economical to have a new contractor brought into the picture.)
2. A letter to the obligee on each bond, requesting that all remaining contract monies be paid over as directed by the surety.
3. A power of attorney authorizing the surety to endorse and deposit all payments of contract monies received on each job and to use such monies to discharge bond obligations.

---

[3] *Federal Interpleader Act,* 28 U.S.C.A. Secs. 1335, 1397, 2361. See also, *Pennsylvania Fire Insurance Co.* v. *American Airlines* [180 F. Supp. 239—EDNY (1960)].

Next the surety should see the owner and his architect and give them the letter of directive (No. 2 above), together with a copy of the application pointing out the sentence which provides for the assignment of all contract monies to the surety. Both should be told that the surety is proceeding as speedily as is possible to obtain the essential facts so that it may properly discharge its obligations. Without making any commitments as to what the ultimate decision may be, the surety might inquire whether or not the owner would be willing to enter into a new contract with a different contractor to finish the project. (Readers are reminded that the surety in such a case would already have a letter from the principal admitting inability to perform.) The surety should be certain to assure the owner that any completion costs in excess of the remaining contract monies will be paid by the surety subject to the terms and the limits of the performance bond. In some cases, particularly if the owner is a governmental body, this method may be neither possible nor feasible because of the resultant time lag where there is a statutory requirement to advertise for new bidders.

Relations with Subcontractors. The surety's next and most pressing problem is that presented by the subcontractors. The sheets showing the original bidding estimate of the principal should give a fairly clear picture as to how much of the original project was subcontracted and how much was to be performed with the principal's own work force. Particular attention should be given to those subcontractors having work remaining to be done. Each of these should be advised, either by letter or telegram, that all of the principal's rights in the contract, including all subcontracts, have been assigned to the surety. Each should be asked to furnish the surety with an itemized statement of account, in duplicate, with as much detail as may be necessary. If an agreement can be reached with the principal as to what is due to each, and the amount can be verified from the principal's books, payment should be made or guaranteed. If some amounts are in dispute, a good procedure is to pay or guarantee that which is not questioned, with assurance that any rights the subcontractor may have as to the unpaid balance are in no wise prejudiced. Simultaneously, there should be obtained from each subcontractor a letter, saying that, in consideration of the payment or guaranty, he will continue to perform, at the subcontracted price, as requested by the surety or its nominee, whether or not the prime contract is in default.

If more than one bonded contract is involved, it is good practice to make a chart, listing all subcontracts on all jobs in one column on the left, all of principal's contracts across the top, filling each interstice with the amount owed and the percentage of subcontract work remaining to be performed. This glorified tit-tat-toe diagram ofttimes is a most potent factor in the ultimate overall decision. Certainly, it is an indication of problems which may arise in connection with subcontractors whose cooperation may be needed, particularly if there is money owed them on contracts other than those presently involved.

"The Moment of Truth." Now comes the "moment of truth." At this point the facts essential for a considered decision have been assembled. All the necessary protective and preventive measures have been taken. The following question must be answered: What then are the possible alternatives, assuming that sufficient "look money" has been spent to keep the job operating and that the owner has not breached the bonded contract so as to relieve the surety?

If the probable cost to complete exceeds the aggregate face amounts of the performance bonds, after taking credit for all contract monies remaining, the decision is relatively simple. The surety should advise the owner that it stands ready to pay, subject to and in accordance with the provisions of the respective bonds, the cost of completion in excess of the remaining contract monies.

If the probable cost is less than the face amounts of the bonds in question, after taking into account the outstanding labor and material bills, the surety must then decide whether or not to finish the contracts. The following considerations are pertinent to the decision:

1. If the principal (*a*) is heavily indebted to outside creditors, (*b*) has an extensive outside work program in which the surety is not concerned, (*c*) has made assignments of contract monies so as to render them unavailable, (*d*) faces unpaid taxes which may result in either a temporary or permanent curtailment of the use of such funds, or (*e*) is incapable of continuing for other than financial reasons, then it is up to the owner to decide whether or not to default the contract since the surety will have taken the position not to finance, due consideration having been given as to the effect such decision will have on any payment bonds involved.
2. On the other hand, if the principal is experienced in the work to be done, is reliable and trustworthy, has a capable organization, both in the field and in his accounting department, and the remaining contract monies are not assigned nor likely to be subjected to tax liens or possible setoffs by the obligee, consideration should be given to financing the principal. The surety must satisfy itself through independent and reliable sources as to a realistic cost of completion and that there is little likelihood of bankruptcy or complications arising from contracts other than those under consideration. If the principal is solvent, but not liquid, and the work remaining, to a considerable extent, is to be done by a bonded or responsible subcontractor, so much the better.

A word of warning is important at this point. No money advanced by a surety to finance its principal reduces the penalty of the performance bond. However, a surety can pay subcontract and material creditors as obligations under its payment bond, thus making it possible to free the remaining contract monies for the completion of the job. To assure this reduction of the penalty, a separate account, preferably in a new bank to which the principal is not indebted, should be established, subject not only to countersignature by representatives of the surety but also to the withdrawal of the balance at any time by the surety alone and at its sole option. At the same time the surety should obtain mortgages or assignments of all of the principal's assets. These arrangements should be reduced to writing, and the agreement should provide that it is terminable at the option of the surety alone, and that it is in addition to any agreements of indemnity previously executed.

In some instances it is advisable, particularly on federal projects where the Assignment of Claims Act[4] is involved, to have the contract monies assigned to a bank as collateral. The bank will then finance the principal but may require the surety's guaranty or it may be satisfied with a pledge of the principal's fixed assets alone.

If the owner has decided to proceed without the principal, relying upon letter No. 1 as an admission by the principal of voluntary default, the owner will look to the surety regarding the next step to be taken. In the meanwhile, the surety should try to obtain a written proposal addressed to the owner, from a new contractor, to finish at a firm price the work remaining to be done. There should be endorsed thereon a request by the surety that this proposal be accepted. When the owner agrees, arrangements can then be made to pay the excess costs to him.

If it is not possible to obtain a new contract for a fixed price, various alternatives remain: One is for the surety to attempt to arrange a new contract for actual cost plus a percentage for overhead and for profit; another, somewhat similar, is to arrange a new contract for actual cost plus a percentage for overhead plus a fixed fee. There should be a guaranteed upset figure. In either event, there should be a clear written understanding of what the term "cost" encompasses, what expenses are chargeable to overhead, and, where necessary, the basis upon which the percentage for profit is to be computed.

In many instances where an agreement is reached as to the upset figure (costs guaranteed not to exceed this amount), it is advantageous to offer to the new contractor a bonus, being a percentage of any savings he might achieve by completing the contract below the upset price.

If a decision must be made before a proposal from a new contractor can be obtained, the owner should be so advised and a request made either to ask for bids or to have the owner proceed independently. In such cases the surety's work is not done, since it is necessary to continue efforts to find a firm proposal to submit to the owner or to secure prospective bidders in case there is a rebidding. Only in these ways is it possible to minimize the loss.

There is a third possible alternative where, after default, the surety performs the contract itself:

1. By entering into a subcontract for all remaining work with the new subcontractor, or

[4] *Assignment of Claims Act*—31 U.S.C.A. Sec. 203; 41 U.S.C.A. Sec. 15 (Oct. 9, 1940, c. 779, 54 Stat. 1029).

2. By using the principal's organization with a superintendent of the surety's own choosing.

This alternative should be approached cautiously for the performance bond penalty can cease to be a "measuring stick" of liability. There is, moreover, every likelihood that the federal government or the trustee in the principal's bankruptcy may joust with the surety for the remaining contract monies. Either the surety will have to advance money for the performance or the obligee will insist that it be indemnified against any adverse claimants before releasing any contract funds. In short, this alternative may turn out to be a modern Pandora's box.

SUGGESTED READINGS

By necessity, the treatment of defaults in suretyship in this chapter has been painted in broad strokes. Much further detail is necessary for a complete picture. However, there are excellent source materials available which merit study in connection with specific problems. Since bibliographies are relatively rare on this topic, a list considerably longer than the lists in other chapters of this *Handbook* is prescribed.

The following articles from *Proceedings of Section of Insurance, Negligence and Compensation Law, American Bar Association.* Chicago: American Bar Center.

Salvage:

DOWNS, WALTER W. "Quia Timet as a Preventer of Anticipated Mischief." 1956, pp. 173–91.

GALLAGHER, EDWARD. "Remedies Available under Indemnity Agreements." 1960, pp. 125–36.

TURNER, MARK N. "Surety's Salvage Sources." 1955, pp. 179–98.

WITHERSPOON, GIBSON B. "Surety Salvage and Subrogation." 1957, pp. 80–88.

Contract Claims:

ANDERSON, NEWTON E. "Liquidated Damages in Construction Contracts." 1958, pp. 110–15.

HUME, ROBERT R. "The Field Attorney's Functions in the Handling of Contract Bond Claims." 1961, pp. 203–12.

KNEPPER, WILLIAM E. (ed.). *Contract Bond Problems.* Syracuse: The Defense Research Institute, Inc., 1962.

CUSHMAN, EDWARD H. *Bonds on Public Works.* New York: National Association of Credit Management, Annual.

Martindale-Hubbell Law Directory. State Law Digest. Summit, N.J.: Martindale-Hubbell, Inc., Annual. Vol. IV.

"Bid Bonds." 70 *American Law Reports* 2d 1370.

"Statute of Limitations." 42 *American Law Reports* 2d 1159.

"Attorneys' Fees." 59 *American Law Reports* 2d 469.

69 *American Law Reports* 2d 1046.

"Conclusiveness upon Surety of Judgment." 59 *American Law Reports* 2d 752.

"Rights of Laborers and Materialmen." 61 *American Law Reports* 2d 899.

"Miller Act Notice." 78 *American Law Reports* 2d 412, 429.

Various articles in the *Insurance Counsel Journal* (Milwaukee, Wisc.: International Association of Insurance Counsel) as follows:

Contract Claims:

BUNGE, GEORGE C. "The Surety Point of View." Vol. 18 (July, 1951), pp. 305–15.

CROSS, J. HARRY. "Federal Tax Claims." Vol. 24 (Oct., 1957), pp. 384–401.

ELGIN, DAVID A. "Notice Requirements of the Miller Act." Vol. 27 (Jan., 1960), pp. 66–72.

FISHER, EDWIN L. "The Government Point of View." Vol. 18 (July, 1951), pp. 297–304.

FLYNN, F. T. "Bond Claims on Public Works Contracts." Vol. 13 (Jan., 1946), pp. 15–21.

HERON, ALEXANDER M. "Federal Tax Claims Again." Vol. 26 (Jan., 1959), pp. 112–16.

KERRIGAN, R. EMMETT. "Recent Developments." Vol. 24 (Apr., 1957), pp. 104–7.

———. "The Surety as Competing Claimant." Vol. 24 (Jan., 1957), pp. 34–46.

MCCAHAN, ELMER B., JR. "Tax Claims under Payment Bonds." Vol. 21 (Apr., 1954), pp. 152–57.

MILLER, H. ELLSWORTH, AND IRETON, HENRY H. "Surety Completing over Protest of Principal." Vol. 22 (Oct., 1955), pp. 472–74.

PARK, ARTHUR. "What Constitutes Labor and Material." Vol. 16 (Jan., 1949), pp. 14–22.

SEDWICK, THEODORE L. "Withholding Tax Claims." Vol. 20 (Apr., 1953), pp. 92–97.

TURNER, MARK N. "Subrogation Possibilities." Vol. 21 (Oct., 1954), pp. 442–51.

WELLS, TROWARD G. "State and Local Contract Bonds." Vol. 16 (July, 1949), pp. 232–34.

Fiduciary Bond Claims:

CROSS, J. HARRY. "Operation of a Business." Vol. 22 (Oct., 1955), pp. 511–15.

FREDERICKS, ALANSON R. "Trustee's Liability for Uninsured Fidelity Losses." Vol. 17 (July, 1950), pp. 286–89.

TURNER, RICHARD A. "Liability of Guardian Surety." Vol. 18 (Oct., 1951), pp. 462–68.

Salvage:

AGER, ROBERT LEE. "Subrogation Pro Tanto." Vol. 29 (July, 1962), pp. 426–35.

HOWELL, CHARLES COOK, JR. "Exoneration of Surety." Vol. 22 (Jan., 1955), pp. 49–56.

PART VIII

The Institution of Property-Liability Insurance

Chapter 58

STRUCTURE OF THE BUSINESS

BY ARTHUR C. GOERLICH

The immense scope of the property-liability insurance business in the United States is best brought into focus by recognition that a total of about *$17 billion* in premiums was received by all types of nonlife companies in 1963. This sum was paid for the diverse personal and commercial protection needs of individuals, families, and business enterprises, large and small. In this chapter attention is given to the makeup of the huge institution providing this critical service.

RANKING BY LINE

The protection afforded ranges from basic coverage on the automobile, coverage on low-cost homes, and health insurance requirements of those with modest incomes to the most intricate programs of protection for the buildings, employees, contents, and business processes of the largest enterprises in the American economy.[1] The growing premium volume of the property-liability business is a faithful mirror of the country's economic and social expansion at all levels.

Specifically, the premiums paid in 1962 were for the following lines of insurance—listed in order of importance as measured by premium volume:[2]

Automobile—all lines
Fire, Extended Coverage, Allied Lines
Workmen's Compensation
Multiple Peril (Commercial, Homeowners)
Health

[1] Virtually all of these coverages except health insurance are described in Parts II–VII of this *Handbook*. (Even though more than $1 billion in health insurance premiums was written annually by nonlife companies in recent years, this subject is left to the *Life and Health Insurance Handbook*, as edited by Davis W. Gregg and published by Richard D. Irwin, Inc. The revised edition appeared in 1964.)

[2] This ranking does not take into account the health insurance premiums collected by life insurance companies or fraternal organizations.

Liability other than Automobile
Inland Marine
Ocean Marine
Surety
Fidelity
Burglary and Theft
Crop-Hail
Boiler and Machinery
Glass
Credit
Other

A comparison of the premium volume for each line is presented later in this chapter.

In recent years marketing and merchandising practices in the United States have led to adoption of the packaging concept by insurance companies. (See Part VI.) Keen competition has accelerated the development and expansion of packages of coverage embodying many if not most of the traditional types of protection. In the foregoing list of lines written by property-liability companies such packages are represented by the category of multiple perils.

While the premium volume in property-liability insurance for the most part represents insurance coverages voluntarily purchased by individuals, families, and business enterprises, it would be misleading to omit mention that certain insurance is—for practical purposes—virtually required by law. Workmen's compensation insurance is the leading example. In some states, nonoccupational disability and automobile liability coverage are in effect required by law. In the case of the automobile, there are not only "compulsory" insurance laws in several states but also financial responsibility statutes which affect purchases of liability protection.

PREMIUM VOLUME

A summary of the premium volume divided conveniently into categories appears in each annual edition of *Insurance Facts* as published by the Insurance Information Institute. Most of the statistics, in turn, come from *Best's Aggregates and Averages,* an annual publication of the Alfred M. Best Company. Table 58–1 shows premium data for 1961, 1962, and 1963.

As can be seen, the automobile lines accounted for almost $7 billion in 1963 or about 40 percent of the total volume. Automobile insurance also is the leader in underwriting losses. During a recent 10-year period it produced a net underwriting loss of about $850 million.

The 1963 property and liability premium volume of approximately $7 billion represents a volume of about eight times that of 1939. This dramatic upward trend in premiums in all property-liability lines for the period of 1939 through 1963 has been traced by the Insurance Information Institute. This record of about a quarter of a century of growth is summarized in Tables 58–2—58–6. The data except as noted otherwise have been taken from the fact book published by the Institute and cited earlier. The data for these tables come from pages 8–10 and 12–26 of *Insurance Facts* (New York: Insurance Information Institute, 1964). Not all of the lines discussed in earlier chapters are included in the tables. A sufficient quantity of data is included, however, to portray the expansion of and relative changes in the structure of the business. Figures for 1963 are estimates.

TABLE 58–1

PROPERTY-LIABILITY INSURANCE PREMIUMS WRITTEN—SELECTED LINES
UNITED STATES COMPANIES
1961–1963

Line	Premiums Written		
	1961	1962	1963 (Estimated)
Auto Bodily Injury Liability	$2,849,764,000	$3,020,496,000	$3,232,000,000
Auto Property Damage Liability	1,172,998,000	1,219,265,000	1,268,000,000
Total for Auto Liability	$4,022,762,000	$4,239,761,000	$4,500,000,000
Physical Damage (Auto)	$1,964,485,000	$2,134,129,000	$2,294,000,000
Liability (other than auto)	1,022,928,000	1,058,871,000	1,080,000,000
Fire Insurance, Extended Coverage and Allied Lines	2,328,606,000	2,338,564,000	2,294,000,000
Multiple Perils (includes Homeowner's Commercial Package Policies, etc.)	965,601,000	1,196,974,000	1,480,000,000
Workmen's Compensation	1,484,010,000	1,603,940,000	1,800,000,000
Surety and Fidelity	327,366,000	338,417,000	366,000,000
Inland Marine	394,567,000	413,978,000	424,000,000
Ocean Marine	229,537,000	237,085,000	245,000,000

SOURCE: *Insurance Facts* (New York: Insurance Information Institute, 1964), p. 8.

The fastest growing of all categories of insurance in the property-liability realm is multiple line. Table 58–7 shows the tremendous growth for the 1955–1962 period.

Readers can observe that this category is traced only from 1955 when credible data on the then relatively limited number of package policies became available. The figures for the ensuing years reflect the addition to this category of numerous other packages.

All signs point to accelerated progress in multiple lines. New habitational and other personal coverages are being written under package forms. Insurers are making available multi-peril packages for a broad spectrum of commercial risks, ranging from the small retail establishments to the giant industrial complex.

The competitive climate in the property-liability business in the past decade has hastened the development and flexibility of package policies, as insurers strive to outdo each other in combining lines to secure the bulk of an insured's business under one cover. The emergence of new packages, in turn, intensifies competition for multiple line business and assures its growth in terms of volume. Its eventual profitability remains to be determined. The plethora of packages includes many on which experience is not sufficient to indicate the loss trend. The question of underwriting results on multiple line coverage is one of the most important to be answered in the next several years.

TABLE 58–2

FIRE, EXTENDED COVERAGE, AND ALLIED LINES INSURANCE PREMIUMS WRITTEN—UNITED STATES COMPANIES
1939–1963

Year	Fire	Extended Coverage	Allied Lines
1939	$ 542,663,000	$ 2,643,000	$ 67,718,000
1940	567,071,000	38,808,000	48,454,000
1941	619,271,000	50,631,000	54,442,000
1942	668,703,000	65,303,000	65,321,000
1943	713,062,000	75,458,000	65,326,000
1944	749,540,000	91,523,000	78,874,000
1945	803,951,000	111,861,000	77,209,000
1946	1,047,167,000	171,673,000	91,946,000
1947	1,197,577,000	199,009,000	103,795,000
1948	1,292,788,000	227,991,000	93,223,000
1949	1,328,391,000	255,956,000	89,401,000
1950	1,407,857,000	296,797,000	81,486,000
1951	1,503,579,000	359,814,000	93,948,000
1952	1,506,946,000	399,824,000	108,669,000
1953	1,534,379,000	434,865,000	112,942,000
1954	1,545,894,000	481,180,000	114,804,000
1955	1,560,549,000	557,523,000	119,858,000
1956	1,582,563,000	597,282,000	117,324,000
1957	1,593,996,000	608,725,000	103,735,000
1958	1,626,167,000	625,977,000	140,619,000
1959	1,709,257,000	632,407,000	147,176,000
1960	1,667,385,000	573,946,000	164,964,000
1961	1,619,076,000	539,414,000	170,116,000
1962	1,623,046,000	522,085,000	183,433,000
1963	1,574,000,000	520,000,000	200,000,000

ASSETS AND SURPLUS TO POLICYHOLDERS

Reliable measures of the strength and stability of property and liability insurers are the companies' assets and surplus to policyholders. The latter expression is insurance jargon to refer to the total net worth which may include capital stock as well as one or more types of surplus. Surplus to policyholders, therefore, is the difference between assets and liabilities.

TABLE 58-3

MARINE AND INLAND MARINE INSURANCE PREMIUMS WRITTEN—UNITED STATES COMPANIES 1939–1963

Year	Inland Marine	(Ocean) Marine
1939	$ 48,646,000	$ 51,156,000
1940	55,785,000	89,889,000
1941	64,427,000	118,675,000
1942	73,309,000	261,221,000
1943	85,390,000	126,708,000
1944	101,229,000	138,716,000
1945	118,447,000	132,870,000
1946	155,172,000	129,904,000
1947	176,363,000	180,082,000
1948	195,600,000	170,731,000
1949	215,752,000	149,248,000
1950	229,883,000	140,872,000
1951	255,473,000	171,085,000
1952	283,287,000	170,862,000
1953	304,025,000	161,841,000
1954	302,931,000	161,333,000
1955	325,636,000	167,999,000
1956	331,539,000	184,930,000
1957	330,170,000	206,504,000
1958	344,464,000	208,633,000
1959	375,698,000	225,556,000
1960	380,919,000	230,429,000
1961	394,567,000	229,537,000
1962	413,878,000	237,085,000
1963	424,000,000	245,000,000

Dramatic evidence of the companies' financial growth from 1939 through 1963 is provided by selecting three 10-year periods and citing the assets and surplus to policyholders at the end of each.

In 1939 the assets stood at $4,831,090,000 and the surplus figure at $2,521,459,000. At the end of 1948 the comparable totals were $10,290,-840,000 and $3,808,836,000. Thus, assets had more than doubled, while the surplus to policyholders had risen significantly.

A comparison of the results for 1948 and 1957 reveals even more rapid growth. Assets had increased more than twofold to $22,870,011,000 and the surplus to policyholders total had matched this performance reaching $8,648,362,000.

A third comparison reveals even greater acceleration of the two figures from 1953 through 1962. At the beginning of this decade the totals were $17,412,366,000 and $6,402,504,000. At the end of the period they were $33,368,191,000 and $13,842,950,000.

From 1961 to 1962 surplus to policyholders declined slightly. This drop in the surplus figure—only the fourth time it decreased in the years 1939 through 1962—was due mainly to plummeting market values of securities.

TABLE 58-4

INSURANCE PREMIUMS WRITTEN BY SELECTED LINES—UNITED STATES COMPANIES 1939–1963

Year	Workmen's Compensation	Liability Other Than Automobile*	Burglary and Theft	Boiler and Machinery	Glass Insurance
1939	$ 248,250,000	$ 101,942,715	$ 28,020,000	$12,300,000	$11,970,000
1940	262,130,000	108,509,821	28,340,000	15,210,000	11,780,000
1941	332,520,000	115,931,188	30,150,000	18,980,000	11,800,000
1942	449,850,000	129,642,546	33,530,000	19,600,000	12,830,000
1943	495,290,000	138,350,432	39,090,000	21,620,000	12,750,000
1944	490,510,000	145,325,344	47,050,000	21,090,000	13,920,000
1945	477,040,000	159,342,559	55,380,000	13,960,000	15,360,000
1946	498,610,000	192,635,302	72,930,000	23,690,000	18,610,000
1947	643,360,000	240,525,231	76,870,000	33,810,000	21,520,000
1948	731,890,000	264,935,417	81,120,000	36,980,000	24,030,000
1949	718,290,000	287,156,783	84,510,000	34,640,000	29,000,000
1950	697,270,000	307,064,871	82,890,000	46,890,000	31,170,000
1951	817,380,000	361,973,995	92,300,000	57,410,000	33,420,000
1952	917,870,000	420,897,197	92,410,000	47,680,000	34,910,000
1953	1,011,140,000	510,561,180	95,130,000	61,980,000	36,700,000
1954	1,016,490,000	571,721,870	101,950,000	66,020,000	37,260,000
1955	1,035,450,000	607,596,485	102,680,000	59,980,000	37,460,000
1956	1,110,740,000	669,560,466	106,980,000	66,280,000	38,570,000
1957	1,199,470,000	726,490,416	114,300,000	69,990,000	45,430,000
1958	1,209,400,000	775,411,310	108,990,000	73,650,000	38,560,000
1959	1,297,000,000	862,131,156	116,500,000	78,000,000	40,100,000
1960	1,419,362,000	962,831,348	115,939,000	85,080,000	47,740,000
1961	1,484,010,000	1,022,926,846	114,304,000	86,397,000	42,705,000
1962	1,603,940,000	1,058,870,683	115,577,000	70,082,000	42,261,000
1963	1,800,000,000	1,080,000,000	115,000,000	75,000,000	45,000,000

* Figures in this column were derived from several annual issues of *Best's Aggregates and Averages* and are the totals of the reported premiums for "B.I. Liability" and "P.D. Liability" for stock and mutual companies. (During the 1939–63 period terminology used in classifying the premium data was changed but the figures in this column are consistent.)

Write-offs of security values were reflected in credits of assets and debits of surplus accounts. The reason that the aggregate asset figures in 1962 did not show a comparable decline is that assets (and liabilities) were increased through new business more than enough to offset the write-offs of security values. It is significant that the then all-time high total of $14,-284,399,000 in surplus to policyholders for 1961 was due to the upward movement of securities. The figure rose again in 1963. (See Chapters 60 and 61 for an explanation of how fluctuations in security values affect financial statements of insurers.) This point should suffice to illustrate without lengthy comment the importance of the investment operations of property and liability insurers.

Because their obligations are of short-term duration, property and liability insurers must invest their assets in a manner that preserves liquidity. (See Chapter 60 for more detail.)

TABLE 58-5

AUTOMOBILE INSURANCE PREMIUMS WRITTEN—UNITED STATES COMPANIES 1939-1963

YEAR	PHYSICAL DAMAGE	LIABILITY	
		Bodily Injury	Property Damage
1939	$ 224,432,000	$ 271,980,000	$ 78,870,000
1940	277,414,000	288,470,000	84,080,000
1941	331,214,000	327,520,000	97,730,000
1942	195,397,000	321,230,000	103,890,000
1943	183,285,000	266,640,000	102,370,000
1944	199,244,000	299,950,000	112,280,000
1945	249,466,000	343,830,000	127,460,000
1946	413,260,000	478,320,000	185,490,000
1947	624,942,000	620,370,000	276,650,000
1948	770,538,000	728,000,000	350,710,000
1949	968,917,000	801,980,000	401,210,000
1950	1,069,840,000	868,920,000	441,350,000
1951	1,263,223,000	1,045,010,000	527,810,000
1952	1,512,463,000	1,276,470,000	641,440,000
1953	1,653,305,000	1,480,750,000	776,690,000
1954	1,573,511,000	1,556,660,000	809,680,000
1955	1,727,710,000	1,655,440,000	839,580,000
1956	1,613,295,000	1,814,010,000	870,260,000
1957	1,748,993,000	2,070,800,000	932,490,000
1958	1,773,832,000	2,295,560,000	1,019,100,000
1959	1,955,196,000	2,563,900,000	1,117,800,000
1960	1,993,930,000	2,725,035,000	1,157,882,000
1961	1,964,485,000	2,849,764,000	1,172,998,000
1962	2,134,129,000	3,020,496,000	1,219,265,000
1963	2,294,000,000	3,232,000,000	1,268,000,000

The yearly growth in assets and policyholders' surplus, which was cited earlier and compared in terms of increase by decades, is presented in Table 58-8.

TYPES OF INSURERS

Insurers in the United States may be divided basically into six classes: stock, mutual, reciprocals (or insurance exchanges), Lloyd's associations, government insurers, and "self-insurers."

Stock Companies

Stock companies predominate in the United States market. They write approximately 70 percent of all property and liability business. As their name implies, these companies are originally capitalized by public purchase of their shares. Premiums received are later added to the original fund, and the total is available for loss payments, as are any accretions to assets. The shareholders, who are the owners of the enterprise, elect a

TABLE 58–6

FIDELITY AND SURETY PREMIUMS WRITTEN
UNITED STATES COMPANIES
1939–1963

Year	Fidelity	Surety
1939	$ 41,030,000	$ 49,980,000
1940	40,940,000	50,090,000
1941	42,080,000	58,500,000
1942	41,390,000	68,380,000
1943	45,420,000	43,670,000
1944	45,390,000	39,100,000
1945	65,050,000	40,530,000
1946	44,980,000	52,530,000
1947	43,210,000	64,160,000
1948	67,560,000	82,810,000
1949	52,460,000	93,580,000
1950	48,510,000	107,990,000
1951	75,650,000	120,290,000
1952	65,900,000	126,180,000
1953	67,070,000	136,760,000
1954	86,340,000	142,470,000
1955	78,640,000	151,810,000
1956	76,930,000	160,480,000
1957	97,570,000	170,380,000
1958	90,600,000	189,030,000
1959	92,800,000	186,000,000
1960	114,757,000	197,692,000
1961	110,229,000	217,137,000
1962	108,572,000	229,845,000
1963	125,000,000	241,000,000

TABLE 58–7

MULTIPLE LINE INSURANCE PREMIUMS WRITTEN—UNITED STATES COMPANIES
1955–1963

Year	*Amount*
1955	$ 68,150,000
1956	196,641,000
1957	269,134,000
1958	374,053,000
1959	560,477,000
1960	819,339,000
1961	965,601,000
1962	1,196,974,000
1963	1,480,000,000

board of directors which, in turn, selects the operating management of the company.

The stock insurance company is in the classic tradition of enterprises formed in all phases of American business to earn a profit. The intent of

TABLE 58–8

Assets and Surplus to Policyholders "Fire and Casualty" Companies—United States 1939–1963

Year	Assets	Surplus to Policyholders
1939	$ 4,831,090,000	$ 2,521,459,000
1940	5,050,807,000	2,586,370,000
1941	5,334,660,000	2,561,052,000
1942	5,684,846,000	2,670,138,000
1943	6,284,606,000	2,995,828,000
1944	6,875,687,000	3,275,926,000
1945	7,706,731,000	3,746,300,000
1946	8,155,484,000	3,485,664,000
1947	9,210,336,000	3,563,404,000
1948	10,290,840,000	3,808,836,000
1949	11,814,403,000	4,609,521,000
1950	13,154,471,000	5,206,666,000
1951	14,395,933,000	5,604,861,000
1952	15,989,530,000	6,099,533,000
1953	17,412,366,000	6,402,504,000
1954	19,904,031,000	8,191,198,000
1955	21,755,697,000	9,246,552,000
1956	22,538,173,000	9,387,560,000
1957	22,870,011,000	8,648,362,000
1958	25,654,029,000	10,444,838,000
1959	27,880,615,000	11,374,121,000
1960	29,357,433,000	11,657,975,000
1961	32,854,822,000	14,284,399,000
1962	33,368,191,000	13,842,950,000
1963	36,705,000,000	15,781,000,000

Source: *Insurance Facts,* op. cit., p. 9.

the stock organization is to realize this profit from the primary business of underwriting property and liability insurance. This goal is not always attained, as the record of recent years attests. However, investment of their tremendous assets in the securities market has yielded an investment income to offset in whole or in part the underwriting losses. Over the years many stock insurers have also been able to pay regular dividends to stockholders.

The stock company organized to do business under the laws of a given state is known therein as a domestic insurer. In other states where it is active, the company is generally designated "foreign." Companies organized outside the United States are usually called "alien."

When a company is admitted to do business within a state, careful control and supervision of its activities are maintained by the insurance department. This control is exercised not only in respect to stock companies but also in respect to all other insurers. Adherence to financial standards and to legitimate operating practices is at all times demanded. Included in these considerations are compliance with capital and reserve requirements, fair claims payment, and ethical advertising. In many instances policies, forms, and rates require approval. State insurance departments maintain complaint bureaus as a check on conformity with its regulations. In addition, the insurers must file an exhaustive annual report each year and are also subject to regular periodic examination by the various states in which they conduct business.

A policyholder of a stock insurer is not involved with the company beyond the payment or denial of indemnity when he suffers a loss. Unlike the policyholder of the mutual company, the second most important type of insurer in the United States, he does not usually share in company profits through dividend payments or otherwise. Some stock companies, however, do issue participating policies and therefore do pay "dividends" to policyholders.

Mutuals

The mutual policyholder automatically becomes one of the owners of his insurer when he places his business with it. The mutual company differs from the stock organization in many vital respects, beginning with the fact that its policyholders are members. Next, there are no shareholders in a mutual. Its directors are named by the policyholder-members and the board then designates the executive officers who are to run the company.

The policyholder pays his premium for his exposures which the company assumes. When there is an excess of funds after all expenses have been met and all losses are paid, this excess may be returned entirely or partially to policyholders in the form of "dividends," thus reducing the protection cost. Readers new to this subject should be careful to notice that "dividends" to a mutual policyholder, being mainly refunds of premiums, are fundamentally different from dividends to stock company stockholders. The latter dividends are of the traditional type, namely, return on an equity investment.

Assessment Mutuals. Mutual companies, themselves, are of different types which entail different methods of premium payment. The assessment mutual, usually a small company, is probably the best example of the original idea of mutuality. Three general methods of premium payment are practiced by these companies. First, the company may charge a modest fee to write and issue a policy and then assess each member when necessary to defray claims and operating expense. Second, the company may, when writing the policy, ask for a payment sufficient to pay ordinary losses and expenses. The policyholders are then asked to sign "premium notes" to be met should loss and expense rise above the original payments. The policyholder's commitment is up to the face of the note. The third and most common premium payment practice is to obtain payment on policy issue of an amount sufficient to pay expenses and smaller claims.

The members are then exposed to assessment up to the amount required to meet the need for additional funds for losses and expenses. As noted, this type of operation is generally a small one and confined to a limited area.

Nonassessment Mutuals. The assessment feature characteristic of these companies is not typical of the mutual insurance companies in general. Quite the contrary is true. The leading mutuals issue only nonassessable policies. These larger companies are known as advance premium mutuals. Companies of moderate and small size may also be among them. As their name implies, these insurers charge at the outset a rate calculated to be sufficient to defray all losses and expense. Computation of such a rate often contemplates the return of a dividend to the insured and also a slight margin for contingencies.

The first insurance company founded in this country was the Philadelphia Contributionship for the Insurance of Houses from Loss by Fire. It represents another type of company—the perpetual. One advance premium is paid for a policy issued in perpetuity. The total of these payments comprises the capital the annual yield of which is enough to pay losses, pay operating charges, and leave a margin for dividends and contingencies. Contracts are subject to cancellation by either party at will.

Factory Mutuals. Although their policies are not available to the ordinary insurance buyer, there are other mutual insurers of a special nature. One is the "factory mutual," a type of organization dating from the 1830's. It was originated to insure factories with the highest standards of operation. These requirements were set up in large part by the insurer which also maintained rigorous inspection and engineering procedures with loss prevention as the objective.

Eight companies now comprise the Associated Factory Mutual Fire Insurance Companies. They continue to operate with loss prevention as one primary consideration. Those seeking coverage are subject to close scrutiny. This scrutiny continues periodically even after acceptance of the applicant. The association has extensive inspection and engineering facilities in the United States and Canada. (See Chapter 64 for more discussion of this organization as well as of the stock insurers' Factory Insurance Association.)

Reciprocals

A reciprocal exchange is an American innovation, dating from the 1880's. It is a device whereby persons combine into a group to insure each other, to obtain protection at relatively low cost, and to obtain relatively broad coverage. An exchange does not issue policies. As its name implies, it provides a device whereby its members "exchange" insurance.

A subscriber receives protection for a certain amount on his own risk. He must then help "underwrite" coverage for the membership. If he has a loss, he will receive payment from all the other subscribers. Each member pays an amount based on his share of losses plus a further sum for expense of operation.

The exchange is often a convenience provided by trade associations. It is managed by an attorney-in-fact who is paid a percentage of premiums received. The attorney-in-fact may be a corporation rather than an individual. Some 75 exchanges are now active with aggregate premium income of more than $500 million annually. About 80 percent of this income is derived from automobile insurance. One of the very large writers of automobile protection in the United States is a reciprocal.

Lloyd's

Lloyd's of London is not an insurance company but a combination of underwriters, each of whom is an individual who undertakes risks for his own accounts. (See Chapter 17 for a brief discussion of the origin and early operation of this institution.) The traditional phrase, "underwriters at Lloyd's," puts the nature of the operation in focus. The underwriters are "at" headquarters known as Lloyd's but the latter does not transact business for itself as an entity.

Underwriting members assume risks for themselves. Nonunderwriting members act as broker-intermediaries in placing business for prospects with the underwriters. In practice, a broker presents a "slip" to underwriters. The slip contains the pertinent details about the risk. Underwriters sign or initial the "slip," indicating the extent of their liability. When the "slip" is 100 percent subscribed, the broker prepares a policy and sends it to the Policy Signing Office. If it meets requirements, the policy is stamped by this office and issued. Syndicates, made up of several individual underwriters, generally do the underwriting today, and each member of such syndicates is individually responsible only for his own share. Traditionally, all Lloyd's underwriters on a particular risk pay if one is held to be liable. Furthermore, syndicate members traditionally contribute to any deficiencies resulting from default of any syndicate member on a claim—in the rare event of such a default.

In the United States a trust fund, originally set up in 1939, is maintained. Premiums paid in dollars are placed in the fund for claim payments on all policies written in dollars. The fund is approximately $250 million. This fund stands in addition to the other guarantees to policyholders in the nature of deposits and funds in England. Lloyd's underwriters are licensed in only two states: Illinois and Kentucky. Separate funds are maintained in these states, in addition to the overall United States fund, for policyholder protection.

There are also organizations known as American Lloyds. These were patterned on the model of London Lloyd's but possibly because their underwriters do not have the same total commitment as those of the original, they have not been particularly successful. Of the 15 American Lloyds in the United States, 12 are domiciled in Texas. New York has a statute forbidding the organization of any new American Lloyds organizations.

Government Insurers

Government insurance operations in other than life and health insurance can be broken down between state and federal areas of activity.

State. In 18 states, workmen's compensation funds are maintained. Seven of these are monopolies. The other 11 funds compete with private insurers, although the coverage on public corporations generally goes to the state fund. The workmen's compensation board or its counterpart usually administers these funds.

Another form of state insurance—in this case a device that benefits employers and their insurers—is the second injury fund now present in most states. This arrangement enables employers to hire a person who has been handicapped by an injury, without exposing themselves to the possibility that another accident will render the employee totally disabled and consequently subject the employer and his insurer to heavy charges. In case of a second injury, the employer pays as though it were the first one, and the second injury fund makes up the difference.

Hail funds are now operative in North Dakota, Colorado, and Montana. Several other states have made provision for such plans to pay losses resulting from hail storms.

Federal. Insurance activity at the federal level embraces such organizations as the Federal Crop Insurance Corporation, the Export-Import Bank, and the Federal Deposit Insurance Corporation which protects commercial and savings accounts.

"Self-Insurers"

"Self-insurance" is a widely discussed phenomenon which is treated briefly in Chapter 72. Since traditionally it is considered in discussions of types of carriers, it is mentioned at this point. Scholars disagree as to its nature—indeed, even as to its existence. Some insist there is no such thing; others say that it is a formal program of premium allocation and loss "payment" within the "self-insured" entity. Readers are left to their own persuasions as to what is meant by the term "self-insurance."

One commonly held concept is that a "self-insurer" must make regular payments into his own fund out of which losses are to be paid. The deposits in this fund will be measured by projections of losses in the years ahead. Officials in a business enterprise should realistically establish the qualifications of the firm as a "self-insurer" before adopting this type of loss treatment. There should be a considerable number of risks of the same type so that loss predictions can be made. Moreover, these units should be scattered so as not to constitute a catastrophe exposure. In short, the "self-insurer" must take into account many of the basic considerations of the commercial insurer.

In addition, he must provide the counterpart of inspection, loss prevention, and engineering services furnished by the private insurer. These facilities are primary parts of any protection program, and if a business cannot afford them, it would do well to approach "self-insurance" warily.

The "self insurer" need not assume the entire burden of the risks of his enterprise. He may use reinsurance and may find particularly attractive an arrangement for payment by the reinsurer of those amounts of loss in excess of a predetermined figure. This excess arrangement is particularly valuable in the case of so-called shock losses.

Talent for the management of a "self-insured" plan is not always plentiful. To offset this scarcity, firms have been set up for the purpose of managing such programs. Making a decision on whether to insure or "self-insure" is a complex matter. On balance, such plans are beyond the reach of all organizations except those in exceptionally sound financial position.

DISTRIBUTION SYSTEM

The preponderance of property-liability insurance in the United States is sold through the independent agency system. An independent agent is a producer who represents a number of companies (stock, mutual, or both) by contractual arrangement. This agent has full control of the business he produces, placing it with one of his companies, and renewing it with another if he chooses and the client does not object.

No company which he represents may solicit this agent's business should he (or the company) terminate his representation. This principle is established by legal precedent in the agents' "ownership of expirations."

This agent is compensated by an agreed scale of commission and is usually paid the full current rate at each renewal of business. Traditionally, this agent has performed certain services—policy writing, billing, and collecting—on behalf of his companies. In later years, the accelerating use of electronic data processing in companies has resulted in some instances of the companies taking over many of the routine tasks formerly discharged by agents.

The exclusive agent, as his title implies, represents only one company. He does not own his expirations; they belong to his company. He is usually compensated on a commission scale somewhat lower than that of the independent agent. Moreover, the exclusive agent's rate of commission return is on a declining schedule. On the other hand, he often enjoys fringe benefits from his company and in other respects has an employee status. His company writes the policies, issues the bills, and collects the premiums. One of the leading stock automobile insurers and two of the top mutual automobile writers operate through exclusive agents.

Another method of distribution is based on employees rather than agents. Some property-liability insurers have salaried representatives who make direct contact with buyers. These organizations are known as "direct writers." The term "direct" is used to indicate that no agent is involved in an insurance transaction with the company. Under these circumstances, the company naturally owns the business. The leading direct writers generally operate through strategically located branch and service offices throughout the United States.

Still another distribution medium is through brokers. They are committed to no company either as agent or employee. They represent the customer for whom they seek the best market in which to place his coverage. Nevertheless, the broker is not paid by the customer directly. He receives a commission from the insurer with whom business is placed.

Since the broker's commission is usually lower than that of the agent (who is under a contractual arrangement with his companies), the agent can place business for a broker and retain the difference in compensation as profit. Brokers may also place business on their own behalf with companies of their choosing. They are most numerous in large metropolitan centers. The leading brokers often have offices countrywide and some are active on an international basis.

ORGANIZATIONS IN THE BUSINESS

The scope and complexity of the property-liability business are emphasized by the number of diverse organizations which serve it. These groups are numerous, indeed, and range from technical bodies providing ratemaking service to advisory units formed on a cooperative basis to advance some broad interest of the business.

There are so many different types of organizations in the insurance industry that a beginner easily can be overwhelmed and utterly confused. To acquaint him—at least superficially—with some of the general types of organizations a list of a few of those active at the national level is presented in Appendix K. Even so, however, the list is only illustrative. Many important organizations because of space limitations are not included in the list. A brief (but strictly unofficial) description of each is included. Where possible, the description includes information about membership, purpose, and pertinent miscellaneous items.[3]

[3] Readers can find more detail about most of these organizations and numerous others in a source book such as the *Insurance Almanac*, published annually by the Underwriting Printing and Publishing Company (116 John Street, New York).

SUGGESTED READINGS

GREENE, MARK R. *Risk and Insurance.* Cincinnati: South-Western Publishing Company, 1962. Chaps. 5, 6, 7.

Insurance Almanac. New York: Underwriting Printing and Publishing Company. Published annually.

Insurance Facts. New York: Insurance Information Institute. Published annually.

KULP, CLARENCE A. *Casualty Insurance.* 3d ed. New York: Ronald Press Co., 1956. Chap. 3.

MAGEE, JOHN H., AND BICKELHAUPT, DAVID L. *General Insurance.* 7th ed. Homewood, Ill.: Richard D. Irwin, Inc., 1964. Chap. 2.

Chapter 59

COMPANY ORGANIZATION AND MANAGEMENT

BY T. E. WALTON, JR.

Company organization and management comprise one of the most fascinating fields for thought in the whole business complex, because here lies the soul of the company. Webster defines *soul* as "the seat of real life, vitality or action; animating or vital principle."[1] In the business world these qualities stem from company management, and the degree to which they can be kept alive and strong depends upon the degree to which the company's organization structure allows them "room to breathe."

Since this area is such a sensitive one within any given business establishment, this chapter deals first with certain principles of organization and management common to any business. Then, with these generalities as a mirror against which to reflect them, the organization and management requirements of property-liability insurance companies are discussed.

GENERAL BACKGROUND

Theory of Organizations

An organization plan of some sort, however informal, is important in any group effort, be it a family picnic or a huge corporate enterprise. Too often in the growth of a business firm the *purpose* of organization becomes sublimated and organizing becomes an aim in itself. If this situation is allowed to occur, Parkinson's laws then tend to take over, "reply by endorsement" comes into usage, and the firm begins to lose its spontaneity. Thus, a timely question could be: what is the purpose of organization and how formal need it be?

In approaching an answer, assume a one-man business. Regardless of

---

[1] *Webster's New Collegiate Dictionary* (Springfield, Mass.: G. & C. Merriam Co., 1961), p. 808.

how small it is, such an operation includes virtually all the problems of a larger business—materials, inventories, customer relations, efficient use of tools, research into new techniques, output schedules, advertising, budgets, and so on through a long list. Yet in the one-man "shop" there is no need for a formalized organization chart or rigidly spelled out definitions of responsibility. Staff meetings are not required to reach decisions, nor must a chain of memoranda be circulated to start an action. The reason, of course, is that this proprietor is his own president, salesman, controller, plant operator, and so forth. When he has a new idea or decides to take an action, his thoughts are immediately transmitted to all "parts" of his organization. All the pertinent facts play a part in each decision or are weighed against the idea; the interests of each division of the operation are considered and the basic aims and principles of the enterprise are observed.

In other words, in a one-man business sound decisions and coordinated progress can be quickly made because complete and instant communication is present. Were it possible to maintain similar communication, identity of objectives, and motivation in a firm employing 10,000 people, this firm, too, could be operated without organization charts, responsibility limits, and the like.

Purpose of Organization

The organization plan, therefore, should be thought of as a tool to maintain communications and to channel responsibility and effort into the areas best suited to each particular endeavor, rather than as an end in itself. Similarly, it follows that the organization plan should be no more formal than necessary to accomplish these aims, lest its requirements slow up effort and hamper initiative. If there is an unnecessary link or clearance point in the flow of work orders, the order will take longer to process. If the perimeters of responsibility are too rigidly defined, the members of one segment of the operation will be discouraged from lending the weight of their thinking to the problems of other areas and to the aims of the total effort.

Management

It is at this point that the force of management must be felt. If the management (1) has a set of clear, all-embracing principles, (2) is consistent in following them, and (3) keeps them well circulated, then decision making can be delegated much more deeply down the line—and action will be much more timely—than will be the case if principles are kept secret or frequently set aside for expediency.

If top management fully communicates the current and long-range aims of the organization, and encourages the interest of all in them, there is less danger that the defining of responsibilities will result in a confining of interests. Responsibility will be more readily accepted and will tend to gravitate to the proper center with less need for specific direction.

The foregoing should not be interpreted as indicating that a sizeable company can be run without any division of responsibility or without documentation of plans and checkpoints for clearance of ideas. The point is made, however, that these are but tools to keep the lines of communication flowing freely and effectively. The extent to which they can be kept minimal and flexible will determine how quickly the decisions of the company can be made and management's desires at any given time be reflected in appropriate and coordinated action.

It is scarcely possible to specify in detail how any one company's organization plan should look on paper. Each business enterprise has its own personality and its own set of aims and principles. These are determined by its management who necessarily take into account the mix of skills and characteristics represented by the total of its employees. It is possible, however, from the products or services to which a particular enterprise devotes itself, to determine the functions involved and to examine the interrelationship of these functions. The remainder of this chapter is addressed to these functions and their interrelationship in a property-liability insurance company.

CLASSIFICATION OF FUNCTIONS

Property and liability insurance is provided by a variety of insurers, principal among which is the traditional capital stock type of company dealt with here. There are also, of course, mutual companies, state funds, reciprocals, underwriting syndicates, and other types of insurers. Some do an across-the-board business, while others are "specialty" in nature. Most of what is presented here is also applicable to these other types of carriers.

A capital stock property-liability insurance company is owned by the stockholders, who are in turn represented by the board of directors. This body is directly responsible to the owners—the stockholders—and elected by them; in turn it elects the chief executive and other officers.

If the board of directors elects a chairman, he is sometimes named chief executive officer, with the president being named chief administrative officer. In many companies, however, the president also chairs the board. How the chairman and the president share the details of this senior area of responsibility varies considerably among companies. In many cases the chairman's role is purely honorary.

Assuming for the purpose of illustration that the president is the chief executive officer, he sits at the top of the management pyramid with respect to the day-to-day performance of the company. He enunciates company policy and establishes the necessary organization to carry it out.

Three Types of Functions

The many functions for which the president must provide within the company can be grouped roughly as follows:

1. Those necessary to preserve the identity and well-being of the organization as a living corporate entity.
2. Those without which an insurance carrier cannot offer protection, accept risks, and service policyholders.
3. Those which in essence are services to enable the other functions, principally those in the second group, to be performed successfully.

The functions as grouped above are by no means exclusive to the respective groups. In many cases—and especially in larger corporations where the economy of centralized services becomes possible—there are overlaps of interest and of actual work performed. For broad purposes of emphasis and relationship, however, these groupings compose a logical pattern.

Outline of Functions

The pattern referred to in the preceding paragraph is spelled out in a bit more detail in Figure 59–1. It classifies activities as they might be in a property-liability company.

Group I and II functions are essential to the very existence and basic purposes of the property-liability insurance corporation, and as such retain independently recognizable identities. Within these areas the corporate decisions affecting policy, profit, owner, and customer are made.

As indicated earlier, the functions included in Group III facilitate the accomplishment of other functions. The extent to which these service functions exist as separately identifiable spheres of activity—or exist at all—depends upon management policy and the size of the company.

Similarly, the preference of officials of individual companies will determine who is assigned the responsibility for what functions, and in what combination. For example, the company from which many of the illustrations in this chapter are drawn combines the office of secretary and treasurer. In addition, the incumbent in this combined office is given responsibility for other activities which could just as logically be assigned elsewhere.

GROUP I FUNCTIONS

Secretary-Treasurer

Since the secretary-treasurer has custody of the corporation's assets, including buildings, furniture, fixtures, and the purse strings, it is quite

Group I—Functions required to maintain corporate identity and well-being:

SECRETARY-TREASURER

Maintenance of official records of the corporation, board of directors, stockholders and employees; custody of corporate assets; and dispersal of corporate funds, including payroll.

CONTROLLER

Documentation of all transactions involving corporate assets; and establishment of controls to prevent or detect fraudulent or careless handling of corporate assets.

INVESTMENT

Investment of those corporate funds deemed available for this purpose.

Group II—Functions inherent to the property-liability insurance operation:

UNDERWRITING

Determination of the types of risk the corporation is willing to assume and the extent of possible loss to which the corporation's assets can be subjected in a given class of risk or on a particular line; determination of the rates deemed necessary to produce a profit within each class; protection of the corporate assets from catastrophe losses beyond their capacity; formation of contracts to reflect the risks assumed and protection provided; and maintenance of bulk reserves commensurate with the liabilities inherent in the risks assumed.

PRODUCTION

Selling the types of protection made available to the insuring public by the corporation; maintenance of satisfactory proportions among types of insurance and insureds within those limits deemed necessary by the underwriters to achieve a profit and to minimize the effect of possible catastrophes on the corporation's assets; and establishment and servicing of sales outlets.

CLAIMS ADJUSTMENT

Investigation and settlement of all just and proper claims; defense of insureds in accordance with policy terms; resistance of claims for which the corporation deems itself not liable and defense of the corporation against suits arising therefrom; and setting of individual case reserves for claims pending settlement.

Group III—Principal internal services:

General Counsel	Personnel
Statistics	Education
Actuarial	Public Relations and Advertising
Safety and Audit	Data Processing
Inspection and Engineering	Other*
Marine Service	

* A listing of the many other possible services might include:

Addressograph	Library	Research
Archives	Mail	Supply
Budget Control	Medical	Telephone
Building Maintenance	Printing	Transcribing
Cafeteria	Purchasing	Transportation
Employees' Association	Real Estate	Work Standards
Job Evaluation	Record Storage	

FIG. 59–1. Outline of functions in property-liability insurer.

logical to place under his supervision those activities which deal with the care and use of these assets and the expenditure of funds to provide them. When a company is small, the purchasing of supplies may be left to individual segments of the operation, but the economies of bulk purchase will soon lead to a centralized purchasing department. Formation of branch offices will lead to a real estate department. A printing department may be warranted as form and manual needs expand. A maintenance department to care for the home office building will be needed. Perhaps the use of dictating equipment will prompt the formation of a centralized transcribing service. The list of such services will expand as the company grows, and the secretary-treasurer is in an excellent position to coordinate them into an effective overall force.

Controller

The controller is charged with the responsibility of a careful documentation of all transactions involving corporate assets and the establishment of controls to prevent or detect fraudulent or careless handling of them. The investigatory activities of the controller and his staff are sometimes received by other departments of the company with something less than enthusiasm. Where this attitude exists the situation is an unfortunate one, because the controller's studies can be of tremendous value to all others in the corporation. The manager of any area of activity has a prime interest in efficient, honest, and high quality performance on the part of his employees, including adherence to time-tested procedures tailor-made to the best interests of all. The controller and his internal auditors, through their periodic auditing of a department's accounts and records, can help a manager or supervisor uncover weak spots and determine the best ways to strengthen his operation.

In a property-liability company one of the most intricate tasks of the controller's office is the allocation of expense, since both the insurance laws and sound rating techniques require a meticulous allocation of all expenses back to the functions for which they were incurred. This involvement with expense figures enables the controller to provide valuable expense analyses. Also, if the corporation operates on a formal budget, the controller's office is an appropriate area in which to assemble the budget forecasts and conformance reports.

Investment

The principal responsibility of the investment department is to invest corporate funds free for this purpose and, by putting this money "to work," to increase the size of company's assets and thus its surplus. This increase, of course, strengthens the company's capacity to take risks. The activities of this department should remain clearly separated from the insurance functions of sales, underwriting, and claims. To operate otherwise can lead to pressures being exerted by the investment officials upon the insurance officials or vice versa, resulting in a dilution of the judgments of each.

A property-liability insurer's assets available for investment are considerably larger than premiums written from year to year. Moreover, the annual income from investments generally exceeds by a fair amount the income from pure underwriting profit. Particularly in times when insurance competition is extreme, this fact tempts some company officials knowingly to accept insurance offerings with little concern for loss ratios, in the thought that investment income will obscure underwriting deficiencies.

Property and liability insurance rates, however, are based on the relationship between premium income on the one hand and losses plus loss adjustment expenses plus general operating expenses on the other. There is generally no provision for investment income in the statistics required by regulatory authorities to justify rates. One must remember here that property-liability insurance stands in sharp contrast to life insurance in this regard. In life insurance the fact is known that all mortals must someday die; ages of death can be reasonably well predicted; premium monies are turned over by the insured to the company for investment for him against that day. In property-liability insurance the loss can occur at any moment and does not lend itself nearly so well to prediction; it will strike only a relative few; the insured's payment to the company represents his share of the losses anticipated and reflects the degree in which the conditions inherent in his risk are expected to contribute to the total loss. Thus, it becomes apparent that, while the investment function is an integral part of life insurance ratemaking, it has little place in property-liability ratemaking or underwriting.

GROUP II FUNCTIONS

Underwriting

Attention is turned now to the Group II functions, those essential and peculiar to the insurance operation of the company. The underwriting function must be discussed first because it is the key to the company's profit possibility. Since the term "underwriter" is loosely used today, some qualification is required to avoid confusion. "Underwriting" is used here in its broadest sense to mean (1) determining the extent to which the corporation's assets can be subjected to risk in a given class and (2) formulating and administering the rules, line settings, and reinsurances required to maintain the risks assumed within these predetermined limits. As the above outline indicates, this usage must include determination of rates, formation of contracts, maintenance of adequate reserves, and so on. (Readers are reminded that at several other places in this *Hand-*

book the term is used in a more narrow sense so as not necessarily to include any or all of the activities mentioned in the preceding sentence.)

Ultimate Responsibility for Profit. The underwriting function has the ultimate responsibility for profit. It naturally follows, therefore, that, if there is disagreement as to the acceptability of a particular risk developed by the producers, or if the policy language leads to disagreement within the company as to liability for a particular claim, the final decision should rest with the underwriter.

This very point emphasizes the importance of communicating to all employees knowledge about and interest in the total aims of the company regardless of particular function. For example, if the salesman or producer, along with his primary interest in selling an increased volume of his company's product, is acutely interested in making a profit for the company and understands the underwriter's problems, he will not try to force the underwriter to accept an inferior piece of business just for the sake of sales volume. By the same token, if the underwriter knows that the producer thinks in these terms, he—the underwriter—will listen with a much more open mind to a special request for consideration of what might appear at first glance to be a marginal risk. In some companies the producer is thought of as the "Yes" man and the underwriter is thought of as the one who always says "No." This dichotomy puts the two in competition with each other and is detrimental to the overall effort. A sensitive knowledge of each other's problems and mutual confidence that each is basically interested in the company's success are important to build and maintain between underwriter and producer. Similarly, this mutual knowledge and confidence should include the claims adjuster who also has special problems.

Effect of Multiple Line Legislation. There can be considerable variety in the ways in which the underwriting responsibility is divided among the company's underwriting officers. Until recent years, however, the historic divisions of fire, marine, and casualty tended to prevail. The passage of multiple line legislation in the 1940's, however, permitted fire and marine companies to write casualty insurance and casualty companies to write fire and marine insurance. (See Part VI of this *Handbook.*) This legislation is leading to a change in organization of company underwriting departments. Package policies now contain protection against fire, wind, theft, liability, and numerous other perils often grouped into one contract and offered for a single indivisible premium. From this metamorphosis there will probably emerge a more logical breakdown of underwriting responsibilities in the years immediately ahead.

Administrative Patterns. The administration of the underwriting function varies among companies. Some have underwriting centralized in the head office. This arrangement appears logical, since in its broad sense underwriting deals with the use of the company's total assets. Other companies, however, operate on a regional or departmental basis and allow these regions or departments considerable autonomy in subjecting the company's assets to risk.

Whatever the type of administrative organization, there is the problem of seeing that the company's established underwriting rules and rates are followed. At this level, underwriting can be thought of in terms of individual risk examination. Such examination of the acceptability of individual risks is, for many classes, susceptible to being delegated right down to the company producer and agent. The degree to which a company desires to delegate its examining function will depend upon the desires of management, the skill of the employees and agents, and the company's capacity.

Production

Production, as the selling operation in a property-liability company is usually termed, is generally accomplished at the customer level in either one of two ways: (1) directly to the public with the company's own employees acting as the salemen or (2) to the public through independent local agents.

Agency System. The property-liability company being discussed in this chapter operates through the independent local agency system. This system was started in the United States in 1807 when the Insurance Company of North America appointed its first independent local agent in Lexington, Kentucky.

The typical independent local agent represents a number of companies. Each of these companies encourages the agent, through the value of its service and products, to sell more of its policies than policies of the other companies he represents. This agent is the individual who deals with the customer, with the latter quite frequently never even remembering the name of the company issuing his contract of insurance.

The primary sales emphasis of companies operating through the local agency system, therefore, is in the nature of sales service to and for the agent. Thus, the company's underlying interest is to equip and encourage the agent to provide maximum service to his policyholders. The variety of service activities ranges from advice on office routines to formalized insurance schools and extensive market research. In addition to agency service, the production department is responsible for the appointment of agents and maintenance of agency operations in accordance with company policy.

Special Agents. Agency service is generally provided by the company's special agents. These are men located in strategic spots throughout the areas in which the company is seeking business. A property-liability company doing an across-the-board business generally has more than one special agent operating within a given territory. If these men are specialized in their respective knowledges, but are still to operate as an effective team, thorough communication of interest and of company endeavor is of particularly great importance. For this reason, as well as to coordinate more efficiently the services provided the agents, these men and their clerical staffs are generally headquartered together in a service office under the direction of a manager.

Since it is important that the producer thoroughly understand the company's underwriting requirements and policy, it would appear logical to have production supervision centralized in the head office along with the underwriters. In this way information about the needs of the insuring public and the agent can be "funneled" up through the special agents into the head office. In such a system the production and underwriting departments can be coordinated immediately in respect to such information. Here again, if the communication of company spirit and interest is effective within the organization, the senior production staff and the senior underwriting staff will be working together consistently in meeting the consumer needs in the best possible way.

Claim Adjustment

The adjustment of claims has often been termed the "payoff" end of the business. When a customer receives his policy and pays his premium, he is buying more than an insurance policy. He is purchasing a claims check should the occasion arise in the future when he has a claim covered by the policy. Thus, the claims adjuster is in effect the man who is delivering to the customer the article which he bought.

For a company operating through independent local agents, the most important one of its few opportunities to deal directly with the public is when a claim is being adjusted. At no time is an insured more sensitive to his own problems than immediately following a loss; hence, this is a time when the company's reputation can be made or broken.

It is customary for a property-liability insurance company to have its own staff of claims adjusters for the handling of third-party liability claims. It is not so common, however, for companies to employ their own claims adjusters for the handling of such first-party losses as fire, extended coverage, inland marine, and so forth. For these losses, many companies employ the services of various adjustment bureaus or independent claim adjusters.

In some circumstances it can be beneficial for a company to have its own staff of claim adjusters to handle all kinds of losses. Particularly if a company is an independent (that is, if it uses its own policies, forms, and rates rather than those of a rating bureau), its own staff can perhaps more easily understand peculiar features of its contracts and appreciate more readily their intent.

The claim adjusters of some companies specialize in particular lines of insurance, whereas those of other companies are trained to adjust claims across-the-board. Across-the-board adjusters are particularly useful to a company which handles its own losses and which sells multiple line contracts. Moreover, when a major hurricane or comparable disaster occurs, a company is suddenly faced with a tremendous number of claims concentrated in a single area. To the extent that each of the company's adjusting staff is capable of handling any type of claim, the company is in a better position to move emergency claims forces into the area to handle the extra load.

GROUP III FUNCTIONS

Legal Counsel

As can be seen from the outline, the Group III functions in a property-liability company can cover a large variety of services. Depending to a considerable degree on the size of the company and the breadth of its operation, these services may or may not be organized departmentally. For example, many small businesses manage to handle their legal problems by acquiring the services of outside law firms. In a property-liability insurance company, however, such an arrangement is not practical because of the complexities of the business. Property and liability insurance in the United States is subject to the regulations of 50 states and the District of Columbia and deals with hundreds of different types of protection. In a sense it is a law-oriented business, with each policy a legal contract and each comma and semicolon having to be studied and placed with care. Thus, in addition to the normal problems of corporate law and the charter powers of the corporation, a vast number of other problems is encountered in the field of insurance law itself. Skill is particularly important in this area if the property-liability company in question elects to follow a course independent of a rating bureau in forming its contracts and setting its rates. The legal staff will be called upon to prepare new contracts for filings, write briefs to advance a position or counter an opponent's arguments, guide the company through numerous insurance department hearings, and perform other commensurately difficult tasks. To some extent work of this type has to be done in virtually every property-liability insurance company.

The general counsel and his staff are not necessarily involved in questions of claim liability, since this type of legal question is generally handled by a company's claim department and outside defense counsel. In smaller companies, however, it is not unusual for the legal department to handle resulting litigation when claims cannot be adjusted amicably.

Statistics

Statistics are required in any insurance operation, but in a small company the statistical activities for a particular line of business may be accomplished within the department responsible for that line. As the company grows in size, however, it may well be more economical to establish a central statistical department. This department can gather the data from all parts of the company's activity and assemble them into reports tailor-made for the particular line of business involved.

Actuarial

The same is true of the actuarial department, although it should be noted that formalized actuarial services are relatively new in the property-liability insurance corporations in America. This activity can be expected to continue growing as competition increases. The growing variety of insurances calls for additional rating schedules and risk analysis and requires forecasting in greater depth—activities for which the actuary is especially prepared.

Safety, Payroll Audit, Inspection, and Marine Service

Safety, payroll audit, inspection, and marine service activities provide technical assistance at the customer level. These activities vary tremendously by company, customer, and type of insurance contract being serviced. For example, safety experts and engineering representatives both include among their activities the analysis of hazardous conditions at the individual risk level, and recommendations for their elimination or control. The safety expert's activities will continue throughout the life of the policy, his primary interest being to maintain the profitability of the account. The bulk of the engineer's work, on the other hand, will normally occur prior to the writing or renewal of the account, his initial interest being to provide technical advice which, while making the account more acceptable to the underwriters, will assist the agent and the company in securing and writing it.

The function of the payroll auditor is to assure the company that it secures the agreed premiums for those lines of business in which the rates are applied to total payroll, sales, or other business activities of the insured. This assurance is accomplished by an examination of the insured's records.

The marine service experts work in the areas of marine and inland transportation. They are loss prevention oriented and maintain an active interest in the insured throughout the life of the policy. Marine service departments on a formally organized basis are less prevalent in property-liability companies than are safety, payroll audit, and inspection departments.

Personnel

The services of a centralized personnel department have an increasing value as a company grows in size. The primary responsibilities of any supervisor or manager include maintaining an adequate staff of personnel to get the work done and, in addition, making certain that the personnel needs of the future are anticipated. As each particular sphere of activity grows and requires more people, the task of recruiting can become quite burdensome. A centralized personnel service to do initial recruiting, counseling, exit interviewing, and related work can save much time for those who otherwise would have to do it.

In addition, as a corporation grows there is always the danger that its "personal touch" will be lost. Little areas or "empires" can spring up with self-developed personnel concepts that may not be in line with those of the total corporate personality. Not only can this splintering be detrimental per se, but it can also hinder the optimum transfer of people across departmental lines as needs arise or opportunities develop. A skilled staff of personnel administrators in a centralized personnel department can be very useful in keeping alive and well-known throughout the corporation the company's basic concepts of personnel administration. Experts in this department also can assist all departments in administering a merit system of salary and responsibility recognition. A corporation cannot expect to be any better than its people and the spirit they bring to their work.

Education

Just as personnel administration is an inescapable activity in any company, so also is education, whether formal or otherwise. This activity exists to some degree in every operation within the corporation. Here again, the degree to which it is formalized into an education department will depend in great measure on management's desires and the size of the company. The range of activities may cover a wide area, including anything from the training of keypunch operators to providing formal schools for local agents.

Some companies prefer to train their own special agents. Talent, of course, can be purchased in the open market by hiring experienced people from the outside. Officials in these companies feel, however, that a corporation's own personality, spirit, ideals, and approach to problems can only be learned by someone who "lives" in the corporation over a long period of years. In such an atmosphere one is likely to find the company tending to recruit its future field and other management personnel from among inexperienced younger people, and providing intensive training for them.

A relatively new training need is that of computer programmers, operators, and systems people. Being new and highly specialized, if such training is provided within the company, it probably will be conducted initially within the methods and electronics departments. The day may come when this training will be incorporated into the activities of the centralized education department.

Public Relations and Advertising

The proportion of income spent on advertising and public relations in the property-liability business is considerably smaller than is the case in many other industries. Increasing emphasis, however, is being placed on these activities. If the company decides to attempt an effective job in the use of advertising, a full-fledged public relations and advertising department is of considerable importance. Advertising and the philosophies involved in public relations have grown to specialist proportions in business generally. Successful competition in this medium requires personnel skilled in this art.

The public relations and advertising department is of principal value to the production efforts of the company. Close liaison with the underwriting areas must be maintained, however, lest the company's advertising and news releases inadvertently encourage production in a direction inconsistent with the underwriting aims of the corporation.

DATA PROCESSING

Discussion of data processing services has been reserved for treatment last in this chapter. The term "data processing" is relatively new and its importance in the insurance mechanism has been undergoing considerable change in recent years. Until recently the work of assembling the data necessary to provide management reports, statistical data, statutory statements, and other information was considered a clerical operation. Much of this work was done usually within the various departments requiring the services. The same could be said of policy preparation, billing, and renewals. Two developments, however, have given a new perspective to this kind of work, to the point where in many respects it is beginning to rank along with the other three Group II functions. Perhaps the time is already here when data processing should be added to underwriting, production, and claims adjustment as being a fourth function basic to insurance.

The two conditions producing pressure for such reclassification are (1) the development of electronic equipment and (2) the profit squeeze resulting from the continuously rising costs of doing business.

By its very nature the insurance business calls for a vast quantity of activity along the lines of computing, recording, and analyzing information. In recent years, the magnitude of this clerical effort has been growing rapidly because of new coverages and increased competition, each requiring a greater variety and volume of statistical data. At the same time, insurance regulations have become more complex and the advent of withholding taxes, unemployment compensation records, "social security," and employee fringe benefits have added tremendously to the clerical burden. During this period wages have been rising. As a result, the mountain of detail work and its accompanying expense has been threatening to grow at a faster rate than the insurance industry's capacity to write premiums to pay for it. Until the advent of electronics, it appeared as though there was no permanent solution to this problem. The specialty of electronic computers, however, is computing, analyzing, and recording information. Electronic developments, therefore, have presented the insurance business with an opportunity to bring this mounting expense load under control once more.

The electronic computer, however, is an expensive mechanism and requires a large volume of data to make its use economical. There was a time when each of several departments within an insurance company might have done a substantial amount of its own statistical work by using its own departmental punched card equipment, policywriters, and general typists. It is not possible, however, for each department to have its own electronic equipment. The natural result has been a centralization of all this work within a company or even by means of recently-emerging outside data processing services.

Some of this data processing work is still more economically handled with relatively inexpensive equipment of an electrical type operated within a particular department. Efficient coordination of *all* the information flows within a company, however, calls for development of a total systems complex with procedures extending from the data source to the final report. Numerous companies, therefore, are establishing a single area of responsibility for all data processing and systems work, with these services cutting across departmental lines throughout the entire company.

It can be observed that among a given group of similar sized insurance companies doing an across-the-board property-liability business, the loss ratios of each will tend to compare rather closely at the year's end. Similarly, acquisition cost is likely to vary from one company to another by only a few points. Thus, the extent to which one company achieves a materially better profit performance than other similar companies depends to a great degree upon the company's ability to control and reduce its other expenses of operation. A large part of these other expenses arises out of data processing. When viewed in this light, it becomes relatively easy to see the data processing function occupying a role equally as important as underwriting, production, and claims adjustment.

CENTRALIZATION

From the foregoing it can be seen that a property-liability insurance company will incur increasing problems in communication and coordination as it grows and as its departments and services—both to the public and to itself—become more varied. Somewhere along the line of this growth a point will be reached where it becomes more economical to centralize some of these activities. At first glance it may seem that centralization would somewhat reduce the communication problem, but such is not the case because this centralization cuts across departmental lines. Consequently, problems of the varying departments utilizing these services must be thoroughly communicated to the service areas, and the coordinating problems of the service areas must be thoroughly understood by the people in each department being served. As centralization occurs, therefore, it becomes exceedingly important to engender in all individuals an informed interest in the aims of the corporation. In this process a danger point is reached, sometimes reflected in an impulsion to "get organized." It is at this point that the company's efforts to organize can get out of balance, and care must be taken to keep the *purpose* of organization in clear perspective.

SUGGESTED READINGS

GOSHAY, ROBERT C. *Information Technology in the Insurance Industry.* Homewood, Ill.: Richard D. Irwin, Inc., 1964.

LUCAS, GEORGE G. R., AND WHERRY, RALPH H. *Insurance Principles and Coverages.* New York: Rinehart & Co., Inc., 1954. Chap. 4.

MEHR, ROBERT I., AND CAMMACK, EMERSON. *Principles of Insurance.* 3d ed. Homewood, Ill.: Richard D. Irwin, Inc., 1961. Chaps. 3, 4, 23, 24, 27.

MICHELBACHER, G. F. *Multiple-Line Insurance.* New York: McGraw-Hill Book Co., Inc., 1957. Chaps. 9, 12, 14, 15, 16, 20.

MOWBRAY, ALBERT H., AND BLANCHARD, RALPH H. *Insurance: Its Theory and Practice in the United States.* 5th ed. New York: McGraw-Hill Book Co., Inc., 1961. Chaps. 22, 23, 27, 28, 29, 30.

Chapter 60

FINANCIAL STRUCTURE OF INSURERS

BY HAROLD C. KROGH

The purpose of this chapter is the presentation of a brief description of the financial structure of insurers. In the process attention is given to the nature of assets, liabilities, and equity of insurers. Attention is also given to statutory control of investment and to insurer investment practices. Detailed consideration of insurance accounting procedures, income and expense classifications, contents of annual statements, and related insurance accounting matters is postponed until Chapter 61. Suggestions for analyzing the financial and other strengths of insurers are the subject of Chapter 74.

ASSETS

Assets (things of value owned) of property-liability insurance companies come from several major sources. These sources include premium payments, earnings on invested assets, gains on disposal of assets, and, in respect to stock companies, contributions of capital.

With the premiums generally being paid in advance of the payment of claims, assets of companies are considerably larger than would otherwise be the case. Two exceptions to this generalization are (1) the assessment concept still used in some companies today—mostly small mutuals—and (2) the payment of premiums on an "audit" basis after the policyholder's premium base (or bases), such as size of payroll, has been determined as of the end of the policy period. While a deposit premium is ordinarily required in advance, it may be too low if estimates of the size of the base are understated.

The fundamental objective in the operation of an insurance company is quite simple, namely, to acquire and use these assets in such a way as to pay claims, expenses, and taxes and leave a residue. Some of this residue normally is passed to stockholders and/or policyholders. The remainder of it is kept in the corporation to support expansion of activities. Growth is a well-nigh universal (and is normally an admirable) objective. Given this objective, the problems of acquiring, using, and preserving assets are quite similar in a general way to such problems in other types of enterprises.

Some peculiar problems arise, however, because of the nature of the insurance business and because of the governmental regulation to which insurance is subjected. One such problem is that insurance companies are prohibited by law from showing certain types of assets at all on their financial statements. The general idea is that solvency and the ability promptly to pay all claims are the characteristics of overriding importance. Hence, only those assets readily convertible into claims-paying and expense-paying currency are "admitted" by regulatory authorities for listing on the Annual Statement. An example of an "admitted" asset is a high-grade corporate bond; a "nonadmitted" asset could be the furniture and equipment in the company's home office building. More discussion of this point appears in Chapter 61.

TABLE 60–1

STOCK COMPANY

AN ILLUSTRATIVE BALANCE SHEET*

ADMITTED ASSETS		
Bonds (amortized value)		$ 57,011,170
Stocks (market value)		52,158,915
Mortgages		304,990
Real estate		1,002,665
Cash		5,316,175
Premium balances		8,383,500
Other assets		3,227,805
Total Admitted Assets		$127,405,220
LIABILITIES		
Losses—Adjustment expenses		$ 29,649,130
Commissions, taxes, etc.		1,918,990
Federal income taxes		485,875
Unearned premiums		33,679,075
Unauthorized reinsurance		563,005
Other liabilities		2,627,615
Special reserves		403,130
Total Liabilities		$ 69,326,820
Capital	$ 6,000,000	
Surplus	40,000,000	
Voluntary reserves	12,078,400	
Policyholders' Surplus		58,078,400
Total		$127,405,220

*Compiled from *Best's Fire & Casualty Aggregates and Averages* (New York: Alfred M. Best Co., Inc., 1964 Edition).

Another peculiar problem in respect to assets of insurance companies is in their manner of evaluation for purposes of official Annual Statements. The laws of the several states prescribe in some detail the manner of evaluation. The laws, therefore, naturally influence to a great extent the investment policies and practices of insurance companies. In a later section of this chapter this problem is discussed in more detail.

Still another special problem regarding insurance company assets lies in the fact that the insurance codes of the several states pose numerous limitations on the ways funds of insurance companies can be invested. These codes also limit in various ways the uses to which the assets are put. The range of uses is also limited of course by the corporate charter which the company possesses. Types of eligible investment are treated later in

TABLE 60–2

MUTUAL COMPANY

AN ILLUSTRATIVE BALANCE SHEET*

ADMITTED ASSETS		
Bonds (amortized value)		$23,116,810
Stocks (market value)		6,585,910
Mortgages		434,625
Real estate		877,125
Cash		1,446,650
Premium balances		1,467,125
Other assets		617,605
Total Admitted Assets		$34,545,850
LIABILITIES		
Losses—Adjustment expenses		$11,891,850
Commissions, taxes, etc.		637,395
Federal income taxes		157,075
Unearned premiums		8,350,690
Dividends to policyholders		338,045
Reinsurance treaty funds		175,415
Other liabilities		465,930
Special reserves		546,450
Total Liabilities		$22,562,850
Surplus	$10,512,400	
Voluntary reserves	1,470,600	
Policyholders' Surplus		11,983,000
Total		$34,545,850

*Compiled from *Best's Fire & Casualty Aggregates and Averages* (New York: Alfred M. Best Co., Inc., 1964 Edition).

this chapter. Furthermore, the investment "mix" normally used to support various types of insuring activities is discussed in general terms in this later section of the chapter. This mix varies considerably from company to company and from time to time. Likewise, the absolute values change (usually upward) over time.

A rough assessment of aggregate relative investments can be gleaned from Table 60–3 which appears in this chapter. Two hypothetical balance sheets are provided for sake of illustration. One is of a hypothetical stock company. The other is of a hypothetical mutual company. These balance sheets show some general financial characteristics of property-liability insurers. Further, the balance sheets are useful references in the study of detailed points.

LIABILITIES

As the foregoing discussion suggests, the nature and use of property-liability insurance company assets are not unduly difficult to understand. Liabilities are another matter, however, and require considerably more attention.

A point worthy of early emphasis is that in insurance terminology a liability may be called a "reserve," such as the unearned premium reserve discussed in a subsequent section. Thus, there is a variation from traditional accounting terminology where reserves are offsets against assets (such as a reserve for bad debts) or an "earmarking" of an equity account (such as a reserve for contingencies). To make matters even more confusing, not all insurance reserves are liabilities. Some may be, in fact, an earmarking of an equity account. Not as much attention seems to be paid to the liability versus equity distinction in insurance as in noninsurance finance. Perhaps the existence of mutual companies contributes in part to a blurring of this distinction.

Another point is that many authors use the term "reserve" rather loosely and speak of a reserve as though it were an asset. These same authors, by the way, frequently refer to "surplus" in a similar vein as though expense, claims, or cash dividends could be paid from surplus or reserves. Such payments, of course, can be made only out of assets. Another frequently made statement is that reserves constitute the chief source of funds for investment. In a precise sense, this statement, too, is incorrect. The funds are assets. The reserves which represent a claim against such funds are liabilities of the company.

As intimated previously, state laws (and they vary somewhat from one state to another) require property-liability insurance companies to show various types of reserves (liabilities) in their official statements. Each major type of reserve along with the reasons for such requirements is discussed below. Attention is given also to some of the problems which these requirements create.

Unearned Premium Reserves

The laws of all states require property-liability companies (except some local mutuals in some states) to maintain unearned premium reserves. The reason for this legal requirement is simple to explain. The insurer collects the whole premium in advance (or at least has the right to the whole premium), whereas the protection can only be given as time elapses during the policy period, which may be as long as five years. The unearned premium is simply that portion which the company has not yet had time to earn. Premium is earned—under the law—strictly on a "straight line" basis. The insurer must show as a reserve the unused portion of the premiums of all policies on the books as of the date of the financial statement.

An Example. As an example, the unearned premium for a one-year fire insurance contract, requiring an annual premium of $120 payable at or soon after the inception of the policy, would be $90 at the end of three months, $60 at the end of six months, and $30 at the end of nine months. Thus, the insurer does not "earn" the full annual premium during any intermediate stage of the policy year but earns it only in the proportion that the policy reaches its maturity. At the end of the first month, 1/12 of the term has elapsed. The company is then justified in considering 1/12 of the premium, $10, as earned; 11/12 or $110, at that stage of time must be considered unearned, inasmuch as the company has not yet furnished protection for the 11 months remaining in the term. Moreover, in the event the company canceled the policy (see Chapter 5), this sum would be refundable to the insured. At the end of six months, ½ of the premium, or $60, is earned. Eventually, at the end of the twelfth month, the company has furnished the full year's insurance, and has earned the full premium. On a three-year policy, the amount earned per month is 1/36 of the gross premium; on a five-year policy, it is 1/60.

Ascertainment of the unearned premium reserve actually takes place in connection with the preparation of annual or intermediate financial statements. If a company's business is uniform month by month throughout a year, the unearned premium reserve remains constant. On the other hand, if business is increased month by month, the unearned premium reserve must also be increased by properly calculated additions. In the event of a reduction in the company's volume, the unearned premium reserve can be reduced. Of course, any change in the "mix" of business also changes this reserve.

Formulas. Computations for the unearned premium reserve are made by formula, rather than by computing the reserve on each policy separately. In using the semiannual formula (also called the "annual pro rata method"), the assumption is made that the policies are issued at an even rate throughout the calendar year. For a December 31 evaluation, it is assumed that all policies were issued on July 1, the average date of issue for the calendar-fiscal year. At the valuation date the unearned premium reserve for one-year policies will be ½ of the premium income attributable to these policies. On three-year policies, this reserve will be 5/6 of the premium income for the first year, ½ for the second year, and 1/6 for the third year. The formula is particularly useful for fire insurance companies whose business proves to be relatively even throughout the year.

In contrast, an insurer may not issue policies uniformly throughout the year. An insurer, for example, may sell a pronounced volume of automobile insurance policies in the spring when automobile sales may reach a seasonal peak. For other insurers the automobile insurance volume may be influenced by the time of the year when the financial responsibility laws became effective. For this reason, the semimonthly method (known also as the "monthly pro rata method") of calculating unearned premium reserve may represent a more nearly accurate valuation procedure than would the semiannual method. For the purpose of a December 31 valuation date, the semimonthly method would portray for all one-year policies issued the previous January an unearned premium reserve of $1/24$ of the premium income. The assumption is that the January policies were issued at "mid-month." Similarly, policies issued in March, June, and September would show an unearned premium reserve, as of December 31, of $5/24$, $11/24$, and $17/24$, respectively. (Taking the September policies as an example, one can see that 17 of the 24 half-month units fall beyond December 31 of the year of issue.) For three-year policies issued in the previous January, the unearned premium reserve would be $49/72$ of the premium. For three-year policies issued two and three Januarys ago, the unearned premium would be $25/72$ and $1/72$, respectively.

With the advent of the computer, some companies have started computing the unearned premium reserve on a daily pro rata basis.

Excess Valuation in the Unearned Premium Reserve. Inasmuch as the unearned premium reserve is calculated on the basis of gross premium, there is a considerable excess in the legally required reserves established as a necessary measure for maintaining solvency. Another way of putting this idea is that the reserves required by law are higher than the "actual" debt owed by the company. The law requires that premiums be "earned" on a "straight line" basis. Expenses, in fact, do not fall on a "straight line" basis. The bulk of the expenses is incurred upon or soon after the inception of the policy. Acquisition expenses, including agent's commissions, are incurred early. Only relatively small expenses are normally incurred later. Hence, the "straight line" assumption is not realistic for an insurer which is a "going concern." The result is sometimes referred to as the "redundancy of the reserve." The amount of the excess represents the difference between total or gross premium and the amount which is actually needed to pay claims.

In underwriting new business the statutory requirement for establishing an unearned premium reserve on a gross premium basis has some serious repercussions on the balance in the surplus account. Assume that a company using the semimonthly valuation basis writes a one-year policy in December for a premium of $144. Suppose further that it incurs expenses of $40 in producing and recording the business. Assets and ultimately surplus are decreased by that amount. Further, the insurer has to show a reserve (a liability) of \$138 (23/24 of \$144). Thus, of the \$144 new premium only \$6 can be considered as earned and, therefore, as properly an increase in the surplus (or equity) account as of December 31. The combined effect on the December 31 valuation date is that the sale of this new policy produced paradoxically a decrease in the balance of the surplus account. Once again, the reason is that the premium is presumed to be earned on a pro rata basis over time, whereas expenses occur disproportionately heavily at the inception of the policy.

Rapid expansion of volume can cause such a severe decline in surplus (equity, not assets) as to push a company into technical insolvency. The result is that it has to increase its equity by capital contributions or slow down its expansion. The capacity problem was particularly widespread and intense among property and casualty insurance companies in the immediate post–World War II period in the United States. In this era the premium volume in all branches of insurance expanded beyond the ready capacity of the insurance industry in terms of its limited capitalization and stringent reserve requirements.

Equity in the Account. The unearned premium reserve, with its element of excess valuation, gives a property-liability company a considerable margin of safety. Some authorities suggest that on the average there may be an "equity" of some 35 percent in this reserve.

Among many companies doing predominantly a fire business the reserve represents 70 percent or more of all liabilities. The reserve makes up a lower percentage of total liabilities of companies which are predominantly liability insurers. The figure is about 40 percent. The difference is attributable to the fact that liability and related policies are usually issued for shorter periods than are fire policies. For virtually all companies the unearned premium reserve and the loss reserve constitute the bulk of the liabilities—often 90 percent or even more.

Loss Reserves

Loss reserves are estimates of amounts which will be needed to pay claims for losses which have occured and to pay expenses associated with such claims. Loss reserves, as liabilities of the insurance company, include specifically: (1) claims for which loss reports have been filed, but on which losses have not yet been paid, and (2) claims arising from losses that have occurred, but which have not yet been reported. These amounts may be shown separately. In addition, reserves for loss adjustment expenses may be shown separately. Remarks made about loss reserves in the remainder of this section apply with equal pertinency to reserves for loss adjustment expenses. (See Chapter 61.) If the reserve is overly generous, the company has an equity in this reserve and has understated underwriting profit or overstated underwriting loss for the period or periods involved. Contrariwise, understatement of the loss reserve means that underwriting profit has been overstated or underwriting loss understated. (As explained elsewhere in this chapter, "underwriting profit" refers to the excess of earned premium over incurred losses and expenses.)

Individual-Estimate Method. Whenever a loss is reported to an insurance company, a reserve is "set up" in the amount estimated to be adequate to settle the claim. The individual-estimate method is utilizable in fire insurance where protracted settlements are not the usual thing and a reasonable estimate of the value of a fire insurance claim immediately following a loss is not difficult. Often claims registers are used for consolidating these claims and estimating the probable amount necessary to settle each one. When the Annual Statement is prepared, a factor may be added for the unreported claims in fire insurance which usually consist almost entirely of losses occurring so recently that notice has not reached the company.

Average-Value Method. In liability insurance the situation is quite different. Experience is not nearly so good a guide to what amounts in individual cases will be required for settlement of claims. Some claims may be paid in installments over a period of years and possibly may involve litigation which also extends over a considerable period of time. Moreover, in workmen's compensation, liability, and crime insurance, claims may arise under policies which have expired. Therefore, the loss reserve must also embrace claims that arose, or will arise, from prior reporting periods.

The individual-estimate method for fixing the amount of the reserve results sometimes in the tendency to underestimate the value of claims and produce inadequate reserves. In an attempt at improvement some companies have experimented with the average-value method. Today some companies use an averaging procedure on all claims for, say, the first 90 days and then convert to an individual-estimate method for claims over 90 days in process. Other companies use averages only for physical damage and minor property damage liability claims. Still other companies attempt to superimpose an average system on individual estimates which have been made. There is a wide variation as to the extent of use of average reserves.

The average method generally involves the computation of the average value of the claims of various types. For each category this figure is multiplied by the number of unsettled claims of that type to secure an approximation of the value of such claims outstanding. Presumably, the method does away with the individual judgment and greatly reduces the expenses of individual estimation when large numbers of claims have to be considered. Incidentally, expenses involved in loss settlement vary widely with the type of insurance involved. Expenses for legal defense in liability and workmen's compensation policies have the tendency to result in loss expenses at somewhat higher figures than for fire and marine policies.

Loss-Ratio Method. A number of years ago the Schedule P formula reserve system was created by statutes in most states and applies to bodily injury liability and workmen's compensation claims. The reserves are based on an assumed loss ratio for the particular line of insurance. In most states the statutory reserve for liability insurance is based on a 60 percent loss ratio less any amount already paid for losses and loss expenses. For workmen's compensation insurance the statutory reserve is at the 65 percent loss ratio level less claims already paid out of the earned premium involved. The statutes require that loss reserves with respect to the liability and workmen's compensation claims shall be carried, less losses paid, for a minimum of three years after a premium is earned. Thus, the statutory reserve is 60 (or 65) percent of the earned premium of the particular line for each of the three most recent years less losses paid arising from such premiums.

The reserve ascertained in this fashion by formula is compared with the company's estimate of the value of each claim for the same three-year period. This latter method is referred to as "case basis" method, although in reality it is similar to the individual-estimate method. The higher figure produced by use of these two methods must be used. As losses develop beyond a three-year period, any excess of statutory losses over "case basis" estimates reverts to surplus.

The minimum amounts required depend, of course, upon the stipulations of each particular state. Average values are used for suits pending under policies written three or more years prior to the statement date. Usually, an increasing dollar value is assigned with each passing year after the third, until a maximum value of, say, $1,500 is assigned for each outstanding suit pending against policies written 10 or more years prior to the statement date.

Unauthorized Reinsurance. The loss reserve of the primary insurer—the ceding company—does not normally include the reinsured portions of estimated claims. On some occasions, however, the reinsurer is not licensed to do business in the domicile of the primary company. (See Chapter 63.) In such cases in some states this primary company may be required to show as a liability the amount of reinsurance recoverable from such unauthorized reinsurer for claims which are outstanding. Some other states permit ceding companies to take credit for reinsurance, provided the reinsurer is licensed in the state where the insured property is located. Still other states permit the credit as long as the reinsurer is licensed in any state of the United States.

Equity in the Account. Similar to the equity in the unearned premium reserve, there may be an equity in loss reserves. Thus, where the statutory loss reserve provides for an amount consistently in excess of the loss experience of a company, there will be, from time to time, a balance available for transfer to surplus. The amount reflects the difference between actual experience and statutory reserve.

Voluntary Reserves

The "statutory reserves," that is, the unearned premium and loss reserves, are usually supplemented by various voluntary reserves. Some of these are accrued liabilities, such as reserves for taxes, dividends, and the like. There is little which is really peculiar to insurance companies in the treatment of these items. Hence, no further treatment is given here. As noted in the next section, some of the voluntary reserves are equity accounts. In the main they are not significantly different (except perhaps in name) from similar accounts in other types of firms.

Readers are referred to the next chapter for additional treatment of the general subject of reserves and additional attention to accounting aspects of unearned premium reserves and loss reserves.

CAPITAL AND SURPLUS ACCOUNTS

The capital and surplus of an insurance company represents the excess of assets over liabilities. Stock companies have net worth consisting of the capital stock and surplus accounts. Mutual companies, since they are owned by their policyholders, have no capital stock accounts. For them net worth is synonymous with surplus.

Paid-in Capital

Paid-in capital refers to the amount paid in by the organizers either at the time of formation of the company or at some later additional capital contribution date. In respect to stock companies, most states require that all stock be issued at a premium (such as 50 or 100 percent of par value) so as to create a paid-in surplus balance as well as a capital stock balance. The effect is to buttress the assets and the equity of the company before it begins underwriting operations.

Earned Surplus

Property-liability insurance companies established in successful operations over a period of years will build an earned surplus by retaining profits. A company's earned surplus derives from two main sources of profit for the company: (1) "underwriting profit," arising from the insuring operations, and (2) "investment profit," arising from earnings on, or appreciation of, the firm's investments. The statutory underwriting profit or loss for a given year is determined by finding the difference between earned premium and incurred losses and expenses for that year of insurance operation. ("Statutory" is used in this sense to mean that the premiums are considered as being earned on the "straight line" basis.)

Earned premiums are computed, therefore, on some sort of "straight line" basis—such as annual pro rata, monthly pro rata, or daily pro rata. Incurred losses are estimated on the basis of claims reported plus anticipated incurred-but-not-reported losses. The "loss ratio" is the quotient resulting from dividing incurred losses by earned premiums. Expenses are also computed on the incurred (accrued) basis. When this figure is divided by the earned premiums, the result is the "expense ratio." Addition of the loss ratio and expense ratio gives an indication of the *relative* underwriting profit or loss. If the combined ratio is less than 100 percent, an underwriting profit was enjoyed; if over, an underwriting loss was suffered. Loss and expenses ratios computed in this manner are deemed more realistic than those based on premiums received and losses and expenses paid.

Even so, there is still the matter of probable redundancy in the unearned premium reserve. (The loss reserve, of course, may be in error in either direction, since the past by any measure may be a poor guide as to the size of claims.) For informal evaluation purposes the statutory loss reserve can be "adjusted" by reflecting an appropriate figure for the equity in the unearned premium reserve (generally calculated as 40 percent in the case of fire insurance and 35 percent with respect to liability insurance). The adjusted loss ratio is combined with an "adjusted" expense ratio which is based on expenses incurred to premiums *written* during the period, in order to arrive at a more "realistic" estimate of underwriting results. This analytical process is described in more detail and is illustrated in Chapter 74. The results, of course, influence an analyst's opinion as to the size of "real" surplus.

It has been traditional among both stock and mutual companies in the property and liability insurance business to invest the entire underwriting profit in the business. This practice provides an additional factor of safety and enlarges the facilities for underwriting. Dividends, in general practice, have been restricted to a part of the earnings derived from investment. Steady growth of the insurance industry has been identified with strength and stability of companies following the practices of adding underwriting profits, together with a portion of the investment income, to surplus.

INVESTMENT REGULATION AND PRACTICES

Property-liability companies diversify their investment portfolios for the very reason that sound insurance is based on the reduction of risk. Geographic, investment media, and industry diversification of investments can be attributed in large part to statutory requirements. State diversification statutes limit investment in any one person, corporation, or institution to a stated percentage (typically 5 to 10 percent) of the insurance company's admitted assets. Such restrictions help to protect insurance companies from financial ruin by the failure of an investment commitment, and rather effectively prevent the insurer from securing voting control of the company in which investment has been made. This type of statute does not apply to obligations of federal and state governments. As investment funds move from the relative safety of secured debt to risk or equity capital, percentage limitations in issues and classes become more stringent.

The primary rationale in investment regulations is solvency of insurance companies. Management policy of individual insurers usually imposes additional safeguards beyond the minimal requirements of state regulation.

Table 60–3 shows in percentages the aggregative investment structures of stock companies and mutual companies for a recent year.

Comments about New York Statutory Provisions

Informative examples of legal requirements relating to state regulation may be found in the insurance law of New York. The New York statutes in this respect are about the most stringent in the country. New York traditionally has been the largest source of premiums; thus, it has important influence. Its influence is accentuated by the "Appleton rule," set forth in 1939. The rule requires that a "foreign" insurer—that is, one domiciled in a state other than New York—be obligated to comply with New York's regulations in respect to *all* its business in the United States *if* it is to be granted a license to write business in New York.

With respect to minimum capital assets (those equal to the minimum net worth prescribed by law) of an insurer licensed in New York, only the following types of investments are eligible: (1) obligations of the United States government or those guaranteed by it, (2) obligations of New York state and its political subdivisions (out-of-state insurers may substitute municipal bonds of their own states for those of New York), (3) obligations of other states, but not including their political subdivisions, and (4) real estate mortgages upon New York state real estate. At least 60 percent has to be in types (1) and (2).

Funds equivalent in amount to the unearned premium reserves and loss reserves can be invested in obligations qualifying under the minimum capital assets requirement. Such funds can also be invested in obligations of states and their political subdivisions or in obligations of solvent corporations with a restriction that there may not be investment of more than 10 percent of an insured's admitted assets in any one corporation. Obligations suitable for investment include: mortgage bonds, debenture bonds, adjustment or income bonds, equipment trust certificates, acceptances and bills of exchange eligible for purchase by the Federal Reserve

Banks, mortgage loans (not more than 40 percent of admitted assets may be invested in mortgages in the aggregate), stocks and debentures in housing developments, obligations of the International Bank for Reconstruction and Development (up to 5 percent of admitted assets), savings and loan association investments (up to 25 percent of admitted assets). An insurer may own home office property or real estate for purposes of transacting business; the aggregate amount is not to exceed 10 percent of admitted assets. Furthermore, the firm may have foreign (other country)

TABLE 60-3

INVESTMENTS OF "FIRE AND CASUALTY" COMPANIES PERCENTAGE BY CATEGORY 1963

809 Stock Fire & Casualty Companies			358 Mutuals		
BONDS			BONDS		
U.S. Government	16.2		U.S. Government	20.9	
State, Municipal, etc.	15.1		State, Municipal, etc.	23.1	
Others	15.1		Special Revenue, etc.	14.8	
			Utility	5.3	
			Others	3.7	
Total		46.4	Total		67.8
COMMON STOCKS			COMMON STOCKS		
Utility	7.5		Utility	3.3	
Bank	3.1		Bank	1.4	
Insurance	9.2		Insurance	2.7	
Others	15.6		Others	8.1	
Total		35.4	Total		15.5
PREFERRED STOCKS			PREFERRED STOCKS		
Utility	1.5		Utility	1.9	
Others	1.2		Others	0.8	
Total		2.7	Total		2.7
MORTGAGES		0.2	MORTGAGES		1.0
REAL ESTATE		1.2	REAL ESTATE		2.6
CASH		4.3	CASH		4.1
PREMIUM BALANCES		7.0	PREMIUM BALANCES		4.3
OTHERS		2.8	OTHERS		2.0
Grand Total		100.0	Grand Total		100.0

SOURCE: *Best's Fire & Casualty Aggregates & Averages*, 1963.

investments of a similar nature to United States investments, with certain limitations—for example, Canadian investments cannot amount to more than 10 percent of admitted assets. If a company is doing business in the countries where the investments are being made, the investment is limited to 1½ times the unearned premium and loss reserves of business done in foreign countries.

Companies cannot invest in securities of an insolvent corporation, or in mortgages which do not meet certain qualifications. Some flexibility is permitted through the provision of the New York act which permits companies to invest not more than 5 percent of their assets in securities of any type other than those listed in the statutes.

Comments about Statutory Provisions Generally

Statutory regulations place emphasis on stability of principal in the portfolio. The taxing powers of the federal and state governments serve to make their obligations prime investments for insurance companies. As a result, most statutes require that such obligations constitute the bulk of the investment assets.

A common stipulation is that the obligation, whether issued by federal, state, or local subdivision, not be in default of principal or interest at any time prior to time of investment. Percentage limitations are also placed on this type of investment. Similar percentage limitations are applied to railroad and public utility corporation obligations and contain the further requirement that there be a history of at least three to five years of full payment of principal and interest on the obligation. A more strict percentage limitation exists for insurance company admitted assets which may be invested in obligations of private corporations. For such corporate bonds and debentures there is a strict solvency requirement, a debt paying history on both principal and interest, and a dividend paying history. Similar requirements are made for investment in equities, with stringent solvency requirements and stringent percentage limitations on the class of investments. Statutes typically contain a restriction on how much can be invested in equities. The New York "5 percent rule" cited in the previous section is an extreme example. Generally, however, the freedom for investing assets equal to the minimum capital requirements is more stringent than for investment of assets in excess of this figure.

A number of states permit assets to be invested to a prescribed extent in mortgages. Usually, the investment must be of first mortgage nature. Further, the property must be otherwise unencumbered and the insurance company alone, or in combination with other insurance companies, must possess all the mortgages or bonds secured thereby. Most state insurance codes limit the purchase of real estate, and improvements on real estate, to buildings as convenient accommodations for home and branch office transactions.

It should be observed that the federal Securities and Exchange Commission under the Securities Act of 1933 through its "Regulation SX" and its "10–K" reporting form may be influencing to an increasing degree the financial structures of stock insurers—firms issuing securities to the public. Prospectuses of stock company insurers making recent public offerings are cases in point.

Each concern with listed securities must file annually with the Securities and Exchange Commission a form (10–K for most companies) which contains a balance sheet and an income statement in prescribed detail. This form also calls for information to bring the registration statement up to date. Similar requirements are imposed with respect to unlisted securities registered for sale under the Securities Act of 1933 if the amount involved exceeds $2 million.

Valuation Practices

In general, legal requirements affect the valuation of assets which comprise the investment portfolio of the insurer. Real estate items are usually carried at the market value as determined by appraisal. Mortgage loans and collateral loans, if properly secured, are carried at the amount loaned. If the security is not up to that standard, the amount is reduced or written off completely with a charge to surplus. Stocks are valued at market, but because of the fluctuating character of their market value, a "reserve" item is often carried in the surplus account to provide for possible decreases in value. Bonds amply secured and not in default as to principal and interest are valued by the process of amortization of premium or discount, depending on whether they were purchased at a price above or below par. Their value gradually approaches par as they age to maturity. Bonds not in "good standing" are valued on the basis of whatever market or other pertinent information is available. The Committee on Valuation of Securities of the National Association of Insurance Commissioners publishes *Valuations of Securities as of 19—* which is an *annual* list of stocks and bonds with the respective valuation figures acceptable for use in the Annual Statement.

Other Factors Affecting Investment Practices

Management investment practices reflect essentially a defensive position. The prime objective of property-liability insurers is a solvency to provide the best possible protection to their insureds for payment of claims. Relative size of the company will have some influence on the composition of its portfolio. The time a company has been in business is also a factor in portfolio composition and management. A relatively new company has a position quite different in terms of investment flexibility than the position of a larger company with a fairly substantial net worth. Furthermore, the volume of a company's premium affects investment practice.

Taxation. Investment activity is also affected by taxes, especially the federal income tax, payable by insurance companies on income from investments. State and municipal taxation of insurers, usually consisting of a percentage levy upon the amount of premiums written within the tax jurisdiction, is not nearly as important a factor for investment income. Such taxes are levied on essentially the same basis for stock and mutual insurers.

There is a delineation, however, in the application of federal income taxation between stock insurers and mutual insurers. This taxation is described in Chapter 66. The point of interest here is that nontaxability of income on various municipal and state obligations is a matter of considerable importance to the investment activities of insurance companies.

Interest Rate Levels. Maturity spacing of bonds is an important consideration and the tendency is to have bond maturity spaced over an extensive period. Most property-liability insurance companies are sensitive to interest rates since bond prices rise when interest rates fall and vice versa. Proper spacing of maturities tends to minimize these fluctuations. Investment practices differ within the insurance industry to a marked degree. For example, a sizeable segment of the property-liability industry places major stress on ownership of bonds, and another segment has followed a more aggressive investment activity by placing relatively greater emphasis on equities.

Types of Insurance Written. The type of business written by an insurer has a pronounced influence on its investment portfolio. In fact, the tradition has been to classify companies as "fire and marine" or "casualty and surety" and then generalize accordingly. The two classes of companies historically have had distinctly different patterns of investments. The growth of multiple line underwriting, however, has tended to obscure this distinction.

Perhaps the better approach now is simply (1) to point out the differences in liquidity which the broad lines of underwriting dictate and (2) to suggest that to the extent an insurer writes one line or another it should plan its investments accordingly.

Generally speaking, insurançe providing indemnity for direct damage type losses requires the availability of large sums of money on relatively short notice. Moreover, payment of losses on an "actual cash value" basis means that changing price levels can influence significantly the amount of the claims. This situation is contrary to a fixed dollar obligation—such as in the usual life insurance settlement. The result is that insurers writing fire, allied lines, marine, or other direct damage insurance need substantial blocks of investments which can be converted quickly into cash without serious loss in value. These investments often comprise more than 50 percent of the portfolio. Such investments take the form of bonds and stocks. The emphasis is on quality and marketability. Hence only "high grade" securities are generally held. Real estate mortgages, despite the adequacy of the security, are not generally held to support direct damage underwriting. The reason apparently is the uncertainty of being able to convert them to cash on a large scale without loss, should exigencies warrant. Some farm mutuals, however, have made sizeable investments in mortgages.

United States government bonds often have represented over half of the bond portfolio of companies writing predominantly fire, allied lines, and inland marine business. Corporate stocks represent the next largest type of investment for most companies in this field—as much as 50 percent for some companies. Listed stocks which have a ready market are emphasized. Stock insurance companies traditionally have held relatively more stocks in their portfolios than have mutuals.

Claims on workmen's compensation, some types of liability insurance (such as rehabilitational claims), and surety claims, while large, may be paid out in installments. For this reason and for other reasons investments to support liability insurance do not have to be as liquid as those supporting direct damage insurance. Therefore, insurers with a heavy liability business can give attention to mortgages and to bonds which are not as liquid as those discussed in the preceding paragraphs. The "classic" generalization has been that "casualty and surety" portfolios do not have to be as liquid as those of "fire and marine" insurers. As mentioned, however, multiple line underwriting renders such generalizations a bit out-of-step with the times. To the extent that a corporate group does its multiple line underwriting by using separate firms within the corporate family for the several coverages, perhaps the generalization still holds.

SUGGESTED READINGS

DAVIS, SHELBY CULLOM. "How U.S. Fire & Casualty Companies Invest," *Financial Analysts Journal*, Vol. 17 (November–December, 1961), pp. 19–20, 22–23.

HUEBNER, S. S., AND BLACK, KENNETH, JR. *Property Insurance*. 4th ed. New York: Appleton-Century-Crofts, Inc., 1957. Chap. 38.

KENNEY, ROGER. *Fundamentals of Fire and Casualty Insurance Strength*. 3d ed. Dedham, Mass.: The Kenney Insurance Studies, 1957.

MEHR, ROBERT I., AND CAMMACK, EMERSON. *Principles of Insurance*. 3d ed. Homewood, Ill.: Richard D. Irwin, Inc., 1961. Chap. 27.

MICHELBACHER, G. F. *Multiple-Line Insurance*. New York: McGraw-Hill Book Co., Inc., 1957. Chap. 21.

MIDDENDORF, J. W., II. *Investment Policies of Fire and Casualty Insurance Companies*. New York: Wood, Struthers & Co., 1954.

MOWBRAY, ALBERT H., AND BLANCHARD, RALPH H. *Insurance: Its Theory and Practice in the United States*. 5th ed. New York: McGraw-Hill Book Co., Inc., 1961. Chap. 27.

Property and Casualty Insurance Companies: Their Role as Financial Intermediaries. American Mutual Insurance Alliance; Association of Casualty and Surety Companies; National Board of Fire Underwriters; monograph prepared for the Commission on Money and Credit. Englewood Cliffs, N.J.: Prentice-Hall, Inc., 1962.

SJOSTROM, ROBERT A. "Which Fire and Casualty Stocks?", *The Analysts Journal*, Vol. 13 (May, 1957), pp. 79–82.

SNIDER, H. WAYNE (ed.). *Readings in Property and Casualty Insurance*. Homewood, Ill.: Richard D. Irwin, Inc., 1959. The following articles:

Best, Alfred M. "Rating the Financial Structure of Insurance Companies," Chap. 10.

Ridgway, William C., Jr. "Investment Policy," Chap. 17.

Fougner, Arne. "The Capacity Problem," Chap. 18.

Chapter 61

INSURANCE ACCOUNTING

BY J. S. PIERINGER, JR.

The purpose of this chapter is to present a brief description of some aspects of insurance accounting. As a part of their study of the subject, readers are encouraged to refer also to Chapters 60 and 74. Both of the chapters bear particularly on matters of insurance accounting.

EARLY REGULATION OF INSURANCE ACCOUNTING

Insurance accounting principles and practices have evolved as a result of statutory enactments and regulations governing the industry. In the early days, regulation was limited and financial statements were relatively simple exhibits of income and outgo on a cash basis, supplemented by a listing of assets and liabilities. Assets included only cash, stocks, bonds, and premiums due but unpaid. "Liabilities" included only reserves for reported but unpaid losses and capital stock. Each state determined the type of financial report needed to encourage solvency and thus protect its insurance-buying citizen. As the insurance business grew and became a more important segment of American business, various state supervisory officials began to require additional financial data. With each state determining its own requirements, it soon became extremely difficult for a company to complete financial statements for each state in which it operated. Obviously, some uniformity in these statements was a necessity if the companies were to continue to grow and do business in several states.

In 1871, the Superintendent of the New York Insurance Department called a meeting of the supervisory officials of 20 states to discuss uniform procedures for state supervision of insurance companies and a uniform Annual Statement blank. As a result of this meeting, the Annual Statement for fire insurance companies was adopted and the National Insurance Convention of the United States was formed. This organization later became the National Association of Insurance Commissioners. In 1930, a uniform "miscellaneous" Annual Statement blank for casualty insurers was adopted by the Association.

In the years which followed, numerous changes were made in the Annual Statement blanks, particularly in the casualty blank. Special schedules were added in the casualty blank for workmen's compensation and liability insurance to check on the adequacy of the reserves for losses. Moreover, other itemized schedules were developed to set forth the details of assets and liabilities.

Two Annual Statement blanks, one for fire insurance companies and one for casualty insurance companies, continued to be required until 1950 when the National Association of Insurance Commissioners adopted a combined fire and casualty blank, which is in use today.[1]

VARIATIONS FROM NONINSURANCE ACCOUNTING

Public accountants often say that fire and casualty insurance accounting violates many of the accounting principles in normal use by other businesses. Insurance accounting principles and practices do vary from those generally accepted, but there is a reason for each variation. Insurance, although a private enterprise, is vested with a public interest and, as such, is subject to strict regulation which determines the applicable accounting principles and procedures. The primary concern of regulators is maintenance of solvency of insurers, and the reporting requirements are designed to present the financial position of a company strictly on this basis and not on the basis of a going concern.

Nonadmission of Assets

As a consequence of the emphasis on solvency, the statutory regulations prohibit including as assets many items that are normally included by other business. Only assets which are readily realizable in cash may be included in the assets of an insurance company. These are considered "admitted assets." For example, no value may be included for furniture and equipment in the insurance company's statement, except for large electronic computers which have recently been given special treatment. The depreciated values of furniture, office machines, automobiles, and other equipment which are assets for most other businesses are considered "nonadmitted" assets. Notes and other accounts receivable which are not secured by collateral of the same type that would be a legal investment for an insurance company are "nonadmitted" regardless of the

---

[1] Throughout Part VIII of this *Handbook* the term "property-liability" is used generally to refer to "other than life" insurers. Since the expression "fire and casualty," however, is still used officially in reference to the Annual Statement, this expression will be used in this chapter. See also footnote 1 in Chapter 66.

worth of the signer. Any premium which is over 90 days due is considered a bad debt and is excluded from assets without regard to the net worth of the person or corporation who owes the premium.

No Deferral of Expenses

Among the major items considered good and valuable assets by most businesses which are not so considered by insurance companies are prepaid expenses and deferred charges. All commissions, premium taxes, bureau fees, and other expenses involved in connection with writing insurance must be treated as current expenses and charged against income. The income from premiums, however, can be translated into earnings only at the rate which corresponds exactly with the passage of time as the contract moves from inception to maturity. On three- and five-year policies, the expense normally exceeds the premium income earned in the first year, resulting in a statutory underwriting loss. (See Chapter 60 for a hypothetical illustration of this point.) In a period of increasing premium volume, statutory underwriting results are thus penalized by this method of recording expenses. There is no matching of cost and income as in other businesses.

Liquidation Values for Assets

Another major area of variance is investments. Insurance companies must invest their funds only as prescribed by the various statutes (see Chapter 60) and any investment not conforming to regulations is not an admitted asset. In addition to prescribing how the funds shall be invested, the regulations specify the methods of valuing certain investments which depart from generally accepted accounting practice. In general terms they are evaluated at the amount for which they could be liquidated. These evaluation guides are discussed briefly in Chapter 60. The point here is that their use means that valuation practices in insurance accounting necessarily are different from those in ordinary noninsurance.

PREMIUM INCOME AND PREMIUM RESERVE

Types of Premium Income

The principal source of income of an insurance company is the premium received from the sale of insurance policies. Accounting for premium income involves several types of transactions. Direct premiums, plus premiums received for reinsurance assumed, less premiums paid for reinsurance ceded, indicates the premium income of a company.

Direct premiums are premiums on policies issued by the company to afford primary insurance coverage. The premium may be received in advance for the full term of the contract, on an installment basis under a financing arrangement, or on audit after the policy has expired. Audit premiums are normally developed where the premium is based on an exposure (such as payroll on workmen's compensation policies) which cannot be accurately determined in advance.

Reinsurance assumed premium is another major premium income item. This type of transaction arises when one company assumes part or all of the liability of another insurance company which has issued its policy to cover the risk. There are many types of reinsurance agreements governing the assumption of business by one company from another. (See Chapter 63.) The assuming company normally pays a commission to the ceding company sufficient to cover the acquisition cost and other expenses incurred by the company which issues the policy.

Reinsurance ceded premium is the premium due another insurance company for the purchase of a policy or coverage which transfers part or all of the liability to another company.

Other types of premium income arise from endorsements. Such endorsements may provide additional premiums by changing the existing policy or necessitate a return premium as a result of the cancellation or reduction of the coverage.

Accounting for Premiums

The procedure for recording premium income varies with the type of company and its method of operation. There are two major classifications, the direct billing company and the agency billing company.

Direct Billing Company. The direct billing company collects the premium directly from the policyholder. Premium bills are prepared by the company and sent directly to the policyholder, who remits to the company. This type of billing is used by many of the large speciality writers. As a by-product of recording the premium item, a collection or accounting card is produced which is used to prepare the billing notice and to generate an awaiting payment or due file. As premiums are received, proper cards are extracted from the due file. The remaining cards represent unpaid premiums. The billing and collection procedure is handled by computers in many of the larger companies.

Agency Billing Company. In an agency billing operation the company sends the agent a monthly statement of all policy transactions recorded during the month. The total premium, agent's commission allowance, and net amount due the company are indicated and the agent remits to the company on the basis of this statement. Some agency companies receive a monthly statement from the agent called an "Account Current." This statement generally provides space for listing policy numbers and several columns for premium classified by rate of commission. The gross premium is totaled; the commission allowance is determined; and the net balance due the company is indicated. Where this system is used, it is necessary to establish an "Agent's Difference" account to reconcile or control the difference between the items reported on the agent's "Account Current" and the company entries. Other companies bill the agent on an item per item basis. The agent remits on an individual policy basis and any item which is not paid is carried forward to the next month's billing. Under this system the month's business cannot be treated as a unit for collection purposes and a premium due file is maintained as in the direct billing operation.

Accounting for the Unearned Premium Reserve

When a company issues a policy obligating it to pay for loss, it incurs a contingent liability. As the obligation extends over a period of months or years, a "reserve" for the potential liability is required by statute. The reserve, called the "unearned premium reserve," is based on the theory that if the premium is sufficient to pay losses and expenses and provide a margin of profit over the term of the policy, the pro rata part of the premium representing the unexpired term should be adequate to pay the losses and expenses which will be incurred during the unexpired term. The reserve also provides the approximate amount to be returned to the policyholder if the policy is cancelled.

The statutes specify that the liability for unearned premiums may be computed on the annual pro rata fraction, provided this method produces an adequate reserve. The supervising authorities may, in their discretion, require the calculation of a monthly pro rata basis if the annual pro rata method does not produce an adequate reserve. (See Chapter 60 for a description of these methods and a discussion of the concepts involved.)

The basic data for computing the unearned premium reserve are provided in the punched cards used to record the premium transactions. The detail cards of original entry are sorted by line of business, by term, and by month and year of expiration and are summarized to produce a premium-in-force file. The premium used is the full term premium or original premium. When a policy is cancelled, the original premium rather than the return premium must be taken out of the premiums in force. When a policy change is made resulting in either an additional or return premium for the remaining term of the policy, the full term premium must be used for the premiums-in-force files.

As the premiums-in-force file is in summary form on an original premium basis, a system of controls is generally employed to provide a check on the accuracy of the in-force file. Normally, additions to the premium-in-force file each month are carefully analyzed in relationship to the actual premium and any abnormal fluctuations in the relationship of the unearned premium to written premium are analyzed to determine the cause.

Various methods are used to calculate the unearned premium reserve.

A punched card multiplier, a computer, or a hand-operated calculator can be used to compute the reserve. Some ingenious methods and formulas have been devised to short-cut this involved calculation.

LOSS DISBURSEMENTS AND LOSS RESERVES

The primary purpose of an insurance company is to pay losses that occur under the contract and, in the case of liability coverages, to protect and defend the insured against financial loss for which he may be liable because of personal injury or damage to the property of others.

Recording Losses

Losses and loss adjustment expenses are the largest single element of expense and one of the most difficult to determine accurately. Losses are recorded in the statement as "Paid Losses" and "Incurred Losses." A paid loss is the disbursement for the partial or total payment of a claim. An incurred loss is the amount of the loss both paid and unpaid for which the company is liable. The estimate of the amount to be paid on a claim presents the real difficulty. When a notice of loss is received, someone in the loss department determines that the policy provides coverage for the type of loss reported and sets an estimate of the probable cost of the claim. This estimate is based on the facts of the claim and the experience of the adjuster. The total of these estimates is generally called "Unpaid Loss Reserves." The estimated cost is also the "Incurred Loss" until the claim is closed. Partial payments are not taken into consideration. When the claim is closed, the unpaid loss reserve is eliminated and the total cost of the claim becomes the "Incurred Loss."

There is a simple formula for determining incurred losses for statement purposes. Paid losses for the period are added to unpaid losses at the end of the period. From that total, the unpaid losses at the beginning of the period are subtracted. The result equals the incurred losses for the period. The use of this formula correctly reflects changes in the value of reported claims and eliminates the redundancy in loss estimates when claims are closed for less than the original estimates.

The Unpaid Loss Reserve is often difficult to determine accurately at the time the loss is reported to the company. Personal injury and workmen's compensation losses require extensive investigation and often a medical examination to determine extent of injury before an accurate estimate can be made.

Generally, an estimate of cost is made at the time the loss is reported and subsequent adjustments are made as the facts develop. Because of the difficulty in accurately estimating the value of each individual loss, most companies use loss development data to assist in the exercise of judgment on reserve estimates. The various methods for estimating loss reserves are described in Chapter 60.

Accounting for Loss Payments

Loss payment procedures vary by companies. Some companies pay all claims by the use of drafts. When claims are paid by drafts, two procedures are in common use. The first ("Issue Basis") involves drafts which are recorded when the draft is issued. They are considered the same as a check and recorded as losses paid at the time of issue which permits the file to be closed, although the draft has not been presented for payment. This method reduces the inventory of claims on hand and reduces the losses incurred by any redundancy in the claim reserve. When this method is used, a "Draft Payable" liability account is established for drafts issued but outstanding. The second procedure ("Paid Basis") involves drafts handled on a paid basis where the loss payment is not recorded until the drafts are presented by the banks. The open claim file must be maintained with the proper reserve until the drafts are presented for payment. As the Unpaid Loss Reserve represents one of the major liabilities of an insurance company, it is extremely important that the reserve be as accurate as possible. Most companies maintain a very close check on the development of the loss reserve by line of business to test the adequacy of reserves and to develop trends in the cost of claims.

Handling Incurred-but-Not-Reported Losses

In addition to the reserve for reported losses, a reserve is established for losses incurred but not yet reported. The amounts are determined by formula based on statistics of prior periods and modified by trend factors.

Reserve for Loss Adjustment Expenses

A reserve for loss adjustment expenses is established for both reported and unreported losses. Loss adjustment expenses include allocated expenses—those which are directly identifiable with a particular claim such as legal fees and court costs; and unallocated—those which cannot readily be allocated to a particular claim. Unallocated expenses are the expenses of company adjusters and claims personnel such as salaries, travel, rent, and so on. Allocated loss expense reserves are frequently recorded on an individual case basis, the same as the loss. Some companies use a formula relating allocated paid loss expenses by lines to unpaid loss reserves at the end of the year. Reserves for unallocated loss expenses are normally estimated based on a ratio of unallocated loss adjustment expense paid to paid losses for a prior period, applying such ratios to unpaid losses at the end of the year.

Voluntary Loss Reserves

In addition to the statutory formula loss reserve (see Chapter 60) many companies establish voluntary loss reserves as added protection against adverse loss developments on these hazardous lines of business.

Salvage and Subrogation

Salvage is a recovery made by a company after a loss has been paid and is treated as a reduction of the amount of loss paid. Subrogation is the legal right of an insurance company to recover from a third party who may be wholly or partially responsible for the loss. Subrogation recovery, similar to salvage, is applied as a reduction to the amount of loss paid.

EXPENSES

Uniform Accounting Instructions

Since 1949, fire and casualty insurance companies have been required to allocate expenses in accordance with Uniform Accounting Instructions adopted by the National Association of Insurance Commissioners. The instructions provide for 21 basic expense classifications with subdivisions by three functional groups, "Loss Adjustment Expense," "Other Underwriting Expense" [separated into (1) acquisition, field supervision, and collection expenses; (2) general expenses; and (3) taxes, licenses, and fees], and "Investment Expense."

The purpose of the Uniform Accounting Instructions is to bring about more nearly uniform results in the allocation of expenses, which will render comparisons of company expenses meaningful and will permit determination of expenses for equitable ratemaking purposes.

Prior to the adoption of Uniform Accounting Instructions only meager details were issued by the supervisory authorities as to what expense items should be charged to the various accounts. As a result, there was no uniformity among companies in handling expense charges. Comparisons of expenses by companies were of little or no value.

Uniform Accounting Instructions are divided into five parts:

Part I provides the 21 operating expense classifications with 3 subdivisions by functional group, as reported in the Annual Statement in part 4, "Expenses." Each classification of expense is defined in the instructions, listing the expenses to be included and expenses not to be included.

Part II covers the allocation of joint expenses where two or more companies operate as a group and one company, usually the parent company, performs certain work for all the companies in the group. The instructions require a proper distribution of expenses by company and by expense grouping.

Part III provides the rules for allocation of expenses to the following expense groups for reporting in both the Annual Statement and the Insurance Expense Exhibit: (1) investment expense; (2) loss adjustment expense; (3) acquisition, field supervision, and collection expense; (4) taxes; and (5) general expenses.

Part IV provides the rules for allocation of expenses to lines of business as required by the Insurance Expense Exhibit.

Part V provides special instructions for acceptable methods of allocation of salaries and other expenses with examples of special studies which form the basis of allocation.

Principal Expenses

The principal expenses in an insurance company are salaries, commissions and brokerage, travel expense, equipment, printing and stationery, rent, postage, and telephone and telegraph. Expense disbursements are coded to indicate the kind of payment, company, major expense class, minor expense class, expense group, department, line of business, and state. Subclassifications may be established to permit a more detailed expense exhibit for the purpose of expense budgeting and control by individual departments. Control of expense is of prime importance. Extensive use is made of monthly expense budget reports which indicate by major departments and major expense classifications the budget expenditure for the period, the amount disbursed for the month, the amount budgeted for the year to date, and the percentage of paid expense to the budget. The format of the budget varies by individual companies from elaborate exhibits, which attempt to budget every minute item of expense to more simple groupings of major items of expense over which the department has direct control. Budget forecasts are an important tool of management because of the importance of the expense element.

Insurance Expense Exhibit

On or before some specified annual date, usually May 1, the Insurance Expense Exhibit must be filed with the insurance department of each state in which the company is authorized to transact business. The exhibit develops the gain or loss from underwriting by line for the previous calendar year on a countrywide basis and provides the data for compilation of the loss and expense experience of all the companies by line of business and by expense function within each line.

The exhibit consists of four parts:

Part I shows the operating expenses by expense group for all lines of business combined, the same data required by part 4 of the Annual Statement, except that "Other Underwriting Expenses" are segregated into 3 groups.

Part II of the exhibit shows the allocation to major lines of business. This part is divided into 2 sections: Section *A* reports premiums, losses, expenses, underwriting gain or loss, and ratios to earned premium; Section *B* reports adjusted direct premiums, expenses, and ratios to written and earned premium.

The principal purpose of Section *B* is to develop expense data on the direct basis related to written premium.

Part III develops the workmen's compensation expense ratio on a standard premium basis. Standard premium is the premium before the application of premium discount or retrospective rating.

Part IV is an exhibit of direct workmen's compensation earned premiums and direct losses by states. This part is included with the expense exhibit because the information is normally not available at the time of filing the Annual Statement.

INVESTMENT INCOME

A general discussion of investment policies and practices of property-liability companies is presented in Chapter 60. A brief comment about the accounting treatment of investments and investment income is made in this chapter. Although the principal purpose of an insurance company is the business of insurance, investment earnings are an important part of an insurance company's operation and pose problems as to accounting treatment. For mutual companies which return a substantial part of the underwriting profit to the policyholders, investment income is the principal source of increasing surplus necessary for growth of the company. In a stock company, investment income provides for dividends to stockholders.

Investment income consists of interest on bonds, which are normally carried on the books at amortized value, and dividends on stocks. Dividends declared but unpaid at year-end are included in the market value of the stock and accrued dividends are, therefore, not included in income. Realized capital gains or losses on the sale of securities are included in the investment income statement with the gain or loss calculated on the amortized value of bonds and the cost of stocks.

Investment expenses as defined by the Uniform Accounting Instructions are deducted from earned investment income in arriving at net investment income. A complete disclosure of each security owned at the end of the year as well as of all details of securities acquired or sold during the year is required by the supplemental schedules in the Annual Statement.

ANNUAL STATEMENT

Every company is required to file at least annually with the state supervisory authorities of each state in which it is licensed to do business, an Annual Statement which sets forth the financial position and operating results in complete detail, under oath of responsible officers of the company. The form of the Annual Statement is prescribed by the National

Association of Insurance Commissioners and, with minor exceptions, is uniform in all states. Changes in the Annual Statement blank are under the supervision of the Blanks Committee and the Committee on Examinations of the National Association of Insurance Commissioners.

The Annual Statement is a 39-page document consisting of the balance sheet, income statement, and statement of surplus supplemented by a series of parts and schedules supporting the balance sheet and income statement. One page of the statement is devoted to 30 pertinent questions regarding the financial status and method of operation of the company.

The balance sheet shows the financial condition as of December 31. The principal asset items are bonds (usually on an amortized basis), stocks (usually at market value as established by the Securities Valuation Committee of the National Association of Insurance Commissioners), mortgage loans on real estate, real estate less encumbrances, collateral loans, cash and bank deposits, agency balances less than three months due (less reinsurance ceded and net as to commission), bills receivable taken for premiums (which are installment premium notes), reinsurance recoverable on paid losses (which is the amount due from reinsurers), interest and dividends, and real estate income due and accrued.

The principal liabilities are: (1) losses (which are a reserve for net unpaid losses); (2) loss adjustment expense (which is a reserve for expenses on unpaid losses); (3) other expenses (which are a reserve for accrued salaries, rents, and such, separated into underwriting and investment expenses); (4) taxes, licenses, and fees (which are a reserve for premium taxes, fees, and federal income taxes); (5) unearned premium reserve; (6) dividends declared and unpaid to stockholders and policyholders; (7) funds held under reinsurance treaties; (8) excess of bodily injury liability and compensation statutory and voluntary reserve over case basis and loss expense reserve (Schedule P); and (9) surplus to policyholders composed of paid-in capital (for stock companies), special surplus such as reserve for security fluctuations, and unassigned surplus.

The underwriting and investment exhibit develops the net underwriting and investment income for the year on an earned basis before federal income taxes.

The capital and surplus exhibit develops the surplus to policyholders at the end of the current year by starting with the surplus at the end of the previous year and adjusting for the gain or loss during the current year, the net income, net unrealized capital gain or loss, change in nonadmitted assets, change in unauthorized reinsurance, change in statutory reserves, capital changes (both paid in and transferred from surplus), and cash dividends to stockholders and policyholders.

The summary of surplus to policyholders compares capital, special surplus, and unassigned surplus as of December 31 of the current year with that of the previous year and depicts the net increase or decrease.

Supplementary parts and schedules covering some 30 pages of detailed premium writings, loss payments, unearned premium reserve calculations, unpaid loss reserves—all by lines of business—are included. Other schedules give complete detail for investments indicating cost, market value, and income received by individual securities. Supplementary schedules also set forth the detail of calculation of statutory reserves and the development of loss reserves over a period of years to test the accuracy of the reserves in the past.

The statement is complicated because of the mass of details included and the many types of transactions reflected. The statement is designed to provide sufficient detail so that supervisory authorities in the various states can determine the solvency of the company. The statements are carefully scrutinized by officials of the insurance departments before a Certificate of Authority is issued to the company permitting it to continue to do business.

The Annual Statement provides the basis for preparing the federal tax return and must be attached to the tax return. Various adjustments in the Annual Statement must be capitalized for tax purposes and depreciated. An adjustment must be made for tax-exempt interest included in the underwriting and investment exhibit of the Annual Statement and case loss reserves must be substituted for statutory reserves.

ANALYSIS OF FINANCIAL STATEMENTS

Because statutory regulations require insurance companies to present financial data on a solvency or liquidating basis, it is necessary to look beyond the statutory results to determine the true financial position and earnings record of an insurance company. (See Chapter 74 for additional discussion of this point.) Supplementary statements adjusting statutory results are frequently included in reports to stockholders and policyholders to reflect the value of the company as a going concern.

Supplementary Statements

Supplementary statements are frequently prepared for management review to eliminate distortion brought about by statutory requirements, and thus present more clearly the true results of the insurance operation. The balance sheet is restated to include assets not admitted by statutory regulations such as the value of equipment and furniture, uncollected premium balances over 90 days due, and loans not collateralized by a security in which the company may invest. These assets are acceptable assets for most businesses in general.

The liabilities are restated to eliminate such statutory items as the excess of Schedule P or formula basis reserves over the actual case estimates. The income statement is restated to reflect the equity in unearned premium reserve created by the prepayment of commissions, premium taxes, and bureau fees. In a period of increasing premium income, prepayment of expenses by statutory provisions must be treated as current expenses and thus can severely penalize statutory underwriting results. During a period of declining premium income, statutory underwriting results would be benefited by earned premium income without related expenses. The equity in unearned premium is one of the most important items to be considered in analyzing the results of the company, as it can change an underwriting loss to a profit.

Another item to be considered is the effect on net income of realized gains or losses on sales of investments which are included in statutory net income.

Unrealized capital gains or losses resulting from a change in market appraisal of securities owned are required to be treated as direct charges or credits to surplus. When the market is on the upswing, substantial amounts may be added to surplus offsetting underwriting losses. Conversely, when there is a sharp decline in the market, surplus may be reduced even though the underwriting results show a satisfactory profit.

Adjustments of Published Information

Although supplemental statements are necessary to make a complete analysis, some adjustments can be made in the published results to obtain a more realistic picture of the company's progress. See Chapter 74 for a discussion of the general topic of analyzing the financial strength of a carrier by the use of published information.

SUGGESTED READINGS

GOSHAY, ROBERT C. *Information Technology in the Insurance Industry.* Homewood, Ill.: Richard D. Irwin, Inc., 1964.

Insurance Accounting: Fire and Casualty. Philadelphia: The Spectator, 1954. (Prepared by and published for the Insurance Accounting and Statistical Association. A revision is in progress at the time of writing of this chapter.)

Chapter 62

MARKETING METHODS

BY JOHN S. BICKLEY

A marketing revolution has occurred in the property-liability insurance business since World War II. In this chapter brief attention is given to this revolution and its results. Specifically, the following topics are discussed: the marketing concept involved; the changing market; the distribution system; the product, prices, and design; the agent and the broker in marketing; company organization for sales; and continuing problems.

THE CONCEPT

The concept of marketing embraced in this discussion is the total process whereby insurance service is rendered the public. This broad viewpoint has been increasingly accepted within the business, and the firms achieving the greatest success in terms of profit and market penetration are those whose officials attach the utmost importance to serving the buyer most effectively. The marketing function in this sense is not limited to the sales or agency department. The nature, availability, and price of the insurance product are the work of underwriters and actuaries. Claims personnel play a vital role in establishing and maintaining the insurer's personality. Competitive efforts in the area of service derive in part from the skill and salesmanship of company engineers and auditors. Any lack of sales consciousness in these functional areas will inevitably affect the insurer's place in the market.

THE CHANGING MARKET

The market for property-liability insurance is changing in numerous ways. Some of these changes are discussed in this section.

More Knowledge

The increasing level of public knowledge of risk and insurance poses problems for insurers. Through articles in the press, the efforts of agents and companies, university courses in insurance, high-school units in insurance, and exposure to the insurance policies they are pressured to buy, the public is becoming increasingly sophisticated about insurance. Potential buyers are now better prepared to raise the question of how a particular contract fits into their total security picture. Buyers recognize the value of competent advice on insurance matters and expect this from sales representatives. They are better able to understand the rationale of price differentials between companies. The situation is even more pressing in the business insurance market because of the growing numbers of corporate risk managers.

Increasing Consciousness of Price

Price consciousness on the part of the insuring public is a vital factor in the insurance market. Many established insurers until recently considered the price of insurance relatively unimportant. High-quality service was considered sufficient to offset the low-price policies of the exclusive agency and direct-selling insurers. The failure of independent agency companies to grow as fast premium-wise as other types of companies and the rash of studies which confirmed public price consciousness finally prompted competitive pricing actions. When surveys showed that the public had no fear of low prices but rather attributed them to the economies of scale and superior management, the die was cast. This price consciousness demands that companies be competitive if they are to retain their share of the market. Rate differentials have narrowed as insurance executives have accepted this view.

Pressure for Service

The danger of basing company growth solely upon the quality of agents' services was suggested in the many conclusions of several postwar surveys of insurance buyers. As was already recognized by many company executives and agents, such studies showed that agents were not servicing their clients as frequently as sound standards of service demand. There were indications that policyholders were practically never contacted by telephone or by personal visits on the part of the agent. These studies helped persuade independent agents that increased sales and service activities were essential. Their response to this challenge gave renewed vigor to the independent agency system.

Built-in Growth

Much of the excitement about the future of the property insurance business lies in the growth which inevitably will occur. Population and gross national income are moving upward. Assets requiring protection will grow. Forecasts show rising levels of income available for discretionary spending, which is the portion of the family budget from which insurance premiums come. This increased capacity to buy, coupled with a growing understanding of the significance of and need for insurance, offer a market well worth the strongest competitive efforts of all types of insurers.

THE DISTRIBUTION OF PROPERTY-LIABILITY INSURANCE

The traditional approach to the sale of property-liability insurance has been through the personal sales efforts of agents, sales representatives, and brokers. There are two major systems of distribution, each with several modifications.

Agency System

One major system centers on agents. This system, itself, is divisible into two principal patterns.

One pattern, which has long been predominant in the United States, is known as the independent agency system or the "American agency system." The agent typically represents a number of insurers, writes his own policies, bills his policyholders, collects from them, and owns the renewal rights on the policies he has solicited and sold. This approach is used by most major stock insurers, but many mutuals employ the same method. Companies employing the independent agency system normally will also accept business from brokers. These representatives of insureds have no contractual tie with insurers but select the company based upon the particular needs of the client.

The second pattern—and the one which has provided the most substantial challenge to the established order—may properly be designated as the exclusive agency or sole representation system. The agent represents a single insurer and has no or very limited ownership rights in the policies he has put on the company's books. He generally receives a lower rate of commission than the independent agent (perhaps 8 to 10 percent versus 15 to 20 percent for the independent agent) in part because of the services the company provides for him, such as policy-writing, billing, and collecting. Because of the resulting lower acquisition cost, as well as because of generally more strict underwriting, the exclusive agency companies have until recently enjoyed a price advantage over the independents. This approach to insurance distribution is often called the direct writing or captive agency approach. In fact, it is neither. The company does not deal directly with the consumer but operates through agents who typically are not acquiescent enough to company desires to be called "captive."

The price advantage of the insurers using exclusive agencies has brought about serious efforts on the part of the independent agency companies to modify their methods of operation. The result has been a general lowering of their operating costs and of their rates. At the same time, many of the exclusive agency companies have faced pressures which have increased their costs. The overall result has been a narrowing of price differentials and a more competitive relationship among insurers using these two agency approaches.

Recent Changes in the Independent Agency Pattern. Recent adaptations include direct billing and collecting by the company rather than by the agent, policy-writing by the company, lower commissions for the agent, the requirement that the premium accompany the application, more select underwriting, and lower-cost insurance. Not all of these techniques need be found in a single insurer. Many independent agency companies have established separate companies to operate on this basis as management sought a product which would be more competitive with those of the exclusive agency companies. Substantial numbers of agents have resisted this trend. Reduced commission schedules squeeze their profit margins and they fear the eventual loss of ownership rights to their business. In spite of such resistance, many independent agency companies have reduced commission rates and have assumed many of the administrative details once performed by the agent.

The basic attribute of an independent agency system is the prohibition on the insurer from soliciting renewal of coverage from the agent's policyholders. There is no indication of a move from this fundamental concept of the agent's ownership of the business he produces in these modified agency systems. However, insurers are establishing closer ties with agents. Many offer the direct billing, collection, and policy-writing indicated above. Some provide advice on agency accounting and others will even perform this service. At least one company maintains a team of consultants to advise agents on sound agency management. Several sponsor cooperative advertising programs in which they share the cost of the agent's advertising. Some will finance new agents recruited into the independent agencies. Many offer substantial training courses in the home office and the field. Still others will assist in working out detailed programs for the perpetuation of agencies. (See Chapter 69.) The price asked of the agent by companies providing such support is an increased percentage of the agent's low-loss-ratio business. Many agents have responded by decreasing the number of companies represented. Where an agent (mainly, to get capacity) might once have represented 15 to 20 companies, many now prefer as few as three to six insurers. This trend is not without benefit to the agent, as he is thus freed from the considerable detail which grows out of contracts with many insurers.

Recent Changes in the Exclusive Agency Pattern. The exclusive agency companies have not remained static in their distribution techniques. Their agents long have viewed the apparently greener pastures of the independent agency system with its higher commission level. Although the companies have lost sales personnel for this reason, they still have maintained adequate numbers of agents to support substantial growth. Their appeal has been based on (1) the monetary value of the services they perform for the agent; (2) the greater ease of selling their policies because of price differentials; (3) liberal provision of sales-supporting services, such as advertising and sales promotion materials; and (4) close sales supervision to aid the agent in his production efforts. Recent efforts to reduce agent turnover include the provision of such fringe benefits as group insurance and, in at least one company, a payment to the agent for his business when he retires. This arrangement equates closely with the independent agent's opportunity to sell his agency at retirement for a figure such as one and one-half times his annual commission income. Efforts such as the above have produced rising acquisition costs for the exclusive agency companies—a trend that has helped reduce materially the price advantage of the exclusive agency companies.

Direct-Selling System

Direct selling is a system of distribution which does not use agents. Insurance is written directly by the insurer for the insured. Typical means for bringing about the company-customer relationship include mail-order selling; contacts made in locations such as department stores, airports, and filling stations; solicitation through newspaper advertisements; and sales through vending machines.

Direct selling does not preclude the use of sales personnel. Some companies handle customers' accounts directly but employ salaried sales representatives to solicit and service the business. These men are company employees and are generally paid on the basis of a salary plus bonus. They represent the single company and enjoy the same advantage indicated above for the exclusive agent. A further appeal to the salesmen of these companies is the opportunity they have to move into sales management.

Brokers

Insurance contracts are also effected through brokers who technically are agents of the insured. As brought out in Chapter 6, a producer who normally is an "agent" may for certain transactions be a "broker." Many individuals, particularly in large cities, operate strictly as brokers in handling large and complicated accounts. Many of the comments made in this chapter about agents apply also to brokers.

Combinations

A confusing note for the student of insurance marketing is that companies—or at least corporate groups—may use combinations of the above distribution techniques. One insurer, for example, may use the independent and direct-selling systems. Another may have within its corporate family independent and exclusive agency operations and also receive considerable business through brokers. This eclectic approach is not restricted to the insurance business. It represents a sound reaction to changing circumstances in the marketplace and often serves a useful purpose in improving the firm's competitive position.

PRODUCTS, PRICES, AND SERVICE

Products, pricing policy, and service are becoming increasingly significant in today's insurance market. Those insurers with the most substantial growth curves in recent years typically have been those which have made innovations in their product line, have offered the buyer below-average prices, and have rendered a wide range of services to their policyholders and sales personnel.

Product Development

Insurance people traditionally consider the insurance contract to be a legal document setting forth the obligations and privileges of the insured and insurer. Only recently has enough attention been given to the buyer and his attitudes to stimulate concern about the policy as a "product." The extent of this change in attitude is clearly evident in the developments indicated below.

Packaging. Numerous "package" contracts have been developed. They grew from simple combinations, such as an automobile contract embracing both liability and physical damage covers, to those covering practically all property and liability exposures of the business firm. These packages offer the buyer greater convenience, more nearly complete coverage, and reduced costs. The agent may gain through a greater average premium income per insured and from reduction in his paper work. The problems which seem to grow out of well-established packages include the tendency toward inadequate rates and the failure to relate the contract to the specific needs of the insured. Efforts to package the automobile and homeowners contracts have been made. Thought is even being given to packaging life, health, property, and liability insurance in a single contract.

Packaging eventually might alter distribution techniques. Properly designed packages might reduce or eliminate the need for highly trained technicians who can visualize and solve all the needs of the buyer. Sales made with package contracts might require less sales effort than survey selling. Another effect might be a reduced number of insurers as the insured is tied to one insurer for the major part of his insurance.

Design. Modern merchandising places considerable emphasis on product design to attract consumer interest. Both the product and its package are created with this objective in mind. To the extent that proper design simplifies the sales process, the increased design cost may be more than offset by reduced selling costs. This approach has been ignored rather generally in the insurance field, although increasing concern is being shown for simplification of contract terms and improvement of the policy format. Steps have been taken in the direction of reducing the length of contracts, and many insurers have increased the attractiveness of their forms, even including illustrations.

Opposition to contract simplification is based largely on the fear of legal problems. However, concerted action within the insurance business could do much to change laws which interfere with the evolution of policies. What is often ignored is the effect of poorly constructed and poorly written contracts on buyers' attitudes toward insurance. An increasingly sophisticated insurance-buying public may eventually *demand* contracts which are readily understandable, easy to handle, and attractive to view.

Other Developments. Product development has manifested itself in ways other than contract simplification. One example is the use of continuous contracts, which were created to reduce policy handling costs. Another example is contracts which will embrace all family needs in one package which automatically adjusts to the changing needs of the family.

Competitive Pricing

Not enough theoretical work has been done in the area of insurance pricing. More study in this area is imperative. Competitive pricing is a fundamental fact in the economics of the insurance business where rates are not based simply on losses and expenses. Many policy decisions, such as the competitive situation for a given line and the need to build volume, must enter into the calculation.

Competitive pricing is possible because of (1) selective underwriting, (2) reduced acquisition cost, (3) reduced administrative cost, and (4) rating procedures which give the insured the lowest possible rate consistent with experience.

Selective Underwriting. This device has been a major factor in the growth of the exclusive agency and direct-selling companies. The independent agency companies have sought to do the same, but they have less effective control over their agents and often must accept some poor business to get good business. Furthermore, highly selective underwriting poses a serious problem for the business as a whole. If applicants for insurance cannot find an insurer willing to write the line requested, pressures gradually develop for state action to eliminate the problem.

Voluntary assigned risk plans offer a solution, but continued highly selective underwriting may place these plans in jeopardy.

Other problems of selective underwriting include (1) the development of rating classifications which permit proper evaluation of the exposure's loss potential, (2) the long-run impact on the insurance market of youthful drivers, and (3) the availability of adequate information for the underwriter seeking to make a decision.

Rating Techniques. Underwriters seeking to gain or retain a favorable piece of business being bid upon by another insurer have many means by which they can develop the lowest possible rate for the exposure. A wide range of discounts, experience ratings, cost-plus approaches, expanded rating classifications, and special filings are all available to the knowledgeable underwriter.

Competition in pricing has been further encouraged by the use of dividends and deviations. These are not rating methods but are ways of passing cost savings to the insured. From the standpoint of serving the marketing function, there are diverse opinions concerning the advantages of each approach. Many favor the dividend approach on the theory that payment of the dividend at the end of the policy year promotes a high renewal rate. Also, agents prefer the initial high rate because the commission percentage yields a higher return. Deviations give insureds lower initial costs and result in lower handling costs for the insurance company.

Acquisition and Administrative Costs. Reductions in acquisition costs have been achieved largely at the expense of the agent and his commission scale. Although differences in commission rates continue to exist among companies within a given distribution system and between distribution systems, these differences have declined. Many independent agency companies have reduced commission scales. It appears that retention of the ownership of renewal rights is of greater importance to many agents than is any specific commission rate. Also, many agents recognize not only the need for a more competitively priced product but also that reduced commissions are a means to that end.

The reduction of administrative expenses has been a constant goal of many insurers in recent years. Its contribution to lower insurance rates is clear, but the consensus seems to be that the margins for substantial saving in the future are so slight that only near-negligible gains from this source are likely in the future.

Service Facilities

The insurance business is generally classified as one involving monopolistic competition. There are many competitors, each charging about the same rate, so customers must be attracted largely through product differentiation, which means either a superior product or superior service.

Much of today's competition takes place in the realm of services, various types of which are discussed below.

Installment payment plans represent an increasingly popular approach to policyholder service. Early concern over costs of administering such plans, increased opportunities to lapse, and the liability of the insurer in case the insured failed to pay an installment has disappeared almost entirely.

Certain insurers historically have relied on engineering and medical services as a means to establish their corporate personality. Loss ratios also have improved as a result of these efforts. The cost of such programs has been a limiting factor for small insurers, but increasingly even these insurers are providing such services. Efforts by workmen's compensation insurers to assist in the rehabilitation of injured workers have become more evident; in time this interest may be applied to victims of automobile and other nonindustrial accidents.

Although the auditing of business insurance accounts hardly seems a part of the marketing picture, the auditor can have a substantial effect on the insurer's relationship to its client. His attitude while on the insured's premises, his efficiency, his knowledge about the premium base for the contract being audited, and his general reflection of his company's integrity are examples in point.

The loss adjustment policy of an insurer and procedures for claims administration have an impact on the insurer's place in the market. Dissatisfied claimants are poor advertisements for a company. Several trends in claims procedures have grown from insurers' desires to serve their clienteles better. Drive-in claims service gives insureds an opportunity for quick and convenient settlement of automobile physical damage claims. Material damage estimators are being employed by many insurers to save the insured the inconvenience of seeking competitive bids. Decentralization of the claims function has produced better service for clients and lower cost operations for many companies.

The underwriter's role in competitive pricing has been discussed. Underwriting attitudes within an insurance organization also are a significant part of the service picture. Positive underwriting embodying definite plans for improving the character of the exposure broadens the market. Special risks departments and a willingness to accept extraordinary exposures have helped create a favorable public image for several firms. Insurers adopting substandard underwriting procedures have provided a needed service and have profited by so doing. The growing interest of many agents in account selling has prompted at least a few insurers to establish account underwriting procedures. If the bulk of the insurance needed by a prospective insured is submitted as a unit by the agent, the exposure will be reviewed as a unit, and the profit potential of the entire package will be evaluated. The problem of training underwriters for this approach is sizeable, but the rewards make the effort worthwhile.

THE AGENT AND BROKER IN INSURANCE MARKETING

Most property and liability insurance contracts are sold by the efforts of individuals in direct contact with the prospect. Concern for the cost of this approach has led various insurers to consider substitute distribution channels. The results invariably show that there is no effective substitute for personal sales and service efforts. The mail-order and vending-machine approaches have been successful when used with certain cohesive groups and for selling particular forms of cover, but their validity for the mass market has yet to be proved. The group insurance concept as utilized in life insurance has been considered by property insurers, but rating laws have hampered such moves.

The person selling and servicing insurance faces many choices. Should he represent a single insurer or many? Should he specialize in certain lines of insurance or seek to handle all property and liability insurance matters for his clients? Should he encompass life and health insurance sales and service in his activities? Should he strive for the standing of a professional in the business? Should he operate as an individual or seek to become part of an insurance firm?

Single- versus Multiple-Company Representation

Adherents of the independent agency system readily admit their disadvantage in the marketplace because of lack of effective control by insurers over their agency force. The agent represents several companies and is thus not bound by the desires or dictates of any one of them. In spite of this, the system of multiple-company representation offers advantages for the company as well as for the agent. The commission cost is the major cost facing the insurer as agents perform most duties associated with insurance sales and service work themselves. Administration of an exclusive agency system generally produces lower commission costs but considerably higher acquisition costs of other types. The advantages of multiple-company representation to the agent include (1) his ability to place a client's insurance in the company best geared to the buyer's needs; (2) his ability to place a degree of pressure on the insurer; (3) his capacity to handle large-sized risks; and (4) his degree of independence from company control. On the other hand, proponents of the sole representation system point to the value to the agent or sales representative of the sales help the company provides through training, sales promotion assistance, and advertising. However, the advantage of exclusive agency companies on this point is diminishing as independent agency companies provide their agents similar benefits.

As indicated earlier, agents representing several companies are tending to establish relatively close ties with certain of their insurers. Many feel that the inevitable result of this will be that in time each personal lines agent will represent a single company. They point to the success of this system in the life insurance business. The answer may lie in the contribution of the independent agency system, with the agent owning renewal rights but with only a few companies in his office. If this path is followed, the impact on companies will be marked. Each insurer will have to recruit aggressively to maintain its full complement of agents. Company mergers may continue to take place.

Specialization or Account Selling

The move of property insurers during the 1940's to multiple line underwriting has been followed by a trend among agents toward account selling. The costs of contacting and selling a client a single line of insurance have been recognized. It is substantially more economical to sell and service the full range of the buyer's insurance needs when a call is made. The commission from selling several lines supports the service activities necessary for account selling. Fewer calls are necessary to achieve a given level of income as the average commission per contact is increased. Clients served on this basis are insulated in large measure from competitors. The buyer also gains in that he is given an opportunity to review at one time and with one person his total property and liability insurance needs.

Officials of both independent and exclusive agency companies have had difficulty in convincing agents of the validity of account selling. In spite of the pressures the latter type of insurer can bring on sales personnel, specialization is still the predominant approach. The answer may be that established agents will continue in their accustomed mold, while the younger generation will turn primarily to account selling. It appears to be the economic approach to agency operations. A further point is that development of package programs has changed the account-selling practices and opportunities. If the package covers the total property-liability insurance needs of the insured, account selling has taken place in a specialized sale. Perhaps it is through this approach that account selling will become the prevailing pattern for agency sales and service efforts.

A corollary to account selling is the question of whether the property insurance agent should also sell life and health insurance. It is claimed that the contacts of property agents with their clients are of such a nature that the sale of life and health insurance would be almost routine if a need exists. The advantages claimed for account selling might be even more applicable if the account included life and health protection.

Another corollary to account selling relates to the agent's attitude with respect to the level of knowledge he wishes to attain in the insurance business. Fully qualified technicians can be found among those who sell single covers and packages, as well as among those who sell on the account basis. However, observation of the total agency operation suggests that most highly trained agents employ the latter approach. The growing public knowledge of insurance and its role in the financial life of the family and business firm suggest that agents will have to be increasingly well educated on all aspects of insurance in the future. Pressure in this direction already is being exerted by a number of state regulatory authorities through licensing requirements. The desire for insurance knowledge also is leading many agents to efforts to achieve the professional stature embodied in the Chartered Property and Casualty Underwriter designation offered by the American Institute for Property and Liability Underwriters, Inc.

Agency Administration

Declining commission rates have forced independent agents to operate their agencies efficiently. This growing sophistication in agency management plays an important role in insurance marketing. The ability of the independent agent to respond to the competition of exclusive agents and direct writers depends in large part upon his ability to function profitably. Many independent agents have not been successful in this regard—they have either left the business or have merged with other agents. Recent merger activity has resulted in larger-sized agencies and has generally reflected the survival of the fittest.

The application of sound management principles to agency operation has made such organizations more aggressive and competent in the marketplace. Effective planning and office management have freed the agent for increased sales and service activity. Efforts to establish a personality for the agency in the eyes of the public have paid off in increased sales. Advertising programs have produced new business. The application of sound collection procedures has strengthened the financial position of many independent agents. Concern for perpetuating agencies has brought new manpower into the independent agency system.

Agents operating under the exclusive agency system and sales representatives of direct writers similarly must apply sound management principles to their own operations. Their problem is a bit less pressing as the company provides so many of the services the independent agent must establish himself. One of the great competitive advantages of the exclusive agents has been their freedom from the detailed office work which has kept the independent agent from spending more time in sales activities. (See Chapter 69 for more treatment of agency management.)

COMPANY ORGANIZATION FOR SALES

The sales or agency department in many insurers is being assigned increasing responsibilities and is being broadened to embrace a growing spectrum of marketing activities. One approach has been to assign all activities related to the sale of insurance service (such as advertising, sales promotion, product development, and market research) to one section of the marketing department, with the administration of the agency plant assigned to another section. Using another approach, other companies have established line and staff organizations in which branch managers have complete responsibility for the production of a satisfactory volume of profitable business in their territories. These managers thus have ultimate responsibility in their territories for sales, underwriting, claims, and engineering efforts. Management thinking is increasingly being directed to studies as to how the organization of the company can most effectively serve the persons responsible for sales.

In addition to organizational questions, top management is faced with decisions on a number of questions pertaining to the marketing function. Some of these are reviewed below.

Creation of Adequate Capacity

It is generally conceded that growth in sales is a function of the size of the sales force. Acceptance of this concept has been a vital factor in the sales planning of many property insurers. Officials in many exclusive agency and direct-selling companies are seeking greatly expanded numbers of agents and other sales representatives. Officials in many independent agency companies are trying to persuade their agents to bring new people into their agencies and are recruiting, selecting, training, and compensating new agents in efforts to bolster their sales organizations.

Another approach to the problem of capacity for increased sales has been the creation of insurance groups. The combination of several companies into a group provides the agent a full range of insurance contracts through the single organization. Internal economies are also available as the management of all companies in the group can be unified.

Affiliations have appeared in growing numbers both among property-liability insurers and between them and life insurance companies. Combinations within the property insurance business have been motivated largely by a desire for economies of scale and for access to new markets. Combinations of life and property insurers have spread rapidly and have been created to provide full-line facilities to agents interested in all-lines selling. They have also provided an attractive form of diversification for property-liability insurers concerned with continuing underwriting losses.

Sales Management

The sales management responsibilities of recruiting, selecting, training, and supervising a sales force present real problems to independent agency companies. Traditional ties with their agency force have precluded vigorous efforts to perform sales management functions. Many agents have resented interference. As indicated earlier, this attitude on the part of agents and company sales officers has been changing. Many agents are showing increasing willingness to work with companies and to accept help in the sales management area.

The independent agency company has maintained contact with its sales force through special agents or fieldmen who are assigned the responsibility for developing a prescribed territory. Their function is to serve the agent by interpreting company policy, assisting in administrative details, instructing on technical insurance problems, participating on joint sales calls, and persuading the agent of the merits of the company. The fieldman's work is directed either from the home office agency department or from a branch office. A "state agent" may be his first-line supervisor. The state agent, despite his label, normally is an employee of the insurer and is in charge of the branch office. In territories where population is widely scattered or where the insurer has too small a volume of production to support a fieldman, a general agent may be appointed. General agents are sometimes known as "managing general agents." Such an agent agrees to develop the insurer's business in his operating territory for a commission scale approximately 5 to 10 percentage points higher than is paid the local agent. This service includes appointing agents, supervising their work through his own field force, underwriting the business submitted, and settling claims within the limit of authority given him. The general agency system has been an important factor in the growth of many insurers, but the branch office approach has been gaining at the expense of general agents. The branch office performs about the same functions, but the manager works on a salary and calls upon the company for the type of services the general agent provides himself. When the volume of business available in a geographic area reaches a given point, processing of business may become less expensive and the company may have greater control over it by using a branch office as opposed to a general agency.

Sales management activities among exclusive agency companies and those employing sales representatives are virtually the same as those found in the typical business firm. A home office sales department selects regional and district sales managers who use established procedures for recruiting, selecting, training, and supervising their sales forces. By virtue of the control such insurers have over the sales personnel, they are able to impose relatively strict procedures for the performance of each of these sales management functions. It is this advantage which is eyed so longingly by many sales executives among the independent agency companies.

Sales-Support Efforts

In both the independent and exclusive agency companies increasing attention is being given to means by which the company can support more effectively the selling efforts of agents. Both types of organizations are employing consumer advertising in magazines, newspapers, and radio-television to sell the company image and the services of its agents. Sales promotion materials, such as point-of-sale literature, direct mail pieces, and display materials are being prepared in abundance. Sales interviews are being supplemented by visual aids tied to the sales presentation. Training programs in the field and at the home office are being oriented to both product knowledge and sales techniques. Policyholder relations programs have been instituted to strengthen ties between the company and consumer.

CONTINUING PROBLEMS

As might be expected in any period of intense competition, insurers face a wide variety of different questions relating to the marketing function. Space limitations prevent any detailed analysis, but policy decisions on each of the points indicated below should be made. How far can the independent agency company go in assisting the agent in his work without incurring his displeasure and losing his support? Should the company move toward expanding its product lines or remain a specialist in certain lines? To what extent are certain natural markets open to the firm into which expansion might be accomplished at reasonable cost? Should administration be centralized at the home office or are sales, service, and cost-saving opportunities available through decentralization? To what extent would the application of sales incentive programs for both the sales force and sales managers yield an increased volume of profitable business? Should research activities in the organization be centralized in one department or centered in each of the major functional areas of the firm? Are all avenues for cost control known to management, and have all been explored to determine their potential for gain to the firm? Have adequate management development programs been introduced to assure a continuing flow of trained people to executive positions? Do the home office recruiting policies give ample attention to the need for intelligent and creative people? Is the impact of every change of company policy on the policyholder, employee, agent, stockholder, and community taken into account before moves are made? Are appropriate steps being taken to reduce the prospects of further governmental controls and intervention into areas private insurers can handle effectively and economically?

This partial listing of company problems which are oriented to the marketing scene suggests the burden placed on insurance company management. Survival demands continuous appraisal of the direction in which insurance marketing is moving. The encouraging discovery to the person observing the property and liability insurance business is that executives of the calibre needed to meet these challenges are appearing in increasing numbers. Agency forces are being upgraded. Every sign points to a higher level of service for the insurance buyer and for an expanding and more meaningful position for insurance companies in the total economy.

SUGGESTED READINGS

Denenberg, Herbert S., *et al.* *Risk and Insurance.* Englewood Cliffs, N.J.: Prentice-Hall, Inc., 1964. Chap. 29.

Greene, Mark R. *Risk and Insurance.* Cincinnati: South-Western Publishing Co., 1962. Chap. 5.

McGill, Dan M. (ed.). *All Lines Insurance.* Homewood, Ill.: Richard D. Irwin, Inc., 1960. Chap. viii. "Impact of All Lines Insurance on Marketing," by Kenneth O. Force.

Snider, H. Wayne (ed.). *Readings in Property and Casualty Insurance.* Homewood, Ill.: Richard D. Irwin, Inc., 1959. Chap. 15. "Marketing Revolution," by Thomas C. Morrill.

Chapter 63

REINSURANCE

BY ROBERT L. BRADDOCK

Reinsurance is the assumption by one insurance company of all or a part of a risk undertaken originally by another insurance company. The company buying the reinsurance is called the ceding company or the reinsured; the one selling it is the reinsurer. The ceding company buys reinsurance to reduce liability, to provide financial support to the primary company, or to gain underwriting capacity. Therefore, reinsurance is both (1) insurance and (2) a management device vital to the effective operation of the primary insurance industry.

An Example

Reinsurance can be illustrated most effectively by considering the role it fulfills for a newly formed insurance company. Organizers of an insurance company must figure out how the company can best achieve the purpose for which it is to be created. Suppose that a company is organized and that its principal purpose is to write automobile insurance in a broad sense. It is unlikely at the outset that the company could handle all classes of automobile business. Specific classes of risk and territories would be selected, maximum policy limits would be established, and projections of premium volume would be made. These decisions and this projection would be influenced by the company's financial structure. Rating plans would then be adopted and the method of producing business determined. The sum of the decisions would become the foundation of the underwriting program and would reflect the company's purpose. After the underwriting program was established, a plan of reinsurance would have to be developed to enable the company to accomplish its objectives. This reinsurance would limit the per risk exposure to a level retention. (By "retention" is meant the amount of coverage retained by the reinsured for its own account.) Reinsurance permits the company to handle gross writings (total business after returns and adjustments but before deductions for commissions, taxes, and reinsurance) which otherwise would be out of line with its financial structure. Reinsurance provides a safety valve to the underwriting program for risks which by their class or exposure the company could not otherwise underwrite.

Functions

There are two prime functions of reinsurance; one is financial and the other is technical. There are many variations and combinations of coverages applied to meet individual situations, but basically they serve either to lend financial strength (the financial function) or to accomplish spread of loss (the technical function).

In performing the financial function the reinsurer assumes a part of the reinsured's responsibility to maintain the statutory premium and loss reserves. (See Chapters 60 and 61 for discussion of unearned premium reserves and loss reserves.) Increasing premium income depletes an insurance company's surplus. This surplus can be restored by passing over the unexpired liabilities to a reinsurer in return for a ceding commission sufficient to recapture the prepaid expense. Thus, provided the business is profitable, this reinsurance procedure enables the company to continue normal activity. Some people consider that all treaty reinsurance (see below) in the area of normal experience (that business producing an expected loss pattern) is serving the financial function. This conclusion—perhaps a bit overdrawn—is reached because over a limited rating period, often three years but rarely more than five years, the premium paid by the reinsured must absorb the loss experience, pay the expenses incurred by the transaction, and provide a profit to the reinsurers.

The "pure" technical function is performed only by facultative reinsurance and by treaty reinsurance which covers the area of exceptional or catastrophic loss. Losses recovered under these programs are truly absorbed by the reinsurer who spreads the cost over his entire portfolio.

TYPES AND USES OF REINSURANCE

Reinsurance generally falls into two general classes: treaty and facultative.

Treaty Reinsurance

In treaty reinsurance the reinsured and the reinsurer agree that the former will cede and the latter accept liability on a block of future exposures according to a pattern set forth in the contract. Broadly speaking, there are three types of treaty reinsurance, each widely used and each fulfilling a specific need of the reinsured. They are: (1) quota share, (2) surplus share, and (3) excess of loss. On some occasions two of the three are applied together within the same pattern of cession.

The underwriting of treaty reinsurance involves a fundamental departure from the practices familiar to primary insurance. This departure lies in the procedure by which the company undertakes the assumption of risk. Acceptance of liability by the primary company follows detailed study of each risk. Evaluation of this detail leads to the decision of whether or not to underwrite and the rate to be charged in case the decision is positive. The treaty reinsurer, on the other hand, knows nothing about the individual risk and relies almost entirely on assessment of the primary company's management and judgment of its underwriting program. Once a reinsurance treaty is accepted, the reinsurer blindly follows the fortunes of the reinsured under a procedure of summary accounting. Almost every insurance company buys treaty reinsurance.

No such program can correct bad selection of risk, inadequate rate structure, or poor management. At best, the solution of these problems can only be postponed by reinsurance. Aside from basic uses discussed above, reinsurance can only enforce management decisions, as for example, excluding coverage on a type of risk or providing a specific method under which a class may be covered by the reinsurer. It is well to remember reinsurance is neither a mystery nor a cure-all.

Quota Share. Quota share and surplus reinsurance are almost as old as insurance. Both involve the pro rata sharing of premium and loss. In quota share the reinsurer agrees to accept a fixed percentage of the gross writings of the reinsured for which the reinsurer allows a ceding commission to cover prepaid expenses and hopefully a profit to the reinsured. For example, the reinsurer may agree to accept one third of the insurance in each policy of a given type. The reinsurer then relieves the reinsured of this proportion of the unearned premium reserve and loss reserves, and the two parties participate according to their respective proportion in future losses and loss expense. Sometimes this type of reinsurance is also arranged to apply to the net account remaining after application of either a surplus share or excess of loss reinsurance contract (see following paragraphs for discussion of these terms). If the reinsurer is approved by the jurisdiction in which the reinsured is operating, the reinsurance is termed "admitted" and full credit is taken in the financial statement of the reinsured. (See Chapter 61.) Quota share is basically use of the capital structure of the reinsurer; it may or may not have an element of risk to the reinsurer.

Surplus Share. This type of reinsurance differs from quota share only in its function, not in its operation. Instead of ceding a percentage of gross premiums as in quota share the reinsured establishes a pro rata retention or "line" on the individual risk and then cedes a fraction or a multiple of that line. For example, for business of a given type the primary insurer may keep the first $10,000 per risk plus one third of each additional $10,000 (or fraction thereof), the other two thirds being ceded. In some cases a minimum net line figure is inserted to prevent adverse selection to the treaty. Once reinsurance is ceded, the reinsured and the reinsurer participate on each risk according to their respective established percentages in all losses and loss expense from the ground up. Usually there is a limit as to the number of lines which may be ceded. Often there is more than one surplus treaty and in such cases the treaty receiving the cessions immediately after the retention is known as the "first surplus." As additional surplus treaties are arranged, they become known as the "second surplus" and "third surplus," and so on. These additional treaties are generally arranged to handle peak risk exposures with use restricted to situations where a portion or all of the capacity of the first surplus has been exhausted. The great advantage of surplus share is that it enables the company to maintain the sharing principle of reinsurance without the necessity of reinsuring small risks on which reinsurance is not required. Its fundamental disadvantages lie in the fact that it (1) is the most complicated in application, (2) requires extensive detail work on the part of the reinsured, (3) is subject to errors both of judgment and oversight, and (4) provides a false crutch for some underwriters who either fear or lack knowledge to face the responsibilities of their job.

In fire and allied lines where insurance protects against the physical loss of the property insured, pro rata (surplus and quota share) has been the traditional method used. It has also been the traditional method in reinsuring contract bonds. However, it can be and is applied to any line. This approach is common where any loss is likely to be total and where in addition the reinsured needs the financial resources of the reinsurer for underwriting capacity or support. There are many possible applications of the share method to balance a reinsurance program, provide capacity, or lessen the impact of a new or expanding portfolio.

Excess of Loss. In "excess of loss" reinsurance the reinsured bears on his own account all loss up to the retention agreed upon; the reinsurer assumes all loss above the retention. Some contracts protect on a per risk basis and some on risks involved in a single event. There has also been use of this type of reinsurance to limit aggregate loss in any one year. This type of coverage enables the reinsured to confine fluctuations in loss ratio to a low or so-called "working level" of his portfolio where it is more likely to be stable. Obviously the shock of the catastrophic event is eliminated.

No problem in using excess of loss reinsurance is more difficult to solve on a rational basis than fixing the retention. Ideally, no retention selected should be subject to frequent penetration. The reason is that, at the working level of cover, trading dollars with a reinsurer who will load them for expenses and profit is too costly. If it is necessary because of the financial structure of the reinsured to require the reinsurer's participation in working level losses, excess of loss reinsurance is not the type of reinsurance needed. Plotting losses by number and size for three to five years on a graph will clearly show where the retention should be pitched. It will be that point where the frequency drop is sharp. When factors other than the "loss curve" must enter the decision (for instance, where the indicated retention is too high for the financial structure), the retention should be set at the highest possible point where the cutoff has a reasonable effect on the overall net loss ratio. If there is no such point, excess of loss should not be used.

Most liability reinsurance is written on excess of loss. Increasingly, the method is being adapted to fire and allied lines in those cases where financial support is not needed. There is also application in fidelity, aviation, health, marine, inland marine, burglary, boiler and machinery, and fire catastrophe covers. The essential difference in excess of loss over pro rata reinsurance (quota share or surplus share) is the fact that little or no financial support is given the reinsured and no additional underwriting capacity is provided. The reinsured must become a gross line underwriter whereas share reinsurance fosters net line underwriting.[1] Excess of loss reinsurance does not fit all situations and its application to all or part of the reinsured's portfolio requires intimate knowledge of management, objectives, financial structure, and record of the ceding company.

Use of the excess of loss method of reinsurance in many lines, notably fire and allied, provides a necessary place in a reinsurance program for surplus reinsurance. Often excess of loss reinsurance (where limits per risk are high and possibilities of total loss exist) is applied to the working level[2] only and surplus reinsurance attaches after the excess is exhausted. As is true in any case, the size of the retention and of the excess is arbitrary. This device has the advantage of permitting the reinsured and the reinsurer to share in the premium above the working level of loss—an advantage to both, for any excess premium in that level would require a rate closely approaching the primary premium collected and would not provide the benefits of pro rata reinsurance.

Handling Reinsurance on Package Policies. The dream of simplified procedures to cover a number of hazards, some unrelated to each other, led to the development of package policies. This development brought about many complications, not the least of which was reinsurance of the package. Traditionally, the primary company reinsured its property lines on a surplus basis and liability lines on an excess of loss basis. A choice as to reinsurance method had to be made by the primary company, particularly after the single or indivisible premium (see Chapter 51) became the normal pricing method. The total liability of the package policy was beyond the capacity of most primary companies and beyond what many

[1] In "net line" underwriting the underwriter attempts, by passing off portions of an undesirable risk to a reinsurer, to make the smaller retained portion more palatable. In "gross line" underwriting the underwriter looks only at the characteristics of the risk and ignores the fact of reinsurance in his commitment. His retention will be the same on the best and worst risks. The concepts are radically different.

[2] The area of cover immediately above the retention which is expected to be penetrated frequently and on which there is normally a regular pattern of loss.

large companies wished to assume net. As a result, the use of excess of loss on a per risk basis has become the normal way to reinsure and has pushed many companies to that method in property lines much earlier than would have been otherwise possible.

Facultative Reinsurance

Facultative reinsurance is a transaction involving a specific risk or a well defined group of risks and its underwriting is similar to that done in primary insurance. On occasions a reinsurer will issue a contract at predetermined rates with complete option on the part of the reinsured to declare individual risks as subject to its terms. This type of agreement is called an "optional facultative treaty"—a misnomer and, unless great care is exercised, an undertaking dangerous to both parties. Facultative reinsurance can be undertaken under all patterns used in treaty reinsurance. There is an extremely broad and flexible worldwide market in all lines for facultative and its proper use is essential in the operation of most primary companies.

Reinsurance through Pools

The pool concept for reinsurance is a natural outgrowth of share coverage. The theory that many underwriting units can combine to cover exposures too large for any one of them is sound. This soundness of the pools has been successfully demonstrated by their use in handling tremendous exposures in the oil industry, trunk airlines, the railroads, and other industries where huge exposures to loss are concentrated. An excellent illustration of pools is found in the solution to the insurance problem arising out of commercial uses of atomic energy. (See Chapter 64.) Here limits required are so high, the hazards are so poorly defined, and experience is so totally lacking of credibility that the pool concept is a practical method of marshalling capacity.

Most successful pools in the primary business are run by professional and competent staffs and relate to types of business which members of the pool do not write except through their participation in the pool. The results of their participation in the pool are isolated and do not influence the results of their regular business. When the pool principle is applied to reinsurance, however, the situation changes because the two classes of results are not kept separated. Factors inconsistent with the concept of pooling must be considered. While there is still no doubt that risk can be reduced, any loss suffered by the pool will probably affect the net business of the members. There is a strong argument—which the author generally endorses—that such an arrangement usually is not reinsurance. The argument goes (1) that reinsurance is basically more volatile than primary insurance; (2) that catastrophic events fall unevenly; and (3) that, if every pool member feels the effect of every catastrophe through both his net account and the pool participation, such system of distributing losses is not reinsurance. Most pools eventually break down because some members feel other members are not sufficiently skilled in risk selection and thereby contribute disproportionately to pool losses. Ideally, a reinsurance pool has its best chance of success if none of its members underwrites the lines of business reinsured by the pool.

THE REINSURANCE CONTRACT

The reinsurance contract has traditionally been considered to be a gentlemen's agreement undertaken by a literate seller and a literate buyer. In this climate extensive detail of contract provision and protective language is not required. Certain broad provisions set forth the intention of the parties—in most instances in uncomplicated and simple language.

Modern types of reinsurance treaties covering several classes of business eliminate duplication of language by using a two-part approach. The first part or main body of the agreement contains clauses of general application; the second part contains an exhibit for each class of business ceded along with terms and rating procedure applicable thereto. The main body includes several broad provisions describing arbitration procedures, claims handling, cancellation provisions, and rights in case of insolvency.

The arbitration clause provides for compulsory arbitration of disputes between reinsurer and reinsured. The usual provision is that each party name an arbitrator and the two selected choose a third. Both parties agree to be bound by the decision of the arbitrators.

The contract normally provides that the reinsurer is to be informed of all claims promptly and completely. In the event of litigation he may, at his own expense, employ counsel and participate in the case. This option is rarely exercised. Usually the reinsured controls the litigation and retains counsel. The reinsurer usually participates in allocated loss expense (generally that incurred to "outside" lawyers and adjusters) as their respective interests in the claim ultimately develop. Unallocated loss expense (generally that of the reinsured's own employees) is normally not reimbursed by the reinsurer but is a factor in the rate charged or commission allowed in the same way as other overhead items of the reinsured.

While there are exceptions, most reinsurance contracts permit cancellation by either party as to new business ceded, subject to a specified period of notice—from 30 days to one year. Normally, business ceded prior to the effective date of cancellation continues to be reinsured until expiration of the direct policies unless both parties agree to a "cutoff" cancellation discontinuing the reinsurance as to losses occurring after the cancellation date or some subsequent date. A "cutoff" cancellation generally provides for return of the unearned premium portfolio by the reinsurer; a "runoff" cancellation does not.

All states either by statute or by administrative practice provide that no statement credit (see Chapter 61 for discussion of the Annual Statement) be given to a ceding company licensed in such state for unearned premiums or outstanding losses reinsured unless the contract carries an "insolvency clause." This clause provides that the reinsurance is payable by the reinsurer on the basis of the liability of the ceding company under the direct contract without diminution because of the insolvency of the ceding company. It is an accepted principle that, in absence of specific language to the contrary, a claimant under the direct policy is not a party or privy to the reinsurance contract and has no right of direct action against the reinsurer. In the event of insolvency, the undiminished claim payments to the receiver become part of the general assets of the insolvent company and are applied for the benefit of all creditors and not to payment of the specific claims which gave rise to the reinsurance recovery.

The fundamental underlying philosophy, whether stated in the treaty or left unstated, in all reinsurance transactions is that the reinsurer follows the reinsured as to the latter's fortunes in handling claims or coverage disputes on such direct contracts as are covered by the treaty.

RATEMAKING[3]

In determining the price or rate for a reinsurance treaty or transaction the reinsurer is free of all control other than that produced by competition. A specific price is negotiated for each contract and ratemaking procedures are not comparable to those used in the primary field.

Rates of Quota Share and Surplus Share

Quota share and surplus share contracts follow the rates used on the primary business, but the net cost of the business to the reinsurer is controlled by the commission arrangements, which vary greatly. A fixed commission, often with a contingent, is the simplest arrangement but it requires the most precise judgment. Partly to overcome this difficulty, partly to eliminate frequent negotiations of change in commission terms, and partly to reduce the influence of competitive bids, commission scales are frequently used instead of a flat commission. This practice is particularly common in fire and allied lines. In essence the commission scale plan is one whereby a provisional commission is allowed on premium as ceded and this figure is adjusted on the earned premium of each year. The final commission payable for the year on premium earned is determined within a maximum and minimum by the ratio for the year of incurred loss to earned premium. The wider the range the less risk there is to the

[3] This term is used here out of deference to the editors and for the sake of consistency with the remainder of the *Handbook*. Since pricing methods in reinsurance are so diverse, "unscientific," and even at times intuitive, "rating" is a better word.

reinsurer provided the middle of the scale is set near the expected loss ratio. The National Association of Insurance Commissioners has adopted guide rules on examination which permit credit being allowed in the reinsured's statement on account of commission received on unearned premium for five points more than the minimum commission in the scale. The guide rule is not universally applied and many companies take expense credit for the entire provisional commission which is normally pitched midway in the range.

Rates for Excess of Loss and Catastrophe

Rating of excess of loss and catastrophe covers[4] presents an involved problem to the reinsurer. No book of excess can be considered as balanced unless the premium it generates is sufficient to cover at least two maximum losses in a calendar year. Since few individual risks can generate that premium volume standing alone, they are basically unbalanced accounts. There are a number of ways the reinsurer can improve the position. The use of excess of loss reinsurance can be confined to a relatively narrow layer above the retention and this excess can be self-rating over a selected number of years. A surplus treaty can then be used for larger risks. Sometimes this arrangement is accompanied by a second excess[5] the rating for which is based on the reinsurer's total "book" or on industry average losses in the level reinsured. No matter what method is used to obtain balance, unless the book is broad, the writing of excess can be extremely hazardous. Since large losses can fall indiscriminately, any reinsurer which has relatively few excess of loss accounts, each one of which can produce a large claim, is indulging in plain gambling. The primary carrier has the law of large numbers as protection against severe fluctuations in his loss ratio beneath his retention. The reinsurer, on the other hand, is exposed for 20, 30, or 40 times the retained net loss with a fraction of the primary premium. It is important that the excess rate be a highly educated determination and that no more "guess" than necessary be in the end product. Complete reliance upon experience rating is doomed to failure.

The rating technique for excess of loss reinsurance involves selection of factors and their evaluation. Important factors are class, exposure, administration, volume, risk experience, industry experience, inflation, expected incidence of loss, maximum probable or possible loss, limit of

---

[4] A "catastrophe cover" is that area between the top of the automatic treaty reinsurance and whatever limit the reinsured feels necessary to buy to protect itself against an unusual incidence of small losses. For example, a company might hold $10,000 per risk and an east coast hurricane might produce 20,000 individual losses of, say, about $200 each. The sheer number of such losses would produce an aggregate loss far higher than the company would want to absorb.

[5] An excess above an excess.

liability provided, and contingency. A discussion of two of these factors, risk experience and inflation, may help readers visualize how such factors enter into rate determination. In considering risk experience the reinsurer must recognize that the average length of time before an excess liability loss is reported to the reinsurer is nearly one year from the occurrence of the loss. Even then the reserve of the ceding company is only about 50 percent of the ultimate value and is not fully determinable until some 30 months after the date of accident. (The figures cited in the preceding sentence are supported by the author's personal observation.) It can be seen that quite heavy development factors and incurred-but-not-reported factors must be applied to any loss pattern.

The effect of inflation on underwriting of excess of loss reinsurance has been a problem since 1939 and continues to be so. Reinsurers must recognize that average claim cost for many years has been rising. The base should be adjusted to current values and then loaded for expected further inflation during the period of cover. Although this process is imperfect, it should be used. Failure to take recognition of the inflation factor will result in a seriously inadequate rate.

Another point about rating fire and wind excess of loss reinsurance should be noted. The assumption that a loss pattern of any sort will provide a burning cost rate for the entire cover is a serious error. For instance, the largest loss might be $200,000 and the cover might be for $1,000,000. A rate obtained by applying normal factors to such a loss pattern can at best only provide a charge for $200,000 of cover and gives the top $800,000 free. To obtain a premium for this hitherto loss-free area it is essential to add a judgment charge to the burning cost rate.

Fire and wind catastrophe reinsurance covers for large companies are usually written to provide the reinsurer with a recapture within a fixed period of years of losses paid by the reinsurer as well as the reinsurer's overhead and profit. Such a contract is called a "spread loss excess." Excess of loss reinsurance which provides for spread of cost and for stability of its Annual Statements is attractive to the reinsured. The complexity of this rating problem has again led to the use of provisional rates and the application of experience debits and credits to determine final cost. In some examples adjustment formulas are applied directly to net premium rates. In others net rates are converted to a gross basis and commission scales are employed in a similar manner to that described for quota share and surplus treaties.

Retrospective Plans

Because of the delay in developing the true loss data in liability lines, there is wide use of retrospective plans where rates are a function of experience in the period being rated. These plans provide for a provisional premium to be paid currently with the assumption of exposure.

Rates are subject to adjustment annually within maximum and minimum limits after the rating period, usually three years, has expired. Adjustments are based on losses incurred within the limits of the plan during the period of coverage. They are made continuingly for each rating period until all losses with accident dates within the rating period are finally disposed of by settlement or court action. There is no precise timing which has to be followed. Rather, when and how adjustments are made are matters to be negotiated by the parties to the contract.

Prospective Plans

Prospective plans are also used, principally in the property field. Minimum and maximum rates are established for a specified period—usually five years. The rate for the first year is determined by using the loss pattern of the risk for a specified number of past years, the losses being divided by a factor to obtain a rate loaded for reinsurer's overhead, profit, and contingency. In subsequent years the oldest year is dropped from the formula and the newest year is added and the rate for the new year must be between the maximum and minimum rates and is guaranteed. The plans are normally noncancellable for the selected period (usually five years) and, where the loss pattern can easily be established, have appeal because the reinsurance charge is prospectively established.

In summary the methods of rating and the variety of plans are limited only by the imagination of the principals.

THE MARKET

Reinsurance is a worldwide business. As civilization becomes more complex and values increase, the demands for insurance protection tax total world capacity. Just as a primary company buys reinsurance to stabilize its net loss experience and gain capacity, so does the reinsurer. Purchase of reinsurance by a reinsurer is known as retrocession, with the buyer known as the retroceder and the seller known as the retrocessionaire. Within the American market exists the largest potential capacity in the world. One of the great challenges facing the insurance industry is its effective marshalling and use in combination with foreign markets.

Reinsurance at Lloyd's

Any outline of foreign markets must start with Lloyd's of London. Since 1687 this great association has been a dominant factor in world marine insurance and through the years it has expanded into all other lines of insurance and reinsurance. (See Chapters 17 and 58.) The central factor in its operation is the principle of individual responsibility. Each "name" or underwriter who might represent a syndicate of names, signs "slips" setting forth the share of the slip he or the syndicate will underwrite. The slip is merely a description of the cover required and is presented by a broker licensed by Lloyd's to do so. The broker attempts to obtain as the first signature on the slip one who is experienced in the cover and who will by his underwriting induce the other underwriters to follow his lead. It can be seen this is an extremely flexible method and almost any proposal can attract the interest of some underwriters. Liability of underwriters is not joint. However, as a practical matter, the failure of one underwriter has been assumed by the others. When an individual becomes a "name" at Lloyd's, he risks not only his deposit but his entire personal fortune. Lloyd's is used by the world market in the primary, excess, and reinsurance fields.

Professional Reinsurers

In Great Britain and Europe there are many old and sophisticated professional reinsurance companies. The professional reinsurer is one whose only business is reinsurance or excess lines. The largest professional reinsurer is in Switzerland and the second largest is in West Germany. All countries in Europe and, in fact, most in the free world, have a domestic reinsurance industry writing business on a worldwide basis. In addition to the professional market, many primary companies write reinsurance accounts and, in fact, some engage in active solicitation. While it is difficult to generalize, the professional reinsurers usually "write direct" and the nonprofessional reinsurers usually recognize and operate through reinsurance intermediaries or brokers.

The insurance business in the United States is subject to severe regulation. Accounting, forms, financial structure, and ratemaking are vital areas supervised by the several states. Professional reinsurance companies must subject themselves to all regulation other than as to rates and forms. Because of the international character of the reinsurance business, any attempt to establish domestic rate regulation would kill the American market, for such regulation would be impossible to impose on the foreign reinsurers. The advantage of regulation to the domestic reinsurer is that he is then admitted or licensed and the reinsurance is completely creditable in the financial statement of the reinsured. Its cost is an allowable expense to the ceding company, its reserves are accepted, and its capacity recognized. (See Chapter 61 for a discussion of the effect of reinsurance on reserves of ceding companies.) Some foreign reinsurers elect to become admitted by submitting to regulation through establishment of American subsidiaries, though most operate on a nonadmitted basis.

There are disadvantages as well as advantages in either method. Regulation is expensive to the regulated company and freedom of action is curtailed. Status as a licensed carrier is the reward. A nonadmitted company has maximum latitude. Regulatory bodies, however, do not permit primary insurers ceding business to them to reduce loss reserves to reflect the reinsurance. Hence, the nonadmitted reinsurers must resort to funding of losses, collection of reinsurance premiums on an earned basis, and other devices to mitigate the attendant penalties of that status. The vast bulk of primary companies by number will only deal with admitted carriers, since only the largest can afford the disadvantages which may otherwise arise. The small specialty companies and the less successful primary insurers constitute a market where the nonadmitted reinsurers are able to operate because of their flexibility.

The domestic professional market dates from the World War I period. Until World War II its main activity was competition with the nonadmitted foreign market. Since the end of World War II, there has been a tremendous expansion of available reinsurance capacity both here and abroad. Many primary insurers have established reinsurance departments and many others regularly accept reinsurance participations. This new capacity is in addition to huge growth in the already substantial professional market. Neither capacity nor competition is in short supply.

NEW PROBLEMS

Recent years have seen the emergence of many reinsurance problems. Aviation has moved from commercial planes worth $150,000 to jet airliners which at the time of this writing cost $6 million each. Planes costing more than double that figure are on the drawing boards. When coverage on the crew, liability coverage for upwards of 125 passengers, and personal accident insurance are added to the hull values, the needed amount is between $10 and $20 millions. The unit base on which to charge the premium required is quite narrow; and, as far as airline business is concerned, it is concentrated in just a few entities. It became apparent that the primary companies could not compete for the aviation insurance business on an individual basis. Pools were organized. The participants hold a small individual percentage of the total retention and reinsurance is purchased for the remainder. The large limits needed, the huge losses, and the natural fear of underwriters to chance the unknown, combined to create a tight market. Gradually this tightness abated, however, as experience developed. The market is now adequate.

The fantastic industrial expansion of the past 20 years has put unremitting pressure on limits most of which has fallen on the reinsurance market. Products liability, boiler and machinery, liability, atomic energy, building and contents values, and concentration of exposure all make their contribution.

Market mobilization has become and will continue to be of primary importance to the reinsurer. Under regulation, a reinsurer can assume liability on an individual exposure of only 10 percent of surplus to policy holders. The ability to meet the requests of its customers require it to maintain retrocessional facilities both broad enough and stable enough to reinsure much more than the statutory limit. The professional reinsurer can offer skilled management to a retrocessionaire coupled with a substantial spread both as to volume and variety. Other methods of market mobilization are pools, co-indemnity agreements,[6] and splitting of reinsurance accounts. Thus far the needs have been met, not always without distress, and in spite of ever higher demands there is every reason to believe the industry will adapt itself to whatever lies ahead. Reinsurance is an important key to a private and competitive insurance market.

SUGGESTED READINGS

BLANCHARD, RALPH H. (ed.). *Dictionary of Insurance Terms.* Washington, D.C.: Chamber of Commerce of the United States, 1949.

KULP, CLARENCE A. *Casualty Insurance.* 3d ed. New York: Ronald Press Co., 1956. Chap. 16.

MICHELBACHER, G. F. *Multiple-Line Insurance.* New York: McGraw-Hill Book Co., Inc., 1957. Chap. 10.

STURHAHN, E. M. *Reinsurance.* 5th ed. New York: Metropolitan Fire Assurance Co., 1941.

THOMPSON, KENNETH. *Reinsurance.* 3d. ed. Philadelphia: Chilton Company, 1951.

[6] An arrangement by which two or more insurers divide a risk between themselves in some fixed percentage, each taking his percentage of premium and becoming responsible for his percentage of loss and loss expense.

Chapter 64

INSURANCE POOLS

BY CHARLES J. HAUGH

In this chapter another important element of the institution of insurance, namely pooling, is treated. The organization and operation of intercompany pools are quite extensive within the insurance industry. Familiarity with this activity is necessary to an understanding of the structure of the business.

NATURE OF AN INSURANCE POOL

The term pool is used in insurance to designate an association of insurers organized for the purpose of sharing among the members the premiums and losses of one or more specified insurances, subject to such conditions as are determined by the association. In this connection, the terms pool and syndicate are synonymous.[1]

In its simplest form, a pool may have a very small staff to whom the members periodically report their premiums and losses for such class of business as is to be pooled. This reporting permits the pool staff to redistribute such premiums and losses among the members in such proportions as are provided for by the pool agreement. Where business to be pooled is written by the individual pool member and then reported to the pool for redistribution, it is essential that all members use a common manual of classifications, rates, and rating plans.

At the other extreme, a pool may be so staffed as to underwrite, issue policies, and furnish inspection and claim adjustment services much as an individual company functions. Under such conditions, the pool may issue policies in the names of *all* of the pool members, showing for each such member its proportionate share of the total amount of insurance afforded

[1] The Automobile Assigned Risk *Plan* quite incorrectly is frequently referred to as the Assigned Risk *Pool*. That plan is not in any sense a pool. It is merely a procedure whereby individual insureds who are unable to secure insurance are assigned to individual insurers each of which writes such insurance solely for its own account and does not pool either premiums or losses. In the field of workmen's compensation insurance there are a few voluntary and several statutory pools for assigned workmen's compensation risks.

under the policy. In some instances the pool may be permitted to issue policies in the names of individual members. In such event, the premiums and losses, of course, are pooled among the members. Usually, but not always, when policies are issued in the names of all of the pool members, the liability of the individual members is several and not joint, that is, each for itself and not one for another.

Frequently, pools are authorized to call upon individual members to perform inspection, claim, or other services on behalf of the pool and where this is done the member is reimbursed for expense so incurred. A pool also may be empowered to secure reinsurance in order to increase the pool's capacity or as a means of protecting the members from a catastrophic loss.

REASONS WHY POOLS ORGANIZED

The formation of pools may be attributed to a number of reasons, such as:

1. To afford a market for insureds seeking extraordinarily large amounts of insurance to be provided in a single policy, which amounts the member companies are unwilling or unable to provide individually.
2. To afford a market for classes of insureds whose operations are such as to require special service facilities not ordinarily furnished by many individual insurers.
3. To afford a market for insureds whose operations present an exceptionally great hazard, especially in instances in which there are relatively few insureds engaged in such operations.
4. To afford a market for insureds whose insurance is not acceptable to the individual insurers which comprise the pool.
5. To afford a medium for insuring special classes of insureds at rates and under rating procedures which differ from those used by the individual company members.
6. To afford a medium for automatically reinsuring on a coinsurance basis classes of business which the individual members of the pool wish to write as a service to their own producers and insureds but prefer to exclude from coverage under their individual reinsurance treaties.
7. To afford small companies a means of competing with large ones by making available to each pool member the combined capacities of the group.

Usually, but not always, pooling agreements (1) require the individual members to place in the pool all business of the class to which the pooling agreement applies and (2) prohibit the members from writing such business for their own account. This arrangement is imposed to prevent adverse selection against the pool by "dumping" into the pool the less desirable business while retaining the more desirable. Exceptions to mandatory pooling may be made in instances where the coverage being afforded by the individual member is so broad as to include as a relatively minor part of the total coverage insurance which, if written separately, would have to be pooled. In some pools which write classes of business not customarily written by individual companies, there may not be an actual mandatory pooling requirement, but the pool in such cases relies upon the unwillingness or inability of the individual members to write the coverage afforded by the pool. Successful operation of this type of pool depends in large part on the continuation of this unwillingness or inability of members to write the coverage individually.

Some types of pools, however, have no need for a mandatory pooling requirement. An example is a pool created as a medium for writing reinsurance in the general reinsurance market and which does not limit its writings to its members and is not required to write such business for members.

Many more pools exist than can be discussed individually in this chapter. Failure, however, to cite the existence and operation of any specifically named pools would render the discussion sterile. Consequently, the discussion reflects a decision to mention several pools merely as illustrative of the several types in operation. Readers are cautioned that the list is by no means exhaustive but rather is arbitrary. Specifically, then, those discussed illustrate the several types of pool, the purposes for which such institutions are created, and significant variations in methods of operation.

NUCLEAR FISSION POOLS

The development of nuclear fission for peaceful purposes confronted industry with an appalling potential liability as well as a new property hazard not contemplated by existing rates. Consequently, there arose a demand for much greater limits of liability insurance than had heretofore been written or sought. To meet this demand the insurance companies of the United States set about to assemble the greatest possible capacity not only in this country, but worldwide. The capital stock companies organized two pools, the Nuclear Energy Liability Insurance Association (NELIA) and the Nuclear Energy Property Insurance Association (NEPIA). The mutual companies organized the Mutual Atomic Energy Reinsurance Pool (MAERP) to handle both liability and property insurance for such risks.

From inception these three pools have afforded a total aggregate liability insurance capacity of $60 million and property insurance capacity of $65 million per risk.[2] It should be borne in mind that a nuclear incident which might result in a liability loss of $60 million or more

[2] For a detailed account of developments leading to the organization of these pools, their operation, and the coverages afforded see Richard H. Butler "Liability Insurance For The Nuclear Energy Hazard," *Proceedings of the Casualty Actuarial Society,* Vol. XLVI (1959), pp. 23–57 and a discussion of the article on pp. 336–38 of the same volume.

probably also would result in the total loss of the reactor itself. For a large reactor, then, such a loss could reach the combined capacity of the three pools of $125 million.

Insurance for the nuclear hazard is further limited to the pools because concurrently with their formation standard policies were amended to exclude the nuclear hazard.

It is of interest to note that approximately 70 per cent of the total capacity of each of these pools is furnished by member companies and approximately 30 percent by foreign reinsurers. The total capacity available from these foreign reinsurers is allocated among the three pools in proportion to their respective domestic capacities and is used by accepting them as quota share reinsurers.

Nuclear Energy Liability Insurance Association

In organizing this pool an invitation to participate was extended to every capital stock insurance company rated in *Best's Insurance Reports.* Actual participations of members range from a minimum of $25,000 up to as much as $3,500,000. Every member is required to agree to retain the entire amount of its participation so as to avoid the possibility of reinsurers being overburdened. The liability of the members is several and not joint. Members may not afford the coverage except through the pool.

Coverage afforded is limited solely to nuclear liability (both bodily injury and property damage) and is purchased principally by operators of nuclear reactors who are required by the Atomic Energy Commission to furnish evidence of financial responsibility. Under the terms of the policy, coverage is not limited to the named insured, but is extended to any one liable for nuclear loss, but excluding damage to or destruction of the reactor and its appurtenances. The pool also writes nuclear liability coverage for others such as fabricators of reactor fuels and transporters of such fuels.

The pool maintains a small staff which issues policies under the guidance of an underwriting committee comprised of representatives of member companies. The policies are issued in the names of all of the members and show for each its proportionate share of the insurance afforded by the policy. Inspection and claim services for the policyholders are made available by the pool through arrangements with individual company members.

Thus far there are as yet relatively few nuclear reactors in operation. Since it is quite desirable to maintain both the stock and mutual pools pending the time when there will be a much greater number, NELIA and MAERP have agreed to reinsure with one another, in proportion to their respective liability capacities, all business written. NEPIA and MAERP have a similar agreement with respect to property insurance.

Nuclear Energy Property Insurance Association

This pool is also comprised of capital stock companies and was organized for the purpose of affording property insurance on nuclear reactors and other operations involving nuclear fission. As in the case of NELIA the liability of the members is several and not joint. However, unlike NELIA, the coverage it writes is not confined to the nuclear hazard. Instead, its policy is a broad type of property insurance which includes fire, extended coverage, and boiler and machinery, together with coverage for loss of or damage to the insured property arising out of the nuclear fission hazard, including meltdown and loss from contamination. NEPIA does *not* offer coverage for the nuclear fission hazard alone. Members are not prohibited from writing the coverage independently of the pool.

The pool has not up to the time of this writing issued business interruption insurance nor has it written insurance for insureds who may seek coverage because of their proximity to a nuclear reactor.

The pool does not maintain a staff of its own, but is operated on behalf of the members by the Factory Insurance Association, another property insurance pool discussed later in this chapter.

Mutual Atomic Energy Reinsurance Pool

This organization, made up of mutual insurance companies, is a reinsurance pool which distributes among its members the nuclear liability and property insurance which is written and serviced on behalf of the pool by a group of six mutual companies operating as Mutual Atomic Energy Liability Underwriters (MAELU). Its coverages and rates are identical with those of NELIA and NEPIA. The liability of the individual companies is several and not joint. As mentioned in connection with NELIA, liability business written by MAELU is shared with NELIA via reinsurance and vice versa. A similar reinsurance agreement exists between NEPIA and MAELU in connection with property insurance.

The operations of MAERP and of MAELU are conducted on behalf of those organizations by the staff of a mutual reinsurance organization, the American Mutual Reinsurance Company, under the guidance of committees comprised of representatives of the six member companies of MAELU.

OTHER EXAMPLES OF PRIMARY WRITING POOLS

Many pools are in operation for the writing of primary (as opposed to reinsurance) nonnuclear coverages. A few of them are discussed for the sake of illustration.

American Foreign Insurance Association

This association is an organization established by a group of capital stock companies for the purpose of writing property-liability insurance in foreign countries. Arrangements usually are made for one or more member companies to be admitted to transact business in a country and such business is actually conducted by the association in the name of the company. Where this is not feasible, business may be written in a local company and reinsured by the AFIA members. All business from all of the countries in which the organization operates is pooled and redistributed among the members.

This pool is staffed both in its home office and its field offices to solicit, underwrite, and service the business much in the manner in which an individual company functions. Such a pool enables the member companies to participate in foreign insurance as well as to offer coverage for foreign operations of domestic insureds, and thereby affords the members an opportunity to secure a greater spread of business at much less expense than would be incurred were each member to attempt to set up the same facilities for itself.

American International Underwriters

A comparable organization to the AFIA but one more recently organized is the American International Underwriters, Inc. This organization functions as the underwriting manager for foreign operations of its subscribing companies. Aside from a few individual companies which operate independently in foreign countries, most domestic companies writing business outside of North America do so through the facilities of the AFIA or the AIU.

American Hull Syndicate

This pool was created as a United States market for ocean marine insurance, principally hull insurance. Its members consist of a group of insurance companies each of which authorizes the Syndicate to write on its behalf such types of ocean marine insurance as are prescribed in the agreement. Members may not write such coverage independently of the Syndicate except where they may wish to afford additional amounts of insurance on hulls on which the Syndicate already has extended its total capacity. Under such circumstances a member wishing to afford additional amounts of insurance must do so at rates no lower and commissions no greater than those of the Syndicate.

The Syndicate, acting as underwriting manager for ocean marine insurance for its members, functions as would an individual company in writing and servicing the business which comes within the scope of its operations, including arranging for reinsurance on business written. Policies are written in the names of the several members showing for each its proportionate share of the amount of insurance afforded by the policy. The liability of each member is several and not joint.

American Negative Film Syndicate

The pool was established by capital stock companies as a medium to provide a market to afford the large amounts of insurance covering the concentrated hazard encountered in insuring negative films for motion picture producers. Original negative film is insured during production of the motion picture, and thereafter while stored in vaults or used to produce prints.

The pool is managed under contract by an organization which does the underwriting, issues policies in the names of the member companies showing the extent of the participation of each member, collects the premiums, and adjusts losses. Here, again, the liability of the pool members is several and not joint.

Factory Insurance Association

This organization was established in 1890 by a group of capital stock companies for the purpose of assembling the necessary capacity to afford in one policy the exceptionally large amounts of insurance required by industrial operations. As originally conceived, it has limited itself to writing fire and allied lines for highly protected risks. In many states it has special filings for highly protected risks under which special treatment is given as respects coverage and rates. It operates as a distinct entity and as such maintains its own underwriting, inspection, and loss adjustment facilities. The policies are issued in the names of the member companies showing for each its share of the amount of insurance afforded by the policy. The liability of the member companies is several and not joint.

Associated Factory Mutual Fire Insurance Companies

This group of mutual companies antedates the Factory Insurance Association. The companies have combined to insure highly protected manufacturing operations for fire and allied lines. Each policy issued by a company member is reinsured by the several companies comprising the group. Inspection service is afforded through the Factory Mutual Engineering Division maintained by the group. Rates are set at such a level that the group is able to pay very large dividends. (See also Chapter 58.)

Foreign Credit Insurance Association

This is one of the few pools which includes in its membership both capital stock and mutual companies. It was organized in 1962 for the purpose of writing credit insurance for manufacturers and exporters selling goods to customers in foreign countries. The pool maintains a staff which does the underwriting, issues policies, and adjusts losses. The policies issued by the pool are described in Chapter 42.

Policies are issued by the pool in the joint names of the Foreign Credit Insurance Association and the Export-Import Bank of Washington. The Export-Import Bank is a coinsurer as respects the coverage for commercial hazards and assumes the entire coverage for political hazards. The liability of individual company members of the Association is several and not joint, and the proportionate share of each member is shown in the policy.

Railroad Insurance Underwriters

The unique underwriting problems and large amounts involved in writing property insurance covering the rolling stock and fixed properties of railroads led to the formation of Railroad Insurance Underwriters by a group of capital stock companies. This pool functions as a joint underwriting organization and also as an advisory organization in those states where provision is made for such. It conducts inspections and adjusts losses. Rates are obtained from the rating bureaus for the respective coverages involved. Each policy is issued in the name of an individual company member and the business is subsequently pooled and distributed among the member companies in proportion to their individual subscriptions.

Oil Insurance Underwriters

Affording property insurance for oil refineries presents special problems of rating, capacity, and inspection service which have led to the creation of pools to write this class of business. The Oil Insurance Underwriters operates for a group of capital stock companies. The agent or broker originating the business may request that the policy be issued in the name of a specific company member of the pool. Otherwise, the pool itself may designate the company in whose name the policy is written. All business written is distributed among the members in proportion to the degree of participation to which they have subscribed to the pool.

United States Aircraft Insurance Group (USAIG) and Associated Aviation Underwriters

The USAIG, a pool comprised of a group of capital stock companies, writes property-liability insurance covering aviation hazards. The pool is managed by the United States Aviation Underwriters, a corporation formed for the purpose of underwriting and servicing the business written by the pool. In practice, USAU designates an individual company member to service each insured. Policies may be issued in the names of all member companies showing the proportionate share of each or upon request a policy may be issued in the name of the servicing company. In the latter event the premiums and losses are also redistributed among the pool members.

The principal markets in this country for writing aviation insurance, especially for commercial aircraft are afforded by the USAIG and by the Associated Aviation Underwriters, another pool of capital stock companies operating in a similar manner.

Other Pools

It must be apparent that the foregoing illustrations of primary writing pools could be expanded to include insurance on other concentrations of property values such as cotton and grain as well as hail insurance on growing crops. As has been illustrated, two or more competing pools exist in many instances.

The primary writing pools cited conduct the underwriting and generally function as would an individual company. The business is placed directly with the pool by an agent or broker. The servicing of the risk and adjusting of claims may be performed by an individual company member of the pool or by the pool's own staff, depending upon the facilities maintained by the individual pool.

REINSURANCE POOLS

Reinsurance pools are of two general types, each of which differs from the types of pools considered in the previous section. (As mentioned previously, NELIA, NEPIA, and MAERP engage in reinsurance activities.) In one type of reinsurance pool the policy issued to the insured is underwritten and issued by and at the discretion of an individual company member and is then automatically reinsured by the pool in accordance with the pooling agreement. In the other category, the pool functions as a general reinsurer writing reinsurance for direct writing companies, regardless of whether they are or are not members of the pool. Examples of each type are found below.

Excess and Casualty Reinsurance Association

This organization is a reinsurance pool, or, more properly, a group of three pools established for the purpose of conducting a reinsurance business. It is managed by Excess Treaty Management Corporation and competes in the open market for reinsurance business of direct writing companies whether members of the pool or not. Separate pools are maintained for property, liability, and bonding lines. Members may participate in one, two, or all of the pools and for varying numbers of shares.

Excess Bond Reinsurance Association

This pool, comprised of a group of member companies of the Surety Association of America (a rating organization maintained by capital stock companies writing fidelity and surety bonds—see Chapter 56) affords to its members a facility to offer for commercial banks $1 million of fidelity coverage in excess of prescribed underlying amounts which vary with the total deposits of the bank. These required underlying amounts range from $50,000 for banks with deposits of less than $750,000 to $6 million for banks with deposits of $2 billion or more. This underlying amount may be uninsured or may be insured in whole or in part. The excess policy is issued by and in the name of the member company selling the coverage. It is reinsured in full by the pool which redistributes among the pool members 70 percent of the premiums and 100 percent of the losses. This arrangement allows 30 percent to the direct writing member for its expenses, including taxes. The liability of the individual members of this pool is joint and several.

Workmen's Compensation Reinsurance Bureau

As the name implies, this pool affords workmen's compensation reinsurance to its members. Members uniformly retain the first $50,000 of loss per accident and are reinsured for loss in excess of that amount. Membership is limited to capital stock companies. The liability of the pool members is joint and several.

Registered Mail Central Bureau

This pool is a facility for redistributing among the capital stock company members the premiums and losses on policies written by the individual members to cover currency, securities, and other valuable property transported by registered mail and first class mail. (See Chapter 24.) It is also applicable to coverage of shipper's interest in such property transported by armored cars. Reinsurance of the individual member in excess of a prescribed retention is automatic up to the maximum capacity of the pool. The participation of each member is determined annually as the ratio of the member's volume of written premiums on such business to the total such volume of all members. The liability of each member is joint and several.

ASSIGNED RISK POOLS

In the field of workmen's compensation insurance there are in effect in many states plans whereby employers who have been unable to secure insurance may be assigned to a company which is required, under the terms of the plan, to write the business. With few exceptions, companies are free to, and in fact must, retain such business for their own account. In the states of Arkansas, Illinois, Indiana, Massachusetts, Minnesota, New Mexico, Texas, and Wisconsin legislation has been enacted creating pools for the handling of such business. Actually, in Indiana and Massachusetts the insurance companies operate voluntary plans which afford a market for all risks. Consequently, the statutory pools in those two states are inoperative. In Arkansas and Illinois provision is made for separate pools for stock and for nonstock (mutual and reciprocal) insurers. For each of the other four states there is a single pool embracing all admitted insurers. In these same four states, provision is made for the appointment, from among the pool members, of servicing companies to write and service these assigned risks. Each servicing company is entitled to retain a specified portion of the premium to cover its expense and the balance of the premium and all the losses are pooled among the entire membership. The liability of pool members in each of these pools is both joint and several.

A voluntary organization of capital stock companies limited to members of the National Bureau of Casualty Underwriters and known as the Assigned Risk Pool exists for the purpose of pooling on a joint and several basis assigned workmen's compensation risks not within the scope of statutory pools. Participants are required to pool all such risks in all states in which the pool functions, excepting only coal mining risks.

Separate pools, called the Coal Mine Assigned Risk Pools, to afford workmen's compensation insurance for assigned coal mine risks are operated by the National Council on Compensation Insurance (a ratemaking organization for this type of insurance—see Chapter 36) which includes in its membership capital stock, mutual, and reciprocal insurers. This coal mine business is handled by servicing companies. The liability of the pool members is both joint and several.

THE FUTURE

Pooling affords the most useful medium for meeting problems of abnormal capacity or those requiring specialized service facilities for classes of business or types of coverage for which the available volume of business is inadequate to warrant their being written by individual companies. Pooling of some type probably will continue indefinitely. However, increased capacities of individual insurers to meet the insurance needs of the public may well result in an eventual lessening need for pools.

SUGGESTED READINGS

HUEBNER, S. S., AND BLACK, KENNETH, JR. *Property Insurance*, pp. 336–39. 4th ed. New York: Appleton-Century-Crofts, Inc., 1957.

RODDA, WILLIAM H. *Fire and Property Insurance*, pp. 528, 531. Englewood Cliffs, N.J.: Prentice-Hall, Inc., 1956.

SNIDER, H. WAYNE (ed.). *Readings in Property and Casualty Insurance.* Homewood, Ill.: Richard D. Irwin, Inc., 1959. Chap. 19. "Principles of Company Underwriting and the Mechanics of Reinsurance," by Otis Clark.

See also the following articles in the *National Underwriter:*

"New Facility for Commercial Risks." Vol. 65 (Sept. 1, 1961), p. 4.

"New Pool to Manage Aviation Insurance." Vol. 66 (Jan. 12, 1962), p. 1.

"U.S. Insurers Now Use More of Their Capacity." Vol. 66 (Feb. 9, 1962), p. 1.

Chapter 65

GOVERNMENTAL REGULATION OF INSURANCE

BY JOSEPH S. GERBER

Every man, woman, and child in the United States is affected one way or another by the business of insurance. Insurance thus is vested with great public interest. Quite obviously, government concerns itself with the stability and growth of a business which so clearly touches the lives of every citizen.

In this chapter a brief account is given of governmental regulation of insurance in this country. The account is divided into: early phases, the development of the National Association of Insurance Commissioners, federal-state relations prior to the South-Eastern Underwriters Association decision, such relations after this decision, and some speculation about the future of insurance regulation.

EARLY PHASES OF REGULATION

The first administrative agency regulating the business of insurance was found in a Florentine statute of 1523. As the business grew in importance, regulation kept pace with its growth. Insurance regulation in England came in the sixteenth century with the expansion of the business of insurance. In many respects, English regulation influenced insurance regulation in the United States. The first American insurance company, the Philadelphia Contributorship, was incorporated in 1768 by the Pennsylvania legislature, but no regulation of this corporation accompanied the legislative enactment.

Early Statutes

In 1794 the first capital stock insurance company, the Insurance Company of North America, was organized. The statute under which the company was incorporated required (1) that funds be invested in certain stock and (2) that deposits of money be made in the Bank of Pennsylvania. There were several other requirements. This statute probably represents the first attempt by a state to regulate the business of insurance.

The special chartering laws under which insurance companies were created are still effective in few states today. These laws basically reflected concern for protection of policyholders. Such protection still remains one of the principal responsibilities and obligations of insurance regulatory agencies. The second objective of insurance regulation was revenue. Raising of revenue remains one of the chief purposes of regulation. The increase of control over activities of insurance companies was a gradual one, and regulation was imposed piecemeal. The first statute transferring regulation from the legislative branch to administrative agencies occurred in New Hampshire in 1851, when a "Board of Insurance Commissioners" was established. The first individual commissioner assumed regulatory control in Massachusetts in 1866.

State Insurance Departments

Over a period of years regulation of insurance has gone through many phases. The creation of authority has varied by states. Most insurance commissioners are now appointed by the governor with senatorial confirmation. Some insurance commissioners are elected. Some act in dual or multiple capacities, holding other governmental posts in the state.

No matter how the commissioners attain office, the fact is that insurance departments are a division of the executive branch of government but are vested also with judicial and legislative powers. Basically, departments carry out legislative intent as an administrative branch of government, but do have rule-making power which is legislative in character. They have quasi-judicial power to hold hearings to determine violations of laws or rules. There is, however, judicial review by the courts of all departmental actions.

With the principal objectives of regulation of insurance being protection of policyholders and production of revenue, regulatory activities take numerous directions. They involve the insurance department's regulation of company investments; periodic examinations; approval of policies and rates; licensing of companies, agents, brokers, and adjusters (in some states); and in general checking on a multitude of insurance operations. One of the difficult tasks performed by the insurance department of a particular state, in addition to the licensing of domestic companies, is the admission and regulation of foreign insurers from other states and alien insurers from other countries.

NATIONAL ASSOCIATION OF INSURANCE COMMISSIONERS (N.A.I.C.)

The most prominent vehicle in the regulation of the business of insurance by the several states is the National Association of Insurance Commissioners. This association was organized in 1870 and was then known as the National Convention of Insurance Commissioners. It is an organization which limits its membership to the heads of state insurance departments. Its importance can be determined by a study of the N.A.I.C. proceedings. The N.A.I.C. provides the only means by which the several states can effectively produce uniformity to permit the flow of insurance business into the several states. It offers insurance commissioners an opportunity to acquire knowledge from the experience of others.

Edwin W. Patterson, Professor of Law at Columbia University, described this phase of the Association's work as follows:

> The significance of the National Convention of Insurance Commissioners is not to be measured by the statutory provisions in which it is given recognition. It is a school of instruction in which a new and inexperienced commissioner may pick up many useful hints, for the discharge of his duties. It develops professional *esprit de corps* among the commissioners through the personal contacts of the members and engenders mutual respect.[1]

Committees

The N.A.I.C. operates on a committee basis. It has standing committees and numerous subcommittees which are charged with the responsibility of studying and making reports on many subjects. Among the more important committees is the Committee on Valuation of Securities. (See Chapter 60 and 61.) This committee maintains a full-time staff of security analysts in New York City. The purpose of this committee's work is to maintain the highest degree of uniformity on evaluation of securities for insurance companies. It would be disastrous if state officials exercised individual judgment in determining the value of securities carried by the insurance companies in their investment portfolios.

The Committee on Blanks is charged with the responsibility of developing the uniformity of insurance company Annual Statement blanks for reporting financial information. It is obvious that without this uniformity a company operating in various states would be faced with an irreconcilable problem of filing multiple and dissimilar Annual Statements in the several states.

The Committee on Rates and Rate Regulation is especially active because of the tremendous impact rate regulation has had by virtue of the South-Eastern Underwriters Association case (discussed later in this chapter).

One of the more formidable objectives of the N.A.I.C. is achieved by the Examination Committee. It is evident that no one state could adequately examine an interstate insurance company operation. Accordingly, the N.A.I.C. has divided the country into six zones. Examinations of

---

[1] Edwin W. Patterson, *The Insurance Commissioner in the United States: A Study in Administrative Law and Practice* (Cambridge, Mass.: Harvard University, 1927), p. 462.

companies are conducted on a zone basis with one state examiner acting for and on behalf of all of the states in the particular zone in the execution of the examination. Thus, it is possible for a company doing business in 50 states to be examined by six examiners. This phase of N.A.I.C. work is considered the most important function of the association and of the greatest value to the several states.

Model Laws

All committees and subcommittees are presented with timely problems which result in surveys, public hearings, and the development of model laws. Two recent specific examples can be cited. The first was the adoption in 1958 by the N.A.I.C. of a model "Credit Life and Credit Accident and Health Bill"[2] which as of the time of this writing is law in 34 states. This bill was of the utmost significance. It created rate regulation, full disclosure, and refunding of premiums. Furthermore, it offered the public the general type of protection deemed necessary. The second example occurred in 1962 when the N.A.I.C. adopted a model "Fire and Casualty Rating Bill." [3] The purpose of this model bill was to (1) merge the current fire and casualty rating statutory articles and (2) amend the aggrieved party and deviation sections of the rating articles by making them compatible with current needs. The bill also solved some of the procedural problems arising out of the new concept of packaging of insurance coverages.

Over a period of years the National Association of Insurance Commissioners has recommended to the states model laws covering trade practices, accident and health standard provisions, life insurance mortality tables, and many other important subjects. The most recent act by the N.A.I.C. was the creation of a Central Non-Admitted Insurers Information Bureau in New York City. (See also Chapter 67.) In response to a need for some measure of control by the states over nonadmitted insurers, more commonly known as surplus line writers, a model bill was proposed to the association. After a great deal of study, the N.A.I.C. set it aside and created the aforementioned office. The chief purpose of this office is to supply information on nonadmitted insurance companies to agents, brokers, insurance department officials, and other interested parties.

Meetings

The N.A.I.C. holds two formal meetings annually. At these meetings members of the committees and subcommittees discuss and attempt to solve their respective committee problems. In addition, these committees and subcommittees hold executive sessions or public hearings during the

---

[2] N.A.I.C. *Proceedings,* Vol. I (1959), p. 126.

[3] N.A.I.C. *Proceedings,* Vol. I (1963), p. 221.

year. They (1) hear spokesmen from the insurance industry, insurance departments, and other organizations present divergent opinions; (2) discuss the various points of view; and (3) prepare recommendations.

FEDERAL-STATE RELATIONS: "PRE–S.E.U.A."

There are two United States Supreme Court decisions of profound significance which have left their mark on governmental regulation of insurance. They concern the relationship of federal and state governments in this field. Their ultimate historical significance is yet to be determined.

The Precedent of Paul v. Virginia

In the case of *Paul* v. *Virginia,* 8 Wall 168 (1869), the United States Supreme Court held that insurance was not commerce as contemplated by the United States Constitution and, therefore, that insurance transactions were local transactions to be governed by local laws. Accordingly, the states were given full authority to regulate and tax the business of insurance on a state level.

An interesting aspect of this case was that it was conceived by insurance agents for the specific purpose of obtaining a decision favoring the concept of insurance as interstate commerce. The agents bringing the suit anticipated the ultimate take-over of insurance regulation by the federal government.

For 75 years thereafter the several states continued to exercise regulatory authority in the insurance business, but not without periods of adversity and investigations. Several of the more consequential investigations were the Armstrong investigation in 1905, the Missouri rate case in 1938, and the Temporary National Economic Committee investigation which occurred in 1938. They exerted profound influence upon state regulation.

Following the stock market crash of 1929 and the depression years of the early thirties, the federal government embarked upon a program to exercise greater national authority. Necessarily, some areas under state regulation and influence succumbed to federal priority. Virtually every segment of business in the American economy, with the exception of insurance, was subjected to some sort of regulation by the federal government, or dually by the federal government and the several states.

South-Eastern Underwriters Association Case

The socioeconomic aspects of the business finally resulted in a United States Supreme Court decision of the greatest magnitude. Prior to 1944, few states exercised substantial rate regulatory powers in the fire and casualty field. This function was performed in the fire field by local groups commonly referred to as underwriters, such as the South-Eastern

Underwriters Association. These groups exercised great authority, even to the exclusion of participation of nonmember companies, agents, and brokers. The stock company agencies controlled most of the fire premiums in the United States.

On June 5, 1944, in a 4–3 decision, the United States Supreme Court handed down a decision in the case of *United States* v. *South-Eastern Underwriters Association*, 322 U.S. 533. The S.E.U.A. controlled the rate-making processes in eight states in the southeastern part of the United States. The basic issue presented in this case was whether or not the South-Eastern Underwriters Association was maintaining monopolistic practices in the fixing of rates. In this most significant case the Supreme Court reversed its former ruling and held that the conduct of an insurance business across state lines was interstate commerce and therefore subject to federal laws and regulation—and specifically to the Sherman Antitrust Act. The majority and minority opinions should be studied in the greatest detail because the decision resulted in a complete revamping and revitalization of state regulation.

FEDERAL-STATE RELATIONS: "POST–S.E.U.A."

A series of developments of unique and vast consequence followed the S.E.U.A. decision.

The McCarran Act

United States Senators McCarran and Ferguson proposed a public law to retain insurance regulation in the states. In 1945 the Senators introduced a bill which, after amendments, became Public Law 15 of the 79th Congress, First Session. The law was approved March 9, 1945. It reads as follows:

[PUBLIC LAW 15—79th CONGRESS]
[Chapter 20—1st Session]
S .340
AN ACT
To express the intent of the Congress with reference to the regulation of the business of insurance.

Be it enacted by the Senate and House of Representatives of the United States of America in Congress assembled, That the Congress hereby declares that the continued regulation and taxation by the several States of the business of insurance is in the public interest, and that silence on the part of the Congress shall not be construed to impose any barrier to the regulation or taxation of such business by the several States.

Sec. 2. (a) The business of insurance, and every person engaged therein, shall be subject to the laws of the several States which relate to the regulation or taxation of such business.

(b) No Act of Congress shall be construed to invalidate, impair or supersede any law enacted by any State for the purpose of regulating the business of insurance, or which imposes a fee or tax upon such business, unless such Act specifically relates to the business of insurance: *Provided*, That after January 1, 1948, the Act of July 2, 1800, as amended, known as the Sherman Act, and the Act of October 15, 1914, as amended, known as the Clayton Act, and the Act of September 26, 1914, known as the Federal Trade Commission Act, as amended, shall be applicable to the business of insurance to the extent that such business is not regulated by State law.

Sec. 3. (a) Until January 1, 1948, the Act of July 2, 1900, as amended, known as the Sherman Act, and the Act of October 15, 1914, as amended, known as the Clayton Act, and the Act of September 26, 1914, known as the Federal Trade Commission Act, as amended, and the Act of June 19, 1936, known as the Robinson-Patman Antidiscrimination Act, shall not apply to the business of insurance or to acts in the conduct thereof.

(b) Nothing contained in this Act shall render the said Sherman Act inapplicable to any agreement to boycott, coerce, or intimidate, or act of boycott, coercion, or intimidation.

Sec. 4. Nothing contained in this Act shall be construed to affect in any manner the application to the business of insurance of the Act of July 5, 1935, as amended, known as the National Labor Relations Act, or the Act of June 25, 1938, as amended, known as the Fair Labor Standards Act of 1938, or the Act of June 5, 1920, known as the Merchant Marine Act, 1920.

Sec. 5. As used in this Act, the term "State" includes the several States, Alaska, Hawaii, Puerto Rico, and the District of Columbia.

Sec. 6. If any provision of this Act, or the application of such provision to any person or circumstances, shall be held invalid, the remainder of the Act, and the application of such provision to persons or circumstances other than those as to which it is held invalid, shall not be affected.

Approved, March 9, 1945.

The intent of Public Law 15 has been debated since its adoption. The most serious issue was raised in the fire and casualty rating field. Upon the effective date of Public Law 15, various interpretations were expressed concerning the pattern state regulation should take. In signing Public Law 15 President Franklin D. Roosevelt issued the following statement:

> After the moratorium period, the antitrust laws and certain related statutes will be applicable in full force and effect to the business of insurance except to the extent that the States have assumed the responsibility, and are effectively performing that responsibility, for the regulation of whatever aspect of the insurance business may be involved. . . . Congress did not intend to permit private rate fixing, which the Antitrust Act forbids, but was willing to permit actual regulation of rates by affirmative action of the States.

Attorney General Biddle stated for the Congressional Record of June 23, 1944, that "the States must fix or approve insurance rates and that mere State permission without the exercise of control is inimical to the public interest."

All-Industry Rating Bills

It became imperative that action be taken by the several states to meet the demands of Public Law 15. Accordingly, the All-Industry Insurance

Committee, consisting of representatives from all segments of the insurance business, was formed for the specific purpose of considering what state legislation was necessary to satisfy the requirements of Public Law 15 and preserve state regulation. After considerable labor by the committee and by the N.A.I.C., the committee proposed the so-called All-Industry Rating Bills, one covering fire and the other covering the casualty field. These bills were subsequently presented to the National Association of Insurance Commissioners and adopted on June 12, 1946.

The relatively rapid preparation and adoption of this model rating legislation is attributable to the exigencies of the situation. Because of the haste and complexity of the subject, the All-Industry Rating Bills were not regarded by all parties as being properly responsive to all problems which existed or which were likely to arise. Nevertheless, because of the time factor, 45 states adopted the bills with some variations in the years 1946 and 1947. Several others proceeded to adopt what is now commonly known as a mandatory rating law whereby the state makes the rate for many lines of insurance.

The greatest departure from the All-Industry approach was the California law which did not require the filing of any rates and thus set a pattern quite apart from the model bill. The California experience, however, demonstrates that various types of rating laws could be interpreted as satisfying the mandate of Public Law 15.

Subsequent Testing of Public Law 15

Since the advent of Public Law 15 there have been many lawsuits testing the various aspects of state regulation. In the case of *Prudential Insurance Company of America* v. *Benjamin,* 328 U.S. 408 (1946), the United States Supreme Court held that a discriminating premium tax which did not apply to domestic companies could be levied on a foreign company doing business in multiple states although interstate insurance was interstate commerce. The court specifically referred to the McCarran Act, recognized regulation and taxation of insurance by the several states of the business of insurance, and examined the intent of Congress to permit states to tax insurance companies. In the case of *Travelers Health Association* v. *Federal Trade Commission,* 262 F. (2d) 241 (1959), reversed by 362 U.S. 293 (1960), the United States Supreme Court held that the F.T.C. had jurisdiction over the insurance company's advertising flowing across state lines into a state in which the company was not licensed. The commissioner (or other regulatory official) in such state would have no means of exercising jurisdiction over such unlicensed company. This decision resolved the question of authority over mail order insurance business and the McCarran Act was fundamental to the Supreme Court decision.

A more recent case of importance is *State Board of Insurance* v. *Todd Shipyards Corp.,* 370 U.S. 451 (1 ed 2d 620, 82 S. Ct. 1380) 1961. The

United States Supreme Court again held to the basic precept of the McCarran Act and denied the state of Texas the right to impose a premium tax on the Todd Shipyards Corporation properties in Texas when in fact, the insurance was purchased in the state of New York from an insurer which was not licensed in Texas and which did not perform any acts in Texas.

Apparent from a study of these and other cases is quite a distinct philosophical pattern. Public Law 15 was intended to give the states control over insurers and their activities within the borders of their state. Where a state must exercise extraterritorial jurisdiction, the United States Supreme Court seemingly deems the McCarran Act inapplicable.

Activities of Senate Subcommittee

In addition to the legal opinions which have given the states an indication of their authority, there have been a number of legislative investigations—both state and federal—into various phases of insurance regulation. However, the one of greatest impact in terms of the future of state regulation is the activity of the Subcommittee on Antitrust and Monopoly of the U.S. Senate Committee on the Judiciary.

This subcommittee has studied the effectiveness of state regulation in the area of fire and casualty rates, aviation insurance, surplus line insurance, and other aspects of the insurance business. In addition, the subcommittee submitted a detailed questionnaire to the several states. In 1959 the subcommittee staff evaluated the statistical material in the responses submitted.[4] Among its findings were the following observations and recommendations:

1. Salaries paid to insurance department personnel are inadequate.
2. Insurance, being a highly specialized business, should be regulated by departments not charged with other administrative responsibilities.
3. Many states are understaffed and inadequately staffed in terms of qualified personnel. For instance, the questionnaire disclosed that in 15 states the insurance departments had no actuary on their respective staffs. Neither did they engage any consulting actuaries. Nineteen states indicated that no attorneys were on the respective staffs of the insurance departments.
4. Examinations of insurance companies are of the utmost importance. In spite of this fact, however, insurance departments lack sufficient qualified examiners. Furthermore, those serving are inadequately compensated.
5. Budgets of insurance departments are generally insufficient for the responsibilities placed on the office. In a particular period 4.27 percent of the total revenue from premium taxes for respondents as a whole was spent on regulatory activities. The report stated that the states accept premium taxes as a source of revenue and do not in return offer to the taxpayers the high degree of regulation of insurance deemed necessary.

---

[4] *Report of the Committee on the Judiciary, U.S. Senate Subcommittee on Antitrust and Monopoly Reports* (Washington, D.C.: U.S. Government Printing Office, Aug. 29, 1961).

On August 29, 1960, the late Senator Joseph C. O'Mahoney, who directed the study, expressed the sentiment of the subcommittee members on the issue of state versus federal regulation accentuated by the work of his subcommittee. He wrote:

> The hearings and the study have not produced any substantial support for an over-all revision of our national policy for the regulation of insurance by substituting Federal power for State power. Nevertheless, in the course of the study it became evident that there were basic defects in the kind of rate regulation which has evolved in the States.

FUTURE OF GOVERNMENTAL REGULATION

Congress has seen fit to appropriate additional sums of money to the subcommittee for further study and review of many phases of the business of insurance and its regulation. Unquestionably there will be a nibbling away of state regulation through circumstances over which the states may have no control. The question of regulating the flow of mail advertising by nonlicensed companies clearly is a case in point. The Todd Shipyards case suggests that the U.S. Supreme Court—where many of the insurance regulatory questions will ultimately be decided—is sympathetic to state regulation. Where the states, however, have, in fact, no modus operandi to control acts of insurers affecting their citizens, the states' regulation under Public Law 15 apparently will be preempted by federal regulation. Judicially, however, where the states do exercise regulation there remains no question as to the applicability of Public Law 15. Of course, Congress can amend Public Law 15 setting forth in more exact terms what it expects of the several states.

Attorney General William G. Clark, of the State of Illinois, suggested in December, 1962, at a meeting of the National Association of Insurance Commissioners, that the Council of State Governments might well be the vehicle for requesting Congressional legislative enactments to cure doubts among the states and the insurance companies as to the full impact of Public Law 15. As an alternative, Congress can repeal Public Law 15 and take over the regulation of insurance which falls within the broad mantle of interstate commerce.

The several states continue to exercise concern over their responsibilities. An examination of legislative action in the states indicates a desire to offer a higher degree of protection and service to the citizens. Increasing budgets are permitting commissioners to retain able employees and hire competent new staff members. Career manpower is being emphasized. Some progress is being made toward basing insurance department appropriations on a formula relating to premium growth and to increases in the amount of premium taxes collected as a means of maintaining a proper relationship between budgets and responsibilities.

In 1957 a Commission on Money and Credit was established by the Board of Trustees of the Committee on Economic Development to study public and private financial institutions of the United States. The section of the report referring to the business of insurance reads:

> Life insurance companies today enjoy greater investment flexibility than that accorded to mutual savings banks, saving and loan associations, and credit unions, although less than that available to private pension funds. While life insurance companies may invest in many credit and equity instruments, limits are set on their holdings of particular assets and each type of asset must meet specified minimum standards before it may be acquired.
>
> During the last decade some states have devised "leeway" or "basket clauses" in their life insurance company regulatory laws. These allow added flexibility and mobility of investment by enabling life insurance companies to invest in types of assets not otherwise permitted, up to some proportion of assets or of capital and surplus. They facilitate direct lending to small businesses and aid them indirectly by allowing life companies to invest in state development credit corporations. They afford life companies an opportunity to experiment and innovate in their lending while at the same time assuring protection to their policyholders. The Commission favors this balanced approach to promoting economic growth, and recommends that other states follow this practice.[5]

Since the issuance of this report, the language in the passage cited above and in other passages has been interpreted by numerous informed persons as a step toward federal chartering of insurance companies if preferred by an insurer doing an interstate business. The possibility for dual regulation therefore arises and unquestionably can be legally sustained.

Many people believe that the states would soon lose all control in this area if dual regulation became a reality. Associate Justice William O. Douglas of the United States Supreme Court had this to say on the subject of dual regulation: "Dual regulation . . . both by state and Federal laws . . . may be logically permissible but practically unsound. Dual regulation may be inherently so disruptive of the policy of the Federal law that the purpose of Congress to foreclose state action may be implied."[6]

More recently, the Honorable William O. Dodd, U.S. senator from Connecticut, introduced a bill which would permit federal chartering of surplus line companies. This bill would require surplus line companies to obtain a federal license which would then permit them to function anywhere within the several states. The National Association of Insurance Commissioners is hopeful that the creation of the Non-Admitted Insurers

[5] *Report of the Commission on Money and Credit* (New York: Committee on Economic Development, 1961), Section on Private Financial Institutions.

[6] Monrad G. Taulsen (ed.), *Legal Institutions Today and Tomorrow* (New York: Columbia University Press, 1959), p. 274. (This was a report of: Conference Marking the Centennial of the Columbia Law School, New York, 1958.)

Information Bureau[7] will give state insurance departments the information necessary to evaluate the financial structure of nonadmitted insurance companies.

THE CHOICE

It must be clearly understood that as long as the several states continue to regulate the business of insurance there will be, by necessity, differences in the regulation of the business. The social, political, and economic variations among states will cause atypicality in the enactment and interpretation of laws. As an illustration, the state of New York and the state of Montana may well have special problems which require varied laws and implementation. A highly populated industrial state, for example, has problems with the automobile insurance business which vary markedly from comparable problems in a sparsely populated agricultural state. On the other hand, the pressure for uniformity in insurance regulation from one state to another is increasingly strong.

Insurance commissioners, therefore, have to walk the thin line between public interest within the state and a free competitive interstate (as well as intrastate) insurance business in their respective states. In practical terms the choice is state regulation or federal regulation. Dual regulation is not an alternative.

SUGGESTED READINGS

AMERICAN MANAGEMENT ASSOCIATION. *Insurance Trends and Guides.* New York: A.M.A. Management Report No. 52, 1960.

CENTER, CHARLES C., AND HEINS, RICHARD M. (eds.). *Insurance and Government.* Madison: University of Wisconsin Fund for Insurance Education and Research, 1962.

DENENBERG, HERBERT S., *et al.* *Risk and Insurance.* Englewood Cliffs, N.J.: Prentice-Hall, Inc., 1964. Chaps. 31–32.

PATTERSON, EDWIN W. *The Insurance Commissioner in the United States: A Study in Administrative Law and Practice,* p. 462. Cambridge, Mass.: Harvard University, 1927.

Report of Committee of Judiciary, U.S. Senate Subcommittee on Antitrust Monopoly Reports. Washington, D.C.: U.S. Government Printing Office, August 10, 1960 and August 29, 1961.

SAWYER, ELMER WARREN. *Insurance as Inter-State Commerce.* New York: McGraw-Hill Book Co., Inc., 1945.

STATE OF NEW YORK. *Report of the Joint Legislative Committee on Insurance Rates and Regulation.* Albany, 1962.

U.S. FIDELITY AND GUARANTY COMPANY. *The Case for the All-Industry Bill.* Baltimore, 1946.

---

[7] N.A.I.C. *Proceedings,* Vol. II (1963) p. 358.

Wilker, Julius, and Knowlton, Donald. *State Regulation of Insurance*, a statement submitted to the U.S. Senate Committee on the Judiciary, Subcommittee on Antitrust and Monopoly. N.A.I.C. *Proceedings*, Vol. I (1960), pp. 53–131.

Chapter 66

TAXATION IN PROPERTY AND LIABILITY INSURANCE[1]

BY VESTAL LEMMON

Everyone is familiar with the adage, ". . . nothing is certain but death and taxes." While medical science has made great strides in lengthening man's life span, political science has been losing the battle for reduced taxes.

Because the very nature of the insurance business requires that insurance companies develop considerable gross income and amass substantial assets, officials from every level of government continually look to this industry for additional taxes. Insurance companies have long been subject to a multitude of taxes, licenses, and fees by the federal, state, and municipal governments. The author estimates that the total paid in taxes by fire and casualty insurance companies amounts to almost half a billion a year. This amount does not include the numerous licenses, fees, and miscellaneous taxes the insurance industry is also required to pay.

The purpose of this chapter is to present a brief discussion of the following matters: (1) historical background of the taxation of "fire and casualty companies"; (2) the present basis of taxation of stock and nonstock companies by the federal government; and (3) a review of the principal types of state and municipal taxes, fees, and licenses applicable to insurance companies. Other state and municipal taxes are mentioned to show the variety of taxes borne by insurance companies.

TAXATION BY THE FEDERAL GOVERNMENT

Historical Notes

Except for the income tax levied during the Civil War, early attempts by the federal government to tax income failed to be adopted or, if

[1] Terminology is somewhat of a problem in this chapter. Much of the literature on the subject pertains to "fire and casualty companies"; some of it to "property and casualty companies"; some of it to "nonlife companies"; and some of it to companies

adopted, were repealed or declared unconstitutional. In 1909, a special corporation tax of 1 percent was imposed on all corporations including stock insurance companies. The right of the federal government to tax income was declared constitutional in 1913 when the Sixteenth Amendment was passed. It provided that "the Congress shall have the power to levy and collect taxes on income. . . ." The tax law passed that same year continued this 1 percent rate (for insurance companies, gross premiums written were considered as income). Until 1921, fire and casualty companies were taxed on the same basis as other corporations. (The reference here is to the technical "basis" for determining income.)

The Revenue Act of 1921 classified insurance companies into three main groups: life insurance companies, mutual companies other than life, and stock companies other than life. The act provided that taxable income be computed from the underwriting and investment exhibit of the Annual Statement approved by the National Association of Insurance Commissioners. In effect, this act established the present basis for taxation of fire and casualty companies.

Most mutual insurance companies were exempt from taxation prior to 1942, claiming exemption as nonprofit organizations. The Revenue Act of 1942 provided that mutual companies be taxed under either of two special formulas, whichever produced the larger tax. These formulas were:

1. Regular corporate rates applied to net taxable investment income from rents, interest, dividends, royalties, and nonrelated business income, plus net realized capital gains; or,
2. One percent of gross investment income plus premium income after deducting policyholder dividends.

Mutual fire and casualty companies were taxed on this basis until passage of the Revenue Act of 1962. Mutual marine insurance companies requested and were granted the right to be taxed on the same basis as stock insurance companies by the Revenue Act of 1941.

Taxation of Stock Fire and Casualty Insurers—1954 Revenue Code

Federal income taxation of stock fire and casualty insurance companies is basically similar to that of other industrial or commercial corporate enterprises. Thus, the net result is that such companies are taxed on both underwriting and investment income at regular corporate rates. Furthermore, the averaging concept applied to all corporate taxpayers is applicable to fire and casualty insurance companies by means of net operating loss carry-back and carry-forward provisions of the Code.

Computation of Taxable Income. Congress has recognized that the business of assuming risks has certain unique features and problems.

labeled in still other ways. In this chapter for the sake of consistency with ordinary usages by those dealing with the subject of taxation, the expression "fire and casualty companies" is often used.

Therefore, the computation of taxable net income of stock fire and casualty insurance companies is governed by separate sets of sections (principally Sections 831 and 832) of the Internal Revenue Code included in Part III of Sub-chapter L of Chapter 1. The computation of taxable net income is based upon the underwriting and investment exhibit included in the Annual Statement as submitted to the insurance departments regulating these companies. In fact, reference is made to the "annual statement approved by the National Convention of Insurance Commissioners" both in Internal Revenue Code Section 832 and in the accompanying regulations promulgated by the Commissioner of Internal Revenue.

Although the basis of the net taxable income determination is as set forth in the underwriting and investment exhibits of the Annual Statement, there are certain differences in the preparation of the tax return relating to allowable deductions from taxable gross income. A simplified formula (based on the 1962 Annual Convention Form Statement) for the computation of taxable net income for federal income tax purposes may be stated as follows:

1. Net income (Line 20 Statement of Income)

   plus

2. Federal and foreign income taxes incurred (included on Line 19, Statement of Income)

   minus

3. Dividends to policyholders (Line 32)
4. Tax exempt interest (principally from obligations issued by states, counties, and municipalities)
5. *a*) 85 percent of dividends from most domestic corporations,
   b) 62.115 percent of dividends on certain preferred stocks of public utilities

   equals

6. Net income subject to federal income tax.

The taxable income as determined above is subject to a tax rate of 30 percent on the first $25,000 of income and at a rate of 52 percent on the amount in excess of $25,000. If such taxable income includes net realized long-term capital gains, a 25 percent tax rate is applied.

Loss Carry-overs. It is not unusual for a company to experience an unfavorable loss ratio and therefore suffer an underwriting loss greater than net investment income. Thus, the item of "net income" shown above as Line 6 may be negative. If this situation prevails for any year or years, such net loss may be applied to reduce taxable income of specified preceding years to produce a refund of federal income taxes already paid, or may be applied to reduce the amount subject to tax in subsequent years. This procedure, which is also available to noninsurance corporations, accomplishes an averaging concept covering a period of nine years.

For example, if a company suffered a net loss for the calendar year 1965, the amount of such loss would be applied to the years shown below in the order designated:

Carry-Back	*Carry-Forward*	
1. 1962	4. 1966	7. 1969
2. 1963	5. 1967	8. 1970
3. 1964	6. 1968	

A net loss may not be carried back beyond three years. The importance of the net operating loss carry-back and carry-forward privileges of the Internal Revenue Code cannot be overemphasized. Fire and casualty insurance companies, by their very nature, are subject to catastrophe losses and cyclical loss trends.

Taxation of Mutual and Reciprocal Fire and Casualty Insurers—1962 Revenue Act

The Revenue Act of 1962 changed the basis (established in 1942) under which mutual and reciprocal fire and casualty insurers pay federal income taxes. With certain qualifications, these companies are now taxed at regular corporation rates on a total income basis—underwriting gain or loss and taxable investment income after dividends to policyholders are deducted. This method of taxation became effective on January 1, 1963.

Protection-against-Loss Account. The primary difference between the formula for taxing stock insurers and the formula for taxing mutual and reciprocal insurers is a special "reserve," referred to in the act as a "protection-against-loss account." Section 824 of the Code allows a deferral of taxable income equal to 1 percent of the losses incurred during the current year plus 25 percent of the underwriting gains for that year to be placed in the protection-against-loss account for a five-year period, during which time it shall be used to cover any excess of underwriting loss over investment income.

If the protection-against-loss account is inadequate to cover such loss, the taxpayer may apply, in general, the same loss carry-back and carry-forward provisions applicable to stock insurance companies. However, there is no loss carry-back to years before January 1, 1963.

In the sixth year, the amount in the protection-against-loss account from the fifth preceding year, except one half of the balance applicable to underwriting gain, is added to current taxable income to the extent not already offset by losses. The other half of the underwriting gain can remain in the protection-against-loss account as a cushion against extraordinary losses. The protection-against-loss account may not be increased above an amount which at the end of any year exceeds 10 percent of the premiums earned during the taxable year, less dividends to policyholders for that year. However, if an insurance company's earned premiums become less than they were in previous years, the protection-against-loss account will not be reduced below the amount in the account at the end of the previous year.

Special Consideration for Small Companies. There are special provisions in the act applicable to small fire and casualty companies. Four separate categories were established. Each category is based on a company's gross receipts; that is, its taxable investment income and net premiums or assessments. The act was designed to afford the most tax relief to the smallest companies, and gradually to diminish this relief as the gross income of the company increases. This special treatment entirely disappears when a company's gross income reaches $1.1 million. These four categories are as follows:

1. Companies whose gross income is less than $150,000. Under the prior law, companies with gross income of $75,000 or less for a taxable year were totally exempt from taxation. This exemption was increased to $150,000 under the act.
2. Companies whose gross income exceeds $150,000, but is less than $250,000. The companies in this category may elect to be taxed on net investment income only with a special provision that the tax computed on its investment income shall be reduced to an amount which bears the same proportion to the tax as the excess of its gross income over $150,000 bears to $100,000. The effect of this provision is gradually to reduce the tax relief as such company's gross receipts approach the upper limit when the relief becomes zero for a company with gross income of $250,000. Such company may also elect to be taxed on the larger company mutual basis. An election once made, however, is binding until the Internal Revenue Service permits a change. The regular basis will apply automatically if there is any amount in the protection-against-loss account, unless the company agrees to bring that amount into income.
3. Companies whose gross income is between $250,000 and $500,000. These companies may elect to be taxed on the regular mutual basis or on their investment income only. The special provision for reducing the tax is not applicable to this group.
4. Companies whose gross income exceeds $500,000, but is less than $1,100,000. These companies are taxed on the regular mutual basis, but they are given a special deduction which amounts to one percent of the difference between $1,100,000 and its lower gross income. As in category two, this provision has the effect of gradually reducing the tax relief as the gross income of the company increases. This special benefit disappears entirely when a company's gross income reaches $1,100,000.

Other Special Provisions. Provisions in the act also pertain specifically to factory mutuals, concentrated risk mutuals, and reciprocals.

The Associated Factory Mutual Insurance Companies are taxed like stock companies, that is, without the special protection-against-loss reserve account. For income tax purposes, however, these companies are permitted to determine their premium income on the basis of a schedule of absorbed premium deposits, plus 2 percent thereof.

The framers of the new tax bill undertook to recognize the unique problem of small and moderate size companies which confine their operations to a limited area and have a significant portion of "windstorm, hail, flood, earthquake or similar hazards" insured. If a company has 40 percent or more of its premium income attributable to these extrahazardous risks in one state, or within 200 miles of a fixed point to be selected by the insurance company, it may set aside an additional amount of underwriting income in a special portion of the protection-against-loss account. This portion of this "reserve" is subject to the five-year limitation, but the 10 percent ceiling is not applicable.

Reciprocals are taxed under the same rules applicable to mutual insurance companies; but they are permitted, in addition to the 1 percent and 25 percent allocations to the protection-against-loss account set forth above, to allocate to such account 25 percent of the net income received by the attorney-in-fact from the reciprocal. Any reciprocal making this election must include in its taxable income the net income received by the attorney-in-fact; however, the reciprocal shall be entitled to deduct from its income tax liability the amount of tax already paid by the attorney-in-fact with respect to this income.

STATE TAXES, LICENSES, AND OTHER IMPOSITIONS

Historical Notes

States began taxing insurance companies in the early 1800's when the legislature of New York passed a series of tax laws applicable to all corporations. At first, these laws did not differentiate between insurance companies and general corporations. In 1824, however, New York passed a special statute which assessed foreign fire insurance companies 10 percent on gross premiums collected within that state. This attempt was the first by a state government to tax insurance companies on a basis different from that for general corporations. This practice spread to other states. Within the next decade or two, both foreign and domestic insurance companies became subject to numerous special tax laws.

Subsequently, this 10 percent gross premium tax was reduced to 2 percent and made applicable to other types of companies. It is interesting to note that this first basis of taxation remains today and, in fact, has become the chief method of taxing insurance companies.

Tax theorists generally recognize two principal purposes of taxation: to raise revenue and to regulate. Initially the production of revenue was a secondary factor in levying taxes upon insurance companies. In most states, taxation was invoked more to strengthen the administrative control and regulation of the business than to produce revenue. Furthermore, in states other than New York, taxation took on the nature of retaliation for the premium tax assessed on foreign fire companies doing business in

New York. Today, however, taxes on insurance companies have become a major source of revenue to state governments. The latest survey made by the Insurance Industry Committee of Ohio shows that almost $625 million in premium taxes, franchise taxes, and fees were collected in 1961 by state governments. This figure includes payments from all types of insurers including life companies. Of this amount, only 4.06 percent was used for operating state insurance departments. The remainder was put into the general fund for other uses.

Opinions differ as to how much insurance companies should be taxed. Since such method of taxation is an indirect tax on policyholders and may, at least theoretically, be included in the base rate, state taxation of the insurance industry is an "easy method" of raising revenue. One fact should be kept in mind: commissions and certain other costs such as assessments for security funds and levies for local taxes are based on gross premiums. This fact means that an insurance company must load the rate about 1¼ percent to recover a 1 percent tax. Consequently, this method of raising revenue becomes a costly one for the policyholders who also are the taxpayers.

There are a few generalizations of state taxation which should be mentioned before some of the individual state practices are reviewed. First of all, there is no uniformity in the rates of taxation or in the bases used. Second, states tend to differentiate between domestic and foreign companies as to the type of tax and to its application. Third, there is a differentiation among types of companies (e.g., life, fire, marine, and casualty). And lastly, there is a prevalence of special purpose charges, licenses, assessments, and fees which are similar to taxes and, for the purpose of this chapter, probably should be placed in this category.

State Premium Taxes

The principal method of taxing insurance companies at the state level is by use of the premium tax. Premium taxes may be divided into "general premium taxes," which are in the nature of franchise taxes, and "special purpose premium taxes" for such services as fire departments, fire marshal's offices, firemen's relief or pension, policemen's relief or pension, and others.

General Premium Tax. This tax is based on the gross direct premiums written within the respective states, less credit for cancellations. As was mentioned earlier, the rate and the base on which such taxes are levied vary not only from state to state but vary within the state itself between domestic and nondomestic companies and by lines of insurance written by these companies. Rates applicable to nondomestic companies vary from 1.75 to 4 percent and for domestic companies from 0 to 2.25 percent. In the majority of the states, however, the rate is at or near 2 percent.

Twelve states—Arkansas, Florida, Illinois, Indiana, Kansas, Michigan,

New York, North Dakota, Ohio, Oklahoma, Oregon and Pennsylvania—exempt domestic insurance companies. Ten of these states impose another form of tax on domestic insurers (Illinois: capital stock tax; Arkansas, Indiana, North Dakota, Oklahoma, Pennsylvania: income tax; Michigan: privilege tax; New York and Ohio: franchise tax; and Oregon: corporation excise tax).

In addition, two states—Kentucky and Wisconsin—exempt all domestic mutual fire and casualty companies, and Maryland exempts "property premiums" of domestic mutual insurance companies. In 16 states, special classes of mutual companies such as county or township mutuals and certain assessment type mutuals are wholly or largely exempt from premium taxes. These are: Colorado, Georgia, Iowa, Minnesota, Missouri, Montana, New Hampshire, New York, North Carolina, North Dakota, Oklahoma, South Dakota, Texas, Utah, Virginia, and West Virginia.

Preferential treatment in the rate of tax paid is afforded domestic insurers in 13 states: Alabama, Alaska, Arizona, Hawaii, Maine, Massachusetts, Mississippi, Nebraska, North Carolina, South Carolina, South Dakota, Washington, and in certain instances in Wisconsin.

Twenty-three jurisdictions tax domestic companies at the same premium tax as foreign companies. In 10 of these states—Colorado, Georgia, Idaho, Louisiana, Montana, New Mexico, Oklahoma, South Carolina, Tennessee and Texas—the premium tax is reducible if an insurer invests a certain percentage of its assets in the taxing state. Another variation of the base is found in Alabama, California, and Florida where some credit against premium tax is given for real estate taxes paid on a regional or principal office building located in the state. California allows the amount of real estate taxes paid on the "principal office in the state" as a credit against the liability for premium tax. This credit is being reviewed and there have been proposals to allow a credit only for a portion of the real estate taxes measured by the amount of space occupied by the insurance company. Alabama allows a credit for ad valorem taxes on real estate owned in Alabama and at least 50 percent occupied by the company. Florida permits any foreign insurance company which maintains a regional home office in the state, as defined in Section 205.43(2), to reduce its premium taxes by 50 percent plus the amount of the ad valorem taxes on the regional home office property, provided the total credit does not exceed 80 percent of the premium tax liability.

These credit provisions are an attempt to encourage insurance companies to locate and invest their assets within the state. To the extent utilized by the companies, it is an effective way of reducing their tax liability. Although generally these provisions apply equally to domestic and foreign companies, in practice they would seem to favor domestic insurers. Table 66–1 summarizes the most important facts regarding state premium tax rates of fire and casualty companies in the various states.

TABLE 66–1

PREMIUM TAX RATES BY STATES—FIRE AND CASUALTY INSURANCE AND INSURERS 1964[1 and 2]

State	Rate on Foreign Insurers, Percent	Rate on Domestic Insurers, Percent	Retaliatory Provision
Alabama	2½[3,28] 3[4,28]	½	Unconstitutional
Alaska	3	1½	No
Arizona	2½[5] 2[4]	1 2 (W.C.)	Yes
Arkansas	2½[34]	Exempt[6]	Yes
California	2.35[30] (2.33 for years 1964–67)	Same	Constitutionality in litigation
Colorado	2¼[28]	Same	Yes
Connecticut	2	2¾[7]	Yes
Delaware	1¾ (W.C., 4)	Same	Yes
District of Columbia	2	Same	No
Florida	2[30]	Exempt[8]	Yes
Georgia	2¼[28]	Same	Yes
Hawaii	3¼	2¼	No
Idaho	3	Same[28]	Yes
Illinois	2	Exempt[9]	Yes
Indiana	2	Exempt[10]	Yes
Iowa	2	Same	Yes
Kansas	2	Exempt	Yes
Kentucky	2	Domestic mutuals exempt; 2% for all other	Yes
Louisiana	Schedule[11,28,32]	Same[32]	Yes
Maine	2	1[31]	Yes
Maryland	2	"Property Premium" of domestic mutual insurers exempt; other domestics 2%	Yes
Massachusetts	2	1[12]	Yes

TABLE 66–1 (*Continued*)

State	Rate on Foreign Insurers, Percent	Rate on Domestic Insurers, Percent	Retaliatory Provision
Michigan	2[13] 3[3]	Exempt[14]	Yes
Minnesota	2	Same	Yes
Mississippi	3	1½[29]	No
Missouri	2	Same	Yes
Montana	2[28] (2¼ for 1963–64)	Same	Yes
Nebraska	2	.6	Yes
Nevada	2	Same	Yes
New Hampshire	2	Same	Yes
New Jersey	2	Same	Yes
New Mexico	2½[28]	Same	Yes
New York	2[15] 1[16]	Exempt[17]	Yes
North Carolina	2½ (W.C., 4)	1[18]	No
North Dakota	2½	Exempt[19]	Yes
Ohio	2½	Exempt[20]	Yes
Oklahoma	4[28]	Exempt[21]	Yes
Oregon	2¼	Exempt[22]	Yes
Pennsylvania	2	Exempt[23]	Yes
Rhode Island	2	Same	Yes
South Carolina	3[24,28]	2% but subject to limit[25]	Yes
South Dakota	2½	½	Yes
Tennessee	2[28,33] (W.C., 4)	Same	Yes
Texas	3.85[28]	Same	Yes
Utah	2¼	Same	Yes
Vermont	2	Same	Yes

TABLE 66-1 (*Continued*)

State	Rate on Foreign Insurers, Percent	Rate on Domestic Insurers, Percent	Retaliatory Provision
Virginia	2¾	Same	Yes
Washington	2	1	Yes
West Virginia	3[26]	Same	Yes
Wisconsin	Reciprocity[27]	Domestic mutuals exempt; domestic stocks pay 1¼%[3]; 2%[13]	Reciprocal law[27]
Wyoming	2½	1½[28]	Yes

EXPLANATORY NOTES:

1 Information for table above obtained from state statutes and *Insurance Law Index Service*, McCombs and Co., Inc.

2 Exclusive of special purpose taxes, such as fire marshal levies. Table incorporates changes enacted in 1963 legislatures.

3 Fire and marine.

4 All other.

5 Auto BI/PD and Auto Physical Damage.

6 Subject to net income tax graduated upon entire net income.

7 Domestic companies also pay a reducing rate of tax on interest and dividends received.

8 Domestic insurers exempt if home office is in Florida.

9 Domestic insurers are subject to "capital stock" tax (on the net value of their assets) applicable to domestic corporations generally.

10 Domestic insurers are subject to state income tax on income from all sources.

11 Fire, marine, and inland marine—$6,000 or less in gross annual premiums, tax is $180 with $200 for each additional $10,000 or fraction thereof; casualty, surety—same basis but tax is $180 with $175 for each additional $10,000.

12 After 1965, presently 2%.

13 Casualty, including all auto, surety, and fidelity.

14 Subject to privilege tax of 5 mills on paid up capital and surplus ($50,000 maximum tax).

15 Fire and allied lines written by foreign and alien insurers, and casualty lines written by alien insurers.

16 Casualty lines written by foreign insurers.

17 Domestic insurers pay 2% franchise tax; foreign fire and alien casualty companies exempt from franchise tax; alien companies pay ½% franchise tax on fire lines, foreign companies pay 1% franchise tax on casualty lines. Premium tax and franchise tax of alien insurers subject to reduction under reciprocal treaties.

18 Or 6% of entire net income, whichever is greater.

19 Subject to income tax on North Dakota transactions.

20 Subject to franchise tax of .2% of smaller of capital and surplus or 8⅓ times Ohio premiums. Minimum tax of $25.

21 Subject to income tax of 4% on Oklahoma transactions.

22 Subject to corporation excise tax of 6% of taxable income.

23 Subject to capital stock tax of 5 mills per dollar of actual value of capital stock and corporate income tax of 6% of taxable net income.

24 Annual license fee 2%; additional annual license fee 1%.

25 Tax shall not exceed 5% of net income under South Carolina Income Tax Act.

26 Rate reduced to 2% if 25% of admitted assets invested in certain West Virginia securities.

27 Foreign insurers pay rate imposed by their states of domicile on Wisconsin companies. Alien insurers pay 2% on casualty lines, 2⅜% on fire.

28 Premium tax rates reducible in accordance with a scale keyed to percentage of insurer's admitted assets (South Carolina—S.C. premium writings, Wyo.—applicable to domestic companies only) invested in taxing state.

29 Real estate taxes deductible up to $20,000.

30 Home or principal office (California) or regional home office deduction (Florida).

31 Subject to franchise tax.

32 All companies subject to 4% income tax. Credit may be taken for premium taxes paid.

33 Franchise tax applicable to both foreign and domestic companies.

34 Tax is reduced to 2% if insurer maintains 50% of reserves (not including loss reserves) on Arkansas business in Arkansas investments.

Special Purpose Premium Taxes. In addition to the aforementioned premium taxes, there are fire department taxes, policemen's and firemen's relief or pension taxes, fire marshal taxes, security fund payments, and assessments to defray the expenses of operating some of the insurance regulatory offices. The theory behind most of these impositions is that these services provide a benefit for the insurance industry by reducing losses or by improving law enforcement. To the extent these services are efficient, policyholders do benefit; however, all or most of these services also benefit uninsured members of the public. For example, fire protection is provided for everyone regardless of whether he has insurance or not. Since fire protection is a state function it should be supported by regular revenue. To the extent policyholders are required to pay more for a service than the amount of the loss it eliminates, such assessment destroys the ability of companies to collect an equitable premium. If the philosophy behind these special purpose impositions were carried to its ultimate, insurance would soon be paying for most public services and insurance protection would become priced far beyond the ability of many people to pay.

Another problem the industry faces with these special purpose payments based on premiums is the proper allocation of the fire portion of homeowners, commercial multi-peril, and other package premiums. Although some work has been done on the problem, some states still use an arbitrary percentage in breaking down the component parts of these coverages. Table 66–2 summarizes these special purpose premium taxes.

State Income Taxes

Alaska and Mississippi are the only states which have an income tax law applicable to both domestic and nondomestic insurance companies and which do not allow a credit for premium taxes paid.

Louisiana and Minnesota have an income tax law applicable to all companies but both states give insurance companies a credit against their premium taxes. In Louisiana the premium tax offset against this tax usually relieves direct writing insurance companies from obligation to pay this tax but licensed professional reinsurance companies customarily have some income tax to pay.

Six other states have income tax laws applicable to domestic companies only (Arkansas, Indiana, North Carolina, North Dakota, Oklahoma, and Pennsylvania). In five of these states, domestic insurers are exempt from the premium tax law; the other, North Carolina, requires domestic fire and casualty insurers to pay an income tax in lieu of a premium tax if the tax developed on a net income basis is greater than the premium tax. State officials generally prefer a premium tax to an income tax since premium income tends to fluctuate less than net income.

TABLE 66–2

SPECIAL PURPOSE ADDITIONAL PREMIUM TAXES
FIRE AND CASUALTY INSURANCE[1]—1964

State	Tax Designation	Premiums Affected[2]	Rate
Delaware	Fire Department Tax	Fire lines	3½%—All insurers
Florida	Fire Marshal Tax	Fire lines	⅜%—All insurers
Georgia	Firemen's Pension Fund	Fire lines	1%—All insurers
Illinois	Fire Marshal Tax	Fire lines	½% maximum—All insurers
Indiana	Fire Marshal Tax	Fire lines	½%—Foreign insurers only
Kansas	Fire Marshal Tax	Fire lines	¾% maximum—All insurers
Kentucky	Fire Department Tax	Fire lines	2%—All insurers
	Rate regulation and Fire Marshal Tax	Fire lines	¾%—All insurers except domestic mutuals
Louisiana	Fire Marshal Tax	Fire lines	1%—All insurers
	Fire Department Tax	Fire lines	2%—Foreign insurers only
Maine	Fire Investigation Tax	Fire lines	½%—All insurers
Maryland	Motor Vehicle UCJ Fund	Auto BI/PD	½% maximum—All insurers
Minnesota	Fire Marshal Tax	Fire lines	½%—All insurers
	Firemen's Relief Fund Surcharge[3]	Fire lines	2%—All insurers
Mississippi	Fire Marshal Tax	Fire lines	½%—All insurers
	Insurance Commission Fund[4]	Casualty lines	Pro rata share of expenses—All insurers
	Municipal Firemen and Policemen Disability and Relief Fund	Fire lines	½%—All insurers
Montana	Fire Marshal Tax	Fire lines	¼%—All insurers
Nebraska	Fire Marshal Tax	Fire lines	½%—Foreign insurers; ¼%—Domestic insurers
New Jersey	Fire Department Tax	Fire Prem.	2%—Foreign insurers
	FR Law Administration Expenses	Auto BI/PD Liability	Pro rata—All insurers
	Motor Vehicle Liability Security Fund (subject to ceiling)	Auto BI/PD Liability	1%—All insurers
	Motor Vehicle UCJ Fund	Auto BI/PD Liability	½% maximum—All insurers
New York	Fire Department Tax	Fire lines	2%—Foreign insurers only
	Insurance Department Expenses	All lines	Pro rata—Domestic

[1] Information for table above obtained from state statutes and *Insurance Law Index Service*, McCombs and Co., Inc. Table exclusive of workmen's compensation insurance. Municipal levies not included.

[2] Other levies on "allied fire lines" not included.

[3] Collected severally in Duluth, Minneapolis, and St. Paul on premiums written in each of these cities.

[4] For administration of casualty rating law.

TABLE 66-2 (*Continued*)

State	Tax Designation	Premium Affected[2]	Rate
New York (*Cont'd*)			Insurers and U.S. Branches of alien insurers domiciled in New York
	Motor Vehicle Liability Security Funds	Auto BI/PD Liability	1%—All insurers
	FR and Compulsory Laws Administration Expenses	Auto BI/PD Liability	Pro rata—All insurers
	Motor Vehicle Accident Indemnification Corporation Expense	Auto BI/PD Liability	Pro rata—All insurers
North Carolina	Firemen's Relief Tax	Fire lines	½%—All insurers
	Firemen's Pension Fund Tax	Fire lines (automobile excluded)	1%—All insurers
North Dakota	Fire Marshal Tax	Fire lines	½%—Domestic companies only
Ohio	Fire Marshal Tax	Fire lines	½%—All insurers
Oklahoma	Fire Marshal Tax	Fire lines	5/16%—All insurers
Oregon	Fire Marshal Tax	Fire lines	½%—All insurers
South Carolina	Fire Marshal Tax	Fire lines	1/10%—All insurers
	Fire Department Tax	Fire lines	1%—All insurers
South Dakota	Fire Marshal Tax	Fire lines	½%—All insurers
Tennessee	Fire Marshal Tax	Fire lines	½%—All insurers
Texas	State Board of Insurance Maintenance Taxes	Fire lines	1¼% maximum—All insurers
		Casualty lines	.4% maximum—All insurers
		Motor Vehicle insurance	.2% maximum—All insurers
Virginia	Maintenance of Bureau of Insurance	Fire and Casualty lines	.1% maximum, pro rata —All insurers
West Virginia	Fire Marshal Tax	Fire lines	½%—All insurers
Wisconsin	Fire Department Tax	Fire lines	2%—Domestic and alien insurers only

Income taxes in the various states have never become a real problem to the insurance industry either because of the "in lieu of" provision or because the individual state's income tax laws exempt insurance companies.

Real Estate and Personal Property Taxes

Until recently, ad valorem taxes on real estate and personal property were not a significant factor in the insurance business. However, within the last few years the need for additional revenue, especially at local levels, has prompted officials to find new sources of revenue and to place on the tax rolls taxpayers who were never there before. The result has been an increased tax burden for the insurance industry. In most areas, both the base and the rate of assessment for real estate and personal property taxes have increased substantially. In the past, only counties assessed real and personal property taxes but now both city and county have entered the field in some states—such as Missouri and Texas. The Louisiana Tax Commission requires a filing of premiums written by line of business for the entire state of Louisiana for purposes of ad valorem taxes.

The "in lieu of" provisions curtail these increases in expense to some extent, but not in states which add the clause "except real and personal property taxes" to these provisions.

Miscellaneous State Taxes, Licenses, Fees, Assessments, and Other Impositions

In addition to the aforementioned levies, insurance companies are required to pay numerous other miscellaneous taxes, licenses, and fees. Most of these are self-explanatory and will therefore not be discussed. The following list contains some of the various types of taxes, licenses, fees, and other assessments and impositions to which insurance companies are subject:

State and Local Taxes:

- Capital Stock Tax
- Sales Tax and Use Tax
- Franchise Tax (Other than measured by premiums)
- Excise Tax on Documents
- Transfer Tax
- License Tax
- Assessment for Maintenance of Bureau of Insurance
- Insurance Rating Commission Assessment
- Interest and Dividends Tax
- Ocean Marine Profits Tax

Special Workmen's Compensation Assessments and Payments:

- Stock Workmen's Compensation Security Fund
- Mutual Workmen's Compensation Security Fund
- Children's Additional Death Benefit Fund
- Second Injury Fund
- Curative Centre Fund
- Industrial Administrative Fund (Industrial Commission Assessments)
- Veterans' Second Injury Fund
- Assessment for Safety Devices

Insurance Department Licenses and Fees:

- Company Examination Fee
- Agents', Brokers', and Solicitors' Licenses
- Fee for Certificate of Authority
- Renewal of Certificate of Authority

Filing Power of Attorney
Filing Annual Statement
Filing Amended Articles and/or Bylaws

Other Assessments and Payments:

Motor Vehicle Liability Security Fund
Public Motor Vehicle Liability Security Fund
Administration of Safety Financial Responsibility Law
Motor Vehicle Financial Security Act Expense
Motor Vehicle Accident Indemnification Corporation Expense
Unsatisfied Claim and Judgment Fund
Statement Publication Fee
Advertising Required by Law

Retaliatory or Reciprocal Laws

As may be seen from Table 66–2, most states have a retaliatory or reciprocal statute. It is not important for the purposes of this chapter to explain the theoretical difference between the two laws. The effect of both is retaliation.

Although retaliatory or reciprocal statutes can be applied to other areas, they have largely been made applicable to the field of taxation of insurance companies. Fundamentally, a retaliatory statute provides in effect that, ". . . the retaliating state says to all other states—If you tax or regulate our insurance companies in excess of the standards that we have set up for your insurance companies here, we shall tax or regulate yours here to the same degree."[2]

A retaliatory law is not designed in most cases to be a revenue-raising statute; rather, it is designed to protect domestic companies from impositions which might be put upon them by other states. Basically, retaliatory laws are designed to equalize the burdens imposed on domestic and foreign companies.

After the South-Eastern Underwriters Association decision[3] and before the passage of U.S. Public Law 15 (McCarran Act) in 1945, many state officials suspected the retaliatory laws would be declared unfairly discriminatory and thus held to be unconstitutional. However, after U.S. Public Law 15 and the *Prudential Life Insurance Company* v. *Benjamin* decision,[4] it was generally accepted that these laws did not violate the federal constitution. This decision did not preclude the possibility of such laws being in violation of individual state constitutions. To date, one state (Alabama) has declared its statute unconstitutional, and another state (California) at the time of this writing is testing the validity of its law.

There are several important and interesting facets to these laws. The first is whether a commissioner of insurance shall be required to invoke

[2] H. Harold Leavey, "Retaliatory Laws in the United States Relating to Insurance," *Insurance Law Journal* (February, 1953), p. 110.

[3] 322 U.S. 533 (1944)—see chapter 65.

[4] 328 U.S. 408 (1946)—see chapter 65.

the statute or whether he has an option of enforcing such a statute. A few states permit the insurance commissioner to use his discretion, but the most common practice is mandatory enforcement.

Another important facet is the method of computation—an aggregate or an item-by-item basis. In most states, the total taxes of that state are compared with the aggregate taxes of another to determine whether a company pays its taxes under the retaliatory law or the premium tax law. In principle this comparison sounds relatively easy, but in practice it is difficult because states tax on different bases.

Wisconsin is the only state with a truly reciprocal law. Under the Wisconsin statute, foreign companies pay upon their Wisconsin business the amount of taxes imposed by the laws of their home states upon Wisconsin companies. However, the minimum tax on fire and marine lines is 3/8 of 1 percent of gross direct premiums plus a 2 percent fire department tax. This minimum does not apply to the casualty lines.

TAXATION BY MUNICIPALITIES

Municipalities derive their taxing authority from their state statutes, their state constitution, or both. When properly authorized, such ordinances may or may not be applicable to the insurance business because of the "in lieu of" provision. Many municipal levies affecting the insurance business are applicable solely to agents. Some, however, are applicable to companies as well as agents.

Some states in authorizing the imposition by municipalities of license taxes on insurers specify that such impositions shall be based on premiums written; other states prohibit levies of this type and limit such impositions to flat fees; in still other states the local levy is based on a flat fee which is graduated upwards with the volume of business written.

Some municipal levies are based on premiums written within the municipality, regardless of where the property or risks insured may be located. Others are based on premiums written for insurance on property or risks located within the municipality; still others are based on premiums on property or risks located within the municipality regardless of where the premiums are written. It is evident that, where varying bases are applied by different municipalities within the same state, insurers' tax liability for the same premiums may be subject to pyramiding or duplication.

These taxes have resulted in a grotesque growth of bookkeeping techniques in order to keep track of where each piece of business is written and where the property or risk is located.

Municipal ordinances are often changed without prior, and frequently without subsequent, notice. Since these ordinances are not usually widely disseminated by the taxing authorities, it is obvious that insurers do not have an easy time of it. Attempts to resolve the serious problems involved have all too frequently met with firm and unaltering resistance from the municipalities, which are especially zealous about safeguarding all their current taxing prerogatives.

At the time of this writing about 14 states permit their municipalities to tax the insurance industry. Most of the problems in this area stem from the southeastern states: Alabama, Florida, Georgia, Kentucky, Louisiana, and South Carolina.

In Alabama, cities assess casualty companies a flat fee of $10 to $50 based upon the size of the city plus 1 percent of premiums written in the municipality. Fire companies are assessed a flat minimum license fee at the beginning of the year adjustable at the end of the year upon a fixed percentage up to a maximum of 4 percent. The fee and the tax are levied on the company and not the agent. There are over 400 municipalities which have passed such laws. Florida municipalities assess a flat fee on either the agent, the company, or sometimes both. Georgia taxes insurance companies a flat fee based on the kind of business written and in accordance with the number of agents in each location. Some municipalities charge in addition a premium tax of at least 2 percent.

The problem has become most vexing in Kentucky where last year over 100 municipalities assessed a license or occupation tax against insurance companies. One city levied a tax of 20 percent of the premium. Louisiana municipalities have a license fee based upon the amount of premiums written by class. There are four classes and the maximum fee is $9,000. South Carolina cities assess on both the bracket system and a percentage of premiums. The tax is levied on all premiums written or collected in a city, and preference is given to that city wherein the property is located. Note that this is only a preference and not a requirement as in most other states.

SUGGESTED READINGS

DENNEY, RICHARD L., AND RUA, ANTHONY P. *Federal Income Taxation of Insurance Companies.* New York: Ronald Press Company, 1961.

Insurance Accounting: Fire and Casualty. Philadelphia: The Spectator, 1954. Chaps. vii, xiv. (Prepared by and published for the Insurance Accounting and Statistical Association. A revision is in progress at the time of writing of this chapter.)

MCCOMBS AND COMPANY, INC. *Insurance Law Index Service,* Vols. 1–7.

STATE OF NEW YORK INSURANCE DEPARTMENT. "Fees and Taxes Charged Insurance Companies Under the Laws of New York Together With Abstracts of Fees, Taxes and Other Requirements of Other States," 1962.

Chapter 67

NONADMITTED MARKETS

BY CAMERON BROWN

To many persons within and outside of the insurance industry the most confusing and mysterious subject in insurance is the nonadmitted market. The purpose of this chapter is to dispel some of this confusion and mystery. The discussion is divided into the following major sections: definitions; growth and scope of the nonadmitted market; types of surplus line regulation; taxation of nonadmitted insurers; principal nonadmitted markets; access to nonadmitted markets; and principal business written in the nonadmitted market.

DEFINITIONS

Each state uses its police power to control the operations of insurance companies, brokers, and agents located within its boundaries. Its control over insurance companies chartered elsewhere and not licensed by it, but providing coverage within the state or for its residents, is far less well established. The federal constitution provides individual insureds and corporations with certain rights of contract which the states may not invade. These situations give rise to the use of companies which operate beyond the jurisdiction of the state. Several reasonably synonymous terms are currently used when referring to the placing of insurance with, or the activities of, such companies.

Nonadmitted

A nonadmitted market is being used in the effecting of insurance when coverage is placed with an insurer (1) not licensed in the state where the insured property is located, or (2) if other than property insurance is involved, not licensed in the state in which the insured conducts his principal business. "Nonadmitted" refers to the fact that the company has not been admitted or licensed by the state to conduct business within such state and is therefore not subject to the insurance laws and insurance department of the state. A nonadmitted company operates outside of the insurance laws of the state, although it may, in certain limited areas, agree voluntarily to furnish information to the state or to limit its operations within the state. "Nonadmitted" is the term most frequently used to describe these activities. For instance, proposed uniform legislation recently considered by the National Association of Insurance Commissioners (N.A.I.C.) was known as the "Non-Admitted Insurance Bill." (See Chapter 65.)

Unauthorized

"Unauthorized" as applied to an insurer or insurance has the same meaning as nonadmitted and the terms are used interchangeably. The official body of the N.A.I.C., which has been studying this subject in recent years, is designated as the Unauthorized Insurance Committee.

Unlicensed

This term refers to the fact that the insurer is unlicensed by the state and is therefore nonadmitted or unauthorized to act within its jurisdiction.

Surplus Line

While often used synonymously with the foregoing terms, surplus line originally had a more limited meaning. It referred to amounts of coverage which exceeded the capacity of the admitted market. For instance, the licensed companies might be capable of writing most, but not all, of a large hazardous fire risk. The portion of the coverage beyond or in excess of the capacity of the admitted market, and therefore placed with a nonadmitted carrier, would be called a surplus line. This term is now used, however, also to denote a type of coverage which no admitted carrier is prepared to write. Legislation in a state, regulating the use of nonadmitted markets, is often known as the surplus line law.

Excess Line

While this term once referred principally to the placing with a nonadmitted insurer of a layer of coverage excess of that written with an admitted insurer, it is now used interchangeably with surplus line. For instance, the New York Insurance Code refers to the licensing of "Excess Line Brokers."

Excluded Classes

Regulation of nonadmitted insurance usually does not apply to certain classes which states have chosen to exempt from control. Some, or all, of the following classes may, under specified conditions, be excluded: reinsurance, (ocean) marine, aviation, health, export credit, and risks of any nature located outside the boundaries of the state.

GROWTH AND SCOPE OF NONADMITTED MARKETS

Rights of Insurance Buyers

Nonadmitted markets exist only because of the regulation of insurance by the several states. If there were no such regulation, all markets, regardless of location, would be available to the insurance purchaser and his broker. Under the federal constitution, trade is unrestricted between the states. Commerce can be regulated by a state within its borders but not beyond; nor can a state interfere with interstate trade. Only the federal government has the authority to regulate commerce between the states. The right of an insurance purchaser to negotiate for coverage where and under whatever terms he wishes, outside of his state boundaries, was first confirmed by the United States Supreme Court in 1897 in *Allgeyer* v. *Louisiana* (165 U.S. 578). Many years later, in 1922, this position was restated by the same court in the *St. Louis Cotton Compress Co.* v. *Arkansas* (260 U.S. 346). The Supreme Court did not specify whether insurance was or was not in interstate commerce. It merely said that an insurance purchaser had the right to contract as he wished and the state could not fine or tax him. The *State Board of Insurance* v. *Todd Shipyards Corporation* decision in 1962 (370 U.S. 451) reconfirmed parts of this position.

Early History

Capacity problems had long existed quite apart from rate and form control. As licensing procedures developed, with the concomitant control of companies, states became more concerned with the activities of insureds, brokers, and agents where unlicensed companies were involved.

The first known example of such concern occurred in New York state in 1884. The garment industry was having trouble placing adequate amounts of fire insurance. The New York legislature in that year took cognizance of the problem in reverse by enacting a statute prohibiting any agent or broker from aiding the transaction of business by any company that had not been licensed by the state. Such action, of course, did not solve the problem. Insureds still had to get insurance to meet their commercial requirements. In 1890 the same legislature passed a law authorizing the licensing of producers to write fire insurance in nonadmitted companies, subject to the filing of an affidavit stating that the risk could not be covered by the conventional market. The law was limited to the control of the producer. Legislators apparently recognized that they probably could not prevent an individual from contracting for coverage outside the state boundaries if he so wished.

In 1893, the National Convention of Insurance Commissioners appointed a Committee on Underground Insurance. This term "underground insurance" was the one then used to describe coverage placed outside of the state's jurisdiction. The committee urged that contracts with such companies be void, a recommendation of dubious constitutionality. A year later the N.C I.C. took note in its proceedings of the progress being made in studying this problem further and in checking companies indulging in the practice.

Other states acknowledged the same problem by the passage of various types of surplus line legislation, generally limited to the control of agents and brokers and providing for the payment of a special surplus line tax. Illinois, for instance, enacted its first statute of this type in 1903.

Effect of the Depression

Up to the great depression of 1929–34, the amount of coverage placed with nonadmitted carriers was relatively small. Exact figures are not available for those years but the premiums written in the nonadmitted market for surplus line reasons are estimated to have been well below 1 percent of the total. The pace of placing risks with Lloyd's and other "off-shore" unlicensed insurers accelerated very considerably starting with the depression years of the early 1930's. The fall in equity prices, plus unsatisfactory underwriting results, forced a number of domestic carriers into liquidation or out of business. Because of the diminution of their assets, admitted companies generally had a much smaller capacity to write the risks offered to them. Also, underwriters in the companies were hesitant to take on any unusual hazards, since they wished to be as nearly certain as possible of underwriting profits. On the other hand, the insurance purchasers, whose businesses in most cases had also suffered from the ravages of the depression, were anxious to purchase the most attractive coverage at the most reasonable prices available anywhere. As a result of these temporary and abnormal circumstances, insureds intensified their search for competitive and capacity markets in unlicensed companies both within the United States and abroad.

Activities of this type became so prevalent that many state legislatures updated their control or established control for the first time, insofar as they could, over the activities of nonadmitted carriers, producers, and insureds. For instance, California, which has the largest known volume of surplus line business at the present time, enacted its first comprehensive law in 1937. Illinois revised its statute on this subject the same year. Additional regulatory legislative activity slowed during the war years and only burgeoned again after the passage of Public Law 15.

Public Law 15

Prior to 1944, regulation of insurance—as explained in Chapter 65—had never been undertaken by the federal congress. The South-Eastern Underwriters Association case of 1944 (322 U.S. 533) and the subsequent passage of Public Law 15 are discussed in Chapter 65. The implications of this decision and this law on the nonadmitted market are particularly pertinent to this chapter.

Many of the practices in the insurance business, such as the fixing of the rates in concert through rating bureaus, were contrary to the Sherman Act and unless regularized through state laws would have had to be abandoned. Public Law 15 did not stipulate that the state laws had to be consistent with the philosophy of the Sherman Antitrust Act and other federal regulatory laws. The principal efforts of the insurance industry were directed towards the enactment of state laws that would enable the practice of fixing rates in concert to be continued. To this end, most states adopted complex and detailed rating laws which required the filing of rating scales, policies, and forms for essentially all types of property-liability insurances with the various insurance departments, and the obtaining of departmental approval before they could be used. The filing requirements were applicable both to rating bureaus and companies fixing their rates in concert as well as to those companies operating independently. As a result of these laws many insureds could no longer solve their coverage problems with licensed insurers.

Postwar Problems

The end of World War II found insureds under pressure to use unlicensed companies for two principal reasons. First, there were the many new rate and form control laws being passed by the states as a consequence of Public Law 15. Second, there was the great growth of industrial plants and values following the end of the war. Licensed companies, whose assets had grown little during the war and which were now operating under more restrictive control than ever before, were unable to accept all of the business which was offered to them. Again insurance buyers were forced, as they had been during the depression, to find markets elsewhere for both their capacity and special risk needs. The growth of these activities brought a rather quick reaction in many of the states. In the late 1940's and the early 1950's, additional states passed laws or amended existing ones in an effort to regulate surplus line business.

N.A.I.C. Action

In the mid 1950's, the National Association of Insurance Commissioners took further cognizance of the nonadmitted problem. After considerable work and discussion, a set of "Guiding Principles Relating to Surplus Line Laws" was adopted in 1957. It was for use by states whose legislators were either contemplating initial surplus line laws or wishing to amend laws already on the books. Many were dissatisfied with the generality of these principles. Following the pattern of the development of the all-industry bills, the N.A.I.C. took on the task of developing a uniform surplus line bill which could be proposed in those states which either had inadequate laws or no legislation at all on this subject. An "All-Industry Committee" assisted the N.A.I.C. in considering this problem. Many possible approaches were proposed and eventually, in 1962, a final draft was presented to the N.A.I.C. convention. It was strongly opposed by many elements within the insurance industry and almost solidly opposed by a large group of insurance buyers. The draft bill was accepted but not adopted. Adoption by the N.A.I.C. of the uniform bill would not have been mandatory on the states but it would have provided a set of provisions from which each state could have taken those desired. One of the most important provisions in the proposed uniform bill was one which would have enabled admitted companies to write business which would have otherwise been surplus line. This provision had substantial support and was an attempt to recognize that much of the surplus line business could be written by admitted companies if they were not subject to restrictive form and rate regulation.

Congressional Review of Public Law 15

In 1960–61 the Senate Antitrust and Monopoly Subcommittee held many hearings to determine the sufficiency of state regulation. (See Chapter 65.) Considerable attention was focused on nonadmitted markets, their regulation, and the type and volume of business flowing to them. Questions were raised regarding the effects of state rate and form control and their relation to business fleeing these restrictions. This subcommittee investigation is continuing at the time of this writing.

Status of State Laws

In 1964 only two states, Delaware and Wyoming, were without special legislation regarding unlicensed companies and the handling of surplus line business. All of the other states had some type of surplus line legislation. Officials of many of these states, however, are not presently satisfied with their own regulations and are considering amendments. This process is a rather steady one as the states attempt to keep up with the actual activities of both their own citizens and the unlicensed companies.

More than 20 states also have statutes which provide for a tax to be paid directly by the insured when a nonadmitted market is used without the services of a resident surplus line broker. At least one state, Michigan, prohibits the use of a nonadmitted market, unless prior approval is received from the insurance department.

Recent Developments concerning the Insurance Buyer

Throughout all of these years of legislative activity, one area of control continued to remain ambiguous. Most surplus line laws were limited in scope to regulation of agents and brokers within the state and to those holding nonresident licenses. As already noticed, however, states attempted to control, through tax measures or otherwise, the insurance-buying activities of their citizens. In 1962, the Supreme Court handed down a most significant decision. In the Todd Shipyards decision, previously referred to, it held that Texas could not tax an insured in respect to insurance on its property in the state when every aspect of the transaction with an unlicensed company took place outside of the state. This decision appears to limit the power which many of the states have assumed in the taxation and regulation of surplus line business. Therefore, based upon the Todd Shipyards case, the regulation of surplus line activities within a state seems to be limited mainly to the licensing of agents and brokers, the collection of surplus line taxes from them, and regulation of companies which may wish to qualify as nonadmitted carriers, where provision is made for such qualification.

Some states have attempted to exercise certain control over nonadmitted companies and their financial stability in particular, by providing that agents and brokers can only effect surplus line business with a nonadmitted company which has been approved by the state. These lists normally contain both foreign and domestic companies, although at least one state, Missouri, will presently only approve an alien company, that is, one chartered in a foreign country. An insurance buyer may still use an unapproved company, but the insurance department assumes no responsibility regarding the solvency or claim paying practices of that company.

TYPES OF SURPLUS LINE REGULATION

Licensing of Surplus Line Agents and Brokers

Despite the fact that no two state surplus line laws are identical, the ultimate results are not too dissimilar. Control is exercised principally through resident agents and brokers, specially licensed to handle business placed with nonadmitted companies. Only one state with surplus line laws, South Carolina, does not require a special license. In every state with such a law, however, the agent or broker, whether specially licensed or not, must report to the state and is accountable for the premium tax on all insurance written with nonadmitted companies. Provisions are generally found which govern the annual license fee to be paid by the surplus line broker, the type of reports to be rendered, and the frequency with which the taxes are to be paid. In most states the surplus line licensee is required (1) to post a bond, the amount ranging from $200 to $25,000, and (2) to pay an annual licensee fee which may be as much as $300.

Due Diligence

Many of the states, of which New York and Illinois are good examples, provide that risks may be placed with nonadmitted companies by a licensed surplus line broker only after a diligent effort has been made to place the coverage with admitted companies. This act of due diligence may be confirmed through the filing of an affidavit listing the admitted companies from which the coverage was sought unsuccessfully. The state may go further and require a number of letters of declination of the risk by admitted insurers. It has turned out to be difficult for framers of surplus line laws and regulations to foresee all of the circumstances under which a citizen may require coverage from a nonadmitted carrier. Due diligence may, therefore, refer to policy, form, or capacity. The law usually prohibits a broker from placing coverage with a nonadmitted carrier for the sole purpose of securing rate advantage. This particular type of proviso has been strongly opposed by insurance buyers.

Export List

A more specific procedure is to provide for the establishment of a list of coverages which may be exported, that is, placed with an unlicensed out-of-state company, without affidavits or without a due diligence search. Florida, California, and New Jersey are typical of states with this type of law. Generally, once a year, at an open hearing, officials in the state insurance department hear arguments for and against various classes being added to or deleted from the list. Any serious objection from even a few licensed companies will prevent a class from being added to or maintained on the export list. Classes not on the list may either be prohibited or writable on an affidavit basis.

Stamping Offices

Some states provide for offices through which copies of all surplus line placings are routed. These are frequently quasi-public bodies, useful to the insurance commissioner in policing surplus line activities. California was the first state to establish an office of this kind. It operates outside of, but in close conjunction with, the office of the insurance commissioner. Its costs are borne by a special charge on each policy. Detailed regulations are published and the activities of its members are closely supervised. This arrangement gives the insurance department a good tool, practically cost-free, to check rates and forms against export lists and other surplus line regulations. In Illinois, the secretary of the Surplus Line Brokers' Association operates a similar office, outside of the direct supervision of the insurance department, but only in regard to coverages placed with Lloyd's. (All references to "Lloyd's" in this chapter are specifically to Lloyd's of London.) In Florida and Georgia, for example, this activity is conducted directly by insurance department personnel.

List of Approved Companies

An increasing number of states are providing that resident surplus line brokers may place coverage only with companies which have been approved or certified by the insurance department. Approval is usually based upon the submission of current financial statements, translated into United States dollars in the case of alien companies. Normally, to be put on the approved list, a company must show that it could have met the minimum financial standards for admittance to the state. Provision is frequently made that if coverage cannot be arranged with an admitted insurer or with nonadmitted insurers on the approval list, it may then be placed with any other company. In these cases the insured may be required to confirm in writing to the insurance department that such other insurers are acceptable to him.

The failure of a few companies writing surplus line business, both alien and domestic, has resulted in increasing interest in the establishment of a nationwide list of nonadmitted companies. Many insurance departments officials have found burdensome and difficult the task of accurately assessing the worthiness of alien and foreign companies. At the 1962 Convention of the National Association of Insurance Commissioners, an N.A.I.C. Central Non-Admitted Insurers Information Bureau was proposed. This bureau would provide to each of the insurance commissioners, and to other interested persons, information on the financial stability and claims-paying ability of nonadmitted carriers. Such a bureau could, in time, replace the individual state lists. It would be limited to alien companies not chartered in any of the states, it being assumed that regulation by a state, of a company chartered by it, is sufficient protection in regard to domestic companies. See Chapter 65 for more discussion of this information office.

TAXATION OF NONADMITTED INSURERS

Federal

Since 1918, the *federal* government has imposed a tax on premiums written by an alien insurer in any state in which that alien insurer is not licensed. It is now 4 percent on all classes of coverage other than reinsurance, life, and accident and health. In these cases the tax is 1 percent. This is an excise tax and is payable through the purchase and cancellation of documentary stamps by the broker arranging the insurance. Should the coverage be effected directly between the insured and a foreign broker or company, then it is up to the insured to purchase and cancel the stamps. In any event, the purchaser of the insurance is ultimately responsibile for compliance with the law.

State

All of the states with a surplus line law provide for the payment of a tax which varies from 2 percent to 6 percent, occasionally with an additional half of 1 percent for a filing or stamping fee. This tax is at least as large as the franchise tax for admitted companies and is frequently considerably larger. When a tax is charged against an insured directly, it is payable by that insured to the state. A copy of the insurance document must also be filed. The Todd Shipyards case raises a question regarding the applicability of such state taxes under certain conditions.

PRINCIPAL NONADMITTED MARKETS

Domestic Companies

Activities of domestic companies writing nonadmitted business fall into two categories. In the first group are those whose business is of a regular nonsurplus line nature but who choose not to be licensed in all the states from which they accept insurance. Many companies have come to specialize in a particular type of activity or product. These companies frequently do without the services of an agent and develop their business either through a traveling representative or by mail, more frequently the latter. There are many examples, including companies sponsored by church organizations, grain elevator operators, sawmill and lumber producers, greenhouses, and cannery groups. Such companies may not find sufficient reason to enter additional states, thereby obligating themselves to pay license and franchise taxes and generally submit to restrictive rating and form control. They thereby enjoy a greater freedom of operation and a lower overhead cost. They are subject only to the jurisdiction of their home state and any others which they enter.

The second group is the growing list of about 30 companies which are licensed in one or only a few states and write surplus line business in other states. These companies compete for the special risk business which has been going abroad. United States companies of this type usually try to become qualified as surplus line insurers in those states where lists of approved companies are maintained. They attempt to avoid pressures from insurance commissioners in other states on this official in their home state; in doing so, they accept business only from qualified surplus line brokers within the state. They are then assured that the state tax is paid and the statutory report made, thereby avoiding regulatory criticism. Companies in this category may write admitted business in one or more states and in the others do business on a surplus line basis. The decision whether to operate as an admitted or a surplus line carrier in a given state depends upon the ease of making special filings or regular filings with sufficient flexibility to meet the problems of the insurance buyer.

Alien Insurers

Historically, the largest volume of surplus line business has gone to English and other alien insurers. Lloyd's of London provided one of the earliest substantial markets for surplus line placings. Around 1900 the first binding representatives were appointed in the United States. Direct placements took place between insureds and Lloyd's brokers in London even earlier, for it long has been known as the principal market for the special, unusual, or capacity risk.

As a result of changes in state insurance laws prior to World War II, Lloyd's became fully licensed in Kentucky. Special syndicates of Lloyd's underwriters have been licensed in Illinois since 1912. The regular Lloyd's syndicates are also qualified as a surplus line insurer so that, under certain conditions, Lloyd's operates as both a licensed and an unlicensed insurer. In all other states, it is a surplus line insurer. In testimony before Congress in 1960, the Chairman of Lloyd's reported the annual volume of direct business done in the United States at $200 million.[1] Its share of the total has been declining as both domestic and alien insurers compete for this business. In one important state its share of the total surplus line business declined from 81 percent in 1955 to about 50 percent in 1963.

In the early post-World War II years, other alien companies began to write this class of business in significant volume. For the most part they were brought into the nonadmitted market by London brokers who found that Lloyd's alone was unable to furnish all of the capacity that was required. For underwriting or other reasons, some of these companies have withdrawn from the American market; new ones are constantly coming into it. About 40 alien companies are active at the present time and at least another 100 take risks occasionally. They may be licensed in one or more states; often they are not licensed in any. In the latter case, all of their operations in this country are on a nonadmitted basis. Being entered in a state means that certain minimum financial requirements have been met. This situation is a manifest advantage to the insurance buyer.

Trust Funds of Alien Companies

Many of these companies, whether licensed in any state or not, have seen fit to establish trust funds in this country. These funds are maintained in dollars, have United States trustees, and are for the purpose of meeting the obligations of the company and giving the policyholder increased confidence. The size of the trust fund of any one company is not necessarily related to its premium volume. The fund may be static or it may have all premiums written in this country paid into it; losses are then usually paid out of the same funds. These trust funds are not under the companies' direct control although the trust document provides for the termination of the trust either at a given time or under certain conditions. Lloyd's is the foremost example of such a trust arrangement. Even though

[1] See *Hearings on Senate Resolution 238 before the Subcommittee on Antitrust and Monopoly of the Senate Committee on the Judiciary* (86th Cong., 2d sess.), pt. 10 at pp. 5980–6012 (1960).

it was then licensed in two states, Lloyd's saw fit to establish a substantial trust fund in this country just prior to World War II. Initially, $40 million was set up in the trust. All premiums are paid into the trust and losses are paid out of it. At the end of 1963, this fund stood at $436,827,000. It is by far the largest of the trust funds established by an alien insurer; other funds range down to the minimum of $300,000.

There are still many alien companies, however, which are not licensed in any state and which do not maintain trust funds in this country. An insured uses these companies on a caveat emptor basis. They may be very substantial insurers in their home country but no guarantee can be given that funds will flow freely to the United States for the payment of policy obligations. Local government currency restrictions may prevent monetary transfers for loss or premium refund payments.

ACCESS TO NONADMITTED MARKETS

Types of Placement

Insureds may purchase insurance from companies not admitted in their state in one of three ways. The normal practice is to use the services of a licensed surplus line broker, resident in the same state as the insured. This procedure gives the insurance buyer the maximum protection and service, since he is dealing with a bonded producer responsible to the state insurance department.

In the second situation, coverage is arranged in another state or even in a foreign country with a representative of the nonadmitted carrier. Such were circumstances in the Todd Shipyards case. This procedure is usually followed either to escape the state surplus line tax or because the coverage is written on a basis which would not qualify under the surplus line laws of the insured's home state.

The third method involves what is termed a direct placement. Coverage is arranged between the insurance buyer and the insurer without the service of a broker or company representative. Mail order business is an example of this method. So also are the contracts entered into directly between an insured in this country and an insurance company abroad.

Surplus line brokers within a state may or may not directly represent the nonadmitted carrier as a binding agent. It depends both upon the state law and the wishes of the nonadmitted insurer. Most states permit the representative of the nonadmitted insurer to be an agent and to have regular binding authority. Some states, New York being the major example, do not. In these cases, the surplus line broker must go to the nonadmitted carrier to place the risk and secure specific evidence that the risk is bound. He operates, therefore, as an intermediary rather than as an agent.

Surplus Line Brokers

A surplus line broker may be a specialist in nonadmitted markets and not do business directly with the insurance buyer. He represents or has access to a number of these potential insurers. His business comes to him from a regular broker or agent. On the other hand, the latter producing organization, doing business directly with the public on behalf of admitted companies, may have a significant volume of surplus line business and hold its own surplus line license in order to service its clients' needs. In numbers, there are more of this type, but the larger volume of surplus line business is done by those specializing in it. Surplus line licensees of both types have joined together in some states to form local associations for purposes of self-policing and unity of action.

Usually the insured's broker determines that a nonadmitted market is required. He knows his client's requirements and in trying to fulfill them discovers that the admitted market cannot offer the required coverage. He then goes to a surplus line broker with his problem. Many states recognize that this is the normal procedure and require that this originating broker also sign an affidavit that he has used diligent effort to place the coverage with admitted carriers. Where this is not a part of the law, the surplus line broker, who may have far less acquaintance with the admitted market, will frequently require that the originating broker give an affidavit or other evidence that the risk is truly surplus line.

Placing a Surplus Line Risk

The surplus line broker, upon receipt of an inquiry, either binds the risk under authority extended to him by a nonadmitted carrier or goes to one or more surplus line insurers and offers the risk for acceptance or rejection. If he has authority to bind, he immediately issues a certificate, usually with a full policy wording, giving evidence of the coverage. The document is then sent to the originating broker who in turn delivers it to the insured. It is the only document that the insured receives.

Where the surplus line broker does not have authority to bind, he gets evidence of binding either in a cable or document form. Based upon this evidence, he then issues a binder or cover note which may outline only the barest essentials of the risk covered. In these instances a formal policy with full wording eventually is delivered to the insured through the surplus line broker and the originating broker.

Throughout the United States there are approximately 700 regularly operating surplus line brokers. Of these, a quarter are specialists, not doing business directly with the public; the others are the regular brokers and agents who do a surplus line business in conjunction with their admitted facilities.

PRINCIPAL CLASSES OF BUSINESS WRITTEN IN THE NONADMITTED MARKET

Volume of Nonadmitted Business

As mentioned, the nonadmitted business can be divided into three categories, depending on the way the insurer is reached. The first is that business which is written through licensed surplus line brokers and on which state taxes are paid. This category totals about $125 million annually. Approximately 75 percent of this business is in liability and related lines, the balance is fire and allied property classes. The composition of this business is well known because several states have published figures giving rather detailed breakdowns. The amount of declared surplus line business varies considerably among the states. California alone reports about 25 percent of the total, its volume being $20,900,000 in 1963. New York has about $17,000,000 and Illinois $12,500,000. Some of the smaller states have only a few thousand dollars a year.

Geographical location makes a considerable difference in the distribution of this business between classes. For instance, in Oregon workmen's compensation coverage written on a surplus line basis accounts for more than 15 percent of the total, while in New York State it is an insignificant class. Western states generally have a large volume of accident and health business; in eastern states this business is not as important a surplus line class. On the other hand, fire and similar property lines account for as much as 40 percent of the surplus line business in the Middle West and about 30 percent in New York, whereas they are just over 10 percent on the West Coast. Local conditions, rating laws and other circumstances determine the flow of any given piece of business into the surplus line markets.

The second group comprises business going to nonadmitted markets, both domestic and foreign, directly or through an intermediary other than a surplus line broker licensed in the state where the risk is located. Since the total volume of surplus line business has been estimated to be as high as $400 million annually, as much as $275 million may be going into the nonadmitted market in this manner. This volume attests to the advantage which insureds have taken of their apparent freedom to contract for insurance wherever they wish.

Excluded from these figures are those in the third category, the premiums written directly with domestic class and speciality writers, especially those in the accident and sickness fields which secure their business principally through the mail. This amount has been gauged to be an additional $150 million. Therefore, using these estimates from industry sources, one finds that nonadmitted property-liability business in the

United States may amount to $550 million annually. This figure compares with a total admitted business of approximately $18 billion in 1964. Surplus line writings are as of the time of this writing, therefore, approximately 2 percent of admitted business and all nonadmitted business accounts for about 3 percent.

Property Risks

In the fire and allied lines area there are risks which seek a nonadmitted market for additional capacity. The absolute size of the risk is not necessarily the ultimate test. The willingness of the admitted market to write the business is the essential criterion. When a risk is considered average for its class, the portion written in the surplus line market is frequently at the same rate as that charged by the admitted companies. Substandard risks are usually surcharged when the coverage is assumed by surplus line writers. The surplus line company, not being subject to the filing of rates and forms, can set its own price.

Then there are those risks which require or fit a special form which admitted companies do not or cannot offer. These include valued business interruption contracts, special deductible forms, nonstandard coinsurance, terms, difference-in-conditions, parasol, and similar contracts. In a final group are risks placed with nonadmitted companies, either as a direct placement or through a surplus line representative in another state, for competitive price considerations.

Liability

The largest volume of business written in the surplus line market is composed of liability risks. They cover an almost infinite variety of individual classes. Automobile and general excess liability, physical damage on long haul and special hazard vehicle risks, many varieties of malpractice, nursing homes, loggers' property damage, products liability, various errors and omissions forms, and some compensation coverages are a few of the lines which find their way to the surplus line writers. For instance, slum properties often are insured on a surplus line basis at rates well above those filed by admitted companies.

Of special interest are the very large excess liability contracts, some as high as $50 million for any one accident, which go far beyond the capacity of the entire admitted market. (See Chapter 40.)

Unusual Lines

There are some coverages which are written so rarely, or for which there is such a small demand, that no admitted company cares to file policies, forms, and rates. Hence, these almost automatically go to a surplus line market. Examples include twin insurance, hole-in-one coverages, 300-score bowling games, kidnapping insurance, nonappearance contingency for public figures, and television transmission failure.

The use of a nonadmitted market can best be summed up by the advertisements of the surplus line brokers which read, "when your regular companies can't write it, come to us."

SUGGESTED READINGS

De Wolf, G. E. "The Proposed Surplus Line Law: Constructive or Destructive?" *Insurance Law Journal* (April, 1961), pp. 259–64.

Hearings on Senate Resolution 56 before the Subcommittee on Antitrust and Monopoly of the Senate Committee on the Judiciary (88th Cong., 1st sess.) pt. 11—Surplus Line Insurance (1963).

Hearings on Senate Resolution 238 before the Subcommittee on Antitrust and Monopoly of the Senate Committee on the Judiciary (86th Cong., 2d sess.) pt. 10, pp. 5980–6012 (1960).

Kuvin, Herbert A. "Surplus Line Insurance," *Insurance Law Journal* (1957), pp. 381–89.

Lockwood, James C. "Case Note," *Michigan Law Review*, Vol. 61 (April, 1963), pp. 1171–75.

Chapter 68

LEGAL AND PROFESSIONAL RESPONSIBILITIES OF AGENTS AND BROKERS

BY GERALD E. MYERS

The law distinguishes between agent and broker, defining the former as a member of the agent-insurance company relationship and the latter as a member of the broker-insured relationship. Unfortunately, the activities of these two types of insurance producers sometimes lead them out of these clear-cut relationships. In determining the legal and professional responsibilities of each, therefore, it is first necessary to determine carefully his exact and individual relationship with the insurance company and the insured in the given transaction. As brought out in the following pages, a producer may be an agent in one transaction and a broker in the next. The term "agent-broker" is coming into use. This chapter reflects an analysis of these relationships and presents a description of these legal and professional responsibilities.

TYPES OF INSURANCE PRODUCERS

The public, generally, makes little distinction among an insurance agent, an insurance broker, and an insurance company employee who is selling insurance. The ordinary insured considers the middleman acting between him and the insurer as his "insurance man" and is little concerned with the legal status of this middleman.

In the insurance industry the salesman is considered in the broadest sense to be an insurance producer. The court in determining the rights of the insured and the insurance company in relation to the insurance producer looks first to the duties or obligations which the insurance producer owes to each party. For this determination it depends on the common law applying to principal and agent, but it also considers the custom and usage within the business.

The insurance industry operates with four distinct types of insurance producers, all licensed by the various states to sell insurance. A fifth type known as the insurance consultant, who may be licensed in some states, is included in this list because of the close relationship between such consultant and the purchaser of insurance.[1] These five types of producers are as follows:

1. The insurance company employee who is a solicitor of insurance for his employer on a salary or salary and commission basis, operating within the "Direct Selling System."
2. The exclusive company agent usually licensed as a solicitor and under a contract with his company which limits his representation to that company and which reserves to that company the ownership, use, and control of policy records and expiration data. This relationship is known as the "Exclusive Agency System."
3. The independent agent representing one or more companies, compensated solely on a commission or fee basis, and operating to a large extent as an independent contractor. He is recognized as the owner of his policy records and expirations and is considered a part of the "Independent Agency System."
4. The insurance broker, also a part of the "Independent Agency System," an agent of the insured and acting for the insured in arranging for and purchasing insurance contracts. In some few instances such as delivery of a policy and collection of the premium he may be considered by common law or designated by statute as an agent of the insurance company.
5. The insurance consultant who does not place insurance contracts, nor receive a commission based on premium, but acts as an adviser and may receive a fee as compensation from the insured. He acts in an expert capacity similar to that frequently undertaken by agents and brokers.

The exclusive company-agent relationship in the first two categories above makes the determination of the agent's responsibility relatively simple. In the area of his business activity, the agent's authority is usually implied, if not expressed. His sole duty as an agent is to his principal, the insurance company, and his status is fairly typical of the employee in an employer-employee relationship in a business enterprise. Similarly, the responsibility of the insurance consultant is solely to the insured, and if he is in an agency capacity, it is exclusively as an agent of the insured.

The independent agent, on the other hand, cannot be said to be acting solely for his principal, the insurance company, because he usually represents more than one company, that is, more than one principal. While he does have authority to bind each of his principals and act for each in a variety of circumstances, he will be found often to be acting as a representative of the insured, that is as a broker, and his obligations and duties will be determined to a large extent in his capacity as broker. Similarly, the insurance broker frequently acts as agent for the insurance company

[1] See Chapter 62 for discussion of various marketing systems and philosophies.

although his principal responsibility will be to the insured. Thus, the independent agent or broker, acting alternately for the insured and the insurance company, must be acutely concerned with legal and professional responsibilities. This overlapping relationship is increasingly frequent as agents function as brokers, and as brokerage firms function as agents.

THE LAW OF AGENCY

Creation of an Agency

The authority of the agent to act for his principal must come from the principal. The third party may not rely upon the agent in determining whether that agent has authority to act. The authority may be "actual" or "apparent"; if "actual," it may be expressed or implied.

The agency relationship may arise out of an oral agreement or a written agreement between the parties which contains specific provisions outlining responsibilities, duties, and obligations, or it may be a mere "understanding" leaving many duties and obligations to be determined by business practices. It may be a mere appointment with no promise of consideration to the agent. It may be subject to revocation by either party at will.

Where the principal by his action or inaction has led a third person to believe that an agent is authorized to act for him, the courts will declare an "agency by estoppel" to exist even though there had been no intention to create an agency. For example, if an insurance company has placed blank policies and forms in the hands of a producer, merely for inspection, it will be estopped to deny the agency when the individual, without any authority to do so, issues a policy to a third party.

Where the authority of the agent is express or implied, there may be further implied or incidental powers resting with the agent. For example, if he has authority to issue a policy of insurance, he will have the implied power to issue an endorsement to modify that policy and to issue a renewal. If he has authority to accept a fire risk, he will have incidental power to make an inspection of the insured property on behalf of the insurer and to perform such other acts as are appropriate to the specific authority granted him.

In determining the agent's apparent authority, custom and practice in the insurance business must be considered. Secret limitations imposed by the company on the agent which are contrary to usual business practices will not be binding on the third party unless he is or should be aware of them.

The establishment of the agency binds the principal under the terms of the contract entered into between the agent and a third party and at the same time relieves the agent of any liability under the contract. This point is not to suggest that the agent has no liability arising out of the transaction, but rather that he is the vehicle by which this principal becomes a party to the contract and the agent is not a party to it himself.

Agent's Liability to His Principal

The agent's primary responsibility to his company is to be true to his appointment and his agency contract. He must obey his instructions and act within the scope of his authority. He must exercise good faith and be loyal to his principal. He is obliged to use due care and reasonable diligence in the transaction of his business and he will be held liable for his mistakes when he fails so to act. For example, an agent who is required to inspect a risk before binding his company will not be liable if he accepts after inspection a risk containing a prohibited hazard, provided he was not negligent in overlooking the hazard during his inspection. On the other hand, if he failed to exercise due care in his inspection and thereby overlooked a hazard, then he will be liable to his principal for his negligence.

As mentioned, the rights of the insured against the insurance company under the policy depend upon the actual or apparent authority of the agent. If the agent had actual authority and if he acted within that authority, then he has no contractual obligation to the insured. If he did not have actual authority or if he exceeded his authority, the principal may still be bound to the third party, provided the third party had the right to rely upon the agent's authority. This latter situation may give rise to a claim by the principal against the agent.

Agent's Liability to the Third Party

On the other hand, if the agent had neither actual nor apparent authority so that the principal is not bound under the contract with the third party, the agent becomes liable as a principal under the contract which he made. It is a fundamental rule that the agent warrants the competency and capacity of his principal to contract and, further, that he warrants his own authority to represent his principal. Therefore, if an insurance agent violates his duty to his company or exceeds his authority as agent, he will render himself liable (1) to his company if his company is held liable under the contract, or (2) to the insured if the company is not liable under the contract.

THE LAW APPLIED TO THE INSURANCE RELATIONSHIPS

Legal Distinction between Agent and Broker

The courts define (1) an insurance agent as one who is an agent of the company with express or implied authority to act for it in dealing with insureds, and (2) a broker as one who acts as a middleman, soliciting insurance from insureds but in no principal-agent arrangement with any particular insurance company. The agent when acting as such is expected to place insurance with his principal, whereas the broker places the insurance with a company selected by the insured or one selected by the broker himself.

The broker may also, on occasion, be an agent of a company if (1) he is soliciting insurance for a specific company or companies, (2) a company holds him out as being a solicitor of insurance for that company, or (3) he is directed by that company to solicit insurance from an insured. Similarly, agents may and frequently do act in the capacity of brokers, that is, as agents for the insured.

Dual Capacity of Agents and Brokers

The general rule of law is that, when an agent acts for both parties, the contract may be rescinded by one party or the other on the theory that, since the agent owes loyalty to his principal, he cannot work at the same time for two people with adverse interests and still properly serve both. There are many exceptions to this general rule and in insurance transactions the exceptions are far more numerous than are the applications of the rule. The principal exceptions are cases where (1) the interests of the two principals are not incompatible; (2) both parties consent to or ratify the transaction even though their interests are conflicting; (3) the duties of the agent to one principal are purely ministerial, that is, involve no exercise of judgment; and (4) the actions of the agent for the respective principals occur at different times and in connection with different aspects of the transaction. For example, the agent may represent the insured in ordering a policy from the underwriter and subsequently represent the insurer in collecting the premium, and faithfully perform for both principals.

Generally, insurance companies operating under the independent agency system may not claim a dual agency because the agent, by custom, is known to, and expected to, represent more than one company and to act on behalf of the insured in many instances. Similarly, the insured is not in a position to take advantage of the dual agency rule because he knows that the agent has authority to represent and bind several companies. Furthermore, the two principals usually ratify the agent's acts, the company by agreeing to the issuance of the policy and the insured by accepting the policy bearing the agent's signature.

The Insurance Agent as Agent of the Insured

Most liability on the part of agents to insureds results from transactions in which the agent is an agent of the insured. If on the occasion of a visit with a client the agent holds himself out as representing one particular company which in fact he does have authority to represent, then his promise to provide certain insurance immediately binds that company. If, however, he promises to find a company to take the risk or if he mentions no specific company or if he holds himself out as representing several companies, then he has not bound any certain company but he has in fact become an agent of the client promising to make a binding contract with some company which he will later choose. If he fails to place the risk with a specific company, he has violated a duty to the client. In this and similar cases of liability by an agent to an insured, the agent is in almost the identical situation as a broker and the legal responsibilities are essentially the same.

LIABILITY OF AGENT OR BROKER

Any liability which does exist rests upon a duty. This duty may be an obligation arising out of contract or it may be the type of duty the breach of which can be considered a tort. An agent may make an oral agreement with the client to secure a policy of insurance. The consideration for this agreement is the commission to be paid to the agent. If the agent fails to perform and the insured suffers an uninsured loss, the agent may be held liable for breach of his oral contract. On the other hand, one who is appointed merely to act for another with no express or implied consideration has a duty either to resign that appointment or to act diligently and with reasonable care. If he neglects to do so, he will be liable for the resulting damages. Frequently, the courts do not distinguish between contractual liability and tort liability. In the case of the relationship of an insurance agent or broker to a client it is probable that both liabilities will be found to exist where the agent or broker has failed to perform.

Liability of Insurer's Agent to the Insured

Where the insurance agent or broker is clearly the agent of the insurance company in a given transaction, the company will be bound by his actions in contract as well as in tort. That is, the insurance company will be bound by the terms of the contract which he made. If he has been guilty of negligence, fraud, misrepresentation, slander, or libel, the company will also be bound under the doctrine of "respondeat superior." These insurance company responsibilities will almost always result from agents' actions in the exclusive agency-company relationship because here the agent has only one principal and all of his business activities will concern the business of his principal.

The agent will not be liable to the third party under the contract where he owes no agency duty to the insured but he will not be excused for his torts even though his principal may be liable also. The tort most closely related to the contract itself for which the agent might be held liable to the insured is misrepresentation or fraud. This consists of a false representation of a fact or a representation made with reckless disregard as to its truth or falsity, and it may include false representation of an opinion if made fraudulently. The representation must be one which the insured has a right to rely upon and it must be relied upon. Relatively few cases of this type reach a court, probably because the insured believes a judgment against the insurance company will be of greater value to him.

Liability to the Insurer

A somewhat larger number of lawsuits is brought by insurance companies against agents who have exceeded their authority and involved their companies in losses they would not otherwise have incurred, or who have committed torts in the course of their duties for which their companies have been held liable. The measure of damages is the amount the insurer has been required to pay in excess of the loss which would have been incurred if the agent had not breached his duty. For example, an agent who issues a policy for $25,000 when his company's underwriting limit on the type of risk involved was $10,000 might be held liable for any loss required to be paid in excess of $10,000. Similarly, an agent who fails to cancel a policy in accordance with his company's order may be liable to the company for any subsequent loss incurred under the policy.

Liability as Agent of the Insured

The vast majority of cases of legal liability on the part of an agent or broker to an insured involve a breach of a duty owed to the insured under the agency relationship. The liability results from a (1) failure to obey instructions or to perform as agreed, (2) failure to exercise the required degree of care and diligence, or (3) failure to exercise the degree of skill and professional judgment which the situation requires. A division of the responsibilities into nonprofessional and professional categories is purely arbitrary, but it does help to emphasize a distinct trend of the courts to hold insurance producers as well as salesmen and practitioners in other fields of business activity to a progressively higher level of performance.

Nonprofessional Acts of Liability. The agent of the insured owes to the insured the duty of obeying his instructions and of using reasonable diligence and care in the performance of his duties, measured by standards common to the business in which he is engaged. He must keep the insured informed in connection with his undertaking of providing coverage and he will be held liable for his failure to procure insurance or for his failure to notify the insured of his inability to procure insurance. He may be found negligent in not securing proper insurance coverage in accordance with his instructions or not securing it on the most favorable terms reasonably available. He may be liable to the insured for failing to point out a warranty or condition which must be complied with or for misrepresenting terms or conditions of the policy. He is not excused from these obligations merely because the insured has failed to read the policy and thereby failed to discover a defect in coverage himself.

While he is not a guarantor of the financial condition of the insurance company, he must use reasonable diligence and care in selecting a financially sound company. By common law in some states and by statute in others a special obligation is placed upon him in connection with the placing of insurance in unauthorized foreign insurance companies. (See Chapter 67.) He will be held liable, generally, for the insured's failure to recover under a policy, provided the insured had no knowledge that the company was not authorized to do business in his state and provided that it was not financially sound.

A gratuitous agent, that is, one to whom no compensation or other consideration has been promised, may under certain circumstances be held liable even though by contract he has no obligation to undertake to provide the insurance. The courts hold that, if there is no consideration for his promise and he makes no effort to secure the insurance, he is not bound because of lack of consideration—but that, if he makes an attempt to secure insurance and fails to do so and also fails to notify the insured, he may be held liable.

He is required to be conversant with the formal and ordinary details necessary to effect coverage and with standard policies, forms, and conditions. A distinction has been made between ordinary or unprofessional agents and those who represent themselves as possessing a high degree of skill. Most courts draw no clear line of demarcation between the two but hold both to a degree of care and skill based upon what might reasonably be expected from one in his situation. It has been suggested that professional conduct requires not only the exercise of due care but also of skill. Certainly this theory forms a basis for distinction between nonprofessional and professional liability of agents and brokers.

Professional Acts of Liability. The general rule that an agent or broker must exercise such reasonable skill and diligence as may fairly be expected for a person in his situation is subject to wide variation of standards. Where he is known to be a specialist or an expert or holds himself out to be such, then certainly higher degrees of care and skill are required. In one recent case, a federal district court in assessing damages for liability against a broker who had represented himself as an expert, said that as occupational groups strive toward professional recognition the law will impose an even higher standard of care in the performance of their duties than it would otherwise. The particular duty charged against this broker, if he had performed it, might well have subjected him to a complaint for unauthorized practice of the law. Even so, the court assessed liability against him because he had represented himself as an expert. He was held to that degree of care which might be expected from other highly skilled insurance salesmen in the community.

If the agent or broker is to be held to this standard without regard to his real competency, he is being subjected to the standards of a professional man, even though insurance selling may not be recognized as a profession.

ETHICAL AND PROFESSIONAL RESPONSIBILITIES

Historically, a profession has come to be known as a vocation in which the practitioner has special training or professes special knowledge which he uses in serving others. The vocation must involve a learning in which there is a special body of knowledge from which the practitioner may draw. The training must be intellectual in character and not merely the development of a skill. The vocation must be pursued in large part for the benefit of others and the pursuit of personal profit must be secondary. The practitioners of the profession must have established, as a group, certain standards of proficiency or a code of ethical practices. (See Chapter 70 for an extended discussion of professionalism.)

The Insurance Agent or Broker as a Professional

These criteria are difficult to reconcile with the activities involved in selling insurance or, for that matter, the activities in most commercial and business enterprises. Whether an agent or broker practices professionalism in accordance with these criteria seems to be much less important than the creation of ethical standards by which he may operate and the public good which can come from any effort he makes to improve his knowledge of the business, and through this, his service to the public.

Evidence that the property-liability insurance fraternity has striven for high ethical standards is the variety of creeds and codes of ethics adopted by various insurance producer groups over the last half-century. The tenor of these creeds and codes is exemplified in one of the most recent such declarations, the C.P.C.U. charge adopted by the American Institute for Property and Liability Underwriters, Inc., in 1942. (See Chapter 70.) This charge is required to be subscribed to by all persons to whom the C.P.C.U. designation is awarded by the American Institute. It reads as follows:

> In all of my business dealings and activities, I agree to abide by the following rules of professional conduct:
>
> I shall strive at all times to ascertain and understand the needs of those whom I serve and act as if their interests were my own; and
>
> I shall do all in my power to maintain and uphold a standard of honor and integrity that will reflect credit on the business in which I am engaged.

Agents' and Brokers' Licensing Laws

All of the states have provision for the licensing of insurance agents and many also provide for licensing insurance brokers. The licensing requirements are all based upon the theory that licensing is necessary for protection of (1) the interests of the insurers and (2) especially, the interests of the public. The amount of knowledge of the insurance business necessary for qualifying for a license varies considerably. Generally, the standards of examinations are quite low. Nevertheless, they do constitute some indication of the minimum degree of skill required of an insurance agent or broker. There is a noticeable trend toward high standards of proficiency.

Professionally Acceptable Conduct

The practice of courts in regard to all professions is to require that degree of skill ordinarily possessed and exercised by members of the profession. The tendency is toward an average "professionally acceptable conduct." The result is that each profession sets its own standards.

As insurance licensing laws are strengthened, as examinations standards are raised, as ethical codes relating to selling and servicing of insurance clients are more widely accepted, and as a higher degree of proficiency is attained by the insurance producer, a higher standard of performance will be required. But the standard of performance which the individual agent or broker establishes for himself in relation to his clients will still to a considerable degree determine his personal responsibility.

SUGGESTED READINGS

American Jurisprudence. San Francisco, and Rochester, N.Y.: Bancroft Whitney Co., and The Lawyers Co-operative Publishing Co., 1960. Vol. 29, Sections 134–82.

Corpus Juris Secundum. Brooklyn, N.Y.: The American Law Book Company, 1945. Vol. 44, Sections 136–74.

COUCH, GEORGE J. *Cyclopedia of Insurance Law* (2d ed. by RONALD A. ANDERSON). Rochester, N.Y.: The Lawyers Co-operative Publishing Co., 1960. Vols. 3 and 4, Sections 25 and 26.

MECHEM, FLOYD R. *Outlines of the Law of Agency* (4th ed. by PHILIP MECHEM). Chicago: Callaghan & Co., 1952.

ROADY, THOMAS G., JR., AND ANDERSEN, WILLIAM R. *Professional Negligence.* Nashville, Tenn.: Vanderbilt University Press, 1960.

Chapter 69

AGENCY MANAGEMENT

BY LAURENCE J. ACKERMAN

The independent agent is a classic illustration of that interesting phenomenon of the American business system—the small businessman. Like his contemporaries in other types of business, he is a sorely tried, beleaguered individual. Prior to World War II, the American agency system provided a comparatively calm, profitable, and stable occupation. It was often termed the "old man's annuity." The end of the war set the stage for a marketing revolution in property-liability insurance. It has had a shattering impact on the financial security, the work load, and the job attitude of the typical agent. As the profit margin eroded, the agent was compelled to evaluate his role as a businessman. He began to study seriously and continuously the managerial process in the conduct of his agency. "Agency management" came of age as an integral part of any agency venture. Today, virtually every agents' convention has a topic on the subject. It has developed its corps of experts. A "mystique" has emerged around the subject of agency management which more often confuses than reveals. But its vital role in agency profitability is denied by no one.

Within the confines of a single chapter one cannot successfully examine the subject microscopically. Such a task must be bequeathed to the future scholar who will write the definitive text on agency management. In this chapter the subject is viewed in its broad outlines with emphasis on current issues.

AN OVERVIEW

The agent as a businessman is normally involved in the activities described in Table 69–1. If a quick glance at the table frightens the agent, a more critical examination will reveal to him that he engages in virtually all of these areas in varying degrees and within a broad spectrum of sophistication and skill. This table serves as an outline for treatment of the subject in this chapter.

OFFICE OPERATIONS

Location, Layout, and Organization

Location of the agency office has been the subject of considerable attention in the postwar era. One major issue is the ground-floor versus the upper-floor office location. In fact, there is no cause for debate. The decision will depend on the nature of customer relationships and the sources of new business. If the bulk of the agency's business is developed by personal visitation and the use of the telephone, the additional cost of a

TABLE 69–1

THE AGENT—A BUSINESSMAN

AN OVERVIEW

Office Operations	*Financial Control*	*Marketing*	*Legal Problems & Perpetuation*
1. Office location, layout, and organization 2. Office equipment 3. Selection and training of employees—office and sales 4. Compensation of employees	1. Accounting process 2. Data processing 3. Expense control and analysis 4. Collections	1. Market research 2. Sales management 3. Account analyses and surveys 4. Advertising	1. Form of business organization 2. Perpetuation problems and techniques 3. Agency valuation 4. Legal liability

ground-floor location may not be warranted. If the agency relies on window displays and institutional advertising, and through such media develops a sufficient number of walk-in customers, then the increase in rental cost of a street-floor site may be justified.

The suburban versus city location has stirred even greater controversy. Like most moot issues, there are plus values and minus values. On the positive side of a suburban location is the argument of convenience. If a substantial part of the agency's business is in personal lines, then the agency producers' travel time to prospects and customers is greatly reduced. Prospects and customers may be more willing to visit the office when the incentive is a short trip and free off-street parking. There may also be time savings to the agency principals in commuting time. The suburban office usually places the principals closer to their homes, if not in miles at least in time. Suburban locations may bolster employee morale and make employee recruitment an easier task. It may reduce square-foot costs.

On the negative side, the agency may lose easy accessibility to some valuable accounts. The move may inconvenience some employees. The agency may lose the advertising value of doing business in the same location for a period of years. One cannot indulge in generalizations about this question. Each agency has to formulate its own reaction in the light of the array of arguments on this issue.

Space is a significant item in an agency budget. Thus, the question as to how much space the agency needs is a critical one. Cost of space consumes on an average from 3 to 5 percent of gross agency income. The author has observed that the average agency with a volume of $100,000 will require about one square foot for every $107 in premium volume. If the agency is in the $250,000–$499,000 class, it will need on the average about one square foot for every $256 in volume. A volume of $500,000–$999,000 will average about one square foot for each $349 in volume. These are only approximations. This subject calls for careful research.

Office organization and layout also need critical research and analysis. It is axiomatic that before an agent selects or builds an office, there must be a careful study of function and work flow. When a policy is written, the following steps are involved: preparing the order blank, checking the rate, calculating the premium, selecting the proper form, preparing the policy, checking the completed policy, preparing the invoice, recording the expiration, posting the accounting data, filing the daily report, and dispatching the policy and the company copy of the daily report. The work will be more efficient if those responsible for related operations are in close proximity to each other when a straight-line process is utilized.

The office should provide for consistency and continuity in design and furnishings. The acid test is the potential impact on customers and employees. It may sound trite and euphemistic, but an office should reflect success without ostentation, comfort without conspicuous self-indulgence, dignity without dullness.

Office layout should be constructed around utilities. It is amazing how often agency office designers overlook little details such as electrical outlets, air-conditioning vents, radiators, and telephone connectors. Desks are frequently located in the part of a draft from overhead ceiling vents. Furniture is sometimes placed next to a radiator.

Lighting is vital. This fact calls for consideration of the appropriate amount of light and the control of glare and reflection. It is said that most agents' offices are 50 percent underlighted.

Office layout is too sensitive a need to be handled casually. The best practice is to construct an office-planning check list as a control device.

Equipment

Office equipment poses a dilemma for the typical agency. Not only is there the decision of the type of equipment needed, but also the agent must discriminate among models and manufacturers. In calculators, the agent faces a bewildering display of virtuosity and beauty, and no independent unit has evaluated conclusively and finally the respective types of calculators in terms of their cost-benefit ratio. The same conclusion applies to bookkeeping machines, copy machines, dictating and transcription equipment, mailroom paraphernalia, office furniture, and typewriters. The agent must wander through a tangled wilderness, and his best companion is luck.

Selection and Training of Employees

Shifting attention to personnel, one finds that great strides have been made in the selection, training, compensation, and supervision of agency personnel. Today, agents' associations, companies, and other educational resources have developed recruitment kits which contain a series of simple aptitude tests, application forms, and guided interview tracks. These kits are inexpensive. They should save the agency money and reduce effort in employee recruitment and selection. Specifically, it is contended that the use of these kits will produce for the agent:

1. More efficient selection of employees.
2. Better use of specific skills and abilities of present employees.
3. Faster and improved service to insureds.
4. Greater output of work per employee.
5. Better communications with customers.
6. Greater accuracy in keeping office records.
7. More time available for the agent to "sell."
8. More profit because of improved selection and efficient use of the office employees.
9. "Upgrading" of the image of the whole agency system in the eyes of the public.
10. —And, as some agents have already observed, "fewer worries and more sleep at night."

Education for agency personnel has also grown in scope and effectiveness. There are company schools, local agents' association educational forums, and correspondence opportunities. These educational opportunities, of course, do not relieve the agent of all training responsibilities, but they do provide him considerable help in training his employees.

Compensation of Employees

Compensation patterns for agency personnel vary also by geographical areas. As a result, agencies can gear their compensation patterns to a competitive scale. There has been widespread adoption, primarily through state and national association media, of fringe benefits—group life insurance and the health coverages. Less has been done in pensions and profit sharing. Some agencies, however, have even ventured into this costly, complex domain in the fringe benefit world. Qualified and unqualified plans, under the Internal Revenue Code, are on the increase.

A solicitor is an employee of the agency whose major function is to produce new business, and service both new business and old business. The solicitor, in agency management, has been the subject of hot debate. More heat and less light, more movement and less progress have been achieved in this area than in most of the areas of concern in agency management. Compensation is the axis on which the major debate revolves. Other sources of controversy are production standards, protection for the agency if the solicitor leaves it, and his eventual ownership role in the agency.

Generally speaking, the solicitor's compensation is either straight salary, salary plus commissions, or commissions with a drawing account. Production standards are difficult to establish but eventually the agency must make money on its sales representative or abandon him. Controversy centers about the period of time necessary to amortize the financial investment in the solicitor. A properly drawn noncompeting covenant offers some protection against the solicitor who leaves the agency to compete with it. These covenants are not popular with the courts. To optimize their effectiveness, they must be reasonable and drawn in the light of the law of the particular jurisdiction.

Although there are exceptions, one might generalize and say that solicitors rarely prove satisfactory, in the long run, unless they are given an opportunity to acquire some ownership interest in the business. The sales representative is a piece of unfinished business in agency management. Careful research should be done on this whole problem. It might develop guidelines for action.

FINANCIAL CONTROL

The major objective of an agency is profit. The basic vehicle to this goal is a planned sales program which is fully implemented. The benefits of such a program can be fully realized if it is supported by an economical and efficient accounting and financial control system. Such a system will provide prompt and accurate preparation and delivery of policies, new and renewal; expeditious billing of customers; careful supervision of the collection process to assure ultimate collection of the premiums; an accurate method to check company accounts and determine balances due; appropriate control over cash and the various accounts; and meaningful summarization of the financial operations of the agency through the profit and loss statement and the balance sheet.

Accounting

Traditionally, the accounting functions of agencies have been performed manually. The system has three major defects. It is expensive. It often leads to an incomplete set of records (for instance, rarely is a profit and loss statement made except annually). It is slow.

The tremendous hue and cry over the new electronic devices has profoundly influenced agency leaders. To illustrate the dramatic appeal of these systems, it has been demonstrated that every posting made in a manual system is subsequently handled, on the average, about 5½ times. When posted and proved on a machine, it is made once. For example, in a posting to cash received, the amount is first entered in the proper column of the cash received sheet. If is then posted to the customer's ledger account. The columns of the cash received sheet are totaled at the end of the day or period and the columns cross-totaled. The individual ledger accounts are totaled for accounts receivable reconciliation. Frequently one or more of the totals must be done over where the balances are off.

By machine, the posting to the cash received sheet and the customer's ledger account is done at the same time. By the proving action, corrections are made immediately.

If an agency has 5,000 postings a year, a manual system would require some 27,500 handlings. A machine holds the number to the 5,000 and does the handling accurately. If each figure posting is done in one minute, the elimination of 22,500 handlings involves a saving of about 400 hours or 10 normal work weeks.

Data Processing

Agents have been intrigued by the potentiality of electric and electronic data processing, and much investigation is under way. Three approaches have been developed. Some agencies (larger ones) have purchased equipment. Some have rented equipment. Many more have engaged the services of a data processing company on a fee basis.

These companies offer substantial services to the agent. Within a narrow range, they provide itemized monthly statements of all charges, payments, and credits by customers; they age the accounts receivable; they account for the production of and commissions due the solicitors; they prepare a complete summary of brokered business by broker, indicating balances due, commissions due, total brokerage business, brokerage expense; they itemize monthly account currents for each company represented; they prepare a check register and summary, as well as a cash receipts summary and a formal entries summary; they present a profit and loss statement and balance sheet; they furnish periodic general ledger reports listing transactions affecting general ledger accounts; and they give a list of expirations.

The accounting transformation to a service center approach is not a matter of a day. For example, the dailies may have to be arranged alphabetically by last name for personal accounts and by company for commercial accounts. Further, the agency will have to supply the center with a list of its companies, solicitors, and brokers, and a complete record of accounts receivable. Usually the center will return up-to-date records five or six days after monthly figures are submitted.

The mass data processing approach embodies several advantages. Records are accurate. They are completed promptly. The process forces an agency to maintain up-to-date records. It eliminates heavy dependence on a trained bookkeeper and may solve many of the agency's personnel problems. It requires no more effort than a manual system. It frees agency personnel for sales activities. It leads to a more efficient collection system. It furnishes information for sound managerial decisions—for instance, volume by solicitors, types of business produced, and so on.

Of course, such a system does not relieve the agency of the tasks of record keeping and accounting. In fact, it places a premium on careful record maintenance. The accounting output is no better than the accounting input.

In making a cost analysis of a change-over, the agency must recognize three sources of expense: (1) the immediate costs of supplying the necessary data ("start-up costs"), (2) the cost of the new set of records, and (3) the processing cost itself. The third item, on the average, for a typical \$100,000 volume agency runs about \$90 a month; a \$500,000 volume agency might spend about \$150 a month.

There appears to be no clear-cut "break point" below which it is not financially sound to utilize automated accounting procedures, but two observations can be made. The larger the agency, the greater the financial advantages. The growing agency which may need more personnel may accept the process more readily than the stable agency with a seasoned staff.

Cost Analyses and Control

With the monotonous upward spiral of the operations cost curve and the downward trend in insurance contract pricing and in commission rates, agencies must maintain sensitive and persistent controls over expense items. Fortunately, there are studies which permit cost comparisons among agencies of similar size. One organization (the Rough Notes Company) produces periodic and regular studies which permit an agency not only to view costs historically, but also to obtain a current comparison. These studies are detailed and provide averages by agency size of such items as average commission per policy, average earnings per producer, and office and sales costs per policy. Without such a comparison, an agency has no fact base from which to project its own cost control policies.

Credit and Collections

The credit and collection policy of an agency plays a vital role in its profitability. A disproportionate percentage of receivables tends to freeze the use of agency capital. Furthermore, past due accounts consume an agent's time. A poor credit and collection policy impairs the sales value of an agency. Finally it produces psychological handicaps for the agent as he engages in a perennial struggle with his insureds to force payment of overdue premiums. Therefore, every agency must develop a clear-cut collection policy. The more successful agents, in dealing with new customers, obtain a definite commitment on premium payment at the time of sale. The budget plans of the various companies and banking institutions have helped to resolve the collection problem for the agent. On renewals, agents are tending to communicate with their insureds well in advance of the renewal date. This helps to avoid the costs of cancellation and establishes a method of payment of the renewal premium. Furthermore, this has added sales advantages in the sense that it may lead to a discussion of adequate values and increased coverage. As part of the collection procedures, agents should have a simple automatic billing system and an effective set of collection letters. These aids will support the basic collection philosophy of the agency.

MARKETING

Property-liability insurance has not developed the comprehensive body of sales planning and sales methods literature found in life insurance, but in the past few years companies and agents have given increased attention to marketing. Competition has forced this attention. The wildfire growth of exclusive agents and direct writers in the personal line field has had an explosive impact on independent agency forces.

Market Research

Comparatively few property insurance agencies do any thorough and continuous market research. Yet such research is a vital and urgent necessity in the dynamic, swift-paced economy of today. Every agent, regardless of the size of his agency, should, at the minimum, study business conditions in his area. Then, against this broad canvas, he should establish the agency's best markets and the most logical approach to each. In addition to making intermediate and long-range sales plans, an agent should make day-to-day sales plans.

Sales Management

The typical sales managerial function includes the following responsibilities:

1. Market analysis.
2. Regular sales meetings with the internal employees and the solicitors.
3. Supervision of the training of solicitors and direction of their activities.
4. Planning and supervision of periodic sales campaigns.
5. Maintenance of adequate sales records.
6. Encouragement of sales consciousness on the part of the office staff.
7. Direction of all advertising, publicity, and public relations efforts.

Sales meetings, properly planned and effectively organized and supervised, are becoming increasingly popular facets of the sales planning activities of agencies. Usually at these meetings attention is concentrated in the following areas:

1. General review of sales results since the last meeting, including a breakdown of prospects secured, number of calls made, number of sales made, and premium per sale for each producer.
2. Review of new policies, forms, and rate changes.
3. Development of special sales campaigns—for instance, business interruption; or concentration on a special stratum of the market, such as physicians.
4. Idea exchange on meeting competition and emphasis on the most effective sales idea.
5. Integration with the current advertising material of the companies.
6. Plans for the next work period in terms of prospects, solicitations, and premium quotas.

For the bulk of agencies, the most lucrative source of increased premium income is present customers. Further, the contributions of current customers are not spread equally. A limited segment produces the largest volume of new premiums. Therefore, many progressive agencies are studying their accounts and grouping them in terms of their profitability and potential volume increase. This process places a premium on the most valuable asset of the agency producer—his time.

About 10 percent on the average of an agency's business is estimated to be lost annually as a result of competition, death, moving from the community, and so on. No matter how well an agency is organized to retain the "business on its books," the agent must prospect for new customers. Property-liability agents do not prospect as intensively or as systematically as their life insurance counterparts, but today's competitive framework may soon outmode such diffidence. However, the amount of servicing work required of a self-sufficient agency (as contrasted with agencies whose principals report to a company-operated branch service office) cannot accurately be compared to the typical life insurance agency. Among other dissimilarities is the fact that a life policy, once issued, remains essentially unchanged for a generation and customarily results in only one claim.

Account Analyses and Surveys

Customer account analysis has become an important phase of many agents' sales activities. It involves a systematic and periodic review of a customer's account in quest of improvements in the customer's insurance program. There are four major steps. First, there is a careful search for unprotected exposures. Second, the adequacy of present coverage is weighed in terms of its loss impact on the capital structure of the insured. The third step is an effort to combine or simplify present coverages.

Finally, the agent attempts to improve his customer's insurance record keeping and buying habits. This last function is an adventure in customer insurance education.

Akin to customer account analysis is the emphasis on survey selling. This technique involves (1) a presentation in writing of the hazards that a person or a company may face; (2) a study of the insured's existing coverages; and (3) recommendations for improving the coverages to meet the hazard array. In the personal risk, the survey might take the form of a narrative letter. In the commercial situation, it might be a lengthy, detailed report. Surveys—from the producer's and the buyer's standpoints—are treated at length in Chapter 75.

Advertising

Advertising is one of the major selling tools of the agent. About 3 percent of total income is the average expenditure, but this figure is only a statistic. An agent must weigh such influences as the age and prestige of the agency, the rate of community growth, competition, and participation in trade association campaigns. All of these variables will affect the individual agency's budget.

Specialized advertising media employed by agencies include: displays (signs, window decorations, and billboards), direct mail, newspaper and magazine advertising, radio advertising, agency slogans, and good will items (calendars, diaries, pencils, matches, and such). To avoid waste, the wise agent studies his market and his sales objectives before he embraces an advertising program. He may survey his customers to check on the basis of their purchase from him. He should run short tests of various advertising techniques to appraise their relative effectiveness. (See also Chapter 71 for additional discussion of advertising.)

LEGAL PROBLEMS AND PERPETUATION

A basic problem facing any agency is the legal form of business organization. One can state categorically that there is no universally "best" form of organization. Rules of thumb and easy formulas are dangerous, or at least useless, in this type of decision. There must be a precise, detailed, and arduous individualized study in each case. There are, however, guide lines of inquiry.

Forms of Business Organization

The basic choice is between the unincorporated firm (the sole proprietorship or the partnership) and the incorporated firm. The first line of investigation involves the legal considerations: formalities and cost of organization, extent of personal liability, life span, and state supervision. Then there are considerations of credit, flexibility of investment, management's role, and tax implications. The latter is the significant factor in the majority of decisions. It is also the most difficult to define in terms of generalities, calling as it does for many avenues of analysis, seasoned judgment, and prophetic skill.

In 1958 a new type of tax organization came into being, as provided for in Section 1371, subchapter S of the Internal Revenue Code. It permits a corporation, fulfilling certain conditions, to elect to be treated for federal income tax purposes substantially as a partnership. Other than its change of tax status, the electing corporation retains all of the characteristics of a regular corporation but the income of the corporation—whether or not distributed—is taxed to the stockholders in proportion to each stockholder's interest in the corporation. Many agencies have utilized this new form of operation.

Perpetuation Problems and Techniques

One of the ironies of the property-liability agent's life is that while he retails security, he has done comparatively little to insure for his family the perpetuation of the capital values he has worked so assiduously to build. There are two sides to the perpetuation coin. The agent, by his failure to act, can deprive himself and his family of the full material benefit to be obtained from his agency. The other side finds the companies represented suffering from the unplanned dislocations of death, disability, or superannuation.

The time for perpetuation planning is when the agency principal(s) is in his prime. A saying is that "the time to get a partner is before you need one." This timing gives adequate opportunity to develop an appropriate long-range plan.

It is said that about 75 percent of all agencies involve a one-man principal. In this situation three successors are available. First, there is the widow. If she was associated with her husband in the business, she may be able to carry it on; but if she was not, the agent is imposing a terrific burden upon her. Further, if there are children at home, the task becomes overwhelming. It may be argued that the widow could hire a manager, but immediately her return is decreased by the manager's salary. In addition, if the customers become dependent upon him, the manager can hardly be prevented from setting up his own agency and soliciting these same people whom he was serving.

A second solution is to leave the business to a member of the family—preferably a son. The junkyards of industry are well populated with agencies left to sons who were too young, too incompetent, or too disinterested to carry on the business. Careful preparation during one's lifetime must be made for this type of contingency.

The third solution is to hire a younger man, train him, and prepare him to succeed to the agent's interest.

Agents are reluctant to follow this line of perpetuation. There are three major reasons for the philosophy of delay. The first is the agent's dread of the adjustments necessary when a new man comes into the agency. The second is the fear of loss of time, money, and energy should the new man not succeed. Finally, there is the apprehension that if the new man does succeed, he may leave the agency and compete with his former employer. These cautions are legitimate, but careful planning can minimize each hazard.

The first deterrent can be overcome through frank exploration, perhaps in writing, of the respective roles of each party. The second fear can be ameliorated through a rigorous plan for careful selection, continuous supervision, and appropriate compensation. The last objection can be contained through a properly drafted noncompeting covenant.

The advantages of a perpetuation plan are many:

1. A guaranteed market for the business is provided at time of death, disability, or retirement.
2. If there is a valid buy-and-sell agreement, binding during lifetime as well as at time of death, and created in an arm's-length framework, the value of the agency can be pegged for federal estate tax purposes.
3. A perpetuation agreement arranging for continuity of management and agency personnel strengthens the agency's relationships with its companies and its customers.
4. Such a plan contributes to efficiency by serving as an incentive for the new man's performance. The more effective his contribution to the welfare of the agency, the more ownership he can buy, and perhaps at a better price.
5. If the plan is funded, an asset is created which might be employed to purchase the agent's interest prior to death.
6. For the benefit of the agent's family, a comparatively nonspeculative source of cash is substituted for an uncertain, speculative business interest. This substitution is especially significant when the plan is funded.

Every agent should concern himself with the problem of perpetuation. The time to do it is today. Tomorrow may be too late. There is no "best" perpetuation technique. The writer, who has served several hundred agencies in this problem, has used many devices either exclusively or in combination. The classic and most talked about approach is the buy-and-sell agreement funded by insurance. Often this approach is inappropriate, unusable, or unacceptable to the principal. A few other methods which can be employed are the private annuity, use of a qualified profit-sharing plan as a buy-out vehicle, reorganization as an incorporated agency with voting common stock and nonvoting dividend-bearing preferred stock, or deferred compensation arrangements.

Agency Valuation

A fascinating offshoot of perpetuation is agency valuation. To ask the question "What is value?" in respect to an insurance agency is like asking the question "What is truth?" Courts, attorneys, judges, writers, scholars, and others have sought for years to discover some magic formula to price a closely held business enterprise—often where tangible assets and inventory loom high. In an insurance agency, where there is no inventory and little in the way of tangible assets, the difficulty is compounded. One approach, advocated by Professor John D. Long, a careful student of this problem, is to estimate the net income the buyer estimates the agency will yield and to establish a present value by using an assumed discount rate.[1]

Some of the factors influencing the market price are:

1. The amount of political business controlled by the agency.
2. The amount of business of a target variety.
3. The amount of business sold through religious, fraternal, or nationality relationships.
4. The balance between large and small accounts.
5. The amount of the agency's business that originates through brokers.
6. Companies represented and commission scales applicable, including contingent arrangements.
7. Loss ratios experienced recently in the agency and their impact on contingent commissions.
8. Division between automobile and other lines.
9. Age of accounts.
10. Collection experience and the bad debt ratio.
11. Office location, layout, and equipment in use.
12. Personnel and their compensation.
13. The accounting system in use.
14. Type of the lease.
15. Size of the agency.
16. Method of payment for the agency.
17. Character of the community.

Legal Liability

An interesting development in agency life is the rapidly expanding scope of the agent's legal liability. It is commensurate with his professional recognition. Errors and omissions coverage affords some protection, but this coverage is found in a limited market and could be volatile. (See Chapters 33 and 68 for a discussion of professional liability insurance and the legal and professional responsibilities of agents and brokers.)

CRITICAL FACTOR

Effective agency management in the future will be the critical factor in agency profitability. It may be the agent's principal survival weapon. Costs of operation will continue to mount. There is no reasonable expectation that commissions will again approach the prewar level.

[1] See John D. Long, *Methods of Agency Continuation* (Bloomington: Bureau of Business Research, Indiana University, 1954), chap. iv.

SUGGESTED READINGS

Agency Management Primer. New York: National Association of Insurance Agents.

ATHEARN, JAMES L. *General Insurance Agency Management.* Homewood, Ill.: Richard D. Irwin, Inc., 1965.

BELING, OSCAR. *Profitable Insurance Agency Management.* Englewood Cliffs, N.J.: Prentice-Hall, Inc., 1946.

"Blueprint for Agency Progress." *Journal of Insurance Information,* Vol. XXV (March-April, 1964), pp. 1–48—a Special Issue.

Bulletins on Effective Agency Management. Indianapolis: Rough Notes Company. Continuous.

LONG, JOHN D. *Methods of Agency Continuation.* Bloomington: Bureau of Business Research, Indiana University, 1954.

"Profitable Agency Operation." Illinois Association of Insurance Agents, 1963.

"Project 100—A Study of Agency Management Problems in Personal Lines." Aetna Casualty and Surety Company, 1963.

What It Costs to Run an Insurance Agency. Indianapolis: Rough Notes Company. Annual.

"Your Office—1962." Insurance Companies of North America.

Chapter 70

PROFESSIONAL EDUCATION

BY EDWIN S. OVERMAN

Professional education may be defined in broad terms as organized learning or disciplined study designed to direct the student toward greater proficiency in his knowledge and understanding of a particular field of thought. Professional education may also be defined, in more succinct terms, as the advanced study of a specific field of knowledge.

Improved understanding leading ultimately to mastery of any advanced discipline of thought is achieved, by and large, through intensive and extensive study of the body of literature which constitutes each separate field of knowledge. This literature consists of textbooks, articles in scholarly journals, monographs explaining discovered principles, and treatises formulating various concepts and newly found theories.

These items of literature, in each field of thought, compose the "mass" of cumulative experiences drawn together from the lifetime findings of generations of professional practitioners. The literature also reflects the results of the myriad of trial and error experiments performed by the many practitioners extending throughout the entire history of the profession.

In this chapter, attention is given to the concepts of a profession and of education; next, education is contrasted with training; then, university and industry sponsored professional education for insurance is traced; and, finally, some of the benefits to be derived from professional education programs are cited.

THE MEANING OF THE "PROFESSIONAL" CONCEPT

Any treatment of the subject of *professional education* must, of necessity, explore in some detail the meaning and significance of the term, "professional." Although there are no universally agreed upon characteristics necessary to the establishment of a profession, there are nevertheless a number of fundamental requisites cited by many writers who have concentrated their attention on the subject of identifying the "profile" of any given profession.

Altruism

First, most writers would agree that *altruism* stands as one of the basic characteristics of any established profession. (A profession, therefore, is said to be altruistic, or nonselfish, in nature.) Each member is guided by and dedicated to the humanitarian principle of service-to-others and does not think only in terms of self-interest or personal gain. Although livelihood is necessarily of importance to the professional man, just as to everyone else, the income from professional pursuits simply follows as the resulting reward for performing acts of dedicated professional assistance. True professionals tend to focus their major attention on providing unselfish and dedicated service to others. The paramount object of every profession, therefore, is *public service* with monetary enrichment or affluence relegated to a secondary role in the order of motivating influences.

Code of Ethics

A second criterion of a profession is the adoption and enforcement by its members of a *code of ethics*. A standard for measuring and judging ethical behavior is essential to success in achieving, from among members of the general public, a high degree of respect and professional regard. The code of ethics, adopted by the profession, serves as the "guiding principles" for decision making by the members and as the protector or guardian of the profession's reputation. Failure to live up to the accepted code is tantamount to failure in functioning as a true professional and thus subjects the guilty person to a variety of sanctions from the group and perhaps to ultimate expulsion from the profession.

Body of Knowledge

A third characteristic of a profession is its possession of a distinctive, systematic, and *well-defined body of highly specialized knowledge*. This body of knowledge is the foundation or backbone of the profession and embodies not only facts but also "chains" of principles and concepts which interlace the facts. This body of interrelated theory, which describes a distinctive department of learning, is scientifically organized, developed, and recorded so as to be readily transmittable to others. The media used for transmitting this body of knowledge, as described previously, are textbooks, monographs, journal articles, and scientific treatises. The central and all-pervading reason for one's learning this body of knowledge is to improve his capacity to *apply* these principles in the daily practice of his profession. The practice of a profession involves independent discretion and professional judgment which are mastered more effectively when conducted on a high intellectual plane. In other words, the techniques and tools used in decision making in the professions are largely based upon theory and principles rather than on routine, trial-and-error practices.

Study of Man

A fourth essential of a profession is that it tends to deal directly with people. As such, it tends to identify itself with their desires, needs, and goals. Thus, the professional practitioner has a far more significant effect on human beings than on material things. For this reason, the professional aspirant should become knowledgeable in the *study of man.* This study means, among other things, a familiarity with those disciplines making up the humanities, and in a broader sense, an understanding of the entire range of the social sciences. An interdisciplinary understanding of the "generalized" knowledge contained in the social studies of philosophy, psychology, sociology, anthropology, and economics provides the professional practitioner with the broad educational background to deal effectively with the numerous "human" problems he faces in his daily practice. A working acquaintance with "general knowledge" helps each practitioner formulate for himself a sound system of humanitarian principles and ethical values. A profession thus calls for not only a *technical* education in the specifics of the discipline but also a *general* education in the liberal arts.

Examinations

A fifth aspect to a profession is the extended or long-range preparation which it requires. This preparation is necessarily of a formal nature. It involves a recognized educational process for acquiring the necessary specialized and generalized knowledge. It suggests a college- or university-type program of organized study culminated by searching and comprehensive *examinations* to test the degree of mastery of the discipline's subject matter by each candidate who seeks entry into the profession. Without a system of rigorous and discriminating examinations, there is no scientific basis for distinguishing professionals from nonprofessionals. A simple, dictionary definition of a profession is "an occupation which one professes to be *skilled in* and to follow." Thus, a formalized educational process accompanied by a battery of discriminating examinations is designed to determine whether or not the candidate is indeed "skilled in" the theory and applied knowledge (the practices) of the discipline he professes and follows.

Formalized Group

A sixth and final qualification for a profession is the existence of a *formalized group* of members often referred to as an association or society. The two principal functions performed by professional societies are (1) to establish and police high standards of ethical behavior and practice among the members, and (2) to encourage and preserve a high quality of technical performance through programs of continuing education sponsored by the society. True professionals strive—through continuing study—to raise their profession's high standards of unselfish and dedicated service to others. They undertake research in both theory and applied knowledge in order to enlarge their total professional capability. Improved understanding, by each member, of the satisfactions derived from moral and ethical behavior coupled with continuing and expanding knowledge of the technical discipline surrounding the profession will produce for the society's members a maximum of respect, admiration, and status among all the persons whom they supply with professional services.

THE MEANING OF "EDUCATION"

Now that the "professional" concept has been explored at least in summary fashion, attention is turned briefly to an analysis of the term, "education." Education may be defined as the impartation or acquisition of knowledge, understanding, and sound reasoning ability through prescribed study or scheduled discipline. Education involves, fundamentally, the development of one's capacity for "rationality" through rigorous, mental discipline. Through education, an individual should be better disciplined to control erratic and unpredictable emotions and thus engage in sound and orderly "reasoning." Education may also lead to more sophisticated decision making. Education is a mind-stretching process which extends through one's entire lifetime.

Education is not merely a method for filling the mind with a mass of information. A person might be characterized as a "walking encyclopedia" and yet not be educated. As suggested above, education involves not merely collection, storage, and recall of facts—it also involves rigorous reasoning. The primary purpose in gathering facts is not to see how long a list one can memorize. Fact gathering permits one to sift and organize *useful* knowledge from trivial information. The person possessing this useful knowledge can then draw appropriate conclusions and make defensible decisions. Thus, it is largely through learning the process of sound reasoning and how to sift out those things really worth reasoning about that "education" has significance and meaning for the individual.

The opposite of the term "educated" is the term "uneducated." A synonym for the latter is "ignorant." One of the most frightening phenomena in the world today is ignorance. Ignorance is not merely the lack of information. It is the lack of ability to understand and to reason, and also is neither knowing nor caring about the possibilities for improvement. Ignorance robs a person of his natural right (1) to establish a set of ideals to be sought after, (2) to develop a sense of important values, and (3) to live up to them in order to experience a more rewarding, meaningful life.

Education allows its possessor to decide what are the really important values in life; it thus improves the ability of a person to form proper and meaningful value judgments. Education provides the opportunity to pursue the true, the beautiful, and the good in the world. It assists one to differentiate the pure from the vulgar, the real from the superficial, and the true from the false by establishing meaningful standards by which to separate wholesomeness from base tendencies.

Education also permits the educated to grasp the full import in the meaning of such words as "empathy," "rapport" or the Spanish term, "simpatía." This harmonious or sympathetic relation with other humans (fellow-feeling) tends to set man clearly apart from the beasts. The ability to imagine oneself literally "in the flesh" of all human counterparts throughout the world is a clear mark of being truly educated. Broad educational understanding thus produces greater capacity to view ethical actions and attitudes with healthy respect and full appreciation. And as ethical considerations become more pronounced in the individual, the character-building process is begun and will surely flourish as education continues throughout life.

Through education, an individual will come closer to the underlying philosophy of the "professions" as contained in the Golden Rule of human conduct. Eventually, perhaps through education, each person will see the wisdom of that statement which calls for man to do unto others that which he would have others do unto him. Then those persons so educated will likely follow, in each of their respective pursuits, the "professional creeds" which admonish all professionals to "act as if the interests of others were their own."

The education of a people, in summary, is measured by its established ideals, its moral principles, and the state of its combined character. The educational level of a group, stated differently, is measured by the sum total of its "rationality." Education of each separate person, on the other hand, will largely be measured by the authority of his conversation, the confidence of his decisions, the conviction of his beliefs, the assurance of his judgments, or, in brief, the combination of his total satisfactions and his fullness of life.

DISTINCTION BETWEEN EDUCATION AND TRAINING

Considerable confusion arises between the two terms: education and training. Many persons no doubt consider them synonymous. Yet each is designed for a different, although no doubt equally important, purpose; and there is usefulness in keeping the distinctions clearly in mind.

Long Run versus Short Run

While education is long-range in pursuit and extends over a period of years, training on the other hand is designed for achievement in a matter of weeks or, at most, a few months. Education involves pursuit of subjects in depth which only "time" will permit. Emphasis extends behind and beyond the obvious details to the underlying "reasons why." In training, one concentrates attention on "know-how" techniques, whereas in education he delves into "know-why" explanations. This distinction between "know-how" and "know-why" suggests that both training and education are necessary if one is to become a well-rounded individual. Moreover, this distinction suggests that education takes up where training leaves off. Thus, after a person learns, through training, the skill of how to perform a task, he will have reached a point in his development which is sure to lead to stagnation unless he begins to "study" *why* the task was done in the manner he was trained originally to do it. No doubt this conclusion prompted the oft-stated axiom that "the man who knows 'how' to do a job will always find employment—working for the man who also knows 'why'." Whether there is truth in this axiom or not, it stands to reason that mere routine how-to-do skills, as important as they are, lack perspective and dimension unless they are supported by the "know-why" knowledge which education epitomizes.

An Illustration

Perhaps an illustration from the field of property-liability insurance will help to dramatize the distinction between training and education. In the area of fire insurance, for example, each person exposed to insurance training is taught no doubt by formula *how to* work various coinsurance problems and *how to* determine the portion of a loss to be borne by the insured when the insured fails to meet the coinsurance percentage requirement. The explanation of "why" the coinsurance concept exists in the first place probably would not be explained, at least not in depth, in a training program. Some statement might be made that such requirement encourages insureds to increase their coverage to a figure more closely approximating the value of their property.

The reason for the existence of the coinsurance concept would likely be reserved until later in the student's career when he undertakes a program of long-range insurance education. Before he could possibly grasp the reason *why* coinsurance exists, the student would need to comprehend the theory of probability and its role in fire insurance ratemaking. He would then need to understand the requisites of a sound insurance rate; particularly the requisite pertaining to equity of rates. He would next need an understanding of the frequency and severity experience of hostile fires and the effect of this experience on the "equitability" requisite in fire insurance rating. Finally, he would need to see the relationship which exists between the theory of probability and the coinsurance concept. After the student comprehended this entire reasoning process based upon an understanding of the underlying "principles" involved, then and only then would he comprehend the full import and significance of the "why" explanation of coinsurance. And it is largely through long-range education, rather than short-term training, that involved and abstract reasons can be grasped and their significance understood by the student.

The Setting

Programs involving insurance education tend to operate through college- or university-type institutions which can provide the elements of longer-term treatment and gradualism of presentation and absorption. The more intricate, involved, and difficult the subject matter, the greater the need for extending the period of study in order to present the subject in smaller segments per session. In training programs, such as those operating in each of the major insurance companies, students are exposed to continuous classroom training in insurance techniques and procedures throughout the entire day, plus evenings in some cases, over a period of weeks or even months. An educational program at the collegiate level, however, would seldom operate effectively unless limited to one or two hours, at most, in the classroom each day with the balance of the time devoted to lengthy reading and writing assignments conducted largely outside of class. Classroom work, in an educational program, depends largely upon the reading and reflecting on the subject done by the student before class. Training, however, which consists largely of exercises, visual aid presentations, work routines, solution of specific problems, and so on, possesses such a variety of "doing" activities that considerably less outside-of-class preparation is required.

A Quotation

No doubt the clearest and most succinct distinction between education and training was developed by the late Dr. David McCahan, president of the American College of Life Underwriters and Professor of Insurance at the Wharton School of Finance and Commerce. He summarized the distinction between these endeavors when he observed:

> We popularly associate the word "education" with the instructional activities in colleges and universities and the word "training" with the instructional activities of companies and associations, even though in a broad sense there is necessarily much overlapping. We associate the word "education" with the impartation and acquisition of knowledge, principles, understanding and the like, whereas we associate the word "training" with exercises or practices to develop skills, techniques, facility in application, proficiency. The emphasis in "education" is on *thinking*—a grasp of the "whys"; contrariwise, the emphasis in "training" is on *doing*—a grasp of the "hows." Ordinarily the goal in the former

is long range and concerns itself with the mental growth of the individual; in the latter it is of short range and concerns itself primarily with the immediate productive efficiency of the person.[1]

COMPANY TRAINING PROGRAMS

Most of the major insurance companies conduct high-quality training programs for their personnel. Many of these companies have training departments consisting of as many as a dozen full-time instructors. Some companies conduct not only home office programs but also branch office programs and other "training center" activities away from the home office. Hundreds of companies have at least one or two training directors with responsibility to conduct company training for such groups as underwriters, special agents, and, frequently, local agents brought in to the home office for training. Most of the training directors in the property-liability companies are joined together in a national organization known as *Insurance Company Education Directors' Society* (*I.C.E.D.S.*). This organization is in the forefront in studying and improving methods for visual aids presentations, techniques for teaching insurance coverage, and the review of new learning techniques such as "*programed learning.*"

Insurance companies are far more efficiently equipped than are any outsiders to conduct company training. In each program, the instructors have developed keen insight into the company's underlying philosophy, its products, its services, and its methods for doing business. No other institution can provide, for new employees as well as experienced personnel, as effective "orientation" training in these subjects as can the company's own training department. The subject matter involved in a company's operations includes technical detail, skills, procedures, methods, routines, and problem solving, all of which require considerable repetition and practice. Company instructors have acquired unusual proficiency in teaching these "know-how" techniques. Highly effective visual aids have been developed to fix indelibly in the minds of the students certain understandings which the instructors wish to impart. Through continuous exercises in "recall," through the use of such remembering techniques as "mnemonics," and through considerable practice in repetitive procedures, the student obtains a firm foundation in basic insurance which is bound to help him constantly throughout his career. Much of the insurance business involves continued repeating of well-established procedures. Thus, the student who learns these skills quickly and lastingly is certain to fill an immediate need for such talent the moment he reports for full-time work in the insurance business.

---

[1] David McCahan, "The Half-Century in Insurance Education," *Journal of the American Association of University Teachers of Insurance*, Vol. XVIII, No. 1 (March, 1951), pp. 54–72.

The most important contribution made by insurance company training experts lies in their ability to teach new employees the skills, techniques, and facility in application so necessary for them to become "productive" on the job *immediately*. It is most unlikely that insurance education, as opposed to training, could fulfill to any appreciable extent this important function. As pointed out earlier, education merely takes over where training leaves off. Education and training, therefore, must never be thought mutually exclusive; they are rather highly complementary and necessary counterparts of each student's overall capacity for functioning on the job as an efficient, well-rounded employee.

PROFESSIONAL INSURANCE EDUCATION—COLLEGE- AND UNIVERSITY-SPONSORED PROGRAMS

Development of a profession is highly unlikely, if not impossible, if it fails to operate through the established institutions of higher learning—colleges and universities. Numerous writers support this conclusion by pointing to the widely accepted professions of divinity, medicine, law, accounting, architecture, and engineering whose early development, present strength, and general acceptance resulted primarily from their close affiliation with the higher educational institutions throughout the country.

Colleges and universities provide, for the professions, the intellectual environment plus the research stimulation so vital to the creation of subject matter in any profession. Full-time college teachers produce, in most of the professional disciplines, the bulk of the textbook subject matter as well as the research articles upon which the profession is based. The teaching of prospective candidates for admission to the profession rests primarily upon the college or university teachers in the various professional schools which make up the total university facility. The professional examinations are often developed on the campus of the college or university by the teaching staff members and they also frequently serve as the persons who set the professional standards of academic excellence so necessary in the examination grading process. Moreover, they often serve on the panel of graders who actually mark the papers in order to judge those competent to enter the profession.

An introductory course in property insurance was offered in 1904 by Dr. S. S. Huebner at the Wharton School of Finance and Commerce of the University of Pennsylvania. Dr. Huebner later became Professor of Insurance and Chairman of the Insurance Department at this professional school of business, widely known as the Wharton School. In 1905, a basic course in life insurance was added to the curriculum in insurance and the start of a full professional program in insurance was underway on this campus. This modest beginning opened the way for similar courses in insurance at other leading colleges and universities throughout the country. A recent survey by the S. S. Huebner Foundation for Insurance Education at the University of Pennsylvania shows that 549 colleges and universities currently offer at least one insurance course for college credit granted toward the bachelor's degree. Moreover, at least a dozen major universities offer a full graduate curriculum in insurance leading to the master's and doctoral degrees.[2]

The American Risk and Insurance Association

The American Risk and Insurance Association (commonly known as A.R.I.A.) is a learned society, the purpose of which is to develop and extend the discipline of risk and insurance through education, research, publication, and communication. More specifically, its objectives are as follows:

1. To foster academic instruction in risk and insurance at the collegiate level.
2. To encourage basic and applied research in risk and insurance.
3. To provide an open forum for the free exchange of information and views concerning risk and insurance matters.
4. To facilitate the personal and professional growth and development of its members.

A.R.I.A. is made up of members from the academic community and other persons interested in the academic approach to insurance education.

PROFESSIONAL INSURANCE EDUCATION—INDUSTRY-SPONSORED PROGRAMS[3]

American Institute for Property and Liability Underwriters, Inc., and the C.P.C.U.

The launching of professional insurance education in property-liability insurance leading to a formal designation can be traced to the date,

[2] At least three important insurance educational foundations have been organized by universities for the express purpose of encouraging, through fellowship and scholarship funds, graduate students to undertake studies leading to advanced degrees in insurance. The fundamental purpose of these foundations is to produce more teachers of insurance with terminal degrees in this field. The oldest and largest foundation is the S. S. Huebner Foundation for Insurance Education of the University of Pennsylvania. It has been estimated that upwards of 100 professors of insurance received, through this foundation, reimbursement for part or all of the expenses incidental to their graduate work in insurance. More recently, the Charles W. Griffith Foundation for Insurance Education at The Ohio State University and the J. Edwin Larson Foundation for Insurance Education at Florida State University have been established to further the cause of professional education in insurance on their respective campuses. The Griffith Foundation, however, also extends its financial support to undergraduate and graduate students in insurance in the professional schools of business in the other state universities throughout Ohio.

[3] The origin of professional insurance education sponsored and supported by the insurance industry can be traced to a day in 1914 in Baltimore, Maryland, during a speech before a life underwriter association meeting presented by Dr. S. S. Huebner,

May 16, 1941, when representatives from a number of major insurance associations met in New York to lay the groundwork for establishing the professional examining organization to be known as The American Institute for Property and Liability Underwriters, Inc. Credit for the establishment of this new professional insurance educational program is probably due three men. Dr. S. S. Huebner, of the Wharton School, and Mr. John A. North, of the Phoenix of Hartford Insurance Companies, were largely responsible for obtaining unanimous support from all segments of the property-liability industry. Dr. Harry J. Loman, then and still Professor of Insurance at the Wharton School, deserves the major credit for organizing and developing the actual educational program leading to professional distinction in property-liability insurance. The professional designation, decided upon at the outset of the program in 1941, became known as Chartered Property Casualty Underwriter and has become even better known over the years as C.P.C.U.

Source Materials. The founders and subsequent leaders of the C.P.C.U. program developed the subject matter to be mastered from a wide variety of sources. The reading matter consists of numerous sets of technical procedures, and systematic or general rules appropriate to the practice of a new professional calling in insurance. These "fundamentals of knowledge" include facts, ideas, concepts, theories, principles, procedures, and rules. They have been organized systematically into weekly segments of study and discussion lesson plans designed with a view toward helping the practitioner apply his broadened knowledge to the practical problems involved in professional service.

Three Objectives. Professional education in insurance unites in a single curriculum a variety of separate subjects intended to accomplish, fundamentally, three important improvements in each candidate who seeks professional status. These are: (1) improvement of the candidate's intellectual comprehension of the discipline plus those fields of learning related to it; (2) improvement of the candidate's practical skills as they apply to the rendering of improved technical service to clients; and (3) improvement of the candidate's "professional attitude" or conviction as to ethical conduct so essential if the profession is ever to become established and flourish. These three objectives, then, serve as the continuous challenge to the administrators of the C.P.C.U. programs. The ultimate success of these programs will depend upon how well the objectives are accomplished.

---

then Professor of Insurance at the University of Pennsylvania. Dr. Huebner proposed that ". . . a life insurance course of study leading to a degree or designation comparable to that of Certified Public Accountant, might ultimately be created and centered in a college of standing, commensurate with other degree-granting educational institutions." Thirteen years after this initial proposal, the C.L.U. professional insurance program was launched with the founding, in 1927, of the American College of Life Underwriters in Philadelphia, Pennsylvania.

These objectives spill over into the "other disciplines" of thought closely related to insurance. It became crystal clear at the outset of each of the two professional programs that knowledge and understanding or "awareness" above and beyond the field of insurance, *per se*, would be absolutely essential if the professional man in insurance could hope to develop intellectual understanding coupled with applied skills combined with personal integrity. Thus, interdisciplinary study was called for in such fields as economics, government, English language, insurance law, business law, management, accounting, and finance. It quickly became evident also that studies in the disciplines concerned with human behavior, applied psychology, business ethics, and philosophy were essential in the well-rounding of the C.P.C.U. candidate. Thus, these topics were subsequently added to the curriculum of study. Moreover, these study materials have undergone a continuous process of revision and refinement in order to relate the appropriate concepts and principles more closely to the professional man in insurance.

In all of this interdisciplinary study, the candidate is sure to pick up ideas, concepts, principles, analogies, reasoning processes, and methodology which will more than likely have their impact on his intellectual development and, coincidentally, on his efficiency on the job. Moreover, improved intellectual equipment coupled with greater skill to do a better job is most likely to have its long-range impact upon the candidate's overall maturity. Maturity, in this respect, includes his sense of moral and ethical responsibility to himself as well as to others.

Society of Chartered Property and Casualty Underwriters

The Society of Chartered Property and Casualty Underwriters was officially organized on January 4, 1944, as a professional association whose membership consists of men and women who have attained the C.P.C.U. designation. The Society is dedicated to the continuous professional and ethical development of its members. This development is accomplished through the Society's national activities and the activities of its local chapters including, among others, the publication of its professional journal—*The Annals*, C.P.C.U. Forums, C.P.C.U. Clinics, and the Annual Meeting and Seminars. About 100 local chapters are currently in existence.

Insurance Institute of America, Inc.

The Insurance Institute of America, Inc., offers two educational programs. Each one embodies a combination of "education" and "training" as the terms have been used in this chapter. The first one is the Program in General Insurance, which consists of three examinations and leads to the award of the Insurance Institute Certificate. The second one is the Program for Adjusters, which consists of six examinations and leads to the I.I.A. Diploma in Insurance Adjusting.

BENEFITS FROM PROFESSIONAL EDUCATION PROGRAMS

A brief analysis of each of several important benefits likely to derive from professional education should not only prove informative but also serve as a satisfactory summary of the purpose and advantage of professional education in insurance throughout the United States.

Useful Body of Facts and Technical Procedures

One of the first important benefits derived from professional education is the acquisition of an abundance of useful technical information. In any formalized study there is, of necessity, a considerable body of facts and technical procedures which must be studied and understood. Mastery of specific facts and procedures provides the practitioner in insurance with a high degree of "know-how" knowledge. To this extent, professional education overlaps or parallels technical insurance training described earlier in this chapter. A certain amount of "how-it-works" detail is essential to enable one to look behind technical procedures for reasons "why." To illustrate the importance of each person's being in possession of technical information, reference is made to the problem of coverage analysis in the field of property-liability insurance. Before an individual can analyze "why" certain provisions are in a policy or why certain others are omitted, he must first have a technical acquaintance with the coverage detail in the contract. In other words, an insurance technician must know *what* is in a contract before he can begin to draw conclusions as to *why* it appears there in the first place.

Understanding Why

Formalized study in a professional education program also helps the practitioner acquire "know-why" understanding about the internal functioning of the profession. The person who can develop sound reasons for or logical explanations of current practices has in his possession far greater knowledgeability, in both depth and breadth, than one who simply knows *how* something works. Reason-why explanations of the theory behind a given technical procedure introduce the student to the process of abstract reasoning. This abstraction, in turn, provides him with the technique for thinking symbolically. Reasoning through the use of abstract symbols or analogies is frequently a far more direct, revealing, and meaningful process than actually "viewing" an operation through its concrete or physical manifestations. To illustrate, a complex electronic mechanism might well be understood by a process of "visualizing" it through abstract reasoning, whereas mere physical inspection might produce no answers whatsoever to its complex operation. In the field of insurance ratemaking, abstract or symbolic reasoning is similarly necessary in order to comprehend many of the complex rating applications and processes.

Problem-Solving Proficiency

Professional education also helps the person develop greater proficiency in problem solving. Continuous exposure, in the professional programs, to hypothetical problem situations to be solved is bound to exercise and strengthen the mental powers by working, through the force of logic, toward sound solutions to the problems presented. Repetition of problem solving by the use of logical reasoning is certain to energize and sharpen mental responses and analytical thought patterns. Students who are thus subjected to hypothetical case problems and who practice repeatedly the techniques of solving problems through analytical reasoning should be able without particular difficulty to transfer these newly developed talents and skills to the actual problems faced on the job. Professional education, therefore, is a mental conditioning process designed to bring out improved capabilities of the mind to cope with difficult situations and to reason systematically toward sound and logical solutions to these problems. Improved proficiencies in "logic" thus simultaneously improve the individual's ability to assume important decision-making responsibilities on the job.

Improved Communicative Skills

Another important benefit derived from professional insurance programs is the improvement of a person's communicative skills. Management consultants or specialists generally agree that one of the major weaknesses among top and middle management personnel is their failure to transmit effectively their thoughts to others. This weakness often may be traced to management's inability, in the first place, to understand thoroughly the complex ideas they wish to transmit to others. In other cases, it may simply result from lack of *practice* in receiving and then transmitting abstract concepts to superiors, subordinates, or other associates. Then, too, it may be that their associates are incapable of "receiving" or comprehending a complex analysis, a difficult concept, or an intricate methodological procedure.

Failure of communication is not limited to oral transmission and receiving. Communication by the written word also reflects serious handicaps on the part of superiors and subordinates alike. Reading deficiencies may also be a major stumbling block in effective communication.

Communication has generally been found to improve largely through practice in more effective reading, speaking and writing. Francis Bacon once observed that "reading maketh a full man, conference [discussion] a ready man, and writing an exact man." And it should be emphasized that professional education consists essentially of these three learning media. Reading assignments in the subject matter are conducted outside of class; discussion over the material is treated in class; and written exercises through examinations, notetaking, and outside reports tend to round out this educational trilogy. This process is repeated over and over again throughout several years of professional study. Professional education would indeed seem to be the ideal vehicle for polishing, exercising, and improving the student's all-around communicative capabilities.

Ability to Discriminate

Professional education also provides for each person an increased capacity to separate important facts from trivial ones. It also affords the student a sound basis for systematizing and organizing data into useful categories. The ability to sift through masses of descriptive detail and pull out "essential" information is a feat sure to stand anyone in good stead in a highly complex business society. Skill in boiling down information into essentials, thereby producing useful concepts or generalizations, is a talent possessed by far too few persons in business today. The possession of such capacity is certain to provide that fortunate person with a deeper sense of confidence in himself. Increased confidence is a particular advantage in the pursuit of extended study which leads ultimately to professional recognition and personal distinction.

Compacting Time through Compressed Experience

An equally important benefit derived from professional education may be stated, in summary fashion, as that process whereby "time" can actually be compacted by compressing "experience." The process works as follows: Experience in business is an element sought after, indeed revered, by almost everyone involved in business today. The major problem, however, is that by the time one gets thoroughly "experienced" in business, the age-65 compulsory retirement rule forces him out of the job. Moreover, when an individual does attain experience late in life, generally his vitality, drive, and ambition have passed their peak. Increasingly, business leaders paradoxically are seeking a method for obtaining men with a wealth of experience but who, at the same time, are sufficiently young in age to possess vitality and enthusiasm for the job.

Many business leaders are turning to professional education as the most probable answer to this paradox. They realize that there are two types of experience: direct and indirect. In some respects, direct experience is superior to learning about the "experiences" of others through studying the basic literature of a given field of thought. Yet in another sense, direct experience suffers in comparison with vicarious experience because the person who must "live" experiences before he can learn them soon discovers the narrowing effect of this method. Most of the business experiences learned in the course of a given business day no doubt tend to be mere "repeats" of previously learned experience. Because of specialization and interdependence in a complex society "learned" experiences in a given, narrow activity are insufficient to equip a person for broad-gauged management responsibilities. He must, therefore, look about him for more *generalized* experience.

The most efficient method for gaining such generalized experience is through systematic study of the experiences of others. Textbooks, treatises, monographs, and journal articles—which, in effect, summarize the "mass" of cumulative experiences of others—have proven by far the best sources for gaining broad experiences from among hundreds of persons—both contemporaries as well as those of earlier generations. A formalized professional educational program, therefore, in either a university-sponsored or industry-sponsored facility would seem a truly effective method for obtaining broad-guage experience, by an employee, who at the same time possesses youth, vitality, and inner drive to succeed in business. Thus, professional education is indeed a most effective experience-compressing and time-compacting process.

Self-Fulfillment

A final, and perhaps the most important, benefit derived from professional education involves the psychological impact it is likely to make on the morale of the student who pursues such study. Psychologists have been in frequent, if not unanimous, agreement that one of the most important psychological needs in life is the desire to feel significant or *worthy*. Achieving "worth," as a human being, might well rank number one among all motivating forces in our society. The need to feel important, the desire to be admired and respected, the drive to amount to something significant are all corollary aspects of the general tendency to seek worth as an individual and as a member of society.

The noted author, Leo Rosten, aptly expressed the essence of true satisfaction which can be gained from this life. He observed:

> The purpose of life is to *matter*, to be productive, to have it make some difference that you lived at all. Happiness, in the ancient, noble sense, means self-fulfillment—and is given to those who use to the fullest whatever talents God or luck or fate bestowed upon them.
>
> Happiness, to me, lies in stretching, to the farthest boundaries of which we are capable, the resources of the mind and of the heart.[4]

---

[4] Leo Rosten, "Words to Live By—the Real Reason for Being Alive," *This Week Magazine* (January 20, 1963), p. 2.

SUGGESTED READINGS

CHILDS, MARQUIS W., AND CATER, DOUGLASS. *Ethics in a Business Society.* New York: Harper & Bros., The New American Library, 1954.

COGAN, MORRIS L. "The Problem of Defining a Profession," *The Annals of the American Academy of Political and Social Science,* Vol. 297 (January, 1955), pp. 105–11.

———. "Toward a Definition of Profession," *Harvard Educational Review,* Vol. 23 (Winter, 1953), pp. 33–50.

DEWEY, JOHN, AND TUFTS, JAMES H. *Ethics.* New York: Henry Holt & Co., 1908.

KOZELKA, RICHARD L. "Education for Business Administration," from *Education for the Professions,* U.S. Department of Health, Education, and Welfare Publication. Washington, D.C.: U.S. Government Printing Office, 1955.

OVERMAN, EDWIN S. "The Professional Concept and Business Ethics." Bryn Mawr: Monograph of The American Institute for Property and Liability Underwriters, Inc., n.d.

POUND, ROSCOE. "What is a Profession—the Elements of a Profession," from *The Lawyer from Antiquity to Modern Times.* St. Paul, Minn.: West Publishing Co., 1953.

SHAFFER, DALE E. "An Analysis of the Attributes of a Profession," *The Deltasig Magazine of Delta Sigma Pi* (November, 1962), pp. 8–11.

SILK, LEONARD S. "The Education of Businessmen," *Is Business a Profession?* Supplementary paper No. 11. New York: Committee for Economic Development, 1960.

STANS, MAURICE H. *The Profession of Accounting.* New York: American Institute of Accountants, 1954. (Reprint from Chapter 1 of *The CPA Handbook.*)

Chapter 71

PUBLIC RELATIONS

BY J. CARROLL BATEMAN

This chapter concludes Part VIII and treatment of the institution of property and liability insurance. A brief general discussion of public relations in business is followed by attention to (1) the public relations standing of insurance, (2) insurance organizations for public relations, (3) public relations at the company level, and (4) public relations for the agent.

PUBLIC RELATIONS IN BUSINESS

"Public relations" is an often-used phrase in the contemporary business world. It is also widely misused. Public relations in business is neither a form of mysticism nor a magic amulet. It is not a cure-all for the multitudinous problems of business management.

Four Basic Functions of Public Relations

Public relations is an essential function of management and with other key functions helps management to achieve its three universal objectives: (1) corporate survival, (2) profits, and (3) growth. In the optimum situation the public relations executive in business has four basic functions.

1. To *evaluate* public attitudes, with reference to his business or industry and its products and services.
2. To *counsel* his management or his industry on the public relations aspects of its policies and actions, so that these will conform to the public interest.
3. To *communicate* pertinent facts and understandings to all kinds of people who have relationships with the business or industry.
4. To *motivate* others who are employed in the business or industry to participate in the public relations activities and so, by extension, magnify the impact of the total public relations effort.

Thus, the public relations function in business includes evaluation, counselling, communication, and motivation. Many people are inclined to think of it primarily as communication (or publicity, which is a common misnomer). But this is an incomplete concept. Good public relations cannot be built out of words alone. An effective public relations posture may be achieved only through the testimony of policies and deeds as well as of words.

The "Publics"

At the risk of oversimplifying matters, it might be said that business public relations is an organized, planned effort to create a generally constructive relationship between a company or an industry and the various groups of people who are related to it in one way or another.

For the property-liability insurance business as a whole, these groups include policyholders, employees, legislators, the "gatekeepers" of the mass media of communication, staff members of the various state regulatory departments, insurance agents, educators concerned with the teaching of insurance, their students, and so on. For individual insurance companies these "publics" might typically include its own stockholders, policyholders, employees, agents, the press, radio and television, and such. For the insurance agent, such "publics" might be made up of his employees, his clients, and his neighbors in his community or hometown.

The Fundamentals of Sound Public Relations

For different businesses at different times, the public relations goals or objectives will vary. Generally speaking, however, the broad objective of business public relations programs is to earn public acceptance of and confidence in the business and its products or services. It goes almost without saying that the *sine qua non* for achieving acceptance and confidence is to operate in a manner which conforms to the public's concepts of its interests. In short, to operate not only in conformity with the law, but also in conformity with commonly accepted principles of fairness, equity, morality, courtesy, and good taste. As someone once said, "Good public relations is, for a business, what morals and good manners are for an individual."

However, in this complex modern society, model behavior on the part of a business must be supplemented with effective communications between a business and its publics, if the desired end result is to be achieved. Thus, in any public relations program, communications play an important role.

While the extent and nature of a public relations program may vary according to the size of an organization, the basic elements remain the same: fair and ethical practice *plus* effective communication. This is as true for the individual insurance agent or broker as it is for the companies he represents, or for the industry at large. Questionable practices engaged in by only a few companies may ruin the reputation of a whole industry.

The insurance business has a good foundation upon which to build its public relations effort, for the business makes a valuable contribution to society; it is a business with a very real social purpose and with a deep sense of social responsibility. Furthermore, it has widespread economic influence which is used to good ends. It contributes, through insurance protection and through investment of its reserves, to the stability and growth of the American economy.

It must be recognized that any business will have only the public relations standing it deserves—no better. All who gain their livelihood in insurance share in the responsibility for seeing that it deserves the best.

PUBLIC RELATIONS STANDING OF INSURANCE

Property and liability insurance coverages—particularly such lines as homeowners, automobile, and workmen's compensation—have a close relationship to the daily lives of most people. Yet public opinion surveys indicate that the business of property-liability insurance as a whole has not made a deep impression upon public consciousness. While some aspects of the business (notably, the steady increases in automobile insurance rates since the end of World War II) have come to public attention and brought strong reactions, generally speaking the public knows little about the business and has few strong impressions pro or con.

Further, what attitudes the public does have are often outdated. For example, the public does not consider the property-liability insurance business to be highly competitive, whereas anyone who has been in this business since World War II knows otherwise.

Some Basic Attitudes

Some of the highlights of the results of a national public opinion survey conducted by the Insurance Information Institute in the early sixties (the first national opinion survey of its kind) may be summarized as follows:

The public image, or profile, of the business of property and liability insurance is weaker than the images of other major service businesses (the airlines, the telephone company, gas and electric utilities, railroads, trucking—and life insurance).

The public does not give the business of property and liability insurance a high rating for progressiveness, for service, for explaining its coverages, for management, or as an employer or a good business in which to invest. To some extent, the business of property and liability insurance is deemed to be monopolistic, and it is not looked upon as a highly competitive industry. The public is not highly critical of the property and liability insurance business—people are just less familiar with it.

Public awareness of insurance-industry sponsorship of fire prevention, highway safety, and other public service activities is not extensive. Only 16 percent of the public recognizes insurance industry sponsorship of fire-prevention activities, and only 12 percent recognizes insurance sponsorship of highway safety programs.

Generally speaking, the public has broad contact with insurance rates in only two areas: fire insurance and automobile insurance. There is little feeling on the part of people that fire insurance rates are too high. About 50 percent of the public believes that automobile insurance rates are too high. However, people tend to fix most of the blame upon increased numbers of accidents, higher repair costs, fraudulent or padded claims, and payment of unjustified claims by companies.

Individuals who have had actual claims experience report very favorably on it. That is, almost all of them are satisfied with the way in which their claims were settled. Even among third-party claimants in automobile insurance cases a substantial majority expressed satisfaction with the handling of the claims. However, the public at large is far more dubious about how promptly and fairly the insurance companies settle claims. Only a little over half feel that companies settle fairly and promptly.

There is much confusion and ignorance among the public concerning the regulation of the insurance business. Only a few of the people know that the business is regulated by the state governments; most of the rest do not know it is regulated. Almost one half think it should not be regulated, and only one third think it should.

If given a choice between buying fire and auto insurance from private companies or a government agency, one third (36 percent) of the public would prefer to buy from the government; 43 percent said they would prefer to continue buying from private insurance companies.

The underlying attitudes revealed by this study generally are not subject to sharp fluctuations; they are likely to change only slowly over long periods of time.

Growing Need for Better Public Relations

This survey (with others of more limited scope) has indicated the need for greater emphasis upon public relations and upon public communication by the property-liability insurance business. The industry is alert and is responding to this need. Programs of public education and information are being conducted by such organizations as the Insurance Information Institute, the National Association of Independent Insurers, and the American Mutual Insurance Alliance, all of which are supported by the various kinds of property-liability insurance companies. Since 1950, numerous state and regional public information offices also have been established with company support. In the last decade, many individual companies have initiated public relations departments or have expanded and intensified existing public relations programs. This development has resulted from a growing realization that today's highly competitive situation requires a greater emphasis upon establishing individual corporate identity. Associations of producers at the national, state, and local levels also have become active in public relations.

All in all, the industry as a whole has an extensive public relations movement underway. What it lacks in coordination is perhaps made up to some extent in zeal.

Nevertheless, a word of caution is in order. Much of the public relations effort of the business is defensive in nature. It seeks to preserve the past rather than to prepare for the future. Certainly, it is not sufficient for the insurance industry to defend the status quo. If leaders in the business of insurance want to have public understanding and support, they must emphasize those things which the public can understand as being in its interest and which the public will support.

INSURANCE ORGANIZATIONS FOR PUBLIC RELATIONS

Numerous organizations designed in whole or in part to carry out public relations activities on behalf of the property-liability insurance business have been established, most of them since the end of World War II.

Insurance Information Institute

In 1960, the capital stock companies that market through the independent agency system founded the Insurance Information Institute, a national organization with four regional offices devoted exclusively to public information and education. The Institute is supported directly or indirectly by about 300 such companies. In addition, the Institute's membership includes eight boards, bureaus, and associations which are supported generally by these same companies. These eight member boards and bureaus include the American Insurance Association, the Fire Insurance Research and Actuarial Association, the Inland Marine Insurance Bureau, the Inland Marine Underwriters Association, the Multiple Line Insurance Rating Bureau, the National Automobile Underwriters Association, the National Bureau of Casualty Underwriters, and the Surety Association of America.[1] From time to time, the Institute also serves other organizations supported by its member companies, such as the National Automobile Theft Bureau, the General Adjustment Bureau, and the various state fire insurance rating organizations. For all of these company-supported organizations the Institute acts as a public information agency, disseminating news and other information relating to their respective interests and activities.

In addition, the Institute implements a broad program of general public education about property-liability insurance. Its activities include the providing of information to press, radio, and television; the development of printed aids, sample policy kits, slide films, and motion pictures

[1] Before they were merged into the American Insurance Association, the Association of Casualty and Surety Companies and the National Board of Fire Underwriters were members of I.I.I.

for the use of educators at the high school and college levels; the publication of a magazine (*The Journal of Insurance Information*) for the independent agents and brokers who represent its supporting companies; the preparation of booklets and exhibit materials for the use of companies and agents; the publication of an annual statistical handbook and other reference pieces; and the development and supervision of insurance speakers' bureaus for which it prepares manuals. The Institute also acts as coordinator for the activities of the fieldmen's associations, which are statewide organizations of stock company fieldmen. The fieldmen's groups carry on a variety of public relations activities at the grass roots, sometimes in liaison with the state associations of independent agents.

American Mutual Insurance Alliance

The mutual property and liability companies through the American Mutual Insurance Alliance have for many years maintained a public relations program to serve their interests. More than 100 mutual companies support the Alliance and its affiliated organizations—the National Association of Automotive Mutual Insurance Companies, the National Association of Mutual Casualty Companies and the Federation of Mutual Fire Insurance Companies.

The Alliance program is conducted from its Chicago headquarters, with AMIA branch offices in New York, Boston, Washington, San Francisco, Atlanta, and Denver supporting and furthering public relations as the need or opportunity arises in their areas.

The Alliance and its affiliated organizations and member companies sponsor forums, schools, symposiums, conferences, scholarships, and special events, including the National Truck Roadeo. Such activities relate to safety and loss prevention in many areas—public welfare, health and accident, rehabilitation, fire, streets and highways, industry, construction, and engineering. The Alliance also conducts a comprehensive study course in property and liability insurance for students in specialized college insurance courses and reaches a large audience with specialized educational and public relations material in the form of motion pictures, booklets, leaflets, and the like.

A principal medium in the Alliance program is the *Journal of American Insurance*, a 32-page award-winning magazine published monthly, for distribution to a controlled circulation of opinion leaders in insurance, law, medicine, banking, education, and public affairs. Copies also are distributed to the daily press, magazines, and radio and television stations. The *Journal* was established in 1924. The Alliance also publishes the weekly *Mutual Memorandum* to inform executives of its companies about current developments.

A regular monthly service of specially prepared releases is supplied to the press, radio, and television, with additional releases as needed on current matters.

Other Organizations

The National Association of Independent Insurers also conducts a public relations program for its member companies, including both stock and mutual organizations which generally operate independently of the traditional rating bureaus.

The Public Relations Department of N.A.I.I. functions as a combination information and service bureau. Its officials handle relations with the trade press, magazines, and general newspapers. They also work with writers and editors who are researching articles in depth, providing them with source material and arranging for interviews with member company officials and staff experts who can speak with authority in the various fields.

Member companies may call on the department for counseling on speeches, news releases, magazine articles, movie projects, printing, typography, special events, and graphic arts. Newsletters, bulletins, reports, and reprints of newspaper and magazine articles are circulated to member companies at frequent intervals. A supply of pamphlets, significant reprints, speeches, and other material is maintained for distribution on request. Press packets and speakers' kits are prepared to deal with specific situations.

At the national level also both the National Association of Insurance Agents and the National Association of Mutual Insurance Agents are active in public relations. The former provides a variety of materials to assist its member associations and affiliated local boards, as well as individual agents, in conducting public relations (and advertising) activities. Agents may also look to their state associations for ideas and materials to implement their public relations efforts. The 1300 local boards of independent agents for many years have been active in community service projects designed to win public recognition for the independent insurance agent. The National Association of Insurance Agents publishes a monthly bulletin entitled *Independent Agents in Action,* which is a report on successful public service projects conducted by local boards, on public relations projects of individual agents, and on new public relations tools available from various companies and industry organizations. The National Association of Mutual Insurance Agents provides public relations materials for its members (including guides for public speaking and press relations). It also sponsors a "National Alert Youth Award" program, a community-relations endeavor to recognize acts of heroism by children under 16 years of age.

The Insurance Advertising Conference (an organization of insurance company advertising directors) each year makes awards to agents who have conducted outstanding advertising and public relations programs. Reports about these winning programs are available from the conference secretary.

State and Regional Organizations

Since 1950, ten statewide and two regional insurance information offices have been established by various groups of companies. Some of these, such as those in Connecticut, Minnesota, New Hampshire, and Pennsylvania, are supported by life companies and by property and liability companies and hence represent all lines of insurance. Others, in Michigan, Illinois, Indiana, Ohio, North Carolina, and Georgia, represent only property-liability lines. Company support of these organizations varies from state to state. Some are supported only by companies headquartered within the state, others by both domiciled and "foreign" companies; some are supported by both "direct writing" companies and agency companies, stock or mutual.

In addition, there are two regional insurance information services which are independent of the regional offices of the Insurance Information Institute. These are the Western Insurance Information Service, with headquarters in Los Angeles, which operates in eleven states (Arizona, California, Colorado, Idaho, Montana, Nevada, New Mexico, Oregon, Utah, Washington, and Wyoming) and the Southwestern Insurance Information Service, with headquarters in Dallas, which is active in Oklahoma and Texas.

The organization called "The Casualty Insurance Companies Serving Massachusetts" also conducts some public relations activities within that state. It is located in Boston. The Texas Insurance Advisory Association, which has headquarters in Austin, Texas, also has a public relations department.

What to Expect

The addresses of all of these organizations may be found in Appendix L. Individuals in company and agency ranks who are interested in public relations may look to these organizations for authoritative information, guidance, and specific communications tools, such as printed matter, exhibit materials, slide films, and motion pictures. Educators, students, journalists, librarians, and others outside the business of insurance also will find that their inquiries are welcomed by these organizations.

PUBLIC RELATIONS AT THE COMPANY LEVEL

Some of the larger companies writing property-liability insurance lines have their own public relations departments, staffed by communications specialists. Sometimes these departments are the counterparts of the advertising departments. In the other companies, the public relations function (where it exists) is sometimes subsumed into the advertising department or into the personnel department. Ideally, the public relations function should stand alone and the person responsible for it should have access to top levels of management. Where this is not the case, the ability of the public relations staff adequately to serve the needs of management may be impaired. Conversely, where the head of the public relations staff is in day-to-day contact with the members of top-level management, he can become acquainted with the public relations and communications problems that are of concern to them. In such a situation he is in a strong position to suggest sound proposals for dealing with these matters.

Organizing the Company Department

In a very large company the public relations department itself may be subdivided. Sometimes, this division is made on the basis of audiences or "publics." For example, one division may be responsible for communications addressed to agents or policyholders; another for communications addressed to the press, radio, and television; still another for educational work with schools and colleges.

Sometimes the division of labor within the public relations department of the large company is based on techniques. That is, one section may be responsible for printed publications (for employees, agents, policyholders, or stockholders); one section may be responsible for publicity and press relations; and still another for the production of motion pictures. A few of the large companies also have established regional public relations offices at strategic points around the country.

Public Relations Functions in the Company

Some of the customary functions of a company public relations department include:

1. Counseling of management on public relations aspects of its policies and actions.
2. Preparation and dissemination of publicity and the answering of press inquiries.
3. Publication of periodical bulletins or magazines for employees or agents.
4. Publication of materials for agents and policyholders.
5. Production of motion pictures about the company and its services, or about insurance and related topics.
6. Development of plans and materials for exhibits and displays.
7. Preparation of special publications, such as corporate histories.
8. Preparation of speeches for company executives.
9. Planning of special events, such as anniversaries, and employees' social and sports activities.
10. Cooperation in civic activities, including fund-raising for welfare organizations.

PUBLIC RELATIONS FOR THE AGENT

It is not possible to outline a public relations program for the "typical" property-liability insurance agent in these pages—or anywhere else, for that matter. For one thing, the "typical" insurance agent or broker is difficult to define. Many agents sell life and health insurance as well as the property and liability coverages. Others may "double in brass" as realtors. Some, although they spend full time in selling general coverages, may devote most of their energies to commercial lines, while still others may be concerned largely with personal lines. No canned public relations program will serve the interests of a number of different agents. Instead, it is better to offer a few simple guidelines for the agent who is interested in conducting his own public relations effort.

The prerequisites for good public relations at the agency level are for the agent to know his business well and to serve his clients properly. Knowledge and service are indispensable. No amount of "public relations" will make up for their lack.

With these prerequisites, however, the individual agent is in a position to plan for his own public relations effort. Few agencies or brokers are large enough to justify the employment of a full-time public relations specialist. Large agencies, however, may find it feasible and desirable to retain a public relations counsellor who is located in their community. A counsellor of this type is set up to serve several clients on a fee basis. Thus, where the public relations effort is not elaborate, the economics of the situation may favor retaining a public relations counsellor rather than building an internal public relations staff.

For the great majority of agents and brokers the public relations effort will be in the do-it-yourself category. In such a case, their public relations efforts must of necessity be simple. Their efforts will be circumscribed by lack of time, by limited funds, and by their personal abilities and interests. But this is not to say that such efforts will be nonproductive.

Some Objectives for Agents' Programs

With proper planning and with economy of effort, the individual property-liability insurance producer can develop for himself a public relations program that will help him to achieve one or more of the following objectives:

1. To identify the agent (or broker) as a responsible citizen interested in the welfare of his community.
2. To solidify his relationship with his existing clients by demonstrating his interest in continuing to serve them.
3. To place his name and his business before the attention of other potential clients in his community.

4. To identify him among the companies that he represents—and with other companies as well—as a sound, progressive, and productive agent, of the type they want to have.

Techniques of Communication

In the pursuit of these goals, the agent or broker has several means of communication available to him:

1. Publicity (in his hometown newspapers and on local radio stations).
2. Advertising (in local newspapers, on local radio and television outlets, on roadside billboards, and in such local publications as Chamber of Commerce magazines).
3. Direct mail (including personal letters, a periodic "newsletter," pamphlets, and brochures).
4. Public speaking on insurance and related subjects (before local civic and service clubs, such as the Rotary, Kiwanis, Lions, Women's clubs, Chamber of Commerce, etc.).
5. Exhibits and displays at local home shows, county fairs, and other events.

Publicity. Newspaper editors generally desire news about the business people and the businesses in their community.

They will appreciate submission of worthwhile news items in written form, and with *good* news photographs when such are available. While the rules for preparing news releases are relatively simple (they are not being repeated here because virtually every library has at least several books on the art of publicity writing), the local editor often will not insist that publicity be in a ready-to-use form. If he is given the facts, he can have the story edited or rewritten by a member of his staff.

What kinds of stories will the editor deem newsworthy? Here are some possibilities:

1. Announcement of the opening of a new agency.
2. Expansion of an existing agency through the opening of a branch office or the purchase of another agency.
3. Appointments of new officers or new staff members in the agency.
4. Speeches by members of the agency staff.
5. Awards to agency staff members for outstanding production or service.
6. Participation by staff members in business conventions or meetings.
7. Promotions or retirements of staff members.
8. Participation by staff members in civic activities (for example, as chairman of a community chest campaign or a hospital building fund drive).
9. Planning of unusual insurance programs. (For example, for a new factory or building under construction, or for unusual coverages. Such publicity efforts, of course, must have the approval of the client.)

Special publicity materials sometimes are made available by companies to the agents who represent them. In addition, agents representing capital stock companies can obtain publicity materials from the National Association of Insurance Agents and the Insurance Information Institute. The National Association of Mutual Insurance Agents publishes a concise publicity guide for its members, entitled *You Are News.*

Advertising. While few agents or brokers may have the funds for an extensive advertising effort, a small advertising budget properly used can be productive. The key concept for advertising of this type is *frequency*. For example, it is better to have very small advertisements in the local paper every week than to have a full page once a year. When budgets permit, it is sometimes better to employ several advertising media (newspaper ads *plus* spot announcements on radio or television *plus* one or more billboards) than to devote the complete budget to one medium.

Much of the advertising naturally may be devoted to achieving identification for the agency. But it is not necessary to stop at that point. Ads describing the special services that the agency has rendered to certain clients also may be valuable. Also, the agent may find it worthwhile to tie in his advertising at the appropriate times to insurance-industry-sponsored programs, such as "Fire Prevention Week," "Protection Week," or highway safety campaigns. The National Association of Insurance Agents provides advertising mats and other materials to its members for use in connection with "Protection Week" and its "Big I" program. Individual companies frequently make advertising materials available to permit their agents to tie in with special company promotions. The National Board of Fire Underwriters has materials for use in connection with "Fire Prevention Week" and other fire-prevention programs. (See Chapter 69 for additional discussion of agency advertising.)

Direct Mail. For the agent with limited means, direct mail to clients and prospects offers the most economical means of communication. Unlike advertising and publicity, direct mail involves little "waste" audience. The mail can be directed specifically only to those individuals or groups that the agent or broker wants to reach with a specific message. For his direct mail effort, the agent will find printed materials available from the companies he represents, from agents' associations, or from some of the public relations organizations listed in Appendix L. Some commercial organizations also provide such materials. A wise first step is for the individual agent to write to these companies and to the public relations organizations representing him or his companies requesting samples of the available printed materials. From these he can then select the items of interest for the audience he has in mind. Such materials are usually available to the agent at low cost—certainly lower than the cost of preparing comparable materials on his own. Sometimes, these materials allow space for the agent to imprint his own name and address.

Some agents have developed periodic newsletters or bulletins for their customers and prospects. Such newsletters may be printed or produced inexpensively by mimeograph or multilith. They provide an opportunity for the agent to express his own personality in writing and he can discuss insurance developments of local interest to his audience. Furthermore, he can call upon his companies and on the appropriate insurance public relations organizations for authoritative background information. Where the agent or someone on his staff has a flair for writing, the once-a-month newsletter is a highly personalized medium for keeping the agency's name and its services before a limited but important audience.

It goes almost without saying, of course, that direct mail includes the day-to-day correspondence that every agency must undertake with its clients. Far too much of this correspondence lacks the warmth and the personal touch that would add immensely to its effectiveness. Many manuals on effective letter writing are available in libraries and from companies and other organizations.

Public Speaking. The use or nonuse of this channel of communication will be dictated by the capabilities of the agent. If he has a flair for public speaking, he would be remiss not to exploit it; but if he has no talent in this direction, then he will do best to devote his energies elsewhere.

For those who chose this medium, however, a great deal of help is available. Many of the company-sponsored public relations organizations at the state and national level provide "speakers' manuals" and other background materials. Numerous local and statewide speakers' bureaus (which help to promote speaking assignments) are sponsored by these organizations and by the agents' associations. "Protection Week," "Fire Prevention Week," and other fire prevention and highway safety drives offer focal points for speechmaking.

In addition, a variety of motion pictures and slide films are available, dealing with various aspects of insurance and with such related subjects as fire prevention, highway safety, bicycle safety, water safety, driver education, and so forth. Educators frequently are desirous of having speakers and films on such subjects. In many communities, local organizations of agents carry out continuing programs of speaking before driver education classes in the high schools.

Exhibits and Displays. Sometimes exhibits at home shows, fairs, and other similar functions are sponsored by agents' associations or by individual companies or company organizations. However, on some occasions an individual agent may find it worthwhile to sponsor his own exhibits. He should be forewarned, however, that good exhibits can be expensive and also that they may draw heavily on manpower. An exhibit at a home show, for example, is not of much value to the agency if representatives of the firm are not on hand to talk to prospects and answer inquiries. On the other hand, window displays are less expensive to put together and require no one to be on hand. Agents interested in such exhibits should survey the companies they represent and the appropriate public relations organizations to ascertain the availability of exhibit materials and give-away literature.

Public Service

Apart from the foregoing activities, the local agent will find that participation in civic affairs will add to his status in the eyes of the community, while at the same time it will provide considerable personal satisfactions. The agent who participates in civic affairs only because he wants to improve his business may be disappointed; but the agent who shows a genuine interest in the advancement of his community and his neighbors cannot help but enjoy corollary benefits in his business. For independent agents, membership in local boards or state agents' associations may provide opportunities for participation in public service projects sponsored by such organizations.

A Note for All-Lines Agents

Many thousands of agents now are engaged in handling all lines of insurance—life, health, property, and liability. Those who are interested in the life and health business will find it to their advantage to read the excellent chapter on "Public Relations for the Underwriter and Agency" which appears in the revised edition of *Life and Health Insurance Handbook* (1964), a companion volume to this one, edited by Davis W. Gregg and published by Richard D. Irwin, Inc. It covers considerable ground not included in this chapter.

SUGGESTED READINGS

COSGROVE, JOHN N. *Competition in Insurance Marketing.* Cincinnati: National Underwriter Publishing Co., 1960. (See especially chap. 20, "Public Relations.")

CUTLIP, SCOTT M., AND CENTER, ALLEN H. *Effective Public Relations.* 3d ed. Englewood Cliffs, N.J.: Prentice-Hall, Inc., 1964. (See especially chap. 15, "The Community Publics.")

FINN, DAVID. *Public Relations and Management.* New York: Reinhold Publishing Corp., Reinhold Management Science Series, 1960.

LESLY, PHILIP. *Public Relations Handbook.* 2d ed. Englewood Cliffs, N.J.: Prentice-Hall, Inc., 1962.

LUNDBORG, LOUIS B. *Public Relations in the Local Community.* New York: Harper & Bros., The American Series of Public Relations Books, 1950.

PART IX

Risk Management

Chapter 72

FUNDAMENTALS OF RISK MANAGEMENT

BY JAMES C. CRISTY

Risk management is the aggregate effort of a business or institution to conserve earning power and assets by controlling the risk of accidental loss. This function goes considerably beyond insurance and has much more cost reduction potential than does insurance management. Its essence is the prevention of accidental loss. While insurance may be the last resort of this conservation activity, rather than the first, this *Handbook* covers risk management because insurance is the dominant tool for treating risks.

This chapter deals with some of the fundamentals of risk management. These fundamentals may be applied generally to personal, as well as business risks, but the term "risk management" is usually associated with business.

While risk management relates principally to insurable risks, it extends to all risks of accidental loss, whether insurable or not. Risk of accidental loss means the possibility of an event which unexpectedly results in personal injury, or damage to or loss of property.

NATURE OF RISK MANAGEMENT

The essence of risk management is both accident prevention and control of accidental loss. The functions include recognition of risk, control of risk, and meeting losses. Recognition includes both identification and appraisal of risk.

Control begins with an attempt to eliminate or avoid risks. Inescapable risks are controlled as far as possible by accident prevention. Loss minimization through protection is a necessary sequel, since the prevention effort is never perfect. Small losses are normally absorbed as direct expense. Losses too large to be absorbed painlessly are met by leveling techniques which may involve use of loss stabilization reserves, captive or wholly owned insurance companies, or commercial insurers.

When a business acquires an asset which is subject to large loss, the risk manager will waste no time arranging adequate insurance. If he is astute, he will select an insurer which will provide top flight engineering service to aid in loss prevention. Hence it might be asked: "Why is insurance last in the logic of risk management when everyone knows that insurance is the prime tool for meeting risk?"

The reasoning is about as follows:

1. Insurance is necessary and economical when the consequence of loss would be more than the owner could easily bear. It is unnecessary and wasteful to cover losses below the maximum tolerable level.
2. Insurance is a costly method of meeting losses the buyer could bear himself, since for most insureds the cost of insuring exceeds the losses suffered. Risk managers find that insurance transfers only the risk of catastrophe loss because the premiums they pay must, in the long run, cover all losses in addition to the insurer's expense.
3. Finally, since insurance never makes the buyer completely whole after a loss, the best way to control the risk of accidental loss is to prevent the accidents.

Insurance should be bought only after other methods of controlling the risk are found wanting. But because of the insurer's fee and the imperfections of insurance, management's responsibility to avoid accidental loss continues for both insured and uninsured risks. The buyer never escapes the ultimate responsibility for loss prevention.

PRACTICE OF RISK MANAGEMENT

Risk managers seek answers to questions like these: What are the causes of accidental loss to the firm's assets or earning power? What are the normal frequency and level of such losses? What are the maximum foreseeable losses in case normal protective measures fail? Can any risks of such losses be eliminated or avoided? How can risks which cannot be eliminated or avoided be controlled? How can losses which cannot be prevented be minimized? (For example, how can one extinguish fires when they are small or at least keep them small?) Since some losses are inevitable, how best can they be absorbed? How shall the decision be made as to which risks to retain without insurance and which to insure? Finally, how best can insurance costs be minimized?

Recognizing Risks

The risk manager asks: What assets does the firm have? What could happen to them? What accidents could impair the firm's earning power? What company activities could possibly create liability to others because of personal injury or damage to property?

These questions point the way to a comprehensive analysis of the risks which threaten any organization. In the course of this analysis someone considers each asset in the light of each peril or hazard, and evaluates the loss potential in terms of frequency and severity. This job is one for an expert, but the required expertise is an intimate and comprehensive knowledge of the company and its activities plus a lively imagination, rather than simply a skill in risk and insurance.

Risk Identification—Assets. In considering the risk of damage to or destruction of physical assets the risk manager might match assets with exposures by listing each as completely as possible and systematically checking one against the other. To be thorough, such an analysis requires the careful attention of persons who know the company intimately.

In seeking to identify risks, the risk manager should look for sources of consequential and indirect loss as well as for the sources of the more obvious direct losses. For example, damage to critical processing equipment which stops production could result in spoilage of materials in process and to loss of earnings due to interruption of business. The indirect loss is often many times larger than the cost of restoring the damaged equipment. In evaluating the loss potential of such bottlenecks, the risk manager should learn whether replacements of equipment could be made from existing stocks or would have to be built to order. One of the largest insured business interruption losses occurred because custom manufacture of a patented part for repair of a critical machine had to await the end of a strike.

The alert risk manager is constantly on the lookout for production bottlenecks, large and small. In one case the bottleneck may be an entire plant, in another a single mold or die. The risk of indirect loss may be off premises if the firm relies on a sole supplier. Dependence on a single source of raw material, catalyst, packaging material, water, fuel, or power can create even more critical bottlenecks than exist on the manufacturer's premises. The firm which depends on a single customer runs the same kind of risk.

Risk Identification—Activities. The risk of accidental loss exists to some degree in every activity of every organization. Thus, in addition to a review of the firm's assets, risk identification requires a comprehensive study of corporate activities.

The risk of injury to employees, customers, and others may be created both by what is said and by what is done. Loss can arise from: the salesman who is overenthusiastic about his product; the sales manager who goes in for unusual customer entertainment; the development technicians who yield to pressures to market incompletely tested products; the employment manager who is indiscreet in replying to an inquiry about a former employee. All of these situations and numerous others can create substantial liability for business firms.

Contracts are a notorious source of liability—sometimes because they fail to define the responsibility of the parties and sometimes because they force unwarranted assumptions of responsibility. Risk managers know from experience that contract negotiators often miss the significance of indemnity agreements while attorneys may review only legal form. To avoid unnecessary assumption of contractual liability by their employers, risk managers should try hard to obtain permission to review contracts.

Instructions for operation or use of products, even though given orally, may be a source of liability. There is a malpractice liability exposure in the activities of the company physician or nurse. The company's responsibility for injury to others or damage to their property goes as far afield as its products, its advertising, and its employees. It accompanies employees through all modes of travel including owned, nonowned, leased, chartered, or borrowed cars, trucks, buses, aircraft, or watercraft.

A study of the activities of every corporate division or department may reveal sources of liability peculiar to the organization which are not apparent to outsiders even after they are well acquainted with the operations. While outside counsellors or brokers can help in suggesting possible sources, a thorough job of risk identification demands careful analysis by an employee with intimate and extensive knowledge of the company.

Risk Appraisal. Insurance professionals can help the firm's technicians estimate normal loss probability, as well as maximum foreseeable loss. The most effective risk evaluation will come from a closely coordinated team of the firm's technicians and experienced insurance counsellors.

Controlling Risks

The steps in risk control are simply the systematic application of common sense to the job of preventing accidents. Going into business means assuming risk, but the businessman can invest more in speculative risk if he can minimize the risk of accidental loss which inevitably accompanies the undertaking. The risk of accidental loss could be eliminated by going out of business. Short of this, the aim is to keep it as small as possible within the limits of reasonable cost. Thus, cost controls are used in the ascending order of costs—lowest cost controls first and highest cost controls last. This order accounts for the sequence of the various steps: elimination, avoidance, control through accident prevention, and control through loss minimization.

It should be emphasized that the objective of risk control is to help the business and not hinder it. For every company there is a practical limit in the length to which management can go in risk control. Some of management's most difficult decisions involve the question of how far to go. The risk manager will bear in mind, however, that risk control is likely to be much less expensive than any other way of approaching losses. Since insurance premium credits for preventive measures may not be realistic, the value of a risk control step can best be assessed by its effect on the maximum foreseeable loss.

Elimination of Risk. Some risks can be eliminated entirely and this approach should be tried first. The risk of fire damage to a building is eliminated, obviously, if the building is constructed so as to resist heat and not burn. This technique, which works in many situations, involves the general idea of *substitution* so as to eliminate one of the essential ingredients for combustion: fuel, oxygen, and heat. (See Chapter 12.) In the foregoing example fuel is eliminated by the substitution of incombustible building materials for combustible materials.

In an operation involving a flammable solvent, one can eliminate the fire risk by finding a satisfactory, substitute, noncombustible solvent. In some chemical reactions the oxygen is eliminated by substitution of carbon dioxide or an inert atmosphere such as nitrogen. In other circumstances substitution might provide the means of eliminating the heat source from a combustible situation.

The conditions essential to vapor explosions are fuel, heat, and oxygen plus the factor of confinement. Such a generalization does not hold, however, in respect to chemical explosions. However, since confinement is nearly always present to some degree, the explosion risk may be eliminated by removal of the chance of pressure buildup. Risk of explosion, like fire, may be eliminated by substitution of fuels, substitution of some other condition for heat, or substitution of inert atmospheres for air.

While risk elimination may not justify disruption of operations in a given case, the advantages are significant and should always be considered.

Avoidance of Risk. Many risks which defy elimination—once they have come into being—can be effectively avoided by planning, separation, or duplication. While planning is, of course, involved in separation and duplication, planning is posited specifically because it may go far beyond the other two.

1. *Planning.* An obvious, but often neglected, tool in risk avoidance is planning. In site selection, for example, foresight may show that building on a river bottom will cost more in the long run than might be inferred from the low cost of the land. While earthquake-resistant structures can be built, much earthquake risk can be avoided by building at sites five miles or more from known fault lines.

Other risks which could be avoided through planning in site selection include: risk of falling aircraft near airports, condemnation (for public works, etc.), demolition (by public ordinance), dust fumes or smog, off-premises conflagration or explosion, and vehicle damage. There are still others but these should be enough to suggest the importance of site selection planning in risk avoidance.

Planning can also be an effective risk avoidance technique in building construction; process engineering; and equipment layout, design, and construction.

2. *Separation.* Another effective technique in risk avoidance is separation. This term may mean separation of the ingredients of combustion, when substitution or elimination are impossible. Examples include: sepa-

ration of welding operations from combustibles; isolation of hazardous operations in expendable buildings; and separation of the power house from the plant. The term "separation" can also mean "not putting all your eggs in one basket." In practical terms the axiom can be translated into not putting "all your executives in one conveyance" or "all your inventories in one warehouse." It means separating production facilities when a second production line or plant becomes necessary.

3. *Duplication.* Separation is closely aligned to duplication. Duplication is aimed at avoiding bottlenecks. The value of duplicating raw material sources seems obvious but it should be investigated and not taken for granted. Duplication of critical dies, molds, or equipment may remove bottlenecks, particularly when it is followed by separation. When a firm sells to other corporations, duplication of customers may be vital as well as profitable. Duplication of power sources, either on or off premises, may be vital to continued operation of the business, and the risk of accidental loss may be virtually eliminated if there is separation as well as duplication.

Duplication and separation of valuable papers is a simple and obvious form of risk avoidance, but risk managers learn from experience that they must frequently prompt their associates to do the obvious.

Prevention of Loss. In order to "live with" the risks he cannot escape, the risk manager does his best to minimize them and thereby to prevent accidents. "Accident prevention" as used here is different in meaning from "avoidance of risk" as used in the previous section. Accident prevention also differs from "protection against loss," to be discussed in the next section. Avoidance of risk is an attempt to escape it. Accident prevention is the attempt to control inescapable risks and forestall losses. Protection consists of the steps taken to minimize losses. Loss prevention precedes the accident; protection comes into play after the accident.

True loss prevention has been neglected. Prevention is frequently confused with protection and discussions of the former are likely to shift to the latter subject. Supporters of "Fire Prevention Week" recommend correction of faulty wiring but much time and attention in home inspections is given to fire extinguishing. The latter is protection, not prevention.

It is easy too, for corporations to protect without really trying prevention. Knowing that prevention is imperfect, one can busy himself with protection and the ways to meet losses and thereby miss the rich potential of loss prevention. For example: a fire started by a careless employee is extinguished by automatic sprinklers. The conclusion is : good protection but poor prevention. Another example is when the collision caused by momentary inattention of a driver results in only minor injuries because of seat-belt protection. Again the verdict must be: protection is fair but prevention has failed. Of course people and property must be protected from the results of accidents, but it is much more important to prevent the accidents themselves. Safety hats have saved many lives, but they cover only the head. It would be better to prevent the brick's fall from the stage above.

These examples suggest a truth seldom recognized. Whereas protection involves devices, prevention essentially involves people. Many fires said to be caused by electrical accidents or failures should be credited to human failure. In fact, increasing numbers of experts recognize that human failure is the basic cause of nearly all accidents. But blaming people is not enough. The most fertile ground for accident prevention is with people. While much remains to be learned about practical psychology, much can be done to prevent these human failures.

Accident prevention starts with the enthusiastic leadership and example of top management. It depends on continuing enthusiasm, constant alertness, and careful work habits. It is a way of life which must infiltrate the entire organization. (This point is strongly emphasized in Chapter 44.)

In a company which "lives" loss prevention, the way of life influences the selection and training of employees. They are trained for both normal operations and emergencies. They are instructed not just at induction, but constantly through the examples of their supervisors. When an organization follows this way of life, it is apparent in maintenance and housekeeping, in the observance of safe practices, and especially in employee morale.

Accidents resulting from human failure are preventable. They may have resulted from ignorance, horseplay, anger, jealousy, insecurity, worry, stress, illness, maliciousness, or dishonesty; but they could have been prevented.

The real challenge of risk management is to motivate people to work safely not just to save their skins and their jobs but because they take pride in their work. As more is learned about people and psychology, risk control should become increasingly successful.

While loss prevention depends predominantly on people, there are some devices to assist them. Ignition sources may be removed through grounding. Explosive concentrations of dust or vapors may be avoided through ventilation. Chemical operations can be automated to "self-correct" before things go wrong.

Protection against Loss. The next precept is: "Keep the losses small. If you can't avoid explosions, at least channel them in the right direction." Therefore, if fires are inevitable, either confine them or put them out quickly.

The principles of loss protection are well known. When properly applied, they are most effective. With respect to fire, early detection and prompt extinguishment backed up by confinement are the tried and true methods. Automatic sprinklers are extremely effective in all three of these objectives. Fire departments can be most effective but they are not automatic. On the other hand, most failures of automatic sprinkler systems are traceable to human rather than mechanical shortcomings.

Other ways to keep losses small involve various aspects of confinement, such as barriers to create small fire areas, roof monitors to vent heat and retard the spread of fire, and special construction or devices for pressure relief to prevent or vent explosions.

Planning obviously is vital to keeping losses small. It is a part of making structures resistant to fire, lightning, explosion, windstorm, earthquake, and to some extent even floods. Avoiding heavy concentrations of value, whether of buildings, equipment, or contents is usually simpler and less costly if considered in the planning and layout stages.

Disaster planning is especially valuable in life and property conservation. The biggest dollar savings accomplished by disaster planning, however, may be in the business interruption area: planning on how to get back into production after the fire is out.

Meeting Losses

Every business absorbs some small accidental losses as direct expense and insures to level the cost of some large losses. But even within a single firm there may be no uniformity in the application of the principle of assuming small losses and insuring large ones. The level of loss assumption varies from zero to millions within corporations. For example, a company insuring $100 direct damage losses may have no coverage for a multimillion dollar business interruption exposure. Such a corporation might assume losses to motor vehicles worth $5,000 and insure parcel post shipments worth $50.

Such inconsistency in level of risk retention implies management by expediency rather than plan. Of course, one firm may use deductibles to escape adjusting small losses, and another may take a calculated risk in leaving business interruption uninsured. The former, however, misses much of the savings potential of deductibles, and the latter practices false economy while imprudently exposing corporate earning power to risks of catastrophic loss.

A General Rule. The answer to the question "When to insure?" is simple to state but may be hard to apply. A firm should retain as much risk as it can afford and insure against the chance of losses going above this amount. To apply this rule the risk manager must know how much accidental loss his company can stand at one time and in one year. The prudent risk manager goes to top management for this decision. In establishing a level of permissible risk retention a company creates a valuable guide for the risk manager. The question "When to insure?" is then half answered.

The rest of the answer is complicated by practical considerations and the need for judgment. Insurance covering losses the firm could afford to bear may be tied to needed services, such as loss prevention or adjustment. Deductibles may be unavailable or unattractively priced, especially at the full amount of risk retention permitted by management. Or the demand for coverage, such as earthquake insurance, may be so thin that the price does not accurately reflect the risk. The risk manager needs sound judgment to decide whether the price is right, and great caution to avoid being unduly influenced by price in deciding whether to insure or not. Price usually indicates loss probability or frequency, whereas the need for insurance depends on loss potential or severity.

Noninsurance. The abstention from use of insurance should be thoughtful and intentional. If risk identification is thorough, the uninsured risks are known and insurance has been considered. Planned noninsurance differs from "self-insurance." (See the discussion of this point in Chapter 58.) Most insurance managers consider "self-insurance" to be a self-administered plan to level losses by means of a stabilization reserve. Uninsured losses, to the contrary, are absorbed as direct expense. While firms may budget for them, budget allocations are not reserves and unused portions do not carry forward to the next year.

When management sets a level of permissible risk retention, it opens the door to systematic noninsurance. Risk with loss potentials below this level can then be retained without insurance. Risks having greater loss potentials can then be insured with deductibles or retrospective rating.

While the level of permissible loss assumption limits the amount of deductible, it does not determine the deductible. Subject to the retention limit, the deductible level is based on the premium reduction offered, and the optimum level is a matter of judgment. Premium credits are greatest for deductibles covering areas of high loss frequency. However, the graphic projection of deductibles and credits is a parabolic curve which flattens gradually and there may be attractive savings for deductibles above the level of most frequent losses.

Some insurance managers advocate choosing deductible levels for two or more lines simultaneously. Savings are estimated as though the lines were pooled. Net estimated savings are premium credits less expected normal losses. These are compared with losses expected in the area above normal frequency levels but within the deductible amount. Proponents believe this procedure improves the predictability of experience under a deductible program and permits adoption of higher deductibles than they could justify if considering the lines separately.

The insurance manager who sets up a program of planned noninsurance is usually alert enough to consider the vital area above the corporation's maximum insurance limits. It seems obvious that, while an omission in the small loss area will not be critical, oversight or false economy involving upper insurance limits could lead to a noninsurance catastrophe. Insurance producers often stress this by recommending that the premiums removed from the bottom by means of deductibles be reapplied at the top to increase maximum limits. Such reapplication of premiums may produce dramatic improvements of protection without added expense.

Companies accepting the concept that risks be retained to the allowable limit and insured above that level may find themselves seeking coverage for previously neglected or ignored risks. This effort is quite proper. A manager does a poor job of conserving corporate assets if his decision to insure is influenced by assumed loss frequency rather than possible loss magnitude.

Use of Insurance. When management decides to insure, it usually turns to professional insurers. Commercial insurance is the most important way to treat risks of accidental loss. Some corporations operate their own insurance companies, and when these insurers limit operations to the property and activities of the owner company, they are called "captive insurers." Captive insurance companies perform a legitimate and worthwhile, though limited, function.

"Self-insurance" (as opposed to "noninsurance") attracts many firms because of the chance of savings, but most of these transfer catastrophe risks by buying excess insurance. Those considering "self-insurance" should give careful attention to tax aspects, administrative costs, and insurance company services before deciding. There is another reason for caution before dropping commercial insurance. While captive insurers and self-insurance have strong supporters, there are few detractors, perhaps because those who have tried such techniques and discarded them are reluctant to advertise their experience.

Nearly all insurance offered to corporate or institutional buyers can be adapted in some degree to meet special needs. Even in such a standardized product as fire insurance many modifications are available. The astute buyer will, therefore, set objectives based on results of the activities described earlier in this chapter and seek the broadest available coverage for possible dollar losses.

Buying insurance on the basis of objectives puts the burden on the underwriter to say what he will not insure. This comprehensive approach is much safer and more logical for the buyer than trying to select specific coverages.

The fewer contracts the better. Risk managers look forward to the day when a corporation's insurance needs can be met in one contract. When one contract replaces two, there may well be a net gain in coverage. Certainly, gaps and overlaps are avoided. Improvement was achieved with introduction of the Homeowners contract. Comparable improvement will be realized when insurers offer industry a combined fire and boiler and machinery breakdown contract. Combined contracts have other advantages. Greater premiums and thus reduction of risk give underwriters more latitude to include substandard business in the "package" or to "ride out the storm" when losses make part of the contract unprofitable. Administration is simpler for both parties to the contract. While reduced cost is a secondary objective, it may result. For example, flood and earthquake insurance each has a thin market by itself but is becoming less costly as interest grows in "difference of conditions" insurance.

As contracts become broader and more flexible, it is increasingly important that the parties to the contract—specifically the buyer and underwriter—understand each other's intent. Such understanding is sometimes hard to attain through an intermediary. Consequently, an alert producer will recognize that, since he will not be a party to the contract, it is his job to encourage a meeting of the minds of the principals. (See Chapter 73.)

The best insurance is that which covers losses at the lowest *long-term* cost. Put another way, the point is: broad coverage will be the best buy in the long run. In these days of broad and complex contracts, the experienced buyer avoids tight specifications and lets the underwriter exercise some ingenuity. Before seeking competitive bids, he scouts the market to find where the best proposals are likely to be and limits the number of bids he requests. Quality of loss prevention service should be considered when the business is awarded, since loss control is the best cost control. A firm with a poor loss record cannot escape higher insurance costs indefinitely by switching insurers. Underwriters tend to load for the unknown; thus it is better for the risk managers to disclose the shortcomings of the risk than to leave them to the underwriter's imagination. It is easier to adjust losses before they occur. Consequently, an hour's discussion of contract terms before the loss may save weeks of wrangling and possible litigation afterwards.

Risk managers who like to "sleep at night" take advantage of automatic features offered by insurers, such as automatic extensions to cover new properties or contracts. They insure two or more properties on a blanket basis to avoid separate limits on the units. They seek agreements with underwriters as to amount of insurance to carry thereby avoiding coinsurance. (See, for example, Chapter 9.) They realize that monthly reports of value are not always essential to cover fluctuating property values.

Skillful risk managers are careful readers of contracts and alert to word meanings such as "all risk" and "comprehensive." They distinguish "occurrence" from "accident," "personal injury" from "bodily injury" (see Chapter 32), and various types of "value" (such as "book," "sound," or "market") from "replacement cost."

When losses occur, the risk manager should meticulously observe contractual requirements. In cases of property loss he will find that scrupulous honesty and careful attention to detail are the most important things he can contribute to fair, fast, and friendly adjustment.

RISK MANAGERS AS SPECIALISTS

Risk management is the aggregate effort of a business or institution to conserve earning power and assets by controlling the risk of accidental loss. If the effort is to be successful, it, of course, involves everyone in the organization. Beyond this general cooperation, however, is the need for guidance, coordination, and motivation. The question of precisely whose job this is remains to be answered. Such leadership should start in top management and should be the specific responsibility of someone near the top.

Small Companies

Although specialization may be desirable, it is not a necessity in small companies. Risks can be controlled successfully by the generalists who manage these companies, provided they recognize the importance of the risk management function and take time to discharge it. The small company manager may need help from insurance advisers to identify and evaluate risks but he should not turn the whole job over to nonemployees. The firm's own people are the best ones to control risk, since such control is simply application of common sense to a knowledge of the company and what might happen to it. Insurance buyers for small companies are seldom insurance technicians. Virtually any manager who has analyzed his risks and grasped the principles of meeting losses can in time find his way through the maze of blanket coverage and coinsurance.

Large Firms

Larger firms which can afford more specialization usually divide the responsibility between an insurance manager and a safety engineer. Few feel the need for a loss prevention specialist except for safety, and only a handful have acknowledged the common goal by integrating the functions. This separation of activities has no serious disadvantage provided there is coordination. But when, for example, the insurance manager reports to the treasurer, the safety engineer to the industrial relations chief, and the loss prevention specialist, if any, to the manufacturing vice president, coordination is difficult, if possible. The lines of authority for risk management will join at the general manager level. Coordination, if any, will cross organizational lines and if one of these specialists shows initiative outside his designated responsibility, his motive will no doubt be questioned. Risk management can result, but overlaps and omissions will occur even in firms which enthusiastically support loss control.

The best arrangement would bring the various specialties under an able and interested executive who knows about all company activities and has ready access to major division heads. This arrangement would permit effective coordination of all aspects of risk control, particularly at the all-important planning stage. While the number and training of specialists will vary with the size and nature of each firm, coordination of risk control under the direct supervision of one top-level executive is desirable in companies of all sizes.

Evolution

The term "risk management" appears to have been proposed in the early 1950's. It caught on with insurance managers who had already begun to analyze, evaluate, abate, and control risks of accidental loss. Most of them had been instructed only to buy and administer corporate insurance, but they went beyond their assignments because they recognized insurance fills only part of the need. But not all the insurance managers realized then (or now) that control of risk of accidental loss is more than buying insurance.

In the early 1920's only a few of the largest corporations in the United States employed insurance specialists. The normal way to handle insurance was to assign the buying to an officer. The policies were turned over to a clerk for accounting and safekeeping. Gradually there appeared a class of specialists known as insurance buyers. When the American Management Association Insurance Division was formed in 1931, its purpose was to provide a forum for insurance buyers, producers, and suppliers. The insurance manager was a rarity in 1931. By 1949 the activity had evolved to "buying and administering corporate insurance"[1] and the specialist had become "Insurance Manager." But while the title sounded impressive, the job was small in many big companies, and some insurance managers were still being paid like clerks.

At the time of this writing many corporations, perhaps 1,000, employ managers who devote a third or more of their time to insurance. While most of these are reasonably well qualified as insurance buyers, some were given the responsibility without prior training and are insurance amateurs. There is a small and growing number who are risk managers in fact but insurance managers in title. A few so-called insurance managers have so little authority after several years of experience that one wonders if their employers really intended them to be part of management. Thus, while the field of insurance management is growing, it is far from mature, and many of the practitioners are hardly qualified as insurance managers, let alone as risk managers.

---

[1] See, for example, R. B. Gallagher, *Buying and Administering Corporate Insurance* (New York: American Management Association Research Report # 15, 1949).

Need for Better Understanding

Practitioners use the term "risk management" loosely. Most specialists in the field realize there is some distinction between insurance management and risk management, but the terms are often used interchangeably. It appears that many consider risk control to be insurance management with a dash of loss prevention. This failure to distinguish between the terms reflects the lack of an accepted definition of risk control or risk management. If risk management is the firm's aggregate effort to conserve its earning power and assets by controlling the risk of accidental loss, the risk manager must be the one who manages or correlates the aggregate effort. This definition drastically limits the number which merit the designation and it leaves without suitable title all those who manage more than insurance but less than the whole risk control activity. But this new activity will serve management more effectively if its full scope comes to be implied in its title.

Management has not accepted the term. While the term "risk management" is probably 10 years old and while there is real need for a title which implies responsibilities beyond insurance administration, management has not used this term. The following is typical of management's reaction: "I do not wish to disagree with the term Risk Management. However, the whole of corporate management is engaged in evaluating the risk it takes in making profits for stockholders. There is no area of corporate endeavor which does not involve some degree of risk."[2] This feeling that only the general manager should be called risk manager might appear inconsistent since top management grants the titles of "controller" and "personnel director" to persons other than the general manager. More likely, it reflects misunderstanding of the term.

A definition will not only clarify the difference between risk management and insurance management; it will also make the activity more saleable to top management by setting limits. Some scholars see the risk manager of the future taking an active part in control of speculative as well as pure risk. While this may come to pass as knowledge of risk and probability develops, the thought tends to confuse the issue at present. Risk management will be much more acceptable to management in the short run if the risk manager's attention is confined to the risks of accidental loss.

Risk Management Distinguished from Insurance Management

The insurance manager buys and administers insurance as economically as he can. The risk manager seeks the most economical ways to

[2] See John P. Schlick, "The Important Role of the Insurance Manager," *The National Insurance Buyer,* Vol. 9 (March, 1962), pp. 10, 24–25 for an exposition of this point of view. The passage quoted appears on p. 10.

control risk of accidental loss and follows a program in which insurance is the last resort rather than the first.

In theory, a risk manager or director of risk control might supervise both an insurance manager and a loss prevention manager. In practice, we find so-called insurance managers whose responsibilities beyond insurance vary from risk recognition to the full spectrum of risk management.

The man responsible for insurance alone busies himself with insurance techniques and coverages. He may be a good candidate for risk manager some day but his horizons will have to broaden. When he has the full responsibility for risk control he must be more manager than technician.

Risk manager is a title which many covet but few have earned. It is in the interest of both insurance managers and risk managers to distinguish between the two terms and emphasize this distinction in communications. Risk management will start "coming into its own" when management realizes the size of its responsibility to stockholders for control of accidental losses. In many firms recognition of the common goal of safety, loss prevention, and insurance management will bring attempts to correlate the total conservation effort without organizational changes. But pressures for cost reduction and efficiency will surely bring ultimate integration. With such top management acceptance and support, risk management will contribute significantly to earnings and free added capital for assumption of speculative risk.

SUGGESTED READINGS

AMERICAN MANAGEMENT ASSOCIATION. *The Growing Job of Risk Management.* New York: Management Report Number 70, 1962.

———. *Identifying and Controlling the Risks of Accidental Loss.* New York: Management Report Number 73, 1962.

ATHEARN, JAMES L. *Risk and Insurance.* New York: Appleton-Century-Crofts, 1962. Chaps. 14–19, 25.

BLUM, ALBERT A. *Company Organization of Insurance Management.* New York: American Management Association Research Study, Number 59, 1961.

BOBBITT, H. RANDOLPH, JR. "Risk Management," *Annals of the Society of Chartered Property and Casualty Underwriters*, Vol. 14 (Summer, 1961) pp. 143–62.

CRIDDLE, A. HAWTHORNE. "Education and Risk Management—The Seller," *The National Insurance Buyer*, Vol. 10 (May, 1963), pp. 24, 78–80.

CRISTY, JAMES C. *Corporate Insurance Manuals, Reports and Records.* New York: American Management Association Research Report Number 25, 1955.

———. "Education and Risk Management—The Buyer," *The National Insurance Buyer*, Vol. 10 (May, 1963), pp. 22, 73–78.

GALLAGHER, RUSSELL B. "A Practical Approach to Risk Management," *Business Horizons* (Summer, 1960), Vol. 3, pp. 78–86.

GREENE, MARK R. *Risk and Insurance.* Cincinnati: South-Western Publishing Co., 1962. Chap. 4.

MEHR, ROBERT I. "Education and Risk Management—The Critic," *The National Insurance Buyer*, Vol. 10 (May, 1963), pp. 28, 51, 53, 55–57, 61, 63.

———, AND HEDGES, BOB A. *Risk Management in the Business Enterprise.* Homewood, Ill.: Richard D. Irwin, Inc., 1963.

MOWBRAY, ALBERT H., AND BLANCHARD, RALPH H. *Insurance: Its Theory and Practice in the United States.* 5th ed. New York: McGraw-Hill Book Co., Inc., 1961. Chap. 36.

NATIONAL INDUSTRIAL CONFERENCE BOARD. *Company Insurance Administration.* New York: Studies in Business Policy, Number 81, 1956.

OVERMAN, EDWIN S. "Education and Risk Management—The Teacher," *The National Insurance Buyer*, Vol. 10 (May, 1963), pp. 26, 81–85.

WILLIAMS, C. ARTHUR, JR., AND HEINS, RICHARD M. *Risk Management and Insurance.* New York: McGraw-Hill Book Co., Inc., 1964. Chaps. 1–9.

Chapter 73

SPECIAL PROBLEMS OF RISK MANAGERS

BY RUSSELL B. GALLAGHER

With the fundamentals of corporate risk management having been reviewed in the previous chapter, attention is now given to some of the special problems faced by risk managers. The major problems of risk managers are related to procedures and, therefore, to people. Consequently, the principal sections of this chapter have to do with education and training, lines of authority, communications, interdepartmental relationships, external relationships, ethics, corporate policy, loss prevention, and the balance between specialization and generalization on the part of risk managers.

EDUCATION

Only in very recent years have any opportunities for formal education in risk management, per se, become available. Moreover, only recently has authoritative textbook literature been published.[1] For these reasons numerous lawyers, accountants, and engineers were pressed early into risk management service. As the function developed, it naturally took on some color of their respective specialties. At a later date, because of the highly technical nature of the work, the function became the province of those educated in insurance theory and practice. Learning in detail the practical needs of risk management became for these persons an "on-the job" requirement.

In the future a substantial number of risk managers may be drawn from insurance agencies, brokerage firms, and companies where business administration graduates have been trained in insurance. However, others whose education has been in law or engineering may be developed into risk managers through such programs as are made available by the

[1] See, for example, Robert I. Mehr and Bob A. Hedges, *Risk Management in the Business Enterprise* (Homewood, Ill.: Richard D. Irwin, Inc., 1963), and also C. Arthur Williams, Jr. and Richard M. Heins, *Risk Management and Insurance* (New York: McGraw-Hill Book Co., Inc., 1964).

American Management Association, the American Society of Insurance Management, and, lately, a number of colleges and universities. The development of the risk manager, whether through formal education or "on-the-job" experience, will provide top management with a decision-maker capable of carrying out broad assignments entirely apart from the risk field.

LINES OF AUTHORITY

Usually, risk management is a financial staff function. Even though the risk manager has line responsibilities, as will later be discussed, his basic accountability is for financial rather than physical assets.

Independent studies made over the past 15 years—the period of major growth of the function in its executive sense—show that most companies which have recognized the risk management function have centralized it under the principal financial officer. Earlier, lines of authority frequently descended from nonfinancial officers in general management, manufacturing, or industrial relations. These earlier lines reflected the then current thinking about the principal nature of the risk management function.

Today, it is recognized that risk management, a highly specialized field, requires education and training across an extremely wide base. Because the ultimate concern of the risk manager is the conservation of the firm's assets and earning power and because no other executive department has as direct an access to all of the functions related to risk management, the evolutionary movement to the financial department was a natural step. The following opinion cannot be supported as a categorical statement, but the author believes that, when the line of responsibility is derived from any other department, the result is inhibiting. This result appears to arise from the fact that other departments have relatively more narrow "missions" than does the financial department.

COMMUNICATIONS

Communications in risk management must be permitted in their broadest aspect, if the operations are to attain a high degree of efficiency. The risk manager must be able to communicate directly, crossing all of the vertical channels which, too often, have acquired hallowed status. It is not to be inferred that unilateral corrective action should be taken by the risk manager, beyond the development of information, except when the expressed policy of the company so permits or requires.

Adherence to Corporate Policy

The risk management department is a staff department with certain line functions. While the judgment of the risk manager may indicate that a certain course of action is warranted, he may advise only, unless corporate policy definitely requires action. Corporate policy, for example, may dictate that insurance be bought immediately on any newly acquired building, but guidelines for selection of the agent, broker, or company, in most instances, will have been determined in advance. As another illustration of the advisory nature of his function, the risk manager may initiate recommendations for loss adjustments or legal action, but usually no action is permissible except with the concurrence of other affected departments, unless specific permission is granted through corporate policy statements.

The foregoing illustrations emphasize the need for a definitive corporate policy for the purpose of avoiding confusion. When concurrence of another department is required by corporate policy as a precedent to action, the policy should require the contributing department's action, whether positive or negative.

Many companies which have the most carefully developed personnel, purchasing, manufacturing, and accounting manuals have not exhibited the same determination and imagination with respect to the risk management function. This very real problem of confusion and indeterminacy exists mainly as a result of inaction on the part of the risk manager and because of the peculiarity of the risk management function.

Terminology

Only the risk manager is in a position to recommend policy and procedure pertaining to his activity. These recommendations must be unequivocally clear because they are intended for review and action by executives of widely divergent operating interests. The normal nontechnical terminology of business must be used. It is not wise to adhere to insurance nomenclature which in many instances is not understood even by all insurance practitioners. For example, depreciation has several different meanings depending upon whether taxes, production, finance, or insurance matters are under consideration. In each instance the effect is different. Warranty and public relations subjects tend to become confused with questions relating to negligence in production, distribution, advertising, labeling, and sales because of conflict in popular and technical word meanings. The insurable extent of physical damage or loss of use of facilities is not readily determinable except in the presence of carefully delineated economic philosophies. These philosophies are not easily appreciated by one without an insurance background. The concepts must be divorced from the insurance idiom.

Sources of Information

One of the most serious problems facing risk managers is obtaining information about company activities.

The financial department usually possesses the most nearly complete and accurate flow of communications in the company. Its line functions exist, to some degree, in every facility, even the "one man–one secretary" branch office. Frequently, every step of its operations is subject to strict written control and carefully devised corporate policy. This condition permits the risk manager to have access to data which are not readily available from other sources. For example, an appropriation request which precedes the purchase order, acquisition, or installation may set in motion an inquiry which results in widespread adjustments of the insurance program. Or a disclosure by the internal audit department of a deviation from standard procedures can require counterbalancing insurance efforts. As another illustration, when a "Manager's Cash Account" is set up, investigation sometimes will reveal an operation, perhaps with serious risk management implications, which otherwise might not have been noticed.

The major source of information for the risk manager is the accounting records. This source should be cultivated extensively. Even so, however, the risk manager may still have difficulty in learning all he needs to know about company exposures to loss. Accounting data usually involve receipt and expenditure of funds but only infrequently involve detail about change in design, production methods, and materials. Such changes may not involve an accounting entry. For this reason it is important that manufacturing, purchasing, and other departmental manuals recite procedure which will generate the flow of proper data to the risk manager. For example, he must have a way of finding out about changes from domestic to foreign suppliers or from multiple sources of supply to limited sources. He must be able to learn about changes of purchase order and acceptance conditions because such changes may require compensating action. Decisions to manufacture products for use in aircraft or watercraft or in nuclear facilities can have an enormous risk coefficient. A "make or buy" decision may have repercussions as to risk control. To do his job properly, the risk manager must be the beneficiary of an information system whereby he is apprised of change. The burden of taking the initiative to obtain the information often rests with him.

In short, information about change from the normal or established order is the signal for review. It is not possible to create an exhaustive checklist of all the ways by which the risk manager can set up the flow of information toward the risk management. A few fruitful and practical devices, however, are suggested. The risk manager can study the operating manuals of the various departments and can work toward inclusion of a provision that he be notified of change. He can conduct periodic briefing seminars for other departments. He can use news bulletins to highlight appropriate topics and to request information about them.

Interdepartmental Relations

A special problem of risk managers is the creation and maintenance of productive and harmonious relationships with managers and staffs of other departments in the company. The problem extends beyond communications and embraces the whole subject of human relations.

The working relationships between the risk manager and the managers of the other departments in the company sometimes unfortunately are limited to communications. To be fully effective, however, the risk manager must have a relationship which produces action. He must be able to convince others that a problem exists, that it is susceptible of solution, and that his recommendations are reasonable. He will find himself more successful if he undertakes to learn the problems of others before he attempts the promotion of his own ideas. If he is an alarmist, if he is a "wolf" crier, or if he promotes a questionable program or one primarily for his own benefit, his administration and his company will suffer. The same will be true if he attempts unilateral action, if he "makes end runs," or if he "goes over the head" of other managers. These conclusions are pertinent to all managerial personnel; but, because the risk manager is dependent in so many ways on other people in the company for cooperation, he is more vulnerable simply as a result of the number of dependencies.

Consider, as a case in point, his relationship with the legal department. In the determination of policy relating to the legal position of the company in any matter, that department is paramount. Its interpretation of documents usually is final. However, there are areas in which the risk manager has a superior position. He makes the business judgments: to insure or not insure, to increase limits, to defer settlements. The risk manager must, on occasion, be able to convince the lawyer of the need for including particular phraseology in a given type of contract or agreement. This convincing cannot be done unless there is a definite rapport in their relationship.

In another situation officials in the purchasing department might argue that it is beneficial from the cost standpoint to purchase all material, even from foreign suppliers, on an F.O.B. supplier's plant basis. Others may hold the contrary viewpoint, namely, that all purchases should be F.O.B. buyer's warehouse. Neither viewpoint is always correct. Where there is an unusual susceptibility to loss or damage, it may be wise to keep the risk with the seller. On the other hand, where foreign purchases are involved, it may be particularly important to have the contractual control which the buyer's insurance provides. An adamant pro or con position is useless in such controversies; negotiation within the company is required.

In many respects the risk manager must spend as much time building and maintaining his internal relationships as he does in discharging his technical responsibilities. The test of the risk manager is his ability to keep the normal interdepartmental confusion of effort at the minimum.

EXTERNAL COMMUNICATIONS

Another problem facing risk managers is the creation and maintenance of productive and harmonious relationships with each of several classes of people outside the firm.

The principal external relationships of the risk manager are with producers[2] and insurance companies.[3] Minor relationships may include those with people in state insurance departments, rating bureaus, industrial commissions, legislatures, and, occasionally, insurance consulting firms.

The risk manager's relationships with producers and companies are usually quite satisfactory insofar as general intent is concerned. Universally, it is agreed that there is little negative thinking in these circles at high levels. It is true that all real or fancied needs are not filled by currently available insurance coverages. The fact remains, however, that very few areas of exposure stay even relatively unprotected.

The most prominent sources of discontent stem from cost and service. The producer is responsible for a number of services of which procurement is only one. These services extend from engineering advice to the preparation and review of statistics and the analysis of reserves. The insurance company provides safety, loss prevention, and claims services in addition to the payment of claims.

Ideas as to the extent of necessary service and as to the proper qualifications of those who render it vary sharply among producers and among insurance company officials. Moreover, the service acceptable to one insured may be totally unacceptable to another. The timeliness of the service may be important to one party but not to the other. An almost infinite number of situations arise which, if not handled properly, can build animosities. Consider, for example, the case where a workmen's compensation claim is not investigated and acted upon at once. The reason for the inaction may be that the case required a 90-mile round trip and was the only case which could be investigated upon such a trip. This reason, however, may not be particularly persuasive to the insured.

In another situation the recommendations of an inspector, having been adjudged impractical by the risk manager, may remain on the report submitted by the insurer to the insured month after month. They act as a constant irritant. The irritant should be removed. Other types of friction arise when audits which should be made immediately following the end

[2] The word "producer" in the sense in which it is used includes agents, brokers, and representatives of direct writing companies and cooperatives.

[3] "Companies" is intended to embrace all organizations to which insurable risk may be transferred.

of the year are delayed. Such delay creates accounting problems for the insured. Failure by the producer to review a coverage and include all the changes endorsed on the expiring policy is another reason for being at odds.

With Insurance Companies

Minor matters can become major causes for discontent with insurance companies because of the difference in points of view of insured and insurer. Much of the data required of the producer and the insurance company becomes tools for the insured. Time is of the essence in the usual situation. A report delivered in June of an inspection made in April is largely valueless. At best it is the source of additional work to determine whether it is currently correct. Again, when the internal auditor puts the risk management department "on report" because of its failure to obtain needed endorsements, audits, billings, or claim settlements within a reasonable time, a compensating action is necessary.

Many risk managers leave such matters in the control of the producer unless the lack of action becomes embarrassing. The producer, in turn, may have passed the responsibility to the insurance company, hence the ensuing turmoil.

With Producers

The risk manager's principal and most common complaint about producers relates to the competency of the persons who are responsible for his account. Often, it is found that the actual work of placement, the development of the insurance contract, and the processing of losses is by persons of less than maximum competency despite the availability of fully competent personnel in the producer's offices. This situation arises from the emphasis placed on new business production and from the producer's giving greatest attention to emergencies. The best qualified employees are used in these capacities.

In a broad sense, the producer has a three-level staff. At the top is the account executive—the contact man. Usually, he is a man of competence though not necessarily a technically trained one. His major qualification is his ability to obtain the information which is acted upon by the second level. He is well paid. At the second level are the technicians. These people are also well paid, are educated, and are experienced in insurance theory and practice and in the mechanics of policy development. The technicians are the heart of the producer organization. If they are spread too thinly in their supervisory capacity, the client will suffer accordingly. At the bottom level are the staff members supervised by the technicians. There is a wide gulf in most producers' offices between the qualifications of the technician and those of the men he supervises. Possibly this gulf exists because the supportable salary at the third level is not particularly attractive to men with maximum technical qualifications. Producer personnel, further, are trained according to specialties. An employee may be a "casualty man" or "marine man," for example. The specialties may be, and frequently are, broken down still further so that activities of certain individuals are limited to boiler insurance, to bonds, or even to bonds of certain kinds. For this reason the specialists are not prepared to recognize the effect of a change in their client's operations on the entire insurance program. There is little interchange of information and cross-fertilization in the average producer's organization.

As a result of the specialization, which amounts to compartition, many areas of exposure are protected on a "one-sided" basis. In the parlance of the risk manager this weakness is known as "falling through the cracks." Situations such as these, if continued over significant periods, can reach such critical proportions as to become explosive. They can be avoided through education in basic principles, rotation in training for the purpose of familiarization, weeding out of the unadaptable employees, and the requirement that the account executive be familiar with every change in conditions or coverage.

In fairness it must be agreed that the risk manager is at least equally responsible for inadequate attention by the producer. He must constantly be alert for situations which have risk implications. It is not reasonable to charge the producer with responsibility for having such knowledge of internal company affairs as is required to develop the optimum insurance program. This responsibility is basic to the risk manager. He is obligated to communicate relevant information to the producer. It then behooves the producer to make appropriate recommendations. They may apply to coverage, cost, service, and/or procedures. The risk manager cannot permit inaction, lest it become habitual.

Complications of Corporate Policy

Many external relationships are not directly controllable by the risk manager because the selection of the insurance producer, hence of the insurance company, is determined by corporate policy. Many obscure but important reasons govern this selection. Among the negative factors are family or social connections and pressure by directors who also have banking, insurance, or other related ties. The positive and recognizable factors include satisfactory service records and long association. Whether positive or negative, the risk manager seldom is able to bring about a change of producer or insurer even though definite future benefits to his company would result from such a change.

The risk manager places his tenure in jeopardy when he challenges such entrenched interests because they, too, have access to the ear of management, often the more sympathetic ear. The risk manager, then, must channel his corrective efforts in one of several directions. He may persistently cultivate the producer principals by carrying all problems, large and small, directly to them. This approach will be resisted, however, first by the principal, who wishes to be relieved of such detail, and second, by the subordinate who is subjected to criticism. Such approach is, of course, a flank attack but it has the questionable virtue of avoiding an overt act. A frontal attack may be made by the painstaking development of evidence as to how the insurance program has been improperly handled. Proof must be submitted of inadequate attention, excessive time lags, and failure to develop coverage and cost on a truly competitive basis. Should this approach be resorted to, however, the relationship will deteriorate to a test of strength between the risk manager and the producer and at best they will remain at odds. This approach is to be avoided except in the most extreme cases.

The risk manager is better advised to bring the offending subordinate producer into periods of consultation with the subordinate's immediate superior. Thus, the insured's requests become part of a cooperative effort. If necessary, the procedure can be repeated, each time at a higher level until the problems are met in a satisfactory manner. Usually this procedure will result in a gradual change of accountability in the producer's office.

Relationship with Others

When a form is specially devised by the risk manager, it is possible it will be rejected by insurance companies to which it is offered, because of the problem of filing. Prior discussions with the state insurance department employees, on an exploratory basis, may prevent the impasse. Many state departments' officials are receptive to this method of developing coverage forms. Any attempt to curry favor or use political leverage with these organizations should be discouraged. It is almost certain to bring about an involvement with a future state administration if not a minor scandal with the present one.

Officials of rating bureaus, particularly those with jurisdiction over workmen's compensation, will discuss reclassification, even new classifications, when substantial evidence of the need can be presented. They, just as the industrial commission personnel of other states, do attempt to arrive at equitable judgments.

Correspondence with state legislators and congressmen should be developed if only for the purpose of giving notice of interest in legislation, hearings, and investigations having either a direct or indirect connection with risk management. Because of laws which govern lobbying, the correspondence should be screened by competent legal counsel.

The insurance function is as much in need of periodic audit as is any other financial activity. An audit, if only financial, may be conducted by the internal audit department. Internal auditors, however, do not usually possess the special knowledge of exposure and of the methods for reducing or transferring risk which should be a part of the audit. The risk manager may have lived with his problems so long that he has become inured to the potential threat. A fresh viewpoint should be encouraged. In some situations insurance audits are conducted by outside insurance consultants. These people, many of whom are very knowledgeable, can be a source of great strength to the risk manager. In most instances the insurance consultant is ethical and objective. If, on the other hand, the risk manager resists the audit, he will court criticism by his superiors even though his program may be technically perfect.

ETHICS

The risk manager's ethics must be above reproach; otherwise his problems will multiply in geometric progression. He can be made or broken by forces outside his company, depending upon his reputation. Many risk managers subscribe to an unwritten code which includes the following points:

1. Both producer and insurance company will be free from competition so long as they do a completely adequate job.
2. When making a request for coverage, the risk manager, to his best knowledge and belief, will make available all relevant data.
3. Offers to insure and the accompanying rates and conditions will be held privileged and will not be disclosed to any competing producer or company.
4. Within the confines of corporate policy, the first offerer of a proposed new coverage will receive the placement of the business, all else being equal.
5. In the preparation and adjustment of claims the risk manager will impose on himself the restrictions which apply to fiduciaries.
6. The risk manager will not participate in any manner in the producer's commissions, directly or indirectly, whether in cash or otherwise.

It is axiomatic that he who will cheat to benefit one man can be bought by another.

CORPORATE POLICY ON INSURANCE

Many problems of risk managers stem from efforts to determine corporate policy and to "live with" such policy once it has been determined.

Corporate practices frequently are confused with policy because they are of such long standing that no one remembers distinctly how they came into being. Among firms generally, for example, in the not too distant past, it was the practice to insure on a somewhat standardized basis. A company would carry "fire, boiler, and liability" insurance. If customary in a particular industry, transportation and perhaps business interruption coverages would be included. Later, probably because of aggressive salesmanship as much as need, the insurance portfolio would include practically every available coverage which had application to the business.

Risk management denies the propriety of this approach. As pointed out in the preceding chapter, it is necessary first to recognize and identify the exposure and evaluate the loss potential either as a single occurrence or as a series. In the event the exposure cannot be reduced or eliminated the economic equivalent of the loss potential becomes the governing factor. When the equivalent is so great as to indicate a disruption of ordinary dividend practices or dangerous reductions in working capital, the risk must be transferred. The risk manager's problem is to decide what corporate policy dictates in each particular case.

In general risk managers will resort to commercial insurance:

1. When an exposure has catastrophic possibilities.
2. When there is a need for specific services which may be provided by an insurance company.
3. When the maximum loss even short of catastrophe exceeds the capabilities of a "self-insurance" or "noninsurance" program.

In all other instances he will transfer the risk to a "self-insurance" program or assume the risk on a "noninsurance" basis. Each decision (or recommendation to a superior) must be made, as already indicated, within the framework of corporate policy. It is the responsibility of the manager to recommend the implementing procedure to his superiors.

One difficult problem of the risk manager is to avoid confusing probability and possibility in arriving at his recommendations. He knows that the experience of one company, unless it is extremely large and widely spread in its operations, is unpredictable as to the future. Statistics are reliable only as to the mass of similar risks and have no individual relationship to the single risk. For this reason, most practitioners resort to a combination of means of risk transfer: deductibles, excess of loss, straight excess, excess of annual aggregate, and similar coverages. (See Chapter 40.) Thus, he arrives at a predictable and acceptable annual expense without the possibility of ballooning losses which can exhaust his insurance fund or eliminate net income.

The purpose of insurance is to provide for the loss which, if it should occur, could be crippling. When the effectiveness of the program is gauged by the ratio of premiums to the sums paid out by the insurance company, the best of programs can be seriously undervalued.

LOSS PREVENTION ACTIVITY

A problem for risk managers results from the fact that in the majority of companies the insurance and loss prevention functions are disassociated. This disassociation comes about as a result of the early relationship between accident prevention and personnel or industrial relations and between plant protection and manufacturing. At times the accident prevention and plant protection responsibilities likewise are separate.

The risk management concept requires that these responsibilities be among those charged to the risk management department. If they are not, loss prevention work will be duplicated. The recognition of exposure requires evaluation, a risk management task. Its elimination, reduction, or transfer pertains more to risk management than to other activities. (See Chapter 72 for a discussion of loss prevention.)

When the risk management department supervises the operations, the other departments act as checks and balances. The result is not the same when the situation is reversed. Finally, the risk manager's approach is likely to be more objective because of his wider perspective.

That the foregoing is the risk manager's opinion is not disputed. It is, however, the consensus of the majority of successful risk managers and is borne out in the results of their programs.

Changes in the responsibility for these activities are unlikely except over a long period of time. The risk manager is well advised, therefore, to inject himself into this field, if he is not currently a part of it. The evolutionary process may bring about a realignment, because his reports to management on cause and effect will not be ignored.

DANGERS OF SPECIALIZATION

"Bridging the gap," an old fire insurance expression, may be used in reference to the final dilemma which faces the risk manager. An insurance manager may or may not be a risk manager. "Risk manager" is not simply a title which descends like a blessing on the bearer. The term is indicative of a state of mind and action which stems from education and training in cause, effect, and stabilization and which matures in experience.

These characteristics, while channeled for the specific purpose of risk management, need not end in a blind alley. Yet this is precisely the situation in which most risk managers find themselves. This situation is quite understandable. As risk managers mature in experience, they find ways and means to do more work with less expenditure of time, personnel, and expense. In a relatively static situation this discovery will lead to a reduction of the work force. Conversely, in the presence of incremental activity the work force will absorb the increase without corresponding expansion. In other words, the capacity to process a greater number of work units in a given time, increases with experience. From the short-term economic viewpoint, it is then desirable to continue the function without changes of any nature. The risk manager becomes a part of a static organization which may expand its assimilation but not its scope. He is locked into his job, simply because he does it so well!

"Rescuing" forces, however, are also at work. The uniqueness of the risk manager's experience, education, and training permits, in fact demands, his employment both in collateral and in general fields of management. That this is recognized by top management is evidenced in the current trend toward the placement of the real estate management function among his responsibilities. Fixed asset control is another area in which his capabilities may be utilized. Facility planning, distribution, and capital investment analysis are other likely fields. However, realignments such as these will not take place unless the risk manager aggressively cultivates their acquisition.

The problem of the risk manager is to escape the bonds of specialization when he has reached the point where his capabilities exceed his responsibilities. Because each company differs from all other companies in its alignment of responsibilities, there is no pat answer to the question, "How can I do it?" Each risk manager should review his company's organization chart or, better still, its organization manual. He should ask himself: "What are the characteristics of another job which may also be found in my job?" In answering this question, he should recognize that he does not have to be able to carry out each and every facet of the work of every subordinate in an activity. The clerk, the secretary, and the assistant each has special abilities which permit the more efficient programming of work. Actually, management follows a mental rather than a physical concept. The manager has the all-inclusive approach to an activity which is lacking in the specialist who cannot rise above his day-by-day occupation.

As the risk manager finds a community of interest, he would be wise to learn the maximum that he can of the subject. He is then in the position of having greater personal assets to place on the developmental scales. Modern business calls for fewer generals and colonels, but more majors, captains, and lieutenants. It is recognized that the ranks will do the work but guidance and leadership are at a premium. This recognition, rather than a blind trust in the inevitability of automatic reward, is the risk manager's compass.

SUGGESTED READINGS

GALLAGHER, RUSSELL B. "Position of the Risk Manager in a Business Organization Structure," *Risk Management* (ed. H. WAYNE SNIDER). Homewood, Ill.: Richard D. Irwin, Inc., 1963, pp. 1–15.

WILLIAMS, C. ARTHUR, JR., AND HEINS, RICHARD M. *Risk Management and Insurance*. New York: McGraw-Hill Book Co., Inc., 1964. Chap. 6.

Chapter 74

ANALYZING THE INSURER

BY CHESTER M. KELLOGG

The fundamental purpose in analyzing or evaluating the financial position of a property-liability insurer necessarily dictates the approach to the problem. Evaluation from a policyholder's point of view naturally differs from evaluation from a stockholder's position. For example, corporate risk managers, responsible for the proper protection of millions of dollars in assets, must exercise great care in the selection of the insurance company or companies to underwrite the various risks. No matter how excellent the engineering, broad the coverage, or low the price, the insurance company must be financially sound and able to function should a loss occur. This point is basic. On the other hand, a stockholder is interested not only in a company's ability to meet all claims and remain in business but also in its growth and earnings potential, quoted market price, and yield. Still other factors must be considered when an evaluation is made in connection with a merger or consolidation.

Selecting the proper yardstick with which to measure the financial position of an insurance company and the ability of its management must be done with great care and with some specialized knowledge or outside professional assistance. Insurance accounting differs from general commercial accounting in important details, but to understand insurance accounting one must have at least a basic knowledge of general accounting.

ANNUAL STATEMENT

Insurance accounting requirements (such as described in Chapter 61) are drawn partly from the field of fiduciary accounting. They perhaps are best described as a modified cash basis of accounting. This characteristic is reflected in the Annual Statement filed each year with the insurance departments of the states in which each company is licensed to transact business.

The present combined "fire and casualty" Annual Statement blank was adopted by the National Association of Insurance Commissioners at its June, 1950, meeting in Quebec, effective for the returns of 1950. (By that date most states had adopted multiple line legislation permitting property and liability lines to be written in a single company.) The Annual Statement may be amended on recommendation of the Committee on Blanks, subject to approval of the N.A.I.C. at its June meeting each year. Since 1950 numerous minor changes have been made. The Annual Statement of some 38 pages, 12″ × 19″ in size, is truly a formidable document.

Professional analysts work from this statement. For any detailed evaluation it is usually advisable to seek their assistance and rely at least in part on their experienced judgment. However, it is possible to gain a very good general knowledge of a company's position by careful study and evaluation of a simplified statement of assets and liabilities backed up by key operating figures and balance sheet items for several years, as reported in standard insurance reference works. The purpose of this chapter is to provide a few guidelines for such an analysis. Since the subject matters of Chapters 60 and 61 are quite closely related to this topic, readers are invited to review these chapters.

BACKGROUND ESSENTIAL TO ANALYSIS

Before one becomes involved in analyzing the financial standing of an insurance company, he must have at least a general idea of its relative position among those of other companies. Evaluating a single company without some knowledge of basic industry trends is looking at something taken out of context. Moreover, credible conclusions cannot be reached by looking at a single year's results or even comparing them with the previous year's results. In order to avoid placing undue importance on chance variations in evaluating an underwriting trend, one should study a three-year span at the minimum. A five-year study with greater emphasis on the three latest years is still better. Although the importance of earnings can hardly be overemphasized, it is still necessary (1) to ascertain that assets are sound and (2) to evaluate liabilities carefully because of the effect that reserves have on reported underwriting results and surplus.

Any financial statement is as of a specific date and made up in conformity with statutory requirements. Therefore, to evaluate a company as a going concern it is necessary (1) to include all sound assets at market values, (2) to eliminate unnecessary statutory liabilities, and (3) to allow for equities or shortages in reserves. In looking at a statement of assets and liabilities one must find out what a company really holds in sound marketable assets and the extent of its adjusted liabilities. In short, one must determine the company's "adjusted net worth." For the results to be favorable, this margin of adjusted assets over adjusted liabilities must be in sound proportion to the insurance liability assumed and include a sufficient margin of liquidity.

EVALUATION OF ASSETS

A substantial portion of thé assets in possession of property-liability companies is held solely because the companies transact an insurance business. They come into existence, first, because insurance protection is paid for in advance and companies find themselves in the position of "trustees" of substantial unearned premiums for insurance running into the future. They arise, secondly, as returns on assets which have been invested. Other sources include capital contributions plus gains on disposals of assets.

Bonds

Because of the quasi-fiduciary nature of these assets held to cover reserve accounts and the need for liquidity, it is not surprising to find that bonds constitute the major investments for most companies. Over a period of years, industry averages indicate that cash and bonds have been generally kept at a level comfortably exceeding total adjusted liabilities. In evaluating a company it is necessary to check the quality of its bond portfolio carefully to be sure that it does not include speculative holdings or large blocks of questionable issues. With rare exceptions, bond portfolios are beyond question as to investment quality. They may be said to represent maximum security with only a "money-rate" risk, that is, a danger of decline in principal because of an increase in the interest rate.

Bonds are normally carried at amortized values in accordance with statutory requirements. Essentially, this amortization procedure entails writing a bond up or down to par value at maturity. Thus, two bond portfolios could be identical but priced differently for statement purposes because of different market values prevailing on different purchase dates. In analyzing an insurer, one should ascertain the current market prices of the bonds.

Stocks

The next largest asset holding is usually in common stocks. Property-liability companies own many different stocks with largest holdings concentrated in recognized "blue chip" issues. Many of these holdings were acquired years ago and have increased substantially in market value. Preferred stock holdings are normally small and concentrated in high quality money-rate issues whose market values tend to follow the trend of the bond market rather than that of the stock market.

In evaluating the quality of the stock portfolio an analyst should watch for any single investment which is too large. He should also bear in mind that existence of a subsidiary insurance company may reduce the liquidity and distort the financial appearance of the parent company. The reason is that the parent company's statement includes as assets the subsidiary's stock owned by the parent. This stock is generally carried on the parent's statement at the subsidiary's book value. This practice may hide important additional equities. Stockholdings may seem relatively large, even though the subsidiary may invest heavily in bonds. Such holdings may also obscure the true relationship between total resources and insurance liability assumed. A consolidated statement is the best approach in evaluating one or more companies in a corporate group.

Other Assets

Mortgages or collateral loans are held by some companies and represent assets which in most instances could be sold fairly readily. However, they should be carefully checked if they appear at all unusual or are sizeable.

Real estate usually comprises home or branch office property and is therefore nonliquid but, more often than not, is carried at depreciated cost rather than at appraised or market value.

Premium balances (premiums in course of collection) average between 10 percent and 20 percent of annual net premiums written for most stock companies and lower for most mutual companies. High premium balances deprive a company of potential investment earnings and could indicate a loss of confidence in the company by its agents.

Additional assets which are not normally considered in evaluating a company from a policyholder's point of view may be important in an evaluation for purposes of an investment or a merger. As brought out in Chapter 61, premium balances over 90 days due are charged out of the statement assets as "nonadmitted," although the bulk of such premiums is normally collectible. Office furniture and automobiles, often sizeable and of definite value, are likewise carried as "nonadmitted" under insurance statutory regulations. Uncollected accrued or earned premiums and gains from salvage or subrogation are examples of other items that should be taken into account. In this type of evaluation it would also be necessary to consider the status of pension funds, stock option plans, the value of the agency plant, and other pertinent items. Finally, federal income taxes would have to be estimated in respect to unrealized gains on which no tax had been paid and prepaid expense which had already been deducted from taxable income.

General Comment

The analyst, in evaluating the liquidity and distribution of assets of any company, should compare the relationship of classes of investments at market values to adjusted liabilities rather than to total assets. A company may have a higher than average percentage of assets invested in real estate or in common stocks yet maintain better overall diversification and greater liquidity in relation to liabilities than another company with more normal diversification of assets but larger liabilities.

EVALUATION OF LIABILITIES

The two largest and most important items among the liabilities of the average property-liability company are the reserve for unearned premiums and the reserve for losses. (See Chapter 60.) These two reserves are peculiar to the insurance business and the relative size of each varies according to the classes of business underwritten and the plan of operation followed by each company.

It is a difficult and complicated problem for management to ascertain the amount of loss reserves sufficient to absorb all claims. Yet establishment of adequate reserves is vital. If such reserves are too low, surplus is overstated and reported underwriting results are more favorable than actual results. Regardless of whether the reserves are inadequate through ignorance, lack of technical competence, a sharp rise in the price level, or deliberate policy, the company is headed for serious trouble. If loss reserves are too high, surplus is penalized and so is underwriting.

Sudden Changes in Loss Reserves

It is also very helpful to understand the reasons behind any sudden change in loss reserves. Should a company sharply increase its loss reserves in a single year, its loss ratio might jump several points, its reported underwriting results deteriorate, and its surplus shrink. Interpretation of such a development poses a problem. Various questions may confront the analyst: Does the change mean that the normal business underwritten by the company has suddenly run into trouble? Does it mean that the company has put a block of inferior business on its books? Does it imply that current business is satisfactory but simply that loss reserves previously set up have proven inadequate? Any or all of these questions may have affirmative answers. Moreover, still other variables, such as a change in reinsurance treaties or retentions, could contribute to the change in the reserves.

Property Claims

Property claims are usually promptly reported, readily estimated, and quickly settled. Hence, they are not likely to create analytical difficulties. There is usually little argument as to the amount of the loss or whether the company is liable. Therefore losses in process of settlement are normally small in number and loss reserves relatively small and reasonably accurate. Only in case of some widespread disaster, such as a major hurricane, when a multitude of losses temporarily overwhelms loss adjustment facilities, do property loss reserves present any real problem.

Third-Party Claims

Third-party liability claims present many loss reserve problems for the analyst. There may be delay in reporting third-party claims. The claims are likely to be much more difficult to investigate than property claims. It is often difficult to determine the degree of liability of the insured and to reach a settlement agreement with a sometimes unreasonable claimant. Often, considerable delay ensues in settlement. Sometimes it is necessary to go to court to make a final settlement. In addition, the analyst must take into account any administrative changes in the company's reserve procedures and its general philosophy regarding the handling of claims. One company may try to settle all claims with unusual dispatch while another may prefer to let questionable claims go to litigation.

While it is less difficult to estimate the amount of loss under workmen's compensation insurance policies, losses are frequently payable over a long period of time. For example, should disability be total and permanent, reserves would have to be established in an amount equal to the present value of estimated payments over the life of the injured worker. Thus, compensation reserves tend to be rather substantial. However, mere size of loss reserves in relation to current premium volume is not an accurate gauge as to their adequacy. Not only does loss experience vary among companies but also among patterns of business. For example, a company writing a decreasing volume of business would normally report relatively higher reserves than one writing an increasing volume of business.

The deferred and uncertain nature of third-party liability claims makes their proper evaluation particularly difficult. Unfortunately, there is no rule of thumb by which they can be judged. Expert analysis of reserve schedules in the Annual Statement is required to arrive at a proper evaluation.

Schedules P and O

Schedule *P* is the source of information on bodily injury liability and compensation reserves from the date a company started to write business in these lines. Information about each of the last eight policy years is shown separately. The analyst should be familiar with various parts of this schedule. Parts 1 and 2 are statistical exhibits showing the losses paid, the reserves set up, incurred loss ratios, number of liability suits, and additional data of significance to the trained analyst. Parts 5, 5–A, and 5–B show the development of incurred losses, the reserve originally set forth by policy year, as computed at the close of the past six years. The data here indicate whether a company has enjoyed a favorable or unfavorable run-off of reserves. Schedule *O* shows some of the run-off, during the calendar year, of loss reserves (on lines other than bodily injury liability and workmen's compensation) carried at the end of the preceding year. Property damage liability losses still outstanding two years or longer after the calendar year of occurrence, however, can not be traced in Schedule *O*.

Reinsurance

Types of reinsurance contracts in force or their terms often make quite a difference in evaluating a company. While this is quite obvious regarding catastrophe losses, it may be overlooked on portfolio reinsurance. The primary company should always be judged in relation to gross as well as net writings when any substantial portfolio reinsurance is in force. Moreover, excess of loss reinsurance arrangements for liability and workmen's compensation insurance should be considered carefully.

Under the laws of many states a primary company may not take credit in its financial statement for reinsurance recoverable from a reinsurance company not licensed in the state. Therefore, the item "Unauthorized Reinsurance Recoverable" set up as a liability unnecessarily depletes surplus when the reinsurance company is financially responsible. It is wise to check the financial standing of each primary company's chief reinsurance companies.

Unearned Premiums

The reserve for unearned premiums is a "fiduciary" type formula reserve (usually monthly pro rata) subject to refund on cancellation of policies. (See Chapter 60.) As this reserve is calculated upon the net amount of premiums under all policies in force at the statement date, it follows that a company will realize an equity in the run-off of the business (remaining in force until normal expiration) equal to that portion of unearned premiums not needed to meet claims. The analyst should remember that this equity fluctuates from year to year and may vary from, say, 20 percent on workmen's compensation to 50 percent on fidelity and surety. As brought out in Chapter 60, a workable rule of thumb often used is 40 percent "fire and allied business" and 35 percent for "casualty lines."

Differences in unearned premium reserve exist not only because of differences in classes of business underwritten but because of differences in operating plans. One company writing mainly term business may report unearned premiums of one-and-a-half times its annual net writings, while a company with similar risks on a yearly or installment basis may have unearned premiums of less than half its net volume. A third company may write business on a monthly reporting basis so there may be only nominal unearned premium liability. The first company has three times as much equity in its unearned reserve as the second carrier. The third company not only has very little equity but also, to be placed on a comparable basis, should be charged an estimated amount for the run-off cost of the business on its books. In practice an estimate of a half year's incurred losses works out reasonably accurately.

When premium volume is either advancing or receding, statutory underwriting results (which are calculated on premiums earned) are distorted. This distortion occurs because the major portion of expense is incurred when the policy is written. Therefore, unless underwriting results are adjusted for the estimated change in equity in unearned premiums, profits will be understated when unearned premiums rise and overstated when they decline.

EXAMPLE OF CALCULATION OF UNDERWRITING RESULTS

Probably the best way to emphasize the necessity of adjusting statutory underwriting results is to set up a simple hypothetical case and trace the course of a premium dollar through the accounts of a company. (A related illustration appears in Chapter 60.) With the danger of possible oversimplification, assume that on June 30 a fire insurance policy is written to cover a period of five years for a total premium of $10,000. Immediately the company sets up an asset, "Premium Balances" (premiums in course of collection) of $10,000 and a liability of $10,000, "Reserve for Unearned Premiums." However, the agent gets his commission not over the term of the policy but at once. Therefore, assuming a flat 25 percent commission cost, an expense of $2,500 is incurred. In addition to the agent's commission, other expenses are incurred in connection with the acquisition of the business, such as state premium taxes, the cost of placing the business on the books, overhead, and so on. These additional expenses may run to $1,500 which, together with commissions, make a total underwriting expense of $4,000. Assume further that during the first six months of the policy term there was a small loss under the policy which, with loss adjustment expenses, cost the company a total of $500.

With the additional assumption that this single policy represented the total business for the year, the company's records as of December 31 can be closed. Abbreviated for clarity, the report required from the company would be as follows:

Premiums Written		$10,000
Deduct Unearned Premiums		9,000
Premiums Earned		$ 1,000
Losses Incurred	$ 500	
Expenses Incurred	4,000	
Total Losses & Expenses		4,500
Statutory Underwriting Loss		$ 3,500

The statutory underwriting loss of $3,500 would be reflected in a charge against surplus. This example shows clearly why and how a rising volume of business is a drain on surplus and points up the problem faced by property-liability companies in setting up the required reserves on a rising volume of business. However, it does more. It demonstrates the necessity of calculating either an *adjusted* underwriting profit or loss or using some other method to arrive at an accurate appraisal of actual operating results, a very important factor in evaluating a company.

METHODS FOR ADJUSTING STATUTORY UNDERWRITING RESULTS

The analyst has a choice of two principal methods in his efforts to arrive at a reasonably accurate assessment of underwriting results of the company under scrutiny.

Method Number One

The hypothetical company in the preceding example increased its reserve for unearned premiums by $9,000 during the year. Allowing an estimated equity of 40 percent, the correction factor would be $3,600 detailed as follows:

Statutory Underwriting Loss	$3,500
Increased Equity in Unearned Premiums	3,600
Adjusted Underwriting Profit	$ 100

Method Number Two

This adjustment method involves use of ratios. Earned premiums are an accurate measure of exposure to loss. Therefore, losses incurred (including loss adjustment expenses) are divided by earned premiums to produce the loss ratio. In the hypothetical case, incurred losses of $500 "ratioed" to earned premiums of $1,000 would produce a loss ratio of 50 percent.

The next step in the use of this method is the estimate of an expense ratio. The major portion of expense is incurred when the policy is written but such items as commissions and state premium taxes apply to the whole premium at inception whether it be a one-year policy or a five-year policy. Therefore, expenses incurred are "ratioed" to net premiums *written*—as opposed to premiums *earned*. In the hypothetical company, expenses incurred amounted to $4,000 which when "ratioed" to premiums written of $10,000, produces an expense ratio of 40 percent.

Use of this method by the analyst indicates a loss ratio of 50 percent and an expense ratio of 40 percent, leaving an indicated profit margin of 10 percent, the very same percentage of profit as arrived at by adjusting the statutory underwriting account with an allowance for increased equity in unearned premiums. That method of adjustment indicated $100 profit on $1,000 earned premiums or 10 percent.

General Comment

It is just as important to use an adjusted underwriting figure or the combination of loss and expense ratios, outlined above, in a period of declining volume, as in a period of increasing volume. The statutory figure in a period of decline is similarly distorted but on the side of overstating rather than understating profits. When premium volume is either advancing or receding, statutory underwriting results are distorted and "ratioing" both losses and expenses to earned premiums or both to written premiums makes for equal distortion. The analyst should always either correct the statutory underwriting figure for change in unearned premium reserve equity (Method One) or "ratio" losses incurred (plus loss adjustment expenses) to earned premiums and underwriting expenses incurred to written premiums (Method Two). The resulting ratios in Method Two, of course, are added and the total is compared with 100. If the total is less than 100, there is an indicated profit; if it is more than 100, there is an indicated loss.

OTHER SIGNIFICANT DIFFERENCES

In evaluating a company there may be other significant variables to consider. Some classes of business are inherently more hazardous than others or subject to a catastrophe hazard or to rather wide swings in loss experience. One company may have an excellent spread of business by territory and by class, while another may specialize or concentrate its risks in a single locality or class. Reinsurance arrangements can vary from one company to another and materially alter the impact of catastrophe losses. Different investment policies may be followed ranging from the ultraconservative to the speculative.

There are participating companies and nonparticipating; standard rate companies and deviating rate companies; those which obtain business directly and those which operate through agents. Since each one of these variations can complicate comparisons between companies, the analyst should be conscious of them. For example, when he makes comparisons of operating results, it is advisable to treat dividends to policyholders as a deduction from underwriting income to place participating and nonparticipating companies on a more nearly comparable basis. He has to recognize, of course, that regardless of classes of business written, territory served, or plan of operation, final operating results may vary widely.

THE IMPORTANCE OF PROFIT

Earnings, or lack of earnings, in an insurance company stem from two sources: underwriting and investments. No matter how sound the assets, adequate the reserves, or large the surplus, a company in order to survive must, over a period of years, demonstrate an ability to make at least a modest profit.

Two companies may present almost identical statements. At first glance they may appear of equal strength. However, one operates consistently at a profit while the other is just as consistently in the red because of poor underwriting. The first company not only has a higher estimated equity in its unearned premium reserve but adds to its surplus each year, while the second company grows progressively weaker as unprofitable operations eat into its surplus. For practical purposes, the profitably operated carrier is unquestionably stronger than the other and may safely write a larger volume of business in relation to its resources than the company showing poor underwriting results and general unprofitable operation.

Although the primary function of an insurance company is the business of insurance, the investment function is also very important and investment earnings and gains from investments must be considered. A very well-capitalized company usually enjoys not only greater latitude in investment policy but consistently reports relatively higher investment income than one with only modest margins of assets over liabilities. The yearly plow-back of a portion of investment earnings plus both realized and unrealized gains from investments have been major factors in making insurance companies largely self-financing and able to underwrite the tremendous increase in premium volume.

OVERVIEW

Size alone is no guarantee of successful operation. Many small companies, writing specialized lines, are carefully and efficiently managed and have a comfortable excess of assets over liabilities. The assets are adequate to support the volume of business underwritten.

In estimating the value of an insurance company as a going concern, it is necessary to adjust all assets to market value, include sound "nonadmitted" assets, eliminate unnecessary statutory liabilities, adjust reserves for equities or shortages, and provide for federal income taxes on unrealized gains and prepaid expense. Furthermore, the analyst should consider the many differences among companies; study the adjusted underwriting results and trends; ascertain the quality of assets, liquidity position, and spread of liability; and relate these findings to the company's adjusted net worth to see how it compares with that of other companies. In this comparison averages are very useful.

Finally, the analyst should look to the future and attempt to answer questions such as the following: What are the company's prospects? How solid is its growth? What may reasonably be expected in earnings from underwriting and from investments? Where will the company stand financially one year or two years from now? Is the management competent to meet future challenges?

SUGGESTED READINGS

BELL, S. ALEXANDER. "Financial Statements of Fire and Casualty Insurance Companies," *Federation of Insurance Counsel Quarterly,* Vol. 10 (Summer, 1960), pp. 6–19.

Best's Insurance Reports, Fire and Casualty. New York: Alfred M. Best Co., Inc. Annual Editions.

Examination of Insurance Companies. Albany: New York State Insurance Department, 1953–55. (7 vols.)

HOFFMAN, ARTHUR L. "Policyholders' Surplus—Its Analysis and Adjustments," *The Annals of the Society of Chartered Property and Casualty Underwriters,* Vol. 11 (February, 1959), pp. 111–18.

Insurance Accounting: Fire and Casualty. Philadelphia: The Spectator, 1954. (Prepared by and published for the Insurance Accounting and Statistical Association. A revision is in progress at the time of this writing.)

OSBORN, GRANT. "Teaching the Analysis of Financial Statements," *The Journal Of Insurance,* Vol. XXVIII (June, 1961), pp. 35–39.

STOCKHAM, REGINALD P. "Financial Statements of Foreign Fire and Marine Insurance Companies," *Best's Insurance News* (Fire and Casualty Edition), Vol. 41 (March, 1941), pp. 21–22, 38–40.

TARBELL, THOMAS F. "The Combined Fire and Casualty Statement Blank," *Proceedings of the Casualty Actuarial Society,* Vol. XXVII (November, 1950), pp. 74–81; Vol. XXVIII (November, 1951), pp. 113–40.

Chapter 75

INSURANCE SURVEYS

BY A. HAWTHORNE CRIDDLE

The marketing concept of the insurance survey is increased sales through rendering a superior service to the buyer. The professional concept is the employment of insurance principles and practices for the maximum economic benefit of the client. In the ultimate sense these concepts merge along the lines set forth in this chapter.

REQUISITES OF A SURVEY

Implementation of a survey under either concept requires:

1. A system for the recognition or identification of all insurable loss exposures or risks.
2. A set of guidelines to be employed in the design of a recommended program for dealing with such insurable loss exposures.
3. A method of auditing existing insurance policies with respect to coverage provided; applicability to the client's exposures; interrelationship of policies to one another; and rates, premiums, and rating plans applied.
4. Coverage and service specifications, negotiations for pricing, and placing the selected program.

When applied to the risk facts developed for a specific client, the insurance survey will usually disclose important program deficiencies. For example, the omission of kinds of insurance essential to the subject matter at risk, through inaccurate or insufficient supporting data; failure to use the best policy and form for the purpose; inadequate or excessive amounts of insurance; failure to integrate related policies thereby creating nonconcurrency; duplication of coverage; gaps or overlaps in protection; unimportant or unnecessary insurance carried; and excessive or otherwise improper premium costs. The discovery and correction of any of these inadequacies is of substantial benefit to the insurance buyer. Surveyed accounts are usually the best handled, have the highest average premiums, create a more nearly permanent relationship between producer and client, and are the most profitable to the sellers. Thus, the added time and expense inherent in the survey procedure is normally fully justified. It adds a significant "plus" to the insurance transaction for both buyer and seller.

RISK RECOGNITION AND IDENTIFICATION

Questionnaire

The most commonly employed system of risk recognition or identification is the insurance survey questionnaire. Forms for this purpose are supplied by many insurance companies in conjunction with survey procedures they have developed as an aid to their agents. They are also available from a few publishing houses that specialize in insurance publications and some survey practitioners have developed their own. Essentially, a company-provided survey questionnaire begins with a section of general information. These items include: name and address of the insured; organizational form—i. e., proprietorship, partnership, or corporation; names and locations of subsidiary or affiliated companies; general description of the business operations; a schedule of all locations from which the business is conducted; and a listing of other properties owned or leased. The sections which follow are substantially a set of underwriting information forms for all currently available kinds of insurance. These forms are designed to reveal the insurable loss exposures of the client and to provide the information necessary to underwrite and rate each coverage. Understandably, they do not attempt to develop similar information on risks for which insurance is not currently available. These questionnaires have undergone substantial revision as the business of insurance has changed and will undergo more as the multiple line package policy becomes the dominant insurance document.

Some companies have several questionnaires, each especially designed to meet the particular requirements of certain classes of business. A retail store questionnaire does not develop the information required to survey a bank. Neither does a manufacturing questionnaire meet the needs of a long-haul truck operation. As more special purpose multiple line package policies are developed, the special questionnaire will become increasingly important.

The questionnaire is the best instrument currently available. Logically, its utility increases with the insurance knowledge and skill of the user, as well as with his knowledge of the characteristics of the business being surveyed.

Physical Inspection

The second important element in developing loss exposures is physical inspection of properties and operations. These take the form of orientation inspections by the surveyor and technical inspections by representatives of companies and rating bureaus with respect to particular aspects such as fire, workmen's compensation, public liability, automobile fleets, plate glass, boilers, and machinery. The orientation inspection is "the picture worth a thousand words" to the surveyor and the technical inspections are essential to accuracy and comprehensiveness.

Property Values

Ascertainment of insurable property values is also an important function of the survey, both from the standpoint of providing indemnity for the client and testing compliance with coinsurance clauses. Both replacement and depreciated values should always be ascertained from the most reliable source. On new property, current cost is adequate for both values. As to older buildings, machinery, and equipment, the sources in order of reliability are (1) a current professional appraisal; (2) an out-of-date appraisal modified to reflect subsequent depreciation, additions, and retirements; (3) on buildings, a current builder's estimate of reproduction cost less depreciation, and on machinery and equipment, a listing priced by a dealer in new and used similar machinery and equipment; (4) on buildings, an estimate of insurable value based on a square or cubic foot method; and (5) an estimate based on original cost or book values modified by judgment. Values of inventories, raw materials, supplies, money, automobiles, and similar personal property are usually readily ascertainable from the client's books.

Development of Facts

The fully completed questionnaire on a current and applicable form, supplemented by the inspection reports and reliable value information, will provide substantially all the data required to recognize and identify the insurable loss exposures of the client. However, the surveyor should keep firmly in his mind that the fundamental purpose of the procedure is to develop and record information about *all* risks of an insurable nature within three broad categories:

1. Property: the risk of physical damage or destruction or the loss of possession.
2. Consequential: the additional loss which follows or is attendant upon the occurrence of another loss-causing event such as deprivation of use of property, spoilage or reduction in value for certain other reasons of otherwise undamaged property, or increased cost of repair or replacement required by ordinance.
3. Liability: the risk of becoming legally obligated to pay monetary damages to another because of personal injuries or property damage.

To the extent that a questionnaire fails to develop facts concerning any such loss of an insurable nature, it is deficient and the surveyor has a duty to expand it on the basis of this broad concept of potential loss and his own knowledge. Insurance availability is constantly changing. A hundred years ago the insurability of windstorm was heatedly debated by underwriters; today it is a matter of course. Years ago "all risk" insurance on buildings was rare; today it is routine. Currently, flood is generally uninsurable on a universal basis, but is frequently dealt with in the professional survey. The rapid advance toward the "all risk" concept in insurance is a compelling reason for converting survey questionnaires to develop all loss exposures. Questionnaires should be oriented to the broad categories of "property," "consequential," and "liability" risks, instead of by specific lines of insurance such as fire, extended coverage, crime, general and automobile liability, workmen's compensation, and other self-limiting classifications.

RECOMMENDING INSURANCE PROGRAM

From the viewpoint of the ordinary insurance buyer the simple purpose of insurance is to indemnify against loss of an accidental or fortuitous nature in exchange for a reasonable premium outlay.

Many such risks will involve loss possibilities so small in amount that they may be conveniently and economically absorbed as an ordinary expense of living or doing business. Other risks involve the possibility of crippling financial consequences. The decision to insure or not insure should be predicated upon the amount of maximum possible loss rather than the probability of the occurrence of the event. The objective of every recommended insurance program should be (1) to provide adequate insurance against every risk of significant financial consequence; (2) to offer choices of insurance or noninsurance on loss amounts which may be properly insured or retained according to client preference; and (3) to propose noninsurance with respect to those risks which involve small potential amounts of loss whether of frequent or infrequent occurrence.

Guidelines

The suggested guidelines are as follows:

A) Recommend insurance when:

1. Insurance is required by law or under a loan agreement, bond issue, construction contract, or other written legal agreement.
2. The amount of possible loss is too large to be safely or conveniently absorbed.
3. The incidence of occurrence of significant financial loss is so irregular that assumption would result in unacceptable annual cost variation (for example, the average fire loss for 10 years may be $10,000 but it may be represented by a $100,000 loss in only one of the 10 years).
4. The accessory services required, in addition to the indemnity, may be more economically provided by an insurance company (widespread or skilled claims service, boiler and pressure vessel inspections, and so on).

B) Recommend retention when:

1. The distribution of exposures is sufficiently widespread; the amount of possible loss is so relatively small that it can be conveniently treated as a normal operating expense; and the cost of insurance appears excessive over a period of time when related to losses incurred and services received. (Consideration should be given to both the maximum loss potential in a single event and the possible aggregate annual cost.)
2. The frequency probability is so high that some loss is almost certain to occur; the annual variation of sustained losses is within acceptable range; and no special services are required in loss settlement, inspection, and loss prevention activities, nor is insurance required by law or legal agreement.
3. The probability of occurrence is so remote that the ordinarily prudent business man will not incur any amount of premium expense for insurance (such as earthquake in areas where no damage by earthquakes has ever occurred; flood in arid or elevated regions where no flood has ever been recorded).

C) Recommend a combination of insurance and retention through the use of deductibles, franchises, excess plans, or retrospective rating procedures when:

1. The premium saving offers a lower estimated combined net cost to the client over a period of time without impairing either the availability of essential advisory services or indemnity against serious loss.
2. Customer relationships and business self-interest of the client are so interwoven with claim settlements that the client's best interest can be served by the control of payment of claims within an acceptable cost range. (Principally encountered in respect to products liability.)

Application of Guidelines

When applied to a specific set of risk facts, these guidelines provide a logical and supportable basis for a recommended course of action. For example, under Point *A*–2, a one-location operation consisting of building, machinery, equipment, furnishings, fixtures, raw materials, supplies, and finished product, represents a loss possibility too large to be safely absorbed as an operating expense with respect to perils of a total loss potential. Such perils include fire, windstorm, riot, civil commotion, colliding aircraft, boiler or other explosion, earthquake, and flood. However, this conclusion could be subject to modification as to earthquake and flood in terms of Point *B*–3. Alternatively, the suggested insurance could be provided on a deductible basis by applying Point *C*–1.

For contrast, assume that the business owned buildings and equipment consisting of 200 hamburger stands of good construction, territorially widespread, with an approximately uniform insurable value of $10,000 each. Assume also that the cost per year to insure fire and extended coverage perils was $100 per unit, producing a total annual premium expense of $20,000 and that the five-year average losses totalled $5,000 per year, the highest having been $13,000 and the lowest $2,000. Point *B*–1 might well be applied because the maximum possible loss in a single event is $10,000, the arithmetical average $5,000, and the historical maximum annual aggregate $13,000. These amounts could be absorbed by the business without insurance and in any year, when the actual losses equalled or were less than the expected, an economy would result. Alternatively, Point *C*–2 could be applied at any deductible level which would introduce a limitation of aggregate annual loss for greater safety. In practically all states Point *A*–1 would dictate the recommendation for workmen's compensation insurance, and in some states the need for an automobile financial responsibility filing would dictate automobile insurance. If the premises contained steam boilers or pressure vessels, which required inspection under state or city law, insurance might well be recommended under Point *A*–3.

Point *B*–3 violates Point *A*–2 in theory, but must be employed to permit conformance with practical management philosophy. For example, the earthquake rate in the City of Philadelphia is $.04 per $100 with 80 percent coinsurance on a fire-resistive office building. There are substantially no buyers and the recommendation of this coverage by an insurance professional might cast an air of doubt upon his other recommendations. Like many other sound guidelines, Point *A*–2 cannot be rigorously applied until time and circumstances make it acceptable. The trend toward "all risk" policies is making it increasingly easy to dispense with Point *B*–3 through the consolidation of perils and price because the charge for remote hazards will be negligible.

It is evident that these guidelines are derived from the professional concept of client needs as distinct from the original sales concept of the insurance survey. Recommending noninsurance or "self-insurance" reduces the volume of commission-producing insurance sales but there are other compensations. In the majority of cases insurance provides the only reliable solution to the risk problem. Insurance sold in this manner is more securely held by the surveyor who has dealt objectively with the areas where insurance is not to the advantage of his client. "Overselling" is recognized as a quick and easy way to lose a customer, and the professional approach to the insurance survey avoids this danger.

After these guidelines have been applied, a schedule of the *recommended program* should be prepared in outline form which will become part of the survey report. Essential data consist of a brief description of the recommended coverage, amounts or limits to be provided, insurance companies proposed, policy period, and quoted premiums.

AUDITING EXISTING INSURANCE

As an opening step, a schedule of existing insurance should be prepared and verified. It will serve as a valuable point of future reference in judging the results achieved by the survey. The visible index book included in most survey systems is an excellent medium for this purpose. An insured is usually quite pleased to receive an attractive summary of his present insurance and will normally be quite cooperative in checking its accuracy. An alternate method is to prepare a typed schedule for similar verification. Minimum information consists of coverage descriptions, amounts or limits, policy numbers, companies, policy period, and premium. Because of the time interval from start to finish of a survey and changes which may be made during the interim, but forgotten, the beginning summary provides the only reliable basis for measuring total survey accomplishments. This summary or schedule will also form a part of the survey report.

There is, of course, the necessity for verifying in every policy the accuracy and completeness of all inserted information. Such information includes the name and address(es) of the insured, the description and location of property or operations, and statements, including representations and other declarations on behalf of the insured.

Knowledge of the Contracts

A prerequisite of good auditing is extensive knowledge of all the elements of each kind of insurance involved, preferably reduced to written guides for each policy and form. Where policies and forms are subject to regulation by states or state approved bureaus, the auditing problem is simplified. This simplification is particularly common with respect to fire insurance. The standard fire contract is the basic document, supplemented by required forms which vary according to the nature of the property and regional rating bureau practices, a variety of amendatory endorsements which are mandatory for certain classes, and optional endorsements which are available and which affect coverage or premium. The guide sheet for checking a fire insurance contract consists of a topical outline which directs the attention of the examiner to all the things that *should* be done to the particular contract of this client, as well as the things which *could* be done. This method of examination is comprehensive and forces consideration of the variety of permissible alternatives, such as (1) higher versus lower coinsurance percentages, (2) blanket insurance versus specific, (3) reporting forms versus fixed amounts, (4) higher versus lower deductibles, (5) market value versus actual cash value, (6) repair and replacement coverage versus actual cash value, and (7) consequential loss assumption endorsements versus only direct damage coverage.

Most liability insurance contracts are not prescribed by state law but some uniformity exists through adoption of the "standard forms" program by bureau companies. The basic contract is the Comprehensive General Liability Insurance Policy. (This contract can be modified to include automobile—see Chapter 34.) There is considerable latitude for amending the contract materially to expand the scope. For example, the insuring clause may be amended to an "occurrence" instead of an accident basis; personal injury may be added to bodily injury; the territorial limits may be extended to a worldwide basis; assumed or contractual liability may be covered on a blanket instead of a defined basis; employees may be included as additional insureds; and certain exclusions may be deleted such as those relating to water damage liability, third-party beneficiaries, liquor law liability, and watercraft liability. The care, custody, and control exclusion may be deleted or materially modified. (See Chapter 32 and 34 for discussion of such topics.) It is axiomatic that under any comprehensive or "all risk" type of policy the elimination of exclusions broadens coverage and is for the benefit of the insured. The guide sheet for auditing policies should contain notations of all the amendments that can be made in order to produce the broadest and best policy available. For certain businesses restrictive endorsements may be mandatory. An example is the exclusion of coverage for professional liability for architects and engineers. These restrictions often identify the need for special kinds of liability insurance.

Where policies and forms are nonstandard, such as is frequently found in the uncontrolled inland marine lines, the guide sheet should be prepared on the basis of the broadest and best contract known to be available for the purpose, supplemented by clauses designed for special attention.

Auditing of Individual Contracts

A prepared or acquired policy-checker of this type, adjusted to the territory and market facilities of the surveyor, is an invaluable aid to the audit procedure. It will assure maximum technical excellence in the utilization of policies, forms, and rules. However, to add the touch of the expert the surveyor should put aside his presumed general knowledge of the policies and forms and read each policy carefully *in terms of the exposures of the specific account under review.* It is remarkable how many times the routine conditions and other provisions of a well-known policy will take on a new meaning when applied to some specific set of risk facts. In such a case modification may be required.

Interrelationships

After each contract has been audited, it should be studied as an interrelated part of the whole program. Some kinds of insurance should always be placed with the same company to avoid disagreements between insurers in case of loss. Examples include employee dishonesty and merchandise theft as well as liability and workmen's compensation. Policies covering the same subject matter should be harmonious with one another. If fire insurance—as an illustration—is on a repair and replacement basis, the boiler and machinery should be also. If stock in a warehouse is insured for market value, the transportation coverage should be on a similar basis. Complete concurrency of all policies covering the same perils and subject matter is a must! Consolidation through packaging or otherwise should be considered to increase the purchasing power of the client. This discussion is necessarily brief but touches several of the significant elements of program planning which are in the province of the coverage expert.

RATES AND PREMIUMS

The common denominator of the businessman—price—is applied to insurance in much the same fashion as it is to all other purchases. Understandably, the objective is the most for the least, and meticulous rate auditing is a critical element of the insurance survey because of its dominance in decision making. In general, there are manual rates, minimum class rates, schedule rates, experience rates, and judgment rates which are initially applied to a policy at issuance. All of these rates may vary in initial application among classes of companies, such as stock company bureau members, stock or mutual independent companies, or reciprocals. The final premium after expiration may also vary among participating companies which pay dividends, whether stock, mutual, or reciprocal. Larger premium risks may also be subject to retrospective rating plans or participating dividend plans based on loss ratios.

The first step in rate auditing is examination for correct application of rates at the time of policy issuance in accordance with the filings of the issuing company, including adjusted premiums developed by audits or reports. The second auditing step is to explore for possible rate reductions through physical or system improvements. The final auditing step is to test the rates against those currently available from the issuing company and those available competitively through a different kind of company, special filings by classification of business, or discounts built into package policy filings. The requisite ability to perform this aspect of policy auditing is a current and thorough knowledge of rates and rating plans.

It might be thought unnecessary to point out that all cost comparisons should be made in terms of identical coverage, but experience has demonstrated that the insured is often technically unqualified to evaluate coverage differences. If a policy is designated as "Comprehensive General and Automobile Liability Policy," it is the same to him as another bearing the same designation. The fact that one may be an unmodified "standard" policy and the other a broader policy on an "occurrence" basis, with personal injury included, contractual liability on a blanket basis, the water damage exclusion removed, and so on, often escapes attention of the buyer in comparing premium charges. Regardless of what is to be recommended, the audited cost comparison should always be on an "apples and apples" basis.

COMPETITIVE MARKETING OF RECOMMENDED INSURANCE PROGRAM

Practices in respect to arranging for placement of recommended insurance necessarily vary among surveyors. The "captive agent" is theoretically limited to the company he represents and the "independent agent" to his several companies. The broker, consultant, and insurance administrator are free of all contractual restraints and have access to all the markets in the world which have the facilities for handling the account. Each insurance practitioner must operate in accordance with his particular environment to produce the lowest cost consistent with adequate coverage and service requirements.

PREPARING THE SURVEY REPORT

Significant results and conclusions of the survey must be communicated to the client in an appropriate manner. The essence of every survey report is "What is wrong?" and "What should be done about it?" Comments and recommendations usually relate to the absence of essential protection, indemnity inadequate in scope or amount, errors in policies and forms, and premium costs. A verbal report may be made on the small, uncomplicated account. A letter may be the medium for a larger account. For the very large and complex commercial or industrial account, the written report may run 50 pages or more and include technical data and other exhibits as an appendix. The controlling objective in the selection of report media is to inform the client and to induce corrective action. Verbosity is a greater sin than brevity. Among the learned professions the techniques of the doctor are more to be emulated than those of the lawyer or minister. If one is having a complete physical examination, the doctor will require a variety of tests, such as urinalysis, blood, X-ray, fluoroscope, basal metabolism, gastrointestinal series, and electrocardiogram. When these have been analyzed by qualified technicians and evaluated by him, he will give a brief summary, usually verbal, telling what was found to be wrong and what should be done about it, supplemented when necessary by written prescriptions and instructions. If the doctor followed the practices of some insurance surveyors, he would spend hours or days with the patient going through the detail of each highly technical report, with the result that the patient would be only slightly better informed, very confused, and probably frightened half to death. The insurance buyer or top corporate executive is rarely interested in a play-by-play account of the tedious technical studies which are the basis of the survey report. Essentially, he wants to know in the medical sense "What did you find wrong and what should I do about it?" and in the business sense "Can you save me money without impairing my coverage?"

Regardless of the size of the account, the technical work must be well done and will involve considerable paper work. This work is the foundation of the report. The succeeding step should be to reduce this mass of data to a comprehensive, but considerably less voluminous, report which, in most instances, need not be put into finished form. This condensed report should then be studied and the essence extracted in the form of succinctly stated conclusions of "What's wrong and what should be done" which then becomes the condensed "Survey Summary" to be typed and delivered. When consolidated with the previously completed "Summary of Insurance Prior to Survey" and the "Schedule of Recommended Insurance," the report to the client or management is complete. Where the insured has a professionally qualified corporate risk manager, the survey report may be a complete typing of the first summary to permit elaboration upon the basis of the comments and recommendations. Because of his greater technical knowledge and his corporate responsibility, the risk manager requires a report in considerably more depth than does the general corporate executive.

DELIVERY OF THE SURVEY REPORT

Written survey reports submitted by mail have a notoriously low success ratio. Sometimes they are set aside until there is "more time." At other times they are used by the insured as a basis for bargaining with his present insurance representatives for better coverage or lower rates, and the surveyor is uncompensated for his work unless he has had the foresight to provide for fee compensation for the survey.

The better delivery method is the prearranged interview at which all persons interested or involved are present, with adequate time available for the necessary discussion. The three parts of the survey report serve as an agenda for the meeting.[1] As previously mentioned, it is advisable to have both the detailed survey and the underlying work papers available for reference but none of this information should be volunteered—nor provided—unless the insured requests further data or rejects a recommendation. In the latter event, the underlying data may contain convincing analytical material which can be used to achieve the objective. Decisions made should be recorded by notation on the working copy of the Survey Summary and if possible, initialed by the client. All authorizations essential to carrying out the accepted recommendations should be obtained at the interview, such as "Broker of Record" letters, rating board authorizations, and so on.

As soon as practicable after the meeting, the surveyor should write a letter fully setting forth the decisions which have been made. This letter

[1] These parts are: "Schedule of Insurance Prior to Survey," "Comments and Recommendations," and "Recommended Program."

serves the dual purpose of businesslike confirmation and affords the client the opportunity of correcting misunderstandings or rescinding any decisions which, upon further reflection, he would prefer to change.

Confirmation should be followed by prompt execution and delivery of the authorized changes. Records of expirations should be made on those items which are not taken over by the surveyor to serve as a future reminder for further solicitation. A revised Insurance Record Book, reflecting the changes made, should be delivered to the insured and, according to the size and activity of the account, a survey review schedule should be established for future servicing.

SALVAGING THE UNSUCCESSFUL SURVEY

Not all surveys are economically successful for the practitioner. Sometimes this outcome is due to the fact that he did not have a valid competitive opportunity from the beginning because the insurance account was handled by some close friend or relative who could not be displaced. Sometimes it is because the account was already in such excellent condition that no major improvements were possible. Finally, the surveyor may not have done a good technical job or may have done a good job but erred in his method of presentation or salesmanship. There is much to be learned from failures and, to avoid a total waste of time, the surveyor should analyze each one in the hope of learning a valuable lesson. If he fails a few times because he did not have a chance from the beginning, he will soon learn to ferret out such situations before beginning his work. Perhaps he may even go so far as to require a letter of commitment from the insured to the effect that if major improvements result the surveyor will get the business or a fee for his services. If the account has been well handled by the present insurance representatives, the surveyor should say so forthrightly and go on to the next job. People and conditions change constantly; and, if he has left a good impression, he stands a better chance of future business than if he becomes a disgruntled loser. If failure is attributable to poor technical work or poor salesmanship, better techniques must be learned to avoid duplicating either of these mistakes in the future. Finally, after making an adverse decision, the client often will feel sufficient obligation to the surveyor to candidly tell him where he made his mistakes. Human nature being what it is, this approach will often leave the door open to an account for a second try or result in a referral to another prospect.

TRENDS

From its inception the insurance survey has demonstrated its value as a medium of more and better sales of insurance, thereby fulfilling the marketing concept. In recent years professionalism, as distinct from pure sales motivation, has been increasingly introduced by a number of surveyors who were sufficiently independent to have such freedom—principally brokers and consultants. Currently the questionnaire forms are being studied as a potentially suitable basic document for risk recognition by the corporate risk manager. The maturing of the "all risk" trend is lending realism to the broad categories of "property," "consequential," and "liability" losses. "Package" policies are compelling unified consideration of entire programs. As a result, the employment of insurance survey principles will expand and techniques will be simplified and improved for the benefit of all concerned.

SUGGESTED READINGS

CRIDDLE, A. HAWTHORNE. "Evaluation of Risk," *Risk Management* (ed. H. WAYNE SNIDER). Homewood, Ill.: Richard D. Irwin, Inc., 1964. Chap. 2.

DENENBERG, HERBERT S., *et al.* *Risk and Insurance.* Englewood Cliffs, N.J.: Prentice-Hall, Inc., 1964. Chap. 6.

WILLIAMS, C. ARTHUR, JR., AND HEINS, RICHARD M. *Risk Management and Insurance.* New York: McGraw-Hill Book Co., Inc., 1964. Chaps. 7–9 plus review cases.

Chapter 76

INSURING AMERICAN RISKS ABROAD

BY E. A. G. MANTON

Americans are to be found all over the globe and there are considerable American investments in foreign lands. Officials in the Department of State say that in January, 1963, there were some 1,750,000 U.S. citizens abroad—with about 1,050,000 in the Armed Forces, some 100,000 civilian employees of the U.S. Government, and about 600,000 private citizens.[1]

Department of Defense figures for January, 1963, show that members and employees of the United States Armed Forces and their dependents owned more than 170,000 private automobiles overseas.[2] At least 150,000 automobiles are owned by other U.S. citizens abroad. The number of American tourists abroad is estimated at over a million annually. These Americans require the usual range of personal insurance—on automobiles, residences, household goods, personal effects, accident and health, personal liability, and so on.

According to the U.S. Department of Commerce private U.S. investments in plants and property abroad in 1963 totaled over $40 billion, whereas in 1950 it was less than $12 billion![3] Roughly a third is invested in Canada, territorially (and about a fourth in the petroleum industry, industrially). This figure leaves the Western Hemisphere excluding Canada with $9,875,000,000; the United Kingdom with $4,216,000,000; the European Common Market with $4,471,000,000; the rest of Europe with $1,664,000,000; Africa with $1,423,000,000; Asia with $2,784,000,000; Australia with $1,277,000,000; and another $1,919,000,000 in some combination of these places.

American contractors annually undertake hundreds of millions of dollars of work all over the world. These projects range from large public

[1] This information was included in a letter dated Jan. 15, 1963, from the Chamber of Commerce of the United States.

[2] This information was included in a letter dated Jan. 16, 1963, from the Chamber of Commerce of the United States.

[3] *Survey of Current Business*, Vol. 44, No. 8 (August, 1964), pp. 10–11.

works, to construction of oil refineries and industrial plants of all kinds, to erection of private homes. Thus, the American foreign stake is huge, involving considerable insurance requirements and an estimated $250,-000,000 of annual premiums.

CHOICE OF MARKET

An insured with foreign exposures may chose to "self-insure" (with a few exceptions of compulsory insurance) or to insure. (See Chapters 58 and 72.) If insuring, he must choose between admitted and nonadmitted insurance, or perhaps choose a combination of both, with the following criteria prominently in mind:

1. *Type of Carrier*—Are the proposed carriers organized so as to be able to provide the type and extent of insurance needed?
2. *Policies and Forms*—Do contracts offered cover the hazards involved and are amounts of insurance and limits of liability adequate?
3. *Service*—Do proposed agents, brokers, and carriers offer reasonable services of risk analysis, inspection, loss prevention, and claims service?
4. *Solvency*—Are proposed carriers able to meet all obligations?
5. *Price*—Are premiums charged reasonable in relation to the hazards involved and to policies, forms, and services offered?

Admitted Insurance

In the context of this chapter the term "admitted insurance" refers to that which is placed locally in the country in which the property is located or other exposure exits. (For a slightly different usage of the term, see Chapter 67.)

The arguments usually advanced for placing risks locally are:

1. Local management is better equipped to buy protection against local hazards than is home office management which, presumably, cannot be fully familiar with all local requirements and other local conditions. (There is some truth in this contention provided that local management has technically competent insurance advice.)
2. Local placement generates goodwill. (This argument, logically extended, would cover all procurement. At some point such goodwill, if created at all, would come only at the expense of considerable sacrifice of corporate profit.)
3. If the risk is in a soft currency area, insurance should be placed locally to utilize otherwise unuseable currency. (If, however, the property can only be replaced for hard money, recovery in inconvertible currency will not provide funds for replacement.)
4. If nonadmitted insurance is illegal, local insurance is necessary.
5. If there is local shareholding in the affiliate, an understanding may exist that insurance will be placed locally. If local insurance companies lend money to the affiliate, they may demand the insurance.

Nonadmitted Insurance

As its name implies, nonadmitted insurance is placed with insurers not licensed in the territory where the risk is located.

There may be substantial advantages to nonadmitted insurance. These may include: contracts in English and insurance in U.S. dollars; advantageous policies and forms compared to those available locally which may not satisfy the insured's requirements (for instance, many local markets do not issue deductible forms); economical premiums compared to those in local markets; a single coordinated coverage which may be cheaper for risks in several territories; and avoidance of the possibility of excessive commissions for business placed in the local market.

There are also disadvantages to nonadmitted insurance. Many countries prohibit nonadmitted insurance or levy a special tax on the premiums. Some countries do not permit nonadmitted premiums to be expensed for income tax. Some jurisdictions prohibit insurance agents and adjusters from rendering any service on nonadmitted insurance. Claims service, consequently, may be impeded, especially with respect to liability coverages.

Most American corporations operate overseas through locally incorporated subsidiaries. Some of the foregoing disadvantages in using nonadmitted insurance formerly were overcome by the parent insuring under the so-called "holding company clause" its interest in the capital stock of the uninsured subsidiary. If the subsidiary, being uninsured, sustained a loss, its net worth was diminished by the amount of that loss. The parent company suffered a diminution of its ownership. The parent recovered such diminution under the holding company clause. However, the U.S. Internal Revenue Service now rules that such recoveries constitute an involuntary dividend and are taxable as income.

There are thus pros and cons to admitted and nonadmitted insurance. In either case there is a wide choice of markets available.

LOCAL MARKETS

Even when the broad choice is made to place the insurance locally—that is, in the foreign country—numerous questions remain as to the operation of the carrier, type of contract, service rendered by the carrier or its affiliated organizations, solvency, and price. In this section of the chapter some of these details of local placement of insurance of American risks abroad will be considered.

Carriers

Most of the countries in which Americans visit, own property, or transact business permit the operation of private insurers. Most countries, however, do pose restrictions of one sort or another. For example, several countries, such as Peru, permit private carriers but only if they are locally incorporated. Frequently there is a limit on the percentage of foreign ownership permitted in national companies. Most of such companies are permitted to maintain reinsurance connections with American or other foreign companies.

Other countries, such as Uruguay, permit operation only of companies which were established there before a certain date. Some countries, such as Sweden, will not permit creation of new companies unless necessity or convenience is proved. Others, like Chile, permit new domestic companies only. Such limitations effectively discriminate against U.S. insurance companies whose interest in the foreign field is comparatively recent. Fortunately, many countries still freely admit foreign companies provided they meet reasonable legal requirements.

Operation in Less Developed Countries. As an illustration of how these carriers may operate in "less developed" countries, consider a "typical" small country in this "less developed" category. There may be, say, 30 companies operating in this country with 10 or so being companies incorporated locally (the term "national" will be used in this chapter to refer to such firms) and the remainder being foreign (that is, alien) admitted companies. Of the latter group three or four are likely to be American. A few of the foreign companies will operate through branch offices; the majority through general agencies. These offices and the head offices of the national companies are likely to be located in the capital of the country.

Some national companies may be owned wholly or partly by foreign companies. The leading national companies are almost invariably owned by wealthy and influential local families and their associates.

Normally there is some sort of organization known as the "Association of Insurance Companies" or by some similar name, to which possibly all will belong. This organization is the center for discussing matters of common interest and deciding common problems such as drafting standard contractual provisions and revising tariffs or rate manuals.

The local association may be linked with the "Fire Offices Committee (Foreign)" and "Accident Offices Association (Overseas)" in London which provide technical information and advice. These British organizations make available to the local association and the local companies their highly valuable experience gained through operation in many countries over many years.

The local association will be governed by a committee with rotating membership. The principal national companies and perhaps leading foreign companies will normally be permanent members of this governing committee. As a general pattern, the governing committee establishes several subcommittees. Usually, one of these subcommittees handles rating matters.

In the typical market in a "less developed" country, insurance intermediaries are likely to be primarily producers and not necessarily qualified to provide services such as risk analysis and inspection. The leading national companies often write the business of their principal shareholders without an intermediary. Moreover, in numerous instances, foreign (for example, American or British) companies write certain business such as mercantile directly. Thus, much business, which might call for a technically qualified intermediary, is tied to a specific carrier. Whether or not the business is written directly, rating and inspection generally are handled by the companies. The intermediaries generally secure commissions primarily for introducing business.

Companies operating in the "less developed" countries normally have agents in the provinces with limited authority to accept and issue simple policies; but any unusual risks must be referred to the principal office (in the capital). On occasion, in foreign companies the proposals must be referred to the home office. An American, intending to place his insurance locally, may find it difficult to locate a qualified intermediary. Conditions, however, are rapidly changing. At one time there were no real brokers in South America, for instance, but today there are many, including several U.S. brokers with branch offices or correspondents.

In some of these small countries competition involves increased commissions rather than reduced rates. When commissions are excessive for production services, producers rebate to clients. This condition is deplorable but still a fact of life in many countries.

Operation in More Advanced Countries. In many countries which could not comfortably be classified as "less developed" the insurance market is not essentially different from that just described. The Fire Offices Committee and Accident Offices Association in London, for instance, perform much the same services as local associations but are fully equipped with a technical staff, and the rating systems are more elaborate as becomes an industrialized country.

There is often a substantial "nontariff" market which sometimes makes its own rates; but "nontariff" rates are usually a discount from the tariff, justified perhaps by the preferred nature of the risks underwritten.

Britain and the more advanced countries of Europe have excellent brokerage houses which give first class service. Local agencies also exist, and sometimes large brokerage firms with provincial branches act as agents. (The difference between agent and broker today often seems to be that the agent gets more commission!)

In Britain some companies write business directly and even pay the insured a commission as a so-called "own case" agent, but most large firms employ brokers, feeling the need of professional advice and assistance.

British companies introduced direct writing when they began to operate overseas. As indicated in the previous section, direct writing is a substantial activity in less developed countries. The increasing complexity of risks, however, seems to be causing companies in advanced countries to move away from direct writing—perhaps in order to provide more service to policyholders.

Policies

Local policies are naturally in the language of the country involved and may occasion serious difficulty if English translations are not available.

It is unwise to rely upon a general description, such as that a policy covers fire, because, for instance, the policy may exclude fire following windstorm, earthquake, riot, and such. Failure to appreciate and provide for such local peculiarities may be costly. As another example of difficulty, one finds that limits of liability under local automobile and general liability policies may appear adequate for local purposes but may leave the American insured improperly protected if sued in some U.S. court. Generalizations in this chapter and on this subject are dangerous as evidenced by the fact that in some countries automobile policies are unlimited—at least for bodily injury claims.

Many gaps in coverage in local policies are curable for additional premium; but any policy offered abroad needs careful scrutiny to determine whether it covers the exposure to which the insured is subjected.

The policy normally provides that claims are payable in local currency. If the currency is freely convertible, no particular difficulty arises; but, if it is nonconvertible or subject to exchange restrictions, it may not be suitable for property which can only be replaced from the U.S.A. Ability to replace rapidly may be vital. If hard currency is not readily available, delay may be serious. Unfortunately, exchange control countries often prohibit U.S. dollar insurance.

Service

Good agency and brokerage service is available in more advanced countries and the quality of service worldwide has tended to improve. In some countries it is advisable to consider carefully the choice of an intermediary because many offer mostly placement service and the minimum of other services.

Engineering and loss prevention services are generally well behind comparable services offered by the U.S. insurance industry. With some exceptions, underwriters tend to insure risks as they are and not to engage in risk improvement and accident prevention.

Claims for losses to the insured's own property are normally settled promptly. Third-party claims service varies widely and is in part dependent upon the legal system of the country involved. There is a wide variance between the best service available and poor or even average service. Before selecting a carrier the insured *should investigate its repu-*

tation for claims service! This point is relatively more important in insuring American risks abroad than it is in insuring risks in the United States.

Sometimes carriers deem their obligations limited to reimbursement and leave insureds in effect to settle their own claims. Some carriers deliberately delay settlement of third-party claims when high interest rates make it worthwhile to hang on to money.

Any American who is subject to suit in the U.S.A. or contemplates early return home should make certain that the carrier will defend him in state and/or federal courts in the United States and that it is equipped to do so. Local carriers sometimes do not cover suits outside their own courts.

Solvency

Most carriers operating outside the United States are solvent and of high repute. Yet there are enough of questionable standing to make caution advisable. Often, too little heed is paid to the financial standing of the carrier. Premiums spent with a carrier unable to respond to its liability is, at best, money wasted. At the worst it can also lead to catastrophic failure to cover losses.

Published balance sheets of foreign companies are not always sufficiently informative, and publications like *Best's* are not usually available. In many cases there is no insurance "commissioner" to whom to appeal and even where there is such an official, his standard of supervision may be perfunctory. A small company undertaking big risks and relying extensively on reinsurance may get into difficulties if something goes wrong with the reinsurer. Moreover, reinsurance provides no direct protection to the insured in case of insolvency of the fronting company.

It is usually possible to ascertain a company's condition through careful inquiry, for example through the banks, and it is certainly advisable to check a carrier not already well known to the insured.

Pricing

While consideration of price to the exclusion of policy, form, service, and solvency may be poor economy, the rate charged is obviously of major concern. The ratemaking process is never entirely satisfactorily resolved in the foreign field. Few companies have sufficiently credible volume to make their own rates.

The typical local association (referred to earlier) is the center of ratemaking in most foreign countries. Frequently, the statistical information available is sketchy partly because members may have inadequate statistical departments or may be reluctant to present information to a committee including competitors and partly because the total experience for a given class may lack credibility.

Generally, local associations make only rates for fire (and allied perils such as riot and civil commotion, windstorm, and earthquake), automobile, and workmen's compensation (if workmen's compensation may be transacted by private insurers). Since these lines in the aggregate probably represent 80 percent or more of the premium income of the country, the pricing of the remaining lines is normally left to the discretion of the writing companies.

The Fire Offices Committee (Foreign) and Accident Offices Association (Overseas) of London still provide technical assistance or actual ratemaking service to many local associations. With the development of so many territories and national companies, however, this help is a waning factor.

Fire and Windstorm Rates. While some exceptions exist, fire business is normally class rated in most countries other than the United States. This system is reasonably satisfactory for simple risks but is unsatisfactory for industrial risks which vary markedly in construction, layout, protection, size, and management. For such cases special rates are sometimes promulgated by the rating committee. Such special rates normally must be supported by an application of the submitting company. The company officials are often armed with an inspection report and with information about similar risks in other countries. Much depends upon the ingenuity and standing of the submitting company. The more it is respected in the market, the more likely the application is to be approved. Sometimes considerations of reciprocity count and a special rate may be more readily approved if committee members feel that they will share in the risk.

In territories susceptible to windstorm there may be a windstorm tariff, with rates based upon construction and classification of contents according to susceptibility to damage. In earthquake areas there will usually be rates for fire following earthquake, but shock damage is frequently not tariff rated.

The problem of inadequate statistics looms large. Inevitably, a large element of judgment is involved. Basic class rates are revised infrequently, and the tendency is toward proliferation of special rates which do rough justice among risks, mitigating somewhat the apparent injustice of class rates.

Automobile Rates. Automobile rating procedures are basically no different from those for fire in most countries. The typical automobile tariff is based on the so-called comprehensive policy denoting a coverage of fire, theft, collision, and third-party liability. Theft is often limited to theft of the entire vehicle. Sometimes such policies may be extended for extra premium to additional named perils.

Rates for these comprehensive policies appear in two basic sections—private passenger automobiles and commercial vehicles. They are scaled according to the horsepower of the vehicle and to the value insured. For limited coverage a reduction is allowed—one third if collision is eliminated and one half if coverage is third-party only. There are reductions for deductibles. Deductibles, by the way, frequently apply to the whole policy, including third-party liability claims.

Often rating plans allow a "no-claim bonus" for not submitting claims. A typical "no-claim bonus" schedule is as follows:

Period without Claim	*Discount on Renewal Premium*
1 year	10%
2 years	15
3 years	20

In most cases rates apply to the whole country. Even large countries have few rating territories. Tariffs usually allow fleet reductions according to the number of vehicles but often provide no adequate means of rating large fleets, for which the rating committee may promulgate special rates.

Inadequate statistics mar automobile rating just as they mar other rating. Revisions are relatively infrequent and the automobile business tends to be unprofitable, particularly where inflation is rampant. When the situation becomes intolerable, it is met by across-the-board increases. Since statistical refinements may be almost wholly lacking, selectivity according to experience is seldom built into the revisions.

Workmen's Compensation Rates. The third major class of business subject to local tariffs is workmen's compensation insurance. Ratings are normally on payroll in simple occupational classifications. Experience ratings are usually absent from tariffs, but large or unusual risks may be specially rated in some countries. Retrospective rating is quite unusual.

Workmen's compensation insurance by private carriers is gradually disappearing outside the United States. Many countries have incorporated workmen's compensation into their social security systems. A few have competitive state funds.

Marine Insurance Rates. Marine insurance is traditionally not subject to tariffs but there are certain schedules and principles of general application. The most obvious are the "War Risk" rates. "War Risk" rates promulgated in London are generally observed in most overseas markets. A few countries, notably in South America, do issue marine tariffs. The "Joint Hull Understanding" generally applies to hulls rated in London. Since the London market provides much capacity for ocean fleets, this agreement plays an important role in rating of such business. As marine risks are often insured in two or more carriers, the leading underwriter is often highly influential in fixing rates.

Control of Rates. Government supervision varies widely from country to country. Many countries—as already noted—have no insurance "commissioner;" others, although possessing such an official, exercise no official control over rates. They may exercise control unofficially when politically expedient. A few countries require filing but exercise no rate control. A growing number require filing with and prior approval by the insurance "commissioner." The efficacy of supervision varies with the technical resources at the "commissioner's" disposal. At times, because of the lack of staff and money, supervision is perfunctory.

Many countries in Latin America and Asia have "Reinsurance Banks" with which writing companies are compelled to reinsure. These institutions, owned in whole or in part by the state, frequently join in the ratemaking process, sometimes to the point of being in effect the final arbiter of rates to be applied.

Rate regulation in the overseas field thus runs the gamut from a fairly general "free-for-all" on rate structure under casual government aegis, as in Belgium, to a rather rigid control of rates, as in Brazil. In virtually every country, however, some form of rate competition exists. In the markets where tariffs do not exist—or are not observed even if they do exist—about the only restraint on reducing rates to the near-vanishing point is the difficulty in finding other insurers or reinsurers willing to follow the lead. In other markets where the government or the reinsurance banks take rate regulation more seriously, competition takes many ingenious approaches. As has been observed, "special rates" are heavily used to obtain and retain business. Enterprising brokers, agents, or underwriters may be able to secure lower rates by reclassifying risks or by suggesting improvements in layout and/or protection. Furthermore, in many countries rates are nominally maintained at the "proper" level but are, in fact, undermined by rebates. In one way or another competition manifests itself.

The "International Markets" (in the U.S., London, and on the Continent) may be used to advantage, especially by an insured having exposures in several different countries, and yet still retain the character of local placement. A coordinated program can be arranged between international insurers and companies admitted in the various countries where exposures exist on the understanding that the business will be placed by reinsurance or other means in these insurers operating in the international market.

NONADMITTED MARKETS[4]

As opposed to being placed locally, a risk may be offered on a nonadmitted basis. Lloyd's is primarily a nonadmitted market.

The nonadmitted markets offer substantial advantages to corporations with exposures in several different countries. Such an arrangement en-

[4] Readers are reminded that this term is used from the point of view of the country where the exposure exists. Thus, in respect to, say, Turkey a U.S. insurance company not "admitted" to write insurance in Turkey is a part of the "nonadmitted market."

ables the corporation-insured to take maximum advantage of buying power because the carrier can average the good and the bad. The nonadmitted insurer—where judicious—can arrange to have some of the business placed in the local market. This "judiciousness" may arise through convenience or legal necessity.

The major nonadmitted markets are now found in London, on "the Continent," and in the United States. Each market is described briefly in this section.

London Market

The London market is at one and the same time a market for risks in Britain and a great international market with large capacity for insuring virtually any risk anywhere. It consists of British companies, American companies operating in Britain, other foreign (to Britain) companies operating in Britain, and Lloyd's.

The market may be divided into "marine" and "nonmarine," with the latter being subdivided into "tariff" and "nontariff." The marine market retains its position of preeminence. No other market can compare in size, range of commitments, and capacity. It is very competitive, with the degree of competition depending largely upon the brokers' ingenuity in formulating and presenting proposals to underwriters. Except for small risks, brokers must place business among many underwriters. The brokers usually first establish terms with a leading underwriter and then "peddle" their risks. Usually, two or three underwriters acquire special knowledge of a particular type of risk and a broker may find it impossible to complete his placement unless it is led by one of these recognized leaders. Thus, although the marine market is very large, a dozen or so underwriters practically determine the terms applicable to all except relatively small risks. (See also Chapter 17 for a discussion of British marine underwriting.)

A good deal of nonmarine business is written in the marine market. This market is used to provide additional capacity for large "shore risks." No "nationwide definitions" differentiate the large marine from the nonmarine market, and sometimes nonmarine underwriters complain that their marine colleagues are poaching.

The nonmarine market deals with every conceivable kind of risk that is not definitely marine. The tariff side is handled by the major British insurance companies and many commonwealth and foreign companies entered in Great Britain. These companies belong to the Fire Offices Committee for fire business and the Accident Offices Association for automobile and "casualty" business. The nontariff market consists of Lloyd's and numerous small companies, many controlled by brokerage firms. There are also a few large nontariff companies.

For a variety of reasons tariff companies play the more important role in the nonmarine market. The principal reason is that with numerous branch offices and agencies throughout the world, the larger companies constitute a formidable production organization which most nontariff companies and Lloyd's can scarcely match. The nature of Lloyd's, incidentally, precludes branch offices. Although numerous producers can effect Lloyd's covers, this arrangement is not the equivalent of a branch system.

Continental Markets

No market on the continent of Europe can compare to London in capacity or scope. Nevertheless, many fine insurance companies headquartered in Europe have a long history of international operations and capacity for coverage of American risks, especially if these are concentrated on the Continent.

Frequently, this capacity is mobilized as part of a London placement. It is not unusual for part of such placements to be with European companies through their branch offices or representatives in London.

Insurance companies incorporated in one Common Market country are still treated as foreign in the other Common Market countries. Eventually, there is supposed to be a Common Market for services as well as for exchange of goods. Committees currently are studying how companies may operate freely throughout the Common Market.

United States Market

Americans seeking to cover risks overseas need not rely upon local, London, or continental markets because there is a strong market in the United States.

The interest of American insurers in overseas business is comparatively recent. Before World War I, American companies took little interest in foreign business except in contiguous territories—Canada, Mexico, and the Caribbean.

When the war ended, many officials in the American industry felt that the industry ought to play a more important international role. No company had sufficient experience or suitable personnel to engage substantially in overseas business on its own. The natural development seemed to be some venture on a cooperative basis. Accordingly, the American Foreign Insurance Association was formed in New York in 1919 by some important American insurance companies. Originally a fire and marine organization and later extended to include casualty and surety, the AFIA rapidly reached the front rank of insurance organizations operating on an international scale, and today remains the senior American organization offering foreign coverage.

A somewhat similar organization grew out of a general agency called American Asiatic Underwriters founded in December, 1919, in Shanghai,

China, where the United States with several European powers then enjoyed extraterritorial rights. The New York organization, American International Underwriters, was organized in 1926.

In addition to the AFIA and AIU, some individual groups, notably the Insurance Company of North America and certain foreign admitted companies such as the Royal Group, now write insurance on American risks abroad.

These organizations maintain branch offices throughout the United States through which the American insured and his broker or agent may cover risks abroad. They are admitted or have arrangements with locally incorporated companies in every country of the free world.

Several large U.S. brokerage firms have emulated the American insurance companies in creating overseas branches or establishing correspondent arrangements with local brokerage firms.

The existence of a strong market in the U.S. for overseas risks is of paramount interest to the U.S. broker or agent. The American companies cover the free world, thereby enabling the broker or agent to provide for overseas exposures with full confidence they will be adequately serviced and covered in accordance with a program which is worked out and coordinated at every stage. The ability to deal with companies "across the street," as it were, is of great advantage. Time was when any risk overseas had to be placed overseas for lack of an American market, but now there is a wide choice available for coverage of American risks overseas.

CAPTIVE COMPANIES

Captive insurance companies, that is, companies closely controlled by an industrial organization are also used for covering risks abroad. In a sense these fit into the "local market" as previously discussed but are important enough to warrant this special discussion.

The idea of using a captive company for insuring risks abroad is not new and has been used expecially in those countries where wealth has tended to be concentrated in a relatively few hands or families. Thus, for instance, it seemed natural to the prewar Zaibatsus of Japan controlling steel mills, shipping lines, textile factories, banks, etc., that they should also own an insurance company with which to insure the business generated by their other interests. This type of company is not necessarily limited to the business of its owners but is run as an insurance enterprise. It is distinguished from its competitors only in ownership and in possession of a portfolio of preferred business which is invulnerable to competition.

Another type of captive company is one which does not operate as an insurance company in the usual sense. These captives write only business of their owners and usually retain, without reinsurance, amounts exceeding normal retentions of professional insurers. These companies treat risk differently from the way it is usually treated by professional insurers. These companies may reinsure with the professional market on an excess of loss basis, retaining a large deductible. There are several such captive companies now operating, some owned by major international oil companies. There is much current discussion—based largely upon assumed tax savings—concerning the establishment of additional companies of this type. To the extent that captives are based on income tax savings, they are in the long run vulnerable because, in a never-ending game, loopholes eventually get plugged. In the short run, professional insurers will lose business to these captive companies. However, the more the latter are proliferated, the more likely it is that the run will be short.

THE CHOICE

In summary, huge American investments and some 1,750,000 American citizens overseas generate substantial insurance requirements ranging from the simplest forms of personal insurance to the most complicated programs for coverage of large industrial complexes.

The private insurance industry is well able to provide for these insurance needs wherever private insurance enterprise is permitted to function. Fortunately, it is so permitted in most countries where American investment is substantial.

The insured has a wide choice of markets available to him for the coverage of his overseas exposures and should be able to decide on the market which suits him best from the standpoint of carrier, form, service, solvency, and price.

Most importantly, the American insured is able to cover his needs in the American market itself through his own broker or agent but is not confined to that single choice. He may, if he prefers, entrust his insurances to one of the other international markets or place his insurance in the country where the risk is located. In most instances he will probably find it most convenient to arrange his coverages through the American market.

SUGGESTED READINGS

Benedict, Lloyd. "What's Ahead for the International Insurance Manager," *The National Insurance Buyer*, Vol. 10 (July, 1963), pp. 3, 20, 22, 24.

"Insurers' View: Common Market," *The Spectator*, Vol. 170 (June, 1962), pp. 5–8.

"Report on Insurance," *The Monetary Times* (May, 1963), pp. 25–78.

See also articles in the *International Insurance Monitor* and in the following British publications:

Journal of Chartered Insurance Institute
Post Magazine
Review

Appendixes

A. Standard Fire Policy

Standard Fire Insurance Policy for Alabama, Alaska, Arizona, Arkansas, Colorado, Connecticut, Delaware, District of Columbia, Florida, Georgia, Hawaii, Idaho, Illinois, Indiana, Iowa, Kansas, Kentucky, Louisiana, Maryland, Michigan, Mississippi, Missouri, Montana, Nebraska, Nevada, New Hampshire, New Jersey, New Mexico, New York, North Carolina, North Dakota, Ohio, Oklahoma, Oregon, Pennsylvania, Rhode Island, South Carolina, South Dakota, Tennessee, Utah, Vermont, Virginia, Washington, West Virginia, Wisconsin and Wyoming.

No.

CAPITAL STOCK COMPANY

RENEWAL OF NUMBER

UNIFORM PRINTING PRINTED IN U.S.A. AUTHENTIC AND SUPPLY DIVISION

SPACE FOR COMPANY NAME, INSIGNIA, AND LOCATION

Insured's Name and Mailing Address

SPACE FOR PRODUCER'S NAME AND MAILING ADDRESS

Inception (Mo. Day Yr.) Expiration (Mo. Day Yr.) Years

It is important that the written portions of all policies covering the same property read exactly alike. If they do not, they should be made uniform at once.

INSURANCE IS PROVIDED AGAINST ONLY THOSE PERILS AND FOR ONLY THOSE COVERAGES INDICATED BELOW BY A PREMIUM CHARGE AND AGAINST OTHER PERILS AND FOR OTHER COVERAGES ONLY WHEN ENDORSED HEREON OR ADDED HERETO.

AMOUNT	RATE	PREPAID TERM PREMIUM DUE AT INCEPTION	ANNUAL PAYMENT DUE UNDER DEF. PREM. PAY. PLAN	PERIL(S) Insured Against and Coverage(s) Provided (Insert Name of Each)
$	$	$	$	FIRE AND LIGHTNING
XXXXXXX	$	$	$	EXTENDED COVERAGE
	$	$	$	
	$	$	$	
$ TOTAL PREMIUM FOR POLICY TERM UNDER D. P. P. P.		TOTAL(S) $	$	

Item No.	Amount Fire or Fire and Extended Coverage, or Other Peril	Per Cent of Co-Insurance Applicable	DESCRIPTION AND LOCATION OF PROPERTY COVERED **Show construction, type of roof and occupancy of building(s) covered or containing the property covered. If occupied as a dwelling state number of families.**
1. -	$		

Subject to Form No(s). INSERT FORM NUMBER(S) AND EDITION DATE(S) **attached hereto.**

Mortgage Clause: Subject to the provisions of the mortgage clause attached hereto, loss, if any, on building items, shall be payable to:

INSERT NAME(S) OF MORTGAGEE(S) AND MAILING ADDRESS(ES)

Agency at

Countersignature Date

________________________________ Agent

IN CONSIDERATION OF THE PROVISIONS AND STIPULATIONS HEREIN OR ADDED HERETO AND OF the premium above specified, this Company, for the term of *years specified above* from *inception date shown above* At Noon (Standard Time) to *expiration date shown above* At Noon (Standard Time) at location of property involved, to an amount not exceeding the amount(s) above specified, does insure *the insured named above* and legal representatives, to the extent of the actual cash value of the property at the time of loss, but not exceeding the amount which it would cost to repair or replace the property with material of like kind and quality within a reasonable time after such loss, without allowance for any increased cost of repair or reconstruction by reason of any ordinance or law regulating construction or repair, and without compensation for loss resulting from interruption of business or manufacture, nor in any event for more than the interest of the insured, against all **DIRECT LOSS BY FIRE, LIGHTNING AND BY REMOVAL FROM PREMISES ENDANGERED BY THE PERILS INSURED AGAINST IN THIS POLICY, EXCEPT AS HEREINAFTER PROVIDED,** to the property described herein while located or contained as described in this policy, or pro rata for five days at each proper place to which any of the property shall necessarily be removed for preservation from the perils insured against in this policy, but not elsewhere.

Assignment of this policy shall not be valid except with the written consent of this Company.

This policy is made and accepted subject to the foregoing provisions and stipulations and those hereinafter stated, which are hereby made a part of this policy, together with such other provisions, stipulations and agreements as may be added hereto, as provided in this policy.

OTP 14-O-T

Standard Fire Policy (Continued)

Concealment, fraud. This entire policy shall be void if, whether before or after a loss, the insured has wilfully concealed or misrepresented any material fact or circumstance concerning this insurance or the subject thereof, or the interest of the insured therein, or in case of any fraud or false swearing by the insured relating thereto.

Uninsurable and excepted property. This policy shall not cover accounts, bills, currency, deeds, evidences of debt, money or securities; nor, unless specifically named hereon in writing, bullion or manuscripts.

Perils not included. This Company shall not be liable for loss by fire or other perils insured against in this policy caused, directly or indirectly, by: (a) enemy attack by armed forces, including action taken by military, naval or air forces in resisting an actual or an immediately impending enemy attack; (b) invasion; (c) insurrection; (d) rebellion; (e) revolution; (f) civil war; (g) usurped power; (h) order of any civil authority except acts of destruction at the time of and for the purpose of preventing the spread of fire, provided that such fire did not originate from any of the perils excluded by this policy; (i) neglect of the insured to use all reasonable means to save and preserve the property at and after a loss, or when the property is endangered by fire in neighboring premises; (j) nor shall this Company be liable for loss by theft.

Other Insurance. Other insurance may be prohibited or the amount of insurance may be limited by endorsement attached hereto.

Conditions suspending or restricting insurance. Unless otherwise provided in writing added hereto this Company shall not be liable for loss occurring

(a) while the hazard is increased by any means within the control or knowledge of the insured; or

(b) while a described building, whether intended for occupancy by owner or tenant, is vacant or unoccupied beyond a period of sixty consecutive days; or

(c) as a result of explosion or riot, unless fire ensue, and in that event for loss by fire only.

Other perils or subjects. Any other peril to be insured against or subject of insurance to be covered in this policy shall be by endorsement in writing hereon or added hereto.

Added provisions. The extent of the application of insurance under this policy and of the contribution to be made by this Company in case of loss, and any other provision or agreement not inconsistent with the provisions of this policy, may be provided for in writing added hereto, but no provision may be waived except such as by the terms of this policy is subject to change.

Waiver provisions. No permission affecting this insurance shall exist, or waiver of any provision be valid, unless granted herein or expressed in writing added hereto. No provision, stipulation or forfeiture shall be held to be waived by any requirement or proceeding on the part of this Company relating to appraisal or to any examination provided for herein.

Cancellation of policy. This policy shall be cancelled at any time at the request of the insured, in which case this Company shall, upon demand and surrender of this policy, refund the excess of paid premium above the customary short rates for the expired time. This policy may be cancelled at any time by this Company by giving to the insured a five days' written notice of cancellation with or without tender of the excess of paid premium above the pro rata premium for the expired time, which excess, if not tendered, shall be refunded on demand. Notice of cancellation shall state that said excess premium (if not tendered) will be refunded on demand.

Mortgagee interests and obligations. If loss hereunder is made payable, in whole or in part, to a designated mortgagee not named herein as the insured, such interest in this policy may be cancelled by giving to such mortgagee a ten days' written notice of cancellation.

If the insured fails to render proof of loss such mortgagee, upon notice, shall render proof of loss in the form herein specified within sixty (60) days thereafter and shall be subject to the provisions hereof relating to appraisal and time of payment and of bringing suit. If this Company shall claim that no liability existed as to the mortgagor or owner, it shall, to the extent of payment of loss to the mortgagee, be subrogated to all the mortgagee's rights of recovery, but without impairing mortgagee's right to sue; or it may pay off the mortgage debt and require an assignment thereof and of the mortgage. Other provisions relating to the interests and obligations of such mortgagee may be added hereto by agreement in writing.

Pro rata liability. This Company shall not be liable for a greater proportion of any loss than the amount hereby insured shall bear to the whole insurance covering the property against the peril involved, whether collectible or not.

Requirements in case loss occurs. The insured shall give immediate written notice to this Company of any loss, protect the property from further damage, forthwith separate the damaged and undamaged personal property, put it in the best possible order, furnish a complete inventory of the destroyed, damaged and undamaged property, showing in detail quantities, costs, actual cash value and amount of loss claimed; **and within sixty days after the loss, unless such time is extended in writing by this Company, the insured shall render to this Company a proof of loss,** signed and sworn to by the insured, stating the knowledge and belief of the insured as to the following: the time and origin of the loss, the interest of the insured and of all others in the property, the actual cash value of each item thereof and the amount of loss thereto, all encumbrances thereon, all other contracts of insurance, whether valid or not, covering any of said property, any changes in the title, use, occupation, location, possession or exposures of said property since the issuing of this policy, by whom and for what purpose any building herein described and the several parts thereof were occupied at the time of loss and whether or not it then stood on leased ground, and shall furnish a copy of all the descriptions and schedules in all policies and, if required, verified plans and specifications of any building, fixtures or machinery destroyed or damaged. The insured, as often as may be reasonably required, shall exhibit to any person designated by this Company all that remains of any property herein described, and submit to examinations under oath by any person named by this Company, and subscribe the same; and, as often as may be reasonably required, shall produce for examination all books of account, bills, invoices and other vouchers, or certified copies thereof if originals be lost, at such reasonable time and place as may be designated by this Company or its representative, and shall permit extracts and copies thereof to be made.

Appraisal. In case the insured and this Company shall fail to agree as to the actual cash value or the amount of loss, then, on the written demand of either, each shall select a competent and disinterested appraiser and notify the other of the appraiser selected within twenty days of such demand. The appraisers shall first select a competent and disinterested umpire; and failing for fifteen days to agree upon such umpire, then, on request of the insured or this Company, such umpire shall be selected by a judge of a court of record in the state in which the property covered is located. The appraisers shall then appraise the loss, stating separately actual cash value and loss to each item; and, failing to agree, shall submit their differences, only, to the umpire. An award in writing, so itemized, of any two when filed with this Company shall determine the amount of actual cash value and loss. Each appraiser shall be paid by the party selecting him and the expenses of appraisal and umpire shall be paid by the parties equally.

Company's options. It shall be optional with this Company to take all, or any part, of the property at the agreed or appraised value, and also to repair, rebuild or replace the property destroyed or damaged with other of like kind and quality within a reasonable time, on giving notice of its intention so to do within thirty days after the receipt of the proof of loss herein required.

Abandonment. There can be no abandonment to this Company of any property.

When loss payable. The amount of loss for which this Company may be liable shall be payable sixty days after proof of loss, as herein provided, is received by this Company and ascertainment of the loss is made either by agreement between the insured and this Company expressed in writing or by the filing with this Company of an award as herein provided.

Suit. No suit or action on this policy for the recovery of any claim shall be sustainable in any court of law or equity unless all the requirements of this policy shall have been complied with, and unless commenced within twelve months next after inception of the loss.

Subrogation. This Company may require from the insured an assignment of all right of recovery against any party for loss to the extent that payment therefor is made by this Company.

IN WITNESS WHEREOF, this Company has executed and attested these presents; but this policy shall not be valid unless countersigned by the duly authorized Agent of this Company at the agency hereinbefore mentioned.

INSERT SIGNATURES AND TITLES OF PROPER OFFICERS

B. Development of Guiding Principles for First-Party Property Losses and Claims

BY W. D. SWIFT[1]

Loss adjustment problems are created when two or more insurance contracts provide overlapping coverages. The insurance industry, consequently, has developed a statement on "Guiding Principles" for handling such overlaps. The statement is dated November 1, 1963, and its full name is *Guiding Principles: Casualty—Fidelity—Fire—Inland Marine; First-Party Property Losses and Claims.* The statement sets forth the general pattern by which losses are shared between or among the insurers whose coverages overlap. Readers interested in the details (which are formidable) of this statement are urged to obtain a copy and study it.[2]

The purpose of this appendix is: (1) to review briefly the background, development, and general nature of these "Guiding Principles"; (2) to present excerpts from the formal statement of "Guiding Principles"; (3) to intersperse within these excerpts brief general comments; and (4) to provide a brief summary suggesting the major import of the "Guiding Principles." Ideally, the full statement, instead of excerpts, would be reproduced. Limitations, however, preclude such an approach. The full statement has numerous and extensive examples which are very helpful but also very lengthy. They are recommended to interested readers.

BACKGROUND

In these days of complex insurance coverages and frustrating overlap it is hard to realize that until a few years ago apportionment problems were confined almost exclusively to the fire side of the business. Most of those difficulties, which by comparison now seem minor, were resolved by way of recommended rules of apportionment laid down by the Committee on Adjustments of the National Board of Fire Underwriters. That was in 1934—four years before the appearance of the Extended Coverage Endorsement.

With the growth of inland marine business and the advent of "all risk" insurance, new questions arose among the inland marine companies

[1] Deputy General Adjuster, American Insurance Association.

[2] Persons interested in a copy can make their wish known to the author of this Appendix at 85 John Street, New York City.

as to how to apportion two or more of their policies covering the same property and interest. Similarly, disputes arose over apportionment of losses involving an inland marine policy and a fire or casualty policy. Rules were made and "principles" pronounced as needs arose, with little thought being given to orderly development.

This arrangement worked very nicely until the introduction of package policies. After that, multiple-line underwriting resulted in an assortment of broad coverages, the fringe areas of which created an unprecedented variety of overlapping situations. An effort was made to update the existing principles, but one of the major stumbling blocks was an inability to classify the contracts such as Homeowners Policies.

DEVELOPMENT OF A NEW STATEMENT

The problems were discussed by representatives of the various insurance associations, who came to the conclusion that joint action was necessary. The coverage afforded by many of the new policies crossed and recrossed the old jurisdictional lines, rendering it no longer practical to group policies by "segments" of the industry. Accordingly, a committee was assigned the task of developing an overall set of "Guiding Principles." The full committee was not to concern itself about overlapping situations limited to one kind of insurance, that is, fire or the many overlapping situations involving solely casualty or inland marine policies. The aim was to preserve the basic concepts of the then current agreements but at the same time expand them to accommodate most first-party overlapping situations which existed or which could be anticipated. If and when suitable principles were developed, a third-party section was to be incorporated. It was with this philosophy that the first meeting of the committee was held on June 23, 1959.

The new principles were developed by a nine-man committee of company representatives from the Association of Casualty and Surety Companies, the Inland Marine Underwriters Association, and the National Board of Fire Underwriters. This group was assisted by technical advisers from the National Automobile Underwriters Association, the National Bureau of Casualty Underwriters, and the Surety Association of America as well as by staff representatives and consultants from these associations.

Their objective was to find solutions which were to the best long-run interest of the public and the industry, even though some temporary disadvantages might accrue to some particular company or industry group. The thought was that, if the principles were adhered to consistently in all cases, the result over a substantial period of time would offset any inequities growing out of specific apportionments not wholly satisfactory to the particular companies involved. This broad-minded spirit of give-and-take finally brought about an equitable result which lent itself to administration at the field level.

NATURE OF THE STATEMENT

Foreword

The foreword sets forth the major objectives. It reads as follows:

Under practices predating these Guiding Principles, where an overlap in coverage existed between or among policies in the casualty, fire or inland marine classifications of insurance, each such classification participated as a group in the adjustment (subject to extent of available insurance and limiting conditions) without regard to the number of policies involved under each classification.

With the advent of multiple-line policies which cross and re-cross jurisdictional lines, the Associations recommending these Guiding Principles have concluded that, excepting overlap between boiler-machinery policies with any other classification of insurance, it is no longer practical to group policies by "segments" of the industry; rather that each policy should contribute as an individual policy unless it be concurrent with another policy or policies, in which instance such *group of concurrent policies* should contribute as if it were a single policy, subject to the Specific Principles and General Conditions contained herein.

However, retention of the classification concept *is* necessary to determine under which of the Principles certain overlaps are apportioned; namely, casualty, fidelity, fire, inland marine; casualty-casualty, fire-fire, inland-inland. For this purpose, and not to determine concurrent policies, the component coverages found in multiple-line policies should be identified on the basis of their traditional underwriting classification; i.e., the burglary and theft coverages of homeowners policies are casualty; the all-risk personal property coverage found in certain homeowners policies is inland marine.

One idea embodied here is that (1) if two nonconcurrent fire policies overlap with any contract (except a boiler and machinery policy,) (2) if there are no peculiar restrictions on liability, and (3) if all policies are for the same amount, each fire insurer could be responsible for one third of the loss. Under earlier allocation procedures the fire insurers would have been responsible for one half as between themselves.

The Purpose

The purpose, prefaced by a note that the "Guiding Principles" supercede all earlier statements, reads as follows:

Whereas from time to time disputes arise in the adjustment and apportionment of losses and claims because of overlapping coverages, which disputes require litigation or arbitration, and

Whereas the occurrence of such disputes is against the interests of the insuring public and the companies, and

Whereas it is desirable to lay down certain Principles for the Elimination of these disputes,

Therefore Be It Resolved that the Association of Casualty and Surety

Companies, the Inland Marine Underwriters Association, the National Automobile Underwriters Association, the National Board of Fire Underwriters, the National Bureau of Casualty Underwriters and the Surety Association of America recommend to their respective members and subscribers their concurrence in adopting the following Guiding Principles, effective as to losses and claims, other than losses and claims involving retrospective rated policies, occurring on and after *November 1, 1963*.

Unlike some of the previous "Guiding Principles," there are no signatories to the new statement. The various associations will "recommend to their respective members and subscribers their concurrence in adopting them." Adherence is voluntary, as has been the case in the past except for the "Inland Agreements" to which there were signatories. The principles are applicable to losses and claims occurring on and after November 1, 1963.

Retrospectively rated policies are excepted because the insured would be adversely affected when the final premium is calculated.

In the past there has been a tendency on the part of some adjusters and even company officials to apply the "Agreements of Guiding Principles" to spell out coverage under a given contract. This approach is erroneous. The principles were not designed for the purpose of interpreting, adding, or reducing coverage in any given situation. They are solely intended to assist insurance companies in deciding among themselves where the primary liability for loss shall fall in cases involving overlapping coverage. Naturally, the insured may elect to file a claim under any policy affording him the most favorable recovery.

The Plan

Special problems are created by apportionment, excess, pro rata liability, and other clauses. These problems are disposed of as follows:

These Principles provide for the equitable distribution of available insurance. As among insurance companies, the "other insurance" clause(s) which is (are) contained in a policy(ies) of insurance, and which may include an excess provision, shall be set aside and be inoperative to the extent that it is (they are) in conflict with the purpose of these Principles. Otherwise, these Principles will not change coverage or other conditions under any policy(ies) of insurance.

Further, the application of these Principles shall in no event operate to reduce recovery to the insured below that which would have been obtained under any policy or policies covering the risk.

Part I

This part deals "with first-party property losses and claims, except those situations more specifically provided for in Part II (Specific Principles—casualty-casualty, fire-fire, and inland-inland) and the General Conditions." Part I includes: "General Principle 1" (with subdivisions A through G), "General Principle 2" (with subdivisions A through E), and nine "General Conditions."

"General Principle 1" is really an expansion of Principles I–VI of the old "Fire–Inland Agreement." It probably embodies the most important matters of philosophy and probably will be the vehicle for resolving the majority of the questions to arise. General Principle 1 is as follows:

1. Insurance covering same property and same interest:
   - A. Insurance covering a specifically described article or object, whether or not for an express amount, at a designated location shall be primary to any other insurance. (See Notes 1 and 2.)
   - B. Insurance covering a specifically described article or object, whether or not for an express amount, without designation of location shall be excess as to "1–A" but primary as to any other insurance. (See Notes 1 and 2.)
   - C. Insurance covering a specifically described group or class of related articles or objects, whether or not for an express amount, at a designated location shall be excess as to "1–A" and "1–B" but primary as to any other insurance. (See Notes 1 and 2.)
   - D. Insurance covering a specifically described group or class of related articles or objects, whether or not for an express amount, without designation of location shall be excess as to "1–A," "1–B," "1–C" but primary as to any other insurance. (See Notes 1 and 2.)
   - E. Insurance covering at a designated location and not specific as to an article or object or as to group or class of related articles or objects shall be excess as to "1–A," "1–B," "1–C," and "1–D" but primary as to any other insurance. (See Notes 1 and 2.)
   - F. Insurance without designation of location and not specific as to an article or object or as to group or class of related articles or objects shall be excess to "1–A," "1–B," "1–C," "1–D" and "1–E." However, as between insurances without designation of location and not specific as to an article or object or as to group or class of related articles or objects, the policy for the more limited purpose (other than peril) to which the insurance applies shall be primary. (See Notes 1 and 2.)
   - G. Two or more policies providing coverage as set forth in "1–A" through "1–F," respectively, shall be contributing. Contribution shall be as follows:
     - (1) Whether or not deductibles are involved, contribution shall be on the basis of the Limit of Liability Rule except that, in the event there is an area of common coverage under two or more policies and separate coverage under any one or more such policies, the policy or policies affording separate coverage shall respond first to that loss it alone covers and the remainder of its limit of liability shall contribute to the common loss on the basis of the Limit of Liability Rule.
       - (*a*) When one of the policies is subject to a deductible, the amount of loss in excess of the deductible will be considered as the common loss. The policy(ies) without a deductible shall first respond to the loss which it alone covers to the extent of its limit of liability, thereafter the remainder of its limit of liability will contribute with the other insurance to the common loss on the basis of the Limit of Liability Rule.
       - (*b*) When two deductibles are involved, the amount of loss in excess of the higher deductible will be considered as the

common loss. The differential between the higher and lower deductible shall be assessed to the limit of liability of the policy(ies) subject to the lower deductible. The remainder of its limit of liability will contribute with the insurance subject to the higher deductible to the common loss on the basis of the Limit of Liability Rule. Where there are more than two deductibles, the same procedure shall apply. (See Notes 1 and 2.)

NOTE 1. In overlapping situations involving boiler-machinery policies, classifications "1–C," "1–D," "1–E" and "1–F" shall not consider other insurance primary. Therefore, losses will be apportioned in accordance with General Principle 1–G.

Insurance effected on a specifically described article or object as defined in General Principles 1–A and 1–B shall be primary to the boiler-machinery policy. However, a building is not construed in overlapping situations involving boiler-machinery policies as a specifically described "article" or "object."

NOTE 2. In overlapping situations involving burglary policies the term "article" or "object," wherever used in these Principles, is not construed to include Buildings or structures.

Readers can see that in subdivisions A through G the order of precedence as to payment is based on the degree of specific identification of property insured and location. That is, the coverage which is most specifically identified with property and location is most "primary." When the degree of such specific identification is equal as between two policies, they stand in the same order of precedence.

"General Principle 2" in essence covers bailee situations and extends also to "quasi-bailee" and moral obligations. Its wording is:

2. Insurance covering same property and different interests:
   - A. Bailee's customers insurance shall be primary to other insurance effected by the same named bailee-insured. (See General Conditon 8.)
   - B. Insurance secured by a custodian covering property belonging to others shall be primary to any other insurance. Where there is more than one custodian, the insurance of the custodian in possession of the property shall be primary. (See General Condition 8.)

     NOTE: Bankers and brokers blanket bonds, and fidelity, burglary, theft, and jewelers block insurance providing coverage on property "held by the insured in any capacity whether or not the insured is liable for the loss thereof," or with equivalent verbiage, are not construed as insurance covering "different interests" and are not bailee's customers insurance or insurance secured by a custodian covering property belonging to others.

     Exceptions:

     General Principle (2–B) shall not apply:

     (1) when the custodian's insurance is afforded under a policy provision containing the words "property for which the insured is liable," ". . . may be liable," ". . . is legally liable," or equivalent verbiage:

     NOTE: For the purpose of these Guiding Principles the above verbiage is construed to provide liability coverage.

(2) when the owner and custodian of the property have stipulated otherwise by written agreement prior to the loss.

C. Contents policies insuring at the place of the loss and covering "employees'," "partners'" or "executives'" personal property, except in 2–B(1) above, shall be primary to any off-premises coverage available under the employee's insurance. However, insurance covering a specifically described article or object, whether or not for an express amount, shall be primary.

D. Coverage for property "used" or "worn" by the insured, for the property of servants or guests, and insurance afforded by the "physical damage to property" coverage, shall be primary to any available insurance in the name of the owner of the involved property, except insurance covering a specifically described article or object, whether or not an express amount, shall be primary.

E. Installment-Sales or Deferred-Payment Merchandise Insurance:

(1) Evidence of insurance issued by a vendor to a vendee under the provisions of a dual-interest policy specifically or generally describing the article or articles and their values individually or in total as invoiced under a conditional-sales contract shall be deemed to be insurance on specifically described property.

(*a*) Above-described insurance shall be primary when overlapping with other contents policy(ies).

(*b*) Above described insurance shall contribute on the basis of the Limit of Liability Rule when overlapping with insurance expressly describing an article(s) or object(s) whether or not an express amount of insurance applies to each such article(s) or object(s).

(2) When no such evidence of insurance has been issued, the dual-interest policy shall be deemed to be blanket floating insurance.

(*a*) Above-described insurance shall be excess to other contents insurance in those cases where loss occurs at the location shown in the contents policy.

(*b*) Above-described insurance shall contribute on the basis of the Limit of Liability Rule when overlapping with a floater policy. It is to be noted that the ten percent (10%) optional extension of the fire policy is floater coverage.

The nine "General Conditions" amplify "General Principle 1" and "General Principle 2" as follows:

As to General Principles 1 and 2, and any additional Principles or amendments as may hereafter be adopted, it is AGREED that:

1. To provide the greatest recovery to the insured, the insurance declared to be excess or noncontributing under the governing Principle shall not include, in applying any coinsurance, average, or distribution clause(s) contained in any policy(ies), the value or loss on property covered under the insurance declared to be primary. However, it shall include any excess value not covered by the primary insurance and the loss unrecoverable under the primary insurance. When a coinsurance (not reduced rate contribution or average) clause is present in any or all policies, it shall be applied as if it were a reduced rate contribution or reduced rate average clause. However, if by this procedure the insured collects less than he

would collect under the terms of the coinsurance clause, the coinsurance clause shall be applied as such.

2. "Contribution," unless otherwise as specified in General Principle 1–G, shall be on the basis of the applicable limit of liability under each respective policy or group of concurrent policies as though no other insurance existed, and the limit separately determined under each policy or group of concurrent policies shall be the smallest of the following:

    (*a*) the amount of insurance,

    (*b*) the amount of loss, or

    (*c*) the amount payable after applying any policy limitation(s).

   The limits so determined of all policies or groups of concurrent policies herein declared contributing shall be added and, if the total amount exceeds the whole loss, each policy or group of concurrent policies shall pay such proportion of the loss as its limit bears to the sum of all the limits, but if the sum of the limits of liability is less than the whole loss, then each policy or group of concurrent policies shall pay its limit of liability. The determined liability of a group of concurrent policies shall be apportioned pro rata among the policies of the group.

3. Insurance covering property both scheduled and blanket, or both specific as to location and floating, shall be deemed to insure each item or portion separately, and the loss shall be apportioned in accordance with the Principle applying to each item or portion declared to be separately insured. In applying such Condition:

   A. Extensions of coverage in the name of the same insured, whether optional, those creating additional insurance, or based upon a percentage of the principal building or contents policy(ies), whether "permitted" or not, and without reference to inception date, shall be considered as excess to any specific coverage applying to the involved property. However, in the absence of specific insurance, the extensions shall be considered as:

      (1) Blanket insurance for on-premises losses.

         Examples:

            Private structures.
            Rental value.
            Additional living expenses.
            Improvements and betterments.
            Replacement cost coverage.
            Debris removal.

      (2) Floater insurance for off-premises losses.

         Examples:

            Contents while "elsewhere."
            Property removed for preservation from damage caused by the perils insured against.
            Livestock, farm and dairy produce while "elsewhere."

4. When the owner of a building is also the owner of the contents of the building and any overlapping coverage exists involving items of building equipment and fixtures essentially in the nature of *real* property, the building policy(ies) shall be primary.

   Examples: Covered under building policy(ies).

   Antennae and towers—TV, detached—*not* affixed to the building or to an outbuilding.

   Porandas—demountable screened enclosures.

Readily removable equipment and fixtures that are included in the realty mortgage.

Wall-to-wall carpeting only when included in the realty mortgage.

Note: The building policy(ies) shall include, whether in position or stored on the premises, storm doors, storm sash, shades, blinds, wire screens, screen doors and awnings.

5. When the owner of a building is also the owner of the contents of the building and any overlapping coverage exists involving items of building equipment and fixtures essentially in the nature of *personal* property, the contents policy(ies) shall be primary, except when such items are included in the realty mortgage, in which event the policy(ies) covering building shall be primary.

   Examples: Covered under contents policy(ies).

   Antennae and towers—TV, affixed to the building or to an outbuilding.

   Fuel.

   Laundering machines whether or not attached to the realty.

   Portable air-conditioning and ventilating units.

   Refrigerators.

   Stoves.

   Wall-to-wall carpeting when not included in the realty mortgage.
6. Tenant's improvements and betterments insurance shall be primary to building insurance when the insured is owner and occupant of a cooperative apartment. However, the tenant's insurance shall first be made available to the loss on his own property and to property not otherwise insured.
7. The Principle specifically providing the basis of apportionment shall prevail over any Principle more general in scope.
8. Where a bailee's policy(ies) covers his own property, as well as property of others, the bailee's policy(ies) shall first be made available to the loss on the bailee's own property and to property not otherwise insured. Such claim or claims will be adjusted subject to all policy conditions affecting the adjustment, except that value and loss of otherwise insured property shall be deleted from the adjustment. A second statement of loss should then be prepared by the adjuster including all values and loss covered by the terms of the bailee's policy(ies) as written to determine the maximum liability under the policy. Distribution should then be made
   (*a*) to the loss on the bailee's own property and to the loss on otherwise uninsured interests,
   (*b*) to the otherwise insured interests for the difference, if any, up to the maximum liability under the bailee's insurance.

   While right of action under subrogation is retained by the bailors' insurers, the inclusion of the bailee insurer's name in any action against the bailee is contrary to the intent of these Principles. Claim filed by other insurers with the bailee insurers after payment or advance to owners shall be recognized to the same extent as if directly presented by the owner through the bailee in order to fulfill the purpose of these Principles, except where the bailee insurer may have certain facts in connection with a specific claim that justify reimbursement in a sum less than the amount paid by the bailor insurer.
9. Differences of opinion respecting the application or effect of these Principles shall be submitted for arbitration in the manner determined by the

participating Associations. Payments of loss, or advances under loan agreements, or otherwise, shall be without prejudice to the rights of the insurers under these Principles.

Part II

Certain situations involving solely two or more fire policies, two or more inland marine policies, or two casualty policies do not automatically fit into "General Principle 1" or "General Principle 2." Therefore, limited "Specific Principles," designated as Part II of the statement, have been developed.

Readers are reminded that Part II (as well as Part I) pertains to *first-party* losses. When and if a statement is prepared for handling overlapping third-party claims, it will appear as Part III.

Specific principles as to treatment of overlapping *first-party* coverages between or among casualty coverages will be in accordance with procedures set forth in Part I.

The "Fire-Fire Section" takes the place of the old "Non-Concurrent Apportionment Rules," and reads as follows:

Overlap of first-party coverage situations occurring between or among fire coverages only are to be resolved in accordance with General Principles 1–A through 1–G; 2–A through 2–E; General Conditions; Specific Principles and Definitions.

Overlap of first-party coverage situations occurring between or among fire coverages only are to be resolved in accordance with General Principles 1–A through 1–G; 2–A through 2–5; General Conditions; Specific Principles and Definitions.

Explantory Notes and Examples

Under overlapping situations between fire-fire coverages:

1. A building is construed to be an object.
2. The following are construed to be a group of related articles or objects and come within the provisions of General Principle 1–C or 1–D:
   (*a*) stock (merchandise),
   (*b*) machinery,
   (*c*) furniture and fixtures,
   (*d*) improvements and betterments.
3. Coverage on any combination of the above in 1 or 2 and coverage on CONTENTS or on personal property are not construed to be coverage on a group of related articles or objects, but come within the provisions of General Principle 1–E or 1–F.

As an example, suppose that a furniture and fixtures policy has been declared to cover a group or class of related objects. It is, therefore, primary to a contents policy covering the same (plus other) objects. Readers are cautioned to keep in mind that these provisions, and any that may be subsequently added, pertain, as the heading states, solely to overlap between two or more fire policies. In other words, the various "segments" have reserved the right to establish whatever "ground rules" they deem advisable, so long as they do not affect other classifications of insurance.

Considerable thought was given to the underwriting impact of eliminating full contribution by other nonconcurrent insurance, as was formerly done through "Class A and B apportionments." Briefly, the theory was that if an insurer accepted a more limited classification of risk, such as, for example, insuring only "machinery" rather than blanket on "all contents," which would include "machinery," that insurer should expect to respond as a primary insurer to a loss on machinery with the other insurance being excess. Obviously, such insurance written on a specific item or classification may become exhausted before the excess is called into play. For policies written with a Coinsurance Clause, this treatment is not quite as radical as it may sound because noncompliance with the coinsurance requirement (first applied as a reduced rate average clause) will be enforced as to such policy and loss payment reduced accordingly.

The "Inland-Inland Specific Principles" cover another important type of overlap of coverages and are worded as follows:

> Overlap of first-party coverage situations occurring between or among inland coverages only are to be resolved in accordance with General Principles 1–A through 1–G; 2–A through 2–E; General Conditions; Specific Principles and Definitions, subject to the following specific exceptions:
>
> 1. Policies issued to common or contract carriers covering their legal liability for cargo shall be deemed to insure independently of any policy issued to a shipper, consignee, owner or agent to the same extent as if no other insurance existed, subject, nevertheless, to pro rata contributions from and with other similar policies issued to the carrier.
> 2. Overlapping insurance shall be deemed to exist in the case of termination, by expiration or cancellation, of a motor truck cargo liability policy with Interstate Commerce Commission and State Endorsement(s) expiring subsequent thereto, and a succeeding motor truck cargo liability policy whose ICC and State Endorsement(s) attach upon the termination dates of the endorsement(s) attached to the succeeded policy. In the case of such overlapping insurance between a succeeded insurer's unexpired ICC or State Endorsement(s) and a succeeding insurer's ICC and State Endorsement(s) whether issued or not: It is agreed that the succeeding insurer shall assume any liability under ICC or State Endorsement(s) from the date of attachment of the succeeding policy but not in excess of the limits stated in the ICC or State Endorsement(s).
> 3. Overlapping insurance shall be deemed to exist whenever insured loss or damage may have occurred during continuous coverage under successive policies of two or more companies and the date of loss cannot be determined but may be presumed to have been during the existence of such policies, the loss shall be prorated between the companies on the basis of time each company was at risk prior to discovery of loss, the total of such time in no case to exceed thirty-six months nor to extend in the case of missing property beyond the time the property was last seen nor in the case of damage beyond the time the property was last known to be in sound condition.

4. When a furriers customers policy has been extended to cover excess legal liability and the amount charged the bailor for storage or services and insurance was predicated on the declared valuation stated in the receipt issued by the furrier for the article lost or damaged, the bailor's insurer shall accept in final settlement the amount of the loss or damage not exceeding such declared valuation, unless such loss or damage was due to unauthorized use or disposition of the article by the bailee. When one bailee sends property to another bailee, insurance covering the bailee in possession of the property at the time of the loss is to be considered primary in relation to the first bailee's insurance. The measure of liability under the insurance declared to be primary shall be determined as follows notwithstanding any limitation of subsequently determined excess liability stated in the original bailee's contract of bailment with the owner or agent:
   A. If a receipt shall have been issued by the bailee in custody, with a declared valuation, or stated limitation of liability, the measure of liability shall be such declared valuation, or stated limitation, but in no event exceeding the actual cash value of the property.
   B. If a receipt shall have been issued by the bailee in custody with no declared valuation, or no stated limitation of liability, or if no receipt shall have been issued, the measure of liability shall be the actual cash value of the property, unless there is in effect a signed contract or other agreement in writing between the parties specifically providing for a lesser liability between the parties.

Definitions

The final section of the statement consists of a definition of each of 10 troublesome terms:

AFFIXED—A television aerial or antenna is affixed to the building or outbuilding when substantially attached with the weight of the antenna borne principally by the building.

BLANKET—(Casualty)—When a policy covers at a stated location and any number of other unstated or non-scheduled locations as well, it is said to be "blanket."

(Fire and Inland Marine)—When a single amount of insurance covers several unrelated items, the policy is said to be written "blanket."

Example

One amount of insurance covering two or more buildings or a building and its contents.

CONCURRENT POLICIES—Concurrent policies are those insuring the same interest and the identical property involved in the loss or claim, which divide the risk of a specific major hazard between or among policies or companies, even though policy dates and amounts vary and certain policies contain reduced rate contribution, average, coinsurance, or deductible clauses, while others do not.

Examples

Two or more standard fire policies.
Two or more contractors installment floaters.
Two or more furriers customers policies.
Two or more mercantile theft policies.

A policy(ies) providing coverage under more than one underwriting classification; i.e., casualty—fidelity—fire—inland marine or multiple-line, shall *not* be considered concurrent to policy (ies) limited to one classification.

Examples

A standard fire policy and a homeowners or MIC.

A boiler-machinery and a fire policy.

A special multi-peril motel policy and a mercantile theft policy.

EXCESS PROVISION—A provision in a policy which stipulates that the policy is liable only after other insurance, covering the risk, has been exhausted—not to be confused with "pure excess" insurance. However, depositors forgery insurance which by its terms is primary to employee dishonesty coverage shall remain so.

FLOATER POLICY (FLOATING)—A policy under the terms of which protection follows movable property, covering it wherever it may be.

Example

A policy on tourist's baggage.

LIMIT OF LIABILITY RULE—As described in *General Condition 2.*

LIMITED PURPOSE—A policy (ies) is said to be for a more limited purpose when it is designed to provide coverage for a specific exposure as contrary to one which includes that exposure and other exposures as well.

Example

A trip transit policy is a more limited purpose policy than a household furniture policy with off-premises coverage.

LOCATION—A site specifically defined in the policy.

OVERLAPPING—When two or more types of insurance cover the same risk, the insurance is said to be "overlapping."

RETROSPECTIVE RATING—A plan under which the final premium for a risk is adjusted on basis of its own loss experience during the policy period.

MAJOR POINTS

The document in its entirety is quite comprehensive. It is worthy of systematic study. There is really no shortcut to grasping its full import. Readers who are unable to study it in detail, however, may find helpful the following summary of several of the major points:

1. There *must* be an *overlap* of direct coverage on the same property under two or more policies. The "General Principles" have no application to the adjustment of loss under a single policy, either in respect to coverage afforded (such as on wall-to-wall carpeting) or precedence of payment to different interests insured thereunder. (See Paragraph 1 of "The Purpose.")

2. For the "General Principles" to apply, coverage *must* be admitted by respective insurers and thus be "available" insurance. "General Principles" do not create coverage where it is denied by an involved company. (See Paragraph 1 of "The Plan.")

3. "Other Insurance" clauses *shall* be set aside and declared inoperative unless a reasonable premium consideration has been granted for an excess provision ("pure excess"). (See Paragraph 1 of "The Plan.")

4. Application of the "General Principles" *shall* not reduce the overall

recovery otherwise available to the insured nor shall it adversely affect his future premiums. Since the insured is not a party to the agreement and is not bound thereby, there is no intention for it to be discussed with him. If he specifically requests payment be made under certain policies contrary to "General Principles," reapportionment can later be worked out between the involved companies. (See Paragraph 2 of "The Plan" and Paragraph 4 of "The Purpose.")

5. Overlap *must* involve *first-party* coverages only. If one policy is direct coverage and the other insures legal liability, the "General Principles" do not apply. (See Paragraph 1 of "The Procedure.")

6. If the same interest in the same property is insured, the order of precedence of coverages *shall* first be determined upon degree of specific identification of the property insured and the location. (See General Principle 1, A to F.)

7. Losses under policies falling within the same precedence category *shall* be apportioned under the "Limit of Liability Rule." A group of concurrent policies will prorate after their limit of liability as a group has been determined. Also, fire policies contribute as a group (even though nonconcurrent) in an overlap with boiler-machinery coverage. (See General Principle 1–G.)

8. If different interests in the same property are insured, the separate coverages *shall* be classified as either primary or excess. (See General Principle 2, A to E.)

9. Coinsurance Clauses *shall* initially be applied as though each were a reduced rate contribution clause to primary coverage. The value and loss covered by primary insurance is then deducted before coinsurance is applied to the remaining loss under the excess coverage. (See General Condition 1.)

10. When coverage is afforded under both building and contents insurance on building equipment and fixtures "essentially in the nature of *real* property," the *building* insurance *shall* be considered primary. If such equipment and fixtures are "essentially in the nature of *personal* property," the *contents* insurance is primary. (See General Conditions 4 and 5.)

11. In overlap between bailee customer's insurance and the bailee's own coverage, the bailee's own policy *shall* first pay the loss to bailee's own property and otherwise uninsured customers; and then the excess, if any, of bailee's customer's insurance is available as primary insurance to pay otherwise uninsured customer's losses. (See General Condition 8.)

12. After payment of loss to the insured without prejudice, all differences of opinion between companies respecting the application of "Guiding Principles" *shall* be submitted to arbitration.

C. Marine Insurance

American Hull Insurance Syndicate

Policy of Insurance

PART I

THE SUBSCRIBERS listed in PART III hereof, hereinafter referred to as the Underwriters, each severally, but not jointly, and not on the part of one for the ther or any of the others, for their respective proportions as set forth therein, do make insurance and cause to be insured, lost or not lost, the Assured named 1 respect of the Vessel named in PART II hereof, subject to the conditions, warranties and other terms of this Policy, including any endorsements now or ereafter attached to any part hereof.

Beginning the adventure upon the said Vessel, and so shall continue and endure during the period aforesaid, as employment may offer, in port and at sea, in ocks and graving docks, and on ways, gridirons and pontoons, at all times, in all places, and on all occasions, services and trades whatsoever and wheresoever, nder steam, motor power or sail; with leave to sail or navigate with or without pilots, to go on trial trips and to assist and tow vessels or craft in distress, but f without the approval of Underwriters the Vessel be towed, except as is customary or when in need of assistance, or undertakes towage or salvage services under pre-arranged contract made by Owners and/or Charterers, the Assured shall notify Underwriters immediately and pay an additional premium if required but no uch premium shall be required for customary towage by the Vessel in connection with loading and discharging. With liberty to discharge, exchange and take on oard goods, specie, passengers and stores, wherever the Vessel may call at or proceed to, and with liberty to carry goods, live cattle, &c., on deck or otherwise.

Touching the Adventures and Perils which we, the said Underwriters, are contented to bear and take upon us, they are of the Seas, Men-of-War, Fire, ightning, Earthquake, Enemies, Pirates, Rovers, Assailing Thieves, Jettisons, Letters of Mart and Counter-Mart, Surprisals, Takings at Sea, Arrests, Restraints nd Detainments of all Kings, Princes and Peoples of what nation, condition or quality soever. Barratry of the Master and Mariners and of all other like Perils, osses and Misfortunes that have or shall come to the Hurt, Detriment or Damage of the said Vessel, &c., or any part thereof; excepting, however, such of the fore-oing Perils as may be excluded by provisions elsewhere in the Policy or by endorsement. And in case of any Loss or Misfortune, it shall be lawful and necessary or the Assured, their Factors, Servants and Assigns, to sue, labor and travel for, in and about the Defense, Safeguard and Recovery of the said Vessel, &c., or any art thereof, without prejudice to this Insurance, to the Charges whereof the Underwriters will contribute their proportion as provided elsewhere in this Policy. nd it is expressly declared and agreed that no acts of the Underwriters or Assured in recovering, saving or preserving the property insured shall be considered as waiver or acceptance of abandonment.

This insurance also specially to cover (subject to the Average Warranty) loss of or damage to the subject matter insured directly caused by the ollowing:—

Accidents in loading, discharging or handling cargo, or in bunkering;

Accidents in going on or off, or while on drydocks, graving docks, ways, gridirons or pontoons;

Explosions on shipboard or elsewhere;

Breakdown of motor generators or other electrical machinery and electrical connections thereto, bursting of boilers, breakage of shafts, or any latent defect in the machinery or hull, (excluding the cost and expense of replacing or repairing the defective part);

Breakdown of or accidents to nuclear installations or reactors not on board the insured Vessel;

Contact with aircraft, rockets or similar missiles, or with any land conveyance;

Negligence of Charterers and/or Repairers, provided such Charterers and/or Repairers are not Assured(s) hereunder;

Negligence of Master, Mariners, Engineers or Pilots;

provided such loss or damage has not resulted from want of due diligence by the Assured, the Owners or Managers of the Vessel, or any of them. Masters, Mates, Engineers, Pilots or Crew not to be considered as part owners within the meaning of this clause should they hold shares in the Vessel.

In the event of accident whereby loss or damage may result in a claim under this Policy, notice shall be given in writing to the Underwriters, where practicable, prior to survey, so that they may appoint their own surveyor if they so desire. The Underwriters shall be entitled to decide the port to which a damaged Vessel shall proceed for docking or repairing (the actual additional expense of the voyage arising from compliance with Underwriters' requirements being refunded to the Assured) and Underwriters shall also have a right of veto in connection with the place of repair or repairing firm proposed and whenever the extent of the damage is ascertainable the majority (in amount) of the Underwriters may take or may require to be taken tenders for the repair of such damage. In the event of failure to comply with the conditions of this clause 15 per cent. shall be deducted from the amount of the ascertained claim.

In cases where a tender is accepted with the approval of Underwriters, an allowance shall be made at the rate of 30 per cent. per annum on the insured value for each day or pro rata for part of a day from the time of the completion of the survey until the acceptance of the tender provided that it be accepted without delay after receipt of Underwriters' approval.

Marine Insurance (*Continued*)

No allowance shall be made for any time during which the Vessel is loading or discharging cargo or bunkering.

Due credit shall be given against the allowance as above for any amount recovered:—

(a) in respect of fuel and stores and wages and maintenance of the Master, Officers and Crew or any member thereof allowed in General or Particular Average;

(b) from third parties in respect of damages for detention and/or loss of profit and/or running expenses;

for the period covered by the tender allowance or any part thereof.

Notwithstanding anything herein contained to the contrary, this Policy is warranted free from Particular Average under 3 per cent., or unless amounting to $4,850., but nevertheless when the Vessel shall have been stranded, sunk, on fire, or in collision with any other Ship or Vessel, Underwriters shall pay the damage occasioned thereby, and the expense of sighting the bottom after stranding shall be paid, if reasonably incurred, even if no damage be found.

Grounding in the Panama Canal, Suez Canal or in the Manchester Ship Canal or its connections, or in the River Mersey above Rock Ferry Slip, or in the River Plate (above a line drawn from the North Basin, Buenos Aires, to the mouth of the San Pedro River) or its tributaries, or in the Danube or Demerara Rivers or on the Yenikale Bar, shall not be deemed to be a stranding.

Average payable on each valuation separately or on the whole, without deduction of thirds, new for old, whether the Average be Particular or General.

No claim shall in any case be allowed in respect of scraping or painting the Vessel's bottom.

The warranty and conditions as to Average under 3 per cent. or unless amounting to $4,850. to be applicable to each voyage as if separately insured, and a voyage shall commence at the Assured's election when the Vessel either begins to load cargo or sails in ballast to a loading port. Such voyage shall continue until the Vessel has made not more than three passages or not more than two passages with cargo (whichever first occurs) and extend further until the Vessel thereafter begins to load cargo or sails (which first occurs), but such extension shall not exceed 30 days in port. A passage shall be deemed to be from the commencement of loading at the first port or place of loading until completion of discharge at the last port or place of discharge, or, if the Vessel sails in ballast, from the port or place of departure until arrival at the first port or place thereafter other than a port or place of refuge or a port or place for bunkering only. Each period in port of 30 days in excess of 30 days between passages shall itself constitute a passage for the purposes of this clause. When the Vessel sails in ballast to effect damage repairs such sailing or passage shall be considered part of the previous passage. In calculating whether the 3 per cent. or $4,850. is reached, Particular Average occurring outside the period covered by this Policy may be added to Particular Average occurring within such period, providing it occur on the same voyage as above defined, but only that portion of the claim arising within the period covered by this Policy shall be recoverable hereon. A voyage shall not be so fixed that it overlaps another voyage on which a claim is made on this or the preceding or succeeding Policy. Particular Average which would be excluded by the terms of this Policy shall not be included in determining whether the 3 per cent. or $4,850. is reached.

No recovery for a Constructive Total Loss shall be had hereunder unless the expense of recovering and repairing the Vessel shall exceed the insured value.

In ascertaining whether the Vessel is a Constructive Total Loss the insured value shall be taken as the repaired value, and nothing in respect of the damaged or break-up value of the Vessel or wreck shall be taken into account.

In the event of Total or Constructive Total Loss, no claim to be made by the Underwriters for freight, whether notice of abandonment has been given or not.

In no case shall Underwriters be liable for unrepaired damage in addition to a subsequent Total Loss sustained during the period covered by this Policy.

General Average, Salvage and Special Charges payable as provided in the contract of affreightment, or failing such provision, or there be no contract of affreightment, payable in accordance with the Laws and Usages of the Port of New York. Provided always that when an adjustment according to the laws and usages of the port of destination is properly demanded by the owners of the cargo, General Average shall be paid in accordance with same.

And it is further agreed that in the event of salvage, towage or other assistance being rendered to the Vessel hereby insured by any Vessel belonging in part or in whole to the same Owners or Charterers, the value of such services (without regard to the common ownership or control of the Vessels) shall be ascertained by arbitration in the manner below provided for under the Collision Clause, and the amount so awarded so far as applicable to the interest hereby insured shall constitute a charge under this Policy.

When the contributory value of the Vessel is greater than the valuation herein the liability of these Underwriters for General Average contribution (except in respect to amount made good to the Vessel) or Salvage shall not exceed that proportion of the total contribution due from the Vessel that the amount insured hereunder bears to the contributory value; and if because of damage for which these Underwriters are liable as Particular Average the value of the Vessel has been reduced for the purpose of contribution, the amount of the Particular Average claim under this Policy shall be deducted from the amount insured hereunder and these Underwriters shall be liable only for the proportion which such net amount bears to the contributory value.

In the event of expenditure under the Sue and Labor Clause, this Policy shall pay the proportion of such expenses that the amount insured hereunder bears to the insured value of the Vessel, or that the amount insured hereunder, less loss and/or damage payable under this Policy, bears to the actual value of the salved property; whichever proportion shall be less.

If claim for total loss is admitted under this Policy and sue and labor expenses have been reasonably incurred in excess of any proceeds realized or value recovered, the amount payable under this Policy will be the proportion of such excess that the amount insured hereunder (without deduction for loss or damage) bears to the insured value or the sound value of the Vessel at the time of the accident, whichever value was greater.

And it is further agreed that if the Vessel hereby insured shall come into collision with any other Ship or Vessel and the Assured or the Charterers or the Surety in consequence of the insured Vessel being at fault shall become liable to pay and shall pay by way of damages to any other person or persons any sum or sums in respect of such collision, we, the Underwriters will pay the Assured, or the Charterers, or the Surety, whichever shall have paid, such proportion of such sum or sums so paid as our respective subscriptions hereto bear to the value of the Vessel hereby insured, provided always that our liability in respect to any one such collision shall not exceed our proportionate part of the value of the Vessel hereby insured. And in cases where the liability of the Vessel has been contested, or proceedings have been taken to limit liability, with the consent in writing of a majority (in amount) of Hull Underwriters, we will also pay a like proportion of the costs which the Assured or Charterers shall thereby incur, or be compelled to pay; but when both Vessels are to blame, then, unless the liability of the Owners or Charterers of one or both such Vessels becomes limited by law, claims under the Collision Clause shall be settled on the principle of Cross-Liabilities as if the Owners or Charterers of each Vessel had been compelled to pay to the Owners or Charterers of the other of such Vessels such one-half or other proportion of the latter's damages as may have been properly allowed in ascertaining the balance or sum payable by or to the Assured or Charterers in consequence of such collision; and it is further agreed that the principles involved in this clause shall apply to the case where both Vessels are the property, in part or in whole, of the same Owners or Charterers, all questions of responsibility and amount of liability as between the two Vessels being left to the decision of a single Arbitrator, if the parties can agree upon a single Arbitrator, or failing such agreement, to the decision of Arbitrators, one to be appointed by the Managing Owners or Charterers of both Vessels, and one to be appointed by the majority (in amount) of Hull Underwriters interested; the two Arbitrators chosen to choose a third Arbitrator before entering upon the reference, and the decision of such single, or of any two of such three Arbitrators, appointed as above, to be final and binding. Provided always that this clause shall in no case extend to any sum which the Assured, or the Charterers, or the Surety, may become liable to pay or shall pay for removal of obstructions under statutory powers, for injury to harbors, wharves, piers, stages, structures, or any other objects (excepting other Vessels and property thereon), consequent on such collision, or in respect of the cargo, baggage or engagements of the Insured Vessel, or for loss of life, or personal injury. And provided also that in the event of any claim under this clause being made by anyone other than the Owners of the Vessel hereby insured, he shall not be entitled to recover in respect of any liability to which the Owners of the Vessel as such would not be subject, nor to a greater extent than the Owners would be entitled in such event to recover.

Marine Insurance (*Continued*)

THIS SPACE FOR ATTACHMENT OF RIDERS AND ENDORSEMENTS

Unless physically deleted by the Underwriters, the following warranty shall be paramount and shall supersede and nullify any contrary provision of the Policy:

F. C. & S. CLAUSE

Notwithstanding anything to the contrary contained in the Policy, this insurance is warranted free from any claim for loss, damage or expense caused by or resulting from capture, seizure, arrest, restraint or detainment, or the consequences thereof or of any attempt thereat, or any taking of the Vessel, by requisition or otherwise, whether in time of peace or war and whether lawful or otherwise; also from all consequences of hostilities or warlike operations (whether there be a declaration of war or not), but the foregoing shall not exclude collision or contact with aircraft, rockets or similar missiles, or with any fixed or floating object (other than a mine or torpedo), stranding, heavy weather, fire or explosion unless caused directly (and independently of the nature of the voyage or service which the vessel concerned or, in the case of a collision, any other vessel involved therein, is performing) by a hostile act by or against a belligerent power, and for the purpose of this warranty "power" includes any authority maintaining naval, military or air forces in association with a power; also warranted free, whether in time of peace or war, from all loss, damage or expense caused by any weapon of war employing atomic or nuclear fission and/or fusion or other reaction or radioactive force or matter.

Further warranted free from the consequences of civil war, revolution, rebellion, insurrection, or civil strife arising therefrom, or piracy.

If war risks are hereafter insured by endorsement on the Policy, such endorsement shall supersede the above warranty only to the extent that their terms are inconsistent and only while such war risk endorsement remains in force.

Additional insurances as follows are permitted:—

(a) DISBURSEMENTS, MANAGERS' COMMISSIONS, PROFITS OR EXCESS OR INCREASED VALUE OF HULL AND MACHINERY, AND/OR SIMILAR INTERESTS HOWEVER DESCRIBED, AND FREIGHT (INCLUDING CHARTERED FREIGHT OR ANTICIPATED FREIGHT) INSURED FOR TIME. A sum not exceeding in the aggregate 25% of the insured value of the Vessel.

(b) FREIGHT OR HIRE, UNDER CONTRACTS FOR VOYAGE. A sum not exceeding the gross freight or hire for the current cargo passage and next succeeding cargo passage (such insurance to include, if required, a preliminary and an intermediate ballast passage) plus the charges of insurance. In the case of a voyage charter where payment is made on a time basis, the sum permitted for insurance shall be calculated on the estimated duration of the voyage, subject to the limitation of two cargo passages as laid down herein. Any sum insured under this Section shall be reduced as the freight or hire is earned by the gross amount so earned.

(c) ANTICIPATED FREIGHT IF THE VESSEL SAILS IN BALLAST AND NOT UNDER CHARTER. A sum not exceeding the anticipated gross freight on next cargo passage, such sum to be reasonably estimated on the basis of the current rate of freight at time of insurance, plus the charges of insurance. Provided, however, that no insurance shall be permitted under this Section if any insurance is effected under Section (b).

(d) TIME CHARTER HIRE OR CHARTER HIRE FOR SERIES OF VOYAGES. A sum not exceeding 50% of the gross hire which is to be earned under the charter in a period not exceeding 18 months. Any sum insured under this Section shall be reduced as the hire is earned under the charter by 50% of the gross amount so earned but where the charter is for a period exceeding 18 months the sum insured need not be reduced while it does not exceed 50% of the gross hire still to be earned under the charter. An insurance under this Section may begin on the signing of the charter.

(e) PREMIUMS. A sum not exceeding the actual premiums of all interests insured for a period not exceeding 12 months (excluding premiums insured under the foregoing Sections but including, if required, the premium or estimated calls on any Protection and Indemnity or War &c. Risk insurance) reducing pro rata monthly.

(f) RETURNS OF PREMIUM. A sum not exceeding the actual returns which are recoverable subject to "and arrival" under any policy of insurance.

(g) INSURANCE IRRESPECTIVE OF AMOUNT AGAINST: — Risks excluded by the F. C. & S. Clause, and risks enumerated in the American Institute War and Strikes Clauses and General Average and Salvage Disbursements.

Warranted that no insurance on any interests enumerated in the foregoing Sections (a) to (f), inclusive, in excess of the amounts permitted therein and no insurance subject to P.P.I., F.I.A. or other like term, on any interests whatever excepting those enumerated in Section (a), is or shall be effected to operate during the currency of this Policy by or for account of the Assured, Owners, Managers or Mortgagees. Provided always that a breach of this warranty shall not afford Underwriters any defense to a claim by a Mortgagee who has accepted this Policy without knowledge of such breach.

IN WITNESS WHEREOF, the **SUBSCRIBERS** listed in **PART III** hereof, each severally, but not jointly, and not on the part of one for the other or any of the others, have caused this Policy to be signed by their Attorney at New York, N. Y., but this Policy shall not be valid unless PART II hereof is countersigned by a duly authorized Agent of each of the Subscribers.

Executed in New York, N. Y.

Attorney for the Individual Subscribers to
AMERICAN HULL INSURANCE SYNDICATE

AMERICAN INSTITUTE
TIME (HULLS)
January 1, 1964
PART I

Marine Insurance (*Continued*)

PART II

SUM INSURED $.. **POLICY No.**

PREMIUM $..

THE ASSURED..

FOR ACCOUNT OF THEMSELVES

but subject to the provisions of this Policy with respect to change of ownership.

In the event of any change, voluntary or otherwise, in the ownership of the Vessel or if the Vessel be placed under new management or be chartered on a bareboat basis or requisitioned on that basis, then, unless the Underwriters agree thereto in writing, this Policy shall thereupon become cancelled from time of such change in ownership or management, charter or requisition; provided, however, that in the case of an involuntary temporary transfer by requisition or otherwise, without the prior execution of any written agreement by the Assured, such cancellation shall take place fifteen days after such transfer; and provided further that if the Vessel has cargo on board and has already sailed from her loading port, or is at sea in ballast, such cancellation shall be suspended until arrival at final port of discharge if with cargo or at port of destination if in ballast. This insurance shall not inure to the benefit of any such charterer or transferee of the Vessel, and if a loss payable hereunder should occur between such transfer and such cancellation the Underwriters shall be subrogated to all the rights of the Assured against the transferee, by reason of such transfer, in respect of all or part of such loss as is recoverable from the transferee and in the proportion which the respective amounts insured bear to the insured value. A pro rata daily return of net premium shall be made. The foregoing provisions with respect to cancellation in the event of change in ownership or management, charter or requisition shall apply even in the case of insurance "for account of whom it may concern".

Loss, if any, (excepting claims required to be paid to others under the Collision Clause), payable to ....

....

.... **or order**

Sum Insured Hereunder .... **Dollars**

at and from the .... **day of** .... **19**........, ... **time**

to the .... **day of** .... **19**........, ... **time**

Provided, however, should the Vessel at the expiration of this Policy be at sea, or in distress, or at a port of refuge or of call, she shall, provided previous notice be given to the Underwriters, be held covered at a pro rata monthly premium to her port of destination.

On the Vessel called the ....

(or by whatsoever name or names the said Vessel is or shall be called).

The said Vessel, for so much as concerns the Assured, by agreement between the Assured and Underwriters in this Policy, is and shall be valued at as follows

Hull, tackle, apparel, passenger fittings, equipment, stores, ordnance, munitions, boats and other furniture $..................

Boilers, machinery, refrigerating machinery and insulation, motor generators and other electrical machinery, and everything connected therewith . . . . $**.................. **$..................

Donkey boilers, winches, cranes, windlasses and steering gear shall be deemed to be a part of the hull and not of the machinery.

Special Conditions and Warranties

Held covered in case of any breach of warranty as to cargo, trade, locality or date of sailing, provided notice be given and any additional premium required be agreed immediately after receipt of advices of breach or proposed breach by Owners.

The Underwriters to be paid in consideration of this insurance the premium as shown in the margin hereof, being at the rate of .... **per cent.**

In event of non-payment of premium thirty days after attachment this Policy may be cancelled by the Underwriters upon five days written notice being given the Assured. Such proportion of the premium, however, as shall have been earned up to the time of such cancellation shall be due and payable; but in the event of Total or Constructive Total Loss occurring prior to cancellation full annual premium shall be deemed earned.

To return cents per cent. net for each uncommenced month if it be mutually agreed to cancel this Policy. **and arrival**

For each period of 30 consecutive days the Vessel may be laid up in port:—

cents per cent. net not under repair.

cents per cent. net under repair.

Provided always: (a) that in no case shall a return be allowed when the Vessel is lying in a roadstead or in exposed or unprotected waters or in any location not approved by Underwriters.

(b) that in the event of a return being recoverable for special trade, or for any other reason, other than for lay-up periods, the above rates of return of premium shall be reduced accordingly.

(c) that in no case shall a return be allowed when the Vessel is used as a storage ship or for lightering purposes.

If, for account of the Assured, the Vessel is laid up for a period of 30 consecutive days, a part only of which attaches to this Policy, Underwriters shall pay such proportion of the return due in respect of a full period of 30 days as the number of days attaching hereto bears to thirty. Should the lay-up period exceed 30 consecutive days, the Assured shall have the option to elect the period of 30 consecutive days for which a return is recoverable.

Countersigned in New York, N. Y.

this .... **day of** .... **19**......

AMERICAN INSTITUTE
TIME (HULLS)
January 1, 1964
PART II
FORM 203-2 3M 1-64

Agent for the Individual Subscribers to
AMERICAN HULL INSURANCE SYNDICATE
As Named in PART III hereof.

Marine Insurance (*Continued*)

PART III

Subscribers	Proportion	
The Aetna Casualty and Surety Company, Hartford, Connecticut	4.3750	
Aetna Insurance Company, Hartford, Connecticut	7.5000	
Agricultural Insurance Company, Watertown, New York	1.6875	
Alliance Assurance Company, Limited, London, England	1.3125	
Alpina Insurance Company, Limited, Zurich, Switzerland	.9375	
American and Foreign Insurance Company, New York, New York	2.6250	
The American Insurance Company, Newark, New Jersey	4.4375	
Atlantic Mutual Insurance Company, New York, New York	10.5625	
Bankers & Shippers Insurance Company of New York, New York, New York	1.5000	
Boston Insurance Company, Boston, Massachusetts	4.3125	
The British and Foreign Marine Insurance Company Limited, Liverpool, England	2.8750	
Buffalo Insurance Company, Buffalo, New York	.5625	
Caledonian Insurance Company, Edinburgh, Scotland	.6875	
The Camden Fire Insurance Association, Camden, New Jersey	.6875	
Centennial Insurance Company, New York, New York	2.1250	
The Century Insurance Company Limited, Edinburgh, Scotland	2.6875	
Christiania General Insurance Corporation of New York, Tarrytown, New York	.7500	
Commercial Union Insurance Company of New York, New York, New York	10.3750	
The Connecticut Fire Insurance Company, Hartford, Connecticut	1.3125	
The Continental Insurance Company, New York, New York	5.4375	
Eagle Star Insurance Company, Limited, London, England	2.5625	
The Employers' Fire Insurance Company, Boston, Massachusetts	1.0000	
Federal Insurance Company, Short Hills, New Jersey	12.8750	
Fidelity-Phenix Insurance Company, New York, New York	5.3750	
Fireman's Fund Insurance Company, San Francisco, California	14.1875	
Firemen's Insurance Company of Newark, New Jersey, Newark, New Jersey	4.4375	
General Insurance Company of America, Seattle, Washington	1.6875	
General Reinsurance Corporation, New York, New York	.5625	
Glens Falls Insurance Company, Glens Falls, New York	5.3750	
Great American Insurance Company, New York, New York	6.4375	
The Hanover Insurance Company, New York, New York	2.4375	
Hartford Fire Insurance Company, Hartford, Connecticut	9.1250	
The Home Insurance Company, New York, New York	9.6875	
The Indemnity Marine Assurance Company Limited, London, England	1.3750	
Insurance Company of North America, Philadelphia, Pennsylvania	21.9375	
The Liverpool and London and Globe Insurance Company Limited, Liverpool, England	3.4375	
The London Assurance, London, England	2.6250	
The Marine Insurance Company, Limited, London, England	2.0000	
Maritime Insurance Company, Limited, Liverpool, England	1.1250	
Merchants Fire Assurance Corporation of New York, New York, New York	3.2500	
National Fire Insurance Company of Hartford, Hartford, Connecticut	1.6250	
The New Zealand Insurance Company Limited, Auckland, New Zealand	.5000	
Newark Insurance Company, Holland Township, New Jersey	3.0625	
Niagara Fire Insurance Company, New York, New York	3.1250	
The Northern Assurance Company of America, Boston, Massachusetts	1.8750	
The North River Insurance Company, New York, New York	2.5625	
Pacific Indemnity Company, Los Angeles, California	.2500	
Phoenix Assurance Company of New York, New York, New York	.6250	
The Phoenix Insurance Company of Hartford, Connecticut, Hartford, Connecticut	2.8750	
Providence Washington Insurance Company, Providence, Rhode Island	2.7500	
Provident Insurance Company of New York, New York, New York	1.2500	
Queen Insurance Company of America, New York, New York	3.8750	
The Reinsurance Corporation of New York, New York, New York	1.8125	

CONTINUED

Marine Insurance (*Continued*)

Subscribers	Proportion		
Reliance Insurance Company, Philadelphia, Pennsylvania	2.0000		
Reliance Marine Insurance Company, Limited, Liverpool, England	1.6875		
Royal Exchange Assurance, London, England	1.2500		
Royal Insurance Company, Limited, Liverpool, England	4.1875		
St. Paul Fire and Marine Insurance Company, St. Paul, Minnesota	8.1250		
The Sea Insurance Company, Limited, Liverpool, England	2.6875		
Security Insurance Company of New Haven Connecticut, New Haven, Connecticut	1.1875		
Standard Marine Insurance Company, Limited, Liverpool, England	3.0625		
Sun Insurance Company of New York, New York, New York	1.5000		
Sun Insurance Office Limited, London, England	1.5000	254.75ths	of Sum Insured
Switzerland General Insurance Company, Limited, Zurich, Switzerland	.6875		
Thames and Mersey Marine Insurance Company, Limited, Liverpool, England	2.0625		
Transcontinental Insurance Company, New York, New York	.5625		
The Travelers Indemnity Company, Hartford, Connecticut	2.2500		
Union Insurance Society of Canton, Limited, Hong Kong	.7500		
The Union Marine and General Insurance Company, Limited, Liverpool, England	1.3125		
United States Fire Insurance Company, New York, New York	3.5000		
Universal Insurance Company, Holland Township, New Jersey	5.8750		
Washington General Insurance Corporation, New York, New York	3.2500		
Westchester Fire Insurance Company, New York, New York	2.8750		
Total	254.7500		

Provisions required by law to be stated in this Policy:—

As to

ALL SUBSCRIBERS EXCEPT THE ATLANTIC MUTUAL INSURANCE COMPANY — "This policy is in a stock corporation."

As to

ATLANTIC MUTUAL INSURANCE COMPANY, NEW YORK, N. Y. — "This policy is in a mutual company, is non-participating and non-assessable."

As to the ST. PAUL FIRE AND MARINE INSURANCE COMPANY, ST. PAUL, MINN.—"This policy is issued under and in pursuance of the laws of the State of Minnesota relating to Guaranty Surplus and Special Reserve Funds." Chapter 437, General Laws of 1909.

Marine Insurance (*Continued*)

AMERICAN INSTITUTE CARGO CLAUSES

1. This insurance attaches from the time the goods leave the Warehouse and/or Store at the place named in the policy for the commencement of the transit and continues during the ordinary course of transit, including customary transhipment if any, until the goods are discharged overside from the overseas vessel at the final port. Thereafter the insurance continues whilst the goods are in transit and/or awaiting transit until delivered to final warehouse at the destination named in the policy or until the expiry of 15 days (or 30 days if the destination to which the goods are insured is outside the limits of the port) whichever shall first occur. The time limits referred to above to be reckoned from midnight of the day on which the discharge overside of the goods hereby insured from the overseas vessel is completed. Held covered at a premium to be arranged in the event of transhipment, if any, other than as above and/or in the event of delay in excess of the above time limits arising from circumstances beyond the control of the Assured. Warehouse to warehouse clause.

It is necessary for the Assured to give prompt notice to these Assurers when they become aware of an event for which they are "held covered" under this policy and the right to such cover is dependent on compliance with this obligation.

2. Including transit by craft and/or lighter to and from the vessel. Each craft and/or lighter to be deemed a separate insurance. The Assured are not to be prejudiced by any agreement exempting lightermen from liability. Craft, &c., clause.

3. This insurance shall not be vitiated by any unintentional error in description of vessel, voyage or interest, or by deviation, over-carriage, change of voyage, transhipment or any other interruption of the ordinary course of transit, from causes beyond the control of the Assured. It is agreed, however, that any such error, deviation or other occurrence mentioned above shall be reported to this Company as soon as known to the Assured, and additional premium paid if required. Deviation clause.

4. Warranted free from Particular Average unless the vessel or craft be stranded, sunk, or burnt, but notwithstanding this warranty these Assurers are to pay any loss of or damage to the interest insured which may reasonably be attributed to fire, collision or contact of the vessel and/or craft and/or conveyance with any external substance (ice included) other than water, or to discharge of cargo at port of distress. **The foregoing warranty, however, shall not apply where broader terms of Average are provided for hereon or in the certificate or policy to which these clauses are attached.** F.P.A. clause.

5. Notwithstanding any average warranty contained herein, these Assurers agree to pay any landing, warehousing, forwarding and special charges for which this policy in the absence of such warranty would be liable. Also to pay the insured value of any package or packages which may be totally lost in loading, transhipment or discharge. Warehousing & Forwarding Charges, Packages totally lost loading, etc.

6. In case of damage affecting labels, capsules or wrappers, these Assurers, if liable therefor under the terms of this policy, shall not be liable for more than an amount sufficient to pay the cost of new labels, capsules or wrappers, and the cost of reconditioning the goods, but in no event shall these Assurers be liable for more than the insured value of the damaged merchandise. Labels clause.

7. When the property insured under this policy includes a machine consisting when complete for sale or use of several parts, then in case of loss or damage covered by this insurance to any part of such machine, these Assurers shall be liable only for the proportion of the insured value of the part lost or damaged, or at the Assured's option, for the cost and expense, including labor and forwarding charges, of replacing or repairing the lost or damaged part; but in no event shall these Assurers be liable for more than the insured value of the complete machine. Machinery Clause

8. General Average and Salvage Charges payable according to United States laws and usage and/or as per Foreign Statement and/or as per York-Antwerp Rules (as prescribed in whole or in part) if in accordance with the Contract of Affreightment. G/A clause.

9. Including the risk of explosion, howsoever or wheresoever occurring during the currency of this insurance, unless excluded by the F. C. & S. Warranty or the S. R. & C. C. Warranty set forth herein. Explosion clause.

10. Where this insurance by its terms covers while on docks, wharves or elsewhere on shore, and/or during land transportation, it shall include the risks of collision, derailment, overturning or other accident to the conveyance, fire, lightning, sprinkler leakage, cyclones, hurricanes, earthquakes, floods (meaning the rising of navigable waters), and/or collapse or subsidence of docks or wharves, even though the insurance be otherwise F.P.A. Shore Clause

11. The Assured are not to be prejudiced by the presence of the negligence clause and/or latent defect clause in the Bills of Lading and/or Charter Party. The seaworthiness of the vessel as between the Assured and these Assurers is hereby admitted and the wrongful act or misconduct of the shipowner or his servants causing a loss is not to defeat the recovery by an innocent Assured if the loss in the absence of such wrongful act or misconduct would have been a loss recoverable on the policy. With leave to sail with or without pilots, and to tow and assist vessels or craft in all situations, and to be towed. Bill of Lading &c., clause.

Marine Insurance (*Concluded*)

12. This insurance is also specially to cover any loss of or damage to the interest insured hereunder, through the bursting of boilers, breakage of shafts or through any latent defect in the machinery, hull or appurtenances, or from faults or errors in the navigation and/or management of the vessel by the master, mariners, mates, engineers or pilots. **Inchmaree Clause**

13. Warranted free of claim for loss of market or for loss, damage or deterioration arising from delay, whether caused by a peril insured against or otherwise, unless expressly assumed in writing hereon. **Delay clause.**

14. Where goods are shipped under a Bill of Lading containing the so-called "Both to Blame Collision" Clause, these Assurers agree as to all losses covered by this insurance, to indemnify the Assured for this policy's proportion of any amount (not exceeding the amount insured) which the Assured may be legally bound to pay to the shipowners under such clause. In the event that such liability is asserted the Assured agree to notify these Assurers who shall have the right at their own cost and expense to defend the Assured against such claim. **Both to Blame clause.**

15. No recovery for a Constructive Total Loss shall be had hereunder unless the property insured is reasonably abandoned on account of its actual total loss appearing to be unavoidable, or because it cannot be preserved from actual total loss without an expenditure which would exceed its value when the expenditure had been incurred. **Constructive Total Loss Clause**

16. Warranted that this insurance shall not inure, directly or indirectly, to the benefit of any carrier or bailee. **Carrier clause.**

17. The following Warranties shall be paramount and shall not be modified or superseded by any other provision included herein or stamped or endorsed hereon unless such other provision refers specifically to the risks excluded by these Warranties and expressly assumes the said risks:—

(A) Notwithstanding anything herein contained to the contrary, this insurance is warranted free from capture, seizure, arrest, restraint, detainment, confiscation, preemption, requisition or nationalization, and the consequences thereof or any attempt thereat, whether in time of peace or war and whether lawful or otherwise; also warranted free, whether in time of peace or war, from all loss, damage or expense caused by any weapon of war employing atomic or nuclear fission and/or fusion or other reaction or radioactive force or matter or by any mine or torpedo, also warranted free from all consequences of hostilities or warlike operations (whether there be a declaration of war or not), but this warranty shall not exclude collision or contact with aircraft, rockets or similar missiles or with any fixed or floating object (other than a mine or torpedo), stranding, heavy weather, fire or explosion unless caused directly (and independently of the nature of the voyage or service which the vessel concerned or, in the case of a collision, any other vessel involved therein, is performing) by a hostile act by or against a belligerent power; and for the purposes of this warranty "power" includes any authority maintaining naval, military or air forces in association with a power. **F. C. & S. Warranty.**

Further warranted free from the consequences of civil war, revolution, rebellion, insurrection, or civil strife arising therefrom, or piracy.

(B) Warranted free of loss or damage caused by or resulting from strikes, lockouts, labor disturbances, riots, civil commotions or the acts of any person or persons taking part in any such occurrence or disorder. **S. R. & C. Warranty.**

Special Terms and Conditions:—

D. Inland Marine

INLAND MARINE POLICY

No. IMP

RENEWAL OF NUMBER

TYPE OF COMPANY

Inland Marine Insurance Policy

Named Insured and Address: (No., Street, Town, County, State)

Policy Period: (Mo. Day Yr.)
From to
at noon, standard time at place of issuance

$ PREMIUM RATE $ AMOUNT

In consideration of the stipulations herein named and of the premium above specified the Company does insure the above Named Insured, hereinafter called the Insured, whose address is shown above, from the inception date shown above, at noon (standard time), to the expiration date shown above, at noon (standard time), at place of issuance to an amount not exceeding the amount(s) above specified, on property described below or in schedule attached.

This policy is made and accepted subject to the foregoing provisions and stipulations and those hereinafter stated, which are hereby made a part of this policy, together with such other provisions, stipulations and agreements as may be added hereto, as provided in this policy.

Agency at

Countersigned:

Agent

Ptd. in U.S.A.

Inland Marine (*Continued*)

CONDITIONS

1. **MISREPRESENTATION AND FRAUD.** This entire policy shall be void if, whether before or after a loss, the Insured has concealed or misrepresented any material fact or circumstance concerning this insurance or the subject thereof, or the interest of the Insured therein, or in case of any fraud, attempted fraud, or false swearing by the Insured relating thereto.

2. **CHANGES.** Notice to any agent or knowledge possessed by any agent or by any other person shall not effect a waiver or a change in any part of this policy or estop the Company from asserting any right under the terms of this policy, nor shall the terms of this policy be waived or changed, except by endorsement issued to form a part of this policy.

3. **COLLECTION FROM OTHERS.** No loss shall be paid or made good hereunder if the Insured has collected the same from others.

4. **NOTICE OF LOSS.** The Insured shall as soon as practicable report in writing to the Company or its agent every loss which may become a claim under this policy and shall also file with the Company or its agent within ninety (90) days from date of discovery of loss a detailed sworn proof of loss. Failure by the Insured to report the said loss and to file such sworn proof of loss as hereinbefore provided shall invalidate any claim under this policy for such loss.

5. **SUE AND LABOR.** In the event of loss to property covered under this policy, the Insured, his employees, factors and assigns shall sue, labor and travel in efforts to recover, safeguard and defend the said property. Such action shall not prejudice this insurance or constitute a waiver of any rights of the Insured.

6. **EXAMINATION UNDER OATH.** The Insured, as often as may be reasonably required, shall exhibit to any person designated by the Company all that remains of any property herein described, and shall submit, and in so far as is within his or their power cause his or their employees, members of the household and others to submit to examinations under oath by any person named by the Company and subscribe the same; and, as often as may be reasonably required, shall produce for examination all writings, books of account, bills, invoices and other vouchers, or certified copies thereof if originals be lost, at such reasonable time and place as may be designated by the Company or its representative, and shall permit extracts and copies thereof to be made. No such examination under oath or examination of books or documents, nor any other act of the Company or any of its employees or representatives in connection with the investigation of any loss or claim hereunder, shall be deemed a waiver of any defense which the Company might otherwise have with respect to any loss or claim, but all such examinations and acts shall be deemed to have been made or done without prejudice to the Company's liability.

7. **NO BENEFIT TO BAILEE.** This insurance shall in no wise inure directly or indirectly to the benefit of any carrier or other bailee.

8. **ABANDONMENT.** There can be no abandonment to the Company of any property.

9. **PAIR, SET OR PARTS.** In the event of loss to:
   (a) any article or articles which are a part of a pair or set, the measure of loss to such article or articles shall be a reasonable and fair proportion of the total value of the pair or set, giving consideration to the importance of said article or articles, but in no event shall such loss be construed to mean total loss of the pair or set; or
   (b) any part of property covered consisting, when complete for use, of several parts, the Company shall only be liable for the value of the part lost or damaged.

10. **VALUATION.** The Company shall not be liable beyond the actual cash value of the property at the time any loss occurs. The loss shall be ascertained or estimated according to such actual cash value with proper deduction for depreciation, however caused, and shall in no event exceed what it would then cost to repair or replace the same with material of like kind and quality.

11. **APPRAISAL.** If the Insured and the Company fail to agree as to the amount of loss, each shall, on the written demand of either, made within sixty (60) days after receipt of proof of loss by the Company, select a competent and disinterested appraiser, and the appraisal shall be made at a reasonable time and place. The appraisers shall first select a competent and disinterested umpire, and failing for fifteen (15) days to agree upon such umpire, then, on the request of the Insured or the Company, such umpire shall be selected by a judge of a court of record in the state in which such appraisal is pending. The appraisers shall then appraise the loss, stating separately the actual cash value at the time of loss and the amount of loss, and failing to agree shall submit their differences to the umpire. An award in writing of any two shall determine the amount of loss. The Insured and the Company shall each pay his or its chosen appraiser and shall bear equally the other expenses of the appraisal and umpire. The Company shall not be held to have waived any of its rights by any act relating to appraisal.

12. **COMPANY'S OPTIONS.** It shall be optional with the Company to take all, or any part, of the property at the agreed or appraised value, or to repair, rebuild or replace the property destroyed or damaged with other of like kind and quality within a reasonable time, on giving notice of its intention so to do within sixty (60) days after the receipt of the proof of loss herein required.

13. **OTHER INSURANCE.** The Company shall not be liable for loss if, at the time of loss, there is any other insurance which would attach if this insurance had not been effected, except that this insurance shall apply only as excess and in no event as contributing insurance, and then only after all other insurance has been exhausted.

14. **SETTLEMENT OF CLAIMS.** All adjusted claims shall be paid or made good to the Insured within sixty (60) days after presentation and acceptance of satisfactory proof of interest and loss at the office of the Company.

15. **SUIT.** No suit, action or proceeding for the recovery of any claim under this policy shall be sustainable in any court of law or equity unless the same be commenced within twelve (12) months next after discovery by the Insured of the occurrence which gives rise to the claim, provided, however, that if by the laws of the state within which this policy is issued such limitation is invalid, then any such claims shall be void unless such action, suit or proceedng be commenced within the shortest limit of time permitted by the laws of such state.

16. **LOSS CLAUSE.** Any loss hereunder shall not reduce the amount of this policy.

17. **SUBROGATION.** In the event of any payment under this policy the Company shall be subrogated to all the Insured's rights of recovery therefor against any person or organization and the Insured shall execute and deliver instruments and papers and do whatever else is necessary to secure such rights. The Insured shall do nothing after loss to prejudice such rights.

18. **CANCELATION.** This policy may be canceled by the Insured by mailing to the Company written notice stating when thereafter such cancelation shall be effective. This policy may be canceled by the Company by mailing to the Insured at the address shown in this policy written notice stating when not less than five (5) days thereafter such cancelation shall be effective. The mailing of notice as aforesaid shall be sufficient proof of notice and the effective date of cancelation stated in the notice shall become the end of the policy period. Delivery of such written notice either by the Insured or by the Company shall be equivalent to mailing.

If the Insured cancels, earned premiums shall be computed in accordance with the customary short rate table and procedure. If the Company cancels, earned premiums shall be computed pro rata. Premium adjustment may be made at the time the cancelation is effected and, if not then made, shall be made as soon as practicable after cancelation becomes effective but payment or tender of unearned premium is not a condition of cancelation. The Company's check or the check of its representative mailed or delivered as aforesaid shall be a sufficient tender of any refund of premium due to the Insured.

19. **CONFORMITY TO STATUTE.** Terms of this policy which are in conflict with the statutes of the state wherein this policy is issued are hereby amended to conform to such statutes.

In Witness Whereof, the Company has executed and attested these presents, but this policy shall not be valid unless countersigned by a duly authorized agent of the Company at the agency hereinbefore mentioned.

INSERT SIGNATURES AND TITLES OF PROPER OFFICERS

Inland Marine (*Continued*)

MUTUAL POLICY CONDITIONS

This policy is issued by a Mutual Company having special regulations lawfully applicable to its organization, membership, policies or contracts of insurance, of which the following shall apply to and form a part of this policy.

This policy is nonassessable. The policyholder is a member of the company and shall participate, to the extent and upon the conditions fixed and determined by the Board of Directors of the Company in accordance with the provisions of law, in the distribution of dividends so fixed and determined.

The Assured is hereby notified that by virtue of this policy he is a member of (Insert full name of Insurance Company), and is entitled to vote either in person or by proxy at any and all meetings of said company. The annual meetings are held at its home office on the (____________) day of (____________________) in each year, at (__________) o'clock (A.)M.

(B)

Inland Marine (*Continued*)

ANNUAL TRANSPORTATION FLOATER

(Named Peril Form)

Attached to and forming part of Policy No.

of the

issued to

at its Agency. Dated

1. **THIS POLICY COVERS:**

(a) on property consisting principally of..

....

shipped by or to the Insured at Insured's risk, in transit at and between points and places within the limits of the continental United States and Canada (excluding Alaska), by rail or air carrier, railway or air express, freight forwarders, public or private truckmen (including vehicles owned or operated by the Insured), and including such shipments while waterborne on ferries or lighters,

(b) from the time such property leaves the factory, store, or warehouse at initial point of shipment until such property is delivered at its destination, including while in or on docks, wharves, piers, bulkheads, depots, stations and platforms, awaiting shipment and after arrival, but only while the property is in due course of transit in the custody of a common carrier incidental to transportation.

2. **LIMITS OF LIABILITY**

The liability of the Company shall in no event exceed the individual limits of liability set forth in the following schedule of limits:

$..........................while in the custody of public or private truckmen;

$..........................while in the custody of any rail carrier or railway express agency;

$..........................while in the custody of any air carrier or air express company;

$..........................while in or on vehicles owned or operated by the Insured.

Nor shall this Company be liable for more than $..........................in any one casualty, either in case of partial or total loss, or salvage charges, or any other charges, or expenses, or all combined.

3. **PREMIUM ADJUSTMENT**

(a) The premium charged in this policy is based on estimated annual shipments of $..........................and is calculated at the rate of $..........................per $100.00 of the value of said shipments.

(b) The Insured agrees to keep an accurate record of all property shipped hereunder during the term of this policy and to report to the Company at the end of such term the actual insured value of shipments covered hereunder, and all records pertaining to such shipments shall at all reasonable times be open to inspection by any duly authorized representative of the Company; in the event of the annual shipments being less than the estimate, a return premium on such deficiency shall be paid to the Insured at the rate stated in Paragraph 3(a) above, or in the event of the annual shipments being greater than the estimate, an additional premium shall be paid by the Insured on such excess at the same rate.

(c) The minimum annual premium on this policy or minimum earned premium in the event of cancelation shall be $....................

4. **DEDUCTIBLE CLAUSE**

The first $..........................of any one loss is not insured hereunder and the Company is liable only for loss in excess thereof, subject to all other applicable limits of liability.

5. **THIS POLICY INSURES AGAINST DIRECT LOSS OR DAMAGE CAUSED BY:**

(a) fire and lightning;
(b) cyclone, tornado and windstorm;
(c) flood (meaning rising of navigable waters);
(d) the collision, overturning or derailment of transporting conveyance;
(e) collapse of docks, bridges or culverts;
(f) theft, of an entire shipping package only, excluding all pilferage;
(g) perils of the seas, lake, rivers and/or inland waters while on ferries or lighters.

6. **THIS POLICY DOES NOT INSURE AGAINST LOSS:**

(a) To accounts, bills, deeds, evidences of debt, currency, money, coins, bullion, notes, securities, stamps;
(b) To jewelry, watches, silverware, furs or articles trimmed with fur, unless shipped in sealed packages by railway express;
(c) To animals, unless specifically insured hereunder, and then only against death caused by, or destruction rendered necessary by injuries due to a peril insured hereunder;
(d) Of profit, loss of use or loss of market, however caused;
(e) Caused by improper packing, rough handling or unexplained shortage;
(f) Caused by moth,,vermin or inherent vice;
(g) To export shipments which have been laden on board export conveyance or have come under the protection of marine insurance, whichever first occurs;
(h) To import shipments until fully discharged from import conveyance or until marine insurance has ceased to cover, whichever last occurs;
(i) To shipments by mail or parcel post;
(j) By nuclear reaction or nuclear radiation or radioactive contamination, all whether controlled or uncontrolled, and whether such loss be direct or indirect, proximate or remote, or be in whole or in part caused by, contributed to, or aggravated by the peril(s) insured against in this policy; however, subject to the foregoing and all provisions of this policy, direct loss by fire resulting from nuclear reaction or nuclear radiation or radioactive contamination is insured against by this policy;
(k) Caused by or resulting from:

(1) hostile or warlike action in time of peace or war, including action in hindering, combating or defending against an actual, impending or expected attack, (A) by any government or sovereign power (de jure or de facto), or by any authority maintaining or using military, naval or air forces; or (B) by military, naval or air forces; or (C) by an agent of any government, power, authority or forces;

(2) any weapon of war employing atomic fission or radioactive force whether in time of peace or war;

(3) insurrection, rebellion, revolution, civil war, usurped power, or action taken by governmental authority in hindering, combating or defending against such an occurrence, seizure or destruction under quarantine or customs regulations, confiscation by order of any government or public authority, or risks of contraband or illegal transportation or trade.

Inland Marine (*Continued*)

tion by order of any government or public authority, or risks of contraband or illegal transportation or trade.

'. SPECIAL CONDITIONS

(a) The valuation of the property covered hereunder shall be the actual invoice cost, including prepaid freight, together with such costs and charges since shipment as may have accrued and become legally due thereon, and all premiums under this policy shall be paid on this basis. If there is no invoice, the valuation of the property insured hereunder shall be the actual cash market value of the property insured at point of destination on the date of the disaster.

(b) In case of damage affecting labels, capsules or wrappers, this Company, if liable therefor under the terms of this policy, shall not be liable for more than an amount sufficient to pay the cost of new labels, capsules or wrappers, and the cost of reconditioning the goods, but in no event shall this Company be liable for more than the insured value of the damaged merchandise.

(c) When the property insured under this policy includes a machine consisting when complete for sale or use of several parts, then in case of loss or damage covered by this insurance to any part of such machine, this Company shall be liable only for the proportion of the insured value of the part lost or damaged, or at the Company's option, for the cost and expense, including labor and forwarding charges, of replacing or repairing the lost or damaged part; but in no event shall this Company be liable for more than the insured value of the complete machine.

(d) Any act or agreement by the Insured, prior or subsequent hereto, whereby any right of the Insured, to recover the full value of, or amount of damage to, any property or interest lost or damaged and insured hereunder, against any carrier, bailee or other party liable therefor, is released, impaired or lost, unless specifically authorized by endorsement, shall render this policy null and void, but the Insurer's right to retain or recover the premium shall not be affected. This Company is not liable for any loss or damage which, without its consent, has been settled or compromised by the Insured.

(e) In event of cancelation, the Insured agrees to furnish the Company with an accurate statement showing the total value of all shipments, covered by this policy between the date of its attachment and up to and including the date of cancelation, and further agrees to pay premium on such amount at the rate stated in Paragraph 3(a) of this policy; if the premium thus determined exceeds the initial premium paid, the amount of such excess shall immediately become due and payable to this Company. If the earned premium is less than the original premium, this Company shall return the difference to the Insured subject to the minimum premium requirements stated elsewhere in this policy.

(f) Cancelation of this policy does not prejudice any risk in transit on the effective date of the cancelation.

All other terms and conditions of this policy remain unchanged.

....Agent

Inland Marine (*Continued*)

SCHEDULED PROPERTY FLOATER POLICY

No. SP

RENEWAL OF NUMBER

CAPITAL STOCK COMPANY

AUTHENTIC

SPACE FOR COMPANY NAME, INSIGNIA, AND LOCATION

Insured's Name and Address: (No., Street, Town, County, State)

SPACE FOR PRODUCER'S NAME AND MAILING ADDRESS

Policy Period: (Mo. Day Yr.)

From to

$__________ PREMIUM __________ RATE $__________ AMOUNT

In consideration of the stipulations herein named and of the premium above specified the Company does insure the Insured named above, hereinafter called the Insured, whose address is shown above, from the inception date shown above, at noon, to the expiration date shown above, at noon, Standard Time at place of issuance, to an amount not exceeding the amount(s) above specified, on the following described property:

This policy is made and accepted subject to the foregoing provisions and stipulations and those hereinafter stated, which are hereby made a part of this policy, together with such other provisions, stipulations and agreements as may be added hereto, as provided in this policy.

Agency at

Countersigned:

____________________ **Agent**

Ptd. in U.S.A.

Inland Marine (*Continued*)

(Attach Schedules and Endorsements Here)

CONDITIONS

Misrepresentation and Fraud. This entire policy shall be void if, ether before or after a loss, the Insured has concealed or misrepre- ıted any material fact or circumstance concerning this insurance the subject thereof, or the interest of the Insured therein, or in case any fraud or false swearing by the Insured relating thereto.

Notice of Loss. The Insured shall as soon as practicable report in ting to the Company or its agent every loss, damage or occurrence ich may give rise to a claim under this policy and shall also file h the Company or its agent within ninety (90) days from date of covery of such loss, damage or occurrence, a detailed sworn proof loss.

Examination Under Oath. The Insured, as often as may be reason- y required, shall exhibit to any person designated by the Company that remains of any property herein described, and shall submit, d in so far as is within his or their power cause his or their em- yees, members of the household and others to submit to examina- ns under oath by any person named by the Company and subscribe e same; and, as often as may be reasonably required, shall produce examination all writings, books of account, bills, invoices and other uchers, or certified copies thereof if originals be lost, at such sonable time and place as may be designated by the Company or representative, and shall permit extracts and copies thereof to be ide. No such examination under oath or examination of books or cuments, nor any other act of the Company or any of its employees representatives in connection with the investigation of any loss or im hereunder, shall be deemed a waiver of any defense which the mpany might otherwise have with respect to any loss or claim, t all such examinations and acts shall be deemed to have been ade or done without prejudice to the Company's liability.

Valuation. The Company shall not be liable beyond the actual h value of the property at the time any loss or damage occurs and e loss or damage shall be ascertained or estimated according to such ual cash value with proper deduction for depreciation, however used, and shall in no event exceed what it would then cost to repair replace the same with material of like kind and quality.

Settlement of Loss. All adjusted claims shall be paid or made od to the Insured within sixty (60) days after presentation and ceptance of satisfactory proof of interest and loss at the office of e Company. No loss shall be paid or made good if the Insured has llected the same from others.

No Benefit to Bailee. This insurance shall in nowise inure directly indirectly to the benefit of any carrier or other bailee.

Subrogation or Loan. If in the event of loss or damage the Insured all acquire any right of action against any individual, firm or rporation for loss of, or damage to, property covered hereunder, the sured will, if requested by the Company, assign and transfer such im or right of action to the Company or, at the Company's option, ecute and deliver to the Company the customary form of loan re- ipt upon receiving an advance of funds in respect of the loss or mage; and will subrogate the Company to, or will hold in trust for e Company, all such rights of action to the extent of the amount id or advanced, and will permit suit to be brought in the Insured's me under the direction of and at the expense of the Company.

Reduction in Amount of Insurance. The amount of insurance and e applicable limit of liability, upon the occurrence of any loss vered hereunder, is reduced by the amount of such loss.

Pair, Set or Parts. In the event of loss of or damage to:

(a) any article or articles which are a part of a pair or set, the measure of loss of or damage to such article or articles shall be a reasonable and fair proportion of the total value of the pair or set, giving consideration to the importance of said article or articles, but in no event shall such loss or damage be construed to mean total loss of the pair or set; or

(b) any part of property covered consisting, when complete for use, of several parts, the Company shall only be liable for the value of the part lost or damaged.

10. **Protection of Property.** In case of loss, it shall be lawful and necessary for the Insured, his or their factors, servants and assigns, to sue, labor, and travel for, in and about the defense, safeguard and recovery of the property insured hereunder, or any part thereof, without prejudice to this insurance, nor shall the acts of the Insured or the Company, in recovering, saving and preserving the property insured in case of loss be considered a waiver or an acceptance of abandonment. The expenses so incurred shall be borne by the Insured and the Company proportionately to the extent of their respective interests.

11. **Suit.** No suit, action or proceeding for the recovery of any claim under this policy shall be sustainable in any court of law or equity unless the same be commenced within twelve (12) months next after discovery by the Insured of the occurrence which gives rise to the claim, provided however, that if by the laws of the State within which this policy is issued such limitation is invalid, then any such claims shall be void unless such action, suit or proceeding be commenced within the shortest limit of time permitted by the laws of such State.

12. **Appraisal.** If the Insured and the Company fail to agree as to the amount of loss, each shall, on the written demand of either, made within sixty (60) days after receipt of proof of loss by the Company, select a competent and disinterested appraiser, and the appraisal shall be made at a reasonable time and place. The appraisers shall first select a competent and disinterested umpire, and failing for fifteen (15) days to agree upon such umpire, then, on the request of the Insured or the Company, such umpire shall be selected by a judge of a court of record in the State in which such appraisal is pending. The appraisers shall then appraise the loss, stating separately the actual cash value at the time of loss and the amount of loss, and failing to agree shall submit their differences to the umpire. An award in writing of any two shall determine the amount of loss. The Insured and the Company shall each pay his or its chosen appraiser and shall bear equally the other expenses of the appraisal and umpire. The Company shall not be held to have waived any of its rights by any act relating to appraisal.

13. **Cancelation.** This policy may be canceled by the Insured by surrender thereof to the Company or any of its authorized agents or by mailing to the Company written notice stating when thereafter such cancelation shall be effective. This policy may be canceled by the Company by mailing to the Insured at the address shown in this policy or last known address written notice stating when, not less than five (5) days thereafter, such cancelation shall be effective. The mailing of notice as aforesaid shall be sufficient proof of notice. The time of surrender or the effective date of the cancelation stated in the notice shall become the end of the policy period. Delivery of such written notice either by the Insured or by the Company shall be equivalent to mailing.

If the Insured cancels, earned premiums shall be computed in accordance with the customary short rate table and procedure. If the Company cancels, earned premium shall be computed pro rata. Premium adjustment may be made at the time cancelation is effected and, if not then made, shall be made as soon as practicable after cancelation becomes effective. The Company's check or the check of its representative mailed or delivered as aforesaid shall be a sufficient tender of any refund of premium due to the Insured.

14. **Changes.** Notice to any agent or knowledge possessed by any agent or by any other person shall not effect a waiver or a change in any part of this policy or estop the Company from asserting any right under the terms of this policy, nor shall the terms of this policy be waived or changed, except by endorsement issued to form a part of this policy.

15. **Conformity to Statute.** Terms of this policy which are in conflict with the statutes of the State wherein this policy is issued are hereby amended to conform to such statutes.

In Witness Whereof, the Company has executed and attested these presents, but this policy shall not be valid unless countersigned by a duly thorized agent of the Company at the agency hereinbefore mentioned.

INSERT SIGNATURES AND TITLES OF PROPER OFFICERS

Inland Marine (*Concluded*)

INLAND MARINE

PAF 1204

PERSONAL ARTICLES FLOATER

Attached to and forming part of Policy Number

issued to

by at its Agenc

located (city and state) Date

This policy covers only with respect to such and so many of the following classes of property as are indicated by a specific amoun of insurance applicable thereto, and a premium therefor, which property is owned by or in the custody or control of the Insure and members of the Insured's family of the same household:

Class of Property	Amount of Insurance	Premium
1. Jewelry, as scheduled herein.	$	$
2. Furs and garments trimmed with fur or consisting principally of fur, as scheduled herein.		
3. Cameras, projection machines, films and articles of equipment pertaining thereto, as listed herein.		
4. Musical instruments and articles of equipment pertaining thereto, as listed herein.		
5. "Silverware", meaning silverware, silver-platedware, goldware, gold-platedware and pewterware.		
6.		

SCHEDULE

THIS POLICY INSURES AGAINST:

All risks of loss of or damage to the insured property except as hereinafter provided.

THIS POLICY DOES NOT INSURE:

(a) Against loss or damage caused by wear and tear, gradual deterioration, moths, vermin, or inherent vice;

(b) Against loss or damage caused by or resulting from:

(1) hostile or warlike action in time of peace or war, including action in hindering, combating or defending against an actual impending or expected attack, (a) by any government or sovereign power (de jure or de facto), or by any authorit maintaining or using military, naval or air forces; or (b) by military, naval or air forces; or (c) by an agent of any suc government, power, authority or forces;

(2) any weapon of war employing atomic fission or radioactive force whether in time of peace or war;

(3) insurrection, rebellion, revolution, civil war, usurped power, or action taken by governmental authority in hindering, com bating or defending against such an occurrence, seizure or destruction under quarantine or customs regulations, confisca tion by order of any government or public authority, or risks of contraband or illegal transportation or trade;

(c) Against loss by nuclear reaction or nuclear radiation or radioactive contamination, all whether controlled or uncontrolled, and whether such loss be direct or indirect, proximate or remote, or be in whole or in part caused by, contributed to, o aggravated by the peril(s) insured against in this policy; however, subject to the foregoing and all provisions of this policy, direct loss by fire resulting from nuclear reaction or nuclear radiation or radioactive contamination is insured against by this policy.

SPECIAL CONDITIONS:

(a) As to Musical Instruments:

The Insured represents and agrees that none of the instruments insured hereunder will be played for remuneration during th term of this policy, unless otherwise endorsed hereon and additional premium paid at the current rates of the Company

(b) As to "Silverware":

This policy does not insure, as "Silverware", pens, pencils, flasks, smoking implements or accessories or articles of persona adornment.

ADDITIONALLY ACQUIRED PROPERTY

The following clause is applicable only to jewelry, watches, furs, cameras and musical instruments when such property is insure hereunder.

In consideration of the agreement by the Insured to report additional property of the kind insured hereunder, acquired by th Insured subsequent to the attachment date of this policy, within thirty (30) days from the date acquired and to pay full premiur thereon from the date acquired at pro rata of the current rates of the Company for such insurance, this policy covers on eac separate class of such additionally acquired property for not exceeding 25%, or $10,000. whichever is the lesser, of the amoun of insurance on such class exclusive of this provision. It is specifically understood and agreed by the Insured that this policy sha cease to cover such additionally acquired property if it is not reported to the Company within the stated thirty (30) day period.

This additional coverage does not apply to property of a class not already insured hereunder.

TERRITORIAL LIMITS

Unless otherwise endorsed hereon this insurance covers wherever the property may be located.

....Agent

E. Comprehensive General Liability Policy

COMPREHENSIVE GENERAL LIABILITY POLICY

No. CGL

RENEWAL OF NUMBER

TYPE OF COMPANY

UNIFORM'S CASUALTY SERVICE

A UNIFORM [AUTHENTIC] BASIC POLICY

UNIFORM PRINTING AND SUPPLY

Division of COURIER-CITIZEN COMPANY

SPACE FOR AGENT'S STICKER OR IMPRINT

DECLARATIONS

Item 1. Named Insured and Address: (No., Street, Town or City, County, State)

•

Item 2. Policy Period: (Mo. Day Yr.) (Months)

From to

12:01 A.M., standard time at the address of the named insured as stated herein

Locations of all premises owned, rented or controlled by named insured (ENTER "SAME" IF SAME LOCATION AS ABOVE ADDRESS)

Interest of named insured in such premises (CHECK "OWNER," "GENERAL LESSEE" OR "TENANT") and part occupied by named insured (ENTER BELOW)

☐ OWNER ☐ GENERAL LESSEE ☐ TENANT

The named insured is (CHECK INDIVIDUAL, CORPORATION OR PARTNERSHIP) Business of the named insured is (ENTER BELOW)

☐ INDIVIDUAL ☐ CORPORATION ☐ PARTNERSHIP

Item 3. The insurance afforded is only with respect to such and so many of the following coverages as are indicated by specific premium charge or charges. The limit of the company's liability against each such coverage shall be as stated herein, subject to all the terms of this policy having reference thereto.

COV.	ADVANCE PREMIUMS	LIMITS OF LIABILITY					COVERAGES
		each person	each accident	aggregate products			A Bodily Injury Liability
A	$	$	$	$			
		each accident	aggregate operations	aggregate protective	aggregate products	aggregate contractual	B Property Damage Liability
B	$	$		$	$	$	
	$	Form numbers of endorsements attached to policy at issue					
	$	Total Advance Premium					

If Policy Period more than one year:

$ Gross Premium $ Discount $ Net Premium

Premium is payable on:

$ Effective date $ 1st Anniv. $ 2nd Anniv.

Item 4. The declarations are completed on attached schedules designated

Item 5. The schedules disclose all hazards insured hereunder known to exist at the effective date of this policy, unless otherwise stated herein:*

Item 6. During the past three years no insurer has canceled insurance, issued to the named insured, similar to that afforded hereunder, unless otherwise stated herein:*

* Absence of an entry means "No Exceptions."

Countersigned:

By______________________

Ptd. in U.S.A. Authorized Representative

Comprehensive General Liability Policy (*Continued*)

RESERVED FOR YOUR COMPANY'S NAME

(A ______________ insurance company, herein called the company)
"Stock" or "Mutual"

Agrees with the insured, named in the declarations made a part hereof, in consideration of the payment of the premium and in reliance upon th statements in the declarations and subject to the limits of liability, exclusions, conditions and other terms of this policy:

INSURING AGREEMENTS

I. Coverage A—Bodily Injury Liability: To pay on behalf of the insured all sums which the insured shall become legally obligated to pay as damages because of bodily injury, sickness or disease, including death at any time resulting therefrom, sustained by any person and caused by accident.

Coverage B—Property Damage Liability: To pay on behalf of the insured all sums which the insured shall become legally obligated to pay as damages because of injury to or destruction of property, including the loss of use thereof, caused by accident.

II. Defense, Settlement, Supplementary Payments: With respect to such insurance as is afforded by this policy, the company shall:

(a) defend any suit against the insured alleging such injury, sickness, disease or destruction and seeking damages on account thereof, even if such suit is groundless, false or fraudulent; but the company may make such investigation, negotiation and settlement of any claim or suit as it deems expedient;

(b)(1)pay all premiums on bonds to release attachments for an amount not in excess of the applicable limit of liability of this policy, all premiums on appeal bonds required in any such defended suit, but without any obligation to apply for or furnish any such bonds;

(2)pay all expenses incurred by the company, all costs taxed against the insured in any such suit and all interest accruing after entry of judgment until the company has paid or tendere or deposited in court such part of such judgment as does nc exceed the limit of the company's liability thereon;

(3)pay expenses incurred by the insured for such immediate mec ical and surgical relief to others as shall be imperative at th time of the accident;

(4)reimburse the insured for all reasonable expenses, other tha loss of earnings, incurred at the company's request;

and the amounts so incurred, except settlements of claims and suits are payable by the company in addition to the applicable limit c liability of this policy.

III. Definition of Insured: The unqualified word "insured" include the named insured and also includes any executive officer, director o stockholder thereof while acting within the scope of his duties as such and any organization or proprietor with respect to real estate manage ment for the named insured. If the named insured is a partnership, the unqualified word "insured" also includes any partner therein but only with respect to his liability as such.

IV. Policy Period, Territory: This policy applies only to accident which occur during the policy period within the United States o America, its territories or possessions, or Canada.

EXCLUSIONS

This policy does not apply:

(a) to liability assumed by the insured under any contract or agreement except (1) a contract as defined herein or (2) as respects the insurance which is afforded for the Products Hazard as defined, a warranty of goods or products;

(b) to any obligation for which the insured may be held liable in an action on a contract or an agreement by a person not a party thereto;

(c) except with respect to operations performed by independent contractors and except with respect to liability assumed by the insured under a contract as defined herein, to the ownership, maintenance, operation, use, loading or unloading of (1) watercraft if the accident occurs away from premises owned by, rented to or controlled by the named insured, except insofar as this part of this exclusion is stated in the declarations to be inapplicable, (2) automobiles if the accident occurs away from such premises or the ways immediately adjoining, or (3) aircraft;

(d) to injury, sickness, disease, death or destruction due to war, whether or not declared, civil war, insurrection, rebellion or revolution, or to any act or condition incident to any of the foregoing, with respect to (1) liability assumed by the insured under any contract or agreement or (2) expenses under Insuring Agreement II (b) (3);

(e) to liability imposed upon the insured or any indemnitee, as a person or organization engaged in the business of manufacturing, selling or distributing alcoholic beverages, or as an owner or lessor of premises used for such purposes, by reason of any statute or ordinance pertaining to the sale, gift, distribution or use of any alcoholic beverage;

(f) under coverage A, to any obligation for which the insured or any carrier as his insurer may be held liable under any workmen's compensation, unemployment compensation or disability benefits law, or under any similar law;

(g) under coverage A, except with respect to liability assumed by the insured under a contract as defined herein, to bodily injury to or sickness, disease or death of any employee of the insured arising out of and in the course of his employment by the insured;

(h) under coverage B, to injury to or destruction of (1) property owned or occupied by or rented to the insured, or (2) except with respect to liability under sidetrack agreements covered by this policy, property used by the insured, or (3) except with respect to liability under such sidetrack agreements or the use of elevators or escalators at premises owned by, rented to or controlled by the named insured, property in the care, custody or control of the insured or property as to which the insured for any purpose is exercising physical control, or (4) any goods, products or containers thereof manufactured, sold, handled or distributed or premises alienated by the named insured, o work completed by or for the named insured, out of which the acci dent arises;

(i) under coverage B, to injury to or destruction of buildings c property therein, wherever occurring, arising out of any of the follow ing causes, if such cause occurs on or from premises owned by c rented to the named insured: (1) the discharge, leakage or overflo of water or steam from plumbing, heating, refrigerating or air-cond tioning systems, standpipes for fire hose, or industrial or domesti appliances, or any substance from automatic sprinkler systems, (2 the collapse or fall of tanks or the component parts or supports therec which form a part of automatic sprinkler systems, or (3) rain or snov admitted directly to the building interior through defective roofs leaders or spouting, or open or defective doors, windows, skylights transoms or ventilators; but this exclusion does not apply to loss du to fire, to the use of elevators or escalators or to operations performe by independent contractors;

(j) under coverage B, to injury to or destruction of any property arising out of (1) blasting or explosion, other than the explosion o air or steam vessels, piping under pressure, prime movers, machiner or power transmitting equipment, or (2) the collapse of or structura injury to any building or structure due (a) to grading of land, excava tion, borrowing, filling, back-filling, tunneling, pile driving, coffer-dar work or caisson work, or (b) to moving, shoring, underpinning, raising or demolition of any building or structure or removal or rebuilding o any structural support thereof; provided, however, this exclusion does not apply with respect to liability assumed by the insured under any contract covered by this policy, to operations performed for the namec insured by independent contractors or to completed or abandonec operations within the meaning of paragraph 2 of the Products Hazard and provided further that part (1) or part (2) of this exclusion does not apply to operations stated, in the declarations or in the company's manual, as not subject to such part of this exclusion;

(k) under coverage B, to injury to or destruction of wires, conduits pipes, mains, sewers or other similar property, or any apparatus i connection therewith, below the surface of the ground, if such injur or destruction is caused by and occurs during the use of mechanica equipment for the purpose of grading of land, paving, excavating o drilling, or to injury to or destruction of property at any time resulting therefrom; provided, however, this exclusion does not apply with respec to liability assumed by the insured under any contract covered by thi policy, to operations performed for the named insured by independen contractors, to completed or abandoned operations within the meanin of paragraph 2 of the Products Hazard, or to operations stated, in the declarations or in the company's manual, as not subject to this exclusion

Comprehensive General Liability Policy (*Continued*)

(ATTACH ENDORSEMENTS HERE)

CONDITIONS

Premium: The premium bases and rates for the hazards described the declarations are stated therein. Premium bases and rates for zards not so described are those applicable in accordance with the anuals in use by the company.

The advance premium stated in the declarations is an estimated emium only. Upon termination of this policy, the earned premium all be computed in accordance with the company's rules, rates, ratg plans, premiums and minimum premiums applicable to this insurce. If the earned premium thus computed exceeds the estimated vance premium paid, the named insured shall pay the excess to the mpany; if less, the company shall return to the named insured the earned portion paid by such insured.

When used as a premium basis:

(1) the word "admissions" means the total number of persons, other than employees of the named insured, admitted to the event insured or to events conducted on the premises whether on paid admission tickets, complimentary tickets or passes;

(2) the word "cost" means the total cost to (a) the named insured with respect to operations performed for the named insured during the policy period by independent contractors, or (b) any indemnitee with respect to any contract covered by this policy, of all work let or sub-let in connection with each specific project, including the cost of all labor, materials and equipment furnished, used or delivered for use in the execution of such work, whether furnished by the owner, contractor or subcontractor, including all fees, allowances, bonuses or commissions made, paid or due;

(3) the word "receipts" means the gross amount of money charged by the named insured for such operations by the named insured or by others during the policy period as are rated on a receipts basis other than receipts from telecasting, broadcasting or motion pictures, and includes taxes, other than taxes which the named insured collects as a separate item and remits directly to a governmental division;

(4) the word "remuneration" means the entire remuneration earned during the policy period by proprietors and by all employees of the named insured, other than drivers of teams or automobiles and aircraft pilots and co-pilots, subject to any overtime earnings or limitation of remuneration rule applicable in accordance with the manuals in use by the company;

(5) the word "sales" means the gross amount of money charged by the named insured or by others trading under his name for all goods and products sold or distributed during the policy period and charged during the policy period for installation, servicing or repair, and includes taxes, other than taxes which the named insured and such others collect as a separate item and remit directly to a governmental division.

The named insured shall maintain for each hazard records of the formation necessary for premium computation on the basis stated in e declarations, and shall send copies of such records to the company the end of the policy period and at such times during the policy riod as the company may direct.

Inspection and Audit: The company shall be permitted to inspect e insured premises, operations and elevators and to examine and dit the insured's books and records at any time during the policy riod and any extension thereof and within three years after the final rmination of this policy, as far as they relate to the premium bases the subject matter of this insurance.

Definitions:

Contract. The word "contract" means, if in writing, a lease of premises, easement agreement, agreement required by municipal ordinance, sidetrack agreement, or elevator or escalator maintenance agreement.

Automobile. The word "automobile" means a land motor vehicle, trailer or semitrailer, provided:

(1) The following described equipment shall be deemed an automobile while towed by or carried on an automobile not so described, but not otherwise: if of the crawler-type, any tractor, power crane or shovel, ditch or trench digger; any farm-type tractor; any concrete mixer other than of the mix-in-transit type; any grader, scraper, roller or farm implement; and, if not subject to motor vehicle registration, any other equipment not specified in (2) below, which is designed for use principally off public roads.

(2) The following described equipment shall be deemed an automobile while towed by or carried on an automobile as above defined solely for purposes of transportation or while being operated solely for locomotion, but not otherwise: if of the non-crawler type, any power crane or shovel, ditch or trench digger; and any air-compressing, building or vacuum cleaning, spraying or welding equipment or well drilling machinery.

(c) **Products Hazard.** The term "products hazard" means

(1) goods or products manufactured, sold, handled or distributed by the named insured or by others trading under his name, if the accident occurs after possession of such goods or products has been relinquished to others by the named insured or by others trading under his name and if such accident occurs away from premises owned, rented or controlled by the named insured or on premises for which the classification stated in division (a) of the declarations excludes any part of the foregoing; provided, such goods or products shall be deemed to include any container thereof, other than a vehicle, but shall not include any vending machine or any property, other than such container, rented to or located for use of others but not sold;

(2) operations, including any act or omission in connection with operations performed by or on behalf of the named insured on the premises or elsewhere and whether or not goods or products are involved in such operations, if the accident occurs after such operations have been completed or abandoned and occurs away from premises owned, rented or controlled by the named insured; provided, operations shall not be deemed incomplete because improperly or defectively performed or because further operations may be required pursuant to an agreement; provided further, the following shall not be deemed to be "operations" within the meaning of this paragraph: (a) pick-up or delivery, except from or onto a railroad car, (b) the maintenance of vehicles owned or used by or in behalf of the insured, (c) the existence of tools, uninstalled equipment and abandoned or unused materials and (d) operations for which the classification stated in division (a) of the declarations specifically includes completed operations.

(d) **Assault and Battery.** Assault and battery shall be deemed an accident unless committed by or at the direction of the insured.

4. Limits of Liability—Coverage A: The limit of bodily injury liability stated in the declarations as applicable to "each person" is the limit of the company's liability for all damages, including damages for care and loss of services, arising out of bodily injury, sickness or disease, including death at any time resulting therefrom, sustained by one person as the result of any one accident; the limit of such liability stated in the declarations as applicable to "each accident" is, subject to the above provision respecting each person, the total limit of the company's liability for all damages, including damages for care and loss of services, arising out of bodily injury, sickness or disease, including death at any time resulting therefrom, sustained by two or more persons as the result of any one accident.

5. Limits of Liability—Products: Subject to the limit of liability with respect to "each accident," the limits of bodily injury liability and property damage liability stated in the declarations as "aggregate products" are respectively the total limits of the company's liability for all damages arising out of the products hazard. All such damages arising out of one lot of goods or products prepared or acquired by the named insured or by another trading under his name shall be considered as arising out of one accident.

6. Limits of Liability—Coverage B: The limit of property damage liability stated in the declarations as applicable to "each accident" is the total limit of the company's liability for all damages arising out of injury to or destruction of all property of one or more persons or organizations, including the loss of use thereof, as the result of any one accident.

Subject to the limit of liability with respect to "each accident," the limit of property damage liability stated in the declarations as "aggregate operations" is the total limit of the company's liability for all damages arising out of injury to or destruction of property, including the loss of use thereof, caused by the ownership, maintenance or use of premises or operations rated on a remuneration premium basis or by contractors' equipment rated on a receipts premium basis.

Subject to the limit of liability with respect to "each accident," the limit of property damage liability stated in the declarations as "aggregate protective" is the total limit of the company's liability for all damages arising out of injury to or destruction of property, including the loss of use thereof, caused by operations performed for the named insured by independent contractors or general supervision thereof by the named insured, except (a) maintenance and repairs at premises owned by or rented to the named insured and (b) structural alterations at such premises which do not involve changing the size of or moving buildings or other structures.

Subject to the limit of liability with respect to "each accident," the limit of property damage liability stated in the declarations as "aggregate contractual" is the total limit of the company's liability for all damages arising out of injury to or destruction of property, including the loss of use thereof, with respect to liability assumed by the insured under contracts covered by this policy in connection with operations for which there is an "aggregate operations" limit of property damage liability stated in the declarations.

Comprehensive General Liability Policy (*Continued*)

The limits of property damage liability stated in the declarations as "aggregate operations," "aggregate protective" and "aggregate contractual" apply separately to each project with respect to operations being performed away from premises owned by or rented to the named insured.

7. Severability of Interests: The term "the insured" is used severally and not collectively, but the inclusion herein of more than one insured shall not operate to increase the limits of the company's liability.

8. Notice of Accident: When an accident occurs written notice shall be given by or on behalf of the insured to the company or any of its authorized agents as soon as practicable. Such notice shall contain particulars sufficient to identify the insured and also reasonably obtainable information respecting the time, place and circumstances of the accident, the names and addresses of the injured and of available witnesses.

9. Notice of Claim or Suit: If claim is made or suit is brought against the insured, the insured shall immediately forward to the company every demand, notice, summons or other process received by him or his representative.

10. Assistance and Cooperation of the Insured: The insured shall cooperate with the company and, upon the company's request, shall attend hearings and trials and shall assist in effecting settlements, securing and giving evidence, obtaining the attendance of witnesses and in the conduct of suits. The insured shall not, except at his own cost, voluntarily make any payment, assume any obligation or incur any expense other than for such immediate medical and surgical relief to others as shall be imperative at the time of accident.

11. Action Against Company: No action shall lie against the company unless, as a condition precedent thereto, the insured shall have fully complied with all the terms of this policy, nor until the amount of the insured's obligation to pay shall have been finally determined either by judgment against the insured after actual trial or by written agreement of the insured, the claimant and the company.

Any person or organization or the legal representative thereof who has secured such judgment or written agreement shall thereafter be entitled to recover under this policy to the extent of the insurance afforded by this policy. Nothing contained in this policy shall give any person or organization any right to join the company as a co-defendant in any action against the insured to determine the insured's liability.

Bankruptcy or insolvency of the insured or of the insured's estate shall not relieve the company of any of its obligations hereunder.

12. Other Insurance: If the insured has other insurance against a loss covered by this policy the company shall not be liable under this policy for a greater proportion of such loss than the applicable limit of liability stated in the declarations bears to the total applicable limit of liability of all valid and collectible insurance against such loss.

13. Subrogation: In the event of any payment under this policy, the company shall be subrogated to all the insured's rights of recovery therefor against any person or organization and the insured shall execute and deliver instruments and papers and do whatever else is necessary to secure such rights. The insured shall do nothing after loss to prejudice such rights.

14. Three Year Policy: A policy period of three years is comprised of three consecutive annual periods. Computation and adjustment of earned premium shall be made at the end of each annual period. Aggregate limits of liability as stated in this policy shall apply separately to each annual period.

15. Changes: Notice to any agent or knowledge possessed by any agent or by any other person shall not effect a waiver or a change in any part of this policy or estop the company from asserting any right under the terms of this policy; nor shall the terms of this policy be waived or changed, except by endorsement issued to form a part of this policy.

16. Assignment: Assignment of interest under this policy shall not bind the company until its consent is endorsed hereon; if, however, the named insured shall die, this policy shall cover the named insured's legal representative as named insured; provided that notice of cancelation addressed to the insured named in the declarations and mailed to the address shown in this policy shall be sufficient notice to effect cancelation of this policy.

17. Cancelation: This policy may be canceled by the named insured by surrender thereof to the company or any of its authorized agents or by mailing to the company written notice stating when thereafter the cancelation shall be effective. This policy may be canceled by the company by mailing to the named insured at the address shown in this policy written notice stating when not less than ten days thereafter such cancelation shall be effective. The mailing of notice as aforesaid shall be sufficient proof of notice. The time of the surrender or the effective date and hour of cancelation stated in the notice shall become the end of the policy period. Delivery of such written notice either by the named insured or by the company shall be equivalent to mailing.

If the named insured cancels, earned premium shall be computed in accordance with the customary short rate table and procedure. If the company cancels, earned premium shall be computed pro rata. Premium adjustment may be made either at the time cancelation is effected or as soon as practicable after cancelation becomes effective, but payment or tender of unearned premium is not a condition of cancelation.

18. Declarations: By acceptance of this policy the named insured agrees that the statements in the declarations are his agreements and representations, that this policy is issued in reliance upon the truth of such representations and that this policy embodies all agreements existing between himself and the company or any of its agents relating to this insurance.

***In Witness Whereof,** the company has caused this policy to be executed and attested, but this policy shall not be valid unless countersigned by a duly authorized representative of the company.

*Company's language may be substituted as desired.

INSERT SIGNATURES AND TITLES OF PROPER OFFICERS

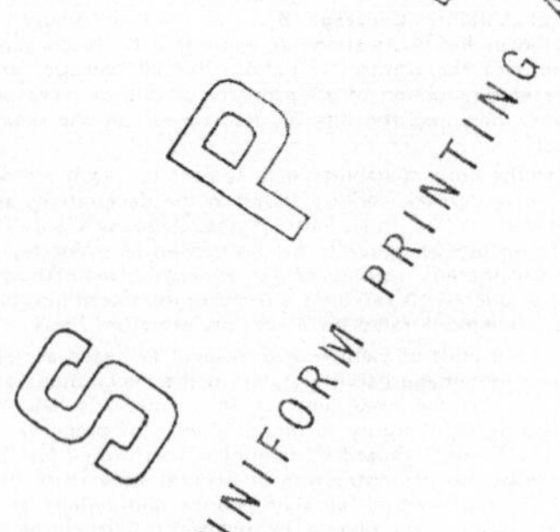

Comprehensive General Liability Policy (*Concluded*)

A&G 661a
NUCLEAR ENERGY LIABILITY EXCLUSION ENDORSEMENT
(BROAD FORM)

This endorsement, effective (12:01 A. M., standard time) forms a part of policy No.

issued to

by

It is agreed that the policy does not apply:

I. Under any Liability Coverage, to injury, sickness, disease, death or destruction

(a) with respect to which an insured under the policy is also an insured under a nuclear energy liability policy issued by Nuclear Energy Liability Insurance Association, Mutual Atomic Energy Liability Underwriters or Nuclear Insurance Association of Canada, or would be an insured under any such policy but for its termination upon exhaustion of its limit of liability; or

(b) resulting from the hazardous properties of nuclear material and with respect to which (1) any person or organization is required to maintain financial protection pursuant to the Atomic Energy Act of 1954, or any law amendatory thereof, or (2) the insured is, or had this policy not been issued would be, entitled to indemnity from the United States of America, or any agency thereof, under any agreement entered into by the United States of America, or any agency thereof, with any person or organization.

II. Under any Medical Payments Coverage, or under any Supplementary Payments provision relating to immediate medical or surgical relief, to expenses incurred with respect to bodily injury, sickness, disease or death resulting from the hazardous properties of nuclear material and arising out of the operation of a nuclear facility by any person or organization.

III. Under any Liability Coverage, to injury, sickness, disease, death or destruction resulting from the hazardous properties of nuclear material, if

(a) the nuclear material (1) is at any nuclear facility owned by, or operated by or on behalf of, an insured or (2) has been discharged or dispersed therefrom;

(b) the nuclear material is contained in spent fuel or waste at any time possessed, handled, used, processed, stored, transported or disposed of by or on behalf of an insured; or

(c) the injury, sickness, disease, death or destruction arises out of the furnishing by an insured of services, materials, parts or equipment in connection with the planning, construction, maintenance, operation or use of any nuclear facility, but if such facility is located within the United States of America, its territories or possessions or Canada, this exclusion (c) applies only to injury to or destruction of property at such nuclear facility.

IV. As used in this endorsement:

"hazardous properties" include radioactive, toxic or explosive properties;

"nuclear material" means source material, special nuclear material or byproduct material;

"source material", **"special nuclear material"**, and **"byproduct material"** have the meanings given them in the Atomic Energy Act of 1954 or in any law amendatory thereof;

"spent fuel" means any fuel element or fuel component, solid or liquid, which has been used or exposed to radiation in a nuclear reactor;

"waste" means any waste material (1) containing byproduct material and (2) resulting from the operation by any person or organization of any nuclear facility included within the definition of nuclear facility under paragraph (a) or (b) thereof;

"nuclear facility" means

(a) any nuclear reactor,

(b) any equipment or device designed or used for (1) separating the isotopes of uranium or plutonium, (2) processing or utilizing spent fuel, or (3) handling, processing or packaging waste,

(c) any equipment or device used for the processing, fabricating or alloying of special nuclear material if at any time the total amount of such material in the custody of the insured at the premises where such equipment or device is located consists of or contains more than 25 grams of plutonium or uranium 233 or any combination thereof, or more than 250 grams of uranium 235,

(d) any structure, basin, excavation, premises or place prepared or used for the storage or disposal of waste,

and includes the site on which any of the foregoing is located, all operations conducted on such site and all premises used for such operations;

"nuclear reactor" means any apparatus designed or used to sustain nuclear fission in a self-supporting chain reaction or to contain a critical mass of fissionable material;

With respect to injury to or destruction of property, the word **"injury"** or **"destruction"** includes all forms of radioactive contamination of property.

....
Authorized Representative

F. Workmen's Compensation and Employers' Liability Policy

STANDARD PROVISIONS FOR WORKMEN'S COMPENSATION AND EMPLOYERS' LIABILITY POLICIES

GENERAL INSTRUCTIONS

1. Standard Language

This form is expressed in standard language which may not be amended and no part of which may be omitted except (a) as indicated by thes instructions, or (b) as indicated in reference notes shown below referring to specific portions of the form, or (c) by an endorsement which stat an amendment or exclusion of some provision of the form in accordance with the provisions of a manual rule, the form of which endorsement ha been approved, if required, by the supervising authority of each state in which such endorsement is applicable.

2. Optional Sequence and Arrangement

The several parts of the form, viz., "Insuring Agreements," "Exclusions," "Conditions" and "Declarations" may appear in the policy in suc sequence as the company may elect and the sequence and arrangement of the several provisions of those parts are also optional with the compan

3. Descriptive Headings—Identifying or Indexing Designations

The descriptive headings of the parts of the form (as quoted above) and of the major insuring agreements ("Workmen's Compensation" ar "Employers' Liability") are standard expressions which may not be amended or omitted, but all identifying or indexing designations (such a "Coverage A," "Defense, Settlement, Supplementary Payments," "Cancelation," etc.), including literal or numerical designations of paragrap or phrases may be amended or omitted at the company's option. When such identifying or indexing designations, used for the purpose of refe ence in the text of the form or any endorsement form applicable thereto, are amended or omitted, descriptive designations shall be substitute therefor.

4. Definition of "Standard Language"

"Standard language" when used in these instructions means the form and endorsements either prescribed or approved by the insurance supe vising authority of the state in which policy forms and endorsements are approved or prescribed. In those states where supervising authorities d not have the authority to approve or prescribe policies, forms and endorsements, the term means the forms and endorsements adopted by th companies for use in such states.

5. Special Conditions for Mutuals, Reciprocals and Participating Stock Companies

When the policy is issued by a mutual company, a reciprocal association or a participating stock company having special provisions applicab to its membership or policyholders, such provisions, when approved by the supervising authority of the state in which the policy is issued if suc approval is required, may be inserted in the policy.

REFERENCE NOTES

1—Matter in brackets may be included, omitted or amended at the option of the company.
2—The effective hour and date of the policy may be typed or printed in this space.
3—Matter in brackets may be omitted.
4—The applicable classifications, including the standard exceptions, may be typed or printed in this space.
5—The capacity of the person countersigning may be stated.
6—Declarations of this type calling for underwriting data and general information may be used at the option of the company.
7—The name and location of the company are to be stated. The type of the company and the word used throughout the policy suitably t designate the company are to be stated.
8—The exclusions may be combined into one or any other number of paragraphs.
9—The language of this paragraph is optional with the company.

Workmen's Compensation and Employers' Liability Policy (Continued)

2

BLANK INSURANCE COMPANY

[Workmen's Compensation and Employers' Liability][1] Policy No.________

DECLARATIONS

Item 1. Name of insured____________________

Address____________________
[No. Street Town or City County State][1]

☐ Individual ☐ Partnership ☐ Corporation ☐ ________ (Other)

Locations—All usual workplaces of the insured at or from which operations covered by this policy are conducted are located at the above address unless otherwise stated herein:____________________

Item 2. Policy Period: From________(See Reference Note 2.)________to________
12:01 A.M., standard time at the address of the insured as stated herein.

Item 3. Coverage A of this policy applies to the workmen's compensation law and any occupational disease law of each of the following states:

____

Item 4. Classification of Operations		Premium Basis	Rates	
Entries in this item, except as specifically provided elsewhere in this policy, do not modify any of the other provisions of this policy.	**Code No.**	**Estimated Total Annual Remuneration**	**Per $100 of Remuneration**	**Estimated Annual Premiums** 3
Loss Constant Expense Constant Loss and Expense Constant Policy Fee 3				
(See Reference Note 4.)				

Minimum Premium $ **Total Estimated Annual Premium $**

If indicated below, interim adjustments of premium shall be made: Deposit Premium $
Semi-Annually ☐ Quarterly ☐ Monthly ☐ 3

Item 5. Limit of Liability for Coverage B—Employers' Liability: $, subject to all the terms of this policy having reference thereto.

[Date and Place of Issue________________][1]

Countersigned [________19____, at________][1] by________
(See Reference Note 5.)

A. Renewal of policy number.
B. Endorsement serial numbers.
C. Rating plan or premium discount.
D. Record of past experience.
E. Cancelation of similar insurance. 6

Workmen's Compensation and Employers' Liability Policy (*Continued*)

[**BLANK INSURANCE COMPANY**
(A________________insurance company, herein called the company)][7]

Agrees with the insured, named in the declarations made a part hereof, in consideration of the payment of the premium and in reliance upon the statements in the declarations and subject to the limits of liability, exclusions, conditions and other terms of this policy:

INSURING AGREEMENTS

I Coverage A—Workmen's Compensation

To pay promptly when due all compensation and other benefits required of the insured by the workmen's compensation law.

Coverage B—Employers' Liability

To pay on behalf of the insured all sums which the insured shall become legally obligated to pay as damages because of bodily injury by accident or disease, including death at any time resulting therefrom, sustained in the United States of America, its territories or possessions, or Canada by any employee of the insured arising out of and in the course of his employment by the insured either in operations in a state designated in Item 3 of the declarations or in operations necessary or incidental thereto.

II Defense, Settlement, Supplementary Payments

As respects the insurance afforded by the other terms of this policy the company shall:

(a) defend any proceeding against the insured seeking such benefits and any suit against the insured alleging such injury and seeking damages on account thereof, even if such proceeding or suit is groundless, false or fraudulent; but the company may make such investigation, negotiation and settlement of any claim or suit as it deems expedient;

(b) pay all premiums on bonds to release attachments for an amount not in excess of the applicable limit of liability of this policy, all premiums on appeal bonds required in any such defended proceeding or suit, but without any obligation to apply for or furnish any such bonds;

(c) pay all expenses incurred by the company, all costs taxed against the insured in any such proceeding or suit and all interest accruing after entry of judgment until the company has paid or tendered or deposited in court such part of such judgment as does not exceed the limit of the company's liability thereon;

(d) reimburse the insured for all reasonable expenses, other than loss of earnings, incurred at the company's request.

The amounts incurred under this insuring agreement, except settlements of claims and suits, are payable by the company in addition to the amounts payable under coverage A or the applicable limit of liability under coverage B.

III Definitions

(a) **Workmen's Compensation Law.** The unqualified term "workmen's compensation law" means the workmen's compensation law and any occupational disease law of a state designated in Item 3 of the declarations, but does not include those provisions of any such law which provide non-occupational disability benefits.

(b) **State.** The word "state" means any State or Territory of the United States of America and the District of Columbia.

(c) **Bodily Injury by Accident; Bodily Injury by Disease.** The contraction of disease is not an accident within the meaning of the word "accident" in the term "bodily injury by accident" and only such disease as results directly from a bodily injury by accident is included within the term "bodily injury by accident." The term "bodily injury by disease" includes only such disease as is not included within the term "bodily injury by accident."

(d) **Assault and Battery.** Under coverage B, assault and battery shall be deemed an accident unless committed by or at the direction of the insured.

IV Application of Policy

This policy applies only to injury (1) by accident occurring during the policy period, or (2) by disease caused or aggravated by exposure of which the last day of the last exposure, in the employment of the insured, to conditions causing the disease occurs during the policy period.

[EXCLUSIONS][8]

This policy does not apply:

(a) to operations conducted at or from any workplace not described in Item 1 or 4 of the declarations if the insured has, under the workmen's compensation law, other insurance for such operations or is a qualified self-insurer therefor;

(b) unless required by law or described in the declarations, to domestic employment or to farm or agricultural employment;

(c) under coverage B, to liability assumed by the insured under any contract or agreement;

(d) under coverage B, (1) to punitive or exemplary damages on account of bodily injury to or death of any employee employed in violation of law, or (2) with respect to any employee employed in violation of law with the knowledge or acquiescence of the insured or any executive officer thereof;

(e) under coverage B, to bodily injury by disease unless prior to thirty-six months after the end of the policy period written claim is made or suit is brought against the insured for damages because of such injury or death resulting therefrom;

(f) under coverage B, to any obligation for which the insured or any carrier as his insurer may be held liable under the workmen's compensation or occupational disease law of a state designated in Item 3 of the declarations, any other workmen's compensation or occupational disease law, any unemployment compensation or disability benefits law, or under any similar law.

CONDITIONS

[The conditions, except conditions 8, 9, 10 and 16, apply to all coverages.][1]
[Conditions 8, 9, 10 and 16, apply only to the coverage noted thereunder.][1]

1. Premium The premium bases and rates for the classifications of operations described in the declarations are as stated therein and for classifications not so described are those applicable in accordance with the manuals in use by the company. This policy is issued by the company and accepted by the insured with the agreement that if any change in classifications, rates or rating plans is or becomes applicable to this policy under any law regulating this insurance or because of any amendments affecting the benefits provided by the workmen's compensation law, such change with the effective date thereof shall be stated in an endorsement issued to form a part of this policy.

Workmen's Compensation and Employers' Liability Policy (*Continued*)

When used as a premium basis, "remuneration" means the entire remuneration, computed in accordance with the manuals in use by the company, earned during the policy period by (a) all executive officers and other employees of the insured engaged in operations covered by this policy, and (b) any other person performing work which may render the company liable under this policy for injury to or death of such person in accordance with the workmen's compensation law. "Remuneration" shall not include the remuneration of any person within division (b) foregoing if the insured maintains evidence satisfactory to the company that the payment of compensation and other benefits under such law to such person is secured by other valid and collectible insurance or by any other undertaking approved by the governmental agency having jurisdiction thereof.

If the declarations provide for adjustment of premium on other than an annual basis, the insured shall pay the deposit premium to the company upon the inception of this policy and thereafter interim premiums shall be computed in accordance with the manuals in use by the company and paid by the insured promptly after the end of each interval specified in the declarations. The deposit premium shall be retained by the company until termination of this policy and credited to the final premium adjustment.

The insured shall maintain records of the information necessary for premium computation on the bases stated in the declarations, and shall send copies of such records to the company at the end of the policy period and at such times during the policy period as the company may direct. If the insured does not furnish records of the remuneration of persons within division (b) of the definition of remuneration foregoing, the remuneration of such persons shall be computed in accordance with the manuals in use by the company.

The premium stated in the declarations is an estimated premium only. Upon termination of this policy, the earned premium shall be computed in accordance with the rules, rates, rating plans, premiums and minimum premiums applicable to this insurance in accordance with the manuals in use by the company. If the earned premium thus computed exceeds the premium previously paid, the insured shall pay the excess to the company; if less, the company shall return to the insured the unearned portion paid by the insured. All premiums shall be fully earned whether any workmen's compensation law, or any part thereof, is or shall be declared invalid or unconstitutional.

[**2. Long Term Policy** If this policy is written for a period longer than one year, all the provisions of this policy shall apply separately to each consecutive twelve months period, or, if the first or last consecutive period is less than twelve months, to such period of less than twelve months, in the same manner as if a separate policy had been written for each consecutive period. The earned premium for each such period shall be computed as provided by Condition 1 of this policy, subject, except as otherwise provided in the manuals in use by the company with respect to classifications of operations for which this policy provides a per capita premium basis, to the following provisions:

(a) The premium rates for the first consecutive period shall be those stated in the declarations and those applicable for such period in accordance with the manuals in use by the company;

(b) The premium bases, classifications of operations, rates, rating plans, premiums and minimum premiums for each such subsequent period shall be those applicable for such period in accordance with the manuals in use by the company.][3]

3. Partnership or Joint Venture as Insured If the insured is a partnership or joint venture, such insurance as is afforded by this policy applies to each partner or member thereof as an insured only while he is acting within the scope of his duties as such partner or member.

4. Inspection and Audit The company and any rating authority having jurisdiction by law shall each be permitted to inspect the workplaces, machinery and equipment covered by this policy and to examine and audit the insured's books, vouchers, contracts, documents and records of any and every kind at any reasonable time during the policy period and any extension thereof and within three years after termination of this policy, as far as they relate to the premium bases or the subject matter of this insurance.

5. Notice of Injury When an injury occurs written notice shall be given by or on behalf of the insured to the company or any of its authorized agents as soon as practicable. Such notice shall contain particulars sufficient to identify the insured and also reasonably obtainable information respecting the time, place and circumstances of the injury, the names and addresses of the injured and of available witnesses.

6. Notice of Claim or Suit If claim is made or suit or other proceeding is brought against the insured, the insured shall immediately forward to the company every demand, notice, summons or other process received by him or his representative.

7. Assistance and Cooperation of the Insured The insured shall cooperate with the company and, upon the company's request, shall attend hearings and trials and shall assist in effecting settlements, securing and giving evidence, obtaining the attendance of witnesses and in the conduct of suits or proceedings. The insured shall not, except at his own cost, voluntarily make any payment, assume any obligation or incur any expense other than for such immediate medical and other services at the time of injury as are required by the workmen's compensation law.

8. Statutory Provisions Coverage A The company shall be directly and primarily liable to any person entitled to the benefits of the workmen's compensation law under this policy. The obligations of the company may be enforced by such person, or for his benefit by any agency authorized by law, whether against the company alone or jointly with the insured. Bankruptcy or insolvency of the insured or of the insured's estate, or any default of the insured, shall not relieve the company of any of its obligations under coverage A.

As between the employee and the company, notice or knowledge of the injury on the part of the insured shall be notice or knowledge, as the case may be, on the part of the company; the jurisdiction of the insured, for the purposes of the workmen's compensation law, shall be jurisdiction of the company and the company shall in all things be bound by and subject to the findings, judgments, awards, decrees, orders or decisions rendered against the insured in the form and manner provided by such law and within the terms, limitations and provisions of this policy not inconsistent with such law.

All of the provisions of the workmen's compensation law shall be and remain a part of this policy as fully and completely as if written herein, so far as they apply to compensation and other benefits provided by this policy and to special taxes, payments into security or other special funds, and assessments required of or levied against compensation insurance carriers under such law.

The insured shall reimburse the company for any payments required of the company under the workmen's compensation law, in excess of the benefits regularly provided by such law, solely because of injury to (a) any employee by reason of the serious and wilful misconduct of the insured, or (b) any employee employed by the insured in violation of law with the knowledge or acquiescence of the insured or any executive officer thereof.

Nothing herein shall relieve the insured of the obligations imposed upon the insured by the other terms of this policy.

9. Limits of Liability Coverage B The words "damages because of bodily injury by accident or disease, including death at any time resulting therefrom," in coverage B include damages for care and loss of services and damages for which the insured is liable by reason of suits or claims brought against the insured by others to recover the damages obtained from such others because of such bodily injury sustained by employees of the insured arising out of and in the course of their employment. The limit of liability stated in the declarations for coverage B is the total limit of the company's liability for all damages because of bodily injury by accident, including death at any time resulting therefrom, sustained by one or more employees in any one accident. The limit of liability stated in the declarations for coverage B is the total limit of the company's liability for all damages because of bodily injury by disease, including death at any time resulting therefrom, sustained by one or more employees of the insured in operations in any one state designated in Item 3 of the declarations or in operations necessary or incidental thereto.

The inclusion herein of more than one insured shall not operate to increase the limits of the company's liability.

10. Action Against Company Coverage B No action shall lie against the company unless, as a condition precedent thereto, the insured shall have fully complied with all the terms of this policy, nor until the amount of the insured's obligation to pay shall have been finally determined either by judgment against the insured after actual trial or by written agreement of the insured, the claimant and the company.

Any person or organization or the legal representative thereof who has secured such judgment or written agreement shall thereafter be entitled to recover under this policy to the extent of the insurance afforded by this policy. Nothing contained in this policy shall give

Workmen's Compensation and Employers' Liability Policy (*Concluded*)

any person or organization any right to join the company as a co-defendant in any action against the insured to determine the insured's liability.

Bankruptcy or insolvency of the insured or of the insured's estate shall not relieve the company of any of its obligations under coverage B.

11. Other Insurance If the insured has other insurance against a loss covered by this policy, the company shall not be liable to the insured hereunder for a greater proportion of such loss than the amount which would have been payable under this policy, had no such other insurance existed, bears to the sum of said amount and the amounts which would have been payable under each other policy applicable to such loss, had each such policy been the only policy so applicable.

12. Subrogation In the event of any payment under this policy, the company shall be subrogated to all rights of recovery therefor of the insured and any person entitled to the benefits of this policy against any person or organization, and the insured shall execute and deliver instruments and papers and do whatever else is necessary to secure such rights. The insured shall do nothing after loss to prejudice such rights.

13. Changes Notice to any agent or knowledge possessed by any agent or by any other person shall not effect a waiver or a change in any part of this policy or estop the company from asserting any right under the terms of this policy; nor shall the terms of this policy be waived or changed, except by endorsement issued to form a part of this policy [, signed by____________ (here insert titles of authorized company officials or representatives); provided, however, changes may be made in the written portion of the declarations by____________ (here insert titles of authorized company representatives) when initialed by such____________ (here insert titles of authorized company representatives) or by endorsement issued to form a part of this policy signed by such____________ (here insert titles of authorized company representatives)][1].

14. Assignment Assignment of interest under this policy shall not bind the company until its consent is endorsed hereon. If, however, during the policy period the insured shall die, and written notice is given to the company within thirty days after the date of such death, this policy shall cover the insured's legal representative as insured; provided that notice of cancelation addressed to the insured named in the declarations and mailed or delivered, after such death, to the address shown in this policy shall be sufficient notice to effect cancelation of this policy.

15. Cancelation This policy may be canceled by the insured [by surrender thereof to the company or any of its authorized agents or][3] by mailing to the company written notice stating when thereafter the cancelation shall be effective. This policy may be canceled by the company by mailing to the insured at the address shown in this policy written notice stating when not less than ten days thereafter such cancelation shall be effective. The mailing of notice as aforesaid shall be sufficient proof of notice. The [time of the surrender or the][3] effective date [and hour][3] of cancelation stated in the notice shall become the end of the policy period. Delivery of such written notice either by the insured or by the company shall be equivalent to mailing.

If the insured cancels, unless the manuals in use by the company otherwise provide, earned premium shall be (1) computed in accordance with the customary short rate table and procedure and (2) not less than the minimum premium stated in the declarations. If the company cancels, earned premium shall be computed pro rata. Premium adjustment may be made at the time cancelation is effected and, if not then made, shall be made as soon as practicable after cancelation becomes effective. The company's check or the check of its representative mailed or delivered as aforesaid shall be a sufficient tender of any refund of premium due to the insured.

When the insurance under the workmen's compensation law may not be canceled except in accordance with such law, this condition so far as it applies to the insurance under this policy with respect to such law, is amended to conform to such law.

16. Terms of Policy Conformed to Statute Coverage A Terms of this policy which are in conflict with the provisions of the workmen's compensation law are hereby amended to conform to such law.

17. Declarations By acceptance of this policy the insured agrees that the statements in the declarations are his agreements and representations, that this policy is issued in reliance upon the truth of such representations and that this policy embodies all agreements existing between himself and the company or any of its agents relating to this insurance.

In witness whereof, the Blank Insurance Company has caused this policy to be signed by its president and a secretary at ____________ and countersigned on the declarations page by a duly authorized agent of the company. 9

(FACSIMILE OF SIGNATURE)
Secretary

(FACSIMILE OF SIGNATURE)
President

G. Family Automobile Policy

FAMILY COMBINATION AUTOMOBILE POLICY

No. ACF

RENEWAL OF NUMBER

TYPE OF COMPANY

UNIFORM'S CASUALTY SERVICE

A UNIFORM [UNIFORM PRINTING AUTHENTIC AND SUPPLY DIVISION] BASIC POLICY

UNIFORM PRINTING AND SUPPLY

Division of COURIER-CITIZEN COMPANY

SPACE FOR AGENT'S STICKER OR IMPRINT

DECLARATIONS

Item 1. Named Insured and Address: (No., Street, Town or City, County, State)

Item 2. Policy Period: (Mo. Day Yr.) (Months)

From to

12:01 A.M., standard time at the address of the named insured as stated herein.

Occupation of the named insured is IF MARRIED WOMAN, GIVE HUSBAND'S OCCUPATION OR BUSINESS (ENTER BELOW)

Item 3. The insurance afforded is only with respect to such of the following coverages as are indicated by specific premium charge or charges. The limit of the company's liability against each such coverage shall be as stated herein, subject to all the terms of this policy having reference thereto.

PREMIUMS CAR 1	CAR 2	LIMITS OF LIABILITY			COVERAGES
$	$		thousand dollars each person thousand dollars each occurrence	A	Bodily Injury Liability
$	$		thousand dollars each occurrence	B	Property Damage Liability
$	$		dollars each person	C	Medical Payments
$	$	$	Actual Cash Value*	D	(1) Comprehensive (excluding Collision)
		$ 100			(2) Personal Effects
$	$	Actual Cash Value less $	deductible	E	Collision
$	$			F	Fire, Lightning and Transportation
$	$	$		G	Theft
$	$	$		H	Combined Additional Coverage
$	$	$ 25	per disablement	I	Towing and Labor Costs
†$	$		thousand dollars each person	J	Uninsured Motorists
††$	All "owned automobiles"		thousand dollars each accident		
$			Form numbers of endorsements attached to policy at issue		
$	$	Total Car 1 - Car 2			
$	Total Premium				

* STRIKE OUT "ACTUAL CASH VALUE" AND INSERT AMOUNT IF POLICY IS WRITTEN ON STATED AMOUNT BASIS.
† ENTER PREMIUM(S) HERE WHEN RATED ON "PER CAR" BASIS.
†† ENTER PREMIUM HERE WHEN RATED ON "PER INDIVIDUAL" BASIS.

Item 4. Description of owned automobile or trailer

	Year of Model	Trade Name	Body Type; Model	Identification Number (I) Serial Number (S) Motor Number (M)	F.O.B. List Price or Delivered Price at Factory	Purchased Month, Year	New or Used	Class & Rating Symbol	Sub-Class (if any)
Car 1									
Car 2									

Item 5. Loss Payee: Any loss under Part III is payable as interest may appear to the named insured and (NAME AND ADDRESS—ENTER BELOW)

Item 6. The owned automobile will be principally garaged in the town or city designated in Item 1 above, unless otherwise stated herein: (ENTER BELOW)

Item 7. During the past three years no insurer has canceled insurance, issued to the named insured, similar to that afforded hereunder, unless otherwise stated herein:

Countersigned:

By____________________
Authorized Representative

Family Automobile Policy (*Continued*)

RESERVED FOR YOUR COMPANY'S NAME

(A____________________insurance company, herein called the company)
"Stock" or "Mutual"

Agrees with the insured, named in the declarations made a part hereof, in consideration of the payment of the premium and in reliance upon the statements in the declarations and subject to all of the terms of this policy:

PART I — LIABILITY

Coverage A—Bodily Injury Liability; Coverage B—Property Damage Liability: To pay on behalf of the insured all sums which the insured shall become legally obligated to pay as damages because of:

A. bodily injury, sickness or disease, including death resulting therefrom, hereinafter called "bodily injury," sustained by any person;

B. injury to or destruction of property, including loss of use thereof, hereinafter called "property damage";

arising out of the ownership, maintenance or use of the owned automobile or any non-owned automobile, and the company shall defend any suit alleging such bodily injury or property damage and seeking damages which are payable under the terms of this policy, even if any of the allegations of the suit are groundless, false or fraudulent; but the company may make such investigation and settlement of any claim or suit as it deems expedient.

Supplementary Payments: To pay, in addition to the applicable limits of liability:

(a) all expenses incurred by the company, all costs taxed against the insured in any such suit and all interest on the entire amount of any judgment therein which accrues after entry of the judgment and before the company has paid or tendered or deposited in court that part of the judgment which does not exceed the limit of the company's liability thereon;

(b) premiums on appeal bonds required in any such suit, premiums on bonds to release attachments for an amount not in excess of the applicable limit of liability of this policy, and the cost of bail bonds required of the insured because of accident or traffic law violation arising out of the use of an automobile insured hereunder, not to exceed $100 per bail bond, but without any obligation to apply for or furnish any such bonds;

(c) expenses incurred by the insured for such immediate medical and surgical relief to others as shall be imperative at the time of an accident involving an automobile insured hereunder and not due to war;

(d) all reasonable expenses, other than loss of earnings, incurred by the insured at the company's request.

Persons Insured: The following are insureds under Part I:

(a) with respect to the owned automobile,
(1) the named insured and any resident of the same household,
(2) any other person using such automobile with the permission of the named insured, provided his actual operation or (if he is not operating) his other actual use thereof is within the scope of such permission, and
(3) any other person or organization but only with respect to his or its liability because of acts or omissions of an insured under (a) (1) or (2) above;

(b) with respect to a non-owned automobile,
(1) the named insured,
(2) any relative, but only with respect to a private passenger automobile or trailer, provided his actual operation or (if he is not operating) the other actual use thereof is with the permission, or reasonably believed to be with the permission, of the owner and is within the scope of such permission, and
(3) any other person or organization not owning or hiring the automobile, but only with respect to his or its liability because of acts or omissions of an insured under (b) (1) or (2) above.

The insurance afforded under Part I applies separately to each insured against whom claim is made or suit is brought, but the inclusion herein of more than one insured shall not operate to increase the limits of the company's liability.

Definitions: Under Part I:

"named insured" means the individual named in Item 1 of the declarations and also includes his spouse, if a resident of the same household;

"insured" means a person or organization described under "Persons Insured";

"relative" means a relative of the named insured who is a resident of the same household;

"owned automobile" means

(a) a private passenger, farm or utility automobile described in this policy for which a specific premium charge indicates that coverage is afforded,

(b) a trailer owned by the named insured,

(c) a private passenger, farm or utility automobile ownership of which is acquired by the named insured during the policy period, provided
(1) it replaces an owned automobile as defined in (a) above, or
(2) the company insures all private passenger, farm and utility automobiles owned by the named insured on the date of such acquisition and the named insured notifies the company during the policy period or within 30 days after the date of such acquisition of his election to make this and no other policy issued by the company applicable to such automobile, or

(d) a temporary substitute automobile;

"temporary substitute automobile" means any automobile or trailer, not owned by the named insured, while temporarily used with the permission of the owner as a substitute for the owned automobile or trailer, when withdrawn from normal use because of its breakdown, repair, servicing, loss or destruction;

"non-owned automobile" means an automobile or trailer not owned by or furnished for the regular use of either the named insured or any relative, other than a temporary substitute automobile;

"private passenger automobile" means a four wheel private passenger, station wagon or jeep type automobile;

"farm automobile" means an automobile of the truck type with a load capacity of fifteen hundred pounds or less not used for business or commercial purposes other than farming;

"utility automobile" means an automobile, other than a farm automobile, with a load capacity of fifteen hundred pounds or less of the pick-up body, sedan delivery or panel truck type not used for business or commercial purposes;

"trailer" means a trailer designed for use with a private passenger automobile, if not being used for business or commercial purposes with other than a private passenger, farm or utility automobile, or a farm wagon or farm implement while used with a farm automobile;

"automobile business" means the business or occupation of selling, repairing, servicing, storing or parking automobiles;

"use" of an automobile includes the loading and unloading thereof;

"war" means war, whether or not declared, civil war, insurrection, rebellion or revolution, or any act or condition incident to any of the foregoing.

Exclusions: This policy does not apply under Part I:

(a) to any automobile while used as a public or livery conveyance, but this exclusion does not apply to the named insured with respect to bodily injury or property damage which results from the named insured's occupancy of a non-owned automobile other than as the operator thereof;

(b) to bodily injury or property damage, caused intentionally by or at the direction of the insured;

(c) to bodily injury or property damage with respect to which an insured under this policy is also an insured under a nuclear energy liability policy issued by Nuclear Energy Liability Insurance Association, Mutual Atomic Energy Liability Underwriters or Nuclear Insurance Association of Canada, or would be an insured under any such policy but for its termination upon exhaustion of its limit of liability;

(d) to bodily injury or property damage arising out of the operation of farm machinery;

(e) to bodily injury to any employee of the insured arising out of and in the course of (1) domestic employment by the insured, if benefits therefor are in whole or in part either payable or required to be provided under any workmen's compensation law, or (2) other employment by the insured;

(f) to bodily injury to any fellow employee of the insured injured in the course of his employment if such injury arises out of the use of an automobile in the business of his employer, but this exclusion does not apply to the named insured with respect to injury sustained by any such fellow employee;

(g) to an owned automobile while used by any person while such person is employed or otherwise engaged in the automobile business, but this exclusion does not apply to the named insured, a resident of the same household as the named insured, a partnership in which the named insured or such resident is a partner, or any partner, agent or employee of the named insured, such resident or partnership;

(h) to a non-owned automobile while maintained or used by any person while such person is employed or otherwise engaged in
(1) the automobile business of the insured or of any other person or organization,
(2) any other business or occupation of the insured, but this exclusion (h) (2) does not apply to a private passenger automobile operated or occupied by the named insured or by his private chauffeur or domestic servant or a trailer used therewith or with an owned automobile;

(i) to injury to or destruction of (1) property owned or transported by the insured or (2) property rented to or in charge of the insured other than a residence or private garage;

(j) to the ownership, maintenance, operation, use, loading or unloading of an automobile ownership of which is acquired by the named insured during the policy period or any temporary substitute automobile therefor, if the named insured has purchased other automobile liability insurance applicable to such automobile for which a specific premium charge has been made.

Financial Responsibility Laws: When this policy is certified as proof of financial responsibility for the future under the provisions of any motor vehicle financial responsibility law, such insurance as is afforded by this policy for bodily injury liability or for property damage liability shall comply with the provisions of such law to the extent of the coverage and limits of liability required by such law, but in no event in excess of the limits of liability stated in this policy. The insured agrees to reimburse the company for any payment made by the company which it would not have been obligated to make under the terms of this policy except for the agreement contained in this paragraph.

Limits of Liability: The limit of bodily injury liability stated in the declarations as applicable to "each person" is the limit of the company's liability for all damages, including damages for care and loss of services, arising out of bodily injury sustained by one person as the result of any one occurrence; the limit of such liability stated in the declarations as applicable to "each occurrence" is, subject to the above provision respecting each person, the total limit of the company's liability for all such damages arising out of bodily injury sustained by two or more persons as the result of any one occurrence.

The limit of property damage liability stated in the declarations as applicable to "each occurrence" is the total limit of the company's liability for all damages arising out of injury to or destruction of all property of one or more persons or organizations, including the loss of use thereof, as the result of any one occurrence.

Other Insurance: If the insured has other insurance against a loss covered by Part I of this policy the company shall not be liable under this policy for a greater proportion of such loss than the applicable limit of liability stated in the declarations bears to the total applicable limit of liability of all valid and collectible insurance against such loss; provided, however, the insurance with respect to a temporary substitute automobile or non-owned automobile shall be excess insurance over any other valid and collectible insurance.

PART II — EXPENSES FOR MEDICAL SERVICES

Coverage C—Medical Payments: To pay all reasonable expenses incurred within one year from the date of accident for necessary medical, surgical, X-ray and dental services, including prosthetic devices, and necessary ambulance, hospital, professional nursing and funeral services:

Division 1. To or for the named insured and each relative who sustains bodily injury, sickness or disease, including death resulting therefrom, hereinafter called "bodily injury", caused by accident,

Family Automobile Policy (*Continued*)

(Attach Endorsements Here)

(a) while occupying the owned automobile,
(b) while occupying a non-owned automobile, but only if such person has, or reasonably believes he has, the permission of the owner to use the automobile and the use is within the scope of such permission, or
(c) through being struck by an automobile or by a trailer of any type;

Division 2. To or for any other person who sustains bodily injury, caused by accident, while occupying
(a) the owned automobile, while being used by the named insured, by any resident of the same household or by any other person with the permission of the named insured; or
(b) a non-owned automobile, if the bodily injury results from
(1) its operation or occupancy by the named insured or its operation on his behalf by his private chauffeur or domestic servant, or
(2) its operation or occupancy by a relative, provided it is a private passenger automobile or trailer,
but only if such operator or occupant has, or reasonably believes he has, the permission of the owner to use the automobile and the use is within the scope of such permission.

Definitions: The definitions under Part I apply to Part II, and under Part II:
"occupying" means in or upon or entering into or alighting from.

Exclusions: This policy does not apply under Part II to bodily injury:
(a) sustained while occupying (1) an owned automobile while used as a public or livery conveyance, or (2) any vehicle while located for use as a residence or premises;
(b) sustained by the named insured or a relative while occupying or through being struck by (1) a farm type tractor or other equipment designed for use principally off public roads, while not upon public roads, or (2) a vehicle operated on rails or crawler-treads;
(c) sustained by any person other than the named insured or a relative,
(1) while such person is occupying a non-owned automobile while used as a public or livery conveyance, or
(2) resulting from the maintenance or use of a non-owned automobile by such person while employed or otherwise engaged in the automobile business, or
(3) resulting from the maintenance or use of a non-owned automobile by such person while employed or otherwise engaged in any other business or occupation, unless the bodily injury results from the operation or occupancy of a private passenger automobile by the named insured or by his private chauffeur or domestic servant, or of a trailer used therewith or with an owned automobile;
(d) sustained by any person who is employed in the automobile business, if the accident arises out of the operation thereof and if benefits therefor are in whole or in part either payable or required to be provided under any workmen's compensation law;
(e) due to war.

Limit of Liability: The limit of liability for medical payments stated in the declarations as applicable to "each person" is the limit of the company's liability for all expenses incurred by or on behalf of each person who sustains bodily injury as the result of any one accident.

Other Insurance: If there is other automobile medical payments insurance against a loss covered by Part II of this policy the company shall not be liable under this policy for a greater proportion of such loss than the applicable limit of liability stated in the declarations bears to the total applicable limit of liability of all valid and collectible automobile medical payments insurance; provided, however, the insurance with respect to a temporary substitute automobile or non-owned automobile shall be excess insurance over any other valid and collectible automobile medical payments insurance.

PART III — PHYSICAL DAMAGE

Coverage D (1)—Comprehensive (excluding Collision); (2)—Personal Effects:
(1) To pay for loss caused other than by collision to the owned automobile or to a non-owned automobile. For the purpose of this coverage, breakage of glass and loss caused by missiles, falling objects, fire, theft or larceny, explosion, earthquake, windstorm, hail, water, flood, malicious mischief or vandalism, riot or civil commotion, or colliding with a bird or animal, shall not be deemed to be loss caused by collision.
(2) To pay for loss caused by fire or lightning to robes, wearing apparel and other personal effects which are the property of the named insured or a relative, while such effects are in or upon the owned automobile.

Coverage E—Collision: To pay for loss caused by collision to the owned automobile or to a non-owned automobile but only for the amount of each such loss in excess of the deductible amount stated in the declarations as applicable hereto. The deductible amount shall not apply to loss caused by a collision with another automobile insured by the company.

Coverage F—Fire, Lightning and Transportation: To pay for loss to the owned automobile or a non-owned automobile, caused (a) by fire or lightning, (b) by smoke or smudge due to a sudden, unusual and faulty operation of any fixed heating equipment serving the premises in which the automobile is located, or (c) by the stranding, sinking, burning, collision or derailment of any conveyance in or upon which the automobile is being transported.

Coverage G—Theft: To pay for loss to the owned automobile or to a non-owned automobile caused by theft or larceny.

Coverage H—Combined Additional Coverage: To pay for loss to the owned automobile or a non-owned automobile caused by windstorm, hail, earthquake, explosion, riot or civil commotion, or the forced landing or falling of any aircraft or its parts or equipment, flood or rising waters, malicious mischief or vandalism, external discharge or leakage of water except loss resulting from rain, snow or sleet whether or not wind-driven; provided, with respect to each automobile $25 shall be deducted from each loss caused by malicious mischief or vandalism.

Coverage I—Towing and Labor Costs: To pay for towing and labor costs necessitated by the disablement of the owned automobile or of any non-owned automobile, provided the labor is performed at the place of disablement.

Supplementary Payments: In addition to the applicable limit of liability:
(a) to reimburse the insured for transportation expenses incurred during the period commencing 48 hours after a theft covered by this policy of the entire automobile has been reported to the company and the police, and terminating when the automobile is returned to use or the company pays for the loss; provided that the company shall not be obligated to pay aggregate expenses in excess of $10 per day or totaling more than $300.
(b) to pay general average and salvage charges for which the insured becomes legally liable, as to the automobile being transported.

Definitions: The definitions of "named insured", "relative" "temporary substitute automobile", "private passenger automobile", "farm automobile", "utility automobile", "automobile business", "war", and "owned automobile" in Part I apply to Part III, but "owned automobile" does not include, under Part III, (1) a trailer owned by the named insured on the effective date of this policy and not described herein, or (2) a trailer ownership of which is acquired during the policy period unless the company insures all private passenger, farm and utility automobiles and trailers owned by the named insured on the date of such acquisition and the named insured notifies the company during the policy period or within 30 days after the date of such acquisition of his election to make this and no other policy issued by the company applicable to such trailer.
"insured" means
(a) with respect to an owned automobile,
(1) the named insured, and
(2) any person or organization (other than a person or organization employed or otherwise engaged in the automobile business or as a carrier or other bailee for hire) maintaining, using or having custody of said automobile with the permission of the named insured and within the scope of such permission;
(b) with respect to a non-owned automobile, the named insured and any relative while using such automobile, provided his actual operation or (if he is not operating) the other actual use thereof is with the permission, or reasonably believed to be with the permission, of the owner and is within the scope of such permission;

"non-owned automobile" means a private passenger automobile or trailer not owned by or furnished for the regular use of either the named insured or any relative, other than a temporary substitute automobile, while said automobile or trailer is in the possession or custody of the insured or is being operated by him;

"loss" means direct and accidental loss of or damage to (a) the automobile, including its equipment, or (b) other insured property;

"collision" means collision of an automobile covered by this policy with another object or with a vehicle to which it is attached or by upset of such automobile;

"trailer" means a trailer designed for use with a private passenger automobile, if not being used for business or commercial purposes with other than a private passenger, farm or utility automobile, and if not a home, office, store, display or passenger trailer.

Exclusions: This policy does not apply under Part III:
(a) to any automobile while used as a public or livery conveyance;
(b) to loss due to war;
(c) to loss to a non-owned automobile arising out of its use by the insured while he is employed or otherwise engaged in the automobile business;
(d) to loss to a private passenger, farm or utility automobile or trailer owned by the named insured and not described in this policy or to any temporary substitute automobile therefor, if the insured has other valid and collectible insurance against such loss;
(e) to damage which is due and confined to wear and tear, freezing, mechanical or electrical breakdown or failure, unless such damage results from a theft covered by this policy;
(f) to tires, unless damaged by fire, malicious mischief or vandalism, or stolen or unless the loss be coincident with and from the same cause as other loss covered by this policy;
(g) to loss due to radioactive contamination;
(h) under coverage E, to breakage of glass if insurance with respect to such breakage is otherwise afforded.

Limit of Liability: The limit of the company's liability for loss shall not exceed the actual cash value of the property, or if the loss is of a part thereof the actual cash value of such part, at time of loss, nor what it would then cost to repair or replace the property or such part thereof with other of like kind and quality, nor, with respect to an owned automobile described in this policy, the applicable limit of liability stated in the declarations; provided, however, the limit of the company's liability (a) for loss to personal effects arising out of any one occurrence is $100, and (b) for loss to any trailer not owned by the named insured is $500.

Other Insurance: If the insured has other insurance against a loss covered by Part III of this policy, the company shall not be liable under this policy for a greater proportion of such loss than the applicable limit of liability of this policy bears to the total applicable limit of liability of all valid and collectible insurance against such loss; provided, however, the insurance with respect to a temporary substitute automobile or non-owned automobile shall be excess insurance over any other valid and collectible insurance.

Family Automobile Policy (*Continued*)

PART IV—PROTECTION AGAINST UNINSURED MOTORISTS

Coverage J—Uninsured Motorists (Damages for Bodily Injury): To pay all sums which the insured or his legal representative shall be legally entitled to recover as damages from the owner or operator of an uninsured automobile because of bodily injury, sickness or disease, including death resulting therefrom, hereinafter called "bodily injury," sustained by the insured, caused by accident and arising out of the ownership, maintenance or use of such uninsured automobile; provided, for the purposes of this coverage, determination as to whether the insured or such representative is legally entitled to recover such damages, and if so the amount thereof, shall be made by agreement between the insured or such representative and the company or, if they fail to agree, by arbitration.

No judgment against any person or organization alleged to be legally responsible for the bodily injury shall be conclusive, as between the insured and the company, of the issues of liability of such person or organization or of the amount of damages to which the insured is legally entitled unless such judgment is entered pursuant to an action prosecuted by the insured with the written consent of the company.

Definitions: The definitions under Part I, except the definition of "insured," apply to Part IV, and under Part IV:

"insured" means:

(a) the named insured and any relative;

(b) any other person while occupying an insured automobile; and

(c) any person, with respect to damages he is entitled to recover because of bodily injury to which this Part applies sustained by an insured under (a) or (b) above.

The insurance afforded under Part IV applies separately to each insured, but the inclusion herein of more than one insured shall not operate to increase the limits of the company's liability.

"insured automobile" means:

(a) an automobile described in the policy for which a specific premium charge indicates that coverage is afforded,

(b) a private passenger, farm or utility automobile, ownership of which is acquired by the named insured during the policy period, provided

(1) it replaces an insured automobile as defined in (a) above, or

(2) the company insures under this Coverage all private passenger, farm and utility automobiles owned by the named insured on the date of such acquisition and the named insured notifies the company during the policy period or within 30 days after the date of such acquisition of his election to make the Liability and Uninsured Motorist Coverages under this and no other policy issued by the company applicable to such automobile,

(c) a temporary substitute automobile for an insured automobile as defined in (a) or (b) above, and

(d) a non-owned automobile while being operated by the named insured; and the term "insured automobile" includes a trailer while being used with an automobile described in (a), (b), (c) or (d) above, but shall not include:

(1) any automobile or trailer owned by a resident of the same household as the named insured,

(2) any automobile while used as a public or livery conveyance, or

(3) any automobile while being used without the permission of the owner.

"uninsured automobile" includes a trailer of any type and means:

(a) an automobile or trailer with respect to the ownership, maintenance or use of which there is, in at least the amounts specified by the financial responsibility law of the state in which the insured automobile is principally garaged, no bodily injury liability bond or insurance policy applicable at the time of the accident with respect to any person or organization legally responsible for the use of such automobile, or with respect to which there is a bodily injury liability bond or insurance policy applicable at the time of the accident but the company writing the same denies coverage thereunder or

(b) a hit-and-run automobile;

but the term "uninsured automobile" shall not include:

(1) an insured automobile or an automobile furnished for the regular use of the named insured or a relative,

(2) an automobile or trailer owned or operated by a self-insurer within the meaning of any motor vehicle financial responsibility law, motor carrier law or any similar law,

(3) an automobile or trailer owned by the United States of America, Canada, a state, a political subdivision of any such government or an agency of any of the foregoing,

(4) a land motor vehicle or trailer if operated on rails or crawler-treads or while located for use as a residence or premises and not as a vehicle, or

(5) a farm type tractor or equipment designed for use principally off public roads, except while actually upon public roads.

"hit-and-run automobile" means an automobile which causes bodily injury to an insured arising out of physical contact of such automobile with the insured or with an automobile which the insured is occupying at the time of the accident, provided: (a) there cannot be ascertained the identity of either the operator or the owner of such "hit-and-run automobile"; (b) the insured or someone on his behalf shall have reported the accident within 24 hours to a police, peace or judicial officer or to the Commissioner of Motor Vehicles, and shall have filed with the company within 30 days thereafter a statement under oath that the insured or his legal representative has a cause or causes of action arising out of such accident for damages against a person or persons whose identity is unascertainable, and setting forth the facts in support thereof; and (c) at the company's request, the insured or his legal representative makes available for inspection the automobile which the insured was occupying at the time of the accident.

"occupying" means in or upon or entering into or alighting from.

"state" includes the District of Columbia, a territory or possession of the United States, and a province of Canada.

Exclusions: This policy does not apply under Part IV:

(a) to bodily injury to an insured while occupying an automobile (other than an insured automobile) owned by the named insured or a relative, or through being struck by such an automobile;

(b) to bodily injury to an insured with respect to which such insured, his legal representative or any person entitled to payment under this coverage shall, without written consent of the company, make any settlement with any person or organization who may be legally liable therefor;

(c) so as to inure directly or indirectly to the benefit of any workmen's compensation or disability benefits carrier or any person or organization qualifying as a self-insurer under any workmen's compensation or disability benefits law or any similar law.

Limits of Liability:

(a) The limit of liability for uninsured motorists coverage stated in the declarations as applicable to "each person" is the limit of the company's liability for all damages, including damages for care or loss of services, because of bodily injury sustained by one person as the result of any one accident and, subject to the above provision respecting each person, the limit of liability stated in the declarations as applicable to "each accident" is the total limit of the company's liability for all damages, including damages for care or loss of services, because of bodily injury sustained by two or more persons as the result of any one accident.

(b) Any amount payable under the terms of this Part because of bodily injury sustained in an accident by a person who is an insured under this Part shall be reduced by

(1) all sums paid on account of such bodily injury by or on behalf of (i) the owner or operator of the uninsured automobile and (ii) any other person or organization jointly or severally liable together with such owner or operator for such bodily injury including all sums paid under Coverage A, and

(2) the amount paid and the present value of all amounts payable on account of such bodily injury under any workmen's compensation law, disability benefits law or any similar law.

(c) Any payment made under this Part to or for any insured shall be applied in reduction of the amount of damages which he may be entitled to recover from any person insured under Coverage A.

(d) The company shall not be obligated to pay under this Coverage that part of the damages which the insured may be entitled to recover from the owner or operator of an uninsured automobile which represents expenses for medical services paid or payable under Part II.

Other Insurance: With respect to bodily injury to an insured while occupying an automobile not owned by the named insured, the insurance under Part IV shall apply only as excess insurance over any other similar insurance available to such insured and applicable to such automobile as primary insurance, and this insurance shall then apply only in the amount by which the limit of liability for this coverage exceeds the applicable limit of liability of such other insurance.

Except as provided in the foregoing paragraph, if the insured has other similar insurance available to him and applicable to the accident, the damages shall be deemed not to exceed the higher of the applicable limits of liability of this insurance and such other insurance, and the company shall not be liable for a greater proportion of any loss to which this Coverage applies than the limit of liability hereunder bears to the sum of the applicable limits of liability of this insurance and such other insurance.

Arbitration: If any person making claim hereunder and the company do not agree that such person is legally entitled to recover damages from the owner or operator of an uninsured automobile because of bodily injury to the insured, or do not agree as to the amount of payment which may be owing under this Part, then, upon written demand of either, the matter or matters upon which such person and the company do not agree shall be settled by arbitration in accordance with the rules of the American Arbitration Association, and judgment upon the award rendered by the arbitrators may be entered in any court having jurisdiction thereof. Such person and the company each agree to consider itself bound and to be bound by any award made by the arbitrators pursuant to this Part.

Trust Agreement: In the event of payment to any person under this Part:

(a) the company shall be entitled to the extent of such payment to the proceeds of any settlement or judgment that may result from the exercise of any rights of recovery of such person against any person or organization legally responsible for the bodily injury because of which such payment is made;

(b) such person shall hold in trust for the benefit of the company all rights of recovery which he shall have against such other person or organization because of the damages which are the subject of claim made under this Part;

(c) such person shall do whatever is proper to secure and shall do nothing after loss to prejudice such rights;

(d) if requested in writing by the company, such person shall take, through any representative designated by the company, such action as may be necessary or appropriate to recover

Family Automobile Policy (*Concluded*)

such payment as damages from such other person or organization, such action to be taken in the name of such person; in the event of a recovery, the company shall be reimbursed out of such recovery for expenses, costs and attorneys' fees incurred by it in connection therewith;

(e) such person shall execute and deliver to the company such instruments and papers as may be appropriate to secure the rights and obligations of such person and the company established by this provision.

CONDITIONS

Conditions 1, 2, 3, 6, 14, 15, 16 and 18 apply to all Parts. Conditions 4 and 5, 7 through 13, and 17 apply only to the Parts noted thereunder.

1. Policy Period, Territory: This policy applies only to accidents, occurrences and loss during the policy period while the automobile is within the United States of America, its territories or possessions, or Canada, or is being transported between ports thereof.

2. Premium: If the named insured disposes of, acquires ownership of, or replaces a private passenger, farm or utility automobile or, with respect to Part III, a trailer, any premium adjustment necessary shall be made as of the date of such change in accordance with the manuals in use by the company. The named insured shall, upon request, furnish reasonable proof of the number of such automobiles or trailers and a description thereof.

3. Notice: In the event of an accident, occurrence or loss, written notice containing particulars sufficient to identify the insured and also reasonably obtainable information with respect to the time, place and circumstances thereof, and the names and addresses of the injured and of available witnesses, shall be given by or for the insured to the company or any of its authorized agents as soon as practicable. In the event of theft the insured shall also promptly notify the police. If claim is made or suit is brought against the insured, he shall immediately forward to the company every demand, notice, summons or other process received by him or his representative.

If, before the company makes payment of loss under Part IV, the insured or his legal representative shall institute any legal action for bodily injury against any person or organization legally responsible for the use of an automobile involved in the accident, a copy of the summons and complaint or other process served in connection with such legal action shall be forwarded immediately to the company by the insured or his legal representative.

4. Two or More Automobiles—Parts I, II and III: When two or more automobiles are insured hereunder, the terms of this policy shall apply separately to each, but an automobile and a trailer attached thereto shall be held to be one automobile as respects limits of liability under Part I of this policy, and separate automobiles under Part III of this policy, including any deductible provisions applicable thereto.

5. Assistance and Cooperation of the Insured—Parts I and III: The insured shall cooperate with the company and, upon the company's request, assist in making settlements, in the conduct of suits and in enforcing any right of contribution or indemnity against any person or organization who may be liable to the insured because of bodily injury, property damage or loss with respect to which insurance is afforded under this policy; and the insured shall attend hearings and trials and assist in securing and giving evidence and obtaining the attendance of witnesses. The insured shall not, except at his own cost, voluntarily make any payment, assume any obligation or incur any expense other than for such immediate medical and surgical relief to others as shall be imperative at the time of accident.

Part IV: After notice of claim under Part IV, the company may require the insured to take such action as may be necessary or appropriate to preserve his right to recover damages from any person or organization alleged to be legally responsible for the bodily injury; and in any action against the company, the company may require the insured to join such person or organization as a party defendant.

6. Action Against Company—Part I: No action shall lie against the company unless, as a condition precedent thereto, the insured shall have fully complied with all the terms of this policy, nor until the amount of the insured's obligation to pay shall have been finally determined either by judgment against the insured after actual trial or by written agreement of the insured, the claimant and the company.

Any person or organization or the legal representative thereof who has secured such judgment or written agreement shall thereafter be entitled to recover under this policy to the extent of the insurance afforded by this policy. No person or organization shall have any right under this policy to join the company as a party to any action against the insured to determine the insured's liability, nor shall the company be impleaded by the insured or his legal representative. Bankruptcy or insolvency of the insured or of the insured's estate shall not relieve the company of any of its obligations hereunder.

Parts II, III and IV: No action shall lie against the company unless, as a condition precedent thereto, there shall have been full compliance with all the terms of this policy nor, under Part III, until thirty days after proof of loss is filed and the amount of loss is determined as provided in this policy.

7. Medical Reports; Proof and Payment of Claim—Part II: As soon as practicable the injured person or someone on his behalf shall give to the company written proof of claim, under oath if required, and shall, after each request from the company, execute authorization to enable the company to obtain medical reports and copies of records. The injured person shall submit to physical examination by physicians selected by the company when and as often as the company may reasonably require.

The company may pay the injured person or any person or organization rendering the services and such payment shall reduce the amount payable hereunder for such injury. Payment hereunder shall not constitute an admission of liability of any person or, except hereunder, of the company.

8. Insured's Duties in Event of Loss—Part III: In the event of loss the insured shall:

(a) protect the automobile, whether or not the loss is covered by this policy, and any further loss due to the insured's failure to protect shall not be recoverable under this policy; reasonable expenses incurred in affording such protection shall be deemed incurred at the company's request;

(b) file with the company, within 91 days after loss, his sworn proof of loss in such form and including such information as the company may reasonably require and shall, upon the company's request, exhibit the damaged property and submit to examination under oath.

9. Proof of Claim; Medical Reports—Part IV: As soon as practicable, the insured or other person making claim shall give to the company written proof of claim, under oath if required, including full particulars of the nature and extent of the injuries, treatment, and other details entering into the determination of the amount payable. The insured and every other person making claim shall submit to examinations under oath by any person named by the company and subscribe the same, as often as may reasonably be required. Proof of claim shall be made upon forms furnished by the company unless the company shall have failed to furnish such forms within 15 days after receiving notice of claim.

The injured person shall submit to physical examinations by physicians selected by the company when and as often as the company may reasonably require and he, or in the event of his incapacity his legal representative, or in the event of his death his legal representative or the person or persons entitled to sue therefor, shall upon each request from the company execute authorization to enable the company to obtain medical reports and copies of records.

10. Appraisal—Part III: If the insured and the company fail to agree as to the amount of loss, either may, within 60 days after proof of loss is filed, demand an appraisal of the loss. In such event the insured and the company shall each select a competent appraiser, and the appraisers shall select a competent and disinterested umpire. The appraisers shall state separately the actual cash value and the amount of loss and failing to agree shall submit their differences to the umpire. An award in writing of any two shall determine the amount of loss. The insured and the company shall each pay his chosen appraiser and shall bear equally the other expenses of the appraisal and umpire.

The company shall not be held to have waived any of its rights by any act relating to appraisal.

11. Payment of Loss—Part III: The company may pay for the loss in money; or may repair or replace the damaged or stolen property; or may, at any time before the loss is paid or the property is so replaced, at its expense return any stolen property to the named insured, or at its option to the address shown in the declarations, with payment for any resultant damage thereto; or may take all or such part of the property at the agreed or appraised value but there shall be no abandonment to the company. The company may settle any claim for loss either with the insured or the owner of the property.

Part IV: Any amount due is payable (a) to the insured, or (b) if the insured be a minor to his parent or guardian, or (c) if the insured be deceased to his surviving spouse, otherwise (d) to a person authorized by law to receive such payment or to a person legally entitled to recover the damages which the payment represents; provided, the company may at its option pay any amount due in accordance with division (d) hereof.

12. No Benefit to Bailee—Part III: The insurance afforded by this policy shall not inure directly or indirectly to the benefit of any carrier or other bailee for hire liable for loss to the automobile.

13. Subrogation—Parts I and III: In the event of any payment under this policy, the company shall be subrogated to all the insured's rights of recovery therefor against any person or organization and the insured shall execute and deliver instruments and papers and do whatever else is necessary to secure such rights. The insured shall do nothing after loss to prejudice such rights.

14. Changes: Notice to any agent or knowledge possessed by any agent or by any other person shall not effect a waiver or a change in any part of this policy or estop the company from asserting any right under the terms of this policy; nor shall the terms of this policy be waived or changed, except by endorsement issued to form a part of this policy.

15. Assignment: Assignment of interest under this policy shall not bind the company until its consent is endorsed hereon; if, however, the insured named in Item 1 of the declarations, or his spouse if a resident of the same household, shall die, this policy shall cover (1) the survivor as named insured, (2) his legal representative as named insured but only while acting within the scope of his duties as such, (3) any person having proper temporary custody of an owned automobile, as an insured, until the appointment and qualification of such legal representative, and (4) under division 1 of Part II any person who was a relative at the time of such death.

16. Cancelation: This policy may be canceled by the insured named in Item 1 of the declarations by surrender thereof to the company or any of its authorized agents or by mailing to the company written notice stating when thereafter the cancelation shall be effective. This policy may be canceled by the company by mailing to the insured named in Item 1 of the declarations at the address shown in this policy written notice stating when not less than ten days thereafter such cancelation shall be effective. The mailing of notice as aforesaid shall be sufficient proof of notice. The time of the surrender or the effective date and hour of cancelation stated in the notice shall become the end of the policy period. Delivery of such written notice either by such insured or by the company shall be equivalent to mailing.

If such insured cancels, earned premium shall be computed in accordance with the customary short rate table and procedure. If the company cancels, earned premium shall be computed pro rata. Premium adjustment may be made either at the time cancelation is effected or as soon as practicable after cancelation becomes effective, but payment or tender of unearned premium is not a condition of cancelation.

17. Cancelation by Company Limited—Part I: After this policy has been in effect for sixty days or, if the policy is a renewal, effective immediately, the company shall not exercise its right to cancel the insurance afforded under Part I unless:

1. the named insured fails to discharge when due any of his obligations in connection with the payment of premium for this policy or any installment thereof whether payable directly or under any premium finance plan; or
2. the insurance was obtained through fraudulent misrepresentation; or
3. the insured violates any of the terms and conditions of the policy; or
4. the named insured or any other operator, either resident in the same household, or who customarily operates an automobile insured under the policy,
   (a) has had his driver's license suspended or revoked during the policy period, or
   (b) is or becomes subject to epilepsy or heart attacks, and such individual cannot produce a certificate from a physician testifying to his unqualified ability to operate a motor vehicle, or
   (c) is or has been convicted of or forfeits bail, during the 36 months immediately preceding the effective date of the policy or during the policy period, for:
      (1) any felony, or
      (2) criminal negligence resulting in death, homicide or assault, arising out of the operation of a motor vehicle, or
      (3) operating a motor vehicle while in an intoxicated condition or while under the influence of drugs, or
      (4) leaving the scene of an accident without stopping to report, or
      (5) theft of a motor vehicle, or
      (6) making false statements in an application for a driver's license, or
      (7) a third violation, committed within a period of 18 months, of (i) any ordinance or regulation limiting the speed of motor vehicles or (ii) any of the provisions in the motor vehicle laws of any state, the violation of which constitutes a misdemeanor, whether or not the violations were repetitions of the same offense or were different offenses.

18. Declarations: By acceptance of this policy, the insured named in Item 1 of the declarations agrees that the statements in the declarations are his agreements and representations, that this policy is issued in reliance upon the truth of such representations and that this policy embodies all agreements existing between himself and the company or any of its agents relating to this insurance.

***In Witness Whereof,** the company has caused this policy to be executed and attested, but this policy shall not be valid unless countersigned by a duly authorized representative of the company.

*Company's language may be substituted as desired.

INSERT SIGNATURES AND TITLES OF PROPER OFFICERS

H. Standard Reporting Procedures for Claim Adjustments as Used by National Association of Independent Insurance Adjusters

GENERAL LIABILITY

(Preliminary) (Interim) (Closing) CLAIM REPORT

FROM

ACE ADJUSTMENT CO.

REPORTING OFFICE __________

COMPANY	XYZ Insurance Co., Chicago, Ill.	REPORT DATE:	July 17, 1959
AGENT	Jones Agency		
POLICY NO.	45678	AGENT'S LOCATION	Mason, Iowa
CO. CLAIM NO.	A 53471	POLICY PERIOD	2/15/59–60
INSURED	Jones Realty Co.	ADJ. FILE NO.	6543
CLAIMANT	Mary Smith		
TYPE	B.I.	DATE OF ACC.	7/10/59

ENCLOSURES	OCCURRENCE	OFFICIAL RECORDS	LIABILITY
ASSIGNMENT	CLAIMS	CONTRIBUTION	REMARKS
COVERAGE	WITNESSES	RISK	FUTURE ACTIVITY

RECOMMENDATIONS FOR USE

The NAIIA recommends that all investigations involving claims under general liability be reported with above headings and captions. All company correspondence on a given claim should follow the outline. After the first report, the interim or final ones should include only the caption "Enclosures," the pertinent sections involved and "Future Activity."

No outline can be prepared which can cover all conceivable situations. Adjusters are encouraged to use additional captions where indicated if the information submitted can not be stated properly under one of those included.

Recommendations concerning the use of the individual captions follow:

Enclosures: All enclosures pertinent to the investigation are to be listed separately.

Assignment: Date, source and method of assignment.

Coverage: Describe the policy in such specific terms that no examination of company records is necessary. Identify premises or equipment involved and if indicated state whether or not described in policy. Discuss policy violations, duplicate coverage and questions of primary and secondary coverage. Mention here reservation of rights, non-waiver agreement and any investigation concerning coverage including any statements taken on the question.

Occurrence: Date, time and place should be stated first followed by a brief but clear description of what took place. A description of the premises or site of the occurrence and a full description of the physical facts should be included. Sketches, diagrams and photographs are reported here.

Claims: Report in separate paragraphs on each claim, listing property damage first, and then injury cases. Begin each paragraph with claimant's name, age, race, address, occupation and employer. On property damage discuss value before accident, salvage value and cost to repair. Describe property insurance and name the carrier and its adjuster. On bodily injury cases state nature and extent of injuries, disability, medical expense, loss of earnings, other expense and possibility of permanent injury. Name hospital and physician and state whether medical reports were obtained or promised. For each claimant show date of first contact and his activity and attitude at time of call. Report here on settlement negotiations, representation by counsel and capability of attorney. If in litigation, give answer date, actions taken and recommendations.

Witnesses: Identify here every known witness, including claimants and other participants, starting a separate paragraph with his name, age, race and address. Report on appearance, apparent reliability, marital status, occupation, availability and relationship to participants. If statement taken, give a brief summary. If not, present his evidence in clear and concise fashion. If not interviewed, state what action is planned. Close this section with a statement as to whether or not canvass for witnesses has been completed or is planned if the occurrence is such that a canvass is practical.

Official Records: Introduce here and comment upon police report, coroner's inquest, criminal trials, weather reports or any other pertinent public record.

Contribution: Discuss other insurance interests which may be involved identifying insureds, types of coverage, carriers and representatives. Describe steps taken to obtain contribution.

Risk: Present all pertinent information as to description and desirability of risk from both physical and moral standpoints.

Liability: The adjuster gives his opinion concerning litigation possibilities and his reasons.

Remarks: The adjuster's comments concerning present and future handling, requests for drafts, settlement authority or other instructions and any other remarks are stated. If litigation is involved and has not been discussed fully under the respective claimant, it should be commented upon.

Future Activity: The report is closed with a precise statement concerning persons to be interviewed and other actions planned. If properly prepared, this section will be a check list for both adjuster and examiner against the next report.

AUTOMOBILE LIABILITY

(Preliminary) (Interim) (Closing) CLAIM REPORT

FROM

ACE ADJUSTMENT CO.

315 W. GRUNT ST. MASON, IOWA

COMPANY	XYZ Insurance Co., Chicago, Ill.	REPORT DATE:	July 17, 1959
AGENT	Jones Agency		
POLICY NO.	87654	AGENT'S LOCATION	Mason, Iowa
CO. CLAIM NO.	A 13579	POLICY PERIOD	3/17/59–60
INSURED	John Doe	ADJ. FILE NO.	7531
CLAIMANT	Richard Roe, et al		
TYPE	B.I., P.D., M.P., Coll.	DATE OF ACC.	7/11/59

ENCLOSURES	ACCIDENT	COLLISION LOSS	RISK
ASSIGNMENT	P.D. CLAIMS	WITNESSES	LIABILITY
COVERAGE	B.I. CLAIMS	OFFICIAL RECORDS	REMARKS
DATE/TIME/PLACE	M.P. CLAIMS	SUBROGATION/CONTRIBUTION	FUTURE ACTIVITY

RECOMMENDATIONS FOR USE

The NAIIA recommends that all investigations involving bodily injury and/or serious property damage be reported with above headings and captions. All company correspondence on a given claim should follow the outline. After the first report, the interim or final ones should include only the captions "Enclosures," the pertinent sections involved and "Future Activity."

This form is not recommended for the typical property damage claim or physical damage loss which does not require the detailed reporting as suggested herein. A special short form has been prepared for such reports.

No outline can be prepared which can cover all conceivable situations. Adjusters are encouraged to use additional captions where indicated if the information submitted can not be stated properly under one of those included.

Recommendations concerning the use of the individual captions follows:

Enclosures: All enclosures pertinent to the investigation are to be listed separately.

Assignment: Date, source and method of assignment.

Coverage: Unless coverage was furnished by direct company correspondence give sufficient information so that no examination of policy records is necessary and state how information obtained. Identify vehicle and state whether or not described in policy. Discuss permissive use, policy violations, duplicate coverage, and questions of primary and secondary coverage if indicated. Mention here reservations of rights, non-waiver agreements and any investigation concerning coverage including any statements taken on the question.

Date/Time/Place: Give date, precise time, and specific location of the accident.

Accident: A first paragraph under this section should describe briefly but accurately the scene of accident including type of intersection, nature of terrain, obstructions to vision, street or highway paving and condition, speed limit, weather and visibility. Photographs and diagrams should be discussed here.

A second paragraph should present a résumé of the facts reported so as to give a brief picture of the accident, including any major discrepancies in the evidence.

* * * * * * * * * * * *

> The next four captions of the report concern the various claims arising. In each case you should present all pertinent information other than his version concerning each claimant and dispose of him fully before proceeding to the next. It is entirely proper, and in many cases desirable, to devote more than one paragraph to a particular person. For purpose of clarity it is suggested that each paragraph concerning any claimant start with his name.
>
> A particular individual may have claims for discussion under more than one section. If such is the case treat his claims separately from the standpoint of information but combine them for discussion of negotiations, litigation, etc.
>
> In these captions concerning claims we do not discuss versions. They should be presented under the caption, "Witnesses."

* * * * * * * * * * * *

Property Damage Claims: A separate paragraph should be devoted to each property damage claimant starting with his name, address and description of property, extent of damage and how determined. If an automobile was damaged, show year, make, model, condition, use and mileage. Discuss value before accident, salvage value and cost to repair. Describe insurance and name the carrier and adjuster. Cover settlement negotiations and litigation, if any.

Bodily Injury Claims: Use a separate paragraph for each claimant starting with pedestrians, then insured's passengers and following with occupants of other automobiles in the same order used under "Property Damage Claims." Start each paragraph with claimant's name, age, address, marital status, occupation, employer and attorney. Describe his exact location when accident occurred. State nature and extent of injuries, disability, medical expense, loss of earnings, other expense and possibility of permanent injury. Name hospital and physicians and state whether medical reports were obtained or promised. For each claimant show date of first contact and his activity and attitude at time of call. Report here on settlement negotiations, representation by counsel and capability of attorney. If in litigation, give answer date, actions taken and recommendations.

Medical Payments Claims: Name each claimant, give a brief description of injury, and an estimate of amount of expense. If settled, explain and detail fully. If claimant previously reported on under "Bodily Injury Claims," discuss here only his medical payments claim under the policy.

Collision Loss: Describe ownership, year, make, model, and report on your inspection including condition, appearance, use and mileage. Give value before accident, salvage value and cost to repair. Submit repair estimates or other verification of damage, including snapshots. Describe previous damage and other reasons for depreciation. State steps taken concerning disposition.

Witnesses: Identify here every known witness, including vehicle drivers and passengers, starting a separate paragraph for each with his name, age, race and address. Report on appearance, apparent reliability, marital status, occupation, availability and relationship to participants. If statement taken, give a brief summary. If not, present his evidence in clear and concise fashion. If not interviewed, state what action is planned. Close this section with a statement as to whether or not canvass for witnesses has been completed or is planned.

Official Records: Introduce here and comment upon police report, coroner's inquest, criminal trials, weather reports or any other pertinent public record.

Subrogation/Contribution: Discuss possibilities of subrogation or contribution naming other carriers and their representatives.

Risk: Present all pertinent information as to desirability and classification of risk including vehicle, named insured and regular drivers.

Liability: The adjuster gives his opinion concerning litigation possibilities and his reasons.

Remarks: The adjuster's comments concerning present and future handling, requests for drafts, settlement authority or other instructions and any other remarks are stated. If litigation is involved and has not been discussed fully under the respective claimant, it should be commented upon.

Future Activity: The report is closed with a precise statement concerning persons to be interviewed and other actions planned. If properly prepared, this section will be a check list for both adjuster and examiner against the next report.

PROPERTY DAMAGE AND/OR COLLISION

(Preliminary) (Interim) (Closing) REPORT

FROM

ACE ADJUSTMENT CO.

315 W. GRUNT ST. MASON, IOWA

COMPANY	XYZ Insurance Co., Chicago, Ill.	REPORT DATE:	July 17, 1959
AGENT	Jones Agency		
POLICY NO.	98765	AGENT'S LOCATION	Mason, Iowa
CO. CLAIM NO.	Not Furnished	POLICY PERIOD	4/14/59–60
INSURED	Joe Taylor	ADJ. FILE NO.	6843
CLAIMANT	James Johnson		
TYPE	P. D.—Coll.	DATE OF ACC.	7/3/59

ENCLOSURES	COVERAGE	P.D. CLAIMS	SUBROGATION
ASSIGNMENT	ACCIDENT	COLLISION LOSS	REMARKS

RECOMMENDATIONS FOR USE

The NAIIA recommends this as a shortened version of the automobile form which is designed for use only on simple property damage claims and collision losses. It is recommended that such reports be short, and in most cases confined to one page.

Recommendations concerning use of individual captions follow:

Enclosures: All enclosures pertinent to the investigation are to be listed separately.

Assignment: Date, source and method of assignment.

Coverage: Unless coverage was confirmed by direct company assignment give sufficient information so that no examination of policy records is necessary and state how information was obtained. Report on vehicle identification and all other questions concerning the insurance involved.

Accident: Give date, time, place and a brief description of accident. Mention witness statements and other documents submitted.

Property Damage Claims: Omit this caption if only physical damage insurance is involved. A separate paragraph should be devoted to each property damage claimant starting with his name, address and description of property, extent of damage and how determined. If an automobile was damaged, show year, make, model, condition, use and mileage. Discuss value before accident, salvage value and cost to repair. Describe insurance and name the carrier and adjuster. Cover settlement negotiations and litigation, if any.

Collision Loss: Omit this caption if only liability insurance is involved. Describe ownership, year, make, model, and report on your inspection including condition, appearance, use and mileage. Give value before accident, salvage value and cost to repair. Submit repair estimates or other verification of damage, including snapshots. Describe previous damage and other reasons for depreciation. State steps taken concerning disposition.

Subrogation: Discuss possibilities of subrogation or contribution naming other carriers and their representatives.

Remarks: If indicated include a brief statement as to liability and reason, recommendations concerning payment or denial, requests for drafts and requests for instructions submitted. If other than a closing report describe future activity intended.

PROPERTY

(Preliminary) (Interim) (Closing)______LOSS REPORT

FROM

ACE ADJUSTMENT CO.

REPORTING OFFICE________________

COMPANY	XYZ Insurance Co., Chicago, Ill.	REPORT DATE:	July 17, 1959
AGENT	Doe Agency	AGENT'S LOCATION	Mason, Iowa
POLICY NO. & AMOUNT	12345—$10,000.	POLICY PERIOD	2/15/59–60
INSURED	Richard and Mary Roe	LOCATION OF RISK	Mason, Iowa
ESTIMATED LOSS	$2,000.00	KIND OF LOSS	Fire
EST. THIS POLICY	$2,000.00	DATE OF LOSS	7/12/59
PROPERTY INVOLVED	Building and Contents	ADJ. FILE NO.	4345

QUESTION SUBMITTED	RISK	SALVAGE
ASSIGNMENT	TITLE/ENCUMBRANCES	RECOMMENDATIONS
COVERAGE	ORIGIN	DRAFT ISSUANCE
POLICY VIOLATIONS	ADJUSTMENT/REMARKS	FUTURE ACTIVITY
INSURED	SUBROGATION	ENCLOSURES

RECOMMENDATIONS FOR USE

The NAIIA recommends to its members that this reporting procedure be used on all formal reports on property losses including particularly those involving coverage for fire and allied lines. The procedure is not intended to replace streamlined reporting on small losses. When this form is used, it should indicate at the blank space at the top whether it is a prelimary, interim, or closing report. The first report on any loss should include all captions. If any one is not involved, it is satisfactory to state "None" or use any other appropriate expression. If a given caption has been fully covered in a previous report it should be omitted in future ones. In some instances it might be advisable to include the caption but state: "Refer to report of (date)." When using a captioned form of reporting, it is not always necessary to make complete sentences. The goal is clarity of expression in submitting all necessary information by using the minimum number of words.

All reports should proceed according to the recommended outline. It is recognized that no outline can be prepared which can cover all conceivable situations. Adjusters are encouraged to use additional captions where indicated if the information submitted can not be stated properly under one of those included. Recommendations concerning the use of the individual captions follow:

Question Submitted: If no questions, state "None." However, in certain cases preliminary reports will submit a question for decision by company officials. It is recommended that when instructions are requested the caption be broken up into three sections in vertical order, viz:

1. Question Submitted: Briefly state the precise question being asked.
2. The Problem: Give an orderly account of the problem encountered, with full information, so that the man sitting behind the desk has no need to ask for further facts in order to reach a decision.
3. Recommendations: The adjuster should suggest a solution or a choice between two or more solutions.

Assignment: Date, source and method of assignment and of confirmation if required.

Coverage: Describe the policy, the forms and endorsements which may affect payment or adjustment of the loss in such specific terms that no examination of company records is necessary. If more than one policy involved, give schedule here or attach as enclosure. If non-concurrency exists, explain fully.

Policy Violations: Describe and explain. Investigate agent's knowledge. Report on any other investigation on question, mentioning any statements taken. State whether non-waiver agreement obtained. If no known violation, state "None."

Insured: Name insured, give age, very brief personal history, previous loss experience and general reputation. If a corporation, give same information concerning principal officers together with brief history of corporation. Report fully on previous losses, business failures and any indication of moral hazard. If indicated, give previous addresses.

Risk: Whether loss involves a building or contents give a brief description as to the age, construction, size, occupancy and general physical condition of the building and risk. Include comment on the suitability of the location, and state whether contents are modern, well maintained and suitable for their required purpose. Describe all physical facts pertaining to the desirability of the risk, and present any suggestions or recommendations for its improvement.

Title-Encumbrances: Describe the nature of insured's interest in the property and any encumbrance or other interests. This can be stated simply but should be authentic. If question exists, county seat records should be checked.

Origin: Describe the time and place of origin and cause as fully as would seem reasonably necessary. This should include a brief history of the loss from its inception, including its discovery. If a fire, the fighting of same, the amount of fire equipment used, and if possible, the amount of water used. Any unusual factors contributing to the spread of the fire such as adjoining construction or physical conditions which may have contributed to the severity of the fire should be described. If the loss is caused by a windstorm or explosion, or similar miscellaneous hazards covered under the policy, this paragraph should, in a similar manner, be employed to describe the manner in which the loss occurred.

Adjustment/Remarks: Report on inspection, describing value before loss, damage, cost to repair and salvage value, if indicated. If experts were used, explain. Reference may be made to estimates or other supporting data, but it is recommended that corrections and reductions on estimates or other papers be plainly and briefly noted on the original and it be made a part of the statement of loss or enclosed. Since the adjustment process will vary according to the coverage, property and amount involved, the information given will also vary, but the facts relating to amount of loss, insured's contribution (if any) and method used in adjustment should be clearly stated. Properly introduced details peculiar to the situation rather than stereotyped generalities can convince the reader of the ability and judgment exercised by the adjuster.

Subrogation: Possibilities of a subrogation recovery should be mentioned and "disposed of" here. If there are none, then so state. If circumstances indicate there could be, then explain why there are none. If subrogation possibilities do exist, explain the circumstances, report what has been and is being done and what is recommended. Report on the wrongdoer's ability to pay and on liability insurance if any.

Salvage: If none, so state. Explain participation of salvor and if authorized by company so state. Previous discussion of salvage submitted under "adjustment" should not be duplicated here, but if indicated state present position of salvage, condition, and arrangements for final disposition.

Recommendations: Report on restoration of loss if known and submit recommendations for continuance on risk including comments on insurance to value and other appropriate items. Here also may be included any other suggestions or recommendations which the adjuster believes will be of value to the company.

Draft Issuance: It is normally correct to recommend that draft be issued and forwarded "In Customary manner." If adjuster's suggestions are at variance with usual procedure, explain fully and give reasons.

Future Activity: The report is closed with a precise statement concerning work to be performed and actions intended. If properly prepared, this section will be a check list for both adjuster and examiner against the next report.

Enclosures: Here should be listed, one beneath the other in order, all enclosures that are to accompany the report. A uniform method of arrangement is recommended.

I. Homeowners Policy

HOMEOWNERS POLICY

No. H TYPE OF COMPANY

DECLARATIONS

Named Insured and P.O. Address (No., Street, Town, County, State)

Policy Term: ______ Years ______ Inception ______ Expiration

The described premises covered hereunder are located at the above address, unless otherwise stated herein: (No., Street, Town, County, State)

Insurance is provided only with respect to those of the following coverages which are indicated by a specific limit of liability applicable thereto.

Premium						Payable:	
Basic Policy Premium	Additional Premium	Total Policy Premium	Credit, if any, for existing insurance	Net Prepaid Premium	Total Premium if paid in installments	At Inception (and)	At each subsequent anniversary
$	$	$	$	$	$	$	$
Premium for Scheduled Property					$	$	$

COVERAGES AND LIMIT OF LIABILITY

SEC I	A. Dwelling	B. Appurtenant Private Structures	C. Unscheduled Personal Property	D. Additional Living Expense	SEC II	E. Personal Liability (Bodily Injury and Property Damage)	F. Personal Medical Payments		G. Physical Damage to property of others
	$	$	$	$		$ Each occurrence	$ Each person	$ 25,000. Each accident	$ 250. Each occurrence

Subject to the following Forms and Endorsements: (INSERT NO. AND EDITION DATE)

The described dwelling of ______ construction is occupied by not more than two families and not more than two roomers or boarders per family.

______ Protection Class ______ Approved Roof ______ Unapproved Roof Not more than ______ feet from Hydrant

______ Zone ______ Premium Group No. Not more than ______ miles from Fire Dept.

Special provisions applicable only in States indicated: $ ______ South Carolina — Valuation Clause

Southern States: ______ Inside City Limits ______ Inside Fire District ______ Inside Protected Suburban Area

N. Y. Coinsurance Clause applies: ______ Yes ______ No ______ Fire District

Applicable when only Form 4 is attached to this policy: $ ______ Annual fire and extended coverage contents rate; Number of apartments in building ______

Described dwelling is not seasonal and no business pursuits are conducted at the premises thereof. Exceptions, if any:* (ENTER BELOW)

Business of Named Insured:

Loss Deductible Clause No. 1 (Loss by windstorm or hail) is ______ applicable.

Loss Deductible Clause No. 2 (Loss by other perils) is ______ applicable.

Section II Only: (a) The described premises are the only premises where the Named Insured or spouse maintains a residence other than business property and farms; (b) Insured employs not more than two full-time residence employees; (c) The Insured owns no outboard motors of more than 24 horsepower for which coverage is desired. Exceptions, if any, to (a), (b) or (c):* (ENTER BELOW)

First Mortgagee: NAME AND ADDRESS

Countersignature Date Agency at:

The words "twelve months" in line 161 of the provisions hereinafter, are changed to "sixty months." ______ Agent

In Consideration of the Provisions and Stipulations Herein or Added Hereto and of the Premium Above Specified (or specified in endorsement attached hereto), this Company, for the term **shown above** from **inception date shown above** (At Noon Standard Time) to **expiration date shown above** (At Noon Standard Time) at location of property involved, to an amount not exceeding the amount(s) above specified, does insure **the Insured named in the declarations above** and legal representatives, to the extent of the actual cash value of the property at the time of loss, but not exceeding the amount which it would cost to repair or replace the property with material of like kind and quality within a reasonable time after such loss, without allowance for any increased cost of repair or reconstruction by reason of any ordinance or law regulating construction or repair, and without compensation for loss resulting from interruption of business or manufacture, nor in any event for more than the interest of the insured, against all DIRECT LOSS BY FIRE, LIGHTNING AND OTHER PERILS INSURED AGAINST IN THIS POLICY INCLUDING REMOVAL FROM PREMISES ENDANGERED BY THE PERILS INSURED AGAINST IN THIS POLICY, EXCEPT AS HEREINAFTER PROVIDED, to the property described herein while located or contained as described in this policy, or pro rata for five days at each proper place to which any of the property shall necessarily be removed for preservation from the perils insured against in this policy, but not elsewhere.

Assignment of this policy shall not be valid except with the written consent of this Company.

This policy is made and accepted subject to the foregoing provisions and stipulations and those hereinafter stated, which are hereby made a part of this policy, together with such other provisions, stipulations and agreements as may be added hereto, as provided in this policy.

*Absence of an entry means "No Exceptions."

Homeowners Policy (*Continued*)

Concealment, fraud. This entire policy shall be void if, whether before or after a loss, the insured has wilfully concealed or misrepresented any material fact or circumstance concerning this insurance or the subject thereof, or the interest of the insured therein, or in case of any fraud or false swearing by the insured relating thereto.

Uninsurable and excepted property. This policy shall not cover accounts, bills, currency, deeds, evidences of debt, money or securities; nor, unless specifically named hereon in writing, bullion or manuscripts.

Perils not included. This Company shall not be liable for loss by fire or other perils insured against in this policy caused, directly or indirectly, by: (a) enemy attack by armed forces, including action taken by military, naval or air forces in resisting an actual or an immediately impending enemy attack; (b) invasion; (c) insurrection; (d) rebellion; (e) revolution; (f) civil war; (g) usurped power; (h) order of any civil authority except acts of destruction at the time of and for the purpose of preventing the spread of fire, provided that such fire did not originate from any of the perils excluded by this policy; (i) neglect of the insured to use all reasonable means to save and preserve the property at and after a loss, or when the property is endangered by fire in neighboring premises; (j) nor shall this Company be liable for loss by theft.

Other Insurance. Other insurance may be prohibited or the amount of insurance may be limited by endorsement attached hereto.

Conditions suspending or restricting insurance. Unless otherwise provided in writing added hereto this Company shall not be liable for loss occurring

(a) while the hazard is increased by any means within the control or knowledge of the insured; or

(b) while a described building, whether intended for occupancy by owner or tenant, is vacant or unoccupied beyond a period of sixty consecutive days; or

(c) as a result of explosion or riot, unless fire ensue, and in that event for loss by fire only.

Other perils or subjects. Any other peril to be insured against or subject of insurance to be covered in this policy shall be by endorsement in writing hereon or added hereto.

Added provisions. The extent of the application of insurance under this policy and of the contribution to be made by this Company in case of loss, and any other provision or agreement not inconsistent with the provisions of this policy, may be provided for in writing added hereto, but no provision may be waived except such as by the terms of this policy is subject to change.

Waiver provisions. No permission affecting this insurance shall exist, or waiver of any provision be valid, unless granted herein or expressed in writing added hereto. No provision, stipulation or forfeiture shall be held to be waived by any requirement or proceeding on the part of this Company relating to appraisal or to any examination provided for herein.

Cancellation of policy. This policy shall be cancelled at any time at the request of the insured, in which case this Company shall, upon demand and surrender of this policy, refund the excess of paid premium above the customary short rates for the expired time. This policy may be cancelled at any time by this Company by giving to the insured a five days' written notice of cancellation with or without tender of the excess of paid premium above the pro rata premium for the expired time, which excess, if not tendered, shall be refunded on demand. Notice of cancellation shall state that said excess premium (if not tendered) will be refunded on demand.

Mortgagee interests and obligations. If loss hereunder is made payable, in whole or in part, to a designated mortgagee not named herein as the insured, such interest in this policy may be cancelled by giving to such mortgagee a ten days' written notice of cancellation.

If the insured fails to render proof of loss such mortgagee, upon notice, shall render proof of loss in the form herein specified within sixty (60) days thereafter and shall be subject to the provisions hereof relating to appraisal and time of payment and of bringing suit. If this Company shall claim that no liability existed as to the mortgagor or owner, it shall, to the extent of payment of loss to the mortgagee, be subrogated to all the mortgagee's rights of recovery, but without impairing mortgagee's right to sue; or it may pay off the mortgage debt and require an assignment thereof and of the mortgage. Other provisions relating to the interests and obligations of such mortgagee may be added hereto by agreement in writing.

Pro rata liability. This Company shall not be liable for a greater proportion of any loss than the amount hereby insured shall bear to the whole insurance covering the property against the peril involved, whether collectible or not.

Requirements in case loss occurs. The insured shall give immediate written notice to this Company of any loss, protect the property from further damage, forthwith separate the damaged and undamaged personal property, put it in the best possible order, furnish a complete inventory of the destroyed, damaged and undamaged property, showing in detail quantities, costs, actual cash value and amount of loss claimed; **and within sixty days after the loss, unless such time is extended in writing by this Company, the insured shall render to this Company a proof of loss,** signed and sworn to by the insured, stating the knowledge and belief of the insured as to the following: the time and origin of the loss, the interest of the insured and of all others in the property, the actual cash value of each item thereof and the amount of loss thereto, all encumbrances thereon, all other contracts of insurance, whether valid or not, covering any of said property, any changes in the title, use, occupation, location, possession or exposures of said property since the issuing of this policy, by whom and for what purpose any building herein described and the several parts thereof were occupied at the time of loss and whether or not it then stood on leased ground, and shall furnish a copy of all the descriptions and schedules in all policies and, if required, verified plans and specifications of any building, fixtures or machinery destroyed or damaged. The insured, as often as may be reasonably required, shall exhibit to any person designated by this Company all that remains of any property herein described, and submit to examinations under oath by any person named by this Company, and subscribe the same; and, as often as may be reasonably required, shall produce for examination all books of account, bills, invoices and other vouchers, or certified copies thereof if originals be lost, at such reasonable time and place as may be designated by this Company or its representative, and shall permit extracts and copies thereof to be made.

Appraisal. In case the insured and this Company shall fail to agree as to the actual cash value or the amount of loss, then, on the written demand of either, each shall select a competent and disinterested appraiser and notify the other of the appraiser selected within twenty days of such demand. The appraisers shall first select a competent and disinterested umpire; and failing for fifteen days to agree upon such umpire, then, on request of the insured or this Company, such umpire shall be selected by a judge of a court of record in the state in which the property covered is located. The appraisers shall then appraise the loss, stating separately actual cash value and loss to each item; and, failing to agree, shall submit their differences, only, to the umpire. An award in writing, so itemized, of any two when filed with this Company shall determine the amount of actual cash value and loss. Each appraiser shall be paid by the party selecting him and the expenses of appraisal and umpire shall be paid by the parties equally.

Company's options. It shall be optional with this Company to take all, or any part, of the property at the agreed or appraised value, and also to repair, rebuild or replace the property destroyed or damaged with other of like kind and quality within a reasonable time, on giving notice of its intention so to do within thirty days after the receipt of the proof of loss herein required.

Abandonment. There can be no abandonment to this Company of any property.

When loss payable. The amount of loss for which this Company may be liable shall be payable sixty days after proof of loss, as herein provided, is received by this Company and ascertainment of the loss is made either by agreement between the insured and this Company expressed in writing or by the filing with this Company of an award as herein provided.

Suit. No suit or action on this policy for the recovery of any claim shall be sustainable in any court of law or equity unless all the requirements of this policy shall have been complied with, and unless commenced within twelve months next after inception of the loss.

Subrogation. This Company may require from the insured an assignment of all right of recovery against any party for loss to the extent that payment therefor is made by this Company.

IN WITNESS WHEREOF, this Company has executed and attested these presents; but this policy shall not be valid unless countersigned by the duly authorized Agent of this Company at the agency hereinbefore mentioned.

INSERT SIGNATURES AND TITLES OF PROPER OFFICERS

Homeowners Policy (*Continued*)

Form 2

(ATTACH FORM AND ENDORSEMENTS HERE)

OTHER PROVISIONS APPLICABLE TO SECTIONS I AND II EXCEPT AS OTHERWISE INDICATED

1. War Risk Exclusion: Under Section I as respects all perils insured against hereunder except the perils of fire and lightning (which are otherwise provided for on page of this policy) and under Section II as respects liability assumed by the Insured under any contract or agreement, as to expenses under any Medical Payments coverage, under any Supplementary Payments provision relating to immediate medical or surgical relief, or as to Coverage F, this policy shall not apply to loss, bodily injury or proper damage caused directly or indirectly by:

(a) hostile or warlike action in time of peace or war, including action in hindering, combating or defending against an actual, impending or expected attack, (1) by ar government or sovereign power (de jure or de facto), or by any authority maintaining or using military, naval or air forces; or (2) by military, naval or air forces; (3) by an agent of any such government, power, authority or forces, it being understood that any discharge, explosion or use of any weapon of war employing nuclea fission or fusion shall be conclusively presumed to be such a hostile or warlike action by such a government, power, authority or forces;

(b) insurrection, rebellion, revolution, civil war, usurped power, or action taken by governmental authority in hindering, combating or defending against such an occu rence; seizure or destruction under quarantine or Custom's regulations, confiscation by order of any government or public authority, or risks of contraband illegal transportation or trade.

2. Nuclear Clause—(Not Applicable in New York) Section I: The word "fire" in this policy or endorsements attached hereto is not intended to and does not embrac nuclear reaction or nuclear radiation or radioactive contamination, all whether controlled or uncontrolled, and loss by nuclear reaction or nuclear radiation or radioactiv contamination is not intended to be and is not insured against by this policy or said endorsements, whether such loss be direct or indirect, proximate or remote, or be whole or in part caused by, contributed to, or aggravated by "fire" or any other perils insured against by this policy or said endorsements; however, subject to the foregoir and all provisions of this policy, direct loss by "fire" resulting from nuclear reaction or nuclear radiation or radioactive contamination is insured against by this policy.

3. Nuclear Exclusion—(Not Applicable in New York) Section I: This policy does not insure against loss by nuclear reaction or nuclear radiation or radioactive contaminatior all whether controlled or uncontrolled, or due to any act or condition incident to any of the foregoing, whether such loss be direct or indirect, proximate or remote, or b in whole or in part caused by, contributed to, or aggravated by any of the perils insured against by this policy; and nuclear reaction or nuclear radiation or radioactiv contamination, all whether controlled or uncontrolled, is not "explosion" or "smoke". This clause applies to all perils insured against hereunder except the perils of fire an lightning, which are otherwise provided for in the Nuclear Clause contained above.

4. Nuclear Exclusion—Section II: This policy does not apply, under Coverage E, to bodily injury or property damage with respect to which an Insured under this policy is als an Insured under a nuclear energy liability policy issued by Nuclear Energy Liability Insurance Association, Mutual Atomic Energy Liability Underwriters or Nuclear Insuranc Association of Canada, or would be an Insured under any such policy but for its termination upon exhaustion of its limit of liability.

GENERAL CONDITIONS

1. MODIFICATION OF TERMS: The provisions on page 2 of this policy as respects uninsurable and excepted property, the exclusion of loss by theft and suspension of insurance are hereby waived. Provisions on page 2, other than those pertaining to waiver, cancellation, concealment and fraud and subrogation, do not apply to Section II of this policy. With respect to subrogation, the provisions are not applicable to Coverage F — Personal Medical Payments.

2. DEFINITIONS:

(a) **Insured:** The unqualified word "Insured" includes (1) the Named Insured and (2) if residents of his household, his spouse, the relatives of either, and any other person under the age of twenty-one in the care of an Insured.

The word "Insured" also includes, under Coverages E and F, (1) with respect to animals and watercraft owned by an Insured, any person or organization legally responsible therefor, except a person using or having custody or possession of any such animal or watercraft without the permission of the owner, and (2) with respect to farm tractors and trailers and self-propelled or motor or animal drawn farm implements, any employee of an Insured while engaged in the employment of the Insured.

The insurance afforded under Coverage E applies separately to each Insured against whom claim is made or suit is brought but the inclusion herein of more than one Insured shall not operate to increase the limit of the Company's liability.

(b) **Premises:** Means the premises described in the Declarations, including grounds, garages, stables and other outbuildings incidental thereto, and private approaches thereto.

(c) **Residence Employee:** Means an employee of an Insured, whose duties are in connection with the ownership, maintenance or use of the premises, including the maintenance or use of automobiles or teams, or who performs elsewhere duties of a similar nature not in connection with an Insured's business.

(d) **Business:** Includes trade, profession or occupation.

3. OTHER INSURANCE: Other insurance covering the described dwelling building (except existing insurance for which credit is given in this policy) is not permitted.

4. APPORTIONMENT:

(a) **Section I—Loss by fire or other perils not provided for in 4(b) below:** This Company shall not be liable for a greater proportion of any loss from any peril or perils included in this policy than (1) the applicable limit of liability under this policy bears to the whole amount of fire insurance covering the property, or which would have covered the property except for the existence of this insurance, whether collectible or not, and whether or not such other fire insurance covers against the additional peril or perils insured hereunder, (2) nor for a greater proportion of any loss than the applicable limit of liability under this policy bears to all insurance whether collectible or not, covering in any manner such loss, or which would have covered such loss except for the existence of this insurance.

(b) **Section I (Coverage C)—Loss by theft or loss of personal property covered o an unspecified peril basis:** Insurance under this policy shall apply as exces insurance over any other valid and collectible insurance which would apply i the absence of this policy.

(c) **Section II (Coverage E)—Loss under Personal Liability:** If the Insured has othe insurance against a loss covered by this policy, this Company shall not b liable under this policy for a greater proportion of such loss than the appli cable limit of liability stated in the Declarations bears to the total applicabl limit of liability of all valid and collectible insurance against such loss, pro vided that with respect to loss arising out of the ownership, maintenance operation, use, loading or unloading of (1) any automobile or midget automobil at the premises or the ways immediately adjoining or (2) watercraft, thi insurance shall not apply to the extent that any valid and collectible insurance whether on a primary, excess or contingent basis, is available to the Insurec

(d) When loss under this policy is subject to a deductible, this Company sha not be liable for more than its pro rata share of such loss in excess of th deductible amount.

5. DEATH OF NAMED INSURED: Upon the death of the Named Insured, this polic shall cover the Named Insured's spouse, if a resident of the same household a the time of such death, and legal representative as Named Insureds from the dat of such death; provided, (a) under Section I, if such legal representative is no a person who was a permanent member of the Named Insured's household at th time of the death of the Named Insured, this policy shall apply as it applied prio to such death but shall not apply to loss of property owned or used by such persor a member of his household or a residence employee thereof, unless such los occurs at a part of the premises occupied exclusively by the original Named In sured's household, and (b) under Section II, if such legal representative was no an Insured at the time of the death of the Named Insured, this policy shall appl to such person only with respect to the premises of the original Named Insurec and those of his spouse, and shall cover as Insured, while a resident of sai premises, any person who was an Insured at the time of the death.

6. LIBERALIZATION CLAUSE: If during the period that insurance is in force unde this policy, or within 45 days prior to the inception date thereof, on behalf o this Company there be adopted, or filed with and approved or accepted by th insurance supervisory authorities, all in conformity with law, any changes in th form attached to this policy by which this form of insurance could be extended o broadened without increased premium charge by endorsement or substitution of form then such extended or broadened insurance shall inure to the benefit of the Insurec hereunder as though such endorsement or substitution of form had been made

7. CONFORMITY WITH STATUTE: The terms of this policy and forms attached heret which are in conflict with the statutes of the state wherein this policy is issue are hereby amended to conform to such statutes.

8. CANCELLATION: The words "five days" in the cancellation provision on page of the policy are deleted and the words "ten days" are substituted therefor.

9. POLICY TERM: This policy applies only to losses or occurrences during th policy term.

Homeowners Policy (*Continued*)

CONDITIONS APPLICABLE ONLY TO SECTION I

1. PERMISSION GRANTED: (a) for such use of the premises as is usual or incidental to a dwelling; (b) for the premises to be vacant or unoccupied without limit of time, except as otherwise provided in this policy for certain specified perils; however, a building in the course of construction shall not be deemed vacant; and (c) for Named Insured to make alterations, additions and repairs, and to complete structures in course of construction.

In the event of loss hereunder, the Insured is permitted to make reasonable repairs, temporary or permanent, provided such repairs are confined solely to the protection of the property from further damage and provided further that the Insured shall keep an accurate record of such repair expenditures. The cost of any such repairs directly attributable to damage by any peril insured against shall be included in determining the amount of loss hereunder. Nothing herein contained is intended to modify the policy requirements applicable in case loss occurs, and in particular the requirement that in case loss occurs the Insured shall protect the property from further damage.

2. CONTROL OF PROPERTY: This insurance shall not be prejudiced by any act or neglect of any person (other than the Named Insured) when such act or neglect is not within the control of the Named Insured.

3. SUBROGATION: This insurance shall not be invalidated should the Named Insured waive in writing prior to a loss any or all right of recovery against any party for loss occurring to the property covered herein.

4. BENEFIT TO BAILEE: The insurance afforded by this policy shall not inure directly or indirectly to the benefit of any carrier or other bailee for hire.

5. PAIR AND SET CLAUSE: If there is loss of an article which is part of a pair or set, the measure of loss shall be a reasonable and fair proportion of the total value of the pair or set, giving consideration to the importance of said article, but such loss shall not be construed to mean total loss of the pair or set.

6. LOSS PAYABLE CLAUSE: Loss, if any, shall be adjusted with the Named Insured and shall be payable to him unless other payee is specifically named hereunder.

CONDITIONS APPLICABLE ONLY TO SECTION II

1. LIMITS OF LIABILITY: The limit of liability stated in the Declarations for Coverage E is the limit of this Company's liability for all damages, including damages for care and loss of services, as the result of one occurrence.

The limit of liability stated in the Declarations for Coverage F as applicable to "each person" is the limit of the Company's liability for all expenses incurred by or on behalf of each person who sustains bodily injury as the result of any one accident; the limit of liability stated in the Declarations for Coverage F as applicable to "each accident" is, subject to the above provision respecting each person, the total limit of the Company's liability for all expenses incurred by or on behalf of two or more persons who sustain bodily injury as the result of any one accident.

2. LIMITS OF LIABILITY; SETTLEMENT OPTIONS — COVERAGE G: The limit of this Company's liability for loss of property arising out of any one occurrence shall not exceed (a) the actual cash value of the property at time of loss, nor (b) what it would then cost to repair or replace the property with other of like kind and quality, nor (c) the applicable limit of liability stated in the Declaration for Coverage G.

This Company may pay for the loss in money or may repair or replace the property and may settle any claim for loss of property either with the Insured or the owner thereof. Any property so paid for or replaced shall, at the option of this Company, become the property of this Company. Payment hereunder shall not constitute an admission of liability of the Insured or, except hereunder, of this Company.

3. NOTICE OF OCCURRENCE — COVERAGES E AND F: When an occurrence takes place, written notice shall be given by or on behalf of the Insured to this Company or any of its authorized agents as soon as practicable. Such notice shall contain particulars sufficient to identify the Insured and also reasonably obtainable information respecting the time, place and circumstances of the occurrence, the names and addresses of the injured and of available witnesses.

4. NOTICE OF CLAIM OR SUIT — COVERAGE E: If claim is made or suit is brought against the Insured, the Insured shall immediately forward to this Company every demand, notice, summons or other process received by him or his representative.

5. ASSISTANCE AND COOPERATION OF THE INSURED — COVERAGE E: The Insured shall cooperate with the Company and, upon the Company's request, assist in making settlements, in the conduct of suits, and in enforcing any right of contribution or indemnity against any person or organization who may be liable to the Insured because of bodily injury or property damage with respect to which insurance is afforded under this policy, and the Insured shall attend hearings and trials and assist in securing and giving evidence and obtaining the attendance of witnesses. The Insured shall not, except at his own cost, voluntarily make any payment, assume any obligation or incur any expense other than for such immediate medical and surgical relief to others as shall be imperative at the time of the accident.

6. MEDICAL REPORTS; PROOF AND PAYMENT OF CLAIM — COVERAGE F: As soon as practicable, the injured person or someone on his behalf shall give to this Company written proof of claim, under oath if required, and shall, after each request from this Company, execute authorization to enable this Company to obtain medical reports and copies of records. The injured person shall submit to physical examination by physicians selected by this Company when and as often as this Company may reasonably require.

This Company may pay the injured person or any person or organization rendering the services and such payment shall reduce the amount payable hereunder for such injury. Payment hereunder shall not constitute admission of liability of the Insured or, except hereunder, of this Company.

7. INSURED'S DUTIES WHEN LOSS OCCURS — COVERAGE G: When loss occurs, the Insured shall give written notice as soon as practicable to the Company or any of its authorized agents, file sworn proof of loss with the Company within ninety-one (91) days after the occurrence of loss, exhibit the damaged property, if within his control, and cooperate with the Company in all matters pertaining to the loss or claims with respect thereto.

8. ACTION AGAINST COMPANY — COVERAGE E: No action shall lie against this Company unless, as a condition precedent thereto, the Insured shall have fully complied with all the terms of this policy applicable to Section II, nor until the amount of the Insured's obligation to pay shall have been finally determined either by judgment against the Insured after actual trial or by written agreement of the Insured, the claimant and this Company.

Any person or organization or the legal representative thereof who has secured such judgment or written agreement shall thereafter be entitled to recover under said Section II to the extent of the insurance afforded by this policy. No person or organization shall have any right under this policy to join the Company as a party to any action against the Insured to determine the Insured's liability, nor shall the Company be impleaded by the Insured or his legal representative.

Bankruptcy or insolvency of the Insured or of the Insured's estate shall not relieve this Company of any of its obligations hereunder.

9. ACTION AGAINST COMPANY — COVERAGES F AND G: No action shall lie against this Company unless, as a condition precedent thereto, there shall have been full compliance with all the terms of this policy applicable to Section II, nor until 30 days after the required proofs of claim have been filed with this Company.

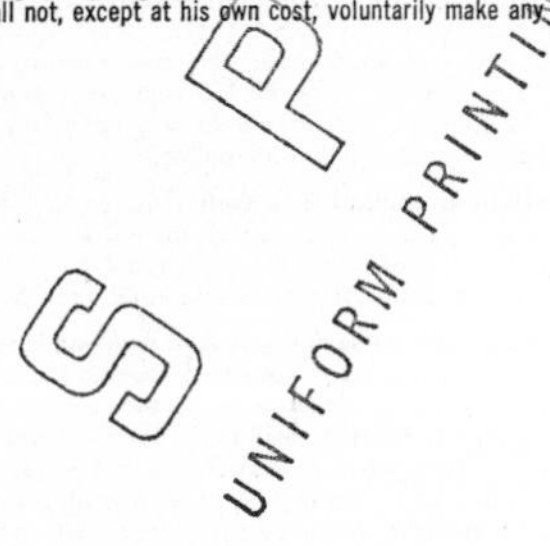

Homeowners Policy (*Continued*)

HOMEOWNERS POLICY — BROAD FORM
PROVISIONS APPLICABLE TO SECTION I

MIC-2
(Ed. 6-63)
Central

DESCRIPTION OF PROPERTY AND INTERESTS COVERED

COVERAGE A — DWELLING.

This policy covers: (a) the building described including additions in contact therewith, occupied principally for dwelling purposes; (b) if the property of the Insured and when not otherwise covered, building equipment, fixtures and outdoor equipment, all pertaining to the service of the premises and while located thereon or temporarily elsewhere; and (c) materials and supplies located on the premises or adjacent thereto, intended for use in construction, alteration or repair of such dwelling. Trees, shrubs, plants or lawns are not covered, except as provided elsewhere in this form.

COVERAGE B — APPURTENANT PRIVATE STRUCTURES.

This policy covers private structures appertaining to the premises and located thereon, including materials and supplies located on the premises or adjacent thereto, intended for use in construction, alteration or repair of such structures. This coverage does not include: (a) any structure used in whole or in part for commercial, manufacturing or farming purposes; or (b) any structures (except structures used principally for private garage purposes) which are wholly rented or leased to other than a tenant of the described dwelling.

COVERAGE C — UNSCHEDULED PERSONAL PROPERTY.

1. On premises: This policy covers unscheduled personal property usual or incidental to the occupancy of the premises as a dwelling, owned, worn or used by an Insured, while on the premises, or at the option of the Named Insured, owned by others while on the portion of the premises occupied exclusively by the Insured.

This coverage does not include: animals, birds, automobiles, vehicles licensed for road use and aircraft; the property of roomers or boarders not related to the Insured; articles carried or held as samples or for sale or for delivery after sale or for rental to others; and property which is separately described and specifically insured in whole or in part by this or any other insurance.

2. Away from premises: This policy also covers unscheduled personal property as described and limited, while elsewhere than on the premises, anywhere in the world, owned, worn or used by an Insured, or at the option of the Named Insured, owned by a guest while in a temporary residence of, and occupied by an Insured or owned by a residence employee while actually engaged in the service of an Insured and while such property is in the physical custody of such residence employee or in a residence temporarily occupied by an Insured. Property pertaining to a business is not covered.

The limits of this Company's liability for such property while away from premises shall be an additional amount of insurance equal to 10% of the amount specified for Coverage C, but in no event less than $1,000.

COVERAGE D — ADDITIONAL LIVING EXPENSE.

This policy covers the necessary increase in living expense resulting from loss by a peril insured against to the property covered hereunder incurred by the Named Insured to continue as nearly as practicable the normal standard of living of the Named Insured's household for the applicable period described in (a) or (b) below:

(a) The time required, with the exercise of due diligence and dispatch, to repair or replace such damaged or destroyed property;

(b) The time required for the Named Insured's household to become settled in permanent quarters.

This coverage includes the fair rental value of the described dwelling and appurtenant private structures with respect to any portion thereof rented or held for rental by an Insured and, as furnished by the owner, for the period of time required with the exercise of due diligence and dispatch to restore same to tenantable condition, less such charges and expenses as do not continue.

The periods described above shall not be limited by the expiration of this policy.

This Company shall also be liable under Coverage D for the period of time, not exceeding two weeks, while access to the premises is prohibited by order of civil authority, but only when such order is given as a direct result of damage to neighboring premises by a peril insured against.

PERILS INSURED AGAINST

This policy insures under Section I against direct loss to the property covered (and additional living expense resulting from such loss) by the following perils as defined and limited herein:

1. Fire and lightning.

2. Removal, meaning loss by removal of the property covered hereunder from premises endangered by the perils insured against, including coverage pro rata for 30 days at each proper place to which such property shall necessarily be removed for preservation from or for repair of damage caused by the perils insured against.

3. Windstorm or hail, excluding:

(a) loss caused directly or indirectly by frost or cold weather or ice (other than hail), snowstorm or sleet, all whether driven by wind or not;

(b) loss to the interior of the building(s), or the property covered therein caused by rain, snow, sand, or dust, all whether driven by wind or not, unless the building(s) covered or containing the property covered shall first sustain an actual damage to roof or walls by the direct force of wind or hail and then this Company shall be liable for loss to the interior of the building(s) or the property covered therein as may be caused by rain, snow, sand, or dust entering the building(s) through openings in the roof or walls made by direct action of wind or hail.

4. Explosion.

5. Sudden and accidental tearing asunder, cracking, burning, or bulging of a steam or hot water heating system, except appliances for heating water for domestic consumption, and excluding loss resulting from freezing while the described building(s) is vacant or unoccupied, unless the Insured shall have exercised due diligence with respect to maintaining heat in the building(s), or unless the plumbing and heating systems and domestic appliances had been drained and the water supply shut off during such vacancy or unoccupancy.

6. Riot, riot attending a strike, and civil commotion, including direct loss from pillage and looting occurring during and at the immediate place of a riot, riot attending a strike or civil commotion.

7. Aircraft.

8. Vehicles, but excluding loss to driveways and walks, caused by any land vehicle owned or operated by any occupant of the premises.

9. Sudden and accidental damage from smoke, other than smoke from agricultural smudging or industrial operations.

10. Vandalism and malicious mischief, meaning only the wilful and malicious damage to or destruction of the property covered, but excluding as respects this peril loss if the described dwelling had been vacant beyond a period of 30 consecutive days immediately preceding the loss.

11. Theft, meaning any act of stealing or attempt thereat and, as to Coverage C (on premises), including theft of property covered from within any bank, trust or safe deposit company, public warehouse, or occupied dwelling not owned or occupied by or rented to an Insured, in which the property covered has been placed for safekeeping.

Upon knowledge of loss under this peril or of an occurrence which may give rise to a claim for such loss, the Insured shall give notice as soon as practicable to this Company or any of its authorized agents and also to the police.

General Exclusions applicable to theft: This policy does not apply as respects this peril to loss: (a) if committed by an Insured; or (b) in or to a dwelling under construction or of materials or supplies therefor until completed and ready for occupancy.

Exclusions applicable while the described dwelling is rented to others: While the portion of the described dwelling customarily occupied exclusively by an Insured is rented to others, this policy does not apply, as respects this peril, to loss from the described dwelling: (a) of money, numismatic property and bank notes; (b) of accounts, bills, deeds, evidences of debt, letters of credit, notes other than bank notes, passports, railroad and other tickets, securities, and stamps including philatelic property; and (c) of jewelry, watches, necklaces, bracelets, gems, precious and semi-precious stones, or articles of gold or platinum; or (d) caused by a tenant of such portion of the described dwelling or any of his employees or members of his household.

Exclusions applicable to property away from described premises: This policy does not apply as respects this peril to loss away from the premises of: (a) property while in any dwelling or premises thereof, owned, rented or occupied by an Insured, except while an Insured is temporarily residing therein; (b) property while unattended in or on any automobile, motorcycle or trailer, other than a public conveyance, unless the loss is the

(OVER)

Homeowners Policy (*Continued*)

result of forcible entry either into such vehicle while all doors and windows thereof are closed and locked or into a fully enclosed and locked luggage compartment, of which entry there are visible marks upon the exterior of said vehicle.

12. Falling objects, but excluding loss to (a) the interior of the building(s) or the property covered therein, caused by falling objects unless the building(s) covered or containing the property covered shall first sustain an actual damage to the exterior of the roof or walls by the falling object; (b) outdoor equipment, cloth awnings, fences, all except as the direct result of the collapse of a building.

13. Weight of ice, snow or sleet which results in physical injury to the building(s) covered or containing the property covered, but excluding loss to (a) outdoor equipment, cloth awnings, fences, all except as the direct result of the collapse of a building; (b) fences, pavements, patios, swimming pools, foundations, retaining walls, bulkheads, piers, wharves or docks, when such loss is caused by freezing, thawing, or by the pressure or weight of ice or water whether driven by wind or not; all except as the direct result of the collapse of a building.

14. Collapse (not settling, cracking, shrinkage, bulging or expansion) of building(s) or any part thereof, but excluding loss to (a) outdoor equipment, gutters and downspouts, cloth awnings and fences, all except as the direct result of the collapse of a building; (b) fences, pavements, patios, swimming pools, foundations, retaining walls, bulkheads, piers, wharves or docks, when such loss is caused by freezing, thawing, or by the pressure or weight of ice or water whether driven by wind or not; all except as the direct result of the collapse of a building.

15. Accidental discharge, leakage or overflow of water or steam from within a plumbing, heating, or air conditioning system or domestic appliance, including the cost of tearing out and replacing any part of the building(s) covered required to effect repairs to the system or appliance from which the water or steam escapes, but excluding: (a) loss resulting from freezing while the described building(s) is vacant or unoccupied, unless the Insured shall have exercised due diligence with respect to maintaining heat in the building(s), or unless the plumbing and heating systems and domestic appliances had been drained and the water supply shut off during such vacancy or unoccupancy; (b) loss if the described property had been vacant beyond a period of 30 consecutive days immediately preceding the loss; and (c) loss to the system or appliance from which the water or steam escapes.

16. Sudden and accidental tearing asunder, cracking, burning, or bulging of appliances for heating water for domestic consumption, but excluding loss resulting from freezing while the described building(s) is vacant or unoccupied, unless the Insured shall have exercised due diligence with respect to maintaining heat in the building(s), or unless the plumbing and heating systems and domestic appliances had been drained and the water supply shut off during such vacancy or unoccupancy.

17. Breakage of glass constituting a part of the building(s) covered hereunder, including glass in storm doors and storm windows, but excluding loss if the dwelling had been vacant beyond a period of 30 consecutive days immediately preceding the loss.

18. Freezing of plumbing, heating and air conditioning systems and domestic appliances, but excluding loss resulting from freezing while the described building(s) is vacant or unoccupied, unless the Insured shall have exercised due diligence with respect to maintaining heat in the building(s), or unless the plumbing and heating systems and domestic appliances had been drained and the water supply shut off during such vacancy or unoccupancy.

19. Sudden and accidental injury from artificially generated electrical current to electrical appliances, devices, fixtures and wiring, except tubes, transistors and similar electronic components.

EXTENSIONS OF COVERAGE

1. Trees, shrubs, plants and lawns: The Named Insured may apply up to 5% of the limit of liability for Coverage A, subject otherwise to the limitations and exclusions applicable thereto, to cover trees, shrubs and plants on the premises (except those grown for commercial purposes), against loss by fire, lightning, explosion, riot, civil commotion, vandalism, malicious mischief, theft, aircraft or vehicles not operated by an occupant of the described premises, but this Company shall not be liable for more than its proportion of $250 on any one tree, shrub or plant, including expense incurred for removing debris thereof. Coverage A shall also apply to lawns. This Company shall not be liable under this Extension of Coverage for loss from the perils (as defined in this policy) of windstorm or hail; or vehicles owned or operated by an occupant of the premises, falling objects; or weight of ice, snow or sleet.

2. Debris removal: This policy covers expenses incurred in the removal of all debris of the property covered hereunder occasioned by loss thereto for which coverage is afforded.

3. Replacement cost — Coverages A and B: This Extension of Coverage shall be applicable only to a building structure covered hereunder, but excluding carpeting, cloth awnings, domestic appliances and outdoor equipment, all whether permanently attached to the building structures or not.

(a) In the event of loss to such a building structure covered under this policy, when the full cost of repair or replacement is both (1) less than $1000 and (2) less than 5% of the whole amount of insurance applicable to such building structure for the peril causing the loss, the coverage of this policy is extended to include the full cost of repair or replacement (without deduction for depreciation).

(b) If at the time of loss the whole amount of insurance applicable to said building structure for the peril causing the loss is 80% or more of the full replacement cost of such building structure, the coverage of this policy applicable to such building structure is extended to include the full cost of repair or replacement (without deduction for depreciation).

(c) If at the time of loss the whole amount of insurance applicable to said building structure for the peril causing the loss is less than 80% of the full replacement cost of such building structure, this Company's liability for loss under this policy shall not exceed the larger of the following amounts (1) or (2):

(1) The actual cash value of that part of the building structure damaged or destroyed;

(2) That proportion of the full cost of repair or replacement (without deduction for depreciation) of that part of the building structure damaged or destroyed, which the whole amount of insurance applicable to said building structure for the peril causing the loss bears to 80% of the full replacement cost of such building structure.

(d) This Company's liability for loss under this policy including this Extension of Coverage shall not exceed the smallest of the following amounts (1), (2), or (3):

(1) The limit of liability of this policy applicable to the damaged or destroyed building structure;

(2) The replacement cost of the building structure or any part thereof identical with such building structure on the same premises and intended for the same occupancy and use;

(3) The amount actually and necessarily expended in repairing or replacing said building structure or any part thereof intended for the same occupancy and use.

This Company shall not be liable under paragraph (b) or subparagraph (2) of paragraph (c) of this Extension of Coverage for any loss unless and until actual repair or replacement is completed.

(e) In determining if the amount of insurance on the building structure insured equals or exceeds eighty percent (80%) of its replacement cost the value of excavations, underground flues, and pipes, underground wiring and drains, and brick, stone and concrete foundations, piers and other supports which are below the surface of the ground shall be disregarded.

(f) The Named Insured may elect to disregard this Extension of Coverage in making claim hereunder, but such election shall not prejudice the Named Insured's right to make further claim within 180 days after loss for any additional liability brought about by this Extension of Coverage.

4. Cellar and Foundation Clause: (Applicable only in Ohio). The Named Insured may apply up to 5% of the limit of liability applicable to Coverage A to cover cellar and foundation walls of the described dwelling building insured thereunder.

5. Fire Department Service Clause: This insurance also covers for an amount not exceeding $100 the Named Insured's liability, assumed by contract or agreement for fire department charges where fire department is called because of a fire in, on or exposing property insured hereunder, while located on the premises described. This extension does not cover Named Insured's liability, by contract or otherwise, to indemnify either a city, municipality or fire protection district, or any other person, firm or corporation against loss, claim or liability arising by reasons of the movement or functioning of fire apparatus or members of a fire department; or by reason of any accident arising out of the performance of services to Insured by any fire department. Coverage afforded under this clause applies only if the property is not located within the limits of the city, municipality or fire protection district furnishing such fire department response.

6. The foregoing Extensions of Coverage shall not increase the limit of liability applying under this policy to the property damaged or destroyed.

Homeowners Policy (*Continued*)

SPECIAL LIMITS OF LIABILITY

1. Loss Deductible Clause No. 1 — Applicable only if so stated in the Declarations: With respect to loss by windstorm or hail to buildings, structures or personal property in the open, this Company shall be liable only when such loss in each occurrence exceeds $50. When loss is between $50 and $500 this Company shall be liable for 111% of loss in excess of $50 and when loss is $500 or more, this loss deductible clause shall not apply. This loss deductible clause shall not apply to Coverage D (Additional Living Expense).

2. Loss Deductible Clause No. 2 — Applicable only if so stated in the Declarations: With respect to loss by any of the perils insured against other than:

(a) fire or lightning, or

(b) windstorm or hail to buildings, structures or personal property in the open,

this Company shall be liable only when such loss in each occurrence exceeds $50. When loss is between $50 and $500 this Company shall be liable for 111% of loss in excess of $50 and when loss is $500 or more, this loss deductible clause shall not apply. This loss deductible clause shall not apply to Coverage D (Additional Living Expense).

No more than one deductible amount shall apply in event of loss by windstorm or hail arising out of any one occurrence.

3. Under Coverage C, this Company shall not be liable in any one loss with respect to the following named property:

(a) for more than $100 on money, bullion, numismatic property and bank notes;

(b) for more than $500 on accounts, bills, deeds, evidences of debt, letters of credit, notes other than bank notes, passports, railroad and other tickets, securities, and stamps including philatelic property;

(c) for more than $1,000 on manuscripts;

(d) by theft for more than $1,000 on any single article of jewelry including watches, necklaces, bracelets, gems, precious and semiprecious stones and any article of gold or platinum or any article of fur or any article containing fur which represents its principal value;

(e) for more than $500 on watercraft, including their trailers, whether licensed or not, furnishings, equipment and outboard motors, nor for any loss by windstorm or hail to such property not inside fully enclosed buildings (except rowboats and canoes on the premises).

SPECIAL EXCLUSIONS

This Company shall not be liable:

(a) as respects Perils 5, 12, 14, 15, 16 and 18: for loss caused by, resulting from, contributed to or aggravated by any earth movement, including but not limited to earthquake, landslide, mud flow, earth sinking, rising or shifting; unless loss by fire or explosion ensues, and this Company shall then be liable only for such ensuing loss; but this exclusion does not apply to loss by theft;

(b) as respects Perils 3, 5, 12, 13, 14, 15, 16, 17 and 18: for loss caused by, resulting from, contributed to or aggravated by any of the following:

(1) flood, surface water, waves, tidal water or tidal wave, overflow of streams or other bodies of water, or spray from any of the foregoing, all whether driven by wind or not;

(2) water which backs up through sewers or drains;

(3) water below the surface of the ground including that which exerts pressure on or flows, seeps or leaks through sidewalks, driveways, foundations, walls, basement or other floors, or through doors, windows or any other openings in such sidewalks, driveways, foundations, walls or floors;

unless loss by fire or explosion ensues, and this Company shall then be liable only for such ensuing loss; but these exclusions do not apply to loss by theft;

(c) for loss occasioned directly or indirectly by enforcement of any local or state ordinance or law regulating the construction, repair, or demolition of building(s) or structure(s) unless such liability is otherwise specifically assumed by endorsement hereon;

(d) for consequential loss of any nature except that loss, to unscheduled personal property covered hereunder, due to change of temperature shall be limited to such loss resulting from physical damage to the described building(s) or to equipment therein or to equipment on the described premises caused by a peril insured against.

SPECIAL CONDITIONS

1. Losses: Loss hereunder shall not reduce the limit of liability under this Policy.

2. Occupancy Clause: It is a condition of this policy that if the described dwelling is associated with and in proximity to farming operations (1) the agricultural products produced on the land are incidental to the occupancy of the dwelling and are principally for home consumption, or (2) that the occupants of the dwelling and buildings appurtenant thereto are not engaged in the operation of the farm and said buildings are in addition to a complete set of farm buildings on the farm and are not exposed within 200 feet by any farm building.

3. Mortgagee Clause — Coverages A and B only — Not applicable in Minnesota — (This entire clause is void unless name of Mortgagee(s) (or trustee(s)) is inserted in the Declarations): Loss or damage, if any, under this policy, shall be payable to the mortgagee (or trustee), named on the first page of this policy, as interest may appear, under all present or future mortgages upon the property herein described in which the aforesaid may have an interest as mortgagee (or trustee) in order of precedence of said mortgages, and this insurance as to the interest of the mortgagee (or trustee) only therein, shall not be invalidated by any act or neglect of the mortgagor or owner of the within described property, nor by any foreclosure or other proceedings or notice of sale relating to the property, nor by any change in the title or ownership of the property, nor by the occupation of the premises for purposes more hazardous than are permitted by this policy; provided, that in case the mortgagor or owner shall neglect to pay any premium due under this policy, the mortgagee (or trustee) shall, on demand, pay the same.

Provided also, that the mortgagee (or trustee) shall notify this Company of any change of ownership or occupancy or increase of hazard which shall come to the knowledge of said mortgagee (or trustee) and, unless permitted by this policy, it shall be noted thereon and the mortgagee (or trustee) shall, on demand, pay the premium for such increased hazard for the term of the use thereof, otherwise this policy shall be null and void.

This Company reserves the right to cancel this policy at any time as provided by its terms, but in such case this policy shall continue in force for the benefit only of the mortgagee (or trustee) for ten days after notice to the mortgagee (or trustee) of such cancellation and shall then cease, and this Company shall have the right, on like notice, to cancel this agreement.

Whenever this Company shall pay the mortgagee (or trustee) any sum for loss or damage under this policy, and shall claim that, as to the mortgagor or owner, no liability therefor existed, this Company shall, to the extent of such payment, be thereupon legally subrogated to all the rights of the party to whom such payment shall be made, under all securities held as collateral to the mortgage debt, or may at its option pay to the mortgagee (or trustee) the whole principal due or to grow due on the mortgage, with interest and shall thereupon receive a full assignment and transfer of the mortgage and of all such other securities; but no subrogation shall impair the right of the mortgagee (or trustee) to recover the full amount of said mortgagee's (or trustee's) claim.

4. Installment Payment — Not applicable if policy is written on a Continuous Renewal basis:

(Not applicable in Arkansas, Ohio and Missouri): If the Insured elects to pay the premium in equal annual payments as indicated on the first page of this policy the premium for this policy is hereby made so payable.

If the Insured is in default of any such premium payment and this Company elects to cancel this policy, notice of cancellation shall be in accordance with the provisions of this policy, but in such case any portions of the premium previously paid shall be earned by this Company.

(Applicable only in Ohio): If the Insured elects to pay the premium in equal annual payments as indicated on the first page of this policy the premium for this policy is hereby made so payable.

Default in making any payment shall be construed as a request of the Insured to cancel this policy, in which case this Company shall, upon demand and surrender of this policy, or after ten days written notice to the Insured, comply with the said request.

If this policy is cancelled, either at the request of the Insured or at the election of this Company, this Company shall refund to the Insured only the excess of paid premium over earned premium. In the event the earned premium exceeds the paid premium the Insured shall pay this Company the difference.

(Applicable only in Arkansas): If the premium for this policy is made payable in annual installments and this Company elects to cancel this policy because the Named Insured is in default of any installment, notice of cancellation shall be in accordance with the policy provisions, but in such case, any portions of the premium previously paid shall be earned by this Company.

If the policy is cancelled, any unpaid installments shall be deducted in determining the amount of return premium due the Named Insured.

(OVER)

Homeowners Policy (*Concluded*)

PROVISIONS APPLICABLE TO SECTION II

THIS COMPANY AGREES WITH THE NAMED INSURED:

INSURING AGREEMENTS

1. COVERAGE E — PERSONAL LIABILITY:

(a) **Liability:** To pay on behalf of the Insured all sums which the Insured shall become legally obligated to pay as damages because of bodily injury or property damage, and the Company shall defend any suit against the Insured alleging such bodily injury or property damage and seeking damages which are payable under the terms of this policy, even if any of the allegations of the suit are groundless, false or fraudulent; but the Company may make such investigation and settlement of any claim or suit as it deems expedient.

(b) **Fire Legal Liability:** Coverage E also applies with respect to all sums which the Insured shall become legally obligated to pay as damages because of property damage to the premises or house furnishings therein if such property damage arises out of (1) fire, (2) explosion, or (3) smoke or smudge caused by sudden, unusual and faulty operation of any heating or cooking unit.

2. COVERAGE F — PERSONAL MEDICAL PAYMENTS: To pay all reasonable expenses incurred within one year from the date of accident for necessary medical, surgical, X-ray and dental services, including prosthetic devices, and necessary ambulance, hospital, professional nursing and funeral services, to or for each person who sustains bodily injury caused by accident.

(a) while on the premises with the permission of an Insured, or

(b) while elsewhere if such bodily injury, (1) arises out of the premises or a condition in the ways immediately adjoining, (2) is caused by the activities of an Insured, (3) is caused by the activities of or is sustained by a residence employee and arises out of and in the course of his employment by an Insured, or (4) is caused by an animal owned by or in the care of an Insured.

3. COVERAGE G — PHYSICAL DAMAGE TO PROPERTY: To pay for loss of property of others caused by an Insured. "Loss" means damage or destruction but does not include disappearance, abstraction or loss of use. This coverage shall not apply if insurance is otherwise provided in Section I of this policy.

4. SUPPLEMENTARY PAYMENTS: With respect to such insurance as is afforded by this policy for Coverage E, this Company shall pay, in addition to the applicable limits of liability:

(a) all expenses incurred by this Company, all costs taxed against the Insured in any defended suit and all interest on the entire amount of any judgment therein which accrues after entry of the judgment and before this Company has paid or tendered or deposited in court that part of the judgment which does not exceed the limit of this Company's liability thereon;

(b) premiums on appeal bonds required in any such suit, premiums on bonds to release attachments for an amount not in excess of the applicable limit of liability of this policy, but without any obligation to apply for or furnish any such bonds;

(c) expenses incurred by the Insured for such immediate medical and surgical relief to others as shall be imperative at the time of the accident;

(d) all reasonable expenses, other than loss of earnings, incurred by the Insured at this Company's request.

5. SUPPLEMENTARY DEFINITIONS:

(a) **"bodily injury"** means bodily injury, sickness or disease, including death resulting therefrom, sustained by any person;

(b) **"property damage"** means injury to or destruction of property, including loss of use thereof;

(c) **premises:** For purposes of Section II, the definition of "premises" appearing in the Basic Policy shall include: (1) all premises where the Named Insured or his spouse maintains a residence and includes private approaches thereto and other premises and private approaches thereto for use in connection with said residence, except business property and farms, (2) individual or family cemetery plots or burial vaults, (3) premises in which an Insured is temporarily residing, if not owned by an Insured, and (4) vacant land, other than farm land, owned by or rented to an Insured. Land shall not be deemed vacant following the commencement of any construction operations thereon unless such operations are being performed solely by independent contractors in connection with the construction of a one or two family dwelling for the Insured;

(d) **"business property"** includes (1) property on which a business is conducted, and (2) property rented in whole or in part to others, or held for such rental, by the Insured. The Insured's property shall not constitute "business property" because of (a) occasional rental of the Insured's residence, (b) rental in whole or in part to others of a one or two family dwelling usually occupied in part by the Insured as a residence, unless such rental is for the accommodations of more than two roomers or boarders per family occupying the dwelling, (c) rental of space in the Insured's residence for incidental office, school or studio occupancy, or (d) rental or holding for rental of not more than three car spaces or stalls in garages or stables;

(e) **"automobile"** means a land motor vehicle, trailer or semitrailer; but the term "automobile" does not include, except while being towed by or carried on an automobile, any of the following: any crawler or farm-type tractor, farm implement or, if not subject to motor vehicle registration, any equipment which is designed for use principally off public roads;

(f) **"midget automobile"** means a land motor vehicle of the type commonly referred to as a "midget automobile", "kart", "go-kart", "speedmobile" or by a comparable name, whether commercially built or otherwise;

(g) **"undeclared outboard motor"** means

(1) an outboard motor of more than twenty-four horsepower, or

(2) a combination of outboard motors of more than twenty-four horsepower in the aggregate and used with a single watercraft,

if not declared and a premium charged therefor.

6. INSURANCE FOR NEWLY ACQUIRED OUTBOARD MOTORS:

Part (3) of Special Exclusion (b) does not apply to a watercraft powered by an undeclared outboard motor, ownership of which is acquired during the policy period by an Insured included within parts (1) or (2) of the definition of "Insured."

SPECIAL EXCLUSIONS

Section II of this Policy Does Not Apply:

(a) (1) to any business pursuits of an Insured, except under Coverages E and F, activities therein which are ordinarily incident to non-business pursuits, (2) to the rendering of any professional service or the omission thereof, or (3) to any act or omission in connection with premises, other than as defined, which are owned, rented or controlled by an Insured, but this subdivision (3) does not apply with respect to bodily injury to a residence employee arising out of and in the course of his employment by the Insured;

(b) under Coverages E and F, to the ownership, maintenance, operation, use, loading or unloading of (1) automobiles or midget automobiles while away from the premises or the ways immediately adjoining, except under Coverage E with respect to operations by independent contractors for non-business purposes of an Insured not involving automobiles owned or hired by the Insured, (2) watercraft owned by or rented to an Insured, while away from the premises, if with inboard motor power exceeding fifty horsepower, or if a sailing vessel with or without auxiliary power and twenty-six feet or more in overall length; (3) watercraft, other than a sailing vessel, while away from the premises and powered in whole or in part by an undeclared outboard motor owned by an Insured, or (4) aircraft; but, with respect to bodily injury to a residence employee, arising out of and in the course of his employment by the Insured, parts (1), (2) and (3) of this exclusion do not apply, and part (4) applies only while such employee is engaged in the operation or maintenance of aircraft;

(c) under Coverages E and F, to bodily injury or property damage caused intentionally by or at the direction of the Insured;

(d) under Coverages E and F, to bodily injury to any person (1) if the Insured has in effect on the date of the occurrence a policy providing workmen's compensation or occupational disease benefits therefor, or (2) if benefits therefor are in whole or in part either payable or required to be provided under any workmen's compensation or occupational disease law, but this subdivision (2) does not apply with respect to Coverage E unless such benefits are payable or required to be provided by the Insured;

(e) under Coverage E, to liability assumed by the Insured under any contract or agreement, but this exclusion as respects Insuring Agreement I (a) does not apply to (1) any indemnity obligation assumed by the Insured under a written contract directly relating to the ownership, maintenance or use of the premises, or liability of others assumed by the Insured under any other written contract;

(f) under Insuring Agreement I (a) of Coverage E, to property damage to property used by, rented to or in the care, custody or control of the Insured, or property as to which the Insured for any purpose is exercising physical control;

(g) under Coverage E, to sickness or disease of any residence employee unless prior to 36 months after the end of the policy period written claim is made or suit is brought against the Insured for damages because of such sickness or disease or death resulting therefrom;

(h) under Coverage F, to bodily injury to (1) any Insured included within parts (1) and (2) of the definition of "Insured" or (2) any person, other than a residence employee, if such person is regularly residing on the premises including any part rented to such person or to others, or is on the premises because of a business conducted thereon, or is injured by an accident arising out of such business;

(i) under Coverage G, to loss (1) arising out of the ownership, maintenance, operation, use, loading or unloading of any land motor vehicle, trailer or semitrailer, farm machinery or equipment, aircraft or watercraft; or (2) of property owned by or rented to any Insured, any resident of the Named Insured's household or any tenant of the Insured; or (3) caused intentionally by an Insured over the age of 12 years.

Sections I and II are otherwise subject to the provisions set forth in the policy to which this form is attached.

J. Fidelity and Surety Bonds

COMMERCIAL BLANKET BOND
Revised to May, 1957

(A Stock Company, herein called the Underwriter)

DECLARATIONS

Item 1. Name of Insured:

(herein called the Insured)

Principal Address:
(NO.) (STREET) (CITY) (STATE)

Item 2. Bond Period: from noon on
(MONTH, DAY, YEAR)
to noon on the effective date of the cancelation or termination of this Bond, standard time at the Principal Address as to each of said dates.

Item 3. Limit of Liability: $

Item 4. The liability of the Underwriter is subject to the terms of the following riders attached hereto:

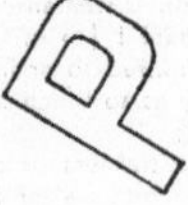

Item 5. The Insured by the acceptance of this Bond gives notice to the Underwriter terminating or canceling prior bond(s) or policy(ies) No.(s)
such termination or cancelation to be effective as of the time this Bond becomes effective.

COMMERCIAL BLANKET BOND

Bond No.

Insured

Fidelity and Surety Bonds (*Continued*)

INSURING AGREEMENT

The Underwriter, in consideration of the payment of the premium, and subject to the Declarations made a part hereof, the General Agreements, Conditions and Limitations, and other terms of this Bond, agrees to indemnify the Insured against any loss of money or other property which the Insured shall sustain through any fraudulent or dishonest act or acts committed by any of the Employees, acting alone or in collusion with others, to an amount not exceeding in the aggregate the amount stated in Item 3 of the Declarations.

GENERAL AGREEMENTS

CONSOLIDATION-MERGER

A. If, through consolidation or merger with, or purchase of assets of, some other concern, any persons shall become Employees, the Insured shall give the Underwriter written notice thereof and shall pay an additional premium computed pro rata from the date of such consolidation, merger or purchase to the end of the current premium period.

JOINT INSURED

B. If more than one Insured is covered under this Bond, the Insured first named shall act for itself and for every other Insured for all purposes of this Bond. Knowledge possessed or discovery made by any Insured or by any partner or officer thereof shall, for the purposes of Sections 6, 7 and 12, constitute knowledge possessed or discovery made by every Insured. Cancelation of the insurance hereunder as respects any Employee as provided in Section 12 shall apply to every Insured. If, prior to the cancelation or termination of this Bond in its entirety, this Bond is canceled or terminated as to any Insured, there shall be no liability for any loss sustained by such Insured unless discovered within one year from the date of such cancelation or termination. The liability of the Underwriter for loss sustained by any or all of the Insured shall not exceed the amount for which the Underwriter would be liable had all such loss been sustained by any one of the Insured. Payment by the Underwriter to the Insured first named of any loss under this Bond shall fully release the Underwriter on account of such loss. If the Insured first named ceases for any reason to be covered under this Bond, then the Insured next named shall thereafter be considered as the Insured first named for all purposes of this Bond.

LOSS UNDER PRIOR BOND OR POLICY

C. If the coverage of this Bond is substituted for any prior bond or policy of insurance carried by the Insured or by any predecessor in interest of the Insured, which prior bond or policy is terminated, canceled or allowed to expire as of the time of such substitution, the Underwriter agrees that this Bond applies to loss which is discovered as provided in Section 1 of the Conditions and Limitations and which would have been recoverable by the Insured or such predecessor under such prior bond or policy except for the fact that the time within which to discover loss thereunder had expired; provided:

(1) the indemnity afforded by this General Agreement C shall be a part of and not in addition to the amount of insurance afforded by this Bond;

(2) such loss would have been covered under this Bond had this Bond with its agreements, limitations and conditions as of the time of such substitution been in force when the acts or defaults causing such loss were committed; and

(3) recovery under this Bond on account of such loss shall in no event exceed the amount which would have been recoverable under this Bond in the amount for which it is written as of the time of such substitution, had this Bond been in force when such acts or defaults were committed, or the amount which would have been recoverable under such prior bond or policy had such prior bond or policy continued in force until the discovery of such loss, if the latter amount be smaller.

THE FOREGOING INSURING AGREEMENT AND GENERAL AGREEMENTS ARE SUBJECT TO THE FOLLOWING CONDITIONS AND LIMITATIONS:

BOND PERIOD, TERRITORY, DISCOVERY

Section 1. Loss is covered under this Bond only if discovered not later than one year from the end of the Bond Period.

Subject to General Agreement C, this Bond applies only to loss sustained by the Insured through fraudulent or dishonest acts committed during the Bond Period by any of the Employees engaged in the regular service of the Insured within any of the States of the United States of America, the District of Columbia, Alaska, Hawaii, Virgin Islands, Puerto Rico, Canal Zone or Canada or while such Employees are elsewhere for a limited period.

EXCLUSION

Section 2. This Bond does not apply to loss, or to that part of any loss, as the case may be, the proof of which, either as to its factual existence or as to its amount, is dependent upon an inventory computation or a profit and loss computation; provided, however, that this paragraph shall not apply to loss of money or other property which the Insured can prove, through evidence wholly apart from such computations, is sustained by the Insured through any fraudulent or dishonest act or acts committed by any one or more of the Employees.

DEFINITION OF EMPLOYEE

Section 3. As used in this Bond, "Employee" means any natural person (except a director or trustee of the Insured, if a corporation, who is not also an officer or employee thereof in some other capacity) while in the regular service of the Insured in the ordinary course of the Insured's business during the Bond Period and whom the Insured compensates by salary, wages or commissions and has the right to govern and direct in the performance of such service, but does not mean any broker, factor, commission merchant, consignee, contractor or other agent or representative of the same general character. The words "while in the regular service of the Insured" shall include the first 30 days thereafter; subject, however, to Sections 12 and 13.

Insured or otherwise, whether such act be committed before or after the date of employment by the Insured.

If, prior to the issuance of this Bond, any fidelity insurance in favor of the Insured or any predecessor in interest of the Insured and covering one or more of the Insured's Employees shall have been canceled as to any of such Employees by reason of the giving of written notice of cancelation by the insurer issuing such fidelity insurance, whether the Underwriter or not, and if such Employees shall not have been reinstated under the coverage of such fidelity insurance or superseding fidelity insurance, the Underwriter shall not be liable on account of such Employees unless the Underwriter shall agree in writing to include such Employees within the coverage of this Bond.

LOSS — NOTICE — PROOF — ACTION AGAINST UNDERWRITER

Section 7. Upon knowledge or discovery of loss under this Bond, the Insured shall: (a) give notice thereof as soon as practicable to the Underwriter or any of its authorized agents, and (b) file detailed proof of loss, duly sworn to, with the Underwriter within four months after the discovery of loss.

Upon the Underwriter's request, the Insured shall produce for the Underwriter's examination all pertinent records, at such reasonable times and places as the Underwriter shall designate, and shall cooperate with the Underwriter in all matters pertaining to loss or claims with respect thereto.

No action shall lie against the Underwriter unless, as a condition precedent thereto, there shall have been full compliance with all the terms of this Bond, nor until ninety days after the required proofs of loss have been filed with the Underwriter, nor at all unless commenced within two years from the date when the Insured discovers the loss. If any limitation of time for notice of loss or any legal proceeding herein contained is shorter than that permitted to be fixed by agreement under any statute controlling the construction of this Bond, the shortest permissible statutory limitation of time shall govern and shall supersede the time limitation herein stated.

Fidelity and Surety Bonds (*Continued*)

LOSS CAUSED BY UNIDENTIFIABLE EMPLOYEES

Section 4. If a loss is alleged to have been caused by the fraud or dishonesty of any one or more of the Employees and the Insured shall be unable to designate the specific Employee or Employees causing such loss, the Insured shall nevertheless have the benefit of this Bond, subject to the provisions of Section 2 of this Bond, provided that the evidence submitted reasonably proves that the loss was in fact due to the fraud or dishonesty of one or more of the said Employees, and provided, further, that the aggregate liability of the Underwriter for any such loss shall not exceed the amount stated in Item 3 of the Declarations.

OWNERSHIP OF MONEY OR OTHER PROPERTY

Section 5. The insured property may be owned by the Insured, or held by the Insured in any capacity whether or not the Insured is liable for the loss thereof, or may be property as respects which the Insured is legally liable.

PRIOR FRAUD, DISHONESTY OR CANCELATION

Section 6. The coverage of this Bond shall not apply to any Employee from and after the time that the Insured or any partner or officer thereof not in collusion with such Employee shall have knowledge or information that such Employee has committed any fraudulent or dishonest act in the service of the

LIMIT OF LIABILITY UNDER THIS BOND AND PRIOR INSURANCE

Section 10. With respect to loss caused by any Employee or in which such Employee is concerned or implicated or which is chargeable to any Employee as provided in Section 4 and which occurs partly during the Bond Period and partly during the period of other bonds or policies issued by the Underwriter to the Insured or to any predecessor in interest of the Insured and terminated or canceled or allowed to expire and in which the period for discovery has not expired at the time any such loss thereunder is discovered, the total liability of the Underwriter under this Bond and under such other bonds or policies shall not exceed, in the aggregate, the amount stated in Item 3 of the Declarations or the amount available to the Insured under such other bonds or policies, as limited by the terms and conditions thereof, for any such loss, if the latter amount be the larger.

OTHER INSURANCE

Section 11. If there is available to the Insured any other insurance or indemnity covering any loss covered by this Bond, the Underwriter shall be liable hereunder only for that part of such loss which is in excess of the amount recoverable or recoverable from such other insurance or indemnity.

CANCELATION AS TO ANY EMPLOYEE

Section 12. This Bond shall be deemed canceled as to any Employee: (a) immediately upon discovery by the Insured, or by

RECOVERIES

Section 8. If the Insured shall sustain any loss covered by this Bond which exceeds the amount of indemnity provided by this Bond, the Insured shall be entitled to all recoveries (except from suretyship, insurance, reinsurance, security or indemnity taken by or for the benefit of the Underwriter) by whomsoever made, on account of such loss under this Bond until fully reimbursed, less the actual cost of effecting the same; and any remainder shall be applied to the reimbursement of the Underwriter.

LIMITS OF LIABILITY

Section 9. Indemnification by the Underwriter for any loss under this Bond shall not reduce the Underwriter's liability for other losses under this Bond whenever sustained. The Underwriter's total liability under this Bond for any loss caused by any Employee or in which such Employee is concerned or implicated is limited to the amount stated in Item 3 of the Declarations.

Regardless of the number of years this Bond shall continue in force and the number of premiums which shall be payable or paid, the limit of liability stated in Item 3 of the Declarations shall not be cumulative from year to year or period to period.

any partner or officer thereof not in collusion with such Employee, of any fraudulent or dishonest act on the part of such Employee; or (b) at noon, standard time as aforesaid, upon the effective date specified in a written notice mailed to the Insured. Such date shall be not less than fifteen days after the date of mailing. The mailing by the Underwriter of notice as aforesaid to the Insured at the address shown in this Bond shall be sufficient proof of notice. Delivery of such written notice by the Underwriter shall be equivalent to mailing.

CANCELATION OF BOND

Section 13. This Bond may be canceled by the Insured by mailing to the Underwriter written notice stating when thereafter the cancelation shall be effective. This Bond may be canceled by the Underwriter by mailing to the Insured at the address shown in this Bond written notice stating when, not less than fifteen days thereafter, such cancelation shall be effective. The mailing of notice as aforesaid shall be sufficient proof of notice. Delivery of such written notice either by the Insured or by the Underwriter shall be equivalent to mailing.

If the Insured cancels, earned premium shall be computed in accordance with the customary short rate table and procedure. If the Underwriter cancels, earned premium shall be computed pro rata. Premium adjustment may be made at the time cancelation is effected or as soon as practicable after cancelation becomes effective, but payment or tender of unearned premium is not a condition of cancelation.

In witness whereof, the Underwriter has caused this Bond to be executed on the Declarations page.

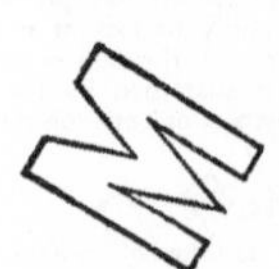

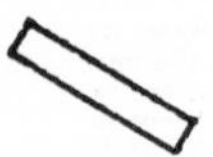

Fidelity and Surety Bonds (*Continued*)

STANDARD FORM 25
REVISED NOVEMBER 1950
PRESCRIBED BY GENERAL SERVICES ADMINISTRATION
GENERAL REGULATION NO. 5

PERFORMANCE BOND

(*See Instructions on Reverse*)

DATE BOND EXECUTED

PRINCIPAL

SURETY

PENAL SUM OF BOND (*express in words and figures*)	CONTRACT NO.	DATE OF CONTRACT

KNOW ALL MEN BY THESE PRESENTS, That we, the PRINCIPAL and SURETY above named, are held and firmly bound unto the United States of America, hereinafter called the Government, in the penal sum of the amount stated above, for the payment of which sum well and truly to be made, we bind ourselves, our heirs, executors, administrators, and successors, jointly and severally, firmly by these presents.

THE CONDITION OF THIS OBLIGATION IS SUCH, that whereas the principal entered into a certain contract with the Government, numbered and dated as shown above and hereto attached;

NOW THEREFORE, if the principal shall well and truly perform and fulfill all the undertakings, covenants, terms, conditions, and agreements of said contract during the original term of said contract and any extensions thereof that may be granted by the Government, with or without notice to the surety, and during the life of any guaranty required under the contract, and shall also well and truly perform and fulfill all the undertakings, covenants, terms, conditions, and agreements of any and all duly authorized modifications of said contract that may hereafter be made, notice of which modifications to the surety being hereby waived, then, this obligation to be void; otherwise to remain in full force and virtue.

IN WITNESS WHEREOF, the above-bounden parties have executed this instrument under their several seals on the date indicated above, the name and corporate seal of each corporate party being hereto affixed and these presents duly signed by its undersigned representative, pursuant to authority of its governing body.

In Presence of:

WITNESS		INDIVIDUAL PRINCIPAL	
1.	as to	....	[SEAL]
2.	as to	....	[SEAL]
3.	as to	....	[SEAL]
4.	as to	....	[SEAL]

WITNESS		INDIVIDUAL SURETY	
1.	as to	....	[SEAL]
2.	as to	....	[SEAL]

Attest:

CORPORATE PRINCIPAL

BUSINESS ADDRESS

BY

TITLE

AFFIX CORPORATE SEAL

Attest:

CORPORATE SURETY

BUSINESS ADDRESS

BY

TITLE

AFFIX CORPORATE SEAL

Fidelity and Surety Bonds (*Continued*)

The rate of premium on this bond is .... per thousand.

Total amount of premium charged, $..

(The above must be filled in by corporate surety)

CERTIFICATE AS TO CORPORATE PRINCIPAL

I, ..., certify that I am the .... secretary of the corporation named as principal in the within bond; that ...., who signed the said bond on behalf of the principal, was then .... of said corporation; that I know his signature, and his signature thereto is genuine; and that said bond was duly signed, sealed, and attested for and in behalf of said corporation by authority of its governing body.

.... [CORPORATE SEAL]

INSTRUCTIONS

1. This form shall be used for construction work or the furnishing of supplies or services, whenever a performance bond is required. There shall be no deviation from this form except as authorized by the General Services Administration.

2. The surety on the bond may be any corporation authorized by the Secretary of the Treasury to act as surety, or two responsible individual sureties. Where individual sureties are used, this bond must be accompanied by a completed Affidavit of Individual Surety for each individual surety (Standard Form 28).

3. The name, including full Christian name, and business or residence address of each individual party to the bond shall be inserted in the space provided therefor, and each such party shall sign the bond with his usual signature on the line opposite the scroll seal, and if signed in Maine or New Hampshire, an adhesive seal shall be affixed opposite the signature.

4. If the principals are partners, their individual names shall appear in the space provided therefor, with the recital that they are partners composing a firm, naming it, and all the members of the firm shall execute the bond as individuals.

5. If the principal or surety is a corporation, the name of the State in which incorporated shall be inserted in the space provided therefor, and said instrument shall be executed and attested under the corporate seal as indicated in the form. If the corporation has no corporate seal the fact shall be stated, in which case a scroll or adhesive seal shall appear following the corporate name.

6. The official character and authority of the person or persons executing the bond for the principal, if a corporation, shall be certified by the secretary or assistant secretary, according to the form herein provided. In lieu of such certificate there may be attached to the bond copies of so much of the records of the corporation as will show the official character and authority of the officer signing, duly certified by the secretary or assistant secretary, under the corporate seal, to be true copies.

7. The date of this bond must not be prior to the date of the instrument in connection with which it is given.

Fidelity and Surety Bonds (*Continued*)

STANDARD FORM 25A
REVISED NOVEMBER 1950
PRESCRIBED BY GENERAL SERVICES ADMINISTRATION
GENERAL REGULATION NO. 5

PAYMENT BOND

(See Instructions on Reverse)

DATE BOND EXECUTED

PRINCIPAL

SURETY

PENAL SUM OF BOND *(express in words and figures)*	CONTRACT NO.	DATE OF CONTRACT

KNOW ALL MEN BY THESE PRESENTS, That we, the PRINCIPAL and SURETY above named, are held and firmly bound unto the United States of America, hereinafter called the Government, in the penal sum of the amount stated above, for the payment of which sum well and truly to be made, we bind ourselves, our heirs, executors, administrators, and successors, jointly and severally, firmly by these presents.

THE CONDITION OF THIS OBLIGATION IS SUCH, that whereas the principal entered into a certain contract with the Government, numbered and dated as shown above and hereto attached;

NOW THEREFORE, if the principal shall promptly make payment to all persons supplying labor and material in the prosecution of the work provided for in said contract, and any and all duly authorized modifications of said contract that may hereafter be made, notice of which modifications to the surety being hereby waived, then this obligation to be void; otherwise to remain in full force and virtue.

IN WITNESS WHEREOF, the above-bounden parties have executed this instrument under their several seals on the date indicated above, the name and corporate seal of each corporate party being hereto affixed and these presents duly signed by its undersigned representative, pursuant to authority of its governing body.

In Presence of:

WITNESS — INDIVIDUAL PRINCIPAL

1. .... as to .... [SEAL]
2. .... as to .... [SEAL]
3. .... as to .... [SEAL]
4. .... as to .... [SEAL]

WITNESS — INDIVIDUAL SURETY

1. .... as to .... [SEAL]
2. .... as to .... [SEAL]

Attest:

CORPORATE PRINCIPAL

BUSINESS ADDRESS

BY

TITLE

AFFIX CORPORATE SEAL

Attest:

CORPORATE SURETY

BUSINESS ADDRESS

BY

TITLE

AFFIX CORPORATE SEAL

Fidelity and Surety Bonds (*Concluded*)

The rate of premium on this bond is .... per thousand.

Total amount of premium charged, $..................................

(The above must be filled in by corporate surety)

CERTIFICATE AS TO CORPORATE PRINCIPAL

I, ..., certify that I am the .... secretary of the corporation named as principal in the within bond; that ...., who signed the said bond on behalf of the principal, was then .... of said corporation; that I know his signature, and his signature thereto is genuine; and that said bond was duly signed, sealed, and attested for and in behalf of said corporation by authority of its governing body.

.... [CORPORATE SEAL]

INSTRUCTIONS

1. This form, for the protection of persons supplying labor and material, shall be used whenever a payment bond is required under the act of August 24, 1935, 49 Stat. 793, as amended (40 U. S. C. 270a–270e). It may also be used in any other case in which a payment bond is to be required. There shall be no deviation from this form except as authorized by the General Services Administration.

2. The surety on the bond may be any corporation authorized by the Secretary of the Treasury to act as surety, or two responsible individual sureties. Where individual sureties are used, this bond must be accompanied by a completed Affidavit of Individual Surety for each individual surety (Standard Form 28).

3. The name, including full Christian name, and business or residence address of each individual party to the bond shall be inserted in the space provided therefor, and each such party shall sign the bond with his usual signature on the line opposite the scroll seal, and if signed in Maine or New Hampshire, an adhesive seal shall be affixed opposite the signature.

4. If the principals are partners, their individual names shall appear in the space provided therefor, with the recital that they are partners composing a firm, naming it, and all the members of the firm shall execute the bond as individuals.

5. If the principal or surety is a corporation, the name of the State in which incorporated shall be inserted in the space provided therefor, and said instrument shall be executed and attested under the corporate seal as indicated in the form. If the corporation has no corporate seal the fact shall be stated, in which case a scroll or adhesive seal shall appear following the corporate name.

6. The official character and authority of the person or persons executing the bond for the principal, if a corporation, shall be certified by the secretary or assistant secretary, according to the form herein provided. In lieu of such certificate there may be attached to the bond copies of so much of the records of the corporation as will show the official character and authority of the officer signing, duly certified by the secretary or assistant secretary, under the corporate seal, to be true copies.

7. The date of this bond must not be prior to the date of the instrument in connection with which it is given.

K. Partial List of Insurance Organizations

Listed below are a few of the many organizations active at the *national* level in insurance. The list is *by no means exhaustive; it is only illustrative.* The purpose is simply to illustrate *some* of the numerous types of organizations which make up the insurance industry. For a larger and more detailed list readers are referred to a source book such as the *Insurance Almanac,* published annually by the Underwriting Printing and Publishing Company (116 John Street, New York.) Much of the information summarized below came from this publication. Numerous additional organizations are described in Chapter 64, "Insurance Pools" and in Appendix L which lists some of the public relations organizations in the insurance industry.

American Bar Association—Section on Insurance

This permanent section of the American Bar Association has a membership of lawyers who are particularly interested in insurance law. Subcommittees cover particular subdivisions of insurance. Annual proceedings are published. The purpose is to provide an opportunity for exchange of views and a sharing of knowledge among members.

American Institute of Marine Underwriters

The members are marine insurance companies and individuals who represent such companies. The general purpose is to exchange information of interest to marine underwriters and to promulgate the general views of marine underwriters through publications and addresses. (See Chapters 17 and 20.)

American Institute of Property and Liability Underwriters, Inc.

This organization established and currently maintains the educational program which leads to the Chartered Property and Casualty Underwriter designation. (See also the description of Society of C.P.C.U.) The activities of the institute extend to the fostering of career education and professionalism generally. (See Chapter 70.)

American Insurance Association

Until January 1, 1965, this organization simply provided a forum for the study of common problems and development of consensuses. On that date it absorbed the Association of Casualty and Surety Companies and the National Board of Fire Underwriters. This merger reflects the increasing industry emphasis on multiple line underwriting.

American Mutual Insurance Alliance

Many mutual fire and casualty companies cooperate through this Alliance to achieve several goals, some of which include research on insurance problems, assistance to state and federal insurance supervisory officials in improving business conditions and ethical standards, encouragement of use of mutual insurance, and stimulation of insurance education.

American Risk and Insurance Association

Membership consists of educators professionally interested in risk and insurance and also of other individuals interested in the improvement of academic education in risk and insurance. The purpose is the encouragement of formal education and research at the professional academic level. This association publishes the *Journal of Risk and Insurance.*

American Society of Insurance Management, Inc.

The membership consists predominantly of large corporations which are represented in the society by their insurance managers. Numerous chapters are active in the United States and Canada. The objective is to foster better understanding among buyers, to work toward development of simpler and better insurance coverages, and to voice interests of corporate users of insurance in respect to legislation affecting insurance. (See Part IX of this *Handbook.*)

Association of Average Adjusters of the United States

Average adjusters (see Part III) have organized this association to encourage use of proper principles in adjustment of averages. Also they are interested in the promotion of uniformity of practice.

Association of Casualty and Surety Companies

On January 1, 1965, this association was merged into the American Insurance Association. Prior to that time, the association was composed of numerous capital stock insurance companies which conducted casualty and/or surety business. The association was the vehicle for discussions of common problems and promotion of common interests of member companies. This function has now been assumed by the American Insurance Association.

Association of Superintendents of Insurance of the Provinces of Canada

The membership is obvious. Since virtually all contract legislation on insurance in the nine commonlaw provinces of Canada (i.e., all provinces except Quebec), is uniform, a principal purpose of the association is to consider amendments which are made on recommendation of Superintendents of Insurance.

Casualty Actuarial Society

Members are "fellows" or "associates," the latter being those who have successfully completed some but not all of the examinations given by the society. The purpose is to "promote actuarial and statistical science." The emphasis is on insurance other than life. The society publishes the *Proceedings of the Casualty Actuarial Society.*

Committee on Interpretation of the Nation-wide Marine Definition

The committee is composed of individuals whose task is to interpret the "Nation-wide Marine Definition" which figures prominently in Part IV of this *Handbook.*

Fire Insurance Research & Actuarial Association

This new organization represents numerous stock insurers as a coordinating medium for fire and allied lines to provide research and actuarial services to rating bureaus and to companies. The organization will also furnish service on reporting form business, continuing this function of the now dissolved Inter-Regional Insurance Conference of which it is a successor body.

Foreign Credit Insurance Association

Membership is open to any insurance company able to participate in providing export credit insurance to U.S. exporters. The association was created as a result of federal legislation which empowered the Export-Import Bank of Washington to establish a program of export credit insurance. The establishment of FCIA permits private insurance facilities to be used with those of the Export-Import Bank. (See Chapter 42.)

Inland Marine Insurance Bureau

The membership, purpose, origin, operation, and other aspects of this bureau are described in detail in Chapter 28.

Insurance Accounting and Statistical Association

This association is "all industry" and international. Individuals from all segments of the industry make up its membership. The purpose is the study and research for development of improved theory and practice in respect to insurance accounting and statistics. A textbook and other publications are issued. (See Chapter 61.)

Insurance Information Institute

The institute's members are other organizations (several of which have been described in this section) which represent generally the interests of stock insurers. The purpose is simply stated as follows: ". . . to attain a better public understanding and acceptance of the insurance business." (See Chapter 71.)

Multi-Line Insurance Rating Bureau

A rating bureau for members and subscribers writing multiple line policies. It makes direct filings countrywide. For certain divisible premium multiple line contracts it makes its filings only after consultation with other national rating units and with local fire rating bureaus. (See Chapter 51.)

Mutual Insurance Advisory Association

Composed of about 150 mutual "fire and casualty" insurance companies, this association acts as an official advisory agency to member companies, particularly in respect to rating problems. It serves also a statistical collection organization.

Mutual Insurance Rating Bureau

This bureau serves a large number of mutual casualty companies in more than 40 states. Its purpose is to file rates, plans, schedules, and forms on behalf of member companies. It is licensed to handle a variety of liability, other casualty, and certain miscellaneous lines. (See Chapter 45.)

National Association of Independent Insurance Adjusters

A large number of individuals who represent independent adjusting firms compose the membership. Regional vice presidents assist the president in the operation of this national organization. The purpose is to impart a dignity to and to maintain high standards for independent adjusting, and to promote increased understanding on the part of the public of the function of independent adjusters.

National Association of Independent Insurers

This association is composed of many "fire, casualty and surety" insurers which do not belong to large rating bureaus. The association distributes considerable information about legislation and litigation. It provides spokesmen to present to various industry and governmental groups the points of view of its members. Also, it serves as an advisory organization and statistical agent.

National Association of Insurance Agents, Inc.

Membership is made up of agents of "fire and casualty" stock insurers who operate as a part of the American agency system, which is defined by the Association to be "the production of insurance premiums and the servicing of insurance contracts by insurance agents operating solely on a commission basis on their own account as independent contractors, who maintain their own offices separate and apart from any production office maintained by an insurance company." The NAIA publishes the *American Agency Bulletin*. Numerous state associations are affiliated with the NAIA. (See Chapters 62 and 68.)

The National Association of Insurance Brokers, Inc.

Drawing members from a large number of brokers, this association represents its members in industry and governmental meetings where brokers' views need to be expressed. Also, it undertakes studies of current and proposed legislation and informs its members on a variety of subjects. (See Chapters 62 and 68.)

National Association of Insurance Commissioners

This one is the organization of state insurance commissioners (some of whom go by other titles). Organized into numerous committees, the NAIC devotes most of its efforts to consideration of actual and proposed legislation pertaining to the regulation of the insurance business. (See Chapter 65.) The organization —under another name—dates back to 1871.

National Association of Insurance Women

Its members consist of career women in the insurance industry. Its purpose is to improve the education, fellowship, loyalty, understanding, and stature of its members.

National Association of Mutual Insurance Agents

Agents representing mutual "fire and casualty" companies make up this association. The general purpose is to promote the sale of mutual insurance through independent agents and, in the process, to foster the well-being, education, and standards of its member agents. Numerous state associations are affiliated with NAMIA. (See Chapters 62 and 68.)

National Association of Mutual Insurance Companies

The members are mutual "fire and casualty" companies, predominantly farm, county, or township mutuals. Its purpose is to protect and improve the institution of mutual insurance generally and its members' interests specifically.

National Association of Surety Bond Producers, Inc.

This association is composed of many prominent surety bond producers in the United States, Canada, and Puerto Rico. It studies matters of general interest pertaining to contract bonds. (See Chapter 55.)

National Automobile Underwriters Association

The NAUA is a rating bureau licensed in nearly all of the states (plus D.C. and Puerto Rico) to file rates and forms for automobile *physical damage* insurance coverages. It serves as a statistical agent also. (See Chapter 45.)

The National Board of Fire Underwriters

Until January 1, 1965, this board provided a professional staff and numerous standing committees (manned by officials from supporting companies). It drew its support from stock "fire" insurers. It was an "educational, factual, and engineering" organization concerned with building-construction standards, fire loss data, arson, legislation, and other technical matters of safety. (See Chapters 12 and 13.) Its functions have been assumed by the American Insurance Association.

National Bureau of Casualty Underwriters

This unincorporated association of stock insurers serves as a rating or advisory organization for its members and subscribers. Its work extends to automobile, general liability, boiler and machinery, glass, burglary, and certain other lines discussed in Part V of this *Handbook.* It is licensed in all states and territories. It prepares and distributes numerous rate manuals. (See Chapter 45.)

National Council on Compensation Insurance

Membership consists of a large number of insurers which write workmen's compensation insurance. Both stock and mutual types of insurers are members. The purpose is to set and file workmen's compensation rates and to improve the rating systems. (See Chapter 36.)

Society of Chartered Property and Casualty Underwriters

This society is composed of individuals who have successfully completed the written examinations offered by the American Institute for Property and Liability Underwriters, Inc. and who have met the experience requirements established by this Institute. Such individuals qualify for the C.P.C.U. designation. The purpose of the society and its many affiliated chapters is generally to foster education and professionalism in "property and casualty" insurance. (See Chapter 70.)

The Surety Association of America

The membership, purpose, origin, operation, and other aspects of this association are discussed in Chapter 56.

Transportation Insurance Rating Bureau

The membership, purpose, origin, operation, and other aspects of this bureau are referred to in Chapters 23 and 28.

Underwriters' Laboratories, Inc.

Sponsored by the National Board of Fire Underwriters (and now by the American Insurance Association), this laboratory tests many materials and products as to how well they meet fire safety standards. The Underwriters' Laboratories label on products such as electrical appliances is familiar to many people. (See Chapter 12.)

United States Salvage Association, Inc.

This association represents major marine insurers and has as its purpose the provision of expert salvage services for marine losses and the supplying of a variety of technical information for marine insurers. It maintains offices in most major world ports. (See Chapter 20.)

L. Insurance Organizations Engaged in Public Relations*

Company-Sponsored

American Mutual Insurance Alliance
20 North Wacker Drive
Chicago, Illinois

Insurance Information Institute
110 William Street
New York 38, New York

National Association of Independent Insurers
30 West Monroe Street
Chicago 3, Illinois

Canadian Underwriters Association
460 St. John Street
Montreal 1, P.Q.
Canada

Agent-Sponsored

National Association of Insurance Agents
96 Fulton Street
New York 38, New York

National Association of Mutual Insurance Agents
827 Investment Building
Washington 5, D.C.

Regional Insurance Information Offices

Midwestern Region, Insurance Information Institute
175 West Jackson Boulevard
Chicago 4, Illinois

Northeastern Region, Insurance Information Institute
110 William Street
New York 38, New York

Southeastern Region, Insurance Information Institute
319 Trust Company of Georgia Building
Atlanta 3, Georgia

Southwestern Region, Insurance Information Institute
2105 Tower Petroleum Building
Dallas, Texas

Pacific Region, Insurance Information Institute
315 Montgomery Street
San Francisco 4, California

---

* See Chapter 71.

Western Insurance Information Service
3440 Wilshire Boulevard
Los Angeles 5, California

Western Insurance Information Service (Branch Office)
Olympia National Life Building
Seattle, Washington

Southwestern Insurance Information Service, Inc.
812 Gibraltar Life Building
Dallas, Texas

State Insurance Information Offices

Insurance Information Office of Connecticut
79 Farmington Avenue
Hartford, Connecticut

Southern Insurance Information Service (Georgia)
41 Exchange Place, SE
Atlanta 3, Georgia

Illinois Insurance Information Service
1712 Board of Trade Building
141 West Jackson Boulevard
Chicago 4, Illinois

Insurance Institute of Indiana
701 Board of Trade Building
Indianapolis 4, Indiana

The Casualty Insurance Companies Serving Massachusetts
8 Beacon Street
Boston 8, Massachusetts

Michigan Insurance Information Service
611 Bank of Lansing Building
Lansing 16, Michigan

Minnesota Insurance Information Center
First National–Soo Line Building
Minneapolis 2, Minnesota

Insurance Information Service of New Hampshire
18 School Street
Concord, New Hampshire

North Carolina Insurance Information Service
P.O. Box 408
Raleigh, North Carolina

Ohio Insurance Information Service, Inc.
8 East Long Street
Columbus 15, Ohio

Insurance Information Office of Pennsylvania
12 South 12th Street
Philadelphia, Pennsylvania

The Texas Insurance Advisory Association
812 Brazos Street
Austin, Texas

Other Organizations

Insurance Advertising Conference
Executive Secretary
51 Birch Road
Longmeadow, Massachusetts

American Institute of Marine Underwriters
99 John Street
New York 38, New York

INDEXES

INDEX OF NAMES

Z

INDEX OF ORGANIZATIONS

INDEX OF COURT CASES

INDEX OF SUBJECTS

H

I

Y